FINCHES & SPARROWS

FINCHES &
SPARROWS

An Identification Guide

Peter Clement

Illustrated by Alan Harris and John Davis

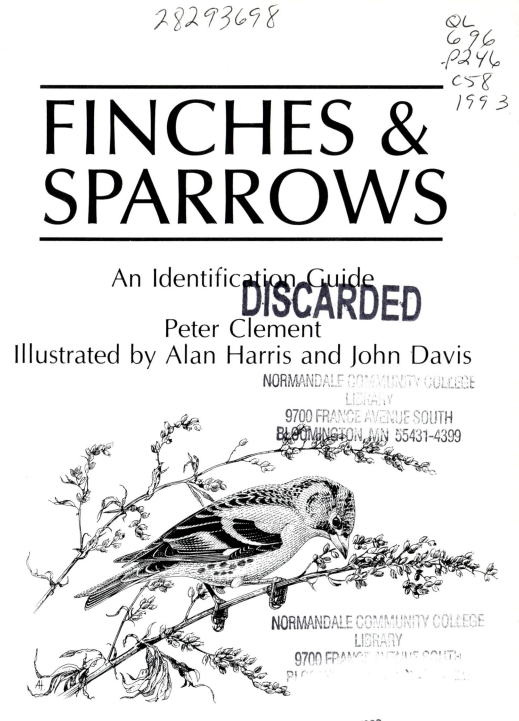

Princeton University Press
Princeton, New Jersey

© 1993 Peter Clement, Alan Harris and John Davis

Reprinted 1994

Maps by Euromap Ltd

Christopher Helm (Publishers) Limited,
a subsidiary of A & C Black (Publishers) Limited,
35 Bedford Row, London WC1R 4JH

ISBN 0–7136-8017–2

A CIP catalogue record for this book is
available from the British Library

Typeset by Rowland Phototypesetting Ltd,
Bury St Edmunds, Suffolk

Originated in Leeds by Gilchrist Bros

Printed and bound in Italy by Arnoldo Mondadori

CONTENTS

FRINGILLIDAE: Fringillinae

FRINGILLIDAE: Carduelinae

ESTRILDIDAE

INTRODUCTION

Finches are widely considered to be among the most attractive of birds. Many are colourful without being gaudy, and are widespread and familiar to the most casual of birdwatchers. The small size, active manner and stout conical bill are features that readily sum up the outlines of a 'typical' finch. But what is a 'typical' finch, since not one of the 256 finches in this book is so widespread in its distribution that it could be considered typical of more than just one continent?

The 'true' finches of the Fringillidae (comprising the Fringillinae and Carduelinae) are perhaps regarded in Europe as typical, since they include such well-known species as Linnet, Goldfinch, Greenfinch and the somewhat notorious Common Bullfinch. However, this family also contains less well-known groups such as rosefinches and grosbeaks. Some groups or genera are more familiar than others: the canaries, serins or seedeaters for instance are well known for their songs and have, within the last hundred years or so, become popular as cagebirds and have been hybridised by aviculturists to produce a variety of strains or 'mules'.

Members of the second finch family, the Estrildidae, are generally small, often brightly coloured seed-eating birds, occurring principally in sub-Saharan Africa (outside tropical forest) and in southeast Asia through the Malay archipelago to the Pacific islands. These highly active finches have, in ornithological terms, suffered from an 'image problem' and have too readily been dismissed outside Africa as purely cagebirds. For many years the only contact ornithologists living in the developed world had with these birds was through the bars of a cage. While this is still true for a large number of people today, we as a whole are far more mobile than ever before in our history and considerable numbers of birders and birdwatchers (the distinction exists but is not for us to make here) have travelled widely in Africa and the Orient and encountered small parties of these active little finches in tropical savannas, semi-desert outbacks, corrals, sheep or cattle ranches, canyons, high-altitude forests or even sun-baked hotel gardens. Very few who have seen them in their natural settings have not been surprised or impressed by their tameness, lively manner, and the range of plumages they exhibit and habitats they occupy.

Not all species, however, are tame or easily found, for the family contains some of the real skulkers of the finch tribes. The crimson-wings, bluebills, and (one or two of) the twinspots of the dense forest and impenetrable thornscrub of Africa, or the high-altitude grassland- or canefield-dwelling munias of New Guinea, are among the most difficult birds to track down. They can offer as much of a challenge to the most dedicated ornithologist or devoted lister as any scrub-dwelling bush-warbler, babbler, pitta or crake.

The third and final family covered by this book, the Passeridae, is linked to the finches in food preference, habitat occupation, distribution and, in some cases, actions and behavioural characteristics. Members of one genus are actually called snow finches and could, were it not for their close links to the rest of the Passeridae in structure, nesting behaviour and choice of nest site, be considered as relatives of the mountain finches *Leucosticte* in the Carduelinae.

The finches and sparrows occupy an important place within the passerines. They occur in almost every type of habitat, from agricultural lowlands to montane plateaux, deserts and savannas to tropical forest, cloud forest and the barren mountain crags and tops of the highest Himalayas. They contain one of the the highest-living passerines, the Red-breasted Rosefinch, which occurs in summer at up to 5450 m (about 18,000 feet); at the other extreme, parts of the Dead Sea Sparrow's breeding range are below sea-level and the House Sparrow has been recorded as living and breeding 640 m (over 2000 feet) below ground down a coal-mine in South Yorkshire, England.

Although this book (unlike most others on finches) is not primarily intended for use in aviculture, it will, it is hoped, greatly add to the wealth of information available to the cagebird enthusiast wishing to know more about the species encountered in captivity. Little or no reference has been made in the texts to birds in captivity or the effects that the taking of finches (and to a lesser extent some sparrows) has had on wild populations, except where the levels of trapping have made excessive demands on the population and outstripped the ability of birds left in the wild to sustain this depredation.

One species of finch, Red Siskin, has been brought to the edge of extinction through the excessive activities of cagebird-trappers. The demands of dealers in small songbirds in Europe, Africa and elsewhere, where birds are taken and housed in poor, overcrowded and inhumane conditions, continue to cause justified outrage. Recent bans by the larger international airlines on the transportation of such shipments have been widely welcomed and applauded in a bid to curtail the trade. More recently, the governing body of aviculture in the United Kingdom has urged people not to buy wild birds when considering buying a pet; this followed a year in which over 130,000 birds (mainly finches and parrots) were imported into the UK alone.

Finches and Sparrows is an identification guide to all the world's species of true finches and sparrows. It describes and illustrates in colour for the first time the plumages (including the most distinctive races) of all 290 species in the Fringillidae, Estrildidae and Passeridae families. It is intended to be an easy-to-use handbook and a definitive work of reference.

This guide will allow the reader to identify unfamiliar species and give some background and insight into species he or she is uncertain about or wishes to know more about. In addition to information we have gathered both in the field and in museums, we have undertaken extensive research, covering both captive and wild birds, of the available literature on the families. However, with such an abundance of papers published in a multitude of journals, some information may well have been overlooked. The author would be extremely grateful to hear of any omissions or errors that may have been made. Please address any correspondence through the publishers.

ACKNOWLEDGEMENTS

Firstly, it has to be said that no book of this nature could ever be the work of just two or three people since it covers almost 300 species in two of the larger groups in the passerines.

We are particularly grateful to the following for their help, advice and comments, given in many ways: Per Alström, Dr John S. Ash, Kevin Baker, Dr Leo Batten, Aldo Berruti, Dave Bishop, George Boobyer, Mark Brazil, Dr Andy Brown, Ian Burrows, Graham P. Catley, David A. Christie, Dr Andy Clements, Nigel Collar, Peter Colston, Chris Dee, E. Dickinson, Euan Dunn, Jon Eames, Chris Galey, Belinda Gillies, Derek Goodwin, Tom Gullick, Dr Colin Harrison, Jo Hemmings, Derek Holmes, Jon Hornbuckle, Steve Howell, Carol and Tim Inskipp, Peter Lansdown, Steve Madge, Bruce Martin, Rod Martins, Chris Mead, David Pearson, Tony Prater, Nigel Redman, James Redwood, Robert Ridgely, Craig Robson, Paul Roper, Phil Round, Ian Sinclair, Tony Smith, J. Dennis Summers-Smith, Bruce Taggart, Don Turner, Bas van Balen, Alan Vittery and Derek Wells.

Particular thanks are due to Linda Burch at the Alexander Library of the Edward Grey Institute, Euan Dunn and Mike Wilson also of the EGI and assistant editors of the *Birds of the Western Palearctic*, Tim Inskipp, Tim Parmenter and Effie Warr of the Natural History Museum, Tring, Malcolm Rush and Dick Seamons at English Nature (formerly the Nature Conservancy Council), and Ian Dawson, librarian at the RSPB, for their help in obtaining copies of references or chasing up obscure papers in foreign journals.

We are indebted to the staff at the Natural History Museum, Tring, particularly Peter Colston and Michael Walters, for helping with access to the national collection and obtaining, on loan, specimens from museums in Australia, Belgium, the Netherlands, South Africa and the United States. Also to the staff in several museums around the world, especially Belinda Gillies at the Museum of Victoria, Australia; Aldo Berruti and Ian Sinclair of Durban Museum, South Africa; Cecilia M. Gichuki of the National Museum of Kenya; K. C. Parkes of The Carnegie Museum of Natural History, Pittsburgh; R. A. Sloss of the American Museum of Natural History, New York; M. Louette of the Musée Royal de L'Afrique Centrale, Belgium; and Karl-L. Schuchmann of the Museum Alexander Koenig, Bonn.

Some of the calls and song transliterations from *Estrildid Finches of the World* are reproduced by courtesy of the British Museum (Natural History), London.

Grateful thanks are due to David A. Christie, Gerda Flumm, Neil Hailey, Miou Helps, Françoise Morgan and Mike Wilson for considerable help with the translation of foreign papers and documents. The author would also like specifically to thank Chris Mead and Dr David Parkin for their extensive comments and help given on the first draft of the introductory chapter, and also Angela Clement, who helped with the word-processing of the entire text.

Especial thanks are due to Robert Kirk and the staff of Christopher Helm (Publishers) Limited, without whom this book would not have been possible.

Finally, the author would like to express grateful thanks to Angela, who has been an extremely patient and completely understanding wife, and to Paul and Louise, who have often forgone parts of family life during the many months this book has been in preparation and production.

HOW TO USE THIS BOOK

This book has been designed and written primarily as an identification guide for use in the field, but also as a reference work for species frequently seen in captivity. The layout of the book has expanded the fieldguide format of text, plates and maps together on facing pages. Most of the information on the species now lies in the species accounts and only a short summary of the critical features, or particular parts of the plumage not readily apparent, together with a distribution map is given on the caption pages facing the plates.

The main text for each species gives a detailed description of its plumage and any variation in the plumages of races or subsequent changes either in non-breeding or in juvenile to adult plumages. Information is also given on voice, the types of habitat where the species is found either permanently or temporarily, and any important aspects such as behaviour and feeding or roosting activities which may be useful for the identification of the species and to distinguish it from confusion species.

No information is given on courtship display or breeding behaviour, since the scope of a book of this size its is restricted by the number of species included and limited to the most essential information required for the identification and ageing of the individual birds. Where such information is relevant for identification, however (for example, distinctive shape of nests built, or whether the bird is a colonial nesting species or has a particularly recognisable display flight), this has been included; at the other extreme, where this information is lacking or entirely unknown, as in the case of some of the more remote montane or forest species, this is stated.

Some explanation of the layout may be useful to help the reader through the various sections of the book.

The Plates

All the main plumages of each species have been included on the plates, together with those of the more recognisable races or geographically distinct forms. In some cases the fresh or non-breeding plumage obscures the breeding plumage and has been depicted, but for the majority of species this is only a transitional or temporary stage. It is included only where it persists for any length of time (in months) or is considerably different from that shown for most of the bird's annual cycle. A few flight illustrations have been included, but these have been kept to a minimum since most finches and sparrows fly so fast that only the brightest or most striking features of the plumage, such as wingbars or a contrasting rump, are likely to be detectable in the field. Where the species is recognisable in flight or has distinctive flight characteristics, however, a black-and-white illustration is included in the main species account.

The plates have been arranged so that groups or assemblages of species, either closely related or similar in appearance, are shown together or follow on for ease of reference and for comparison with similar-looking species. In one or two instances this has not been possible, but the summary caption to the plate and the identification section of the text indicate which other species closely resemble the bird under discussion. Birds are to scale within each plate. Each bird has been numbered to allow easy reference to the summary on the caption page opposite the plate or to the main text. In only one instance, São Tomé Grosbeak (41), is the species illustrated out of sequence or away from the nearest similar species. This is because the bird was rediscovered in July 1991 following a period of a little over 100 years since the previous (and then only the second) sighting.

The Maps

All species have distribution maps showing the main breeding and non-breeding ranges. Nomadic, wandering or migratory birds frequently occur outside or between these ranges, and it may generally be taken that in the unmarked areas between the coloured ranges the particular species could be expected on passage. The maps are intended only as a guideline, and within its range a species may be sparsely, locally or abundantly distributed depending on habitat, population density or seasonal movements. For some species, arrows show areas of very small populations which may otherwise be overlooked on this scale; some areas are indicated with a question mark to denote that confirmation is required as to whether the species is still found there or may have recently expanded its range into that area. Consultation of the main text will help to give a clear idea of the ranges, status and occurrence patterns of all species.

The distribution of species that are resident, mainly sedentary or can reasonably be expected throughout the year is shown in green; this includes those species which breed at high altitudes and winter at lower levels. For practical purposes these seasonal differences in areas of occupancy cannot be shown on these maps; for some species, such movements may not be true of all of the population. Those regions where the species is a breeding-season visitor are shown in yellow; and those areas where the species is a non-breeding visitor are shown in blue. Pale areas or those indicated within a dotted line are where the species occurs in certain years (i.e. limits of irruptions) but not ordinarily.

The Systematic Section

Species Sequence

In recent years, the number of bird species and families and their relationships with other families have received a considerable amount of attention from different taxonomists. The families included within this book, however, have received only sparse or piecemeal attention and, as has been noted by several authorities, lacked an overall comprehensive review.

The sequence of species used in this book (which has not sought to be taxonomically exact) has been drawn up for the convenience of use, and no claims are made for its evolutionary exactness. It is based on regional nomenclature and classification of species and genera within the families. For those species in Fringillidae and Passeridae (except the sparrows) the Holarctic sequence follows Voous (1977), or in certain noted Palearctic exceptions, Vaurie (1959). For sub-Saharan Africa the sequence follows that of Hall and Moreau (1970), with amendments as proposed or included in the revised SAOS Checklist (Clancey 1980). For the Estrildid finches the order is generally as proposed by Goodwin (1982), and the sequence for the sparrows is as that proposed by Summers-Smith (1988) with the exception of Golden Sparrow.

There have been several recent attempts to arrange all bird species into a simple unified classification. Some of these have, however, caused further confusion where they have differed from previous treatments by separating well-marked subspecies into full species, without clearly indicating to which of these the less well-marked subspecies belong. In some cases, this has led to confusion or misunderstanding as to which of the remaining races are allied to which nominate race or 'new' species.

Most recently, Sibley and Monroe (1991) and Sibley and Ahlquist (1991) produced a classification of families using DNA-DNA hybridisation, a molecular method of measuring the degree of genetic similarity between the DNAs of different species as a key to clarifying or establishing the relationships between families. This is a very promising start on what is clearly an enormous task. However, we are still some way from understanding the complexities of such a classification, and indeed Peterson and Stotz (1992) have already pointed out that such a new and untried system is not without its flaws or drawbacks. Further refinement of the DNA technology is undoubtedly the way forward, and will perhaps in a decade or so from now be able to demonstrate significant developments in establishing the exact relationships of families and species. While the present classification of species (particularly birds) is in a state of flux, it would be unwise to put forward yet another set of species classified into an order based on previously available (or at least pre-DNA) information.

The sequence of species within this book is thus largely that of existing or pre-DNA world-list classifications (Howard and Moore 1980, 1991; and Peters et al. 1934–87), with stated exceptions or derogations from those orders. A number of papers have been published which attempt to establish an order for various families, or parts of families, with well-defined geographic boundaries. The classification of the complex relationships of the African Serinus group has been researched and documented by van den Elzen (1985) and to some extent by Erard (1974), yet there appears to be no current accepted treatment of the species and races of canaries, serins and seedeaters of Africa. In fact, in line with present taxonomic trends, further elevation to full species of some forms previously treated (and widely accepted) as races is likely to be proposed by some taxonomic authorities. Whether this splitting, or the previous collective ('lumping') treatment is correct only time and possibly genetic analysis will tell.

At present, the line between clinal races and full species is almost imperceptibly thin and the distinction between these is not always clear. Indeed, it is not well understood either by taxonomists or (perhaps more importantly in terms of consistency of field recording) by amateur birders, birdwatchers or lay ornithologists (i.e. those providing field data relating to occurrences and distribution).

Heading

Each species is given a reference number which identifies it on the plates and in the texts. These numbers are purely for the convenience and purpose of this book, and have no other function. The species' English name is followed by alternative names (in parentheses) and the scientific name, then the plate number and where in the world the species is found. The first scientific name is given to show the earliest documented evidence of the species, followed by the location where the type specimen (i.e. the first recorded specimen collected by those who discovered or named the bird) was taken or in some cases where the specimen is now kept.

Identification

This section contains the essential information on the species' size (given in centimetres and inches), and the features of its shape or plumage most necessary to establish its identity regardless of age, sex or race. Where relevant, the species with which it is most likely to be confused (within and beyond the scope of this book) are described and cross-referenced. For some distinctive or obvious species this may not be relevant (also, a few species are the sole representatives of the finches or sparrows in various parts of the globe and have no similar counterparts).

Description

Following on from the brief outline in Identification, this section gives detailed information on the plumage or range of plumages for breeding and non-breeding adults, juveniles and, where recognisable in the field (or in some cases in the hand), first- or second-summer/winter birds. Unless stated otherwise, the nominate race will be described here. In some species the nominate race has a very small distribution, or is less well known or infrequently encountered compared with another of the races; (in such cases, the nominate race will then be mentioned under Geographical Variation.

For those species that are similar to several others, this section should be used in conjunction with the plates to determine the subtlety of colours shown in shades of yellows, greens, reds or browns, and to determine (if possible) the age of the bird in question. Most individuals, certainly of the smaller and shorter-living species, will be readily identifiable as adult or juvenile. Some species, however, particularly the larger ones, have more complex or intermediate stages, while in others the bright colours of the fresh plumage (or of displaying birds) are lost or obscured in summer or in moult.

This section also gives details of the colours or patterns visible, whether or not all parts of the bird appear on the plates. It also includes details of the bare (or soft) parts: bill, leg and (for some species) eye and eye-ring colours are also given here.

Geographical Variation

As in the classification of species, we have followed those taxonomic authorities who have given racial status to closely allied forms which can be distinguished either in the field or in the hand. Some species have a number of recognisable races (subspecies), and these are detailed here with all the visible features that differentiate them from the nominate race. In some cases there are variations or plumage 'morphs', which are also described here. Some races are clearly more easily separable in the field than others, which may differ only slightly in colour tones or size. For those species with races that are indistinguishable in the field, we have also indicated these but offer no information as to differences in the hand, as in some cases (e.g. Hooded Grosbeak (127)) the details are apparently unpublished.

Some races, particularly those which are clearly different or readily separable from the nominate, may eventually prove to be full species in their own right. If this is so it is mentioned, and the most strikingly different races are given a more complete description. We have avoided the splitting into further races on very minute criteria (perhaps by measurements in millimetres alone) as this seems to us unsafe until the present levels of relationships between the more clear-cut races and species are better understood.

Voice

This section is restricted to the main or most frequent calls or song; it is widely recognised that most of the species within this book (especially the canaries noted for their vocal qualities) are capable of a wide range of variation within their tonal structures, and may make some notes which are of local or dialectal origin. Also, the nest calls of parents to young, most noticeable in Estrildid finches, have not been recorded here, since this is a book for field identification and the complex nature of such calls is more appropriate to a book devoted to the breeding behaviour of these birds: such information is readily found in Goodwin (1982).

Sonagrams are not used as the differences they show between species with very similar calls will convey little to the lay fieldworker not familiar with the range of notes depicted. While it is appreciated that to different human ears some notes or songs will not always resemble the same transcriptions, every effort has been made to detail as closely as possible the renderings of the birds; only with familiarity will some species become recognisable or identifiable by voice alone.

Status, Habitat and Behaviour

The status or abundance of a species is given here together with the habitat occupied by the bird, since the former is often dependent on the availability and distribution of the latter. Most finches (with the exception of a few forest dwellers) and sparrows are birds of open country, though within this broad category some divisions into elevation and types of habitat have to be made. For instance, many species are frequently found at the margins of forest or woods, in savanna or grassland or in scrub. It does not follow that apparently suitable habitat for a particular species will hold individuals of that species. Far more needs to be learned and appreciated before we can fully understand the complex needs of birds in their occupation of habitat niches.

Also, the behaviour, habits or actions of the bird may vary through the year, especially between different seasons. Foraging in wet and dry seasons may differ, not just when it comes to obtaining sufficiency for the individual but also during the breeding season when raising young or when surviving through periods of food shortages. With this in mind, it becomes even harder for us to understand how some species, mainly the very high-altitude rosefinches, mountain finches and snow finches, withstand and endure severe winter weather, frozen ground and deep snowfalls while finding sufficient nourishment in an apparently bleak and inhospitable climate.

The food items given here are principally those which have been recorded as being most commonly taken, or taken seasonally or frequently, by the species in question. It is not an exhaustive list of prey items, since some species, especally the sparrows, will eat anything given the chance. Considerable effort has nevertheless been spent on making this list as comprehensive as possible.

Distribution

Closely linked with both status and habitat is the range of each species, since the extent of the habitat for resident or sedentary species is often that of the distribution. The details of the breeding ranges shown on the maps are expanded and given in detail here.

Movements

This section gives information on movements outside the breeding season, to and from non-breeding areas, or where the species undertakes random or nomadic wanderings. It also outlines the sedentary or resident nature of species and summarises (where available) information on the occurrences of birds outside their normal areas, from the unusual but regular visitor to the extreme vagrant. Almost any species can turn up well away from its normal area of occupancy, especially those species which undertake long movements away from their breeding areas.

Measurements

Apart from the total length given in centimetres and in the Identification section, all measurements given here are in millimetres. Measurements are given as a guide for comparing similar-sized birds in the field. Some species have slight but critical differences in leg or wing length which, with practice, may be recognisable in the field. Differences in the comparative length (or shape) of the bill may be critical when attempting to identify an unknown species.

Wing length is measured from the carpal joint (the bend of the wing) to the tip of the longest primary on the flattened folded wing. For some (mostly Holarctic) species this information relates to live birds captured for ringing (Svensson 1984; Pyle et al. 1987), but for all other species measurements from live birds are not readily available and museum specimens have been used. It should be borne in mind, when comparing museum data with those for live birds, that a 2–3% reduction takes place in dead or prepared specimens owing to the natural processes of skin shrinkage. Also, some measurements may include juveniles, which may be slightly smaller or shorter than adults in fresh plumage (though most immatures will have fully grown feathers within a few days or weeks of leaving the nest and becoming independent), or adults in moult or with worn or abraded feathers, which can also give shorter measurements.

For most species we have credited the source of the measurements (in the References section), but for some we give only data taken ourselves from specimens at the Natural History Museum at Tring, Hertfordshire, England, which houses the largest collection of bird skins anywhere in the world.

Tail length is measured from the tip of the longest feather (except in cases where the bird has elongated central tail feathers, which are given separately) to the point of entry into the body at the base of the central feather. These measurements are taken solely from live birds and those measured before preparation, as measurements taken from prepared specimens are, in our opinion, unreliable and make no allowance for the movement of the tail or the shrinkage of skin.

The tarsus is measured along the back of the leg from the top of the centre of the 'knee' to the base of the middle toe, sometimes (always in finches) characterised as the last scale on the leg before the toes divide.

Bill length is measured from the tip of the bill to the furthest point of the exposed,

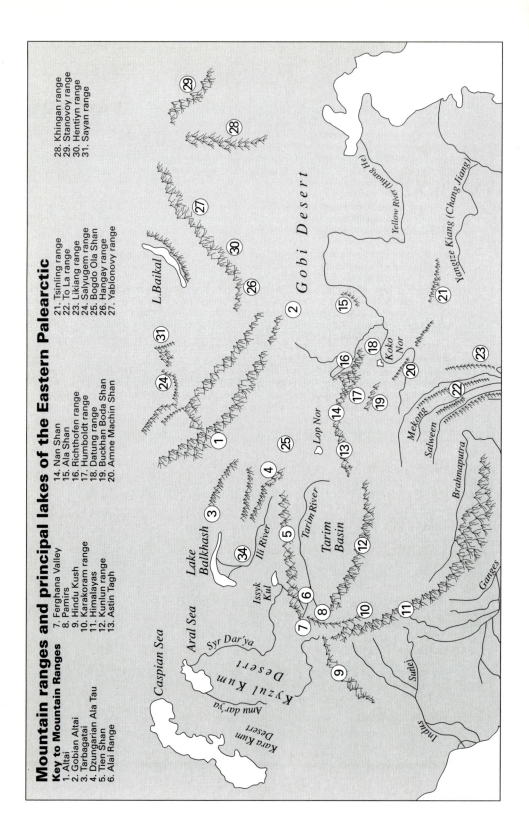

Mountain ranges and principal lakes of the Eastern Palearctic

Key to Mountain Ranges

1. Altai
2. Gobian Altai
3. Tarbagatai
4. Dzungarian Ala Tau
5. Tien Shan
6. Alai Range
7. Ferghana Valley
8. Pamirs
9. Hindu Kush
10. Karakoram range
11. Himalayas
12. Kunlun range
13. Astin Tagh
14. Nan Shan
15. Ala Shan
16. Richthofen range
17. Humboldt range
18. Datung range
19. Buckhan Boda Shan
20. Amne Machin Shan
21. Tsinling range
22. To La range
23. Likiang range
24. Salyugem range
25. Bogdo Ola Shan
26. Hangay range
27. Yablonovoy range
28. Khingan range
29. Stanovoy range
30. Hentiyn range
31. Sayan range

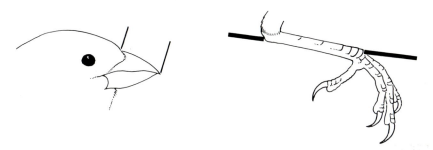

Bill measurement (left): length of culmen is from tip of bill to base of forehead feathers where they meet bill. Standard tarsus measurement: from notch on back of intertarsal joint to lower edge of last complete scale (Svensson, 1992).

unfeathered culmen where it meets the forehead. In some cases difficulties arise where the forehead feathers conceal the base of the culmen, and here the measurement is taken from the base of the feathers.

Weights, where available, are given in grams; they are possibly of little use in an identification book such as this, but some can give an idea of the bulk of the bird in comparison with similar species. All weights have been taken from existing literature and credited with the relevant reference. All weights refer to adults; juveniles and first-winter birds are often smaller or lighter and less bulky than adults.

References

The most useful of existing literature sources for each species are cited. These are mostly papers or reference works concerning identification, ageing, behaviour or distribution, and may be useful as a reference point for anyone wishing to undertake further studies on particular species. These, and details of all references given in the species texts, will be found in the Bibliography on page 485. The reader is also referred to the many regional field guides which do not appear in the bibliography.

GENERAL NOTES ON FINCHES AND SPARROWS AND THEIR RELATIONSHIPS

Vernacular Names

In addition to the current controversies over the assimilation of all species into an agreed taxonomic order, several attempts have been made to establish a uniformity of English names for all species. The purpose of this is primarily to give every bird species an English name which supersedes all those in existence (some of course will remain the same) and, like the scientific name, cannot be confused with any other. While the reasons that lie behind this may well be very sound and laudable, it is possibly too late in the development of ornithology throughout the world to be able to impose such a definitive list. We have therefore made no attempt to adapt or adopt these 'new' names since they are not yet agreed nor are they practical; many are applied purely for naming's sake or serve no purpose of clarification.

These proposals to create a single unified list will, in practical terms, result in the proliferation of lists used at two or more levels. On one level will be the 'official' world-list, used by editors and compilers or writers of ornithological works (books, reports and perhaps, to a lesser extent, scientific papers) but ignored or dismissed by those who wish to pursue at another level their own ideas on bird names. Names in everyday usage by birders and birdwatchers will continue to be in the old or traditional vernacular, if not the colloquial. The addition of the prefix of 'Eurasian' is ungainly, as is to some extent 'Northern' though it has more geographical significance than some proposed alternatives. There is some precedence for this since the nominate race of Common Bullfinch has (since the days of Witherby's *Handbook*) frequently been known as Northern Bullfinch. We have also avoided the use of recently invented names and the use of qualifying adjectives where none yet exists, though other names in occasional or regional use are included in the alternative names.

We feel that any list of new names (created for the sake of uniformity) imposed from a distance is a bureaucratic exercise, and since it makes no provision for local views or usage is more likely to fail in its aims. While there is (or the possibility exists of) some confusion between names used regionally or in different avifaunas owing to traditonal usage or author preference, it is the purpose of the scientific name to be the standard worldwide name for each species. In the extensive travels undertaken by us in the compilation of this book, we have always been able to communicate in different languages at species level by using scientific names.

The English species names used in this book are derived largely from those sources given above under the heading Species Sequence; where (in one or two cases) we have chosen to differ from these, we have stated our reasons why. The use of the name canary or seedeater in the *Serinus* group and mannikin or munia in the *Lonchura* group may seem inconsistent or arbitrary, but we see no reason to impose change or realignment from traditional usage or that used in current works and field guides to the regions.

Characteristics and Relationships

The finches in the subfamilies Fringillinae and Carduelinae are grouped together in the family Fringillidae and classed as true finches. The term 'finch' has been or is currently (according to differing taxonomic authorities) applied to some members of at least seven (and possibly nine) other families or subfamilies of birds – Emberizinae (buntings), Thraupinae (tanagers), Geospizinae (Galápagos finches), Pyrrhuloxinae (cardinals and grosbeaks), Bubalornithinae (buffalo-weavers), Viduinae (whydahs) and Ploceinae (weavers). At one time the Fringillidae also included the Emberizinae, Geospizinae and Pyrrhuloxinae, but these are now widely considered to have evolved separately and are accepted as belonging in their own family, the Emberizidae. There are also some similarities with other families, such as the more distantly related Phytotomidae (plantcutters). All are very similar in actions and appearances and have the same range of bill sizes and structures for dealing with their primary source of food – seeds.

The true finches are primarily arboreal or terrestrial seed-eating birds and have stout or strong (occasionally massive) conical bills, strong skulls with large or powerful jaw muscles and well-developed gizzards. In each wing there are nine large primary feathers and a vestigial or very small outermost first (or tenth in the American numbering system) primary (with the sole exception of Przewalski's Rosefinch *Urocynchramus pylzowi*, which has ten well-developed primaries), in each wing and 12 feathers in the tail. Other characteristics are the cup-shaped nest, and that the hen alone builds the nest and incubates the eggs. Differences between the two subfamilies are apparent mostly in the food fed to the young – insects in the Fringillinae and seeds (or seeds and insects) in the Carduelinae – and in the courtship displays and establishment of nesting territories. The Fringillines find all their food from within their territories, whereas the Cardueline finches have small territories and forage for food both within and beyond the territory; anatomically, the three species of Fringillinae differ from the Carduelinae in lacking a crop.

The Fringillidae are an Old World family, and are well represented in the Holarctic and Africa but are absent from Madagascar, large parts of the Malay archipelago, Australasia (except where introduced) and the South Pacific islands. Several Palearctic species extend their breeding ranges south or east into the Oriental region, but only three species (Mountain Serin *Serinus estherae*, Vietnamese Greenfinch *Carduelis monguilloti* and Philippine Bullfinch *Pyrrhula leucogenys*) are endemic to the region. Within the family, the *Serinus* are most widespread in Africa yet are probably of Palearctic origins, having undergone adaptive evolution to become somewhat more terrestrial in their habits than the closely related *Carduelis* finches. The genus also contains two 'relict' species isolated from the Mediterranean-African region, *Serinus thibetanus* in central Asia and *S. estherae* in a fragmentary range through parts of the Malay archipelago; both of these have at various times been classed as belonging to *Carduelis*, owing to similarities and bill shapes.

Some of the Carduelinae have at some time colonised vacant niches in the New World and several species of *Carduelis*, *Loxia*, *Leucosticte*, *Carpodacus* and *Pinicola* are well established in (mainly western) North America. In the case of the three *Carpodacus* rosefinches found in the New World, this represents a considerable leap in the range of the genus from its origins and stronghold in central and eastern Asia. In the two members of the *Loxia*, one, *L. leucoptera*, has evolved a race (*megaplaga*) endemic to the island of Hispaniola in the Caribbean, where it is now isolated from its nearest relatives in northern North America, presumably through invasion (by irruption) and retreat of the species in the recent past. Perhaps more surprising is the colonisation of Central and South America by 12 of the *Carduelis*, all of them extremely similar in many respects and clearly descended from a very recent common ancestor: a good example of species radiation.

The inclusion of the two New World *Hesperiphona* grosbeaks within the Fringillidae creates several anomalies. The genus has some links firstly with the Old World *Coccothraustes* (in which it is frequently included, though the link here has never been proved – and may be more apparent than real); and, secondly, with the other seven New World genera of grosbeaks (particularly *Pheucticus* and *Guiraca* of North America), which are classed as belonging to the Emberizidae.

It is difficult to be precise about the closest relatives of the Fringillidae as opinions differ widely among taxonomists, but some of the Emberizidae of the New World, particularly the Galápagos finches, the cardinals and the grosbeaks, show close affinities in size, structure, voice, habitat and nest-site choice. There have been numerous attempts to determine the exact relationships and lines of evolutionary emergence and divergence in both the Fringillidae and the Emberizidae; each has included subfamilies or genera later reclassified as belonging to the other, while some authorities have united the Emberizidae within the Fringillidae, resulting in a total of over 680 species. In 1968, the authors of the *Checklist of the Birds of the World* stated that 'the limits of the genera and relationships among the species are less understood – and subject to more controversy – in the cardueines than in any other group of passerines . . .' (Paynter 1968). This situation remains unchanged and is still intriguing.

The Estrildidae, or weaver-finches are treated as a separate family, and, although they clearly have close ties to the weavers (Ploceidae), there are structural, food and behavioural ties to the finches and buntings. They are generally regarded as having diverged from the same ancestral stock as the weavers at an early stage in their development. The smallest of the seed-eaters, they range from 9 cm to 17 cm and include the crimson-wings, waxbills, bluebills, firefinches and parrotfinches. Probably of African origin, they are an Old World family inhabiting the tropics east through Arabia to India and most of the Oriental region, the Malay archipelago, New Guinea, Australia and the islands of the South Pacific. They are characterised by their small size, a diet almost entirely of seeds (with the exception of the two species of *Parmoptila*, which feed almost exclusively on ants) and by being sociable and extremely active with highly developed courtship displays, ritualised nest-building behaviour and responses to nestlings. The nestlings also have characteristic markings (often in a horseshoe shape) on the palate or roof of the mouth and sides of the tongue, and coloured gape markings or flanges on the inside of the lower mandible. These wart-like growths of thickened tissue, known as tubercles or papillae, are present from birth and gradually shrink and disappear soon after the young leave the nest. Many species are brood-hosts to the parasitic indigobirds and whydahs (Viduidae).

The bills of most of the waxbills (*Estrilda*) are bright or waxy red, from which they are named, while the firefinches are so called from the bright or deep reds of the males of most of the *Lagonosticta*. The seedcrackers (*Pyrenestes*) have massive bills and differ from one another mainly in size and coloration, but they have continued to confuse taxonomists as

11

to whether there are three species or just one with a cline in size and plumage. The bluebills are frequently mistaken as belonging to the weavers, particularly the malimbes (*Malimbus*) of west and western-central Africa, because of their bill size, structure, plumage and secretive behaviour; they have some features shared by the seedcrackers, but are probably more closely related to the twinspots (*Euschistospiza* and *Hypargos*).

Both of the *Amadina* species are frequently classed as weavers, since the bills of both are deep at the base and have curved culmens. They are, however, a recent divergence from the *Pytilia* with which (apart from the bill) they share similarities in behaviour, voice and the nestlings' mouth markings. *Lonchura* finches are generally large-billed and more soberly coloured than the brighter waxbills and firefinches in black, brown (including chestnut) and white, though some have yellow on the lower rump and uppertail-coverts. They are principally birds of lowland grassland and edges of cultivation, and include rice among their preferred food items. *Lonchura* finches are, apart from the silverbills and three species of mannikin (Bronze, Black-and-white, and Magpie) of Africa, found mainly in southeast Asia, the Malay archipelago and Australasia; the other exception to this is the Madagascar Munia, which, as its name implies, is endemic to Madagascar, and the only finch to occur there.

Previously included in the genus *Lonchura* were the two species of *Padda*, which include the well-known Java Sparrow, an avicultural favourite, that differs from the sombre *Lonchura* species in its grey and pink plumage, face pattern and pink bill. The parrotfinches of southeast Asia to the South Pacific are predominantly green, with patches of deep blue and red in the plumage. They feed on the seeds of dicotyledonous plants, wild figs and the hard seeds of bamboo, and while they are a very distinctive group their affinities within the Estrildid family are uncertain. The Estrildids found in Australia and parts of New Guinea are frequently referred to as the grassfinches, a name more appropriate to the *Poephila* finches since they are found in grassy savannas and arid semi-desert scrub.

Some of the Australian finches are brightly coloured, particularly with red, such as Crimson Finch *Neochmia phaeton* and Star Finch *N. ruficauda*, while others are more gaudy in their brilliance. The single species of Australian waxbill, the Red-browed Firetail *Aegintha temporalis*, has caused much debate over its exact relationship with the African *Estrilda* finches, to which it bears considerable resemblance yet is widely separated geographically. Several explanations have been put forward as to its apparent convergent evolution in isolation, chief of which is the suggestion that it may be related to those ancestors from which other Australian finches are derived, or that there were invasions of Estrildid finches during the Pleistocene and that this is the sole living representative.

The final family included in this book, the sparrows in the family Passeridae, have also in the past been classed with the finches but are now considered to have closer links with the weavers of the family Ploceidae. The Passeridae is an Old World family (as is the Ploceidae). Most of the species are in Africa, but the range extends north and east to the Palearctic and Oriental regions; introductions elsewhere of the best-known member of the family and possibly the commonest bird in the world (House Sparrow *Passer domesticus*) have taken it to Australasia, Indonesia (and various parts of the Malay archipelago) and the New World. Characteristic of the sparrows is the possession of ten primaries, but the first or outermost is greatly reduced in size (unlike in the weavers). Most *Passer* species are sexually dimorphic and are usually brown, dull buff or grey with distinctive areas of black or white, though the two golden sparrows *P. euchlorus* and *P. luteus* and the Chestnut Sparrow *P. eminibey* might be considered the brighter members. The voices of all the species are poorly developed, with most giving only harsh chirping, buzzing or chattering songs, and calls varied only with higher-pitched squeaks. In the males of the *Passer* and *Montifringilla* species the bill becomes black in the breeding season.

The sparrows in the genus *Passer* are probably the best or most widely known of the group as they have developed a close association with man, and at least eight species regularly nest in or under man-made structures. The rock sparrows or petronias are generally less well marked and more sombre in plain sandy-brown or grey; some show a yellow spot on the throat (usually most prominently in display), but the Rock Sparrow *Petronia petronia* has a striking black-and-white striped head pattern. The high-altitude snow finches (*Montifringilla*) of the Palearctic show large areas of white in the wings and tail, the sexes are almost alike, and they are highly gregarious, often forming large flocks outside the breeding season. Several species are dependent on the holes made by rodents (mostly pikas — mouse-hares) for the nest site, an almost unique example of symbiosis in birds.

HOW TO IDENTIFY FINCHES AND SPARROWS

One of the most important steps in attempting to identify an unfamiliar finch or sparrow is to get an idea of its size and shape. The size and shape of the bill may be critical in distinguishing between the more slender-billed goldfinches or siskins and the blunter-billed serins or seedeaters. It must, of course, be borne in mind that neither the size nor the bill shape alone is enough to settle the identification of a bird, but in some cases it will be the critical factor.

Size may not always be easy to judge, particularly for small birds on their own. Exactly how large or small a bird is may not be established if there are no other birds to compare it with. Thus a Parrot Crossbill seen on its own may appear no bigger than a Common Crossbill (though different in shape) until it is joined by a Common Crossbill, and conversely a Common Crossbill on its own may appear sufficiently large to be mistaken for a Parrot Crossbill. Grant (1980, 1983) also pointed out that, when using powerful optical aids such as a telescope or telephoto lens, the chance of optical size illusion is increased. This is a potential pitfall to the unwary: birds behind the plane of focus tend to appear larger than those in front.

In the identification of finches, as in the case of practically all birds, it will greatly assist the observer to have a thorough knowledge of the common species within his or her area. There is no substitute for knowledge gained from personal observation; books can only enhance the individual impression gained in the field. Once common birds are familiar, it will be easier to make comparative assessments of those further afield.

Recognition of Principal Features

Although most finches and sparrows can be said to be small birds with conical bills, they also show a characteristic shape. They vary in shape of the head (flat or rounded), length of the wings (long or short), and shape of the tail (notched, forked or square-ended). The plumage will also be crucial to a successful identification: Is the bird streaked on the upperparts or only on the breast and flanks? Does it have a supercilium or a moustachial streak, and, if so, are they faint or pronounced? (Are any head markings given emphasis by a thin or broad eye-stripe?). Does it have wingbars or bright patches in the wing, and in flight does it show as a broad wingbar across the whole wing or only part of the way? For some species it is vital to note the colour of hidden parts of the bird while it is settled. On some, the plumage of rump and uppertail-coverts is a critical point to note: Is it uniform with or different from the back and tail, streaked or unstreaked?

It is extremely bad practice and poor fieldcraft to flush a bird just to see an important feature; it may, after all, be a very tired migrant, and any disturbance could be damaging to its chances of survival (and is also not appreciated by others who wish to see the bird). In the identification of the smaller and potentially more confusing waxbills and firefinches, the extent of red on the face or body is critical; with some of the more shy or skulking species the chances of establishing this level of information are fleeting (unless you are very fortunate), so speed and accuracy are essential.

The behaviour of the bird is also a very important clue to its identity. Does it feed mainly on the ground or in vegetation or in the tops of trees? Does it cling to thistle-heads or pine cones, or take grass seeds while on the ground? Does it walk, shuffle or hop (or all three)? Does it keep in flocks or on its own? Does it call frequently or not at all? Does it have a special type of food plant or seed?

It is worth remembering, when identifying a potential wanderer or out-of-range vagrant, that the choice of habitat occupied and the feeding habits may not be at all representative of those of the species within its native range.

Topography

In the descriptions in this book a number of ornithological terms are used. These have been kept to a minimum for ease of reference, and generally follow the system adopted and recommended by Grant and Mullarney (1989) and published in the journal *Birding World*. However, we recognise the cheeks as separate from the ear-coverts, since several species of finch show a distinct mark or patch on the cheeks not found on the ear-coverts. A full glossary of terms will be found on page 483. The drawings on page 14 define the areas of the feather tracts and structural features mentioned in the text.

Plumage Sequences

The way in which full or breeding plumage is acquired is often ignored or misunderstood by those attempting to identify unfamiliar species or individuals. A knowledge of the stages by which full plumage is attained will assist in practically all cases of identification.

BIRD TOPOGRAPHY

HEAD MARKINGS

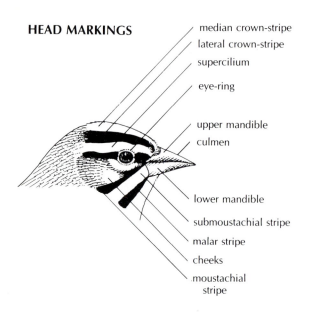

median crown-stripe
lateral crown-stripe
supercilium
eye-ring
upper mandible
culmen
lower mandible
submoustachial stripe
malar stripe
cheeks
moustachial stripe

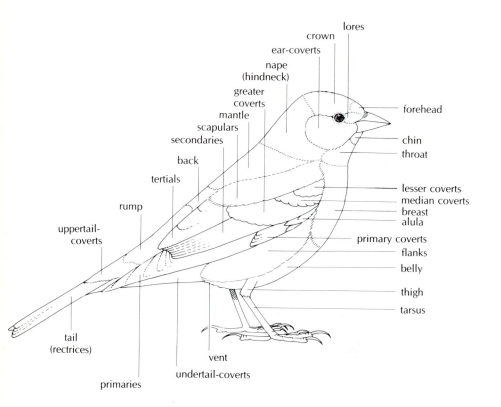

lores
crown
ear-coverts
nape (hindneck)
greater coverts
mantle
scapulars
secondaries
back
tertials
rump
uppertail-coverts
tail (rectrices)
primaries
undertail-coverts
vent
forehead
chin
throat
lesser coverts
median coverts
breast
alula
primary coverts
flanks
belly
thigh
tarsus

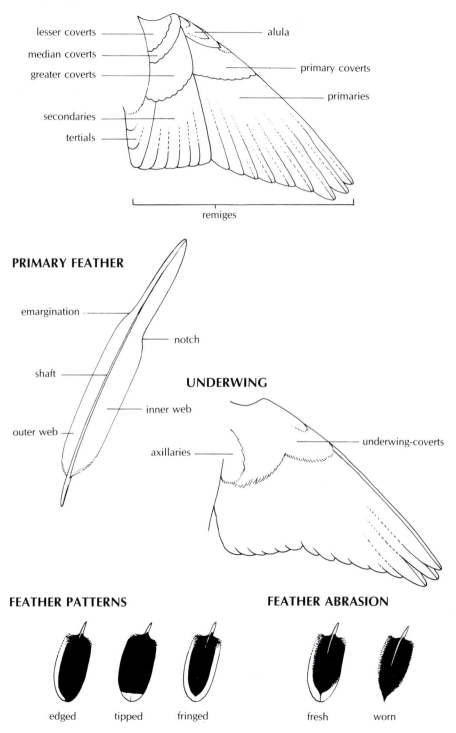

UPPERWING

lesser coverts

median coverts

greater coverts

secondaries

tertials

alula

primary coverts

primaries

remiges

PRIMARY FEATHER

emargination

notch

shaft

inner web

outer web

axillaries

UNDERWING

underwing-coverts

FEATHER PATTERNS

edged   tipped   fringed

FEATHER ABRASION

fresh   worn

The young hatch from the egg naked or covered with a thin layer of fine down, and over the next two to four weeks gradually attain the juvenile plumage. They can fly within a few days of leaving the nest, although they can often be seen still with odd tufts or patches of down on the head and back. The juvenile retains its plumage into the autumn (or non-breeding season for tropical species), and then undergoes a partial moult of body feathers, the median coverts and some or all of the inner greater coverts into first-winter plumage; the strong flight and tail feathers are retained (in Fringillid finches) for up to a full year, although in the south of the range about 5% of juvenile Cardueline finches undergo a complete body and wing moult in their first autumn. In most cases, the first-winter plumage is very similar to that of the juvenile or adult female; in some it may be indistinguishable in the field. In Fringillid finches, the first-summer individual is often recognisable by slightly duller or less complete plumage (or with partially retained pale tips from first winter) than the more brightly coloured adults.

Estrildid finches usually moult from juvenile to adult plumage without any recognisably intermediate stages within a period of six to eight weeks. Some, perhaps most, breed within six months of leaving the nest. In the Fringillid finches and the sparrows, males of most species usually acquire the distinctive characteristics of the plumage through moult or abrasion during their first winter. In some, this will be partial or an incomplete first-summer version of the adult male; others will closely resemble the adult male, but have distinctive pale or dark spots or tips as the last remnant or vestige of first-winter plumage is lost. For some species, particularly the rosefinches *Carpodacus*, fully adult plumage is not attained until the second winter or second summer.

Following the breeding season the adults undergo a full moult, replacing the entire head, body, wing and tail plumage. The flight feathers are replaced sequentially, i.e. one at a time, symmetrically on each wing at the same time, starting with the inner primaries and moving outwards. Soon after the replaced inner primary feathers are full grown, the moult of the secondaries begins from the outermost to the innermost. The tertials may be replaced as a single unit (i.e. they can all be absent from the bird for short periods) during the moult of the secondaries. The tail is moulted from the central feathers outwards, but not always in symmetrical sequence, so birds with missing or partially grown tail feathers may be encountered. Birds in moult are usually recognisable from the presence of both new and old wing and tail feathers.

This final moult results in almost all species having fresh plumage in autumn and winter. In some species, this new plumage has pale edges or tips to the feathers which wear down through the winter to reveal the bright colours for display and courtship at the onset of the breeding season.

Hybrids

Hybrids occurring in the wild between finches or sparrows are rare but not unknown, and hybridisation occurs more frequently in some species pairs (e.g. House x Tree Sparrow) than in others. Some naturally occurring hybrids may show features of either parent or have plumage readily identifiable with neither parent. Hybrids between species of different families are even less likely and, if encountered, are probably the product of aviculture. Hybrids produced by cagebird enthusiasts and practising aviculturists can be the result of more than one hybridised parentage or be a colour variant of a normal species (Greenfinch, Goldfinch etc). Hybrid finches are much more common in captivity than in the wild and many are deliberately produced, with specific crosses or 'mules' created between the most unlikely of species and with the most unlikely or bizarre individuals resulting. This should always be borne in mind when the observer is faced with an individual bearing no resemblance to any naturally occurring species. Female hybrids are particularly difficult to determine and so are more likely to be overlooked or misidentified.

The Problem of Escapes

Finches, particularly Estrildids and to some extent sparrows, are a great favourite with cagebird enthusiasts, and most species of Fringillid and Estrildid finches are (or have been) kept somewhere in captivity. It would be impossible to compile a list of those species which are currently kept in captivity, since this would be somewhat arbitrary and easily become outdated. Recent bans (implemented throughout the world via CITES and in Europe by EC regulations) in the sale or trade of some species has led to their decline (if not total disappearance) from the cagebird markets. However, there is still a considerable trade, particularly in African species from Senegal and Tanzania and in Asiatic species from China. There is also a sizeable black market taking species from the wild illegally to satisfy the demands of aviculture. While this trade concerns particularly the very expensive birds (i.e. those in greatest demand) such as macaws, parrots and birds of prey, it would be naive to think that this did not affect any of the finches or sparrows.

While aviculture does have a part to play in the appreciation of birds at close range and the provision of information on the captive breeding of rare or endangered species, it is in the main conducted in an uncontrolled and uncoordinated fashion, since it is carried out mostly as a hobby or part-time occupation. No records exist anywhere to show comprehensively which species are imported, kept or bred in any country. This clearly presents problems, both for the individual observer when encountering what is ostensibly a great rarity far out of its range, and for the national records committees attempting to compile geographic lists of wild bird sightings. Recent records of Long-tailed Rosefinch *Uragus sibiricus* in Finland and England have given rise to much speculation, but are considered to have concerned escaped birds from captivity. Records involving Pallas's Rosefinch *Carpodacus roseus* may have similar origins, since there is evidence that the species has recently been imported into Europe (Germany); it is also, however, one of the more long-distance migrants among the rosefinches.

Escaped finches and sparrows are not necessarily tame, approachable or ringed, and may, to all appearances, behave as wild individuals. They may also adapt very well to life in the wild (though tropical species invariably fail to survive a severe northern winter), and join flocks of wild finches or sparrows. They may move with them, and even travel considerable distances on their own (even to remote islands) from their points of origin.

Research and Conservation

In some respects research into the relationships of finches and sparrows is urgently required, since there have been numerous attempts to review the families but none has yet arrived at a position agreeable to all taxonomic authorities. It is possible that advances in DNA technology will enable the systematic relationships to be unravelled.

Perhaps more important, in practical terms, is the need for work to be carried out on those species either under threat or about which very little is known. Several species are almost unknown, even to the extent that their nest or eggs have never been found; others have been very little studied in the wild. Some of the high-altitude finches, which spend almost their entire lives in a barren, hostile and often frozen landscape, are very little known, and nothing is known of their abilities to obtain sufficient nourishment or withstand severe cold for long periods. Conversely, some of the Estrildids live on the edge of the hottest deserts, yet we know little of their survival patterns or abilities to cope with droughts.

Conservation of finches, and most sparrows, really concerns the conservation of their habitats. The destruction, depletion and disintegration of habitat, usually for short- or long-term agriculture, has altered or affected the populations of several species. Allied to this are the toxic effects of agricultural dressings, the long-term results of which are only just becoming apparent. In Europe, the decline of once common or abundant species such as the Linnet *Carduelis cannabina* and Tree Sparrow *Passer montanus* caused by modern intensive agriculture has drastically reduced the lowland breeding populations. The live trapping of a number of species continues to give rise to concern: 49 species are listed in the *World Checklist of Threatened Birds* (1990) as being threatened by the trade, and of these at least two (and possibly three) are in acute danger of becoming extinct in the wild. Of the remainder, the continued trapping for food or commercial exploitation will have a cumulative effect on their numbers and distribution with the reduction in habitat, shooting for sporting purposes or the spread of human habitation.

Only those species living in the most remote of the world's remaining wildernesses have yet to feel the effects of man's influence, but for how much longer will they remain unaffected? With this in mind, it is crucial that everyone should support national and international conservation organisations seeking to safeguard both habitats and species. Finches in particular may be helped by subscribing to BirdLife International (Wellbrook Court, Girton Road, Cambridge CB3 0NA, UK) or by joining the Fauna and Flora Preservation Society (1 Kensington Gore, London SW7 2AR, UK).

Rare Species

Several species are considered rare because of their small, fragmentary or restricted distribution, while some are so poorly known or understood that their status is very uncertain. The rarest species is the São Tomé Grosbeak *Neospiza concolor* seen by ornithologists on only four occasions; sightings in 1991 and 1992 were the first for over a hundred years. The population has probably never been high (no more than two have ever been seen together), and any destruction of the rainforest will put its survival severely at risk. In central Ethiopia are three species of serins (and possibly an as yet unnamed fourth) which have very small ranges. One, the Ankober Serin *Serinus ankoberensis* is possibly threatened by the planting of eucalyptus trees for firewood; the other two, Yellow-throated Seedeater and Salvadori's Seedeater *Serinus flavigula* and *S. xantholaema*, are so poorly known as to have no discernible threats.

In South America, the Red Siskin and Yellow-faced Siskin *Carduelis cucullata* and *C. yarrellii* have very restricted ranges and both are considered endangered, the latter has always been very restricted in its distribution, but the former was once widespread. None of the Himalayan or Chinese breeding rosefinches has been well studied, but of them all Przewalski's and Tibetan Rosefinches *Urocynchramus pylzowi* and *Carpodacus roborowskii* remain very rare and extremely little known by western ornithologists. Of the Estrildids, little is known of the Black-faced Waxbill *Estrilda nigriloris*, which has a very small range in central Zaire and for which there are no published records since 1950. In southeast Nigeria, the Anambra Waxbill *E. poliopareia* seems to lead a precarious existence on the banks of the Niger river, as parts of the range are frequently inundated during the annual flooding.

Some of the parrotfinches have extremely small or restricted ranges and some are very rarely recorded by ornithologists. None, however, is as yet threatened by the activities of man, but the depletion of tropical forests on the small Pacific islands for short-term financial gain will seal their fate. The race *malayana* of the Green-tailed Parrotfinch is perhaps as rare as the São Tomé Grosbeak as it remains virtually unknown, having been seen only three times (once when it was collected). None of these species has been studied at all, so it is difficult to propose any conservation measures.

PLATES 1–73

PLATE 1   CHAFFINCHES AND BRAMBLING

1   **Chaffinch** *Fringilla coelebs*   **Text page 165**

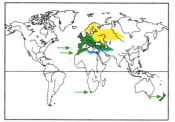

Palearctic (with introductions elsewhere): mostly forest, woods, parks, gardens and hedgerows.

a Adult male breeding plumage: chestnut-brown mantle and back, orange-pink face and underparts; the typical Chaffinch of Europe and the Middle East.

b Adult female breeding plumage: dark grey-brown upperparts, paler grey-brown face and buffish-grey underparts; very little variation throughout the range, some are slightly greyer.

c Adult male: in flight shows broad wingbars and deep green rump.

d Adult male *africana*: pale blue head and face, deep olive-green mantle, back and rump; pale pink underparts.

e Adult male *spodiogenys*: very similar to *africana*, but with blue rump and uppertail-coverts and extensive white wingbars and edges to secondaries and tertials.

f Adult male *maderensis*: deep blue crown and nape, deep green mantle; upper back and rump divided by blue lower back; face to breast pale peach.

g Adult male *moreletti*: very similar to *maderensis* but paler blue; blue lower back and rump, face and underparts pale peach.

h Adult male *tintillon*: dark blue upperparts except for green rump; face to belly pale peachy-buff.

2   **Blue Chaffinch** *Fringilla teydea*   **Text page 167**

Western Canary Islands: pine forest.

a Adult male breeding plumage: entirely slate-blue except for paler wingbars and white undertail-coverts.

b Adult female breeding plumage: brown or dull olive-brown with pale buff wingbars and pale grey underparts.

c Juvenile: slightly darker than adult female.

3   **Brambling** *Fringilla montifringilla*   **Text page 168**

Palearctic, winters discontinuously south to North Africa, the Mediterranean, Iran, northwest India, China and southern Japan: forest, woods and copses, in winter also in fields and scrub.

a Adult male breeding plumage: very striking black and orange with large white rump; lacks white on outer tail feathers.

b Adult male winter: duller than summer, with pale tips to head, nape and upperparts; bill also paler.

c Adult female breeding plumage: similar to non-breeding male, but with browner head and mantle, dull orange scapulars and coverts suffused with brown; large white rump, no white in tail.

d Juvenile: similar to winter female, but browner with pale or buffish-brown tips to head and underparts, pale orange-buff wingbars; rump and underparts tinged dull yellow.

e Adult male: in flight shows large white rump patch; lacks prominent white wingbars of Chaffinch (1).

PLATE 2 EUROPEAN AND ASIAN SERINS

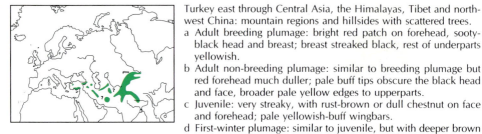

4 Red-fronted Serin *Serinus pusillus*   Text page 170

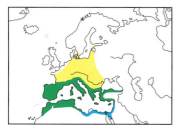

Turkey east through Central Asia, the Himalayas, Tibet and north-west China: mountain regions and hillsides with scattered trees.
a Adult breeding plumage: bright red patch on forehead, sooty-black head and breast; breast streaked black, rest of underparts yellowish.
b Adult non-breeding plumage: similar to breeding plumage but red forehead much duller; pale buff tips obscure the black head and face, broader pale yellow edges to upperparts.
c Juvenile: very streaky, with rust-brown or dull chestnut on face and forehead; pale yellowish-buff wingbars.
d First-winter plumage: similar to juvenile, but with deeper brown on face and heavier streaks edged yellowish-buff on upperparts; breast as adult.

5 Serin *Serinus serinus*   Text page 172

Europe and the Mediterranean to North Africa, Estonia and south-west Russia (Ukraine): hillsides with trees (mainly conifers) parks, gardens, olive groves and edges of cultivation.
a Adult male: small; stubby bill, yellow head and dark-streaked breast, pale yellow wingbars and bright yellow rump.
b Adult female: duller than male, with pale yellow around the face and dull yellow wingbars; underparts heavily streaked.
c Adult male: in flight appears small, with prominent forked tail and bright yellow rump.
d Juvenile: similar to adult female but lacks yellow; rump light olive with dark streaks, wingbars warm buffish-brown.

6 Syrian Serin *Serinus syriacus*   Text page 173

East Mediterranean: lightly wooded (mainly conifers) mountains and hillsides and bushy slopes; in winter in lower-altitude semi-desert thornscrub.
a Adult male: pale yellow and grey with bright yellow face, broad pale yellow wingbars, bright yellow rump; deeply forked tail has yellow edges.
b Adult female: similar to male but duller; paler yellow face, more heavily streaked grey upperparts and slightly streaked flanks.
c Adult male: in flight, shows bright yellow upperparts and tail deeply forked at tip.
d Juvenile: pale buff-brown, warm buff-brown wingbars, yellow edges to flight and tail feathers.

9 Tibetan Siskin *Serinus thibetanus*   Text page 177

Eastern Himalayas to west China: hillsides with forest.
a Adult male: uniform green, with bright yellow supercilium and pale greenish-yellow rump and uppertail-coverts.
b Adult female: duller green than male; streaked crown, mantle and flanks.
c Juvenile: dull olive-green with dark-streaked upperparts; rump dull olive-yellow.

PLATE 3 · AFRICAN SERINS OR CANARIES

7 Canary *Serinus canaria*

Text page 174

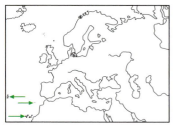

North Atlantic islands (introduced into Bermuda, not shown): valleys, woodland, gardens, orchards and scrub.
a Adult male breeding: grey to greenish-yellow dark-streaked upperparts, yellowish face and dull yellow rump.
b Adult female: greyer than male, with grey-brown mantle and back, dull green rump and slight streaking on flanks.
c Juvenile: pale brown with darker streaks, greenish-yellow forehead, warm buffish-brown wingbars; breast yellowish-buff with dark streaks.

10 Yellow-crowned Canary *Serinus canicollis*

Text page 178

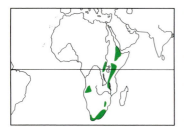

East Africa to eastern South Africa: scattered bushes, grassland, heathland and scrub, also towns and gardens.
a Adult male breeding: crown to mantle grey, yellowish-green rump, face and breast, yellow edges to base of tail.
b Adult female: duller than male, with grey on chin and breast; distinctly streaked on upperparts, more lightly on flanks.
c Juvenile: pale buffish-brown with dark streaks; yellowish wash to underparts, broad pale buff-brown wingbars and yellowish edges to flight feathers.
d Adult male *flavivertex* breeding: much brighter than nominate male (lacks any grey); black wings and broad yellow wingbars.
e Adult female *flavivertex*: duller than male, with greenish tinge.
f Juvenile *flavivertex*: slightly darker than nominate race.
g Adult male *huillensis*: unstreaked golden-yellow; wing-coverts edged pale yellow, bright yellow edges to flight feathers.

21 Yellow-fronted Canary *Serinus mozambicus*

Text page 189

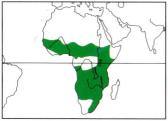

Africa south of the Sahara (with introductions elsewhere, not shown): widely distributed from savannas to scrub, plantations, cultivation and gardens.
a Adult male breeding: distinctive head-and-face pattern (varies among races), bright yellow underparts and rump; tail can appear notched or slightly forked at rest.
b Adult female: upperparts greyer than male, rump yellow, head pattern less well defined.
c Juvenile: similar to adult female, but pale yellow face and breast, dull greenish-yellow rump and spots or streaks on sides of breast.
d Adult male *grotei*: grey crown, poorly defined face pattern.

24 White-bellied Canary *Serinus dorsostriatus*

Text page 193

East Africa, Sudan east to Somalia south to northern Tanzania: open woodland, bushes and thornscrub.
a Adult male breeding: face pattern only lightly defined; white lower belly and flanks diagnostic.
b Adult female breeding: similar to male, but with greenish-olive face and streaks on sides of breast and flanks.

PLATE 4   SOUTH AND EAST AFRICAN CANARIES

15 Forest Canary *Serinus scotops*   **Text page 184**

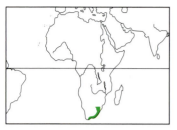

South Africa: highland evergreen forest and thick bush.
a Adult male breeding: variable amount of black on face and chin, otherwise deep green streaked with black; short supercilium and lower throat yellow; short yellow wingbars.
b Adult male breeding: shows variation in extent of black on face.
c Adult female breeding: similar to adult male, but with grey face, streaks on throat and shorter supercilium.
d Juvenile: similar to adult female, but with paler face and underparts and broad yellowish-buff wingbars.

23 Yellow Canary *Serinus flaviventris*   **Text page 192**

South Africa (introduced into St Helena, not shown): semi-arid bush and scrub.
a Adult male breeding: strongly marked head-and-face pattern (southern birds), dark green upperparts and bright yellow underparts.
b Adult female breeding: generally grey with darker streaks; dull greenish rump, face pattern similar to male, underparts whitish-buff streaked with brown.
c Adult female *guillarmodi* breeding: face pattern less heavily defined than nominate, more heavily streaked upperparts.
d Adult male *damarensis*: paler or yellowish upperparts with bright yellow rump and poorly defined face pattern.
e Adult female *damarensis*: paler than nominate female, with yellow on rump and yellowish wingbars.

25 Brimstone Canary *Serinus sulphuratus*   **Text page 194**

Central and southern Africa: scattered trees or bushes, hillsides and edges of forest.
a Adult male breeding: face pattern similar to Yellow Canary (23) but cheek patch more diffuse; larger, with bigger bill, bright yellow wingbars, greenish rump and dull greenish-yellow underparts.
b Adult female breeding: similar to male but duller, with poorly defined face pattern, duller wingbars and pale supercilium.

22 Grosbeak Canary *Serinus donaldsoni*   **Text page 191**

East Africa from southern Ethiopia to northern Tanzania: dry savannas, thornscrub or semi-desert areas.
a Adult male breeding: has similar face pattern to Yellow (23) and Brimstone (25), but pale pink bill, yellow rump, streaked flanks and heavily streaked upperparts are distinctive.
b Adult female: similar to male but green areas replaced with buffish-brown, except for yellow rump and uppertail-coverts.
c Adult male *buchanani* breeding: similar to nominate, but less heavily streaked and lacks face pattern, has a slightly larger bill and is paler with a slightly greener rump.
d Adult female *buchanani* breeding: very similar to male *buchanani* but streaks on breast more extensive.

15a
15b
15c
15d
23a
23b
23c
23d
23e
25a
25b
22a
22b
22c
22d

PLATE 5   EAST AFRICAN SERINS

11 Black-headed Siskin *Serinus nigriceps*

Text page 180

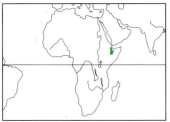

Endemic to Ethiopia: high-altitude grassland and moorland.
a Adult male: distinctive all-black head, bright yellow scapulars and broad pale yellow wingbars.
b Adult female: lacks black head of male except for dark area from forehead to crown; lightly streaked above and below, thinner wingbars than male.
c Juvenile: similar to female, with prominent streaks above and below, dark olive-grey head and pale buffish wingbars.

12 African Citril *Serinus citrinelloides*

Text page 181

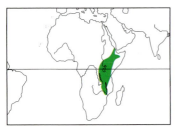

East Africa, Ethiopia to Zimbabwe and northern Mozambique: scrub and secondary growth along edges of lakes, rivers or forest, also plantations and gardens.
a Adult male: black forehead, cheeks, lores and chin; pale yellow thin double wingbar, thin yellow supercilium.
b Adult female: duller than male; dull olive face, short and thin supercilium, more heavily streaked above and below.
c Juvenile: similar to female, but grey-green with pale yellow underparts and buffish-brown wingbars and edges to tertials.
d Adult male *frontalis*: bright yellow from forehead to area over eye.
e Adult male *hypostictus*: black face replaced with dark grey, streaked on throat and breast, lacks supercilium.
f Adult male *brittoni*: differs from all other races in lacking any black on face; very similar to Papyrus Canary (14) but shows thin yellow supercilium and pale yellow double wingbars.

13 Black-faced Canary *Serinus capistratus*

Text page 182

Africa from Gabon to Angola, Zambia and northern Zimbabwe: clearings in evergreen forest, swamps or thickets.
a Adult male: similar to African Citril (12), but has shorter bill, more black on ear-coverts and only faintly streaked underparts.
b Adult female: similar to male, but lacks black face and has some streaks on throat, breast and flanks.
c Juvenile: similar to adult female but paler and more heavily streaked.

14 Papyrus Canary *Serinus koliensis*

Text page 183

Africa, southern Uganda to southwest Kenya and northeast Zaire: papyrus and areas close to papyrus swamps.
a Adult male: very similar above to race *brittoni* of African Citril (12) but lacks supercilium and has dark grey lores and poorly defined wingbars; more heavily streaked underparts and curved ridge to upper mandible.
b Adult female: virtually identical to male but more heavily streaked on underparts; lores grey.

PLATE 6   AFRICAN CANARIES AND SOUTH AFRICAN SERINS

16   White-rumped Seedeater *Serinus leucopygius*   Text page 185

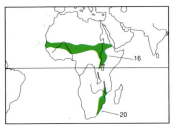

Africa, Senegal to Ethiopia south to Uganda and extreme northeast Zaire: savannas with bushes, woodland, edges of cultivation and gardens.
a Adult: pale grey-brown except for white rump and thin wingbar.
b Juvenile: similar to adult or slightly warmer brown, has more streaks or spots on underparts.
c Adult *riggenbachi*: slightly greyer than nominate, with whiter underparts and distinct brown spots.

17   Yellow-rumped Seedeater *Serinus atrogularis*   Text page 185

East and South Africa: dry-country habitats from thornscrub to open broadleaved woodland, orchards, cultivation and parkland.
a Adult: small and grey-brown; distinctive bright yellow rump, thin pale supercilium, pale buff double wingbars and light buff-brown underparts.
b Juvenile: similar to adult but warmer buff-brown; chin and throat whitish with dark spots, becoming streaks on breast.
c Adult *riechenowi*: browner upperparts than nominate; pale or creamy forehead and supercilium, pale chin and throat, brown spots on breast.
d Adult *xanthopygius*: greyer than nominate; generally lacks any streaks on underparts, chin and throat off-white.

20   Lemon-breasted Canary *Serinus citrinipectus*   Text page 188

Southeast Africa, Malawi to Natal: palm savannas, dry woodland, scrub, grassland and edges of cultivation. Map above.
a Adult male: small, with distinctive face pattern; rump yellow, as is area from chin to breast (may be absent on latter), thin whitish double wingbar.
b Adult female: very similar to male, but paler face pattern, and yellow underparts replaced by pinkish-buff on flanks.

37   Cape Siskin *Serinus totta*   Text page 205

South Africa, Cape Province: macchia scrub and protea bushes of woodland edges and clearings in mountains and rocky hills.
a Adult male: dark brown upperparts, yellowish-brown forehead and olive-yellow face; white tips to flight feathers, tertials and tail.
b Adult female: as male but lacks grey on head; forehead and area from face to breast more streaked.

38   Drakensberg Siskin *Serinus symonsi*   Text page 206

South Africa, east Cape Province to western Natal: valleys, hillsides and grassland of the Drakensberg range.
a Adult male: similar to Cape Siskin (37) (but isolated); lacks white tips to wing or tail, underparts duller or tinged green.
b Adult female: similar to male, but with warm brown head and orange-buff underparts; slight streaking on head and breast.
c Juvenile: similar to female but more heavily streaked.

PLATE 7   AFRICAN CANARIES (1)

26 White-throated Canary *Serinus albogularis*   **Text page 195**

Africa, Angola to South Africa: karoo grassland and dry veld with bush and scrub.
a Adult: fairly large, with prominent bill; drab grey, with white chin and throat and yellow or greenish-yellow rump.
b Juvenile: similar to adult, but browner and more heavily streaked above and on breast.

27 Streaky-headed Seedeater *Serinus gularis*   **Text page 196**

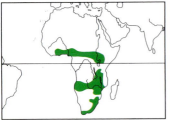

East and South Africa: dry *Brachystegia* woodland, scrub, savanna, edges of cultivation, orchards and gardens.
a Adult: finely streaked crown, broad white supercilium, dark face, white chin and throat; rump plain brown.
b Juvenile: less prominently streaked on crown, paler supercilium, duller than adult; heavily streaked underparts.
c Adult *reichardi*: greyer upperparts, browner face and prominent streaks on pale buff underparts.
d Adult *humilis*: warm buff-brown underparts lack any streaks.

28 Black-eared Canary *Serinus mennelli*   **Text page 198**

Southern Africa, southeast Zaire and southern Tanzania to Zimbabwe and northern Mozambique: dry *Brachystegia* woodland, coastal forest, edges of cultivation and gardens.
a Adult male: crown streaked finely black and white, broad white supercilium and black face; rump grey.
b Juvenile: similar to adult but face brown; underparts heavily streaked.

29 Brown-rumped Seedeater *Serinus tristriatus*   **Text page 199**

East Africa, Ethiopia to northern Somalia: montane scrub, edges of woodland and large gardens.
a Adult: almost entirely brown except for slight streaking on crown; short white supercilium and white chin and throat.
b Juvenile: similar to adult, but with darker streaks on mantle and underparts also streaked.

PLATE 8   AFRICAN CANARIES (2)

36 Protea Canary *Serinus leucopterus*

Text page 204

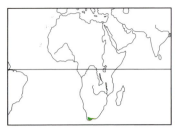

South Africa, endemic to southwest Cape Province: protea bushes and woods in mountains.
    Adult: generally grey-brown; large pale bill, black chin and white throat, faint supercilium and lightly streaked underparts.

33 Streaky Seedeater *Serinus striolatus*

Text page 201

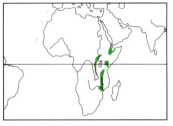

East Africa, Sudan and Ethiopia to northern Zimbabwe: open country, forest or woodland edges, thickets, scrub or edges of cultivation.
a Adult: distinctive head pattern, broad buffish-white supercilium, dark-streaked upperparts and heavily streaked underparts.
b Juvenile: duller than adult, with pale buff streaks on crown and thinner streaks on buffish underparts.
c Adult *whytii*: supercilium, face, sides of neck, chin and throat yellow; edges to flight feathers greenish-yellow.

34 Thick-billed Seedeater *Serinus burtoni*

Text page 202

Central Africa, Cameroon to central Kenya south to southern Tanzania, also in central Angola: high-level forest, bush, open hillsides, grassland with scattered bushes above the tree line.
a Adult: distinctive size and shape; huge bill; generally dark olive-brown, large pale spot on (sides of) forehead, buffish-white double wingbars.
b Juvenile: similar to adult but paler brown; forehead, lores, chin and throat whitish, bill blackish.
c Adult *tanganjicae*: very little (if any) white on forehead, smaller and browner bill than nominate.
d Adult *melanochrous*: smaller, less black, lacks any white on forehead; no green edges to flight feathers and no wingbars, but has heavily streaked underparts.

35 Principé Seedeater *Serinus rufobrunneus*

Text page 203

São Tomé and Principé Islands: forest, dry woodland and plantations to edges of towns and villages.
a Adult: generally warm cinnamon-brown with stout bill; appears short-tailed.
b Adult *thomensis*: greyer-brown than nominate, with pale buffish lower throat and whitish undertail-coverts.

PLATE 9   EAST AFRICAN ENDEMICS AND LINNET

30 **Ankober Serin** *Serinus ankoberensis*   **Text page 199**

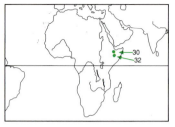

Extremely restricted endemic to the highlands of central Ethiopia: open areas of grass and low vegetation among hill or clifftop boulders.

Adult: heavily streaked on head, face and body, paler cheeks, dark brown wings and tail; fine Linnet-like bill.

31 **Yellow-throated Seedeater** *Serinus flavigula*   **Text page 200**

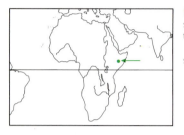

Extremely restricted endemic to southern Ethiopia:
semi-arid desert scrub, hillsides with scattered acacias and thornbush.

Adult: pale grey-brown with dull yellow rump and pale yellow spot on throat, faintly streaked breast, off-white underparts.

32 **Salvadori's Seedeater** *Serinus xantholaema*   **Text page 201**

Extremely rare endemic to southern Ethiopia: semi-arid desert wadis, dry streambeds, scattered acacias, thornbush and scrub. Map above.

Adult: similar to Yellow-throated Seedeater (31), but has white forehead and face, brighter yellow rump and distinctively marked yellow throat with black at edges.

74 **Warsangli Linnet** *Carduelis johannis*   **Text page 251**

Scarce endemic to northern Somalia: high-altitude juniper forest, woodland and scrub.
a Adult male: pale grey upperparts except for rufous-brown upper rump and white lower rump, white supercilium; white lower face and underparts except for rufous-brown lower flanks; thin white panel in wing.
b Adult female: similar to male, but rufous areas paler and upperparts visibly streaked.
c Juvenile: generally pale buffish-brown, with dark to brownish streaks; scapulars fringed warm brown, wings as adult but with buff-brown tips to coverts and edges to tertials; heavily streaked from breast to flanks.

72 **Linnet** *Carduelis cannabina*   **Text page 249**

Palearctic and marginally Oriental: heaths and commons, open areas of hills, moors and areas of gorse, also edges of cultivation, gardens, orchards, plantations.
a Adult male breeding: grey head, warm brown mantle and back, crimson forehead and breast patch; white flash in open wing.
b Adult female breeding: duller brown than male, with darker streaks; pale face and underparts streaked dark brown.
c Adult male non-breeding: duller than in summer, with darker bases to head and upperpart feathers; lacks any crimson on forehead or breast.
d Juvenile: similar to female but generally warm buff-brown, streaked darker brown above and below.

PLATE 10 EUROPEAN AND ASIAN GREEN FINCHES

49 Siskin *Carduelis spinus*

Text page 219

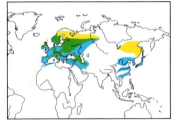

Palearctic and Oriental: forest and conifer woodland, also birch; in winter also heaths, commons, weedy areas, plantations and gardens.

a Adult male: black cap and chin; wingbars and sides to base of tail bright yellow.

b Adult female: lacks black cap and chin; heavily streaked grey-green; underparts dull yellowish, streaked blackish.

c Adult male: in flight, shows bright yellow wingbars, rump and sides to base of tail.

d Juvenile: similar to adult female, but generally buff-brown with dark streaks, pale buff supercilium and warm buff wingbars.

8 Citril Finch *Serinus citrinella*

Text page 175

West and southern-central Europe: subalpine conifer forest, woods and meadows.

a Adult male: grey crown and nape, greyish-green upperparts with paler greenish-yellow rump, broad bright yellowish double wing-bars, face yellowish-green.

b Adult female: duller or darker than male, more grey-green with indistinct streaks on upperparts, thinner wingbars.

c Juvenile: buffish-brown, paler around the eye; warm buff-brown wingbars and dark streaks on underparts.

d Adult male *corsicanus*: mantle, back and scapulars deep brown with indistinct dark streaks; underparts brighter yellow.

44 Greenfinch *Carduelis chloris*

Text page 212

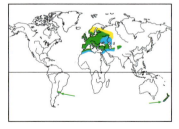

Palearctic (with introductions elsewhere): woods, farms, orchards, hedgerows, plantations, gardens, scrub and weedy areas.

a Adult male: extensive yellow edges to primaries; greater coverts and edges to secondaries and tertials grey; yellow sides to base of tail.

b Adult female: duller than male; grey-brown upperparts and coverts; alula, primary coverts and primaries finely edged pale yellow, less yellow at sides of base of tail.

c Juvenile: buffish head and upperparts and sandy-buff tips to coverts and edges to tertials; yellow in wing as adults; streaked underparts, bill dull or dingy pink.

d First-summer male: as adult, but duller upperparts and brown tinge to underparts.

e First-winter female: almost entirely dull buff-brown, lacking any visible tinges of green; bill dull. Males separable from females by extent of yellow on primaries and outer tail feathers.

49a

49b

49c

49d

8a

8b

8c

8d

44a

44b

44c

44d

44e

J.D.

PLATE 11   EASTERN GREENFINCHES AND MOUNTAIN SERIN

45 Oriental Greenfinch *Carduelis sinica*

Text page 214

East Palearctic: conifer or broadleaved forest, woods on hillsides or in valleys, also scrub, bushes, rice-fields and orchards.
a Adult male: forehead deep olive-green, crown to nape dark grey or dark olive, bright yellow flash in wing and at base of tail, secondaries broadly edged white.
b Adult female: duller than male, with uniform dark head, indistinct dark centres to duller brown mantle and back.
c Juvenile: pale head, nape and streaked underparts, pale brown mantle and back with indistinct darker streaks.

46 Himalayan Greenfinch *Carduelis spinoides*

Text page 216

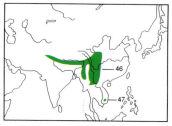

Palearctic and Oriental: broadleaved or conifer forest, rhododendrons, open hillsides with scattered trees, edges of cultivation and gardens.
a Adult male: diagnostic dark olive and yellow face pattern, bright yellow wing flash, yellow rump and underparts.
b Adult female: paler or duller than male, with indistinct dark streaks to upperparts, less yellow at sides of tail.
c Juvenile: similar to juvenile Oriental Greenfinch (45), but lacks warm buff tone to mantle and back, has pale yellow tips to coverts and lacks extensive white edges to secondaries.

47 Vietnamese Greenfinch *Carduelis monguilloti*

Text page 218

Central Vietnam: open woods, forest edges, pine woods and secondary growth, edges of cultivation and gardens. Map above.
a Adult male: black head and face (nape can also be dark), bright yellow rump, yellow median coverts and wing flash.
b Adult female: as male, but more olive, less yellow in wing, dark olive on sides of breast and flanks.

48 Black-headed Greenfinch *Carduelis ambigua*

Text page 218

Southeast Palearctic and Oriental: open conifer and deciduous woodland, open hillsides, forest clearings and meadows.
a Adult male: dark head, pale yellowish rump and pale grey tips to greater coverts; broad yellow base to flight feathers.
b Adult female: as male but paler or duller; head and face blackish-olive, flanks tinged pale buff-brown.
c Juvenile: similar to juvenile Himalayan Greenfinch (46) but darker, with warmer buff wingbars and broad yellow base to flight feathers.

40 Mountain Serin *Serinus estherae*

Text page 208

Parts of Malaysia, Indonesia and the Philippines: alpine and subalpine grassland and meadows with scrub and scattered bushes.
a Adult male: yellow forehead and around eyes, yellow wingbars, rump and breast; spotted underparts, curved ridge to bill.
b Adult female: paler than male, with less yellow on head.
c Adult male *mindanensis*: yellow forehead, chin and throat.
d Adult male *renatae*: yellow on forehead, wingbars and rump.
e Adult female *renatae*: as male, but yellow replaced with bright orange.

45a

45c

45b

46c

46a

46b

47a

47b

48a

40a

40c

48b

40b

40d

AH.

48c

40e

PLATE 12   GOLDFINCHES

68 Goldfinch *Carduelis carduelis*

Text page 240

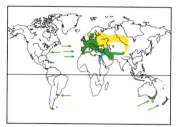

Palearctic and marginally Oriental (with introductions elsewhere): wide variety of habitats, woodland, plantations, cultivated areas, orchards, gardens and weedy patches.

a Adult male: very distinctive; red on face extends slightly behind eye.

b Adult female: as male, but red on face extends only to eye.

c Juvenile: generally pale brown with darker streaks or spots; wings as adult, but with buff-brown tips to coverts, tertials and flight feathers.

d Adult male *parva*: slightly darker upperparts than nominate, with extensive white underparts.

e Adult male *caniceps*: crown to mantle, back and scapulars grey; lacks white sides to crown and face; outer webs of tertials broadly white.

f Adult male *paropanisi*: similar to *caniceps* but paler or whiter on face and underparts; has longer bill than other races.

65 American Goldfinch *Carduelis tristis*

Text page 236

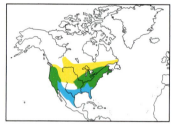

North America: variety of open and woodland habitats, edges of cultivation, weedy areas, gardens and roadside verges.

a Adult male summer: bright yellow; black cap, wings and tail, white wingbars, rump, uppertail- and undertail-coverts.

b Adult female summer: dull green or olive-yellow upperparts and paler or brighter yellow below; white double wingbar.

c Adult male winter: similar to female; black cap obscured by olive-green tips, upperparts brown but rump whitish.

d Adult female winter: dull brown crown and upperparts, face greenish-olive, wingbars and edges to flight feathers buffish; chin pale greenish-yellow, underparts greyish.

e Juvenile: warm brown upperparts, pale buff rump, black wings and buffish-white wingbars, yellowish face and underparts.

67 Lawrence's Goldfinch *Carduelis lawrencei*

Text page 239

Southwest USA: dry chaparral country, grassy slopes, canyons with open oak or pine woods.

a Adult male summer: black forehead, chin and throat, grey face and body, greenish-olive mantle and bright yellow rump and breast; broad yellow wingbars and edges to tertials.

b Adult male winter: similar to summer but greenish-olive on mantle more extensive; wingbars more extensive and greenish.

c Adult female summer: similar to male but lacks black on head; mantle pale brown, underparts and wingbars duller or paler.

d Adult female winter: head and upperparts buffish-brown, underparts duller.

e Juvenile: similar to winter female, but has buff-brown wingbars and lightly streaked underparts.

PLATE 13   NORTH AND SOUTH AMERICAN FINCHES

66   Dark-backed Goldfinch *Carduelis psaltria*

Text page 238

North America south to Ecuador and northern Peru: dry open country, lowlands and foothills, woodland, brush, scrub and farms.
a Adult male summer: glossy black upperparts; wingbar and edges to primaries and tertials white, inner webs to tail also white.
b Adult male *hesperophila* ('green-backed') summer: crown black, pale yellowish double wingbar.
c Adult female: similar to male *hesperophila* but lacks black cap; white wingbars.
d Juvenile: upperparts dark-streaked; buff-brown wingbars and small patch of white on edge of primaries.
e First-winter male ('black-backed'): transitional, with black adult plumage showing through.

50   Pine Siskin *Carduelis pinus*

Text page 221

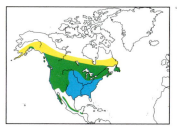

North America south to Guatemala: conifer forest, mixed woods, plantations, thickets and shrubs.
a Adult: extent and intensity of yellow in wing and at base of tail very variable among individuals.
b Adult: in flight, shows broad pale wingbar, dark rump and deeply forked tail.
c Juvenile: as adult, but buffish-brown edges to upperparts and pale buff wingbars.

54   Red Siskin *Carduelis cucullata*

Text page 225

Northern Venezuela and Colombia: forest, dry scrub and grassy areas with scattered trees.
a Adult male: distinctive black and vermilion; white or off-white tips to tertials.
b Adult female: grey from head to back; rump and wingbars bright vermilion, orange-red sides to breast.

58   Saffron Siskin *Carduelis siemiradzkii*

Text page 230

Endemic to Ecuador: lowland humid deciduous forest and woods, brush and dry scrub.
a Adult male: bright saffron-yellow underparts, wingbar, base of primaries, rump and sides to base of tail.
b Adult female: lacks black on head, duller than male; lower belly and vent white, undertail-coverts pale yellow.

PLATE 14   CENTRAL AND SOUTH AMERICAN SISKINS (1)

60 Black-headed Siskin *Carduelis notata*   **Text page 231**

Middle America, central Mexico to Nicaragua: conifer and oak forest, lower edges of cloud forest.

a Adult male: extensive black from head to centre of breast, golden-yellow collar.

b Adult female: less extensive black on head and throat, yellow in wing duller and less extensive.

c Juvenile: lacks black head; has duller upperparts and less yellowish rump, smaller wingbars, and less extensive yellow on base of primaries and sides to base of tail.

55 Thick-billed Siskin *Carduelis crassirostris*   **Text page 226**

Andes of central South America: woodland and shrubs of high Andean steppes and hillsides.

a Adult male: large bill; breast and sides of neck yellow, black head, white belly to undertail-coverts.

b Adult female: duller than male, with dark grey head; lacks bright yellow breast, has dull olive rump.

56 Hooded Siskin *Carduelis magellanica*   **Text page 228**

South America: woods, groves or plantations, edges of cultivation, scrub, parks and large gardens from coastal lowlands to tropical and subtropical zones.

a Adult male: black from head to upper breast; thin yellow collar and yellow underparts, wingbars, rump and sides to base of tail.

b Adult female: dull olive with dull yellow wingbars, brighter on rump and sides to base of tail; greenish-yellow breast and flanks; belly and undertail-coverts whitish.

59 Olivaceous Siskin *Carduelis olivacea*   **Text page 231**

South America: Ecuador to northern Peru and Bolivia:
forest edges and clearings of the subtropical zone.

a Adult male: very similar (if not identical) to *capitalis* race of Hooded Siskin (56, not illustrated, separated on altitude and habitat occupation); smaller, with slightly streaked mantle and back, and less or generally no yellow collar across nape.

b Adult female: very similar to female Hooded Siskin (56), but has brighter yellow rump and yellow (or olive-yellow) underparts.

c Juvenile: darker or dull green; darker-streaked than adult, with dull yellow wingbars, rump and underparts.

60a

60b

60c

55a

55b

56a

56b

59b

59c

59a

J. D.

PLATE 15   CENTRAL AND SOUTH AMERICAN SISKINS (2)

61 Yellow-bellied Siskin *Carduelis xanthogastra*

Text page 232

Central and northern South America: tropical and subtropical forest edges, clearings and pastures.
a Adult male: all black except for yellow base to flight feathers, sides of tail and underparts.
b Adult female: dull olive-green with warmer yellow underparts; tips to wing-coverts paler olive or greenish-yellow.

51 Black-capped Siskin *Carduelis atriceps*

Text page 223

Southern Mexico to northern Guatemala: forest, clearings, pastures and edges of cultivation.
a Adult male: black cap and chin, slightly paler rump than upperparts and small amount of yellow in wing.
b Adult female: much duller or more dusky than male; some streaks on mantle, back, throat and breast.
c Juvenile: duller than female; indistinctly streaked below, yellowish tips to coverts and yellow bases to flight feathers.

63 Yellow-rumped Siskin *Carduelis uropygialis*

Text page 234

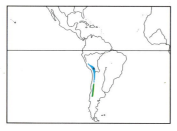

Central and southern South America: tropical- and temperate-zone mountain slopes, woodland, ravines and edges of cultivation.
a Adult male: green or olive-yellow edges to black upperparts; bright yellow rump and sides to base of tail, yellow wingbars and edges to flight feathers and yellow underparts.
b Adult female: as male, but duller or blackish-brown with broader pale edges to upperparts, underparts duller or paler.

62 Black Siskin *Carduelis atrata*

Text page 234

Andes from central Peru to western Argentina: high Andean steppes, puna grassland, rocky slopes, crags, gullies and hillsides.
a Adult male: very obvious black and yellow; pale or abraded tips to secondaries and tertials in worn plumage.
b Adult female: as male but sooty- or blackish-brown; some birds show yellowish tips to median coverts.

61a

61b

51a

51b

51c

63a

63b

62a

62b

J.D.

PLATE 16   CARIBBEAN AND SOUTH AMERICAN SISKINS

57 Antillean Siskin *Carduelis dominicensis*   **Text page 229**

Hispaniola: mountain pine forest.
a Adult male: black head, pale bill, uniform upperparts and underparts; rump and base of tail brighter yellow.
b Adult female: dull olive upperparts, rump paler, pale or dull yellowish wingbars; pale underparts streaked dark brown.
c Juvenile: dark olive, indistinctly streaked above and below; pale buff or yellowish-buff wingbars.

53 Yellow-faced Siskin *Carduelis yarrellii*   **Text page 225**

Northern Brazil: lowland humid forest, woodland and edges of plantations.
a Adult male: black crown; bright yellow face, underparts, wingbars, rump and sides to base of tail.
b Adult female: similar to male, but lacks black crown and is duller yellow.

52 Andean Siskin *Carduelis spinescens*   **Text page 223**

Northern South America: subtropical and paramo zones in scrub, low bushes, elfin forest and open hillsides.
a Adult male: similar to Yellow-faced Siskin (53), but duller (lacks bright yellow) with less extensive black cap and slightly more yellow in wing.
b Adult female: lacks black cap; olive-green with greenish-yellow wingbars and less yellow in wing than male.

64 Black-chinned Siskin *Carduelis barbata*   **Text page 235**

Southern South America, southern Chile to Cape Horn and Falklands: forest, thickets, open country with vegetation, gardens and roadsides.
a Adult male: black from cap to chin and upper throat; bright yellow sides to neck and underparts, bright greenish-yellow rump, thin yellow wingbars and leading edge to primaries.
b Adult female: lacks black from chin to crown; duller green than male, with pale greenish-yellow breast, belly whitish.
c Juvenile: similar to adult female but paler; more streaks on upperparts and pale buffish-yellow wingbars.

57a

57b

57c

53a

52b

52a

53b

64a

64c

64b

J.D.

PLATE 17   REDPOLLS AND TWITE

69 Common Redpoll *Carduelis flammea*   **Text page 242**

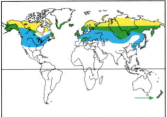

Holarctic (with introductions elsewhere): woodland, plantations, large gardens, dwarf birch, willow thickets.

a Adult male *cabaret* breeding: streaked brown, pink breast, pointed bill; flanks heavily streaked.

b Adult male *cabaret* non-breeding: paler and less heavily streaked than in summer, broad pale buff wingbars, rump brown.

c Adult female *cabaret* breeding: as male, but no pink on face and less on breast and rump; less heavily streaked underparts.

d Adult female *cabaret* non-breeding: as non-breeding male, but duller buffish-brown and no pink tips to breast.

e Juvenile: pale head and face, upperparts as non-breeding adult female.

f Adult male *flammea* breeding: slightly larger and paler (or frosted with grey) than *cabaret*; pale pink rump and white wingbars.

g Adult female *flammea* breeding: as male but lacks pink.

h Adult female *flammea* non-breeding: paler than in summer; whitish-grey rump with variable dark streaks, mantle and flanks tinged with buff.

i Adult female *rostrata* non-breeding: larger version of (d), but with heavier streaks and buff-brown, darker-streaked rump.

70 Arctic Redpoll *Carduelis hornemanni*   **Text page 245**

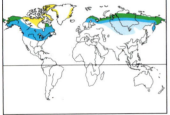

Holarctic: arctic tundra and stunted trees, bushes, willows, dwarf birch and low-spreading shrubs.

a Adult male breeding: pale grey above with white rump, white below, faintly streaked flanks, pink tinge to breast and rump.

b Adult male non-breeding: similar to summer male but whiter on face and upperparts; no pink tinge.

c Adult female breeding: as breeding male but lacks pink tinge; some streaks on flank.

d Adult male *exilipes* non-breeding: variably similar to both nominate *hornemanni* and *flammea* race of Common Redpoll (69); small bill, white rump and unstreaked undertail-coverts.

e Adult female *exilipes* non-breeding: as male, but never shows pink on breast or rump.

71 Twite *Carduelis flavirostris*   **Text page 246**

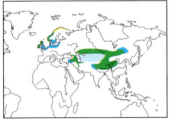

Palearctic to central China: open hillsides, moorlands, mountains and high plateaux; lower in winter to river valleys and the coast.

a Adult male breeding: deep pink rump, underparts dark-streaked.

b Adult male non-breeding: warm buff underparts, pale bill, dull pinkish rump.

c Adult female breeding: as breeding male but rump dark, less white to edge of primaries.

d Juvenile: as female but paler, with broad rich buff wingbar.

e Adult male *montanella* breeding: very pale buff above, whitish below, variably pink rump.

f Adult male *brevirostris* breeding: darker upperparts than *montanella*, with broad dark streaks on sides of breast.

PLATE 18   ARABIAN ENDEMICS

73 Yemen Linnet *Carduelis yemenensis*   **Text page 250**

Arabia: dry mountains, plateaux and hillsides, wadis with rock or scree.
a Adult male breeding: grey head and breast, pale greyish rump and uppertail-coverts; sides of breast and flanks warm brown.
b Adult female breeding: as male but paler; mantle, back and scapulars finely dark-streaked, pale brown on sides of breast and flanks.
c Juvenile: very streaky on head, upperparts and from breast to flanks; pale buff-brown tips to wing-coverts, white primary patch as adults.

18 Arabian Serin *Serinus rothschildi*   **Text page 187**

Arabia: open rocky country with sparse vegetation, shrubs and well-wooded areas.
Adult: very similar to Yemen Serin (19), but greyer, with stouter bill (curved culmen), dull grey-brown breast and poorly defined olive rump; lacks any moustachial streak.

19 Yemen Serin *Serinus menachensis*   **Text page 188**

Arabia: dry stony areas, hillsides and cliffs. Map above.
Adult: very similar to Arabian Serin (18) but paler on underparts; pale area above and below eye, pale cheeks and indistinct dark moustachial stripe; straighter culmen ridge than Arabian Serin, and lacks any pale olive on rump.

180 Arabian Waxbill *Estrilda rufibarba*   **Text page 372**

Arabia: dry wadis, rocky hillsides with thick scrub, thickets or patches of reeds and tamarisk.
a Adult: very distinctive within range; red mask through eye, finely vermiculated above and below, cheeks whitish, warm buff tinge to underparts.
b Juvenile: as adult, but tinged with brown on upperparts, and mask through eye black.

43 Golden-winged Grosbeak *Rhynchostruthus socotranus*

Text page 211

Arabia and extreme northeast Africa (Somalia):
montane wadis, rocky outcrops, acacias, juniper forest and euphorbias.
a Adult male breeding: sooty-black head with whitish ear-coverts, bright golden flash in wing and at sides of tail.
b Adult female breeding: as male, but head dark brown, paler upperparts and less extensive yellow in tail.
c Juvenile: very streaky above and below, pale buff wingbars with yellowish tips, yellow edges to secondaries and sides of tail.
d Adult male *percivali* breeding: brown crown, black from lores to chin; warm gingery-brown throat.
e Adult male *louisae*: dark brown cap, black from lores to chin; pale area below eye.

73a

73b

73c

18

180a

180b

19

43a

43d

43e

43b

43c

AH.

PLATE 19 DESERT, TRUMPETER AND CRIMSON-WINGED FINCHES

79 Crimson-winged Finch *Rhodopechys sanguinea* **Text page 258**

Morocco, central Turkey and Middle East to northwest China: mountains, rocky slopes and boulder fields, scattered scrub.
a Adult male breeding: blackish cap, extensive pink in wings, rump and face, black centres to breast feathers; large pale yellow bill.
b Adult female breeding: duller than male; lacks pink (or pink obscured) on face and rump, less pink in wing.
c Adult male *aliena* breeding: as nominate male, but nape grey, chin and throat white, breast warm brown.

82 Desert Finch *Rhodopechys obsoleta* **Text page 262**

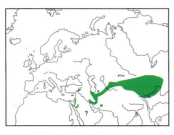

Southeast Turkey, Middle East to western China and Mongolia: dry plains, semi-desert scrub, oases and saxaul stands.
a Adult male breeding: pale sandy-brown, black lores, pink coverts and base of flight feathers, white edges to primaries and outer tail feathers.
b Adult female breeding: as male, but lacks black lores, slightly less pink in wing and flight feathers brownish-black.
c Juvenile: as adult female, but often with very little pink in wing; straw-yellow bill with dark tip.

80 Trumpeter Finch *Rhodopechys githaginea* **Text page 260**

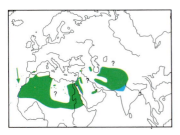

Canary Islands, North Africa, Middle East to Central Asia and northern Pakistan: mountain slopes, dry stony plains, semi-desert wadis, cliffs or hills.
a Adult male breeding: greyish head, bright pink tinge to body and wings, waxy orange-red bill.
b Adult female breeding: pale grey or sandy-grey, with pale (or faint) pink tips to wing-coverts, sides of base of tail, chin and throat; bill pale yellow.
c Adult male non-breeding: very similar to breeding female, but with slightly more pink edges to wing and tail feathers and underparts.
d Juvenile: very similar to breeding female but lacks any pink; pale buffish-brown panel in wing and dull yellowish bill.

81 Mongolian Trumpeter Finch *Rhodopechys mongolica* **Text page 261**

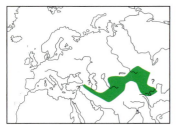

Eastern Turkey to Central Asia, Kashmir, western and northern China, Mongolia: mountainous areas of dry desert, semi-arid scrub or rocky slopes.
a Adult male breeding: similar to male Trumpeter Finch (80), but with frosted white bases to greater coverts and secondaries, grey crown, mantle and back and dull greyish-yellow bill.
b Adult female breeding: similar to male, but with less pink and frosted white in wing; pale whitish-grey underparts.
c Adult male non-breeding: similar to breeding female, but with pink wash to underparts.
d Juvenile: very similar to juvenile Trumpeter Finch (80), with duller bill, darker brown centres to tertials and pinkish-brown edges to primaries.

PLATE 20   MOUNTAIN AND SNOW FINCHES

75 Hodgson's Mountain Finch *Leucosticte nemoricola*   Text page 252

Northern Pakistan, Himalayas to western China: open hillsides and mountainous plateaux to edges of cultivation.

a Adult breeding: sparrow-like size and shape; dark brown with paler streaking, slight supercilium, thin white or creamy-buff wingbars.

b Juvenile: paler or warmer brown than adult; broad wingbars paler or whitish-buff.

76 Brandt's Mountain Finch *Leucosticte brandti*   Text page 253

Central Asia and northern Pakistan to northwest China and Mongolia: high-altitude cliffs, crags, slopes or barren plateaux.

a Adult male breeding: sooty-black head, pale or dingy grey body and edges to wings, lightly streaked upperparts, pale pink lesser coverts and rump.

b Adult non-breeding: pale or buffish-brown with dark brown tips to head and mantle, pink only on tips of rump and lesser-covert feathers; pale buff edges to wings, pale yellow base to bill.

c Juvenile: similar to non-breeding adult, but paler or warm buff-brown, lacks any pink and has dull yellowish bill.

d Adult *haematopygia* breeding: extensively blackish-brown on head and upperparts, dull underparts; pink on median coverts and rump often obscured by paler (medians) or darker feather bases.

284 Snow Finch *Montifringilla nivalis*   Text page 475

Northwest and northeast Spain discontinuously east to Central Asia and western China: high mountains, passes, snow-fields and alpine slopes.

a Adult male breeding: grey head, black bib, rich brown mantle and scapulars, extensive white in wing, distinctive tail pattern (see text).

b Adult male non-breeding: pale chin with dark feather tips, bill yellow with black tip.

c Adult female breeding: as male but bib less well defined; often shows dark bases to medians.

d Juvenile: similar to non-breeding adult, but has buffish-brown head; pale grey chin and white in wing tinged with buff or sandy-buff.

e Adult male *alpicola* breeding: paler than nominate, with grey-brown head, mantle and scapulars; face slightly darker, with more solid black bib, underparts whitish.

285 Adams's Snow Finch *Montifringilla adamsi*   Text page 476

Kashmir to Nepal (Himalayas) and northwest China: barren mountaintops, plateaux and boulder fields.

a Adult breeding: similar to race *alpicola* of Snow Finch (284), but smaller, shows less white in wing, duller underparts, sandy-buff in outer tail feathers and all-black bill.

b Juvenile: similar to adult, but more buff-brown, lacks black bib and white inner secondaries, has pale yellow base to bill.

PLATE 21   SNOW FINCHES

287 Père David's Snow Finch Montifringilla davidiana   Text page 478

Russian Altai to Mongolia and northwestern China:
high-altitude plateau-lands, semi-steppe plains, deserts or valleys.
a Adult: pale brown or sandy-brown; forehead to lores and bib
   black; white bases to primary coverts, white or greyish outer tail
   feathers.
b Juvenile: similar to adult but paler, lacks black on face and bib;
   sandy-buff edges to wings and outer tail feathers.

286 Mandelli's Snow Finch *Montifringilla taczanowskii*   Text page 477

Tibet and western China: high stony plateaux, deserts and barren
steppes.
a Adult: generally pale, with dark brown streaks from mantle to
   scapulars, blackish lores on pale head, large white rump.
b Juvenile: darker or more sandy-brown than adult; pale sandy-buff
   edges to wings and pale buff tips to greater coverts.

288 Red-necked Snow Finch *Montifringilla ruficollis*   Text page 479

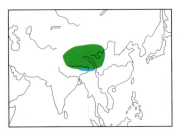

Tibet and western China: alpine grassland and barren stony steppes
and plateaux.
a Adult: black lores, whitish face except for chestnut ear-coverts;
   cinnamon on nape and sides of breast and lower back, white
   tips to wing-coverts.
b Juvenile: paler or duller version of adult, without well-defined
   face pattern; white areas of adult replaced with pale buff.

289 Blanford's Snow Finch *Montifringilla blanfordi*   Text page 480

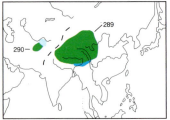

Tibet to western and northwestern China: mountains and plateaux,
dry sandy steppes and hillsides with sparse vegetation.
a Adult: unique face pattern of 'horns' over eye and on centre of
   forehead, sandy-buff nape, very lightly streaked mantle.
b Juvenile: duller version of adult, lacking face pattern; grey crown,
   mantle uniform sandy-brown.

290 Theresa's Snow Finch *Montifringilla theresae*   Text page 481

Afghanistan: stony hillsides and plateaux of mountains and high passes. Map above.
a Adult male: generally grey-brown with darker streaks on mantle; black from lores to eye and chin; white
   edges to flight feathers show well in flight.
b Adult female: similar to male, but tinged buff-brown, face greyer and less well defined, white in wing
   less extensive.

287a

287b

286a

286b

288a

288b

289a

289b

290a

290b

PLATE 22   ROSEFINCHES (1)

107 Red-headed Rosefinch *Pinicola subhimachala*   **Text page 295**

Himalayas to western China and northern Burma:
high-altitude dense juniper or dwarf rhododendron scrub, open
forest.
a Adult male breeding: large; bright crimson forehead, chin and
    breast, reddish-brown tinge to upperparts, deep reddish rump,
    square-ended tail.
b Adult female breeding: red areas of male replaced with olive-
    yellow, upperparts tinged greenish-olive, chin and throat grey
    streaked with black.
c First-summer male: intermediate between the two adults, but has
    red or reddish tinge to head, breast and upperparts.

103 Caucasian Great Rosefinch *Carpodacus rubicilla*   **Text page 289**

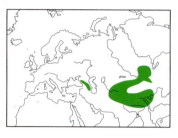

Caucasus, Central Asia, Himalayas to west and northwest China:
high-altitude valleys and plateaux, boulder fields and rocky screes.
a Adult male breeding: deep crimson, with white or pinkish-white
    spots at centres of feathers; face deep crimson, bill pale horn.
b Adult female breeding: pale grey, with dark or brownish streaks
    on slightly darker face; lower back and rump unstreaked.
c Adult male *severtzovi* breeding: apart from lores to chin, much
    paler pink with paler grey back and wings than nominate; rump
    unstreaked pale pink.
d Adult female *severtzovi* breeding: as nominate female, but much
    paler and less heavily streaked.

95 Dark-rumped Rosefinch *Carpodacus edwardsii*   **Text page 279**

Himalayas to western China: forest, juniper, dwarf rhododendron,
bamboo thickets and alpine meadows.
a Adult male breeding: deep mauve-tinged brown, dark-streaked,
    with pale pink supercilium, chin and throat; distal edges to ter-
    tials also pale pink.
b Adult female breeding: dull brown above, buff-brown below,
    with darker streaks above and below; pale buff-brown super-
    cilium.

102 Eastern Great Rosefinch *Carpodacus rubicilloides*   **Text page 288**

Himalayas to central and northern China: high-altitude rocky
slopes, screes, plateaux, bushes and scrub.
a Adult male breeding: similar to nominate male Caucasian Great
    Rosefinch (103), but more extensively dark face contrasts with
    pinkish-red body (with whitish feather centres); grey-brown
    upperparts and wings, pale buff edges to tertials.
b Adult female breeding: grey above, pale buff below, heavily
    streaked all over including rump and uppertail-coverts; tail dark
    brown, no white in outer feathers.

PLATE 23   ROSEFINCHES (2)

104   Red-breasted Rosefinch *Carpodacus puniceus*   **Text page 290**

Central Asia to northern Pakistan, northern India and northwest China: high-altitude alpine meadows, plateaus, boulder fields, scree slopes and cliffs.

a Adult male breeding: large or stoutly built; crimson from forehead to area over eye and from chin to breast; pink rump and streaked underparts.

b Adult female breeding: lacks any red; heavily or broadly streaked above and below.

c Adult male *longirostris* breeding: slightly larger and paler than nominate; less broadly streaked underparts, bill slightly longer.

101   Red-mantled Rosefinch *Carpodacus rhodochlamys*   **Text page 287**

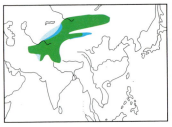

Central Asia, Afghanistan, northwest India, northwest China and Mongolia: forested mountains and alpine meadows.

a Adult male breeding: broad supercilium and eye-stripe, fine white tips to face, streaks on upperparts, unstreaked deep pinkish-red rump.

b Adult female breeding: lacks any red; no supercilium or eye-stripe, heavily streaked above (including rump) and below.

c Adult male *grandis* breeding: deeper mauve on head and face than nominate; upperparts browner, rump duller.

87   Common Rosefinch *Carpodacus erythrinus*   **Text page 269**

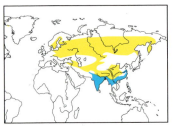

Palearctic and Oriental: widespread at low altitudes; breeds in willows or tamarisks in damp areas, along river banks and forest edges.

a Adult male breeding: bright red head, with red from face (with variable amounts of brown feather bases showing through) to breast; pinkish-red wingbars and rump.

b Adult female breeding: uniform upperparts, some streaks on forehead and crown, pale buff wingbars, streaked to breast.

c Juvenile: similar to adult female, but buffish with darker streaks and with pale buff-brown wingbars, plain buff-brown face; breast to flanks more heavily streaked than female.

d First-summer male: as adult female, but head, face, chin and throat can show variable amounts of red with brown feather bases.

e Adult male *roseatus* breeding: extensively red, deeper in tone than nominate male.

85   Blanford's Rosefinch *Carpodacus rubescens*   **Text page 266**

Himalayas to western China: conifer and birch forest with open areas.

a Adult male breeding: deep red, with brighter red sides to crown and wingbars; dark face, pale grey belly.

b Adult female breeding: uniform upperparts, warm or slightly reddish-brown tinge to lower back and rump, unstreaked underparts.

c First-summer male: as adult male, but duller red and shows more brown on upperparts.

PLATE 24   ROSEFINCHES (3)

97 Pallas's Rosefinch *Carpodacus roseus*   **Text page 282**

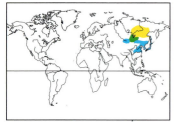

Central Siberia to Sakhalin Island: forest, alpine meadows, thickets and undergrowth.

a Adult male breeding: silvery tips to deep pink crown; chin and throat, lower back and rump deep pink, pale whitish-pink double wingbars.

b Adult female breeding: pale orange forehead, warm brown face and mantle, breast warm buff-brown, pinkish-red rump.

c First-summer male: similar to adult female but more heavily orange-pink from head to breast; grey nape.

d First-winter female: as adult female, but light orange-buff on forehead, lower back and rump.

92 Stresemann's Rosefinch *Carpodacus eos*   **Text page 276**

Southeast Tibet to southwest China: high-altitude alpine plateaux, stony slopes and grassland with boulders.

a Adult male breeding: very similar to adult male Beautiful Rosefinch (91), but found at higher altitudes; generally darker, with deep crimson underparts (paler in 91) and pale pink supercilium.

b Adult female breeding: indistinguishable from female Beautiful Rosefinch (91), except by altitude where found.

105 Tibetan Rosefinch *Carpodacus roborowskii*   **Text page 292**

Northeast Tibet to western China: desolate mountain plateaux with rocky slopes and steppes.

a Adult male breeding: slender yellow bill, long wings and deep crimson head and face.

b Adult female breeding: same shape as male; lacks any red, upperparts and chin to breast broadly streaked.

91 Beautiful Rosefinch *Carpodacus pulcherrimus*   **Text page 275**

Himalayas to central and northern China: forest edges, juniper and rhododendron scrub, slopes with scattered vegetation, edges of cultivation.

a Adult male breeding: similar to male Stresemann's Rosefinch (92); pale lilac-pink supercilium (often invisible in front of eye and flares behind eye), pale pink underparts and rump, white belly.

b Adult female breeding: lacks any pink; heavily streaked on upperparts and underparts, short pale supercilium.

c Adult male *waltoni* breeding: paler than nominate, with deep reddish-pink underparts.

PLATE 25   ROSEFINCHES (4)

100 White-browed Rosefinch *Carpodacus thura*   **Text page 285**

Northeast Afghanistan to northern India, Tibet, west and northwest China: forest edges, alpine meadows, dwarf rhododendron, bamboo and juniper scrub.
a Adult male breeding: forehead and supercilium red, with silvery-white tips at rear of supercilium; heavily streaked upperparts, unstreaked below.
b Adult female breeding: buffish supercilium becomes white at rear; warm brown from chin to breast, pale buffish-brown tips to greater coverts, underparts heavily streaked.
c Adult female *femininus* breeding: as nominate female, but lacks any buff (or buff-brown) in supercilium, wingbar or underparts.

93 Pink-browed Rosefinch *Carpodacus rhodochrous*   **Text page 277**

Himalayas from Kashmir to western Sikkim: forest, undergrowth, willows, dwarf juniper, scrub and grassy slopes.
a Adult male breeding: broad pink forehead and supercilium, broad dark reddish-brown eye-stripe, streaked upperparts (except deep pink rump), unstreaked below.
b Adult female breeding: thin pale buff supercilium, heavily streaked above and below, underparts tinged buff-brown.

99 Spot-winged Rosefinch *Carpodacus rhodopeplus*   **Text page 284**

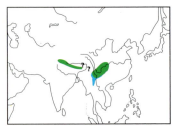

Himalayas from northern India to western China: scrub and bushes on slopes and alpine meadows; in winter in bamboo and mixed forest.
a Adult male breeding: long pale pink supercilium, spots at tips of wing-coverts and outer webs of tertials, deep or dull pink rump and underparts.
b Adult female breeding: lacks any red or pink; heavily streaked, pale creamy-buff supercilium, thin wingbars, pale buff distal edges to tertials.
c Adult male *verreauxi* breeding: as nominate but slightly smaller; paler pink supercilium, rump and underparts.

78 Red-browed Finch *Callacanthis burtoni*   **Text page 257**

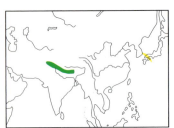

Himalayas from northwest Pakistan to Sikkim: fir and mixed forest with rhododendron.
a Adult male breeding: very distinctive pattern of black head, red face and spots on wing; pale yellow bill with dark tip.
b Adult female breeding: as male, but head blackish, forehead to eyes yellow, upperparts grey-brown; smaller amounts of white in wing.
c Juvenile: as female, but duller brown head, buffish area around eye, buffish wingbars and spots, buffish-brown underparts.

100a

93a

93b

100b

100c

99b

99a

78a

99c

78b

78c

PLATE 26   ROSEFINCHES (5)

86 Dark Rosefinch *Carpodacus nipalensis*   Text page 267

Himalayas from northern India to southern Tibet and western China: oak and fir forest, scrub and bushes above the tree line.
a Adult male breeding: very dark crimson; pinkish forehead, supercilium, face and tips to underparts, ill-defined wingbar, slender bill.
b Adult female breeding: almost uniform dark brown upperparts, with lighter brown wingbars and edges to tertials.

96 Sinai Rosefinch *Carpodacus synoicus*   Text page 281

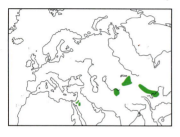

Negev and Sinai deserts, northeast Afghanistan discontinuously east to western China: dry arid mountains, rocky deserts, wadis and cliffs.
a Adult male breeding: pale sandy-brown from crown to back and wings, bright pinkish-red face, paler underparts and rump.
b Adult female breeding: lacks any pink; generally pale sandy-brown.
c Adult male *beicki*: similar to nominate male, but uniform upperparts slightly darker, deep pink from face to breast and silvery-pink from forehead to crown; paler pink rump.

94 Vinaceous Rosefinch *Carpodacus vinaceus*   Text page 278

Himalayas from northern India to northern Burma, southwest Tibet, central China and Taiwan: dense mixed and damp bamboo forest, bushes and scrub.
a Adult male breeding: almost entirely dark crimson; paler rump, pale pink supercilium and tips to outer webs of tertials.
b Adult female breeding: deep tan-brown, upperparts tinged olive with indistinct dark streaks; faint or pale buff tips to outer webs of tertials.

98 Three-banded Rosefinch *Carpodacus trifasciatus*   Text page 283

West and south China: conifer forest, undergrowth and thickets, in winter in orchards and hedges, barley fields.
a Adult male breeding: dark crimson head and blackish face, white edges to scapulars and outer webs of tertials, wingbars pale pinkish-white.
b Adult female breeding: head and upperparts grey or olive-brown streaked with black, rump light olive-brown, wings as male but tips to coverts yellowish-buff.
c First-summer male: duller than adult male, with crimson replaced by reddish-brown; wingbars pale buff or whitish-buff.

PLATE 27   ROSEFINCHES (6) AND BROWN BULLFINCH

83 Long-tailed Rosefinch *Uragus sibiricus*   **Text page 263**

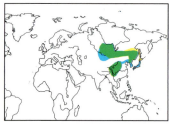

Siberia east to Amurland, Sakhalin, Manchuria, North Korea, northern Japan: damp or dense thickets, woodland with undergrowth, reedbeds.

a Adult male breeding: dark red from forehead to chin and behind eye, pale tips to crown and nape, extensive white edges and tips to wings, white outer tail feathers, yellowish stubby bill.

b Adult female breeding: lacks any pink; head and face to mantle greyish with dark streaks, broad white wingbars and edges to secondaries; rump orange-brown.

c Adult male non-breeding: paler or whiter, with extensive pale buff or whitish tips to crown and underparts.

d First-winter male: similar to adult female, but with orange or orange-brown on breast, scapulars and rump.

e Adult male *lepidus* breeding: shorter tail than nominate; dark grey hindcrown to mantle and scapulars, wingbars less extensive.

f Adult female *lepidus* breeding: warm brown, with dark streaks to head and upperparts; less white in wing than nominate female.

84 Przewalski's Rosefinch *Urocynchramus pylzowi*   **Text page 265**

Eastern Tibet to west-central China: high-altitude bushes, scrub and thickets of dwarf willow or dwarf rhododendron.

a Adult male breeding: long thin tail (graduated in flight), pale upperparts with darker streaking; supercilium, face and chin to lower breast deep pink; lower mandible pale pink.

b Adult female breeding: lacks any pink (except lower mandible); generally pale buffish-brown with darker streaks, base of tail pale pinkish-orange.

113 Brown Bullfinch *Pyrrhula nipalensis*   **Text page 305**

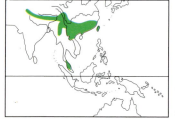

Northern Pakistan east to southern Tibet, northwest Burma, western China and Taiwan: thick forest and dense undergrowth in fir and broadleaved forest.

a Adult: pale grey, with glossy deep blue wings and tail, pale buff patch on greater coverts, orange edge to inner tertial.

b Juvenile: duller than adult (but wings and tail glossy); warm buff-brown tips to greater coverts, buffish underparts.

c Adult *waterstradti*: darker grey forehead and crown; white cheeks and ear-coverts.

d Adult *ricketti*: forehead and lores black, crown dark grey, white immediately below eye.

108 Scarlet Finch *Haematospiza sipahi*   **Text page 296**

Himalayas from central Nepal to northeast India and west-central China: fir and oak forest, edges and clearings.

a Adult male: unmistakable. All bright scarlet except for black (or blackish) lores, wings and tail; bill bright yellow.

b Adult female: dull or dark olive-green, with paler or yellowish tips to feathers, bright yellow rump patch and duller bill.

c Juvenile/First-summer male: duller than adult, with deep orange tips to head, mantle and breast; rump bright orange.

83b

83d

83a

83c

83e

83c

84a

83f

84b

113c

113a

113d

108a

113b

108c

108b

PLATE 28 BULLFINCHES

118 Common Bullfinch *Pyrrhula pyrrhula*

Text page 310

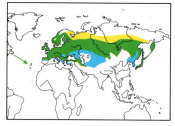

Palearctic, Azores to Japan: forest, woods, copses, hedgerows, gardens, bushes, scrub and orchards.

a Adult male: glossy black cap, wings and tail; broad white rump band, deep pink underparts.

b Adult female: cap blackish-blue, some gloss on wings and tail feathers; grey-brown above with white rump.

c Juvenile: similar to adult female but lacks black cap; broad pale buffish-brown tips to wing-coverts.

d Adult male *griseiventris*: deep pink on ear-coverts, cheeks and throat only, rest of underparts pale grey.

e Adult male 'roseacea': as *griseiventris*, but paler pink extends to breast and belly (overlying grey bases).

f Adult male *cineracea*: lacks any pink; all pale grey face and underparts.

g Adult *murina*: sexes alike; uniform pale brown cheeks and body, with dull or buffish (not white) rump.

116 Red-headed Bullfinch *Pyrrhula erythrocephala*

Text page 307

Himalayas, Kashmir to Bhutan: dense conifer and birch forest with rhododendron.

a Adult male: orange head and underparts; white surround to black forehead, lores and chin.

b Adult female: yellowish-olive from crown to nape, underparts pale grey; face as male.

c Juvenile: generally warm brown, with broad buff tips to wing-coverts; eye to bill and chin blackish.

117 Beavan's Bullfinch *Pyrrhula erythaca*

Text page 308

Southeast Tibet to northwest and northeast China, also Taiwan: mixed conifer and birch forest with willows, rhododendron and buckthorn.

a Adult male: grey head, thin white surround to black forehead, lores and chin, deep orange from breast to belly.

b Adult female: greyish head and sides to nape, body dull brown, dull grey tips to greater coverts; face as male.

c Juvenile: similar to adult female; broad warm buff-brown tips to greater coverts (dull grey on female).

115 Orange Bullfinch *Pyrrhula aurantiaca*

Text page 306

Northern Pakistan, Kashmir and northwest India: fir and mixed forest.

a Adult male: bright orange, except for paler tips to coverts, black on face, glossy blue-black wings and tail, white rump.

b Adult female: similar to adult female Beavan's Bullfinch (117) (but geographically separated), but with more black on face and no white border separating grey of rest of head.

c Juvenile: pale brown head and yellowish-brown face, warm brown body.

118a

118b

118c

118d

118e

118f

118g

116a

116b

116c

117a

117b

117c

115a

115b

115c

J.D.

PLATE 29   PHILIPPINE BULLFINCH AND HAWFINCHES

114 Philippine Bullfinch *Pyrrhula leucogenys*

Text page 306

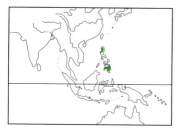

The Philippines, northern Luzon and Mindanao: damp oak forest on hillsides.
a Adult male: white face, black lores and cap, deep crimson outer edge to smallest tertial, thin white rump.
b Adult female: slightly duller than male; face buffish, brown outer edge to smallest tertial.
c Juvenile: similar to adult, but face dark and cap poorly defined, outer edge to smallest tertial and rump pale sandy-buff.

119 Hawfinch *Coccothraustes coccothraustes*

Text page 312

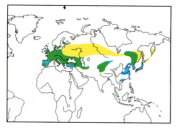

Palearctic, Spain and North Africa to Japan: deciduous and mixed woods, parks, bushes and gardens.
a Adult male breeding: rich brown crown, face orange-brown, black bib, deep brown mantle, secondaries deep glossy blue.
b Adult female: dull brown head and face, dark brown mantle, rump dull brown, secondaries pale blue-grey.
c Adult male non-breeding: as in summer, but duller mantle, dull yellowish bill, darker grey on nape.
d Adult male: in flight, shows broad white wingbars and white tip to tail.
e Adult male: in flight overhead, shows contrasting black-and-white wing pattern.
f Juvenile male: dull version of adult, with brown streaks and spots on underparts; secondaries glossy blue.
g Juvenile female: similar to juvenile male, but dark lores and base of bill not so well defined; secondaries pale grey.

120 Chinese Grosbeak *Eophona migratoria*

Text page 314

Eastern Siberia, North Korea, central and eastern China: mixed or deciduous forest, woods, parks, orchards and gardens.
a Adult male: black head, orange flank patch, deep blue wings with extensive white tips to primaries.
b Adult female: grey head, blackish face, dark brown tertials, broad white fringes to primaries.
c Juvenile: similar to female but duller brown; pale buff tips to median and greater coverts.

121 Japanese Grosbeak *Eophona personata*

Text page 315

Eastern Siberia, Amurland to north-central China and Japan: mixed and deciduous forest, woods, groves, parks and gardens.
a Adult male: black crown and face, pale grey body tinged with brown on upperparts, whitish rump, white patch on primaries.
b Adult female: as male but wings slightly duller; rump grey-brown.
c Juvenile: generally pale brown; lacks black crown; pale buffish tips to median and greater coverts.

114a
114b
114c
119a
119b
119c
119d
119e
119f
119g
120a
120b
120c
121a
121b
121c

PLATE 30 GROSBEAKS (1)

122 **Black-and-Yellow Grosbeak** *Mycerobas icterioides* **Text page 317**

Eastern Afghanistan to northwest India (Punjab): conifer and deciduous forest, woods and scrub.
a Adult male breeding: large; glossy black head, scapulars, sides of mantle, wings and tail; deep yellow body, thighs yellowish-grey or black.
b Adult female breeding: pale grey head and upperparts, warm buff wash to rump and lower underparts.
c Juvenile male: similar to adult female but pale or dull brownish-grey; rump pale yellow.
d Juvenile female: as adult female, but very pale buff or off-white underparts.

123 **Collared Grosbeak** *Mycerobas affinis* **Text page 318**

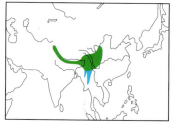

Northern Pakistan east to northern Burma and western China: mixed and conifer forest, rhododendrons and dwarf juniper above the tree line.
a Adult male breeding: very similar to adult male Black-and-yellow Grosbeak (122), but with nape to rump tinged golden-brown; thighs yellow, bill greyish-green.
b Adult female breeding: grey head and face, greyish olive-green from mantle to wings, dull sandy-yellow underparts.
c Juvenile male: pattern as adult male, but dull black, body yellowish-buff.

124 **Spot-winged Grosbeak** *Mycerobas melanozanthos* **Text page 319**

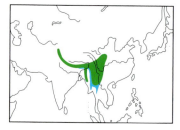

Northern Pakistan to southeast Tibet, western China, northern Burma and northern Thailand: mixed or fir forest.
a Adult male breeding: all-black head, face and upperparts with glossy blue tips; pale yellowish-white tips to greater coverts, secondaries and edges to tips of tertials and primaries.
b Adult female breeding: head, face and body streaked black-and-yellow; wing similar to male, with pale yellow tips to median coverts.
c Juvenile: very similar to adult female, but base colour pale yellow, yellowish-white or buff.

125 **White-winged Grosbeak** *Mycerobas carnipes* **Text page 320**

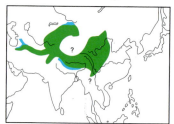

Northeast Iran to Himalayas and Tien Shan to western and northern China: high-altitude juniper and mixed forest with rhododendron and scrub.
a Adult male breeding: sooty-black and dull yellowish; small white patch at base of primaries, yellowish wingbar.
b Adult female breeding: greyer than male, with white streaks from face to breast; smaller white wing patch than male.

PLATE 31 GROSBEAKS (2) AND GOLD-NAPED FINCH

126 Evening Grosbeak *Hesperiphona vespertinus* Text page 321

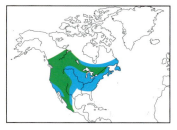

Central and eastern Canada to Mexico: mixed and conifer forest, woods and copses, also gardens and parks.
a Adult male breeding: broad bright yellow forehead and supercilium, head to mantle varies from dark yellow to brown; white inner greater coverts and secondaries.
b Adult female breeding: grey head, mantle and back, yellowish nape, short black submoustachial stripe, small white patch at base of primaries, also white tips to tail.
c Juvenile male: pale yellow throat, extensive yellowish-white or white in wing; no white at base of primaries or tip of tail.
d Juvenile female: less white or yellowish-white in wing than juvenile male, but has small white patch at base of primaries and white tips to tail.

127 Hooded Grosbeak *Hesperiphona abeillei* Text page 323

Mexico: cloud forest and moist woods, also parks and gardens.
a Adult male breeding: all-black head, wings and tail; white inner greater coverts and tertials, and bright yellow bill.
b Adult female breeding: black cap, dull olive-green upperparts, greyish-white inner greater coverts and tertials; dull yellow bill.
c Juvenile male: similar to adult female, but underparts tinged yellow and inner greater coverts bright yellow.

106 Pine Grosbeak *Pinicola enucleator* Text page 293

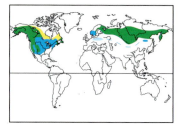

Northern Norway to Siberia, northeast China, Japan, Alaska, Canada and western USA: conifer, alder and birch forest, also orchards and scrub.
a Adult male breeding: deep pink with numerous grey tips; wings black, with white tips to coverts and edges to tertials; distinctive grey face pattern around eye.
b Adult female breeding: pink replaced by dull olive-yellow; grey on scapulars, rump, flanks and underparts; also grey on face and chin.
c Juvenile: similar to adult female, but paler grey with dull olive-yellow head; wingbars buffish.
d First-winter male: as adult female, but with russet head and face; rump orange or yellowish-orange.
e Adult female *alascensis*: dull olive-yellow restricted to head and face only.
f First-winter *alascensis*: russet or rich orange head and face, underparts uniform pale grey.

128 Gold-naped Finch *Pyrrhoplectes epauletta* Text page 324

Himalayas, northwest India to western China: undergrowth in high-altitude fir and rhododendron forest.
a Adult male: all black, with orange sides to breast (epaulettes) and orange from crown to nape; white inner webs to tertials.
b Adult female: grey and olive-green head and face, grey mantle, warm brown underparts, tertials as male.

126a

126c

126d

126b

127a

127b

127c

106a

106c

106e

106b

106d

106f

128a

128b

AH.

PLATE 32 NORTHEAST ASIAN AND NORTH AMERICAN FINCHES

77 Rosy Finch *Leucosticte arctoa*

Text page 255

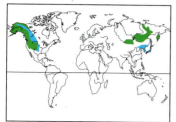

Central Asia (Altai) to eastern Siberia, Japan, Alaska to western Canada and western USA: tundra, plains, cliffs, alpine meadows and scree slopes.

a Adult male breeding: broad silvery-grey edges to flight feathers and pale uppertail- and undertail-coverts.

b Adult male *gigliolii* breeding: entirely dark brown, except for pale buff nape and reddish-brown belly and flanks.

c Adult male *brunneonucha* breeding: extensively blackish; pale golden-yellow nape, pink edges and tips to rump and wings, broad white spots on underparts with pink spots on flanks.

d Adult female *brunneonucha* breeding: browner above than male; whitish edges to flight feathers, grey and black underparts.

e Adult male *littoralis* breeding: black forehead, grey face.

f Adult male *tephrocotis* breeding: grey hindcrown and sides of nape, pink in wings and from flanks to belly.

g Adult female *tephrocotis* breeding: lacks pink in wing.

h Juvenile *tephrocotis*: dark slate-grey, with broad buff-brown edges and tips to wing-coverts and tertials.

i Adult male *australis* breeding: very similar to adult *tephrocotis*, but browner than other races and with slight amount of grey on hindcrown and sides of nape.

j Adult male *atrata* breeding: generally blackish, with extensive pink on rump, wings, flanks and undertail-coverts.

88 Purple Finch *Carpodacus purpureus*

Text page 271

Canada to eastern and western USA south to northern Mexico: conifer forest, mixed woods, parks and suburban gardens.

a Adult male breeding: pale pink supercilium, reddish cheeks and ear-coverts, curved culmen and short primary projection.

b Adult female breeding: similar to female Cassin's Finch (89), but with well-defined face pattern, arrowhead streaks on underparts, shorter wing.

89 Cassin's Finch *Carpodacus cassinii*

Text page 273

Western Canada, western USA to northern Mexico: conifer forest.

a Adult male breeding: bright red from forehead to crown, brown face (no supercilium), brown streaks on mantle and scapulars, pointed bill, longer wing projection than similar male Purple Finch (88).

b Adult female breeding: similar to female Purple Finch (88), but lacks contrasting face pattern and has continuous streaks on underparts, pointed bill, longer wing projection.

90 House Finch *Carpodacus mexicanus*

Text page 274

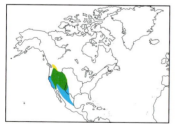

Southwest Canada, USA (except central States), Hawaii and Mexico: canyons, farmland, orchards, suburban parks and gardens.

a Adult male breeding: red forehead, chin, breast and rump; thin pale buffish wingbars, heavily streaked underparts.

b Adult male breeding: red replaced with yellow on some birds.

c Adult female breeding: lacks red in plumage; indistinct wingbars, streaked underparts.

d Adult male *frontalis* breeding: extensively red on head and upper belly.

e Adult male *frontalis* 'yellow phase': red replaced with orange-yellow.

PLATE 33 CROSSBILLS

110 Common Crossbill *Loxia curvirostra*

Text page 298

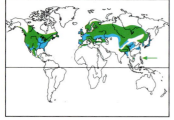

Holarctic and partially Oriental: conifers.
a Adult male: brick-red, with darker upperparts and bright red rump, stout bill with crossed mandibles at tip (not easily seen); more rounded head than other crossbills.
b Adult female: dull olive-green or grey-tinged, rump paler or lighter green; same shape and bill as male.
c Juvenile: similar to female (or darker), but streaked.
d Juvenile: some birds are 'wingbarred', with variable-width pale edges and/or tips to wing-coverts and tips to tertials.
e First-winter male: red adult plumage beginning to show.
f Adult male *poliogyna*: grey face, nape, mantle and crown; orange breast.
g Adult female *poliogyna*: rump and underparts tinged green.

111 Scottish Crossbill *Loxia scotica*

Text page 302

Northern Scotland: Caledonian pine forest.
a Adult male: plumage as male Common Crossbill (110); slightly broader head and heavier bill; tip of lower mandible never prominent as on male Common Crossbill.
b Adult female: plumage as female Common Crossbill (110); slightly heavier bill.
c Juvenile: as juvenile Common Crossbill (110), except for slightly heavier bill.

109 Parrot Crossbill *Loxia pytyopsittacus*

Text page 297

Northwest Europe east to the Pechora (with limit of irruptions to dotted line): conifer forest and woods, also larch.
a Adult male: very thick or heavy bill, often with bulge to lower mandible before tip; usually flat-headed, with no-neck appearance; darker red than very similar male Common Crossbill (110) and well-plumaged birds show grey on ear-coverts and sides of neck, although this may be absent.
b Adult female: size and shape as male, though bill often slightly larger; plumage as female Common Crossbill (110), though often duller or greyer.
c Juvenile: similar to female or paler below, with heavy streaking to upperparts and underparts.

112 Two-barred Crossbill *Loxia leucoptera*

Text page 303

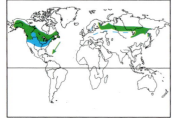

Northeast Europe to eastern Siberia and northern China, Alaska, Canada and northern USA, also Hispaniola: fir forest, cedars and larches.
a Adult male: pinkish-red on head, underparts and rump; black wings (including bases to coverts), with broad white tips to coverts, broadening on inner greater coverts, and white tips to tertials; slender bill with crossed tips.
b Adult female: green or grey-green with dark streaks on mantle and flanks; size, shape and wingbars (including tips to tertials) as male.
c Juvenile: paler than female; broadly but diffusely streaked darker, wingbars and tips to tertials pale yellowish-white.

110a 110b 110c 110e 110f 110g 110d

111a 111b 111c

109a 109b 109c

112a 112b 112c

J.D.

PLATE 34   AFRICAN FINCHES (1): NEGRO-FINCHES

131   White-breasted Negro-finch *Nigrita fusconota*   **Text page 326**

Liberia to Uganda and western Kenya: forest edges and clearings, secondary growth and scrub.
a Adult: glossy blue-black rump and tail.
b Juvenile: duller version of adult; rump to tail darker brown.
c Adult *uropygialis*: pale whitish-buff lower back and upper rump.

132   Chestnut-breasted Negro-finch *Nigrita bicolor*   **Text page 327**

Guinea to Cameroon, northern Zaire and northwest Angola, also Principé: forest clearings and edges, thick bush, scrub, edges of cultivation.
a Adult: slaty grey-brown upperparts, browner wings and blackish tail.
b Juvenile: warm rich buff-brown underparts.
c Adult *brunnescens*: crown to back and wings browner than nominate, underparts also deeper brown.

133   Pale-fronted Negro-finch *Nigrita luteifrons*   **Text page 328**

Ghana to western Uganda, northwest Angola and Fernando Po: forest edges, secondary growth and scrub.
a Adult male: white forehead tinged with pale buff or yellow; red eye.
b Adult female: similar to male, but pale grey underparts, slate-grey or blackish face.
c Juvenile: entirely uniform grey upperparts, brownish-grey underparts, pale eye.
d Adult male *alexanderi*: forehead, crown and nape pale yellow; eye black.

134   Grey-headed Negro-finch *Nigrita canicapilla*   **Text page 329**

Guinea to southern Sudan, Kenya and northern and western Tanzania: secondary and riverine forest and clearings, plantations and tall trees.
a Adult: thin white border between black underparts and grey upperparts from crown to sides of nape; white spots at tips of lesser and median coverts, and tips to greater coverts form an irregular or poorly defined wingbar.
b Juvenile: uniform dark grey with pale tips to wing-coverts and tertials, pale grey eye.
c Adult *candida*: crown, nape and upper mantle white or greyish-white; less white on tips to coverts and tertials.
d Adult *emiliae*: no white on crown or sides of nape; very fine pale tips to wing-coverts and tertials.

PLATE 35   AFRICAN FINCHES (2)

135   Fernando Po Olive-back *Nesocharis shelleyi*   **Text page 330**

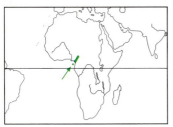

Southeast Nigeria, Cameroon and Fernando Po: mountain-forest clearings and edges, plantations and savanna.
a Adult male: black head, grey nape, olive back and wings, golden-yellow rump and black tail; white sides to throat, yellowish-olive patch on breast.
b Adult female: as male, but white on sides of throat reduced or absent and lacks yellowish-olive breast patch.
c Juvenile: as adult female, but duller with brown-tinged underparts.

136   White-collared Olive-back *Nesocharis ansorgei*   **Text page 331**

Eastern Zaire, western Uganda and northern Rwanda: damp forest, marshes, bushes or thickets near streams or water.
a Adult male: larger, longer-tailed version of male Fernando Po Olive-back (135), with grey nape and white collar from sides of nape.
b Adult female: very similar to female Fernando Po Olive-back (135), but larger and tail longer; less grey on nape than male White-collared.

137   Grey-headed Olive-back *Nesocharis capistrata*   **Text page 331**

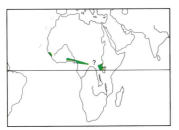

Senegal discontinuously east to northern Zaire, southern Sudan and northwest Uganda: forest edges and clearings, savannas with thickets.
a Adult: grey head, white face, black from chin to sides of neck; olive back and wings, bright yellow flanks.
b Juvenile: dark grey head and face, dull buff-brown flanks.

42   Oriole Finch *Linurgus olivaceus*   **Text page 210**

Southeast Nigeria, Fernando Po to central Kenya, eastern Tanzania and northern Malawi: montane evergreen forest undergrowth, scrub and bamboo.
a Adult male: distinctive black head, yellow body and edges to wings, greenish-yellow mantle and scapulars, yellow edges and tips to tail; bright orange-yellow bill.
b Adult female: olive-grey head and upperparts, bright yellow tips to greater coverts, dull greenish edges to secondaries (tips yellow); tail dull olive-green, bill yellow.
c Juvenile: similar to adult female, but paler below with slight olive streaks; bill brown.
d Adult male *kilimensis*: extensively darker olive-green upperparts, no yellow on nape; less yellow in wings and tail than nominate.
e Adult male *elgonensis*: bright yellow upperparts and edges to wings except for white or whitish tertials; tail yellow.

PLATE 36   AFRICAN FINCHES (3): PYTILIAS

138 Crimson-winged Pytilia *Pytilia phoenicoptera*   **Text page 332**

Senegal and the Gambia east to central Ethiopia: acacia woodland and savanna, edges of forest, bush and scrub.
a Adult male: black bill; crimson wings, rump and tail.
b Adult female: similar to male but paler underparts.
c Juvenile: pale pink base to bill; brownish upperparts, with dull reddish edges to wing, rump and tail.
d Adult male *lineata*: as nominate male, but with bright red bill and heavier barring on underparts.

139 Red-faced Pytilia *Pytilia hypogrammica*   **Text page 333**

Sierra Leone discontinuously east to northwest Zaire: open country savanna with bushes or thickets, edges of cultivation.
a Adult male: golden-yellow in wing; red rump and tail.
b Adult male 'red-winged': orange or reddish-orange in wing.
c Adult female: paler yellow in wing; rump to tail dull red, with fine barring on lower breast and flanks.
d Juvenile: similar to female but duller in wing and tail; paler buff and less heavily barred below.

140 Orange-winged Pytilia *Pytilia afra*   **Text page 334**

Southern Sudan and southern Ethiopia south to Mozambique and northern South Africa: thornscrub and scattered bushes in dry open country.
a Adult male: bright orange in wing, red face, and dull olive-yellow underparts barred whitish.
b Adult female: head and face grey, yellowish-orange in wing, underparts more broadly barred, white belly.
c Juvenile: duller than female; warm buff-brown in wing, underparts barred with pale buff.

141 Green-winged Pytilia *Pytilia melba*   **Text page 335**

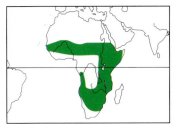

Senegal to Ethiopia south to Mozambique and eastern South Africa: dry or semi-desert thornscrub, acacia woodland or thickets.
a Adult male: greyish lores, uniform olive-green mantle, back and wings; breast green, underparts heavily barred or spotted.
b Adult female: grey head, dull green mantle, back and wings; underparts barred dark grey and white.
c Juvenile: dull olive upperparts and wings with paler green or yellow edges; underparts buffish-brown.
d Adult male *belli*: yellow breast; vent and undertail-coverts white.
e Adult male *citerior*: red face and yellow breast; barring on underparts poorly defined.

PLATE 37   AFRICAN FINCHES (4): TWINSPOTS

142 **Green-backed Twinspot** *Mandingoa nitidula*   **Text page 336**

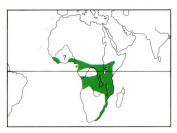

Sierra Leone to southern Ethiopia, south to Mozambique and eastern South Africa: dense riverine or secondary-forest undergrowth, plantations, grassland.

a Adult male: bright red from bill to eye; orange chin, bright olive-green breast and upperparts.

b Adult female: pale yellow from bill to eye; greenish-olive throat and breast.

c Juvenile: pale buff from bill to eye; grey-green upperparts, green wings and tail.

d Adult male *chubbi*: red face and chin, deep orange-brown rump, breast tinged orange.

e Adult male *virginiae*: as male *chubbi*, except for all-red bill, orange-brown back and rump.

f Adult male *schlegeli*: black bill with red cutting edges, orange chin and throat, deeper on breast; lower back and rump orange-brown.

g Adult female *schlegeli*: similar to male, but face yellowish-buff and underparts dark green with whitish spots.

h Juvenile *schlegeli*: darker than nominate, but greyer or with olive-green underparts.

153 **Brown Twinspot** *Clytospiza monteiri*   **Text page 347**

Southeast Nigeria to western Kenya and northwest Angola: grassland, savannas, damp thickets, scrub and clearings or edges of forest.

a Adult male: red stripe on chin and throat.

b Adult female: white stripe on chin and throat.

c Juvenile: underparts unspotted; whitish tips to belly and undertail-coverts.

154 **Rosy Twinspot** *Hypargos margaritatus*   **Text page 348**

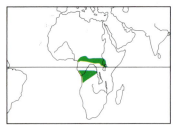

Southern Mozambique to eastern South Africa: forest edges, thickets, bush and dense scrub.

a Adult male: pinkish from face to breast, duller pink from rump to base of tail; underparts black, with erratically spaced pinkish-white spots.

b Adult female: face to breast grey, centre of belly to undertail-coverts buffish-white or grey; rump deep pink.

c Juvenile: as female, but underparts unspotted buffish-brown or grey.

155 **Peters's Twinspot** *Hypargos niveoguttatus*   **Text page 349**

Eastern Zaire to southern Somalia south to Malawi and Zimbabwe: lowland bush or grassland, thickets, acacia scrub and undergrowth.

a Adult male: bright red from face to breast; rump to tail bright red, underparts (except vent and undertail-coverts) spotted with white.

b Adult female: yellowish-buff from face to breast; rump to tail red.

c Juvenile: warm brown or russet-brown underparts; blackish from belly to undertail-coverts.

142a
142b
142c
142d
142e
142f
142g
142h
153a
153b
153c
154a
154b
154c
155a
155b
155c

PLATE 38   AFRICAN FINCHES (5)

156 Dybowski's Dusky Twinspot *Euschistospiza dybowskii*

Text page 350

Sierra Leone to southern Sudan: grassy savanna with thickets, edges of forest and cultivation.

a Adult male: crimson from mantle to uppertail-coverts, white spots on black flanks.

b Adult female: duller than male; crimson upperparts broken by brown feather bases showing through, wings browner than male, generally more spotted on flanks.

c Juvenile: slate-grey body, dull reddish-brown upperparts; unspotted.

157 Dusky Twinspot *Euschistospiza cinereovinacea*   **Text page 351**

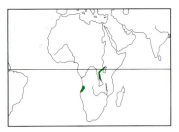

Southwest Uganda to Burundi and central and eastern Angola: grassland with bush or thickets of scrub in mountain valleys and plateaux.

a Adult: mantle and scapulars uniform with head, flanks deep scarlet finely spotted with white.

b Juvenile: dark slate-grey; wings browner, rump and uppertail-coverts crimson, unspotted pink-tinged flanks.

129 Flowerpecker Weaver-finch *Parmoptila woodhousei* Text page 325

Southwest Nigeria to Central African Republic south to southwest Angola: lowland secondary-forest undergrowth, also edges of damp or swamp forest.

a Adult male: reddish-orange forehead, warm brown face, pale shaft streaks on mantle and scapulars; finely but strongly patterned underparts.

b Adult female: as male, but forehead and sides of crown dull brown; generally fewer pale shaft streaks on upperparts; underparts as male, but duller and pattern more interrupted.

c Juvenile: crown and upperparts similar to adult female; face and underparts warm reddish-brown.

130 Red-fronted Flowerpecker Weaver-finch *Parmoptila rubrifrons*

Text page 326

Liberia discontinuously to eastern Zaire and western Uganda: dense foliage and undergrowth of forest edges and clearings.

a Adult male: bright red from forehead to crown; fine white tips to face, rich or deep cinnamon-brown underparts.

b Adult female: similar to Flowerpecker Weaver-finch (129), but lacks ginger face; upperparts darker brown, fine white tips to crown and face and prominently spotted underparts.

c Juvenile: similar to adult male but lacks red forehead patch; has orange-buff face and brown barring on underparts.

PLATE 39   AFRICAN FINCHES (6): CRIMSON-WINGS

143 Red-faced Crimson-wing *Cryptospiza reichenovii*   **Text page 337**

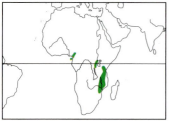

Southwest Nigeria to Uganda south to Mozambique and northern Angola: dense undergrowth, edges or clearings of montane forest.
a Adult male: red face patch and red on lower flanks.
b Adult female: yellowish-buff face patch; dark olive-green feather bases to mantle and back show through.
c Juvenile: duller olive or browner than adult; reddish tinge to flanks, back and edges to wing-coverts and tertials.

144 Ethiopian Crimson-wing *Cryptospiza salvadorii*   **Text page 338**

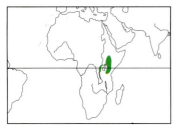

Southeast Sudan and southern Ethiopia to eastern Zaire and north-east Tanzania: thickets, undergrowth and creepers in montane forest.
a Adult male: similar to male Red-faced Crimson-wing (143), but lacks red face patch and red on secondaries.
b Adult female: similar to female Red-faced Crimson-wing (143), but lacks pale buff face patch and body is greyish-olive.
c Juvenile: very similar to juvenile Red-faced Crimson-wing (143), but greyer.
d Adult male *ruwenzori*: pale grey from head to upper mantle and underparts, except for pale buff chin.

145 Dusky Crimson-wing *Cryptospiza jacksoni*   **Text page 339**

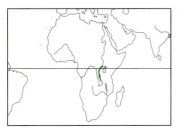

Eastern Zaire to southwest Uganda and Rwanda: dense forest undergrowth and scrub.
a Adult male: red on forehead, crown and face.
b Adult female: red from forehead to face (occasionally absent or can extend to sides of nape).
c Juvenile: lacks red on head and face, red is reduced or absent on flanks.

146 Shelley's Crimson-wing *Cryptospiza shelleyi*   **Text page 340**

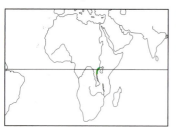

Eastern Zaire to southwest Uganda and southwest Rwanda: dense undergrowth and tangled thickets of montane forest.
a Adult male: reddish-mauve head, face and upperparts.
b Adult female: light olive-green head and face, and from breast to belly.

PLATE 40   AFRICAN FINCHES (7): SEEDCRACKERS

147 Crimson Seedcracker *Pyrenestes sanguineus*   **Text page 341**

Senegal to Ivory Coast: dense undergrowth, swamps, marshes and scrub alongside rivers or streams.

a Adult male: massive bill; rounded or domed glossy red head, red breast and flanks.

b Adult female: red on nape and lower breast duller than male.

c Juvenile: no red on brown head and breast.

148 Black-bellied Seedcracker *Pyrenestes ostrinus*   **Text page 342**

Ivory Coast to Uganda south to northern Angola and northern Zambia: marshes, rice-fields and swamps, also dense woods, forest edges and clearings.

a Adult male: smaller than male Crimson Seedcracker (147); body black.

b Adult female: red on crown, face and upper breast, olive-brown from mantle to wings.

c Juvenile: similar to juvenile Crimson Seedcracker (147) but dark olive-brown, otherwise identical.

149 Lesser Seedcracker *Pyrenestes minor*   **Text page 343**

Southern Tanzania to Malawi and Mozambique: hill forest, dry woodland, thickets and tangled scrub.

a Adult male: similar to female Black-bellied Seedcracker (148) but smaller; bill also smaller and more blunt in profile; some birds show less red on upper breast.

b Adult female: red on forehead, lores, cheeks, chin and upper throat.

147a

147b

147c

148a

148b

148c

149a

149b

PLATE 41   AFRICAN FINCHES (8): BLUEBILLS

150 Grant's Bluebill *Spermophaga poliogenys*   **Text page 344**

North-central Zaire to western Uganda: undergrowth of thick forest.
a Adult male: red-and-blue bill; extensive red on head, breast and upper flanks; rest of underparts jet-black.
b Adult female: red from chin to breast; white spots in pairs on lower breast, belly and flanks.
c Juvenile: red only on rump; face greyish, bill extensively bluish.

151 Western Bluebill *Spermophaga haematina*   **Text page 345**

Senegal and the Gambia to Central African Republic and northwest Angola: edges of forest or clearings, dense thickets and scrub.
a Adult male: bill blue with red tip; red from chin to breast and flanks, broken pale whitish-blue eye-ring.
b Adult female: bill as male but less red at tip; face black, washed red or maroon.
c Juvenile male: all-black underparts tinged red on breast and flanks.
d Juvenile female: as juvenile male but paler underparts.
e Adult male *pustulata*: reddish cutting edges to bill, red underparts extend to lower face.
f Adult female *pustulata*: bill similar to male *pustulata*; less red on forehead than nominate female, but face more prominently red.

152 Red-headed Bluebill *Spermophaga ruficapilla*   **Text page 346**

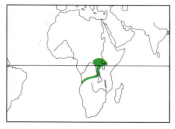

Southern Sudan to northern Tanzania and northwest Angola: forest edges, clearings and thickets in damp areas.
a Adult male: bright red head, face, breast and flanks; bill blue with red tip and cutting edges.
b Adult female: as male but with white-spotted underparts.
c Juvenile female: all dark grey, with red rump and dull base to bill; some birds show pale or poorly defined spots or bars on belly and flanks.
d Adult male *cana*: purple base to bill; pale grey feather bases on sides of head and breast show through.
e Adult female *cana*: as male, but with white spots and bars on underparts.

150a

150b

150c

151a

151b

151c

151d

151e

151f

152a

152b

152c

152d

152e

PLATE 42   AFRICAN FINCHES (9): FIREFINCHES (1)

163 Pale-billed Firefinch *Lagonosticta landanae*   **Text page 357**

Cabinda and lower Congo to northwest Angola: grassland savanna, dry thornbush with acacias.
a Adult male: pale pink bill with black culmen; grey (tinged pink) nape and black undertail-coverts.
b Adult female: bill as male; pinkish-red underparts, blackish undertail-coverts.
c Juvenile: similar to female, but with pale pink base to bill, reddish forehead and pinkish cheeks; lacks white spots on underparts.

162 African Firefinch *Lagonosticta rubricata*   **Text page 356**

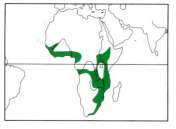

Guinea-Bissau to central Ethiopia south to South Africa: edges of forest, savanna, acacia woodland, scrub or thornbush.
a Adult male: dark grey from crown to nape, pale pink base to bill, black vent and undertail-coverts.
b Adult female: paler or less intensely red than male.
c Juvenile: similar to juvenile Pale-billed Firefinch (163), but whitish at base of bill and lacks pink tinge to face.
d Adult male *polionota*: darker upperparts, deep bluish bill.
e Adult male *haematocephala*: reddish from crown to nape; belly to undertail-coverts black, blue-grey base to bill.
f Adult female *haematocephala*: paler than male; buff-brown from belly to undertail-coverts.

159 Bar-breasted Firefinch *Lagonosticta rufopicta*   **Text page 353**

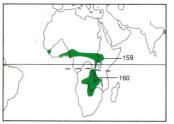

Senegal and the Gambia to southern Sudan, southwest Ethiopia south to northern Zaire and eastern Kenya: grassland, bush, edges of villages and cultivation.
a Adult: deep reddish-pink underparts, small white crescents on sides of breast and flanks, bright reddish-pink bill.
b Juvenile: pinkish wash to breast, dull buff underparts.

160 Brown Firefinch *Lagonosticta nitidula*   **Text page 354**

Eastern Angola to Zambia south to northeast Namibia and northern Botswana: lowland riverine forest or thickets, reedbeds or swamps with bushes. Map above.
a Adult male: grey, with bright pinkish-red from face to breast, white spots on sides of breast.
b Adult female: as male, but grey tips to pink throat and breast.
c Juvenile: lacks pink in plumage; pale pink base to black bill.

161 Red-billed Firefinch *Lagonosticta senegala*   **Text page 354**

Cape Verde Islands, southwest Mauritania, Senegal to southeast Ethiopia and central Somalia south to Angola and central South Africa: acacia grassland and scrub, gardens and cultivated areas in towns.
a Adult male: bright pink bill, pale yellow eye-ring, tiny white spots on sides of breast (may be absent on some birds).
b Adult female: pale pink bill and red spot on lores, white spots on sides of breast and flanks.
c Juvenile: as female but plain face and flanks; bill black.
d Adult female *brunneiceps*: darker or greyer-brown than nominate female, fewer spots on sides of breast.
e Adult male *ruberrima*: deeper red tinge to crown and upperparts.

PLATE 43   AFRICAN FINCHES (10): FIREFINCHES (2)

164 Jameson's Firefinch *Lagonosticta rhodopareia*   **Text page 358**

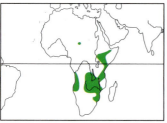

Southern Chad, southeast Sudan, southern Ethiopia and Cabinda south to eastern South Africa: dry grassland, thick undergrowth in lightly wooded areas.

a Adult male: bright red face and underparts, minute white spots on sides of breast; black from belly to undertail-coverts.

b Adult female: bright red lores, warm pinkish-buff underparts, black vent and undertail-coverts.

c Juvenile: as adult female but lacks pink lores; upperparts brown, with pinkish-red from lower rump to base of tail.

d Adult male *jamesoni*: as nominate male, but nape to coverts infused with crimson; face deeper pink.

165 Kulikoro Firefinch *Lagonosticta virata*   **Text page 359**

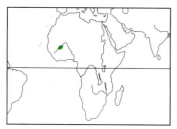

Mali: rocky sandstone with bushes, scrub and grass.

a Adult: grey-brown from crown to back and wings, pale eye-ring, crimson rump and underparts except black undertail-coverts; slate-blue base to dark-tipped bill.

b Juvenile: brown above, pale buff-brown below; pale eye-ring, crimson rump and uppertail-coverts.

166 Black-faced Firefinch *Lagonosticta larvata*   **Text page 360**

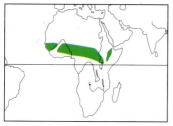

Gambia and Senegal to southeast Sudan and western Ethiopia: tall savanna grassland, thickets of scrub, bamboo and edges of woods.

a Adult male: very dark; face black, crown dark grey, small white spots on pinkish-mauve upper flanks; belly to undertail black.

b Adult female: dull or dark grey-brown head and upperparts, rump to uppertail-coverts crimson, sides of neck tinged pink.

c Adult male *vinacea*: pale pink upperparts and underparts, forehead to crown pale grey, undertail-coverts black.

d Adult female *vinacea*: paler than nominate female; pale grey head and pale pink underparts, upperparts tinged pink.

e Juvenile *vinacea*: similar to nominate female but underparts paler, lacks mauve tinge; no white spots.

f Adult male *nigricollis*: dark grey upperparts, except bright crimson rump and uppertail-coverts; pale lavender underparts, small white spots on sides of lower breast.

g Adult female *nigricollis*: similar to nominate female, but slightly paler brown or grey-brown upperparts with pale or buff-brown underparts.

158 Black-bellied Firefinch *Lagonosticta rara*   **Text page 352**

Sierra Leone and Liberia east to southern Sudan, northern Uganda and western Kenya: grassland savanna with scattered bushes, edges of cultivation.

a Adult male: dull crimson except for brighter rump and uppertail-coverts; centre of lower breast to lower flanks and undertail-coverts black.

b Adult female: grey head and face; bright red spot on lores, pale buff throat, pinkish underparts, blackish from lower belly to undertail.

c Juvenile: generally dull buff-brown, paler below; deep red rump and uppertail-coverts, pale pink base to lower mandible.

d Adult male *forbesi*: brighter crimson body than nominate male.

e Adult female *forbesi*: similar to nominate female but deeper pinkish-red.

PLATE 44   AFRICAN FINCHES (11): WAXBILLS (1)

182 Common Waxbill *Estrilda astrild*   **Text page 374**

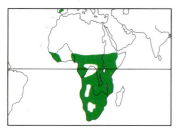

Africa, south of the Sahara (with introductions elsewhere, not shown): tall-grass savannas, edges of cultivation, marshes, gardens, villages and towns.

a Adult: finely barred, except for pale face, bright red eye-stripe, wax-red bill and small pinkish patch on lower breast and belly.

b Juvenile: very faintly barred (looks plain), pale red through eye; black bill, pale buff-brown underparts.

c Adult *minor*: slightly smaller than nominate, with darker or greyer upperparts; face also whiter.

d Adult male *rubriventris*: heavily tinged pink or pinkish-red on upperparts and underparts.

e Adult female *rubriventris*: similar to nominate, but slightly darker with pink wash to belly.

f Adult male *damarensis*: paler than nominate; grey crown, red patch on centre of belly.

g Adult female *damarensis*: as male but lacks red patch on belly; flanks and undertail-coverts barred.

h Adult *peasii*: much darker above, especially on crown; white face, pale pink from breast to belly.

179 Crimson-rumped Waxbill *Estrilda rhodopyga*   **Text page 371**

Sudan to Somalia south to northern Malawi and central Tanzania: lowland grassland with bushes or scrub, acacia savanna and edges of cultivation.

a Adult: very similar to Common Waxbill (182), but with crimson edges to greater coverts, tertials and from rump to uppertail-coverts; bill blackish with pinkish-red base.

b Juvenile: as adult but paler, lacks faint barring and eye-stripe, red of adult replaced with dull pink; bill black.

181 Black-rumped Waxbill *Estrilda troglodytes*   **Text page 373**

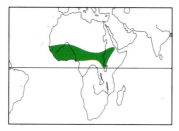

Senegal and the Gambia east to western Ethiopia and western Kenya south to northeast Zaire (with introductions elsewhere, not shown): grassland savannas with thickets, scrub or thornbushes.

a Adult male: very similar to Common Waxbill (182), but rump to tail black; white in outer tail feathers, pale pink tinge to breast and belly.

b Adult female: as adult male, but lacks pink tinge to breast and belly.

c Juvenile: dark band through eye, uniform buff-brown upperparts, lacks barring; bill black.

PLATE 45 AFRICAN FINCHES (12): WAXBILLS (2)

183 Black-faced Waxbill *Estrilda nigriloris*   **Text page 375**

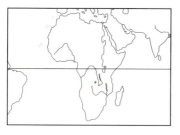

South-central Zaire: open grassland and river banks.
  Adult: all-red bill, black eye-stripe, deep pink tinge to breast and belly.

184 Black-crowned Waxbill *Estrilda nonnula*   **Text page 376**

Southeast Nigeria to southern Sudan, eastern Zaire and northwest Tanzania: grassy clearings and forest edges or clearings, woodland, bushes and gardens.
a Adult male: black-and-red bill, crimson patch on flanks.
b Adult female: as male, but greyer-brown from mantle to wings, less red on flanks.
c Juvenile: paler than adult; lacks fine barring, has dull red rump, pale buff flanks and black bill.

185 Black-headed Waxbill *Estrilda atricapilla*   **Text page 377**

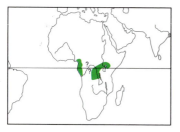

Southeast Nigeria to western and central Kenya, Zaire to northwest Angola: tall grass or bamboo thickets in forest clearings or edges.
a Adult: greyer underparts than Black-crowned Waxbill (184); black from belly to undertail-coverts, reddish base to bill, large red patch on lower flanks.
b Juvenile: duller than adult; black bill, orange-red flanks.
c Adult female *graueri*: pale whitish-grey from face to upper breast.
d Adult *avakubi*: underparts mostly whitish; black undertail-coverts.

186 Black-cheeked Waxbill *Estrilda erythronotos*   **Text page 378**

Southern Sudan and northern Somalia south through East Africa to central and eastern South Africa: savanna with thornbush or acacia thickets, woodland and edges of cultivation.
a Adult male: reddish-pink flanks, black from belly to undertail-coverts.
b Adult female: as male, but with finely barred underparts, pinkish-red flanks.
c Juvenile: as female but bill black.
d Adult male *charmosyna*: paler than nominate; pale silvery border to black face, pale pink underparts.
e Adult male *delamerei*: paler grey from head to mantle; silvery-grey edge to black face, paler grey underparts and whitish undertail-coverts.

PLATE 46   AFRICAN FINCHES (13): WAXBILLS (3)

178 Orange-cheeked Waxbill *Estrilda melpoda*   **Text page 371**

Senegal and the Gambia to northern Congo and northern Zaire south to northern Zambia and northern Angola (with introductions elsewhere, not shown): forest edges, grassy clearings, edges of cultivation.
a Adult: red or deep orange bill, bright orange face.
b Juvenile: as male, but with paler orange face, reddish-brown rump, black bill.

177 Fawn-breasted Waxbill *Estrilda paludicola*   **Text page 370**

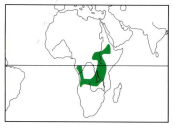

Congo to eastern Sudan south to central Angola, central Zaire, northeast Zambia and western Tanzania: moist grassland or swamps, forest or clearings with streams.
a Adult male: grey head, buffish underparts, pink tinge to belly.
b Adult female: as male but with brown from forehead to crown; lacks any pink on belly.
c Juvenile: black bill, browner rump, whitish-buff underparts.
d Adult male *benguellensis*: dark grey head, deep pink on lower flanks and vent, yellowish tinge to belly.
e Adult male *ochrogaster*: yellowish or golden-brown from face to underparts, pink tinge to vent.
f Adult male *marwitzi*: warmer brown upperparts, pale grey from chin to breast.
g Adult male *roseicrissa*: pale grey underparts, white belly, pink from lower flanks to vent.
h Adult female *roseicrissa*: as male, but lacks pink tinge to lower flanks.

176 Anambra Waxbill *Estrilda poliopareia*   **Text page 369**

Southern Nigeria: tall grass on edges of forest or swamps.
a Adult male: head and face pale brown, tinged grey; rump to tail scarlet, tail dark brown, pale yellowish underparts; bill bright red.
b Adult female: as male but slightly duller.

178a

177a

178b

177b

177c

177d

177e

177f

177g

176a

177h

176b

AH.

PLATE 47 AFRICAN FINCHES (14): WAXBILLS (4)

172 Lavender Waxbill *Estrilda caerulescens*   **Text page 366**

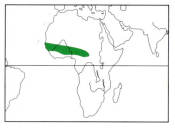

Senegal and the Gambia to northern Central African Republic and southwest Chad (with introductions elsewhere, not shown): flowering shrubs, open country with bushes, thornscrub and dry savanna.
a Adult: almost entirely pearl-grey; black lores, pale pink at base of bill; rump, tail and undertail-coverts crimson.
b Juvenile: undertail-coverts black, tipped with red; poorly defined black lores.

173 Black-tailed Waxbill *Estrilda perreini*   **Text page 367**

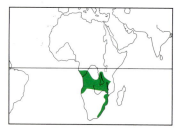

Gabon and lower Congo to western and southern Tanzania south to eastern South Africa: tall grass, thick evergreen scrub, thickets or forest edges.
a Adult: bill grey or greyish-blue with black tip; dark grey or blackish undertail-coverts; black tail.
b Juvenile: duller grey than adult; lacks black over ear-coverts, paler base to bill.
c Adult *poliogastra*: paler grey body and wings.

174 Cinderella Waxbill *Estrilda thomensis*   **Text page 367**

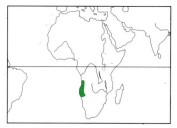

Western Angola to northern Namibia: dry thornbush, scrub, open woodland and riverine forest.
a Adult male: pale or reddish-pink base to bill, rosy pink wash to lower breast, dull crimson lower flanks.
b Adult female: as male, but has reduced (or absent) pink on lower breast and less black on undertail-coverts.

175 Yellow-bellied Waxbill *Estrilda melanotis*   **Text page 368**

Southeast Sudan south to East Africa to western Angola and South Africa: dense grass, bushes or scrub along edges of montane or upland forest.
a Adult male: uniform dull olive-green mantle, back and wings; rufous-orange edges to inner greater coverts and tertials.
b Adult female: as male, but has pale grey not black face with white or pale grey chin and throat.
c Juvenile: duller than female; lacks white on throat, bill mostly black.
d Adult male *bocagei*: finely barred mantle, back, coverts and flanks; underparts bright yellow.
e Adult female *bocagei*: as male but lacks black face.
f Adult male *quartinia*: all-grey head and grey from face to breast; bright yellow from belly to undertail-coverts.

172a

172b

173c

173a

173b

174a

174b

175d

175a

175b

175e

175c

175f

PLATE 48   AFRICAN FINCHES (15): WAXBILLS (5)

189 Zebra Waxbill *Amandava subflava*   **Text page 381**

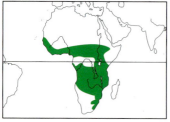

Senegal to southern Sudan, Ethiopia and North Yemen south to eastern South Africa: tall grassland savannas, edges of swamps or reedbeds and edges of cultivation.

a Adult male: bright orange from breast to undertail-coverts.

b Adult female: lacks red supercilium, has pale orange undertail-coverts; rump to tail dull red.

c Juvenile: dull buff-brown upperparts, rump brown, bill blackish.

d Adult male *clarkei*: bright golden-yellow underparts and orange centre to breast.

190 African Quailfinch *Ortygospiza atricollis*   **Text page 382**

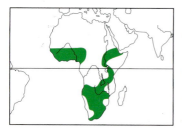

The Gambia to southern Sudan and central Ethiopia south to South Africa: dry sandy plains, riverbeds or swampy areas with grass tussocks.

a Adult male: blackish face but crown and ear-coverts grey; fine white chin, warm brown from breast to belly.

b Adult female: grey face, warm buffish-brown breast, red lower mandible.

c Juvenile: grey-brown from head to throat, warmer brown on breast; indistinct barring on flanks.

d Adult male *muelleri*: blackish from upperparts to throat; white 'spectacles' and chin, broad white bars on breast, light buff underparts.

e Adult male *fuscocrissa*: blackish from head to breast, with lightly streaked upperparts; chin white and underparts deep brown.

f Adult male *ansorgei*: blackish from head to breast, with unstreaked upperparts; chin white and underparts deep brown.

191 Black-chinned Quailfinch *Ortygospiza gabonensis* **Text page 383**

Rio Muni and Gabon to Rwanda, Tanzania and northern Angola: flat moist areas of swamp, also damp grassland.

a Adult male: mottled brown upperparts, black from forehead to throat; no white on chin, bill bright red.

b Adult female: as male, but with grey face and dark upper mandible, reddish-pink lower mandible.

c Adult male *fuscata*: very similar to *ansorgei* race of African Quailfinch (190), but blackish or slate-grey with all-red bill, no white chin and more pronounced streaks on sides of breast.

192 Locust Finch *Ortygospiza locustella*   **Text page 384**

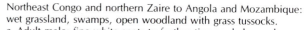

Northeast Congo and northern Zaire to Angola and Mozambique: wet grassland, swamps, open woodland with grass tussocks.

a Adult male: fine white spots to feather tips on dark grey-brown upperparts, flanks and undertail-coverts; deep orange in wings.

b Adult female: no red from face to breast; minute white spots on upperparts, dull orange-brown in wings.

c Juvenile: duller than female; warm brown wings, black bill.

d Adult male *uelensis*: no white tips to upperparts, flanks or undertail-coverts.

189a

189b

189c

189d

190a

190b

190c

190d

190e

190f

191c

191a

191b

192a

192b

192c

192d

PLATE 49   AFRICAN FINCHES (16): CORDON-BLEUS

167   **Cordon-bleu** *Uraeginthus angolensis*   **Text page 361**

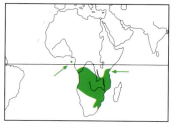

São Tomé, Cabinda and Congo to southeast Kenya south to South Africa: savanna or dry open woodland, rank vegetation, scrub, edges of cultivation and villages.
a Adult male: cerulean blue from face to flanks and from rump to tail; pale grey or pinkish-grey bill.
b Adult female: paler blue from face to breast and from rump to tail than male.
c Juvenile: similar to female but paler blue on breast; bill black.
d Adult male *niassensis*: brighter blue with browner upperparts than nominate; longer tail than other races.
e Adult female *niassensis*: difficult to distinguish from male, as blue underparts are often as extensive.

168   **Red-cheeked Cordon-bleu** *Uraeginthus bengalus*   **Text page 362**

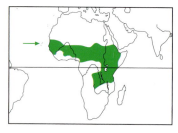

Most of Africa south of the Sahara to eastern Angola and southern Zaire (with introductions elsewhere, not shown): dry acacia woodland, thornscrub, open grassland, villages, gardens and cultivation.
a Adult male: extensive blue underparts, bright red patch on ear-coverts.
b Adult female: blue from face to breast (no red on face) and slightly blue on flanks; belly pale buff.
c Juvenile: as female but duller on breast; no blue on flanks.
d Adult female *katangae*: blue from face to throat, underparts buffish brown; pale pink base to bill.
e Adult male *brunneigularis*: brown head and face, blue from throat to flanks.

169   **Blue-capped Cordon-bleu** *Uraeginthus cyanocephalus*

Text page 363

Southern Somalia to central Tanzania: semi-arid desert, thornbush or open grassland with scattered acacias.
a Adult male: cerulean-blue head, face, breast and flanks; red bill.
b Adult female: brown from forehead to crown, blue on breast not so extensive, belly to vent white.
c Juvenile: pale blue from face to upper breast with paler feather bases showing through; some birds show a wash of blue on breast and flanks; bill black.

PLATE 50   AFRICAN FINCHES (17)

170   Common Grenadier *Uraeginthus granatina*   **Text page 364**

Angola to Mozambique and South Africa: dry thornscrub or acacia woodland and semi-arid desert scrub.
a Adult male: violet or purplish face, black chin; deep blue rump, uppertail and undertail-coverts.
b Adult female: as male, but shorter-tailed, lacks black chin, blue on rump and uppertail-coverts less extensive, underparts pale buff-brown.
c Juvenile: lacks mauve face; bill black, eye brown, rump as female.
d First-winter male: red-and-black bill, face as adult, body plumage as juvenile.
e First-winter female: as first-winter male but lacks black chin.

171   Purple Grenadier *Uraeginthus ianthinogaster*   **Text page 365**

Southern Sudan, southern Ethiopia and Somalia to Uganda, Kenya and central Tanzania: dense thornscrub, scrub and dry brush and undergrowth.
a Adult male: blue face, broken edges to blue underparts.
b Adult female: pale blue around eye, lacks blue underparts.
c Juvenile: as female but face and underparts plain; bill black.
d First-winter male: some blue on face, black tip to bill.
e First-winter female: like adult female but with black tip to bill.

256   Cut-throat Finch *Amadina fasciata*   **Text page 441**

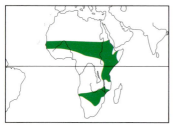

Senegal and the Gambia east to Somalia and south to eastern South Africa: dry brush and mopane woodland, acacia savanna, scrub and edges of cultivation.
a Adult male: crimson-red from ear-coverts to throat; sandy-buff crown with dark-barred upperparts.
b Adult female: as male, but lacks red on ear-coverts to throat, with no chestnut belly patch.
c Juvenile male: red from ear-coverts to throat less extensive and obscured by black; mantle and back almost uniform.
d Adult male *meridionalis*: paler grey head and face, barring darker than nominate; prominent crescents on underparts.

255   Red-headed Finch *Amadina erythrocephala*   **Text page 440**

Northwest Angola to southwest Zimbabwe and South Africa: dry grassland, savanna and thornscrub, edges of woodland, cultivation and villages.
a Adult male: red head and pale grey or sandy-brown lores; pale buff underparts boldly spotted or with dark scallops.
b Adult female: lacks red on head, has some reddish-brown tips to crown and nape; less boldly or heavily spotted below.
c Juvenile: pale version of female; poorly defined blackish edges to white spots on underparts.

PLATE 51 AFRICAN FINCHES (18): SILVERBILLS AND MADAGASCAR MUNIA

219 African Silverbill *Lonchura cantans*

Text page 409

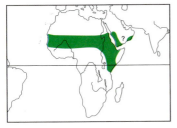

Mauritania to Somalia south to Tanzania, also southwest Saudi Arabia to Oman (with introductions elsewhere, not shown): dry savanna, thornscrub, acacia woodland and edges of cultivation.

a Adult: pale sandy-brown from mantle to scapulars, with pale tertials (the longest finely vermiculated/barred), rump to tail black.

b Juvenile: as adult but slightly paler brown upperparts.

c Adult *orientalis*: slightly darker than nominate; scapulars and tertials pale buff-brown, also with finer dark barring.

220 Grey-headed Silverbill *Lonchura griseicapilla*

Text page 410

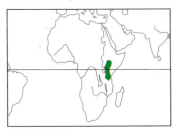

Southern Ethiopia to Tanzania: dry bush grassland, acacia woodland and thornscrub.

a Adult: grey head with white tips to face; rump and uppertail-coverts white or creamy-white.

b Juvenile: no white tips to forehead or face, rump duller creamy-buff.

218 Indian Silverbill *Lonchura malabarica*

Text page 408

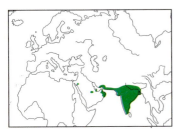

Eastern Saudi Arabia east to Nepal, Bangladesh and Sri Lanka: open grassland, edges of forest, savanna, scrub and semi-desert.

a Adult: very similar to African Silverbill (219), but rump white and pointed tail black.

b Juvenile: as adult, but duller buffish-orange face and underparts; rump buffish-brown.

221 Madagascar Munia *Lonchura nana*

Text page 410

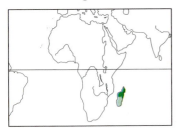

Madagascar: forest or woodland edges, grassland with bushes, scrub, marshes, edges of cultivation and villages.

a Adult: black chin, yellowish tips to rump, poorly defined spots on pinkish-buff underparts.

b Juvenile: uniform brown upperparts and dull buff-brown underparts.

219a

219b

219c

220a

220b

218a

218b

221a

221b

PLATE 52 AFRICAN FINCHES (19): MANNIKINS AND BLACK-HEADED CANARY

222 Bronze Mannikin *Lonchura cucullata*   **Text page 411**

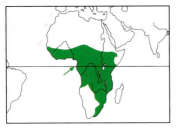

Senegal to western Ethiopia south to northwest Angola and eastern South Africa (with introductions elsewhere, not shown): open woodland with bushes, scrub, edges of cultivation, marshes, villages and towns.

a Adult: Small; dark brown, with darker head and purple-tinged breast; glossy bottle-green patch on scapulars and on barred flanks.

b Juvenile: dull grey-buff head, buff-brown breast and upperparts; bill dark grey.

223 Black-and-white Mannikin *Lonchura bicolor*   **Text page 412**

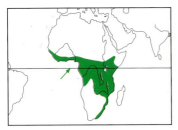

Guinea-Bissau east to Somalia and south to northern Angola and Tanzania: forest edges and clearings, grassland, savanna with bushes, edges of cultivation.

a Adult: glossy black tinged green above and to centre of breast with irregularly barred flanks, small white spots at base of tertials.

b Juvenile: dull brown head and upperparts, tinge of warm peach-buff on flanks.

c Adult *poensis*: as nominate, but rump, uppertail-coverts and (all but tips of) flight feathers barred black and white.

d Adult *nigriceps*: mantle, back, scapulars, greater coverts and tertials warm chestnut-brown; barring on flanks more spotted than nominate.

224 Magpie Mannikin *Lonchura fringilloides*   **Text page 413**

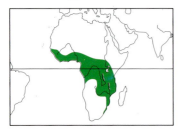

Senegal to southern Sudan south to Gabon and east South Africa: clearings or edges of forest, bamboo thickets, bush, grassland with scrub.

a Adult: larger than Bronze Mannikin (222) and Black-and-white Mannikin (223); bluish-black from head to breast, dark brown mantle and wings, black-and-brown barring on flanks.

b Juvenile: dark head and face, buff-brown upperparts, warm buff patch on sides of breast and upper flanks.

39 Black-headed Canary *Serinus alario*   **Text page 207**

Namibia, Botswana and South Africa: dry scrub and open grassland, upland rocky outcrops, edges of cultivation, gardens.

a Adult male: black from head to sides of lower breast, white collar, rich brown upperparts and tail.

b Adult female: head and face dull grey, tinged brown, with darker streaks, upperparts also streaked; rich brown median coverts and tips to greater coverts.

c Juvenile: similar to adult female but paler, with less rich brown wingbars; streaks continue to underparts.

d Adult male *leucolaema*: distinctive black-and-white face pattern; white collar continues across lower throat.

e Adult female *leucolaema*: as nominate female, but with faint face pattern of male.

PLATE 53   INDO-PACIFIC MUNIAS (1)

226 Javan Munia *Lonchura leucogastroides*   **Text page 415**

Singapore to Lombok Island (with introductions elsewhere, not shown): lowland grassland with bushes, scrub, edges of cultivation, rice-paddies, gardens.
a Adult: blackish-brown head (tinged purple) and upperparts; blackish-brown breast also tinged purple.
b Juvenile: paler than adult, lacks chocolate breast and black undertail-coverts.

227 Dusky Munia *Lonchura fuscans*   **Text page 416**

Borneo to Cagayan Sulu: grassland, scrub, edges of forest, river banks, edges of cultivation, rice-paddies, gardens. Map above.
a Adult: dark brown with black tips forming a scalloped pattern on body and wings; pale blue-grey base to lower mandible.
b Juvenile: as adult but more uniform, with all-dark bill.

228 Moluccan Munia *Lonchura molucca*   **Text page 417**

Indonesia: grassland, rice-paddies, bushes and scrub, also edges of forest and cultivation.
a Adult: black head and breast, brown upperparts, thinly barred rump and underparts.
b Juvenile: head and breast dark brown or dark buffish-brown, fine pale buff tips to face; pale buff underparts with faint dark bars.

229 Spotted Munia *Lonchura punctulata*   **Text page 417**

India to southern China and Vietnam and parts of Malay archipelago (with introductions elsewhere, not shown): grassland or rice-paddies, scrub, edges of forest, parks, gardens.
a Adult: rich brown from face to breast, rump pale brown and finely spotted, yellowish uppertail-coverts; underparts white, with dark brown or blackish fringes forming crescents.
b Juvenile: buffish-brown; warmer on wings and paler buff below, belly whitish or cream.
c Adult *subundulata*: slightly darker than nominate; rump and uppertail-coverts dull olive.
d Adult *topela*: face duller brown, extending to lower throat; underparts finely fringed pale brown, with patterned feather centres.

231 White-bellied Munia *Lonchura leucogastra*   **Text page 420**

Malay peninsula to the Philippines: bushes or scrub, forest, forest edges or clearings, edges of cultivation and villages.
a Adult: generally blackish, with fine buff shaft streaks on upperparts, tail dark brown with broad yellow edges; large blue or blackish-grey bill.
b Juvenile: similar to adult but duller, with dull or off-white underparts, less yellow on tail; bill dark.
c Adult *castanonota*: crown to back and wings chestnut or deep warm brown; blackish-brown from face to breast and flanks.

226a

226b

227a

227b

228a

228b

229c

229a

229b

229d

231a

231c

231b

PLATE 54   INDO-PACIFIC MUNIAS (2)

187 Red Munia *Amandava amandava*   Text page 379

Central Pakistan to Vietnam, also parts of Malay archipelago (with introductions elsewhere, not shown): tall grass, reeds, sugarcane, bushes or scrub.
a Adult male breeding: bright red, speckled with white spots; vent and undertail-coverts dark brown or black, tinged with red.
b Adult female: bright red rump, grey-brown upperparts, white spots at tips of coverts.
c Juvenile: as female, but with dark bill, generally browner upperparts, pale buff wingbars and fringes to tertials.
d Adult male *flavidiventris*: orange-red from head to breast, pale orange belly.

188 Green Munia *Amandava formosa*   Text page 380

Northern India: tall grassland, sugarcane, open forest or woodland with bushes or scrub.
a Adult male: red bill, lime-green body, broad stripes on flanks, undertail bright yellowish.
b Adult female: greyish olive-green above; grey breast, stripes on flanks more widely spaced than on male.
c Juvenile: grey-brown head and upperparts, with yellowish-green tinge to rump; bill dark, with pale pink edges at base.

225 White-rumped Munia *Lonchura striata*   Text page 414

Kashmir to southern China and Taiwan, also parts of Malaysia and Indonesia (introduced Ryukyu Islands): dry scrub and light woodland, grassland, edges of cultivation, rice-paddies, gardens.
a Adult: white rump, belly and flanks; fine pale buff streaks on dark brown head and upperparts.
b Juvenile: slightly paler or browner than adult; white areas duller, streaks poorly defined.
c Adult male *fumigata*: lacks streaks on upperparts; belly creamy or off-white.
d Adult male *acuticauda*: heavily streaked with pale buff on head, face and upperparts; belly has pale brown fringes and shaft streaks.

230 Rufous-bellied Munia *Lonchura kelaarti*   Text page 419

Southwest India to Sri Lanka: grassland with thickets or scrub, edges of forest and cultivation, plantations.
a Adult: brown upperparts, heavily spotted underparts, golden-yellow uppertail-coverts.
b Juvenile: pale tips to face, finely barred chin; throat and underparts faintly spotted.
c Adult *jerdoni*: upperparts finely streaked pale buff; warm rufous rump, pale buff-brown edges and tips to underparts.

187a

187b

187d

187c

188a

188b

225a

225c

188c

225d

225b

230c

230a

230b

PLATE 55   INDONESIAN FINCHES

235 Chestnut Munia *Lonchura malacca*   **Text page 423**

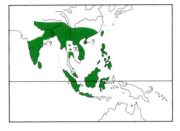

India to Vietnam, Malaysia and Indonesia (with introductions elsewhere, not shown): edges of forest, marshes, reeds, cane-fields, grassland, rice-paddies or scrub.

a Adult: deep chestnut from rump to tail; black from centre of belly to undertail-coverts.

b Juvenile: dull brown face, buffish-brown upperparts, warmer brown wings; less yellow in tail than adult.

c Adult *atricapilla*: as nominate, except warm brown flanks and upper belly.

d Adult *jagori*: forehead, crown and nape dark grey-brown; rich brown underparts, black from belly to undertail-coverts.

e Adult *ferruginosa*: white head; chin to breast black.

f Adult *sinensis*: very similar to *jagori*, but lacks black from belly to undertail-coverts.

234 Chestnut-and-white Mannikin *Lonchura quinticolor* **Text page 422**

Lesser Sunda Islands: coastal scrub, grassland, edges of montane forest, cultivation and rice-paddies.

a Adult: dark chestnut-brown head, with paler shaft streaks on face and greyish tips to nape; golden-yellow from rump to outer tail feathers.

b Juvenile: pale grey face; ear-coverts have fine pale buff shaft streaks.

236 White-headed Munia *Lonchura maja*   **Text page 425**

Southern Thailand to Bali: tall grassland, marshes, swamps, reed-beds, edges of cultivation and gardens.

a Adult: whitish head, pale buff breast, dark chestnut-brown rump, golden-yellow tinge to outer tail feathers.

b Juvenile: generally pale brown above, with warm brown rump; pale buff underparts.

237 Pale-headed Munia *Lonchura pallida*   **Text page 425**

Sulawesi and the Lesser Sunda Islands: paddy-fields, dry scrub, grassland, edges of cultivation.

a Adult: very similar to adult White-headed Munia (236), but has greyer (or tinged buffish-brown) nape and breast, peachy-orange underparts, reddish-brown uppertail- and undertail-coverts.

b Juvenile: very similar to juvenile White-headed Munia (236), but whiter below and lacks warm brown rump.

PLATE 56   PARROTFINCHES (1)

206   Green-tailed Parrotfinch *Erythrura hyperythra*   **Text page 397**

Malay archipelago: forest and bamboo jungle, open clearings or edges, also (in some areas) rice-paddies.
a Adult male: black forehead, deep blue crown, deep green upperparts; rich peachy-orange rump and warm buff-brown underparts.
b Juvenile: pale version of adult; lacks any black or blue on head; black tip to pale yellow bill.
c Adult male *macrorhyncha*: less blue on forecrown, extensively green on flanks, pale peach-buff underparts.
d Adult female *macrorhyncha*: as male above.
e Adult male *brunneiventris*: shorter bill; green sides to nape, sides of breast to flanks deep blue with green tinge.

207   Pin-tailed Parrotfinch *Erythrura prasina*   **Text page 398**

Thailand to Borneo and Java: forest edges and secondary-growth forest, bamboo, also rice-paddies.
a Adult male: deep blue face; bright red from centre of lower breast to belly and from rump to tail.
b Adult male 'yellow variant': as above, but all red replaced with yellow.
c Adult female: blue wash to cheeks and sides of neck; no red on belly and no long central tail projections.
d Juvenile: pale yellow base to lower mandible; dull greenish underparts, dull orange-red from rump to tail.
e Adult male *coelica*: blue from face to breast meets red on lower breast.
f Adult female *coelica*: heavier blue wash from face to centre of breast.

209   Three-coloured Parrotfinch *Erythrura tricolor*   **Text page 400**

Lesser Sunda Islands: eucalyptus forest edges, grassland thickets and bamboo.
a Adult: deep blue forehead; face to breast, sides of breast to belly and flanks paler blue, bright red from rump to tail.
b Juvenile: pale yellow base to lower mandible; dusky face, pale greenish-buff underparts.

210   Mount Katanglad Parrotfinch *Erythrura coloria*   **Text page 400**

Central Mindanao, the Philippines: tall grass in clearings and edges of montane forest.
a Adult: red-and-blue face, otherwise all green except for bright red rump, uppertail-coverts and tail.
b Juvenile: almost entirely dull pale green except for dull reddish-brown uppertail-coverts and tail; pale yellow base to bill.

PLATE 57   PARROTFINCHES (2)

211 Blue-faced Parrotfinch *Erythrura trichroa*   **Text page 401**

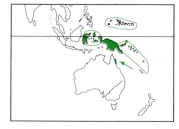

Northeast Australia, New Guinea, parts of Indonesia, western Pacific islands: forest clearings and edges, undergrowth, grassland and edges of cultivation.
a Adult male: deep blue from forehead to crown and face; rich or deep red from rump to tail.
b Adult female: less blue on head and face, rump to tail duller; buff-brown underparts.
c Juvenile: pale green head and underparts, pale yellow base to bill.
d Adult male *sigilifera*: deep blue or violet-blue on head and face, hindcrown to upper mantle tinged yellow.

213 Red-throated Parrotfinch *Erythrura psittacea*   **Text page 403**

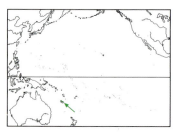

New Caledonia, south Pacific: forest edges or clearings, bushes, edges of cultivation, plantations, gardens.
a Adult: bright red forehead, crown, face and throat and from lower rump to tail; tail has elongated central feathers.
b Juvenile: yellowish wash to sides of chin and throat, dull green underparts; pale yellow base to bill.

215 Pink-billed Parrotfinch *Erythrura kleinschmidti*   **Text page 405**

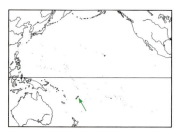

Fiji: mature rainforest or secondary forest.
Adult: very large pale pink bill; black face, blue from crown to nape, short black tail.

214 Red-headed Parrotfinch *Erythrura cyaneovirens*   **Text page 403**

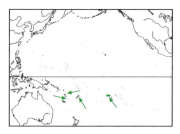

Fiji and south-central Pacific islands: forest or plantations, edges of cultivation, rice-paddies, parks and gardens.
a Adult: deep red from head to nape, bluish wash to chin, throat and nape; green underparts.
b Juvenile: bluish face, red tips to crown; distinctive bill has bright yellow base.
c Adult male *regia*: deep blue nape, sides of neck and underparts.
d Adult male *pealii*: blue from throat to breast; bright or deep green upperparts and underparts.
e Adult female *pealii*: less red on crown and face; green hindcrown and sides of nape.
f Juvenile *pealii*: bluish face and throat, green from crown to nape.
g Adult male *serena*: similar to adult male *regia*, but deep blue restricted to nape, sides of neck and from chin to breast; wing-coverts also tinged with blue.

PLATE 58 PARROTFINCHES (3) AND NEW GUINEA FINCHES

208 Green-faced Parrotfinch *Erythrura viridifacies*   **Text page 399**

The Philippines: forest edges and lowland grassland with thickets or bamboo.
a Adult male: entirely pale green, except for bright red uppertail-coverts and long tail and pale buff undertail-coverts.
b Adult female: as male, but shorter tail and more extensive yellowish-buff from belly to undertail-coverts.

212 Papuan Parrotfinch *Erythrura papuana*   **Text page 402**

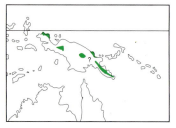

West and central New Guinea: forest, also edges and clearings with tall grass.
a Adult male: very similar to Blue-faced Parrotfinch (211; see Plate 57), but larger and separated on range; blue from forehead to crown, face and chin also blue.
b Adult female: similar to male, but blue less extensive on crown and face and does not extend to pale green chin.

198 Crimson-sided Mountain Finch *Oreostruthus fuliginosus*

Text page 389

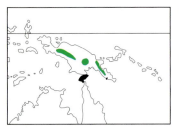

New Guinea: montane forest edges, clearings and undergrowth.
a Adult male: all dark chocolate-brown, except for reddish flanks (with dark brown bases) and bright red rump and uppertail-coverts.
b Juvenile: entirely warm brown, with orange-red base to lower mandible, dull red rump and uppertail-coverts.
c Adult male *hagenensis*: paler brown underparts, and red on flanks less extensive; red tips to mantle and back.

199 Crimson Finch *Neochmia phaeton* (See also Plate 65)

Text page 390

New Guinea to northern Australia: tropical swamps or areas of tall grass, cane grass, dense vegetation or savanna woodland.
a Adult male *evangelinae*: pale bluish-grey base to bill; pale grey lower breast, belly to undertail-coverts white.
b Adult female *evangelinae*: pale blue base to bill; pale grey lower breast, belly to undertail-coverts white.

208a

208b

212a

212b

198a

198c

199a

198b

199b

AH.

PLATE 59   NEW GUINEA MANNIKINS (1)

233   White-spotted Mannikin *Lonchura leucosticta*   **Text page 421**

Southern New Guinea: tall grass, savanna, bamboo, forest edges, clearings, river banks and marshes.
a Adult: heavily streaked head, upperparts and breast; chin and throat pale whitish-buff, rump pale golden-yellow.
b Juvenile: dull brown, warmer below, finely streaked with pale buff on head, face and breast; pale double wingbar.

232   Streak-headed Mannikin *Lonchura tristissima*   **Text page 421**

New Guinea: edges of forest, grass, shrubs, scrub, villages and towns in forest.
a Adult male: almost entirely dark brown, finely streaked or spotted with pale buff on head; golden-yellow rump patch.
b Adult female: slightly paler than male; broad pale streaks on head and face, pale buff spots on breast.

241   Grey-crowned Mannikin *Lonchura nevermanni*   **Text page 428**

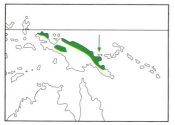

New Guinea: lowland savanna, tall grass and reeds, river banks and rice-fields.
a Adult male: pale buff head with blackish-brown bases showing; chin and throat black, rump rufous-brown, yellow on uppertail-coverts and sides of tail.
b Adult female: as male, but head browner with only pale buff tips; chin and throat extensively dark brown.
c Juvenile: uniform brown head, face and upperparts (excluding warmer brown rump); pale yellowish-buff uppertail-coverts and sides to tail.

247   Black Mannikin *Lonchura stygia*   **Text page 434**

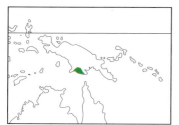

New Guinea: lowland grassland, reeds, swamp grassland, marshes and dry savannas.
a Adult male: all glossy black, except for bright golden-yellow rump and sides to tail.
b Adult female: as male, but mantle, back and wings slightly browner; rump chestnut.
c Juvenile: grey-brown face and upperparts, pale buff streaks on crown, nape, throat and breast; pale yellow sides to tail.

PLATE 60   NEW GUINEA MANNIKINS (2)

246 Chestnut-breasted Mannikin *Lonchura castaneothorax* (See also Plate 63)   **Text page 432**

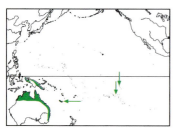

Northeast Australia, New Guinea (introductions on some Pacific islands): grassland with scrub, swamp or marshes, thornbush thickets, edges of cultivation, towns and villages.

a Adult *sharpii*: pale buffish-white forehead, with crown and nape pale buffish-grey, no streaks on black face; deep golden-brown from rump to tail, extensive barring on flanks.

b Adult *ramsayi*: blackish head, with pale buff tips to crown and nape; golden-yellow uppertail-coverts and sides to tail, heavily barred flanks.

238 Great-billed Mannikin *Lonchura grandis*   **Text page 426**

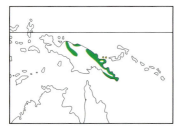

New Guinea: lowland rank grassland, swamps, marshes, cane fields, rice-fields and gardens.

a Adult: huge bill; chestnut sides to lower breast and flanks, yellowish-brown edges to tail.

b Juvenile: bill as adult; dull brown head and face, pale buff-brown from rump to sides of tail.

250 Snow Mountain Mannikin *Lonchura montana*   **Text page 436**

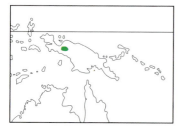

New Guinea: alpine plateaux, montane boggy grassland, stunted scrub and edges of cultivation.

a Adult male: black from face to chin, bright or deep warm brown from sides of neck to breast; pale yellow rump and uppertail-coverts.

b Adult female: as male but slightly duller; black on forehead, paler straw-yellow breast.

c Juvenile: dark face, dull orange-brown breast and dull or dingy buff from belly to undertail.

248 Grand Valley Mannikin *Lonchura teerinki*   **Text page 434**

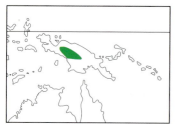

New Guinea: edges of clearings, cultivation, grassland, weed or scrub patches, abandoned gardens.

a Adult male: black from face to breast, fading into brown flanks; bright yellowish-straw rump and uppertail-coverts.

b Adult female: as male, but flanks whiter or streaked with brown.

c Juvenile: very similar to juvenile Snow Mountain Mannikin (250), but warmer brown upperparts and dull or dusky grey-brown breast; pale orange wash to flanks.

PLATE 61   NEW GUINEA MANNIKINS (3)

239 Grey-banded Mannikin *Lonchura vana*

Text page 427

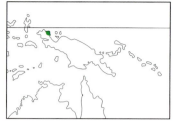

New Guinea: high-level grassland on hillsides or mountain slopes.
a Adult: whitish head, face, chin and breast, brown tips to hindcrown and nape; golden-yellow from rump to tail.
b Juvenile: dull greyish olive-brown head, face and upperparts,
pale yellowish-buff underparts.

249 Alpine Mannikin *Lonchura monticola*

Text page 435

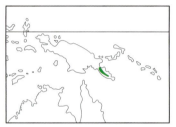

New Guinea: alpine grassland, rocky or boulder-strewn pastures
with stunted bushes.
a Adult: black face and throat; sides and lower breast white, with
black (lower) breast-band and bars on flanks; bright yellow from
uppertail-coverts to base of tail.
b Juvenile: dark brown forehead and face; brown upperparts,
buffish-grey breast, pale buffish-white underparts.

240 Grey-headed Mannikin *Lonchura caniceps*

Text page 428

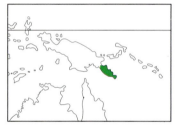

Southeast New Guinea: grassland, savanna, swamp, marshes,
forest edges and clearings, rice-fields, roadsides and gardens.
a Adult: pale grey head and breast, dark chocolate-brown back
and wings; rich bright yellow or orange from rump to tail.
b Juvenile: almost entirely sandy buff-brown, with darker brown
wings.
c Adult *scratchleyana*: paler than nominate; brown back and
wings, warm or reddish-buff underparts with black undertail-
coverts.

244 Hunstein's Munia *Lonchura hunsteini*

Text page 431

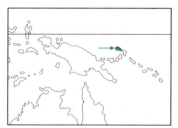

Bismarck archipelago (introduced Micronesia): lowland grassland.
a Adult: all black except for white tips to head and face; bright
chestnut rump, with uppertail-coverts and tail golden-yellow.
b Juvenile: dark grey head and brown upperparts; fine pale buff
tips to crown and face, pale buffish-brown breast and belly.

PLATE 62   NEW BRITAIN FINCHES AND PLUM-HEADED FINCH

242 New Britain Mannikin *Lonchura spectabilis*   **Text page 429**

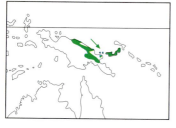

New Guinea to Bismarck archipelago: lowland grassland, savanna and tall grass with scrub, cane grass and gardens.
a Adult: black on head, lower flanks and undertail-coverts, white on rest of underparts; golden-orange from rump to tail.
b Juvenile: black face, chin and throat, brown on crown and upperparts; pale warm or buff-brown from rump to tail.
c Adult *mayri*: warmer brown upperparts than nominate; black sharply defined on nape, creamy-white breast, yellowish rest of underparts, pale yellow from rump to tail.

251 Thick-billed Munia *Lonchura melaena*   **Text page 436**

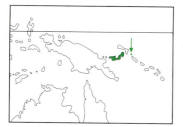

New Britain to Solomon Islands: rank grassland with bushes or scrub and swamps.
    Adult: all black or blackish-brown, except for pale cinnamon or orange patch on belly and rich golden-brown from rump to tail.

243 New Ireland Mannikin *Lonchura forbesi*   **Text page 430**

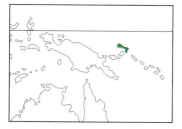

Bismarck archipelago: lowland grassland.
a Adult: similar to New Britain Mannikin (242), but underparts rich cinnamon or reddish-buff, silvery tips to breast in fresh plumage.
b Juvenile: very similar to juvenile New Britain Mannikin (242) but separable on range, and possibly slightly paler brown underparts, with pale yellowish-brown from rump to base of tail.

217 Plum-headed Finch *Aidemosyne modesta*   **Text page 407**

Eastern Australia: open woodland and tall savanna grassland, scrub and thickets.
a Adult male: deep 'plum' reddish-brown from forehead to crown (visible usually only at close range – appears brown at a distance), black upper lores and chin.
b Adult female: slightly reddish or duller plum-coloured on forehead; white supercilium, black lores and whitish chin.
c Juvenile: paler than adults; pale cream double wingbar, faintly or diffusely barred underparts.

242a

242b

242c

251

243a

243b

217a

217b

217c

AH

PLATE 63   AUSTRALIAN FINCHES (1)

252 Pictorella Finch *Lonchura pectoralis*   **Text page 437**

Northern Australia: open woodland, grassland with scattered trees and bushes, spinifex plains, edges of cultivation.
a Adult male breeding: black face and throat, broad white tips and obscure black bases on breast feathers, small whitish tips to wing-coverts.
b Adult female breeding: as male, but shows more black-and-white barring on breast, smaller and fewer white spots to tips of coverts.
c Juvenile: dark brown face, paler buff-brown upperparts; bill blackish, with pale base to lower mandible.

246 Chestnut-breasted Mannikin *Lonchura castaneothorax* (See also Plate 60)   **Text page 432**

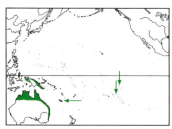

Northeast Australia, New Guinea (introductions on some Pacific islands): grassland with scrub, swamp or marshes, thornbush thickets, edges of cultivation, towns and villages.
a Adult: pale grey from forehead to nape, black face with fine streaks, black bars or crescents on sides of breast and flanks; golden-yellow from rump to tail.
b Juvenile: grey head, brown upperparts, dull buffish orange-brown breast-band, pale buff on rest of underparts.

245 Yellow-rumped Mannikin *Lonchura flaviprymna*   **Text page 432**

Northwest and northern Australia: tall rank grassland, savanna with reeds, mangroves, plains with scattered trees, edges of cultivation.
a Adult breeding: pale buff head, warm dark brown back and wings, deep golden-yellow rump, becoming paler on tail; yellowish underparts.
b Juvenile: pale cinnamon-brown upperparts, paler buffish-brown below, grey lores and bill.

193 Red-browed Firetail *Aegintha temporalis*   **Text page 385**

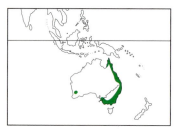

South and eastern Australia: eucalypt forest, clearings in open woodland, mangroves, orchards and gardens.
a Adult: bright red sides to bill, sides of forehead, supercilium, rump and uppertail-coverts; pale greenish-yellow neck patch, olive-green back and wings.
b Juvenile: black bill; no red on head, grey or olive-green upperparts.
c Adult *minor*: brighter green neck patch, back and wings than nominate; face and underparts paler or whitish.

252a

252b

252c

246a

246b

245a

245b

193a

193c

193b

A.H.

PLATE 64   AUSTRALIAN FINCHES (2)

196 Red-eared Firetail *Emblema oculata*

Text page 388

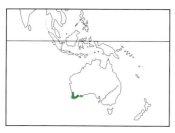

Southwest Australia: undergrowth of thick forest, dense coastal scrub, thickets and paperbark swamps.

a Adult male breeding: black from sides of forehead and lores to eye; bright red ear, belly to undertail black with large white spots or patches.

b Adult female breeding: as male but paler red ear.

c Juvenile: no black on face, pale red base to bill; barred underparts to breast, crescents from belly to undertail.

195 Beautiful Firetail *Emblema bella*

Text page 387

Southeast Australia and Tasmania: thick or dense belts of forest scrub or heathland, undergrowth with bracken, marshes or swamps.

a Adult male breeding: head pattern similar to Red-eared Firetail (196), but lacks red ear; entire underparts finely barred with dark olive, lower belly to undertail blackish.

b Juvenile: no black on face, pale red base to bill; buff from face to breast, finely barred underparts duller than adult.

194 Painted Finch *Emblema picta*

Text page 386

West and interior east-central Australia: stone deserts, gorges and rocky hills with acacia scrub, spinifex, dunes, also (some) gardens.

a Adult male breeding: unmistakable black and red; pale blue base to lower mandible, red face, chin and throat.

b Adult female: as male, but less red on face and belly (if any).

c Juvenile: no red on face; pale pink base to lower mandible, poorly defined white spots on black underparts.

197 Diamond Firetail *Emblema guttata*

Text page 388

East and southeast Australia: eucalypt forest, grassland with acacia scrub, open country or mallee, orchards, parks and gardens.

a Adult male breeding: grey head, black lores and red eye-ring; broad black band across white-spotted breast.

b Adult female breeding: as male, but lores duller or greyer, pale eye-ring and thinner breast-band.

c Juvenile: greyer-brown version of adult; bright red rump, black bill with pale base to lower mandible, flanks barred grey and white.

196b

196a

196c

195a

195b

194a

194b

194c

197b

197a

197c

44

PLATE 65   AUSTRALIAN FINCHES (3)

201 **Zebra Finch** *Poephila guttata*

Text page 392

Indonesia to Australia: dry brush, scrub and open woodland, plains, saltmarsh, edges of cultivation, parks and gardens.
a Adult male: warm orange or light chestnut ear-coverts, grey from chin to breast; thin black breast-band.
b Adult female: lacks orange or warm brown ear-coverts, breast-band and warm brown flank patch also missing.
c Juvenile: as adult female but slightly duller; bill black.
d Adult male *castanotis*: chin to breast finely barred pale grey and black.

199 **Crimson Finch** *Neochmia phaeton* (See also Plate 58)

Text page 390

New Guinea to northern Australia: tropical swamps or areas of tall grass, cane grass, dense vegetation or savanna woodland.
a Adult male: small white spots on upper flanks, bluish-grey or whitish base to lower mandible, black from lower belly to undertail-coverts.
b Adult female: red face, grey body with whitish spots on flanks, pale base to bill.
c Juvenile: generally dull brown, with reddish tips to greater coverts and edges of wings; reddish-brown tail, black bill.
d Adult male *evangelinae*: pale blue base to bill, white from centre of upper belly to undertail-coverts.

200 **Star Finch** *Neochmia ruficauda*

Text page 391

North and east Australia: waterside vegetation, swamps, damp grassland, scattered bushes, rushes, rice-fields and sugarcane.
a Adult male: red face and chin very finely spotted with white; rest of head yellowish-olive, underparts heavily spotted with white.
b Adult female: dull red from bill to eye; duller greyish-olive back and scapulars.
c Juvenile: pale grey-brown head and dull yellowish-olive upperparts, rump to tail warm buff-brown spotted with paler buff; bill black, pale buff-brown breast.
d Adult male *clarescens*: more extensive red on head, brighter yellowish-green upperparts, yellowish breast and flanks.

216 **Gouldian Finch** *Chloebia gouldiae*

Text page 406

Northern Australia: dry grassy plains with scattered trees, tall bushes along rivers or streams, woods and scrub with spinifex.
a Adult male 'black-headed': very distinctive multicoloured finch; black head, chin and throat.
b Adult male 'red-headed': bright red forehead, crown and face, bordered with black.
c Adult male 'yellow-headed': golden-yellow or orange forehead, crown and face, bordered with black.
d Adult female 'black-headed': as male, but lacks long central tail projections and strong blue edge to face; breast patch pink.
e Adult female 'red-headed': as male but base of bill black.
f Juvenile: grey head, dull olive-green back and wings, very short tail; dark grey bill with pale pink base to lower mandible, pinkish-buff breast.

201a

201b

201c

201d

199a

199b

199d

199c

216b

216c

216d

216e

216a

216f

200a

200d

200b

200c

PLATE 66   AUSTRALIAN FINCHES (4)

205 Black-throated Finch *Poephila cincta*   **Text page 396**

Northern Australia: tall rank grassland, reeds near water, mangroves, open plains with scattered trees, edges of cultivation.

a Adult: grey head, black lores, chin and upper breast, patch of black on rear of flanks, warm tan-brown underparts, white rump.

b Juvenile: duller version of adult, with poorly defined blackish-brown on upper breast and rear of flanks.

c Adult *atropygialis*: as nominate, but with black from lower back to tail and pale pink underparts.

202 Double-barred Finch *Poephila bichenovii*   **Text page 393**

North and east Australia: semi-arid country, dry-grass plains with scattered woodland or scrub, edges of cultivation, parks and gardens.

a Adult: all-white face bordered by black, second (lower) breast-band, finely barred pattern on closed wing.

b Juvenile: duller version of adult, with brown tinge to forehead, crown and back; breast-bands less well defined.

204 Long-tailed Finch *Poephila acuticauda*   **Text page 395**

Northern Australia: eucalypt woodland, dry-grass open plains, savanna with scattered trees and bushes.

a Adult: very similar to adult Black-throated Finch (205), but with long thin wispy central tail projection, pale pinkish underparts, yellow bill.

b Juvenile: dark grey chin and upper breast, pale or whitish sides to throat; lacks long central tail projections.

c Adult *hecki*: as nominate adult, but bill bright red.

203 Masked Finch *Poephila personata*   **Text page 394**

Northern Australia: dry open woodland, grassy areas with trees, often around farms or settlements, roadsides and suburbs.

a Adult: bright yellow bill, black forehead and black from lores to chin; deep brown head and upperparts, white rump, and black tail with elongated pointed central feathers.

b Juvenile: dull buffish-brown version of adult; dusky yellow bill.

c Adult *leucotis*: as nominate, but white from ear-coverts to sides of chin.

PLATE 67   SPARROWS

258 House Sparrow *Passer domesticus*

Text page 443

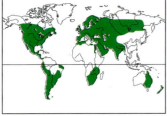

Cosmopolitan: urban, suburban and (some) rural habitats.

a Adult male breeding: grey crown and rump, dull white face, black from chin to upper breast, chestnut sides to crown and greyish nape.

b Adult male non-breeding: similar to breeding plumage, but nape and chin obscured by pale or grey tips; bill yellow.

c Adult female: short pale buff supercilium, pale buff stripes at sides of mantle bordered by darker stripes.

d Juvenile male: similar to adult female, but with whitish stripe behind eye and greyish chin and throat.

e Adult male *indicus* breeding: slightly smaller than nominate; cheeks, ear-coverts and underparts whiter.

259 Spanish Sparrow *Passer hispaniolensis*

Text page 446

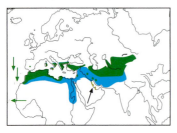

Cape Verde Islands, Canary Islands, discontinuously east through North Africa, Middle East, Central Asia to western China: dry open country, woodland and cultivation.

a Adult male breeding: chestnut crown and nape, black chin and throat with extensive black on underparts; thin white upper lores and white slightly behind eye.

b Adult male non-breeding: breeding plumage obscured by pale yellowish-buff tips; bill yellowish at base.

c Adult female breeding: broad pale buffish or creamy-buff supercilium, broad pale buff stripes at sides of mantle and back; underparts lightly or faintly streaked.

d Adult male *italiae* breeding: head as male Spanish; underparts and rump as male House Sparrow (258).

273 Desert Sparrow *Passer simplex*

Text page 462

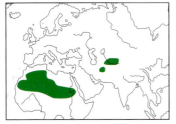

Sahara desert and Turkmenia: edges of deserts, sandy plains and oases, wadis and date palms, also around settlements.

a Adult male breeding: pale sandy-grey, with black lores, chin and bib; white face, wingbars and edges to flight feathers.

b Adult female breeding: pale sandy head and upperparts, very pale sandy-white wingbars and underparts; no marked face pattern.

c Adult male *zarudnyi* breeding: slightly greyer from crown to mantle and rump.

257 Saxaul Sparrow *Passer ammodendri*

Text page 442

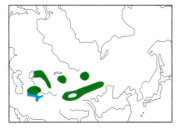

Central Asia discontinuously east to northwest China and Mongolia: deserts, oases, tamarisk or poplar thickets, settlements.

a Adult male breeding: very distinctive head pattern, with pale tawny-brown sides to nape; grey-brown body streaked with black on mantle.

b Adult female breeding: paler or duller version of male; grey face and dark grey smudge to chin and throat.

c Adult male *stoliczkae* breeding: much warmer brown than nominate male, with warm gingery-brown sides to crown and nape.

d Adult female *stoliczkae* breeding: warmer buff-brown than nominate female; prominent pale sandy supercilium, wingbars, and edges to tertials and secondaries.

258a

258d

258b

258c

258e

259b

259d

259a

259c

273a

273c

273b

257c

257a

257b

257d

PLATE 68   ASIATIC SPARROWS

262 Cinnamon Sparrow *Passer rutilans*   **Text page 450**

Northeast Afghanistan to Sakhalin, Taiwan, Laos and northern Burma: forest and oak woods, rhododendrons, alders, scrub and cultivation.
a Adult male breeding: bright russet or cinnamon-brown crown and upperparts, black streaks on mantle, off-white face.
b Adult female breeding: dark sides to crown (greyish centre), long broad creamy-white supercilium and broad dark eye-stripe.
c Adult male *cinnamomeus* breeding: as nominate male, but with yellow face and underparts.
d Adult male *intensior* breeding: similar to *cinnamomeus*, but with paler yellow tinge.

263 Pegu Sparrow *Passer flaveolus*   **Text page 451**

Northern Burma to South Vietnam: edges of forest, open country, plantations, cultivation, villages, towns and city suburbs.
a Adult male breeding: yellow forehead becoming grey on crown and nape, warm brown sides to nape and mantle, whitish or pale median coverts, yellowish underparts.
b Adult female breeding: uniform upperparts, broad pale creamy-buff supercilium, yellowish underparts.

260 Sind Jungle Sparrow *Passer pyrrhonotus*   **Text page 448**

Southeast Iran to northwest India (Indus floodplain): tamarisk and acacia scrub, tall grass along rivers, pools, marshes or rice-paddies.
a Adult male breeding: very similar to male House Sparrow (258; see Plate 67) but has grey crown and nape with chestnut-brown sides to nape, rich brown mantle and back streaked with black.
b Adult female breeding: very similar to female House Sparrow (258), but smaller; long well-defined buff supercilium, pale buff braces bordered with black on sides of mantle, white chin and throat and whitish underparts.

274 Tree Sparrow *Passer montanus*   **Text page 463**

Palearctic and Oriental: open or lightly wooded country, edges of cultivation, hedgerows and parkland. Replaces House Sparrow (258) as a city bird in east of range.
a Adult: rich brown from crown to nape, white collar across nape, black patch on ear-coverts, black on chin and throat only.
b Juvenile: paler or duller version of adult, with dark tips to forehead and face; bill yellowish at base.

262a

262c

262b

262d

263a

260a

263b

260b

274a

274b

PLATE 69 AFRICAN SPARROWS

265 Rufous Sparrow *Passer motitensis*

Text page 453

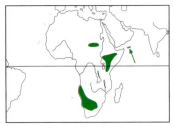

Chad to Somalia south to southern Angola, Namibia and South Africa: dry areas with grassland, acacia savanna with thickets of scrub. In some areas replaces House Sparrow (258; see Plate 67) as a bird of towns and cities.

a Adult male breeding: grey crown and nape, warm rich brown sides to crown and upperparts, bold black streaks on mantle.
b Adult female breeding: grey-brown crown and nape, pale buff supercilium and sides to nape, dark eye-stripe.
c Juvenile male: similar to adult female, but with warm buff-brown supercilium and sides to nape; dark grey bib.
d Adult male *cordofanicus* breeding: paler grey crown and whiter face and underparts than nominate.
e Adult female *cordofanicus* breeding: pale grey crown, whitish face and underparts.
f Adult male *shelleyi* breeding: dark grey crown extends to mantle; supercilium and sides of nape light brown.
g Adult female *shelleyi* breeding: as male but paler, with less extensive supercilium.
h Adult male *insularis* (Socotra Sparrow) breeding: grey crown extends to rump and uppertail-coverts, scapulars warm brown.
i Adult female *insularis* breeding: much duller than other females, with poorly defined supercilium; bill black.
j Adult male *rufocinctus* breeding: similar to *shelleyi*, but with pale eye and no black eye-stripe; cheeks and ear-coverts pale grey.
k Adult female *rufocinctus* breeding: grey crown and mantle, rich brown from rump to tail; dark grey chin and throat.

266 Iago Sparrow *Passer iagoensis*

Text page 455

Cape Verde Islands: dry open desolate lava plains, gorges, cliffs and edges of cultivation.

a Adult male breeding: blackish forehead, crown and eye-stripe; white face, rich cinnamon-brown supercilium and sides to nape.
b Adult female breeding: similar to female House Sparrow (258; see Plate 67) but has white median coverts, mantle and back streaked with black, pale creamy-buff supercilium.
c Juvenile male: warmer brown upperparts tinged with grey on mantle, warm brown supercilium, blackish chin.

267 Cape Sparrow *Passer melanurus*

Text page 456

South Africa: grassland and savanna, acacia woodland, thickets, edges of cultivation, suburban parks and gardens.

a Adult male breeding: diagnostic head-and-face pattern; unstreaked rich brown upperparts.
b Adult female breeding: faint or broken head pattern similar to male, but duller or greyer; unstreaked upperparts.
c Juvenile male: similar to adult female, with poorly defined head-and-face pattern.

265a

265b

265c

265g

265d

265e

265f

265i

265k

265h

265j

266c

266a

267c

266b

267a

267b

PLATE 70   MIDDLE EAST AND AFRICAN SPARROWS

264 Dead Sea Sparrow *Passer moabiticus*   **Text page 452**

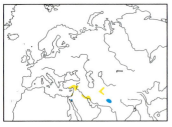

Cyprus to southwest Iran and western Afghanistan: tamarisks, poplars, scrub, bushes and reedbeds along rivers, streams or pools.
a Adult male breeding: ash-grey head with two-tone supercilium, white submoustachial stripe, yellow sides to throat, chestnut panel in wing.
b Adult female breeding: yellowish-buff supercilium, pale yellow sides to throat, buff-brown mantle with pale buff braces or 'tramlines'.
c Adult male *yatii* breeding: yellow wash to underparts.

261 Somali Sparrow *Passer castanopterus*   **Text page 449**

Southwest and eastern Ethiopia, Somalia and northwest Kenya: dry open plains with scattered bushes, cultivation, also rocky coasts with cliffs.
a Adult male breeding: creamy-yellow face, grey mantle, back and tail; underparts pale grey to off-white.
b Adult female breeding: broad creamy-buff supercilium.
c Adult male *fulgens* breeding: yellow tinge to face and underparts.

277 Chestnut Sparrow *Passer eminibey*   **Text page 467**

Western Sudan to southwest Somalia south to north-central Tanzania: dry grassland with scrub, acacia thickets, marshes or papyrus swamps, villages.
a Adult male breeding: dark chestnut; darker face, black bill.
b Adult male non-breeding: fine pale buff edges to upper and underparts, pale base to grey bill.
c Adult female breeding: warm buff-brown supercilium, rich brown chin, throat and scapulars, grey head and face, mantle also grey; pale yellowish bill.
d First-winter male: chestnut upperparts with black streaks on mantle, dark chestnut crescents on whitish underparts.
e Juvenile: rich warm buff supercilium, warm brown scapulars; pale yellowish bill.

275 Sudan Golden Sparrow *Passer luteus*   **Text page 465**

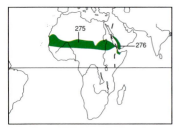

Mauritania to northern Sudan and extreme northern Ethiopia: dry arid scrub and thornbush, sparse savanna, cereal cultivation, towns.
a Adult male breeding: bright yellow head and underparts, rich brown mantle, scapulars, edges to secondaries and tertials.
b Adult female breeding: warm light brown upperparts, pale buff wingbars, yellowish-buff supercilium, yellowish face and breast; pinkish bill.
c First-winter male: similar to female, but with greyer head and rich brown tips to mantle and scapulars; bill dusky or blackish.

276 Arabian Golden Sparrow *Passer euchlorus*   **Text page 466**

Eastern Ethiopia to South Yemen: arid country with thornscrub. Map above.
a Adult male breeding: deep golden-yellow, pale yellow coverts, white edges to flight feathers, black bill.
b Adult female breeding: dark grey-brown crown, yellowish nape, face and breast; greyish upperparts tinged with yellow.

PLATE 71   AFRICAN GREY-HEADED SPARROWS

270 Parrot-billed Sparrow *Passer gongonensis*   **Text page 459**

Southeast Sudan to Somalia south to northeast Tanzania: dry arid thornbush or savanna with scattered acacias.
a Adult: large bulbous bill, grey-tinged brown body, bright chestnut lower back and rump.
b Juvenile: brown tinge to body heavier than on adult; pale chestnut lower back and rump, pale base to bill.

269 Swainson's Sparrow *Passer swainsonii*   **Text page 459**

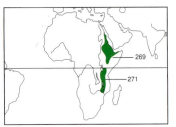

Northeast Sudan to northern Somalia and south to north-central Kenya: arid bush and scrub, plains, savannas, light woodland, towns and villages.
   Adult: grey head and body, dull brown mantle and scapulars, rich brown or chestnut rump and uppertail-coverts.

271 Swahili Sparrow *Passer suahelicus*   **Text page 460**

Southern Kenya to Malawi and northwest Mozambique: grassland with scattered trees, scrub and edges of cultivation, towns and villages. Map above.
   Adult: as Grey-headed Sparrow (268), but greyer-brown mantle and back, darker below from belly to undertail-coverts; chin to throat pale grey.

268 Grey-headed Sparrow *Passer griseus*   **Text page 458**

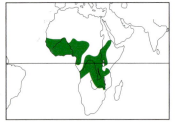

Senegal to northern Ethiopia south to Gabon and Tanzania: dry grassland, open plains, savanna with acacias and thornscrub, edges of cultivation, villages and towns.
a Adult: pale grey head, face and underparts, chin whitish, breast and flanks grey; mantle and scapulars grey-brown, becoming reddish-brown.
b Adult *ugandae*: as nominate adult, but darker grey head and breast with white chin and whitish underparts.

272 Southern Grey-headed Sparrow *Passer diffusus*   **Text page 461**

Angola to Tanzania south to South Africa: dry open plains, grassland with scattered thornscrub, towns and villages.
   Adult: pale grey head and underparts; mantle and scapulars pale brown, tinged with grey.

270a

270b

269

271

268a

268b

272

PLATE 72   PETRONIAS

281   Rock Sparrow *Petronia petronia*   **Text page 471**

Palearctic, discontinuously east from Portugal to western China, also North Africa and North Atlantic islands: barren hills and mountains, rocky outcrops, gorges, ruins and scree slopes.
a Adult: black-and-white head stripes, pale buff braces on mantle, pale yellow spot on lower throat, underparts streaked brown; white tips to tail not always visible at rest.
b Juvenile: as adult, but tinged pale brown and braces less well defined; no yellow spot on throat, dull grey underparts.
c Adult *puteicola*: as nominate adult, but slightly larger and paler; streaks on underparts barely visible in the field.

278   Pale Rock Sparrow *Petronia brachydactyla*   **Text page 468**

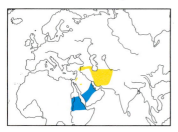

Southeast Turkey to the Caucasus, Middle East to Baluchistan: grassy plains or hillsides with rocky outcrops, stony deserts and wadis.
a Adult: pale, unstreaked, lark-like ground-dweller with long wings, pale bill, pale buff-brown moustachial stripe and darker malar stripe.
b Juvenile: as adult but paler; dark tip and edges to bill.

283   Bush Petronia *Petronia dentata*   **Text page 474**

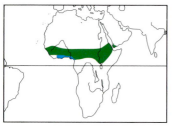

Senegal to central Ethiopia and North and South Yemen: dry or arid country, semi-desert valleys or wadis with scrub or sparse vegetation.
a Adult male: light chestnut supercilium with chestnut running behind eye to rear of ear-coverts; white chin and throat, yellow lower throat.
b Adult female: broad pale buff supercilium, some streaks on mantle, pale throat with light yellow spot.
c Juvenile: browner than adult, resembling female sparrow; pale warm buff supercilium, pale face; dark malar stripes border sides of throat.

279   Yellow-throated Sparrow *Petronia xanthocollis*   **Text page 469**

Southeast Turkey to northwest India and Nepal: dry forest and woods, scrub, groves, oases, orchards, date palms, edges of cultivation.
a Adult male breeding: pale grey head and upperparts, whitish throat with yellow spot; bright chestnut lesser coverts, medians white.
b Adult female: as adult male, but yellow on throat almost invisible, lesser coverts warm brown or grey-brown; pale base to bill.
c Juvenile: similar to adult female, but shows more supercilium; buffish face and breast, white throat and no yellow spot.

281a

281b

281c

278a

278b

283a

283b

283c

279c

279a

279b

PLATE 73

280 Yellow-spotted Petronia *Petronia pyrgita*   **Text page 470**

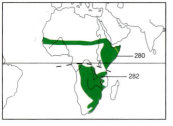

Mauritania and Senegal discontinuously east to Ethiopia south to Uganda and Tanzania: dry grassland with scrub, light woodland, thornscrub and edges of cultivation.
a Adult: almost entirely uniform light grey; white chin and throat, small yellow spot on lower throat (difficult to see in the field).
b Adult *pallida*: paler than nominate; upperparts pale buffish-brown, underparts almost entirely white.

282 Southern Yellow-throated Sparrow *Petronia superciliaris*
Text page 473

Southern Congo to southern Tanzania south to eastern South Africa: grassland with acacias, thornscrub, light woodland, trees near rivers or streams. Map above.
a Adult: broad whitish-buff supercilium (mostly behind the eye), broad dark brown eye-stripe, pale yellow spot on lower throat.
b Juvenile: pale buffish-brown supercilium, warm brown body with darker brown streaks.

254 Java Sparrow *Padda oryzivora*   **Text page 439**

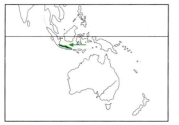

Java to Bawean (with introductions elsewhere, not shown): lowland grassland or open woodland with grass or scrub, edges of cultivation.
a Adult: bluish-grey upperparts and breast, pale pink belly, flanks and vent.
b Juvenile: grey-brown; dull buff face, pale pink base to bill.

253 Timor Dusky Sparrow *Padda fuscata*   **Text page 438**

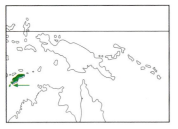

Timor to Roti: lowland scrub, grassland and saltflats, edges of cultivation and rice-paddies.
a Adult: black crown, white face, deep chocolate- or purplish-brown upperparts and breast.
b Juvenile: similar to juvenile Java Sparrow (254), but wholly dark grey bill and warm orange-buff breast.

41 São Tomé Grosbeak *Neospiza concolor*   **Text page 209**

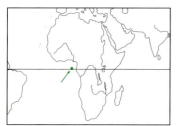

São Tomé: dense rainforest.
    Adult: all dark cinnamon-brown, slightly paler below; bill dark or dusky horn.

280a

280b

282a

282b

254a

254b

253a

253b

41

GENUS *FRINGILLA*

Three species. Robust or sturdy finches with stout bills and a characteristic jerking head movement and shuffling gait. Their distribution is Palearctic, with one species an island endemic. The Brambling is a true migrant and the Chaffinch a partial migrant. They are very similar to Cardueline finches (with which they have been merged in some classifications), but differ in nesting behaviour, feeding of nestlings, and lack of a crop.

1 CHAFFINCH *Fringilla coelebs*   Plate 1
Palearctic

Fringilla coelebs Linnaeus, 1758, Syst. Nat., ed. 10, p. 179, Sweden.

IDENTIFICATION Length of male 14–18 cm, of female 14–17·5 cm (5½–7 in). A medium-sized finch, often appearing quite stocky. The head has a gently peaked crown and the tail is slightly forked; walks with a characteristic jerky hopping gait. Males are very distinctive. **Confusion species:** The closely related but larger Blue Chaffinch (2) is entirely blue- or slate-grey and lacks white medians or tips to greater coverts. Females and immatures are distinguished at all times from the similarly plumaged Brambling (3) by green or greenish edges to brown rump and uppertail-coverts; Brambling is generally more orange and always shows a large white rump.

♂ *Detail: outermost (left) and second outermost tail feathers.*

DESCRIPTION Sexes differ. **Adult male** (all races except North Africa and Atlantic islands) summer plumage: Forehead black or blackish, merging into slaty grey-blue of crown, nape and hindneck; sides of head, lores, area over eye to ear-coverts and cheeks deep pink, tinged deep orange. Mantle and back deep reddish-brown to chestnut, becoming blue-green on scapulars; lower back and rump green or deep green, extending slightly onto uppertail-coverts and becoming blue-grey. Tail has slate-grey centre to otherwise black feathers, all thinly edged green, outer tail feathers white. Median and outer lesser coverts white, inner lesser coverts bluish-grey or green (merging with scapulars); greater coverts black, thinly fringed and broadly tipped white; alula and primary coverts black; flight feathers black or brownish-black, outers (except outermost three) with broad white or yellowish-white bases (shows as small white square on closed wing), all finely edged greenish-yellow; tertials also blackish, broadly edged and tipped chestnut in fresh plumage, but soon becoming pale buff. Chin and throat to breast and flanks deep pink tending to orange, becoming duller on lower breast and belly; ventral region and undertail-coverts white. Bill pale blue-grey (dark tip in summer), becoming yellow or buffish in winter but retaining dark tip. Legs and feet pale pinkish-brown. In winter, a paler or somewhat duller version of summer plumage, especially on head (crown and nape become grey-brown), mantle and underparts; greenish-yellow edges to secondaries become more pronounced. **Adult female** (all races except North Africa and Atlantic islands) summer plumage: Forehead to nape, mantle, scapulars and back dull earth-brown, tinged slightly grey; sides of head and neck washed smoke-grey, quite pronounced on some, but otherwise lores, cheeks and ear-coverts slightly paler than upperparts. Upperparts as male except for rump, which is green or deep green, deepest in centre and browner at edges. Tail as male but brown instead of slate-grey or black, outer tail feathers white. Wings also as male but more brownish-black. Chin and throat pale or dingy buff, becoming dull buffish-grey on breast and upper belly with a tinge of pale grey (or, on some, pink) on breast; belly paler, more off-white, with whiter undertail-coverts. In winter, very similar, but less grey about sides of head and neck and white in wings not so bright. Bill at all times brown or brownish, darkest at tip, palest at base and on lower mandible. Legs pink or pinkish-brown. **Juvenile:** Very similar to winter-plumage female, but with conspicuous pale buff patch on nape; rump shows less green, and is more uniform brown with yellowish wash to underparts. On males, mantle is tinged warm brown and cheeks and ear-coverts more buff than brown. Moults July-September: first-winter plumage as adult, but retains juvenile wing and tail feathers and some outer greater coverts and alula; retained tail feathers are narrower than those of adult. Breeds in first summer.

GEOGRAPHICAL VARIATION Very little variation in plumage among races found in Europe and the Middle East, except for some slight differences in the intensity or depth of colour of head and body, usually undetectable in the field. However, males of British race *gengleri* have brick-red underparts compared with vinaceous-red of nominate race; males of race *schiebeli* are also similar to nominate but paler on underparts, with pale pinkish throat. Males of North African and North Atlantic island races lack chestnut mantle and upper back, and deep pinkish-orange of face and underparts. North African races *africana* and *spodiogenys* have entire head and neck (except chin and throat) bluish-grey, with forehead and upper lores black or blackish (*africana* has a thin white eye-ring and a small pale or whitish spot behind eye), mantle and back olive-green (deeper and extending to rump on *africana*), and blue or bluish-grey scapulars, rump (*spodiogenys*) and uppertail-coverts; *spodiogenys* also shows (quite broadly on some) white edges to secondaries and tertials, the white in outer two tail feathers has a dark outer web for the terminal half of the feather and white on a large area of inner web of next inner feathers. In both races, chin and throat to belly are pink or washed peach. Those on Gran Canaria, Gomera and Tenerife (*tintillon*) have black on forehead becoming deep slate-blue on crown to mantle and back, and dull green or yellowish-green on rump becoming deep slate-grey-blue on uppertail-coverts and tail; outer tail feathers have variable amounts of white, with a blackish terminal half to outer webs, and a white spot on the next feather; the wings are generally black, but median coverts and tips of greater coverts are white, secondaries and primaries edged pale green; underparts peachy-buff or pinkish on lower breast and flanks or whitish on belly and undertail-coverts, but some can be heavily washed yellow; bill virtually all black or dark bluish-horn. On the island of Hierro, *ombriosa* is very similar to *tintillon*, but has dull green on lower mantle, back and rump, a small white patch at base of inner primaries, and fine yellowish edges to secondaries; underparts are very similar, but the peachy-buff is paler and does not always extend onto flanks. Males on Las Palmas (*palmae*) differ from *ombriosa* in having upperparts entirely deep slate-blue and the yellowish-green fringes to inner secondaries, primaries and tertials more pronounced; the central tail feathers are grey; underparts are mostly white, with a light peach or pinkish wash to chin, throat and upper breast, and flanks can be tinged with grey. Birds on Madeira (*maderensis*) and the Azores (*moreletti*) closely resemble the North African races, with deep blue on crown and nape (paler on *moreletti*), green or olive-green across mantle and rump interrupted by blue on lower mantle and back (to the rump on *moreletti*) and buff or yellow fringes to flight feathers; light pink or peach-buff from face to breast (or tinged with brown on some birds on the Azores), becoming pinkish or white on belly and flanks. All the above races have dark or almost black bills; those on the Canaries (and some of the birds on the Azores) have slightly larger and deeper-based bills. Females of the North African and Atlantic island races are generally paler or grey-brown on the upperparts, with olive or grey-green on the rump and with bluish-grey uppertail-coverts; the chin and throat are pale or dull peachy-buff, with sides of throat and breast washed buffish-brown; the wings are paler or duller than in other races, with white tips to median coverts and pale yellowish-buff tips to greater coverts and edges to secondaries. Females on Madeira (*maderensis*) have only one white outer tail feather (all other races have two) and have mantle and back slightly darker or browner; on the Azores (*moreletti*) they are similar to females of the nominate race.

VOICE Call is a distinctive, almost metallic 'pink', 'spink' or 'chink', uttered as either a single or a double note from the ground or perch, also a loud 'wheet', 'whit', 'tsip' or 'tsirrup' (usually in spring) and a thin high-pitched or wheezing 'eeese'; in flight a characteristic quiet 'tap', 'chap' or 'tsup' note. Females on the ground utter a quiet soft 'chip' or 'chirrip'. *F. c. coelebs* has several variations or individual notes such as 'twit' or 'fit', and also a 'hooeed' note not dissimilar in tone to some calls of Willow Warbler (*Phylloscopus trochilus*) or Chiffchaff (*P. collybita*); in many areas of Europe the 'chink' call is unknown. Atlantic island races have local dialect variations, some of which can be described as variations on 'chwee', 'chee-oo' or 'chwoo'; others, e.g those on Tenerife, have one or two notes of their own. Song is a musical rattle of several notes repeated on a descending scale followed by a final rapid flourish, 'chip chip chip tell tell tell cherry-erry-erry tissi cheweeo' (W Garstang), usually given from a tree and repeated several times; birds in northern Europe have a distinctive variation to the song (occasionally heard elsewhere from spring migrants), with the normal song phrase followed immediately by a sharp 'chip' or 'chink' recalling the call of Great Spotted Woodpecker (*Dendrocopos major*). Local variations and dialects exist throughout the range, particularly in North Africa and the Atlantic islands, but song is unmistakably the same. In spring, females often give a repeated soft or feeble 'zi' or 'si-si-si'.

STATUS, HABITAT AND BEHAVIOUR Common, in places abundant. Found in both conifer (native and non-native) and deciduous woods, forest, heaths, copses, parks, orchards and gardens; often in stubble fields in autumn and winter. Most of the Canary Islands races inhabit forests of laurel or chestnut, except on Palma, Hierro and Madeira where pine forests are preferred. In winter, birds in mainland Europe are often found in mixed flocks of Bramblings (3), Greenfinches (44) and sparrows; also in large flocks comprising males only (*coelebs* = bachelor) or females and immatures. The bird has a distinctive short shuffling or jerky step with slightly nodding head in a rather crouched walk or hop; often rather shy or nervous, especially when in company of more aggressive species. Flight is bounding and undulating. Food is principally seeds, beechmast, corn, also buds, fruit, spiders, beetles, insects and their larvae; nestlings are fed on caterpillars.

DISTRIBUTION *F. c. coelebs*: Europe to northern Scandinavia, east through Russia (north to the tree line) to Kazakhstan and about 90°E (Krasnoyarsk), western Siberia, occasionally further east (to the Yenisei) in isolated areas; south to the shores of the northern Mediterranean from Portugal and Spain east to Turkey and northern Lebanon, including the Balearics, Sardinia, Corsica, Sicily and Cyprus.

F. c. gengleri: British Isles.

F. c. transcaspica: southern Caucasus and northern Iran (possibly also Turkmenia, Central Asia).

F. c. alexandrovi: northern Iran.

F. c. solomkoi: Crimea and the Caucasus.

F. c. schiebeli: Crete.

F. c. sarda: Sardinia.

F. c. africana: Morocco east to Tunisia and Cyrenaica (Libya) northwest Africa.

F. c. spodiogenys: northern and eastern Tunisia to Libya (Tripoli).

F. c. tintillon: Gran Canaria, Tenerife and Gomera.

F. c. ombriosa: Hierro (Canary Islands).

F. c. palmae: La Palma (Canary Islands).

F. c. maderensis: Madeira.

F. c. moreletti: the Azores.

The nominate race has also been introduced into New Zealand (where it is widespread) and the Cape Town area of South Africa.

Note: breeding birds in the southern Caucasus may be of the races *transcaspica*, *solomkoi* or *alexandrovi* or intermediates, as considerable interbreeding takes place.

MOVEMENTS Sedentary and migratory. Northern breeders of the nominate race move west, southwest or south to winter mostly within the range in central and southern Europe, around the Mediterranean, Cyprus, the Middle East to Israel, southern Iraq and southwest Iran. Those from southern Norway and Sweden together with some from Finland, Poland and the Baltic States move southwest to winter in the British Isles, and birds from Germany and central Europe winter in France and Spain. Breeding birds in northern Iran and the

southern Caucasus (*solomkoi*) move east to winter in Afghanistan, northern Pakistan, Kashmir and Nepal, also occurring regularly in northwest India. It is a scarce or irregular migrant (presumably *coelebs*) to Libya (in varying numbers annually, occasionally common in coastal areas, also one record from the Libyan desert), Egypt (has occurred in southern Egypt: Aswan, February 1976), and Tunisia. Vagrant to Iceland, Faroe Isles, Saudi Arabia (east to Dharan), Kuwait, United Arab Emirates, Tibet and eastern China – Beidahe, (March–April 1989) Shenyang, Liaoning Province (December 1963), and Beijing (winter 1988/89); birds of race *coelebs* (or perhaps *gengleri*) have occurred as vagrants to the Canary Islands.

It has also been recorded in North America: Massachusetts (April 1961), Newfoundland (February 1967), Louisiana (December 1978) and Maine (April 1980). While these probably relate to escapes from captivity, particularly the Louisiana record, the northeast bias in spring also suggests natural vagrancy. Southward migration in autumn begins in mid-September and continues to the middle or end of November; onward or continuing passage is not unusual in January or February, and some populations also move in front of, or at the onset of, periods of severe winter weather. Return movement northward in spring begins mid-March (occasionally as early as the first week of February) and continues to early May. Young birds and females move further than males and older birds. It is a nocturnal and diurnal migrant, with flocks of 40–50 often visibly moving along coasts, rivers or through passes in autumn; in some areas (e.g. the North Sea coast of Holland) passage can be almost continuous for several days, with up to several thousand arriving at (or passing) headlands and islands.

MEASUREMENTS Wing of male 82–92, of female 77–87; tail 58–68; tarsus 17–21; bill (from skull) 13–14. Weight of male 20·5–24·5.

REFERENCES Dementiev and Gladkov (1951–54), Witherby *et al.* (1938–41).

2 BLUE CHAFFINCH *Fringilla teydea* Plate 1

Canary Islands

Fringilla teydea Webb, Berthelot and Moquin-Tandon, 1841, Hist. Iles Canaries, Ornith., 1836–42, p.20, Tenerife.

IDENTIFICATION Length 16–17 cm (6½ in). A large and rather dark Chaffinch, more robust and longer-legged in appearance than Chaffinch (1); the bill, which is used for prising seeds from cones, is also considerably longer than Chaffinch's. **Confusion species:** Male is very distinctive and easily separated from blue Canary Island races of Chaffinch by entirely slaty grey-blue upperparts and underparts. Females and immatures are larger than female Chaffinch, and brown above with grey underparts.

DESCRIPTION Sexes differ. **Adult male:** Dark or

black forehead band, otherwise entire head and upperparts deep slaty grey-blue, but cheeks and ear-coverts often deep blue; the thin whitish eye-ring is broken in front of eye. Tail black, but central pair of feathers edged deep greyish-blue; outer pair of tail feathers tipped with white (on inner web). Lesser and median coverts are black, with broad whitish or bluish-white tips to medians, and greaters blackish, edged and broadly tipped greyish-white, forming two rather dull wingbars; alula and primary coverts are black; secondaries and primaries black or blackish, thinly edged bluish-white, with a small square of greyish-white at bases of inner primaries on closed wing; tertials as secondaries but more broadly edged. Underparts are greyish-blue or similar to upperparts, but more bluish, becoming white on lower belly, vent and undertail-coverts. Bill stout or deep at base, pointed, metallic steel-blue or bluish-black. Legs and feet slate-grey, tinged pink. **Adult female:** Head and upperparts drab olive-brown or dull deep earth-brown, mantle, back and scapulars washed greenish or olive; also a pale whitish broken eye-ring. Tail is slightly darker than rest of upperparts, brownish-black with paler brown outer feathers. Wings are blackish-brown, lesser and median coverts black with pale buff or whitish tips (not white, but whiter than male), greaters black with broad pale grey tips; tertials, secondaries and primaries blackish-brown, thinly or indistinctly edged buffish; a small amount of buffish-white at base of inner four primaries. Underparts are paler or greyer than upperparts, becoming paler on lower breast, flanks and belly; undertail-coverts whitish. Bill greyish-horn or grey-brown, with a pale pink tinge to base of lower mandible. Legs and feet deep pinkish-brown. **Juvenile:** Very similar to adult female but perhaps slightly darker, with even less white or pale edges to wing feathers.

GEOGRAPHICAL VARIATION Birds on Gran Canaria (*polatzeki*) are similar to nominate race but distinctly duller and greyer on upperparts, and the dark band across the forehead is more pronounced; also, the tips to the median and greater coverts are prominently white. The bill is slightly smaller than that of nominate.

VOICE Call is a 'chirp', sometimes repeated as a double note, also a rather slurred 'che-wir' or 'sdderrer'; *polatzeki* has a softer low 'twee' or 'tui' note. In flight, occasionally gives a fairly sharp 'sipp'. The song is similar to but a poor imitation of Chaffinch's, being slower and consisting of only two to three repeated notes and ending with several harsh notes instead of a flourish: 'chip, chip, chip, wee, weer'.

STATUS, HABITAT AND BEHAVIOUR An African *Red Data Book* species. Formerly rare, but now common or locally common on Tenerife; the race on Gran Canaria is considered to be in decline. A bird of high Canary pine forest, usually found between 300 m and 1800 m, in highest density where there is rich undergrowth, but also in areas where little ground cover is present; it has also been found on tree-heaths and in laurels within pine forest. Family parties band together at the end of the breeding season and form foraging flocks, even associating with flocks of Chaffinches (*F. c. tintillon*) on occasions. Habits and actions are similar to Chaffinch, but flight is heavy and undulating. It often travels some distance (especially in summer) in search of water. It forages in small flocks, often on the ground, in search of flower and pine seeds. The predominant food is seeds of the Canary pine (*Pinus canariensis*), but also insects, principally caterpillars (on which the young are fed), and it will hawk after butterflies and moths.

DISTRIBUTION Restricted to the western Canary Islands (for details of range see Collar and Stuart 1985).

F. t. teydea: Tenerife.
F. t. polatzeki: Gran Canaria.

MOVEMENTS Practically none, but some have been recorded at lower levels in winter when snow or freezing temperatures force birds down from high-altitude forest. There is one extralimital record, northwest Lanzarote (eastern Canary Islands) mid-October 1967.

MEASUREMENTS Wing of male 96–107, of female 89–97. Wing of male *polatzeki* 90–97, of female 85–97.

REFERENCES Bannerman (1963), Collar and Stuart (1985).

3 BRAMBLING *Fringilla montifringilla*

Plate 1

Palearctic

Fringilla montifringilla Linnaeus, 1758, Syst. Nat., ed. 10, p. 179, Sweden.

IDENTIFICATION Length of male 14·5–18 cm, of female 14·5–17 cm (5½–7in). Males are very distinctive, especially in summer: jet-black head, face and mantle contrasting with warm orange from breast to scapulars. Winter male and female have brown mottling on head, mantle and scapulars, with sides of nape and hindneck pale powder blue-grey. It has a distinctive white rump and all-black tail. **Confusion species:** White rump and all-black tail prevent confusion with Chaffinch (1); some young females have rump tinged yellow, but it is always pale.

DESCRIPTION Sexes differ. **Adult male** summer: Forehead to nape, including sides of head, cheeks and sides of neck glossy black. Mantle and upper back glossy black, scapulars pale orange, lower back and rump white; uppertail-coverts dark grey, with pale buff or buffish-brown tips. Tail is entirely jet-black. Lesser coverts as scapulars, contrasting with white median coverts; greater coverts black, tipped white; alula and primary coverts black; flight feathers black, with pale buffy edges to some secondaries and edges and tips of tertials; white base to outer web of third and fourth primaries forms a small white patch at base of primaries; underwing-coverts bright lemon-yellow. Chin pale orange, becoming stronger and deeper (variable) on throat, breast and upper belly and flanks; belly and ventral region white, rear of flanks pale orange with some heavy dark spots; undertail-coverts pale

Spring

coverts are black or blackish, otherwise wing as male except for flight feathers and tail, which are more obviously brownish-black. Winter plumage is similar to adult male, but with paler head, dark or blackish tips to orange scapulars and pale orange tips to median and greater coverts. The edges to tertials and some inner secondaries are warm brown. Underparts are duller or more dirty orange than male; spotting on rear of flanks often more suffused. Bill horn-coloured and paler at base. Legs and feet brown. **Juvenile:** As adult female but browner, with pale buff-brown tips to forehead, crown, nape, mantle and back; rump and belly are tinged with dull yellow, and tips to median and greater coverts are pale orange-buff or pale yellowish-buff. First-winter male as adult male following post-breeding moult (July-September), but outer greater coverts and primary coverts are paler, more grey-brown, not black as adult; lesser coverts paler reddish or rust-brown, often spotted with black. Body and wing feathers are moulted in first autumn, but flight and tail feathers are retained to first summer.

VOICE Call is a sharp or rasping wheeze, 'zweee', 'tsweek' or 'tswee-ik', often loud and repeated monotonously, and given in alarm especially in the breeding season; also a musical Greenfinch-like 'dweee' (sometimes heard in autumn or early spring); occasionally gives a high-pitched note and some variably pitched churring or rattling notes which form part of the song; flight call is a 'chucc' or 'chup', repeated rapidly and frequently. Song is rather sweet and melodious, reminiscent of Redwing (*Turdus iliacus*) with several flute-like notes followed by a long drawn-out 'zweee' or a descending musical rattle; sometimes given in chorus by groups of males before spring migration.

STATUS, HABITAT AND BEHAVIOUR Common or locally common. In summer found in birch woods, also mixed deciduous woods and along edges of conifer belts; further north it occurs in dwarf birch and willow scrub. In winter, it is also found in large open areas of weed or edges of cultivation and in stubble fields. A sturdy robust finch, often found in pairs, small flocks or more rarely (except at migration gatherings) in large communal or mixed foraging flocks with other finches and sparrows; in years of exceptional food shortages up to several million can flock together where food is available (see below). On the ground short jerky movements recall Chaffinch, but it has a strong bounding, undulating flight. Feeds on the ground, but often continually flying up to and down from nearby shrubs or trees. Principal food is seed and is much famed for eating beechmast and hornbeam seeds, but will also take many grass and weed seeds, wheat and occasionally berries, as well as insect larvae. Mature beech forests may provide thousands of tonnes of beechmast, and in years when beechmast is plentiful in central Europe it has been estimated that up to 80 million birds congregate; such large flocks are easily sustained by the abundance of food.

DISTRIBUTION Monotypic. Breeds continuously eastwards from southern Norway, central and northern Sweden, Estonia, Finland and the Kola Peninsula to Kamchatka and the Pacific, with

orange-buff. Bill varies from pale yellow to dark orange at base, with a blackish tip; breeding birds have entirely black bills. Legs and feet dark brown. In winter, head, neck, mantle and back are more mottled, with dark grey or blackish centres to feathers flecked with brownish edges and paler or greyish-brown tips; nape and hindneck pale grey and sides of neck smudged with pale blue-grey. Occasionally shows pale buffy-brown eye-ring or half eye-ring at rear of eye. In late winter, face and head become progressively darker or black; scapulars a deeper or less bright orange. Median coverts become duller, and less white shows on wing-coverts, becoming pale orange on inner feather tips; tertials and inner secondaries are thinly edged warm brown. The rest of the plumage is similar to summer female, but underparts deeper orange on chin, throat and breast. Bill is dark at tip but otherwise noticeably pale yellow or orange, becoming darker all over as spring progresses. **Adult female:** summer: Very similar to adult male in winter, but lacks strong jet-black tones of head, neck and mantle; instead has plain brown forehead, crown and face, with cheeks and ear-coverts grey-brown, hindnape and neck (and sides of neck) pale or soft grey bordered with dark or blackish sides to crown and nape. Feathers of mantle are browner, with broader pale brown fringes or tips. Less orange shows on upper scapulars at shoulder. Lesser the northern limit closely allied to the tree limit (70°N). In the south, to the boundary of the forest steppe at about 55°N, but further south to 45°N in central Siberia, through Mongolia and northern China; also at small outposts in forests in the Alps in Switzerland, and northern Italy. It has also bred in eastern Denmark, Germany, the Netherlands and Scotland (and possibly England).

MOVEMENTS Migratory. Apart from a few birds which remain in central or southern Sweden, the entire population moves south or southeast to winter south of the breeding range in Europe, south to central Portugal and the Mediterranean, North Africa, Turkey and the Black Sea coastlands discontinuously east to the Crimea, the Middle East, southern Caucasus, northern Iran, northern Baluchistan and Afghanistan, parts of southern Central Asia to Kashmir, northwest India, Nepal, most of Tibet and lowland central, eastern and northern China (south to eastern Szechwan, Yunnan, Hunan and northwest Fukien), Korea and southern Japan, Ryukyu and Bonin Islands to Taiwan. It has also occurred on the Faroe Isles, in southern Morocco, central Algeria, Cyprus (occasionally), northern Egypt and Iraq. A vagrant to Iceland, Madeira, Tunisia, Libya, Cyprus, Jordan, United Arab Emirates, Oman, Bhutan (May 1990), Thailand (November 1989), Philippines (Calayan, two records), Pribilof Islands and Alaska, western Canada (British Columbia) and the USA (Oregon, Nevada, Montana, North Dakota, Pennsylvania, New York,

Massachusetts and New Jersey, some of which undoubtedly escapes from captivity); almost annual on the western Aleutians mid-May to late June and mid-September to mid-October. Autumn departure from breeding areas begins mid- to late September and first passage migrants arrive at that time in southern Urals and parts of Europe; passage continues to late October or mid-November. Return passage in spring is from late February or early March to early or mid-May, arrival in some of the more northerly breeding areas often delayed by prolonged cold or winter weather. In periods of cyclic abundance, following a series of successful breeding seasons, massive concentrations involving millions of individuals erupt from their summer ranges and move, seemingly at random, over wide areas, occurring outside the normal winter range. In one extreme instance, a wintering flock of 11 million birds fed on an abundant supply of beechmast in the severe winter of 1946/47 near Porrentruy, Switzerland, and in 1951 an estimated 72 million birds roosted near Thun, Switzerland; other irruption years on a much smaller scale have been in 1937/38, 1974/75 and 1976/77.

MEASUREMENTS Wing of male 84.5–94, of female 83–89; tail 55–66; tarsus 17–19; bill (from feathers) 11–13, (from skull) c16. Weight of male 21–29, of female 19–25.

REFERENCES Dementiev and Gladkov (1951–54), Newton (1972), Witherby et al. (1938–41).

GENUS *SERINUS*

Thirty-seven species. Generally small or slender finches (except one larger and thick-billed species), and predominantly green, greenish-yellow, brown or grey with dark streaks, usually with distinctly bright rump patch and forked or notched tail. The bright green or yellow-tinged birds are frequently referred to as canaries, and the duller or more drab birds as seedeaters, but usage of either term seems optional. The canaries are certainly good songsters, but so are some of the seedeaters; all species eat seeds. A genus of African origin that has now spread to central and southern Europe, Turkey, the Middle East and Arabia, it also contains two species (Tibetan Siskin (9) and Mountain Serin (40)) distantly removed from other members of the family in southern-central Asia and Indonesia, the latter a doubtful member of this genus and probably more closely related to *Carduelis* finches. Within Africa the genus contains several species of extremely restricted distribution and presumably specialised requirements.

4 RED-FRONTED SERIN (Fire-fronted Serin)
Serinus pusillus   Plate 2
Palearctic

Passer pusillus Pallas, 1811, Zoogr. Rosso-Asiat., 2, p. 28, near Caucasus and Caspian Sea.

IDENTIFICATION Length of male 12·5–13 cm, of female 12–13 cm (5 in). Adults are small dark-headed finches with bright red or reddish-orange forehead, with sooty-black nape, face and breast, upperparts streaked brownish-buff, and blackish streaks on pale yellowish flanks and belly. Immatures have rusty-buff faces, with forehead to chin and throat very streaky, and a distinctive trilling

call in bounding flight. A small finch whose plumage and trilling song and call make it unlikely to be confused with any other species.

DESCRIPTION Sexes similar. **Adult male:** Forehead a circular patch of bright red or reddish-orange, when seen well has bright velvety luminous appearance (duller in winter); rest of head and face sooty-black. Nape as head; mantle, back and scapulars black, with broad yellowish-buff or golden-buff edges. Rump bright yellow or yellowish tan-brown, becoming darker on uppertail-coverts. Tail is forked at tip, dark brown with thin orange edges to outer webs. Lesser and median coverts have dark brown feather bases edged warm buff-brown, medians tipped pale orange, greaters similar but paler, buffish-yellow tips on inner coverts forming a double wingbar, and with subterminally warm brown edges; flight feathers and tertials dark brown, with fine deep yellowish-orange edges to primaries, secondaries edged paler buff, becoming duller and wider on edges to tertials. Underwing-coverts pale yellowish-white. Chin, throat and upper breast sooty-black, becoming continuous broad dark streaks on centre of breast, extending to flanks, lower breast with more broken streaks, and base colour of lower breast and belly yellow or yellowish-white; undertail-coverts white. Bill short or stubby, dark brown or black. Legs and feet dark brown. **Adult female:** As male but tends to be duller, and often has only a thin strip or patch of red on upper forehead. Black on face, chin and throat also duller, more brownish-black, and hindcrown and nape have paler grey edges with black centres. Mantle, back and (on some) breast are more yellowish or less extensively black especially in winter. In winter, both sexes have a duller forehead patch and slightly more yellow edges to the wing feathers and underparts; head, face and throat feathers have fine ashy-brown or pale buff edges and tips. The overall appearance is paler than in breeding plumage. **Juvenile:** Forehead to nape, face, sides of neck, chin and throat rust-brown or dark cinnamon with crown and ear-coverts often slightly darker or duller; nape also shows some slightly darker centres. Upperparts are streakier than adults', with broad pale buff-brown or yellowish-buff edges to blackish-brown centres on mantle, back, scapulars and wing-coverts; rump as adult. The sides of all tail feathers (except central pair) are bright yellow. Edges of scapulars and tips to greaters coverts are noticeably gingery in the field; the rest of wing is similar to adult, with white or pale yellowish-buff tips to blackish median and greater coverts; edges of secondaries are yellowish or sandy-brown; the primaries finely edged golden-yellow. Breast brown or washed with light orange, streaked darker on lower breast and upper flanks; belly and flanks are yellowish. First-winter birds have darker brown head and face, some showing red tips to forehead; females are more streaked, and throat is black in males and brown in females, but this may indicate only that males assume adult plumage before females.

VOICE Call is a rather rapid ringing trill, 'trillit-drillt' usually given repeatedly in flight, otherwise a soft 'dueet' or 'tuueet' and a continuous ringing twittering 'bri-ihihihihi'. The song is very similar to that of Serin (5), but softer and more Goldfinch-like in quality, melodious rippling trills interspersed with twittering notes, rather hurried, and many phrases repeated; often delivered from tops of trees or similar prominent places.

STATUS, HABITAT AND BEHAVIOUR
Common or locally common. A bird of the lower or middle mountain ranges and valleys, usually between 2000 m and 4600 m (lower in winter), with scree slopes, alpine meadows and along forest edges of birch, juniper, spruce and pine, rarely in hardwood forest but occasionally in rhododendron zone. Flight is short bounding hops interspersed with rapid wingbeats; often gives trilling call in flight. Rarely settles in trees or on shrubs, preferring open aspects of dead branches, stones or boulders. Found in small flocks of up to 30 birds, but also singly and in small family parties in autumn and early winter. Feeds on the ground, often in company of other finches, principally on seeds of alpine plants and wild roses, also seeds of alder, birch, spruce and juniper; occasionally takes insects.

DISTRIBUTION Monotypic. Breeds in suitable mountainous habitat discontinuously eastwards from central and southern Turkey through the southern Caucasus, Iran to northeast Afghanistan and northern Baluchistan, Pakistan and northwest India (Chitral, Gilgit, Kashmir and the Karakorum range) to Nepal and southwest Tibet; in Central Asia from eastern Turkmenia (north of Bukhara) to the Pamirs and through the Tien Shan range discontinuously northwards to the Tarbagatai range, Sinkiang, northwest China.

MOVEMENTS Altitudinal, descending in winter to lower-lying valleys, rarely more than 40–50 km from the closest mountain range; some move south or southwest beyond the breeding range to winter in southern Turkey (where it reaches the coast in winter) and irregularly to Lebanon, Syria, northern Iraq, Israel (scarce but increasing), southern Iran, southern Afghanistan and northwest India (Punjab). A vagrant to Greece (two records involving several flocks), Cyprus (two records, 1973 and 1992) and Egypt (three records). It has recently (June 1992) occurred in England, but was considered to be an escaped bird. Post-breeding dispersal from breeding areas occurs from late July to August, but longer-distance altitudinal movements to lower levels is from mid-September onwards; return movements in spring from early March to mid-April.

MEASUREMENTS Wing of male 73–83, of female 67–76; tail 58–60; bill (from skull) 9–10; tarsus c15. Weight of male 10·5–12·7, of female 10·5.

REFERENCES Ali and Ripley (1983), Dementiev and Gladkov (1951–54).

Fringilla Serinus Linnaeus, 1766, Syst. Nat., ed. 12, p. 320, southern Europe; restricted to Switzerland by Laubmann, 1913, Verh. Ornith. Ges. Bayern 11, p. 193.

IDENTIFICATION Length of male 11·5–12 cm, of female 11–11·5 cm (4½in). A small, rather dumpy finch with a short stubby bill. Males have bright yellow on head and breast, and females are dull yellow or whitish with blackish streaking; both have bright yellow or yellowish-green rump (absent in immatures). In flight, has small, almost rounded wings and a deeply forked tail. **Confusion species:** Fairly distinctive, bears little true resemblance to any other closely related finch; some females and immatures may be briefly confused with similar-aged Siskins (49), but Serin lacks black on crown to nape, bright yellow wing flash at base of flight feathers and broad bright yellow edges to base of tail; bill also much less pointed than Siskin's. Syrian Serin (6) is paler, has an all-yellow face and pale yellow edges to tail and is virtually unstreaked on the underparts. Immature Serin is heavily streaked below, but same-aged Syrian Serin is unstreaked. In Britain and Europe, 'mules' – avicultural hybrids or crosses of birds, including crosses with Green-finches (44) and Goldfinches (68) as well as Canaries (7) – may look like Serin, but are generally much larger.

DESCRIPTION Sexes differ. **Adult male:** Fore-head, forecrown and supercilium extending around ear-coverts to sides of neck bright lemon-yellow; cheeks and ear-coverts yellowish-green, with small patch or crescent of yellow below eye (some also show small patch of yellow on lower cheeks), moustachial stripe dull or dark green. Crown and upper nape green or yellowish-green, finely dark-streaked; hindneck to sides of nape forms broad half-collar of yellow. Mantle, back and scapulars yellowish or yellowish-green, broadly streaked with black or blackish-brown, with two wide and quite long yellowish 'braces' or 'tramlines' down sides of mantle and back; rump bright yellow or greenish-yellow, but some feathers are more green than yellow and have darker edges; uppertail-coverts dark brown, as is forked tail, feathers of latter having fine yellow outer edges in summer or yellowish-green in winter (not always noticeable at a distance in the field). All wing-coverts have dark or grey-brown centres, but les-sers are yellow or yellowish with slightly darker centres, and medians and greaters have fine yel-lowish-green edges and pale yellow or yellowish-buff tips forming two wingbars; alula, primary coverts and flight feathers dark or greyish-brown, with fine pale yellow or greenish-yellow edges; ter-tials similar but with pale buff edges. Chin to lower breast bright yellow, white or pale yellow on sides of lower breast, belly and undertail-coverts; black or blackish streaks on sides and lower breast, becoming continuous on flanks. Bill short or stubby and conical, brown or dark horn, paler on lower

mandible. Legs and feet brown. Summer plumage, assumed during spring abrasion of winter plumage, is brighter than in winter, with wingbars and streak-ing more prominent; some birds have variable amounts of bright yellow on head, face and breast, depending on extent of yellowish-green tips to feathers. **Adult female:** A much duller version of male, with prominent streaking above and below. Forehead to crown and nape dull or dingy green, finely dark-streaked; thin pale buff or yellowish-buff supercilium, pale yellow cheeks and lower ear-coverts; lores, moustachial area and edges of ear-coverts pale greenish-grey or buffish-brown in worn plumage. Mantle, scapulars and back green-ish, grey-green or greenish-yellow, broadly streaked dark or blackish-brown, has pale 'tram-lines' either side of mantle as male; rump yellow or greenish-yellow (paler on some). Tail is dark brown, with fine pale yellowish-green edges to outer webs. Wings as male, but yellow is replaced by pale green or greenish-yellow on edges to coverts and flight feathers; tips to medians and gre-aters pale buff or faintly yellow, forming two wing-bars; tertials edged buff. Chin and throat pale buffish-yellow, becoming a paler yellowish wash or off-white with fine dark streaks on lower throat and breast; breast and flanks streaked dark brown or blackish, becoming continuous on flanks; centre of belly tinged yellowish, vent and undertail-coverts white. In winter, greyish-green tips to head, mantle and flanks give a much duller overall appearance, and the flanks are less clearly streaked. **Juvenile:** A browner or duller version of female. Upperparts are broadly edged with green-ish-buff on mantle, back and scapulars, with darker brown streaking, rump light olive or brownish with dark brown streaks. Wings and tail dark brown, but tips to median and greater coverts and edges to tertials and tail feathers warm gingery-buff. Underparts are pale yellowish-buff and more finely streaked than adult, with short individual brown or buffish-brown streaks; chin pale yellow or whitish. Some juveniles undergo complete moult in first autumn (mainly in south of range), but most retain old primaries, secondaries and tail feathers through first winter to moult at end of breeding season; thus, some first-summer birds may not always be sexed accurately in spring.

VOICE Call is a rapid or high-pitched twittering trill 'tirrillilit', or a shorter 'titteree', often of a tinny or metallic quality; occasionally a sparrow-like 'tirrup'; anxiety note a high-pitched Canary-like 'tsooee' or 'tsswee'. The song is a jumbled or jan-gling mixture of notes recalling Corn Bunting (*Emberiza calandra*) in overall quality, though somewhat less harsh. Usually sings from a fair height, e.g. top of a tree or telegraph wire; in display has a characteristic stiff-winged songflight recalling the bat-like flight of a Greenfinch (44). Males sing all year round, but only infrequently during autumn and winter months.

STATUS, HABITAT AND BEHAVIOUR Common or locally common. Found in or near gardens, suburban parks (even in the middle of large cities), plantations, orchards and olive groves or open agricultural areas; in Spain, Italy and other countries bordering the Mediterranean more often found in scattered pines or pine woods, but also a bird of hillsides and mountains. Especially fond of pines, and noted nesting sites have been in cedars or cypress trees. On the ground walks or hops with shuffling hopping movement. In flight, short rounded wings are a good field character, flight undulating with rather light bouncing action. Perches on trees, telegraph wires, bushes etc. Commonly feeds in small flocks, usually on the ground or in bushes, shrubs or small trees. Food mainly seeds of various flowers, but alder, birch and pine seeds are taken; also insects and some green vegetable food.

DISTRIBUTION Monotypic. Spain and France (except the north and northwest coastal areas) and erratically through Belgium, Holland and southern Denmark (and possibly southern Sweden) to Estonia, Latvia, Lithuania and Poland, south through the Ukraine to the Black Sea and through the Balkans to Turkey, Cyprus, Lebanon and sporadically into northern Israel and south along the coast to Tel Aviv. In North Africa from Morocco, northern Algeria and Tunisia to northern Libya (Tripoli and Cyrenaica); also on most of the Mediterranean islands except Malta. Now breeds on Tenerife and Gran Canary in the Canary Islands, but the origins of these birds are unclear and may relate to escapes from captivity. The range is slowly expanding north and east: until the early part of the 19th century was entirely restricted to southern Europe (Spain east to Greece) and northwest Africa (Morocco to Tunisia), but by about 1875 had expanded to include most of central Europe from central France to Austria, and by the early 1930s extended to the west coast of France, the Baltic and eastern Europe; by 1960 the range had increased in northern France, through Belgium and Holland to northern Germany and southern Denmark and extensively eastwards through the Baltic States into the former USSR and through Turkey to Cyprus. Although still slowly expanding its range in periods of rapid expansion followed by long periods of consolidation, the next phase, which is likely to include central Sweden, Finland, the coasts of northern France, Belgium and Holland or even southern England (where it has already bred), is awaited.

MOVEMENTS Sedentary and migratory. Breeding birds from northern parts of the range move south to winter within southern Europe, around the Mediterranean (including coastal North Africa), the Balkans (including the Hungarian Plain), Cyprus, Lebanon, Israel, southern Iraq, Libya (Cyrenaica) and northern Egypt. Regularly occurs (and has bred) in the British Isles, where it has also been known to winter. A vagrant to southern Finland and southwest Iran. Post-breeding dispersal begins middle to end of July merging with true migration in early August which continues to middle or end of October. Return movement in spring begins at the end of March or the beginning of April and continues into the middle of May.

MEASUREMENTS Wing of male 68–77, of female 64–71; tail 42–49; bill (to feathers) 7–9; tarsus 11–13. Weight of male 10·8–12·5.

REFERENCES Dementiev and Gladkov (1951–54), Witherby et al. (1938–41).

---

6 SYRIAN SERIN (Tristram's Serin) *Serinus syriacus*   Plate 2
Eastern Mediterranean

Serinus syriacus Bonaparte (ex Hemprich and Ehrenberg MS), 1851?, Consp. Avium, 1 (1850), p. 523, 'ex. As. occ. Bischerra'.

IDENTIFICATION Length 12–14 cm (5–5½ in). A small finch of very restricted range in the Middle East. Similar in size and shape to Serin (5). Has bright yellow forehead, slightly duller chin, throat and area around eyes, and broad yellow wingbars; greyish-buff with dark streaks on mantle, back and scapulars. **Confusion species:** Serin is somewhat shorter-tailed and is much more heavily marked and streaked (especially on underparts); first-winter Syrian Serin is plain, virtually unstreaked on underparts, whereas first-winter Serin is streaked above and below.

DESCRIPTION Sexes differ. **Adult male:** Forehead to forecrown deep golden-yellow (orange on some) becoming paler yellow, broadly encircling the all-dark eye, with lores and chin paler yellow; crown to ear-coverts, lower cheeks and centre of nape pale greyish-buff, very slightly dark-streaked and faintly yellow-tinged. Sides of neck yellow, often quite deep in tone, not extending to nape; mantle, back and scapulars as crown; rump a uniform unstreaked bright yellow, uppertail-coverts also yellow but some streaked dark brown. Tail is short but deeply forked at tip, feather centres blackish-brown, edges quite broadly yellowish at base of inners and becoming pale buff on outers. Lesser and median coverts yellow or pale greenish-yellow, greaters also yellow with blackish inner webs; alula and primary coverts black, the latter finely edged with yellow; flight feathers blackish or blackish-brown, finely edged with yellow on primaries and more broadly on secondaries, which

have white or pale buff tips; tertials as flight feathers, broadly edged pale yellow or buffish. Chin and throat pale yellow, pure yellow on belly and undertail-coverts; some may show slight streaking on flanks. Bill blackish. Legs and feet pale brown. **Adult female:** A duller or less vivid yellow version of male, especially the yellow of head, face and underparts. Crown and nape greyish and dark-streaked; rest of upperparts dull greyish-buff with dark streaks; rump patch as male but duller or paler, occasionally with a few short streaks. Wings as male, but yellow much paler on edges of flight feathers and coverts. Underparts are dull yellow, washed greyer on belly and flanks; some birds are unstreaked, but others show two to three lines of brown streaking on flanks. **Juvenile:** A pale or warm buffish-brown, with yellow edges to flight feathers; base of tail feathers as adult male but not so vividly yellow. Head to nape and sides of neck pale buff-brown, becoming more sandy-brown and lightly streaked on mantle and back. Median and greater coverts broadly tipped warm buff, with bases to greaters pale warm brown or tinged light ginger; flight feathers blackish-brown, broadly edged yellow. Tail as adult, but more dark brown than blackish, with yellow bases to inner feathers and pale buffy edges and tips to outers. Chin, throat and upper breast pale buff or buffish-brown, becoming mottled with buff-brown or light grey-brown on breast; rest of underparts dull whitish. Adult plumage begins to appear on head, face and rump at end of first winter.
VOICE Call is less musical and generally drier in pitch than Serin's (5), 'tearrrh' or 'tirrrh' and 'tsirrr', and a thin or nasal 'shkeep', occasionally gives very low Redpoll-like twitters in flight and a soft

'tree-der-dee' or 'tree-der-doo'. The song is similar to that of Canary (7) or Linnet (72), slightly hesitant or more drawn out, and containing characteristic 'twee', 'tweet', 'siu' or rolling 'drrrr' and chirping notes accompanied by a trill, also frequently repeating phrases and often including the call notes; it is rarely given in flight and usually delivered from the top of a tree.
STATUS, HABITAT AND BEHAVIOUR Uncommon or only locally common. Occurs on open bushy slopes or lightly wooded mountains between 900 m and 1800 m, in trees, principally cedars or junipers, but also in other deciduous trees including orchards; in winter, less dependent on trees and may be found in low-lying acacia thorn, desert or semi-desert scrub. Similar in actions and behaviour to Serin. After the breeding season forms large noisy nomadic flocks of up to several hundred birds, which often remain together during the winter. Forages in trees, bushes and on the ground; feeds mainly on seeds, and occasionally on insects.
DISTRIBUTION Monotypic. Breeding restricted to the Lebanon range in southern Syria and northern Israel (Mount Hermon).
MOVEMENTS Partial migrant; random dispersal in large nomadic post-breeding flocks usually south to southern Israel and irregularly to Jordan (including in breeding season, June 1992), the Sinai and elsewhere in northern Egypt; also recorded in Iraq. Movement or dispersal from breeding areas takes place in September and October, returning to breed at the end of March to early April.
MEASUREMENTS Wing 70–77. Weight: 10–14.
REFERENCES Hollom (1959), Scott (1992).

7 CANARY (Island Canary) *Serinus canaria* Plate 3
North Atlantic Islands

Fringilla Canaria Linnaeus, 1758, Syst. Nat., ed. 10, p. 181, Canary Island.

IDENTIFICATION Length 12·5 cm (5 in). Very similar to Serin (5) (and also other members of family), but is larger, longer-tailed and has pale pinkish bill, grey (dark-streaked) upperparts, pale yellow face, olive-yellow rump and dark or grey-brown tail; underparts are dull greenish-yellow with some slight streaking. Females are duller, with greyer face, brown back and wings, grey breast and streaked flanks. **Confusion species:** Serin, but Canary is bigger or longer-tailed and looks less compact; Serin also has predominantly green or olive-yellow (dark-streaked) upperparts including tail, a brighter, purer yellow rump (male) and is heavily streaked across breast and belly (female) with whiter belly and ventral region. Call of Canary unlikely to be confused with any of the notes uttered by Serin. No other finch from western Europe or North Africa is likely to cause confusion.
DESCRIPTION Sexes differ. **Adult male:** Forehead to supercilium dull golden-yellow, upper

forehead to crown and nape greenish-yellow with some slight streaking; lores dusky olive, this colour extending slightly more heavily down moustachial stripe and around edges of ear-coverts; cheeks and centre of ear-coverts yellow or olive-yellow; sides of nape dusky or dingy yellow. Feathers of mantle, back and scapulars light grey or ashy, with blackish centres and greenish-yellow edges; rump greenish-yellow or dull olive-yellow, uppertail-coverts dark brown tipped grey-brown. Tail is forked or notched at tip, and dark brown edged with pale green. Lesser coverts olive-yellow; medians and greaters black or blackish, edged greenish-yellow and tipped pale buffish-brown; alula and primary coverts black; flight feathers blackish-brown with fine yellow edges, tertials similar but slightly more broadly bordered buff or brownish-buff on inner tertial. Underparts dull golden-yellow washed with olive on chin, throat and breast, becoming (on some) greyish-tinged on sides of breast and flanks;

breast and upper belly yellow or yellowish, with some broken blackish streaking on rear of flanks; lower belly and undertail-coverts pale buff or whitish. Bill pale pink or pinkish-horn with darker or browner upper mandible. Legs and feet brown. **Adult female:** Similar to male, but generally much duller and greyer on face and upperparts. Sides of head from lores and moustachial area to ear-coverts and side of neck much greyer than on male, with small patches of dull yellow from lower forehead to cheeks and eye. Crown to back grey, streaked with black, generally much more heavily streaked than male and tinged with brown; rump and tail slightly duller than male and tinged with green. Median coverts have broad yellowish tips and greaters pale buff-brown tips (becoming paler or whiter in worn plumage); secondaries and primaries are finely edged greenish-yellow, tertials blackish-brown edged pale buff-brown and tipped with buff. Chin and throat yellow or dull yellowish; breast grey, becoming yellowish on belly, with diffuse dark brown or blackish streaks continuing onto greyish or greyish-yellow flanks; undertail-coverts white or off-white. **Juvenile:** Forehead dull greenish-yellow, upper forehead to crown and nape pale brown with dark streaks; face and sides of head and neck plain greyish buff-brown. Upperparts as crown and nape but noticeably dark-streaked (with short broken streaks); rump pale or light brown, slightly dark-streaked; uppertail-coverts dark brown with grey edges and tips. Tail is dark brown, finely edged with pale grey-brown fringes. Lesser coverts are brown; medians and greaters dark brown, with broad warm brown tips forming double wingbar; flight feathers black or blackish-brown edged buffish grey-brown, becoming more broadly edged buffish-brown on tertials. Chin and throat as face but tinged slightly yellow, becoming more strongly yellow on breast and fading to white on belly and flanks are greyish, tinged yellow; short dark brown streaks on sides of breast; undertail-coverts are dingy white. Bill pale horn, but some birds have dark horn on upper mandible, with lower paler, more pink or pale horn. Legs dark brown. Note: There is some variation in plumages of adults, especially males which do not appear to have attained full adult plumage, and it is possible

that birds resembling females or brightly coloured females are first-year males; they are generally detected by a brighter rump and underparts before moulting into fully adult plumage in second winter. **VOICE** Most calls are as those of well-known domesticated birds. Commonest is the contact call, a high-pitched 'sooee' or 'sweee' usually accompanied by a light twittering trill; birds fighting in spring often utter a 'zee-zee-zee' call. The song, often given from cover, is the same series of sweet, melodious fluty whistles and trills of domesticated birds, but often interspersed with twitters or churrs; the Canary has a stiff-winged butterfly-like display flight, ending with the bird planing down with quivering wings half closed to alight on the top of a tree or similar songpost.
STATUS, HABITAT AND BEHAVIOUR Common or locally common. Occurs in a range of habitats (usually at some elevation in the Canary Islands) from the edges of lowland cultivation, including gardens and orchards, to dry valleys (*barancos*), laurel forest, open woodland, mountainsides with scrub and pine forest, from sea-level to 1700 m. Habits similar to Serin, with which it used to be considered conspecific; has same buoyant undulating flight, though not nearly so bouncy, more direct and often at some speed. Gregarious and usually found in flocks, occasionally of many hundreds; in winter, freely associates with Linnets (72) and Goldfinches (68). Feeds on the ground or in short seed-bearing plants, mainly on seeds of weeds and grass but also fond of fig seeds.
DISTRIBUTION Monotypic. Restricted to the Azores, Madeira and the Canary Islands (western islands only, excluding Fuerteventura and Lanzarote). It has also been introduced (probably prior to 1930) into Bermuda, the Hawaiian Islands (Midway), where it is now established, and Puerto Rico.
MOVEMENTS Resident or sedentary. Most movements are of a very localised nature, none long-distance; some disperse in winter from Madeira to neighbouring Desertas.
MEASUREMENTS Wing of male 71−77; tail 53−60; tarsus 16−19; bill (from base of nostrils) 6−6·5, (from feathers) 8·5.
REFERENCES Bannerman (1963), Vaurie (1956).

8 CITRIL FINCH *Serinus citrinella*

Plate 10

West and central Europe

Fringilla citrinella Pallas, 1764, in Vroeg, Cat. raisonné, Oiseaux, adumbrat., p. 3, Holland.

IDENTIFICATION Length 11·5−12 cm (4½ in). A greyish-green, fairly stocky mountain or alpine forest finch with deep yellow wingbars, bright greenish-yellow rump, black flight feathers and tail, and lacking any streaking on underparts. Grey on back of head, nape and sides of neck readily distinguishes adults, males being brighter than females. Immatures buffish grey-brown streaked darker brown above, and pale buff brown below with short streaks on breast, belly and flanks, without any prominent grey, green or yellow in plumage. **Confusion species:** Similar to Serin (5), but longer-tailed and lacking bold streaking above and below. Wingbars and generally slimmer shape and size separate it from similarly plumaged Greenfinch (44). Siskin (49) is also much greener and more heavily streaked, shows bright yellow in wings and tail in flight, and lacks grey areas of head, neck and breast of Citril Finch.

DESCRIPTION Sexes differ. **Adult male:** Forehead to behind the eye yellow tinged with green, lores dull ashy-grey, lower cheeks and ear-coverts ashy-grey but tinged slightly olive on ear-coverts; forecrown olive-green, becoming grey or greyish tinged blue-grey on hindcrown, nape and sides of neck; grey of nape merges into olive-green on mantle, back and scapulars (though some can show grey on scapulars, especially lower scapulars), with some very fine dark brown streaks on mantle and upper back; lower back, rump and uppertail-coverts a brighter unstreaked yellow or greenish-yellow. Tail is deeply forked at tip, blackish, broadly edged with yellow or pale yellow on outer webs and pale buff on inner webs. Lesser and median coverts blackish at base and tipped yellowish-green; greater coverts blackish-brown, finely edged green and with broad yellowish-green tips forming prominent wingbar; alula, primary coverts, primaries and secondaries black or blackish-brown edged with yellow or yellowish-green, outer primaries edged whitish, tertials the same, edged slightly more broadly and tipped pale buff. Chin and throat are yellowish with green or olive tinge, becoming bright yellow on breast and belly (on some, the grey sides of nape extend to sides of throat and breast); sides of breast/upper flanks greenish-yellow, tinged ashy-grey; vent and undertail-coverts whitish or washed yellowish. Bill short, slender and pointed, dark or dark brownish, paler at base of lower mandible. Legs and feet brown. **Adult female:** Slightly duller or darker than male, especially on areas which are green or yellow. Forehead, lores, area around eye and chin much duller green than male; forecrown to nape olive-grey, becoming greyer on sides of neck, ear-coverts and cheeks. Mantle, back and scapulars dark olive, tinged grey with short or fine dark brown streaks on mantle and inner scapulars; rump, uppertail-coverts and tail dull or dingy greenish-yellow, though shows more green edges (yellow on male) to tail. Wings also as male, but tertials edged yellow and have pale grey tips. Chin is dull yellow, becoming suffused with grey on throat, sides and upper breast; breast yellowish grey-green, becoming yellower on lower breast and belly; flanks greyish, vent and undertail-coverts off-white or whitish, washed buff or yellow. **Juvenile:** Forehead, lores and area around eye plain pale brown-buff, forecrown to nape brown. Mantle to scapulars and back brown with darker streaks; rump and uppertail-coverts paler, more tawny-brown, and streaked at sides. Tail is dark brown or blackish with thin pale greenish-yellow edges. Wings have dark brown or blackish centres to coverts, with broad pale brown or buff-brown edges and tips to median and greater coverts; flight feathers are dark brown or blackish with fine buff-brown edges and tips, tertials the same but more broadly edged and tipped. Chin may show some yellow, but is generally warm buff-brown or washed lightly with yellow from chin and throat to belly and rear of flanks, with short brownish

streaks; vent and undertail-coverts pale white or buff. Juvenile body feathers, wing-coverts and inner secondaries are replaced in first autumn, but flight and tail feathers are retained into first-summer plumage. Bill dark horn. First-year birds resemble adults, but are noticeably browner and show heavier streaking on mantle and back; also, edges to coverts, flight and tail feathers are buff, not green as in full adult.

GEOGRAPHICAL VARIATION Adult male and female *corsicanus* have mantle, back and scapulars warm brown with darker brown or blackish streaking; they are also slightly yellower on underparts, especially the male.

VOICE A variety of calls recalling both Serin and Siskin in tone and quality. The most frequent is a metallic 'tiyie' or 'tsiew' and a 'check', 'chwick', 'twick' or 'chit' note in flight, becoming a Linnet-like 'chitt-tit-itt' or 'check-eck-eck'. The song is also very Siskin-like, consisting of liquid or musical notes, often high-pitched, and delivered in short repeated phrases interspersed with harsher twittering notes; usually sings from a treetop, but in spring song is given while in circular display flight with slow butterfly-like wingbeats.

STATUS, HABITAT AND BEHAVIOUR Common or locally common. Occurs in subalpine woods of spruce and larch and montane pine forest, also meadows, up to the tree line in the Alps; breeds above 1500 m in the Alps, but can be as low as 700 m in southern Germany. Found in much the same habitat as Redpoll (69) and Siskin, with which it mixes in winter. In Corsica and Sardinia found in dry montane scrub, woodland and generally more open vegetation. Flight light and undulating, recalling Goldfinch (68). Perches in trees, bushes, on roadside wires and settles freely on rocks etc. Often social and in winter feeds in considerable gatherings. Feeds on seeds of weeds, thistles, fir, spruce and pine; does not cling to pine cone in manner of a Siskin or tit, so seeds have to be extracted on the ground using its pointed bill tweezer-fashion; also does not sit on or climb plants such as thistles in manner of Goldfinch.

DISTRIBUTION *S. c. citrinella* Spain (Cantabrian Mountains, central and eastern Pyrenees and the central and northeastern Sierras), southern France (Massif Central) and northern Italy (hills to the north of Rome), east through southern Germany to western Austria and north to eastern France (Vosges).

S. c. corsicanus: Corsica and Sardinia.

MOVEMENTS Largely altitudinal, in winter descending to lower levels in sheltered valleys (even treeless areas), especially the south and western areas of the Alps, and exceptionally to more arid plains in the north. A vagrant to northern France, Belgium, the Balearics and Algeria; also two recent records in Ceuta, North Africa, of separate individuals in March and April 1991. There are also old (mostly 19th-century) records of vagrancy to Heligoland and England (though some doubts have been expressed about the origins of the English record).

MEASUREMENTS Wing of male 75–79, of

female 73–76; tail 47–51; tarsus 13·5–15; bill (from skull) 8·5–9·5.

REFERENCE Witherby *et al.* (1938–41).

9 TIBETAN SISKIN (Tibetan Serin) *Serinus thibetanus*

East Palearctic

Plate 2

Chrysomitris thibetana Hume, 1872, Ibis, p. 107, borders of Sikkim and Tibet.

IDENTIFICATION Length 12 cm (5 in). Males have bright olive-green crown and upperparts, yellow supercilium and unstreaked bright greenish-yellow underparts. Female duller and dark-streaked on upperparts, with streaks on flanks. Juvenile like adult female, but dull green on crown to back and paler below with streaks on breast, belly and flanks. **Confusion species:** Similar to larger Siskin (49), which closely resembles in many actions and habits, but males are unstreaked and both sexes have a different face pattern; Tibetan lacks black cap of male Siskin, bright band of yellow in wing and yellow sides to base of tail. Female Siskin tends towards a greyer-green back and much brighter pale yellow rump, and has paler yellow but broader wingbars. Separated from Greenfinch (44), Oriental Greenfinch (45) or Black-headed Greenfinch (48) by smaller size and slightly thinner bill, lack of any bright yellow or greenish-yellow flashes in wing or sides of tail, and absence of black head pattern in male.

DESCRIPTION Sexes differ. **Adult male:** Forehead to crown and upper nape light olive-green. Lores blackish; upper lores, supercilium and border behind and below ear-coverts yellow, enclosing greenish-yellow cheeks and ear-coverts; yellow moustachial stripe bordered by thin greenish-yellow submoustachial stripe. Mantle, back and scapulars olive-green, with yellowish edges to lower scapulars in fresh plumage; lower back and rump to uppertail-coverts yellow or pale greenish-yellow. Tail is forked or notched at tip, black or blackish-brown and edged bright yellow on all feathers. Median coverts as upperparts, tips pale greenish-yellow (slightly paler than tips of greaters), and greaters blackish-brown edged and tipped greenish-yellow; alula black, primary coverts also very dark with fine grey edges; flight feathers blackish, edged greenish-yellow, with fine white tips to secondaries; tertials blackish, broadly edged (especially towards tips) yellow, buff on inner web. Underparts deep yellow, tinged with green on breast; belly and flanks paler or whiter from lower belly to undertail-coverts. Bill fairly thin and Siskin-like, with bluish-grey upper mandible and pale fleshy-brown lower. Legs and feet pinkish-brown.

Adult female: Much darker and more heavily streaked than male. Forehead to crown dull olive-green with blackish streaking, hindcrown and nape brighter or paler green and slightly dark-streaked; face pattern similar to male, but with duller olive ear-coverts and moustachial stripe; cheeks yellowish. Mantle, back and scapulars dull olive-green with dark or blackish streaks, most prominent on mantle and upper back; rump and uppertail-coverts pale yellow or yellowish-green, not so heavily streaked as upperparts, with tips of uppertail-coverts deep green. Tail as male, black or blackish-brown, finely edged greenish-yellow. Median coverts blackish, broadly edged and tipped pale yellowish-green, greaters blackish with green edges towards pale yellow tips; flight feathers black or blackish-brown, thinly edged pale lime-green; tertials similar, with broad pale green or greenish-yellow edges and tips, inner webs buff. Chin and throat to breast pale lemon-yellow, streaked on breast and flanks; lower breast and belly paler or creamy-white; undertail-coverts pale yellow, but streaked dark brown or blackish. Bill brownish-horn. Legs and feet deep brown.

Juvenile: Very similar to adult female and not always separable in the field, but generally duller green or tinged buffish-brown from forehead to back and dark-streaked; rump and uppertail-coverts dull olive-yellow. Wings and tail as adult female, but edges and tips to greater coverts and tertials pale buff or buffish-brown. Underparts pale light green with darker or blackish streaks on breast, belly and flanks, but this may vary individualy. First-winter males show contrasting greater coverts with worn juvenile feathers in outer coverts, and some slight streaking on mantle and flanks.

VOICE Call is a soft twittering; in flight utters a series of short finch-like notes; when in flocks keeps up a continuous hard tremulous twittering, at times quite deafening, sounding in the distance like Starlings (*Sturnus vulgaris*) going to roost. Song is a variation of the twittering call, a nasal buzzing two-to-three-note 'zeezle-eezle-eeze' with many trills added.

STATUS, HABITAT AND BEHAVIOUR Locally common or scarce. Inhabits open hillsides and coniferous and birch forest between 2800 m and 4000 m, with an understorey of rhododendron; also in alder, hemlock and mixed fir forest. Breeding data little known. Found in small flocks of up to 50 quietly feeding in treetops, its presence given away only by the twittering contact call; occasionally feeds on the ground, but usually under bushes or scrub. Food is a variety of seeds, principally alder and birch.

DISTRIBUTION Monotypic. Eastern Himalayas from southeast Tibet, Sikkim, Bhutan and Arunachal Pradesh (may also breed in eastern Nepal) to about 95°E and northern Szechwan, western China.

MOVEMENTS An altitudinal migrant. Descends

to between 1000 m and 3000 m (down to 600 m in Burma) in winter and occurs west to central Nepal, found more widely in Assam, Bhutan and Arunachal Pradesh, south to northeast Burma (Myitkyina district) and east to northern Yunnan, western China.

MEASUREMENTS Wing of male 67–72·5, of female 64–70; tarsus 14–15; tail of male 40–43, of female 42–45; bill (from skull) of male 11–14, of female 12–14. Weight: 10–11.
REFERENCES Ali and Ripley (1983), Ludlow (1944).

10 YELLOW-CROWNED CANARY (Cape Canary (South Africa))
Serinus canicollis   Plate 3
Africa

Crithagra canicollis Swainson, 1838 (1837?), Anim. Menag., p. 317, Africa; restricted to Cape of Good Hope by Vincent, 1952, Check List Birds South Africa, p. 115.

IDENTIFICATION Length 13 cm (5–5¼ in). A rather distinctive deep or dull green finch found in South and East Africa and divided into two principal types: males of southern races have a pale grey hindcrown, nape and sides of neck (shawl), while those of East Africa have forehead and crown bright yellow with dull green on nape and mantle. Females are also separable on the amount of yellow or greenish-yellow on forehead. Immatures are less easily separable, being browner and heavily streaked. **Confusion species:** The grey nape or shawl and otherwise dull greenish-yellow plumage of southern males diagnostic; juveniles also unlikely to be confused with similar-plumaged birds within normal limits of range. In East Africa it is the only yellow-headed canary (male), while the duller female shows more yellow on forehead and forecrown than possible confusion species. Both adult Yellow-fronted Canaries (21) have bright yellow forehead and supercilium but a darker crown to nape, with dark or blackish lores to ear-coverts, yellow cheeks and broad black malar stripes. Adult female Black-faced Canary (13) has a greenish-yellow forehead and similar coloured ear-coverts and cheeks, but it also has more prominent streaking on lower throat and breast. Juveniles are distinguished from African Citril (12) by buff-brown (not green) rump, uppertail-coverts and edges to bases of tail. Male Parasitic Weaver (*Anomalospiza imberbis*) resembles a finch, but is more stub-tailed, lacks wingbars, has a browner mantle and back and an all-black bill.
DESCRIPTION Sexes differ. **Adult male:** Forehead to crown deep green, tinged with yellow or golden-yellow; lores to eye and slightly behind eye dusky, ear-coverts dull olive-green; rear of ear-coverts, hindcrown, nape, hindneck (to mantle) and sides of neck (forming a broad collar or shawl) pale grey or ashy-grey. Upper mantle as hindcrown to nape; back and scapulars deep olive-green, finely dark-streaked, and some back feathers tipped with grey; lower back and upper rump yellowish-green; lower rump and uppertail-coverts yellow, tinged green. Tail is blackish, broadly edged bright yellow or greenish-yellow. Median and greater coverts as scapulars, some with pale greenish-yellow tips forming double wingbar; alula and primary coverts also black; flight feathers black or blackish, finely edged with greenish-yellow; tertials black, broadly edged and tipped greenish-yellow. Chin and throat are dull greenish-yellow, with a slightly deeper green wash to sides of breast and flanks (some birds show grey on tips of breast and flanks); lower breast to belly pale yellow, undertail-coverts whitish-yellow. Upper mandible dark brown and lower mandible pale horn to creamy-white. Legs and feet dark brown. **Adult female:** Forehead to forecrown greenish-yellow with heavy narrow dark streaks; crown to nape, sides of neck and ear-coverts grey-green, tinged brownish on nape. Upper mantle grey-green with fine darker or blacker streaking; lower mantle, back and scapulars olive-green and dark-streaked; rump and uppertail-coverts plain bright greenish-yellow. Tail is black with pale yellow or greenish-yellow edges and tips. Median coverts have dark brown or blackish centres and green edges; greaters are blackish on inner webs, with bright yellow-green edges to outer webs and tips; alula and primary coverts black; flight feathers black or blackish-brown with bright greenish-yellow edges, tertials the same but more broadly edged yellow and tipped buff or pale yellowish-buff. Chin and throat are greyish or tinged light green, becoming grey-green or dull greenish-yellow on lower throat, breast and belly, with fine streaking on sides of breast; flanks are paler and yellowish, with light streaking; belly and vent off-white, undertail-coverts yellowish. **Juvenile:** Forehead to crown, nape and mantle pale buff-brown, finely dark-streaked on head and nape. Upperparts as head, but streaks are larger and slightly broader on mantle; lower mantle, back and scapulars tawny-buff (but with some light green edging on inner scapulars), more heavily streaked dark brown; rump and uppertail-coverts warm buff, streaked dark brown. Tail is dark brown, broadly edged pale yellow, brighter on edges of outer feathers. Medians and greaters are blackish-brown, with pale, broad warm buff-brown tips (and edges to greaters); alula and primary coverts black; flight feathers blackish, edged bright yellow; tertials dark brown, broadly edged pale yellowish-buff and tipped buff; tips of primaries also buff. Underparts pale yellowish-buff with heavy dark brown streaks, latter becoming thinner on belly; pale warm buff on

undertail-coverts. Bill dark horn, with paler base to lower mandible.

GEOGRAPHICAL VARIATION Males of race *thompsonae* are very similar to nominate, but are generally darker on upperparts and have forehead and crown brighter or golden-yellow and grey of shawl slightly heavier; the edges of wings and tail are bright yellow; the underparts are also darker, with throat and breast deeper greenish-yellow, occasionally tinged lightly with orange. Females of this race are darker than those of nominate, and the upperparts are light olive-brown with fairly heavy streaks. Males of race *griseitergum* have forehead, crown and face much greener and less yellow than *thompsonae*, and the grey 'shawl' is deeper or bluish-grey in tone; mantle, back and scapulars are green, tinged with grey, and the dark central shaft streaks are more pronounced; the underparts are more greenish and less intensely yellow. Females have crown to lower back cold greenish-grey with darker central shaft streaks, and rump and uppertail-coverts greenish-yellow; the underparts are as *thompsonae*, but with deep grey or bluish-grey on chin and throat. East African birds make up the following three races. Males of race *flavivertex* differ from southern birds in having forehead to crown bright golden-yellow, becoming dingy green on hindcrown to nape; mantle, back and scapulars are bright olive-green, streaked blackish; rump and uppertail-coverts are bright yellow; median and greater coverts are black, with broad bright yellow tips forming two wingbars; the black tertials are broadly edged and tipped with yellow; underparts are bright or golden-yellow on sides of neck, becoming slightly greenish-yellow on sides of breast, with lower belly whitish. Female *flavivertex* is similar to male, but duller and tinged with green, and the yellow wingbars are not so bright; underparts are pale green or washed with yellow, and finely dark-streaked on sides of breast and flanks. Juveniles are similar to those of nominate race, but slightly deeper brown on body. Males of race *sassii* are appreciably smaller, and have tail almost entirely yellow apart from blackish central shafts and dark outer webs of outer feathers; females are similar to nominate, but show more blackish-brown on webs of central tail feathers (only the edges are yellowish). Males of race *huillensis* have forehead to crown (and nape), sides of face, ear-coverts, cheeks and entire underparts golden-yellow, and nape to mantle and back is more yellow than in previous races and completely unstreaked; the wings lack broad yellow wingbars, medians and greater coverts are edged pale yellow and tipped paler, and secondaries and longest tertial edged bright yellow on otherwise black flight feathers. Females (as in *flavivertex*) a duller olive-green version of male, especially on upperparts, with a paler yellow rump and some slight streaking on crown. Juveniles are as *flavivertex*, with bright yellow edges to base of tail feathers and yellowish edges to flight feathers; heavily streaked on underparts to buff undertail-coverts.

VOICE Commonest call is 'sweeet' and a staccato chatter, alarm call a repeated 'tweee', 'pee-eee' or 'twoo-ee' or 'sklereee'; gives a twittering note in

flight. Song is a loud, prolonged and musical series of Goldfinch-like trills and warbles, said to resemble Skylark (*Alauda arvensis*) in tone; in spring frequently delivered from tops of trees, also in slow butterfly-like display flight.

STATUS, HABITAT AND BEHAVIOUR Common or locally common. In the south of the range nominate *canicollis* and *thompsonae* are found in lowland and coastal areas, including towns and gardens, while further north it is a bird of montane grassland with scattered bushes, heathland or bracken-briar, scrub, also in eucalyptus or juniper, above and below the tree line, usually between 2000 m and 3000 m, although *griseitergum* occurs down to 1200 m and *flavivertex* is found between 1450 m and 4300 m in Ethiopia and Kenya; it also favours orchards, scrub, or edges of forest. A very sociable species often found in flocks, especially in winter, often roosting in larger numbers; also breeds in small loose colonies of up to 25 pairs. Feeds low down in vegetation or on the ground, usually on seeds (often green or unripe) of weeds, grasses and small plants and shrubs; occasionally takes insects; *griseitergum* also feeds on pine seeds of *Pinus patula*.

DISTRIBUTION S. c. *canicollis*: western and southern Cape Province, sporadically east to western Orange Free State, Lesotho and Transkei, South Africa.

S. c. *thompsonae*: northern Transvaal, through Natal, western Swaziland and western Zululand to Lesotho and Transkei, northeast Cape Province, South Africa.

S. c. *griseitergum*: highlands of eastern Zimbabwe and adjacent border of Mozambique.

S. c. *flavivertex*: northern Ethiopia (Eritrea) south to central and southern Ethiopia to southeast Sudan (Imatong Mountains) and northeast Uganda, through west and central Kenya to northern Tanzania.

S. c. *sassii*: southern and eastern Zaire, western Uganda, Rwanda, northern Malawi and southwest Tanzania.

S. c. *huillensis*: central Angola.

Intermediates between the first two races occur in overlap areas. Birds of nominate race have also been introduced into Mauritius and Réunion Island.

MOVEMENTS Largely sedentary, but some undertake nomadic wandering in the non-breeding season, while persistent cold conditions in upland and mountainous areas forces birds to lower levels (*griseitergum* has been recorded down to 900 m in June and August); an individual of the nominate race has been recorded once in southeast Transvaal, in October.

MEASUREMENTS Wing of male 75–82, of female 72–79; tail 48–58; tarsus 14–16; bill (culmen) 9·5–11. Wing of male *thompsonae* 78–83, of female 76–79. Wing of male *griseitergum* 73·5–81·5, of female 74–78. Wing of male *flavivertex* 75·5–83, of female 72–80. Wing of male *sassii* 77–78, of female 71–77; tail of male 53–59, of female 52–54; tarsus 13; bill (culmen) 8–9.

REFERENCES Clancey (1964, 1968), Gyldenstolpe (1924), Mackworth-Praed and Grant (1963), Sinclair (1987).

Serinus nigriceps Rüppell, 1840, Neue Wirbelt., Vögel, p. 96, Simen Province, 10,000 ft, Abyssinia.

IDENTIFICATION Length c11–12·5 cm (4¼–5 in). A distinctive endemic finch of the highlands of Ethiopia. The male has an all-black head and green upperparts, with bright yellow scapulars contrasting with dark wings in breeding plumage. Females are similar but duller, the head dark grey, usually with dusky brown forehead, sides to face, ear-coverts or chin, and they lack bright yellow scapulars. **Confusion species:** At all ages dark or sooty-brown or black on head easily separates it from Yellow-crowned Canary (10) found in similar habitat; immatures of the two are similar, but Black-headed Siskins are dull olive or olive-green on upperparts and not generally pale or tawny buff-brown. Male African Citril (12) has black restricted to face only and lacks bright yellow scapulars and wingbar; females are much more heavily streaked, also lack the bright yellow wingbar and generally show a slight supercilium.

DESCRIPTION Sexes differ. **Adult male:** Entire head to hindneck, sides of neck and throat sooty-black. Mantle and back dull olive-yellow, scapulars brighter yellow or paler yellowish-green, rump brighter and less olive, and uppertail-coverts also yellowish. Tail is notched at tip, black and narrowly edged and tipped yellowish or buffish-white. Median and greater coverts are black, broadly tipped pale lemon-yellow; alula, primary coverts and flight feathers black or blackish, edged thinly pale yellow; tips to tertials and secondaries whitish or pale buff. Black extends onto chin, lower throat and upper breast, otherwise underparts are yellowish, tinged more heavily with olive-green on sides of breast and flanks; belly and undertail-coverts pale yellow. Black bill is thin and pointed (more typically Siskin-like). Legs and feet very dark blackish-brown. In worn plumage male becomes much duller, with bright yellow areas of scapulars and body generally dull green or greenish-yellow; there is variation in the plumage of spring males, with some more advanced towards breeding plumage (presumably first-summer). **Adult female:** Similar to male but head is duller, grey, greyish-brown or dull greyish-olive usually on lores, cheeks, forehead and crown, and tends to be less well defined or pale greenish-yellow on nape and ear-coverts; dull greenish-yellow or yellowish-olive on mantle

and back and less contrasting or paler on scapulars, with indistinct darker streaking; rump is bright yellowish-green. Tail is blackish-brown, with pale yellow or greenish-yellow edges to base. Wings as male, but with duller yellow and yellowish-buff tips to tertials and flight feathers. Dull greyish-olive on throat extends as a wash to yellow breast; belly and flanks are also yellow or yellowish with thin dark streaks on flanks, undertail-coverts pale yellow. Bill dark brown. Legs and feet black. **Juvenile:** Very similar to adult female, but generally dull olive with heavier or darker streaking on entire head, becoming a dull olive with suffused streaking on mantle, back and scapulars; pale buff tips to median and greater coverts. Underparts are dull white or off-white, heavily dark-streaked.

VOICE Call is a variety of high-pitched musical twitters and trills recalling those of both Serin (5) and Goldfinch (68). The song is a pleasant series of musical trills in frequently repeated phrases, recalling Goldfinch but without the buzzing quality, often delivered from the top of a dead weed-head or other prominent perch such as roadside telegraph wires. Birds in non-adult plumage also sing.

STATUS, HABITAT AND BEHAVIOUR Local or locally common to abundant. A high-altitude bird of grassland, open areas within montane forest and moorland of the plateaux of central and northern Ethiopia, rarely below 1800 m and up to 4100 m; usually occurs in areas of giant lobelia, alchemilla and giant heath, as well as its preferred food plants. Outside the breeding season occurs in flocks, often up to 100 or more individuals, roving upland areas and feeding on a variety of available seeds. Behaviour similar to Siskin's (49), with nervous or excitable movements and actions but also recalls Goldfinch or Linnet when singing. Feeds on the ground while clinging to vegetation in Siskin-like fashion; takes mostly seeds of small plants, particularly St John's wort and hagenia.

DISTRIBUTION Monotypic. Endemic to northern and central highlands of Ethiopia.

MOVEMENTS Apparently none, but birds from higher regions of the range may move to lower levels in times of severe weather.

MEASUREMENTS Wing 74–80.

Serinus citrinelloides Rüppell, 1840, Neue Wirbelt., Vögel, p. 95, Simen, Abyssinia.

IDENTIFICATION Length 11·5–12 cm (4½–4¾ in). A small finch with bright but variable plumage. Considerable racial variation: can show a black face and bright yellow supercilium or none at all; upperparts are green, dark-streaked or blackish, underparts of males are bright yellow or dull yellowish-green with rather heavy streaking on breast and flanks. Some birds may be indeterminate intermediates. **Confusion species:** Black-headed Siskin (11) is similar, but has an all-dark or black hood; where hood is incomplete (females), the bright yellow supercilium and edges to wing-coverts of African Citril should be distinctive. The southern range of race *frontalis* and western range of *hypostictus* adjoin (but are not known to overlap) that of similarly plumaged Black-faced Canary (13), which, like male *frontalis*, has a black lower forehead below a bright yellow upper forehead and supercilium; Black-faced Canary has more black on face, while African Citril has black (not dusky brown) flight and tail feathers. Females are very similar, but both sexes of *frontalis* can be told by the long and more sharply attenuated bill. Race *hypostictus* has a grey or dark grey-brown face and lacks yellow supercilium. Juvenile birds have green or greenish-yellow rump, uppertail-coverts and base of tail feathers, not warm or pale buff as in juvenile Yellow-crowned Canary (10). For differences between *brittoni* and the very similar (but widely separated in habitat) Papyrus Canary (14), see latter species.

DESCRIPTION Sexes differ. **Adult male** (*citrinelloides*): Lower forehead, lores, cheeks and chin black or blackish (on some, dusky, drab or olive-green), ear-coverts either blackish towards cheeks or entirely olive-green; supercilium is a very thin (may be absent) line of bright yellow over eye and ear-coverts; upper forehead to nape pale green, finely dark-streaked. Mantle, back and scapulars as nape, with short dark streaks (quite heavy on some); lower back, rump and uppertail-coverts paler, more yellowish, and unstreaked. Tail is black or blackish, edged thinly pale greenish-yellow on outer webs. Median and greater coverts black, with pale yellow edges extending to tips and forming thin double wingbar; alula, primary coverts and flight feathers black, with secondaries and tertials broadly edged pale yellowish-green, and in fresh plumage primaries have pale buff tips. Throat, sides of neck to breast and belly are bright yellow (some have sides of neck, throat and breast tinged with green); flanks yellow or yellowish, streaked black, undertail-coverts yellow. Pointed bill is thin or fairly slender, upper mandible dark horn in colour, lower mandible pale flesh to yellowish. Legs and feet light brown, tinged pinkish. **Adult female** (*citrinelloides*): Face and ear-coverts are dull green or slightly olive-green, extending to

chin and sides of neck; supercilium pale yellow, very thin and rather short extending to just beyond eye. Upperparts are dull or pale green with short, blackish streaks from forehead to lower back, heaviest on mantle and back; rump and uppertail-coverts plain or lighter yellowish-green. Tail is blackish, edged pale yellowish-green on outer webs. Median and greater coverts are black, edged with light green, greaters tipped bright yellow forming single wingbar; secondaries and primaries blackish-brown, finely edged yellowish-green; tertials the same but more broadly edged, especially at tips. Chin and throat whitish, breast and upper belly pale greenish-yellow, with short dark streaks on throat, breast and flanks; lower belly and vent paler yellow, with undertail-coverts washed yellow. The upper mandible brown, horn on lower. Legs and feet brown. **Juvenile:** Face dull greyish-olive with fine dark streaks. Upperparts are darker and duller buffish-olive than adult female (some appear brown or brownish in the field); rump and uppertail-coverts dull greenish-yellow. Tail is dark brown, with greenish-yellow edges to outer feathers. Wings have pale or light buff tips to median and greater coverts and edges to tertials; flight feathers are edged greenish-yellow or buff. Chin and throat are buff, becoming buffish-yellow on throat and breast, with dark brown streaks on throat, breast and flanks. No racial differences known among juveniles or immatures.

GEOGRAPHICAL VARIATION Adult male *kikuyuensis* has much more distinct and pronounced yellow supercilium, often narrowly crossing forehead above black band, also tends to have heavier streaking on mantle and back, with upperparts darker or more olive-green than *frontalis*; female *kikuyuensis* is similar to adult female *citrinelloides* but duller olive-yellow, with quite heavy streaking on throat, breast and flanks. Adult male *frontalis* also as nominate, but with bright yellow band broadly across forehead joining supercilium (brighter and more extensive in male than female); upperparts are brighter green than in other races (but only in comparative terms), underparts are purer yellow and often lack green tinge to breast; bill is more slender and pointed, rather Siskin-like (*frontalis* is considered by some authorities to be a separate species). Adult female *frontalis* differs from females of all other races in distinctive bright yellow across forehead onto supercilium, and in pure yellow underparts lacking any streaking. Adult male *hypostictus* has black of face replaced by grey or dark grey (or restricted to lores, cheeks and chin in this race and the next), but in the hand it shows dark brown or black bases to feathers overlaid with a greyish tinge; it lacks bright yellow supercilium and band across the forehead, and some birds have short dark streaks on

throat and breast. Adult female *hypostictus* very similar to male, with grey or pale grey on face and chin; on some, streaks on throat and breast extend to flanks. Adult male and female *brittoni* are very similar to *hypostictus* and adult female *citrinelloides*, with hardly any blackish or grey areas on face and ear-coverts, these being replaced by dark green: differ from *hypostictus* in having a narrow yellow supercilium from upper lores (more prominent in males than females), upperparts much brighter green than *hypostictus* and streaking on mantle, back and scapulars usually much finer (but individual variation, as some can show heavily streaked upperparts); chin greyish-yellow and green tinge to sides of breast and flanks, otherwise warm yellow below, very heavily streaked on chin, throat and upper breast, less so on lower breast and flanks (but area of streaking may be variable).
VOICE Call is a soft clicking 'cheep', alarm call a soft 't,t, tee', and there is also a subdued twittering note, often given in flight. Song is loud and Canary-like or Linnet-like, but sweeter in tone, with a clean piping whistle of three or four notes, 'tweet-ti-tu', which carries for some distance and is usually given from the top of a tree or post, telegraph wire etc.
STATUS, HABITAT AND BEHAVIOUR Common and widespread. Found in most open habitats, generally above 1000 m (but see Distribution), especially in areas of high rainfall; frequently in rank growth along streams, rivers or edges of lakes, also edges of forest, clearings, secondary bush and scrub, cultivated areas such as eucalyptus plantations, gardens and rough patches. Usually occurs in small groups, even in the breeding season. Feeds on the ground and in or on grow-ing vegetation taking a variety of seeds; has a preference for black jack (*Bidens pilosus*), sunflowers, thistles and similar flower-heads, also takes some grass seeds; has been recorded taking flying ants in flight. Race *brittoni* is often found in banana plantations and on other fruit trees.

DISTRIBUTION *S. c. citrinelloides:* southern Eritrea through Ethiopia and extreme southeastern Sudan (Imatong, Dongotona and Didinga Mountains) to northern Kenya.

S. c. frontalis: western Uganda, eastern Zaire, western Kenya and northwest Tanzania, usually between 1000 m and 2100 m, but has been recorded at up to 3300 m in Zaire.

S. c. kikuyuensis: endemic to highlands of south and southwest Kenya.

S. c. brittoni: endemic to western Kenya, Mount Elgon to Kongelia and the Kakamega Forest, at altitudes between 1200 m and 2800 m; overlaps with *kikuyuensis* in western Kenya, apparently without interbreeding.

S. c. hypostictus: southern Kenya, south through central and eastern Tanzania to Malawi, Zimbabwe and northern Mozambique; in Malawi occurs from 700 m up to 1800 m.

MOVEMENTS None recorded, but possibly some of the higher-level breeding birds make altitudinal or dispersive movements in non-breeding season.
MEASUREMENTS Wing of male 64–70, of female 64–67·5; tail 49; tarsus 14·5–15; bill (culmen) 11–11·5. Wing of *frontalis* 64; tail 54; tarsus 13; bill (culmen) 10·7. Weight of male *hypostictus* 11·5–15·4, of female 14·7.
REFERENCES Mackworth-Praed and Grant (1960), Sclater and Moreau (1933).

13 BLACK-FACED CANARY *Serinus capistratus*   Plate 5
Southern-central Africa

Crithagra capistrata Finsch and Hartlaub, 1870, Vög. Ost-Afr., p. 458, Golungo Alto, 1800–2800 ft, Angola.

IDENTIFICATION Length 11·5 cm (4½ in). A small, stubby-billed, brightly coloured finch. **Confusion species:** Males greatly resemble *frontalis* race of African Citril (12), while females are very similar to nominate female African Citril, the range of which it adjoins on its eastern boundary but does not overlap; nor does it generally come into contact with African Citril, being found at lower elevations. Black-faced Canary is blacker on face, especially from lower forehead to under and behind eye, and somewhat blacker on sides of lower cheeks and chin. It also has a very short stubby bill, while *frontalis* has a very fine, pointed Siskin-like bill. Flight feathers of African Citril are blacker than on Black-faced Canary, which has broader greenish-yellow edges to tertials. Female also resembles a small Brimstone Canary (25), but has dark streaking on chin, throat and breast.
DESCRIPTION Sexes differ. **Adult male:** Base of forehead, lores, around eye and fore ear-coverts and cheeks to chin black; rear of ear-coverts and sides of neck greenish-yellow; upper forehead to supercilium broadly golden-yellow. Crown to nape, mantle, back and scapulars light greenish-olive, bright in tone and finely streaked blackish; rump and uppertail-coverts are unstreaked yellowish, tinged with green. Tail is black or deep brown, edged (and tipped on some) greenish-yellow. Median and greater coverts black, edged and broadly tipped bright greenish-yellow, forming double wingbar; alula, primary coverts and flight feathers dark brown, broadly edged greenish-yellow on secondaries and tertials. Underparts are bright golden-yellow, slightly washed green on flanks and finely dark-streaked. Bill short and very stubby, with a pinkish-brown upper mandible and pale whitish-horn lower. Legs and feet brown or pinkish-brown. **Adult female:** Lacks black face,

and supercilium is paler yellow; lores form a dusky or grey-brown smudge; lower cheeks are yellowish, becoming greener on ear-coverts. Forehead (frontal band of yellow is streaked) is slightly greener than on male and somewhat more heavily streaked blackish; rump is brighter green than yellow, as are edges to dark brown tail. Chin and throat to breast yellowish-green, streaked dusky or blackish; rest of underparts yellow or olive-yellow, sides of breast and flanks washed green and with fine dark streaks. **Juvenile:** As adult female but paler olive or dull green in tone, lacking bright greenish-yellow of adult, and heavily streaked above and below.

GEOGRAPHICAL VARIATION Birds of race *hildegardae* have forehead and supercilium more greenish-yellow, fading over ear-coverts, and more greenish-yellow underparts.

VOICE Call is a variety of 'chissick' notes. The song is a jumble of high-pitched Canary-like phrases.

STATUS, HABITAT AND BEHAVIOUR Uncommon or locally common. Very little is known of its habits or breeding ecology. Occurs from sea-level to 1500 m (rarely to 1700 m in southeast Zaire); mainly on edge of or at clearings in moist evergreen forest, swamps or thickets, usually near water. Fairly sociable, gathering in small flocks or mixed parties with weavers (*Ploceus* spp.). Food is a variety of grass and plant seeds.

DISTRIBUTION *S. c. capistratus:* southern Gabon to northern Zaire and west Burundi, south to northern Angola and east to Zambia and northern Zimbabwe.

S. c. hildegardae: southern Angola.

MEASUREMENTS Wing 59–65; tail 39–42.

14 PAPYRUS CANARY (Van Someren's Canary) *Serinus koliensis*
Plate 5

East Africa

Serinus capistratus koliensis Grant and Mackworth-Praed, 1952, Bull. Brit. Ornith. Club, 72:1, Onyulu's, Koli river, Lango, Uganda.

IDENTIFICATION Length 10·5–11 cm (4¼ in). Found almost exclusively in papyrus, either along streams and rivers or in large floating swamps. A deep greenish-yellow finch with a short stubby bill and a considerable amount of streaking above and on throat and breast. Usually separable from most other serins through habitat preference. **Confusion species:** Differs from most races of African Citril (12) in streaked underparts on both male and female. Race *brittoni* of African Citril is virtually identical, but is somewhat brighter yellowish-green on upperparts, its flight feathers (including tertials) and tail are blacker, it has a fine or narrow yellow supercilium (absent in *koliensis*), more prominent wingbar, and slightly more pointed bill with less markedly curved ridge to upper mandible, and *brittoni* is also restricted to high ground above 1200 m; race *hypostictus* of African Citril has a dark greyish face (or at least chin and cheeks) and has duller upperparts. It differs from Black-faced Canary (13) in lacking any black on face and in having heavily streaked underparts.

DESCRIPTION Sexes similar. **Adult male:** Forehead, crown and nape to sides of head and face deep green, finely but prominently dark-streaked on forehead and crown; cheeks, ear-coverts and sides of neck uniform deep green, cheeks with some very slight streaking, and sooty lores encircling lower mandible. Mantle, back and scapulars are deep green and heavily dark-streaked; rump and uppertail-coverts plain green (almost lime-green on some). Tail is black or blackish-brown, with yellowish-green edges to outer webs. Median and greater coverts are black or blackish, with green or deep green edges and tips to medians, greaters with fine paler yellow edges and tips form-ing poorly defined wingbar; alula, primary coverts and flight feathers are black, the latter finely edged with greenish-yellow; tertials the same, but tipped paler green. Underparts are deep yellow or yellowish-green, with dark streaking on throat, breast and flanks, heaviest on throat. Bill short and rather stubby, the upper mandible pinkish-brown, lower mandible paler and more horn-coloured. Legs and feet pale brown. **Adult female:** Very similar to adult male, but with grey on lores, cheeks and lower forehead; the underparts are paler yellow (throat can be off-white or lemon), and streaks on breast are heavier than on male and extend to flanks. **Juvenile:** Very similar to adult female, but with olive-brown upperparts broadly dark-streaked; rump, uppertail-coverts and tail as female, wings also as female but with pale buffish-white edges and tips to coverts and tertials. Underparts are warm buff with broad dark brown streaks, becoming yellow on belly with fine or narrow dusky streaks.

VOICE Generally silent, but has a variety of soft wheezing and slurring notes; song 'see-see-see-surr', with emphasis on last syllable (Turner *et al.* in prep.).

STATUS, HABITAT AND BEHAVIOUR Local but occasionally common. Very poorly known, the nest and eggs have never been found. An Appendix C (near-threatened) species in the African *Red Data Book*, owing to possible threats of habitat destruction. It is virtually restricted to papyrus between 900 m and 1600 m or in adjacent areas of cultivation (bananas, sorghum, maize), but returns to papyrus to roost. Usually found alone or in pairs, but up to about 15 have been seen feeding together. Feeds principally on seeds of papyrus, but will also take small seeds from edges of adjacent cultivated areas.

DISTRIBUTION Monotypic. Southern Uganda (Kigezi and Ankole) to southwestern Kenya and northeast Zaire.

MOVEMENTS Resident.

MEASUREMENTS Wing of male 61–67, of female 63–65.

REFERENCE Collar and Stuart (1985).

15 FOREST CANARY *Serinus scotops*

South Africa

Plate 4

Crithagra scotops Sundevall, 1850, Ofv. K. Sv. Vet.-Akad. Forh., 7, p. 98, lower Caffraria; type from Pietermaritzburg, Natal, *fide* W.L. Sclater, 1930, Syst. Av. Aethiop., p. 816.

IDENTIFICATION Length 13 cm (5 in). The South African counterpart of African Citril (12) and Black-faced Canary (13), which it closely resembles in habits and behaviour. The darkest and most heavily streaked of the canaries. Males have black or blackish lores, cheeks and ear-coverts, with heavy streaking on sides of throat, breast and flanks (heaviest on birds in the Transvaal), and dark or deep olive-green upperparts with a bright unstreaked green lower rump. Females and juveniles are similar but lack black or blackish face.

DESCRIPTION Sexes differ. **Adult male:** Lower forehead to cheeks, ear-coverts and chin variably blackish to dark olive (lores and chin always black); short and thin bright yellow supercilium from upper lores to area over ear-coverts. Upper forehead to crown, nape, mantle, back, scapulars and upper rump dark or deep olive-green with blackish streaks to centres of feathers; lower rump and uppertail-coverts uniform bright yellowish-green. Tail is blackish or blackish-brown, edged light green. Median and greater coverts are blackish, with yellow edges and tips forming thin double wingbar, slightly broader and brighter on greaters; alula, primary coverts and flight feathers blackish-brown, finely edged yellow or, on some, broadly so on secondaries. Upper throat as face or dull olive, lower throat plain yellow in centre; breast is olive or dusky-green, fairly heavily and diffusely streaked blackish, especially at sides, streaks continuing broadly and distinctly to flanks; finely streaked on belly, but otherwise belly to undertail-coverts deep yellow. Bill rather stout and robust-looking, with brown upper mandible and paler pinkish-brown lower. Legs and feet dark brown. **Adult female:** Similar to adult male, but has smaller or poorly defined supercilium, lacks black on chin and around base of bill, has grey, dark grey or olive lores to cheeks (to ear-coverts on some) and chin, and yellow on lower throat is streaked with black; rest of underparts as male, but has greenish breast

and paler yellow flanks and vent (streaked blackish, heaviest on sides of breast and flanks). **Juvenile:** Closely resembles adult female, but is generally duller or deeper olive where female is green and pale yellow where female is bright; chin and throat pale yellow with thin dark streaks; median and greater coverts and tertials are tipped yellowish-buff.

GEOGRAPHICAL VARIATION Males of race *transvaalensis* are prominently streaked blackish on entire underparts, and black on face is restricted to lower forehead and base of bill to chin.

VOICE Call is a low 'tsik' or 'tsisk', also a thin, plaintive 'tweetoo, twee-ee' repeated frequently. The song is a rich and brisk high-pitched warble; also has a quiet jumbled song.

STATUS, HABITAT AND BEHAVIOUR Uncommon or locally common. Inhabits clearings or edges in thick evergreen highland forest or dense bush up to 1800 m. Actions and behaviour as African Citril and Black-faced Canary, but much harder to see, generally shy and keeps to cover, more often heard than seen. Forages in pairs or small parties, either at mid-tree level or on the ground, feeding on a variety of seeds, buds and fruit; also gathers at flowering or fruiting shrubs, and comes to feeders and tables in gardens close to forest.

DISTRIBUTION *S. s. scotops*: south and southeast Cape Province (north to the Amatole range), where local, to Transkei, South Africa.

S. s. transvaalensis: eastern Griqualand, western and northern Transvaal to western Swaziland, South Africa.

MOVEMENTS Makes local movements in search of food and is attracted to seasonally unpredictable fruiting shrubs.

MEASUREMENTS Wing 64–68; tail 48–53; tarsus 14–16; bill (culmen) 10–12.

REFERENCES McLachlan and Liversidge (1978), Newman (1983), Sinclair (1984).

16 WHITE-RUMPED SEEDEATER (Grey Canary) *Serinus leucopygius*
Plate 6

Africa

Crithagra leucopyga Sundevall, 1850, Ofv. K. Sv. Vet.-Akad. Forh., 7, p. 127, Sennar.

IDENTIFICATION Length 10–11·5 cm (4–4½ in). A small ground-dwelling finch of dry or arid semi-desert areas south of the Sahara and northeast Africa. Virtually all pale grey-brown with browner mottling or streaks on the upperparts, except for distinctive all-white rump and pale buff wingbar. Chin to breast are greyish or buffish, slightly mottled with brown on throat and breast, remaining underparts whitish. **Confusion species:** Dull grey-brown plumage rules out other canaries within range, and plain head, face and nape distinguish it from otherwise similarly plumaged Streaky-headed Seedeater (27). In northern Ethiopia to southern Sudan range overlaps with Yellow-rumped Seedeater (17), from which it is easily separated at all ages by colour of rump.

DESCRIPTION Sexes alike. **Adult:** Forehead, crown and nape pale grey-brown with dark brown streaks, paler and less streaked across nape. Face pale ashy-grey with an indistinct dark eye-stripe. Mantle, back and scapulars pale grey-brown with dark brown streaks or feather centres; rump white, uppertail-coverts whitish with dark tips. Tail is brown, edged grey-brown. Median coverts are brown or mid-brown, edged pale or greyish-buff, greater coverts the same with off-white tips forming wingbar; alula and primary coverts dark brown or black, the latter white-tipped; flight feathers are also brown, primaries narrowly edged with white, slightly broader edges on secondaries. Chin and throat are ashy-grey or pale buff, slightly mottled browner at sides and across lower throat and breast; lower breast and belly white or off-white, becoming greyish-brown on flanks, where streaked lightly with brown; undertail-coverts white. Bill fleshy pinkish-brown or dark brown at tip and along culmen, with a pale or whitish base. Legs and feet pale fleshy-pink to very pale brown. **Juvenile:** Similar to adult, but paler or warmer brown and more heavily streaked on upperparts and noticeably mottled and spotted on breast and flanks.

GEOGRAPHICAL VARIATION Birds from Niger and northern Nigeria, *pallens*, are paler or greyer on upperparts, but this is not always noticeable without direct comparison. In *riggenbachi* and *pallens* the chin and throat are whitish, with dusky tinge to breast and belly; the breast spots on *riggenbachi* are much browner and more obvious, while *pallens* has fine streaks on sides of throat and breast.

VOICE Call is undescribed. The song is rather subdued but clear, sweet and Canary-like in quality.

STATUS, HABITAT AND BEHAVIOUR Common or locally common. Found in dry open bush or savanna below 1000 m, also in cultivated land, farms and gardens and woodland or bushes on the outskirts of villages. Usually found in pairs or often in company of other small finches and waxbills, particularly with Yellow-fronted Canary (21); tame and often approachable. Forages on the ground and in tall grass and feeds on a variety of seed-bearing plants, including millet.

DISTRIBUTION *S. l. leucopygius:* central and southern Sudan (mostly along the Nile) south to extreme northeastern Zaire and northwest Uganda to western and northwest Ethiopia.

S. l. pallens: Niger (Air province) to northern Nigeria (Kano).

S. l. riggenbachi: Senegal (to about 16½°N) and Gambia, east through Mali, Burkina Faso (few published records), northern Guinea, Niger, northern Nigeria, northern Cameroon, Central African Republic (uncommon) and Chad to western Sudan.

MOVEMENTS None long-distance, but becomes locally abundant when millet is ripening.

MEASUREMENTS Wing 62–70; tail 37–45; tarsus 13; bill 7–8.

REFERENCE Mackworth-Praed and Grant (1963).

17 YELLOW-RUMPED SEEDEATER (Black-throated Canary (South Africa)) *Serinus atrogularis*
Plate 6

Africa

Linaria atrogularis A. Smith, 1836, Rept Exped. Centr. Africa, p. 49, about and beyond Kurrichaine, western Transvaal.

IDENTIFICATION Length 11–12 cm (4¼ in). The southern African counterpart of White-rumped Seedeater (16). A small brown or brownish-grey finch with a short conical bill, thin pale buff supercilium, a black or greyish smudge on chin and throat, streaking on sides of breast and flanks and a bright yellow rump. There is considerable variation in plumage tones throughout its range and at least eight races are currently recognised, some readily separable in the field. **Confusion species:** Small size and rump colour instantly distinguish it from otherwise similar-looking species. Within its range, other species with yellow rumps are best separated by colour of entire upperparts; only

185

White-throated Canary (26), which is about one-third larger and looks a chunkier bird, has a bright yellow rump, but (as its name implies) lacks any black on chin and throat and has a slightly different face pattern, a much larger and more pointed bill, and also lacks any streaking on underparts.

DESCRIPTION Sexes similar. **Adult male:** Forehead and crown to nape pale buff-brown, tinged grey; sides of head buffish-grey, with narrow or indistinct pale buff supercilium from mid-lores to area over ear-coverts; cheeks and ear-coverts greyish-brown, finely streaked with black. Mantle, back and scapulars as crown, or slightly darker, with broad dark streaks; rump bright yellow, and uppertail-coverts pale brown, edged and tipped white. Tail is dark brown with tips to all feathers buffish-white, extending along outer feathers for about the distal third. Median coverts are dark brown with buffish-white or pale buffish-brown edges and tips, greater coverts browner, edged pale brown and tipped buffish, not so pale as tips to medians; alula, primary coverts and flight feathers dark brown, finely edged dull yellowish-green or buffish-yellow, tertials broadly edged and tipped light buffish-brown, secondaries more finely tipped pale buff. Chin whitish or pale buff, throat and upper breast dark grey, variably smudged or mottled darker brown or black; rest of underparts whitish or washed with buffish-brown. Bill short and conical, brownish-horn, paler at base of lower mandible. Legs and feet pinkish-brown. **Adult female:** Females have chin, throat and breast buff with indistinct small dark spots, sides of breast to flanks warm buff-brown, streaked darker brown or blackish, and lower breast and belly either dull white or buffish-white. **Juvenile:** Like adult, but generally warmer buff-brown and spotted on chin, throat, breast and flanks, varying in intensity among races; some have fine streaks on sides of breast and flanks, with a pale yellow wash to breast and upper belly.

GEOGRAPHICAL VARIATION Upperparts of *xanthopygius* and *deserti* are as nominate, but greyer in *semideserti, seshekeensis, somereni* and *lwenarum* or intermediate in *impiger*; crown slightly ashy-grey in *impiger*. Some birds appear very dark on upperparts at a distance owing to heavy streaking. Race *reichenowi* is the most distinctive of the races as it is browner on upperparts, and both sexes have a pale buffish-white or creamy-buff forehead and supercilium and also lack black or dark smudging on throat and upper breast, this being replaced with brown spots or streaks on breast and flanks. The underparts are highly variable: the markings on throat and upper breast can be either black (*somereni*) or mottled blackish, the dark grey broken into spots, or smudged (*impiger, deserti, semideserti*), or even only faintly indicated (*xanthopygius*); but even within races there is variation in the intensity of black, which is most likely to be present/heaviest on males in the breeding season. Underparts of females of *xanthopygius, deserti, semideserti* and *reichenowi* are as nominate, but slightly tinged pinkish on *impiger*, and entirely warm buff-brown on *somereni* and *lwenarum*. Note: Another race,

kasamaensis from Zambia (formerly northern Rhodesia), described by Benson (1955), has dark-streaked grey forehead to nape, dark-streaked brown mantle, back and scapulars, black chin, throat and upper breast (only lightly indicated on some) and is deep buff or tawny-buff on breast and upper flanks; it is now considered by some authorities to be inseparable from *lwenarum*.

VOICE Contact call is a rising 'tswee' or 'tsuii'; in flight gives a double chirrup note. It has a strong and clear Canary-like song, sustained and rambling with repeated phrases, often delivered from a tree-top, and is one of the most persistent songsters of southern Africa.

STATUS, HABITAT AND BEHAVIOUR Common in the south, local in northern and eastern parts of range. A dry-country species found in a wide range of habitats, from savanna with thornscrub to broadleaved woodland, orchards, cultivation, grassland and open parkland; in the more arid parts of its range usually found close to waterholes, which it visits regularly. A sociable bird, nesting in some areas in loose colonies; feeds in pairs or small parties. Perches freely in trees and bushes but more usually on the ground, searching for seeds of a variety of grasses and plants, especially flower-heads of the Compositae; known to take insects, particularly termites, and also tree sap.

DISTRIBUTION *S. a. atrogularis*: Zimbabwe (south of 17°S), eastern Botswana south to northern Cape Province, South Africa.

S. a. deserti: southern Angola (where it occurs along the coast) and Namibia south to northern Cape Province, South Africa.

S. a. semideserti: northeast Namibia, southern Angola and southwest Zambia, through northern Botswana to west and northwest Zimbabwe and south to northwest Transvaal, South Africa.

S. a. lwenarum: Angola, southern Zaire, Zambia to northern Zimbabwe and southwest Tanzania.

S. a. impiger: southern Transvaal to northern Cape Province, South Africa.

S. a. seshekeensis: southwest Zimbabwe.

S. a. somereni eastern Zaire, western Uganda to western Kenya (Kakamega-Siaya region).

S. a. reichenowi: central and southern Ethiopia, eastern Uganda to Kenya and northeast Tanzania.

S. a. xanthopygius: northern Ethiopia.

Note: Arabian Serin (18) is also considered by some authorities, including Mackworth-Praed and Grant (1960) and Howard and Moore (1980), to be a race of Yellow-rumped Seedeater.

MOVEMENTS A partial migrant. In the non-breeding season forms large nomadic flocks which rove about at random, often over large areas of its range, in search of food; occasionally wanders to southeast Sudan and coastal areas of South Africa (especially the Cape).

MEASUREMENTS Wing of male 65–72, of female 64–67; tail 41–47; tarsus 11–14; bill (culmen) 8–9.

REFERENCES Benson (1955), Clancey (1964), Ginn *et al.* (1990), Mackworth-Praed and Grant (1960), McLachlan and Liversidge (1978), Newman (1983).

Serinus rothschildi Ogilvie-Grant, 1902, Bull. Brit. Ornith. Club, 13, p. 21, Ichaf ravine, Hamerah, and Dthubiyat, upper Haushabi.

IDENTIFICATION Length 11·5 cm (4½ in). A small, dull brown or grey-brown, greenish-tinged finch endemic to highlands of southwest Arabia. It has a characteristic bill shape, dusky head and face, a small olive-green, yellow-tinged rump patch and a dark tail. **Confusion species:** Very similar to Yemen Serin (19), which is slightly browner and has paler face with a pale spot below eye, a thin moustachial streak and no green or yellowish-green on rump; Yemen Serin also has a shorter tail, a thinner pointed bill with straight culmen and dark upper mandible contrasting with paler lower, and longer primary projection two-thirds the length of tertials (Arabian Serin's is only one-third). Much duller and browner than brightly coloured and heavily streaked Serin (5), and lacks large bright yellow rump patch and well-marked face pattern of Yellow-rumped Seedeater (17), but neither is likely to occur within the range.

DESCRIPTION Sexes similar. **Adult:** Forehead to crown, nape and sides of neck dull or dingy olive-brown, tinged grey, with diffuse dark streaks; face is slightly paler or greyer, but lores, ear-coverts and cheeks are pale grey-brown and it has a short and indistinct (often scarcely visible) eyebrow. Mantle, back and scapulars as crown and nape, but with browner centres to feathers; rump green or olive-green, variable in extent and often only on a small area of upper rump, bordered by brown or greyish-brown as on uppertail-coverts. Tail is dull dark brown. Median and greater coverts dull brown, edged slightly paler, and in fresh plumage with buff tips forming poorly defined double wingbar; flight feathers and tertials the same, with slightly broader pale buff or buffish-brown edges to tertials. Chin and throat pale buff (though some are whiter on chin), greyer or buff-brown on breast, with short brownish streaks or spots of varying intensity (some visible at close range) continuing onto flanks, which are either buff or warm buff-brown; belly and undertail-coverts buff or off-white. Bill has a characteristic shape, deep at base with a curved ridge to both mandibles, variable in colour from brown to dull pinkish-brown or horn to brownish-grey, but uniform on both mandibles. Legs and feet pink or light pinkish-brown. Adult females are very similar but slightly paler or buffer (less olive) on upperparts, and at close range show pale buff streaks on crown and nape. **Juvenile:** As adult, from which it is virtually indistinguishable.

VOICE Call is a quiet 'tsit-tsit', frequently given in flight. The scratchy song is a slow and warbler-like 'zi juu chi-chi chichi' or 'ti-tiiu-tui-tsu', beginning with a rising trill and tapering off with a jumble of notes; recalls Common Rosefinch (87) in its musical quality.

STATUS, HABITAT AND BEHAVIOUR Uncommon or locally common, but fairly widespread (especially in North Yemen) within its limited range. A bird of high ground between about 1000 m and 2800 m, in a variety of habitats from open rocky country with sparse vegetation to more cultivated land or shrubs, bushes and well-wooded areas. A typical serin in feeding habits, perching mostly in bushes, shrubs and trees as well as on the ground. It has a characteristic habit of gently pumping or flicking its tail. It occurs in pairs or small (family?) groups. Feeds on the ground and actively in or on vegetation, mainly on a variety of seeds including millet and grass, also seeds and buds of shrubs such as aloe and agave, occasionally insects such as caterpillars are taken.

DISTRIBUTION Monotypic. Endemic to the Hejaz and Asir highlands of southwestern Saudi Arabia (to about 26°N) through the highlands of North Yemen and the western Hadramawt of South Yemen. Considered by some authorities to be a race of Yellow-rumped Seedeater (17), but since it has notable plumage and structural differences and is geographically isolated we consider it a full species.

MOVEMENTS Resident.

MEASUREMENTS Wing of male 69, of female 63.

REFERENCES Everett (1987), Hollom *et al.* (1988).

19 YEMEN SERIN (Menacha Seedeater) *Serinus menachensis* Plate 18
Arabia

Poliospiza menachensis Ogilvie-Grant, 1913, Bull. Brit. Ornith. Club, 31, p. 90, Menacha, Yemen.

IDENTIFICATION Length 11·5 cm (4½ in). A small and rather nondescript little finch of limited distribution in southwest Arabia. Very similar to Arabian Serin (18), with which it shares many features and a similar though slightly smaller range. It has grey-tinged brown upperparts, brown rump and lightly streaked underparts. **Confusion species:** The only confusion species likely to occur within natural range is Arabian Serin, which is very similar but stockier and larger-headed, greyer on upperparts and with a short primary projection, longer tail, green rump, darker face, and a larger bill with more curved culmen and virtually uniform in colour. Yemen Serin has a slightly more pronounced supercilium and a dark moustachial stripe in front of pale-streaked cheeks, and the bill is more pointed; ground colour of underparts is cleaner than the dull or dingy buff of Arabian Serin's breast and flanks. More likely than latter to be encountered in a flock, and does not flick or wag tail. Yemen Serin also favours rocky hillsides or drier habitat at higher elevations, but there is considerable overlap between the two species' ranges.
DESCRIPTION Sexes alike. **Adult:** Forehead, crown and nape grey-brown, with some fine darker streaks on crown; pale, ill-defined buff supercilium; lores brown, cheeks and ear-coverts pale tan or buffish (slightly browner at rear), pale buff crescent immediately below eye; lightly defined pale olive-brown moustachial stripe from lower lores to sides of mid-throat, but varies in tone and extent among individuals. Mantle, back and scapulars are grey-brown, with indistinct dark streaks on mantle and back; rump and uppertail-coverts uniform brown or grey-brown. Tail is brown to dark brown. Median and greater coverts are brown, finely edged and tipped buffish-brown, occasionally showing pale buff wingbars (probably through abrasion); alula and primary coverts brown to dark brown; flight feathers brown, thinly edged buff, tertials more broadly edged buffish-brown; shows long primary projection. Underparts are pale buffish or whitish, with pale brown streaks (some quite heavily or densely streaked on lower throat) on sides of neck to lower breast and flanks; belly and undertail-coverts white. Bill small and stout, and more slender than Arabian Serin's (lacks pronounced curve to culmen); upper mandible is pale brownish-horn, the lower slightly pinkish, but can be brown or even orange-yellow. Legs and feet dull pinkish-brown. **Juvenile:** Very similar but noticeably duller than adult.
VOICE Call is 'teee-oo', with the first note drawn out; typical flight call a dry 'dweep' or 'wheep', sometimes repeated several times, slightly Redpoll-like (flocks sound like Redpolls (69) in flight); also a faint twittering note in flight, a rapid 'twi-twi-twi-twi' (or ending in 'tuu') and 'ti-ti-ti', with various notes often combined. The song sounds like 'chew-chee-chee-chwee'.
STATUS, HABITAT AND BEHAVIOUR Common or locally common. Inhabits dry stony areas with little vegetation, also hillsides and cliffs in towns and villages (including the middle of Sana'a, North Yemen), between 2000 m and 3200 m, but has also been recorded at over 3600 m. Occurs in small flocks, occasionally with Yemen Linnet (73), feeding in low vegetation or on the ground, where it freely perches on rocks. Feeds on a variety of seeds, principally of millet and grass, but also seeds of other types of plants and shrubs.
DISTRIBUTION Monotypic. Restricted to highlands of southwest Saudi Arabia (southern Asir, north to about 20°N), North Yemen and northwest South Yemen.
MOVEMENTS None known.
MEASUREMENTS Wing 70–75.
REFERENCES Everett (1987), Hollom *et al.* (1988).

20 LEMON-BREASTED CANARY *Serinus citrinipectus*   Plate 6
South Africa

Serinus citrinipectus Clancey and Lawson, 1960, Durban Mus. Novit., 6:61–64, Panda, southern Mozambique.

IDENTIFICATION Length 12 cm (4½–5 in). Not described until 1960 and widely believed to have originated as a product of hybridisation between Yellow-fronted Canary (21) and Yellow-rumped Seedeater (17), but now considered to be a full species within a small range (see Irwin 1981, Hall and Moreau 1970). Males have bright lemon-yellow chin to breast and characteristic facial markings, with a bright yellow spot on base of ear-coverts; lower underparts white. Female and juvenile are similar, but with rather diffuse or indistinct face markings. Both sexes have a bright yellow rump. **Confusion species:** Similar to bright green-and-yellow Yellow-fronted Canary, with which it often forms mixed flocks, but has a different head-and-face pattern which is not so strongly defined and a well-defined supercilium. Brimstone Canary (25) is much larger, has green (male) or yellow (female) upperparts and is more extensively uniform yellow on underparts. Female separated from initially similar but much larger (and out of range) White-throated Canary (26) and Yellow-rumped Seedeater by face pattern, faint wingbars and colour of underparts. [Hall and Moreau (1970) describe this species as being highly variable in the amount and extent of yellow on face, extent of white in tail and bill colour; of 15 specimens examined by them, no two were found to be alike. They also noted that some recently captured birds at a dealer's shop in Mozambique had been identified as Yellow-rumped Seedeater x Lemon-breasted Canary hybrids. The range of Yellow-rumped Seedeater adjoins but does not overlap that of Lemon-breasted Canary.]

DESCRIPTION Sexes separable. **Adult male:** Forehead to crown grey or greyish-brown, streaked slightly darker, less heavily streaked on nape; white or whitish spot at sides of lower forehead; lores are black or dark grey with a white or whitish spot at side of base of lower mandible (not present or visible on all birds); cheeks, moustachial stripe and slightly onto ear-coverts dark grey, with a circular yellow or yellowish-white spot in centre of ear-coverts, and a very thin or slight pale yellow supercilium behind eye. Mantle, back and scapulars are greyish-brown, streaked dark brown or with blackish feather centres; rump and tips of uppertail-coverts bright yellow, base of uppertail-coverts dark grey or blackish. Tail is fairly short and square-ended, dark grey or blackish with white, pale buff or greenish-yellow edges and pale buff or whitish tips to outer two feathers. Median and greater coverts are dark grey-brown, with thin buff or off-white edges and tips forming thin but distinctive whitish wingbars; alula, primary coverts and flight feathers also very dark grey-brown, with pale greenish-yellow edges to secondaries and primaries. Chin, throat and breast are usually deep bright yellow, variable in extent, sides of breast

and flanks buffish; rest of underparts pure white, or tinged warm peachy-buff on flanks. The small but relatively stout bill has a greyish-horn upper mandible and greyish-horn tip to lower, the latter with a paler grey base. Legs and feet pinkish-brown. **Adult female:** A slightly paler or duller version of adult male; lacks bright yellow underparts. Face pattern as male but paler or greyer, with yellow tones on sides of lower forehead and centre of ear-coverts (present on some males) replaced by pale or sandy-buff. Median and greater coverts are black or blackish-brown, edged and tipped sandy or pinkish-buff, with tips to greaters paler, plain buff or whitish; rest of wing as male. Pale buff or pale buffish-brown chin, throat and breast, often with short, dark streaks on breast and upper flanks; belly and lower flanks white or very pale yellow, with pale pinkish-buff or yellow undertail-coverts. **Juvenile:** Similar to adult female, but with paler rump and with little or no yellow on throat; breast and flanks are streaked with brown.

VOICE Call is similar to Yellow-rumped Seedeater's but higher-pitched. It has a pretty song with a rather sparrow-like tone.

STATUS, HABITAT AND BEHAVIOUR Local and uncommon within limited range; occasionally abundant in some areas. A bird of lowland palm savannas, clearings in dry woodland, *Brachystegia* scrub, grassland, gardens, road verges and edges of cultivation, invariably below 750 m. Gregarious and often forms flocks with Yellow-fronted Canary; the largest number ever seen together is 160. Feeds on the ground on a variety of seeds, mostly small weed seeds and flowering grasses.

DISTRIBUTION Monotypic. Southern Malawi (lower Shire valley), southeast Zimbabwe, southern Mozambique to Zululand and northern Natal, South Africa; also recently recorded in Zambia.

MOVEMENTS In non-breeding season, nomadic flocks move at random in search of feeding areas of flowering grasses.

MEASUREMENTS Wing of male 62–71; tail 37·5–41; tarsus 13–14; bill (culmen) 11–13.

REFERENCES Clancey (1985), Hall and Moreau (1970), Irwin (1981), Mackworth-Praed and Grant (1963), McLachlan and Liversidge (1978), Sinclair (1984).

21 YELLOW-FRONTED CANARY (Yellow-eyed Canary, Green Singing Finch (avic.)) *Serinus mozambicus*   Plate 3
Africa

Fringilla mozambica S. Muller, 1776, Natursyst., suppl., p. 163, Mozambique.

IDENTIFICATION Length 11–13 cm (4¼–5 in). A small green canary, widely distributed throughout most of Africa. It has a very strongly marked face pattern and variable green or greenish-yellow forehead and crown to lower back, with bright or deep yellow rump and underparts. Sexes similar, but female and juvenile slightly duller or less bright, juveniles also streaked on underparts. **Con-**

fusion species: The well-defined face pattern and green or greenish-yellow upperparts separate Yellow-fronted from larger Yellow (23) and Brimstone Canaries (25), both of which have more diffuse black through eye; Yellow-fronted also has a grey or greyish nape (not present on the other two) and a yellow rump (not present on Yellow Canary). Face pattern of female also much better defined than on either male or female Lemon-breasted Canary (20), which has a grey-brown mantle and back. Juvenile Yellow-fronted has streaking on breast and flanks (lacking on Yellow and Brimstone), and its smaller size, bill shape and pale tip to tail are also good distinguishing features. Escaped Yellow-fronted Canaries are very similar to and possibly confusable with Serin (5), but Yellow-fronted is slightly larger, with a square-ended tail (but can appear slightly forked when perched); when seen well, the lack of streaking on underparts (except for juveniles, which are faintly streaked), stronger face pattern, bright yellow forehead to supercilium, prominent moustachial stripe and faintly streaked mantle and back should readily separate Yellow-fronted Canary.

DESCRIPTION Sexes differ. **Adult male:** Lower forehead and supercilium deep yellow; lores to upper ear-coverts black, becoming greyer towards rear of ear-coverts; cheeks and lower ear-coverts deep yellow, contrasting with blackish or dusky moustachial stripe; sides of nape and neck grey or pale grey. Upper forehead to nape grey or greyish-olive or dull green, variable according to race, but usually finely streaked with black on upper forehead to hindneck; nape to sides of neck a plain grey or tinged greyish-green. Mantle, back and scapulars green or greenish (some tinged buffish or light brown) with dark brown streaks in southern races, to more yellow or a yellowish-green and only lightly streaked in northern races; rump and uppertail-coverts bright or deep yellow (some tinged greenish). Tail is black or blackish, finely edged with yellow and tipped buff or buffish or yellowish-white (but some birds lose tips through abrasion, and not all races have the same width of pale yellow at feather tip). Median and greater coverts blackish-brown, in fresh plumage broadly edged and tipped yellow (greaters less broadly edged) forming indistinct double wingbar; alula, primary coverts and flight feathers blackish, finely edged pale green. Underparts are rich or bright yellow on chin, throat and breast, washed slightly green on sides of breast (in winter becomes greyish), rest of underparts pale yellow or whitish. Bill is small and pointed, with a dark brown or horn-brown upper mandible (mostly on culmen) and pale horn or greyish-horn lower mandible. Legs and feet dark brown. In worn plumage, the tips to coverts are only very slightly yellowish and wingbars become even less distinct; abrasion also reduces coverts and secondaries to their dark or black centres, and sides of breast become greyish. **Adult female:** A slightly duller or greyer version of male, especially noticeable on upperparts (excluding rump); also, yellow on fresh coverts and flight feathers less pronounced. Underparts are not always so bright as male, and face is greyer (not black) with less contrast. Some show a white chin spot. **Juvenile:** Similar to adult female, but greyer or grey-green on upperparts, with only a tinge of yellow in plumage; rump is dull greenish-yellow. The face pattern is not so well defined, and the moustachial stripe is very thin; very pale yellow or yellowish-buff on forehead. Fairly broad pale buff or yellowish-buff tips to median and greater coverts. Underparts are

very pale yellow, but with some short dusky brown spots (more widespread and heavier on juvenile female than male) and streaking on sides of lower breast and flanks.

GEOGRAPHICAL VARIATION Very difficult to determine in the field, as most are separated by varying degrees of green or yellow (or green progressing into yellow) in plumage of upperparts and underparts; varies from yellowish-green with fine or thin streaks in north of range to greyish-green with heavy streaks in the south. Race *caniceps* has crown to nape grey or pale grey and *santhome* has a grey-brown crown, while *barbatus* lacks any grey on head. In some races, particularly *granti* and *grotei*, the moustachial stripe is greyer than in nominate and often joins grey on sides of nape. In the hand, some races (e.g. *punctigula*) have white on chin. Adult females of *punctigula* and *caniceps* have chin and throat spotted blackish or a necklace of dark spots across lower throat.

VOICE Call is a single or double 'tsssp' note, 'tseeuu', 'swee-et', or 'zeee-zereee-chereeo'. Song is lively and rather canary-like but repetitive, and often delivered in short bursts (males often sing in concert).

STATUS, HABITAT AND BEHAVIOUR Common to locally abundant. Widely distributed throughout range (though may be absent from large areas of suitable habitat), it is frequently persecuted for the cagebird trade. Usually found in small parties on savanna plateaux or plains with occasional trees (though avoids dense thornscrub), woodland savanna, *Brachystegia* woodland, edges of cultivated areas, also reedbeds, plantations, gardens and around houses in villages, often at considerable elevation to between 1800 m and 2100 m but generally well below 1500 m. Tame and rather confiding, and commonly kept in cages both in Africa and throughout Europe and America as the 'Green Singing Finch'. Most behaviour is typical of the serin group; flight is noticeably bouncing in fairly short undulations, but often erratic in direction. Towards the breeding season, it is not uncommon for groups of males to sing in concert from treetops. Perches in trees and on the ground. Feeds mainly on seeds, principally of grasses, but weed seeds also taken; also some buds and flowers of trees.

DISTRIBUTION *S. m. mozambicus*: southeast Kenya to eastern Zambia, Malawi, southeast Tanzania and northern Mozambique, central and eastern Zimbabwe south to southeast Botswana, northeast Namibia (Caprivi Strip), central Transvaal and northern Orange Free State, South Africa.

S. m. granti: eastern Cape Province to Natal and southeast Transvaal, South Africa and southern Mozambique.

S. m. somaliyae: southeast Zaire, Zambia through Malawi to southwest Tanzania.

S. m. tando: northern Angola to western Zaire and adjacent areas of the Congo.

S. m. barbatus: southern Sudan (south of 14°N), south to Uganda, western Kenya, northern Zaire to Rwanda and northwest Tanzania.

S. m. grotei: eastern Sudan and western Ethiopia.

S. m. gommaensis: northern, central and southern Ethiopia.

S. m. vansoni: southern Angola to west-central Zimbabwe, south to northern Namibia and northern Botswana.

S. m. santhome: São Tomé.

S. m. punctigula: central and southern Cameroon.

S. m. caniceps: Senegal (and possibly extreme south Mauritania) to about 17°N, Gambia, southern Mali (north to 15°N) and Burkina Faso (irregularly to extreme southwest Niger) to Nigeria, northern Cameroon and western Central African Republic, but scarce or absent from much of Guinea, Sierra Leone and Liberia.

Note: Considerable interbreeding takes place between races where ranges overlap. It has also been introduced to Hawaiian Islands (Hawaii and Oahu), Puerto Rico, Mauritius, Réunion and Assumption Islands; formerly (1800s) also to Amirante Islands, but now extinct there.

MOVEMENTS As most other African canaries, gathers together in large flocks in non-breeding season, roaming through large areas of suitable habitat in search of food.

MEASUREMENTS Wing 63–73; tail 39–49; tarsus 12–14; bill (culmen) 8–10. Wing of *barbatus* 60–68. Wing of *punctigula* 64–72. Wing of *tando* 62–74. Wing of *somaliyae* 69–73. Wing of *caniceps* 60–70; tail 37–43; bill 8–9.

REFERENCES Hall and Moreau (1970), Mackworth-Praed and Grant (1963), Newman (1983), Serle *et al.* (1977), Sinclair (1984), Williams and Arlott (1980).

22 GROSBEAK CANARY *Serinus donaldsoni*   Plate 4
East Africa

Serinus donaldsoni Sharpe, 1895, Bull. Brit. Ornith. Club, 4, p. 41, Somaliland; type from Darde or Smith river near Sheikh Hussein, Abyssinian Somaliland, *fide* W.L. Sclater, 1930, Syst. Av. Aethiop., p. 817.

IDENTIFICATION Length 14 cm (5½ in); *buchanani* 15 cm (6 in). A large canary of dry thornscrub country of East Africa, more usually found alone or in pairs. The large bill is obvious, and the male's deep green upperparts with broad dark streaks contrast with bright yellow rump; female and juvenile of nominate race are much duller and grey brown with a yellow rump, but lack yellow underparts. In the southern race the sexes are alike. **Confusion species:** Brimstone Canary (25) has a slightly smaller bill, different face pattern, and greenish (not yellow) rump; it also lacks male Grosbeak Canary's heavy dark streaks on upperparts and yellow (or suffused with olive or green) underparts with (on nominate males) some streaks on breast and flanks.

DESCRIPTION Sexes differ (nominate race). **Adult male:** Forehead to nape deep green, finely dark-streaked or blackish (some have nape paler or more yellowish). Bright yellow supercilium reaching base of bill; lores, upper cheeks and ear-coverts olive-green, lower cheeks bright yellow with almost circular or oval patch enclosed by an olive-green moustachial stripe. Mantle, back and scapulars slightly darker than nape, with broad dark or blackish-brown centres to feathers and pale green or greenish-yellow edges and tips (some, perhaps young birds, are more predominantly green, with only bases of feathers black on mantle and back); rump and uppertail-coverts bright or rich yellow. Tail is dark brown, with fine green or greenish-yellow edges to outer feathers. Median coverts are dark brown, edged pale buff or pale yellowish, greaters similar but with broader buff or yellow edges and tips; alula and primary coverts dark brown, with fine pale yellow edges and tips to latter; flight feathers dark brown, finely edged buffish or yellowish on secondaries and tertials.

Chin to belly and flanks deep or rich yellow, sides of breast olive-green, occasionally shows a few dark streaks on flanks; vent white and undertail-coverts yellow. Bill is large or stout, pale flesh or pinkish-orange with paler base to lower mandible. Legs and feet brown or dark brown. **Adult female:** Forehead to crown and nape pale brown with dark streaks, becoming buffish-brown on nape and upper mantle. The supercilium is pale buff; lores and upper cheeks to ear-coverts plain mid-brown with a pale buff oval centre to lower ear-coverts; a broad mid-brown moustachial stripe merges with side of neck, and submoustachial stripe is white. Mantle, back and scapulars are pale to mid-brown, broadly streaked dark brown; rump and uppertail-coverts yellow, tinged orange on some. Tail is brown or dark brown, finely edged very pale yellow (not always visible in the field). Median and greater coverts dark brown, with pale buff fringes forming double wingbar; alula and primary coverts blackish-brown; flight feathers dark brown with fine olive-yellow edges, but some show warm buff-brown edges to secondaries; tertials broadly edged and tipped pale buff. Underparts white or off-white, with dark brown malar stripe, and heavily streaked on breast and flanks. Bill as male or paler and slightly smaller. **Juvenile:** Very similar to adult female, but is more buffish-brown about sides of head and face and lacks cheek patch and moustachial stripe; some are greyer above, while others are more heavily streaked below.

GEOGRAPHICAL VARIATION The sexes of race *buchanani* are alike and much larger, and greener (less heavily streaked or mottled darker) above, especially on mantle and back; rump is slightly greener than nominate. The supercilium is much reduced (absent on some) and restricted to area over lores, eye and slightly over ear-coverts; also lacks pale cheek patch. The yellow of underparts is less bright, and tinged with green on breast, with fine short streaks on sides of throat and breast, usually more extensive on females than males. The bill is salmon-pink and slightly larger than in nominate.

VOICE Usually silent, but has a long drawn-out 'seeeeeek'. The song is short and rather metallic in tone, a rising 'hiki-hiki-hiki-hiki-hiki-hirrer', quite unlike that of other canaries.

STATUS, HABITAT AND BEHAVIOUR Scarce or local. Inhabits dry savanna, thorn acacia, steppe or semi-desert areas (in north of range) or arid bush or thornbush country, generally up to 1300 m and exceptionally to 1600 m, but absent from coastal lowlands. Usually found alone or in pairs, and large flocks unknown. Often feeds in trees on acacia fruit, where it is said to adopt an agile tit-like feeding manner; otherwise feeds on the ground on grass seeds and a variety of weed seeds.

DISTRIBUTION *S. d. donaldsoni*: south and southeast Ethiopia, Somalia (south of 10°N) and northern-central Kenya (north of the Equator), west to Lake Turkana.

S. d. buchanani: central and southern Kenya (east of 35°E and south of the Tana river) south to northern Tanzania.

Note: Considered by some authorities to be two species: Northern (nominate) and Southern Grosbeak Canaries.

MOVEMENTS Mainly resident or sedentary, but non-breeding birds are nomadic and can occur anywhere within range for short periods before moving on.

MEASUREMENTS Wing 76–86. Wing of *buchanani* 81–92.

REFERENCE Benson (1947).

23 YELLOW CANARY *Serinus flaviventris* Plate 4
South Africa

Crithagra flaviventris Swainson, 1828, Zool. Journ., 3, p. 348, Cape of Good Hope; restricted to Berg river, Cape Province, by Vincent, 1952, Check List Birds South Africa, p. 114. Considered by some authorities to be conspecific with White-bellied Canary (24).

IDENTIFICATION Length 13–14 cm (5–5½ in). A medium-sized South African canary with variable green or yellow upperparts, including rump; males in northwest of range are pale green above with bright yellow rump while those in the southeast are green, with a gradual cline in plumage between the two. Yellow northern birds lack the strongly marked face except for the dark moustachial stripe; intermediates have largely yellow upperparts and a strong face pattern; those in the southeast have a dark green face pattern and upperparts. Females are pale or buffish-brown, lacking any bright yellow, and are more heavily streaked or mottled on upperparts and streaked below. **Confusion species:** Similar to both Yellow-fronted (21) and Brimstone (25) Canaries. Differs from Yellow-fronted principally in larger size, relatively smaller bill and face pattern, has a smaller area of yellow on lower cheeks, and nape is yellow or greenish-yellow (not grey). Female Yellow Canaries have white underparts with varying amounts of streaking on breast and flanks. Northern or more yellow birds differ from similarly plumaged Brimstone Canary in more contrasting rump (similar to rest of upperparts on Brimstone) and in deeper or brighter yellow underparts lacking any green. Brimstone has a larger bill, and crown colour extends to top of bill (forehead yellow on male Yellow Canaries). Adult female similar to adult White-throated Canary (26), but separable by streaks on underparts and a distinctively duller rump (generally) and larger supercilium.

DESCRIPTION Sexes differ. **Adult male:** Lower forehead and long supercilium rich or bright yellow; lores, cheeks and ear-coverts olive-green, duller or dusky green (on some, side of neck duller or dusky green); lower ear-coverts bright yellow, bordered by dusky or greyish-green with olive or blackish moustachial stripe (well defined on some). Upper forehead to crown and hindneck green, yellowish-green or dark green, becoming slightly deeper on nape. Mantle, back and scapulars are green or pale yellowish-green with thin dark streaks; rump and uppertail-coverts uniform bright yellow on northern and western birds, becoming green or bright green on southern and eastern populations. Tail is black or blackish-brown, edged yellow or yellowish-green on outer webs. Median and greater coverts are blackish-brown, edged and tipped green (yellowish-buff on some); alula, primary coverts and flight feathers blackish-brown, with greenish or yellow edges on inner secondaries and tertials, the latter tipped with grey. Entire underparts from chin to undertail-coverts golden-yellow, but can show varying amounts of dull green on or across breast. Bill small, but deep at base, stout, blackish or dark horn. Legs and feet dark brown. **Adult female:** Lower forehead and long supercilium (thin and rather indistinct on some) white or off-white; lores, cheeks and ear-coverts ashy-grey, with white spot or oval area on lower cheeks/ear-coverts region bordered by grey or grey-brown moustachial stripe. Upper forehead, crown and nape very dull buffish-grey or grey-brown, thinly dark-streaked. Mantle, back and scapulars similar, but more heavily or broadly dark-streaked or blackish-brown; rump uniform dull green or olive-green (yellow on northern birds), becoming darker or brown on uppertail-coverts. Tail is dark brown, edged pale greenish-yellow on outer webs. Median and greater coverts are dark brown, finely edged pale or yellowish-buff and tipped buff, with edges of bases to greater coverts greenish; alula, primary coverts and flight feathers dark brown, very slightly or thinly edged pale greenish-yellow or buffish-brown; tertials the same, but broadly edged buff. Chin and throat pale buff, rest of underparts off-white or buffish white, streaked with dusky brown on breast and flanks. Bill is paler or greyer on than male's on upper mandible and pale flesh on lower mandible. **Juvenile:** In first-winter plumage, both sexes are very similar to adult female but are separable. Young males have mantle, back and scapulars brown, with darker centres to feathers and buff-brown edges; median and greater coverts fairly broadly tipped with buffish-brown or pale horn; and underparts pale yellow, streaked heavily dark brown or blackish. Young females have greyer or predominantly grey upperparts, and are whiter or more buffish-brown below and rather less heavily streaked than juvenile male.

GEOGRAPHICAL VARIATION Generally, males are darkest or deepest green on the upperparts in southeast of range (*flaviventris*, *quintoni* and *guillarmodi*), while those in north or northwest (*damarensis*) are paler with yellow rumps, with intermediates in between. Females in southeast of range have a less white and more greyish breast, obscuring the streaking, than those elsewhere, while females of *marshalli* have very little streaking and are very slightly yellow below. Male *damarensis* are paler or tinged more heavily yellow on upperparts than other races, have bright yellow rumps, and lack the strong face pattern; in worn plumage they have pale or whitish tips to greater coverts and broad pale edges to tertials. Females of this race are paler or buffish on underparts, have less streaking on breast and flanks, and rump and wingbars are yellow or pale yellow. Both *guillarmodi* and *quintoni* are larger than other races, *quintoni* noticeably so in the field.

VOICE Call is a distinctive and far-carrying deep 'chirrup' or 'tirriyip', often in a jumbled song of 'chissick' and 'cheree' notes. Song otherwise long and varied, a loud or vigorous, sweet-toned twitter; it is delivered from the top of a bush, tree or similar high point or while in a slow, stiff-winged display flight. Several males often sing in concert.

STATUS, HABITAT AND BEHAVIOUR Common or locally common. An abundant resident in some coastal areas but widely distributed, mainly in scrub and bush, extending to the dry semi-arid regions and foothills of mountains. Occurs in pairs and small parties in trees, bushes and more usually on the ground (including the seashore). Feeds on a variety of seeds, either on the ground or directly from the seed heads of flowers; occasionally takes insects such as termites.

DISTRIBUTION *S. f. flaviventris*: western Cape Province, South Africa.

S. f. damarensis: Namibia (except the Caprivi Strip, Ovamboland or the northern Kaokoveld) to western Botswana.

S. f. marshalli: northwest Cape Province to Orange Free State, lowlands of Lesotho and southwest Transvaal, South Africa.

S. f. quintoni: central and southeastern Cape Province, South Africa.

S. f. guillarmodi: highlands of Lesotho.

It has also been introduced (probably nominate race) to Ascension and St Helena in the South Atlantic.

MOVEMENTS Generally sedentary, but non-breeding birds gather in large flocks and wander at random throughout the range in search of food, visiting areas where they do not breed, e.g. birds of race *marshalli* occur annually in Natal. Extralimitally, has been recorded in southern Angola and is a vagrant (one record) to western Zimbabwe.

MEASUREMENTS Wing of male 71–73, of female 68–74; tail 47–57; tarsus 16–20; bill 10–12. Wing of male *guillarmodi* 77–81, of female 76–80; tail 58–60; tarsus 19–20; bill 10–10·5. Wing of male *marshalli* 71–77, of female 71–75. Wing of *quintoni* 71–82.

REFERENCES Clancey (1964), McLachlan and Liversidge (1978).

24 WHITE-BELLIED CANARY *Serinus dorsostriatus* Plate 3

East Africa

Crithagra dorsostriata Reichenow, 1887, Journ. f. Ornith., 35, p. 72, Kagehi, Wembaere, Niansa and Schasche; type from Wembere, Tabora, Tanganyika, *fide* W.L. Sclater, 1930, Syst. Av. Aethiop., p. 815. Considered by some authorities to be conspecific with Yellow Canary (23).

IDENTIFICATION Length 11·5–13 cm (4½–5 in). A medium-sized canary of drier parts of East Africa. The face pattern is similar to that of Yellow-fronted Canary (21) but not so bold; White-bellied has diagnostic underparts, yellow to lower breast or upper belly and white lower belly and flanks, and lacks Yellow-fronted's prominent dark moustachial stripe. Females are similar to males but slightly duller, with streaks on breast and flanks.

DESCRIPTION Sexes differ. **Adult male:** Forehead to lores, supercilium, rear of ear-coverts and sides of neck bright or deep yellow; crown to nape green or deep green, finely streaked with black; lores to sides of chin and throat bright or deep yellow; cheeks and upper ear-coverts olive-green, bordered by thin olive-green moustachial stripe which merges with lower edge of ear-coverts. Mantle, back and scapulars olive-green or greenish, lightly tinged with yellow and streaked with black or dark brown; rump yellow or bright yellow, becoming green on uppertail-coverts. Tail is blackish-brown, finely edged greenish-yellow. Median coverts dark brown or blackish-brown, edged and tipped pale yellow, greaters the same, edged pale green and more prominently tipped pale yellow; alula and primary coverts dark brown; flight feathers also dark brown, with fine yellowish or yellowish-green edges, tertials more broadly edged greenish and tipped buff. Chin and throat to lower breast bright or deep yellow; lower flanks, belly and vent white, undertail-coverts pale yellowish (some show a few dark grey spots on flanks). Bill small and pointed, with upper mandible brown or brownish-horn and lower pale horn. Legs and feet black or dark greyish-horn. **Adult female:** Lower forehead and supercilium from base of bill to rear ear-coverts bright yellow; upper forehead, crown and nape green or olive-green, finely streaked with black; lores, cheeks and ear-coverts dingy greenish-olive, with a diffuse dusky greenish-olive moustachial stripe. Mantle, back and scapulars as crown, with broader or more diffuse streaks; rump and uppertail-coverts bright yellow, tips of longest uppertail-coverts lime-green. Tail is blackish-brown, finely edged with pale yellow or yellowish-green. Median coverts dark or blackish-brown, edged (and broadly tipped) pale yellowish-green or buff, greaters similar with tips forming indistinct double wingbar; alula and primary coverts also dark brown, with fine pale green edges; flight feathers blackish-brown, finely edged yellow or pale yellow, tertials edged and tipped buff. Chin to breast pale lemon-yellow, with some dark brown spots or streaks on lower throat and sides of upper breast and flanks; belly and undertail-coverts white. Legs and feet pale greyish-horn. **Juvenile:** Forehead to crown, mantle and back pale earth-brown or buffish-brown and dark-streaked, often with yellow or green tinge to mantle and back; rump yellow. Flight feathers and tail are dark brown, edged paler or yellowish-green; wing-coverts also brown, edged and tipped pale yellow-

ish-buff or buff. Short pale supercilium and face are off-white, otherwise face is dusky brown with grey-brown moustachial stripe. Chin to breast pale buff-brown, with some dark brown spots or streaks on lower throat and upper breast; lower breast, belly and undertail-coverts white.

GEOGRAPHICAL VARIATION Male *maculicollis* has a narrower band of yellow on forehead than nominate and is slightly greener or greyer-green on upperparts (but not always consistent); white on belly extends to undertail-coverts. Females are as nominate, but with white on breast and belly.

VOICE Call is a shrill 'whee' or 'suweee'. Song is a sweet series of Goldfinch-like notes or trills, interspersed with some harsher phrases, and quite loud.

STATUS, HABITAT AND BEHAVIOUR Widely distributed but locally common. Found in arid and semi-arid bush, woodland and grass savanna areas and also edges of cultivation up to 2100 m, exceptionally to 2650 m on Mount Nyiru in Kenya, but most occur below 1400 m. Usually found in small flocks or parties where suitable food is available. Generally has same habits and behaviour of other small canaries. Feeds in bushes or shrubs, or more usually on the ground on grass seeds.

DISTRIBUTION *S. d. dorsostriatus*: southwest Kenya (Nyanza) and northern Tanzania.

S. d. maculicollis: central and southern Ethiopia to Somalia, northeast Uganda and western, central and coastal northeast Kenya and extreme northeast Tanzania (Mount Meru).

Intermediates occur over a considerable area where ranges overlap.

MOVEMENTS Generally resident, but in non-breeding season large flocks roam throughout the range in search of suitable feeding areas; in some drier parts of the range occurs only after the rains. The race *maculicollis* has occurred (once) in extreme southeast Sudan.

MEASUREMENTS Wing 72–77. Wing of male *maculicollis* 65–74, of female 66–73; tail 47–53·5; tarsus 14·5–15·5; bill (culmen) 8–10.

REFERENCE Nikolaus (1989).

25 BRIMSTONE CANARY (Bully Canary, Bully Seedeater)
Serinus sulphuratus
Plate 4

Africa

Loxia sulphurata Linnaeus, 1766, Syst. Nat., ed. 12, p. 305, Cape of Good Hope.

IDENTIFICATION Length 15–16 cm (6–6½ in). A large or stocky and heavy-billed canary with a rather distinct or broad yellow supercilium. Upperparts can be either deep green and streaked blackish (southern birds), or yellowish, tinged with green and streaked darker (the two northern races). Some have entirely yellow underparts or have deep green on sides of throat and across breast. Con-

fusion species: Yellow (23) and Yellow-fronted (21) Canaries; other species are either smaller, darker or have distinctively marked features. Brimstone lacks well-defined face-and-head pattern of smaller Yellow-fronted, even dark birds having much less clearly marked moustachial stripe and eye-stripe (dark Brimstones also have a pale area on ear-coverts); lacks grey or greyish nape, but has deep green wash either on sides of upper breast or across breast and on flanks. Brimstone also has a much larger bill. Similar to male Yellow, especially northern birds (which have smaller bills), but Brimstone has a less well-defined face pattern, duller greenish-yellow underparts, and bright yellow edges and tips to wing-coverts, while crown colour extends to bill (instead of forehead being bright yellow and joining supercilium).

DESCRIPTION Sexes similar. **Adult male:** Forehead, crown and upper nape deep green, finely dark-streaked, nape and sides of neck more uniform deep green; bright yellow supercilium from base of bill over eye and tapering at rear of ear-coverts; lores, upper cheeks and ear-coverts olive-green, with moustachial stripe dark green, becoming deep green on sides of throat; lower cheeks have an oval patch of bright yellow. Mantle, back and scapulars are green with darker centres (less broadly streaked blackish than females); rump uniform pale yellow; uppertail-coverts dull yellow, becoming duller or greenish-yellow on edges to base of tail. Tail is blackish-brown with pale green edges. Median and greater coverts are blackish, finely edged greenish and tipped with yellow; alula, primary coverts and flight feathers blackish, thinly edged greenish, tertials similar but more broadly edged pale greenish-yellow. Chin and throat are bright yellow, with sides of throat and entire breast deep or heavy green, fading on flanks; belly and undertail-coverts bright yellow. Bill large and heavy for a finch, deep at base with a curved culmen, and dark brown or horn-coloured with paler lower mandible. Legs and feet dusky brown. **Adult female:** Generally paler or duller, particularly supercilium and wingbars; lacks the well-defined face pattern (pale cheek patch is often very small), has slightly more heavily streaked upperparts, and entire underparts are washed with green. **Juvenile:** Very similar to adult but much duller, more greyish-olive in tone on upperparts, with pale yellow tips to wing-coverts; less bright or deep yellow below, with some pale brown streaking on breast and flanks.

GEOGRAPHICAL VARIATION Both northern races, *sharpii* and *wilsoni*, are smaller and paler green or more yellowish-green than nominate. The face pattern is less strongly defined and more diffuse, with dark or deep green being replaced by greenish-yellow or green; the forehead, crown, mantle, back and scapulars are paler yellow than nominate and dark streaking is more restricted to centre of feathers (on some *sharpii* the rump is more yellow). The median and greater coverts have

bright yellow edges and tips which form distinct double wingbar. The underparts are entirely bright yellow or golden-yellow in *sharpii*, or similar to nominate but not so green or with a slightly buff-brown tinge. Both races have slightly smaller bills than nominate, *sharpii* being the smallest.

VOICE Call varies with locality, a harsh or throaty 'chirrup' or 'chee-u-wee'. Song is often delivered from a prominent perch and is sweet and varied in tone, but southern (nominate) birds have a slower, deeper, jumbled and less tuneful song.

STATUS, HABITAT AND BEHAVIOUR Widespread and fairly or locally common, nowhere abundant. Occurs usually in open coastal plain (in South Africa) and bush country with scattered trees, hillsides, gorges or edges of forest up to 2400 m, though most are found between 1000 m and 1500 m, also edges of cultivated areas and gardens. Usually singly or in pairs, very rarely in flocks. A rather quiet and generally less active bird than most canaries; when not feeding, spends long periods sitting unobtrusively in a bush. Flight more direct and less undulating than other similar species. Feeds in trees, bushes and on the ground, on a variety of seeds (the strong bill is used to crack open hard seedcases), berries and buds or even ripe fruit.

DISTRIBUTION *S. s. sulphuratus*: southern and southwest Cape Province, South Africa.

S. s. sharpii: Angola through eastern Zaire to Uganda, southwest, west and central Kenya and south through central and southern Tanzania (where it reaches the coast) to Malawi, Zambia, southern Zimbabwe and northern Mozambique.

S. s. wilsoni: southern Mozambique to Transvaal and south to eastern Cape Province, South Africa.

Note: Some authorities divide the apparently brighter and smaller-billed birds in the southern range of *sharpii* (Angola to eastern Zaire, southwest Tanzania, Zambia, southern Malawi, northern Zimbabwe and northern Mozambique) into separate races, *shelleyi* and *frommi*.

MOVEMENTS Very little known. Generally resident, but also a dry-season visitor in non-breeding season to parts of its range where it does not normally occur.

MEASUREMENTS Wing 76–84; tail 58–64; tarsus 17–19; bill (culmen) 13–15. Wing of *sharpii* 72–79; tail 53–58; tarsus 16–17; bill (culmen) 12–13. Wing of male *wilsoni* 80·5–85·5, of female 79–84.

REFERENCES Mackworth-Praed and Grant (1963), McLachlan and Liversidge (1978), Newman (1983).

26 WHITE-THROATED CANARY *Serinus albogularis*   Plate 7
South Africa

Poliospiza crocopygia Sharpe, 1871, Ibis, p. 101, Otjimbinque, Damaraland; type from Daviljob near Otjimbinque, *fide* W.L. Sclater, Syst. Av. Aethiop., 1930, p. 823.

IDENTIFICATION Length 15 cm (6 in). A typical   bird of karoo grassland and dry veld of the northwest Cape. A rather large, dull or drab brown canary, unstreaked below (adults), with white chin and throat (not always easy to see except under good conditions); it has a large or prominent bill, a slight or short white supercilium to just beyond eye, and either a greenish-yellow (in the south) or a bright yellow rump (in northern parts of the range).

Confusion species: Differs from Protea Canary (36) and Streaky-headed Seedeater (27) in lack of strongly defined head pattern, dark brown on face and bright green or yellow rump. Initially similar to female Yellow Canary (23), but lacks streaking below and is browner above with a shorter supercilium. Larger bill and colour of throat distinguish juvenile from similar juvenile Yellow-rumped Seedeater (17).

DESCRIPTION Sexes alike. **Adult:** Forehead, crown and nape a pale greyish-brown, finely dark-streaked; hindneck and sides of neck paler, more plain buffish-brown; thin off-white supercilium tapers behind eye; lores, cheeks and ear-coverts greyish-brown, lower cheeks and ear-coverts slightly grey-tinged; indistinct moustachial stripe grey-brown or plain pale brown, with thin white submoustachial stripe and dark malar stripe. Mantle, back and scapulars dull grey-brown to earth-brown, streaked darker brown; rump dull green or slightly tinged greenish-yellow (duller on females), uppertail-coverts brown with greenish-yellow or yellow tips. Tail is dark grey or grey-brown, thinly edged paler. Median and greater coverts are dark brown or blackish-brown, edged and tipped pale greyish-brown; flight feathers, primary coverts and alula dark brown, thinly edged buffish-brown on secondaries (especially towards the base). Chin is white, with a few brown spots or tips, throat is pure white, becoming dingy, buffish or greyish-brown on breast, (stronger on some than on others); flanks more heavily buffish-brown; belly and undertail-coverts white, but duller than throat. Bill is large and deep at base, and pointed, the upper mandible brown or brownish-horn, the lower mandible pale yellowish or horn. Legs and feet brown or pinkish-brown. **Juvenile:** Very similar to adult but noticeably browner above, with heavier streaks on mantle, back and scapulars; also some brown spots or streaks on breast.

GEOGRAPHICAL VARIATION Rump of *crocopygius* bright yellow, by far the brightest of the races, extending across entire rump; *hewitti* has duller, more greenish-yellow rump, while other races have yellow on rump confined to centre and bordered with green or greenish-yellow. Upperparts of both *crocopygius* and *sordahlae* much paler, more greyish-buff or fawn-brown, with dark brown streaks. Underparts of *crocopygius* much paler greyish or whiter than others, lacking buff-brown tones; also, supercilium on this race and *hewitti* much less noticeable. Race *crocopygius* is the largest, but this is not especially noticeable in the field without direct comparison with others.

VOICE Call is a deep-throated double note, 'squee-yik', typically given when taking off, otherwise a mixture of typical canary- or sparrow-like notes. Song is a strong and tuneful 'weetle, weetle, frrra, weetle, frree, tee, chipchipchipchip'.

STATUS, HABITAT AND BEHAVIOUR Common resident of the Great Karoo, a large expanse of dry grassland with bush and scrub; also found on edges of deserts, hillsides, dunes and thornscrub, also dry river courses, and extends to edges of cultivation or occasionally gardens; usually found near water. Occurs alone, in pairs or in small flocks of up to ten birds which roam over suitable habitat in search of food. On the ground hops in typical finch fashion. Feeds on the ground or in vegetation, on seeds, berries and buds, and is especially attracted to euphorbias.

DISTRIBUTION *S. a. albogularis*: southwestern Cape Province, South Africa.

S. a. hewitti: western and central Cape Province, South Africa.

S. a. sordahlae: southern Namibia (Great Namaqualand) to northwest Cape Province, South Africa; one record outside this range, of a single at Philipstown in the northern Cape Province.

S. a. orangensis: northern Cape Province, Orange Free State, lowlands of Lesotho and southern Transvaal, South Africa.

S. a. crocopygius: southwest Angola to the Damara highlands of northern Namibia.

MOVEMENTS Outside breeding season wanders widely throughout the range, becoming periodically common before deserting the area in search of food elsewhere.

MEASUREMENTS Wing 74–81; tail 53–61; tarsus 20–22; bill (culmen) 12–15. Wing of *sordahlae* 75–82. Wing of *crocopygius* 78–86.

REFERENCES McLachlan and Liversidge (1978), Newman (1983), Sinclair (1984).

27 STREAKY-HEADED SEEDEATER *Serinus gularis*   Plate 7

Africa

Linaria gularis A. Smith, 1836, Rept Exped. Centr. Africa, p. 49, Cape Colony; restricted to Latakoo, near Kuruman, Bechuanaland, by W.L. Sclater and Mackworth-Praed, 1918, Ibis, p. 468.

IDENTIFICATION Length c15 cm (c6 in). A common and widespread African finch with a distinctive head-and-face pattern. A broad white supercilium and finely streaked crown; dark brown lores, cheeks and ear-coverts contrast with white chin and buffish underparts; upperparts are indistinctly streaked, and rump is plain brown. **Confusion species:** Similar to Black-eared Canary (28), but face is never black, deep brown or so well defined on lower face. Streaky-headed has a slightly weaker-looking bill, is grey or earth-brown (not dark brown) on upperparts, and most (except *reichardi*, which overlaps with Black-eared) lack prominent streaks on underparts (though, on some *reichardi* the streaks are not always strongly defined). In north of range Brown-rumped Seedeater (29) is similar, but face and head pattern, particularly forehead to crown, is less prominently streaked brown and white than Streaky-headed, the supercilium is thinner and shorter, the upperparts lack any streaks, and the primary projection is much shorter than on Streaky-headed.

DESCRIPTION Sexes similar. **Adult male** (*gularis*): Forehead to hindcrown/hindneck dark brown, heavily streaked white or whitish (all feathers white at base with dark brown tips). Nape and sides of neck brown or dusky brown, with some fine white streaks at tips of feathers; lower forehead often white, broad white supercilium from base of bill, tapering at rear of ear-coverts; lores, cheeks and ear-coverts dark brown, sides of neck similar or paler buff-brown, moustachial area and chin often slightly spotted (visible only at close range). Mantle, back and scapulars brown, streaked faintly or indistinctly dark or dusky brown (some more distinct than others); rump and uppertail-coverts uniform brown. Tail is dark brown with thin white edges. Median and greater coverts are dark brown, medians edged and tipped paler brown, greaters with broad pale buff-brown edges and tips (but scarcely of sufficient contrast to form wingbar); alula and primary coverts dark brown; flight feathers the same, thinly edged buffish, more broadly on secondaries and tertials in winter. Chin and throat white (some have a few small black spots on chin); rest of underparts vary from warm buff to sandy-brown or grey-brown, undertail-coverts white. Bill large, stout or heavy, sharply pointed, with a dark horn upper mandible and tip to lower mandible; the base of lower is paler and pinkish or pinkish-brown. Legs and feet pale flesh to dark brown. **Adult female:** As adult male, but some show slight streaking on lower throat and breast. **Juvenile:** Similar to adult female, but less streaked with white on crown and nape. The supercilium is dull buff or off-white; mantle and scapulars are prominently streaked, and greyer underparts have much heavier streaking on breast, flanks and belly.

GEOGRAPHICAL VARIATION Differs mostly in tone of upperparts (and streaking on mantle, back and scapulars) and underparts. Races *endemion*, *reichardi* and *elgonensis* are slightly greyer or grey-brown on upperparts, while *benguellensis*, *striatipectus*, *humilis*, *montanorum* and *canicapilla* are browner above with *montanorum* warmest in tone; *humilis* also lacks or has greatly reduced streaks on mantle and scapulars. In *reichardi* the streaks on breast are always distinct, fading on flanks, while in all other races they are generally less distinct or absent (as in *endemion* and

elgonensis) or present only on chin (some *benguellensis*) a white, whitish-buff or (as in *elgonensis*) on a buffish grey-brown base colour. Race *striatipectus* is streaked more diffusely brown on chin, throat, breast and flanks; *reichardi* has darker or browner cheeks and a slightly smaller bill; *humilis* has warm buff-brown underparts (except for white chin and throat), the darkest of all the races; *benguellensis* has a slightly larger bill than nominate race.

VOICE Call is a rather thin or high-pitched 'tsee-ee' or 'see-e-ee', also a chirrup note, or a soft or weak 'trrreet'. Song is a soft or quiet, pleasant canary-like 'wit-chee-chee-chee-cha, cha, cha, cha, cha, chip', rising in tone and often interspersed with mimicry of other birds' calls and songs; in breeding season a repetitive 'tweu, tweu tirrirrit-tirik' is often given in slow-motion display flight.

STATUS, HABITAT AND BEHAVIOUR Common, locally common or uncommon. Found in a variety of habitats, from dry *Brachystegia* woodland, scrub and savanna to gardens, often in suburban areas, orchards and edges of cultivation up to 2100 m; *montanorum* occurs only between 1200 m and 2000 m and *striatipectus* between 1600 m and 1800 m. Usually found in pairs or small flocks, but occasionally in large gatherings, also in mixed flocks with other canaries, particularly Black-eared. A quiet or rather shy and unobtrusive bird, perching inside the tops of trees and bushes as well as on the ground; has a habit of frequently raising its crown feathers when perched. Feeds on a variety of seeds, including sunflower, millet and corn, (large flocks have been known to do considerable damage to crops), also takes soft fruit, weed seeds and buds of flowers and trees; has been known to take termites and caterpillars.

DISTRIBUTION *S. g. gularis*: Botswana, southern Zimbabwe, south to northeast Cape Province, western Orange Free State, western and northern Transvaal, South Africa.

S. g. humilis: southwest and southern Cape Province, South Africa.

S. g. endemion: eastern Cape Province to Lesotho, Natal, eastern Transvaal, Swaziland, South Africa, Zimbabwe and southern Mozambique.

S. g. benguellensis: central Angola to western Zambia.

S. g. reichardi: southern Tanzania and northern Mozambique to Malawi, Zambia and southern Zaire.

S. g. elgonensis: northeastern Zaire, southern Central African Republic, northern Uganda and western Kenya.

S. g. striatipectus: southern Ethiopia to western and central Kenya and northeast Zaire.

S. g. montanorum: central Cameroon highlands.

S. g. canicapilla: Ivory Coast, southern Mali and southern Niger to Nigeria and northern Cameroon.

Other races have been described. Some East African authorities consider *reichardi* and *striatipectus* to be a separate species (Stripe-breasted Seedeater).

MOVEMENTS In non-breeding season, flocks

wander at random throughout the range into areas where it is not known to breed; birds of races *elgonensis* and *striatipectus* occur north into southern Sudan between November and March (*elgonensis*) or May (*striatipectus*).

MEASUREMENTS Wing 73–82; tail 58–68; tarsus 14·5–16·5; bill (culmen) 12–13·5. Wing of *benguellensis* 84–86. Wing of male *elgonensis* 81–84, of female 79.

REFERENCES Mackworth-Praed and Grant (1963), McLachlan and Liversidge (1978), Newman (1983), Nikolaus (1989), Sinclair (1984).

28 BLACK-EARED CANARY *Serinus mennelli*

Plate 7

Southern Africa

Poliospiza mennelli Chubb, 1908, Bull. Brit. Ornith. Club, 21, p. 62, Tjoko's Kraal, Shangani river, (Southern) Rhodesia.

IDENTIFICATION Length 13–14 cm (5–5½ in). A big-billed grey-brown canary of southern (but not South) Africa. Both adults and juveniles have a striking black-and-white head pattern of black crown streaked with white, white supercilium and black or brown face; white underparts fairly heavily streaked with short dusky streaks. **Confusion species:** It has a much bolder or stronger face pattern than Streaky-headed Seedeater (27), is also slightly paler on upperparts and has grey, not brown or grey-brown, rump. Adults and immatures are very similar to *reichardi* race of Streaky-headed (which has streaking on breast and flanks), but Black-eared has more extensive area of streaking and blacker face, well-defined or broader white supercilium and a more substantial-looking bill. Ranges of the two species overlap, but Black-eared is more likely to be found in pristine or untouched woodland, whereas Streaky-headed is more catholic in its preferences.

DESCRIPTION Sexes alike. **Adult:** Lower forehead and supercilium to rear of ear-coverts white; upper forehead to crown and nape black, with fairly heavy white streaks or edges to feathers; lores to ear-coverts and cheeks black or sooty (male) to brown or deep brown (female). Mantle, back and scapulars are uniform grey-brown, with centres of feathers brown or dark brown; rump and uppertail-coverts paler or plain grey, with darker centres to uppertail-coverts. Tail is dark brown, with paler brown or mid-brown outer feathers. Median coverts are dark brown, lightly tipped buff; greaters similar but more prominently tipped buff-brown and whitish at tip, forming indistinct wingbar; primary coverts, alula and flight feathers dark grey, with fine buff edges to secondaries, more broadly buff on outer edges and tips to tertials. Chin and throat to sides of neck white, with some small black spots on chin; breast and sides of breast to flanks silvery-white (female slightly duller) with short brown streaks, latter extending more finely to lower flanks; belly and vent pale buff, undertail-coverts white. Bill short or stubby, pointed, pink or pinkish-horn, sometimes paler on lower mandible. Legs and feet dark brown or blackish-brown. **Juvenile:** Similar to adult, with brown face, rather heavily streaked underparts and pale buff-brown edges and tips to wing-coverts and inner secondaries.

VOICE Call is a three- or four-note 'ess-ee-dee'. Song is given either from a high, prominent perch or during courtship display flight and consists of a series of uneven twittering whistles, 'teeu-twee-teu-twiddy-twee-twee', the second note higher than the rest. Males spend a considerable time singing from the tops of tall bare branches, and in courtship flight rise to some height before diving down in a series of twisting spirals and butterfly flaps.

STATUS, HABITAT AND BEHAVIOUR Common or locally common. Occurs up to 1950 m and usually above 600 m throughout most of its range, in dry *Brachystegia* (miombo) woodland but also in some wooded hillsides, coastal forest, around gardens (inland) and edges of cultivated fields. Generally shy or unobtrusive except in the breeding season, when males sing almost incessantly. Often found in mixed parties or in pairs or small groups. Feeds mostly in trees and rarely on the ground, principally on a variety of seeds, also some soft fruit, flowers, nectar and insects.

DISTRIBUTION Monotypic. Southeast Zaire (possibly extreme southeast Angola/northeast Namibia – Caprivi Strip) and extreme northeast Botswana to Zimbabwe, Malawi, southern Tanzania and Mozambique (north of the Limpopo river).

MOVEMENTS In the non-breeding season undertakes local movements in search of food.

MEASUREMENTS Wing 79–86; tail 48–56; tarsus 12·5–14·5; bill (culmen) 10–12·5.

REFERENCES Ginn *et al.* (1990), Mackworth-Praed and Grant (1963), McLachlan and Liversidge (1978), Vincent (1936).

29 BROWN-RUMPED SEEDEATER *Serinus tristriatus*

Plate 7

East Africa

Serinus tristriatus Rüppell, 1840, Neue Wirbelt., Vögel, p. 97, Taranta Mountain passes, 8000 ft, Abyssinia.

IDENTIFICATION Length 13 cm (5 in). A small brown seedeater endemic to the highlands of eastern Ethiopia and northern Somalia. Almost entirely brown or warm buff-brown with some streaking on head, short white supercilium, white chin and throat; has fairly short wings. **Confusion species:** Similar in all respects to race *reichardi* of Streaky-headed Seedeater (27), the range of which it adjoins but does not overlap. Brown-rumped is generally smaller and smaller-billed, forehead to crown is less heavily streaked black-and-white, the primary projection is very short, the underparts are white only on chin and throat, and adult also lacks any streaking on breast and flanks (present in *reichardi* race of Streaky-headed); underparts in general are more buff, warm buff or duller brown than on Streaky-headed. Both Brown-rumped and Streaky Seedeater (33) have confusingly similar canary-like calls and songs to the unwary (see Voice).

DESCRIPTION Sexes alike. **Adult:** Forehead, crown and nape dull, dingy brown or washed slightly grey, with fine indistinct brown streaks on upper forehead and crown; pure white supercilium from base of bill tapering over ear-coverts; lores brown or dark brown, slightly paler cheeks, ear-coverts and sides of neck. Mantle, back and scapulars are uniform brown; rump and uppertail-coverts similar, but slightly browner. Tail is dark brown. Median and greater coverts dark brown, with edges and tips slightly paler brown; alula and primary coverts are darkish brown; flight feathers similar, with paler buff-brown edges to secondaries and tertials. Centre of chin and throat white (some have a few small dark spots or streaks on side of throat); rest of underparts buff or with dull grey-brown wash, centre of belly whitish, with dark centres to undertail-coverts. Bill small and pointed, horn or pale pinkish-horn with darker tip. Legs and feet flesh-brown. **Juvenile:** Generally similar to adults, but more clearly streaked on crown, mantle and scapulars; entire underparts are buffish, with short dark streaks.

VOICE Call is a shrill 'tsooee' or 'swee' with a rising inflection, also a 'sip' or 'siss' note which is probably part of the song. Song is a high-pitched but rather weak three-to-four-note 'sip-sip-twis-twis', also 'sis-sis-sissis', very distinctive but confusable with some similar notes of Streaky Seedeater.

STATUS, HABITAT AND BEHAVIOUR Locally common to abundant. Found on high ground between 1060 m and 3330 m in montane scrub, juniper or other woodland, also in large gardens with suitable habitat; occurs commonly in centre of Addis Ababa, Ethiopia. Usually found in pairs or small flocks, perching in low trees and on the ground. Little is known of its food or breeding behaviour beyond that it has been found nesting from April to October; food is mainly the seeds of herbs, small plants or shrubs.

DISTRIBUTION Monotypic. Highlands of west, northeast and southeast Ethiopia and northern Somalia.

MOVEMENTS Nothing known of any long-distance movements. Loose flocks sometimes wander in search of food in the non-breeding season.

MEASUREMENTS Wing of male 66–68, of female 66–69; tail 51–57; tarsus 16–17; bill 9·5–10·5. Weight 12·2–19·4.

30 ANKOBER SERIN *Serinus ankoberensis*

Plate 9

Northeast Africa

Serinus ankoberensis J.S. Ash, 1977, Ibis 121: 1–7, 3 km north of Ankober, Shoa Province, Ethiopia.

IDENTIFICATION Length 12–13 cm (c5 in). A small, heavily-streaked serin with dark brown wings and tail and a fine Linnet-like bill. Endemic to a very small area of the highlands of central Ethiopia. Relatively little known; discovered only in 1976 and very few individuals and records exist. **Confusion species:** Heavily streaked head and body and lack of white supercilium make Ankober Serin distinctly different from Brown-rumped Seedeater (29), which occurs in the same area but is streaked (but less heavily so) only on underparts and only in juvenile plumage. It is separated from the initially very similar Streaky Seedeater (33), which also occurs quite commonly in the same area, by lack of clearly defined supercilium or strong face pattern; is much more Linnet-like in actions and flight compared with rather sluggish or bunting-like Streaky Seedeater. Considered to be a close relative of the geographically isolated Yemen Serin (19), from which it is distinctively different in having much more streaking on the body.

DESCRIPTION Sexes alike. **Adult:** Forehead to

crown dark or blackish-brown, feathers thinly edged with buff or light fawn-brown. Nape off-white or tinged light fawn, broadly streaked blackish, appears in the field as a pale or ill-defined collar; face also heavily streaked brown or olive-brown, with slightly paler or greyer cheeks (which stand out well as a pale area in the field) and an indistinct olive moustachial streak (females lack pale cheeks and show no contrast with the moustachial area). Mantle similar to crown, with pale buff edges giving thinly streaked appearance; back and rump paler brown, streaked blackish. Tail is short and slightly forked, dark brown with fine pale grey edges to the outer webs. Median and greater coverts are dark brown, thinly edged and tipped buffish-brown; primary coverts, alula and flight feathers also dark brown with buff-brown edges, tertials broadly edged grey-brown and tipped grey. Chin and throat are white or whitish-grey with small dark spots or ovals, becoming pale buff-brown, fairly heavily streaked grey or grey-brown (brown in the hand) especially on breast, flanks and undertail-coverts. Bill is elongated and Linnet-like in shape, with greyish-horn upper mandible and paler lower mandible. Legs and feet flesh-brown. **Juvenile:** So far as is known (only two specimens), juveniles are similar to adults.
VOICE Call is either a double note, 'treet-treet', or 'chree', quite high-pitched, also a soft sparrow-like 'witchu' or 'weetchu'; flight call 'twi-ti-twi-twi' or even 'tchweet-weet-lu', as well as a nasal 'chirp'. The song is a musical chirruping, often in concert with others.

STATUS, HABITAT AND BEHAVIOUR A relatively little-known finch, recorded only seven times since its discovery in 1976 (1977 twice, 1981, 1989 three times, and 1991); and from only two sites. Has been seen in pairs or small flocks, with maximum of 60 together on any one occasion; only two specimens have been collected, both in 1976. A ground-feeding and ground-nesting species occurring among lichen-covered boulders and rocks, with open areas of grass and other low-lying vegetation, on high ground and broken cliffs between 2980 m and 3200 m, though further work within and around its known range may reveal a wider occupation of plentiful adjacent identical habitat. Often found in company of or loosely associated with Streaky or Brown-rumped Seedeaters. The flight is buoyant and dashing, recalling Linnet (72); when flushed, rises high and circles around before returning. Spends most of its time on the ground, where it feeds on seeds, predominantly of grass but also herbs and other locally available plants.
DISTRIBUTION Monotypic. Endemic to a very small area of approximately 25 km² of the central highlands of Shoa Province, Ethiopia.
MOVEMENTS None known, but large numbers present at one site on one occasion suggest movement, at least locally, from other areas.
MEASUREMENTS Wing 74–75; tail 51–53; tarsus 16; bill (culmen from skull) 12·5–14. Weight 14–15.
REFERENCES Ash (1979), Ash and Gullick (1989).

31 YELLOW-THROATED SEEDEATER *Serinus flavigula*   Plate 9
Northeast Africa

Serinus flavigula Salvadori, 1888, Ann. Civ. Mus. Genova, 26, p. 272, Ambokana, Shoa Province, central Abyssinia.

IDENTIFICATION Length c10–11·5 cm (4–4½ in). An extremely rare and little-known finch of very restricted distribution in southern Ethiopia. Very similar to Yellow-rumped Seedeater (17) of race *xanthopygius*, but smaller; a pale grey-brown finch with a dull yellow rump, brown wings and tail and distinctive yellow spot on throat. **Confusion species:** Likely to be confused only with Yellow-rumped Seedeater, and has been considered a hybrid between latter and White-bellied Canary (24) by some authorities. Yellow-rumped Seedeater lacks any yellow on underparts and is more prominently streaked above, with a pale supercilium.
DESCRIPTION Sexes similar. **Adult:** Forehead to crown and nape pale grey-brown or tinged fawn or buff; lores brown, cheeks, ear-coverts and sides of neck pale buff with fine brown streaks. Mantle, back and scapulars pale buffish-brown or tinged light grey and dark-streaked (with darker brown feather centres); lower back and rump pale or dull yellow; uppertail-coverts pale brown. Tail is brown, fairly broadly edged pale buffish-brown. Median

and greater coverts are dark brown; alula, primary coverts and flight feathers dark brown, very thinly edged buffish-brown (more broadly so in worn plumage). Chin whitish; centre of throat (possibly to centre of upper breast) has a yellow or pale yellow spot, sides and centre of lower breast a gorget of faint streaks, slightly smudged at sides of breast; rest of underparts whitish or pale buffish-white. Bill typical of seedeater in shape, and pale brown. Legs and feet pale brown. **Juvenile:** Unknown.
VOICE Virtually unknown, but 'typical serin calls' given by birds in flight.
STATUS, HABITAT AND BEHAVIOUR An African *Red Data Book* species (published prior to 1989 sighting). Extremely rare and virtually unknown: recorded (collected) on three occasions in 19th century (1880, 1885 and 1886), then not seen again for a hundred years; seen once in 20th century, in 1989 (when also photographed). Occurs in fairly arid semi-desert, rocky hillsides with scattered acacias, scrub and thornbush; the 1989 sighting was from one of the three 19th-

century sites, which is characterised by a small stream regularly used by the birds for drinking. Food is presumably small seeds or possibly grain.
DISTRIBUTION Known only from one very small area, about 30 km² of Shoa Province, central Ethiopia, on the escarpment of the west highlands and edge of the Danakil desert and the central highlands; approximately 30 km from another finch endemic to Ethiopia, Ankober Serin (30), and close to areas where Salvadori's Seedeater (32) occurs.
MOVEMENTS Poorly known. Not always present at the site where half of the records have originated; presumably makes daily local movements in search of food or water.
MEASUREMENTS (Three specimens). Wing 66·5–67·5; tail 49·5–50·5.
REFERENCES Ash and Gullick (1990), Collar and Stuart (1985), Erard (1974).

32 SALVADORI'S SEEDEATER *Serinus xantholaema*   Plate 9
Northeast Africa

Serinus xantholaema Salvadori, 1896, Ann. Mus. Civ. St. Nat. Giacomo Doria (2) 16: 43–46, between Wabi Shabelle and Lake Stephanie, southern Ethiopia.

IDENTIFICATION Length 11 cm (4½ in). A small but distinctively marked species, which is mostly grey-brown on the upperparts except for a bright yellow rump; it has white underparts with a bright yellow throat partially broken or bisected by a band of black. The plumage of throat and breast is diagnostic. Discovered in 1880 but remains very little known (nest, eggs, and juvenile plumage unknown), and has probably been seen since on only about 12 occasions.
DESCRIPTION Sexes alike. **Adult:** Base of forehead to lores white or whitish; forehead to crown and nape pale grey, indistinctly dark-streaked; faint white stripe from forehead to eye; face also ash-grey, darker on ear-coverts, with short dark eye-stripe behind eye. Hindneck grey-brown; mantle, back and scapulars streaked greyish-brown; rump bright yellow, becoming duller on uppertail-coverts. Tail is notched or slightly forked at tip, and pale brown or fawn-brown with olive-green edges to base of outer feathers. Median and greater coverts dark brown, edged and tipped slightly warmer brown; alula and primary coverts black or blackish-brown; flight feathers also blackish-brown, primaries edged olive-green, secondaries and tertials edged more broadly pale buff-brown, extending to tips on tertials. Underwing-coverts are yellow or pale yellow. Chin white (or white restricted to sides of base of bill; chin can also be yellow, continuous with breast); throat and centre of upper breast bright yellow, bisected by fairly broad but broken (incomplete in centre) band of black or blackish-brown; lower breast and belly off-white or very pale grey, faintly dark-streaked, lower belly white. Bill fairly stout or substantial, pale brown or brownish-horn. Legs and feet brown or pale brown. **Juvenile:** Unknown.
VOICE Call is a fairly sharp or abrupt 'tsip'; song a typical canary- or Linnet-like 'chweep-widdy' (Ash pers. comm.).
STATUS, HABITAT AND BEHAVIOUR Extremely rare; an African *Red Data Book* species, included in Appendix C as near-threatened and 'though rare, is probably spread widely enough to be at no risk'. First discovered in 1880 and seen on about 12 occasions since (last in March 1989); about nine specimens exist in collections. Occurs in semi-arid desert wadis, rocky gorges and dry streams or watercourses with scattered acacias, thornscrub and bush. Its habits are little known but said to be as those of other seedeaters, with which it has apparently occurred (but details lacking). Feeds on the ground, presumably on small seeds of a variety of dry-country plants.
DISTRIBUTION Monotypic. Endemic to southern Ethiopia, where known only from central Harrar, northern Bale and Sidamo Provinces.
MOVEMENTS Probably wanders throughout the range in the non-breeding season.
MEASUREMENTS Wing 64–69·5; tail 45–49; bill 9–10; tarsus 15. Weight 11–12.
REFERENCES Ash and Gullick (1989), Collar and Stuart (1985), Erard (1974).

33 STREAKY SEEDEATER *Serinus striolatus*   Plate 8
Africa

Pyrrhula striolata Rüppell, 1840, Neue Wirbelt., Vögel, p. 99, Halai and Simen, 8000 to 10,000 ft.

IDENTIFICATION Length 15 cm (6 in). An aptly named, heavily streaked and fairly big-billed, medium-sized seedeater. Identified by its conspicuous creamy or white supercilium, brown dark-streaked upperparts, all-brown wings and tail and heavily streaked underparts. Southern birds (*whytii*) have supercilium, face and sides of neck to throat deep yellow. **Confusion species:** More heavily streaked than any other seedeater, with the possible exception of smaller Ankober Serin (30); presence of supercilium distinguishes it from latter, and strongly streaked underparts and lack of bright yellow rump from Yellow-rumped Seedeater (17). All-brown forehead, finely streaked crown and nape and heavy streaking on underparts, together with build and bill shape, distinguish it from both Brown-rumped (29) and Streaky-headed (27) Seedeaters.

DESCRIPTION Sexes alike. **Adult:** Forehead to crown brown, finely dark-streaked and tipped white, nape paler brown with broad pale buff feather edges; broad white or buffish-white supercilium over eye and tapering down behind ear-coverts; lores blackish, becoming deep brown across ear-coverts, with pale white or whitish crescent below eye, and lower ear-coverts to lower cheeks white or whitish-buff; dark brown moustachial stripe, broadening below cheeks and ear-coverts. Mantle, back and scapulars slightly paler than crown, heavily or broadly streaked blackish-brown and warmer buff-brown, feathers edged with buffish-white; rump pale brown and dark-streaked, uppertail-coverts similar with dark brown centres. Tail is fairly long and thin, blackish-brown with fine greenish-yellow edges to all except central pair of feathers. Median and greater coverts dark brown, very finely edged paler or warm buffish-brown; alula and primary coverts blackish-brown; flight feathers similar, but edged buff or yellowish-buff on secondaries and tertials. Chin and throat dull white or yellow-tinged, becoming buff or pale sandy on lower throat to belly and flanks and heavily streaked dark or blackish-brown; lower belly, vent and undertail-coverts buffish-white or whiter than breast. Bill is quite large or stout, with slightly decurved upper mandible, blackish or dark horn in colour. Legs and feet a deep reddish-brown or light brown. **Juvenile:** Similar to adult but generally less heavily marked, the forehead to crown has pale buff edges and tips, and the face pattern is duller or buffish; the upperparts are more tawny-brown; throat is streaked, but streaking generally narrower on underparts, which are tinged buffish-yellow.

GEOGRAPHICAL VARIATION Birds of race *graueri* are slightly darker above and below, more heavily streaked on breast, and have underparts much deeper or rich buff-brown and indistinct green edges to flight feathers. Southern birds of race *whytii*

have pale areas of head, face, neck, chin and throat yellow; the supercilium and chin and throat are bright yellow except for some small black spots on chin; edges to wing and tail feathers are dull yellow or greenish-yellow. Other races have been described, but there is considerable individual variation and differences exist among birds of the same population. However, those on the slopes of Mount Kilimanjaro in northern Tanzania, which have been separated as *affinis* (a doubtful race), show brighter yellowish-green edges to flight feathers and some are prominently buff on underparts and have a yellowish tinge to sides of forehead, fore supercilium and chin and throat.

VOICE Call is soft, three high-pitched notes (the first often uttered on its own and higher-pitched), a 'sooee', 'seeeeeeit' or 'suwee-ip' with a rising inflection, not unlike call of Brown-rumped Seedeater, with which it overlaps in north of range. The song is a fairly monotonous extension of the call, 'sweee' or 'chwee-chip-chip-chip-chip'.

STATUS, HABITAT AND BEHAVIOUR Common or very common. Resident in open country and woodland edges between 1300 m and 4300 m, also in moist secondary forest, thickets, scrub, gardens and edges of cultivated areas. Not especially fond of trees, usually found in low cover, bushes or scrub, where it gives away its presence by its repeated call. Often regarded as a pest in gardens, as it apparently does damage to growing crops or flowers. Race *whytii* is less common, local, and restricted to the edges of evergreen forest at high altitude. Usually occurs alone or in pairs or small groups, feeding in low vegetation or on the ground on a variety of seeds; also known to take some fruit such as blackberries.

DISTRIBUTION *S. s. striolatus:* southern Sudan (Imatong and Dongotona Mountains) and Ethiopia to central and southwest Kenya and northern Tanzania.

S. s. graueri: southwest Uganda, northeast Zaire (Ruwenzori Mountains).

S. s. whytii: southern Tanzania to eastern Zambia, Malawi and northern Zimbabwe.

At least two other races have been described.

MOVEMENTS None long-distance, but wanders in non-breeding season throughout the range in suitable habitat.

MEASUREMENTS Wing 66–73; tail of male 59–65, of female 56·5–65; tarsus 18–22; bill (culmen) 11·5–14. Weight 18·9–26·5.

REFERENCE Sclater and Moreau (1933).

34 THICK-BILLED SEEDEATER *Serinus burtoni*   Plate 8

Africa

Strobilophaga burtoni G.R. Gray, 1862, Ann. Mag. Nat. Hist. ser. 3, 10, p. 445, Cameroon Mountains, 7000 ft, West Africa.

IDENTIFICATION Length 18 cm (7 in); length of *tanganjicae* 15 cm (6 in). Very distinctive: a large-

billed and robust seedeater with dark olive-brown upperparts except for a diagnostic white patch or oval on forehead (absent in two races), double wing-bar, and paler brown underparts becoming buffish on belly and undertail-coverts. Unlikely to be confused with any other canaries or seedeaters.

DESCRIPTION Sexes alike. **Adult:** Pale spot each side of forehead above lores or, on some, a broad white band across forehead; lores to ear-coverts dark brown (but appear blackish). Crown and nape to rump deep olive-brown and dark-streaked, with blackish feather bases to mantle and back; uppertail-coverts brown, edged paler or olive. Tail is dark brown, finely edged dull greenish-yellow. Median and greater coverts dark or blackish-brown, edged olive-green or paler and becoming white or buffish-white at tips, forming double wing-bar; alula and primary coverts blackish-brown, finely edged olive; flight feathers similar, but very finely edged greenish-olive or dull yellow. Chin and throat to sides of neck dark brown or blackish, sometimes interspersed with occasional white feathers; breast and sides of breast to flanks, paler more dusky or olive-brown, becoming pale buff on belly, flanks and undertail-coverts; upper belly and flanks broadly streaked dark brown. Bill is large with a noticeably curved culmen, blackish or dark horn on upper mandible and paler or whitish-horn on lower. Legs and feet dull pinkish-brown. **Juvenile:** Similar to adult, but generally paler brown on upperparts; forehead to crown whitish, streaked with black; has pale buff or light buffish-brown edges to wing-coverts and some secondaries; lores to chin and throat whitish with dark brown tips, rest of underparts warm brown and diffusely dark-streaked. The bill is virtually all-black.

GEOGRAPHICAL VARIATION Birds of race *tanganjicae* have a slightly smaller and weaker bill, more brown than black on upperparts and are extensively browner on underparts; they have very little (if any) white on forehead. Race *albifrons* either lacks white on forehead or has just a line of white across base of upper mandible, and (together with *kilimensis)* shows more bright green edges to flight feathers; *albifrons* also has a yellowish or pale wash to upperparts, which are not so black as nominate, has dark streaks on crown, mantle and scapulars, and is also paler on belly and flanks, the latter having dark streaks becoming smaller towards undertail-coverts. Race *kilimensis* is very

slightly darker above than *burtoni* and *albifrons*, and shows very little (if any) white on forehead. The very distinctive race *melanochrous* is smaller, and lacks white on forehead, bright greenish-yellow edges to flight feathers and pale wingbars; the throat is white or pale yellow, and breast, belly and flanks pale buff, heavily streaked dark brown.

VOICE Generally silent, but occasionally utters a soft or squeaky 'pleet'. The song is a soft or weak warbling series of squeaky notes.

STATUS, HABITAT AND BEHAVIOUR Local or uncommon. A bird of high forest or bush, usually between 1500 m and 3000 m, exceptionally down to 1200 m in Kenya; in West Africa, the nominate race is found on the edges of montane forest or in broken forest on open hillsides and heath with grass-land and small or scattered bushes, well above the tree line. Mainly a bird of dense undergrowth, though often found high in tree canopy. Occurs in pairs or small parties, but is slow or sluggish and shy, unobtrusive, and easily overlooked. Usually detected by habit of appearing as if from nowhere and clambering about in creepers in search of food, usually silently but occasionally uttering the plaintive contact call. Feeds on fruit, hard seeds of trees or shrubs, but also forages on the ground.

DISTRIBUTION *S. b. burtoni*: highlands of Cameroon, possibly also on the Obudu Plateau, eastern Nigeria.

S. b. tanganjicae: eastern Zaire to southwest Uganda and western Kenya (west of the Rift Valley), also found on Mount Moco, west-central Angola.

S. b. kilimensis: southwest Kenya to northern Tanzania.

S. b. albifrons: highlands of central Kenya (east of the Rift Valley).

S. b. melanochrous: Nyombe highlands, southwest Tanzania, east to Chita, Kigogo and Dabaga Forests, Uzungwa Mountains, southeast Tanzania.

MOVEMENTS None known, but generally a little-studied species.

MEASUREMENTS Wing 85–97; tail 62–74; bill 15.5–17. Wing of *tanganjicae* 80–86; tail 70; tarsus 19; bill 14.

REFERENCES Chapin (1954), Williams and Arlott (1980).

35 PRINCIPÉ SEEDEATER *Serinus rufobrunneus*   Plate 8

West Africa, an island endemic

Linurgus rufobrunneus G.R. Gray, 1862, Ann. Mag. Nat. Hist., ser. 3, 10, p. 444, Western Africa [Principé Island, *fide* Hartlaub, in Dohrn, 1866, Proc. Zool. Soc. London, p. 328].

IDENTIFICATION Length 11–12·5 cm (4½–5 in). A medium-sized seedeater found on three small islands in the Atlantic; generally deep cinnamon-brown all over, with a stout bill and short tail. Within its natural range there are no similar species with which it is likely to be confused;

birds in captivity may be confused with Thick-billed Seedeater (34), but lack of forehead spot, smaller bill and much shorter tail are distinctive.

DESCRIPTION Sexes alike. **Adult:** Head entirely dark cinnamon-brown, darker on face, and entire upperparts warm cinnamon-brown, with dark brown streaks on crown and nape and less distinctly on mantle and back; rump uniform rufous-brown, uppertail-coverts slightly warmer or more rufous. Tail is short and slightly notched at tip, brown, finely edged rufous. Wings are long (tips of primaries reach to more than half of tail length): median and greater coverts dark brown or blackish-brown, edged and tipped rufous-brown; alula, primary coverts and flight feathers blackish-brown, secondaries edged warm rufous and tertials also tipped light rufous-brown. Chin and throat are plain or slightly pale rufous, rest of underparts slightly darker or browner, with brown centres to feathers of breast, belly and flanks; can also be bright rufous or light chestnut from breast to undertail-coverts. Bill is small or stubby and rather sparrow-like, dark horn above and slightly paler on lower mandible. Legs and feet brown. **Juvenile:** Similar to adult, though lacks warm rufous tones and is generally duller dark brown.

GEOGRAPHICAL VARIATION Race *thomensis* is much duller or greyer-brown, with very little rufous in plumage; much duller brown below than nominate, has a conspicuous pale off-white or buffish lower throat patch and is whitish from vent to undertail-coverts.

VOICE Call is a clear 'tweet', often given as part of a trill. The song is Canary-like, containing several syllables of twittering notes and a trill.

STATUS, HABITAT AND BEHAVIOUR Endemic to islands of São Tomé, Princípe and Caroco (south of Princípe). Race *thomensis* is common on São Tomé, occurring virtually everywhere, while *rufobrunneus* is more scarce; however, it may be that the populations fluctuate, as ornithologists visiting the islands in the past have described it as rare in one year but common two years later. On São Tomé it occurs in a variety of habitats from town and city centres to forest, plantations and dry woodland, while on Princípe it appears to be less of a city or suburban bird; found from sea-level to 900 m. A noisy bird, it calls frequently and usually occurs in pairs feeding high up in trees along forest or plantation edges. Feeds on seeds and a variety of vegetable matter.

DISTRIBUTION *S. r. rufobrunneus*: Princípe Island.

S. r. thomensis: São Tomé Island.

S. r. fradei: Ilheu Caroco.

MOVEMENTS Little known or studied.

MEASUREMENTS Wing 77–82; tail 42–48; tarsus 18–19; bill 12–13. Wing of *thomensis* 78–85; tail 48–53; tarsus 20–22.

REFERENCES Jones and Tye (1988), Mackworth-Praed and Grant (1963).

36 PROTEA CANARY (Protea Seedeater, White-winged Seedeater, Layard's Seedeater) *Serinus leucopterus* Plate 8

South Africa

Crithagra leucoptera Sharpe, 1871, Ann. Mag. Nat. Hist., ser. 4, 8, p. 235, South Africa; restricted to Paarl, southwest Cape Province, by Vincent, 1949, Ostrich, 20, p. 150.

IDENTIFICATION Length 15–16 cm (5½–6 in). A medium-sized brown canary with a large pale bill, dark chin and contrasting white throat with slightly streaked underparts, dark brown wings with buffish wingbars at tips to coverts. An endemic localised resident of woods and protea bush of mountains of the southwest Cape. **Confusion species:** Differs from White-throated Canary (26), the only species which is likely to cause confusion, in lack of yellow or green on rump; instead has brown rump and uppertail-coverts, pale wingbars, large pale bill, indistinct pale supercilium and white lower chin and throat.

DESCRIPTION Sexes similar. **Adult:** Forehead to crown and upper nape brown or grey-brown with fine darker brown streaks; ill-defined pale buff supercilium from mid-lores and fading over ear-coverts (not always visible); lores and cheeks dusky or blackish, ear-coverts to sides of neck grey-brown with faint or slightly darker streaks. Upperparts as crown and nape, becoming paler or unstreaked on lower nape; mantle, back and scapulars the same, with darker centres to feathers; rump and uppertail-

coverts as back, with fine whitish or buff tips to uppertail-coverts. Tail is dark brown, finely edged dull greenish-yellow or pale buffish-white. Median and greater coverts dark brown, finely edged greyish-buff and tipped buffish or whitish, forming double wingbar (but in worn plumage this becomes rather indistinct); alula, primary coverts and flight feathers dark brown, edged slightly olive, with pale buff or buffish-brown edges to secondaries; tertials also finely edged and tipped pale whitish-buff. Chin is blackish or heavily mottled with blackish spots, merging with those on lores; lower throat to upper breast white; lower breast, flanks and belly buff-brown, with darker or grey-brown streaks on centre and sides of breast and lower flanks; vent and undertail-coverts whitish or tinged buff, with buff-brown bases and shaft streaks. Bill is large and rather heavy, generally pale buff, flesh-coloured or yellowish on lower mandible, upper mandible darker at base and along culmen. Legs and feet black or blackish-brown. **Juvenile:** Similar to adult but more heavily streaked.

VOICE Call or contact note a distinctive 'tree-leeloo' or 'twee-oo' and a more familiar 'sweet'. In the breeding season males sing from tops of bushes: fairly typical canary-like song, rather loud, with a varied assembly of notes and trills; it is also an excellent mimic.

STATUS, HABITAT AND BEHAVIOUR Uncommon or locally common. Occurs in bush (particularly protea bush), woods and evergreen forest and pines on slopes of mountains of the southwestern Cape. Differs from most canaries and seedeaters in being shy and retiring, often overlooked; spends much of its life in thick vegetation. Flies fast, low and direct and soon dives into cover. In flight, pale wingbars (even when present on perched bird) are not always obvious. Usually alone, but also occurs in pairs or small parties, feeding in low cover or on the ground, usually under cover. Feeds on a variety of seeds, particularly protea seeds and those of *Othonna amplericaules* (especially following the breeding season) and *Rhus anarcardia*, also some buds, shoots and nectar of various plants; occasionally takes insects.

DISTRIBUTION Endemic to southwestern Cape Province from the northern Cedarburg to Banaankloof, west of Port Elizabeth (does not reach the coast), South Africa.

MOVEMENTS Resident.

MEASUREMENTS Wing 70–76; tail 56–59; tarsus 18; bill (culmen) 12·5.

REFERENCES McLachlan and Liversidge (1978), Newman (1983).

37 CAPE SISKIN *Serinus totta*

South Africa

Plate 6

Loxia totta Sparrman, 1786, Mus. Carlsonianum, fasc. 1, pl. 18, Hottentot country, i.e. Cape Province.

IDENTIFICATION Length 13 cm (5–5¼ in). A small and rather drab finch, endemic to mountains of southern South Africa. Dull greenish-yellow below, streaked on chin to breast (female), head and face olive (male) or brownish (female) with dark streaks; brown on mantle, back and wings. Diagnostic white tips to otherwise dark brown or blackish primaries, tail also broadly tipped white.

Confusion species: Very similar to Drakensberg Siskin (38), with which it does not overlap; best separated by smaller size, white tips to flight and tail feathers and uniform upperparts, while females are also more yellow on underparts than the virtually all-brown female Drakensberg Siskin. Other finches of the region are paler or light brown, with noticeable darker streaking.

DESCRIPTION Sexes differ. **Adult male:** Forehead, crown and upper nape dull olive-brown, finely dark-streaked, fading on nape to greyish-olive and slightly buff-brown on sides of neck; indistinct and rather short dull yellowish-brown supercilium over lores, fading over ear-coverts; lores and cheeks dusky olive, paler or olive-yellow washed with brown on ear-coverts and sides of throat. Mantle, back and scapulars rich or warm brown, tinged lightly with olive; rump yellowish-olive, uppertail-coverts brown, some with thin white tips. Tail is black, with broad white terminal band. Median and greater coverts dark brown or blackish-brown (some have medians chocolate-brown) with fine buff edges and tips; alula, primary coverts and flight feathers blackish, finely edged brown especially on inner secondaries and tertials; tips of primaries, outer secondaries and tertials white or pale buff. Chin is spotted with brown, becoming yellow or tinged with brown on lower chin and throat; breast and sides of breast yellow, washed (heavily on some) with olive; belly and flanks are browner; vent and undertail-coverts greyish-brown, tipped paler. Bill is sharply pointed, with blackish or dark horn upper mandible and a paler pinkish-brown base to lower. Legs and feet brown. **Adult female:** Very similar to adult male but browner on forehead to crown and nape, dark-streaked, becoming darker on mantle, back and scapulars. Face greyish-brown, 'with paler lores and cheeks streaked buffish-brown. Wings as male, with very thin or fine off-white tips to primaries, secondaries and tertials which are soon lost through wear. Chin, throat and breast are dull olive-yellow or buffish-brown, becoming dull yellow on lower breast and belly; heavily streaked with dark brown to mid-breast and flanks; undertail-coverts dull whitish with darker centres. **Juvenile:** Very similar to adult female but duller, and underparts are darker or browner and more heavily streaked buff-brown. Young males show more yellow on throat and breast than young females. Adult plumage is acquired within the first three months.

VOICE Call, most frequently uttered in flight, is a 'pee-chee' or 'pitchee'; otherwise has a high-pitched metallic 'tchwing, tchwing, tchwing, tchwing'. Song is a pleasant but weak warble, similar to Yellow-fronted Canary's (21), incorporating several 'pee-chee' notes.

STATUS, HABITAT AND BEHAVIOUR Common or locally common. Endemic to mountains, rocky hills, fynbos and valleys of southern Cape Province; inhabits clearings or woodland edges and scrub, particularly macchia scrub and protea bushes, also plantations of pines or other exotics. Common in areas of coastal cliffs on the Cape peninsula, where it breeds in the rock crevices; also occurs in towns and the suburbs of Cape Town. Usually found in pairs or small parties of up to 15 together, rarely alone; a shy and unobtrusive bird, moving quietly among the bushes or shrubs.

Feeds in bushes and on the ground, on a variety of seeds, buds and insects.

DISTRIBUTION Monotypic. Endemic to mountains of southwest Cape Province, from Klaver south and east to the eastern Cape west of Port Elizabeth, South Africa. The ranges of this species and Drakensberg Siskin do not meet.

MOVEMENTS Very little known but numbers may move to lower levels in winter.

MEASUREMENTS Wing 68–72; tail 49–53; tarsus 14–15·5; bill (culmen) 9–10·5.

REFERENCES McLachlan and Liversidge (1978), Newman (1983), Sinclair (1984).

38 DRAKENSBERG SISKIN *Serinus symonsi*   Plate 6
South Africa

Spinus symonsi Roberts, 1916, Ann. Transvaal Mus., 5 (3), suppl. 1, p. 1; redescribed, 1917, Ann. Transvaal Mus., 5 (4), p. 257, Sangebetu Valley.

IDENTIFICATION Length 13–14 cm (5–5½ in). A small finch of high-altitude grassland of southeastern South Africa. Males are dark-streaked with green and yellow on head and nape, with a dull brown mantle and dark-streaked back; wings and tail black. Chin and throat bright yellow, greenish across breast; lower flanks and undertail-coverts warm buff-brown. Females are virtually all-brown and heavily streaked above and warm buff below. **Confusion species:** Likely to be confused only with Cape Siskin (37), but the ranges do not overlap. Drakensberg Siskin lacks white on wings and on tip of tail, but has streaking on mantle and back, a dark greenish crown and nape, with a green wash to underparts (male), while female lacks yellow below and is generally a warm buff-brown with more or heavier streaking than female Cape Siskin.

DESCRIPTION Sexes differ. **Adult male:** Forehead, crown and nape yellowish-green, finely dark-streaked, especially on crown; thin pale or indistinct yellow supercilium from base of upper mandible to behind eye; lores dark grey or dusky, becoming paler and more greenish-yellow on cheeks, ear-coverts and sides of neck. Mantle, back and scapulars are dark brown, tinged warmer or rusty-brown and indistinctly dark-streaked; rump slightly grey-brown, lower rump an indistinct band of dull green, uppertail-coverts grey with paler edges and tips. Tail is black or blackish, with white inner web to outer feathers. Median and greater coverts are dull brown with fine pale buff edges and tips; alula, primary coverts and flight feathers black or blackish-brown, with fine ashy-grey edges to secondaries and tertials. Chin and throat are bright yellow, tinged slightly greener at sides of throat; breast and belly also tinged green, becoming pale brown on flanks, heaviest on lower flanks; undertail-coverts pale buff to whitish. Bill is sharply pointed, dark horn, brownish or blackish. Legs and feet pale brown. **Adult female:** Forehead, crown and upper nape to sides of neck and face warm or rich tan-brown, streaked with dark brown. Mantle, back and scapulars are dull brown, with indistinct

darker brown feather centres; rump and uppertail-coverts slightly paler than back. Tail is black or blackish. Median coverts are blackish-brown with dull brown edges and buffish tips, greater coverts also blackish-brown with fine buff-brown edges and tips; alula, primary coverts and flight feathers black or blackish, with fine pale edges to inner secondaries and pale brown edges to tertials. Chin, throat and sides of throat and breast warm orange-buff, fairly heavily spotted or streaked, becoming richer buff on breast and flanks with longer brown streaks continuing to lower flanks; lower breast, belly and undertail-coverts pale buff-brown, with some brown streaking on sides of undertail-coverts. **Juvenile:** Very similar to adult female, but generally duller in tone and more heavily streaked about head and on chin, throat, breast and flanks; rear of flanks warm buff-brown, belly pale buff.

VOICE Calls are similar to those of Cape Siskin, the most usual contact note being a Canary-like 'schwee'. The song is a lively jumble of buzzy 'cheez' notes and melodic chirps; a lively and vociferous songster, sings all day in the breeding season.

STATUS, HABITAT AND BEHAVIOUR Common or local. An endemic resident of higher (above 2400 m) parts of Drakensberg range of South Africa. As its closely allied relative Cape Siskin, it inhabits scrub in valleys, hillsides and grassy areas on the plateau. Found in pairs or small flocks, often in company with Yellow (23) or Black-headed (39) Canaries, and, like Cape Siskin, is shy or unobtrusive. Feeds on the ground, on a variety of seeds (including proteas), buds and insects.

DISTRIBUTION Monotypic. Endemic to mountains of Drakensberg range of extreme northeastern Cape Province, Transkei, Lesotho and western Natal, South Africa.

MOVEMENTS Descends to lower levels and valleys in winter.

MEASUREMENTS Wing 73–78; tail 54–59; tarsus 16–17; bill (culmen) 10·5–11.

REFERENCES Ginn *et al.* (1990), McLachlan and Liversidge (1978).

39 BLACK-HEADED CANARY *Serinus alario* Plate 52

South Africa

Emberiza alario Linnaeus, 1758, Syst. Nat., ed. 10, p. 179, Cape of Good Hope.

IDENTIFICATION Length 12–15 cm (4¾–6 in). Males of nominate race have all-black head to nape, chin, throat and upper breast extending down to flanks; northern race has a black crown and distinctive dark grey or black-and-white face and a band of black on lower throat/upper breast. The mantle to rump and tail is rich chestnut, with blacker-brown flight feathers. Females have black on head replaced with brown and finely dark-streaked, blackish-brown chin, and warm rich brown on wing-coverts, rump and tail. **Confusion species:** Males bear a passing or superficial resemblance to red-backed form of Black-and-white Mannikin (223) (known locally as Red-backed Mannikin), but the ranges do not overlap and the two have very different behaviour and characteristic actions. Females are separated from other female and immature canaries by warm brown tones of upperparts. Confusion possible with Cape Sparrow (267), but male Black-headed Canary has greater extent of warm brown or chestnut (and lacks grey mantle and white in wing) on upperparts and tail, and has more black on breast and flanks; female Black-headed Canary has a streaked head and mantle, is generally warmer brown on upperparts and tail, and lacks white edges to feathers of wing.
DESCRIPTION Sexes differ. **Adult male:** Entire head to sides of neck jet-black (in fresh plumage, some show pale buff tips to hindcrown, nape or lower ear-coverts), lower nape and sides of neck form a collar of white or whitish-buff. Mantle to scapulars, rump and uppertail-coverts rich chestnut-brown, slightly richer or deeper on rump and uppertail-coverts. Tail is rich or deep chestnut, with fine black centres on shafts near tips. Median and greater coverts are chestnut; secondaries also chestnut; progressively blacker at base towards outer edges, tertials chestnut with black bases to inner webs; alula, primary coverts and primaries black. Chin and throat to centre of breast jet-black, tapering in a V onto flanks (with rufous edges in fresh plumage), with a thin band of white from sides of lower neck to sides of breast; lower breast, belly and flanks buffish-white or faintly tinged buffish-brown; undertail-coverts white, tinged warm brown. Bill is short, stubby and pointed, brown, grey-brown or brownish-horn. Legs and feet black or dark grey. **Adult female:** Forehead, crown and nape dull grey, tinged with brown, slightly warmer or more rufous-brown on nape; face plain grey-brown, slightly paler over lores, eye and ear-coverts (some may show small pale crescent below eye); sides of neck greyish, tinged brown, becoming slightly warmer on sides of nape. Mantle and back as nape, with thin dark brown or blackish streaks; scapulars warmer brown and dark-streaked; lower back, rump and uppertail-coverts rich brown or pale chestnut. Tail is chest-

nut, with dark or blackish shafts towards centre. Median coverts warm brown or light chestnut; greaters blackish or dusky brown at base, broadly tipped light brown or chestnut; alula, primary coverts and flight feathers blackish or blackish-brown, edged rufous or chestnut-brown on inner secondaries and tertials. Chin and throat blackish or dark grey, fading into greyish-brown on lower throat/upper breast; sides of breast greyish-brown, tinged brownish or warm buff-brown and extending onto flanks; centre of belly and vent buffish-white or light buffish-brown; undertail-coverts pale buff or brown-tinged (some show warm brown feather centres). **Juvenile:** Very similar to adult female, but less warm brown, greyer and more heavily streaked on mantle and back; underparts are more uniform warm buff, with dark spots or streaks on throat, breast and flanks; also has broad dark feather centres to distal half of tail. First-winter males acquire the black feathers of head and the chestnut of mantle and back by a gradual moult from a fairly early age.
VOICE Call is a low 'tseet', 'tweet' or 'swea'. Song is a rather unmelodious jumble of gargling, twanging and 'skizzing' notes; only the male sings.
GEOGRAPHICAL VARIATION Males of race *leucolaema* have white at base of forehead, thin white supercilium to rear of ear-coverts, and white crescent below eye joining at base of bill with white on chin and throat; ear-coverts greyish or streaked with black or with a central patch of white; also a black crescent across breast, tinged warm buff on upper breast. The amount of black on sides of breast is variable and there are many intermediates between pure *alario* and *leucolaema*, especially in the amount of black on head and sides of breast/flanks area. Female *leucolaema* is similar to female *alario*, but has white on chin and throat and a pale or whitish supercilium similar to adult male, and a pale cinnamon breast.
STATUS, HABITAT AND BEHAVIOUR Locally common. An endemic resident of southwest South Africa, found in a variety of dry habitats from scrub and upland grassland, open grassland of the Karoo to rocky outcrops, edges of cultivation and in suburban gardens. Found in pairs or small parties; nests loosely colonially, and in winter forms flocks of up to 200. Forages in lower parts of bushes and trees, but mainly a ground-feeder on seeds of a variety of plants and grasses.
DISTRIBUTION *S. a. alario*: western, central and eastern Cape Province, southern Orange Free State and the highlands of Lesotho, South Africa.
S. a. leucolaema: north and northwest Cape Province, Namibia (north to about 24°S but absent from the sandveld), southern Botswana, western Orange Free State and southwest Transvaal.
MOVEMENTS In non-breeding season wanders

widely at random over the entire range, and irruptive flocks appear from time to time; has been recorded in the coastal grassland of the eastern Cape.

MEASUREMENTS Wing of male 62–71, of female 63–67; tail 42–49; tarsus 13–15; bill (culmen) 8–9.

REFERENCES MacLean (1988), McLachlan and Liversidge (1978), Sinclair (1984).

40 MOUNTAIN SERIN (Malay Goldfinch, Malay Serin, Malaysian Finch, Sunda Serin, Indonesian Serin, Javan Greenfinch)
Serinus estherae   Plate 11
Mountains in Malaysia, Indonesia and the Philippines

Crithagra estherae Finsch, 1902, Notes Leyden Mus., 23, p. 151, Mount Pangrango, 6000 ft, western Java.

IDENTIFICATION Length 11 cm (4¼ in). A very scarce or rarely seen finch of alpine meadows and mountain forest of Indonesia and the Philippines. Similar in size, shape and basic coloration to Serin (5), but males of nominate race have the crown and nape to rest of upperparts olive-brown (rump bright yellow), and two thin yellow wingbars; the underparts are pale yellow, becoming buffish-white, with dark spotting on breast and some streaks on flanks. Females are similar to males but duller, with less yellow on forehead and no yellow underparts. There is considerable variation among races, most noticeably in face markings. The only olive-coloured finch of its kind within its native range, and unlikely to be confused with any other species.

DESCRIPTION Sexes differ. **Adult male:** Forehead and slightly onto sides of crown yellow or bright yellow (but with darker bases to feathers and some may appear slightly spotted); crown and nape grey-brown; lores to cheeks white or whitish-buff, becoming pale grey-brown on ear-coverts, with moustachial region light yellow. Mantle, back and scapulars olive-brown, tinged with grey; rump bright or deep golden-yellow, uppertail-coverts the same with dark centres. Tail is short and slightly forked at tip, and dark brown or blackish-brown. Lesser, median and greater coverts are blackish-brown, with pale yellow tips on median and greaters forming double wingbar; alula and primary coverts blackish-brown or slightly darker; flight feathers blackish-brown, secondaries thinly edged with pale yellowish-white in fresh plumage and tertials edged pale yellow on outer webs in fresh plumage. Chin is yellow, lower chin and throat light brown or brownish; breast yellow or pale buffish-white, heavily streaked with dark or brown centres to feathers (appears closely spotted), streaks extending onto flanks; belly (unstreaked) and undertail-coverts white. Bill is short, deep at base, fairly stubby with a curved culmen, dark or olive-brown on upper mandible and pale brown on lower. Legs and feet brown or dark brown. **Adult female:** Very similar to adult male, but yellow on forehead either lacking or greatly reduced, yellow on rump also paler or duller; has white lores and a thin white eye-ring. The yellow in wing is much paler, and breast is generally buffish-white with only a slight tinge or wash of yellow; also lacks any suggestion of a moustachial stripe. **Juvenile:** Juvenile of nominate race is unknown, but see *vanderbilti* below.

GEOGRAPHICAL VARIATION Birds of race *vanderbilti* have small bills (the smallest of any race), dark lores, a small area of white around eye, all-dark or brown chin and throat, secondaries and inner primaries narrowly edged with white, and the breast is yellow with dark brown spots. Females are similar to males, but have less yellow and are more brown on chin; throat and upperparts are less olive. The juvenile of this race is very similar to adult female, but with bright yellow on rump and uppertail-coverts; it has a pale grey-brown collar or shawl and lacks any yellow on breast. Both sexes of race *orientalis* closely resemble nominate, but have only a small amount of yellow on malar area (does not cross chin), dark lores and a small area of white around eye, the wingbars are pale yellow and base colour of breast is yellow streaked with black; of the two known females of this race, one is as male but the other lacks any yellow on underparts. Birds of race *mindanensis* are the darkest of all races, with blackish-brown upperparts and greenish-olive edges to mantle, back and scapulars; rump and uppertail-coverts are bright yellow or golden-yellow, forehead to crown also golden-yellow, as are cheeks, malar area, throat and breast, and area around eye is dark olive; tips to wing-coverts are bright yellow; underparts generally dull or off-white, with thin or fine dark brown streaks on flanks. The bill in this race is blunter than in other races. Birds of race *renatae* are very similar to *vanderbilti*, but they have much larger bills (the largest of all races), dark lores, little or no white around eye, and tips to median and greater coverts are deep or bright yellow, as are edges to tertials; chin and throat are dark brown, and rest of underparts white or whitish with brown streaks on breast and flanks. A few individuals of this poorly known race are erythristic (and may yet prove to be a further race), and have the yellow of forehead to crown, rump, uppertail-coverts, base of tail, tips of wing-coverts and edges of tertials replaced with brilliant reddish-orange.

VOICE Call is a dull, metallic chittering note. In flight it gives a short tinkling song similar to that of Black-capped White-eye (*Zosterops atricapilla*).

STATUS, HABITAT AND BEHAVIOUR Very scarce or rare and infrequently recorded. Has been seen in the wild on only a few occasions and photographed only once. The nominate race was discovered in 1901, *vanderbilti* and *orientalis* in 1939, *mindanensis* in 1960 and *renatae* in 1980. Occurs in alpine or subalpine grassland and heather-dominated meadows with scattered bushes or scrub above the tree line, between 1400 m and 3400 m. In Sulawesi, western Java and on Mindanao, occurs in montane rainforest or dwarf ericaceous forest. It has been found alone or in small groups of up to eight; generally shy and retiring, it spends long periods sitting unobtrusively low in a bush or on the ground. Flight is swift and typically undulating. Food items are practically unrecorded, most probably a variety of seeds and berries; has been seen foraging on flowers of a large white terrestrial orchid.

DISTRIBUTION *S. e. estherae*: mountains of western Java. Most recent records have come from the Cibodas-Gunung Gede Nature Reserve, the site where the bird is most easily seen.

S. e. orientalis: Tengger Mountains, eastern Java.

S. e. vanderbilti: Mount Leuser and the Gunung Leuser National Park, northern Sumatra.

S. e. mindanensis: Mount Apo and Mount Katanglad, Mindanao, Philippines.

S. e. renatae: Gunung Rantekombola, northern Sulawesi.

There are also at least four other records from the Lore Lindu National Park, Sulawesi, which may refer to another, as yet undescribed, subspecies.

MEASUREMENTS Wing of male 65–71, of female 67–68; tail of male 43–46, of female 40–45; tarsus of male 12–15, of female 9–15; bill 9. Race *renatae* as above, except: tail 58; bill (culmen) 8. Wing of male *mindanensis* 70, of female 72; tail of male 39, of female 45; bill (culmen) of male 9, of female 7.

For a table of measurements for all races see Schuchmann and Wolters (1982).

REFERENCES Bishop and King (1986), de Schauensee and Ripley (1940), Schuchmann and Wolters (1982).

GENUS *NEOSPIZA*

One species. A virtually unknown grosbeak of uncertain affinities; it has long been considered a weaver, but is classed here as closer to the finches. Possibly of extreme antiquity, never common or widespread, and unable to adapt to change in specialised habitat. An island endemic restricted to a very small area of rainforest.

41 SÃO TOMÉ GROSBEAK (São Tomé Canary, Grosbeak Weaver, Grosbeak Bunting, São Tomé Grosbeak Weaver) *Neospiza concolor*
Plate 73

São Tomé

Amblyospyza concolor Barboza du Bocage, 1888, Jorn. Sci. Math. Phys. Nat. Lisboa, p. 229, Angolares, Sancti Thomae.

IDENTIFICATION Length 19–20 cm (7½–8 in). An all-dark chestnut-brown grosbeak with warm cinnamon underparts, a large bull-head and massive bill, restricted to dense rainforest of São Tomé. Discovered in 1888 and seen again in 1890 and 1891, when a total of three specimens was collected; not seen again until August 1991, despite several attempts to find it in 1928, 1963–73, 1988 and 1990. **Confusion species:** Within its natural range, its distinctive size, shape and coloration make it unlikely to be confused with any other species.

DESCRIPTION Sexes presumed alike. **Adult:** Almost entirely dark chestnut-brown, slightly darker or blackish-brown on mantle to scapulars and wings; at close range, crown to nape and ear-coverts have short blackish streaks. The massive bill is typically grosbeak-like, with strong mandibles recalling Thick-billed Seedeater (34) and curved ridges to both upper and lower; dark horn in colour. Legs and feet are probably dark brown or blackish. **Juvenile:** Unknown.

VOICE Call is a brief series of four or five short thin whistles given in a canary-like fashion.

STATUS, HABITAT AND BEHAVIOUR Extremely rare, the entire population is probably fewer than several hundred individuals. It has been seen on only four or five occasions, and only once in the 20th century, on 4 and 5 August 1991; possibly also seen in 1992, at a different locality from the 1991 sighting (P. Roberts pers. comm.). Found in dense primary forest on slopes of the Cabume massif, where it feeds in the closed canopy of tall trees. The 19th-century locations are coastal and may at that time have been forest; most of the lowland forest has since been cleared and cultivated with cocoa plantations. It was considered to be extinct following the destruction of forest, but a faint hope remained that it had survived. Clearance of the forest for cultivation ceased in 1975 (following independence), and there is now considerable hope for the survival of the bird. Behaviour and food unknown, but the possible sighting in 1992 was on the ground, so it may take hard-shelled seeds from trees or when fallen. Between 1888 and 1891 three specimens were collected from São Tomé, but only one now remains (in the collection at Tring); the other two were destroyed by a fire in the Bocage Museum, Lisbon, in 1975.

DISTRIBUTION Monotypic. Endemic to primary forest of southwest São Tomé.

MEASUREMENTS Wing 104; tarsus 20; bill (from feathers) 21, depth 17.

REFERENCES Collar and Stuart (1985), Sergeant et al. (1992).

GENUS *LINURGUS*

One species. A brightly coloured and little-known or little-studied finch of the tropical forest of central Africa. It has no direct relationship with any other African genus, but bears some passing resemblance to orioles (*Oriolus* spp.).

42 ORIOLE FINCH *Linurgus olivaceus*   Plate 35
Africa

Coccothraustes olivaceus Fraser, 1842, Proc. Zool. Soc. London, p. 144, Clarence, Fernando Po.

IDENTIFICATION Length 13 cm (5 in). The adult male is like a miniature Black-headed Oriole (*Oriolus larvatus*), with all-black face, chin and throat, bright orange-yellow bill, light greenish-yellow upperparts including tail and wings, with black primaries; sides of neck and underparts bright or deep yellow, slightly orange on breast. Female duller and more green, lacks black head but has a yellow wingbar. **Confusion species:** Males are similar, at least superficially, to several of the weavers, especially those with black heads or masks and particularly Brown-capped Weaver (*Ploceus insignis*), but latter has a black bill, warm brown crown (male) and black wings and tail lacking any yellow or green edges. Also, the different habits, behaviour and thinner and orange-yellow bill of Oriole Finch should separate it from all similar weavers. Confusion with the larger true orioles is also a possibility, but the restricted amount of black on head, size and shape of bill and absence of black in tail should separate it.

DESCRIPTION Sexes differ. **Adult male:** Forehead to hindneck, sides of head, face to chin and upper throat jet-black; nape bright yellow. Lower nape, mantle, back and scapulars light yellowish-green, becoming more yellow on lower back, rump and uppertail-coverts. Tail is light olive, broadly edged and tipped with yellow. Median coverts greenish-yellow as scapulars; greater coverts blackish, broadly edged greenish-yellow and tipped bright yellow; alula, primary coverts and flight feathers black, but secondaries and tertials very broadly fringed yellow, forming a panel; tips to primaries and some secondaries and outermost tertial are creamy-white. Golden-yellow from sides of nape to undertail-coverts, tinged with orange on upper breast, slightly greenish-yellow on flanks. Bill is bright orange-yellow, large or prominent, with deep base and with curved ridge to upper

mandible. Legs and feet orange-brown. **Adult female:** Forehead, crown and nape to sides of head, face, chin and throat dull grey or dingy olive-green, darker or more dingy green on forehead and lores. Mantle, back and scapulars dull greenish-olive, becoming slightly paler on rump and uppertail-coverts. Tail is olive or olive-green. Median coverts dull green as scapulars; greaters blackish, finely edged green and broadly tipped yellow; alula, primary coverts and flight feathers black, but secondaries and tertials edged green or dull green and tipped bright yellow, inner primaries and outer secondaries tipped finely with white. Throat and sides of throat generally dull grey-green, tinged or streaked brownish or olive-brown and occasionally yellow on some feathers, becoming plain greenish-yellow on belly and bright yellow on undertail. Bill is yellowish or more yellow than male. **Juvenile:** Very similar to adult female but much duller green, and head is not so dark green but more uniform with or slightly darker than dark olive-green mantle and back; wing-coverts have pale greenish-yellow tips; underparts are very pale yellow, streaked with dull green on breast and flanks. The bill is entirely brown. Legs and feet brown or purplish-brown.

GEOGRAPHICAL VARIATION Only males of nominate race have a yellow collar below black nape. Other racial differences are generally indeterminate in the field, involving mostly the intensity of yellow or green on the upperparts. Male *elgonensis* is bright golden-yellow on upperparts, tinged with brown or golden-brown on mantle, back and scapulars, has broad silvery-white inner webs to tertials and secondaries and creamy-white tips to primaries, with tail and underparts bright yellow; females are similar to nominate, generally dull olive suffused with a yellowish wash on underparts and with bright yellow outer webs to secondaries. Both sexes of *kilimensis* are much darker, or olive, on upperparts and underparts, and males can have black of face extending to centre of upper breast and green or greenish-olive on breast and flanks (and from chin to flanks on female); the tail is almost entirely deep or dark olive, edged and tipped finely with yellow. Birds of race *prigoginei* are tinged with orange-brown on underparts.

VOICE Generally a silent bird, but occasionally utters a wheezy 'tssip', 'twee' or 'tzit-tzit' or 'sip-sip' call. The song is a soft churring ending with a soft or melodious whistle.

STATUS, HABITAT AND BEHAVIOUR Uncommon or locally common. Inhabits evergreen forest in mountains and upland areas, mainly above 1700 m and up to 3000 m, although nominate race occurs down to 1000 m on Mount Cameroon. Fairly shy and restless; usually seen at forest edge, feeding in undergrowth in low scrub or bamboo clumps to mid-level or in the canopy. Occurs alone, in pairs or small scattered groups of up to about 15, feeding on seeds of trees (particularly albizias) or large shrubs, also millet and other grasses; occasionally takes caterpillars.

DISTRIBUTION *L. o. olivaceus*: Obudu and Mambilla plateaux, southeast Nigeria, west Cameroon (Mount Cameroon north to Oku and Genderu) and Fernando Po.

L. o. prigoginei: Impenetrable Forest, southwest Uganda to eastern Zaire.

L. o. elgonensis: southeast Sudan (Imatong Mountains) to western and central Kenya.

L. o. kilimensis: eastern, southeastern and southwestern Tanzania to northern Malawi.

MOVEMENTS Sedentary.

MEASUREMENTS Wing of male 72–81, of female 70–76; tail 48–53; Tarsus 20; bill 13–14.

REFERENCE Chapin (1954).

GENUS *RHYNCHOSTRUTHUS*

One species. A robust and large-billed finch with limited distribution in parts of northeast Africa and Arabia. Most probably a relict descendant from the larger-billed finches in east Asia, but little studied and has no direct affinities with any other genus.

43 GOLDEN-WINGED GROSBEAK *Rhynchostruthus socotranus*
Plate 18

Arabia and East Africa

Rhynchostruthus socotranus P.L. Sclater and Hartlaub, 1881, Proc. Zool. Soc. London, p. 171, Goehel Valley, Socotra.

IDENTIFICATION Length 14·5 cm (5–6 in). A robust or plump, large-headed and very large-billed bird with a short tail. Males are black or brown on top of head, with white ear-coverts, greyish-brown upperparts, black wings with a broad bright golden-yellow panel, and a black tail with yellow feather edges (except central and outermost feathers). The base of the bill, chin, throat and upper breast are black or blackish-brown, becoming greyish-buff on belly and flanks. Females are similar but less strongly or intensely coloured, and generally have less black on head, and ear-coverts are duller or greyish-white. Confusion with any other species unlikely.

DESCRIPTION Sexes differ. **Adult male:** Forehead black, becoming blackish-brown on crown and nape, this colour extending down lores and cheeks to chin and throat, and entirely encircling white ear-coverts. Mantle, back and scapulars grey-brown, becoming plain grey on rump and uppertail-coverts. Tail is notched at tip, with broad yellow edges to all outer feathers (especially at base) showing as two yellow panels each side of black or blackish-brown central feathers. Median coverts grey or dark grey, tipped with yellow; outer greater coverts all bright yellow, innermost black

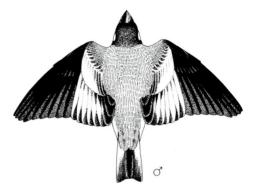

or blackish, tipped pale buff and edged pale grey; alula, primary coverts and flight feathers black, but edges to secondaries (and lower tertial) broadly yellow or golden-yellow, some with white or whitish-buff tips, and tertials edged pale yellow or white. Chin and throat to upper breast black or blackish-brown; lower breast, belly and flanks are washed pale greyish or light buff; undertail-coverts white. Bill is stout, very deep at base, black or dark slate-grey. Legs and feet pale flesh-brown. **Adult female:**

Very similar to adult male, but less intensely black and much more brown on head and nape; ear-coverts greyish-white. Mantle, back and scapulars are paler and tinged with brown. The upper breast is brown, and on some the belly is slightly greyer. Yellow at sides of base of tail is less extensive. **Juvenile:** Lacks black head and face and white ear-coverts, and has forehead to crown and nape brown and dark-streaked, lores dark, cheeks and ear-coverts dull yellowish-buff and faintly dark-streaked. Mantle, back and scapulars are grey-brown or greenish-brown, broadly streaked darker brown. Wings and tail similar to adult, but yellow paler and less extensive, restricted to tips of coverts and edges of secondaries. Chin and throat to breast pale buff, streaked darker brown; centre of breast, belly and flanks buffish with darker streaks continuing (but becoming smaller or finer) on belly and vent; undertail-coverts whitish-buff. Bill is almost entirely black, except for a pale or grey base to lower mandible.

GEOGRAPHICAL VARIATION Male *louisae* has crown and forehead dark brown with black on lores, cheeks and chin, and grey or greyish ear-coverts with white upper and fore edges. Mantle, back and scapulars are uniform grey-brown, contrasting with grey rump; underparts are paler, belly to undertail-coverts white or whitish. The bill is conspicuously smaller in this race. Females have black across face and chin. Male and female *percivali* have warm brown forehead to crown and upper nape, fading over lower nape and merging with grey-brown of mantle. The black on face is restricted to lores, fore cheeks and chin. The ear-coverts and hindcheeks are white or tinged with grey (on some, the white is restricted to lower ear-coverts); throat and sides of neck brown or warm gingery-brown, becoming greyish-buff on belly. Females are similar, but black of face is an ill-defined blackish-brown.

VOICE Has a variety of musical Goldfinch-like calls, including 'wip' or 'wink', 'tzee', a rippling 'tut-tut-tut-tut' or 'did-ee' or 'did-did-ee', a soft 'tlyit', often repeated, and a rapid 'dy-dy-dy' followed by a harsh dry 'drrrt' trill; also 'si-si-si ooo tzee'. The song is liquid, musical and discordant or jangling, often from a concealed perch in a tree (usually acacia) or in rapid bat-like display flight: phrases include 'whit-whee-oo', 'whee wee-ooo whee', 'sit-eeee-did-oo-ee' or 'tviit-te-vyt-te-viit', interspersed with Linnet-like or Goldfinch-like notes; also has a subsong.

STATUS, HABITAT AND BEHAVIOUR Uncommon. An elusive and shy resident found in mountains or upland areas, wadis or rocky outcrops between 1060 m and 2800 m, in acacias and euphorbias, also in juniper forest and scrub. Flight is direct and only slightly undulating; often flies some distance when disturbed (appears quite short-tailed in flight). Occurs singly or in pairs, and in small groups of up to about 30 in the non-breeding season; roosts communally. Feeds on a variety of seeds, buds and fruit, particularly of euphorbias, acacias and also junipers.

DISTRIBUTION *R. s. socotranus*: Socotra Island.
R. s. louisae: locally in northern Somalia from about 43°E to 48°E and south to 9°N.
R. s. percivali: southwest Saudi Arabia (Asir Mountains) and the Hadramawt in northern North Yemen (though range fragmentary here), possibly also in South Yemen; also in Dhofar, southwest Oman.

MOVEMENTS Poorly known; possibly only local, roams throughout the range in winter.

MEASUREMENTS Wing 83–95; tarsus 16; bill (to skull) 15·2, (to feathers) 9·9.

REFERENCES Ash and Miskell (1983), Hollom *et al.* (1988), Martins (1987).

GENUS *CARDUELIS*

Thirty-one species. Medium-sized finches with slender or strong-looking bills depending on the foraging method: siskins and goldfinches have thin bills for extracting seeds while greenfinches have more substantial bills for opening seedcases. A widely dispersed genus, occurring throughout the Holarctic to north of the Arctic Circle and south through the Neotropics; almost entirely absent from Africa (only one species with restricted range in extreme northeast Africa).

44 GREENFINCH *Carduelis chloris*   Plate 10
Palearctic

Loxia chloris Linnaeus, 1758, Syst. Nat., ed. 10, p. 174, Europe; restricted to Sweden by Hartert, 1903, Vögel pal. Fauna, p. 61.

IDENTIFICATION Length 14·5–16 cm (5–6¼ in). A stoutly built finch with distinctive plumage and familiar call, common and well known as a garden bird over much of its range. Males are olive-green or brighter green with bright yellow and grey edges to wing and tail feathers. Females and first-years are greyer, tinged brown or green on upperparts with paler or duller yellow in wing and tail edges. Juveniles are slightly streaked below. **Confusion species:** Males are unlikely to be confused with any other species when seen well; the yellow patches in wing and base of tail are very distinctive. Siskins (49) are smaller, with a black cap (males) and a different wing pattern. Male Serin (5) is smaller, and much more yellow and streaked on the underparts. Female Greenfinches can be as dull and nondescript as female/juvenile House Sparrow (258), but lack strong streaks and have pale uniform heads without well-defined supercilium. For differences from geographically widely separated Oriental Greenfinch (45), see that species.

DESCRIPTION Sexes differ. **Adult male:** Forehead to crown and nape deep green or olive-green, slightly paler or brighter green on sides of crown, hindneck and neck; lores black, cheeks and sides of neck yellowish-green or green, ear-coverts green or variably tinged grey-green, especially towards rear. Mantle, back and scapulars deep green or olive-green; lower back and rump brighter or pale lime-green; uppertail-coverts olive-yellow, edged and broadly tipped grey. Central feathers of tail are entirely black; all others have basal half yellow and distal half black. Median coverts are olive-green as scapulars, greater coverts ash-grey; alula black, with outer webs bright yellow, becoming grey at tip; primary coverts black or blackish, finely edged olive-yellow or yellowish-buff; primaries dusky brown or blackish-brown or grey-brown, broadly edged bright yellow (to shaft) at base and blackish towards tip; secondaries broadly edged pale grey or lead-grey, as are tertials, which are blackish on inner web. Chin is often pale yellow; breast and belly yellowish-green in centre but otherwise almost entirely olive-green; flanks tipped dusky grey, lower belly whitish, and undertail-coverts whitish washed yellow or yellowish. Bill is fairly stout and deep at base, coming to a point, and flesh-pink or pale pinkish-horn. Legs and feet are brown. In winter, olive-green of plumage is duller and often concealed by buff-brown or grey-brown feather tips to all or some of upperparts and green or deep green tips to underparts. **Adult female:** Forehead to crown pale green, becoming deeper green or olive on nape; upper lores and base of forehead blackish or dark grey, lower lores, cheeks and onto ear-coverts pale green; rest of face uniform pale ash-grey, extending onto sides of neck and to sides of breast and flanks. Mantle, back and scapulars vary individually, from greyish-buff to grey tinged green or dull green streaked with grey; lower back and rump pale green, uppertail-coverts ash-grey with dark or olive-green at bases of feathers. Blackish-brown tail, with all but central pair of feathers thinly edged yellow or pale yellow towards base. Median coverts are dull olive-grey, becoming greyer or dull grey on greater coverts, tips paler; alula and primary coverts edged green and tipped pale grey; flight feathers blackish or blackish-grey, thinly edged with pale yellow (not reaching feather shaft) at base of primaries and outer secondaries, inner secondaries greyish, tertials broadly greyish on outer web and blackish on inner. Chin and throat pale yellow, with green or deep green tinge to centre of breast and belly; flanks washed brown and lightly streaked darker brown; vent off-white, undertail-coverts white. Bill is similar to adult male's but greyer, especially

towards tip. **Juvenile:** Superficially similar to adult female (but differences in sexes apparent in wing and tail feathers), but much more buff-brown on head, face, mantle and back, with faint but noticeable darker brown streaking; alula brownish grey-green, finely edged off-white, pale sandy-buff tips to median and greater coverts. Underparts also very pale buff or pale buff-brown, streaked darker on breast, belly and flanks. Post-juvenile moult variable: in southern populations up to 50% of birds may have complete moult, whereas northern populations always retain juvenile primaries, secondaries and tail feathers; also, late (i.e. second- or third-brood) juveniles may retain all greater coverts (recognisable as a sandy-buff bar across tips). First-winter coverts, however, are never so clear a yellow or dove-grey as those on adult male. Pale horn bill with dull flesh-pink base to lower mandible.

GEOGRAPHICAL VARIATION Southern populations, irrespective of race, have noticeably larger or heavier bills. There are very few differences between races that are obvious in the field, most being of value in direct comparisons (except in extreme or more obvious cases); considerable individual and clinal variation exists and intermediates between the races are not unknown. Race *aurantiiventris* is very slightly smaller and more brightly green above, with less grey on wings and brighter or golden-yellow belly; *turkestanicus* is slightly paler (as is *chlorotica*) or greyer than European birds (differences are very subtle), especially on underparts, with a deeper grey on wings and a paler yellow at bases of flight feathers, and also has more yellow than green from forehead to area over eyes.

VOICE Most frequent call is a harsh twittering 'twichit' or 'twichichichit', occasionally given as an individual 'chit', 'chip' or 'teu, teu' or variations, and a sharp, rising 'swee-it' or 'tsooeet' is frequently uttered when disturbed or alarmed; young birds in autumn give a hard 'chip' or 'chip chip' call resembling (sometimes almost identical to) explosive note of Common Crossbill (110), or a softer 'chee', 'chi' or 'chwii' when being fed. In spring and summer, displaying or territory-holding males give a persistent nasal 'tsweeee' or 'zweee', occasionally just 'weee'; call of nestlings is a soft version of adult's trilling call. The song is a repeated collection of phrases incorporating the call notes, usually beginning with a dry nasal trill and continuing with a slowly rising 'teu-teu-teu-teu', interspersed with a 'tswee' or 'zeee' note; delivered from a high perch or in slow stiff-winged bat-like flight around top of a tree etc. Song period late February to June.

STATUS, HABITAT AND BEHAVIOUR Common throughout most of its range. Found in a variety of habitats, breeding mainly in low forest or edges of woodland, scrub, plantations, groves, orchards, parks, edges of cultivated areas and gardens. Winters in similar habitat but spreads into farmland, stubble fields and weedy areas including open coast where sufficient food is available. Sociable, often found in small flocks or larger groups and mixed with other ground-loving foragers such as Tree Sparrows (274), Linnets (72), Yellowhammers (*Emberiza citrinella*) and Reed Buntings *E. schoeniclus*). Pairs nest alone or in loose groups. Perches in trees and bushes, as well as on the ground; hops in cautious manner. Flight slightly undulating and quite fast (very distinctive thickset shape in flight, with yellow in wings and short notched tail prominent). Roosts communally in hedgerows, preferably evergreens. Feeds on a variety of weed seeds, and often gathers in numbers to exploit ripening seeds of particular plants; seeds of dog's mercury, sainfoin, clover, turnip seed, blackberries, hips, yew berries and hornbeam buds, also takes chickweed, dandelion, *Persicaria*, burdock and charlock; occasionally, and also when feeding young, takes insects such as ants and aphids, a few beetles and some spiders. In most of western Europe readily comes to garden feeders, where it is particularly fond of peanuts.

DISTRIBUTION *C. c. chloris*: Northern Europe from the British Isles, southern Scandinavia, Finland and western CIS (USSR) north to the southern shores of the White Sea, east to the central Urals and south to northern France, southern Germany, Switzerland, Corsica, Sardinia, Austria, northern Hungary and northern Romania.

C. c. aurantiiventris: Southern Europe and North Africa from Spain and Portugal to southern France, Italy, Yugoslavia to southern Hungary, southern Bulgaria, Greece and western Turkey, also the western Mediterranean islands (except Corsica and Sardinia), Crete and Cyprus; in North Africa, from Morocco to northern Algeria and northern Tunisia.

C. c. chlorotica: Syria and Lebanon to central Israel, Jordan and northern Egypt (Nile Delta).

C. c. turkestanicus: Crimea and the Caucasus to northern Iran; in southern CIS (USSR) discontinuously through Central Asia in parts of Turkmenia, southern Kazakhstan, Kirghizia and Tadzhikstan.

Other races have been described but very few are distinct in the field. It has also been introduced into: Azores (*aurantiiventris*); Uruguay (mainly coastal Colonia to Rocha) and northeastern Argentina (race not known); and nominate race into southern Australia (resident in southeast South Australia, through Victoria to southeast New South Wales and Tasmania), New Zealand (widely but unevenly or locally distributed) and Chatham Islands, from where it has spread to several subantarctic islands.

MOVEMENTS Sedentary and migratory. Birds from northern areas of breeding range move south and southwest to winter mostly within or slightly to the south of the range, with nominate race regular in winter in southern Spain, southern France, Italy (possibly also Malta) and southwest CIS (USSR); *aurantiiventris* is largely sedentary, but some move south to reach Malta, Cyprus, Libya and northern Egypt south to the Suez Canal and the northern shores of the Red Sea; *chlorotica* winters south to southern Israel and northern Egypt (Sinai); *turkestanicus* winters within the range and south to Afghanistan, west and southwest Iran and Iraq (an uncommon winter visitor to Iraq and northwest Saudi Arabia). It has occurred as a vagrant in the Faroes, Madeira, Canary Islands (*aurantiiventris*), northern Scandinavia, and western Siberia at Semipalatinsk (probably *turkestanicus*). Has also occurred in Mauritania (May and June 1980), but this may have been an introduced bird or an escape from captivity. In the British Isles in winter it is highly mobile (dependent on food supply), with evidence of movements from east and southeast to southwest England; there is also an established pattern of movements between southern Norway and northeast Scotland. A diurnal and nocturnal migrant, with flocks on the move often noted at coastal stations. In autumn, most southward migration takes place between late September and mid-November, with occasional movements later in the year often induced by severity of the winter or shortage of food; return passage in spring from mid-March to the end of April.

MEASUREMENTS Wing of male 82–91, of female 82–85; tail 55–60; tarsus 17–19; bill (from feathers) 12–14. Wing of *turkestanicus* 85–98.

REFERENCES Browne (1981), Witherby *et al.* (1938–41).

45 ORIENTAL GREENFINCH (Chinese Greenfinch, Grey-capped Greenfinch) *Carduelis sinica* Plate 11

Southeast Palearctic

Fringilla sinica Linnaeus, 1766, Syst. Nat., ed. 12, p. 321, China; restricted to Macão by Jacobi, 1923, Abh. Ber. Mus. Dresden, 16, p. 25.

IDENTIFICATION Length 12·5–14 cm (5–5½ in). Smaller and more slender than Greenfinch (44). Male has a dull grey-green head with dark face mask, warm brown back and scapulars, yellowish-green rump and grey uppertail-coverts; wings and tail black, with bright yellow flashes on wing and sides to base of tail; breast and flanks are brown, cinnamon or tinged with yellow, belly and undertail-coverts yellow. Female similar but duller, and browner on face and head; rump and base of tail are duller and not so yellow. In flight, yellow wingbar along whole length of wing is very distinctive. **Confusion species:** Similar to Greenfinch but ranges widely separated; Oriental Greenfinch is much browner above and below, and confusion with all deep green male Greenfinch or paler female or juvenile very unlikely. More likely to be confused with Black-headed Greenfinch (48), especially females and juveniles, but Oriental lacks well-defined head pattern and has darker underparts.

DESCRIPTION Sexes differ. **Adult male:** Forehead to lores, cheeks, ear-coverts (and, on some, chin and throat) deep or dark olive-green. In full breeding plumage, lores, sides of lower forehead, and cheeks to around eye are blackish, and crown to nape and (on some) ear-coverts become darker grey or blackish-olive. Mantle, upper back and scapulars are rich warm brown, often with a wash of olive or grey-green on upper mantle; upper rump paler warm buffish-brown, lower rump yellow or yellowish-brown, edged with green, uppertail-coverts tipped ash-grey. The tail is forked at tip, black or blackish-brown, with bright yellow outer edges to all but central feathers forming prominent panels at sides of base; edges to central tail feathers broadly grey. Lesser and median coverts olive-brown, tinged with bright green in fresh plumage; greater coverts similar but slightly warmer brown, outermost greater coverts yellow or yellowish, all with fine buff or grey tips; alula black, with broad yellow outer edge; primary coverts jet-black; flight feathers black, all with bright or deep yellow at base, more extensive on primaries than secondaries, the latter broadly edged greyish or buffish-white (forming panel on closed wing) in fresh plumage and broadly tipped pale buff; tertials black, with extensive buff-brown or greyish-white outer edges and tips. In flight shows a broad bright yellow wingbar across base of all flight feathers; underwing-coverts pale yellow. Chin, throat and sides of neck as face or slightly yellow or greenish-yellow, merging into a warm brown or rich cinnamon on upper breast; lower breast and flanks deeper or warmer brown; belly yellow, whitish on vent, undertail-coverts bright yellow. Bill as Greenfinch, pale pink or pale horn colour. Legs and feet pale or bright flesh-pink. In winter, slightly more grey-brown above, crown to nape and (on some) ear-coverts pale grey, and flight feathers have pale buff-brown edges and tips; much paler or more buff-brown on underparts. **Adult female:** Similar to male but much duller, head more uniform with brown mantle or washed heavily with grey; face as head, but tinged with green or olive-yellow on upper lores, ear-coverts and over eye; mantle, back and scapulars as male, but duller brown with dark shaft streaks; rump paler or yellowish-brown, especially in centre; uppertail-coverts pale grey. Tail as male, but yellow at sides of base much less extensive. Median and greater coverts brown, edged pale yellowish-brown on medians, and pale buff or very slightly yellowish at tip of greaters; alula black, thinly edged yellowish-green, primary coverts black; flight feathers much as male; tertials are black on inner webs, edged pale brown on outer and tipped pale buff or pale greyish. Chin and throat are yellowish or yellowish-green, breast and flanks dull or warm buff-brown washed with yellow; belly and lower flanks pale yellow or buff, vent whitish and undertail-coverts pale or bright yellow. **Juvenile:** Lacks dark head and face of adults; head and nape generally pale yellowish (except for dark lores and plain buffish-brown

cheeks and ear-coverts), with indistinct dark streaks on crown, nape, mantle, back and scapulars. Median coverts are dark brown, fringed with paler or warmer brown, and greater coverts are broadly fringed warm buff; wings otherwise as adult. Underparts pale yellowish-buff with short brown streaks, the chin, throat and breast often tinged pale green.

GEOGRAPHICAL VARIATION Males of race *kawarahiba* have head and face to chin and throat deep green, tinged grey, with a grey moustachial streak, mantle and back are chocolate-brown and rump green or lightly washed with yellow, breast, belly and flanks are deep or rich cinnamon, tinged with yellow, undertail-coverts bright yellow; females are like nominate, but generally darker or more dingy-brown, and have head and face to chin, throat and breast paler and much more buffish-brown. Juveniles have fairly heavily streaked upperparts and underparts. Males of race *ussuriensis* are paler and greyer, especially on crown, nape and sides of nape, with underparts much paler or more extensively yellow or yellowish-brown than in other races; females are similar to or as pale as *kawarahiba*. Male *chabarovi* is generally dark brown on upperparts, with a tinge of grey on head, and yellow in wing is more extensive (onto alula); females are probably indistinguishable in the field from female *ussuriensis* or *kawarahiba*. Birds from southern Japan, *minor*, are more closely allied to nominate, but have forehead and lores deep blackish-green and upper forehead to upper mantle deep grey; nape, sides of nape and underparts are deep green; in breeding plumage, rump of adult male is green tinged with yellow or with yellow in the centre.

VOICE The calls of this species and of Himalayan Greenfinch (46) are fairly close to those of Greenfinch. Oriental Greenfinch has distinctive twittering 'dzi-dzi-i-dzi-i' flight call, with a slightly more metallic or Redpoll-like quality; also utters the characteristic nasal 'dzweee' or 'djeeen'. Song is very similar in tone and phrases to Greenfinch but with some harsher or coarse notes, including 'kirr' or 'korr'.

STATUS, HABITAT AND BEHAVIOUR Common or locally common. The preferred habitat is valleys with scrub or bushes, rice-fields, orchards, wooded or open hillsides of lower elevations to about 2400 m, along river banks, edges of conifer or broadleaved forest and edges of cultivation; in winter occurs on plains and on edges of urban areas. Found in pairs or small groups, or in larger flocks of up to 1,000 in winter. Acts and behaves in typical Greenfinch fashion, feeding and perching in trees, bushes, shrubs or on the ground. Feeds on a variety of seeds, from buckwheat, rice or other grain to sunflowers and a range of other weed and shrub seeds; occasionally takes insects. In parts of the range (Japan), readily comes to feeders and birdtables.

DISTRIBUTION *C. s. sinica*: eastern and central China from southern Manchuria south to Kwang-tung, west to Szechwan, eastern Tsinghai and southern Kansu.

C. s. chabarovi: northern Manchuria to Amur-

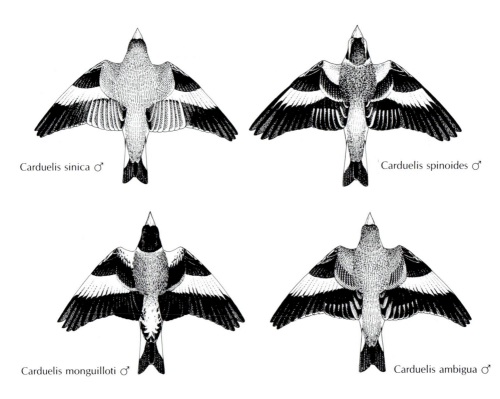

Carduelis sinica ♂

Carduelis spinoides ♂

Carduelis monguilloti ♂

Carduelis ambigua ♂

land (Khabarovsk) and northeast Mongolia (Khingan).

C. s. ussuriensis: eastern Mongolia and northeast China (Hopei) to eastern Manchuria, Korea, southern Ussuriland and probably southern Amurland.

C. s. kawarahiba: Kamchatka, Sakhalin and Kurile Islands.

C. s. minor: Quelpart Island, South Korea, east through Japan to the northern Ryukyu and Izu Islands.

C. s. kittlitzi: Ogasawara (Bonin) and Iwo Islands.

MOVEMENTS Sedentary and migratory. Some northern breeders move south in September and October to winter at lower altitudes, mostly within the range or slightly to the south, returning to breeding areas in April and May; birds of race *kawarahiba* move south or southeast to winter in Japan south to Okinawa. A vagrant to Taiwan (November 1932) and the western Aleutians (Attu, Shemya and Buldur, four records 1976–82).

MEASUREMENTS Wing of male 76–84, of female 76·5–85; tail 55–60; bill 10–13; tarsus 13–19; bill (culmen) 10·5–12. Weight 17–22.

REFERENCE Brazil (1991).

46 HIMALAYAN GREENFINCH (Black-headed Greenfinch, Yellow-breasted Greenfinch, Himalayan Goldfinch)
Carduelis spinoides   Plate 11
Southeast Palearctic and marginally Oriental

Carduelis spinoides Vigors, 1831, Proc. Zool. Soc. London, p. 44, Himalayas; restricted to Simla by Baker, 1921, Journ. Bombay Nat. Hist. Soc., 27, p. 730.

IDENTIFICATION Length 14 cm (5½ in). Males of nominate race have distinctive face pattern, with blackish-olive crown to nape, ear-coverts and moustachial stripe; other races have all-black heads, with rest of face and entire underparts yellow or pale yellow. The upperparts are blackish or blackish-olive or tinged bright yellow; rump and sides to black-centred tail also yellow. Wings black or blackish-brown, with broad yellow double wingbar and bases to primaries. Female is duller olive above and has some smudges or streaks on sides of breast and flanks. **Confusion species:** Black-headed Greenfinch (48) where ranges overlap in Burma: male Himalayan has blackish-olive mantle and back, bright yellow rump and uppertail-coverts, a different wing pattern and bright yellow (not dull greenish) underparts; female lacks dark brown head or face of female Black-headed. Juveniles are also similar to same-aged Black-headed Greenfinch, but have pale supercilia and yellow on underparts is more prominent on sides of neck. Tibetan Siskin (9) is similar but smaller, with a thin bill, and lacks any yellow or greenish-yellow in wing.

DESCRIPTION Sexes differ. **Adult male:** Lower forehead yellow (but can be lacking), spotted with black; centre and upper forehead to upper nape black or blackish-olive, nape paler or lightly tipped yellow or yellowish, forming a slight collar; super-cilium from lores to rear of ear-coverts bright or deep yellow, extending below eye to cheeks and moustachial stripe; submoustachial stripe blackish-olive; ear-coverts and lower cheeks blackish-olive (some variation in amount of black on face and in length of supercilium, and some show pale yellow). Mantle, upper back and scapulars blackish-olive, lower back dull yellow, rump and uppertail-coverts bright yellow. Tail, forked at tip, is dark or blackish-brown, outer feathers edged bright yellow, central feathers entirely black. Lesser and median coverts bright yellow with olive-brown bases, greaters black with broad yellow edges and tips; alula black, finely edged yellow, primary coverts black; flight feathers black, with bases to all primaries and (less extensively) outer secondaries yellow, in worn plumage (midsummer) tips to sec-ondaries greyish-white becoming edged white on tips, tertials the same. Underparts are almost entirely bright yellow, sides of breast and upper flanks tinged with green or greenish-yellow (on some, becoming duller on flanks). Bill is more slen-der than Greenfinch (44), pointed, the upper man-dible brown or brownish-pink, lower paler or pinkish with a brownish tip. Legs and feet pinkish or pinkish-brown. In winter very little difference, but generally duller with yellow areas of plumage duller, or tinged with green on rump; moulting birds in autumn can show a complete yellow collar around nape and sides of neck. **Adult female:** Very similar to male in general pattern, but dark olive on head, face, mantle and scapulars and yellow on face, wings, rump and base of tail are much paler or duller; extent of yellow on edges of wing-coverts, flight and tail feathers is also reduced. Mantle, back and scapulars have faint dark streaks. Underparts are duller yellow than male, and there is often smudging or small dull olive streaks on sides or centre of breast; flanks are tinged light brown. **Juvenile:** Lacks dark olive plumage of adults, is paler and streaked darker on head and upperparts, which can be tinged slightly buffish-yellow on nape, mantle and rump. Ear-coverts, cheeks and submoustachial stripe pale or light buff-brown, sides of neck bright yellow or buffish-yellow, thinly streaked brown; thin pale yellowish-buff supercilium from base of bill to rear of ear-coverts. Median coverts are blackish-brown, tipped pale yellow, greater coverts the same or tipped yellowish-buff, forming two wingbars; flight feathers blackish or blackish-brown, tipped buff,

with yellow or pale yellow bases (not so extensive as on adults); tertials edged pale grey. Tail as adult but blackish-brown, not black. Chin and throat pale or dull yellow, buffish-yellow tinge to breast and flanks, with thin brown streaks to sides of throat, breast and flanks; lower belly, thighs and undertail-coverts pale buff or tinged with yellow. Juvenile or first-winter males show more yellow on underparts and more extensively in wing than adult female. This plumage is retained into first summer, when (exceptionally among passerines) it under-goes a pre-nuptial moult.

GEOGRAPHICAL VARIATION Birds of race *heinrichi* are generally darker; males have crown and ear-coverts black and lack yellow moustachial stripe and area below cheeks (but retain yellow supercilium).

VOICE The call notes are similar to those of Greenfinch: a characteristic light twittering fol-lowed by or including a harsh 'tsswee', 'dzwee', 'beez' or 'zeez', but noticeably shorter and with a melodious or metallic quality; the long and drawn-out 'sweee-tu-tu' is more sparrow-like and drops slightly in pitch at the end; also has similar twit-tering flight notes to Greenfinch; immatures have a hard 'chit chit' note. The song, uttered from the tops of trees or in typical slow and stiff-winged bat-like flight, also recalls Greenfinch but is some-what higher-pitched.

STATUS, HABITAT AND BEHAVIOUR Common, locally common or very common. A bird of open or edges of oak, rhododendron or conifer forest, open hillsides, edges of cultivation, gardens and scrub, often above the tree line; usu-ally breeds between 1600 m and 4400 m, but has been recorded possibly breeding down to 1100 m in Simla. Found in pairs or small groups, or in larger flocks of up to 100 in winter often mixed with Goldfinches (68), feeding in trees and bushes. A much more tree-loving bird than other green-finches, often feeding at the tops of pines or alders; in winter less arboreal, and occurs on ter-raced hillsides with scattered bushes. Feeds on a variety of seeds, including hemp, sunflower, and tree seeds such as pine and alder; millet, buckwheat, some berries and small insects also taken.

DISTRIBUTION *C. s. spinoides*: Pakistan (poss-ibly also eastern Afghanistan), Kashmir and north-west India, through Nepal to the eastern Himalayas in Bhutan and marginally to the extreme south of Tibet.

C. s. heinrichi: southern and eastern Assam (Nagaland and Manipur) to northwest Burma (south to Mount Victoria).

MOVEMENTS Partial migrant. Some populations are resident, but others from higher altitudes descend in winter to foothills and lower valleys of adjacent plains to between 1300 m and 1500 m (but winters at 2700 m in Sikkim). Moves to lower altitudes in September and October, and returns to breeding areas in late May and June.

MEASUREMENTS Wing of male 76–83, of female 72–80; tail of male 43–51, of female 46–50; tarsus 14–16; bill (from skull) 14–16. Weight of male 18·5–20·5, of female 16–18·5. Wing of male *heinrichi* 72–77, of female 70–74. Weight 15–16.

REFERENCES Ali and Ripley (1983), Whistler (1940).

47 VIETNAMESE GREENFINCH *Carduelis monguilloti*　　Plate 11
Oriental

Hypacanthis monguilloti Delacour, 1926, Bull. Brit. Ornith. Club, 47, p. 20, Dalat, Annam. Note: Previously considered as a race of Himalayan Greenfinch (46), but classification here follows the list proposed by the Oriental Bird Club (UK) (in prep.).

IDENTIFICATION Length 14 cm (5½ in). A distinctive greenfinch from southern Vietnam, unlikely to be confused as it is the only Cardueline finch of the region. Males are blackish above, apart from some yellow or green tinges and bright yellow flashes on wing and rump, and bright yellow below; females are duller, with only head and face black and with paler or duller yellow underparts.

DESCRIPTION Sexes differ. **Adult male:** Forehead to hindcrown/upper nape, lores, cheeks and ear-coverts black. Thin band of pale yellow, often flecked or obscured with black, across nape. Mantle, back and scapulars black with blackish-olive feather bases (appear uniform black in the field); rump and uppertail-coverts deep olive or blackish-olive, with bright yellow centre to rump (variable and not always obvious). Tail is black, with yellow at base of all outer feathers (amount of yellow declines inwardly). Lesser and median coverts bright yellow, but can be black or blackish-olive with bright yellow edges; greater coverts black, with thin olive or dull yellow tips; alula black, with yellow edge on largest feather; primary coverts black; flight feathers black, with bright and deep yellow bases for about half the primary length; tertials uniform blackish-olive. Chin and throat to sides of neck yellow or deep yellow; rest of underparts the same, but heavily infused with olive or blackish-olive on centre or sides of breast and flanks (amount varies individually). Bill has a pinkish-brown upper mandible, with a brown tip to lower. Legs and feet pinkish or pale pinkish-brown. **Adult female:** Forehead to hindcrown and face to below cheeks and ear-coverts black or blackish-olive, often shows a paler ring around eye. Nape and sides of neck pale yellow but flecked with olive, merging into dark-olive on mantle, back and dark-streaked scapulars; rump and uppertail-coverts bright yellow. Tail is notched at tip, central pair of feathers and tips to all outers black, bases of outer feathers broadly yellow. Lesser and median coverts as scapulars, but tips to medians spotted with yellow or pale yellow; greater coverts blackish-brown; alula blackish, finely edged dull yellow, primary coverts blackish-brown; flight feathers black or blackish-brown, with bright yellow bases to secondaries and primaries (paler and not so broad as on adult male); tertials blackish. Underparts yellow on chin and throat, becoming pale yellow on belly and undertail-coverts; breast, flanks and sides of belly are obscured or streaked with dark olive. **Juvenile:** Very similar to adult female, but lacks black on forehead and face, and has pale yellow underparts and sides to neck extending to sides of nape.

VOICE Call is a light canary-like series of three to four notes run together (often descending in tone), interspersed with slightly more musical notes and harsher twittering 'chi-chi-chi'; also a dry or nasal 'zweee'. The song is a series of instantly recognisable greenfinch-type notes, a slowly rising 'seeuuu-seeuuu-seeuuu' or 'teoo-teoo-teooo' followed by a dry nasal 'weeeee' or 'chweee', much harsher than Greenfinch (44).

STATUS, HABITAT AND BEHAVIOUR Local or locally common. Occurs in open wooded areas of *Pinus insularis*, forest edges and secondary growth, also on edges of cultivated areas and gardens, usually above 1000 m. Habits and food probably as Himalayan Greenfinch, but otherwise generally little known and poorly studied; possibly more of a canopy feeder, apparently spending little (if any) time on the ground. Favours seeds of *Pinus insularis*; has been seen flycatching recently hatched termites.

DISTRIBUTION The Da Lat Plateau of south Annam, central Vietnam.

MEASUREMENTS Wing 65–76; bill (from feathers) 10·5; tarsus 11.

REFERENCE Eames and Robson (1992).

48 BLACK-HEADED GREENFINCH (Tibetan Greenfinch, Yunnan Greenfinch) *Carduelis ambigua*　　Plate 11
Southeast Palearctic and marginally Oriental

Chrysomitris ambigua Oustalet, 1896, Bull. Mus. Hist. Nat. Paris, 2, p. 186, Mienning; Yun Chou and banks of Sang pi Kiang river, Yunnan.

IDENTIFICATION Length 12·5–14 cm (5–5½ in). A dark greenfinch of eastern Asia. Male has all-black or blackish-brown head (except chin and throat), dull olive-green upperparts including wing-coverts, and black wings with broad bright yellow band across bases of flight feathers; the tail is black with yellow bases to all outer feathers. Females similar, but have blackish-brown restricted to face; crown and upperparts are dull olive. **Confusion species:** The all-black or all-brown head is distinctive within range (the isolated Vietnamese Greenfinch (47) has black head with yellow chin and throat), and a good distinguishing feature from similar but browner Oriental Greenfinch (45) and the more distinct head pattern of adult Himalayan Greenfinch (46). Both sexes of Black-headed at all ages also have green or olive-green underparts with some yellow, and are not brown or brownish like Oriental. Female and juvenile Himalayan have distinctive face pattern and usually show dull or pale yellow underparts; immature Black-headed also has more yellow in wing than same-aged Himalayan.

DESCRIPTION Sexes differ. **Adult male:** Forehead to crown, upper nape and face black or deep blackish-olive (some show an indistinct paler olive supercilium restricted to area over eye). Hindneck, mantle, back and scapulars dull olive, becoming paler or green on lower back; rump olive-green with yellow bases to feathers, uppertail-coverts greyer. Tail is slightly forked at tip and black, central pair of feathers finely edged grey, outers broadly edged yellow at base forming distinct panels each side of tail (very obvious in flight). Median coverts as scapulars or with paler yellowish-green bases; greater coverts black or blackish, tipped light grey becoming olive-green on outer coverts; alula black, edged pale yellowish; primary coverts black; flight feathers black, with bases to primaries and outer secondaries bright yellow, tips of outer secondaries and inner primaries grey or off-white; tertials black, broadly fringed grey or buffish-white. Underparts are almost entirely green or olive-green, slightly paler or mottled with yellow on throat and uniformly pale yellow on undertail-coverts; belly to vent and thighs whitish or pale buff. Bill similar to that of other greenfinches, pale flesh or horn-brown. Legs and feet pale brown or flesh to pinkish-brown. **Adult female:** Very similar to adult male, but has face and sides of neck blackish-olive, with some slightly darker or blackish streaks or tips on crown (at a distance can appear dark-hooded, but not so black as male). Mantle, back and scapulars are dull green or olive-green, slightly paler on rump; uppertail-coverts grey or greyish. Wings as male, tips to tertials broadly pale whitish or grey. Underparts are virtually all dull olive with a wash of pale or light green, flanks tinged pale

buff-brown, belly to vent and thighs pale buff or off-whitish, undertail-coverts the same or tinged yellow. **Juvenile:** Generally pale or buffish-brown and dark-streaked. Upperparts are broadly streaked with brown or dark brown; rump and uppertail-coverts pale buff or buffish-brown with darker streaks. Wing-coverts are edged brownish-buff and tipped pale or warm buff-brown; base of primaries and outer secondaries broadly bright yellow. Underparts are dull buffish lemon-yellow, with brown streaks from chin to belly and flanks; pale yellow wash on centre of throat and undertail-coverts; lower belly whitish, flanks washed with buff, thighs and undertail-coverts unstreaked.

GEOGRAPHICAL VARIATION Males of race *taylori* have more sooty-black on head and are much duller olive-green or tinged slightly with brown on mantle and back; rump is green or pale green with yellow bases to feathers. The underparts are yellow, and undertail-coverts are pale green on males and pale buff or buffish-grey on females. Lone females are unlikely to be separable racially in the field.

VOICE Call is a short, thin, high-pitched metallic twitter, 'tit-it-it-it-it', usually given in flight and repeated; also a rising wheezy Greenfinch-like 'twzyee' or 'tzyeee'. The song is similar in style to Greenfinch, but with more metallic notes and shrill high-pitched trills and a dry or sharp sounding 'screee' or 'treeee-tertrah'.

STATUS, HABITAT AND BEHAVIOUR Locally common resident or partial migrant. Occurs between 1200 m and 3100 m, but winters at slightly lower altitudes. Found in both open coniferous and deciduous forest, also forest edges, clearings, open hillsides, scrub and meadows, occasionally edges of cultivation. Usually in pairs or small family parties, but in larger numbers (100+) in winter, when found in weedy fields. Feeds on a variety of seeds.

DISTRIBUTION *C. a. ambigua*: south-central China, southeast Szechwan to northern Yunnan (Likiang range) south to Kunming and the Tengchung region (possibly east to Kweichow), and northern Burma; also northern Laos to northwest Tonkin, North Vietnam.

C. a. taylori: southeast Tibet (Pome and Kongbo districts).

MOVEMENTS Partially migratory. Breeding birds from higher altitudes move to lower levels within the range in winter; also a rare winter visitor to northwest Thailand (but in large flocks in some years). Vagrant to Hong Kong (flock of ten in December 1975).

MEASUREMENTS Wing of male 81; tarsus 11; bill 11.

REFERENCES King et al.(1975), Lekagul and Round (1991).

49 SISKIN *Carduelis spinus*   Plate 10
Palearctic

Fringilla spinus Linnaeus, 1758, Syst. Nat., ed. 10, p. 181, Europe; restricted to Sweden by Hartert, 1903, Vögel pal. Fauna, p. 71.

IDENTIFICATION Length 11–12 cm (4½ in). A   small finch with a distinctive sharply pointed bill, bright green plumage with darker streaks, bright yellow wingbars, greenish-yellow rump, and a wheezy call. Males are easily distinguished by black cap and chin and bright yellowish-green face, underparts and sides to tail. Females lack black cap and chin and are more streaked greyish-green, with yellow wingbars; juveniles are similar to adult females, but duller. **Confusion species:** Greenfinch (44) is much larger, with a bigger, more robust bill, and adults lack streaking or yellow wingbars. Serin (5) lacks sharply pointed bill, dark wing-coverts with contrasting bright yellow wingbars and yellow at sides of base of tail (and also lacks black cap of adult male). Citril Finch (8) lacks streaking and yellow at base of tail. Separated from Tibetan Siskin (9) at all ages by wedge of yellow at bases of flight feathers; female Tibetan Siskin lacks yellow panels at base of tail. For differences from the very similar but geographically separated Pine Siskin (50), see that species.

DESCRIPTION Sexes differ. **Adult male:** Forehead to hindcrown and upper lores black; upper nape green or greenish-yellow with some grey or black tips. Bright yellow supercilium begins above or just behind eye and continues behind earcoverts to sides of neck; thin dark eye-stripe; lower lores, cheeks and ear-coverts yellow, washed with green. Lower nape to mantle, back and scapulars rich or deep green, with blackish-brown feather centres on mantle, back and scapulars; rump bright yellow, becoming yellowish-green or greenish on uppertail-coverts. Tail is short, notched or forked at tip, and black, with rich or deep yellow edges to bases of all but central pair of feathers forming two prominent side panels. Median coverts are black, broadly tipped pale greenish-yellow, greater coverts black, edged and fairly broadly tipped pale green; alula and primary coverts black with fine greenish edges; flight feathers black or blackish, inner primaries and all secondaries yellow at base with yellow edges for about half their length; tertials black, fringed pale yellow or whitish. Chin black; throat and breast yellow, becoming tinged with green on sides of breast; upper belly yellow, flanks yellow or tinged with green; lower belly and flanks to undertail-coverts white or whitish; midflanks to undertail-coverts streaked blackish. Bill is thin and sharply pointed, upper mandible dark brown, brownish-horn or greyish-horn, lower mandible paler horn. Legs and feet dark brown. In winter, has some grey or greyish-yellow tips to crown, nape, sides of neck, ear-coverts, chin, throat, mantle and back; is generally much duller or more dull green than yellow, and wingbar on greater coverts is much less bright than in summer. **Adult female:** Forehead to nape grey-green, tinged buffish-brown, becoming slightly more greenish on nape, all streaked darker or brownish, finely on forehead and crown. Pale or dull yellowish-buff supercilium over eye and ear-coverts; lores dusky or ashy-grey; cheeks and ear-coverts yellow, washed greenish. Mantle, back and scapulars as nape, heavily streaked blackish or blackish-brown; rump greenish-yellow, boldly streaked with black; uppertail-coverts dull greenish-yellow or olive-green. Tail as male but very dark brown, with fine

yellow or pale yellowish edges to base of outer feathers. Median and greater coverts as male, but tips pale yellowish-green, creamy or whitish; flight feathers very similar to male, but with bases and edges to feathers very pale or dull yellow; upper two tertials are fringed creamy or white, lower fringed yellowish. Chin and throat to sides of neck off-white or dull yellowish; lower throat, breast and upper flanks tinged yellow, with broad blackish streaks on breast and flanks; lower breast, belly and undertail-coverts buffish-white or whitish. In winter, becomes greyer about head and upperparts, and yellow areas are more green-tinged or duller. **Juvenile:** Very similar to adult female, but has forehead, crown, nape, mantle, scapulars and back to uppertail-coverts buff-brown with dark brown streaks. Supercilium and sides of neck are dull whitish or pale buff, ear-coverts pale brown and dark-streaked. Wings and tail as adult female, but base of primaries often paler or whitish and tips to greater coverts warm buff, buffish-yellow or yellowish-white on outers when worn. Underparts dull greyish-buff or off-white; black spots on upper breast and throat become streaks on rest of underparts. First-winter plumage is assumed after post-juvenile moult from late August, but outer three to six greater coverts and all primaries, secondaries and tail feathers are retained from juvenile plumage: first-winter males resemble adult male, but are streaked more heavily on mantle and back and yellow at base of flight feathers is not so extensive; first-winter females closely resemble adult female, but retain buff-brown feathers on face, head and mantle.

VOICE The most typical and characteristic call is a ringing or tinny 'toolee' or 'tsuu-ee', also a dry 'tet' or 'tet-tet'; in flight, gives a trilling 'tirrillilit' or a variation of this, 'twillit', 'tittereee' etc.; birds feeding in trees utter a soft chirp or chipping twitter as a contact note; anxiety or alarm call is a sharp canary-like 'tsooeet'. The song is a jumbled mixture of jangling notes not dissimilar in style to Corn Bunting (*Emberiza calandra*), though softer and clearly finch-like, with many metallic twitters, trills and wheezy notes interspersed. Usually given from a high vantage point or in slow-winged bat-like display flight on prospective breeding territory; often sings in short bursts or subsong in late winter prior to return migration.

STATUS, HABITAT AND BEHAVIOUR Common or locally common. Usually breeds in conifers, chiefly spruce, but also feeds in alders (especially in winter), larch and birch; also known to roost in tall hedges. Found in virtually any habitat with suitable trees, especially heaths, commons, forest, weedy thickets also orchards and gardens. A social or gregarious bird, associating in small parties or mixing freely with other small finches, usually Common Redpolls (69), at a common source of food. An active or restless bird, constantly on the move and frequently uttering its plaintive and distinctive note, especially in its undulating and bounding flight. Usually keeps to trees where it feeds high up in conifers, hanging acrobatically tit-like upside-down while extracting seeds with its fine bill; not unknown to feed on the ground, especially on migration when main food is not available, and at such times readily takes seeds of plants such as thistles or dandelions. Also a regular visitor to gardens, both rural and suburban, to feed on peanuts (particularly during February to April, when building up fat reserves for migration). In addition to conifer, alder, birch and larch seeds, feeds on seeds and buds of many other deciduous trees, including eucalyptus and juniper berries; small amount of insects also taken, including small beetles. The young are reared on insects, predominantly aphids, for the first few days of life.

DISTRIBUTION   Monotypic.   Discontinuous through Europe to central CIS (USSR), with a separate population in eastern Asia. In Europe, from Ireland, Scotland and parts of England east through southern Scandinavia, Finland and Russia (north to the Kola Peninsula and the White Sea) to about 70°E, though isolated small populations breed to about 80°E in western Siberia and in the mountains east of Lake Baikal; in central Europe, continuously eastwards from France (Massif Central and the Vosges) to northern Holland, Denmark, Germany and eastern Europe north of 50°N; in the south, isolated populations in the Pyrenees, Sardinia, Switzerland, central and southern Italy, Yugoslavia, Hungary, Bulgaria and Romania, the Crimea, Cyprus, northern Turkey, the southern Caucasus and northern Iran to the southeastern shore of the Caspian. In eastern Asia, from northwest Amurland and Ussuriland to the southern coasts of the Sea of Okhotsk, Sakhalin Island and northern Japan (eastern Hokkaido and northern Honshu).

MOVEMENTS Sedentary and migratory. In the west of the range, those breeding in the northern regions move south and southwest to winter within and south of the breeding range to southern Spain, Balearic Islands, throughout France and the British Isles, Italy, the Balkans to Greece, Cyprus, Turkey, central Iran and southern Central Asia; also occurs irregularly or rarely in Iceland, Faroe Isles, Sicily (has bred), Malta, Lebanon, Israel, Jordan, Tunisia, Libya (Tripoli), northern Egypt, Iraq, southern Iran, United Arab Emirates, Bahrain and Kuwait. There are also at least 15 records in the USA, mostly from the coastal northeast or the Aleutians, and all are considered to relate to escapes from captivity (the species is not included on the 1983 *Check-list of North American birds*); attempts were made to introduce the species into Oregon and Ohio at the beginning of the 20th century. In the east of the range, moves south, southeast and southwest to winter in Mongolia, Korea, southern China (middle Yangtze valley to Kwangtung), Taiwan, Japan, Ryukyu and Bonin Islands; a vagrant to India (Himachal Pradesh, one record), Nepal (one record, April), southern Szechwan and Yunnan (January-February 1985), Hong Kong (two records, December-February) and the Philippines (two records, Calayan and Batan Islands, October and November). Post-breeding dispersal begins from mid-July, but longer-distance southward migration begins in mid-September (occasionally late August) and continues to early November; in spring, northward movement is from the end of March to early May. In years of food shortage, it occasionally irrupts in large numbers into the wintering range. Individuals do not necessarily winter in the same area in successive years: one individual wintered at two locations 3200 km apart in successive years.

MEASUREMENTS Wing of male 66−75, of female 64−74; tail 42−49; tarsus 12−14; bill (from skull) 7−10·5. Weight of male 11−14, of female 11−17.

REFERENCES McLaren *et al.* (1989), Newton (1973), Witherby *et al.* (1938−41).

50 PINE SISKIN *Carduelis pinus*   Plate 13

North and Middle America

Fringilla pinus Wilson, 1810, Amer. Ornith., 2, p. 133, Bush Hill, Nr Philadelphia, Pennsylvania.

IDENTIFICATION Length 11−13 cm (4¼−5 in). A small streaky-brown finch of North America, a grey-brown equivalent of Siskin (49). It has a thin or finely pointed bill, and dark wings and tail with variable amount of yellow in wing and at base of tail. It also has a distinctive single or double call note. Usually associated with conifers or mixed woods. **Confusion species:** Common Redpoll (69) has red forehead to forecrown, and lacks yellow in wings and tail and bold streaking on underparts. Female Purple Finch (88), Cassin's Finch (89) and House Finch (90) have larger and more stubby bills, only a small notch in tail, and female Purple Finch has a pronounced broad white supercilium. All the above lack yellow or buffish-yellow in wing and at base of tail. Juvenile Pine Siskins have much less yellow at base of flight feathers and lack greyish head and face of same-aged Black-capped Siskins (51). For differences from very similar female Siskin (49), see Geographical Variation below.

DESCRIPTION Sexes differ. **Adult male:** Forehead to nape pale buffish-brown, finely dark-streaked and tinged with grey on nape. Ill-defined or pale buff-brown supercilium over eye and ear-coverts underlined by an indistinct eye-stripe; cheeks and ear-coverts buff or buffish-brown, finely dark-streaked. Mantle, back and scapulars to rump pale greyish earth-brown (some show a greenish tinge: see below), broadly streaked darker; uppertail-coverts the same or darker brown, with pale brown or yellowish-brown tips.

Tail is notched at tip, dark or blackish-brown, with bases to outer feathers yellow or pale yellow and increasing outwards (variable in extent individually and may not be obvious). Median coverts dark brown or blackish, tipped light buffish or warm buffish-brown, greaters similar with inners buff or paler on edges and tips; alula and primary coverts blackish; flight feathers black or blackish-brown, finely edged pale buff or buffish-yellow with a small patch of yellow at base of outer primaries (this and the amount of pale or buff on greaters is variable); tertials the same, edged pale buff or whitish. Chin, throat and sides of neck pale buff or whitish, slightly streaked or darker-spotted, becoming predominantly streaked on rest of underparts (some are more streaked than others). Bill is thin and sharply pointed, pale or light brown to greyish with a dark tip. Legs and feet dark brown or blackish. In winter, the body plumage, especially upperparts, is slightly warmer brown, and pale tips are slightly broader. **Adult female:** Very similar to male, but also tends to have paler or whiter tips to median and greater coverts, and on average has a smaller pale or yellow area at base of second-aries. **Juvenile:** Very similar to adult, but softer or more loosely feathered (fluffy) in appearance, lightly or thinly streaked darker above and edged with pale buff; median and greater coverts are also tipped whitish; underparts tinged buff and thinly dark-streaked, especially on breast.

GEOGRAPHICAL VARIATION Birds of race *macroptera* are not so prominently streaked above or below, and streaks on breast and belly are paler brown and less distinctly defined; males also show much brighter or deeper yellow at base of flight feathers and sides of base of tail. Both sexes of *perplexus* are distinctively paler or greyer than either of the other races and only faintly or lightly streaked on underparts, appearing more washed with grey. In the south of the range, *perplexus* hybridises with Black-capped Siskin. A small number of males of nominate race appear as 'green morphs' and show a considerable or noticeable tinge of green on the upperparts, brighter or more extensively yellow wing and tail patches, and little or no streaking on underparts. As such, these birds closely resemble female Siskins and are best separated by: (a) the yellow in the wing is too bright for Siskin; (b) female Siskin has two pale yellow wingbars (on tips of coverts), while Pine Siskin has a greater extent of yellow at base of flight feathers; (c) female Siskin invariably has broad or prominent dark brown streaks on flanks, whereas 'green-morph' birds examined to date lack these; (d) the yellow patches at sides of tail are less intense and not so extensive on Siskin; (e) the undertail-coverts of 'green-morph' Pine Siskins are yellow or yellow-ish, but pale buff or off-white on Siskin. Absence of yellow on an otherwise 'green-morph' bird, however, does not necessarily indicate a female Siskin.

VOICE Call is a loud 'clee-ip' or 'chlee-it', a nasal rising 'sweeeet' or 'zwee-e-e-e-e-t', also a short chatter or twittering 'tit' or 'twit-it-tit' similar to Common Redpoll (69). The song is a long or rambling jumble of nasal and chattering notes with rising, trilling 'zzzhreeee'.

STATUS, HABITAT AND BEHAVIOUR Erratically or irregularly common or locally common, nesting in abundance in one year and none at all the next. Inhabits conifers (mainly spruce), mixed woods and forest, alder thickets, deciduous or ornamental trees, and feeds in shrubs in some suburban areas. Very social and colonial, and found in flocks of various size throughout the year, occasionally up to 1,000 together in winter; also mixes freely with other small finches, and commonly associates with post-breeding and winter flocks of American Goldfinches (65). Distinctive flight pattern of flocks: when disturbed, birds bunch together then disperse in strong undulating and fairly swift flight. Feeds on a variety of seeds or buds, mostly of spruce, hemlock, white cedar, birch and alder, which are taken in the trees; also on a variety of plant seeds taken on the ground and occasionally small insects. Also takes salt from the surface of roads in parts of the United States as do several other finch species.

DISTRIBUTION *C. p. pinus*: southern Alaska, through Canada south to central Ontario, central Quebec and east to Newfoundland and Nova Scotia, south in USA to northern New England in the east and east of the Rockies to southern California, southern Arizona, southern New Mexico and southwest Texas.

C. p. macroptera: Baja California to the central volcanic belt of central Mexico to western Veracruz.

C. p. perplexus: mountains of northern Chiapas, Mexico and Guatemala. Hybridises extensively with Black-capped Siskin.

MOVEMENTS Partial migrant. Birds from northern parts of the breeding range in Alaska and northern Canada move south to winter throughout the southern breeding range and most of the United States to Baja California and most of northern Mexico, south to northwest Durango and Tamaulipas, and along the Gulf coast east to southern Florida. Movements are largely dependent on food availability; extremely mobile and highly nomadic in autumn and winter. Birds of the two southern races are largely sedentary but some move to lower altitudes in winter, even reaching the coast in Sonora, Mexico. Has also occurred irregularly on the Pribilof Islands, Unimai in the Aleutians and several other islands in the Bering Sea; accidental or vagrant to north Manitoba, southern Baja California and Bermuda.

MEASUREMENTS Wing of male 68−79, of female 66−76; tail 44·5−48; tarsus 13·5−15; bill (exposed culmen) 9·5−11.

REFERENCES Farrand et al. (1985), Godfrey (1979), McLaren et al. (1989), Peterson (1980).

51 BLACK-CAPPED SISKIN (Guatemalan Siskin) *Carduelis atriceps*
Plate 15

Middle America

Chrysomitris atriceps Salvin, 1863, Proc. Zool. Soc. London, p. 190, near Quetzaltenango, 8000 ft, Guatemala.

IDENTIFICATION Length 11–13 cm (4½–5 in). A small, virtually all-green finch with restricted distribution in mountains in southern Mexico and Guatemala. Males have a black cap but are otherwise dark olive-green with pale yellow flashes in wings and at base of tail. Females are similar, but generally duller above and paler on underparts. Virtually unique in adult plumage: all other siskins either have more black on head and breast or are predominantly yellow. For differences from same-aged immatures of Pine Siskin (50), see that species.

DESCRIPTION Sexes differ. **Adult male:** Forehead and upper lores to crown and hindcrown black, rest of face dark greenish-olive. Nape, mantle, back and scapulars uniform green or deep green, becoming slightly paler green on lower back and rump; uppertail-coverts dull olive-green. Tail is forked at tip, black or blackish, feathers edged bright yellowish-green, and bases to all but central feathers bright yellow. Median and greater coverts are blackish, tipped bright olive-green (greaters can be tipped yellowish-green); alula and primary coverts black; flight feathers also black, edged greenish-yellow (broadest towards tips of secondaries), with base of outer secondaries and inner primaries bright yellow; tertials black or blackish, edged olive-green and tipped whitish-buff. Chin and throat blackish, becoming green on breast; belly and undertail-coverts yellow. Bill thin and sharply pointed (typical siskin shape), and pale flesh-pink. Legs and feet greyish or dark horn-brown. In winter, the plumage is tinged or washed light greyish. **Adult female:** Similar to adult male, but head and upperparts much duller, with sooty

or dusky brown cap to head; face and nape pale greyish-green, becoming deeper olive-green on mantle, back and scapulars, which are noticeably dark-streaked; rump pale green, uppertail-coverts greenish-olive. Pale or dull green on chin, throat, breast and flanks, faintly streaked on throat and breast; belly and undertail-coverts paler or whiter. **Juvenile:** As adult female, but generally more buffish-brown, tinged green, with upperparts streaked darker, forehead to crown greyish-green; median and greater coverts have yellowish tips, and outer secondaries and inner primaries have bright yellow bases. Chin and throat pale buff, becoming paler or yellowish-buff and indistinctly streaked with dark brown on sides of neck and upper breast.

VOICE Call is a rising buzzing trill 'zree-ee-ee'. Song is a rambling series of buzzes and trills, very similar to Pine Siskin.

STATUS, HABITAT AND BEHAVIOUR Scarce or uncommon; very little known. Occurs at high altitude, between 2350 m and 3050 m, in oak and alder forest, also in conifer woods and in adjacent fields, pastures and edges of cultivation. Usually found in pairs or small flocks; hybridises widely with Pine Siskin (race *perplexus*) in overlap areas. Feeds on the ground or in treetops, on a variety of tree and plant seeds (particularly of genus *Salvia*).

DISTRIBUTION Monotypic. Highlands of Chiapas, southeast Mexico south to the western highlands of Guatemala.

MOVEMENTS None known.

MEASUREMENTS Wing 71–72.

REFERENCE Land (1970).

---

52 ANDEAN SISKIN *Carduelis spinescens*
Plate 16
South America

Chrysomitris spinescens Bonaparte, 1851?, Consp. Avium (1850), p. 517, Santa Fé de Bogota, Colombia.

IDENTIFICATION Length 9·5–10 cm (c4 in). A small green-and-yellow finch from northern South America, with deep green upperparts and black-and-yellow wings and tail; male has a distinctive black cap. Female lacks cap and is generally duller olive, and has white belly to undertail-coverts. **Confusion species:** Female differs from female Yellow-bellied Siskin (61) in being paler and brighter, also lacks olive throat and yellow undertail-coverts. Female Hooded (56) is also very similar,

but female Andean has white ventral region to undertail-coverts, olive or olive-green rump and uppertail-coverts (*nigricauda* and *capitanea* only), and face is tinged with green, not grey.

DESCRIPTION Sexes differ. **Adult male:** Forehead and crown to centre of upper nape black, forming a cap; face uniform dull or dingy green, slightly paler or yellowish on cheeks. Lower nape, hindneck and sides of neck to mantle, back and scapulars deep green (often finely dark-spotted);

♂

rump brighter or paler yellow, contrasting with duller greenish-yellow uppertail-coverts. Tail is black, with yellow at base of all but central pair of feathers and on edges of all outer feathers, and is notched at tip. Median coverts are black, broadly edged and tipped green, greaters also black but tipped bright greenish-yellow; alula and primary coverts black; flight feathers black, with inner primaries and secondaries bright yellow at base (forming prominent wingbar in flight), inner primaries and outer secondaries also broadly edged bright yellow; edges of tertials white or whitish-yellow at tips. Chin to breast and belly greenish-yellow, becoming paler or duller yellow on sides of breast and upper flanks; undertail-coverts pale yellow. Bill is thin and pointed, fairly typical siskin shape, brown or brownish-horn with a paler base to lower mandible. Legs and feet brown or dark brown. **Adult female:** Very similar to adult male, but duller and lacks black cap (but see below). Face greenish-grey, forehead to crown and nape is uniform (some have forehead and lores slightly darker) with dull green or olive-green mantle, back and scapulars (or slightly darker-mottled with dark centres and tips to feathers); lower back and rump greenish-yellow or pale yellow. Wings and tail as adult male, but duller and with less extensive areas of yellow to bases of flight feathers. Underparts as male or paler, greenish-grey, but belly, vent and undertail-coverts white or yellow-tinged. Note: Several females collected (and sexed on dissection) from the western slope of the eastern Andes in Carchi, Ecuador, were in full adult male plumage (Ridgely pers. comm.). **Juvenile:** A paler or more buffish version of female, with uniform buff or sandy-buff on head, face and upperparts with the exception of paler yellow rump. Tail is dark or blackish-brown, with pale yellow panels at sides. Wings as adult, but tips to medians and inner great-

ers brown or buffish-yellow. Chin and throat to breast and flanks buffish or sandy-buff, becoming paler or more yellowish on belly and undertail-coverts.

GEOGRAPHICAL VARIATION Male *nigricauda* is generally duller or darker green on upperparts, including rump, and underparts are dull green lacking any tinge of yellow; the tail is all-black, and the wings lack greenish-yellow tips to median and greater coverts but retain bright yellow bases to inner primaries and secondaries. Females are similar, but have the cap dusky and rather ill-defined. Race *capitanea* is similar to *nigricauda*, but the upperparts are generally paler olive without any of the darker olive centres to feathers; it has yellow at sides of base of tail and on tips to median and greater coverts; the undertail-coverts are unstreaked. Females are similar to nominate but paler or greyer.

VOICE Call is a typical Goldfinch-like 'tswee' or similar variation, frequently given in flight. The song is a lively rambling series of Goldfinch-like notes, high-pitched and interspersed with rolling trills.

STATUS, HABITAT AND BEHAVIOUR Common or locally common. Occurs in subtropical and paramo zones of the northern Andes, mostly between 1800 m and 3700 m (occasionally down to 1500 m in Colombia); in scrub or low bushes in open cloud or elfin forest or edges of forest, also open hillsides with scattered trees or bushes, occasionally to edges of cultivation. Usually found in pairs or small flocks of up to 20, occasionally mixed with other finches; in northern Ecuador occurs in mixed flocks with Hooded Siskins. Often perches high in tops of trees, but generally keeps low or feeds on the ground. Feeds on a variety of plant seeds and is particularly fond of *Espletia* seeds and flowers.

DISTRIBUTION *C. s. spinescens:* coastal mountains of northeast Aragua (Colonia Tovar), northern Venezuela, the Andes of western Venezuela (Merida and Tachira) through the Perija Mountains and the eastern Andes in Colombia south to Valle (and the eastern slope of the western Andes), Cauca, Putumayo, Nariño and northern Ecuador (Carchi south to Pichinca).

C. s. capitanea: Santa Marta Mountains, northern Colombia.

C. s. nigricauda: northern, central and western Andes (Antioquia, Paramillo Mountains) south to Caldas and possibly northern Tolima, Colombia.

MOVEMENTS Not well understood, but erratic in occurrence and wanders widely throughout the range.

MEASUREMENTS Wing 64; bill 11.

Carduelis yarrellii Audubon, 1839, Syn. Birds N. Amer., p. 117, 'Upper California' [in error]; Bahia, Brazil, designated by Todd, 1926, Ann. Carnegie Mus., 17, p. 32.

IDENTIFICATION Length 10 cm (4 in). A small yellow finch from northern Brazil, very similar to Andean Siskin (52) (but ranges widely separated), the male having a black cap but with bright yellow face, underparts and rump and olive-green mantle and back; the female lacks black cap and has an olive-yellow crown and mantle. Both sexes show bright yellow wingbars and bases to flight feathers.
Confusion species: The only possible confusion likely to arise is with Andean Siskin, which, as its name implies, is a bird of very different range and habitat. Female Yellow-bellied Siskin (61) is duller or olive, tinged with grey, has paler yellow on face and underparts and centre of belly and undertail-coverts are white.
DESCRIPTION Sexes differ. **Adult male:** Upper lores and forehead to crown and upper nape black; lower nape and hindneck green; face and sides of neck bright yellow. Mantle, back and scapulars deep green or olive-green (some show dark or blackish feather bases), becoming bright yellow on lower back, rump and uppertail-coverts; longest uppertail-coverts dark green, edged and tipped paler. Tail is black, with broad yellow outer edges to all outer feathers. Median coverts olive with black centres, greaters black and broadly tipped yellow; alula and primary coverts black; flight feathers black with very bright yellow bases to all feathers forming a broad wingbar; tertials black with pale greenish-yellow edges towards tips, which can be white or whitish-buff. Underparts bright yellow, tinged with green on sides of breast and flanks. Bill short and pointed, dark brown or dark horn. Legs and feet brown or dark brown.
Adult female: Slightly different from male. Face bright yellow; forehead to crown, nape, mantle, back and scapulars dull-green or olive-green; rump and uppertail-coverts paler, greenish-yellow or

brighter pale yellow. Tail as male. Median coverts olive or dark olive; greaters blackish, tipped greenish or pale yellow; alula and primary coverts black, as are flight feathers, which have dull yellow (duller than male) at base; primaries finely edged yellow; tertials blackish, edged whitish. Underparts bright yellow, brightest on centre of breast and belly or with a greenish wash on sides of throat, breast and flanks. **Juvenile:** Very similar to adult female but much duller, with yellow of plumage replaced by pale buff-brown, and is lightly or thinly streaked above and below.
VOICE Undescribed.
STATUS, HABITAT AND BEHAVIOUR Rare or restricted and very little known; no population estimates but apparently locally common in Pernambuco and Alagoas. Occurs on edges of lowland humid forest, secondary-growth woodland and edges of cultivation and coffee plantations of northeastern Brazil up to about 500 m, but little current information exists on its present status, behaviour, voice, or breeding behaviour. The only food items known to be taken (from one specimen collected) are small fruits; doubtless it also takes small seeds. The species is considered to be at risk: it is still illegally hunted and widely trapped throughout its small, poorly documented and fragmentary range, and up to 800 appear every week in the bird markets of Brazil despite its being a protected species.
DISTRIBUTION Monotypic. Northern Brazil (Ceara, Paraiba, Pernambuco and Alagoas to northern Bahia); records from separate localities in northern Venezuela are considered to relate to escapes from captivity.
MEASUREMENTS Wing 68; tarsus 9; bill 9.
REFERENCES Collar *et al.* (1992), Ridgely and Tudor (1989).

Carduelis cucullata Swainson, 1820, Zool. Illus., pl. 7, Spanish Main; Cumana, Venezuela, designated by Todd, 1926, Ann. Carnegie Mus., 17, p. 43.

IDENTIFICATION Length 10 cm (4in). Virtually unique plumage for a small finch. Male has black head, chin and throat, tips of flight feathers and tail, a whitish belly and undertail-coverts, and the rest of the plumage a deep or rich red. Female and immature are grey or greyish-brown on head and upperparts (except for red rump and uppertail-coverts); breast, tips to wing-coverts and base of

flight feathers pale red or orange-red. Unlikely to be confused with any other species.
DESCRIPTION Sexes differ. **Adult male:** Entire head, face, sides of upper neck, chin and throat jet-black. Hindneck, mantle, back and scapulars rich or deep scarlet (with black feather bases); lower back and rump paler or brighter pinkish-vermilion, and uppertail-coverts deep vermilion.

Tail is black, edged pale vermilion at base (probably not visible in the field). Median coverts are black, tipped deep or dark vermilion, and greaters black, broadly tipped with vermilion; alula and primary coverts black; flight feathers black with vermilion bases, paler at bases of outer primaries; tertials black, edged pale pink or pinkish, becoming white at tip. Sides of lower neck, breast, flanks and undertail-coverts rich vermilion; belly and vent white or whitish tinged with pink. Bill is slightly larger or deeper than that of typical siskins, with a slight curving ridge to upper mandible, pointed, and is dark or greyish-horn on upper mandible and paler on lower. Legs and feet brown or dark brown.

Adult female: Forehead, crown and nape plain grey or very slightly dark-streaked; face and sides of neck plain pale grey, slightly paler on lores. Mantle, back and scapulars pale grey, slightly dark-streaked, and tinged reddish-pink on back; rump and uppertail-coverts vermilion-red, tips of longest coverts grey. Tail is blackish-brown, finely edged with red at base. Wings as male, but median coverts blackish and greaters more extensively black, with tips paler orange-red; flight feathers blackish-brown with pale orange-red bases; tertials similar, with white or whitish-buff tips. Chin and throat whitish, or speckled with red on lower throat; breast and flanks (occasionally to upper belly) washed heavily with orange-red; lower breast and belly to undertail-coverts white or whitish. **Juvenile:** Young females resemble adult female but are paler or greyer, with only pale tinges or tips of red or orange-red in the plumage. Young males are similar to adult male but red or vermilion areas are brown, with adult plumage assumed with age and gradual abrasion of brown feather tips; the tips of wing-coverts are yellowish or buffish, and flight feathers black with pale or creamy-yellow bases; the underparts are deep ochre-brown, but black feathers of throat and vermilion of breast and belly soon begin to show through.

VOICE Call is a high-pitched twitter and a sharp distinctive 'chi-tit' or 'chut-chut', recalling Indian Silverbill (218). The song is a long series of repeated Goldfinch-like phrases broken with twitters and trills.

STATUS, HABITAT AND BEHAVIOUR An extremely rare species following relentless and excessive persecution by bird-trappers to satisfy the demands of aviculture and the cagebird trade. Included in the *ICBP World Check-list of Threatened Birds* (Collar and Andrew 1988). The species has a history of exploitation by man owing to its popularity as a cagebird: it hybridises with (already domesticated) canaries to form 'red-factor' variants (mules). In 1981 the world population (in the wild) was estimated at 600–800 birds. Present opinions, however, are divided and uncertain as to the exact number remaining in the wild; several recent estimates disagree on the population within northern Venezuela, which may be as high as 6,000 birds. The trapping continues, and considerable numbers are still being taken (illegally) from the wild. In 1975 almost 3,000 were known to have been caught, but by 1982 (the year after it was estimated that only up to 800 remained) this figure had dropped to just over 1,000. The true population will probably never be known until it can be counted in tens, shortly before its ultimate and inevitable extinction in the wild. The species inhabits open country or edges of evergreen forest, dry scrub or grassy areas with occasional trees, bushes or shrubs, between 280 m and 1300 m. Following the breeding season, family parties used to band together and form large flocks (which were easily lured to baited areas and taken by trappers), but in recent years it has been seen only alone or in pairs. Feeds on a wide variety of seeds, mostly of trees or shrubs, also on seeds of grasses and flower-heads; birds in Trinidad were also known to take the fruits of some cacti.

DISTRIBUTION Monotypic. Now very reduced in range and restricted to fragments of the upper tropical zone of the northern Cordillera in extreme northeast Colombia and northern Venezuela between 300 m and 1200 m (one record from 1700 m), and also on the islands of Gasparee and Monos. Introduced (or a small population became established from escaped cagebirds) on Trinidad, where last seen in the wild in 1960; similarly, a few records from Cuba also suggest escapes from captivity. It was also introduced into Puerto Rico in the 1920s or 1930s, but is extremely rare in the dry hills of the south of the island; the last documented sighting was in 1982.

MOVEMENTS Undertakes daily movements away from the breeding and roosting areas to feed. Otherwise semi-nomadic or a partial migrant with non-breeding-season dispersal away from breeding areas, usually roaming in search of food. It has occurred up to 50 km from its nearest known breeding area. On the offshore island of Monos it is apparently common at times, suggesting seasonal influxes from the mainland.

REFERENCES Collar and Andrew (1988), Collar et al. (1992).

55 THICK-BILLED SISKIN *Carduelis crassirostris*   Plate 14

South America

Chrysomitris crassirostris Landbeck, 1877, Zool. Garten, 18, p. 254, near passes of Uspallata and Portillo, high cordillera of Mendoza, Argentina.

IDENTIFICATION Length 13·5–14·5 cm (5¼–5½ in). An obvious or noticeably thick- or large-billed finch from the high Andes. It has a black or grey head, olive or greyish-olive mantle and back, pale greenish-yellow rump, black wings and tail with bright yellow flashes at bases; underparts of male yellow or tinged with green, and whitish on centre of belly, underparts of female pale yellow, becoming white. The thick bill of the nominate race is diagnostic (but not always easy to see in the field). **Confusion species:** Extremely similar to smaller (less plump) and smaller-billed male Hooded (56) and Olivaceous (59) Siskins, both of which, however, have much finer, more siskin-like bills and lack any white from centre of belly to vent. Also similar to Yellow-rumped Siskin (63), which has more extensive amounts of black on breast and upperparts and much finer or typical siskin-like bill. Juveniles probably not always safely separated in the field on their own.

DESCRIPTION Sexes differ. **Adult male:** Entire head to nape, chin and throat black; sides of neck bright yellow. Hindneck, mantle, back and scapulars olive-green, indistinctly streaked with blackish feather centres; rump and uppertail-coverts greenish-yellow, becoming yellower on uppertail-coverts. Tail is notched at tip, black, with deep yellow bases to all outer feathers forming side panels. Median coverts are blackish-brown with dull yellow or yellowish-green tips, greaters blackish-brown with fine dull yellow tips (absent in worn plumage); alula and primary coverts black; flight feathers black, with basal half of primaries yellow, this extending to bases of secondaries, distal edges of secondaries finely fringed pale buff or light olive; tertials black, with pale buff outer edges and tips. Lower throat, breast (centre of upper breast can be black, as throat) and upper flanks bright yellow, tinged greenish on sides of breast and upper flanks; belly, vent and undertail-coverts white. Bill is thick and deep at base but comes sharply to a point, and is black with brown or brownish-horn on lower mandible. Legs and feet dark grey or blackish. **Adult female:** Much duller than adult male, with grey or dark grey head to nape and chin, dull or greyish-olive upperparts with some paler buff flecking, except for olive-yellow wash on rump; tail has less extensive yellow at sides of base. Wings as adult male, except for yellowish-buff tips (in fresh plumage) to median and greater coverts and less extensive yellow at base of flight feathers. Except for dark or blackish chin and throat, the underparts are dull or dingy yellow with some dark streaks on flanks, becoming dull white or off-white from belly. Bill horn-brown or greyish, with a paler tip and base to lower mandible. Legs and feet dark brown. **Juvenile:** Very similar to adult female, but with buffish-brown on upperparts and underparts, except for pale yellow undertail-coverts.

GEOGRAPHICAL VARIATION Birds of race

amadoni are generally much duller olive and have slightly smaller bills. Male's black head usually lacks any gloss, yellow on underparts is much duller or tinged with green, and yellow bases to flight feathers are restricted to bases of inner primaries and secondaries; the rump is olive and uppertail-coverts have grey tips, while tail is all dull or dark brown and lacks bright yellow panels at sides. Female as nominate, but has no contrast on rump and uppertail-coverts except for tinge of green at base of tail (invisible in the field); generally greyish-white below, and has dusky brown streaks on lower flanks and undertail-coverts.

VOICE Call is a hoarse and drawn-out 'wheeep', also a coarse 'chler-ee'. Song a typical siskin-like twitter but lower-pitched and slightly faster than in other siskins, often given in concert with others.

STATUS, HABITAT AND BEHAVIOUR Rare to locally common; infrequently recorded. Occurs in high Andean steppe country between 3000 m and 4800 m in *Polylepis* shrubs and woodland, also brush-covered slopes and hillsides. Usually found in pairs, small family groups or flocks of up to 30, occasionally in company with Black (62) and Hooded Siskins. Feeds actively and acrobatically, often hanging upside-down in bushes or in trees, almost exclusively on buds, shoots and seeds of *Polylepis* trees.

DISTRIBUTION *C. c. crassirostris*: Andes of western Bolivia (Potosi and Cochabamba), Chile (Aconcagua, Santiago and Colchagua) to western Argentina (Jujuy, Salta, Catamarca, La Rioja and Mendoza).

C. c. amadoni: discontinuously through the Andes of west and south Peru from Ayacucho and Apurimac to northwest Oruro, west Bolivia; may also be more widely distributed through northern Chile and western Bolivia (first record for Cochabamba: August 1988). Also, an unnamed subspecies in northern Peru (Ancash, Pasco, Lima and Ayacucho); intergrades in the south (Ayacucho) with *amadoni*.

MOVEMENTS Sedentary and partially migratory, an austral migrant. Movements not well known, but southern birds of nominate race move north to winter within the range; otherwise appears to be nomadic outside breeding season, but (possibly only immatures) may well be an altitudinal migrant to lower elevations.

MEASUREMENTS Wing of male 76–80, of female 74–82; tail of male 48–52, of female 46–51; bill 12. Wing of male *amadoni* 79–83, of female 81–82; tail of male 49–53, of female 52–54. Weight 19.

REFERENCE Fjeldså and Krabbe (1990), George (1964), Ridgely and Tudor (1989).

56 HOODED SISKIN *Carduelis magellanica*   **Plate 14**
South America

Fringilla magellanica Vieillot, 1805, Ois. Chant., pl. 30, Southern America and vicinity of Straits of Magellan [error]; Buenos Aires, Argentina, designated by Todd, 1926, Ann. Carnegie Mus., 17, p. 61.

IDENTIFICATION Length 11–12 cm (4¼–4¾ in); *urubambensis* and *tucumana* 14 cm (5½ in). A smaller (and smaller-billed) version of Thick-billed Siskin (55), widely distributed over large areas of South America. Males have all-black heads, black extending to centre of breast, greenish-olive upperparts, bright yellow rump, black wings and tail with yellow wingbars, and yellow bases to flight feathers and sides of tail; underparts yellow, but tinged light orange-buff or slightly greenish. Females are less well marked, with green, olive-green or greyish-green on head, and have less yellow in wings; underparts vary among races from dingy yellow to pale greyish-white. **Confusion species:** The very similar but larger Thick-billed Siskin has a very distinctive large bill, and a very restricted range and habitat preference. Olivaceous Siskin (59) is very similar to race *capitalis*, but is smaller and has differing habitat preference and range, being mainly a subtropical species (but hybridises with Hooded where ranges meet). In small area of overlap similar to Andean Siskin (52), but Hooded (race *capitalis*) separable by all-black head of males and dull greyish or white (not yellow) underparts of females.

DESCRIPTION Sexes differ. **Adult male:** Entire head to nape, most of sides of neck, chin, throat and, on some, centre of breast or upper breast black (but amount of black on cheeks, chin and throat is variable); thin yellow collar extends up sides of neck and across hindneck. Mantle, back and scapulars olive-green with faint or indistinct dark feather centres (but in worn plumage shows quite heavy dark streaks); rump bright yellow, uppertail-coverts olive-green. Tail is black with pale yellow base. Median coverts black with pale olive-green tips, greaters also black, tipped with pale or bright yellow; alula and primary coverts black; flight feathers black or blackish-brown, with bases bright yellow and forming a broad wingbar;

tertials black or blackish-brown, edged bright yellow, becoming whiter towards tip. Underwing-coverts also bright yellow. Sides of neck and breast to undertail-coverts bright yellow; some have tinges of warm orange on sides of breast or are tinged with green or greenish on flanks and belly. Bill thin, pointed, and almost entirely black. Legs and feet dark grey or blackish. **Adult female:** Forehead, sides of face and neck to nape, mantle, back and scapulars dull or pale olive-green, tinged grey; rump yellow or tinged pale green, becoming plain green on uppertail-coverts. Tail is blackish, with yellow bases to all feathers (but some usually concealed below uppertail-coverts). Median and greater coverts black or blackish, variably tipped buff, pale yellow or pale greenish-yellow; flight feathers as male, but yellow less extensive and secondaries finely edged pale yellow (whitish or whitish-buff when worn). Chin pale greyish; throat and breast pale yellow, greenish or greenish-yellow, becoming whiter on belly and undertail-coverts. Bill grey. Legs and feet dark brown. **Juvenile:** Very similar to adult female, but head and upperparts light grey or buffish-olive with fine dark streaks on crown, nape, mantle and back; rump and uppertail-coverts pale olive-green, tips of longest coverts greyish. Tips of median coverts dull yellow, tips of greaters bright yellow, bases of flight feathers bright yellow; tips of tertials whitish on outer web. Chin and throat as face but can be greenish or yellow, rest of underparts as adult female or washed with grey; undertail-coverts tinged with yellow.

GEOGRAPHICAL VARIATION There is considerable variation in the amount or intensity of olive or yellow in the upperparts and the degree to which dark or dusky centres to feathers are visible in the field. Apart from males in full breeding plumage, very few birds are racially separable in the field (except by geographic location) owing to the variability of the plumage. Males of race *capitalis* have black on head extending only to chin and throat, are darker olive above, with rump more uniform with upperparts, have white tips to flight feathers and obvious yellow bases to all tail feathers, and are deeper yellow or more golden-yellow on underparts; females are also generally yellow above, with underparts pale grey with only a light olive or yellowish wash on throat to breast (on some, belly and undertail-coverts are white). Birds of race *paula* are similar, but males have mantle and back less streaked or mottled darker, rump is yellow, and the yellow in wings and tail is more extensive; females are greyer above, with a yellow rump, and both sexes have greenish-yellow underparts. Race *peruana* is similar to *paula*, but males are more green on upperparts and rump is duller yellow; females are more olive than grey on upperparts. Race *urubambensis* is similar to *peruana* but larger; females are variable and can also resemble nominate, with chin to belly pale grey to greenish, tinged with pale yellow or white on vent and undertail-coverts. Males of race *boliviana* have black of throat (usually) extending well onto breast and sides of breast, mantle and back are prominently streaked with black, uppertail-coverts are blackish, and tail has broad yellow edges. Male *tucumana* has black on chin and throat only, paler yellow underparts and white flanks. Note: Hybridises with Olivaceous Siskin where ranges overlap in eastern Peru and apparently widely with Yellow-rumped Siskin (63) in southern Peru, where hybrids can usually be separated by yellow patch on sides of neck.

VOICE Call is a long trilling 'trrrrrr' or a repeated 'djey, djey'. Song is a variety of short twittering 'tseet-tseet', 'tseet-weet' or 'tseet-weet-a-weeta' notes with frequently repeated phrases, uttered with speed either from a perch or in flight; usually sings constantly or with pauses, males often singing in concert.

STATUS, HABITAT AND BEHAVIOUR Common or locally common. Found in a range of habitats from coastal lowlands, temperate, tropical or subtropical zones up to 5000 m, from woodland or savanna with small woods, poplar groves, palm plantations, swamp woods, edges of cultivation, bush or scrub to parks and large gardens in towns. Usually found in pairs or small parties, but in non-breeding season in larger gatherings or flocks often with other siskins (including Thick-billed). Not shy, but restless and quick in actions, and has a rapid undulating flight. Feeds in trees and bushes and on the ground on a variety of seeds (including thistles), buds and leaves (including lettuces) and occasionally insects.

DISTRIBUTION *C. m. magellanica*: Uruguay and eastern Argentina.
  C. m. icterica: southeast Para and Piaui, central Brazil, to eastern and southern Paraguay.
  C. m. longirostris: Apure and Bolivar, southeast Venezuela, Guyana and Roraima, northwest Brazil.
  C. m. alleni: southeast Bolivia, Paraguay, northeast Argentina.
  C. m. sanctaecrucis: eastern and central Bolivia.
  C. m. tucumana: Jujuy to Mendoza, northwest Argentina.
  C. m. boliviana: highlands of central and southern Bolivia.
  C. m. urubambensis: Cuzco, southern Peru, to Atacama, northern Chile.
  C. m. peruana: Huanuco to Ayacucho and Cuzco, central Peru.
  C. m. paula: southern Ecuador, along western Andes to Arequipa, southern Peru.
  C. m. capitalis: central and southern Colombia, through Ecuador to northwest Peru.

MOVEMENTS In some areas of the range erratic in its appearances. Some wander in the non-breeding season, birds of race *tucumana* occuring east to Buenos Aires in winter.

MEASUREMENTS Wing of male *magellanica* 70–74, of female 68–72; bill 9. Wing of male *icterica* 66–71, of female 65–72. Wing of male *urubambensis* 67–78, of female 67–72. Wing of *longirostris* 60–64, of female 58–61. Wing of male *paula* 60–62, of female 61–66·5. Wing of male *capitalis* 61–68, of female 62–66. Wing of male *peruana* 65·5–73, of female 68–72. Wing of male *tucumana* 70–76, of female 60–69.

REFERENCES Fjeldså and Krabbe (1990), Koepcke (1964), Sclater and Hudson (1888).

57 ANTILLEAN SISKIN *Carduelis dominicensis*   Plate 16
Caribbean

Chrysomitris dominicensis Bryant, 1868, Proc. Boston Soc. Nat. Hist., 11 (1866), p. 93, Port au Prince, Haiti.

IDENTIFICATION Length 11–12 cm (4½ in). An island endemic, unlikely to be confused with any other species and the only siskin found in the Caribbean. The male is predominantly black-headed and yellow, and the female is olive tinged, with brown and white above, streaked darker below; both have a pale brown or straw-coloured bill.

DESCRIPTION Sexes differ. **Adult male:** Forehead to upper nape, sides of head to chin and upper throat black. Nape, hindneck, mantle, back and scapulars uniform olive-green, tinged with yellow; rump and uppertail-coverts brighter or olive-yellow. Central pair of tail feathers black; bases to all outers broadly yellow, forming two panels at base of tail, tips of all outers black. Median coverts

yellowish-olive, greaters similar but broad olive-yellow edges obscure dark centres; alula and primary coverts black; flight feathers black or blackish-brown, finely edged with olive or olive-yellow; tertials the same or paler, with broader edges. Underparts are yellow or bright yellow on sides of neck and breast, below this washed with olive, heaviest on flanks. Bill short and rather stubby but pointed, distinctively whitish or pale straw. Legs and feet brown or dark brown. **Adult female:** Forehead to crown, nape, mantle, back and scapulars uniform olive-green, or tinged slightly brownish on mantle and scapulars; rump and uppertail-coverts paler, olive-green tinged with yellow; face paler than crown, pale olive-yellow on lores, cheeks and ear-coverts. Tail is dark or blackish-brown, with pale yellow edges to outer webs. Median and greater coverts black or blackish-brown with yellow or dull yellowish tips forming double wingbar; alula and primary coverts black or blackish-brown; flight feathers also black or blackish-brown with light green or olive-yellow edges, broadly so on tertials. Chin and throat buffish-yellow or tinged with grey becoming more yellowish on breast, which is streaked with brown; flanks and belly whitish, flanks paler than belly but more prominently streaked dark brown; undertail-coverts white or off-white. Bill as male. **Juvenile:** Very similar to adult female, but duller and browner and broadly but indistinctly streaked darker on upperparts, with dull yellowish-olive underparts streaked broadly darker. First-year males show more yellow on underparts than same-aged females.

VOICE Flight note is a soft or low 'chut-chut' or a higher-pitched 'swee-ee' and a siskin-like 'seee-ip' or 'e-see-ip', also a 'chit chit, chee-ee-o'. Song is a low chittering trill or a jumble of notes

resembling song of American Goldfinch (65) or the warbling song of a Ruby-crowned Kinglet (*Regulus calendula*).

STATUS, HABITAT AND BEHAVIOUR Locally common. A bird of upland pine forest (usually above 1500 m), where it is usually found in flocks or loosely associated groups of up to 25, even in the breeding season. Perches freely in trees and forages in shrubs, in substantial seed-bearing plants or on the ground. Feeds on a variety of seeds and is particularly fond of the seeds of docks.

DISTRIBUTION Monotypic. Endemic to mountain pine forest of Hispaniola (Haiti and Dominican Republic).

MOVEMENTS Not well known, but appears to be nomadic outside the breeding season. May be an altitudinal migrant to lower elevations.

MEASUREMENTS Wing of male 64–65·5, female 62–65; tail 39–43; tarsus 14–16; bill (culmen) 8–10.

REFERENCES Bond (1979), Wetmore and Swales (1931).

58 SAFFRON SISKIN *Carduelis siemiradzkii*   Plate 13
South America

Chrysomitris siemiradzkii Berlepsch and Taczanowski, 1883, Proc. Zool. Soc. London, p. 551, Guayaquil, Ecuador.

IDENTIFICATION Length 11 cm (4¼ in). A small siskin with a very restricted range. Males have all-black head to chin and throat, greenish-yellow back and bright yellow rump, black wings with yellow wingbar and base of flight feathers, black tail with a bright yellow base, and rich or deep saffron-yellow underparts. Females lack black head, and upperparts are uniform greenish-olive with greenish-yellow rump; underparts a deep saffron-yellow. **Confusion species:** The male is similar to the slightly larger adult male Hooded Siskin (56), but lacks latter's dark centres to mantle and back and also has much richer or deeper yellow underparts. Females and juveniles are particularly alike, but those of Saffron are generally much brighter.

DESCRIPTION Sexes differ. **Adult male:** Entire head, face, chin and throat glossy black. Nape, mantle, back and scapulars uniform bright olive or greenish-yellow; rump and uppertail-coverts bright or deep yellow. Tail is short and forked, all feathers pale or bright yellow at base (but mostly visible only on outers), with distal half black. Lesser and median coverts black, edged greenish-yellow as scapulars; greater coverts black, tipped with yellow; alula and primary coverts black; flight feathers black, but bases of primaries bright or deep yellow, yellow extending narrowly across secondaries; outer edges to tertials white or pale buff. Underparts rich saffron-yellow, slightly paler on flanks and vent or tinged green on flanks. Bill is short and pointed, dark brown or horn, paler along

cutting edges. Legs and feet brown or dark brown. **Adult female:** Forehead pale yellow, crown and nape olive-green and faintly dark-streaked; face pale olive-green, with a paler or slightly yellowish area over and behind eye and on cheeks. Mantle, back and scapulars as crown and nape; rump and uppertail-coverts yellow, tinged with green. Tail is pale or light yellow at base (usually visible only on outers), with rest black. Median and greater coverts as male, but tips duller; rest of wings as male but duller, with yellow at bases of primaries and secondaries not so extensive. Chin and throat to sides of neck and breast greenish-yellow; centre of breast, upper belly and flanks saffron-yellow, vent white, undertail-coverts pale yellow. **Juvenile:** Very similar to adult female, but duller.

VOICE Undescribed. Calls and song apparently very similar to those of Hooded Siskin (56).

STATUS, HABITAT AND BEHAVIOUR Rare or uncommon within its extremely restricted range; very little known but considered possibly threatened. Occurs in pairs or small (family?) groups in lowland deciduous forest or woodland, brush and dry scrub up to about 800 m, also in tall grasses and plants on forest edges and in similar habitat along roadsides etc. In most actions and habits identical to Hooded Siskin. Feeds low down on seed-bearing plants, shrubs and grasses or on the ground.

DISTRIBUTION Monotypic. Ecuador from Machalilla National Park, Manabi, to Chongon Hills, Guayas and Puna Island, also southwest

Loja, and in adjacent Tumbes department, Piura, extreme northwest Peru. Note: Regarded by some authorities as a race of Hooded Siskin.

REFERENCE Collar *et al.* (1992), Ridgely and Tudor (1989).

59 OLIVACEOUS SISKIN *Carduelis olivacea*   Plate 14
South America

Spinus olivaceus Berlepsch and Stolzmann, 1894, Ibis, p. 387, Vitoc, Junin, Peru.

IDENTIFICATION Length 11 cm (4¼ in). Identical to *capitalis* race of Hooded Siskin (56) (of which it may be only another race), but found at higher elevations and in different habitat where the two occur together. In areas where ranges overlap, field characters to note on male Olivaceous are: smaller size, blackish-streaked mantle and back (streaks poorly defined on Hooded except in worn plumage), less obvious yellow collar or band across nape and sides of neck, and generally duller or more olive-yellow underparts; females are also very similar. Note: Olivaceous is considered by many authorities to be a race of Hooded Siskin, but this treatment follows Ridgely and Tudor (1989) in giving it tentative species status; differs principally in range and habitat preference, but the two readily hybridise where the ranges overlap.

DESCRIPTION Sexes differ. **Adult male:** Entire head to nape, sides of face, chin, throat and breast black; sides of neck to lower nape a thin strip of yellow, forming a collar. Hindneck, mantle, back and scapulars olive-green, streaked with blackish feather bases, becoming plain or bright yellow on rump and uppertail-coverts. Tail is blackish-brown, with bases of all outer feathers bright yellow, forming two panels. Median coverts blackish, edged greenish-olive and tipped with yellow; greaters black or blackish, tipped with bright yellow; alula and primary coverts black; flight feathers black with fine pale buff or whitish edges, and bases to all flight feathers bright yellow, forming a wing panel with greater coverts; tertials also black, but more broadly edged and tipped pale buff. Sides of breast and upper flanks olive, becoming dull yellow on lower breast, flanks and belly; bright yellow or saffron-yellow undertail-coverts. Bill greyish or greyish-horn. Legs and feet brown or flesh-brown. **Adult female:** Forehead to crown greenish or olive-yellow; face a dull or dark olive-green, with lores slightly darker or dull-grey; mantle to scapulars as crown, rump and uppertail-coverts bright or contrasting yellow but tips of uppertail-coverts occasionally greenish. Tail and wings as male. Chin, throat and sides of neck olive-yellow, becoming bright yellow on breast, belly and undertail-coverts. **Juvenile:** Similar to adult female but duller, more brown, and yellow in plumage is less bright, generally more buffish or tinged pale buff-brown and streaked with brown on upperparts and underparts.

VOICE Call is similar to that of Hooded Siskin and is frequently given, especially when in large flocks. Song is also similar to Hooded Siskin's.

STATUS, HABITAT AND BEHAVIOUR Uncommon or locally common. A bird of the subtropical zone between 1200 m and 3000 m, at forest edges and adjacent clearings in montane, subtropical forest. Usually found in pairs, small groups or family parties, or in winter in larger flocks; an active and gregarious bird, with flocks continually on the move. Actions and behaviour as Hooded Siskin. Feeds in trees and on the ground on a variety of seeds, mainly of low ground-loving plants but also some tree and bush seeds.

DISTRIBUTION Monotypic. Eastern slope of the Andes in southeast Ecuador, north to Napo, also Amazonas, northern Peru, south through the Andes to La Paz and Cochabamba, Bolivia. Has also been found recently in Santa Cruz, Bolivia.

REFERENCE Bates *et al.* (1992).

60 BLACK-HEADED SISKIN *Carduelis notata*   Plate 14
Middle America

Carduelis notata Du Bus, 1847, Bull. Acad. Roy. Sci., Bruxelles, 14, p. 106, Mexico; Jalapa, Veracruz, designated by Todd, 1926, Ann. Carnegie Mus., 17, p. 68.

IDENTIFICATION Length 10–12 cm (4–4¾ in). The only siskin of Middle America. All black from head to centre of breast, with greenish-yellow upperparts and bright yellow underparts; females similar to males, but with paler yellow underparts and dull greenish upperparts, and have paler yellow edges to coverts. **Confusion species:** Within range likely to be confused only with female and juvenile Black-capped Siskin (51), which are much duller overall, predominantly green and lack black hood; juvenile Black-headed is browner on upperparts, with a yellowish rump, and lack obvious streaks. Juvenile Black-capped has greater resemblance to juvenile Pine Siskin (50).

DESCRIPTION Sexes differ. **Adult male:** Entire head to lower nape, chin, throat and upper breast

♂

black (amount of black varies, and may extend to centre of lower breast); sides of lower neck almost to hindneck a dull golden-yellow. Mantle, back and scapulars olive, tinged with yellow (or with black bases to feathers), becoming brighter yellow on rump; uppertail-coverts black, as is tail, which has broad yellow bases to all but central pair of feathers forming two bright side panels. Median and greater coverts, alula and primary coverts black (greater coverts tipped yellow); flight feathers also black, with bright yellow bases to primaries (about one-third of length) and slightly onto bases of outer secondaries forming a bright wing panel. Underparts from sides of breast and belly golden-yellow, with flanks slightly more greenish-yellow; undertail-coverts yellow. Bill sharply pointed, bluish-grey. Legs and feet brown or brownish-horn. **Adult female:** Very similar to adult male but generally paler or duller, with blackish-brown hood extending only to lower throat or occasionally with pale yellow tips on throat. Mantle, back and scapulars dull olive-green; rump yellow or dull yellow, uppertail-coverts olive. Tail as male, but with less extensive yellow side panels. Wings also as male, but with less extensive yellow at base of flight feathers. Underparts almost entirely pale lemon-yellow. **Juvenile:** Forehead to crown, mantle, back and scapulars light olive-brown; rump and uppertail-coverts paler dull olive-yellow. Tail blackish-brown, with small amount of yellow at sides of base. Wing (including coverts) blackish, with buff or pale buffish-white or yellow tips to median and greater coverts; yellow bases to primaries not so extensive or as bright yellow, and on some (perhaps first-years) pale yellow; tips of ter-

tials pale yellow or buffish-white. Yellowish or olive-yellow on cheeks and ear-coverts, becoming more uniform yellow on chin, throat and sides of neck; breast similar but with a green or light olive-green wash, warmer in tone on flanks and undertail-coverts; faint streaks on breast and flanks.

GEOGRAPHICAL VARIATION Very little difference among races noticeable in the field, as they are only weakly differentiated, based on intensity of green or olive above and yellow below. Race *oleacea* is apparently darker above and below, but birds from Mexico can also approach these in tone. Male and female *oleacea* are almost identical, except that females are slightly darker or greener in fresh plumage than males and black on head appears not to extend so far onto lower throat/upper breast.

VOICE Call is a nasal 'teu', similar to Dark-backed Goldfinch (66), a drawn-out 'tseeeu' or 'djeein', a dry 'jeh-jeht' and a nasal 'ti-chie'. Song is a varied and rapid jangling or twittering warble, often prolonged, a repetition of phrases with occasional nasal or metallic notes.

STATUS, HABITAT AND BEHAVIOUR Common or locally common. Occurs in the highland and subtropical zones, rarely lower in the breeding season (except in Guatemala). Inhabits large conifer and oak forests and also lower edge of cloud forest and secondary forest, mostly between 1000 m and 2750 m; in eastern Guatemala and elsewhere, occurs in lowland pine forest and in pines on open savanna down to sea-level. Usually found in pairs, small groups or family parties; in the non-breeding season in much larger numbers, up to 200 together. Feeds in manner of a Goldfinch (68), clinging to seedheads and taking the seeds of small plants; also feeds in pines.

DISTRIBUTION *C. n. notata*: San Luis Potosi south to Chiapas, eastern and central Mexico, to northern Guatemala.

C. n. forreri: northeast Sonora, Chihuahua and Durango, western Mexico.

C. n. oleacea: Belize to northern Nicaragua.

MOVEMENTS Birds breeding in north of range move south to winter in south of range. In non-breeding season occurs at lower levels; some move down to sea-level and occurs in lowland rainforest.

MEASUREMENTS Wing of male 61–68, of female 60–66.

REFERENCE Howell and Webb (in prep.).

61 YELLOW-BELLIED SISKIN *Carduelis xanthogastra*   Plate 15
Central and South America

Chrysomitris xanthogastra Du Bus, 1855, Bull. Acad. Roy. Sci., Bruxelles, 22, p. 152, Ocana, Colombia.

IDENTIFICATION Length 10–11·5 cm (4–4½ in). Males are all black from head to breast and uppertail-coverts. Wings and tail are also black, but with typical siskin patches of yellow at sides of

base of tail and at base of flight feathers; rest of underparts are bright yellow. Females have dull olive-green upperparts with yellow wing and tail flashes; underparts dull greenish-yellow from chin to breast, white on the remainder. **Confusion species:** Yellow-rumped Siskin (63) is very similar but, as its name implies, has a bright yellow rump in both sexes. Female and immature Yellow-bellied are similar to same-age/sex Hooded (56) and Andean (52) Siskins, but are darker olive on upperparts and show more contrast with yellow in wings and tail. Male Dark-backed Goldfinch (66) has black or bluish-black upperparts, with white at base of primaries and on tips to all tertials, and uniform yellow underparts; 'green-backed' females are also similar, but white in wing is a good character and they also have white or whitish belly and undertail-coverts.

DESCRIPTION Sexes differ. **Adult male:** Entire

♂

upperparts from head and face to rump and uppertail-coverts glossy black; tail also black, with yellow at sides of base forming two side panels. Wings entirely black, but with bright yellow bases to flight feathers (except outermost primary and inner three secondaries) for about a third of their length, forming a bright wing panel and a short wingbar in flight. Chin and throat to centre of breast glossy black; sides and lower breast, flanks, belly and undertail-coverts yellow, slightly tinged with olive on lower flanks; thighs black. Bill is deeper at base than on typical siskins, pointed at tip, dark brown or blackish. Legs and feet dark brown. **Adult female:** Forehead to crown dull olive-green; face pale olive-green, tinged greyish or slightly yellower on lores and around eye. Mantle, back and scapulars uniform dull olive-green, paler or lighter on rump and uppertail-coverts. Tail is dusky or dark blackish-brown, edged broadly with olive or yellowish-green, with yellow at base of all outer feathers (paler and less extensive than on male). Median and greater coverts black or blackish with pale olive or greenish-yellow tips; alula, primary coverts and flight feathers dusky black, finely edged with pale green or slightly olive-green, bases to primaries and outer secondaries (as male) yellow

and forming panel in closed wing. Chin and throat greyish-olive; breast and flanks olive-yellow, becoming paler, buffish or yellowish-white on belly and undertail-coverts. **Juvenile:** Very similar to adult female on upperparts, but paler or more yellow on underparts. Lacks yellow at base of tail or in flight feathers, but median and greater coverts have pale buff tips forming wingbars, secondaries are edged with pale buff and tertials broadly edged and tipped off-white; underparts pale buffish-yellow or tinged with olive, belly often yellowish.

GEOGRAPHICAL VARIATION Race *stejnegeri* is slightly larger, with longer bill. Males have larger or broader patch of yellow at base of flight feathers, and greater coverts are tipped with yellow; the tertials are lightly tipped (and slightly edged) white or whitish-buff. The black on sides of breast is slightly more extensive than in nominate, and rest of underparts, including thighs, are paler or brighter yellow. Females of the same race are slightly duller olive than nominate, the greater coverts are tipped with yellow, and throat and upper breast are dull olive or greenish-yellow with yellow on rest of underparts.

VOICE The song is a thin and variable musical twitter.

STATUS, HABITAT AND BEHAVIOUR Fairly or locally common; scarce in Ecuador. In parts of the range has become uncommon to rare owing to intense persecution for the cagebird trade. Found in subtropical and upper tropical zones, where it inhabits clearings with scattered trees or bushes and edges of humid forest, plantations or high pastures between 800 m and 3700 m, most occurring at 1400–2000 m. Usually found in pairs or small parties of up to 30 birds, occasionally in mixed flocks with Black Siskin (62). Spends most of its time in trees, mainly mid-height to treetop level, also (but less frequently) low down or on the ground. Feeds Goldfinch-fashion on seeding thistles and a variety of plant, bush or tree seeds.

DISTRIBUTION *C. x. xanthogastra:* Cordillera Central to Cordillera Talamanca, Costa Rica, to western Chiriqui, western Panama, Andes of Colombia (except Nariño) and Perija Mountains, Colombia/Venezuela, also coastal mountains (west to Yaracuy) and Andes, south of Merida, Venezuela; also irregularly recorded in El Oro and Pichincha, western Ecuador.

C. x. stejnegeri: extreme southeast Peru (Puno) to central Bolivia (La Paz and Santa Cruz).

MOVEMENTS Generally sedentary or resident, though erratic in occurrence in some areas.

MEASUREMENTS Wing of male 64–67, of female 61–66; tail of male 36–43, of female 34–40; tarsus 12–15; bill (culmen) 9–11.

Carduelis atratus Lafresnaye and d'Orbigny, 1837, Mag. Zool. [Paris], 7, p. 83, La Paz, Bolivia.

IDENTIFICATION Length 12–13 cm (4¾–5 in). A bird of the high Andes, generally occurring at higher altitudes than other siskins except Thick-billed (55). The only virtually all-black (male) or brownish-black (female or juvenile) finch of the region, easily distinguished by its typical yellow flashes in wing and at sides to base of tail. **Confusion species:** Yellow-bellied Siskin (61) has a clearly defined yellow breast, belly and flanks, while female is olive-green and lacks any deep brown in plumage. Yellow-rumped Siskin (63) is similar, but both sexes and juveniles show more yellow on lower breast and belly and have clearly defined bright yellow rump and uppertail-coverts.

DESCRIPTION Sexes differ. **Adult male:** Entire

head and body (except bright yellow vent and undertail-coverts) jet-black or glossy black. Tail is slightly notched at tip, black but with bright yellow flashes to basal two-thirds of all except central pair of feathers forming two side panels. All feathers in wing black, except for bright yellow tips to greater coverts and extensively across bases to flight feathers, less on secondaries; tertials all black, except for white outer web and tip to lower tertial (and pale edges in worn plumage). Underparts black, except for brown or dark brown belly (occasionally shows a few yellow tips), becoming bright yellow on vent and undertail-coverts. Bill is thin and sharply pointed, with dark brown upper

mandible and pale or whitish lower. Legs and feet dark brown or blackish-brown. **Adult female:** Similar to adult male, but black of upperparts is slightly sooty or brownish-black and tips to median as well as greater coverts can be pale yellow or buff; flight feathers also pale yellow at base, and finely edged pale yellow or yellowish towards tip. Underparts are often more extensively yellow or pale yellow from throat to undertail-coverts, but breast and flanks are heavily mottled or obscured with brown or dark brown. **Juvenile:** Very similar to adult female, but generally a duller brown or brownish-black with only pale yellow in wing and base of tail.

VOICE Not recorded, but song apparently similar to that of Yellow-rumped Siskin. Sings with wings hanging, from prominent perches such as tops of bushes or small trees; also performs display flights.

STATUS, HABITAT AND BEHAVIOUR Uncommon or locally common. A bird of the high Andean steppes, puna grassland and temperate zones of the Andes between 1800 m and 4800 m, mostly towards higher end of the range in the north and lower towards south; found on rocky or stony slopes, crags, gullies or hillsides with light or scattered vegetation, woodland or bushes, also occasionally around farms and villages. Usually found in pairs or small parties, occasionally in larger gatherings (especially when not breeding) or in mixed parties including Thick-billed or Yellow-bellied Siskins. Occasionally perches on telephone wires. Feeds mostly on the ground on a variety of seeds, predominantly of low-growing plants or bushes, and some insects.

DISTRIBUTION Monotypic. Andes of Huanuco and southern Ancash in central Peru to La Paz, Cochabamba and Potosi in central or western Bolivia, northern Chile (Antofagasta, occasionally to Colchagua and Santiago), and Jujuy south to Mendoza, western Argentina.

MOVEMENTS Generally sedentary or resident, but some altitudinal movement in the non-breeding season.

MEASUREMENTS Wing 85; tail 50; bill 9.

Chrysomitris uropygialis P.L. Sclater, 1862, Cat. Coll. Amer. Birds, p. 125, Chile.

IDENTIFICATION Length 12·5–13 cm (5 in). Male and female are similar in plumage, with most of head, upperparts (to lower back) and chin to

breast black or blackish mottled with olive, and bright yellow on rump, uppertail-coverts and lower underparts. Females are more brownish-black, with yellow paler in tone. It has been known to hybridise with Hooded Siskin (56) in Peru. **Confusion species:** Similar to Yellow-bellied Siskin (61), but ranges do not meet (Yellow-bellied found mostly at lower elevations), and to Black Siskin (62), with which it overlaps. Yellow-bellied lacks bright yellow rump and female is distinctly different in plumage; both sexes of Black Siskin lack bright yellow rump and uppertail-coverts and have far less yellow on underparts.

DESCRIPTION Sexes differ. **Adult male:** Entire

head to sides of neck, nape, mantle, upper back and scapulars sooty-black, with feathers of hind-neck, to back and scapulars edged or mottled with olive or olive-yellow (but this is not always present, owing to wear and abrasion); rump bright yellow or tinged lightly with green; uppertail-coverts black or blackish with yellow edges and tips. Tail is long and slightly notched, black with all but central pair of feathers yellow at base, forming two side panels for about two-thirds of tail length. Median coverts black with fine yellow edges and tips; greater coverts black, broadly tipped yellow; alula and primary coverts black; flight feathers also black, but with bright yellow bases forming broad wing panel across primaries and narrowly on bases of secondaries; tertials black, with whitish or very pale yellowish edges and yellow tips. Black of head

and neck extends to centre of upper breast; rest of underparts bright yellow, tinged slightly green on flanks. Bill thin and pointed, dark brownish or blackish-brown. Legs and feet dark brown or black. **Adult female:** Very similar in plumage but duller, with upperparts, head and breast blackish-brown and with broader olive-greenish edges to mantle, back and scapulars; rump and underparts are slightly paler or duller yellow. **Juvenile:** Similar to female, but plumage is brown or tinged brown and streaked brown on mantle, back, breast, flanks and belly.

VOICE The song is a rich and melodious Goldfinch-like warble mixed with various twitters.

STATUS, HABITAT AND BEHAVIOUR Rare in Peru and Bolivia and common or locally common in Chile. Inhabits tropical and temperate zones of the Andes between 2500 m and 3500 m, lower in non-breeding season, on mountain slopes, heaths, lightly wooded plains (especially *Polylepis* woodland) and bushy ravines, or even edges of cultivation; in Chile, breeds in desert scrub and on vertical cliff faces. Occurs in pairs, small groups or parties, occasionally in company with other siskins. Feeds in bushes or on the ground on a variety of plant seeds, and occasionally a few insects.

DISTRIBUTION Monotypic. The Andes of Ancash and Lima through central and southern Peru to La Paz and Potosi, western Bolivia, south to Mendoza in western Argentina also northern and central Chile (where common from Atacama southwards) south to Bio Bio. Commonly hybridises with Hooded Siskin in Arequipa, southern Peru.

MOVEMENTS A partial or altitudinal migrant; from April to October occurs erratically north to central Peru and western Bolivia. In the non-breeding season occurs down to 500 m, rarely down to sea-level, or even ascends to 4000 m. Wanders widely and erratically in search of food; some movements are also initiated by weather.

MEASUREMENTS Wing 81–83; tail 49; tarsus 12; bill 9–10.

REFERENCE Fjeldså and Krabbe (1990).

64 BLACK-CHINNED SISKIN *Carduelis barbata*   Plate 16
South America

Fringilla barbata Molina, 1782, Saggio Stor. Nat. Chile, pp. 247, 345, Chile; restricted to Valparaiso by Todd, 1926, Ann. Carnegie Mus., 17, p. 81.

IDENTIFICATION Length 12–13 cm (4¾–5 in). The southernmost siskin. Males are easily told by dark cap, chin and throat and a yellowish-green face, olive-green back and yellow rump; the bases of flight feathers are also yellow. Females are generally duller and lack black cap and chin, but in fresh plumage have a bright yellow forehead, supercilium and neck sides. **Confusion species:** Similar to Andean (52) and Thick-billed (55) Siskins, neither of which it overlaps in range. Hooded Siskin (56) overlaps in Chile, but male Hooded has black hood to centre of breast, while female lacks

bright yellow supercilium and sides of neck of female Black-chinned.

DESCRIPTION Sexes differ. **Adult male:** Forehead to crown and upper nape black; supercilium from behind eye to nape yellowish-green (can be bright yellow in fresh plumage); lower lores, cheeks and ear-coverts olive or green, washed lightly with yellow; sides of neck pale yellowish-green. Mantle, back and scapulars olive-green with dark feather centres and greyish tips; rump and uppertail-coverts yellow or yellowish-green (tips of some uppertail-coverts can be grey). Tail is black with slight greyish edges to outers, with all feathers except central pair yellow at base, showing as short side panels. Median coverts black or blackish, broadly edged pale olive-green and with dull yellow tips; greaters black, broadly tipped bright yellow; alula and primary coverts black; flight feathers also black, but yellow at base of outer primaries forming small square on closed wing and a longer yellow panel at base of secondaries; tertials black, edged pale buff or pale greenish-yellow, broadly so on lowest feather. Chin and centre of throat black; sides of throat, breast and flanks bright yellow or washed lightly with green on flanks; belly white or whitish, undertail-coverts yellow with dark tips (not always visible in the field). Bill is short and conical, upper mandible dark brown or blackish, lower pale brown or flesh-brown. Legs and feet brown or pale flesh-brown. **Adult female:** Similar in many respects to adult male, but lacks black crown, chin and throat, though in fresh plumage has pale or bright yellow lower forehead and supercilium, becoming paler yellow on rear of ear-coverts and sides of neck, enclosing dull greenish-yellow or olive-yellow cheeks and ear-coverts. Crown and nape to mantle, back and scapulars similar to olive-green upperparts of male but streaked darker green. Wings as male, but less extensively yellow on tips of greater coverts and bases to flight feathers. Chin and throat dull yellow, becoming washed or tinged with green or grey, belly white or whitish, flanks tinged buffish-brown. **Juvenile:** Very similar to adult female, but thinly streaked pale brown above, lacks bright yellow areas on face and sides of neck, is generally paler or much more buff than yellow, and has prominent pale buff tips to median and greater coverts; underparts are pale yellow, with greyish-olive on breast and flanks.

VOICE Uses a variety of call notes, a rising canary-like 'tsooeet' and a sparrow-like abrupt 'chit' or 'chi-tip', also a subdued 'tsi-tsi-tsi' and a constant twittering contact note while feeding, and a 'chup' flight note. Song is loud, a sustained musical mixture of phrases and trills involving many of the call notes and other typical siskin or more melodious (Chaffinch-like) notes; usually delivered from a high perch or in display flight.

STATUS, HABITAT AND BEHAVIOUR Common and widespread; local in the Falklands. Inhabits the temperate zone of South America, rarely above 1500 m, in a range of habitats from high forest, mostly conifers but also broadleaved, to thickets, brush or open country with scattered vegetation; in some areas a bird of suburban gardens and roadsides. In the Falklands, inhabits areas of introduced trees and shrubs and areas of tall tussac (tussock-grass). Found in pairs or small groups, family parties or occasionally in the non-breeding season in flocks up to 100 strong; associates with Hooded Siskin in Chile. Many habits and actions as Siskin (49). Feeds mostly on the ground, in weed patches or other areas of seed-bearing plants, on small seeds and insects or their larvae; also known to feed in trees, often at a considerable height.

DISTRIBUTION Monotypic. Copiapo valley, Atacama, southern Chile and Neuquen and western Rio Negro, Argentina, south to Strait of Magellan, Tierra del Fuego, and east to the Falkland Islands. Has also occurred in La Pampa, Argentina.

MOVEMENTS Partial migrant; a non-breeding-season visitor to plains and valleys in lower parts of the range.

MEASUREMENTS Wing 73; tail 48; tarsus 13; bill 10–11.

REFERENCE Woods (1982, 1988).

65 AMERICAN GOLDFINCH *Carduelis tristis*   Plate 12
North America

Fringilla tristis Linnaeus, 1758, Syst. Nat., ed. 10, p. 181, Northern America; restricted to South Carolina by Amer. Ornith. Union, 1931, Check-list North Amer. Birds, ed. 4, p. 326.

IDENTIFICATION Length 11·5–14 cm (4½–5½ in). Male in summer is very distinctive, with brilliant yellow plumage except for black cap, tail and wings and white rump, tail-coverts and wingbars; in winter, black cap is lost or shows only on forehead, upperparts are generally buffish-brown, and face and throat still retain some yellow, but otherwise it is rather drab. Female lacks black cap, and is greenish or olive-yellow on head and upperparts and pale yellow below; in winter becomes drab and dull, loses most of yellow and is generally brown or grey-brown. Juveniles are similar to adult male in winter, but wingbars and rump are yellowish-buff. **Confusion species:** Females are very similar to female Dark-backed Goldfinch (66), but their bright yellow rump or white undertail-coverts are distinctive. Juv-enile American is much browner than green or greenish-yellow juvenile Dark-backed.

DESCRIPTION Sexes differ. **Adult male summer:** Forehead to crown black, forming black cap. Entire face, hindcrown to mantle, back and scapulars bright lemon-yellow; rump pale yellow, uppertail-coverts pure white. Tail is black, with most feathers (except central pair) edged and tipped white on inner web. Lesser coverts lemon-yellow, medians pale or whitish-yellow; greaters black, with white tips forming a wingbar (this is gradually abraded throughout the summer); alula, primary coverts and flight feathers glossy black, with inner secondaries and tertials broadly edged and tipped white. Underparts are almost entirely bright or deep lemon-yellow except for white vent, thighs and undertail-coverts. Bill is sharply pointed and pale brown or straw-coloured. Legs and feet orange- or yellowish-brown. In winter, the forehead can be black (or black-tipped), but on some, perhaps most, it is uniform with the crown; face pale yellow or yellowish except for olive or brownish-buff tinge to cheeks and ear-coverts; crown olive-green; nape, mantle, back and scapulars buff or warm earth-brown, tinged with yellow; rump and uppertail-coverts yellow or whitish, tips of latter often greyish. Tail as in summer, but with broad whitish or pale buff-brown edges to feathers; wings as summer with yellowish-buff lesser coverts, but white tips to greaters more extensive in fresh plumage and edges to secondaries and tertials pale buffish. Chin and throat to sides of neck yellow, becoming dingy grey or warm buff-brown on breast and flanks; belly and undertail-coverts white or whitish, washed with yellow. Bill is duller brown than in summer, with a dark tip. **Adult female** summer: Forehead, crown, nape, mantle, back and scapulars olive or light buffish-brown, tinged with yellow; rump, bright yellow, becoming paler and greyer or whitish on uppertail-coverts. Tail is black, but edged with white on inner web of all but central pair of feathers. Median coverts black with buffish edges and whitish tips, greater coverts black, tipped more broadly with white, forming double wingbar; alula, primary coverts and flight feathers blackish-brown, secondaries and tertials edged whitish. Face and sides of head as crown, but more yellowish (some have darker or greenish-olive ear-coverts). Sides of neck to chin and throat yellow or pale lemon-yellow, this colour extending to breast and becoming greener or tinged buffish-brown on flanks and belly; undertail-coverts white. Bill as adult male. In winter, a duller, browner or greyish-brown version of summer plumage: head is olive-tinged, but sides of neck and breast to flanks are greyish; wingbars and tips to secondaries and tertials buffish or off-white; rump and uppertail-coverts dingy white or buffish; chin and throat tinged yellow or greenish-yellow, rest of underparts greyish. **Juvenile:** Similar to winter adults, but much browner or more warm brown on upperparts (darker on head) and has rump and uppertail-coverts buff or pale brown. Tail is black, feathers broadly edged white or greyish-white. Lesser coverts yellowish-olive; median and greater coverts black or blackish, with buff, sandy-buff or buffish-white tips forming double wingbar; flight feathers blackish, all edged and tipped sandy or buff-brown, more broadly on tertials. Face is similar to upperparts, but paler or more yellowish. Chin and throat yellowish, becoming sandy or buff-brown on rest of underparts; belly whitish. Bill brown.

GEOGRAPHICAL VARIATION Very little variation noticeable in the field. Race *pallida* is slightly larger than nominate, and adult female, winter male and juveniles are paler or whiter below than *tristis*; *salicamans* is intermediate between nominate and *pallida*; and *jewetti* is browner or darker overall in winter plumage. Some birds of race *salicamans* have a prolonged and irregular moult, and some individuals never attain the brilliant plumage of others.

VOICE Call is a light twittering 'chi-dup, chi-dee-dup', or 'ti-dee-di-di' or 'per-chic-o-ree', frequently given in flight, also a high-pitched 'chi-eee' or 'zwee-zeeeee'. The song is a mixed jumble of melodious and 'wee' or 'swee' notes with thin twittering trills.

STATUS, HABITAT AND BEHAVIOUR Common and gregarious throughout entire range. Found in a variety of open or woodland habitats, where it perches freely in trees, shrubs and tall plants such as sunflowers and thistles, but also more commonly on the ground in weed fields, thickets, edges of cultivation, woodland edges, orchards, gardens and roadside verges. Usually found in pairs, family parties or, in winter, large flocks, often mixed with Common Redpolls (69), Arctic Redpolls (70) and Pine Siskins (50). It has a bounding or undulating flight. Feeds on a variety of plant seeds, particularly thistles, teasel, burdock and those of the dandelion family, occasionally some buds and berries, and in winter also feeds in alder, spruce, willow, hemlock and larch trees; also takes a number of insects, small grasshoppers and beetles.

DISTRIBUTION *C. t. tristis*: eastern Canada and central and eastern USA from southern Quebec and central Ontario south to Nebraska, eastern Colorado, central Oklahoma to northeast Texas and the Gulf States east to central Georgia and South Carolina.

C. t. pallida: western Canada and central USA from southern British Columbia and central Alberta through Saskatchewan to southern Manitoba and southwest Ontario, south to Oregon, Nevada, central Utah, western Colorado and northwest Nebraska.

C. t. jewetti: southwest Canada to northwest USA, from southwest British Columbia to southwest Oregon.

C. t. salicamans: central California, west of Sierra Nevada range, to northern Mexico (Baja California).

Intermediates occur between the first two races.

MOVEMENTS Moves south and southeast in late autumn, to winter within the eastern and western parts of the range or south to northern Mexico (northern Coahuila, Nuevo Leon, Tamaulipas and Vera Cruz), the Gulf coast and Florida; coastal-state populations are probably resident, with most central and northwestern populations leaving the interior for the winter. Birds of race *salicamans* are largely resident, but move east to winter in the Mohave and Colorado deserts and on the San Quintin plains (30°N); birds of race *pallida* probably move the furthest distances into Mexico south to central Veracruz. Nominate race has been recorded north to northern Ontario, northern Quebec, southern Labrador and Newfoundland; a vagrant to Cuba and Bermuda. Race *salicamans* has been recorded as a vagrant to northeast California and Arizona.

MEASUREMENTS Wing of male 68–78, of female 65–74; tail 42·5–51·5; tarsus 12·5–14·5; bill (exposed culmen) 9·5–11.

REFERENCES Farrand et al. (1985), Godfrey (1979), Peterson (1980).

66 DARK-BACKED GOLDFINCH (Lesser Goldfinch, Arkansas Goldfinch, Green-backed Goldfinch) *Carduelis psaltria*   Plate 13

Nearctic and Neotropical

Fringilla psaltria Say, 1823, in Long, Exped. Rocky Mountains (Philadelphia ed.), 2, p. 40, Arkansas River near mountains [Colorado Springs], Colorado.

IDENTIFICATION Length 9–11 cm (3–4¼ in). Male is either glossy black on upperparts, wings and tail, or has a black forehead and crown, olive-green nape, mantle and back, with a yellow rump; both have white patches at base of primaries, and underparts are all bright yellow. The female is a pale greenish-yellow above, lightly streaked heavier green and paler or yellowish on the rump; tail and wings black, with two pale wingbars and a small white patch at base of primaries. **Confusion species:** Female American Goldfinch (65) is similar but somewhat larger, and, except for a very few pale birds or juveniles, has white (not yellow or pale yellow) undertail-coverts. The white patch at base of flight feathers is diagnostic of Dark-backed, which also has a dull green or olive rump (white or bright yellow on American Goldfinch).

DESCRIPTION Sexes differ. **Adult male** (*psaltria*): Head, face to nape and mantle to tail are black or glossy black; the tail has (variable amounts of) white on inner webs of all feathers except central pair (visible only in flight). Wings also entirely black, except for white tips to greater coverts (in fresh plumage), white at base of inner primaries forming square panel on closed wing, and broad white edges and tips to all tertials. Lower lores, chin and throat to belly bright yellow, paler on vent and undertail-coverts. Bill is sharply pointed, pale brown or pinkish-brown with a grey tip, and greenish-yellow at base of lower mandible. Legs and feet dark brown. **Adult female:** Forehead to crown, nape, mantle, back and scapulars dull olive or greenish-yellow with faint streaks; rump and uppertail-coverts paler or slightly greener. Tail is dusky or blackish-brown with white on inner webs of all but central pair (as male). Lesser coverts as scapulars, medians brownish-black edged with pale greenish-olive, greaters black or blackish edged with buff and tipped white; alula and primary coverts dark brown; flight feathers dark brown edged whitish or pale buff, but also with thin patch of white at base of primaries; tertials dark brown, broadly edged and tipped white or whitish-buff. Face, lores and cheeks yellow or yellow tinged with green, yellow often extending across forehead; ear-coverts slightly darker or more green. Underparts and sides of neck pale yellow, with a tinge of green on breast or olive, brown or buffish-brown on flanks. **Juvenile:** Resembles adult female, but is generally duller or greyer above and paler with buffish-brown on underparts, and with duller wingbars. First-winter males can be told from a fairly early age by black bases to feathers of forehead, crown and nape to scapulars.

GEOGRAPHICAL VARIATION Males of race *hesperophila* have lores, forehead and crown black, and ear-coverts, nape, mantle, back and scapulars a deep green or olive-green, with a paler or yellowish rump and uppertail-coverts; tail is black, with white inner webs to all outer feathers and fine pale green edges; wings as nominate, but with white only at bases of flight feathers and broadly on edges and tips of tertials; tips of greater coverts pale yellow, becoming pale olive or buffish with wear. Underparts are yellow, but less bright than in black-backed races. Males of races *jouyi*, *witti* and *columbiana* are all black-backed; females of these races are inseparable from nominate females. Males of *columbiana* and *witti* can show a green mantle and back in fresh plumage; *witti* have black of upperparts extending beneath eye onto cheeks and lower lores.

♂ black-backed form. Detail: outer tail feather.

VOICE Typical call is a curious or questioning rising 'pee-yee', 'cheeo' or 'choo-ii', also a plaintive 'jee', 'ee-ee' or 'ch-ch-ch-ch' often given when disturbed or in flight. The song consists of a rising musical twittering with notes often in paired phrases, usually incorporating a variety of imitations of other birds (including flicker, wrens and pewees), similar to that of Lawrence's Goldfinch (67) but not so clear or so long.

STATUS, HABITAT AND BEHAVIOUR Common or locally common. Occurs in lowlands and foothills up to 3100 m in dry open country, brush, woodland or roadside edges, plantations, farms, gardens and orchards. Usually in pairs or small flocks, but in winter also in groups of up to 50, exceptionally to 300 or 400; often in company with seedeaters and Dickcissels (*Spiza americana*). A restless and shy finch, not often giving its presence away by calling, unlike the more persistently noisy American Goldfinch. Perches freely in trees, often at the top, in bushes and shrubs, but also feeds on the ground. Feeds on a variety of seeds taken from trees (also flowers of cottonwood trees), shrubs including mistletoe, sunflower and thistle seeds and grass seeds on the ground; also some buds and berries. A commonly taken cagebird in Central America.

DISTRIBUTION *C. p. psaltria*: southwest USA from eastern Arizona, northern Colorado, northern Texas south to northern and central Mexico to Guerrero, Oaxaca and central Veracruz.

C. p. hesperophila: northwest USA from southwest Washington (Vancouver) and western Oregon, northern Nevada, northern Utah south through California (though less plentiful along Pacific coast) and central Arizona to northwest Mexico in southern Baja California and southern Sonora.

C. p. jouyi: southeast Mexico, Yucatan.

C. p. witti: Tres Marias Islands and Islas Mujeres, Mexico.

C. p. columbiana: southern Mexico from southwest Chiapas discontinuously south through the highlands of Middle America to the eastern Andes of northern and central Colombia, also lowlands and coastal mountains and Andes of northern Venezuela to northwest and west Ecuador and the Andes of northern Peru south to La Libertad.

It has also been introduced into Cuba, but there is no recent information and it is considered probably extinct there.

MOVEMENTS Mostly resident, but breeding birds at high elevations descend to lower levels. In USA, nominate race a partial migrant and winters mostly within southern parts of the range in Mexico but also north in USA to northern Texas. Has also been recorded in British Columbia, Southern Wyoming, eastern Oregon, Kansas, Missouri, Louisiana, Kentucky and southern New Mexico.

MEASUREMENTS Wing of male 57–69, of female 58–66; tail 39–47; tarsus 11–12; bill (culmen) 9–10·5. Wing of male *columbiana* 57–66, of female 55–58.

REFERENCES Farrand *et al.* (1985), Grant (1964), Peterson (1961).

67 LAWRENCE'S GOLDFINCH *Carduelis lawrencei*　　Plate 12

North America

Carduelis lawrencei Cassin, 1852, Proc. Acad. Nat. Sci. Philadelphia (1850), p. 105, Sonoma and San Diego, California.

IDENTIFICATION Length 10–11·5 cm (4–4½ in). A greyish-brown finch with bright yellow in wing, yellowish rump and black tail. The male has very distinctive black face and, in summer, black wingbar and bright yellow breast and belly; at other times of the year the yellow is less extensive and underparts are as female, white or whitish-buff with brown flanks. **Confusion species:** Easily separated from other North American goldfinches by the amount of yellow in wings. Black face to chin and throat of male diagnostic. Juveniles are distinguished from those of other goldfinches by dull brown plumage, thinner and ill-defined wingbars and streaks on head, nape and upperparts (except pale rump). It bears a superficial resemblance to thinner-billed Virginia's Warbler (*Vermivora virginiae*).

DESCRIPTION Sexes differ. **Adult male:** Forehead to crown, lores, chin and centre of throat black; hindcrown and nape to sides of neck pale ashy-grey, paler or pearl-grey on cheeks and ear-coverts, grey of nape merging gradually across upper mantle into greenish or light olive-yellow on lower mantle and back, but olive variable in extent and scapulars often grey; lower back and rump golden or greenish-yellow, becoming greyer (especially on tips) on uppertail-coverts. Tail is black, finely edged grey, with white patches on inner webs of all but central feathers. Lesser and median coverts bright yellow or greenish-yellow with black bases (not visible in the field); greater coverts have a black basal half with broad bright yellow tips (some, usually tips of inner greaters, paler or whitish); alula and primary coverts black; flight feathers also black, but inner primaries and all secondaries broadly edged with bright yellow at base forming square panel on closed wing, yellow on outer secondaries becoming white towards tip; tertials black, broadly edged pale yellow and tipped whitish. Breast and belly bright yellow or golden-yellow, sides of breast and flanks pale whitish, buffish or tinged brownish; belly and undertail-coverts white. Bill bright pink or pinkish-flesh. Legs and feet pale brown or pinkish-brown. In winter, the greenish-yellow on mantle is more extensive, yellow in wings is paler than in summer and more extensive on edges of greater coverts, the flight feathers have extensive yellow edges and pale whitish tips, and the tail is extensively white on inner webs of feathers; yellow on underparts is restricted to breast, and rest of underparts are white or whitish-buff, becoming browner on sides of breast and flanks. **Adult female:** Very similar to male at all times of the year, but lacks any black on head and face, this being replaced by an even or uniform grey or grey-brown (extending to chin, throat and sides of neck), becoming pale brown on nape and mantle. **Juvenile:** Entire head to back a dull buff or pale olive-brown; sides of face paler buff-brown than crown; rump and uppertail-coverts pale buffish, tinged yellow or light-brown. Tail is dark or blackish-brown, edged and tipped pale buff. Median and greater coverts dark brown, broadly edged and tipped buffish-brown, forming two wingbars; alula and primary coverts dark brown, finely edged paler; flight feathers blackish, edged olive-yellow or pale brown (more noticeable on secondaries) and tipped whitish or pale buff; tertials black, but broadly edged and tipped whitish or pale buffish-brown. Chin, throat, sides of neck and breast pale buff-brown, sides of throat and breast lightly streaked with pale brown on young males (streaking absent on young females); belly dull white or off-white, becoming duller on undertail-coverts.

VOICE The call is a distinctive 'tink-oo' or 'tink-il', usually in flight, also a sharp 'kee-yerr'. The song is a musical tinkling twitter, and as in the previous species incorporates mimicry of other birds, but Lawrence's more often sings for an extended period.

STATUS, HABITAT AND BEHAVIOUR Common or locally common. Found in the drier regions of the southwestern States or northern Mexico, on dry grassy slopes or dry chaparral country, open oak or pine (piñon/juniper) woods. A bird of erratic occurrence in some regions as it does not always breed in the same area in successive years. In winter often in company with other finches, e.g. Dark-backed Goldfinch (66) and

House Finch (90), or Lark Sparrows (*Chondestes grammacus*). Feeds either in trees or shrubs, but spends most of its time foraging on the ground for a variety of plant seeds and some insects; makes regular visits to water (in drought years often flying some distance); has a fondness for salt in breeding season.

DISTRIBUTION Monotypic. Southwest USA, southern California (Los Angeles county), west of the Sierra Nevada and western Arizona, and northwest Mexico (northern Baja California to Sierra San Pedro Martir).

MOVEMENTS In winter wanders throughout the range from north-central California, San Francisco and southern Nevada southwards, and is a casual visitor to central Arizona, central and southwestern New Mexico, western Texas, south to northern Sonora and irregularly south to southern Baja California. Has also occurred in southern Oregon and southern Nevada.

MEASUREMENTS Wing of male 64–71, of female 61–68.

REFERENCES Farrand *et al.* (1985), Peterson (1961).

68 GOLDFINCH *Carduelis carduelis*

Palearctic

Plate 12

Fringilla carduelis Linnaeus, 1758, Syst. Nat., ed. 10, p. 180, Europe; restricted to Sweden by Hartert, 1903, Vögel pal. Fauna, p. 67.

IDENTIFICATION Length 13–15·5 cm (5–6 in). An obvious and distinctive finch with a red face, black crown and nape (lacking on eastern birds), white sides to face and throat, pale brown or deep buff-brown above with a paler or whitish rump, deeply-forked black tail, and black wings with bright yellow wing flash and white tips to flight feathers. **Confusion species:** Juveniles may be confused with juvenile Greenfinches (44) and Siskins (49) both of which, however, are greener and have bright yellow at sides of base of tail.

Detail: outer tail feather.

DESCRIPTION Sexes alike (or very slightly different, though this not appreciable in the field). **Adult:**

Forehead to crown and chin to cheeks rich red, broken by broad black lores from base of bill to eye (slightly brighter red on male extends beyond level of eye; red reaches only to lower eyelid in female); rest of face from side of head to side of upper neck and throat white or whitish. Crown and upper nape to sides of nape black; lower nape whitish; hindneck, mantle, back and scapulars uniform light sandy-brown; rump paler buffish, becoming white on uppertail-coverts. Tail is deeply notched or forked, black with white tip to each feather, greatest in extent on central pair of feathers and decreasing in size outwards; outermost two feathers have broad white inner webs (extending as a spot onto the third). Lesser and median coverts are black or blackish (lessers show broad grey tips on female); greater coverts bright yellow except outermost, which is black; alula and primary coverts black; flight feathers black with basal half of secondaries and primaries golden-yellow, all tipped white (often lacking in midsummer owing to abrasion); tertials also black, with white or buffish-white tips. Lower throat white or tinged buffish-brown, becoming brown (similar in tone to upperparts but darker) on the upper throat and sides of breast and extending to flanks (but extent variable); centre of breast, belly and undertail-coverts white, the latter tinged buffish-brown. Bill is fairly thick at base but sharply pointed, pale horn above and below; in winter assumes a dark tip. Legs and feet pale brown or pinkish-brown. In the hand,

240

males have black rictal bristles and females brown.

Juvenile: Lacks head-and-face pattern of adults, has rather drab or pale greyish-brown head and upperparts with fine dark streaks on crown and nape (red of face assumed in moult into first-winter plumage in August-September), streaks becoming broader and more continuous on mantle, back and scapulars (often looks rather more spotted than streaked). Wings and tail as adult (not usually moulted before first summer), tips buff or buffish-brown, including broadly on tertials; greater coverts and bases of flight feathers pale yellow or creamy-yellow (not bright yellow). Face very pale buffish or pale yellowish-brown, especially on forehead, lores, cheeks and ear-coverts, with fine dark streaks on rear of ear-coverts and sides of neck. Underparts are pale buffish or yellowish-brown, browner on breast and flanks, which are also streaked with brown. First-winter and first-summer plumage as adult but slightly duller, with blackish or blackish-brown wings and tail (probably not discernible in the field) and buff tips.

GEOGRAPHICAL VARIATION Most races in Europe and the Western Palearctic closely resemble *C. c carduelis* described above, and little difference is noticeable in the field without direct comparison; most differences relate to clinal variation in tone or depth of colour of upperparts or underparts, red and white on head, and wing and bill length and depth. Race *britannica* averages slightly darker brown on mantle, back and sides of breast, while *niediecki* is paler or greyer on mantle and back; races on Atlantic islands are smaller in size and have reduced white tips to wings, and birds of race *loudoni* are noticeably very dark earth-brown on upperparts and on breast patches. Eastern races *subulata*, *paropanisi* and *caniceps* have black of head replaced by pale grey, this colour continuing to sides of neck and onto mantle, back and scapulars, palest of all in *subulata* and greyest or heaviest in *caniceps*; *paropanisi* has a longer and slightly heavier bill.

VOICE Call is a shrill or ringing 'pee-uu' or 'tsee-yu', occasionally followed by a twittering note in flight; alarm or aggression call is a harsh or grating 'zeez' or 'eeez'. Song is a pleasant and very characteristic rapid tinkling 'tsswit-witt-witt' repeated with various twittering, buzzing 'zee-zee' notes added, creating a fast and liquid canary-like song, usually given from a prominent songpost such as a treetop, post or telegraph wire etc. Song period from end of February to mid-July and again from late September to December.

STATUS, HABITAT AND BEHAVIOUR Common and widely distributed; less commonly encountered in eastern parts of range, where it breeds at higher levels (up to 4250 m), often above the tree line. Found in pairs, small flocks, family parties at the end of the breeding season, and in winter in larger flocks, not usually in mixed flocks. Occurs in a wide variety of habitats from cultivated areas such as gardens and orchards, roadside verges and parks, often in the centre of large urban or built-up areas, to small mixed and coniferous woods, forest and plantations, scrub, steppe (avoiding large extensive forest), sparsely wooded areas, or even semi-desert; in the east, usually along forest edges, clearings or river valleys. Flight very characteristic of goldfinches, light, bouncing and with short undulations, usually accompanied by its constant and distinctive twittering call note. Feeds mostly on plants rather than in trees or on the ground, perching acrobatically on seedheads or hanging upside-down on longer plants such as sunflowers, teasels or thistles; a wide variety of plant seeds is taken, including those of dandelions, docks, agrimony, sorrel and teasels, and young in the nest are fed on insects collected from fruit trees.

DISTRIBUTION *C. c. carduelis*: west and central Europe (Pyrenees, northern Spain east to northern Italy, central Yugoslavia, Hungary and Romania and the Black Sea, north to southern Scandinavia (north to about 64°N) and southwest Finland east to the Urals.

C. c. britannica: Britain, Channel Islands and the Netherlands.

C. c. parva: Azores, Madeira, Canary Islands, Spain (south of the Pyrenees), extreme southwest France, Balearic Islands, Morocco, northern Algeria, northern Tunisia and northern Libya.

C. c. tschusii: Corsica, Sardinia, Sicily.

C. c. balcanica: central and eastern Romania south to Thrace, Greece, Crete, Albania and southern Yugoslavia (Dalmatia and Macedonia).

C. c. niediecki: Rhodes, Karpathos, Cyprus, Turkey, northern Iraq, Iran, Syria and Lebanon south to southern Israel (Negev) and northern Egypt (Nile delta, western oases and northern Sinai).

C. c. major: western Siberia east of the Urals to the western Altai mountains and the Yenisei River, south to about Semipalatinsk.

C. c. brevirostris: Crimea and the Caucasus to northeast Turkey and northwest Iran.

C. c. loudoni: extreme southern Caucasus (Azerbaijan) and northern Iran (to the southern Caspian districts).

Grey-headed races: *C. c. paropanisi*: southeast Iran through Afghanistan and Central Asia east to the Tien Shan and the Dzungarian Ala Tau in northwest Sinkiang, China.

C. c. subulata: southern central Siberia north to about 60°N east to Lake Baikal and northwest Mongolia and south to the southern Altai ranges.

C. c. caniceps: southern Central Asia, extreme south of Turkmenia and Tadzhikstan (Pamirs) to Afghanistan, Pakistan, Kashmir, western Himalayas and Nepal (to southwest Tibet?).

At least seven other races have been described. Considerable interbreeding occurs between races (even between black-crowned and grey-crowned, principally *major/subulata* and *loudoni/paropanisi*) in overlap areas. Goldfinch has also been introduced into: various parts of the USA (Oregon, Missouri, Ohio, Massachusetts, New York and New Jersey), but remains rare and not well established except perhaps on Long Island, New York State; Bermuda; Uruguay (Colonia to Maldonado), and has occurred in northeast Argentina; Australia (now fully established throughout Victoria, southern South Australia and southeast New South Wales and Tasmania, also in one or two small areas near Perth); and New Zealand, from where has extended its range to the Kermadec Islands (also occurs regularly on Campbell Islands and other subantarctic islands.

MOVEMENTS Sedentary and migratory; birds breeding in northern parts of the range move south and southwest to winter mostly within the southern boundaries of the range or occasionally just beyond. Nominate race regularly (annually?) reaches the Mediterranean, Malta, North Africa and southern Israel; about two-thirds of the British breeding population moves south to winter from Belgium to southern Spain, but some remain even in the northernmost parts of the British Isles; *niediecki* regularly winters to northwest Saudi Arabia and may have bred near Tabuk in 1990; birds of race *major* regularly occur in Turkmenia, southern Uzbekistan, Tadzhikistan, Afghanistan and northeast Iran; *loudoni* regularly occurs on Cyprus and has been recorded in southern Iraq; *paropanisi* winters south to southern Iran, southern Afghanistan and Baluchistan; and *subulata* regularly wanders to the northwest, west and south of its breeding range to Afghanistan and Baluchistan. Individuals of races *major* (once) and *subulata* (twice) have been collected in Quetta, western Pakistan. A vagrant to Libyan desert, eastern Saudi Arabia, Kuwait, Bahrain, United Arab Emirates and Oman. Southward movements in autumn (both short- and long-distance) take place from the end of September to the beginning of November, but onward passage of occasional flocks continues throughout the winter. Return movements to the breeding area occur in March and April.

MEASUREMENTS Wing of male 74·5–87·5, of female 73–84·5; tail 47–51; tarsus 13–15; bill (from skull) 12·5–13·5. Wing of male *britannica* 76–82. Bill of male *parva* 15–18, of female 14–16·5. Wing of male *major* 85–89, of female 76·5–85·5. Wing of *brevirostris* 75–82. Wing of *subulata* 79·5–85. Wing of male *caniceps* 77–87·5, of female 76–81; bill 16–19. Wing of male *paropanisi* 78–84, of female 74–83. Weight 16–22.

REFERENCE Jennings (1991).

69 COMMON REDPOLL (Redpoll, Lesser Redpoll (*A.f. cabaret*)
Carduelis flammea   Plate 17
Holarctic

Fringilla flammea Linnaeus, 1758, Syst. Nat., ed. 10, p. 182, Europe; restricted to Norrland, Sweden, by Hartert, 1903, Vögel pal. Fauna, p. 77.

IDENTIFICATION Length of *flammea* 12·5–14 cm (5–5½ in); of *cabaret* 11·5–12·5 cm (4½–5 in). *A. f. cabaret* is the smallest of the races. Generally a small brown or grey-brown dark-streaked finch (apart from some individuals of race *islandica*) with a very distinctive metallic call and song; bright red from forehead to crown, black chin, and pale pinkish, pinkish-brown or brownish rump; pink or reddish-pink wash to breast (not present on all females). Underparts whitish, with varying amount of dark streaking on breast and flanks.
Confusion species: Much care is needed in the separation of races, especially when also considering the possibility of the very similar race *exilipes* of Arctic Redpoll (70). For differences from Arctic Redpoll see that species. Linnet (72) has pale grey or buffish head and warm brown upperparts. Twite (71) is similar, but warmer or darker brown overall, and has a small area of pale pink on lower rump, but is unlikely to be found in the same habitat as Common Redpoll; it also (as Linnet) has a noticeable white flash in wing.
DESCRIPTION Sexes differ. **Adult male** (*cabaret*) 'Lesser Redpoll' summer: Upper forehead to fore-crown deep red or crimson (rarely, orange or even yellow); hindcrown to lower nape streaked brown, russet-brown or darker, with pale buffish or greyish-brown feather edges. Lower forehead and lores blackish, pale supercilium over (or just in front of) eye; short thin dark eye-stripe behind eye; cheeks and ear-coverts buffish-brown (can be tinged pink); sides of neck greyish-white, finely streaked dark brown. Mantle, back and scapulars similar to nape, but more broadly streaked and with paler feather edges; rump bright pink or concealed by brown tips, variable in extent among individuals, usually brightest or most pronounced in centre but can extend from lower back to brown or dark brown uppertail-coverts. Tail is noticeably forked or notched, blackish-brown with fine narrow buff or buffish-brown edges on outer webs (white or whitish on inner webs). Median coverts dark brown or blackish-brown, finely tipped buff or buffish-white, greater coverts the same but more broadly buff-tipped, forming two thin pale wingbars usually visible at all times on tips of greaters but can be virtually absent or completely abraded by mid-summer; alula and primary coverts blackish-brown; flight feathers dark brown or blackish-brown, finely edged pale buff, broadly or more prominently so on tertials. Chin black; throat, breast and, on some, upper flanks tinged rosy-pink; flanks or lower flanks buff or buffish-brown with dark or blackish-brown streaks; belly and undertail-coverts white, the latter streaked brown, some tinged pinkish. In autumn and winter, following moult, paler or more tawny-brown on head, neck and upperparts, with darker streaking, sides of neck more buff than greyish-white, and pink on rump is less bright and more extensively covered by larger buff or buff-brown tips to feathers; wings have a slightly greater extent of pale or whitish edges, and wingbars (especially tips to greater coverts) become much more prominent; pink on

242

throat and breast becomes almost a wash on centre of breast, with throat and sides of breast pale tawny or buffish-brown, lightly streaked with brown at edges. Summer plumage acquired by abrasion of tips and fringes of feathers. Bill is short and sharply pointed, dull yellowish or straw with a dark culmen and tip. Legs and feet black or blackish-brown.

Adult female summer: Similar to adult male, but generally darker or duller with brown or grey-brown face and paler or less pink on rump and underparts, though at close range some show a fairly prominent pink wash on breast or a light tinge of pink on lower back (otherwise rump is brownish or buffish-brown and dark-streaked); underparts are whitish, dull off-white or buffish-brown on sides of breast, streaked or heavily streaked (especially in winter) brown or buff-brown on sides of breast and flanks and thinly in centre of breast. Following autumn moult, browner, paler or tawny-brown, with dark streaks on sides of neck, nape and mantle; wingbars broad, buff or whitish-buff, as are edges to secondaries and tertials, with tips to flight feathers finely buff; chin is black and, on some, slightly more extensive than on males.

Juvenile: Similar to adult female in summer plumage, but lacks black forehead and red on forecrown; forehead, crown and nape are warm or dark brown, but with broad pale buffish-white edges and bases to feathers. Face is rather plain, chin and lores grey or dark-grey, ear-coverts buffish-brown, lightly or thinly dark-streaked. Mantle and back are similar to crown, with slightly darker centres to feathers and the edges more warm buffish-brown; rump and uppertail-coverts buffish with brown or dark brown streaks, becoming darker overall towards tail. Wings and tail as adults, but tips to median and greater coverts almost white or pale buff, forming double wingbar; edges to secondaries and tertials warm brown, becoming pale buff on tips to tertials. Throat, breast and flanks buffish or greyish-white, streaked or spotted quite heavily with dark brown, rest of underparts greyish or off-white. Bill is pale straw with dark tip. First-winter birds variable; many are inseparable in the field from adult females, but some males acquire a considerable amount of colour during the winter.

GEOGRAPHICAL VARIATION C. f. flammea 'Mealy Redpoll': Sexes alike. Adult is slightly larger than cabaret, with a bright crimson, occasionally orange or even yellow forehead and forecrown. Hindcrown, nape and sides of neck pale 'frosted' grey or pale greyish-buff, coarsely dark-streaked, and mantle and scapulars pale tawny-brown, streaked with black (in late summer the pale edges are mostly abraded and birds can appear very dark). Rump is usually greyish-white to buff or very slightly pink (summer males), streaked darker with brown or grey-brown feather centres, but this is variable and can be reduced or partly absent, at least on some adult males, with rump partly whitish. Tail is very dark, grey finely edged pale greyish-white or buffish-white. Wings as cabaret, but flight feathers are slightly darker, tips to median and greater coverts are broader and paler, normally off-white to pale buff, and edges to tertials are very

pale grey or whitish. Face is similar to cabaret but greyer and slightly more black on chin (of males), but this varies among individuals. Throat and breast pink or pinkish on males or variably buff or greyish-white, becoming paler buffish or greyish-white on upper flanks; belly and flanks to undertail-coverts the same or whiter, but streaked with brown or dark grey-brown, streaks heavier and more extensive on females. The winter plumage is slightly paler than summer, greyer and streaked with buff-brown on mantle and back; pink (if or where present) on throat, breast and rump is concealed by off-white or whitish-buff tips to new feathers, with darker tips to feathers on rump; flanks are paler, as are edges of coverts and tail feathers. Juvenile as cabaret, but slightly larger and much darker (darker than adult female); assumes first-winter plumage (which is very similar to adult) in late August-September. Note: In race cabaret (and possibly flammea), birds with tinges or traces of pink or light red on face and breast may not necessarily be males, as some females can show this in summer (breeding) months. 'C. f. holboellii' is now considered to be a longer-billed variation of flammea, discernible by differences in food and feeding behaviour. C. f. rostrata ('Greenland Redpoll') closely resembles flammea but is larger, and the upperparts are browner (not grey) and heavily streaked or edged pale or tawny-buff on mantle, back and scapulars; also heavily and broadly streaked dark on sides of buff breast and flanks. In summer males are almost dimorphic, with some lightly washed pink on breast while others have no pink at all (none so heavily pink as flammea). Rump as flammea but more usually streaked, or partially streaked with brown or buff-brown centres to feathers. Bill is noticeably heavy-looking and less angular or sharply pointed, with a rather curved ridge to upper mandible, but this character is more useful in the hand than in the field and may not be consistent throughout. C. f. islandica populations are intermediate in size between rostrata and flammea and contain both pale and dark birds closely resembling race hornemanni of Arctic Redpoll and pure rostrata respectively. Individuals vary from frosted pale grey to dark grey-brown on upperparts with variable dark streaking, and the rump is white or whitish and ranges from unmarked to variable amounts of dark centres to some or all feathers. Underparts vary from practically all-white with only light streaking on sides of breast and flanks to more extensive streaking on breast and flanks with only lower breast and belly white or whitish. The bill is short and rather stubby in shape, recalling rostrata, with a slight curve to upper mandible; in the hand, the wing is marginally shorter than rostrata and hornemanni. The subspecific identity of Common Redpolls, especially those out of their normal range, is not to be undertaken lightly: some birds will show strong or classic features of their race, while others will appear intermediate or show features of more than one race. The specific and subspecific status of redpolls has been considerably reviewed in recent years; this classification follows that of Knox (1988) and Lansdown et al. (1991), but for other

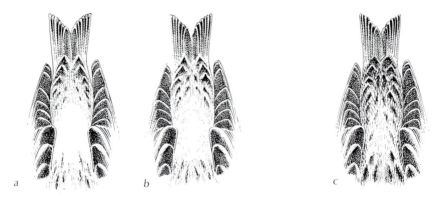

Rump patterns of redpolls (after Svensson, 1992): (a) Arctic Redpoll C. hornemanni (typical); (b) Arctic Redpoll (poorly marked individual); (c) Common Redpoll (C. f. flammea (Mealy Redpoll)).

treatments of the species complex see References below.

VOICE Call is a distinctive metallic twitter, 'chuch-uch-uch-uch' or 'chut-ut-ut-ut', varying in pitch from soft to harsh, also a plaintive 'teu-teu teu-teu' and a 'tooee'; in alarm or defence of territory has a sharp grating Goldfinch-like 'eeeeze'. The song is a short rippling trill, which includes the flight call drawn out and interspersed with a buzzing 'errr errrr', in flight display around territory; song otherwise delivered from song perch or in looping or circular display flight, often involving several males together.

STATUS, HABITAT AND BEHAVIOUR Common or locally common; subject to annual fluctuations in both summer and winter. Inhabits a variety of woodland, both coniferous and broadleaved, including willow, birch, alders, hawthorn scrub to plantations, copses and large gardens. In central and northern Europe it is more likely to be found in upland or montane areas, also alpine habitat above the tree line. Northern birds (Mealy, Greenland and Iceland Redpolls) occur in dwarf birch, willow thickets, spruce and juniper or low-spreading shrubs, often on the tundra itself. Usually found in pairs, small groups or parties, or in larger flocks; flocks of Common Redpolls (occasionally of more than one race) join together in winter with mixed flocks of Goldfinches (68), Siskins (49) and Tree Sparrows (274). It has a very fast or rapid bouncing flight during which it invariably gives its typical metallic call. When feeding on the ground in flocks it appears nervous, frequently flying up to the top of a nearby tree or bush; on the ground hops or shuffles and appears rather short-legged. Feeds in an acrobatic, often tit-like manner, on alders or birch catkins, on a variety of plant and tree seeds mainly of birch (in eastern Canada, the staple winter food is seeds of white birch *Betula papyrifera*), alder, willow and juniper, together with a variety of seasonally available plant or grass seeds including those of dandelion and fat hen, often taken on the ground; a few insects are taken in early spring. Introduced birds in New Zealand have developed the habit of removing seeds from strawberries and have become pests to fruit-growers.

DISTRIBUTION *C. f. flammea*: a broad band across Scandinavia, the Baltic Republics south to east Germany and Poland, across CIS (USSR) south to about 55°N (but to about 50°N in Kamchatka), Mongolia, Amurland and Ussuriland and possibly the borders of northern Manchuria, Sakhalin Islands, Aleutians, Alaska and northern Canada south to about 46°N in Newfoundland.

C. f. rostrata: eastern Baffin Island and west and east coasts of Greenland.

C. f. islandica: Iceland.

C. f. cabaret: British Isles discontinuously eastwards through southern Norway, Denmark, Belgium, northern France, Germany and parts of Czechoslovakia, and the Alps in Switzerland.

It has also been introduced into Lord Howe Island and New Zealand, from where it has since spread to Campbell and Macquarie Islands, and many other subantarctic islands.

MOVEMENTS Sedentary and migratory. Races *cabaret*, *islandica* and *rostrata* are mostly sedentary or make only short-distance movements: *cabaret* regularly occurs south to the Mediterranean, including southern Spain, Malta and Sicily; *islandica* may occasionally wander to Scotland; *rostrata* moves southwest, south or southeast to winter in eastern Canada and northeast USA west to Iowa and Illinois and south to New Jersey, also Iceland and probably Ireland and Scotland. Northern breeders of nominate race move south in varying numbers from year to year to winter (mostly north of 40°N) in central Europe from southern and northern France, northern Italy east through eastern Europe, the northern Caucasus and northern CIS (USSR) to northwest China (west Sinkiang and the Tien Shan range), northeast China (Manchuria south to Kiangsu), Korea and Japan (Hokkaido and northern Honshu). In North America a few remain in the north of the breeding range, but the majority move south to winter throughout most of USA south to northeast California, northern Nevada, Utah, Colorado to Indiana, Ohio and Virginia; has also occurred irregularly in most of the southern

States. A vagrant to Bermuda (frequent but scarce October to early February), Morocco, Malta, Sicily, Cyprus, Turkey, Iraq, central (eastern Kansu) and southern China (Fukien), Ryukyu, Izu and Bonin Islands. Post-breeding dispersal occurs from July into August, and longer-distance southward movements begin in early to mid-October and extend through to late November but numbers and extent of movement dependent on availability of food in home range (in some years very few move far south of the breeding limits); southward movement may also be initiated by onset of severe weather. Return movements take place from mid-March to May.

MEASUREMENTS Wing of male 70–81, of female 67–78; tail 49–58; tarsus 14–16; bill (from skull) of male 8·5–10·5, of female 8–10. Wing of male *cabaret* 67–76, of female 63–73; tail 47–55; tarsus 13–15; bill (from skull) of male 8–10, of female 7·5–9·5. Wing of male *rostrata* 72–82·5, of female 75–81; tail 56–63; tarsus 15–17; bill (from skull) 8–11. Wing of male *islandica* 74–82, of female 72–81; tail 55–64; bill 8–10. Weight of male *flammea* 11–14, of female 11–17.

REFERENCES Herremans (1990), Knox (1988), Lansdown *et al.* (1991), Molau (1985), Troy (1985), Williamson (1961).

70 ARCTIC REDPOLL (Hoary Redpoll) *Carduelis hornemanni*
Plate 17

Holarctic

Linota hornemanni Holboell, 1843, Naturhist. Tidsskr., 4, p. 398, Greenland; type from Ameralikfjord, *fide* Salomonsen, 1928, Vidensk. Medd. Dansk naturhist. Foren., 86, p. 170.

IDENTIFICATION Length 11·5–14 cm (4½–5½ in). Very similar to some of the northern races of Common Redpoll (69), but paler on average. Adults are pale or 'frosted' grey with slightly darker streaking on upperparts; rump white or very slightly streaked; and white or nearly all-white below, with some fine streaking on sides of breast and flanks. Bright red from forehead to crown, and black on chin 'bib'; summer males also have a very pale pink wash on breast and rump. *C. h. hornemanni* is larger and far more distinctive than race *exilipes*, and much caution is needed in the identification of the latter race at all times because of the potential confusion with races *flammea* and *islandica* of Common Redpoll (69). **Confusion species:** The characters to note in separating *exilipes* from Common Redpoll are: its generally paler appearance, in particular the nape, while the centre of the mantle is white or buff (streaked darker) and the white rump is generally unstreaked (except in worn plumage); the short, stubby, conical bill; almost entirely white or whitish underparts, with thin or sparse streaking on flanks (rarely to lower flanks), and unmarked undertail-coverts with the exception of a dark centre to longest feather. Any individuals not meeting one or more of these criteria are best left unidentified. See also Lansdown *et al.* (1991) and Svensson (1992).

DESCRIPTION Sexes similar. **Adult:** Lower forehead dusky or dingy white; upper forehead to forecrown deep blood-red (though some have orange or yellow admixed). Lores blackish; cheeks and ear-coverts whitish or tinged light buff and pale grey or with grey-brown surround; supercilium and sides of neck white or off-white. Crown, nape to mantle, back and scapulars white or whitish, tinged with buff or grey, and with dark grey or blackish centres forming isolated arrowheads or thin central streaks to feathers; lighter and slightly

broader streaks on mantle and upper back; lower back and rump white or tinged pinkish (mainly summer adult males), or white, often with a few thin greyish tips (females and first-year birds); uppertail-coverts also white with greyish centres. Tail is notched or slightly forked, blackish or dark brown, edged with white or pale grey. Median coverts dark or with blackish centres and broad buffish-white tips, greaters the same or whiter, and tips to both coverts form prominent double wing-bar; alula and primary coverts black; flight feathers also black, but thinly edged whitish or pale grey, becoming broadly white on edges and tips of tertials. Chin black; rest of underparts mainly white (or males in summer have a pale pink tinge mainly on centre of breast), most having some streaking on flanks but its extent depends on how much is concealed by the white body feathers; undertail-coverts usually appear all white, but most have thin or slender dark or dark grey centres to longest feathers, usually visible only when the bird is perched overhead. Bill is short and noticeably stubby, bright orange or deep yellow with a black tip, and the distal culmen in summer becomes more extensively dark. Legs and feet black or blackish-brown. In autumn and winter, birds generally lose all pink on breast and rump, latter becoming basally white or whitish; upper rump likely to show some dark centres to feathers in worn plumage (late winter-early spring). **Juvenile:** Very similar to adult female, but lacks any pink on breast and lacks deep red forecrown; some are slightly more buffish on upperparts, but as with adults variable, and some cannot be reliably aged in the field (or even in the hand).

GEOGRAPHICAL VARIATION Many individuals occur which cannot always be identified with certainty or distinguished from the paler, less streaked races *flammea* or *islandica* of Common

Redpoll. Race *exilipes* is very similar to *hornemanni* except in size, but is less white overall, with pale buff to buffish-brown feathers on head and face and greyish-white edged with pale buff on nape, mantle and back; the upper rump is often streaked with small dark centres to feathers (especially in worn plumage), and males are also tinged with pink on lower rump in fresh plumage; the median coverts have buff or pale buff tips, and greater coverts have broad white or buffish-white tips. Underparts are white or faintly tinged pink in fresh plumage; the flanks are more likely to be streaked (finely) in *exilipes* than in nominate, but streaks much finer or narrower than on most races of Common Redpoll and rarely extending to lower flanks; undertail-coverts are white, often unstreaked or with only a single dark central streak to the longest undertail-covert. Overall, *exilipes* is not such a white bird but more buff or greyish than the bright or white 'snowball' individuals of nominate *hornemanni*.

VOICE Call is very similar to that of Common Redpoll but with a degree of variation, said to be more metallic or coarser than Common's, but to anyone not in frequent contact with such calls the degree of variation is probably not easily detectable. Some Arctic Redpolls (*exilipes*), when present with both *cabaret* and *flammea* Common in parts of Europe, have been detected by their slightly higher-pitched calls, but this may not be consistent. The song is identical to Common Redpoll's.

STATUS, HABITAT AND BEHAVIOUR Uncommon or locally common. Occurs in the high Arctic on tundra, ravines and slopes with some stunted trees or bushes; further south and in winter, occurs in dwarf birch, willow thickets, spruce and other low-spreading shrubs. Usually found in pairs or loose family parties or in larger flocks of up to 100, often in company with Common Redpolls (69) where the ranges overlap; breeds loosely communally. Most habits and actions as Common Redpoll. Feeds on small seeds, primarily of shrubs or trees (see also food items of Common Redpoll); the young are fed principally on insects until they fledge.

DISTRIBUTION *C. h. hornemanni*: Ellesmere Island to Baffin Island, Canada, to northern Greenland from about 72°N.

C. h. exilipes: almost circumpolar on northern tundras of North America, Asia and northern Europe: in Europe, from extreme north of Norway and Sweden, islands in the Arctic Ocean, the Kola Peninsula east through tundra belts of northern Russia, northern Siberia to Anadyrland and the Chukotski Peninsula, northern Kamchatka and the coasts of the Sea of Okhotsk, south to Khabarovsk and northern Sakhalin Islands; in North America, west and north Alaska to Yukon and the Mackenzie range to northeast Manitoba, northern Quebec and northern Labrador.

MOVEMENTS Sedentary and migratory. Northern breeders of race *exilipes* move south to winter within and south of the breeding range in Scandinavia, northern Europe, northern CIS (USSR), the eastern Tien Shan in Sinkiang, northwest China, northwest Mongolia, and Manchuria; in northern North America, nominate race moves south to northern Michigan, southern Ontario and in eastern Canada to Labrador, and *exilipes* moves further south to winter in southwest Canada, central USA (Illinois, Indiana and Ohio) and east to the New England states. A rare visitor to Sakhalin Island, northern Japan, Spitsbergen (summer), Jan Mayen Island (summer), Faroes; *exilipes* is rare or scarce but almost of annual occurrence in very small numbers in British Isles in winter (often in flocks of Common Redpolls, particularly *flammea*), and has also been recorded south to Czechoslovakia, Austria, Romania and Hungary; birds of both races have been recorded in most of the maritime states of the eastern north Atlantic (from France – five records – northwards), but *hornemanni* remains extremely rare. Southward post-breeding movements occur from August to October, but many roam in nomadic fashion in search of feeding areas and may not settle to winter in one area until late October or November. Return movements northwards take place from February to late March, but some birds may linger *en route* when encountering adverse weather further north.

MEASUREMENTS Wing of male 80–88, of female 79–85; tail 57–67; tarsus 15–18; bill (from skull) 8·5–11. Wing of male *exilipes* 71–79, of female 68–77; tail 56–64; tarsus 13·5–16; bill (culmen) 7–9·5.

REFERENCES Knox (1988), Lansdown *et al.* (1991), Svensson (1992).

71 TWITE *Carduelis flavirostris*   Plate 17
Palearctic

Fringilla flavirostris Linnaeus, 1758, Syst. Nat., ed. 10, p. 182, Europe; restricted to Sweden by Hartert, 1903, Vögel pal. Fauna, p. 76.

IDENTIFICATION Length 13–13·5 cm (5–5½ in); *altaica* 14–15 cm (5½–6 in). A small and generally dark streaky-brown finch found almost exclusively in open country. Has a diagnostic call (from which its name is derived), frequently uttered in flight, pale creamy wingbars, and white flashes in wing and at base of tail, male has variable amount of pink on rump and (in winter) a distinctive pale yellow bill. Mountain or eastern races are generally paler or more frosted in appearance often with dark or blackish patches on sides of breast or flanks. Amount of pink shown on rump varies among individuals and races. **Confusion species:** In Europe Linnets (72) are superficially very similar, but lack warm orange-buff tones to face, chin and throat to flanks and the streaked upperparts and have warm orange-brown or light chestnut, almost uniform mantle (only very slightly streaked), back and scapulars; the head and face are mostly greyish (paler over eye, on cheeks and chin) and the underparts lightly streaked. Linnet's bill is slightly heavier than the small, rather stubby bill of Twite and is never yellow, appearing grey or pale greyish-horn. Linnet also has more white in wing (on leading edge of all primaries), white (streaked dark brown) rump and more white at sides of base of tail; male in summer has red forehead to crown and orange-red breast, while females and juveniles have streaks on chin and throat. Common Redpoll (69) is smaller, shorter-tailed and more compact: adults have red on forehead and black on chin, and most likely confusion is with juveniles, especially of race *cabaret* (as other races are more likely to show white on rump); paler or more obvious streaks on upperparts, chin and throat (as well as more heavily on rest of underparts) of *cabaret*, and call, if given, should be distinctive.

DESCRIPTION Sexes similar. **Adult** summer: Forehead to crown dark brown, darkest on forehead, finely or lightly streaked paler buff-brown; nape and hindneck lighter brown with broad buff streaks. Lores to sides of forehead, supercilium and cheeks rich or warm buff-brown, finely dark-streaked on lower cheeks, ear-coverts and sides of neck; thin dark brown eye-stripe behind eye and over ear-coverts. Mantle, back and scapulars heavily streaked, with broad dark brown centres to feathers and pale or warm buff edges; rump pink or bright pink, variable in extent possibly depending on age, and paler or pale buff on females (some show variable amount of dark centres or tips to feathers); uppertail-coverts brown or dark brown with buff or buff-brown edges and tips, slightly paler on females. Tail is deeply notched, blackish-brown with thin pale or whitish edges and tips to outer webs, buff on inners (in flight, shows little or no white in tail). Lesser and median coverts dark brown with light buff-brown tips, greaters similar with pale buff or warm buff tips, creating prominent wingbar; alula and primary coverts blackish-brown, finely tipped buff; flight feathers also blackish-brown, with white on leading edges of outer primaries (less extensive or prominent on females) which appears as a thin panel on closed wing; secondaries edged buff at about mid-length; tips of all flight feathers finely edged buff (in fresh plumage); tertials also blackish-brown, broadly edged and tipped brown or pale buff-brown. Chin and throat are plain, warm orange-buff, this colour extending to breast and upper flanks; sides and lower centre of breast to flanks heavily streaked brown or blackish-brown (but varies in intensity among individuals); belly, lower flanks and undertail-coverts white or washed buff (some are lightly streaked on sides of undertail-coverts). Bill is short and fairly stubby but pointed, blackish in summer or with a dull yellow base to lower mandible. Legs and feet black. After the

autumn moult, the face, sides of neck, chin, throat and sides of breast to flanks and pale feather edges of streaked upperparts become much warmer buff (the pale edges conceal the colour which is acquired through abrasion in spring); male's rump retains pink bases and centres to feathers but is more heavily overlain with brown edges and tips obscuring the pink, while females have rump uniform with mantle and back; streaks on sides of breast and flanks are more diffuse brown or dark brown, tips of greater coverts are more extensively pale buff-brown, edges to all but the outer two to three primaries are entirely white, and tips to all secondaries and most primaries are pale buffish-white. Bill is almost entirely orange-yellow, except for brown base. **Juvenile:** Very similar to adult female, lacking any pink on rump, but is slightly warmer brown and not so dark on mantle, back and scapulars; warm buff-brown or gingery-brown tips to greater coverts and tertials and edges to secondaries. The crown and nape feathers are edged greyish and the face is not so deep buff as on adult, and is generally paler on lower throat and breast, which is fairly heavily streaked; chin can be very lightly streaked. First-winter (as adult winter) plumage attained in moult in July-September. Bill as adult winter. Legs dark brown.

GEOGRAPHICAL VARIATION Note: Twites of Central Asia wander at random over great distances in winter and it is extremely difficult to separate races with certainty outside the breeding season; also, birds in worn plumage may not always be identifiable. Race *pipilans* is similar to nominate but slightly warmer on upperparts, including buff edges on crown to mantle, but in worn (late-winter) plumage loses buff edges and tips and looks very dark brown; also buff on face, throat and breast is more warm or tinged with orange; tail and flight feathers black. Race *brevirostris* is much paler on upperparts, and face is paler, with more creamy-buff on lores, supercilium, cheeks, chin and throat; it has broad pale buff or whitish edges to brown centres of mantle and back, the edges of the coverts and secondaries are brown or pale buff-brown, and bases of secondaries and edges to all outer primaries white; male's rump is deeper or brighter pink than nominate, and uppertail-coverts have very dark centres with broad white edges and tips. On some, the chin, throat and breast is white or whitish-buff; the sides of lower throat and breast have bold blackish-brown centres and fine buff tips; the lower flanks are streaked pale brown, and lower breast, belly and undertail-coverts are buffish-white. In winter, this race is much browner above and brown tips often obscure pink rump. Race *korejevi* is generally paler buff on upperparts than *brevirostris* and is heavily streaked on underparts, with dark on sides of breast broken into streaks; rump varies from whitish tinged lightly with pale pink to pink; all tail feathers (especially in winter plumage) are edged white or pale buffish-white. In worn plumage, has broad pale whitish or buff tips to greater coverts and flight feathers. Race *montanella* is very pale buff (the palest of all races) on upperparts and white or whitish below; intensity of pink on rump varies from whitish-pink to pale buff or tinged brown (latter especially on females) to reddish-pink. Race *altaica* is very similar to both *korejevi* and *montanella*, but the rump of some males is deeper pink and in winter both sexes have very white edges to tail feathers and pale brown or browner streaks to lower flanks. Race *miniakensis* has pale buff edges to brown streaks on upperparts, broad white flashes on edges of primaries, and the male's rump is white or pale pink; on females, the rump is a prominent band of white or pale pinkish-buff. Males of race *rufostrigata* are very warm brown on mantle, with bold dark lines; they have bright or deep pink rump, blackish wings and tail with broad pale or whitish wingbars and white edges to outer tail feathers (not so broad as *brevirostris*), and a warm brown or rufous-tinged vent and undertail-coverts with streaks continuing from flanks.

VOICE Call in flight is a jumbled twitter of notes very similar to Linnet but interspersed with a very distinctive 'tweee', 'chweee' or 'chwaiie', rather nasal and quite harsh in tone, often given on its own or in a short twitter from birds on the ground; eastern birds (including *brevirostris*) sound particularly nasal or more metallic, and *rufostrigata* has a rather distinctive 'ditoo' or 'didoo', 'didoowit' and a twanging 'twayee'. Song is an extension of the call but somewhat more chattering, alternating with short quiet trills.

STATUS, HABITAT AND BEHAVIOUR
Common or locally common. Breeds on open hillsides, moorland and mountains and high plateaux up to 4850 m, usually in open terrain or on cliffs, scree slopes or boulder-strewn plateaux with little or sparse vegetation but also in alpine meadows and low bushes, Tibetan furze (*Caragana*) or *Hippophae* scrub or dwarf birch; some *pipilans* nest in heather at low altitude close to the coast and on some Scottish islands. In winter, most descend to lower altitudes at the onset of severe weather and frequent lower pastures, open hillsides, river valleys, plains and the coast. Usually occurs in summer in pairs or is loosely colonial, but in late autumn gathers in flocks some of which may by midwinter be large (flocks of over 1,000 not unknown). Roosts communally in the open, or in short bushes, scrub or reedbeds. Flocks fly fairly fast with distinctive undulating flight in short bounds with occasional unexpected twists and turns, accompanied by excited twittering calls. Hops or shuffles on the ground (generally shows less tarsus length than Linnet). Forages on the ground and in or on vegetation; perches on rocks, boulders and in small bushes. Feeds on seedheads of sea-lavender, *Salicornia*, thistles, asters and other small weed seeds, and has been known to feed in stubble fields; also takes some insects and larvae.

DISTRIBUTION Two distinct and discrete populations: one in northwest Europe, and the other, the ancestral population, on high ground and mountain ranges of central and eastern Asia.

A. f. flavirostris: west and north coast of Norway north to Lapland and the Kola Peninsula, occasionally in northern Sweden and northern Finland.

A. f. pipilans: northern Britain and Ireland.

A. f. brevirostris: eastern Turkey, Caucasus, northwest Iran.

A. f. korejevi: Kirghiz steppes north to about 50°N, Russian Altai (Turkestan) south through the Tarbagatai range and the Dzungarian Ala Tau to northern Afghanistan, east through the Tien Shan range to the Bogdo Ola Shan range in Sinkiang and the northwest Nan Shan range in Tsinghai, west China.

A. f. altaica: eastern Central Asia, from the Tannu Ola river, northwest Mongolia, through central and southeast (Gobian) Altai range.

A. f. montanella: Russian Turkestan (Alai and Pamir ranges) south to northern Pakistan east to Gilgit, also from Kashgar through the Kunlun range, Sinkiang to the northern Nan Shan range, Tsinghai, western China.

A. f. miniakensis: western and central China, from southern Nan Shan ranges, eastern Tsinghai and southwest Kansu south to Sikang, west and northwest Szechwan and possibly eastern Tibet.

A. f. rufostrigata: northern Pakistan, Kashmir and the northern Himalayas to southwest Tibet east to Gyangtze.

Some races (notably *montanella* and *rufostrigata*) intergrade where the ranges meet or overlap.

MOVEMENTS Sedentary and migratory. In Europe, most of the breeding population moves south and southwest to winter in the coastal lowlands and estuaries around the North Sea and the Baltic, from southern England and northwest France east to Poland, north along the coasts of the Baltic Republics to southwest Finland and southern Sweden; in Norway, some may remain within the breeding range but at lower altitudes. It has also been recorded in central Spain, southern France, Hungary, Romania and in the CIS (USSR) around Leningrad and Moscow. Eastern populations are widely nomadic, moving or dispersing altitudinally to lower levels in winter, but erratic or unpredictable in their occurrence or abundance within the range; in northern Pakistan and Kashmir occurs down to 1500 m and probably lower in the river valleys east of the Caspian Sea in Central Asia; *korejevi* also occurs south of the Caspian in northeast Iran, and *altaica* in the central Gobi desert; *rufostrigata* winters south to Sikkim. Southward or altitudinal movements in autumn take place mostly from late September to November, but severity of winter weather and availability of food supply may determine earlier or later departures. Return movement northward in spring is in March and April.

MEASUREMENTS Wing of male *flavirostris* 71–82, of female 70–79; tail 63–66. Wing of male *pipilans* 73·5–80, of female 72–78·5; tail 55–61; tarsus 15·5–17; bill (from skull) 8·5–10. Wing of male *rufostrigata* 80–81, of female 73–81. Weight 14·5–20·5.

Fringilla cannabina Linnaeus, 1758, Syst. Nat., ed. 10, p. 182, Europe; restricted to Sweden by Hartert, 1903, Vögel pal. Fauna, p. 73.

IDENTIFICATION Length 13–14 cm (5¼ in). A familiar, attractive and rather brightly coloured finch with a distinctive twittering call and melodic wheezing song. Males are distinctive, with bright chestnut-brown upperparts, grey head with a bright red patch on forehead and breast and no black on chin. **Confusion species:** Females, non-breeding males and juveniles are more likely to be confused with similar Common Redpoll (69) or Twite (71): for differences from Twite see that species. Common Redpolls are smaller, paler and invariably more streaky, and lack white edges to tail feathers and prominent white leading edges to primaries; they also have a small yellow bill and black on chin (except juveniles of race *cabaret*, which can also be separated from juvenile Linnet by prominent pale buff-brown tips to greater coverts).

DESCRIPTION Sexes differ. **Adult male** summer: Lower forehead pale buff, forecrown rich crimson, often finely tipped with black; crown to upper nape grey, grey extending to face, with pale buffish-white upper cheeks and area over eye, and light buff centres to ear-coverts; sides of neck and nape grey (some are streaked darker, with fine pale buff edges to hindcrown and centre of nape). Mantle, back and scapulars cinnamon-brown or light chestnut, with very fine dark streaks and darker brown edges to some feathers of mantle and scapulars; lower back and rump slightly paler or sandy on some (or with a pinkish tinge). Uppertail-coverts black, with fine pale buff or whitish edges and tips. Tail is deeply notched, all outer feathers black and finely edged pale or whitish-buff. Median and lesser coverts as scapulars, edged slightly paler on some; outer greater coverts black with pale buff fringes, inners as scapulars; alula and primary coverts black; flight feathers black, primaries edged broadly white on outer web (most noticeable in flight as it forms a panel in wing); secondaries broadly edged warm buff-brown; tertials dark brown, edged warmer buff-brown. Chin and throat pale, whitish-buff, lightly spotted or streaked with brown on malar stripe, enclosing a whitish-buff submoustachial stripe; breast crimson or crimson-pink (with brown bases to some feathers), occasionally or rarely absent (breast is then pale or whitish-buff with pale brown spots); sides of lower breast (and, depending on age, sides of upper breast) and flanks warm buffish-brown, with darker buffish-brown mottling on flanks; centre of lower breast pale buffish or pale pinkish; belly and vent dull white, undertail-coverts similar or washed light sandy-buff. Bill blackish-brown, with grey at base of both mandibles. Legs and feet dark pinkish-brown. In autumn moult, crimson on new feathers of forehead is obscured by buffish-brown tips and

crown and nape are edged with pale buff; mantle, back and scapulars are slightly darker brown with darker brown or blackish streaks; breast is rich warm or brownish-buff (obscuring crimson bases to feathers) and streaked blackish-brown, continuing onto flanks. **Adult female:** Forehead to hindcrown brown or grey-brown, finely dark-streaked; nape, hindneck and sides of neck uniform dull grey-brown, slightly streaked paler on sides of neck. Mantle, back and scapulars chestnut-brown with dark or brown centres to feathers; coverts similar, but with paler brown edges and buffish-brown tips; rest of wing as adult male, but white in wing not so broad (less than half the outer web of inner primaries) and forms a broken panel on closed wing. Rump and uppertail-coverts as adult male, but with heavier brown bases and tips to feathers; tail as adult male, but central feathers edged buffish-brown, outers edged white. Face has a distinctive pale buff area on cheeks and around eyes (as male), but otherwise is greyish buff-brown. Chin and throat pale buff-brown (some are tinged pinkish), streaked with dark olive-brown on malar stripe; breast, upper belly and flanks deep or dirty buffish-brown, heavily streaked dark brown; centre of belly to undertail-coverts paler buff. Bill as male but slightly browner, more horn-coloured at base. In winter, very little change except for a slightly more streaky appearance, with pale buffish-brown edges and tips to mantle, back, scapulars and median and greater coverts; edges and tips to primaries finely buff. **Juvenile:** Very similar to adult female but generally browner, warm buff-brown on head; mantle, back and scapulars all streaked dark brown; wings and tail as adults (sexes separable at an early age), and underparts more sandy or light buff (lighter than adult female) and streaked dark brown. First-winter birds as adult female. First-summer males can show variable amounts of pinkish or red on breast (including none at all), but red probably never so rich or extensive as on older (second-summer) birds.

GEOGRAPHICAL VARIATION Most variation concerns the colour of brown upperparts. Race *harterti* is generally paler, more light cinnamon above (males), with whiter flanks. Race *bella* is paler above and below and summer male has very pale grey crown and nape; most distinctive feature is the pale, almost white uppertail-coverts and lower rump; pink on forehead and breast is deeper on average. Madeiran and Canary Island races *nana* and *meadewaldoi* are unlikely to be separable in the field on plumage.

VOICE Call a rapid, trilling 'chi-chi-chi-chit', usually uttered in flight with other twittering notes and similar to Twite but without latter's distinctive 'tweet' note; also gives a very soft or subdued 'too-tee' or 'too-hwee', uttered in the breeding season at or near nests or young; a sharp 'tsooeet' is given as an alarm or anxiety call, and a similar note is given by newly fledged young but often harsher and somewhat more of a 'twit' note, occasionally recalling Common Crossbill (110). Song is a soft and varied musical warble interspersed with twitters and trills, usually from exposed top of bush, tree or spray of gorse etc., occasionally from the ground.

STATUS, HABITAT AND BEHAVIOUR
Common or relatively common, more local in northern areas. A bird of hills or high ground (usually below 2000 m), typically on open commons or heathland with scattered trees and usually fairly mature gorse or other suitable thick growth in which to nest; it occurs also in gardens, orchards, hedgerows, plantations, woodland edge and edges of cultivation; in Turkey and Central Asia, race *bella* prefers even rocky mountain slopes, maquis or valleys with low shrubs and weedy patches, often among rocky fields. In winter most *cannabina* form large flocks, often in company with Greenfinches (44), Common Redpolls and Tree Sparrows (274) and roam widely in search of food, feeding in stubble fields, weedy patches, plains, deserts and along the shoreline. Flight is undulating and fairly fast, and slightly more purposeful and direct than the more wavering or erratic flight of Twite. Usually detectable by very noticeable and characteristic jangling twitter similar to Twite. On the ground it hops. Feeds mainly on the ground but freely perches in trees, bushes and on fences etc., taking a variety of weed seeds and garden-flower seeds but also buds and some insects; nestlings are fed on insect larvae for the first few days, but mostly on seeds until fledging.

DISTRIBUTION *A. c. cannabina*: British Isles, Europe to southern Scandinavia (approximately 65°N), east to the Urals, central Kazakhstan and western Siberia; in the south to North Africa, Morocco (south to edge of Sahara), northern Algeria, northern Tunisia and parts of Libya (Tripoli

and Cyrenaica) and most of the Mediterranean islands including the Balearics, Corsica, Sardinia, Sicily, Crete, Cyprus, to western Turkey, north to Romania and the Crimea.

A. c. bella: (Turkestan Linnet) central and eastern Turkey, through Middle East to southern Israel, the Caucasus, discontinuously in Iran (isolated areas in the Elburz Mountains and the southwest) and the southern shores of the Caspian Sea, northwest through Central Asia and Afghanistan to the Altai, Tarbagatai and Tien Shan ranges to the Bogdo-Ola Shan, Sinkiang, west China.

A. c. nana: Madeira.

A. c. meadewaldoi: western Canary Islands, Tenerife, Gran Canaria, Gomera, Hierro and Palma.

A. c. harterti: eastern Canary Islands, Lanzarote, Fuerteventura, Graciosa and Allegranza.

MOVEMENTS Sedentary and migratory. Northern breeders of races *cannabina* and *bella* move south and southwest to winter mostly within the range around the Mediterranean and Iran, Iraq and northern Baluchistan, also to coastal areas of North Africa, the Negev, northern Egypt and exceptionally (perhaps regularly) to northern Sudan (Nile areas only). Has also occurred in eastern Saudi Arabia, northern Pakistan, Kashmir (Gilgit and Ladakh) and northwest India (Punjab). A vagrant to Lapland, Senegal (March 1971), Libyan desert, Kuwait, the United Arab Emirates and Nepal. In Europe, southward movement in autumn is from mid-September to the end of October or exceptionally into November; return movement in spring is from late March to mid-April or occasionally into May. A diurnal and nocturnal passage migrant, with flocks often noted arriving at headlands and migration points during daylight hours.

MEASUREMENTS Wing of male 74–86, of female 75–79 (for a more comprehensive range of male wing lengths see Vaurie 1956); tail 50–57; tarsus 16–17; bill (from skull) 10–11. Weight 16–18.

REFERENCES Vaurie (1956), Witherby *et al.* (1938–41).

73 YEMEN LINNET *Carduelis yemenensis* Plate 18

Arabia

Pseudacanthis yemenensis Ogilvie-Grant, 1913, Bull. Brit. Ornith. Club, 31, p.89, Menacha, Yemen.

IDENTIFICATION Length 11·5–12 cm (4½–5 in). A distinctive endemic found at high levels in southwest Arabia; similar in plumage to Linnet (72), from which it is geographically isolated. **Confusion species:** Confusion with species other than Linnet (which is a winter visitor to parts of Egypt and southern Israel) unlikely. Yemen Linnet has all-grey head, bright chestnut upperparts, grey breast (male), no red on forehead or breast, white wingbar or small square of white on generally black primaries, and shorter, more stubby bill.

DESCRIPTION Sexes differ. **Adult male:** Entire head to hindneck, chin, throat and centre of breast light grey, with very fine or faint dark eye-stripe or (on some) a slightly paler area over lores and below eye recalling Linnet. Mantle, back, scapulars and wing-coverts deep chestnut (some, perhaps first-summer birds, show slightly darker streaks on feather centres), lower back often brightest or most chestnut; rump greyish-white or greyish-brown, uppertail-coverts dark greyish-brown with paler buffish-grey edges and tips. Tail is deeply notched, black, edged broadly with white at base of all outer

feathers (very conspicuous in flight). Flight feathers black, with all (except first three primaries) edged white at base forming a broad wingbar in flight and small patch on closed wing; edges to secondaries light chestnut-brown, tipped paler buff brown; tertials black or blackish, edged chestnut or light chestnut and tipped whitish. Chin to upper breast light grey, sides of lower breast chestnut or rich brown, becoming paler on belly and flanks; rest of underparts white or washed light cinnamon-brown. Bill as Linnet but blunter, with a definite curve to upper mandible, dark horn upper and paler or yellowish-horn lower mandible. Legs and feet brown or dark brown. In winter, the grey is duller, the rich brown of upperparts is somewhat duller, and buff tips to wing and tail feathers more prominent. **Adult female:** Similar to adult male but separable in the field, being paler or duller. Grey of head duller and merges with the brown of mantle, back is tinged with brown; crown to mantle and back streaked finely with black. Greater coverts have dark or blackish-brown centres or bases, with brown or buff-brown edges and tips; white edges at base of primaries less extensive or prominent than on male. A light brown or buff-brown patch on sides of lower breast, on some to upper flanks, otherwise underparts light buff with belly and undertail-coverts white or whitish-buff. **Juvenile:** Very little known. Has pale brown crown streaked finely darker, and pale buff crescents below eye; brown ear-coverts and dark brown upperparts all dark-streaked; greater coverts and scapulars edged and tipped pale chestnut or warm buff-brown; chin and throat whitish with faint streaks, breast warm buff and streaked with dark brown on breast and flanks.
VOICE Call is a musical 'tirrrit' or 'wid-lee-ee', also a Goldfinch-like abrupt and soft rippling 'vliet'. The song is a lively and rapid musical twittering interspersed with notes reminiscent of both Canary (7) and Goldfinch (68), delivered either from top of a bush or tree or in circular display flight often in pursuit of female.

STATUS, HABITAT AND BEHAVIOUR Common or locally common resident. Found between 1800 m and 3660 m in dry mountains, plateaux or hillsides, in wadis with rocks or scree but with scattered vegetation of thornscrub, acacias, euphorbias or junipers; occasionally in or near areas of cultivation, including orchards or plantations. Nests semicolonially in bushes or trees. Outside breeding season occurs in flocks, often mixing with Yemen Serin (19) especially at communal roosts. Hops on ground; flight fast and lightly undulating, perches (and sings) on bushes or trees. Feeds mostly on the ground, though does take seeds from bushes and suitable plants. Food seems to be entirely seeds, usually of grass and small weeds but also of herbs, barley and sorghum.
DISTRIBUTION Monotypic. Endemic to the Hejaz and Asir Mountains of southwest Saudi Arabia, through the highlands of North Yemen and, according to Meinertzhagen (1954), into northern South Yemen (to around Taiz) though its presence there now requires confirmation.
MOVEMENTS In the non-breeding season nomadic or wandering flocks have been observed in the Asir Mountains, Saudi Arabia; has been seen down to 590 m in November.
MEASUREMENTS Wing of male 78–80, of female 68–73; tarsus 13·9–14·9; bill (to skull) 10–12·8; bill (to feathers) 6–6·8. Weight 13·4–15.
REFERENCES Bowden and Brooks (1987), Hollom et al. (1988), Meinertzhagen (1954), Stagg (1984).

74 WARSANGLI LINNET *Carduelis johannis* Plate 9
Northeast Africa

Warsanglia johannis Clarke, 1919, Bull. Brit. Ornith. Club, 40, p. 48, Mush Haled, 4000 ft, about 250 miles west-southwest of Cape Guardafui, Warsangli country, British Somaliland.

IDENTIFICATION Length 12·5–13·5 cm (5–5¼ in). A little-known and poorly studied species restricted to montane forest of northern Somalia. Distinctive almost black-and-white plumage makes it very unlikely to be confused with any other finch: upperparts grey, with white forehead and chestnut rump and flanks; wings and tail black with a large white patch at base of primaries; underparts white.
DESCRIPTION Sexes similar. **Adult male:** Forehead and supercilium white; lores black, eye-stripe from bill to area over ear-coverts dark or blackish-grey, becoming paler towards sides of nape; cheeks white, ear-coverts pale grey. Crown pale grey, becoming darker on hindcrown and nape (in worn plumage nape becomes paler or whitish); mantle, scapulars and lower back grey; upper rump chest-nut, becoming white on lower rump; uppertail-coverts dark grey, tipped white. Black tail is slightly notched. Median and greater coverts black (tipped white in fresh plumage); flight feathers black, with white edges to basal half of all primaries except outermost two (shows as large white wing flash in flight). Chin, throat and rest of underparts (except lower flanks) white, or washed with buff on breast, with lower flanks rich brown or chestnut. Bill dark grey, slightly paler greyish-horn on lower mandible. Legs and feet dark brown. **Adult female:** Similar to adult male but separable in the field; generally has less white on forehead and over eye. Crown, nape and most of upperparts (except rump) a pale greyish-brown, streaked or washed dull brown; centres to scapulars also darker; rump as male or slightly duller; uppertail-coverts broadly

tipped white. Chin and throat white, flecked with grey; flanks tinged reddish as on rump or slightly paler; rest of underparts white or whitish-buff. Bill is paler grey than male's, especially on lower mandible. **Juvenile:** Head, face and upperparts pale greyish-buff, heavily streaked with brown; forehead and rump paler cream-buff, spotted with dark brown; underparts pale buff-brown, with fine dark brown streaks on upper breast becoming spots on sides of breast and flanks. Wings as adult but blackish-brown, with broad pale buff-brown tips to coverts, secondaries and tertials.

VOICE A single Goldfinch-like high-pitched 'tsee-wit' or a *Phylloscopus*-like 'tweek', a twittering 'sis-sis-sis' and a clear 'sweet-ee'. The song is a jumble of typically Serin-like notes.

STATUS, HABITAT AND BEHAVIOUR
Locally common endemic resident. An African *Red Data Book* species; has been seen about a dozen times by Western ornithologists since being first described in 1919, but remains poorly known and its habitat preference is still little known. Occurs within a restricted range of montane juniper forest between 1200 m and 2400 m; found principally in (but not restricted to) open or degraded juniper forest but also in other woodland and scrub. Observers have been unable to agree on whether the population is stable, increasing or endangered, but the destruction and continual degradation of the forest zones where it has been found are likely to be highly detrimental to its future. Usually seen alone or in pairs or small groups. Flight fast and direct. Prefers high exposed perches at tops of trees

♂

or the ends of dead branches. Feeds mainly on grass, plant and shrub seeds, including green seeds of *Salvia*. Nest and eggs unknown; the juvenile is known from only a single specimen.

DISTRIBUTION Monotypic. Restricted to highlands of Mijjertein and Warsangli regions of northeast Somalia, where it occurs discontinuously for approximately 250 km, from about 100 km east of Mush Aled west to Daloh (principally the Daloh Forest Reserve).

MEASUREMENTS Wing 70–80; tarsus 13; bill (from feathers) 9. Weight 11·8–15.

REFERENCES Armani (1983), Ash and Miskell (1981, 1983), Collar and Stuart (1985), Mackworth-Praed and Grant (1960).

GENUS *LEUCOSTICTE*

Three species. Dark-plumaged sparrow-like finches of east Asia and North America. Live mostly in alpine or high-altitude habitats but one species, Rosy Finch (77), ranges widely from tundra to mountain plateaux and spans two continents.

75 HODGSON'S MOUNTAIN FINCH (Hodgson's Rosy Finch, Plain Mountain Finch) *Leucosticte nemoricola*   Plate 20

Palearctic

Fringilauda nemoricola Hodgson, 1836, Asiatic Researches, 19, p. 158, central and northern Nepal.

IDENTIFICATION Length 15 cm (6 in). Distinctly and characteristically nondescript and recognisable by its sparrow-like shape and featureless dull or grey-brown plumage. A high-altitude finch found not below 1800 m on alpine meadows and hillsides with dwarf scrub, above and below the tree line. Occurs in flocks in summer and winter and recognisable by the constant swooping movement of the flock in flight. **Confusion species:** Brandt's Mountain Finch (76) is darker about the head and face, is generally plain or more uniform and less streaked than Hodgson's, and has pale grey wing-coverts and pink or brownish-pink tips

to rump feathers. Similar to female House Sparrow (258), but lacks bright stripes on upperparts and prominent buffish-brown supercilium.

DESCRIPTION Sexes alike. **Adult:** Forehead to crown, nape, lores, cheeks and ear-coverts brown or gingery-brown, slightly paler, lighter buffish or grey over eye and ear-coverts. Nape and sides of neck dark brown (or buffish-brown on lower nape). Mantle, back and scapulars dark or warm brown, with paler or tawny-buff edges to feathers in fresh plumage (when also shows pale buff braces or 'tramlines' at sides of mantle and back); lower back and rump plain ash-grey or lightly tinged with brown; uppertail-coverts dark grey or blackish, tipped slightly paler, longest feathers tipped white. Tail is slightly notched, dark brown or blackish-brown, with feathers finely edged with buff. Median coverts brown, with blackish centres and white tips (broadly in fresh plumage); greater coverts dark brown, lighter or warmer brown on outer edge and finely tipped white or creamy-buff; alula and primary coverts blackish-brown, the latter edged buff or light buff-brown; flight feathers dark brown, all edged mid or warm brown (except bases to secondaries), inner secondaries edged pale buff or whitish; tertials dark brown, broadly edged warm brown and tipped light buff. Chin whitish, otherwise generally uniform dull grey or ash-brown below (in fresh plumage can show plain or dingy brown on upper breast, flanks and belly), with vent and undertail-coverts paler or whitish with some black streaks. Bill is sparrow-like but finer and slightly longer, brown or brownish-horn on culmen and tip, paler at base of lower mandible. Legs and feet dark brown. Eye bright red. In winter, somewhat duller than summer, with abrasion causing the pale or buff tips and edges to be markedly reduced or absent, giving a more 'uniform' appearance. **Juvenile:** Similar to adult, but crown, cheeks and ear-coverts are darker or rufous-brown and finely streaked paler; mantle and back gingery-brown, less heavily streaked, and lacks braces or 'tramlines'; median and greater coverts have fine white tips forming double wingbar. Underparts are reddish-brown or tinged with ginger on breast and belly, lower belly whitish-buff, whiter on undertail-coverts. First-winter birds more like adult, but retain rufous feathers on crown and ear-coverts.

GEOGRAPHICAL VARIATION Racial separation in the field doubtful. Race *altaica* generally more rufous-brown, becoming deep ginger and often with darker feather centres (but some cannot be identified racially by this character), with paler underparts; juvenile and first-winter birds of this race may be deeper ginger or rich warm brown on underparts. In the hand, axillaries bright or deep yellow in nominate and pale grey in *altaica*.

VOICE Call is a soft sparrow or Redpoll-like twitter, 'chi-chi-chi-chi'; also has a shrill whistling double-note call. The song is a sharp twitter, 'rick-

pi-vitt' or 'dui-dip-dip-dip', usually delivered from the top of a boulder or prominent stone.

STATUS, HABITAT AND BEHAVIOUR Common. Occurs on mountains, hillsides, plateaux and alpine meadows above 1800 m, in summer not below 3600 m and regular around Everest base camp at 5150 m. In winter, found at edges of cultivation, on open fields or even in and around small villages. Usually in flocks, in some areas containing up to 200 birds, in trees or feeding on open ground or among rocks or screes and occasionally on ground in open woodland. Hops or runs sparrow-like on ground, but restless and often takes flight in large flocks; flight is fast, wheeling and frequently changing in direction, recalling Starlings (*Sturnus vulgaris*) at roost. Gregarious and sociable at all times. Feeds on a variety of small seeds, particularly *Artemisia*, also barley and some insects.

DISTRIBUTION *L. n. nemoricola*: Himalayas from Nepal and southern Tibet, south to Sikkim and Bhutan, discontinuously east to northern Yunnan (Likiang range), eastern Szechwan (Wa Shan) and eastern Tsinghai and northwest Kansu to southern Shensi (Tsinling Shan), western China.

L. n. altaica: northeast Afghanistan (Badakhshan) to Chitral, northern Pakistan, Kashmir east in the Himalayas to Garhwal and Kumaon, north to the western Kunlun ranges, Tarbagatai and Altai mountains, western Sinkiang, China.

MOVEMENTS Partial and altitudinal migrant. Immatures wander or descend to lower levels than adults; birds of nominate race recorded in winter in Adung valley, extreme northern Burma. Moves down to about 1800 m in winter, all returning to above 4300 m in summer. Noted on southward passage in Turkestan in early November and northward in southeast Tibet in early May; considerable numbers still on passage in valleys of southwest Tibet in late May and early June.

MEASUREMENTS Wing of male 94–105, of female 90–108; tail of male 65–72, of female 64–69; tarsus 19·5–21·5; bill (from skull) 12–15. Weight 20–25·5.

REFERENCES Ali and Ripley (1983), Dementiev and Gladkov (1951–54), Ludlow (1951), Ludlow and Kinnear (1933), Smythies (1985), Whistler (1925).

76 BRANDT'S MOUNTAIN FINCH (Black-headed Mountain Finch)
Leucosticte brandti　　　　　　　　　　　　　　　**Plate 20**

Palearctic

Leucosticte brandti Bonaparte, 1851?, Consp. Avium 1 (1850), p. 537, eastern Siberia; amended to Turkestan by Hartert, 1904, Vögel pal. Fauna, p. 137; restricted to Zailiski Ala Tau by Vaurie, 1959, Birds Pal. Fauna, Passeriformes, p. 621.

IDENTIFICATION Length 16·5–19 cm (6½–7½ in). A finch of high altitudes and alpine meadows. Similar to Hodgson's Mountain Finch (75), but much blacker or greyer and has a much wider dis-

tribution. **Confusion species:** Likely to be confused only with Hodgson's Mountain Finch, but it is much darker, with a sooty-black forehead and crown, grey or grey-brown nape and mantle, distinctive pale wing-coverts with bright pink on lesser coverts and (in fresh plumage) pink on rump; some races lack pink on lesser coverts. All snow finches (284–290) are paler and generally have white underparts.

DESCRIPTION Sexes similar. **Adult male:** Forehead to crown sooty-black, hindcrown and nape paler or dark grey, lores black, cheeks and ear-coverts blackish-grey; in fresh plumage ear-coverts and sides of nape and neck are tinged with yellow. Lower nape and upper mantle dull or dark brown and grey-tinged, lower mantle and upper back grey, washed with pale buff or yellowish, scapulars pale grey or grey-brown with fine or thin dark streaks; lower back, rump and uppertail-coverts pale pearl-grey with rosy-pink edges and tips (abrasion in summer may reduce these partially or totally). Tail is blackish-brown on central pair of feathers, with all outers finely edged and tipped whitish or whitish-buff, slightly broader on outer web of outer pair (very prominent in flight). Lesser coverts pale grey, tipped pale pink, median and greater coverts grey, broadly edged pale frosted grey; alula and primary coverts black, the latter finely edged pale grey; flight feathers blackish or dusky blackish, edged pale grey on primaries and whitish on tips and edges of secondaries; tertials pale buffish-grey on outer web, brown on inner web. Underparts are almost entirely pale or dingy grey; belly to undertail-coverts tinged buffish. Bill is rather sparrow-like but more slender and pointed towards tip, black in summer plumage, dark brown with yellow base in winter. Legs and feet black. In winter, the dark head and mantle to back and scapulars is much more tawny or warm buff-brown, with black of summer appearing only through abrasion, while the lesser coverts are broadly edged rosy-pink, which disappears before the summer plumage is assumed. **Adult female:** As adult male, but at all times rump is much duller grey and pink on rump is less marked even at close range. **Juvenile and First-summer:** Juveniles lack black on forehead to crown and have sandy-brown upperparts with dark brown feather centres to mantle and back; rump and uppertail-coverts also dark with orange-buff fringes; wings and tail feathers have buff-brown edges, but some show a faint pink tinge on lesser coverts as winter adults. First-summer birds have generally tawny or buff-brown head with black feather bases to forecrown; mantle and upper back are dingy brown, but feathers of nape to lower back are all tipped with pale or yellowish-buff, becoming golden-buff on lower back and scapulars; rump grey or pale grey, with faint pink or rosy-pink edges and tips. Lesser and median coverts pale ashy with rich golden-buff edges, tips to greater coverts creamy or pale buff-brown. Throat whitish or pale buff, breast, belly and flanks grey or buffish-brown, rest of underparts paler buff. Bill has a grey-brown upper mandible, while lower is pale yellow with a dark tip.

GEOGRAPHICAL VARIATION There is considerable variation in the intensity of the upperparts colour and the extent of black on crown. Summer-plumage *haematopygia* has blackish-brown fore-

head (blackest) to nape, mantle and scapulars are distinctly darker with dark brown streaks continuing to upper back, lores and chin are nearly as black as forehead, and cheeks and ear-coverts to sides of neck are black or deep or dull brown. Race *pallidior* is similar to nominate *brandti* on mantle and back, but has extensive black on crown to hindcrown, brown or dark brown upper nape, and variably dark brown to black lores and brown cheeks and ear-coverts; the chin and throat are grey or pale buff. Race *pamirensis* is closer to nominate in extent of black on crown, but has darker grey nape and mantle and also has heavier streaks on mantle and back; the face is generally pale grey but lores to below eye can be black; also has deep red tips to rump and is slightly greyer on breast, belly and flanks. Both *pallidior* and *haematopygia* lack pink tips to lesser coverts, which are replaced with plain pale grey. Race *margaritacea* has plainer grey plumage, with forehead and underparts pale grey or silvery-grey; pink in wing extends to edges of primaries.

VOICE Call is a loud 'twitt-twitt', 'twee-ti-ti' or 'peek-peek', often given in flight, also a harsh distinctive 'churr' recalling a grosbeak or a stonechat. The song is undescribed, and some authors consider that it has no song.

STATUS, HABITAT AND BEHAVIOUR Generally common (abundant in some areas in winter). Found on high-altitude cliffs, crags, scree slopes and desolate or treeless areas of barren stony mountaintops or plateaux; has a preference for wet or boggy areas and also edges of streams. Occurs generally at higher elevations than Hodgson's, in summer from 3950 m to 6000 m and lower in winter (though many remain in summer breeding areas). Frequently tame and most habits very similar to Hodgson's, with birds in colonies or large flocks (often of one sex) during the year; occasionally associates with Adams's Snow Finch (285). Flight strong, undulating and swift. Perches on bushes, boulders and stone walls. Feeds on the ground, commonly in areas of melting snow, on seeds of small alpine plants, shoots of *Sedum* plants or, in winter, in fallow barley fields.

DISTRIBUTION *L. b. brandti*: Dzungarian Ala Tau and the western Tien Shan to about 85°E in western Sinkiang.

L. b. margaritacea: Tarbagatai range, northwest Sinkiang and the Altai range from eastern Kazakhstan east to western Mongolia.

L. b. pamirensis: western Tien Shan, Tadzhikstan (south of nominate) to the Pamirs, northeast Afghanistan and extreme western Sinkiang.

L. b. haematopygia: northern Pakistan, Kashmir, northwest Punjab north to the Karakoram range and east to Nepal and northern Sikkim, also through southern Tibet to northern Szechwan and Tsinghai north to the Buckhan Boda Shan.

L. b. pallidior: Humboldt range, west Nan Shan (and possibly Tatung Shan and the mountains of the Koko Nor range) in northern Tsinghai, west through the Astin Tagh (north to Lop Nor) and the Kunlun and Tien Shan ranges, southwest Sinkiang.

Note: Other races (*walteri, audreyana, incerta*

and *intermedia*) have been proposed, but the level of variation is not considered separable from *haematopygia* (see Vaurie 1949). Two specimens of mountain finch collected in western Tibet as long ago as 1929 were recently (1992) described as a new species, *Leucosticte sillemi* (*Bull. Brit. Ornith. Club.* 112: 225–231); no other individuals are known, however, and the possibility that the specimens – a juvenile and a worn adult – are in fact aberrant examples of Brandt's Mountain Finch cannot be excluded.

MOVEMENTS Sedentary (at lower levels of breeding range), altitudinal migrant and nomadic. Moves down to 3000 m and exceptionally down to 2100 m in winter, but, unless winter severe, many remain at higher elevations; otherwise nomadic throughout the range. Occurs in northern Pakistan (Chitral to Gilgit), central Nepal and Sikkim (mostly *haematopygia* and *pamirensis*); *brandti* is a vagrant to Gilgit and *pallidior* a vagrant to Sikkim.

MEASUREMENTS Wing of male 110–125, of female 105–117; tail of male 73–82·5, of female 69–75; tarsus 20–22; bill (from skull) of male 13–14·5, of female 14–15. Weight 26–29.

REFERENCES Ali (1962), Ali and Ripley (1983), Fleming *et al.* (1979), Osmaston (1925), Vaurie (1949), Whistler (1925).

77 ROSY FINCH (Rosy Mountain Finch, Arctic Rosy Finch)
Leucosticte arctoa   **Plate 32**

Holarctic

Passer arctous Pallas, 1811, Zoogr. Rosso-Asiat., 2, p. 21, Yenisei River and eastern Siberia; restricted to Russian Altai by Kozlova, 1934, Ibis, p. 293.

IDENTIFICATION Length 14–18 cm (5½–7 in). Widely distributed, mostly in easily recognisable races, across much of eastern Siberia to Kamchatka, Aleutians, Pribilofs, Alaska and western USA to Baja California. Variable in plumage, from black or blackish-purple to brown or pinkish-brown on body, with black on face, chin or forehead and/or pale or warm brown or grey on crown to nape. The wings, rump and underparts are also variably pink or pinkish; birds from central Asia have pale grey in wings and tail. Females are much less brightly coloured, but still as variable in body plumage as males. Unlikely to be confused with any other species; all races are equal in size except *griseonucha*, which is much larger.

DESCRIPTION Sexes differ. **Adult male** (*L. a. arctoa*): Lores black; forehead to crown and upper nape, face and ear-coverts dark brown, finely streaked or flecked paler or whitish; pale buffish 'supercilium' behind eye and over ear-coverts to sides of nape joins with buffish-brown or pale buffish-brown or grey hindneck. Mantle, back and scapulars dark chocolate-brown or tinged a deep rust-brown, often with paler feather edges to mantle and back; paler, greyer or greyish-white on rump, uppertail-coverts, and all of tail feathers except central shafts, which are blackish, with tips of all feathers dark brown or blackish; tail is notched or forked. Lesser coverts as scapulars but tipped lightly with grey, median coverts grey with black shafts and tips to feathers; greater coverts, alula, primary coverts and flight feathers all pale silvery-grey with darker or blackish-brown tips; tertials the same, with dark brown inner webs. Chin black, becoming dark chocolate-brown on rest of underparts, paler on sides of breast, lower breast, belly and flanks and with a faint pink or light purple tinge; thighs and undertail-coverts grey or grey-brown with dark tips and shaft streaks. Bill is fairly deep at base and pointed, black in summer, pale

brown or straw-yellow with a dark tip in winter. Legs and feet black. **Adult female:** Very similar to adult male, but generally much paler brown on head and body, with paler buff-brown edges and tips to many feathers on upperparts and underparts; head and face slightly darker, without pale flecking (but some are streaked on crown in worn plumage); wings and tail are as adult male but less intensely silvery-white. **Juvenile:** Overall much paler and more uniform brown or greyish-brown with buff or sandy edges and tips to feathers, and pale buff wingbars formed by pale buff tips to median and greater coverts; mantle and back feathers have dark centres, face and underparts have pale grey edges, and belly is paler buff-brown.

GEOGRAPHICAL VARIATION Males of race *sushkini* are more heavily tinged pink, and greater coverts, flight and tail feathers are grey or greyish-brown; females also have wings and tail darker. Male *cognata* is deeper pink or more rosy-pink on body than *arctoa* (but not so deeply pink as *sushkini*); females are also paler on head and body than *arctoa*; wings and tail as *sushkini*. Sexes of race *gigliolii* are almost alike: males have dark brown head except for grey or greyish cheeks and ear-coverts (in winter forecrown to crown becomes paler or pale buff and forehead is red or deep red), nape and hindneck are pale buff or buffish-brown, mantle and back rich brown becoming reddish-brown on rump, chin and throat dark brown or grey-brown, flanks and belly dark reddish-brown, or rosy-pink, wings and tail blackish-brown, and uppertail- and undertail-coverts are black or blackish-brown, finely edged pale brown; females are drab grey-brown with paler or buffish-brown (streaked brownish) mantle, back and scapulars, and in winter have broad pale buff edges to median and greater coverts and edges of tertials. Males of *brunneonucha* differ from nominate in having forehead to crown black, blackish or obscured by grey centres; nape and sides of neck are golden or tawny-yellow, mantle and scapulars dark brown with rich tawny or sandy-brown edges, and lower back to uppertail-coverts blackish-brown but obscured by deep pink tips and whitish centres to feathers; tail is blackish-brown with paler or buff-brown edges; median and greater coverts are dark brown, edged pink or bright pink (more prominently on greaters); flight feathers black or blackish, edged with pink (broadly on bases to secondaries); throat and upper breast are black with white or pearl-grey tips, lower breast, belly and flanks blackish-brown with white or pale pink tips. In winter much more sandy or buff overall, with body feathers (including head) having pale sandy fringes, the only rose or pink at this time of year is on tips of median and/or greater coverts (edges are pale grey), breast, belly and flanks. Juveniles are very similar and lack any pink on rump. Female *brunneonucha* are much duller, browner or more grey-brown (especially on underparts) than males, and lack prominent pink edges to wing feathers (but flight feathers edged whitish) or underparts except for light pink edges to outer medians and pale or orange-pink on sides of lower flanks and undertail-coverts (which may be invisible in the field). Both sexes of *griseonucha* are similar to *brunneonucha* but much larger (the largest of the races), and have black or blackish chin and throat and deep brown breast lacking any white tips, but lower breast and belly is prominently tipped with rosy-pink; forehead to crown black, cheeks, ear-coverts, sides of neck, hindcrown and nape silvery-grey; mantle, back and scapulars are deep brown, rump and uppertail-coverts blackish-brown with pale pink tips; wings and tail blackish-brown, tips of medians and greaters bright pink but fading to dull or whitish-buff in worn plumage. Juveniles of this race are generally sooty-brown, tinged with ash-grey, with median and greater coverts dull grey, edged paler, and flight feathers black, narrowly edged whitish or pale buff-brown on secondaries and broadly so on tertials. Race *umbrina* is very similar (if not identical in the field) to *griseonucha* but darker above and below, especially on head and throat. Males of race *tephrocotis* have forehead to fore-crown black, and sides of crown, hindcrown and nape grey; cheeks, ear-coverts, nape to mantle, back, scapulars and the entire underparts warm brown, slightly darker on chin to lower breast; scapulars and back indistinctly dark-streaked; rump, uppertail-coverts, flanks (and sometimes to lower belly and undertail-coverts) are broadly tipped pink; median coverts pink, tipped paler or whitish, greater coverts black and tipped pale pink, flight feathers also black, edged pink or light crimson (becoming pale buff or yellowish-buff in winter or when worn); tail is black, finely edged pale buff. Female generally duller or browner, with less distinct pale pink or buff tips in worn plumage and to most of body in winter; the grey on hindcrown and nape can be reduced or even absent. Race *littoralis* is very similar to *tephrocotis*, but has whole head (except black forehead to crown, chin and upper throat) ash-grey. Race *atrata* has same head markings as *tephrocotis* (but hindcrown and nape

slightly paler grey) otherwise is almost entirely black or blackish or tinged with brown on body (except for pinkish-red tips to lower belly), with wings, rump and tail as *tephrocotis*; females are more brownish-black, and grey on nape is not always distinct. Race *australis* is by far the brownest of the races, usually lacking any grey on head (but some in fresh plumage in January-April show greyish-buff centres to sides of nape or hindneck): the body plumage of male, apart from pink lower belly, rump, uppertail- and undertail-coverts, is a warm brown, streaked slightly darker on mantle, back and scapulars and edged paler below, with crown blackish and ill-defined; females are darker, more dusky or dingy brown, with no clear cap or darker crown, and pink on body and wings greatly reduced.

VOICE Call is a single 'chew' or 'cheew' repeated continuously, also a hoarse or dry 'pert' and a high-pitched sparrow-like 'chirp'. The song consists of a slow descending series of the 'chew' note, delivered either from the ground or during circular, undulating flight.

STATUS, HABITAT AND BEHAVIOUR
Common or locally common, and in winter or on migration abundant in some areas; *atrata* is apparently uncommon throughout its range. In summer found in a variety of habitats, from tundra, grassy maritime plains or high cliffs, stony plateaux, rocky screes and alpine meadows to tops of snow-clad mountains and glaciers above the tree line. In winter found in foothills, along river banks, valleys and coastal plains, where it occurs in a variety of open habitats including roadside verges, farmyards and streets of towns and villages and has been seen at garden feeders. Tame and approachable; on the ground walks, and does not hop. Flight undulating or in long bounds, erratic and prone to sudden movements or changes in direction. Mostly terrestrial, usually in pairs or flocks; nests loosely colonially, and in winter large numbers (up to 1,000) occur together at communal roosts in caves, mineshafts etc. Feeds on the ground on small seeds of various plants; some grain is taken in winter, also some insects and their larvae from flotsam along tideline; the nestlings are fed entirely on insects.

DISTRIBUTION *L. a. arctoa*: central, southern and southeastern Altai range, Mongolia, possibly south into Sinkiang, northwest China.

L. a. cognata: Sayan ranges, southwest Siberia, to northern Mongolia and the mountains southwest and southeast of Lake Baikal.

L. a. sushkini: Khangai, northern Mongolia.

L. a. gigliolii: northwest and northeast of Lake Baikal to the Yablonovy range in eastern Transbaicalia (possibly also in Mongolia in the Hentiyn range and around Ulan Bator).

L. a. brunneonucha: northeast Siberia, east of the Lena river to the Sea of Okhotsk, Stanovoy range, western Manchuria and northern Amurland east to Kamchatka, Commander and Kurile Islands; it has also bred in Hokkaido, northern Japan.

L. a. griseonucha: Aleutian, Nunivak, Kodiak, Unga and Semidi Islands and Alaska peninsula.

L. a. umbrina: Pribilof and St Matthew Islands.

L. a. irvingi: northern Alaska.

L. a. littoralis: mountains of central, eastern and southeast Alaska and western Canada (western British Columbia) south to the mountains of Washington, Oregon and northern California.

L. a. tephrocotis: northern Alaska (Seward Peninsula and the Brooks range) to northwest Canada, central Yukon south through the Cascades and Rocky Mountains to southeast British Columbia, western Alberta and northwest Montana.

L. a. dawsoni: Sierra Nevada mountains, eastern California.

L. a. wallowa: northeast Oregon.

L. a. atrata: west and central USA, from central Idaho, southwest Montana and north-central Wyoming through the Rockies to northern Nevada and central Utah.

L. a. australis: western USA from southeast Wyoming to Colorado and central-northern New Mexico.

Treated by some authorities as three separate species: *L. tephrocotis* as Grey-crowned Rosy Finch; *L. atrata* as Black Rosy Finch and *L. australis* as Brown-capped Rosy Finch; while other authorities have merged all North American races into a single species, American Rosy Finch *L. tephrocotis*, and all Asian races into the Asian Rosy Finch *L. arctoa*.

MOVEMENTS Sedentary, partial (altitudinal) migrant or wholly migratory. Breeding birds from the northern areas of the range move southwest, south or southeast to winter either at lower levels or well to the south of the breeding range; some move only short distances, while others travel further. Races *cognata* and *gigliolii* winter at lower levels and extend to the shores of Lake Baikal, the former occasionally along the upper Angara river, while the latter more frequently occurs in northern

Mongolia; *brunneonucha* winters in Ussuriland, southern Manchuria south to Hopeh, central China, north Korea, Sakhalin and Hokkaido to central Honshu, central and southern Kyushu, Japan. In North America, *littoralis* winters from southern Alaska and the Aleutians through western Canada to Montana, northern California and central New Mexico; *tephrocotis* winters from southern British Columbia to southwest Manitoba, south to southwest South Dakota and northwest Nebraska west to northeast California and east to northern New Mexico; *wallowa* moves south to winter in western Nevada; *atrata* winters from central Idaho and the mountains of northwest and southeast Wyoming to eastern California and infrequently to Nevada, northern Arizona, southern Colorado and northern New Mexico. Species has also been recorded in central Siberia (Krasnoyarsk and Semipalatinsk) and South Korea (*brunneonucha*); within USA, *littoralis* has been recorded in Minnesota and Maine, *tephrocotis* in Wisconsin, Iowa and southern California, and *atrata* in eastern Oregon and eastern Montana. Migrants appear in wintering areas from late October onwards and return to breeding areas from late March to mid-April; midwinter movements not unusual, as most birds wintering in Japan occur in January and February.

MEASUREMENTS Wing of male 111·5–112·5, of female 102–109. Wing of male *brunneonucha* 114–123·5, of female 114·4–118. Weight of male 27·4–48, of female 22·4–35. Wing of male *tephrocotis* 102·5–109, of female 101–104; tail 62–73; tarsus 19–21; bill (exposed culmen) 11–12.

REFERENCES Dementiev and Gladkov (1951–54), Farrand *et al.* (1985), Godfrey (1979), Peterson (1961).

GENUS *CALLACANTHIS*

One species. Very distinctive, with a bright red or yellow eye patch. Closely related to the true rosefinches *Carpodacus* and of similar Himalayan distribution to several members of that genus.

78 RED-BROWED FINCH (Spectacled Finch) *Callacanthis burtoni*
Plate 25

Southern Palearctic

Carduelis burtoni Gould, 1838, Proc. Zool. Soc. London, 1837, p. 90, Himalayas; restricted to Srinagar, Kashmir, by Baker, 1921, Journ. Bombay Nat. Hist. Soc., 27, p. 729.

IDENTIFICATION Length 17–18 cm (6½–7 in). A very distinctive but shy or retiring Himalayan finch. Males are generally reddish or reddish-brown, with black wings (spotted with white) and tail; broad red or yellow 'spectacles' around eyes meet across forehead. Females are similar but paler, and lack red tinges to body feathers; the head is black or blackish but broken by paler or pale grey bases to feathers, and has pale yellow or deeper

'spectacles'. Spends much of its time on the ground under bushes in forest. **Confusion species:** Confusion possible (if seen briefly) with Spot-winged Rosefinch (99), which has pale pink spots at tips of median and greater coverts and tertials; it also has broad pink supercilia (not meeting over forehead) and a pale pink rump, but lacks black on head, wings and tail (though it is generally dark) and lacks white at tip of tail.

DESCRIPTION Sexes differ. **Adult male:** Forehead, lores and broad area encircling eye scarlet, paler or slightly paler pinkish around eye and lores (on some, red continues over ear-coverts to sides of nape). Crown to nape, sides of neck, lower cheeks and ear-coverts black or finely grey-streaked. Mantle, back and scapulars greyish-olive, extensively fringed maroon or reddish-brown; rump and uppertail-coverts paler or cinnamon-brown; tail black, with a white tip to each of the central feathers increasing outwardly, outermost with a wedge-shaped spot of white. All coverts black, with pinkish-white spot at tip of each of greaters forming a broad wingbar; alula black, lower feather with a large white spot at tip, and primary coverts black at base with outer half of tip white; flight feathers black, secondaries and primaries all tipped white, and tertials broadly tipped with pinkish-white on outer webs. Chin is dusky, black or blackish-brown; throat black, tipped scarlet, breast buff-cinnamon and broadly fringed pinkish-red, becoming cinnamon-brown on flanks and belly (or tinged slightly reddish-pink); thighs warm brown, undertail-coverts pale buffish-brown. Bill is fairly stout and pointed, yellow with a darker yellow cutting edge and dusky brown tip. Legs and feet pinkish or flesh-brown. **Adult female:** Generally olive (or browner than male) and lacks bright red tones. Lower forehead and lores to behind eye pale to bright yellow. Crown, nape, sides of neck and face blackish or dusky brown. Mantle and scapulars to rump and uppertail-coverts paler olive, tinged grey-brown. Tail browner than male, all feathers with a white spot at tip increasing to a wedge on outer pair. Lesser coverts uniform with scapulars or slightly darker, median coverts dark olive with slightly paler tip, greater coverts black with white or buffish-white spots at tips forming a wingbar; tips of primary coverts have less white at tip than male; flight feathers as male but not so jet-black. Underparts almost entirely pale grey-brown, with yellowish or straw-coloured wash on throat and upper breast. Bill as male but paler. **Juvenile:** Like adult female but duller brown, head pattern less distinct, with area around eye pale buffish-cinnamon or buffish-brown with dark brown ear-coverts; generally darker brown (not so

olive) on mantle, back and scapulars; edges to greater coverts buff or pale buffish-brown and tips to secondaries and tertials the same (whiter on tips to primaries), but all smaller than on adults. Underparts dull buffish, cinnamon or gingery-brown. Bill pale yellowish-horn.

VOICE Call is a loud, clear Bullfinch-like whistle but higher in tone, 'pweee' or 'chew-ee', often followed by a melodious, descending 'pweu, pweuweu' or 'chipeweu'; contact note a light 'chip', alarm a rising 'uh-eh' or 'twee-yeh'. Song is similar to trilling 'til-til-til' notes of Goldfinch (68) but louder, also a monotonous song consisting of a single note repeated; usually given from high up on a bare branch.

STATUS, HABITAT AND BEHAVIOUR Locally common to scarce, and erratic in occurrence in some parts of its range. Inhabits birch, deodar, rhododendron and fir forests, and in winter oak and hemlock forest, between 2270 m and 3330 m. A quiet, unobtrusive or tame bird, spending much of its time on the forest floor or under bushes. Occurs in pairs in breeding season, but otherwise in small flocks of up to 12 (exceptionally to 30). Hops on the ground, and when disturbed usually flies only short distances. Feeds mostly on seeds of trees (deodars), but has also been known to eat the bark of rhododendron and has been seen pecking deep into flower-heads.

DISTRIBUTION Monotypic. Northwest Pakistan, Chitral and Safed Koh (possibly also into extreme eastern Afghanistan) southeast along the Himalayas to Sikkim; erratic in occurrence in parts of the range, very local east of Kumaon, Uttar Pradesh, India.

MOVEMENTS Poorly known or understood, and probably only of short distance or altitudinal; of seasonal occurrence in parts of the range where it is not known to breed. Recorded at lower levels in winter in Kashmir and down to 2300 m, elsewhere to 1800 m (exceptionally to 800 m), and up to 3350 m in Nepal.

MEASUREMENTS Wing of male 96–104, of female 97–100; tail of male 63–65, of female c61; tarsus c19; bill (from skull) c18.

REFERENCES Ali and Ripley (1983), Bates and Lowther (1952), Fleming et al. (1979).

GENUS *RHODOPECHYS*

Four species. Medium-sized finches, generally pale or sandy with pale or brightly coloured wings and bills. Probably of central Asian origin, has now spread west to Turkey, the Middle East and into North Africa.

79 CRIMSON-WINGED FINCH *Rhodopechys sanguinea*   Plate 19
Palearctic

Fringilla sanguinea Gould, 1838, Proc. Zool. Soc. London, 1837, p. 127, Erzurum, Turkey.

IDENTIFICATION Length 15–18 cm (6–7 in).   A bright and distinctively coloured finch of mountaintops and scrub-covered slopes, not usually below 1280 m. Identified by combination of pale yellow bill, dark brown or black cap, streaked brown upperparts and streaked or spotted underparts, together with bright pink wings and base of tail. In flight appears quite long-winged.

Confusion species: Trumpeter Finch (80) is similar in overall pink tones of plumage, but male is mottled red on forehead and underparts, lacks a dark crown or streaks on upperparts and has a bright red bill, while female is generally drab brown with only a small amount of pink on rump and also lacks dark crown, streaked upperparts and pink in wing. Juvenile and immature Trumpeter Finches have no pink in plumage. Desert Finch (82) is smaller and dull sandy-brown, with an all-black bill and white flashes in primaries and sides of tail.

DESCRIPTION Sexes differ slightly. **Adult male:** Forehead, crown and hindcrown black or blackish-brown, in fresh plumage tips of each feather very finely edged buffish-brown, those on forehead often forming a paler or buffish front to cap. Lores to above eye and cheeks bright deep rose-pink, fading into sandy-brown on lower cheeks and ear-coverts; supercilium behind eye sandy or sandy-buff and curving behind ear-coverts to sides of neck, which are tinged warm buff-brown and finely spotted darker. Upper nape pale buffish-brown; hindneck, mantle, back and scapulars warm or rus-set-brown with darker feather centres, lower back uniform warm brown; lower rump and uppertail-coverts rosy-pink with sandy-brown feather bases. Central pair of tail feathers entirely black with fine white tip, all outers broadly pink or pale pink on outer edges except for broad black subterminal band, all tipped with white; outermost pair almost entirely white. Lesser and median coverts warm brown or brownish on inner web, with black shaft streak, and edged and tipped pale pink; greaters similar, but with blackish-brown inner webs and bright pink edges to outers and tips to all feathers; alula and primary coverts black, the latter finely edged bright pink; flight feathers black or blackish-brown, but outer webs broadly bright pink for about two-thirds length of primaries and entire length of secondaries, forming broad wingbar in flight, and secondaries tipped white; tertials black-ish-brown, broadly edged pale or warm brown and tipped buffish-white. Underwing-coverts notice-ably silvery-white in flight. Chin and throat warm sandy-brown with faint dark spots or streaks, becoming larger on lower throat; upper breast as throat with prominent blackish bases to feathers, becoming creamy or white and often with a light or faint pinkish wash on lower breast; flanks sandy-brown, finely streaked blackish; belly to undertail-coverts white. Bill quite deep at base and stout in appearance, yellow with brown at tip and along cutting edge. Legs pale brown, feet blackish. In winter more sombre and browner, with pink of lores, cheeks and tips to crown replaced by a dull sandy-buff. Bill changes to greyish-horn. **Adult female:** Similar to male, but crown deep brown and lightly streaked or edged with sandy-brown; pinkish-red on lores is often obscured by sandy-

brown, which extends to cheeks and ear-coverts, and pink in wing is less extensive and paler, with tips and edges to greater coverts warm brown and bases of secondaries and inner primaries very pale pink or whitish; rump and uppertail-coverts sandy-brown, tipped faintly with white, and underparts less heavily spotted or streaked than male. **Juvenile:** Similar to adult female, but crown, face, cheeks and ear-coverts uniform sandy-brown, mantle and back similar but with some dark centres to feathers; very little pink shows on closed wing apart from bases to secondaries, and leading primaries are brown. Bill is dark horn-yellow or brownish towards tip.

GEOGRAPHICAL VARIATION Males of race *aliena* have grey or greyish-buff on nape and hind-neck, the upperparts are paler pink except for deeper brown rump and uppertail-coverts, the wings are duller and the inner secondaries tipped off-white; outer tail feathers have outer web white and inner web brown; chin and throat are white, faintly tinged with pink. Females are similar, but have paler crown or more brown and less pink on face; chin and throat white.

VOICE The contact note is a fairly soft but musi-cal, almost chat-like 'wee-tll-ee' or 'wee-tell-er', and the flight call a soft 'chee-rup', 'chilip', 'tlweep' or 'toik' and a Woodlark-like 'dy-lit-dy-lit'. Song is a repeated, clear and melodious, quiet, grating and sparrow-like 'tchwili-tchwilichip', delivered from tops of bushes or grass tussocks, and a rippling 'turdel-edel-weep-ou' in circling and undulating songflight, often high in the sky.

STATUS, HABITAT AND BEHAVIOUR Wide-spread but generally scarce or locally common. A ground-loving bird, rarely seen on bushes or trees (except in spring when singing). Found on bare mountaintops and slopes, also boulder-fields, occasionally in areas of sparse or scattered scrub, usually above 2000 m, but in winter at lower levels in stony wastes along foothills or on edges of culti-vated areas. Often tame and approachable, usually in pairs or small groups; in non-breeding season forms larger flocks. On the ground has very upright stance and often hops, but also has a rather wad-dling walk. The flight is strong, fast and undulating (pink shows well in flight, as does white underwing). Feeds on a variety of small seeds, mainly of grass or small alpine plants.

DISTRIBUTION *R. s. sanguinea*: discontinuously from central, southern and eastern Turkey through the southern Caucasus to Iran and Afghanistan and Central Asia to Tadzhikstan (Ferghana), the Russian parts of the Tien Shan range and the Tarbagatai range in northwest Sinkiang, China; also southern Lebanon (Lebanon range) to Mount Hermon, Israel.

R. s. aliena: high Atlas Mountains, Morocco, and possibly northeast Algeria (though may be only a winter visitor here (recent information lacking)).

MOVEMENTS Mostly altitudinal, to lower levels in winter; in the Middle East, birds from Lebanon and Mount Hermon are found at lower levels and possibly occur in Syria. Breeding birds from eastern end of the range in China move east to winter in north-central China; has also been recorded in the northern Caucasus to North Ossetia and twice in Kashmir, in Chitral (July) and Ladakh (April).

MEASUREMENTS Wing of male 105–111, of female 97–103; tail 55–63; tarsus c19; bill 11·5–12, (from skull) c17. Weight of male 34–44, of female 32–33.

REFERENCES Ali and Ripley (1983), Hollom (1959), Paludan (1959).

80 TRUMPETER FINCH *Rhodopechys githaginea*   Plate 19
Palearctic, Arabia and Africa

Fringilla githaginea Lichtenstein, 1823, Verz. Doubl. zool. Mus. Berlin, p. 24, Afghanistan.

IDENTIFICATION Length 14–15 cm (5½–6 in). A medium-sized, plain or uniformly coloured finch which blends well into its desert or semi-desert habitat. It has a broad head, stout and often bright bill, short tail, and a characteristic buzzing call. The adult male has a bright waxy-red bill, yellow on female; both sexes lack any wingbars or pale areas in tail. **Confusion species:** For differences from the initially similar Mongolian Trumpeter Finch (81), Crimson-winged Finch (79) and Sinai Rosefinch (96), see those species. Similar to Desert Finch (82) in overall appearance, but bright red, orange or yellow bill (black on Desert) and lack of bright pink on coverts or white flash on primaries, together with its frequently uttered call, make it distinctive.

DESCRIPTION Sexes differ. **Adult male:** Forehead grey, with bright red tips to feathers (often appearing as a red frontal band), forecrown to nape and hindneck pale ashy or grey-brown; cheeks and ear-coverts as crown and nape, lores and moustachial area to sides of neck similar or washed light pink. Mantle, back and scapulars light grey-brown or light sandy-brown, tinged with pink; rump and uppertail-coverts paler or plain pinkish. Tail is brown or greyish-brown, edged pinkish on outer webs. Median and lesser coverts similar to scapulars but edged with pale pink, greater coverts pale grey edged with pink; alula and primary coverts blackish-brown, the latter finely edged a pale pink; flight feathers dark brown, edged pink or deep pink on primaries, paler on secondaries, latter also finely tipped pale buff or whitish; tertials brown or light brown, edged with pinkish-buff on outer webs. Chin and throat grey, but all feathers tipped pink or pinkish-buff; breast and belly brighter pink, often mottled with pale or grey bases to feathers; flanks pale brown or greyish-brown with a tinge of pink; thighs and undertail-coverts whitish, washed light pink. Bill is short and stubby or blunt at tip, waxy bright orange-red in breeding plumage, yellow in winter, on some (sub-adults?) orange-yellow, or brownish at base of mandible. Legs and feet fleshy-brown. In winter, pink tips of forehead, face and underparts are abraded and birds are much paler, duller or greyer on head, mantle, back and underparts; bill is yellow. **Adult female:** Similar to winter-plumage male or a paler or slightly duller sandy version; overall much more uniformly light brown or sandy, with pale buff or pinkish-buff edges and tips to coverts and secondaries contrast-ing with brown primaries. Rump, uppertail-coverts and fringes of greater coverts and flight feathers vary from pale pink to pinkish-orange; some pale pink on lores, ear-coverts, moustachial area, chin, throat and breast, with rest of underparts dull sandy or buffish, occasionally streaked slightly darker. Bill pale yellow. **Juvenile:** Generally browner than adults, lacking any pink, with all wing-coverts and flight feathers edged pale brown; rest of plumage is very similar to adult female, and many cannot be aged with certainty. Bill dull or dark yellowish to brownish-horn.

GEOGRAPHICAL VARIATION Birds of race *crassirostris* are generally much lighter or paler pink than those elsewhere. All differences between races are very slight, not always constant, and are of relatively little use in the field without comparative material (for racial separation in the hand, see Vaurie 1956). However, birds of race *zedlitzi* from Algeria and Air Province, Niger, are undoubtedly the brightest or deepest in body colour and in pink in wings.

VOICE Call is a short or abrupt 'chee' or 'chit', often used as a contact note; the flight call is a soft 'weechp'. Song is a very distinctive and characteristic drawn-out nasal wheeze or monotone buzz, 'cheeeee' or just 'eeeeeeeee', rising slightly in scale and often followed by short tin-trumpet-like phrases, or interspersed with short high-pitched metallic clicks and whistles.

STATUS, HABITAT AND BEHAVIOUR Common or locally common (occasionally abundant in places). A desert or semi-desert bird, preferring dry desolate hills, mountain slopes, stony plains, cliffs or wadis, but absent from areas of open sand and scrub; rarely found above 1700 m. Spends most of its time on ground, foraging, but not averse to perching on trees, bushes or roadside wires. On the ground it shuffles or hops, rapidly at times, often with upright stance. Flight fast and undulating or bouncing, and usually fairly low. Social and loosely colonial in breeding season; in winter gathers in large flocks, comprising all ages, and which can number several hundred. Feeds mainly on small wind-blown seeds and seedlings of grasses or green shoots, leaves and buds of desert plants; also some insects, principally grasshopper larvae. Makes regular journeys to drink, especially at sunset.

DISTRIBUTION *R. g. githaginea*: Egypt (mostly

Nile valley, eastern and western Sahara desert oases) to northern Sudan (to about 20°N).

R. g. zedlitzi: southeast Spain (Almeria, rare and very localised though has recently spread to the Cartagena Mountains), North Africa from Morocco, Algeria and central and southern Tunisia discontinuously eastwards through Libya possibly to northwest Egypt (where it has been obtained), south to Mauritania and east through northern Mali to Niger (Air Province) and Chad (Tibesti and Ennedi Provinces).

R. g. crassirostris: northern Egypt (Sinai) and southern Israel to Jordan, southern Iraq and discontinuously north to Azerbaijan and east through south, east and northeast Iran to Afghanistan and Central Asia (Bukhara and the Kara-Kum desert) east to western Sind, northern Baluchistan and northern Pakistan (Chitral and Peshawar); in northwest and west Arabia (to the southern Hejaz) and the central desert (Tuwaiq escarpment) of Saudi Arabia (may also breed in parts of the eastern province).

R. g. amantum: Canary Islands, Tenerife, Gran Canaria and most of the eastern islands.

MOVEMENTS Resident, nomadic or partially migratory; outside the breeding season some populations dispersive and wander within the range,

these movements largely determined by the presence of food. In the east is a regular migrant, with birds from Iran and Afghanistan moving south into Baluchistan, Sind, the Punjab south to the Makran Coast and Rajasthan, western India. It has also bred in southern Turkey and probably Armenia (but not recently), where otherwise rare (though several records in the late 1980s from southeast Turkey); scarce or infrequent to southern Italy, Sicily (14+ records 1952–79), Malta (possibly annual; large influx in 1977, with flocks up to 50 in late summer), Greece, Cyprus and northern Israel, a scarce winter visitor in small numbers to Lebanon, Jordan (Azraq), the eastern Gulf states (has also occurred, May 1990 and April 1992, in the UAE), North Yemen and Oman, where it may be a scarce resident; *amantum* is a non-breeding visitor to Hierro. A vagrant to Gibraltar, southern France, Switzerland, British Isles (six records), Channel Islands, Denmark, Sweden, Germany, Austria and Cyprus (seven records). Most records away from breeding range fall between October and May.

MEASUREMENTS Wing of male 80–93, of female 83–89; tail 47–55; tarsus 16–19; bill (from skull) 12–13. Weight: 19.

REFERENCES Hollom *et al.* (1988), Jonsson (1992), Mild (1990), Vaurie (1956).

81 MONGOLIAN TRUMPETER FINCH *Rhodopechys mongolica*
Plate 19

Palearctic

Carpodacus mongolicus Swinhoe, 1870, Proc. Zool. Soc. London, p. 447, Keming, between Kalgan and Nankow, southern Chahar, China.

IDENTIFICATION Length 14–15 cm (5½–6 in). Similar to Trumpeter Finch (80), with which it forms a species-pair. Generally pale sandy, with a well-defined pink rump, pinkish supercilium, white outer edge to tail and an obvious white panel across base of flight feathers. Prefers more dry mountainous or plateau terrain than Trumpeter, moving some distance to lower altitudes in winter.
Confusion species: Differs from Trumpeter at all times in being slimmer and longer-tailed; lacks pink on upperparts, has prominent pale buff panel at base of secondaries and, in summer, pinkish edges to primaries and tips to greater coverts; white edges to black tail, has prominent pink on rump and over eye (in fresh plumage), and is whiter below, lacking bright pink; also, bill is yellowish or dull yellow, never red or orange-red as on male Trumpeter. Desert Finch (82) has pale white flash in wing and bright pink on secondaries but always black or blackish bill and much more deeply notched tail.
DESCRIPTION Sexes differ. **Adult male:** Forehead to hindcrown grey or tinged sandy-brown, with slightly darker feather bases; paler or pale buffish-brown on nape and sides of neck (some show light pink tinges on sides of forehead and nape). Eye-ring pale buff or greyish-white; lores

and supercilium light pink, fading over ear-coverts, which are light sandy-brown towards rear edge, with cheeks and fore ear-coverts (to sides of chin) pale sandy or greyish, washed with pale pink. Mantle, back and scapulars greyish, tinged with sandy-brown, with broad or ill-defined darker bases; rump pale sandy-brown, tinged pink or reddish-pink; uppertail-coverts pale sandy-brown tipped grey-brown. Tail is black or blackish-brown with white outer edges (except central feathers), slightly broader on outer feathers. Lesser and median coverts as scapulars (or with darker bases to medians), tipped with pink; greater coverts black or blackish on inner web, broadly edged whitish at base and pale pink towards tip (but pink often deepest on or confined to edges of outer coverts); alula black; primary coverts black or blackish-brown, finely edged pale buff or pinkish; flight feathers blackish, all primaries edged pale pink, inner secondaries broadly edged whitish and forming a contrasting pale panel in closed wing; tips of primaries finely white; tertials dark brown, edged whitish. Chin and throat to lower breast and flanks washed with pale lilac-pink or pinkish-grey; belly and undertail-coverts white or whitish. Bill as Trumpeter Finch but not so red or striking, pale or greyish-yellow. Legs and feet brown or pale brown.

In late summer much plainer or duller, and abrasion or bleaching of feathers reduces pink on wings and rump, but still retains ill-defined pink supercilium, pale buffish-brown panel on inner edges to flight feathers and white edges to tail; in worn plumage, tips of tail feathers become white. **Adult female:** Like adult male in summer but duller or plain, with much less pink in supercilium and wings; mantle to scapulars, rump and underparts more uniform buffish-brown than pink; wings edged whitish at base of greater coverts and secondaries, with only a faint tinge of pink on tips of greater coverts and edges of primaries. In fresh plumage sexes may not always be separable. **Juvenile:** Similar to adult female but is sandy-brown overall, lightly streaked (slightly darker feather bases) on crown, nape, mantle and back; wing-coverts edged with pale sandy-brown, secondaries broadly edged pale buff or whitish-buff at base and forming a pale panel, becoming sandy towards tips; edges of primaries brown or pinkish-brown, all tipped broadly pale or whitish-buff; tertials black at base, broadly edged pale buff-brown and tipped paler or whitish. Lower throat, breast and flanks pale buff or buffish-brown; belly pale buff very slightly dark-streaked. Bill brown or dull yellowish-brown.

VOICE Usually silent. Call is a soft 'dju-vud' or 'djudjuvu', also a constant twittering 't'yuk-t'yuk-t'yuk-t'yuk' when feeding in a flock. Song is a pleasant slow 'do-mi-sol-mi', with many phrases repeated and interspersed with chirps, usually given from the ground.

STATUS, HABITAT AND BEHAVIOUR Widely distributed, but locally common only in Mongolia and parts of Tibet and scarce or sporadic throughout much of rest of range. Occurs in fairly high, arid desert or semi-desert and mountainous plateaux up to 4200 m, on stony or rocky slopes or on steep cliffs, screes or ravines. In winter descends to lower levels. Social or gregarious, and in winter gathers in flocks; regularly flies some distance to water. Quite tame and confiding. Perches on bushes, but more usually on the ground. Feeds on the ground, on a variety of small seeds and shoots, possibly also takes small insects and their larvae.

DISTRIBUTION Monotypic. Eastern Turkey discontinuously to Armenia and Azerbajan, northern Iran (Elburz Mountains) and possibly also in the southwest, through Afghanistan to northern Pakistan (Chitral), and possibly in Transcaucasia, to Kashmir (Gilgit and Ladakh) to the Karakoram range; in Central Asia, from the Kyzyl-Kum desert, Uzbekistan, east to the Pamirs, north to eastern Kazakhstan, through the Tarbagatai and Dzungarian Ala Tau ranges to the Altai range in Mongolia (to northeast Gobi), in the south to the Tien Shan, Bogdo Ola Shan and northern Kunlun ranges, Sinkiang (possibly also in the northern Chang Tang, Tibet, but no recent confirmation), east to the Nan Shan range in southwest Kansu and eastern Tsinghai, west China. First recorded in eastern Turkey in 1915, but only very infrequently since until the first breeding record, near Asagi Mutlu in 1990; also present at this site and at three others in summers of 1991 and 1992. Only recently confirmed breeding (alongside Trumpeter Finches) in Azerbaijan.

MOVEMENTS Sedentary and partially migratory. Occurs at lower altitudes in areas adjacent to breeding ranges, the foothills of the Tien Shan and Kunlun ranges, edges of the Takla Makhan desert, through eastern Mongolia to southwest Manchuria south to northern Hopeh, Ningsia and Kansu, China; also to Ladakh and central Pakistan (Quetta) and possibly Sind. A vagrant to northwest India (Punjab), Nepal and Bahrain (three records, all in winter of 1970/71). Recorded at lower levels between October and May.

MEASUREMENTS Wing of male 83·5–96, of female 84–94; tail of male 51–58, of female 51–52; tarsus c17; bill (from skull) c12. Weight of male 18–24, of female 19–23.

REFERENCES Barthel et al.(1992), Dementiev and Gladkov (1951–54), Hollom et al. (1988), Paludan (1959), Panov and Bulatsova (1972).

82 DESERT FINCH (Black-billed Finch) *Rhodopechys obsoleta*

Plate 19

Palearctic and marginally Arabian

Fringilla obsoleta Lichtenstein, 1823, in Eversmann, Reise von Orenburg nach Buchara, p. 132, Kara-ata spring, near Bokhara.

IDENTIFICATION Length 14·5–15 cm (c6 in). A slim, sandy-coloured finch with distinctly marked wings and tail and (in spring and summer) a large black bill; females are duller than males. Has a very characteristic call in flight. A desert-edge bird occurring in irrigated and cultivated areas. **Confusion species:** For differences from initially similar Trumpeter (80) and Mongolian Trumpeter (81) Finches, see those species. Crimson-winged Finch (79) is clearly bigger or heavier in appearance, darker and with streaked upperparts, and has a contrasting dark crown and darker face.

DESCRIPTION Sexes differ. **Adult male:** Forehead to scapulars and rump pale or greyish sandy-brown, tinged warmer on head and face on some; distinct broad black line from base of bill to eye; cheeks and ear-coverts slightly paler or more sandy than upperparts. Uppertail-coverts warm brown. Tail is forked at tip, black, quite broadly edged and tipped white except outermost feathers, which have only thin (if any) white edge, central pair having broad pinkish-white edges. Lesser coverts as upperparts, with warmer edges and tips; median coverts sandy, edged and tipped deep pink; greaters blackish on inner webs, broadly bright pink across outer webs, thinly tipped paler; alula black or blackish-brown, finely edged pink; primary coverts black, edged with pink at base; primaries blackish, with broad white outer edges except on outer two to three feathers, which have very fine pale edges; secondaries similar, broadly edged pale or bright pink, tips white or whitish-pink; tertials black, broadly edged and tipped white or very pale sandy-buff. On closed wing, edges to primaries form a long white panel contrasting with pink edges to secondaries and greater coverts; in flight shows pale primaries and pink secondaries, from below both appearing very pale, almost translucent. Underparts pale sandy-brown, often lightly washed pink on breast; flanks sandy-brown, belly and undertail-coverts white. Bill is deep at base, stout, conical and black. Legs and feet dark or deep fleshy-brown. In worn plumage much duller or drab, with upperparts becoming much greyer or more pale grey than sandy-brown and uppertail-coverts uniform with (or slightly darker sandy-brown than) rest of upperparts. Bill pale yellowish or brownish-horn, with a dark tip. **Adult female:** Similar to adult male but paler or dull in overall tones; white in primaries is tinged greyer, pink on coverts and secondaries is not so extensive or so bright as on male, rump and uppertail-coverts are uniform with rest of upperparts, and lacks black across lores. Bill as adult male. In winter as male, but much greyer on head and upperparts. **Juvenile:** Similar to adult female, but wings duller and have buff-brown edges to coverts and tertials. Bill dull straw-yellow or paler, with a dark tip. First-winter birds closely resemble adult winter female.

VOICE Call is a rather soft rippling or purring, almost Bee-eater-like 'r-r-r-r-ee', 'prruii-prruii', 'prrryv, prrryv' or 'prrrt-prrrt', also a fairly harsh 'turr' and a sharp 'shreep' given in flight. The song is a pleasant rambling or chattering jumble of disconnected notes incorporating many of the call notes with some harsher trills and rolls, reminiscent of both Linnet (72) and Greenfinch (44) but usually harsher or more nasal.

STATUS, HABITAT AND BEHAVIOUR Common or locally common; scarce or intermittent in places. Prefers dry plains or semi-desert areas, avoids 'true' open sandy or stony deserts, and usually found in open country with scattered trees or bushes such as oases or saxaul stands and edges of cultivation such as orchards and vineyards; in Central Asia, found in orchards and gardens in the middle of large cities (e.g. Frunze). An active bird but can also be fairly secretive, especially in breeding season. Flight is fast and lightly undulating usually accompanied by characteristic purring call. Frequently perches in trees and bushes but feeds on the ground, on a variety of small seeds (including those of thornscrub), buds, leaves and insects.

DISTRIBUTION Monotypic. Southeast Turkey, northern Syria, southern Israel (erratically), southern Jordan and northwest Saudi Arabia (northern Hejaz Mountains) and possibly central Arabia, southern, central and northeast Iran (and probably elsewhere in the north and southeast), Afghanistan and northern Pakistan (south to Quetta); in Central Asia, from the southeast Caspian in Tadzhikstan east through the foothills of the Tien Shan to the western Kunlun range (to about 80°E) in the south, and discontinuously in the north through western Sinkiang, northeast Tsinghai and Kansu to the Gobi desert, Inner Mongolia.

MOVEMENTS Sedentary and partially migratory; makes short-distance dispersal movements away from breeding areas during October to March. Recorded in Iraq and the southern Sinai in winter and in northern Jordan (Azraq) in April. A vagrant to Egypt (four records).

MEASUREMENTS Wing of male 80·5–92, of female 75·5–87; tail of male 56–65, of female 54–61; tarsus 16–18; bill (from skull) 13–14. Weight 23–26.

REFERENCES Ali and Ripley (1983), Dementiev and Gladkov (1951–54), Hollom et al. (1988), Jennings (1991).

GENUS *URAGUS*

One species. A slim, long-tailed rosefinch of east Asia. Possibly related to other rosefinches, but, as the bill is similar to that of the bullfinches, it possibly has some affinities with *Pyrrhula*.

83 LONG-TAILED ROSEFINCH *Uragus sibiricus*   Plate 27
Eastern Palearctic

Loxia sibirica Pallas, 1773, Reise versch. Prov. Russ. Reichs, 2, p. 711, near montane rivers and streams of southern Siberia.

IDENTIFICATION Length 16–18 cm (6¼–7 in); races *lepidus* and *henrici* 14 cm (5½ in). A small and long-tailed rosefinch with a tiny bullfinch-like bill. The long tail gives it a distinctive shape but is shorter in some races, and there is considerable racial variation in plumage. In breeding plumage, males are deep pink on face, rump and underparts, with frosted grey or white on crown, nape and wings (latter appear mainly white), and tail is long and black, with white outer feathers; males of races *henrici* and *lepidus* are much browner on upperparts. Females are generally pale grey or sandy-brown, streaked, and lack bright pink or frosted grey on body. **Confusion species:** Przewalski's Rosefinch (84) is similar, but both sexes lack frosted white areas of head, extensive white in wing and deep pink on face and rump; Przewalski's is more streaked above, has a finer pointed bill and pale orange-pink (not white) outer tail feathers.

DESCRIPTION Sexes differ. **Adult male:** Lower forehead and lores deep crimson, concealed by silvery-pink feather tips in fresh plumage; supercilium pearl-white, fading over ear-coverts; cheeks and ear-coverts deep pink, concealed in fresh plumage by silvery-white tips. Upper forehead and crown to nape pearl-grey, tinged with pink and streaked with blackish to some feathers; nape and hindneck also show reddish-pink tips. Mantle and back have black feather bases with pink fringes (in fresh plumage feathers have pale grey tips), becoming uniform deep pink on lower back and rump; uppertail-coverts dusky or blackish at base, fringed dull pink. Tail is long, each feather quite thin and rounded at tip, black, edged finely with white, with outer three feathers white (in the hand, black bases to inner webs increase inwardly to centre of tail). Lesser coverts pink; median and greater coverts black with broad white edges and tips, appearing mainly white on closed wing, otherwise broadest on greaters and forming broad (merging) double wingbars; alula and primary coverts black with fine white edges; flight feathers blackish, broadly edged white on inner secondaries and tertials; inner webs of tertials black. Chin and throat crimson, with silvery-white or pale pink tips to lower throat; breast, flanks and upper belly rose-pink, lower flanks tipped white (in fresh plumage); lower belly and undertail-coverts white, washed pale pink; thighs ashy-white. Bill is short, stubby and bullfinch-like, yellow in spring and summer, otherwise brown on upper mandible and pale or whitish-horn on lower. Legs and feet dark brown. In winter, becomes generally paler or dirty-white, with pale pearl-grey forehead to upper mantle with slightly duller tips (lower forehead may still be crimson); mantle, back and scapulars have black bases fringed with white or very pale pink; wing-coverts and flight feathers have slightly more extensive white or off-white edges; underparts are also paler, and the pink feathers are obscured by pale grey or white tips and edges. The upper mandible is dark horn in non-breeding plumage. **Adult female:** Lower forehead and lores pale grey or ashy-white; upper forehead to nape and upper mantle light grey, finely dark-streaked; ear-coverts pale buffish-brown with fine dark streaking. Lower mantle, back and scapulars dull sandy-brown with diffuse dark grey feather centres; rump orange-brown, becoming duller or darker on tips of uppertail-coverts. Tail is blackish-brown, with outer two feathers white. Lesser and median coverts blackish-brown at base, medians tipped with white; greater coverts black, broadly tipped

white; alula and primary coverts dark grey or blackish; flight feathers blackish-brown, edged buff, with inner secondaries edged pale buff or whitish and tipped with white, tertials the same, more broadly edged white. Chin and throat ashy-white or buffish, slightly dark-streaked; rest of underparts dull buff-brown, with streaks on lower throat and breast, breast and flanks warm buff or sandy-buff, streaked dark brown; belly, thighs and undertail-coverts white. **Juvenile:** Very similar to adult female, but greyer on upperparts and underparts. On juvenile and first-winter males, mantle, back and scapulars are warm brown or reddish-brown with blackish centres, unstreaked rump is orange or light reddish, cheeks and ear-coverts have pale or off-white tips, lower throat, breast and flanks are washed light orange or pinkish with occasional silvery-white tips on throat and whitish tips to breast and upper belly, and flanks are pale or warm buff and diffusely dark-streaked. First-winter females resemble adult female, but lack orange rump.

GEOGRAPHICAL VARIATION Considerable variation throughout the range. Both sexes of *ussuriensis* are darker than nominate: males are darker red, with mantle, back and scapulars browner and the pink more intense or deeper in tone; females are more heavily streaked, have pink on rump and often show a tinge of pink on breast. Both sexes of race *sanguinolentus* are darker than either nominate or *ussuriensis*: in fresh plumage tips to head, face, nape, mantle and back are brownish (not grey), and as the tips wear the upper forehead, ear-coverts to chin and throat become white or very pale pinkish-white; females are generally plainer sandy or sandy-buff about head and face in winter, also comparatively shorter-tailed than either of previous two races (though still appears long-tailed in the field). Race *lepidus* (has very restricted range) is darker than the previous races: crown to back greyer, with only a slight tinge of pink on edges to feathers, has pale silvery-pink feathers on front half of crown extending to area over ear-coverts, wing-bars narrower and restricted to tips of feathers, with less extensive white across flight feathers, and shorter tail than nominate, with white in outer tail reduced to outer two feathers; females are warmer brown than nominate, with less white in wing, and are less streaked on underparts. Race *henrici* has hindcrown and nape tipped buff-brown, becoming sandy-brown on mantle, with back and scapulars heavily streaked with black, median and greater coverts dark brown or blackish with white tips, flight feathers also dark brown or blackish, edged pale brown, tail has blackish-brown central feathers with outer three feathers white (outermost) or mostly white, breast to belly deep pink, and flanks and sides of belly buffish-brown with some darker streaks; females are darker or more sandy-brown than females of previous races and heavily streaked on upperparts and underparts, rump is pale cinnamon, and also has white outermost tail feather with a small wedge of white at tip of next inner feather. Tail of both sexes of *lepidus* and *henrici* much shorter than in *sibiricus* or *sanguinolentus*.

VOICE Call is a melodious and accentor-like (particularly like Dunnock *Prunella modularis*), liquid, three-syllable warble, 'pee-you-een' or 'su we, su wee, sweeoo, cheweeoo', also a rising 'sit-it-it'; *sanguinolentus* has a soft, fluty 'hwit-hwot'; alarm similar to the sharp 'pink' of Chaffinch (1). The song is a pleasant and rippling variety of trills resembling song of Common Crossbill (110), but more resounding.

STATUS, HABITAT AND BEHAVIOUR Common but nowhere numerous; rare or scarce in parts. Inhabits damp or dense thickets, grassland, reedbeds and wet meadows, also woodland or forest with well-developed undergrowth, up to 3400 m; found in deciduous riverine woods or forest, principally of pine, birch and alder, but also thornscrub, willow, larches and poplars. Usually seen singly or in pairs; recently fledged juveniles form small flocks of up to 15. Flight is weak and rather fluttering, and wingbeats make a 'frrrrp frrrrp' sound. Actions and behaviour recall Long-tailed Tit (*Aegithalos caudatus*); feeds almost like Goldfinch (68), pecking at seeds while clinging to seed heads. Feeds on small seeds, but also takes larger ones such as wormwood.

DISTRIBUTION *U. s. sibiricus*: southern Siberia (north to about 59°N), west to foothills of western Altai in eastern Kazakhstan, east through northern Sinkiang and northern Mongolia to northern Manchuria and Amurland.

U. s. ussuriensis: Ussuriland and Amurland (to about 50°N), central Manchuria to northern Korea.

U. s. sanguinolentus: Sakhalin, southern Kurile Islands and northern Japan (Hokkaido, occasionally to northern Honshu).

U. s. lepidus: Shansi to southern Shensi (Tsinling Mountains), also southeast Kansu (Wu Shan range), northwest China.

U. s. henrici: southern Szechwan, west to extreme southeast Tibet and south to northern Yunnan (Likiang range).

MOVEMENTS Sedentary and migratory. Breeding birds in north of range (mostly nominate, *ussuriensis* and *sanguinolentus*) move south or southeast to winter at lower levels; *sibiricus* winters west to central Siberia (Omsk) and in Dzungaria, south to northern Tadzhikstan and the Tien Shan in Sinkiang, China; *ussuriensis* moves south to north-central China (Kansu to northern Hopeh), southern Korea and southern Japan (Honshu, occasionally to Shikoku and southern Kyushu); *sanguinolentus* leaves Hokkaido to winter in northern and central Honshu, occasionally to Kyushu.

Immatures gather in small flocks which forage throughout the breeding range before undertaking longer-distance movements to wintering areas. Departs from breeding areas mid-September to October (usually at onset of first snowfall), and returns in April and early May. Has also occurred in Europe, in Finland (April 1989), Sweden (May 1992), England (August 1991) and the Netherlands (November 1991), but all are considered to relate to escapes from captivity.

MEASUREMENTS Wing of male 70–79, of female 68–76; tail of male 75–85, of female 67–84; bill 8–9. Weight (one female) 16. Wing of male *ussuriensis* 65–75, of female 65–73·5; tail of male 72–86, of female 65–81; tarsus 15–16·5. Weight 16–26. Wing of male *sanguinolentus* 65–71, of female 63–66; tail of male 62–68, of female 55–65. Wing of male *henrici* 68–74, of female 67–73; tail 64–70. Wing of male *lepidus* 64–68, of female 66.

REFERENCES Brazil (1991), Dementiev and Gladkov (1951–54).

GENUS *UROCYNCHRAMUS*

One species. A slim, long-tailed rosefinch of very limited distribution in central China. Similar to Long-tailed Rosefinch (83), but differing in habitat occupation and altitude, and bill shape is closer to that of *Carpodacus* rosefinches.

84 PRZEWALSKI'S ROSEFINCH (Pink-tailed Rosefinch)
Urocynchramus pylzowi
Plate 27

Eastern Palearctic

Urocynchramus pylzowi Przewalski, 1876, Mongol. i Strana Tangut., 2, p. 99, sources of Tatung River, Nan Shan, northeastern Tsinghai, China.

IDENTIFICATION Length 15·5–16·5 cm (6–6½ in). A shy and little-known species from central China, similar to Long-tailed Rosefinch (83) but with significant differences. Bill is fine, slender and more pointed than on any other rosefinch, upperparts are brown and strongly dark-streaked, and wings are very short and rounded. Male is pink on lores, supercilium and from breast to belly; the tail is long and graduated, and largely pink or reddish-pink. Female is similar, but with pink in tail only. **Confusion species:** Likely to be confused only with Long-tailed Rosefinch, which has pink or silvery-white on forehead (male), a broad white double wingbar (both sexes), a small stubby bill and white outer tail feathers. Przewalski's tail is graduated, that of Long-tailed square-ended.

DESCRIPTION Sexes differ. **Adult male:** Centre of forehead, crown and nape buff-brown, finely streaked with black, slightly paler or greyer on nape and hindneck; sides of lower forehead, lores and supercilium a deep rose-pink, with pale pink eye-ring; ear-coverts to sides of neck grey or grey-brown finely dark-streaked. Mantle, back and scapulars buff or light sandy-brown, with broad blackish streaks on centres of feathers; rump and uppertail-coverts similar, but not so heavily streaked. Tail is long (and graduated at tip, visible only at close range or in flight), central feathers dark brown, narrowly edged whitish, outer feathers brown and broadly edged pale pink or reddish-pink, the outermost completely pink (from above closed tail appears mainly dark, from below mainly pink). Median and greater coverts edged warm brown, tips of greaters buff-brown or paler buff on inner feathers; primary coverts dark brown, edged with buffish-brown; flight feathers dark brown edged sandy or warm buff-brown; tertials similar, but broadly edged and tipped pale buff. Chin and throat (including cheeks and sides of throat) to upper belly and upper flanks deep pink or rose-pink, with white tips to sides of throat and breast in fresh plumage; lower flanks and belly white, washed pink; undertail-coverts deep pink.

Bill is fairly long and rather slender, upper mandible dark brown, lower mandible pink. Legs and feet brown or dark brown. **Adult female:** Forehead to crown and nape pale brown, streaked darker brown, becoming slightly paler on nape and neck; lores pale buff or whitish, extending in short and slight supercilium over eye and ear-coverts; cheeks and ear-coverts pale buff, slightly dark-streaked. Mantle, back and scapulars as crown, with broadly darker feather centres; rump slightly paler, but streaks continue to uppertail-coverts. Central feathers of tail are brown with pale buff or whitish-

buff outer edges, and outer three feathers white or whitish at tip and pale pinkish-orange at base, fading midway along each feather. Median coverts dark brown, edged and tipped light warm brown, greaters the same, edged and tipped pale buff; alula and primary coverts dark brown, edged buff; flight feathers and tertials the same, finely edged buff on former and more broadly on latter. Chin and throat pale buff or buffish-white finely streaked with brown extending to rest of underparts; breast is often tinged pink, and flanks are washed buffish-brown. Bill as male. **Juvenile:** Unknown; probably very similar to female. Immature males have tail dark brown with pink edges to all feathers (can breed in this plumage).

VOICE Call is generally quiet, but in flight or when alarmed gives a clear and ringing 'kvuit, kvuit'. The song is a short, hurried, chattering verse, 'chitri-chitri-chitr-tri' or 'chitri-chitri-chitri-chitri'.

STATUS, HABITAT AND BEHAVIOUR Rare or uncommon. Very little known. Occurs between 3050 m and 5000 m in bushes and scrub on hillsides, with a preference for *Potentilla tenuifolia* or thickets of dwarf willows or dwarf rhododendrons, usually near water. Mainly in pairs or singly, but outside the breeding season small flocks of five to ten occur. Flight is fluttery and rather weak. Feeds in bushes and on the ground in open areas of scrub; also perches on tops of bushes. Food is presumably small seeds of alpine plants.

DISTRIBUTION Monotypic. Eastern Kansu and eastern Tsinghai (Koko Nor to the Nan Shan range) south to central Szechwan (west of the upper Yangtze and Mekong rivers), China, and eastern Tibet (Chamdo region).

MOVEMENTS Sedentary.

MEASUREMENTS Wing of male 68·5−74, of female 71; bill (from feathers) 10.

REFERENCES Przewalski (1876), Schäfer (1938).

GENUS *CARPODACUS*

Twenty-one species. True rosefinches: males are generally red, pink or deep rose with grey or brown upperparts, and females are brown and dark-streaked. Medium-sized to fairly large; the bill is large or strong, developed for cracking hard seeds. Usually high-altitude birds, able to withstand extremely low temperatures even in winter; some species occupy mountainous areas supporting the sparsest vegetation, while others are forest-dwelling. This genus has the highest-breeding passerine — Red-breasted Rosefinch (104). Probably of Himalayan origin (or slightly north of this), and one member, Common Rosefinch (87), now occurs widely throughout the Palearctic and breeds at low altitudes. Three species occur, and are widespread, in parts of North America.

85 BLANFORD'S ROSEFINCH (Crimson Rosefinch) *Carpodacus rubescens* Plate 23

Southern Palearctic

Procarduelis rubescens Blanford, 1872, Proc. Zool. Soc. London, 1871, p. 694, Sikkim.

IDENTIFICATION Length 15 cm (6 in). A scarce rosefinch of the central Himalayas, Tibet and southwest China. Males have deep crimson head, darker crimson upperparts except for rump, crimson double wingbar and unstreaked red or pinkish-red underparts. Females and immatures have unstreaked underparts and uniform olive-brown upperparts. **Confusion species:** Lack of supercilium eliminates similar-sized rosefinches. Male Dark Rosefinch (86) has a dark breast and dark line through eye and ear-coverts to nape; females are similar to female Blanford's but latter has crimson on rump and uppertail-coverts and unstreaked mantle and back. Both Blanford's and Dark Rosefinches have finer or more slender bills than others of genus.

DESCRIPTION Sexes differ. **Adult male:** Forehead, crown and nape (including sides of crown and nape) bright or deep crimson; lores to under eye dusky; cheeks, ear-coverts and sides of neck crimson or dark crimson. Mantle, back and scapulars dark crimson with darker feather bases; rump and uppertail-coverts reddish-crimson, edged paler or more red. Tail is slightly notched, and dark brown, edged dull crimson. Median and greater coverts dark brown with crimson edges, broadly tipped bright crimson; alula, primary coverts and flight feathers dark brown, edged wine-red or brownish; tertials similar, edged broadly paler or crimson. Chin, throat and breast a light pinkish-crimson, becoming paler or pink on lower breast, flanks and belly but variable, with dark or grey bases to feathers; lower belly, thighs, vent and undertail-coverts ashy-grey, often with pale pink tips. Bill is short, both mandibles curving to a point, with pale horn on upper mandible and yellow on lower. Legs and feet light brown or yellowish-brown. **Adult female:** Forehead to crown dark brown or reddish-brown; lores and around eye ashy, ear-coverts dark brown, cheeks as underparts or lightly streaked with buff. Nape, mantle, scapulars and upper back olive-brown, faintly washed with crimson or reddish-brown; lower back, rump and uppertail-coverts as mantle, with brighter crimson. Tail is dark brown, edged light or warm buff-brown. Median coverts dark brown, edged light olive-brown, greaters similar but broadly tipped light buff-brown; alula, primary coverts and flight feathers dark brown, finely edged warm brown or, in worn plumage, paler buff-brown; tertials the same, with broader edges. Chin and throat to breast and flanks pale brown or with buff-brown wash; centre of lower breast, belly and vent to thighs and undertail-coverts pale grey or smoky-grey. **Juvenile:** Similar to adult female, but lacks dark brown or reddish tinge to upperparts or rump and uppertail-coverts; throat and breast are also slightly paler than adult female, as are rest of underparts.

First-summer males resemble adult male, but have duller red tinges to head and upperparts and rich rufous edges to median and greater coverts (with deep pink tips) and scapulars; underparts are dull or dingy brown, with pinkish-red tips to lower lores, chin, throat, breast, belly and flanks.

GEOGRAPHICAL VARIATION No subspecies, but birds from Yunnan (formerly separated as *saturatior*) are generally darker, and red or crimson is less bright and more brownish.

VOICE Call is a short, thin and high-pitched 'sip', also a series of short or abrupt but quickly rising and falling 'pitch-ew, pitch-it, chit-it, chit-ew' etc. notes, which are also given individually. The song is unknown.

STATUS, HABITAT AND BEHAVIOUR Scarce or rare; generally little known, with nothing known of its breeding biology. Found in open areas in coniferous or mixed conifer and birch forest. Occurs in pairs in breeding season; in winter forms flocks of up to 30 birds. Feeds chiefly on the ground, but nothing is known of its preferred food items.

DISTRIBUTION Monotypic. Himalayas of central Nepal and southern Tibet, east through Sikkim, Bhutan and Arunachal Pradesh, northeast India, to west and northwest Yunnan, west and central Szechwan and southeast Kansu, western China.

MOVEMENTS An altitudinal migrant, recorded at up to 4000 m in Tibet and Sikkim in summer and down to 1500 m in winter, possibly exceptionally at latter level as most winter records are above 2500 m.

MEASUREMENTS Wing of male 80–85, of female 76–81; tail of male 49–55, of female 49–52; tarsus 17–19; bill (from skull) 13–15.

REFERENCE Ali and Ripley (1983).

86 DARK ROSEFINCH (Dark-breasted Rosefinch, Nepal Rosefinch)
Carpodacus nipalensis   **Plate 26**

Southern Palearctic

Carduelis nipalensis Hodgson, 1836, Asiatic Researches, 19, p. 157, central and northern Nepal.

IDENTIFICATION Length 15–16 cm (6–6¼ in). One of the darkest rosefinches, with most of upperparts from nape, lores and ear-coverts dark brown washed with crimson. Male has bright crimson forehead, supercilium, cheeks and ear-coverts, and its distinctive dark maroon breast is a useful feature. **Confusion species:** Male Dark and Dark-rumped (95) are the only rosefinches with all-dark breast, but Dark-rumped has bright pink on lower forehead and supercilium and dark crimson upper forehead and crown. Lack of obvious streaks and wingbars and of red or crimson on rump separates Dark Rosefinch from generally paler Blanford's (85) and Common (87) Rosefinches. Females and juveniles are separated from those of all other rosefinches by pale unstreaked underparts and lack of any warm brown, red or crimson wash on rump; indistinct streaks on upperparts distinguish females from paler female Blanford's. Both Dark and Blanford's Rosefinches have thinner or more slender bills than other Himalayan rosefinches.

DESCRIPTION Sexes differ. **Adult male:** Forehead to forecrown deep pinkish-crimson; pale or deep pink supercilium behind eye, (often joins forehead, but some have a dark area above eye); lores blackish, continuing broadly as an eye-stripe across upper ear-coverts to sides of neck; lower cheeks and lower ear-coverts pale or rosy-pink (slightly paler than forehead), extending to sides of chin and throat. Crown, nape and hindneck dark brown, washed with crimson; mantle, back and scapulars to rump and uppertail-coverts similar, edges to scapulars more visibly crimson, mantle darker. Tail is slightly indented or notched, blackish-brown but finely edged dull reddish-brown or purple. Median and greater coverts as back but darker, except for slightly paler edges and tips to greaters; alula, primary coverts, flight feathers and tertials blackish, finely edged dull crimson, paler on edges of some secondaries; edges and tips to tertials crimson or dull crimson. Chin and throat pale pink or rosy-pink; sides of lower throat, breast, upper belly and upper flanks maroon or dark brown with crimson wash (variable in extent, see Geographical Variation); lower flanks, sides of belly and undertail-coverts pinkish or with tips lightly washed crimson. Bill is pointed, dark brown, paler or fleshy-brown at base to lower mandible. Legs and feet flesh-brown. **Adult female:** Forehead, crown and nape dull or dusky dark brown, Entire face slightly paler than crown. Mantle, back and scapulars dark dull brown, broadly but indistinctly streaked pale or warm buff-brown; rump and uppertail-coverts uniform warm buff-brown. Tail is dark brown with paler or warm buff-brown edges. Lesser coverts as scapulars; median and greater coverts dark brown at bases, with broad pale or warm buff-brown tips forming indistinct double wingbar; alula, primary coverts and flight feathers dark brown, edged paler brown or buffish on secondaries, with tips and edges to tertials pale or warm buff-brown. Chin and throat as face, becoming paler brown on breast and upper flanks; belly and undertail-coverts paler buff or lightly washed brown. Bill is slightly paler brown than male's. **Juvenile:** Very similar if not identical to adult female, but has more of an olive-brown wash to upperparts and paler (less noticeable at any distance) brown streaks (or spots) on mantle and back; first-winter and first-summer males often show reddish-brown on upperparts. Adult plumage is attained in second winter.

GEOGRAPHICAL VARIATION Although three races have been described and one of these widely accepted, it should be noted that this reflects a cline of increasing depth (saturation) of colour: birds in the west (kangrae) are somewhat paler, browner or less blackish on upperparts and breast, and those in the east are darker. In addition those from central (Nepal) and eastern (Sikkim) parts of the range show variable amounts of dark or maroon on breast, which on some is reduced or restricted to lower neck/upper breast area and can be more brown than maroon.

VOICE Call is a characteristic and plaintive wailing double whistle, also a sparrow-like twitter and a 'cha-a-rrr' alarm note. The song is a monotonous chipping.

STATUS, HABITAT AND BEHAVIOUR Common or fairly common. Occurs principally in high-altitude mixed oak or conifer and rhododendron forest but also in scrub, including stunted bushes, grass or weed patches among rocks or boulders or in ravines above the tree line; in winter descends to forest clearings, undergrowth and edges of cultivation. An active but fairly shy bird, keeping to cover in bushes or on the ground, usually in pairs or small flocks (often of single sex), occasionally in larger numbers in spring; also occurs in mixed flocks with Red-headed Rosefinch (107). The nest has never been found, and the breeding biology is almost unknown. Feeds principally on small seeds and berries, and has also been noted taking blossoms and nectar from rhododendron flower-heads.

DISTRIBUTION *C. n. nipalensis*: Himalayas, from central Nepal and southern Tibet to Sikkim, Bhutan, northern Assam and Arunachal Pradesh, northeast India.

C. n. kangrae: western Himalayas, Kashmir to Garhwal and Kumaon, Uttar Pradesh, northern India.

C. n. intensicolor: discontinuously from south Kansu through Szechwan to north Yunnan, west China.

MOVEMENTS An altitudinal migrant, occurring at up to 4000 m in Nepal and between 3030 m and 4242 m in Sikkim and Bhutan. Descends in winter to 1500–2730 m in Nepal, northern India and Sikkim, exceptionally to 1200 m in severe winters, though in most years the majority are found towards the upper limit. Race *intensicolor* winters (regularly?) in northeast Burma and probably annually (but very scarce) at high altitudes in northeast Thailand.

MEASUREMENTS Wing of male 81–96, of female 74–90; tail of male 53–66, of female 56–58; tarsus 20–23; bill (from skull) 13–16. Weight 22–23·5.

REFERENCES Ali and Ripley (1983), Fleming *et al.* (1979), Vaurie (1956).

87 COMMON ROSEFINCH (Scarlet Rosefinch, Scarlet Grosbeak, Hodgson's Rosefinch (*roseatus* only)) *Carpodacus erythrinus* Plate 23

Palearctic (winters in Oriental region)

Loxia erythrina Pallas, 1770, Nov. Comm. Acad. Sci. Petrop., 14, p. 587, Volga and Samara Rivers.

IDENTIFICATION Length 14·5–15 cm (5¼–6 in). The commonest, least skulking and most widely distributed of the rosefinches. Male in adult plumage has wings and upperparts grey-brown, washed or streaked with red; head and breast bright red (varying in intensity, but red becomes more intense with age), cheeks and ear-coverts often dark. Females are dull grey-brown above, with streaked underparts against a pale buff ground colour. Both sexes lack a supercilium, and females lack any red in plumage. Juveniles are plain buff-brown, almost dull or featureless, but with two pale wingbars and pale tips to tertials, and a small dark eye in plain brown face. **Confusion species:** Males are generally much brighter or more rose-red than other rosefinches (but see comments under Geographical Variation); lack of pale or prominent supercilium and presence of darker cheeks and ear-coverts and white on belly (in most races) eliminates most other similar species. Females have only slight or pale super-cilium (over and behind eye) and two pale buff wingbars (all lone females need careful exam-ination); in Britain and Europe, confusion possible with larger and plump Corn Bunting (*Miliaria calandra*).

DESCRIPTION Sexes differ. **Adult male** (sum-mer): Forehead to crown, nape and hindneck bright red or crimson, variable in extent and often with brown feather bases showing (younger birds not so red or so extensively red as older ones); lores ashy or ashy-brown; cheeks and ear-coverts brown or dark brown, variably washed with crimson (less often on younger birds). Mantle, back and scapu-lars brown or dusky brown with slightly paler edges to feathers, all washed with red or crimson (which is absent in worn plumage); rump variable from pinkish-red to deep red depending on age, some showing brown tips to feathers; uppertail-coverts brown, washed with red. Tail is notched or indented, brown, broadly edged (on all but central pair of feathers) paler, warmer or even reddish-brown. Lesser coverts as scapulars; median and greater coverts dark brown, lightly edged pale brown and tipped pale pink or pinkish-buff, form-ing double wingbar (becomes paler or buffish with wear, and abrasion reduces it to a faint or narrow wingbar); alula, primary coverts and flight feathers dark or deep brown, finely edged paler or buffish-brown (in fresh plumage) and tinged light reddish-buff towards tips of secondaries and primaries; tertials the same, edged paler pink or pinkish-buff. Chin, throat and centre of breast variably crimson or bright crimson (paler or not so extensive on younger birds), sides of breast and belly buffish-white, some with a wash or tinge of crimson, flanks

washed buffish-brown or lightly washed with red; undertail-coverts and thighs whitish or buffish-white. Bill is fairly stout, both mandibles curving to a point, greyish or dark grey-brown, though some full adults show pale yellowish-brown or even pinkish base to lower mandible. Legs and feet brown or pinkish-brown. In winter much duller, with red on crown tinged duller (often with fine pale buff tips), rest of upperparts uniform brown including rump, which can be tinged warmer or reddish, face and underparts much duller or tinged light or pinkish-mauve with paler tips, and wing-coverts are buffish or warm buffish-brown. **Adult female:** Forehead, crown, nape, mantle, back and scapulars olive-brown, tinged light grey, fine dark centres to crown becoming indistinct on mantle, back and scapulars; rump and uppertail-coverts uniform olive-brown or tinged slightly with green. Tail is dark brown, edged with buff or light olive-brown. Lores ashy or ashy-brown; faint or indistinct buff-brown supercilium over eye; cheeks and ear-coverts light olive-brown with faint dark streaks; pale buff moustachial stripe and short, distinct dark or dusky submoustachial stripe. Median and greater coverts deep brown, edged pale brown and tipped pale buff, forming double wingbar; alula, primary coverts and flight feathers deep brown, edged pale brown, paler or buffish-white on edges of primaries. Chin and throat buffish-white with light or faint streaks; breast to upper flanks buff or olive-buff with prominent streaks; belly and lower flanks white, buff or greyish-buff. Bill is slightly paler than male's. In winter much less olive in over-all tone, and streaks on whiter breast less prominent. **Juvenile:** Juvenile and first-winter birds are distinguished by their initial similarity to adult female, but are heavily streaked above (on some, restricted to crown and nape only) and below and are generally less olive and more buff on underparts; appears more dome-headed or round-headed, with a relatively large dark eye in centre of a plain pale buffish or buffish-brown face; broad pale buff tips to median and greater coverts form double wingbar (in autumn, broader and paler or whiter on juveniles than on adult females), with pale buff edges and tips to tertials and pale olive or buff-brown edges to secondaries. Streaks on underparts broader and more extensive (to flanks) than on adult female. Bill has a pinkish-brown base and dark tip to upper mandible and pale horn base to lower mandible. First-summer (and most second-summer) males are generally a browner version of first-winter plumage (and are very similar to adult or first-summer females) and can breed in this plumage, but exceptionally can have red on forehead, dark face and ear-coverts, some red tips on rump and upper breast, and faint streaks on lower breast, belly and flanks. Adult (or what is recognisably more adult than juvenile) plumage is acquired in late summer/early autumn (August-October) of second summer (third calendar-year): forehead to crown feathers become deep red, nape is also tinged deep red, and there is a deep or rich red suffusion to some feathers on mantle; rump is orange, becoming reddish-orange towards uppertail-coverts (which are brown); pale tips to median and greater coverts are broader (in fresh plumage) and more noticeably pinkish-buff; chin, throat and upper breast are red or reddish, but can be lightly tinged or mottled with pink, white, yellow or light orange, lower sides of breast are buff-brown and belly is washed a light pink, flanks are washed warm buff-brown and undertail-coverts are white or whitish.

GEOGRAPHICAL VARIATION Most races are not easily separated (although breeding-plumage *roseatus* should present few problems); most differences refer to intensity and extent of red on head, upperparts and underparts, but it must be borne in mind that this also differs with wear or abrasion irrespective of race. In general, wintering birds cannot be separated with certainty. The following differences relate to breeding plumage only. Male *roseatus* (by far the most distinctive race) is darker red than males of other races, deep or rich carmine or even slightly purple in tone, red wash on upperparts is much more extensive and deeper, and red on breast extends over flanks and belly; females are also much darker and more heavily streaked. Male *ferghanensis* (the least well-defined race) is more rose-red than scarlet or carmine, and has less reddish suffusion to upperparts; on underparts, red does not extend beyond lower breast. Nominate *erythrinus* is comparatively less red on breast and belly, and on predominantly brown upperparts red suffusion is reduced (absent altogether in worn plumage). Both male and female *grebnitskii* are darker than *erythrinus*, and males have more red or carmine (as in *roseatus*) on upperparts, but are less red and more pinkish below than *roseatus*.

VOICE Call is a distinctive, clear rising whistle 'ooeet', 'ueet' or 'too-ee', and alarm a sharp Greenfinch-like 'chay-eeee'. The song is a monotonously repeated, slowly rising, whistling 'weeeja-wu-weeeja' or 'sooee teeew' or variations thereon, 'tiu-wee-tiu' or 'te-te-wee-chew'. Almost entirely silent outside breeding season, but males often begin to sing in early spring before departing for breeding areas.

STATUS, HABITAT AND BEHAVIOUR Common or locally common, also an annual or occasional visitor to non-breeding areas. Widespread at low altitudes throughout most of the range, but in the Himalayas *roseatus* is found most commonly between 2000 m and 2700 m. Occurs in a variety of habitats, breeding in willows or tamarisks, thickets or patches of scrub or bushes in taiga or along river banks, often favours moist or damp areas, forest edges, also orchards, edges of cultivation, on plains or hillsides (up to 4550 m in Himalayas) with junipers, rose or thornbushes. In winter, found in similar habitat in more open foothills and on plains, also in reedbeds, edges of paddy-fields and crops such as mustard and sugarcane. On migration found virtually anywhere. Usually solitary (mostly autumn) or in pairs or small groups, occasionally in company with other finches, sparrows or buntings, either in bushes or on the ground. Has a typical undulating flight, and hops when on the ground. Feeds on a wide variety of plant and tree seeds and buds, including bamboo seeds, also crops such as millet and wheat (see also above), flower buds, fruit and berries, also some insects and their larvae and the nectar of a range of plants; fledglings are fed mainly on seeds.

DISTRIBUTION *C. e. erythrinus*: northern and eastern Europe, from southern Finland, occasionally southern Sweden (has also bred in Scotland, first in 1982, and England, five+ pairs 1992), east through CIS (USSR) (north to about 65°N) and western Siberia (to about 50°N) to the western Altai range, almost to Lake Baikal and Irkutsk north to the upper and middle reaches of the Lena river (birds to the east of this range are intermediate between nominate and race *grebnitskii*); in the south, from the Netherlands discontinuously through Germany and Czechoslovakia to the Ukraine and the lower Volga. The range is spreading slowly (more rapidly in some years than others) northwest, with pairs breeding for the first time in southern Sweden, Scotland, England, and the Netherlands (45+ pairs in 1992) within the last decade; singing males have also held territories in Belgium and northeast France in 1991 and 1992.

C. e. grebnitskii: eastern Siberia, east of the Lena river, Irkutsk and Lake Baikal (north to about 60°N), south to the Altai range in Mongolia, east to Kamchatka, western shores of Okhotsk Sea, northern Sakhalin, northern Ussuriland and Amurland to Manchuria and northern Hopeh, northeast China.

C. e. kubanensis: northern and northeast Turkey (exceptionally west to the Bosphorus), southern Caucasus and Iran east to Gurgan (southeast Caspian), also possibly in the southern Zagros range.

C. e. ferghanensis: northeast Iran (Khorasan), through the Hindu Kush in Afghanistan and northern Baluchistan, Pakistan to Zanskar, Ladak and Baltistan in Kashmir, north through Tadzhikstan in Central Asia to the Tien Shan range, Dzungarian Ala Tau and the Tarbagatai range on the borders of south and southwest Sinkiang, China.

C. e. roseatus: Himalayas, from north Pakistan, Kashmir and Garhwal, northwest India, east through Nepal to Bhutan (possibly Arunachal Pradesh) and southeast Tibet to west and north Szechwan, northeast Tsinghai, Kansu, southwest Ningsia and Shensi and possibly southwest Inner Mongolia south to western Hupeh, west Kweichow and north Yunnan (Likiang range), China.

Note: The ranges of *ferghanensis* and *roseatus* meet in Kashmir, and intermediates between the two races occur.

MOVEMENTS Migrant or partial migrant. Northern races (nominate and *grebnitskii*) are entirely migratory, moving south, southeast or southwest to winter in a broad range eastwards from eastern Iran (Baluchistan) through northern and central

India, the lowlands of Nepal, southeast Tibet, northern Burma, *grebnitskii* principally in northern Thailand and Indochina to North Vietnam and the southern-central regions of China south of the lower Yangtze. Southern races (*ferghanensis*, *kubanensis* and *roseatus*) are partial or altitudinal migrants, descending to much lower altitudes in winter, when all Himalayan birds move to the lowlands of India and Indochina except for a few stragglers in the northern valleys; *roseatus* also winters east to Burma, Thailand, Laos, northern Kampuchea (Cambodia) and south Yunnan. Species regularly occurs on spring and autumn migration in eastern and central Europe (west to Switzerland) and also Norway, British Isles, United Arab Emirates and Oman; in the east in Japan and the Commander Islands; and irregularly to the western Aleutian Islands, Pribilof Islands and western Alaska (mostly in spring). A vagrant to the Faroes (four records), Balearic Islands, Morocco, Malta (six+ records), Cyprus (three records), Israel, northern Egypt, eastern Saudi Arabia (three records), Bahrain (one record), Qatar (one record), Kuwait (one record), Korea (seven records) and Taiwan (one record, August 1986). Northern birds leave breeding areas from mid-August to early October; movements in August usually relate to post-breeding dispersal, and departure of adults begins in late September following completion of moult. Return movements occur from late April to late May (arrivals in Europe not usually before late May); some *roseatus* are found on passage in northern Pakistan in March and early April, but some *grebnitskii* do not arrive on breeding territory until early or mid-June.

MEASUREMENTS Wing of male 81–90, of female 78–90; tail of male 56–61, of female 54–59; tarsus c19; bill (from skull) 14–15, (from feathers) 9·5–11. Wing of male *grebnitskii* 80–89, of female 76–83; tail of male 54–63, of female 52–60; tarsus of male 18–19·5, of female 17·5–19·5; bill (culmen) of male 11–11·5, of female 10·5–11·5. Wing of male *ferghanensis* 78–88, of female 78–84. Wing of male *roseatus* 82–90, of female 78–87; tail of male 54–61, of female 51–60; tarsus 18–20; bill 13–15. Weight of male (summer) 20–32, (winter) 22–28, of female 19–33.

REFERENCES Ali and Ripley (1983), Shaw (1936), Stevens (1925).

88 PURPLE FINCH *Carpodacus purpureus* Plate 32
Nearctic

Fringilla purpurea Gmelin, 1789, Syst. Nat., 1 (2), p. 923, Carolina; amended to South Carolina by Amer. Ornith. Union, 1931, Check-list North Amer. Birds, ed. 4, p. 320.

IDENTIFICATION Length 13·5–16 cm (5¼–6¼ in). A plump or robust-looking finch of North America, with a short tail and a fairly large bill with curved ridge to upper mandible. Males are deep purplish or 'raspberry' reddish-pink on head, face, rump and chin to breast, the mantle and back are suffused with red or purple, wings and tail are brown, and lower underparts are white. Females are grey-brown and heavily dark-streaked above, with a well-marked face pattern, and white or buffish-brown below; western birds are less boldly marked. Has a distinctive flight call. Confusion species: Very similar to the other two American rosefinches, Cassin's Finch (89) and House Finch (90). Males are separable from the slightly larger Cassin's by continuation of deep red on crown to rest of upperparts compared with Cassin's predominantly brown nape and upperparts, and both races of male Purple are more extensively pinkish-mauve on breast; Cassin's also has fine streaks on flanks, belly and undertail-coverts. Male Purple is distinguished from proportionately smaller, slimmer and longer-tailed House Finch by colour of upperparts and lack of bold streaks on sides of breast, belly and flanks. Female is distinguished from female Cassin's by well-defined dark ear-coverts and contrasting pale supercilium (finely streaked on female Cassin's); Cassin's also has shorter and sharply defined 'arrowhead' streaks or spots on throat, breast, flanks and undertail-coverts on white base. Female House Finch is more diffusely streaked, has a small stubby bill and lacks strong facial pattern and pale supercilium. Pine Siskin (50) is smaller, with a finer bill, yellow in wing and at sides of base of tail. Possible confusion with female or juvenile Rose-breasted Grosbeak (*Pheucticus ludovicianus*), which has strongly defined supercilium, larger and darker cheek and ear-coverts patch, paler or more fine streaks on underparts, and bold white spots at tips of median and greater coverts.

DESCRIPTION Sexes differ. Adult male: Forehead to hindcrown raspberry-red or purplish-pink, nape and hindneck (occasionally sides of hindcrown) the same, streaked brown; lores dusky brown (deep pinkish-red in worn plumage), becoming brown washed with crimson on cheeks and ear-coverts; broad pinkish supercilium from over eye, fading on sides of nape; some have one or two dark streaks on sides of crown, others also show thin dark eye-stripe behind eye. Mantle, back and scapulars as nape, with darker brown centre streaks, all washed with crimson or deep pink; lower back and rump unstreaked deep rose-red; uppertail-coverts ashy-brown, but edged and tipped rose-pink or reddish. Tail is deeply notched, dark brown and finely edged warm brown or rufous-brown. Lesser coverts as scapulars; median

271

and greater coverts dark brown, edged and tipped pinkish-buff (in fresh plumage, tips of greater coverts pale buff); alula and primary coverts dusky brown or blackish; flight feathers the same, but finely edged with reddish-brown (buff-brown in worn plumage); tertials as secondaries. Chin, throat and breast pinkish or pinkish-mauve, fading on lower breast/upper belly; flanks buff or dull white, lightly smudged with dark brown or washed orange-red but generally unstreaked; belly and undertail-coverts white, or the latter washed with rose. Bill is conical, with distinct curve to culmen, which is dark horn, as is tip, while cutting edges and lower mandible are yellowish-horn. Legs and feet pale brown. **Adult female:** Forehead to crown and nape pale brown, finely dark-streaked; lores, cheeks and ear-coverts brown (as crown and nape), with broad white or pale buff supercilium from over lores and to rear of ear-coverts; pale creamy ill-defined moustachial area or patch below cheeks and ear-coverts is often lightly flecked with buff-brown. Mantle, back and scapulars as nape or very slightly warmer with darker feather centres; rump and uppertail-coverts paler brown and unstreaked. Tail is dark brown, edged (broadly on outers) pale buffish-brown. Median and greater coverts dark brown, finely edged paler brown and tipped light buffish-brown; alula, primary coverts and flight feathers dark brown, edged finely with paler buffish-brown. Sides of chin and throat (malar stripe) buffish-brown or with small dark feather centres, centre of chin and throat white or whitish-buff; breast and flanks white, heavily streaked (in inverted wedges) dark brown or blackish (older females in east of range can show some pink on breast); central and lower belly to thighs unstreaked; undertail-coverts streaked (often visible only in the hand). Bill pale pink, darker on upper mandible in summer. **Juvenile:** Closely resembles adult female, but more generally warm brown on upperparts except for rump, which is tawny-brown. First-summer males are similar, but have head and rump washed olive-yellow, and chin and throat are plain deep yellow, this extending slightly onto breast, which has small dark brown spots; sings and breeds or holds territory in this plumage and moults into adult plumage in second autumn/winter.

GEOGRAPHICAL VARIATION Male *californicus* is brighter rose or pinkish-red than nominate, generally shows less of a supercilium, and mantle and back are warmer brown and not so strongly washed with crimson. Females are more easily separated by their diffuse streaks (darker feather centres often obscured by buff-brown edges) on buff (not white) underparts.

VOICE Calls vary, but in flight gives a sharp or metallic 'pik', 'pit' or 'pink'; also a musical 'char-lee' or 'chee-wee'. The song is a flowing rising and falling warble of rich, bubbling notes rapidly delivered with most notes in pairs, repeated twice or more, given from regular song perches in tops of trees or during elaborate dancing courtship flight.

STATUS, HABITAT AND BEHAVIOUR Common or locally common. Breeds in conifer forests of Canada and northern USA, also in open mixed woodland, wooded hills, ornamental conifers and canyons or suburbs with open areas such as parks, orchards or gardens with feeders. Flight undulating, and accompanied by distinctive call. Usually found alone, in pairs or in small flocks; often conspicuously numerous or abundant on migration and in winter; occasionally forms post-breeding flocks of up to 30 females and immatures. In winter may also be found with flocks of Pine Siskins and American Goldfinches (65). Rather slow or sluggish in its actions. Feeds in trees or bushes or on the ground, on a variety of conifer and other tree seeds and also on buds, berries and ripening fruit such as cherries, also takes a few insects or their larvae; in some areas comes readily to feeders, where it takes sunflower seeds, hemp and millet.

DISTRIBUTION *C. p. purpureus*: northern British Columbia east to Newfoundland, Canada, and in USA south to northern New Jersey, West Virginia, northern Ohio, northern Illinois and central Minnesota.

C. p. californicus: Cascades and western Sierra Nevada ranges from southwest British Columbia, Canada, and in the USA from Washington to Oregon and California, also the mountains of Sierra Juarez, northern Baja California, Mexico.

MOVEMENTS Partial migrant. Some are present within breeding range throughout the year; numbers wintering south of breeding range depend on the supply of conifer seeds within the breeding area, and species may be common in one area in one year and rare the following year. Birds of nominate race move south to winter south and southeast of the breeding range, mostly in the eastern half of USA south to southeast Texas, the Gulf coast and central Florida. Birds of race *californicus* winter largely within or at lower altitudes adjacent to breeding range, or move to southern Baja California, northern Mexico, or east to southeast California and the mountains of southern Arizona. A vagrant to Bermuda (three records) and north of Labrador (off Resolution Island).

MEASUREMENTS Wing of male 74–87, of female 74–84; tail 51·5–61·5; tarsus 17–18·5; bill (exposed culmen) 10–12. Weight 20–31.

REFERENCES Farrand *et al.* (1985), Terres *et al.* (1980).

Carpodacus cassinii Baird, 1854, Proc. Acad. Nat. Sci. Philadelphia, 7 (3) p. 119, Camp 104, Pueblo Creek, New Mexico.

IDENTIFICATION Length 14·5−16·5 cm (5−6½ in). A bird of the western and mid-western States. **Confusion species:** Both sexes are very similar to Purple Finch (88) and House Finch (90); confusion more likely with Purple Finch. Cassin's is slightly larger than Purple, and males have a distinctive red crown which contrasts with brown on rest of head and neck, a long primary projection and a distinctively different call; for further differences, see Purple Finch. Smaller House Finch is much brighter red on forecrown, rump (red also less extensive) and chin to breast, browner elsewhere (including centre of crown), with well-streaked underparts and plainer brown wings. Female House Finch lacks supercilium and has broader but less well-defined streaks on underparts. Cassin's also has slightly longer and more pointed bill than either species.

DESCRIPTION Sexes differ. **Adult male:** Forehead to crown bright red or pinkish-crimson; lores, cheeks and ear-coverts dusky brown with a pinkish-red tinge, pale pinkish-red area behind eye merges with pinkish sides to neck; dull reddish moustachial stripe bordered by a short dusky submoustachial stripe (not shown by all birds). Nape and hindneck to mantle, back and scapulars brown with darker feather centres, mantle and upper back with fairly broad buff-brown edges faintly tinged with pink in fresh plumage; lower back and rump plain pale pinkish-red (some with slight brown streaks on rump); uppertail-coverts brown, tinged red. Tail is deeply notched, dark brown, edged lighter or warm buff-brown, with red or pinkish tinge in fresh plumage. Median and greater coverts dark brown, edged pinkish-buff and tipped pale pink, greaters edged warmer buff-brown; alula and primary coverts blackish; flight feathers dark brown, thinly edged paler, and in worn plumage with pale buff edges to tips of secondaries and tertials. Chin, throat and centre of upper breast variably pale pink with deeper or crimson tinge, becoming rosy-pink on sides of throat and paler or whiter on sides and lower breast; belly and undertail-coverts off-white, flanks and sides of belly buffish-brown and finely (not always prominently) dark-streaked. Bill is longer and slightly more slender (less deep at base) than that of Purple, with a straighter culmen, dark grey or blackish with a pale yellowish-horn lower mandible. Legs and feet pale flesh-brown to pale brown. **Adult female:** Very similar to slightly smaller female Purple Finch, but has larger or longer pointed bill, faint and finely streaked supercilium, and paler or more tawny edges to upperparts, which are heavily streaked on nape to upper back; pale buff or whitish-buff tips to median and greater coverts (often present only on former); streaks on underparts are sharper and cleaner, becoming dark on undertail-coverts or in lines on a paler or whiter background. **Juvenile:** As adult female, from which not always separable in the field. Male attains full breeding plumage in second winter.

VOICE Call is most frequently uttered in flight, and is a dry double or triple note variously described as 'giddy-up', 'tee-dee-yip', 'kee-yup', 'soo-leep' or 'cheedly-up'. The song is similar to that of both Purple (88) and House (90) Finches, but more varied or less organised and with more pauses between phrases, and is delivered from the top of a tree or in flight.

STATUS, HABITAT AND BEHAVIOUR Common or locally common. Found in open conifer forest, including lodgepole pines, red fir and mountain hemlock, often at considerable altitude, also in drier semi-arid forests of ponderosa pine; less common or scarce towards coastal areas. In winter it occurs in similar habitat at lower levels, but never so suburban as Purple Finch. Usually found in pairs or small flocks, in summer in small flocks of non-breeding males, in winter often in company with Common Crossbills (110) and Evening Grosbeaks (126). Many actions and slow undulating flight recall Purple Finch. Has a habit of often erecting crown feathers to form a short but spiky crest. Feeds either in tops of trees or on the ground, on a variety of tree seeds and buds or shoots, especially those of conifers, also berries and in summer some insects.

DISTRIBUTION Monotypic. Southern British Columbia and southwest Alberta, Canada, and in USA eastern Washington to central Montana, northern Wyoming south to central New Mexico, northern Arizona, parts of interior northwest and southern California and the Sierra San Pedro Martir, Baja California, Mexico.

MOVEMENTS An erratic or unpredictable migrant, dependent on the supply of food within breeding range; many remain to winter within breeding range. Also moves to lower altitudes in winter, and occurs in southern and coastal California, south-central Arizona and the mountains of northern Mexico south to San Luis Potosí and west-central Veracruz south to central volcanic belt (i.e. latitude of Mexico City). Has also been recorded in Nebraska and southeast Colorado, USA, and on the Tres Marías Islands (off Mexico).

MEASUREMENTS Wing of male 89−97, of female 86−92·5; tail 61·5−66; tarsus 17·5−19; bill (exposed culmen) 12−13.

REFERENCE Terres *et al.* (1980).

Fringilla mexicana P.L.S. Muller, 1776, Natursyst., suppl., p. 165, Mexico; restricted to Valley of Mexico by Moore, 1939, Condor, 41, p. 201.

IDENTIFICATION Length 12·5–15 cm (5–5¾ in). The third American rosefinch. Smaller than Purple (88) and Cassin's (89) Finches. Male is bright red on forehead, supercilium, chin to breast and rump, with underparts heavily streaked. Females lack supercilium and the underparts are more diffusely streaked. **Confusion species:** Both sexes are likely to be confused with Purple and Cassin's Finches (for differences see those species); House Finch is proportionately smaller, slimmer and with a longer, square-ended tail, and also has a smaller and more stubby bill than either Purple or Cassin's.

DESCRIPTION Sexes differ. **Adult male** (*frontalis*): Forehead to forecrown, extending to supercilium and rear of ear-coverts, deep or rich red (see note below); lores, cheeks, ear-coverts and sides of neck brown or deep buff-brown (on some, lower lores, cheeks and ear-coverts bright red); moustachial area crimson; centre of crown, nape and hindneck pale brown, variably tinged red or reddish-brown, or lightly edged ashy. Mantle, upper back and scapulars dark brown with fine pale edges, washed with red in fresh plumage; lower back and rump red or rich crimson (see note below); uppertail-coverts brown, with pale or ashy-brown edges and reddish-brown tips. Tail is square-ended, dark brown, finely edged buff or buffish-brown. Median and greater coverts dark brown, finely edged pale or light sandy-buff and tipped pale buff, forming indistinct double wing-bar; alula dark brown; primary coverts, flight feathers and tertials dark brown, finely edged paler or buffish-brown, slightly paler on edges and tips of tertials. Chin, throat and variably to upper breast or upper belly red or crimson in fresh plumage (see note below); sides of throat and breast buff-brown, tinged with red, duller or dingy in tone; rest of underparts dull whitish-buff, broadly or diffusely streaked dark brown (on some, streaks begin on sides of lower breast), flanks and undertail-coverts washed sandy-buff and streaked dark or dusky brown. Short and rather blunt bill has dark brown or dark horn upper mandible and paler yellowish-horn lower. Legs and feet brown or flesh-brown. Note: There is some individual variation in colour or tone of the normally red or crimson parts of male's plumage (as well as in intensity among differing races); some can be more orange than red, while it is not unknown for all red or crimson in the plumage to be replaced by yellow. **Adult female:** Entire upperparts to uppertail-coverts brown or pale brown, finely dark-streaked from mantle to scapulars, occasionally with slight reddish or yellow tinge (on some, rump is ginger or red, tinged light reddish-brown). Tail and wings as adult male, but can show warm buff-brown edges to greater coverts. Lores are

buffish with fine dark feather centres, cheeks and ear-coverts pale buffish-brown, finely dark-streaked. Almost all underparts are buffish-white, and finely dark-streaked with dusky brown on chin and throat (often appears smudged) and broadly or diffusely on rest of underparts.

Bill as adult male, but slightly paler. **Juvenile:** Similar to adult female, but more finely streaked on head, face, nape and upperparts; mantle, back and scapulars slightly paler buff than adult.

GEOGRAPHICAL VARIATION Racial variation is shown by males, and relates to darkness of upperparts and amounts and intensity of crimson on forehead to crown and nape, sides of face and chin to breast. Nominate males from Mexico are slightly darker on upperparts, and crimson on forehead and supercilium is deeper while on underparts it is only present on chin, throat and upper breast; sides and lower breast are grey-brown, and belly and flanks are off-white, streaked with brown. Race *amplus* is larger, with a larger or heavier and deeper base to bill (appreciable in the field), and has crimson extending onto lower lores and cheeks.

VOICE Call is a sweet 'cheeet' or 'queet', often given in flight or as part of a series, also given from perched birds in a rather drawn-out version; occasionally gives a House Sparrow-like 'chirp'. The song is a slow or disjointed jumble of musical notes, higher-pitched than Purple and Cassin's Finches and with a higher last note, 'whee-er' or 'che-err'.

STATUS, HABITAT AND BEHAVIOUR Common to abundant. Well known in some areas as the 'Linnet'. Occurs frequently in and around suburban towns and villages, but also found in farmland, ranches, orchards, scrub, canyons or semi-dry brush country up to 1500 m. Feeds mainly on the ground on a variety of weed seeds, principally thistle and dandelion, but also on blossoms, buds and fruit (cherries, figs, pears or peaches), mostly fallen but also those that are ripe and still on the tree; considered a pest species in orchards and fruit farms of western USA; also sips maple sap and readily comes to garden feeders.

DISTRIBUTION *C. m. mexicanus:* south-central Mexico.

C. m. centralis: central Mexico.

C. m. griscomi: Guerrero, southern Mexico.

C. m. potosinus: extreme southwest Texas (middle Rio Grande valley) and north-central Mexico from Chihuahua to Zacatecas and San Luis Potosí east to Nuevo Léon.

C. m. coccineus: southwest Mexico.

C. m. rhodopnus: central Sinaloa, Mexico.

C. m. ruberrimus: southern Baja California and northwest Mexico from Sonora, southwest Chihuahua and northern Sinaloa.

C. m. amplus: Guadalupe Island (off western Baja California).

C. m. mcgregori: San Benito and Cedros Islands (off central Baja California) (now extinct).

C. m. clementis: San Clemente Island (off southwest California), Los Coronados Island (off northern Baja California).

C. m. frontalis: southern British Columbia, Canada, and in western USA east to Idaho, Wyoming, western Nebraska southeast to Oklahoma and Texas to California and Baja California, Mexico.

In 1940 it was released (accidentally?) on Long Island and has since spread north through New York State to New England States and the Canadian border, west to Illinois and south to South Carolina and Alabama, and apparently its range is still expanding. In the 1980s it was noted in central Chiapas (southern Mexico), where it was fairly common in cities, whether a natural extension of the range or derived from escapes (or introductions) is unknown (S.N.G. Howell pers. comm.). Also introduced to Hawaii in 19th century and is now abundant on all main islands; vagrant to Nihoa.

MOVEMENTS Generally sedentary but some dispersal takes place in winter, with some birds wandering at random throughout the range and south to the Gulf coast of southern Texas and southern Sonora, Mexico. Has also been recorded in Alberta. In eastern part of the USA, some of the population undertake a partial migration to the south and southwest of the range, with adult females moving longer distances on average than males.

MEASUREMENTS Wing of male 74–83·5, of female 70–80; tail 57–65; tarsus 16–18; bill (exposed culmen) 9–11. Weight 21.

REFERENCES Belthoff and Gauthreaux (1991), Godfrey (1979), Pratt *et al.* (1987).

91 BEAUTIFUL ROSEFINCH *Carpodacus pulcherrimus* Plate 24

Southern Palearctic

Propasser pulcherrimus Moore, 1856, Proc. Zool. Soc. London, 1855, p. 216, Nepal.

IDENTIFICATION Length 15 cm (6 in). A medium-sized rosefinch of the Himalayas and southwest China. Male has pink forehead and paler pink supercilium, crown and upperparts are greybrown and dark-streaked, it has two indistinct wingbars and pale pink underparts, slightly deeper in tone on face. Female is pale brown, heavily streaked on both upperparts, and underparts and with a short pale supercilium and two indistinct buff wingbars. **Confusion species:** Both sexes are likely to be confused with Stresemann's Rosefinch (92) and Pink-browed Rosefinch (93). Males are extremely similar to (if not conspecific with) the smaller Stresemann's; fully adult male Stresemann's is much deeper pink, pink on head and supercilium is deeper and more uniform across cheeks, and crown and mantle are tinged with pink in fresh plumage. Females are indistinguishable in the field except by size. Male Pink-browed Rosefinch has deeper pink on forehead, supercilium and underparts, crown to nape is uniform (not streaked) reddish-brown, rest of upperparts are same colour but streaked blackish, pink rump patch is slightly smaller, and it lacks any streaks on underparts; female Pink-browed has larger, unstreaked supercilium and dark earcoverts, with underparts warmer buff on breast and belly. Both male and female Dark-rumped Rosefinch (95) are similar but generally darker: male has pink tips to tertials and greater coverts and dark or maroon on breast; female has long, pale and quite broad supercilium and darker buff-brown underparts. White-browed (100) is larger, and male has conspicuous pink face and white supercilium, pink tips to median coverts and white tips to greaters; female has broad white or whitish supercilium, and rich or warm brown breast is broadly darkstreaked. Male Spot-winged Rosefinch (99) has more uniform upperparts, with white spots at tips of median and greater coverts, and is darker on chin and throat; female is similar to female Pink-browed, with more extensively buff underparts and a larger bill.

DESCRIPTION Sexes differ. **Adult male:** Lower forehead pink, becoming broadly paler lilac-pink behind eye (on flared supercilium) and fading over rear of ear-coverts (pink varies in intensity with the light, at times disappears and can appear to be pale grey); lores to chin deep crimson-red; eye-stripe broadly dark brown (reddish-brown at close range) across top of ear-coverts; small white half eye-ring on lower half of eye; cheeks, ear-coverts and sides of face grey or pale grey, suffused with pink or with some feathers tipped pale silvery-pink in fresh plumage. Upper forehead, crown and nape grey or grey-brown, tinged lightly with pink and streaked with black. Mantle, back and scapulars the same or slightly greyer, with parallel lines of grey and black down sides of mantle and back (tramline fashion), lacking any tinge of pink; rump plain pale pink; uppertail-coverts brown with darker feather centres and edged rose-pink. Tail is slightly notched, dark brown, edged paler or warmer brown. Median and greater coverts dusky or dark brown, edged warm brown and tipped pink or pale pink; alula, primary coverts and flight feathers dark brown, edged paler brown, becoming buff-brown on secondaries; tertials the same, but edged pale buff and tipped off-white. Underparts are rose or pale pink, with some feathers tipped paler on throat and sides of breast, also some dark streaks on sides of breast and upper flanks at close range; centre of belly off-white, lower flanks buffish-brown, sides of belly to undertail-coverts pale pink. Upper mandible of bill is dark brown, lower paler brown. Legs and feet pale fleshy-brown. **Adult female:** Forehead to crown dark brown, rest of upperparts to uppertail-coverts warm buff-brown, paler in worn plumage, all heavily streaked blackish-brown (slightly smaller and thinner streaks on crown and nape), but rump unstreaked pale brown or light tan-brown. Short pale buffish-white supercilium from eye to area over ear-coverts; lores, cheeks and ear-coverts pale or grey-brown, finely dark-streaked, upper edge of ear-coverts dark brown. Tail is dark brown edged paler buff-brown. Median coverts blackish-brown, edged warm brown, with pale or yellowish-buff tips; greaters similar, edged and tipped buffish; alula, primary coverts and flight feathers blackish-brown, edged paler brown, tertials the same but with broad warm buff-brown edges and tips (paler when worn). Underparts pale or tawny-brown, paler on chin and throat, all streaked with dark brown except for lower belly, which is paler whitish-buff and unstreaked; thighs brown, undertail-coverts pale buff-brown with blackish-brown central streaks. **Juvenile:** Identical to adult female, and inseparable in the field. First-winter and first-summer males also as adult female, and sing, display and apparently breed in this plumage. First-summer males begin to acquire adult plumage in late summer (second winter), with a pink suffusion to throat and upperparts and bright pink rump and uppertail-coverts.

GEOGRAPHICAL VARIATION Most racial variation is in depth or intensity or colour in the plumage (of limited use in the field). Male *waltoni* is paler than nominate, with underparts brighter or deeper reddish-pink (in the hand, lack dark shaft stripes), and is also slightly larger; females are said to be paler than nominate birds.

VOICE Call is a soft or subdued 'trip', 'trilp' or 'trillip', also a sparrow-like 'chillip' and a soft tit-

like twitter or trill (recalls Long-tailed Tit *Aegithalos caudatus*); a harsh 'chaaannn' is given in flight. The song is undescribed, apparently seldom uttered.

STATUS, HABITAT AND BEHAVIOUR Common over much of its range, and in northern Nepal the commonest rosefinch. In summer, occurs between 3600 m and 4650 m (lower in Tibet) in rhododendron, buckthorn, oak and juniper scrub and forest edges, also bushes on slopes with sparse vegetation on and above the tree line, and in bushes at the edge of cultivation. Usually found in pairs or small groups feeding low down or on the ground. Often sits motionless in bushes, and when disturbed prefers to 'freeze' until danger has passed; when alarmed, raises short but distinct crest. Feeds on a variety of small seeds and buds.

DISTRIBUTION *C. p. pulcherrimus*: Himalayas from Garhwal, Kashmir and northwest India, east through Nepal and (marginally) southern Tibet and Sikkim to Arunachal Pradesh.

C. p. waltoni: southeast Tibet (Gyangtze) to extreme northwest Yunnan.

C. p. argyrophrys: southern Inner Mongolia south to southwest Kansu and the Koko Nor in east Tsinghai; also Min valley, southern Szechwan, to Likiang range, northern Yunnan, western China.

C. p. davidianus: southwest Inner Mongolia and Ningsia (Ala Shan) south to Hopeh, Shansi and central Shensi, north-central China.

MOVEMENTS An altitudinal migrant, descending in winter to between 2100 m and 3300 m, or to 3600 m in Sikkim.

MEASUREMENTS Wing of male 74–81, of female 74–78; tail 62–64; tarsus c20; bill (from skull) c13; wing of male *waltoni* 76–82. Weight of male 17·5–20, of female 17–19.

REFERENCES Ali and Ripley (1983), Fleming *et al.* (1979).

92 STRESEMANN'S ROSEFINCH (Pink-rumped Rosefinch)
Carpodacus eos
Plate 24

Southeast Palearctic

Erythrina eos Stresemann, 1930, Ornith. Monatsb., 38, p. 75, Sungpan, Szechwan.

IDENTIFICATION Length 12·5 cm (5 in). Slightly smaller and shorter-tailed than Beautiful Rosefinch (91); the females of both species are identical. Some authorities consider this a race of Beautiful Rosefinch, but it breeds at a higher elevation and does not intergrade with closely similar races *waltoni* and *argyrophrys* of Beautiful. **Confusion species:** Male Stresemann's in full breeding plumage can be separated from male Beautiful by colour of underparts and general tone of head and upperparts: pink on underparts is deeper and more extensive and it lacks buff-brown flanks; pink on face is much clearer and more extensive across cheeks and ear-coverts, pink on forehead and supercilium is much paler, and crown and mantle are warmer brown, tinged or washed with pink in fresh plumage. Such males are

very scarce and outnumbered by birds in greyer first- or second-summer plumage (in which they frequently breed). The adult female and juvenile are probably inseparable in the field from those of Beautiful, but, as breeding ranges do not (apparently) overlap, may be identified by altitude at which found; in winter, descends to lower altitudes and mixes with Beautiful Rosefinch. In the hand, female Stresemann's are slightly smaller.

DESCRIPTION Sexes differ. **Adult male:** Forehead reddish-pink, crown and hindcrown deep pink, heavily streaked dark brown; lores and eye-stripe dark reddish-brown; long and broad pale pink supercilium with silvery-white tips towards nape; cheeks and ear-coverts pink with some pale or silvery-white tips. Nape, mantle, back and scapulars grey-brown, broadly streaked blackish or dark brown with warm pink suffusion; rump and uppertail-coverts bright or deep pink, longest feathers brown in centre. Tail is dark brown. Median coverts as scapulars or slightly darker brown, edged and tipped pinkish; greater coverts the same, but edged and tipped pale buffish-pink; alula and primary coverts dark brown; flight feathers dark brown, finely edged pinkish-buff, tertials more broadly edged. Underparts are almost entirely deep pink (or whitish on belly in worn plumage), with some dark bases and streaks to feather centres showing through; some feathers on sides of neck are also pink with silvery-white tips. Bill fairly short, pointed, dark brown or dark horn-brown. Legs and feet pale brown. **Adult female:** Forehead, crown and nape to mantle, back and scapulars pale buff or light tawny-brown, broadly dark-streaked; rump similar but less prominently streaked; uppertail-coverts the same, with dark central streaks. Tail dark brown. Median coverts dark brown, tipped pale buff, greaters the same, edged pale buff; alula and primary coverts dark brown; flight feathers and tertials the same, finely edged buff. Face entirely pale buff, finely streaked with dark brown, except for pale buff supercilium. Chin and throat pale buff, finely brown-streaked, becoming pale buff with heavy dark streaks on breast and flanks, and more finely streaked on belly and lower flanks. **Juvenile:** As adult female, but in fresh plumage has slightly warmer buff tones to head, upperparts and edges to median and greater

coverts, with edges to tertials broadly pale buff; underparts are not quite so heavily streaked as there are more buffish-brown edges to feathers, and face and sides of neck are streaked with buff and brown.

VOICE Call is an assertive 'pink' or 'tink', also a bunting-like 'tsip' or 'tsick'; occasionally a harsher double note, 'piprit', similar to Beautiful Rosefinch, and a tinny rattle, 'tvitt-itt-itt-itt'. The song is undescribed.

STATUS, HABITAT AND BEHAVIOUR Very little known; rare. Found in the same type of habitat as Beautiful Rosefinch, but in more open country, stony slopes or alpine grassland, at higher altitudes of 3950–4880 m; in Tibet, occurs from dry valleys with bushy slopes and edges of agriculture to areas of alpine shrubs. Occurs in pairs or small groups feeding on the ground on seeds; in winter gathers in larger flocks, often mixing (at lower altitudes) with local races of Beautiful Rosefinch. Many habits and actions are as Common Rosefinch (87). Nest and breeding ecology unknown.

DISTRIBUTION Monotypic. Southwest China from southern Tsinghai south to Sikang, southwest Szechwan, extreme northwest Yunnan (To La mountain) and marginally southeast Tibet.

MOVEMENTS An altitudinal migrant; descends to lower levels in winter, and moves south to winter in the Likiang range, northern Yunnan. A vagrant to northern Thailand (October 1968).

MEASUREMENTS Wing 69–76.

REFERENCE Schäfer (1938).

93 PINK-BROWED ROSEFINCH *Carpodacus rhodochrous* Plate 25
Southern Palearctic

Fringilla rodochroa Vigors, 1831, Proc. Committee Sci. Zool. Soc. London, p. 23, Himalayas; restricted to Simla-Almora district by Ticehurst and Whistler, 1924, Ibis, p. 471.

IDENTIFICATION Length 14–15 cm (5½–6 in). A small to medium-sized rosefinch. Males are generally rich warm or reddish-brown with darker streaking on mantle and back, bright pink rump and underparts, and faint (not prominent) wingbar; long supercilium to sides of nape is pale pink with pale silvery or frosted tips, with cheeks and ear-coverts similar. Females are generally dull brown and dark-streaked, with long buffish supercilium and thin buffish-brown tips to median and greater coverts. **Confusion species:** For differences from Beautiful (91) and Stresemann's (92) Rosefinches, see Beautiful. Both sexes of (nominate) Spot-winged Rosefinch (99) are larger, and have pale pink spots on tips (male) or pale buff tips (female) to median and greater coverts and same-colour edges to tertials, and cheeks and ear-coverts are more uniformly dark (lone females of race *verreauxi* are probably indistinguishable). Male Dark-rumped (95) has a dark or mottled dark breast and more uniform upperparts. White-browed (100) and Red-mantled (101) are much larger, with larger

bills: male White-browed has white upper edge to supercilium (over pink) from over eye to sides of nape, and whitish-pink tips to median coverts and edges to tertials; male Red-mantled has not so clearly defined white upper supercilium, less heavily streaked upperparts, and breast and flanks are duller (a more lavender shade of pink). Females on their own may not always be separable, but female White-browed has a more pronounced and paler supercilium, pale buff tips to greater coverts, and buff breast becoming white on belly.

DESCRIPTION Sexes differ. **Adult male:** Pale or bright pink from lower forehead broadly over lores to long supercilium (tapering on sides of nape), with tips of supercilium pale pearl or frosted paler pink in fresh plumage; broad deep reddish-brown eye-stripe from base of bill through eye to sides of neck; cheeks, ear-coverts and sides of face pink or bright pink, with paler or frosted tips to edges of ear-coverts. Upper forehead, crown and nape bright reddish-brown, only very slightly streaked. Mantle, back and scapulars warm or reddish-brown with broad black centres/streaks (in fresh plumage, reddish-brown may be obscured by grey or greyish-buff tips, especially on mantle); rump unstreaked deep pink; uppertail-coverts dull or dingy brown, washed deep pink. Tail is slightly notched or indented, dark brown, edged warm or reddish-brown. Lesser, median and greater coverts dark brown, edged and tipped as scapulars, except for paler or light pink tips to greaters; alula dark brown, edged paler brown; primary coverts and flight feathers blackish-brown, edged warm brown, slightly paler on edges of secondaries and tertials. Underparts almost entirely rich rose or bright pink, deeper or tinged with mauve on breast, belly and flanks, paler pink on undertail-coverts, upper flanks tinged brown and in worn plumage more extensively buff-brown. Bill is short, with both mandibles curving slightly to a point, with a dark brown tip and culmen but paler brown or brownish-horn edges to upper and base of lower mandible. Legs and feet brownish-flesh. **Adult female:** Forehead to forecrown buff-brown, streaked darker brown; crown and nape darker and more heavily black-streaked. Lores blackish-brown; thin, pale creamy or buffish-yellow supercilium from in front of eye tapering towards rear of ear-coverts; cheeks and ear-coverts deep buff-brown, finely dark-streaked. Mantle, back and scapulars warm buffish-brown (paler than crown and nape), streaked dark brown or blackish; rump and uppertail-coverts the same but streaks reduced or faint. Tail dark brown, edged paler warm buff or sandy-brown. Median and greater coverts dark brown or blackish-brown, broadly edged warm buff-brown with slightly paler buff tips; alula and primary coverts blackish, edged pale buff-brown; flight feathers dark or blackish-brown, finely edged warm or pale brown, broadly warmer brown on tertials (in worn plumage becomes pale buff-brown). Chin and throat pale buff, finely streaked dark brown, streaks becoming heavier on sides of upper breast; breast and flanks deeper or warmer buff-brown, prominently streaked dark brown; belly and undertail-coverts pale buff-brown with fine streaks,

thighs buff-brown. Bill as male, but with dull pale pinkish-flesh or bluish tinge to lower mandible. Legs and feet pale flesh-brown. **Juvenile:** Identical to adult female; some may be warmer or more buffish-brown on upperparts in fresh plumage and remain in this plumage throughout first summer. Second-winter males begin (in late first summer) to show reddish-brown of upperparts and pale pink tips to feathers of rump, supercilium and underparts, though latter are generally paler or less intensely pink and often retain dark central streaks.

VOICE Call is a loud 'per-lee' or 'chew-wee', also a canary-like 'sweet'. The song is sweet and lilting.

STATUS, HABITAT AND BEHAVIOUR Common or locally common. Found in summer between 2250 m and 4540 m (possibly to 5150 m) in undergrowth in open mixed forest of birch and fir, breeding in willows, dwarf juniper, rhododendrons and on open grassy slopes, scrub or edges of lowland woods or oak forest; occasionally in gardens in winter. Found in pairs (summer) or in small loose flocks in winter; occasionally flocks comprise only one sex. Often feeds unobtrusively on the ground until flying up into bushes at the last moment; on the ground hops or shuffles. Feeds on a variety of small seeds and berries.

DISTRIBUTION Monotypic. Himalayas, from Kashmir (excluding Ladakh) east through extreme northern Punjab, Uttar Pradesh, India, and Nepal to western Sikkim, occurring mainly in central and southern ranges of Himalayas; possibly also on the adjacent northern slopes and valleys in southern Tibet, and said to be a rare resident in Lhasa, Tibet.

MOVEMENTS An altitudinal migrant; in winter descends to between 1800 m and 2700 m, exceptionally to 910 m. Has been recorded in southwest Tibet in June.

MEASUREMENTS Wing of male 71–75, of female 67–71; tail 58–62; tarsus 19–20; bill (culmen) 10–11·5, (from skull) c15. Weight of male 17–20, of female 16–18·5.

REFERENCES Ali (1962), Ali and Ripley (1983), de Schauensee (1984), Fleming et al. (1979).

94 VINACEOUS ROSEFINCH *Carpodacus vinaceus* Plate 26
Southeast Palearctic and Oriental

Carpodacus vinaceus Verreaux, 1871, Nouv. Arch. Mus. Hist. Nat. [Paris], 6 (1870), p. 39, mountains of Chinese Tibet [probably Ho-pa-tchang, Chengtu, Szechwan, *vide* Verreaux, 1872, Nouv. Arch. Mus. Hist. Nat., 7 (1871), p. 62.

IDENTIFICATION Length 13–16cm (5¼–6¼in). A distinctive dark rosefinch with a high rounded crown and longish tail. Male is darkest of rosefinches (appears black at a distance), almost entirely dark crimson, with bright pink supercilium, pale rose-red rump and distinctive white outer edges to tertials. Female generally deep or rich buff-brown, tinged dark olive, and indistinctly dark-streaked on head and on paler or warmer brown underparts; wings have pale yellowish outer

edges to tertials. **Confusion species:** Males are more uniformly dark or dark crimson than other rosefinches. Both Dark (86) and Dark-rumped (95) have paler chin, throat and belly contrasting with a dark band on breast (though this may be absent or reduced on some Dark, in which case head pattern is distinctive). Spot-winged (99) is initially similar but much larger, and has paler (contrasting) underparts and prominent pale tips or (broken) wingbars on median and greater coverts. Females are much more likely to be confused, but all-dark plumage and lack of prominent or distinct streaking is likely to indicate Dark or Blanford's (85), latter of which is unstreaked and has a rusty-tinged rump, but prominent pale outer webs to tertials on Vinaceous (absent or reduced on some juveniles) diagnostic. Female Pink-browed (93) is paler, heavily streaked, with a broad pale supercilium.

DESCRIPTION Sexes differ. **Adult male:** Upperparts to lower back deep or dark crimson; rump paler, a deep or rich rose-pink, uppertail-coverts dark crimson. Tail is notched, black, edged finely with reddish or reddish-brown. All coverts and flight feathers black, finely edged with reddish-pink; tertials the same, but broadly or prominently edged pinkish-white towards tip of outer web. Lores and eye-stripe blackish, with a bright pale pink supercilium beginning on upper lores, extending over eye and ear-coverts and tapering on sides of nape. Rest of face and underparts deep or dark crimson, slightly or marginally paler on lower breast, belly and flanks, and at close range (or in the hand) shows dark central streaks to feathers; undertail-coverts lighter or buffish, tipped with red or pinkish-red. Bill is short and stout, both mandibles curving to a point, and dark brown or blackish. Legs and feet dark tan or dark horn-brown. **Adult female:** Almost entirely uniform deep or warm earth-brown or tan-brown, tinged olive on upperparts, at close range with slightly darker feather centres to crown, mantle, back and scapulars; rump the same, but unstreaked. Tail dark brown with fine buffish-brown edges. All coverts and flight feathers dark brown or blackish-brown, finely edged as upperparts, with tips slightly paler; tertials have dull yellowish-white or buffish-white outer webs towards tips (in worn plumage, may be totally absent or present on inner-most only). Underparts are very slightly paler or warmer buff-brown than upperparts, paler on chin and throat and with some ill-defined dull or darker brown streaks on breast and belly; lower belly, flanks and undertail-coverts uniform warm buff-

brown. Bill grey-brown. Legs and feet dull pink. **Juvenile:** As adult female, except slightly warmer brown (less olive) upperparts and finely dark-streaked above and below; young males begin to show traces of pale pink supercilium at an early age, and some have reduced amounts of (or totally lack) pale yellow or buff tips to tertials.

GEOGRAPHICAL VARIATION Race *formosana* is slightly darker than nominate; in winter, some males have lower breast and belly brown.

VOICE Call is a hard, assertive 'pwit' or 'zieh' with a whiplash-like quality, sometimes repeated several times, and often precedes the song; also a thin high-pitched 'tip' and faint 'tink', 'pink' or a bunting-like 'zick'. Song is a simple and distinctive 'pee-dee, be do-do' lasting about two seconds.

STATUS, HABITAT AND BEHAVIOUR Scarce or generally uncommon (*vinaceus*); fairly common in Taiwan. Found in summer between 1970 m and 3400 m in fairly dense mixed or damp bamboo forest, bushes or scrub on open hillsides; in Taiwan, *formosana* occurs between 2280 m and 2875 m. Usually found alone (or in small flocks), and sits unobtrusively in a bush or low under-growth for long periods; forages low down in bushes or on the ground, rarely far from the ground. Food unknown, but probably seeds of trees or shrubs as other rosefinches.

DISTRIBUTION *C. v. vinaceus*: Himalayas, from Naini Tal (only two records), Uttar Pradesh, India, through Nepal (where very scarce and thinly distrib-uted), and northern Burma, eastern Tibet and southern China from northwest Yunnan and Kwei-chow through Szechwan north to southern Kansu and southern Shensi (Tapai Shan) and east to Hupeh.

C. v. formosana: mountains of Taiwan.

MOVEMENTS An altitudinal migrant, moving down in winter to between 1065 m and 3050 m.

MEASUREMENTS Wing 69–71; tail *c*58; tarsus *c*20; bill (from skull) *c*14. Wing of male *formosana* 78·5–83; tail 63–68.

REFERENCE Ali and Ripley (1983).

95 DARK-RUMPED ROSEFINCH (Large Rosefinch) *Carpodacus edwardsii*   Plate 22

Southeast Palearctic

Carpodacus edwardsii Verreaux, 1871, Nouv. Arch. Mus. Hist. Nat. [Paris], 6 (1870), p. 39, mountains of Chinese Tibet; type from Moupin, *vide* Verreaux, 1872, Nouv. Arch. Mus. Hist. Nat., 7 (1871), p. 59.

IDENTIFICATION Length 16–17 cm (6¼–6¾ in). A medium-sized dark rosefinch (appears all dark in the field); male lacks any pink on upperparts, but has prominent pale pink supercilium and paler areas of pink on chin, face and belly. **Confusion species:** Similar to male Dark (86), Vinaceous (94) and Spot-winged (99) but easily separable. Females are very similar to female Vinaceous, Beautiful (91) and Spot-winged and separable with care, but some lone females may not always be identified with cer-

tainty. Males can be separated from male Dark by paler pink supercilium and cheeks, lack of reddish tinge to upperparts or underparts and lack of red on forehead to crown; from Vinaceous by larger size, pale chin, throat and sides of face and belly, and dark rump (Vinaceous almost entirely uniform except for pink rump and very prominent broad white tips to tertials); male Spot-winged has pale pink rump, prominent pale pinkish-white tips to median and greater coverts, and (apart from sides of breast) all-pale pink underparts. Male Pink-browed (93) has similar head and back pattern, but bright pink rump and underparts. Females are less easily separable with certainty, but generally darker and heavily streaked plumage and lack of wing spots distinguishes Dark-rumped from Vinaceous, Pink-browed and Spot-winged; female Dark is entirely unstreaked, and female Beautiful has dark forehead to crown, lacks well-defined supercilium and is generally paler or greyer, streaked paler on face, and paler or whiter-buff below.

DESCRIPTION Sexes differ. **Adult male:** Upper forehead, crown and nape dark brown, at close range tinged or washed with deep mauve; sides of forehead and supercilium (tapering on sides of nape) pale pink; lores and broadly below eye to sides of neck dark crimson, cheeks and lower ear-coverts pale or pinkish-red with paler frosted tips in fresh plumage. Mantle, back and scapulars warm brown (or tinged with mauve), noticeably dark-streaked; rump and uppertail-coverts unstreaked, the same colour as mantle, back and scapulars or very lightly reddish-brown. Tail is slightly notched or indented, dark brown, edged with warm chestnut or reddish-brown, more broadly towards base. Median and greater coverts are blackish in centre, edged brown, light chestnut, or (in fresh plumage) crimson-brown and tipped paler deep pinkish-red; alula, primary coverts and flight feathers brown or dark brown, edged warm brown, inner secondaries tinged reddish-brown in fresh plumage; tertials the same, but with broad pale pinkish-buff tips on outer web. Chin and throat pinkish-red with darker feather bases; breast dark crimson or light maroon, becoming paler or more pinkish on lower breast and belly and finely dark-streaked; flanks, thighs and undertail-coverts brown. Bill is short, with both mandibles curving to the tip, fairly stout and pointed, brown on upper mandible and paler or lighter horn on lower. Legs and feet dark flesh-brown. **Adult female:** Forehead to crown and nape dull brown and dark-streaked. Mantle, back and scapulars generally dull or dingy tawny-brown with heavy dark brown streaks; rump and uppertail-coverts uniform tawny-brown. Tail dark brown, edged lighter or buffish-brown. Median and greater coverts dull or dusky brown, edged tawny-brown and tipped pale buffish-brown; alula and primary coverts dark brown; flight feathers dark brown, edged paler, more broadly pale on edges and tips of tertials. Face is very dark or closely black-streaked, with pale buff tips on lores, cheeks and ear-coverts and with a fairly broad but ill-defined pale buff supercilium from upper lores to sides of nape, duller in front of eye and finely dark-streaked; a slightly paler area below cheeks. Chin and throat pale buff,

dark-streaked; breast, upper belly and flanks deeper or heavier brownish-buff, broadly dark-streaked; lower belly and lower flanks to undertail-coverts paler buff-brown with thin or fine dark streaks. **Juvenile:** As adult female or slightly duller brown, darker brown on underparts (except for chin and throat which are pale buff) and streaks are clearly marked. First-summer males are very similar, but have a deep reddish or crimson tinge to crown, mantle, back and uppertail-coverts, and supercilium is paler and pinker, as is face; chin and throat as juvenile, but breast heavily washed deep pink.

GEOGRAPHICAL VARIATION Males of race *rubicunda* are much more heavily washed crimson on entire upperparts, heaviest on crown to mantle, back and rump, with lower belly and undertail-coverts less brownish; females are darker or duller brown and more heavily streaked than nominate.

VOICE Generally silent, but has a metallic 'twink'; also a rasping 'che-wee' alarm call. The song is undescribed.

STATUS, HABITAT AND BEHAVIOUR Uncommon or scarce, locally common in winter. Occurs between 3050 m and 4240 m in birch and fir forest, also in bamboo; breeds in juniper and dwarf rhododendron stands, also bamboo or thornscrub or thickets of rose bushes in alpine meadows and on open hillsides. Usually found alone or in small (family) parties; has been known to associate with Rufous-breasted Accentors (*Prunella strophiata*). Feeds under bushes on the ground. Generally skulking and shy, quickly disappears into thick foliage, rarely found at any height in trees; tends to flick wings and tail when alarmed. Breeding biology unknown. Feeds on seeds of grasses, but also on rose seeds and crab apples.

DISTRIBUTION C. e. edwardsii: Szechwan (west of the Min Ho) to southern Kansu, western China.

C. e. rubicunda: Himalayas from western Nepal to Sikkim, Bhutan and Arunachal Pradesh to southeast Tibet (west to Pome district), southeast Szechwan and northern Yunnan south to the Likiang range.

MOVEMENTS An altitudinal migrant, descending in winter to between 2000 m and 3700 m in Nepal and to 1060 m in Tibet and western China; also winters south to northern Burma.

MEASUREMENTS Wing of male 79–85, of female 77–82; tail of male 61–67, of female 59–66; tarsus 22–25; bill (from skull) 14–16. Weight (one female) 26·5. Wing of male *rubicunda* 78–86, of female 75–79.

REFERENCES Ali and Ripley (1983), Fleming *et al.* (1979).

Pyrrhula synoica Temminck, 1825, Pl. Col., livr. 63, pl. 375, Mount Sinai.

IDENTIFICATION Length 14·5–16 cm (5¾–6½ in). A very distinct, plain or unstreaked pale pink or sandy rosefinch. Males have bright red from face to chin and throat and a deep pink rump and uppertail-coverts; females are generally an unremarkable pale buffish-grey or sandy-brown, lacking any pink or red; both sexes blend in well with their surroundings. Winter flocks often contain birds of various ages and intermediate plumages. **Confusion species:** Unlikely to be confused with brightly coloured male Common Rosefinch (87), which shows deeper red and brown in plumage, while female Common is streaked on underparts and shows two thin wingbars; Sinai's preferred habitat of arid terrain, semi-desert or dry wadis is not favoured by any other rosefinch. Confusion is possible with the slightly smaller and stockier sandy-pink Trumpeter Finch (80), but latter's stubby bright red bill (bright yellow on duller female), generally dull brown tones (greyish in winter) lacking any contrast between upperparts and underparts, different head shape, and dark wings and tail (together with distinctive tin-trumpet-like call of Trumpeter) enable separation. Desert Finch (82) has a conical all-black bill, pink coverts, and white flashes in wing and sides of tail.

DESCRIPTION Sexes differ. **Adult male:** Upper forehead to crown pale pink with silvery-whitish tips; lower forehead, lores, supercilium, cheeks, fore part of ear-coverts to chin and upper throat red or bright pinkish-red; rear of ear-coverts pale pink or pale silvery-pink. Hindcrown, nape and sides of neck pale sandy-brown, faintly dark-streaked, and in fresh plumage can be washed pale pink. Mantle, back and scapulars similarly pale sandy-brown, washed with pink and finely dark-streaked; rump and uppertail-coverts bright pink. Tail is slightly notched, deep sandy-brown, edged pale sandy-brown. Median and greater coverts as scapulars or with slightly warmer buff-brown edges, tips to greaters pale pink; alula and primary coverts sandy-brown, with fine warm brown or rosy-pink edges; flight feathers sandy-brown edged finely with pale sandy-brown or buff-brown, more broadly on secondaries and tertials. Sides of lower throat and/or upper breast red or tipped with pale pink; rest of underparts almost uniform pink (rose-pink in fresh plumage), with ventral region paler, whitish or washed with buff. Bill short and conical, pale yellow or greyish-horn. Legs and feet warm brown. In worn or bleached plumage, the pale or silvery-white tips to forehead and crown are absent and the head is sandy-brown, pink on rest of plumage is much paler or more buff-coloured, wings may be browner, and flanks, thighs and undertail-coverts pale sandy or bleached buff-brown. **Adult female:** Generally pale sandy-brown or tinged greyish above, and pale buff below. Very faintly marked with slightly darker

centres to feathers on crown, nape and mantle. Wings as male, lacks wingbars but edges and tips to coverts paler buff or sandy-brown, as are edges to flight feathers and tertials. Tail has deep sandy-brown central feathers, outers edged pale greyish-buff. The whole face can be warm brown or sandy-brown, or this colour can be restricted to ear-coverts. Birds in worn or bleached plumage are much greyer and closely resemble non-breeding or worn-plumage males, but lack any trace of pink. **Juvenile:** Often inseparable from adult female, plain grey-brown or tinged with sandy on upperparts, warm brown on head and nape; bill is brown. Immature males become more pink about head in first summer, and attain almost full adult plumage in second winter after post-breeding moult.

GEOGRAPHICAL VARIATION Males of race *salimalii* are greyer on mantle and back, with only very slight (if any) trace of pink on mantle, and rose-red on underparts extends only to ventral region, with undertail-coverts white. Male *stoliczkae* is sandy on upperparts, and pink on underparts is paler and less extensive. Race *beicki* has plain pale grey-brown upperparts from hind-crown and nape, lacking any pink except on rump, where less extensive than in other races and does not reach sandy-brown uppertail-coverts.

VOICE In flight gives a distinctive Tree Pipit-like 'trizp', also a bunting-like 'tieu' or a quiet 'pleu', and frequently a 'chig' note given both on the ground and in flight; otherwise 'tsweet', 'tzewt' or 'tweet' high-pitched and metallic recalling a sparrow, calls of female being somewhat softer than male's. The song is a musical jumble often containing buzzing notes, especially during display.

STATUS, HABITAT AND BEHAVIOUR Scarce or locally common; in certain favoured areas becomes occasionally common. Found in dry arid mountains (in Asia breeds up to 3350 m, considerably lower in the Middle East), foothills and rocky deserts, wadis, cliffs and gorges with apparently little or no vegetation, but water is always within or close to breeding territory. Occurs usually in small (family?) groups or parties of about 10–12 (exceptionally up to c50), which travel considerable distances in search of water. Roosts in rocky cliffs or crevices. On the ground is quiet and often overlooked owing to its shy or retiring nature and, despite brilliance of adult male, the sandy-grey plumage blends in well with the habitat. Feeds on the ground on a variety of small seeds, also leaves, shoots, buds or occasionally fruit; in the dry season utilises a variety of water sources, including pools in remote monastery gardens or even garden sprinklers.

DISTRIBUTION *C. s. synoicus*: Negev and Sinai deserts (Israel and Egypt), western Jordan (very local) and northwest Saudi Arabia.

 C. s. salimalii: northeast Afghanistan (Bamian valley to Shibar Pass).

C. s. stoliczkae: Koko Nor, eastern Tsinghai, and Yarkand to foothills of western Kunlun range, southwest Sinkiang, China.

C. s. beicki: Langchow region, northwest Kansu, to the Sining Ho, eastern Tsinghai, China.

MOVEMENTS Sedentary and partial altitudinal migrant; descends to lower levels and coastal areas in winter, otherwise nomadic. In winter usually descends to similar habitat in surrounding plains or valleys, but often occurs in places some distance from the breeding range.

MEASUREMENTS Wing 83–91; bill (from feathers) 8–9; tarsus 17. Weight 17–24. Wing of male *salimalii* 92–101, of female 92–94.

REFERENCES Hollom et al. (1988), Mild (1990), Paludan (1959), Shirihai (1989).

97 PALLAS'S ROSEFINCH (Siberian Rosefinch) *Carpodacus roseus*
Plate 24

Palearctic

Fringilla rosea Pallas, 1776, Reise versch. Prov. Russ. Reichs, 3, p. 699, Uda and Selenga Rivers, Transbaicalia.

IDENTIFICATION Length 16–17 cm (c6½ in), exceptionally 14·5–19 cm (5¾–7½ in). A medium-sized rosefinch, rather stocky and with a longish tail in flight. Breeding males have very distinctive deep pink face, head and almost entire underparts, with white tips to chin, throat and crown; prominent and large area from lower back to uppertail-coverts pink or pale pink (the most extensive of the rosefinches); wings brown, with two pale wing-bars. Females are duller or dingy brown and dark-streaked, with only a red suffusion to face, throat and breast, and rump is bright orange. **Confusion species:** The absence of any supercilium and the large area of pink or pale whitish-pink on rump and uppertail-coverts should be diagnostic at any age or for either sex; the fairly long, thin tail in flight is also a useful character. Male's head pattern very distinctive (when in full summer plumage): White-browed (100) has dark brown, dark-streaked crown, mantle and back lacking any pink; Beautiful (91) and Stresemann's (92) are smaller and slimmer and have darker forehead, crown and face and no pale or white tips to feathers; and all three species have well-defined supercilia and lack prominent wingbars. Red-mantled (101) is much larger, with a dark crown. Female and immature best told by extent of pale lower-back/rump area; pink on head, breast and rump (of adult female), plain face, and relatively small head and conical bill on stocky body are also useful characters; also distinctive at close range are pale buff or pinkish edges to tail feathers.

DESCRIPTION Sexes differ. **Adult male:** Forehead to crown silvery-white with pink bases to feathers; hindcrown and area behind eye to upper nape rich red, tinged with brown or pinkish-brown; lores and below eye dull or dark crimson; cheeks, ear-coverts and moustachial area deep pink, tipped silvery-white in fresh plumage. Lower nape and upper mantle grey, becoming rich pink or rosy-pink with bold black feather centres on lower mantle, scapulars and upper back; lower back, rump and uppertail-coverts rich or deep rose-pink, centres to uppertail-coverts streaked dark or blackish. Tail is notched or indented, blackish-brown, edged pink or pale pink, more broadly so on outer

feathers. Lesser coverts deep crimson; median and greater coverts dark or dusky brown, edged pale pink on outers and buffish on inners, and tipped white (broadly on medians), pale pinkish or buffish-white (on greaters), forming double wing-bar; alula, primary coverts and flight feathers dark brown, edged pale buff or pale pink; tertials the same, but edged pale brown or pale buff-brown at tips. Chin and throat as moustachial area, but chin often streaked finely with black and more uniform pink; rest of throat and breast deep pink, lower breast and belly white or washed pink, flanks pink with whitish or pale grey tips (some show dark central shaft streaks); undertail-coverts whitish, washed pink, often with dark centres. Bill is short and stout but pointed, with a brown upper mandible or culmen and pale yellow or greyish-horn lower. Legs and feet reddish-brown. In winter or in fresh plumage, the pink edges to wings and coverts become buffish-brown and white tips on head and face more concealed by pink. **Adult female:** Forehead to crown reddish or orange-red, becoming brown washed with red and finely dark-streaked on crown to upper nape; lower nape paler or plain brown and less prominently washed with red, often with pale buff feather edges; lores pale buff-brown; cheeks and ear-coverts pale brown or warm brown, tinged reddish and finely dark-streaked. Mantle, upper back and scapulars dark brown, washed or edged with warm brown or rufous-brown (or pink on mantle); lower back and rump pinkish-red or orange-red, lightly streaked with brown; uppertail-coverts brown edged paler. Tail dark brown, edged paler brown (on some, tinged pale rose-pink). Median and greater coverts dark brown, edged pale buff-brown and becoming pale buff or whitish at tips; alula, primary coverts and flight feathers dark brown, edged paler brown or buff-brown on secondaries; tertials edged and tipped broadly pale buff or buffish-brown. Chin, throat and breast pale buffish-brown, washed with pinkish-orange and narrowly dark-streaked; lower breast, belly and flanks buffish or pinkish-brown, streaked darker brown, lower belly, vent and undertail-coverts paler or whitish with dark streaks on belly and vent. Bill as male, but in winter often entirely dark brown or blackish. **Juvenile:** As adult female but considerably duller brown, lacking red on head, chin to breast and rump (which is pale, almost whitish-buff); streaked above, with pale grey or buffish feather edges to mantle, scapulars and upper back; finely streaked below on chin to breast and flanks. First-winter males are very similar to adult female, but with warm orange-buff on head and face to chin and breast often obscured or concealed by brown or buff-brown tips; mantle area is grey with blackish feather centres or edged on back and scapulars with pink, lower back and rump pale orange or whitish-pink, and tips to median and greater coverts and edges to tertials pale buff. First-summer males become pink or orange-pink on forehead, crown, cheeks, ear-coverts, chin, throat, breast and rump, but full adult or nearly adult plumage not attained until second winter (August-October), with silvery tips on forehead and throat present from December onwards; some are not in full breeding plumage until their second summer. First-winter females resemble adult female, but are generally brown or dull buffish-brown with very little orange in plumage (confined to a tinge on forehead, breast and lightly streaked rump).

VOICE Generally silent. The call is a short subdued whistle; the song is similar but with slightly more rising and falling notes, frequently repeating several phrases, usually delivered from cover at some height in a tree but audible for only a short distance.

STATUS, HABITAT AND BEHAVIOUR Locally common or scarce. Occurs in breeding season at up to 3030 m in conifer, birch and cedar forest of northern taiga zone, also in alpine meadows, shrub thickets and undergrowth on sparsely vegetated mountain passes and summits; in winter it is found in deciduous woods or thickets in lowland river valleys, often on or near farmland, in aspens near water, occasionally in gardens or parks. Usually found in pairs, small groups or parties; in parts of Siberia, occurs on migration in flocks of up to 100. Feeds in trees, bushes or on the ground, on a variety of seeds, also shoots, buds and occasionally berries.

DISTRIBUTION Monotypic. South-central Siberia, from the Yenisei basin and the southeast Altai northeast through the Lena basin (to about 67°N or 68°N along the Yana) and east to the Kolyma and the Sea of Okhotsk coast; in the south, through the Sayan ranges to the Tannu-Ola Mountains, and Hangay and Hentiyn ranges, northern Mongolia, northwest through the Stanovoy range (a few pairs may exceptionally breed south to the mountains of northern Hopeh, China, but this requires confirmation), northern Amurland and east to Sakhalin.

MOVEMENTS Migratory or nomadic. Birds from the central and northern areas of the range move south, southeast or east to winter in Ussuriland, southeast Mongolia and northern China from southern Kansu and Shensi to Manchuria and south to Kiangsu; also in Japan (Hokkaido to central Honshu) and the plains of western Siberia and northern Kazakhstan (Tomsk south to Semipalatinsk). Occurs irregularly in Korea, islands in the East China Sea, western Japan and the northern Ryukyu Islands. Has also occurred in Hong Kong (October 1989), but this record must remain in some doubt owing to the numbers of wild individuals exported through the colony. A vagrant to European CIS (USSR) west of the Urals, Kiev and the Crimea, Czechoslovakia, Hungary, Switzerland, Denmark (October 1987), the British Isles (June-July 1988) and the Netherlands (April-May 1991); records from eastern Europe and Switzerland are either mid-19th century or early 20th century (Switzerland, 1930), while those from Denmark, the Netherlands and British Isles may well relate to escapes from captivity. It departs from breeding area in October and November, and returns north in March and April.

MEASUREMENTS Wing of male 82–93, of female 80–91·5; tail of male 61–74, of female 61–72; tarsus 18·5–22; bill (culmen) 10·5–12, (from skull) 15–16. Weight of male 23–35, of female 21–34.

REFERENCES Dementiev and Gladkov (1951–54), Shaw (1936), Stepanyan (1990), Vaurie (1959).

98 THREE-BANDED ROSEFINCH *Carpodacus trifasciatus*   Plate 26
Southeast Palearctic

Carpodacus trifasciatus Verreaux, 1871, Nouv. Arch. Mus. Hist. Nat. [Paris], 6 (1870), p. 39, mountains of Chinese Tibet; restricted to Paohing, Sikang, by Vaurie, 1959, Birds Pal. Fauna, Passeriformes, p. 637.

IDENTIFICATION Length 17–19·5 cm (6¾–7¾ in). A large, well-marked rosefinch with a large deep base to its bill. Males have dark grey upperparts with strong reddish or crimson tinge, more uniform red on rump, black wings and tail, with white edges to scapulars and tertials and pink tips to median and greater coverts. Females and juveniles have deep grey upperparts heavily black-streaked, yellowish-buff or white edges to and tips of tertials, warm orange-brown on throat, breast and flanks, with rest of underparts white. The size, distinctive markings in wing and strongly marked plumage make it unlikely to be confused with other species.

DESCRIPTION Sexes differ. **Adult male:** Forehead white, edged crimson; crown, nape and sides of neck deep crimson-red (appears black at distance) with black feather bases; lores, cheeks and ear-coverts black, edged with crimson, with white shaft streaks. Mantle, back and inner scapulars dark carmine-red with blackish centres and grey edges to some feathers; outer scapulars white, forming a diagonal band above closed wing; rump carmine, (some plain, more uniform red or pinkish-red); uppertail-coverts as rump, tipped dark-grey. Tail is square-tipped and black. Median and greater coverts black or blackish with deep or bright pink tips (on some, the pink is subterminal with actual tip white, forming two broad wingbars); alula, primary coverts and flight feathers black; tertials with broad white outer web at tips. Chin and throat black mixed with buff, in fresh plumage shafts white (as face) but these wear or are retained only at sides or on lower throat; upper breast deep wine-red, with black bases to feathers; breast and flanks carmine or wine-red, sides of breast grey; centre of lower breast, belly and lower flanks white; undertail-coverts also white, with grey centres and black shaft streaks. Bill is stout and Hawfinch-like, with a dark horn culmen and tip to upper mandible, the remainder and whole of lower mandible greenish-yellow or yellowish-horn. Legs and feet dark brown. **Adult female:** Forehead, crown, nape to mantle, back and inner scapulars deep grey, heavily streaked with black; outer scapulars broadly yellowish-buff or whitish; rump deep dull brown or olive-brown; uppertail-coverts blackish-brown. Tail black. Wings as adult male, but median and greater coverts are dark grey, edged paler and tipped yellowish-buff or light orange, with outer webs to tips of tertials white or yellowish-white. Face warm gingery-brown, mottled grey or blackish. Chin and throat yellowish-brown or somewhat duller or mottled with grey at tips; breast and upper flanks warm gingery-brown or tinged yellow; lower flanks and sides of belly washed gingery-buff; belly and undertail-coverts greyish-white. Bill is slightly more slender than male's, with

brownish-horn upper mandible and yellowish-brown lower. **Juvenile:** Similar to adult female. First-winter males have outer edges of scapulars yellowish-white, tips of median coverts orange-yellow, greater coverts tipped yellow, and rump olive or warm reddish-brown; face (but not chin and throat) is more like that of adult male, with long white tips; face, breast and flanks are more chestnut or rust-brown than adult female. Bill as adult female, but more yellow at base of both mandibles.

VOICE Generally silent; song unrecorded.

STATUS, HABITAT AND BEHAVIOUR Scarce or uncommon; locally common in winter. Breeds between 2130 m and 3050 m in undergrowth and thickets in small or light conifer forest; in winter found in orchards, hedges, cotoneaster bushes, crab-apple trees and in barley fields. A sluggish or slow-moving, placid bird, spending long periods motionless concealed in bushes or trees. Feeds on seeds, mainly on the ground but also within bushes, and on crab apples. Breeding biology virtually unknown.

DISTRIBUTION Monotypic. Southwest Kansu to west and south Szechwan (west of the Min Ho) and in northwest Yunnan (Likiang range), western China.

MOVEMENTS An altitudinal and partial migrant. Descends in late autumn or early winter to foothills and valleys down to 1800 m; some also move southwest to winter in southeast Tibet (Pome District) along the Tsangpo river, to 3400 m. Has recently (March 1986) been recorded in Bhutan, the first record for Indian subcontinent, where it may be a scarce visitor or a local winter visitor to some northern valleys. Birds move to lower levels in late autumn and early winter, and return from Tibet mid-March onwards.

MEASUREMENTS Wing 82–88; tail 71–74; bill (from skull) 15–16; tarsus 21–22.

REFERENCE Clements (1992).

99 SPOT-WINGED ROSEFINCH *Carpodacus rhodopeplus*　　**Plate 25**
Southeast Palearctic

Fringilla rodopepla Vigors, 1831, Proc. Committee Sci. Zool. Soc., p. 23, Himalayas; restricted to Simla-Almora district by Ticehurst and Whistler, 1924, Ibis, p. 471.

IDENTIFICATION Length 15 cm (6 in). A medium- to large-sized rosefinch. Males are fairly distinctive with their generally deep crimson upperparts, long pale pink supercilium, pale pink underparts and pink spots on tips to median and greater coverts and tertials. Females are generally dull brown, dark-streaked above, with a buffish supercilium, pale tips to tertials and streaked underparts. **Confusion species:** Male is initially similar to male Vinaceous (94), but larger and with spots on tips of median and greater coverts and paler underparts. Female and immature are more likely to be confused with those of Dark-rumped

(95), Beautiful (91), Pink-browed (93) and Vinaceous, of which only the latter has similar pale buffish outer webs to tips of tertials, though in worn plumage or in moult these may be reduced or absent (in which case head-and-face pattern are useful characters); female Beautiful lacks dark cheeks and ear-coverts or well-defined creamy supercilium; female Dark-rumped has much more streaked face and head (with a dark crown); female Pink-browed is very similar but smaller and paler, with lighter tawny-buff dark-streaked upperparts and pale edges to flight feathers (bill is also smaller).

DESCRIPTION Sexes differ. **Adult male:** Forehead to crown and nape a deep or dark crimson; pale pink supercilium begins over lores and tapers on sides of nape, some feathers tipped finely white; lores, cheeks and ear-coverts very dark crimson; moustachial area pinkish-red with dark or black central shafts. Mantle, scapulars and back similar to crown, with black streaks, and with broad pale pink outer edges to lower inner scapulars; rump tipped paler pink; uppertail-coverts dark crimson. Tail is indented, dark brown, edged with crimson. Median and greater coverts blackish-brown, edged dark crimson and spotted with pink at tip; alula, primary coverts and flight feathers blackish, finely edged with crimson; tertials the same, with broad paler pink or whitish outer webs at tips. Chin and throat as moustachial area, but throat often has pale pink or whitish tips; breast and belly deep pink, sides of breast and upper flanks mottled dark reddish-brown or crimson; flanks tinged brown, with crimson tips; undertail-coverts brown or warm brown, washed crimson. Bill is fairly stout, pointed, with dark brown upper mandible and slightly paler lower. Legs and feet flesh-brown or pale brownish-horn. **Adult female:** Forehead, crown, nape, mantle, back and scapulars brown or warm brown, broadly streaked dark brown, edged slightly paler or yellowish-buff on mantle and back; rump (almost) unstreaked plain brown; uppertail-coverts dull brown. Tail dark brown, edged paler buff-brown, broadly so towards base. Median and greater coverts brown or dark brown, edged paler or tawny and tipped paler buff-brown (finely on tips of medians); alula, primary coverts and flight feathers blackish-brown, finely edged warm brown; tertials the same, edged broadly pale buff on outer webs at tips. Long pale creamy-buff supercilium begins thinly over upper lores and extends to sides of nape; lores, upper cheeks and ear-coverts blackish-brown; lower lores and lower cheeks paler buff, finely black-streaked. Underparts are

almost entirely pale or warm buff-brown and heavily streaked blackish on breast, becoming less heavy at sides of breast and lower breast, with belly and flanks finely streaked; undertail-coverts paler buff-brown. **Juvenile:** As adult female, from which inseparable in the field.

GEOGRAPHICAL VARIATION Race *verreauxi* is somewhat smaller than nominate, and males are brighter or paler (except for crown and face), pink on rump is paler and more extensive, and underparts are slightly paler and more uniform pink; females are identical to nominate.

VOICE Generally silent, but occasionally gives a far-carrying canary-like chirp. The song is unrecorded.

STATUS, HABITAT AND BEHAVIOUR Scarce or locally common. Inhabits rhododendron scrub and bushes on slopes and alpine meadows between 3000 m and 4600 m in summer, in winter at lower levels in bushes, bamboo and mixed forest. Often perches in the open on top of bushes, but generally shy and retiring and very little is known about its breeding biology. Food items virtually unknown except for a variety of small seeds, which it takes on the ground.

DISTRIBUTION *C. r. rhodopeplus*: Himalayas from Garhwal, Kashmir and Uttar Pradesh, northern India, east through central Nepal to Sikkim and extreme southern Tibet.

C. r. verreauxi: west and north-central Szechwan south to northern Yunnan (Likiang range), western China.

MOVEMENTS An altitudinal and partial migrant; in winter descends to between 2000 m and 3050 m. Race *verreauxi* is a winter visitor to northern Burma.

MEASUREMENTS Wing 82−90; tail 67−74; tarsus $c23$; bill (from skull) 14−15. Wing of male *verreauxi* 73−76. Weight (one male) 23.

REFERENCE Ali and Ripley (1983).

100 WHITE-BROWED ROSEFINCH *Carpodacus thura*　　　Plate 25
Eastern Palearctic

Carpodacus thura Bonaparte and Schlegel, 1850, Monogr. Loxiens, p. 21, Nepal.

IDENTIFICATION Length 17 cm (6¾ in). A large, brightly coloured rosefinch, both sexes with distinctive plumage. Male has deep pink rump and underparts, and a long pale supercilium tipped with white; pale pink or whitish tips to median coverts, slightly duller tips to greaters. Female similar to other female rosefinches, but nominate has deep yellow rump and warm brown on breast (whiter in other races). A tame and approachable bird at all times of the year. **Confusion species:** Males are initially similar to (but larger than) Dark-rumped (95), Spot-winged (99), Pink-browed (93) and Beautiful (91), but head-and-face pattern and size should enable separation: also told from Dark-rumped by prominent rose-pink rump and uppertail-coverts patch; from Spot-winged by lack

of prominent pale outer webs to tips of tertials; from Pink-browed, Beautiful and Stresemann's (92) by prominent pale tips to median and greater coverts. Female has distinctive rump and underparts and is likely to be mistaken only for larger female Red-breasted (104), which lacks supercilium.

DESCRIPTION Sexes differ. **Adult male:** Crown, nape and sides of nape deep or rich brown and dark-streaked; forehead and lores bright crimson, joining with deep pink supercilium over eye and ear-coverts (tapering on sides of nape), with white or silky-white tips to upper forehead and upper edge of supercilium (not always easily seen) and whitest at rear; broad dark brown eye-stripe from eye to side of nape; cheeks, lower ear-coverts and sides of face rose-pink, lightly streaked with white. Mantle, back and scapulars as crown, streaked with black; rump and uppertail-coverts deep pink, with dark centres to longest uppertail-coverts. Tail is slightly notched or indented, black, edged with brown. Median coverts blackish-brown, tipped pale or whitish-pink, greaters blackish, edged brown or warm brown and tipped pale buff; alula, primary coverts and flight feathers blackish-brown, edged with dull pink, paler on edges of secondaries; tertials the same, edged pale buff or whitish-buff. Chin and throat crimson or wine-red with paler or less prominent pinkish-white tips; lower throat, breast (occasionally with thin white tips) and belly uniform rose-pink; flanks brown, lightly streaked black; vent and undertail-coverts white, washed pink and with dark shaft streaks. Bill fairly stout or strong-looking, brown or brownish-horn. Legs and feet flesh-grey to dark brown. In worn plumage, dark streaks on mantle and back become indistinct, pale tips to median and greater coverts are reduced or absent, as are white or pale tips on face, chin and throat. **Adult female:** Lower forehead pale brown or buff-brown, streaked with black; upper forehead, crown and nape brown, streaked with black, as are mantle, back and scapulars; rump bright yellow or golden-yellow with blackish feather centres (often partly obscuring gold colour), uppertail-coverts dark brown, tinged with golden-yellow. Tail black, edged with pale brown. Median and greater coverts blackish or blackish-brown, edged brown and tipped with pale buffish-brown, forming double wingbar; alula, primary coverts and flight feathers blackish-brown, finely edged paler brown; tertials the same, but edged pale buffish-brown. Supercilium is creamy-buff and whitish, very finely streaked with black, beginning over or just in front of eye and tapering at rear of ear-coverts; ear-coverts blackish-brown; lores, cheeks and lower ear-coverts buffish-white, strongly streaked with black. Chin, throat and breast warm ginger-brown, streaked dark or blackish-brown; lower breast whiter, also streaked dark brown; belly white, more thinly streaked dark brown; flanks washed buff-brown and streaked brown; undertail-coverts yellowish-white, finely streaked. **Juvenile:** Very similar to adult female. First-winter and first-summer males have lower back and/or rump rich buff-brown or reddish-brown and tips to greater coverts are pale brown; chin, throat and breast base colour is much deeper rufous-brown or even orange-brown than on adult female. First-summer males often breed in this plumage.

GEOGRAPHICAL VARIATION Most racial variation concerns depth or intensity of brown on upperparts and of pink on rump and underparts. Males of race *blythi* have brown mantle, back and scapulars washed or suffused with pink, and generally duller purple-tinged underparts. Male *dubius* are generally light brown on upperparts, streaked fairly heavily with dark brown, ear-coverts are crimson (not dark brown as nominate) and meet supercilium, and dark eye-stripe is reduced or absent. Male *femininus* is very similar to *dubius*, but deeply purple-pink with heavier streaks on

underparts. Females are easily recognisable or separable in the field: those of race *blythi* have rufous or warm brown on chin to breast less intense in tone or slightly reduced (to centre of breast); in races *dubius*, *charmensis* and *femininus*, chin, throat and breast base colour is white or buffish-white and streaked heavily with dark or blackish-brown, and female *femininus* also has paler supercilia and upperparts than nominate *thura*.

VOICE Call is a sharp, buzzing 'deep-deep, deep-de-de-de-de' or a bleating 'veh ve ve ve ve ve ve', also a loud and rapid piping 'pupupipipipi', usually while on the ground. Race *blythi* has a loud or harsh whistling note repeated several times and likened to 'pwit-pwit' call of European Nuthatch (*Sitta europaea*), also a soft 'wid wid' contact note given when feeding. The song is a seldom heard Linnet-like twitter, usually given from a treetop.

STATUS, HABITAT AND BEHAVIOUR Common or locally common. In summer, found only at high altitudes between 2400 m and 3330 m on the Afghanistan/Pakistan border and at 3800–4200 m in Nepal, up to 4250 m in Sikkim and to 4600 m in Tibet and western China, in open or edges of forest or alpine meadows, dwarf rhododendron, bamboo and juniper scrub above the tree line; in winter, open hillsides with scrub; it is fond of berberis bushes. Usually found in pairs or small, loosely scattered parties of up to 20, occasionally mixing with other rosefinches, particularly Dark-rumped, or White-winged Grosbeaks (125); in winter often in single-sex flocks. Tame and very approachable. Feeds on the ground, where it both hops and walks; takes mainly small seeds of a variety of plants and shrubs, also berries, including blackberries, raspberries and junipers.

DISTRIBUTION *C. t. thura*: central Himalayas from western Nepal to Bhutan, north to the Chumbi valley, southern Tibet.

C. t. blythi: Safed Koh, northeast Afghanistan, N.W.F.P., Pakistan, Kashmir and the western Himalayas to Kumaon, Uttar Pradesh, northern India.

C. t. femininus: southeast Tibet from about 93°E, eastern Assam and northern Arunachal Pradesh, northeast India, to western Szechwan, extreme southwest Tsinghai and northern Yunnan (Likiang range), western China.

C. t. dubius: eastern Tibet (Chamdo District), northern Szechwan (Sungpan) and eastern Tsinghai (Tatung River) east to the Ala Shan range in eastern Kansu and Ho Lan Shan, Ningsia, northwest China.

C. t. deserticolor: northeast Tsinghai (east of *dubius*) in the Nan Shan and Buckhan Boda Shan ranges, northwest China.

MOVEMENTS An altitudinal migrant. In winter many descend to lower levels, but some remain at high level even in severe winters when deep snow covers the ground; usually not lower than 2440 m, exceptionally to 1830 m and mainly around 3030–3630 m. Birds of race *femininus* may winter in northern Burma, but this is not confirmed.

MEASUREMENTS Wing of male 81–87, of female 80–83; tail of male c75, of female c65; tarsus c25; bill (from skull) c14. Wing of male *femininus* 83–88, of female 82–85; tail of male 75–

REFERENCES Ali and Ripley (1983), Fleming *et al.* (1979), Schäfer (1938).

101 RED-MANTLED ROSEFINCH *Carpodacus rhodochlamys* **Plate 23**

Eastern Palearctic

Pyrrhula (Corythus) rhodochlamys Brandt, 1843, Bull. Acad. Imp. Sci., St Petersbourg, cl. Phys.-Math., 1, col. 363, Siberia; probably Tarbagatai, *fide* Korovin, 1934, Bull. Univ. Asie Centrale, Tashkent, 19, p. 68.

IDENTIFICATION Length 18 cm (7 in). A large rosefinch with a distinctive large bill. Males are lilac-pink on face, rump and entire underparts; crown, mantle, back and wings are brown, and it has a pink supercilium with pale silvery-white tips. Females and immatures are pale grey-brown and dark-streaked, with a narrow supercilium and tips to wing-coverts. **Confusion species:** Very like a larger version of Pink-browed (93), whose range it adjoins but does not overlap, but with a large bill, paler supercilium with less well-defined white tips and eye-stripe which is not so broad or dark, paler more lilac-pink underparts and less contrasting streaks on upperparts. Females are best separated by size, but female Red-mantled generally has paler buff ground colour to underparts. Beautiful (91) and Stresemann's (92) are initially similar but smaller and slimmer, with heavy streaking on mantle, back and scapulars and no (or fewer) pale or white tips to cheeks, ear-coverts or supercilium. Both sexes of White-browed (100) have pale wing-bars and long white tips to chin, throat and forehead to supercilium. Red-breasted (104) is also initially similar, but brighter red on face and underparts and browner on upperparts; females have rich brown, dark-streaked underparts.

DESCRIPTION Sexes differ. **Adult male:** Upper forehead and crown deep or dark crimson, nape similar, indistinctly dark-streaked; lower forehead and broad supercilium pale pink, with fine silky-white tips usually along upper edge and ending on sides of nape; lores and broad eye-stripe (to nape) dark crimson; cheeks, ear-coverts and sides of face deep pink with some long white or silky-white tips. Mantle, back and scapulars brown, streaked blackish and heavily washed with red; rump uniform bright pink; uppertail-coverts brown, edged reddish-pink. Tail is notched or indented, dark or blackish-brown with reddish-brown or crimson edges. Median and greater coverts dark brown, edged pale brown tinged with pink and tipped slightly paler; alula, primary coverts and flight feathers dull dark brown, edged pale brown tinged pinkish; tertials the same, broadly edged pale pinkish-brown becoming pale pinkish-buff towards tips. Chin and throat reddish-crimson, with white or silky-white tips in fresh plumage; rest of underparts rosy or lilac-pink, flanks tinged brown, undertail-coverts pale lilac-pink. Brown bill is large or stout and deep at base, upper mandible curving to a point, with base of lower mandible yellowish or yellowish-horn. Legs and feet flesh-brown. In worn plumage duller or darker, and red or crimson is deeper and less lilac-pink in tone. **Adult female:** Forehead, crown and nape to mantle, back and scapulars ashy-brown, heavily dark-streaked; rump the same (but some show very faint tinge of pink), and uppertail-coverts brown or grey-brown, darker in centre. Tail is dark or dusky-brown, edged paler, ashy or buffish-brown. Median and greater coverts dark brown or blackish with paler ashy-brown edges and tips; alula, primary coverts and flight feathers dark brown or blackish-brown, edged with ash-grey or buffish, broadly so on tertials. Lores, cheeks and ear-coverts and sides of face pale buff or ashy-brown, finely dark-streaked. Underparts creamy or buffish-white, streaked dark brown or blackish; undertail-coverts pale buffish-brown. Bill has dark brown upper mandible, yellowish-horn lower. **Juvenile:** Both juvenile and first-winter plumages are as adult female.

GEOGRAPHICAL VARIATION Nominate males are much brighter or deeper reddish-pink than race *grandis*, which is larger, browner on upperparts and less noticeably streaked black on centres of feathers; rump of nominate *rhodochlamys* is bright reddish-pink, but in *grandis* it is duller with brown bases to feathers, and *grandis* also has face, chin, throat and underparts darker, more wine-red than nominate; nominate has a variable amount of red across lower forehead tipped silky-white, which is reduced or absent in *grandis* (but more noticeable on supercilium and ear-coverts). Race *kotschubeii* is intermediate in plumage and size between *rhodochlamys* and *grandis*, and lacks red band on forehead and is much more strongly washed with red on upperparts, including crown and rump.

VOICE Call is a single plaintive wheezy or buzzing whistle, 'kwee' or 'sqwee', also a sharp or abrupt 'wir'. The song is undescribed.

STATUS, HABITAT AND BEHAVIOUR Locally common or scarce. In summer, found between 2720 m and 4900 m in upper regions of forested mountains, mainly juniper or deciduous forest, woods or rose bushes in alpine meadows, fond of honeysuckle, caragana and barberry bushes; in winter at lower levels, and found in scrub, rose or thornbush areas, orchards or gardens and edges of cultivation. Usually in pairs or small parties, occasionally alone in winter. Keeps low in bushes or feeds on the ground; raises a small crest when alarmed, generally secretive but often tame and confiding. Feeds mainly on seeds of bushes, roses and flower-heads (including dandelion).

DISTRIBUTION *C. r. rhodochlamys*: Tien Shan range, Russian and Chinese Turkestan from about 71°E, east through Kashgaria to the western Kunlun range, Sinkiang, north through the Dzungarian Ala Tau range to the Tarbagatai and western Altai ranges and northern Mongolia (Hentiyn and possibly Hangay ranges).

C. r. kotschubeii: Altai range south to northern Pamirs, Russian Turkestan.

C. r. grandis: Hindu Kush, northern Afghanistan, northern Baluchistan, Karakoram range, northern Pakistan, and the western Himalayas east to Garhwal region, Kashmir, northern India.

MOVEMENTS An altitudinal migrant; in winter moves down to adjacent foothills and valleys, usually between 2200 m and 2600 m, occasionally as low as 1200 m. Birds of nominate race winter west to Tashkent area and east to Lop Nor and the Bogdo Ola Shan range, Sinkiang, northwest China.

MEASUREMENTS Wing of male 86–91, of female 88–92; tail of male 69–74, of female 65–70; tarsus 20–22; bill (culmen) 14·5–15, (from skull) 18–20. Wing of male *grandis* 91–97, of female 89–92. Weight of male 31–36, of female 31–35.

REFERENCES Ali and Ripley (1983), Vaurie (1949, 1959).

102 EASTERN GREAT ROSEFINCH (Streaked Rosefinch)
Carpodacus rubicilloides Plate 22
Eastern Palearctic

Carpodacus rubicilloides Przewalski, 1876, Mongol i Strana Tangut., 2, p. 90, Kansu.

IDENTIFICATION Length 19 cm (7½ in). A large or robust-looking rosefinch with a large bill; has a full-breasted appearance both on ground and in flight, also long wings and tail; usually found in rocky screes or slopes and plateaux above tree line. Males are bright or deep rich red on forehead, face and underparts, with fine pale pink spots on latter, and have a deep pink rump and grey-brown dark-streaked upperparts. Females and immatures are very drab grey-brown, dark-streaked, and apart from size rather featureless. **Confusion species:** Both sexes are very similar to Caucasian Great Rosefinch (103) and some, especially females and immatures, may be indistinguishable except for white in outer tail feather of Caucasian. Males are generally darker above with dark brown streaks, and red is much more intense, especially on face and underparts, appearing much more frosted pink on Caucasian. Male Red-breasted (104) is similar, but is greyer above, has brown flanks and lacks white spots or streaks on face and underparts. Females are generally much darker brown than Caucasian, which tend to be much more sandy-brown. Female Red-breasted is warm brown below, with an olive or olive-yellow rump. Immatures are less likely to be separable.

DESCRIPTION Sexes differ. **Adult male:** Forehead to forecrown rich or deep strawberry-red with fine white or whitish centre streaks; lores to eye and below eye deep strawberry-red; rest of face bright or deep red with light or fine whitish streaks. Crown, nape and sides of neck brown, heavily tinged reddish. Mantle, back and scapulars brown or grey-brown and dark-streaked, with pink wash in fresh plumage; rump uniform deep pink; uppertail-coverts similar, with darker brown feather centres. Tail is slightly notched, blackish-brown, finely edged with buffish-brown. Median coverts grey-brown with pale pink edges, greaters also grey-brown but with orange or reddish-pink tips; alula, primary coverts and flight feathers dark

brown, with fine pale buff edges to secondaries; tertials the same, with broader or prominently pale buff edges and whitish tips. Chin and throat as forehead and lores; breast paler or bright red with pale or white feather centres; belly and flanks slightly paler or more pinkish-red with white streaks (at centres); undertail-coverts whitish with pink at tips. Bill is large, strong and pointed, with a dark horn upper mandible and paler or yellowish-horn lower. Legs and feet dark brown. **Adult female:** Almost entirely cold grey-brown. Forehead to crown pale or buffish grey-brown, streaked dark brown, paler on face, with cheeks and ear-coverts heavily streaked dark or blackish; a pale or flesh-coloured eye-ring; upperparts also pale buffish or grey-brown, streaked dark brown, lightly on rump; tail dark brown or blackish; wings dark brown, but median and greater coverts have pale buff edges, secondaries are edged pale buff and form pale panel on closed wing; tertials have pale buff or whitish edges and tips. Underparts are entirely pale buff, heavily streaked with dark or blackish-brown. Bill as male in size, uniform dark horn. **Juvenile:** Indistinguishable in the field from adult females.

GEOGRAPHICAL VARIATION Birds of race *lucifer* are slightly larger than nominate, but this unlikely to be noticeable in the field; birds from western end of range are slightly paler and not so intensely red in fresh plumage.

VOICE Call is a loud Chaffinch-like 'twink', 'pink' or 'sink'; also a soft 'sip' note and a melancholy bullfinch-like 'dooid dooid'. The song is a slowly descending 'tsee-tsee-soo-soo-soo', occasionally with the first phrase repeated several times.

STATUS, HABITAT AND BEHAVIOUR Fairly common or locally common. A bird of high, arid rocky slopes, screes and plateaux above tree line, found between 3700 m and 4800 m in Nepal and up to 5150 m in Tibet, in bushes (mainly *Caragana*) or hillside scrub (mainly *Hippophae*); in winter, often in sea-buckthorn thickets and occasionally found around villages or settlements. Somewhat shy or retiring. Flight is strong, fast and bounding, recalling Chaffinch (1) or a bunting. Often roosts communally in willows. Mixes freely with other finches, including Caucasian Great Rosefinch or White-winged Grosbeak (125), in areas where the ranges overlap. Perches in trees or bushes and on rocks; has a habit of flicking wings and tail when alarmed. Feeds on the ground on a variety of small seeds.

DISTRIBUTION *C. r. rubicilloides*: central Szechwan (eastern Sikang) east to Kangting, southern Tsinghai (Jyekundo region), Koko Nor and northeast Tsinghai (Yushu and Nan Shan), through Kansu to central Inner Mongolia.

C. r. lucifer: Himalayas, from eastern Kashmir (Ladakh) east through Nepal to southeast Tibet (Pome District) north to Lhasa and extreme northern Sikkim.

MOVEMENTS An altitudinal migrant; descends in winter to 2200 m in Tibet, generally not below 2800 m in Nepal. Occurs in southern Szechwan and northern Yunnan (Likiang range) in winter.

MEASUREMENTS Wing of male 102–108, of female 97–107. Wing of male *lucifer* 107–115, of female 97–108; tail 84–92; tarsus 24–25; bill (from skull) c18.

REFERENCES Ali and Ripley (1983), Ludlow (1951), Osmaston (1925).

103 CAUCASIAN GREAT ROSEFINCH (Great Rosefinch, Severtzov's Rosefinch) *Carpodacus rubicilla* Plate 22

Palearctic

Loxia rubicilla Güldenstädt, 1775, Nov. Comm. Acad. Sci. Petrop., 19, p. 464, Caucasus.

IDENTIFICATION Length 19–20 cm (7½–8 in). Very similar to Eastern Great Rosefinch (102), but males are generally much paler or frosted pink on face and underparts, and upperparts are much less noticeably or less heavily streaked. Females are also less heavily streaked on mantle than female Eastern Great and are generally more yellowish-buff on underparts, but lone females or immatures may not always be identified with certainty. **Confusion species:** For differences from Eastern Great (with which it overlaps in northern Pakistan and the western Himalayas), see that species. Both sexes are similar to Red-breasted Rosefinch (104), though latter is less bulky, with smaller bill, males have deeper red faces and streaked upperparts, dark crown and belly, while females have warm brown on lower breast to undertail-coverts.

DESCRIPTION Sexes differ. **Adult male:** Forehead to hindcrown crimson or strawberry-red, finely spotted or streaked with white; lores, cheeks and ear-coverts deep crimson (appear dark or blackish-red), with pale or whitish spots at rear of ear-coverts (absent in worn plumage). Nape and sides of neck bright red or crimson. Mantle, back and scapulars brown, tinged red or crimson (especially on mantle), and faintly streaked (most noticeable in fresh plumage); rump deep pink, uppertail-coverts brown, edged and tipped pink or pale pink. Tail is slightly notched, blackish-brown, finely edged warm brown or reddish-brown at sides (some show pale or whitish tip in fresh plumage). Median coverts blackish-brown with edges and tips pinkish-brown as scapulars; greater coverts also blackish-brown, edged pinkish-red and tipped whitish-pink; alula, primary coverts and flight feathers blackish-brown, finely edged reddish in fresh plumage (or pale brown on secondaries), all tipped ashy-white; tertials the same, but more broadly edged pale buff or ashy-white. Chin, throat and breast deep crimson, spotted white or pale pink, smaller spots on throat becoming larger on breast; belly and flanks paler or plain pink with longer white or pale pink streaks (centres); thighs buffish-brown; undertail-coverts pale rosy-pink. Bill is slightly smaller or less deep and more gradually pointed than (but same length as) on Eastern Great Rosefinch, upper mandible dusky or horn-yellow, base of lower as upper but sides and tip grey. Legs and feet dark brown. **Adult female:** Very similar to adult female Eastern Great. Upperparts including forehead to nape grey-brown and dark-streaked, slightly paler grey on unstreaked lower back and rump, uppertail-coverts similar with dark or dusky brown feather centres. Tail is blackish-brown, most feathers finely margined with pale buff-brown, edges of outermost finely white or whitish. Median and greater coverts dark brown, edged pale grey-brown, with pale grey or buff at tips; alula, primary coverts and flight feathers dark brown, edged paler brown, edges of secondaries and tertials whitish-buff. Lores, cheeks and ear-coverts darker than crown, with thin dark streaks. Chin, throat and breast buffish or buffish-brown and dark-streaked; thighs and undertail-coverts whitish-grey, streaked darker, more finely so on belly and flanks. **Juvenile:** Juveniles closely resemble adult female, but are generally more sandy-brown (paler below) than grey females and bill is uniform pale grey. First-winter and first-summer birds become greyer-brown and some are inseparable from adult females, but immatures often show less dense streaking (absent on some) on belly. Birds in first-summer (i.e. female-type) plumage breed and hold territory. Second-winter males are generally red or deep pink on underparts, but may retain streaked upperparts of immature plumage.

GEOGRAPHICAL VARIATION Most racial

variation concerns intensity (or saturation) of pink or red in males and length of wing, tail, bill etc., very little of which is recognisable in the field. Both sexes of race *severtzovi* are paler than nominate, with females also having shorter or thinner streaks above and below (confined to shaft streaks on upperparts and flanks).

VOICE Call is similar to that of Eastern Great Rosefinch, but also has a sharp 'twit, ping'. In flight, gives a short subdued whistle or a brief twitter. Song is a series of loud (especially first two phrases) intermittent whistles, 'tiu' or 'fyu-fyu-fyu-fyu-fyu', fading towards end, also with some shrill whistles often included; has a softer subsong of varied twittering audible only at short range. Song of *severtzovi* is a mournful low 'weeep' and a series of soft chuckles.

STATUS, HABITAT AND BEHAVIOUR Fairly or locally common. Inhabits high-altitude valleys and plateaux of open boulder or rock-strewn areas between 2500 m and 3500 m in the Caucasus and 3630 m and 5000 m (possibly higher) further east, in alpine meadows, treeless foothills, fields near villages or even in sparsely vegetated or desolate areas; in winter, also found in hillside scrub and around village fields. Usually occurs singly, in pairs or (particularly in winter) in small flocks, often mixing with other rosefinches, particularly Eastern Great (which it recalls in habits and actions), where ranges overlap. Flies quite strongly and at times recalls larks. Feeds on the ground or in bushes, mainly on seeds of small alpine plants and *Caragana* bushes, berries and some insects.

DISTRIBUTION *C. r. rubicilla*: central and eastern ranges of the Caucasus.

C. r. diabolica: northeast Afghanistan; known from only one pair in worn plumage from Sanglich.

C. r. kobdensis: central and southeast Russian Altai range east to extreme northern Sinkiang and Mongolian Altai, possibly also to northwest Kansu, also in western Hangay range, Mongolia, and in the Sayan ranges, southwest Siberia.

C. r. severtzovi: central Tien Shan and the Pamirs, Russian Turkestan, east to the Bogdo Ola Shan range, western Sinkiang, in the south through the Kun Lun range east to the Koko Nor and Nan Shan range, east and north Tsinghai, also Yushu and the upper Yangtze, southern Tsinghai; in the south from the Karakorum range in northern Pakistan (possibly west to Wakhan, northern Afghanistan) and Kashmir (Gilgit and Ladakh), through northern Punjab to northern Nepal, northern Sikkim, south and southeast Tibet.

MOVEMENTS An altitudinal migrant; moves to lower altitudes in winter, generally above 2600 m (exceptionally to 1500 m), though many remain at high elevations, to 4240 m in Tibet. Birds of nominate race are casual (infrequent to rare?) visitors to the Crimea.

MEASUREMENTS Wing of male 113·5–121·5, of female 105–112·5. Wing of male *severtzovi* 116–123, of female 111–121; tail of male 86–91, of female 83–92; tarsus 22–23·5; bill (from skull) of male 18–20, of female 19–20, (from feathers) male 13–14·5, female 14·5–15. Weight 39–43.

REFERENCES Dementiev and Gladkov (1951–54), Fleming *et al.* (1979), Schäfer (1938), Vaurie (1959).

104 RED-BREASTED ROSEFINCH *Carpodacus puniceus*   Plate 23

Eastern Palearctic

Pyrrhospiza punicea Blyth (ex Hodgson MS), 1845, Journ. Asiat. Soc. Bengal, 13 (1844), p. 953, Himalayas; type from Nepal, *fide* Vaurie, 1959, Birds Pal. Fauna, Passeriformes, p. 644.

IDENTIFICATION Length 20 cm (8 in). A high-altitude finch, one of the highest-breeding passerines in the Palearctic. Adult male is large and brown, with red forehead (to over eye), red chin to breast, red rump and heavily streaked upperparts, easily distinguished from Eastern Great Rosefinch (102) and Caucasian Great Rosefinch (103). Females are generally brown and dark-streaked, but have yellow or buff on throat and breast, warm brown on lower breast and belly, and may also show yellow on rump. Both have fairly long (for a rosefinch) and pointed bills. **Confusion species:** For differences from both species of great rosefinch, see those species. Male Red-breasted is much browner, with a broad dark band through face, dark crown and nape, and brown belly, flanks and undertail-coverts; females are more olive than grey-brown and streaked darker, some have distinctive yellow or olive-yellow on rump, and lower

underparts are warm brown (dark-streaked). Female Red-mantled Rosefinch (101) is similar but smaller, and has a pale narrow supercilium. All other initially similar rosefinches are smaller and paler (or more generally pink), except for Red-headed Rosefinch (107): latter has a much smaller and more conical bill, males have pale grey on breast, flanks and undertail-coverts, and females have well-defined pale olive or yellowish-olive patches on forehead, sides of breast and rump; very unlikely to occur in same habitat as Red-breasted, being a bird of lower-altitude forest.

DESCRIPTION Sexes differ. **Adult male:** Forehead and short supercilium (to over ear-coverts) crimson-red; lores, area below eye and across ear-coverts dark brown; cheeks and lower ear-coverts crimson. Crown, nape, mantle, back and scapulars dark brown, streaked blackish, lower back unstreaked; rump bright pink, uppertail-coverts brown, edged pink in fresh plumage. Tail is notched at tip, dark brown, edged paler brown. Median and greater coverts dark brown, edged paler brown, edges of greaters warm or reddish-brown and tipped paler or buff-brown; alula, primary coverts and flight feathers dark brown narrowly edged paler or buffish-brown. Chin, throat and breast bright crimson with pale or silvery-white tips to some feathers, lower breast very slightly duller crimson; belly brown with blackish streaks; flanks dark brown, streaked with black; undertail-coverts pink with dark brown streaks. Bill is rather long (or longer than on other rosefinches of similar size), pointed, brown or dark brown at tip. Legs and feet brown. In winter, feathers of forehead, breast and rump are often tipped brown and white centres to throat and breast feathers are abraded, giving a more uniform crimson appearance. **Adult female:** Forehead dark or dull grey-brown with some fine pale buff tips; crown, nape, sides of neck, mantle, back and scapulars dark or dull grey-brown and streaked blackish, heaviest on mantle and back; rump and uppertail-coverts paler or generally more uniformly olive, though some (probably older individuals) have rump yellow or yellowish, finely or narrowly dark-streaked. Tail as male. All wing-coverts and flight feathers dark brown with thin pale brown edges. Face is generally pale buff or buffish-brown, with fine dark streaks. Chin, throat and upper breast pale yellow, streaked blackish, lower breast and belly warm brown, tinged grey and streaked with dark brown; flanks and undertail-coverts grey-brown and dark-streaked. **Juvenile:** Very similar to adult female but generally much browner, lacks grey tinge and is heavily streaked above and below. On first-winter and first-summer birds, throat and breast are buff, becoming yellow (females) or olive-yellow (males) in second winter; immatures also lack warm brown tinge to belly, and rump is grey or grey-brown (uniform with rest of upperparts) in first winter and first summer, yellow in second summer (females and a proportion of males); second-summer males also show pink or reddish-pink on chin, sides of throat and belly. These characters appear to be constant for all races, though immature plumages in this species are not well known.

GEOGRAPHICAL VARIATION Racial variation concerns intensity of plumage colour and/or size. Both *humii* and *kilianensis* are much paler and less crimson than nominate (which is the smallest and has the strongest or darkest streaking on upperparts), and are also paler brown on underparts; male *kilianensis* has (on average) much thinner band of red across forehead and brown on crown extends to forecrown; *kilianensis* is also larger than either nominate or *humii*. Female *kilianensis* has lower throat and brown or buffish-brown breast edged and tipped with yellow, and rump and uppertail-coverts are also bright yellow; in nominate and *humii*, this area is uniform with back. Race *longirostris* is the largest and palest or brightest or most intensely red or crimson of the races, and has on average a slightly longer bill (unlikely to be noticed in the field); some males

also show a very wide band of red on forehead and over eyes, but this is not a constant feature. Race *sikangensis* is intermediate in size and plumage between nominate and *longirostris*, but females are more distinctly different in that the ground colour is paler or whitish on throat and breast and grey on rest of underparts, all dark-streaked as other females.

VOICE Call is a fairly loud, bulbul-like, cheery whistling 'are-you-quite-ready'; also has a cat-like grating 'm-a-a-a-u' and a sparrow-like chirp in flight. Song is a short 'twiddle-le-de', also gives soft short snatches of a warbling song; sings infrequently throughout the year.

STATUS, HABITAT AND BEHAVIOUR Common or locally common, but nowhere numerous. Occurs in extremely high-altitude habitat, one of two of the highest-breeding passerines in the Palearctic. Found between 3900 m and 5700 m, well above the tree line (and almost at the limit of vegetation), in alpine meadows, plateaux, dry valleys, rock screes and boulder-fields, cliffs and glaciers. Usually in small flocks or family parties, approachable but always wary and never flies far when disturbed. Feeds on the ground in rhododendrons, dwarf junipers or stunted scrub, and often at the edge of melting snow. Hops when on the ground. Most food consists of small seeds of alpine plants, but in summer also takes buds, petals and flower-heads.

DISTRIBUTION *C. p. puniceus:* central Himalayas (east of *humii*) from Nepal to Assam, Bhutan, south-east Tibet (Kongbo) and western Szechwan, China.

C. p. kilianensis: Tien Shan and Pamirs, Russian Turkestan, and Kunlun range east to the western Astin Tagh (Keriya range), southwest Sinkiang, west China; also the Karakoram range in northern Kashmir to Ladakh.

C. p. humii: western Himalayas from northern Pakistan (Gilgit to Baltistan) and Kashmir to Kumaon, Uttar Pradesh, northwest India.

C. p. sikangensis: southern Szechwan, western China.

C. p. longirostris: Buckhan Boda Shan, eastern Tsinghai, south to Koko Nor and southern Nan Shan ranges, southern Kansu, and northern Szechwan, northwest China.

Note: Races *humii* and *puniceus* interbreed in overlap areas and intermediates occur.

MOVEMENTS An altitudinal migrant, but is evidently able to withstand prolonged periods of extremely low temperatures as many move no lower than lower limit of breeding range. Descends in winter to between 3000 m and 4575 m, occasionally to 2400 m or exceptionally to 1500 m.

MEASUREMENTS Wing of male 106–120, of female 105–117; tail of male 72–85, of female 70–82; tarsus 23–24; bill (from skull) 17–19, (culmen) 11–13·5 (13–15 in Tibet). Wing of male *humii* 111–120, of female 113; tail of male 76–88, of female 81; tarsus 24–26; bill (from skull) 18–20, (culmen) 11–13. Wing of male *kilianensis* 119–122, of female 115–117; bill (culmen) 12–14·5. Wing of male *longirostris* 117–126; bill (culmen) 15–17. Weight of male 42·8–51·2, of female 43–50.

REFERENCES Ali and Ripley (1983), Fleming *et al.* (1979), Vaurie (1956, 1958).

105 TIBETAN ROSEFINCH (Roborovski's Rosefinch)
Carpodacus roborowskii   Plate 24
Eastern Palearctic

Leucosticte roborowskii Przewalski, 1887, Zapiski Imp. Akad. Nauk, 55, p. 88, mountain pass from Tibetan plateau across eastern Burkan-Budda [Buckhan Boda] Shan, Tsinghai.

IDENTIFICATION Length 17–18 cm (6¾–7 in). A large, long-winged and distinctive rosefinch endemic to high-altitude rocky steppes and mountains of Tibet. Males have a dark crimson face extending to chin and throat, grey upperparts tinged with pink, pale pink rump, and bright lavender-pink underparts, paler on undertail-coverts; females are generally grey-brown, dark-streaked (except for rump and uppertail-coverts), and paler or more buffish-white below with lighter streaking; both have a distinctive yellow bill. General plumage of male and very long wings are distinctive field characters; unlikely to be confused with any other rosefinch. Note: The taxonomic position of this species remains unclear, and several authorities consider it closer to snow (*Montifringilla*) or mountain (*Leucosticte*) finches while others place it closer to the buntings (Emberizidae).

DESCRIPTION Sexes differ. **Adult male:** Forehead, face and crown dark crimson, with red or light crimson tips; hindcrown and nape greyer (or dark grey), with red or light crimson tips. Sides of neck, mantle, back and scapulars pale grey with pale pink or reddish-pink tips (often forming bars or lines); rump and uppertail-coverts light pink. Tail is slightly notched, blackish-brown, finely edged deep pink. Wings are long, extending almost to tip of tail: median and greater coverts pale brown, edged and tipped light pink in fresh plumage (but tips of greaters often whitish); alula, primary coverts and flight feathers dark brown, primaries and outer secondaries edged light pink, inner secondaries and tertials edged pale whitish or buff. Chin and throat blackish, terminally fringed with red and spotted with white at tip; breast, upper belly and upper flanks bright pink or washed with a lavender tinge; lower flanks tinged orange, lower belly whitish; undertail-coverts white, washed with pink. Bill is slender and pointed, bright or pale yellow with a dark horn tip. Legs and feet dark brown. **Adult female:** Forehead to nape and face buffish-brown, finely dark-streaked, lores dark grey. Mantle, back and scapulars warm brown or tawny-brown, streaked with darker brown centres, rump and uppertail-coverts unstreaked. Tail dark brown, finely or narrowly edged buff-brown (or warm buff). Wings are long, as on male: median and greater coverts dark brown, edged and tipped paler buffish or grey-brown; alula, primary coverts and flight feathers dark brown, secondaries and tertials finely edged paler brown. Chin, throat and breast warm buffish-brown, narrowly dark-streaked; belly, flanks and undertail-coverts paler buff, irregularly streaked or spotted (more on flanks than in centre of body). Bill bright or pale yellow. **Juvenile:** Undescribed, but probably similar to adult female.

VOICE Generally silent, but has a short plaintive but pleasant whistle, often repeated as a trill.

STATUS, HABITAT AND BEHAVIOUR Rare and little-known resident. Found on desolate rocky steppes and barren alpine steppe of argillite-slate mountains and plateaux between 4500 m and 5400 m and slightly lower in winter. Occurs alone or in pairs, occasionally in family parties, but inhabits desolate and harsh alpine areas avoided by virtually every other species with the exception of Brandt's Mountain Finch (76). Has a rapid and elegant flight recalling Grandala (*Grandala coelicolor*); short legs give it a rather shuffling gait on the ground. Feeds on the ground among scant plant growth, on seeds and fragments of alpine grasses.

DISTRIBUTION Monotypic. Northeast Tibet, also south and east slopes of the Buckhan Boda Shan, the southern chain of the Amne Machin Shan and the southern Marco Polo chain (Wild Yak steppe), central Tsinghai, western China.

MOVEMENTS Mainly sedentary, but possibly occurs at lower altitudes during sustained periods of extremely severe winter weather.

MEASUREMENTS Wing 121–123; tail 90; tarsus 21; bill (from feathers) 12, depth 6·5.

REFERENCE Neufeldt and Vietinghoff-Scheel (1978).

GENUS *PINICOLA*

Two species. Robust finches with stout bills. They have clear affinities with both *Carpodacus* and *Loxia* finches. Red-headed Rosefinch (107) is clearly more associated with the rosefinches, occupies a similar niche and is of limited distribution; Pine Grosbeak (106), however, has an extremely widespread distribution at lower levels.

106 PINE GROSBEAK *Pinicola enucleator* Plate 31
Holarctic

Loxia enucleator Linnaeus, 1758, Syst. Nat., ed. 10, p. 171, Sweden.

IDENTIFICATION Length 20–25·5 cm (8–10 in). A large, robust or stout finch with a short thick bill. Males are deep raspberry-pink on head, face and most of underparts; mantle and back pinkish but mottled with black, rump uniform bright pink; wings and tail black, with distinctive white tips to coverts (forming double wingbar) and outer webs of tertials. Females generally grey above, with orange or yellowish-brown head and face, and with greenish-yellow wash to underparts. **Confusion species:** Large size and long tail are distinctive field marks. Told from all male rosefinches by obvious pale double wingbar; occurs outside range of Three-banded Rosefinch (98), the only rosefinch with similar wing pattern. Female, too, is unlikely to be confused with female Red-headed Rosefinch (107), which has much brighter yellow in patches on forehead and sides of breast. Plumage is much paler pink (males) or grey-green (females) than corresponding plumages of Common Crossbill (110), which is smaller, while Parrot Crossbill (109) also has a different-shaped bill. Two-barred Crossbill (112) is initially similar, but much redder (males) or a more uniform pale green (females) and with obviously crossed mandibles.

DESCRIPTION Sexes differ. **Adult male:** Forehead to crown, nape and sides of neck deep raspberry-pink, though in worn plumage some show grey or dark brown tips to hindcrown and nape; lores to slightly behind eye dark or dusky brown (some fresh-plumage adults have a small pale grey crescent below eye), in worn plumage ear-coverts also show dull or brownish tips, otherwise face as crown. Mantle, scapulars and upper back similar to crown, pink, prominently mottled with dark or blackish feather centres (some may have mantle, back and scapulars entirely dark grey); lower back and rump uniform bright pink; uppertail-coverts dark grey, edged pinkish or pinkish-white. Tail is long and slightly indented, black, very finely edged pink or pale pink. Median coverts dusky or blackish in centre, broadly edged and tipped pale pinkish-white, greater coverts the same but tips white and extend some way along edges; alula, primary coverts and flight feathers black, very finely edged pale pink, edges to secondaries paler or whitish, becoming quite broadly white on edges and tips of tertials. Chin, throat, breast, upper belly and flanks bright or deep raspberry-pink (often shows grey tips, and in sub-adult plumage flanks often entirely

grey), lower belly whitish, thighs and undertail-coverts pale grey (or latter tipped with white). Bill is stout and rather stubby, often visibly hooked at tip, dark grey or blackish with pink base to lower mandible. Legs and feet dark brown or blackish.

Adult female: Lacks any pink in plumage. Forehead, crown to nape and face variably deep yellowish-green or bright olive-yellow (with orange tinges on some, duller or less extensive on others) and mantle and back generally grey with darker feather centres (but on some upper mantle can be same as nape); scapulars, lower back and rump uniform grey, becoming olive or olive-yellow on lower rump and uppertail-coverts. Wings and tail as adult male but dark or dull brown (not black), and edged finely white or whitish on primaries, more broadly so on secondaries and tertials, and edges to tail are broadly light olive-brown. Face as above, but lores and cheeks often greyish or cheeks to fore part of ear-coverts forming a pale grey crescent below eye. Chin, throat and breast buffish-white or light grey, washed with olive-yellow, orange or yellowish-brown on lower throat and breast; belly and lower flanks dull grey, thighs and undertail-coverts similar or greyish. **Juvenile:** Grey or tinged with yellow or yellowish-olive on head, becoming buff on throat, ear-coverts and breast; rump tinged dull ochre-yellow; wings dark grey, with pale buffish tips to median and greater coverts and occasionally on edges to tertials. First-winter and second-summer males are similar to adult female, with rusty or russet-brown forehead to nape, and with similar tinges to ear-coverts and sides of neck and some tips to mantle and upper back; rump is orange or yellowish-orange with grey tips in first winter, becoming deep pink with olive or greyish-olive tips in second summer; median and greater coverts are (edged and) tipped with white, forming two distinct wingbars; underparts are similar to adult female but paler or duller or tinged orange-buff, with flanks to undertail-coverts grey.

First-winter females are duller than first-winter males, with crown and rump ochre or dull olive-yellow and underparts entirely plain grey.

GEOGRAPHICAL VARIATION Most racial variation is unlikely to be detectable in the field without direct comparison, as it concerns mainly size and the depth or intensity of colour of adult males. In the three Palearctic races, however, dif-

293

ferences in bill shape may be visible in close or good views: nominate race has a large or stout bill, while that of *kamtschatkensis* is shorter and more blunt at tip, and that of *pacatus* is small, thinner and comparatively weaker in appearance, with a slender or attenuated tip. Females of Nearctic races are much greyer (with darker grey or blackish feather bases) on mantle and back, only head and rump are olive (or tinged russet) and underparts are also greyer, lacking olive-green tinge; female *alascensis* has yellow or olive-yellow restricted to head, a larger pale crescent below eye and a short whitish supercilium from base of bill to eye, and chin, throat and breast are plain grey (first-winters are similar to adult female, but have head rich orange or rufous-orange instead of yellow).

VOICE Call is a fluty whistling 'teu-teu-teu' or 'pee-lee-jeh, pee-lee-ju' with the middle note higher than the others, also a quiet chattering twitter when feeding in a flock, and a short subdued musical trill 'pui pui pui' often given in flight, or a rasping 'caree', 'crrru' or 'ca-r-a-r'; alarm note 'chee-vli'; juveniles have a clear bell-like 'tee-klee'. The song is a loud varied musical warble, similar to that of Purple Finch (88), containing high flute-like notes and trills followed by a harsh twanging note. In certain parts of the range local dialects or vocalisations occur, e.g. coastal Alaska, western British Columbia and California.

STATUS, HABITAT AND BEHAVIOUR Fairly common or locally common. A bird primarily of northern conifer (particularly larch or spruce) or alder and birch forest, often along forest edge or marshy areas; in winter more usually in deciduous woods than fir. Favours edges and rides of forests but also occurs in orchards, edges of cultivation and mixed scrub; in Japan, occasionally visits berry-bearing trees in winter. In the breeding season occurs in pairs, but at other times in small flocks though in irruption years considerable numbers flock together. Generally a tame or unobtrusive bird, preferring to stay hidden in foliage when disturbed. In western USA often associates with flocks of Bohemian Waxwings (*Bombycilla garrulus*). Feeds mainly in trees on seeds, particularly beechnuts, also maples, crab apples and apple seeds, ash fruits and flowering buds of spruces, berries (particularly rowans) and in summer on insects (mostly mosquitoes); in western USA in winter not infrequent at bird feeders, where it takes sunflower seeds.

DISTRIBUTION *P. e. enucleator*: northern Norway and northern Sweden south to about 65°N, northern Finland east through the Kola Peninsula in CIS (USSR) to the Yenisei river, western Siberia, south to about 62°N.

P. e. pacatus: Siberia, (east of nominate) to the Kolyma river, south to the Sayan range and Lake Baikal and the Russian Altai range to northern Mongolia, Liaoning, Manchuria, to Stanovoy range, northern Amurland.

P. e. kamtschatkensis: far eastern Siberia, from Anadyrland south to Udskaya Bay (Sea of Okhotsk), Kamchatka, Sakhalin and Kurile Islands, to northern Japan (breeds at high altitudes on Hokkaido).

P. e. alascensis: northwest and central Alaska to western Canada (Mackenzie) and northeast British Columbia.

P. e. flammulus: southern and southeast Alaska (including Kodiak and Kenai Islands) to northwest British Columbia, western Canada.

P. e. carlottae: Queen Charlotte Island, Vancouver Island and coastal British Columbia.

P. e. montanus: central British Columbia and southwest Alberta south through the Cascades and Rocky Mountains to central and southeast Washington, northeast Oregon, central Utah, eastern Arizona and northern New Mexico.

P. e. californicus: Sierra Nevada, eastern California; also recorded in western Nevada in summer.

P. e. leucurus: Canada from the Yukon east through northern Manitoba to northern Quebec and Labrador, in the south to northern Alberta, Saskatchewan and central Ontario.

P. e. eschatosus: southeast Canada from central Quebec east to Newfoundland, south to northern New Hampshire and Maine to Nova Scotia.

MOVEMENTS Sedentary or partially migratory; an erratic or irruptive migrant to regions south, southwest or southeast of breeding range in years when winter food supply is short. In some years very few birds leave the breeding range, while in others whole populations move hundreds of kilometres in search of food; in such irruption years, birds of nominate race move south to southern Scandinavia, western CIS (USSR) and the Baltic Republics to eastern Germany. Race *pacatus* winters south to northern Manchuria, Amur River to Sea of Okhotsk and Ussuriland; *kamtschatkensis* south to western Honshu, Japan; *alascensis* south to southeast Alaska, central Oregon, Montana, northern North Dakota and northwest Minnesota; *flammulus* south to southern Alaska, Washington, Oregon and northwest Idaho, USA; *montanus* from southeast British Columbia to southeast Oregon, western Nebraska, southwest New Mexico and northwest Texas; *leucurus* to Nebraska east to Kentucky and Maryland and New England states in northeast USA, *eschatosus* occurs south in winter to Wisconsin, northern Ohio, Pennsylvania and Virginia, northeast USA, and has also occurred (once) in Connecticut. Species has occurred as an erratic visitor or vagrant in Bermuda (January 1977 and November 1980), Greenland, the British Isles and most of central and eastern Europe south to Spain, Italy, Czechoslovakia and northern Yugoslavia (first record for France, February 1992); in the east, in central China (Szechwan); race *kamtschatkensis* is a vagrant to St George Island, Pribilofs (Alaska); *eschatosus* is a vagrant to Repulse Bay, Northwest Territories, Canada. It departs from breeding territory late September and October (but later movements may be caused by shortage of food), and returns from late February to mid-March.

MEASUREMENTS Wing of male 106–116, of female 105–110; tail 78–90; tarsus 20–23; bill (from feathers) 14–15. Wing of male *eschatosus* 102·5–116, of female 105–110; tail 85–95; tarsus

19–23; bill (exposed culmen) 13·5–16. Weight of male 42·5–62, of female 52–62.

REFERENCES Delin and Svensson (1988), Dementiev and Gladkov (1951–54), Godfrey (1979), Svensson (1992), Witherby et al. (1938–41).

107 RED-HEADED ROSEFINCH (Juniper Finch, Crimson-browed Finch) *Pinicola subhimachala* Plate 22

Southeast Palearctic

Corythus subhimachalus Hodgson, 1836, Asiatic Researches, 19, p. 152, northern Nepal.

IDENTIFICATION Length 19–20 cm (7½–8 in). A large or heavily built finch with a distinctive large or robust bill; female more brightly coloured than most other rosefinches. Male has a bright red face (with dark eye-stripe), chin and throat to breast, with belly to undertail area white or whitish, and upperparts except for forehead and rump (which are red) reddish-brown and dark-streaked. Females have grey head, with mantle and back greenish-olive and indistinctly dark-streaked; forehead, sides of breast and rump are olive-yellow (becoming deeper or orange with age), wings and tail black, edged with yellow, and lower underparts pale grey. **Confusion species:** Fairly distinctive plumage of both sexes at all ages makes confusion with any other rosefinch unlikely. Males are similar to male Red-breasted Rosefinch (104) but are unlikely to occur in same habitat; Red-breasted has brown (not grey) from belly to undertail-coverts, while Red-headed lacks well-defined streaks on upperparts and prominent white spots to lower throat and breast. Bright olive-yellow or orange patches and lack of obvious streaking are distinctive features of female and immature Red-headed. Females are confusable with female Scarlet Finch (108), but latter lacks bright yellow on forehead and sides of breast and has much brighter yellow rump and shorter tail.

DESCRIPTION Sexes differ. **Adult male:** Forehead to supercilium (not reaching rear of ear-coverts) bright red or crimson; lores dusky brown, becoming dark brown below and behind eye; lower lores, cheeks and fore part of ear-coverts bright red or crimson, rear of ear-coverts and sides of neck dark crimson. Crown to nape dark brown, tinged with crimson; mantle, back and scapulars warm brown or reddish-brown, tinged crimson and slightly streaked with dark or blackish feather centres; rump and uppertail-coverts unstreaked deep red or crimson (orange on sub-adults). Tail is slightly notched, dark brown, edged rather narrowly with reddish-brown. Median and greater coverts dark brown, edged orange or pale red (warm brown in worn plumage); alula and primary coverts dark brown or blackish-brown, narrowly edged with dull crimson; flight feathers also dark brown, primaries edged dull reddish-brown and secondaries olive-brown, tertials more broadly edged pale reddish-pink and becoming white or whitish towards tips. Chin and throat to breast bright crimson, but many feathers on lower throat and breast tipped with dark crimson (in worn plumage dark tips are absent, and throat becomes uniform); lower breast duller or browner; flanks to thighs and undertail-coverts grey or pale ashy-grey, sometimes slightly darker on belly. Upper mandible of bill blackish-brown, lower has paler base with blackish-brown tip. Legs and feet dark brown. **Adult female:** Forehead to supercilium (extending over eye) bright olive-yellow, brighter or more yellow on upper lores and forehead (becoming orange on older birds); lores and cheeks pale grey, becoming darker grey on ear-coverts and sides of neck. Crown to nape grey, with some dark feather centres or bases showing (though some can appear plain olive-yellow on nape). Mantle, upper back and scapulars greenish-olive, indistinctly streaked or mottled slightly darker (with brown bases); lower back, rump and uppertail-coverts olive-yellow. Tail dark brown, prominently edged with yellow or yellowish-olive. Median and greater coverts dark brown, edged olive-yellow and tipped the same colour but brighter or more yellow; alula, primary coverts and flight feathers dark brown, secondaries finely edged olive-yellow, becoming greyer on edges and tips of tertials. Chin and throat grey, mottled darker grey; breast and flanks plain or uniform ashy-grey, but sides of breast bright olive-yellow or sometimes orange (often mottled darker); belly, rear flanks, thighs and undertail-coverts paler ashy-grey. Bill dark flesh-brown. Legs and feet brown or dark brown with a reddish tinge. **Juvenile:** First-winter birds are very similar to adult female, but are duller greenish-yellow on breast. First-summer or second-winter males have forehead and sides of breast orange (as on older females) or pink in centre of breast; in second summer almost as adult male, but forehead can be brown and breast may retain yellowish plumage or be partly crimson, the crimson extending to rest of throat and breast with age; retains olive-yellow edges to primaries, secondaries and tail until adult.

VOICE Generally silent, but has a melodic but sparrow-like chirp. The song is a bright and varied warble; also a 'ter-ter-tee'.

STATUS, HABITAT AND BEHAVIOUR Uncommon or locally common. Occurs in thick or dense juniper or dwarf-rhododendron scrub above or near the tree line between 3500 m and 4200 m, also in light or open forest; in winter in thick undergrowth in forests. Usually found in pairs or small parties, a shy, quiet or unobtrusive bird easily overlooked in its preferred habitat. Generally slow-moving or unhurried, forages low down in bushes and undergrowth or on the ground. Feeds on a variety of seeds (including pine), berries, especially barberries, and buds, but also on fruit such as crab apples. Very little is known of its breeding behaviour.

DISTRIBUTION Monotypic. Himalayas from central Nepal east to Sikkim, Assam, Bhutan, Arunachal Pradesh and southeast Tibet to southeast Szechwan and the Likiang range, northern Yunnan, west China.

MOVEMENTS An altitudinal migrant; descends in late autumn to winter between 1975 m (exceptionally to 1800 m) and 3050 m. Also winters south to mountains of northeast Burma.

MEASUREMENTS Wing of male 92–110, of female 91–97; tail of male 74–83, of female 74–79; tarsus 21–25; bill (from skull) 13–18. Weight of male 44–48, of female 44–50.

REFERENCES Ali and Ripley (1983), Fleming et al. (1979).

GENUS *HAEMATOSPIZA*

One species. A stout and robust finch closely linked to both rosefinches and grosbeaks. Male has very distinct, almost uniform plumage. There are no clear affinities, but the plumage of the male suggests ties with *Carpodacus* rosefinches, while bill shape and the diet of hard seeds suggest some relationship with Hawfinch *Coccothraustes* or possibly with the larger yellow-billed finches in *Eophona*.

108 SCARLET FINCH *Haematospiza sipahi*   Plate 27
Southeast Palearctic and possibly Oriental

Corythus sipahi Hodgson, 1836, Asiatic Researches, 19, p. 151, Nepal.

IDENTIFICATION Length 18–19 cm (7–7½ in). In its native range the adult male is unmistakable and the female unlikely to be mistaken for any other species, as both are distinctive in the field. Male is entirely bright or brilliant scarlet, with black wings and tail and a large pale bill. Female is much duller, generally dark or dull olive-green on upperparts with paler or brighter green on head and face and a conspicuous bright yellow rump, and underparts are dingy grey. **Confusion species:** Females may be confused with Red-headed Rosefinch (107), but are generally much duller below with distinctively differing pale areas. The bright rump distinguishes it from all crossbills and grosbeaks; Himalayan Honeyguide (*Indicator xanthonotus*) has similar plumage pattern, but is smaller, thinner and with smaller or flatter bill and has bright yellow forehead and moustachial area.

DESCRIPTION Sexes differ. **Adult male:** Entire head, face and body to uppertail- and undertail-coverts bright scarlet; lower forehead dusky or dull brown, often extending to lores. Tail is short and square-ended or only slightly indented, black or blackish, edged dull crimson. Median and greater coverts black, fringed with scarlet; alula, primary coverts and flight feathers black or blackish-brown, finely edged deep scarlet, broadest (on closed wing) on secondaries and tertials. Undertail-coverts have blackish bases. Bill is large and fairly powerful-looking, with both mandibles curving to tip; upper mandible is pinkish-brown with a pale crimson tinge, lower is yellowish or pale buffish-horn. Legs and feet pinkish-brown. **Adult female:** Forehead to crown and nape olive-yellow, mottled slightly darker or browner; lores and cheeks olive-yellow, ear-coverts darker or browner but washed

with olive-yellow. Mantle, back and scapulars dull olive, tinged with green or olive-yellow in fresh plumage; rump bright yellow, uppertail-coverts olive with dull yellow edges and tips. Tail dark or dusky brown, edged finely with dull olive. Median and greater coverts dark or dusky brown, finely edged pale olive-brown; alula, primary coverts and flight feathers dark or dusky brown finely edged with olive-brown. Chin and throat grey, washed with olive-yellow and mottled with darker feather centres; rest of underparts dull or dingy grey, mottled or scalloped with darker grey and white at base, thighs brownish, undertail-coverts white or whitish and washed or tinged olive-yellow. Bill and legs as male but duller. **Juvenile:** Juveniles and first-winter females are inseparable from adult female. First-summer males have orange rump and a warm rufous or orange tinge to crown; throat and breast and also edges to flight feathers are warm orange. Sub-adult or newly adult males are brightest scarlet, as the intensity fades with age; some adult males (sub-adults?), with scarlet plumage can have olive-yellow edges to flight feathers.

VOICE Call is a loud pleasant 'too-eee' or 'pleeau' and a 'kwee-i-iu' or 'chew-we-auh'. The song is a clear liquid 'par-ree-reeeeeee.

STATUS, HABITAT AND BEHAVIOUR Scarce or uncommon. Inhabits mostly open forest, usually between 1600 m and 3355 m at forest edges or in clearings; in summer prefers fir forest, but in winter also found in bamboo and oak forest. Usually alone or in scattered loose flocks of up to 30 birds; in winter often in single-sex flocks. Forages both low down in bushes or shrubs and on the ground and high up in tall trees; often perches conspicuously on treetops or at end of a branch. The flight is strong and dipping, with rapid wingbeats. Feeds on a variety of seeds, buds, berries and some insects. Breeding biology is little known.

DISTRIBUTION Monotypic. Himalayas from central Nepal east through northern Assam, northeast Arunachal Pradesh and Meghalaya, northeast India, and extreme northern Bangladesh (Khasia hills) to northern and western Yunnan from the Likiang range south to Shweli-Salween divide; possibly also east to Laos and northwest Tonkin, North Vietnam, but most records here are of winter occurrence only.

MOVEMENTS An altitudinal migrant, but

seasonal movements imperfectly known or understood. In winter occurs down to 1400 m in Nepal or lower, down to 600 m in Sikkim. Also occurs more widely south of the Brahmaputra and east to northeast Burma; a scarce or rare winter visitor to northwest Thailand.

MEASUREMENTS Wing of male 98–108, of female 95–103; tail of male 59–70, of female 55–66; tarsus 19–22; bill (from skull) 16–20. Weight of male 38–42.5, of female 39–40.

REFERENCES Ali and Ripley (1983), Fleming *et al.* (1979).

GENUS *LOXIA*

Four species. All have very distinctive and characteristic crossed mandibles for specialised extraction of conifer seeds, and generally red (males) or dull green or olive (females and immatures) plumage. Common Crossbill (110), Scottish Crossbill (111) and Parrot Crossbill (109) are clearly very closely related in size, bill shape and plumage and possibly represent a cline of forms. Probably of Scandinavian or Siberian origins, Common Crossbill now has a wide northern-hemisphere distribution and has cyclic irruptions caused by population peaks and food shortages. Parrot and Two-barred (112) Crossbills also have a slight irruptive tendency but do so less frequently; such irruptions in North American population of Two-barred may have resulted in its isolated Caribbean race.

109 PARROT CROSSBILL *Loxia pytyopsittacus*   **Plate 33**
Western Palearctic

Loxia pytyopsittacus Borkhausen, 1793, Rheinisches Magazin, 1, p. 139, Sweden; designated by Hartert, 1904, Vögel pal. Fauna, p. 122.

IDENTIFICATION Length 17 cm (6¾ in) Generally a larger, stockier and bigger-billed version of Common Crossbill (110), with a large or broad flat-headed and thick-necked appearance; adult males and some females tend to be somewhat darker. **Confusion species:** Easily confused with Common Crossbill and may be initially dismissed or overlooked, especially among mixed flocks. Bill size and intensity of plumage colour vary. In typically big-billed birds bill shapes should suffice, but in others it is the bill combined with shape of head and neck that are the important field characters; also has a variety of calls, some of which are noticeably or distinctly different in tone from those of Common Crossbill; see also Identification section under Common Crossbill. Scottish Crossbill (111) is also extremely similar and has a heavier bill and head shape than Common (and thus more closely resembles Parrot Crossbill), but there are many birds with indeterminate-sized bills; bill of Scottish, though larger than Common's, is never so large, bulky or bulbous as that of Parrot (but beware small-billed Parrot Crosbills), and the rounded forehead and crown never produce such a flat-headed appearance as on Parrot Crossbill. Note that Scottish Crossbill is unknown (and unlikely to be encountered) outside its small and restricted world range).

DESCRIPTION Sexes differ. At all ages the shape of bill, head and neck is an important field charac-

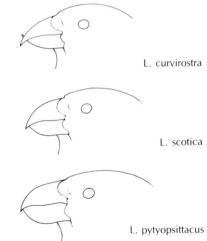

L. curvirostra

L. scotica

L. pytyopsittacus

Crossbills Loxia spp.: typical bill shapes

ter: usually shows a large bulky or bulbous bill with a flat forehead and crown (though when excited or alarmed can temporarily raise a slight crest) and a thick neck. The bill is deep at base and almost parallel for a short distance before curving towards the blunt-shaped tip, but not all have large bills and those with smaller (or less bulky and less parallel-based) bills cannot always be identified with certainty. Adults have a bulbous lower mandible bulging near tip (often seen well in profile) before curving up to tip (less pronounced on immatures); tip of lower mandible is never visible above tip of upper in profile. The head, in addition to being flat-crowned, also looks disproportionately large or broad and is given some emphasis by short thick neck (a useful feature in comparison with Common, as all crossbills can look heavy-headed at times). Bill size increases with age, and males have larger bills than females. At all ages upper mandible is brown or brownish-horn, as is base of lower, but cutting edges and sides (especially towards tip) of lower mandible are pale whitish or buff and present a contrasting area (a good field character but not diagnostic, as Common can also show this). **Adult male:** As adult male Common Crossbill, with very little or no recognisable difference in range of plumages between the two species. Fully adult males, however, tend to be a duller or deeper blood-red or crimson (even chestnut-red) than Common, with a grey or greyish tinge to rear of ear-coverts, nape and upper mantle. **Adult female:** As same-aged Common, but darker or duller green or greenish olive-grey on head, sides of neck, nape and upper mantle, with contrasting bright yellowish-green lower back and rump. **Juvenile:** Generally dark olive-green or grey-green, streaked darker on head, face and underparts; on mantle and back, streaks are often given some emphasis by pale buffish or buffish-yellow edges; has a pale buffish wingbar on tips of greater coverts, often very fine or restricted to tips of feathers, while on others it is prominent only on outer greater coverts (this feature is shared by same-aged Common Crossbills, which can show variable amounts of buff or dull buff tips to coverts). Recently fledged birds have normal (i.e. uncrossed) mandibles.

VOICE The calls of Parrot and Common Crossbills are extremely similar, but can be separated by the experienced ear when the variations in timbre, pitch and strength are known: those of Parrot Crossbill are generally consistently stronger and deeper in tone (but there is overlap between the two) and somewhat more metallic, and usually expressed as 'choop choop', 'chok, chok' or 'clop, clop' (against higher 'chip, chip' of Common) and a softer 'gop' contact note from feeding birds; alarm is a stuttering 'tsu-tsu-tsu-tsu' and a very hard 'cherk-cherk'; juveniles have a shrill 'tee-tu, tit' or 'chit'. The song is very similar to the call notes which are generally incorporated into it, a slow 'chit, chit, chit-chit-chit tcho-ee tcho-ee' and a 'chee-ler chee-ler' refrain.

STATUS, HABITAT AND BEHAVIOUR Common only in northern or northwest part of range, scarce or rare elsewhere, but irruptions occur at frequent intervals when the species becomes nomadic or present in some numbers, temporarily common (even remaining to breed), before retreating northwards. Inhabits northern conifer forest, principally Scots pine (*Pinus sylvestris*) or occasionally larch but only rarely in spruce. Occurs in pairs, small parties or, in irruption years, in large groups (often mixing freely with Common Crossbills). Usually silent while feeding in treetops. Rarely feeds on the ground, but often comes regularly to drink or bathe at small pools or puddles. Feeds on cones of pines (both ripe and green), mainly Scots pine, or larches, from which it easily extracts the seeds using its massive bill, often (if not always) breaks off cone from branch and takes it to where it can be held in one foot while feeding; generally has a much more lethargic feeding action than Common Crossbill; has also been known to take berries (bilberries) and alder catkins; nestlings are fed on regurgitated pine seeds and some insects, particularly saw-fly larvae.

DISTRIBUTION Monotypic. Northwest Europe from southern and central Norway (north of 67°N) to most of central and northern Sweden, Finland to CIS (USSR), north to the Kola Peninsula and east to the Pechora river, south to the Moscow region and to Estonia and Saarema Island. Occasionally breeds further south into southern Baltic Republics, Poland, Germany and has bred in Denmark, England and northern France.

MOVEMENTS Sedentary, partially migratory and nomadic; part of the population moves south or southeast to winter in eastern Europe, southern CIS (USSR) to western Siberia. A vagrant to Belgium, Netherlands, Austria, Hungary, Czechoslovakia, Yugoslavia, northern Italy, Britain and northern France. Much less numerous and consequently less prone to cyclic irruptions than Common Crossbill, but cone-crop failures have resulted in recent smaller-scale invasions (in 1982/83 and 1989/90) into western Europe, where birds remained to breed in 1984 and 1985 (and possibly other years) in Britain and northern France, and possibly also bred in Belgium in early 1992 (following high winter numbers in Belgium and the Netherlands); presumably similar circumstances dictate breeding south of the usual range in eastern Europe.

MEASUREMENTS Wing of male 98–110, of female 99–106; tail 57–66; tarsus 18–19; bill (from feathers) of male 19–22·5, of female 18–21·5, depth 12·5–15·5, juvenile 12–14·5. Weight 47–59.

Delin and Svensson (1988), Gantlett (1990), Harris *et al.* (1989), Olsson (1964), Svensson (1992), Witherby *et al.* (1938–41).

110 COMMON CROSSBILL (Red Crossbill) *Loxia curvirostra* Plate 33
Holarctic, Oriental and marginally Neotropical

Loxia curvirostra Linnaeus, 1758, Syst. Nat., ed. 10, p. 171, Europe; restricted to Sweden by Hartert, 1904, Vögel pal. Fauna, p. 117.

IDENTIFICATION Length 16–17 cm (6¼-6¾ in); *himalayensis* 15 cm (6 in). A medium-sized (but racially variable) stocky finch often appearing large-headed, this reinforced by a thick bill with both mandibles curving towards each other and (though not often visible) crossing at tip. Generally adult males are brick-red or orange-red and females green or greyish-green, but there is considerable variation throughout the many races, in some the males are very dark cherry-red, in others mottled orange (or yellowish-orange) and red or deep grey-green; in some races in which the male is (or does become) red, such males may be very rare. Bill sizes vary, but all races have a prominent and characteristic bill with both mandibles curving seemingly to a point, not especially heavy or bulbous in appearance (but see also Geographical Variation). **Confusion species:** Very similar to closely related Parrot (109) and Scottish (111) Crossbills. It must be emphasised that specific identity is not easy (or always possible) and depends on good or close views and experience of (known) Common Crossbills. The plumages of all three species (arguably proposed by some taxonomic authorities as a single, or at best two, species with a gradual cline in body and bill size) are extremely similar. The following points, however, are generally valid and should be used in conjunction with each other; the identification of an individual showing only one or two points which indicate Parrot Crossbill will not necessarily be conclusive, and unless all points can be satisfied the bird is probably best left unidentified. It is also stressed that these are intended only as guidelines, as there will always be odd individuals showing a variety of characters which defy any determining criteria. Parrot Crossbills have a large and bulky, almost disproportionately sized, bill with parallel-edged base, a large head, thick neck and flat crown; note, however, that not all Parrot Crossbills (adults and immatures) have large, bulky or protruding bills, and some have smaller or less well-developed bills very similar to those of both Common and Scottish Crossbills. Male Parrot are generally darker or deeper blood-red (or even chestnut-red) overall, with grey or greyish tips to ear-coverts, nape, sides of neck and mantle; female Parrot Crossbills are generally duller, green or greyish-olive from crown to mantle, with back and lower scapulars brighter or yellower (than female Common) though mottled slightly grey and olive and with a bright greenish-yellow rump. Scottish Crossbills are much closer to Common Crossbill in size, shape and bill than are most Parrot Crossbills. The most conspicuous differences between the first two species concern head and bill shapes. The bill of Scottish is more sturdy or robust-looking, slightly deeper at base, blunter towards tip (not so rounded or sloping), and the lower mandible often appears to be swollen or bulging, especially at base; if seen well enough, tip of lower mandible on Common points slightly more forwards than that of Scottish, which point upwards. The head of Scottish is bigger, though not so broad or so completely flat-headed as on Parrot Crossbill, and cheeks and ear-coverts often (especially seen head-on) look prominent or

swollen, a combination of features which, together with sturdier bill, gives it a somewhat top-heavy or heavy-headed appearance. Scottish Crossbills are unlikely (unknown?) outside their small, restricted range in the ancient pine forest of highland Scotland, but the widely distributed Common Crossbill can occur (especially in invasion or irruption years) alongside the resident Scottish birds.

DESCRIPTION Sexes differ. **Adult male** (*L. c. curvirostra*): Forehead, crown and nape bright red or brick-red (but varies from deep orange or orange-red), in worn plumage crown and nape showing dark centres; lores dusky brown; cheeks and ear-coverts as crown, variably red or reddish, but some are dusky brown or grey-brown from lores to lower and upper edges of ear-coverts. Mantle and back as crown or slightly paler, but can be mottled slightly darker with dusky feather centres (and/or bases); scapulars brown, washed or tinged (variably) red, brick-red, reddish-brown or orange-red; rump bright pink or brick-red; uppertail-coverts brown, or warm brown edged and tipped with red. Tail is deeply forked, blackish-brown or warm brown, edged with red or reddish-brown. Median and greater coverts brown or warm brown edged with dull reddish-brown; alula, primary coverts and flight feathers blackish-brown, with fine edges of pink or reddish-brown in fresh plumage; tertials also dark or blackish-brown. Underparts almost entirely red, brick-red or orange-red, slightly browner on flanks and thighs; undertail-coverts greyish-white with brown or dark brown feather centres (and/or bases) and faintly washed red. Bill is distinctive, with curving mandibles crossing (or appearing to cross) at tip, some more visibly crossed than others, grey or greyish-horn, some with paler or yellowish cutting edges. Legs and feet brown or dark brown (tarsus noticeably short in good views). Exceptionally, or perhaps very rarely (it has been estimated at 1:1,000), 'wingbarred' individuals (usually males, but not unknown in females) occur which have fairly broad off-white, pale buff or white tinged with pale sandy-brown tips to either median or greater coverts, or this colour is somewhat broken or restricted on either; these pale tips can vary from very thin to up to 3–4 mm (possibly more) and in addition white tips may be present on some or all tertials, producing close resemblance to Two-barred Crossbill (112). Reasons for this are unclear, and may be due to aberration or hybridisation between Common and Two-barred Crossbills. Such birds (previously considered a separate race *rubrifasciata*) can usually be separated from Two-barred by: (a) tips to coverts may not be entirely white or are (b) incomplete (on some) or broken on tips to median coverts, usually strongest or broadest only on tips of greaters but never so broad or bulging on inner greaters as Two-barred; (c) white on tertial tip can be broken by dark central shaft or present only on outermost tertial; (d) plumage is generally more pinkish-red (or bright pink on rump) on Two-barred and less brick- or orange-red, especially on head, mantle, back and rump; (e) Two-barred has a much more obviously rounded head than Common, with a domed crown and a longer, slimmer and generally weaker looking bill. **Adult female:** Generally olive-green or olive tinged with lime-green above and yellowish-green below. Forehead, crown and nape olive, variably tinged green or yellow, and mottled with dark or blackish feather centres; face olive or olive-green, tinged with grey on cheeks and ear-coverts, or washed with light yellow in fresh plumage. Nape often paler or greyer than crown; mantle and back variably lime-green or duller olive with dusky brown centres or bases, scapulars dark olive-green; rump pale olive-green or yellowish-green, uppertail-coverts the same with dull or dark olive centres. Tail and wings as adult male, but edged dull olive (not red); females with pale buff or white tips to median and greater coverts and/or tertials are practically (but not entirely) unknown (see above). Entire underparts olive-yellow, yellowish or tinged lightly with green, occasionally with grey feather bases, belly paler or whiter, thighs and flanks tinged grey-brown; undertail-coverts white or whitish with dark central shaft streaks. **Juvenile:** Forehead to nape and mantle grey-brown, tinged pale green or brown and edged paler or buffish (juvenile male often shows olive tips to crown); cheeks, ear-coverts and sides of neck dark olive, streaked finely with buff on ear-coverts. Back and scapulars as crown, but feathers edged olive-green (males) or brown (females); rump yellowish or pale yellowish-green, streaked with darker centres and tinged brown (more prominently on males); uppertail-coverts dark brown, edged and tipped olive. Tail and wings as adult female, but median, greater and primary coverts tipped with buff (finely or narrowly on primary coverts), sometimes pale or whitish-buff tips to median and greater coverts forming diffuse or occasionally well-defined double wingbar; tips to tertials buffish. Entire underparts dull buffish-grey or pale yellow, streaked heavily blackish-brown, lower throat edged finely with yellow or pale olive-green; less heavily or prominently streaked on belly; flanks brown or buffish-brown, broadly dark-streaked. Note: Nestlings fledge with straight bills. First-winter and first-summer males vary in colour from greenish-yellow to yellowish-orange or orange-red or a mixture thereof on head and body, most prominently on crown, nape, mantle and underparts; the buff tips to median and greater coverts and greenish or olive edges to flight feathers and tail are retained from juvenile plumage, as are streaks on flanks and belly (also on breast on some individuals); in first summer most streaks are lost through abrasion. First-winter and first-summer females are closely similar to adult female, except for buff tips to wing-coverts and broadly streaked upperparts and underparts. The red of adult male is not acquired until at least the second winter or early second summer, and even then may not be so intensive as in older birds; up to that time there is considerable variation among immature males, from very bright yellow or orange to seemingly full adult male plumage but for immature wing and tail feathers. Breeds while in late-immature or sub-adult plumage; in North America has been known to breed within its first year of life.

GEOGRAPHICAL VARIATION Most variation between races concerns the intensity of colour of

Common Crossbill L. curvirostra: *a variant showing two wingbars and while tertial spots; in males these may be tinged pink. Note that the pale tips run diffusely into the dark feathers, not abruptly clear cut as in Two-barred Crossbill* L. leucoptera.

males, the abundance or scarcity of males in red plumage, and size. In nominate *curvirostra*, there is an eastward cline across Russia to paler or brighter and larger birds in Siberia. Race *corsicana* is duller than nominate, and females of this and of race *balearica* are greyer and less olive on crown, mantle and back; *balearica* males are also paler than nominate. Males of *poliogyna* are more orange than red (though red males occur, but are very rare), while females have crown and mantle grey (lacking any olive) and rump is tinged with green or grey-green. Males of race *guillemardi* are similar to those of race *poliogyna* but paler than nominate, with a heavy yellow or orange tinge to upperparts and underparts (and true red males are very rare), while females are dark grey on crown and mantle (similar to Scottish Crossbill); both have distinctly larger or heavier bills (similar to Scottish Crossbill). Male *mariae* is apparently paler and brighter red than nominate, and females are paler, greyer or grey-brown and less heavily streaked. Race *altaiensis* is very similar to nominate but darker, males dark red or blood-red and females dark olive or grey-brown with brown ear-coverts, and with a thinner or more slender bill. Race *tianschanica* also has a slender bill but is paler, males mostly either yellow or greenish-yellow (brown and red males are rare); females are more yellowish than nominate and have a bright yellow rump. Birds of race *japonica* are similar to nominate but both sexes are paler and brighter, with males bright red or scarlet-red with brown mottling reduced; vent and undertail-coverts on both sexes often white. The darkest race is *himalayensis*, with adult males dark cherry-red or brownish-red and females also brown or dark brown tinged with olive. Males of race *meridionalis* have head and body deep or rich scarlet or blood-red and are relatively small in size, as is race *luzoniensis*, in which males are predominantly dull dark pink or pinkish-red and females grey. In North and Middle America, there are eight races which differ from each other mainly in size and the intensity of plumage coloration (mostly adult male); they are unlikely to be separable in the field with certainty, although *sitkensis* is the smallest and has a small stubby bill.

VOICE The typical call is a well-known hard 'chip, chip', variously given as 'jip, jip' or 'glipp, glipp', sometimes explosive in delivery and occasionally run together in a whole series, especially when alarmed or in flight; when feeding, gives a softer subdued 'chip' as a contact note; all calls are very similar to those of Parrot Crossbill but are generally higher-pitched, though there is overlap in timbre and pitch of some calls. The song is a loud series of call notes developing into 'cheeree-cheeree-choop-chip-chip-chip-cheeree' interspersed with a trill, and occasionally a more musical warbling version; often sings from a tree-top, usually a pine, but also in a soaring circular display flight. Both sexes give a subdued subsong, often while feeding, consisting of a rising and falling excited trill, often ending in a softer version of call note.

STATUS, HABITAT AND BEHAVIOUR

Common or locally common. Erratic in numbers or occurrence, as various populations undergo cycles of abundance and scarcity (see below). Inhabits conifer forest throughout its vast and fragmented distribution, chiefly Scots pine (or its varieties), larches or spruces, but also alders and birch. Usually a forest bird, but in autumn, winter or during irruptive migration can turn up in pines anywhere, even in the centre of towns and cities. Usually found in pairs or small parties which often form part of a much larger roaming flock, especially in irruption years; nests loosely colonially. On the ground hops in an uncertain or ungainly fashion. Flight is fast and lightly undulating, frequently accompanied by the distinctive repeated call, especially if in flocks, which can be quite noisy (often the first indication of the bird's presence). Rarely intentionally breaks off the pine cone on which it is feeding (see Parrot Crossbill), preferring to feed acrobatically (in manner of a Goldfinch (68) on a thistle-head), often upside-down, while extracting seeds; has been known to feed on ground on fallen cones, but only in poor cone-crop years. Frequently or regularly drinks at small pools or puddles. Feeds mainly on seeds of conifers (mostly spruces and pines), but also recorded taking seeds of maple trees, Lombardy poplars and willows, also buds and berries (mainly hawthorn and rowan), small insects, caterpillars or even small beetles.

DISTRIBUTION Slowly expanding south and has been for most of 20th century, doubtless as a result of irruptions moving birds into new areas where they remain to breed.

L. c. curvirostra: west and central Europe from parts of British Isles (including Scotland), east through southern and central Norway and Sweden, Finland and northern CIS (Kola Peninsula) and north to about 66°N to eastern Siberia, northern Mongolia, northern Amurland (and Sea of Okhotsk?), in the south to southern Europe, Spain (and probably parts of Portugal), central and eastern France, east and south Germany southeast to the Balkans, Greece, isolated areas in west and central Turkey and more continuously in northeast north to the Caucasus and western Ukraine to the southern Urals. Formerly a rare winter visitor to Israel, but since 1973 has bred on several occasions in three areas (including northern edge of Negev desert).

L. c. corsicana: Corsica.

L. c. balearica: Balearic Islands.

L. c. poliogyna: eastern Morocco, Algeria and Tunisia.

L. c. guillemardi: Cyprus.

L. c. mariae: southwest Crimea.

L. c. altaiensis: Altai range from Russia to Mongolia.

L. c. tianschanica: Dzungarian Ala Tau and Tien Shan ranges, Sinkiang, northwest China.

L. c. himalayensis: Himalayas from northern Punjab and erratically through northwest India and Nepal to Sikkim, Assam, Bhutan, and southeast Tibet to northeast Tsinghai, northwest Kansu south to northern Szechwan and northern Yunnan (Likiang range), western China.

L. c. meridionalis: mountains of southern Annam, Vietnam.

L. c. japonica: northeast Asia, Ussuriland and lower Amur river, Sakhalin and the Kurile Islands, west and south to Mongolia, Shensi, Hopeh and occasionally to the lower Yangtze river, Kiangsu, central China, to Japan (uncommon in Hokkaido and northern Honshu).

L. c. luzoniensis: northwest Luzon, Philippines.

L. c. pusilla: Newfoundland.

L. c. minor: southeast Canada (Ontario to Nova Scotia) and irregularly in northeastern USA (south to Tennessee and North Carolina).

L. c. benti: west and central USA (southeast Montana, western South Dakota south to eastern Utah and northern New Mexico).

L. c. bendirei: western Canada, southern Yukon to southwest Saskatchewan and western USA (east of the Cascades) to Montana, Wyoming, southern Oregon and extreme northern California.

L. c. sitkensis: coastal south and southeast Alaska to northwest California.

L. c. grinnelli: southwest USA (central California, southwest Nevada, southwest Utah to eastern Arizona).

L. c. stricklandi: southern USA (southeast Arizona and southern New Mexico) to Mexico (Baja California south through the tablelands to Chiapas).

L. c. mesamericana: mountain forest of central Guatemala and Belize to northern Nicaragua.

MOVEMENTS Sedentary and partially migratory, mainly nomadic; breeding birds from the northern parts of the range move erratically or unpredictably west and south in irruptive fashion to winter (often remaining to breed) in areas to the south of their normal breeding range, usually within the range of the species but occasionally slightly beyond. These movements are largely determined by the level of the population and the availability of food within the range: a high population level and failure or exhaustion of the pine-cone crop triggers these eruptive movements which, in central and southern Europe, are of irregular occurrence (every three to ten years). Irrupting birds may include family parties with juveniles still fed by their parents many hundreds of kilometres from the natal area. Most races except largely sedentary island ones are irruptive, nomadic or partially migratory within the extremes of the breeding range as described above, but some, principally those in eastern Asia and North America, move more regularly further south beyond the breeding range at the onset of winter. Birds of the nominate race occur irregularly in Sicily and in Israel (in both of which it has bred), and in 1990 considerable numbers reached the Faroes; in the east, invasions often reach the Gobian Altai, Mongolia and northern Tsinghai; birds of race *tianschanica* occur east from western Sinkiang sporadically to Hopeh and Liaoning provinces, central China; *himalayensis* occurs in winter to northeast Burma (and has occurred south to southern Yunnan); *japonica* winters south to eastern central China, Korea (where irregular) and southern Japan, and has occurred in the Izu and Bonin Islands. In North America, *pusilla* winters west to Ontario and in northeast USA from Iowa to New England States, Virginia and occasionally south to Georgia; *minor* winters in central and eastern Canada to southeast USA (Missouri, Georgia and northern Florida); *benti* winters west to Oregon, south to southern California, southeast Texas and western Oklahoma, east to Michigan and north to North Dakota and occasionally southwest Saskatchewan; *bendirei* winters from southeast Alaska to Mexico (Baja California and Guadalupe Island – where it may have bred) east to west Texas and Kansas; *sitkensis* winters sporadically throughout Canada (to southwest Quebec) and USA (to Massachusetts, New York, Virginia and South Carolina); *grinnelli* winters to central Nevada, coastal California, southeast Arizona and northwest Mexico; *stricklandi* winters north to southwest USA (central California, central Nevada, southern Utah, central Colorado and eastern

Kansas). A casual or irregular visitor to the Pribilof and Aleutian Islands. Has also occurred in Faroe Isles, Lebanon, Syria, and Afghanistan. A vagrant to Bermuda (five records), Greenland, Iceland, Bear Island, Jan Mayen, Gibraltar (seven+ records), Canary Islands (January 1991), Madeira, Iran and Libya. Breeds when food is abundant and many pairs have young in midwinter when cones are ripe; irruptions in Britain and West Europe occur in May-June and August-September, coinciding with pine and larch crops. Post-breeding dispersal of family parties and true irruptions occur mainly in April-May (North America) or May-August (Europe), and perhaps later as nomadic groups wander in search of feeding areas. Some movement also occurs later in the autumn, more likely involving short-distance migrants. Return movements northwards may take place at any time in late winter or early spring, depending on favourable weather conditions.

MEASUREMENTS Wing of male 95–100, of female 91–98; tail 54–60; tarsus 15–18; bill (from feathers) 165–21, depth 95–125. Wing of male *himalayensis* 77–91, of female 80–88; tail 50–56; tarsus 15–17; bill (from skull) 18–20. Wing of male *altaiensis* 91–98; bill 15–17, depth 9–95. Wing of male *tianschanica* 89·5–97; bill 13·5–15·5, depth 9–10. Wing of male *japonica* 89–96; bill 14–16·5, depth 9–10. Wing of male *pusilla* 88·5–97·5, of female 87·2–92·3; tail 53–59·4; tarsus 16·3–17·8; bill (exposed culmen) 17–18·6. Bill of *sitkensis* (culmen) 13·5–15. Weight: 43–50.

REFERENCES Catley and Hursthouse (1985), Ehrlich *et al.* (1988), Harrap and Millington (1991), Harris *et al.* (1989), Knox (1990), Svensson (1992), Van den Berg and Blankert (1980).

111 SCOTTISH CROSSBILL *Loxia scotica*   Plate 33
Western Palearctic

Loxia scotica Hartert, 1904, Vögel pal. Fauna, p. 120, east Ross-shire, Scotland.

IDENTIFICATION Length 16·5 cm (6½ in). Extremely similar to Common Crossbill (110) in plumage and bill size. Has previously been treated variously as a race of both Common Crossbill and Parrot Crossbill (109), but since 1975 has been considered a full species. **Confusion species:** In plumage it is identical to Common Crossbill and separable only with careful attention to size and shape of head and bill and a knowledge of Common. Head is somewhat bigger or broader than generally rounded or domed head of Common Crossbill, with cheeks and ear-coverts prominent (or bulging) when seen from front or back. Scottish Crossbill has a larger, more substantial bill which is deeper at base, with a more prominent or slightly bulging base to lower mandible and steeply curving culmen (and thus closer in shape to that of Parrot Crossbill), and which is, in effect, intermediate between those of Common and Parrot Crossbills; the tips of the mandibles, especially that of

upper, are generally thicker or more blunt and not so slender as on Common. Individuals with intermediate bill sizes, however, are likely to cause considerable, if not insoluble, confusion. The calls of Common and Scottish Crossbills are extremely similar, but to an ear familiar with the range of Common's, some of those of Scottish are significantly deeper. Initially similar to the overall larger and heavier-billed Parrot Crossbill, which see for detailed differences, but most confusion likely to be with Common Crossbill. Unlikely to be met with (or identified) in the field outside its native range.

DESCRIPTION Sexes differ. Plumages show no recognisable differences in the field from equivalent plumages of Common Crossbill.

VOICE Very similar to calls and song of Common Crossbill but with certain slight variation in tone and pitch (both higher and lower than Common). The typical 'chip-chip' is often given as a much sharper 'jip-jip', while birds in trees can utter a soft, almost whispered contact 'tip' note; also a 'toop' or 'choop'. The range of Common Crossbill call notes, however, is such (both higher and lower) that satisfactory identification outside Scotland is unlikely or unwise.

STATUS, HABITAT AND BEHAVIOUR Not uncommon within its fairly limited range, which closely parallels that of Scots pine (*Pinus sylvestris*) in the Caledonian pine forest of the highlands of central Scotland; total population probably between 1,200 and 1,500 birds. Usually in pairs or small flocks of up to 20. Feeds on the seeds of Scots pine, which it extracts from cones in the same manner as Common Crossbill. In all other habits and actions similar or identical to Common Crossbill.

DISTRIBUTION Monotypic. Endemic to the ancient native pine woods of northern Scotland (from northern Argyll to Inverness-shire west to Aberdeenshire and south to Perth).

MOVEMENTS None known of any great distance, and rarely recorded outside its native range. Non-irruptive, as the principal source of food, ancient Scots pine, does not have large-scale fluctuations in cone crops from year to year.

MEASUREMENTS Wing of male 96–106, of female 91–99; tail 55–64; tarsus 17–19; bill (from feathers) 17–21, depth (at base) 11–14·5.

REFERENCES Knox (1975, 1976, 1990), Voous (1978).

112 TWO-BARRED CROSSBILL (White-winged Crossbill) *Loxia leucoptera*
Holarctic
Plate 33

Loxia leucoptera Gmelin, 1789, Syst. Nat., 1, p. 844. Based on the White-winged Crossbill, Latham, 1781, Gen. Synop. Birds, 1, p. 108, Hudson Bay and New York.

IDENTIFICATION Length 14·5–17 cm (5¾– 6¾ in). Slightly slimmer or more slender than Common Crossbill (110), with smaller head and neck and thinner, more attenuated bill which is clearly crossed at tip. Both sexes and all immatures show prominent white tips to median and greater coverts (5–12 mm broad on adults, up to 6 mm on juveniles) creating a broad white double wingbar. Males are generally paler or more pink than the deep red of male Common Crossbill, while females and immatures are dull green or olive, dark-streaked and with bright greenish-yellow rumps. In general prefers larches, though often found in mixed flocks of crossbills in pines or spruces. **Confusion species:** Broad white tips to median and greater coverts are diagnostic, but some caution is needed as, rarely, first-winter or sub-adult Common Crossbills can also show pale buff or whitish crescents or tips, though never usually so broad or the same shape as on Two-barred; also, tertial tips of aberrantly marked Common are buff, pale buff or off-white, and not pure white as on Two-barred. Shape of white tips to. median and greater coverts and tertials is a crucial factor, those on 'wingbarred' Common often being broken or incomplete at the feather tip. Common Crossbill is also more intensely red or brick-red than bright or deep pink, and its slightly shorter and comparatively stubbier bill is a further useful field character. Crossed bill tips and broad white tips to wing-coverts distinguish Two-barred from similar Purple Finch (88), and its size and generally smaller or slimmer (crossed) bill from larger, longer-tailed Pine Grosbeak (106).

DESCRIPTION Sexes differ. **Adult male:** Forehead to crown deep pink or pinkish-red with some dark or grey-brown feather bases; lores dusky or mottled with grey, the grey often continuing as an eye-stripe to rear of ear-coverts; cheeks, ear-coverts and sides of neck bright pink or reddish-pink, mottled with grey or grey-brown bases; hindcrown to nape as crown, lacking dark bases, tipped grey in fresh plumage. Mantle and back reddish or deep pink with brown or blackish feather bases, often showing thin band of grey across hindneck/upper-mantle area; scapulars (and sides of mantle) black or blackish, tipped (broadly in fresh plumage) with pink or deep pink; lower back and rump uniform bright or deep pink; uppertail-coverts black, finely tipped with pink or pale pink. Tail is forked, black, finely edged pale brown on inner feathers and whitish on outers. Median and greater coverts black, broadly tipped white (more broadly on inner coverts, thinly on outers); alula, primary coverts and flight feathers black, finely edged pale pink, with prominent white tips to outer webs of tertials and fine pale whitish tips (in fresh plumage) to secondaries and primaries. Chin, throat, breast and flanks bright pink or tinged light reddish, but flanks can be grey; lower flanks lightly streaked with black or blackish-brown; belly, vent and thighs pale ashy-grey, becoming white on undertail-coverts (which have black bases). Bill is slightly longer and thinner or more attenuated than that of Common Crossbill, decurved towards tip and more visibly crossed at tip; blackish-brown with pale yellow or yellowish-horn cutting edges. Legs and feet brown. **Adult female:** Forehead to crown and nape olive, tinged variably with green or yellow and finely dark-streaked, washed with grey on nape; lores dusky or mottled with grey, often continuing through eye into eye-stripe to rear of ear-coverts; cheeks, ear-coverts and sides of neck dull green or olive, or mottled with grey or grey-brown feather bases. Mantle, back and scapulars olive-green or deep green, heavily mottled with dark or blackish centres; rump pale yellow, tinged green; uppertail-coverts dark olive-green or blackish finely tipped paler green. Tail black or blackish, edged with olive or olive-green. Median and greater coverts as adult male, but white tips not always so extensive; flight feathers and tertials as male, but finely edged yellowish or olive; tips of tertials also white but by autumn often reduced in extent by wear and abrasion. Chin, throat, breast, belly and flanks greenish-yellow (or slightly paler) and dark-streaked, quite broadly so on breast and flanks; lower belly, thighs, vent and undertail-coverts pale buff, or lightly washed pale yellowish-green on lower flanks and ventral area. **Juvenile:** Juvenile and first-winter birds are similar to adult female but paler buffish-brown, with pronounced dark brown streaks on crown and nape to mantle and back; rump and uppertail-coverts the same or tinged pale green. Median coverts white; greater coverts black, broadly tipped with white (but may show pale yellowish-white); alula black with pale buff edges, and flight feathers black or blackish with fine yellowish edges (becoming pale buff on first-winters); tertials as adults. Face as adult female or duller, and finely streaked with buffish-brown; pale buff or whitish-buff above and below eyes. Underparts whitish-buff, heavily streaked with dark brown. Bill dark brown with a pale buffish-horn base. Legs dark brown. First-summer males more closely resemble adult males, but head, mantle, back and breast show patches of bright crimson with yellow and/or brownish feather tips; wing and tail feathers retain yellowish edges of juvenile/first-winter plumage, and tips to median and greater coverts and tertials are pale yellowish-white.

GEOGRAPHICAL VARIATION No racial variation that is recognisable in the field without direct comparison; *bifasciata* is slightly larger and has a slightly thinner bill than nominate, and has mantle and back more uniform pink or pinkish-red, lacking dark feather base.

VOICE Call is quite distinct from that of Common Crossbill, generally weaker or softer and not so hard or metallic, 'glip-glip', 'kip-kip', or 'chiff-chiff', also canary-like 'tweet' or 'peet' and a twittering Redpoll-like 'chut-chut' or 'chuch-chuch' often given by feeding flocks. The song is rich, varied and rather Siskin-like, with buzzing trills and harsh rattles; it is delivered from a treetop, usually a conifer, or in slow-motion circular display flight ending on hovering wings.

STATUS, HABITAT AND BEHAVIOUR Common or locally abundant; in southern parts of range less frequently encountered. A bird of the northern conifer forest (except for isolated population in the highlands of Hispaniola), inhabiting principally larches and cedars in northern Europe and Asia, spruce and fir trees in North America. In southern parts of the range it is most usually found in pairs; in the north in loose colonies or in winter in sizable flocks, mostly of up to 50 but 300 is not unknown. Frequently mixes with flocks of Common Crossbills and other finches such as redpolls, Pine Siskins (50) and Evening (126) and Pine

Grosbeaks. Habits and many actions as Common Crossbill. Feeds on a wider variety of food items than other crossbills; in addition to extracting seeds of larches, cedars, spruces and hemlock, it also takes a variety of berries, spiders, and insects and their larvae.

DISTRIBUTION *L. l. leucoptera*: north and central Alaska through the Yukon to northern Alberta, northern Manitoba, northern Quebec and Newfoundland, south through British Columbia to central Alberta and northern Minnesota, northern Wisconsin, Michigan, southern Ontario and southern Quebec to New Brunswick and Nova Scotia. In recent years, the range in western United States has moved further south to the present limits.

L. l. megaplaga: Hispaniola.

L. l. bifasciata: northeast Europe, from extreme east of Finland east through the CIS (USSR) to about 65°N and in Siberia to about 67°N, in the south to about 58°N; in the east occurs in the Sayan range and mountains north of Lake Baikal and possibly also the Mongolian Altai sporadically east to Manchuria and the Amur river. Has also bred in northern Norway, Sweden, northeast Finland and Germany (near Berlin in 1991).

MOVEMENTS Sedentary, partially migratory and irruptive. In winter, birds from the northern areas of the breeding range irregularly wander (or in northeast Europe regularly irrupt approximately every seven years) south and southeast, mostly to southern Scandinavia, Denmark and the Baltic Republics and southern CIS (USSR); some join with the movements of Common Crossbills, especially in irruption years, and occur to the south and southwest of the normal wintering range. In North America, race *leucoptera* occurs south to Washington, Idaho, Colorado, Kansas, Illinois, Indiana, Kentucky, east to southern New Jersey, Maryland and North Carolina; exceptionally to Oregon, southern Utah and northern New Mexico. A rare or irregular visitor to Greenland, Faroe Isles (six records), British Isles (at least 100), eastern France (eight), Denmark, Belgium (at least 30), Holland (six), Germany (at least 60), Switzerland (three), northern Italy (20), Yugoslavia, Czechoslovakia, Hungary, Bulgaria and Romania, also northern China (northern Hopeh and Liaoning), Korea (one), Sakhalin and Japan (Hokkaido and Honshu); a vagrant to Bermuda. As with Common Crossbill, movements away from the breeding area can take place at any time and are influenced largely by food supply during the winter months. Movements south into Europe and Japan (usually in flocks of Common Crossbills) are from late September to December, and return movements from January to April or even May; an early nester in southern parts of the range.

MEASUREMENTS Wing of male 83–91, of female 80–89; tail 57·1–63·5; tarsus 15·9–17; bill (exposed culmen) 15·9–16·9. Wing of male *bifasciata* 87–99, of female 85–91; tail 54–66; tarsus 15–17; bill (from feathers) 16–18, depth 9·5–11.

REFERENCES Harrap and Millington (1991), Van den Berg and Blankert (1980).

GENUS PYRRHULA

Six species. Bullfinches are typified by their large or broad heads and short, stubby or blunt bills. The bill is adapted particularly for feeding on buds.

113 BROWN BULLFINCH *Pyrrhula nipalensis*   Plate 27
Palearctic and Oriental

Pyrrhula nipalensis Hodgson, 1836, Asiatic Researches, 19, p. 155, central and northern Nepal.

IDENTIFICATION Length 16–17 cm (6¼–6¾ in). Upperparts pale grey with a white band across lower rump; upper rump, uppertail-coverts, tail and wings are glossy black; lower forehead to lores and chin dark brown. Underparts are pale buffish or whitish, tinged brown. Typical short and swollen bullfinch-bill; long tail. Sexes separable in the field only if seen well; adults unlikely to be confused with any other species. **Confusion species:** Juveniles resemble female Orange Bullfinch (115), but ranges do not overlap. Latter has a uniform crown and is generally paler or sandy-brown, with a larger amount of white on rump and uppertail-coverts and no blackish-purple band across lower back.

DESCRIPTION Sexes similar. **Adult male:** Forehead, lores to chin dusky or blackish; white or whitish-buff spot or streak across cheeks just below and behind eye; ear-coverts and sides of neck pale buffish-grey. Crown to nape pale ashy or grey-brown, mottled or spotted with darker feather centres. Mantle, back and scapulars dull grey with a band of blackish-purple across upper rump; lower rump a broad band of white; uppertail-coverts black with deep glossy blue tips. Tail is long and notched, glossy blackish-blue with edges and tips velvety-black. Median coverts black, broadly tipped purplish-blue; outer greaters glossy purplish-black, inners (and tips of outer two to three) entirely pale buff, forming small pale patch on closed wing; alula, primary coverts and flight feathers blackish, edged glossy purple, tips of inner secondaries glossy deep blue; tertials the same, the smallest or innermost with crimson-pink outer edge (not always noticeable in the field). Underparts pale grey, tinged buffish, paler on centre of lower breast, belly and undertail-coverts; thighs pale brown. Bill is short, swollen or stubby, grey or greenish-grey with a blackish tip. Legs and feet pinkish-brown or dark greyish-pink. **Adult female:** Almost identical to adult male, but outer edge of innermost or smallest tertial is yellow, whitish (or even entirely uniform glossy black), not red or crimson. **Juvenile:** Similar to adult, but has uniform buff-brown crown and duller grey-brown mantle, back and scapulars; edges of uppertail-coverts and tips of greater coverts are buff-brown; ear-coverts, throat and breast are tawny-brown.

GEOGRAPHICAL VARIATION Most variation concerns depth of colour on crown, mantle and back, and more especially the presence or extent

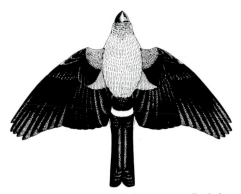

of white on cheeks. Race *ricketti* is generally darker above than nominate and has blackish crown; cheek spot or streak is lacking or only slightly indicated. Race *victoriae* is generally greyer than any other race, with a darker crown and a predominantly scaly appearance like *ricketti*, but has a very prominent white spot or streak below eye. Race *waterstradti* has whole of cheeks and ear-coverts white, pale buffish-brown inner greater coverts, and comparatively more glossy blue on tertials and tail. Race *uchidai* has very pale underparts, with belly almost white, and shafts of central tail feathers are white.

VOICE Call is a mellow 'per-lee', similar to that of Red-headed Bullfinch (116) but more melodious, also a soft whistling twitter while feeding. Song is a repeated mellow 'her-dee-a-duuee', usually given from cover at top of tre.

STATUS, HABITAT AND BEHAVIOUR Fairly or locally common. A bird of thick forest or dense undergrowth in broadleaved or fir forest between 1350 m and 3300 m, particularly favouring oak but also occurs in rhododendron; more rarely in fir forest in Himalayas; *waterstradti* is rarely found away from conifers, inhabits upper montane 'ericaceous' forest. Usually in pairs or small parties, quite tame and approachable. Flight is fast and rather direct. Feeds in tops of trees and bushes, rarely on the ground, on a variety of seeds, blossoms, buds and oak twigs; has also been recorded taking nectar from rhododendron flowers. Breeding behaviour is unknown.

DISTRIBUTION *P. n. nipalensis*: northern Pakistan (Gilgit) and Kashmir to northern Himachal Pradesh, northwest India, Nepal, Sikkim, Assam, southern Tibet (east to Chamdo) and Bhutan.

P. n. ricketti: southeast Tibet and northern Burma (Adung valley and Irrawaddy-Salween divide) to southwest Szechwan and Yunnan, also the mountains of Kwangtung and northwest Fukien, southern China, to northern Tonkin, North Vietnam.

P. n. victoriae: Mount Victoria, Chin hills, northwest Burma.

P. n. waterstradti: mountains of southern peninsular Malaysia (Perak, Selangor and Pahang states).

P. n. uchidai: Mount Arizan, Taiwan.

MOVEMENTS Generally resident (particularly *waterstradti*), but some undertake seasonal or short-distance altitudinal movements; in winter birds move down from higher levels, and are rarely found above 3050 m during this season.

MEASUREMENTS Wing of male 83–90, of female 80–87; tail of male 70–80, of female c70; tarsus c17; bill (from skull) 11–14. Weight of male 26–29, of female 24.

REFERENCES Ali and Ripley (1983), Fleming *et al.* (1979).

114 PHILIPPINE BULLFINCH *Pyrrhula leucogenys*   Plate 29
Philippines

Pyrrhula leucogenis Ogilvie-Grant, 1895, Bull. Brit. Ornith. Club, 4, p. 41, mountains of Lepanto, northern Luzon.

IDENTIFICATION Length 15–16·5 cm (6–6½ in). Endemic to the Philippines, where it is the only bullfinch and unlikely to be confused with any other species.

DESCRIPTION Sexes alike. **Adult:** Forehead to lores black, crown and nape glossy bluish-black; front of cheeks black, hindcheeks and ear-coverts pure white or yellowish-white (can be duller on female). Sides of neck, mantle, back and scapulars deep or rich brown; dark or blackish band across upper rump, lower rump white; uppertail-coverts dark bluish-black, blackest at tips. Tail is long and slightly notched, black with bluish or purplish gloss. Lesser and median coverts as scapulars; greater coverts black, inners broadly tipped light or pale buff-brown, outer two to three tipped slightly paler; outer edge of innermost or smallest tertial deep crimson (male) or pale brown (female) (as with other bullfinches with a similar marking, extremely hard to see in the field); secondaries black with bluish gloss, primaries dull black. Chin to centre of throat black; lower throat, breast, belly and flanks brown, gingery-brown or washed lighter buff-brown, undertail-coverts warm brown or rufous-brown. Bill is short and stubby, yellow or yellowish with black cutting edges and base to lower mandible. Legs and feet brown. **Juvenile:** Fairly similar to adult, but lacks black cap and has brown forehead, crown and nape; rump is pale buff-brown. Rest of plumage as adult, except outer edge of smallest tertial duller or pale sandy-buff, tips to inner greater coverts broadly pale buffish-brown, sides of face buffish-white, with some black on lores and base of bill, and underparts almost entirely dull or dingy brown. Bill paler than adult, with a paler yellowish-horn lower mandible.

GEOGRAPHICAL VARIATION Nominate is larger than *steerei*, but comparatively little or no racial variation in plumage is discernible in the field.

VOICE Undescribed.

STATUS, HABITAT AND BEHAVIOUR Scarce or only locally common. Occurs in moist oak forest on hillsides and in mountain valleys, usually up to 1750 m. Usually in pairs or family groups; small flocks not unusual in non-breeding season. Very little known.

DISTRIBUTION Both races endemic to the Philippines.

P. l. leucogenys: northern Luzon.

P. l. steerei: Mindanao (Mounts Bliss, Apo, Katanglad, Mayo, Malindang and Hilong Hilong).

MOVEMENTS An altitudinal migrant, moving to lower levels in non-breeding season.

MEASUREMENTS Wing 79; tail 66; tarsus 19; bill 12. Wing of *steerei* 77; tail 65; tarsus 17; bill 11.

REFERENCE Ogilvie-Grant (1895).

115 ORANGE BULLFINCH *Pyrrhula aurantiaca*   Plate 28
Southern Palearctic

Pyrrhula aurantiaca Gould, 1858, Proc. Zool. Soc. London, 1857, p. 222, Kashmir.

IDENTIFICATION Length 14 cm (5½ in). An obvious bullfinch by its head and bill and black face, and with generally orange body colour (much duller on adult female). Wings and tail black glossed with blue, pale or buffish wingbar on greater coverts; rump pure white. **Confusion species:** For differences from similar Brown Bullfinch (113), with which it does not overlap, see that species. Female Beavan's Bullfinch (117) is also similar, but has a longer tail, dark band across lower back, and a white border to face mask.

DESCRIPTION Sexes differ slightly. **Adult male:**

Forehead, lores and upper cheeks to chin black; cheeks, ear-coverts and sides of neck bright or deep orange. Forecrown to nape, mantle, back and scapulars rich or deep orange (appears yellow in strong light), often deepest on crown, mantle and back often showing grey bases to feathers; rump white; uppertail-coverts white at base, the longer ones velvety-black. Tail long and slightly notched, glossy blue-black. Median coverts black, edged with pale orange and subterminally greyish; greater coverts black at base, edged ashy-white and broadly (on inners) tipped pale or whitish-orange, forming a broad panel; alula, primary coverts and secondaries glossy blue-black, primaries black, tertials the same with outer web of smallest or innermost orange. Chin black; lower throat, breast, belly and flanks variable from pale to deep orange or orange-yellow; vent, thighs and undertail-coverts white. Bill is typical bullfinch shape, short and stubby, and black. Legs and feet dark brown or dark fleshy-brown. **Adult female:** Forehead to lores and chin black. Crown and nape to sides of neck grey, becoming a buffish-brown or yellowish-brown on mantle, back and scapulars. Rump, uppertail-coverts, wings and tail as male but median coverts are grey with a tinge or wash of pale yellow, and greater coverts are glossy blue-black, tipped buff or pale buffish-yellow, the inners broadly tipped pale buffish-brown with a tinge or wash of yellow. Underparts warm orange or deep peachy buff-brown, paler, greenish or more yellowish on belly and flanks; vent and undertail-coverts white. **Juvenile:** Very similar to adult female, but forehead and crown to nape initially dull tawny-brown, median coverts have pale buff or buffish-brown tips, and face and underparts paler or more yellow than orange. Chin and upper throat brown, belly and undertail-coverts white or yellowish. Young males become deeper orange in first summer.

VOICE Call is a soft, clear low-pitched 'tew'. The song commences with a loud call followed by a rapidly repeated metallic triple note, 'tyatlinka-tlinka'.

STATUS, HABITAT AND BEHAVIOUR Common or very common. Found in open fir, birch or mixed forest, usually between 2700 m and 3900 m. A quiet and relatively unobtrusive bird, often sitting motionless in trees for some time or keeping low in the undergrowth or on the ground; usually alone or in pairs or small flocks. Feeds on a variety of seeds (including grass seeds), berries and buds.

DISTRIBUTION Monotypic. Northern Pakistan (Chitral, Gilgit) to Kashmir and possibly also the northern Punjab, south to Simla, northwest India.

MOVEMENTS An altitudinal migrant; descends to between 1600 m and 2330 m in winter.

MEASUREMENTS Wing 80–83; tail 57–58; tarsus c18; bill (from skull) 13. Weight of male 17–21, of female 18–22.

REFERENCE Ali and Ripley (1983).

116 RED-HEADED BULLFINCH *Pyrrhula erythrocephala*   Plate 28
Southern Palearctic

Pyrrhula erythrocephala Vigors, 1832, Proc. Zool. Soc. London, 1831, p. 174, Himalayas; restricted to Simla-Almora district by Ticehurst and Whistler, 1924, Ibis, p. 471.

IDENTIFICATION Length 17 cm (6½ in). A brightly coloured bullfinch. Both sexes have a black or dark face, broad greyish-white wingbar, white rump and glossy blue-black wings and tail. Males have head and neck rich orange, paler on sides of neck and underparts. Females have hindcrown and nape yellowish-green, with forecrown, mantle and back grey; sides of neck and underparts are lighter grey. **Confusion species:** Adult male is unlikely to be confused with any other species. Lone females or immatures are possibly confusable with those of Orange (115) or Beavan's (117) Bullfinches, but colour of head, face and upperparts should enable separation: adult female has yellow-ish-olive crown and nape, whitish face, grey mantle and back, and lacks black band on lower back of female Beavan's; Orange Bullfinch is warmer or more rufous-brown on upperparts and underparts than Red-headed.

DESCRIPTION Sexes differ. **Adult male:** Forecrown to nape rich or deep orange (varying in intensity individually from very pale orange to almost red); forehead, lores to below eye and chin black, some also having a thin or fine pale band of whitish or pale buff bordering black on forehead; sides of face and neck pale orange or greyish, washed with orange on ear-coverts; cheeks and fore ear-coverts very pale orange or buffish-orange.

Mantle, back and scapulars pale grey or ashy-grey; rump white; uppertail-coverts and tail black, glossed with purple, tail notched or forked. Median coverts ashy or pale grey with black on inner webs and bases; greater coverts black or purplish-black at base, broadly tipped pale grey and with thin or fine band of white at tips (especially on outer two to three); alula, primary coverts and flight feathers black, glossed deep blue, prominently so on secondaries. Throat white or pale buff; breast and flanks orange; lower flanks, thighs and belly pale grey or washed with orange, becoming whiter on vent and undertail-coverts. Black bill is typically short and stubby. Legs and feet pale pinkish-brown. **Adult female:** Forehead, lores and fore cheeks to chin black, edged pale buff or whitish; crown and nape yellowish-olive or light greenish-yellow; hindcheeks and ear-coverts grey, but paler or buffish below eye. Mantle, back and scapulars deep grey, can become greyish-brown on upper rump, lower rump white; uppertail-coverts and tail black, edged and tipped purplish-black. Median coverts grey or grey-brown at base, tipped paler grey; greater coverts black, becoming grey and tipped finely white; alula and primary coverts grey, finely edged black; flight feathers black, inner secondaries and tertials glossed blue-black. Underparts dull grey or brown-tinged, with belly,

vent and undertail-coverts white. **Juvenile:** Like adult female but browner; head and upperparts warm brown or rufous-brown, tinged grey on mantle and back; wing-coverts broadly tipped with warm or rufous-buff; breast pale greyish-olive or yellowish-olive, becoming warm brown or orange-brown (some may have a yellowish wash) in first summer/second winter birds, belly pale grey.

VOICE Call is a soft plaintive whistle, 'pew-pew', very similar (if not identical) to that of Common Bullfinch (118). Song is a low mellow 'terp-terp-tee.

STATUS, HABITAT AND BEHAVIOUR Common or fairly common; sporadic or erratic in occurrence. Inhabits mainly dense conifer forest of cedar, pine or juniper or mixed forest of fir, birch or rhododendron between 2700 m and 4200 m in summer; in winter mainly oak and rhododendron forest, also occasionally in conifer forest and willows. Often found near streams or rivers. Usually in pairs or small parties (often of one sex) feeding low down in bushes or on the ground; quite lethargic and habitually spends long periods in one place, often sitting motionless in bushes. Feeds mainly on plant seeds, buds (also catkins) and berries; also known to take nectar from rhododendron flowers.

DISTRIBUTION Monotypic. Himalayas from southern Kashmir through northern Punjab and the mountains of northwest India, to Nepal, southeast Tibet (Mount Everest to Chumbi valley), Sikkim to eastern Bhutan (Mount Yonpu La).

MOVEMENTS An altitudinal migrant, descending in winter to around the lower levels of breeding range but some to 1000 m; in Nepal generally occurs at highest part of range in summer.

MEASUREMENTS Wing of male 72–81, of female 76–80; tail of male 60–70, of female 63–67; tarsus 17–20; bill (from skull) 10–13. Weight of male 18–22·5, of female 18–21.

REFERENCES Ali and Ripley (1983), Fleming *et al.* (1979).

117 BEAVAN'S BULLFINCH (Grey-headed Bullfinch) *Pyrrhula erythaca*   Plate 28

Southern Palearctic and Oriental

Pyrrhula erythaca Blyth, 1862, Ibis, p. 389, Sikkim.

IDENTIFICATION Length 17 cm (6½ in); *wilderi* 14–14·5 cm (5½-5¾ in). Both sexes have a black face as Red-headed Bullfinch (116), but on male Beavan's the crown to back and throat are pale grey; female has mantle and back dull greyish-brown and only crown or throat grey. Male's black face and chin have a complete white border, which is duller or more buffish and broken on female. Male has underparts variably reddish or deep orange (paler on some), while females are never red and are generally much paler or duller in tone; both sexes have white rump, black tail and wings

with a pale patch on coverts. **Confusion species:** Similar to Red-headed, but male Beavan's has grey (not bright orange) head, nape and sides of neck; female Red-headed lacks black band across lower back and is generally greyer above and below, with yellow or olive-yellow nape/upper mantle. Male and immature Orange Bullfinch (115) are pale or bright orange, while females are duller brown and lack white border to black face and black band across lower back. Brown Bullfinch (113) is somewhat similar to female Beavan's, but has mottled or scaly forecrown and no white band around black

face; also lacks large pale grey patch in wing (but has thin white wingbar), and has only small or thin band of white across rump.

DESCRIPTION Sexes differ. **Adult male:** Forehead and lores to below eye and chin black, finely bordered with white (not always obvious below chin); hindcheeks, ear-coverts and sides of neck pale grey. Crown, nape, mantle, upper back and scapulars dove- or lead-grey; lower back a band of black; rump white; uppertail-coverts glossy black. Tail is forked, black with a slight bluish gloss. Median coverts pale grey with black bases; greater coverts black or purplish-black at base, broadly tipped pale grey or white on outers, forming pale patch or panel across closed wing; alula, primary coverts and flight feathers black, secondaries edged and tertials entirely a purplish, glossy bluish-black. Chin black, thinly bordered with white; throat and slightly onto upper breast grey or greyish-brown; breast to upper flanks variable, from deep orange or reddish-orange or tinged slightly scarlet to yellowish; lower flanks, thighs and belly ashy-brown or tinged grey; vent and undertail-coverts white. Black bill is short and stubby, and typical of bullfinch. Legs and feet pink, grey or grey-brown. **Adult female:** Head and face as adult male, but grey is much duller or obscured by brownish bases on crown and nape. Mantle, back and scapulars dull grey-brown; lower back a band of black, blackish-brown or purplish-black; rump white; uppertail-coverts, tail and wings as adult male. Face as male, with an incomplete white or pale buff surround to black; sides of neck, ear-coverts and cheeks dull grey-brown, pale buffish-brown or warm gingery-brown. Throat pale grey, becoming warm or deep buff-brown on breast, belly and flanks; thighs, vent and undertail-coverts white. Bill dark brown or blackish. Legs and feet pale brown or flesh-brown. **Juvenile:** Very similar to adult female, but crown and nape more greyish-olive than grey-brown; sides of neck to mantle, back and scapulars dull grey-brown or tinged darker or olive; broad buffish-brown tips to greater

coverts. Flight feathers and tail dark blue and slightly glossy. Face has dark grey lores, with pale buff above and below eye. Underparts dull or dingy brown, becoming slightly warmer on flanks and paler or buffish-brown on lower belly and undertail-coverts. Assumes a plumage more closely resembling adult female in first winter.

GEOGRAPHICAL VARIATION Little variation between *erythaca* and *wilderi* noticeable in the field; the latter is slightly smaller and has a smaller bill. Males of race *owstoni* lack warm brown tones of underparts, being soft lavender-grey from lower throat to belly and vent, occasionally tinged light pink or buffish-brown on breast; flanks to undertail-coverts white; also shows black (or blackish-blue) patch on outer median coverts, flight feathers and tail are very glossy bluish-black, and outer web of inner tertial is bright red; has very faint band surrounding black face. Female *owstoni* are more gingery-brown on underparts and deeper grey on crown and nape, with outer web of inner tertial bright yellow.

VOICE The call is a typical slow, bullfinch-like soft 'soo-ee' or 'poo-ee', frequently repeated or given as a triple whistle. The song is undescribed.

STATUS, HABITAT AND BEHAVIOUR Scarce or locally common; very rare in Sikkim and Bhutan. Found in mixed conifer and rhododendron, birch or larch forest between 2500 m and 4100 m, also in willows, poplars, junipers and buckthorn; *owstoni* occurs in temperate or deciduous forest above 2280 m. Often approachable or confiding; usually in pairs in breeding season and small flocks in winter. Feeds in bushes, often low down or on the ground, on a variety of seeds, buds, catkins, insects and their larvae, also nectar of rhododendron flowers. Breeding biology little known.

DISTRIBUTION *P. e. erythaca*: Himalayas from southeast Tibet (Pome District), Sikkim, Bhutan, eastern Arunachal Pradesh, northeast India and extreme northern Burma (Adung valley), and northwest Yunnan and eastern Kweichow north through Szechwan to eastern Tsinghai, Kansu and southern Shensi (possibly also east to Shansi), northwest China.

P. e. wilderi: northern Hopeh to west Peking, northeast China.

P. e. owstoni: Mount Arizan and Mount Morrison, Taiwan.

MOVEMENTS An altitudinal migrant; descends in winter to between 2000 m and 3200 m, exceptionally to 1700 m; occurs more widely in northern Burma in winter. Race *owstoni* appears to be resident.

MEASUREMENTS Wing of male 80–86, of female 79–85; tail of male 67–73, of female 66–74; tarsus 16–18; bill (from skull) 11–13. Wing of male *wilderi* 74·5–78, of female 73·5–77; tail of male 63–67·5, of female 60–66·5; tarsus 15–16·5. Weight 18–21.

Loxia pyrrhula Linnaeus, 1758, Syst. Nat., ed. 10, p. 171, Europe.

IDENTIFICATION Length 14·5–16 cm (5¾–6¼ in). Common and well known. Over much of Europe and western Asia, males have a black cap, grey mantle and back, white rump, black tail and wings, with broad white tips to greater coverts forming a wingbar, with lower face and sides of neck to belly bright pink; females are duller and browner, lacking any pink, and have lower face and underparts warm brown. Eastern birds have pink restricted to face and chin, with most of underparts grey or washed very lightly with pink. Those on the Azores (considered a separate species by some authorities) are warm brown (both sexes) on body and lack any pink, closely resembling females of northern races. Unlikely to be confused with any other species once seen well: the shape, and the plumage of black cap, white rump, and (except *murina*) pink variably on cheeks, ear-coverts to underparts (males) or all-brown underparts (females) is extremely distinctive. The slow, monotonous piping call is common to most races.

DESCRIPTION Sexes differ. **Adult male** (*pyrrhula*): Forehead, lores, chin to crown and upper nape black or very slightly glossy black; hindneck, mantle, back and scapulars plain grey or lightly washed bluish-grey; rump white. Uppertail-coverts and central tail feathers glossy black, outer tail feathers black on inner webs, glossy blue-black on outers; tail rather square-ended. Median coverts grey (as scapulars); greater coverts black or glossy blue-black, tipped buffish- or greyish-white, slightly greyer on inner feathers; alula and primary coverts black, finely edged greyish-white; flight feathers black, edged glossy black, tertials with pinkish-red or orange outer web to smallest or innermost. Cheeks, ear-coverts and sides of neck to throat, breast, belly and flanks bright or deep pink; vent and undertail-coverts white. Bill short, stubby and black. Legs and feet dark brown or blackish-brown. **Adult female:** Forehead, lores, chin, and crown to hindcrown blackish-blue. Nape and hindneck pale grey, extending slightly onto upper mantle; mantle, back and

scapulars grey-brown, greyer in worn plumage; rump white; uppertail-coverts and tail glossy blue-black, outer tail feathers black (outermost often show a buffish-white shaft streak). Median coverts blue-grey; greater coverts black, with outers tipped broadly pale greyish-white, inners grey; alula and primary coverts grey or dark grey; flight feathers as male in fresh plumage, duller when worn; tertials the same, but inner tertial has outer web very pale reddish or pink (very hard to see in the field). Hind-cheeks, ear-coverts and sides of neck in fresh plumage pinkish or mauve-brown or somewhat duller and tinged buffish-brown, extending onto throat, breast, belly and flanks; vent, lower flanks and undertail-coverts white. **Juvenile:** Similar to adult female, but black of face and crown is replaced by dull brown, as mantle, back and scapulars; rump is white, tinged heavily with pale or peachy-buff. Tail and wings as adult female, but median coverts have buffish-brown tips and greater coverts are broadly tipped pale buffish-brown; inner tertial edged with brown. Lores and chin pale yellowish-brown, extending onto underparts, slightly browner on breast (but paler than adult female); vent and undertail-coverts pale buff or washed pale buffish-brown. First-winter birds following post-juvenile moult (August-September) resemble adult, but retain juvenile greater coverts and/or alula. Bill is pale horn.

GEOGRAPHICAL VARIATION Most racial variation concerns size and the brilliance or intensity of plumage coloration, with largest and brightest birds in the north and dullest or brownest in the southwest. Race *pileata* is almost identical to nominate in plumage, but smaller in overall size and size of bill: males are deeper or slightly darker blue-grey above, not so bright or deep pink on face and underparts, with tips to greater coverts greyer on inners and buffish on outers; females as nominate but less grey on both upperparts and underparts, which are generally duller brown. Both sexes of *europoea* are unlikely to be separated from nominate with confidence. Race *rossikowi* is also very similar to nominate, but males are deeper or more intensely red or reddish-pink on face, sides of throat and underparts, and females are greyer above and darker buff-brown below; both sexes have a large or deep-based bill as nominate. Race *caspica* is an eastern progression of *rossikowi* (and intermediates occur), also with a large bill; males are very bright or deep pink or reddish-pink on underparts, females are olive-brown or predominantly brown on mantle and back and pale or greyer on underparts. Male *cassinii* are very similar to nominate, but are paler grey on upperparts and bright pink below, with pure white tips to outer greater coverts; females are similar to those of other races (or can be slightly paler or greyer above and below), and also have white tips to outer greater coverts. Male *griseiventris* (regarded by some authorities as a separate species) are very conspicuous in the field, as red in plumage is deep pink and clearly restricted to ear-coverts, cheeks, sides of neck and throat, below which underparts (except for white vent and undertail-coverts) are soft grey, but on some ('*roseacea/kurilensis*') lower sides of face and breast (or even belly) is often tinged or washed pink or pinkish-orange; mantle and back are grey, but often tinged with brown or russet-brown; also has quite a small bill (but this feature is variable); females are generally pale brown but can show slight reddish or rusty tinge on ear-coverts and/or throat, with pale grey nape and upper mantle contrasting with rest of pale brown upperparts. Male *cineracea* lack all red in the plumage, having grey face, throat and underparts and pale uniform grey mantle and back; females are grey, tinged with brown. In Spain, *iberiae* closely resembles *caspica* in that males are very deep or bright pinkish-orange below and females are slightly paler or greyer above and below than similar birds of race *europoea*. Race *murina* on the Azores (which may be a separate species) resembles females of other races: both sexes are almost entirely brown (males slightly browner than females), but crown to nape, lores and chin, wings and tail are glossy purplish-black; rump is pale buff and uppertail-coverts are dull or dingy grey-brown; face, sides of neck and entire underparts are light brown, tinged warmer on face, flanks and undertail-coverts; wings as nominate, but with very broad greyish or dingy grey tips to greater coverts (slightly greyer than brown scapulars).

VOICE Call is a soft piping 'teu', 'deu' or 'deu-deu', but audible for a considerable distance, given while on wing and at rest; call of young similar, but harsher or more hoarse. The song consists of the call note repeated at intervals, occasionally interspersed with a trisyllabic piping note. Both sexes have a subsong, but it is only a softer version of the piping warble.

STATUS, HABITAT AND BEHAVIOUR

Common. Well known as a garden or suburban bird over much of its range, though some races are uncommon or scarce; race *murina* is extremely rare and considered endangered unless measures to protect its habitat are implemented, although a small reserve has now been established within the main part of its very small range. Most races occur in a variety of woodland or forest habitat, from mixed deciduous woods, copses and scrub to gardens, hedgerows, parks, and especially orchards in spring (where often classed as a pest); northern birds are more commonly found in conifer (including spruce, cedar or larch), birch, yew or even bamboo forest, often at some altitude (to 2900 m); in Japan, breeds between 1000 m and 2500 m. Generally a quiet, shy or unobtrusive bird, giving itself away only by its quiet piping note. Feeds at no great height in trees, bushes or shrubs, and is quite often agile or nimble and acrobatic, feeding upside-down or sideways on seedheads. Fairly short-legged, on the ground moves quite rapidly in short hops. Feeds on a variety of seeds of trees, particularly ash keys, shrubs, weed seeds, docks, berries (including rowan, buckthorn and dried blackberries), also mistletoe and the buds of many trees (particularly fruit trees and bushes); only occasionally are insects taken.

DISTRIBUTION *P. p. pyrrhula*: northern Europe from Scandinavia (about 70°N) and the White Sea, east through CIS (USSR) (to about 65°N, and south to about 48°N) to northern Mongolia, the Stanovoy range and the southern coasts of the Sea of Okhotsk; in the south from eastern France and southern Germany, Switzerland, Italy, the Balkans to Greece, Bulgaria and north to central Romania.

P. p. pileata: British Isles (including the Channel Islands)

P. p. europoea: northwest Spain and the Pyrenees east through France (except the east) to Belgium, Holland, western Germany and Denmark.

P. p. iberiae: northern Portugal and northern Spain (in central and western Pyrenees at higher altitudes than *europoea*).

P. p. murina: Azores (eastern San Miguel Island).

P. p. rossikowi: northern Turkey to the southern Caucasus (Azerbaijan) and probably extreme northwest Iran.

P. p. caspica: northern Iran to south Caspian region.

P. p. cineracea: west of Lake Baikal to northeast Altai range and northern Mongolia.

P. p. cassinii: Kamchatka and Commander Islands west to Ayan, Okhotsk coast, Kurile Islands (Paramushir).

P. p. griseiventris: lower Amur river, Ussuri, Sakhalin to Manchuria, Korea, southern Kurile Islands and Japan (Hokkaido and northern and central Honshu).

Note: Race *griseiventris* also comprises former races *roseacea* and *kurilensis*.

MOVEMENTS Sedentary, migratory and infrequently irruptive. Northern and eastern breeding birds of nominate race and *cineracea*, *cassinii* and *griseiventris* move south or southeast to winter within and south of the breeding range in southern Europe, northern Turkey, northern Iran, Central Asia, northwest and northeast China (from the Tien Shan range in Sinkiang), south to Hopeh (irregularly?) and east to Manchuria, Korea, Kurile Islands and in Japan south to Kyushu and Izu Islands. The nominate race is a passage migrant through central Europe, occasionally reaching the Mediterranean, and irregularly in small numbers through the British Isles (mainly Scotland). Vagrant to Iceland, Gibraltar (two records), Morocco (five records), Tunisia, Sicily (four records), Malta and Jordan (two records, both 1989). Race *cineracea* has been recorded in Korea; *cassinii* and '*roseacea*' form of *griseiventris* in Japan. Also at least ten records (to 1980) in Alaska (including St Lawrence and Nunivak Islands) and the Aleutians, one of which was identified as *cassinii*. Southward movement in autumn is usually between mid-October and November or occasionally into early December, and onward movements can be induced by the onset of severe winter weather or shortage of food; returns northwards in March and April.

MEASUREMENTS Wing of male 88–97, of female 87–95; tail of male 64–73, of female 62–74. Wing of *europoea* (male and female) 77–88·5.

Wing of male *pileata* 78–84, of female 78–83; tail 56–62; tarsus 15–17; bill (from feathers) 8–9.

REFERENCES Bibby and Charlton (1991), Bibby *et al.* (1992), Svensson (1992), Witherby *et al.* (1938–41).

GENUS *COCCOTHRAUSTES*

One species. A large-billed, robust and stocky finch, with unique curled tips to inner primaries. Closely related to grosbeaks, but differs in structure and head shape. The relationship between Old World *Coccothraustes* and the two species of New World *Hesperiphona* is very close, but no links have ever been established.

119 HAWFINCH *Coccothraustes coccothraustes*   **Plate 29**
Palearctic

Loxia coccothraustes Linnaeus, 1758, Syst. Nat., ed. 10, p. 171, southern Europe; restricted to Italy.

IDENTIFICATION Length 16–18 cm (6½-7 in). Large size, dumpy or stocky shape, short tail, short-necked appearance and massive bill are distinctive. The plumage is rich brown with pale or soft grey on nape, black chin, and black wings (except for pale whitish coverts) which have very distinctive curled and pointed tips to primaries (though this feature is not always visible or easy to see in the field). In flight, dumpy shape, short tail and broad white wingbar, together with sharp call note, are diagnostic. Juveniles can be sexed at a very early (nestling) age. Once seen well, unlikely to be mistaken for any other species.

DESCRIPTION Sexes similar but separable. **Adult male:** Lower forehead (top of bill) and lores to below eye black; cheeks and ear-coverts warm orange or cinnamon-brown; forehead to crown warm brown or cinnamon, becoming chestnut on

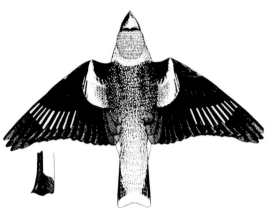

♂ *Detail: Sixth primary.*

hindcrown and upper nape. Lower nape, hindneck, and sides of neck grey or pale grey. Mantle, upper back and scapulars rich or dark chocolate-brown, lower back, rump and uppertail-coverts warm cinnamon-brown. Tail is short, square-ended with slight notch at tip, dark cinnamon-brown with black outer feathers, all broadly tipped white. Median coverts white or pale buffish-white with black or dark grey bases; greater coverts as medians but browner at base, with inners tinged warm brown or light cinnamon; alula and primary coverts black; flight feathers black, but glossed with purple or purplish-blue on inner primaries and secondaries, inner primaries with very distinctive curled tips which form an overlying arrowhead pattern on closed wing. Chin and throat black (forming a bib); sides of throat grey or greyish-brown, breast and flanks to belly pinkish-brown (can be paler or darker on flanks), vent and undertail-coverts white or greyish-white. Bill is massive, deep and broad at base, almost triangular and coming to sharp point; lead-blue with yellowish base to lower mandible in summer, paler or more entirely yellowish-horn in winter, but always slightly darker at tip. Legs and feet pale pinkish-brown. In flight overhead, shows a broad white wingbar at base of primaries (invisible at rest). In winter, often shows fine pale buff tips to throat and breast. **Adult female:** Very similar to adult male but duller, and less warm cinnamon-brown on head, face or underparts; crown dull brown, face pale brown, black on lores and around bill reduced but still present on chin. Hindcrown and nape grey or grey-brown; mantle and scapulars chocolate-brown, slightly paler on back; rump and uppertail-coverts dull brown; tail as male but less white at tip. Median coverts have black centres or bases and white tips, greaters as male but inners tinged grey-brown; secondaries and primaries blackish, but entire secondaries and distal half of primaries are broadly edged dull grey; tertials dark brown. Has distinctive curled tips to inner primaries. Underparts dull or pale brown. In

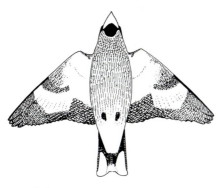

From below.

flight, wingbar is not so white as male's. **Juvenile:**
A paler or duller version of adults, with yellowish-
buff underparts, the breast mottled brown and with
some black spots or barring on sides and along
flanks. Has same mantle, back, wing and tail pattern as adults, though is generally duller, and pale
patch on wing-coverts is dull buffish, not white
(except median coverts, which are palest). Head,
face and nape brown or olive-brown (often with a
yellowish or olive-yellow tinge). Centre of belly,
vent and undertail-coverts pale uniform buff. Juvenile and first-winter males have deep blue secondaries, and a narrow line of black surrounding entire
bill (absent on same-aged females). Juvenile and
first-winter females are whiter on underparts than
same-aged males, and secondaries are pale grey
(deep blue on male) as on adult female. Immatures
of both sexes have bill yellowish-horn to brown,
with darker tip.

GEOGRAPHICAL VARIATION Race *buvryi* is
slightly smaller (not noticeable in the field) and has
a finer or less heavy-looking bill than nominate;
crown, rump and uppertail-coverts are greyer, and
shows less white in wingbar and at tip of tail. Race
nigricans is similar to nominate, but darker or
blackish on mantle and back; males show more
pink on underparts and females are whitish below.
Race *humii* is paler or more yellowish-brown on
mantle and back and pale tawny or warm buffish-
brown on underparts (both sexes) Race *japonicus*
is also paler than nominate, with more white on
belly and less white on tip of tail; bill is slightly
smaller.

VOICE Call is a sharp or abrupt Robin-like 'tick',
'tzik' or repeated as a double note, given both in
flight and from cover, also a shrill 'teee' and a
longer more drawn-out hoarse whistle, 'tzeep', or
a very thin Blackbird-like 'sreeee'; the call is often
the best indication of the bird's presence. Song,
seldom heard, is an intermittent bunting-like 'deek-
waree-ree-ree' or 'tchee-tchee-turr-wee-wee',
beginning with a whistling note and ending with
musical or more liquid notes, usually delivered
from the top of a deciduous tree.

STATUS, HABITAT AND BEHAVIOUR
Common or locally common, generally sparsely
distributed; very faithful to particular habitats.
Occurs at up to 3000 m in old deciduous and
mixed woods in lowlands and mountains, also in
parks, orchards and gardens, and has a noted preference for hornbeams but also found in beech
woods, elms, junipers, oaks, mountain ash and
cherries, both wild and cultivated; in winter,
occurs in more open country with bushes. Usually
found in pairs or small groups or family parties,
occasionally in considerable numbers (in hundreds
or thousands in eastern parts of range). A generally
quiet, wary or shy and unobtrusive bird, sitting high
in trees or feeding on the ground beneath tall trees;
in spring often more noticeable, with frequent calling and display activity by pairs. On the ground,
hops or walks with upright or erect stance. Flight
swift and bounding with rather rapid wingbeats,
often quite high over woods. Feeds on a variety of
seeds, mostly of trees of preferred habitats, and the
kernels of cherries, plums and maples, which it
either seeks in the foliage of trees or forages for on
ground; also takes fallen fruit, walnuts, holly, yew
berries, and at times resorts to feeding in fields and
gardens on crops such as maize, peas, wheat and
cotoneasters and sunflowers in spring; takes buds
and a few insects (nestlings are fed principally on
insects). In parts of Europe, a common species in
city-centre parks (e.g. Vienna) and regularly comes
to feeding stations.

DISTRIBUTION *C. c. coccothraustes:* northern
Europe from Britain, southern Sweden (has bred in
Norway and southern Finland) and Russia (to
62°N) east to the Urals, also in Siberia to
northern Kirghiz steppes, Sayan range (north to
about 64°N), south to southern Lake Baikal,
Russian Altai range and the Tola river, northern
Mongolia, continuing east to southern Amurland
and Ussuriland to northern and eastern Manchuria,
northern Korea and the southern Kuriles (Etorofu);
in the south, from southern Spain to Corsica, Sardinia, Italy, the Balkans and northwest Turkey to
the Caucasus.

C. c. buvryi: northwest Africa, from northern
Morocco to northern Algeria and northern Tunisia.

C. c. nigricans: Crimea, Caucasus, Ukraine and
northern Iran.

C. c. humii: central Russia or southern Siberia,
from the Dzungarian Ala Tau southwest to
Tadzhikstan (possibly also the Pamirs and northern
Afghanistan).

C. c. japonicus: Sakhalin Island and throughout
Japan.

Nominate and *nigricans* races intergrade and
interbreed in overlap areas. Other races have been
described.

MOVEMENTS Sedentary and migratory; birds in
the southern and central parts of the range are
largely resident or make only short-distance movements. Northern breeders migrate south, southeast
or southwest. Nominate race winters from Ireland
to southern Europe mostly around the Mediterranean, including Algeria and Tunisia, northwest
Africa, Malta, Crete and Cyprus, east through the
Balkans and the Black Sea sporadically to west and
central Turkey, northern Iran (to about Tehran),
Central Asia, southern Mongolia to Manchuria,
central and southern China, also Sakhalin; a rare
summer migrant to northern Japan (Hokkaido and
Honshu). Race *nigricans* winters in southern Iran

and occurs erratically (common in some years) west to Iraq, Lebanon and Israel. Race *japonicus* winters from eastern central China (from Hopeh) to Korea, Quelpart Island, southern Japan, Ryukyu, Izu, Bonin and Iwo Islands. Race *humii* winters south to the northwestern Himalayas and uncommonly or locally in the northwest Punjab and northern Pakistan. A scarce or irregular winter visitor to the Balearic Islands, Morocco, southern Tunisia, Libya, Sicily and northern Egypt; may also be an irregular or rare visitor to Hong Kong, but the five records (in December, January and May) during 1934–85 are considered equally likely to have involved escaped cagebirds. Vagrant to Gibraltar, Canary Islands, Madeira, Afghanistan, southwest Iran, Kamchatka, Commander Islands, Taiwan, Aleutians, Pribilofs, St Lawrence Island and Alaska

(12 records to 1980). The timing of migration and the numbers involved vary enormously from year to year, is presumably determined by the presence or likelihood of food throughout the winter. In autumn, most movement is from the end of August to the end of October, but migrants in November and early December are not unknown; in spring, return migration is from the middle or end of March to mid-May.

MEASUREMENTS Wing of male 100–110, of female 95–106; tail 47–54; tarsus 18–20; bill (from feathers) 18–22·5, depth 13–16·5. Wing of male *buvryi* 94–103. Wing of male *nigricans* 101–110, of female 98·5–106; tail of male 49–55·5, of female 46·5–54; bill 20–22. Weight 49·5–57.

REFERENCES Chalmers (1986), Witherby *et al.* (1938–41).

GENUS *EOPHONA*

Two species. Grosbeaks: similar in size, structure and bill shape to *Coccothraustes* (with which they have sometimes been classified), but slimmer, longer-tailed and with closer affinity to some of the *Mycerobas* grosbeaks than to any other large-billed species.

120 CHINESE GROSBEAK (Yellow-billed Grosbeak, Black-tailed Hawfinch) *Eophona migratoria* Plate 29
Eastern Palearctic

Loxia melanura Gmelin, 1789, Syst. Nat., 1(2), p. 853, China.

IDENTIFICATION Length 15–18 cm (6–7 in). A large or stocky and distinctive bird with a large bright yellow bill. Males have a black hood; females and immatures have blackish head and face and grey underparts. Females are otherwise similar to adult male, but mantle and back are warm light brown and rump is a paler grey. Wings are black, but greater coverts, secondaries and tertials are glossy deep blue with white tips to primary coverts; tips to secondaries and primaries are broadly white, very distinctive in flight. **Confusion species:** Japanese Grosbeak (121) is similar but larger and greyer, with a larger and brighter yellow bill; both sexes have a black cap which extends to chin and below eye, but does not extend onto ear-coverts as on male Chinese. Chinese has a paler grey rump and uppertail-coverts, a grey centre to tail (females) and distinctive white tips to primaries; Japanese has a white patch midway along primaries, but all-black tips to primaries and secondaries.

DESCRIPTION Sexes similar but separable. **Adult male:** Head and face to upper nape and chin and throat glossy black, bordered on sides of neck to throat by pale buff. Nape, mantle, upper back and scapulars light brown or dull sandy-brown tinged with grey; lower back and rump pale grey, uppertail-coverts white. Tail is fairly long and noticeably indented or notched at tip, and bluish-black. Median coverts black with bluish gloss;

greater coverts, inner secondaries and tertials blackish with deep blue gloss, tips of tertials white; alula black; primary coverts black, tipped (often quite broadly) with white; primaries and outer secondaries black, but distal third of outer five primaries (declining inwards) white and tips to all secondaries white (form white trailing edge to wing in flight). Breast to belly pale lead-grey or tinged lightly buff or sandy-brown; flanks warm sandy or gingery-brown; vent to undertail-coverts white. Bill is large and very obvious, almost triangular, pointed with yellow, dark grey or blackish at base of both mandibles, along cutting edges and at tip; in summer, base and cutting edges grey or greenish-yellow; in fresh plumage, in November/ December to February, bill is entirely yellow (darkens from tip). Legs and feet brown or pinkish-brown. **Adult female:** Similar to adult male, but black of head and face replaced by grey on forehead to crown and dark grey on lores and face. Mantle and back pale grey-brown, becoming paler grey on rump and uppertail-coverts. Tail as male, but central feathers are pale grey (becoming glossy blue-black on outers). Wings have greater coverts brown, tipped with black, and only tips of primary coverts and secondaries and distal fringes of primaries are white; tertials brown edged, with black and tipped finely with white. Underparts are dull or dingy buff-brown, with flanks warm gingery- or tawny-buff and lower belly and undertail-coverts white. Bill duller yellow than male's, with grey or greyish-horn at base. **Juvenile:** Very similar to adult female, but with dull grey face, buffish lores, white chin, all-dark bill, and pale buff tips to median and greater coverts; tail is mostly grey, with blackish edges and tip.

GEOGRAPHICAL VARIATION Race *sowerbyi* is slightly larger, with a bigger bill, deeper at base and with more noticeably curved culmen, than nominate; is also variably darker sandy-brown on upperparts (both sexes), greyer on throat and breast, and tends to show heavier or more extensive rufous or warm gingery-brown on flanks. Plumage differences, however, are not constant and intermediates occur; races are best separated on size and shape of bill.

VOICE Call is a loud 'tek-tek'. The song consists of a variety of whistles and trills and is apparently similar in tone to that of Linnet (72).

STATUS, HABITAT AND BEHAVIOUR Locally common, scarce or irregular. Occurs in mixed or deciduous forest (including bamboo), also well-wooded hills, river valleys, parks, orchards and gardens, usually on edge of forest or woodland; not found in deep or thick forest. Prefers oaks, birch, alder and beeches. Usually in pairs, but can occur in numbers on migration. Generally stays hidden within foliage, but often quite tame and approachable. Feeds in trees and on the ground on a variety of seeds, mostly those of trees and shrubs, but also in summer on fruits, berries and insects; nestlings are fed mostly on insects.

DISTRIBUTION *E. m. migratoria:* southern Amurland, southern Ussuriland, northeast Mongolia and Manchuria south to northern Hopeh and east to northern Korea.

E. m. sowerbyi: eastern China along the lower Yangtze valley west to southern Szechwan and east to Kiangsu and Shanghai.

MOVEMENTS Sedentary and migratory. Nominate race moves south or south-southwest to winter in southern China from southern Yunnan east to Kwangtung, Hong Kong and Fukien, also to Taiwan (where scarce); also regular in spring and autumn or an annual winter visitor to southern Japan (where bred on Kyushu in 1980) and the Izu Islands. Race *sowerbyi* is more resident, but some wander south and west to central China (Yunnan). Has also been recorded in North Vietnam. A vagrant to northern Burma, northern Thailand (one record), Bonin Islands and northern, central and southern Nansei Shoto (Japan). Leaves breeding areas in CIS (USSR) mid-August to mid-September but arrives in wintering areas from September to November and mid-winter occurrences in Japan not uncommon; return movements are from early May to mid-June. Several recent records in Europe are considered to have involved cagebirds, as the species is widely imported from Hong Kong.

MEASUREMENTS Wing of male 96–109, of female 91–101; tail 70–87; bill (from skull) of male and female 19–26, depth 13–16. Weight 50.

REFERENCES Brazil (1991), Flint *et al.* (1984).

121 JAPANESE GROSBEAK (Masked Hawfinch) *Eophona personata*
Plate 29

Eastern Palearctic

Coccothraustes personatus Temminck and Schlegel, 1848, in Siebold, Fauna Japonica, Aves, p. 91, Japan.

IDENTIFICATION Length 18–23 cm (7–9 in). Similar to Chinese Grosbeak (120) which it partly overlaps in range. Adult has black from forehead to nape, below eyes and chin; ear-coverts and sides of neck pale whitish-grey, upperparts grey (or tinged lightly with buff-brown), and underparts duller, very light grey, flanks washed with gingery or tawny-buff. Wings and tail black except for pale grey on inner coverts; rest of coverts and secondaries glossy blue-black with a distinctive band of white midway across primaries. Juveniles are duller or greyer and lack black cap. Unlikely to be confused with any other species except Chinese Grosbeak (120), which see for differences.

DESCRIPTION Sexes almost alike. **Adult:** Forehead to lores, crown, nape and across face to below eye and chin black, forehead and crown with blue gloss in fresh plumage; hindcheeks, ear-coverts and sides of neck pale whitish-grey, becoming grey. Hindneck, nape, mantle, back, rump and uppertail-coverts grey or dull grey, tinged with buffish-brown (longest uppertail-coverts bluish-black). Tail is long and forked, all central feathers glossy bluish-black, outermost plain black. Median and greater coverts glossy bluish-black, but inner greater coverts grey; alula and primary coverts black; flight feathers also black, secondaries edged glossy blue-black (more extensive on male than female), primaries (except

315

♂   ♂ *from below.*

outers) with broad white bar mid-length (shows as a triangular white patch on closed wing); tertials buff-brown, tinged with grey. Lower throat pale grey or whitish in centre; sides of throat, breast, belly and thighs pale or dull grey; flanks washed pale tawny or gingery-brown; lower belly, vent and undertail-coverts white. Bill is massive, deep and broad at base, pointed and yellow, but can be paler or with pale brown at base of both mandibles. Legs and feet brown, straw-yellow or reddish-brown. **Juvenile:** Similar to adults, but generally pale buffish-brown and lacks black cap; has pale buff-brown forehead, black on lores and below eye to base of bill; chin and throat greyish-buff. Grey plumage of upperparts and underparts duller or paler buffish-brown than adults, and thinly or indistinctly streaked on scapulars; wings as adult, but tips to median and greater coverts pale yellowish-buff, usually broadly on greater coverts; small patch of white on outer primaries; tertials often warm brown.

GEOGRAPHICAL VARIATION Race *magnirostris* is larger than nominate and has a somewhat larger bill; plumage is generally paler or lighter in tone, and white patch on primaries is smaller than in nominate.

VOICE Has a short but hard 'tak, tak' note, given in flight. The song consists of a short series of four to five fluty whistled notes.

STATUS, HABITAT AND BEHAVIOUR Common or locally common (abundant in some places). Occurs in mixed or deciduous forest, more commonly in valleys than on hillsides, also woods and groves of birch and oak, well-wooded parks and gardens; in winter, occurs on edges of cultivation. Usually in pairs or small flocks. Deceptively shy or secretive and often stays hidden in foliage; prefers treetops, its presence given away only by its song or call. Feeds on a variety of seeds and insects; in winter mainly on cedar nuts, but also pine and birch seeds taken (and doubtless other tree seeds) and berries; in summer, insects, including caterpillars and beetles, form main part of diet.

DISTRIBUTION *E. p. personata*: Japan, from Hokkaido to central Honshu and Kyushu.

E. p. magnirostris: eastern Amurland through Ussuriland to eastern Manchuria, south to Hopeh, Beijing and possibly Shantung; also an uncommon summer resident in northeast Korea.

MOVEMENTS Sedentary and migratory. Northern birds of nominate race move south and southwest to winter in southern Japan, Ryukyu Islands and Fukien, eastern China; an occasional visitor to southern Korea (Quelpart Island), Izu and Bonin Islands and a vagrant to Taiwan. Race *magnirostris* is a longer-distance migrant to Fukien, Kwangtung and Kweichow in southern China, and possibly west to the Min Ho and Omei Shan, southern Szechwan; a vagrant to south Korea and Hong Kong (November 1985). Leaves breeding area from September to November, with occasional onward movements in December and January; returns in April and May.

MEASUREMENTS Wing of male 113–117, of female 102–111; tail 83–95; bill of male 24–26, of female 21·5–24·5, depth 17–20·5. Weight of male c80.

GENUS *MYCEROBAS*

Four species. Grosbeaks: closely related to *Coccothraustes*, but larger and of different habitat occupation, with specialised feeding requirements. Clearly of Himalayan origins, and two species have very restricted range.

122 BLACK-AND-YELLOW GROSBEAK *Mycerobas icterioides*
Plate 30

Southern Palearctic

Coccothraustes icterioides Vigors, 1831, Proc. Zool. Soc. London, p. 8, Himalayas; restricted to Simla-Almora district by Ticehurst and Whistler, 1924, Ibis, p. 471.

IDENTIFICATION Length 22 cm (8½ in). A large black-and-yellow (males) grosbeak with a stout bill; both sexes are very similar to Collared Grosbeak (123). Males have all-black head, face, scapulars, wings, tail and thighs; rest of plumage is bright yellow, but some (probably older males) have a wash of orange-buff on upper mantle and sides of neck. Females have head to mantle, back and breast pale or dull grey, wings and tail dark grey, and rump, belly and undertail-coverts dull tawny or buffish-brown. **Confusion species:** Adult males are extremely similar to male Collared Grosbeak, but black of plumage is duller (not glossy) and thighs are conspicuously black (not yellow); has a less pronounced orange 'collar' across upper mantle, and yellow in plumage is also paler than on male Collared. Females are also similar to female Collared but less likely to be confused, having buff-brown rump and belly to undertail-coverts (lack green on upperparts, coverts and tertials and yellowish-green underparts). Calls and songs of the two species are also conspicuously different. Female White-winged Grosbeak (125) is similar, but darker grey on head, mantle and breast, pale green on belly, flanks and undertail-coverts, and has an obvious white patch at base of primaries.

DESCRIPTION Sexes differ. **Adult male:** Forehead to crown, upper nape, face and cheeks to chin and throat (occasionally extending to centre of upper breast), sooty-black. Nape, hindneck and sides of neck yellow or orange-yellow, forming a collar. Centre of mantle, back, rump and uppertail-coverts golden-yellow; sides of mantle, scapulars, back, wings and all wing-coverts black. Black tail is long and square-ended or very slightly indented at tip. Breast to undertail-coverts bright or deep yellow, thighs dark grey-brown or black. Bill is stout and pointed, pale green (yellowish-green in winter), with paler or yellowish-horn cutting edges and tip. Legs and feet pale fleshy-brown or reddish-brown. On old males, upper mantle, sides of neck and occasionally sides of breast are deep yellow, orange or pale orange-buff. **Adult female:** Forehead to crown and nape to face, sides of neck, chin and throat (to upper breast on some) ashy-grey. Mantle, upper back and scapulars also grey, slightly duller than on head and face; lower back and rump pale tawny or light buffish-brown, very lightly washed with grey in fresh plumage; uppertail-coverts pale grey. Tail is ashy-grey with

black shafts on central feathers, all outer feathers black. Median and greater coverts ashy-grey; alula, primary coverts and flight feathers blackish-brown, edged broadly pale grey on secondaries. Breast light ash-grey, belly, flanks and undertail-coverts tawny or fawn buff-brown, thighs grey. Bill is pale green or greyish-green, yellowish at tip and along cutting edges. Legs and feet pale flesh-pink. **Juvenile:** Both sexes initially resemble adult female, but first-winter and first-summer males have black wings and tail as adult, mantle and back are mottled blackish and rump is yellow; throat and breast are mottled grey and yellow, and head can show black tips. Adult plumage is attained in second winter. The bill of young birds is similar to that of adult female or slightly darker, more horn-coloured; legs are either as adult female or slightly more yellowish.

VOICE Male has a high-pitched whistle, 'pi-riu, pir-riu, pir-riu', or a three-note whistle 'tit-te-tew, tit-te-tew', given in short bursts; both sexes also give a short 'chuck' or 'cluck' contact note when feeding. Song is a rich, clear 'prr-trweeet-a-troweeet' or a rich and clear 'tookiyu, tookiyu'.

STATUS, HABITAT AND BEHAVIOUR Common or fairly common. Occurs between 1800 m and 3500 m in conifer and deodar forest, also, less frequently, in oak and scrub at the edge of forest or woods. Found in pairs or loosely scattered flocks. Frequents tops of tall trees, but often feeds low down in undergrowth or on the ground. Often heard more than seen as it has a habit of staying well hidden in the foliage, but can be tame and approachable. On the ground hops in sparrow-like fashion. Feeds on a variety of seeds, chiefly of pine, fir and crab apple, also berries, fruit and shoots or buds; also takes insects, but mainly in breeding season when feeding young.

DISTRIBUTION Monotypic. Safed Koh, east Afghanistan, to Kumaon, northwest India.

MOVEMENTS An altitudinal migrant; descends in winter to 1500 m, exceptionally to 750 m in severe winters, when it remains at low levels well into the spring months. Occurs east into Himachal Pradesh in winter.

MEASUREMENTS Wing of male 126–136, of female 122–133; tail 88–97; tarsus 23–25; bill (from skull) 23·5–29.

REFERENCES Ali and Ripley (1983), Bates and Lowther (1952).

123 COLLARED GROSBEAK (Allied Grosbeak) *Mycerobas affinis*

Plate 30

Palearctic and marginally Oriental

Hesperiphona affinis Blyth, 1855, Journ. Asiat. Soc. Bengal, 24, p. 179, [probably] Alpine Punjab.

IDENTIFICATION Length 22 cm (8½ in). A large black-and-yellow grosbeak; males are very similar to Black-and-Yellow Grosbeak (122). Males have a glossy black head, face, wings and tail; rest of plumage is deep or rich yellow, with a pronounced brown or warm brown collar across upper mantle from sides of neck. Females are also similar to Black-and-Yellow, but are sufficiently different in plumage above and below to cause only minimal confusion. **Confusion species:** For differences from closely similar Black-and-Yellow Grosbeak, which it overlaps in range in northwest India, see that species. Voices of the two species are distinctly different. Females are somewhat similar to female White-winged Grosbeak (125), but much more olive-green on mantle, back and scapulars and lack prominent white patch at base of primaries. Unlikely to be confused with any other grosbeaks, and the stout bill should immediately distinguish both Collared and Black-and-Yellow Grosbeaks from closely similar orioles, particularly Asian Black-headed Oriole (*Oriolus xanthornus*).

DESCRIPTION Sexes differ. **Adult male:** Forehead to crown and nape, sides of face to chin, throat and upper breast black, with gloss on crown, ear-coverts and sides of face. Hindneck and sides of lower neck bright yellow, merging into warm orange-brown collar (deeper or more intense on some) from sides of neck to centre of upper mantle; lower mantle, scapulars and back black, broken or streaked with yellow or orange-yellow down centre of mantle and back; rump and uppertail-coverts deep yellow or golden-yellow, tinged orange, the longest uppertail-coverts black. Tail is black, with central feathers glossy black. All wing-coverts and flight feathers black, edged glossy black on edges of greater coverts, inner scapulars and tertials. Underparts from lower breast (including thighs) bright or deep yellow, paler on belly. Bill is large, deep and broad at base, pointed, bluish-green, grey or steely grey-blue, often with paler cutting edges. Legs and feet fleshy or reddish-brown. **Adult female:** Entire head and face to nape, upper sides of neck, chin and throat grey, slightly paler on face and throat; lores to under eye darker grey. Hindneck to lower sides of neck pale olive-green, becoming duller olive-green on mantle, back and scapulars; paler or brighter green on rump and uppertail-coverts. Tail black or blackish-grey. Median and greater coverts olive-green, slightly paler at tips of greaters; alula black, edged with pale olive; primary coverts and flight feathers black, tertials edged broadly with olive. Lower throat grey; breast olive or olive-yellow, becoming dull yellow (or tinged with olive) on undertail-coverts. Bill as male, but more green or sea-green in tone. **Juvenile:** Juveniles initially closely resemble adult female, but are much duller; rump is slightly yellowish and throat is grey-brown in centre. First-winter and first-summer males are more like adult, but black of head is duller with some brown feather centres or fringes, and yellow of underparts is paler, more dingy or mottled with olive.

VOICE Call is a mellow but rapid 'pip-pip-pip-pip-pip-pip-ugh'; also a sharp alarm note, 'kurr', often rapidly repeated, sounding rather like two stones striking together. Song is a clear, loud and rising musical or piping whistle of five to seven notes, rendered as 'ti-di-li-ti-di-li-um'; also a loud creaky song punctuated with musical bulbul-like notes constantly repeated.

STATUS, HABITAT AND BEHAVIOUR Fairly common, local or scarce. Occurs in summer between 2700 m and 4000 m (occasionally to 4200 m) in mixed and conifer forest, also in maple, oak and rhododendrons and in dwarf juniper above tree line. Usually in pairs or small parties. Normally seen at tops of tall trees, but often feeds in low bushes, undergrowth or on the ground. Flight is fast and fairly direct or slightly undulating, in a tight and compact flock. Breeding behaviour, nest and eggs are unknown. Feeds on a variety of seeds (those of pines extracted from cones with its strong bill), buds or shoots, nuts and fruits (including crab apples), also some insects, mainly caterpillars, and snails.

DISTRIBUTION Monotypic. Himalayas of northern Pakistan and Kashmir through northwest India and Nepal to Sikkim, Assam, Bhutan, southeast Tibet and east to west and central Szechwan, southern Kansu and northwest Yunnan (Likiang range), western China, and Adung valley, northern Burma.

MOVEMENTS An altitudinal migrant, but also undertakes post-breeding wanderings and dispersal of young; wanders nomadically throughout the range. In winter descends to lower levels, occasionally to 1800 m, exceptionally to 1065 m in Nepal, more usually around 2700 m in Sikkim; occurs more widely in northeast Burma. A vagrant to northern Thailand (one record, January 1986).

MEASUREMENTS Wing of male 123–136, of female 121–132; tail of male 88–97, of female 87; tarsus c26–29; bill (from skull) c27. Weight 69–72.

REFERENCES Ali (1978), Ali and Ripley (1983).

124 SPOT-WINGED GROSBEAK *Mycerobas melanozanthos* **Plate 30**
Southeast Palearctic and marginally Oriental

Coccothraustes melanozanthos Hodgson, 1836, Asiatic Researches, 19, p. 150, Nepal.

IDENTIFICATION Length 22 cm (8½-8¾ in). A large, stoutly built black-and-yellow grosbeak with distinctive white spots on wing (both sexes). Male has entire upperparts, wings, chin, throat and upper breast slaty-black, with paler tips to feathers and white spots in wings; underparts yellow. Female has a very bold and striking face pattern, heavily striped black and yellow on upperparts, becoming more uniform dark grey or black on rump and tail; the yellow underparts are spotted with black. **Confusion species:** Possible confusion with similar but duller (less bright yellow) White-winged Grosbeak (125), but male Spot-winged has uniform upperparts (not olive or yellowish-olive on rump) and brighter and more extensive yellow on underparts (on White-winged, black extends to upper belly). Females and immatures are unlikely to be confused with those of White-winged, which are unstreaked.

DESCRIPTION Sexes differ. **Adult male:** Entire head, face, sides of neck to chin, throat and breast, and mantle and back to rump and tail all slaty-black, with paler tips to all feathers (except tail) creating a scaly effect at close range. In fresh plumage tips of crown to mantle and back glossy, and some individuals show white spots on tips of inner scapulars/edge of mantle area. Tail is slightly notched or indented at tip. Median and greater coverts black, greaters tipped broadly cream or pale yellowish-white (can also be finely edged with slate-grey); alula and primary coverts black; flight feathers black, edged brown or grey-brown in worn plumage, with small white patch at base of inner primaries (often concealed on closed wing, becomes prominent in flight); and outer edge of tips of all secondaries and entire outer webs of tertial tips yellowish-white. Underparts from upper breast deep yellow, with some showing a few black spots on sides of breast and flanks. Pointed bill is large or massive, deep and very broad at base, lead-grey or slightly bluish-grey. Legs and feet grey or dull blue-grey. **Adult female:** Forehead to crown and nape yellow, streaked heavily with black; upper lores, supercilium and (on some) to sides of nape yellow, often with a few slight or fine dark streaks; lores and ear-coverts black, but cheeks and lower edge of ear-coverts yellow; moustachial stripe black, with broad yellow submoustachial stripe. Sides of neck yellow, broadly streaked with black. Mantle, back and scapulars yellow, boldly or heavily streaked or spotted with black; rump and uppertail-coverts slate-grey or black. Tail black, finely edged dull yellow. Wings as adult male but with pale yellowish tips to medians and more lead-grey than black, and tips to greater coverts, secondaries and tertials broader than on male and yellowish-white; small square of white

or yellowish-white at base of primaries; edges to primaries and secondaries finely yellow, becoming whitish towards tips. Chin and throat bright yellow, with black malar stripe; rest of underparts bright lemon-yellow, with breast and flanks heavily streaked or spotted with black (largest and heaviest streaks on sides of breast and flanks); belly, vent and undertail-coverts uniform yellow or pale yellow. **Juvenile:** Juvenile and first-winter plumages are similar to adult female but duller on upperparts, more mottled with pale yellowish-white or pale buff, and scapulars and lower back to uppertail-coverts are edged with olive; yellow of underparts is replaced by a pale whitish-buff which is finely spotted, often in continuous streaks or lines on sides of breast and flanks. First-summer males retain this plumage, but the moustachial area, throat and upper breast are tinged with warm buff, reddish or rufous-brown.

VOICE Call is a rattling 'krrrr' or 'charrarauk', rather Magpie-like in tone, also said to be like the shaking of a matchbox containing only a few matches. Song is a loud, melodious whistle consisting of three notes, 'tew-tew – teeeu', also some mellow oriole-like whistles, 'tyop-tiu' or 'tyu-tio', and a rising human-like 'ah. When feeding in a large group (and also when going to or dispersing from communal roosts in autumn), the birds keep up a running cackling chorus.

STATUS, HABITAT AND BEHAVIOUR Uncommon, local or occasional in its occurrences. Found in mixed or evergreen forest, principally of fir and birch, hemlock or maple between 2400 m and 3600 m, or down to 1700–1800 m in Thailand; occasionally in other deciduous forest. Usually in pairs or small flocks of up to 30 (exceptionally 80 together); flocks keep close company in flight, which is heavy and quite laboured. Usually seen sitting or feeding in treetops, but also feeds low down or on the ground. A shy or unobtrusive bird, often overlooked as it sits quite still and without a sound for considerable lengths of time. Feeds on a variety of seeds and fruits (principally those of trees); also takes wild cherry and berries.

DISTRIBUTION Monotypic. Northern Pakistan east through Kashmir, northwest India, Nepal, Sikkim, Assam, Bhutan and southeast Tibet to southern Szechwan and northwest Yunnan (Likiang range), western China, also south through Arunachal Pradesh, northeast India to Nagaland, northern Burma (south to Mount Victoria, Chin Hills) and northern Thailand.

MOVEMENTS An altitudinal migrant, but movements poorly known; in winter descends to around 1200 m in the Himalayas, occasionally as low as

900 m, and to 600 m in Bhutan and about 500 m in northern Thailand.

MEASUREMENTS Wing of male 122–135, of female 119–135; tail of male 71–83, of female 73–77; tarsus of male 22–25, of female 22–24; bill (from skull) of male 24–32, of female 28–31, depth 21–22. Weight (one male) 74, (one female) 50.

REFERENCES Ali and Ripley (1983), Fleming *et al.* (1979).

125 WHITE-WINGED GROSBEAK *Mycerobas carnipes*   **Plate 30**
Eastern Palearctic

Coccothraustes carnipes Hodgson, 1836, Asiatic Researches, 19, p. 151, Nepal.

IDENTIFICATION Length 22–24 cm (8¾–9½ in). A large, long-tailed, dark grosbeak with an obvious dull yellow rump patch and single white wing patch or wingbar on primaries; belly to undertail-coverts dull or dingy yellow. Males are blacker or darker than females and have brighter yellow on rump. Bill is thick at base and massive in size. **Confusion species:** Adult male Spot-winged Grosbeak (124) is much blacker, lacks yellow or olive-yellow rump and has white (or pale yellowish-white) tips to greater coverts, tertials and secondaries; yellow on underparts is more extensive, to sides and centre of lower breast. Female and immature White-winged unlikely to be confused with those of Spot-winged, which are heavily streaked.

DESCRIPTION Sexes similar but separable. **Adult male:** Entire head, breast to centre of belly and flanks and mantle to upper back and scapulars sooty-black or blackish-grey, in fresh plumage bases to scapulars jet-black tipped blackish-grey or dull yellow; lower back and rump mustard-yellow; uppertail-coverts dull black or blackish with yellow tips. Black tail is long or relatively long (in comparison with other grosbeaks) and square-ended, though often looks slightly rounded at tip. Median coverts black or dull black, edged and tipped blackish-grey, greaters the same with deep yellow tips on inners in fresh plumage; alula, primary coverts and flight feathers black, primaries edged finely pale grey but bases of outer four broadly white (forming a small but obvious patch on closed wing, or short wingbar in flight), tertials edged rich or pale yellow on outer edges towards tip. Underparts from centre of belly and lower flanks dull or dingy mustard-yellow; thighs pale grey. Bill is broad and deep at base, blunt-tipped, with a dark grey or blackish-horn upper mandible, lower paler or whitish at base. Legs and feet pale brown or pinkish-brown. **Adult female:** Very similar in general plumage to male, but paler or duller slate-grey (not black, but with black feather bases occasionally showing through); dull yellow on rump and undertail-coverts is also paler. Tail black or blackish-grey. Wings as adult male, but tinged with olive and not so black; greater coverts are edged and tipped olive-yellow (more prominent on inners), and blackish flight feathers are edged with olive-yellow, primaries with a similar (but smaller) dull white patch at base; tertials have pale olive-yellow spot on outer web near tip, becoming greyish-white at tip. In fresh plumage, cheeks and ear-coverts are dark ashy-grey with fine white streaks. Underparts slate-grey, with narrow or fine white streaks or lines on throat and breast (more prominent on some than on others) or greyish-yellow on breast with white centres; belly dull yellow, thighs pale grey. **Juvenile:** Similar to adult female but browner, with pale edges forming crescents on head, mantle and upper back; wing-coverts are brown, and medians and greaters have olive-yellow tips. First-winter birds lose pale tips (and crescents) and are more similar to adult female. First-summer males are also similar to female on head, face, breast and mantle, but rump and undertail area is brighter yellow (though still tinged duller); rest of plumage similar to adult female, but with olive wash to mantle, upper back and wing-coverts; throat and breast often show patches or blotches of dark grey or dull white spots in worn (or moulting) plumage.

GEOGRAPHICAL VARIATION Race *speculigerus* is inseparable in the field; paler (not so black) on upperparts (males) or paler grey above and below (females), and also slightly smaller, though this is difficult to detect without direct comparison.

VOICE Call is a soft nasal 'shwenk' or 'chwenk' contact note or a squawking 'wit' or 'wet', often extended into 'wet-et-et' or 'add-a-dit' notes which also form the basis or beginning of song, continuing into 'un-di-di-di-dit', rest of song also described as 'dja-dji-dji-dju'. Usually calls or sings from a high prominent perch, but the full song is rarely heard.

STATUS, HABITAT AND BEHAVIOUR Common or locally common. Found in juniper forest or dwarf juniper and sparse or scattered scrub near or above the tree line, between 2800 m and

4600 m; also occurs in high-level fir and mixed forest with rhododendrons in mountains, valleys and slopes, also in bamboo undergrowth. Usually in pairs or small, often scattered, flocks of up to 30 or 40, in winter in larger groups of up to 50–60 birds; sociable and often in company with other finches, particularly Red-mantled Rosefinch (101). Approachable, often seen in treetops or in flight between feeding areas, but often sits quietly or unobtrusively for long periods. Has a strong or bounding flight, somewhat reminiscent of a woodpecker, but in rapid alarm flight makes a slight whirring noise. Feeds in treetops and low down in scrub and undergrowth, mainly (some exclusively) on juniper berries (very noisy and detectable when cracking open the stones and discarding the outer kernel), also on other (tree and shrub) seeds and berries (including strawberries).

DISTRIBUTION *M. c. carnipes*: Russian and Chinese Turkestan in the Tarbagatai and Tien Shan ranges east to Kashgaria, western Sinkiang, south

to Tadzhikstan, also the Himalayas from northern Pakistan (Gilgit) east through Nepal, Sikkim to Assam, Bhutan, southern and southeast Tibet, Szechwan to northwest Yunnan (Likiang range), also eastern Tsinghai (Koko Nor), southern Kansu to southern Ningsia (Ala Shan and Ho Lan Shan) and western Inner Mongolia.

M. c. speculigerus: northeast Iran (from south Caspian district) east to northern Afghanistan and northern Baluchistan, Pakistan.

MOVEMENTS An altitudinal migrant; in winter descends to 2400 m, exceptionally to 1500 m, but many stay at high levels unless the winter is particularly severe. May also occur regularly in northern Burma (Adung valley).

MEASUREMENTS Wing of male 103–130, of female 112–123; tail 92–96; tarsus 27–28; bill (from skull) of male 30, of female 28. Weight of male 56–66, of female 54–60.

REFERENCES Ali and Ripley (1983), Fleming *et al.* (1979).

GENUS *HESPERIPHONA*

Two species. Grosbeaks with close similarities to *Coccothraustes* (with which they are frequently classed), but no links between the two genera have been established. Both are New World species: one widespread in North America, the other an uncommon resident in cloud forest of Middle America.

126 EVENING GROSBEAK *Hesperiphona vespertinus*   Plate 31
North and Middle America

Coccothraustes vespertina W. Cooper, 1825, Ann. Lyc. Nat. Hist. New York, 1, p. 220, Sault Sainte Marie, Michigan.

IDENTIFICATION Length 18–21·5 cm (7–8½ in). A distinctive, brightly coloured and rather plump or short-tailed North American grosbeak. The male is very obvious in full plumage; females and immatures are much duller or paler but retain characteristic features. Adult male has bright yellow on forehead and supercilium, black crown and brownish nape, face, and breast, becoming bright yellow on rest of upperparts and underparts; tail and wings are black, but tertials and inner secondaries are white. Female is greyer on head, face and upperparts, lacks bright yellow, and has less white on inner wing but white tip to tail. **Confusion species:** When seen well, the male is unlikely to be confused with any other species. Adult male American Goldfinch (65) is smaller and more lightly built, with black forehead to crown, all-black wings and white rump. Male and female Hooded Grosbeak (127) have all-black heads. All similar species of American orioles (e.g. Black-headed *Icterus graduacauda*) are larger, with finer bills and long tails.

DESCRIPTION Sexes differ. **Adult male:** Forehead, over eye to midway along (or rear of) ear-coverts bright yellow; line above bill, and lores and cheeks sooty-brown or black; ear-coverts and sides of neck brown or dark warm brown, lower ear-

♂

coverts sometimes washed with yellow. Crown black or blackish-brown; nape, mantle to centre of upper back (variable in extent) yellowish-brown to rich dark brown, edges of mantle and back yellow; scapulars, lower back and rump bright or deep yellow; uppertail-coverts black, edged and tipped finely with yellow. Black tail is fairly short and indented at tip. Median and greater coverts black, inner greater coverts, inner secondaries and tertials white, finely edged pale yellow in fresh plumage; remainder of coverts, secondaries and all primaries black. Chin and upper throat black or blackish,

♀ *Detail: outer tail feather.*

becoming browner on lower throat and centre of breast or washed lightly with yellow, becoming gradually yellow on sides of lower breast; belly, flanks and undertail-coverts bright yellow, tinged with brown or golden-brown on flanks; thighs blackish. Bill is large, conical, pale greenish-yellow, or pale buffish-horn in winter. Legs and feet flesh-pink. **Adult female:** Forehead to crown and upper nape grey or grey-brown; lores and line above bill to eye dark grey or blackish, rest of face grey or pale grey with ear-coverts yellow-washed. Nape and sides of neck grey or pale grey, washed with yellow; mantle, upper back and scapulars grey or pale olive-grey, washed yellow or brown on upper mantle; lower back and rump yellowish or buffish-brown; uppertail-coverts black, broadly tipped with white; tail black, with large spot of white at tip of each feather. Median and outer greater coverts black, edged finely with pale grey, inner greaters white; alula, primary coverts and flight feathers black, but bases of all primaries white for about 10 mm (showing as patch on closed wing and a short wingbar in flight); innermost secondaries and tertials white on outer web washed grey or brown (brown on inner web), but some show white tips to tertials. Chin or sides of chin white (some show a short indistinct dark submoustachial stripe); throat, sides of throat, breast, belly to upper flanks dull peachy-buff or drab yellow, sometimes tinged with greenish-yellow on belly or flanks; vent and undertail-coverts white or buffish-white. Bill as male or greenish-yellow. **Juvenile:** Similar to adult female, but duller or browner on head, upperparts and underparts; rump is dull brown and uppertail-coverts are black, tipped with pale earth-brown; tail is black, tipped white (increasing in extent outwards). Wings brown or blackish-brown, with secondaries and tertials edged white, inner greater coverts pale lemon-grey (outers brown or blackish-brown), inner primaries with some white at base on inner webs; undertail-coverts white. Juvenile male as juvenile female, but has more lemon-yellow on throat, lacks white at bases of primaries and has very little, if any, white in tail. First-summer males are more like adult males, but generally duller yellow or greenish-yellow and with dark or blackish central stripe to tertials, which are dull pale brown or brownish-

white; uppertail-coverts and tail have some white tips, and yellow forehead has some fine dark streaks.

GEOGRAPHICAL VARIATION Considerable individual variation in plumage of all races, but females of race *brooksi* average darker on body, as does plumage of some males on head, face, mantle and breast.

VOICE Call is a loud sharp 'cleer', 'cleep' or 'peeer', also a soft clicking or chattering note. The song is a rambling erratic or uneven musical warble ending with a whistle.

STATUS, HABITAT AND BEHAVIOUR Common, locally common or irregularly abundant. Breeds in mixed and conifer woods, forests, clusters of trees (usually alders and maples) or copses; in winter, occurs in similar habitat but more often in suburban gardens and parks, where it regularly takes to feeding stations. A gregarious bird found in small parties or flocks. Has a strong or rapid bounding flight. Feeds mainly on seeds of trees and bushes, but occasionally takes buds, grain, fruit and nuts (especially pinyons) also fond of maple sap; occasionally insects are taken, particularly budworms or small beetles or their larvae; at feeders shows a preference for sunflower seeds.

DISTRIBUTION *H. v. vespertinus*: central and eastern Canada from northeast Alberta, central Saskatchewan, southern Manitoba to central Ontario, central Quebec, Newfoundland and Nova Scotia, south to northern Minnesota, northern Michigan, northern New York, Vermont and Massachusetts, northern USA.

H. v brooksi: western Canada from southwest and central British Columbia to western Montana, Wyoming and central Colorado, south through the Rocky Mountains to northwest and central California, northeast Nevada, central Arizona and central-southern New Mexico, southwest USA.

H. v. montanus: southwest USA from southeast Arizona to the mountains of west and southwest Mexico to Michoacan, west and central Vera Cruz and Oaxaca.

Note: The ranges of *vespertinus* and *brooksi* are still expanding east and south.

MOVEMENTS Mostly resident or partially, erratically or irregularly migratory, depending on availability of food. Birds of nominate race winter south to Kansas, northwest Arkansas, Tennessee, South Carolina and northern Georgia, USA; *brooksi* winters south to southern California, southern Arizona, southern New Mexico, west Texas east to South Dakota and Oklahoma. Has occurred (November-February) in Bermuda and occurs irregularly in southeast Alaska, southern Mackenzie and Newfoundland. Vagrant to British Isles (March 1969, March 1980) and Norway (May 1973, May 1975).

MEASUREMENTS Wing of male 105·5–115·5, of female 104·5–111·5; tail 60–69·5; tarsus 19·5–22; bill (exposed culmen) 16–20. Weight 52–63·5.

REFERENCES Farrand *et al.* (1985), Godfrey (1979), Peterson (1980).

127 HOODED GROSBEAK *Hesperiphona abeillei* **Plate 31**

Middle America

Guiraca abeillei Lesson, 1839, Rev. Zool. [Paris], 2, p. 41, Mexico.

♂

♀ *Detail:*
outer tail feather.

IDENTIFICATION Length 15−18 cm (6−7 in). Similar to Evening Grosbeak (126), but male has entire head and face black and female has only lores and crown black. **Confusion species:** Confusion likely only with race *montanus* of Evening Grosbeak (126) in northern Mexico, where the ranges overlap, but male Evening Grosbeak lacks black head and face and has bright yellow forehead and short supercilium, and is darker on throat and breast. Female Evening is more similar, but generally very dull yellowish-grey with pale grey inner greater coverts and secondaries and broad white tips to tail; female Hooded is more yellow on rump and has a well-defined cap (less distinct on juvenile), against generally grey head or crown of female and juvenile Evening; at close range, female Evening has darker centres or inner webs to white or whitish tertials. Calls of both species are distinctive; habitat and altitude preferences may also separate the two.

DESCRIPTION Sexes differ. **Adult male:** Entire head and face to hindneck, sides of neck, chin and throat to centre of upper breast black. Mantle, back and scapulars yellow or lightly tinged dull yellow, or tinged with olive on mantle and upper back; lower back and rump bright yellow; uppertail-coverts yellow, the longer ones edged and tipped black. Black tail is only slightly indented at tip. Wing-coverts black, as are primaries, inner greater coverts (and sometimes edges of scapulars), secondaries and tertials white or silvery-grey, latter edged with yellow in fresh plumage. Underparts bright or deep yellow or dull yellow, thighs black or blackish but edged with yellow. Bill is large, stout and heavy-looking, deep at base, uniform pale greenish-yellow. Legs and feet pale flesh or pinkish-brown. **Adult female:** Forehead, crown (and sides of crown) to nape black, forming a cap. Mantle, back and scapulars olive or olive-green with a strong wash of yellow (especially in fresh plumage); rump paler or more yellow, as are uppertail-coverts, which are indistinctly tipped whitish. Tail black, but outer feathers tipped with

white. Wings as adult male, but inner greater coverts and (some) scapulars pale grey or greyish-white; also has small square of white at base of inner primaries. Lores blackish; cheeks and ear-coverts pale olive-green washed with yellow, becoming more strongly yellow or greenish-yellow on sides of neck. Chin and feathers at base of lower mandible black or blackish, centre of chin pale buffish-brown or whitish; throat, breast and flanks pale greenish or yellow or yellowish-brown; belly, vent and undertail-coverts light buffish-brown or whitish. Bill as male but slightly duller. **Juvenile:** Young birds closely resemble adult female, but face is brighter yellow and less tinged with olive-green; young males have dark inner webs to tertials, and underparts are brighter yellow or yellowish-buff than on adult females.

VOICE Call is 'beebink' or 'bree-bink', 'bre-bruk', a sharp 'beet beet' or a loud 'clew-clew' or 'tyew-tyew', also a single 'clee' and a harsh 'jerr'. The song is a variation of the call, 'be-be jerr chee' or 'be-be chee', also a buzzing 'wij-ee-er-tee' (last syllable rising) or 'bee-bink-beeaw' with the first two syllables on the same scale and the third descending.

STATUS, HABITAT AND BEHAVIOUR Locally common to rare. Found in high-level forest between 1000 m and 3350 m, especially cloud forest above 1200 m and damp, humid or moist oak woods, also pine, oak and fir forest or edges of forest; also known to frequent gardens, parks or orchards and edges of cultivation. Usually in pairs or loose flocks of up to 40 or 50; often perches at top of dead trees or on exposed perches at tops of trees. Flight high, often covering some distance. Feeds on berries and seeds of trees.

DISTRIBUTION *H. a. abeillei:* central Mexico, Sierra de Juarez, Vera Cruz to northern Oaxaca; also in the highlands of Michoacan east to Puebla, and in the western Sierra Madre del Sur, Guerrero, southern Mexico.

H. a. pallida: Sierra Madre Occidental of southern Chihuahua and western Durango, northwest Mexico.

H. a. *saturata*: Sierra Madre Oriental, southern Tamaulipas and eastern San Luis Potosi, Mexico.

H. a. *cobanensis*: Chiapas, southern Mexico, to central Guatemala and northwest El Salvador.

MOVEMENTS Resident or sedentary, but some may descend to valleys and foothills in the non-breeding season.

MEASUREMENTS Wing of *cobanensis* 100–106. Weight of *abeillei* 46.

REFERENCES Irby Davis (1972), Edwards (1972), Peterson and Chalif (1973).

GENUS *PYRRHOPLECTES*

One species. A generally shy species of the Himalayas and southwest China, of uncertain affinities but possibly most closely related to bullfinches. Within the finch genera, the head patch and black plumage of the male are unique.

128 GOLD-NAPED FINCH (Gold-crowned Black Finch, Gold-headed Black Finch) *Pyrrhoplectes epauletta* Plate 31

Southern Palearctic

Pyrrhula epauletta Hodgson, 1836, Asiatic Researches, 19, p. 156, northern and central Nepal.

IDENTIFICATION Length 15 cm (6 in). A very obvious but shy and infrequently seen finch, but when seen well is very distinctive; even females are unlikely to be confused with any other species. Both sexes have white edges to tertials (forming two short tramlines). Male is almost entirely black, except for bright orange crown and nape and white inner edges to tertials; female is similar, but more generally warm or rufous-brown on body, with deep olive or yellow crown, nape and face; mantle and back are grey and wings (except coverts) are blackish. Note: A species of uncertain affinities; most similar to bullfinches (113–118) in body and bill shape, call and certain actions and habits, but considered sufficiently separate or isolated to warrant its own genus.

DESCRIPTION Sexes differ. **Adult male:** Almost entirely jet-black, relieved only by bright or deep orange on crown (or on some hindcrown) to nape and at sides of breast (hence *epauletta*), though can be absent on latter or appear as a line at edge of bend of wing; wings are slightly glossed black, with inner edges or webs of tertials white and forming two very distinctive longitudinal white lines down back. Underparts slightly duller black or very dark charcoal-grey, with (usually visible only at close range) slight tinge of orange-brown in centre of belly. In flight, shows white on underwing-coverts. Bill short, with curved culmen, slightly pointed, and black. Legs and feet greyish, dark grey or even fleshy-grey. **Adult female:** Forehead to lores and just below eye dark olive-grey; cheeks and ear-coverts similar or slightly paler grey, washed with olive or olive-green. Crown and nape similar but edged and tipped with olive or dark olive-green, more plainly olive-green on nape; sides of neck grey or dark grey. Mantle, upper back and scapulars grey or dark grey; lower back, rump and uppertail-coverts warm brown or chestnut. Tail dark brown or blackish-brown. Median and greater coverts warm brown, edged slightly brighter brown; alula and primary coverts dark brown or blackish-brown; primaries and secondaries black or blackish; outer web of tertials edged bright or warm chestnut, inner edges white. Underparts almost entirely warm rufous or deep cinnamon-brown, breast browner with paler warm brown on belly; thighs greyish, underwing-coverts white. **Juvenile:** As adult female, but generally duller or more dusky brown. First-winter birds resemble adult female but are darker or chestnut on upperparts, with a few yellow-orange feathers showing on nape; throat, breast and belly as adult female, but flecked with black. First-summer birds as adults, but with partial juvenile plumage present in patches in early summer.

VOICE Call is distinctive, thin, high-pitched and repeated whistle, 'teeu', 'tseu' or 'peeuu', also 'purl-lee' and a squeaky 'plee-e-e'. Song is a rapid high-pitched 'pi-pi-pi-pi', but also gives a soft or low Bullfinch-like piping.

STATUS, HABITAT AND BEHAVIOUR Local, fairly common or rare. Inhabits undergrowth in high-level oak and rhododendron forest and breeds between 2800 m and 3900 m, also found in ringal bamboo, usually commonest in or near rhododendron thickets, where it may breed (nest unknown); in winter in Sikkim, it favours patches of nettles. Mostly in pairs in summer or in small flocks of no more than six to eight; shy and secretive, keeps to interior of bushes or undergrowth, often low or on the ground. Frequently mixes with other roaming flocks of finches in winter and often in company of various forest-dwelling rosefinches, notably Red-headed (107) and Dark (86). Feeds on a variety of seeds (including nettles), buds, berries and insects; usually very quiet or unobtrusive when feeding.

DISTRIBUTION Monotypic. Himalayas from

northern Punjab, northwest India, east through Nepal to Sikkim, Assam, Bhutan, Arunachal Pradesh, northeast India to southeast Tibet, southern Szechwan and northwest Yunnan (Likiang range), western China.

MOVEMENTS An altitudinal migrant but also disperses from breeding range, in winter descending to between 1400 m and 3300 m, thus many high-level breeders winter at lower levels of breeding range; also occurs in late winter (February-April) in northeast Burma.

MEASUREMENTS Wing of male 75–80, of female 74–77; tail of male 54–62, of female 53–56; tarsus 19–20; bill (from skull) 12–15. Weight c19.

REFERENCES Ali and Ripley (1983), Fleming *et al.* (1979).

GENUS *PARMOPTILA*

Two species. Ant-peckers, previously placed with warblers, tits and flowerpeckers but now classified as aberrant finches on nesting behaviour and mouth pattern of nestlings. Extremely specialised food requirements are assisted by the development of a slender bill and brush tongue.

129 FLOWERPECKER WEAVER-FINCH (Ant-pecker) *Parmoptila woodhousei*   Plate 38

Africa

Parmoptila woodhousei Cassin, 1859, Proc. Acad. Nat. Sci. Philadelphia, 11, p. 40, Camma River, Gabon.

IDENTIFICATION Length 11 cm (4¼ in). A small, short-tailed and almost warbler-like finch, with a fine thin bill (used largely for feeding on ants) and short rounded wings. Male has warm reddish-brown forehead and dull orange face and throat, dull brown upperparts and mottled brown underparts; female is similar but lacks red forehead. **Confusion species:** The buffish, mottled or spotted underparts distinguish adults from adult male Red-fronted Flowerpecker Weaver-Finch (130) which is also much darker brown above. Female has a warm brown face, chin and throat, lacking on Red-fronted *rubrifrons* (which is finely barred dark brown). Juveniles are probably inseparable in the field on their own where the ranges overlap. Note: Has been considered conspecific with Red-fronted Flowerpecker Weaver-Finch, but ranges overlap in central Zaire apparently without their interbreeding.

DESCRIPTION Sexes similar but separable. **Adult male:** Forehead reddish-orange, becoming warm rich brown on sides of face, chin and throat; lores to slightly behind eye dusky or dingy brown. Crown, nape, mantle, back, rump, scapulars and wing-coverts dull or dark earth-brown with fine pale buff-brown shaft streaks, tips of crown and nape (and on some upper mantle) light buffish or orange-brown; tips of greater coverts finely spotted with warm buff-brown. Flight feathers (including alula and primary coverts) slightly darker earth-brown. Tail dark earth-brown, with paler or warm buff edges to outer feathers. Underparts below throat white or very pale buff and spotted or mottled with brown or olive-brown, occasionally in small crescents on belly, flanks and undertail-coverts. Black bill is thin and fine. Eye red or reddish-brown. Legs and feet variable, from flesh-pink to pale greyish or grey-brown; quite long-legged for a small bird. **Adult female:** Very similar to adult male, but forehead to crown and nape brown with buff tips, at close range showing darker shaft streaks on lower mantle and scapulars; underparts duller than male's, with pattern broken or interrupted with small dark spots. **Juvenile:** Similar to adults, but with slightly duller brown upperparts; has rich or reddish-brown underparts with slightly darker tips to some feathers, and is paler or buff on thighs and undertail-coverts.

GEOGRAPHICAL VARIATION Race *ansorgei* is slightly larger and generally paler or more olive-brown on upperparts; males have less visible red on forehead.

VOICE Call is a loud clicking note of varying pitch or length. The song is unrecorded.

STATUS, HABITAT AND BEHAVIOUR Uncommon, but very secretive and easily overlooked. Found in lowland dense undergrowth of secondary forest, forest edge or damp or swamp forest, occasionally in open scrub, where it feeds low down or on ground. Social, often found in small groups mixing with other species in foraging parties. Feeds on insects, particularly ants and mainly worker ants, which it gathers with its brush-like tongue.

DISTRIBUTION *P. w. woodhousei*: southeast Nigeria east to Cameroon and southern Central African Republic south to central and western Zaire.

P. w. ansorgei: northern Angola to southwest Zaire.

MOVEMENTS None known of any distance, but forages widely when not breeding.

MEASUREMENTS Wing of male 48–53, of female 49–52; tail 36–40; tarsus 14·5–15·5; bill 10–11.

130 RED-FRONTED FLOWERPECKER WEAVER-FINCH (Red-fronted Ant-pecker) *Parmoptila rubrifrons*   Plate 38

Africa

Pholidornis rubrifrons Sharpe and Ussher, 1872, Ibis, p. 182, Denkera, Ghana.

IDENTIFICATION Length 10–11 cm (4–4¼ in). A small warbler-like finch with a short thin bill and rounded wings. The male has dull or dark brown upperparts with a bright red forehead, and chestnut or deep rich brown underparts. Females are similar to Flowerpecker Weaver-finch (129), dull olive or drab earth-brown above with a finely spotted head and face, and with heavily spotted underparts. **Confusion species:** Likely to be confused only with Flowerpecker Weaver-finch: males are quite distinctive, with rich chestnut underparts; females lack Flowerpecker's bright warm brown or chestnut chin and throat and are generally paler below. Juveniles of the two are very similar, separable by the intensity of coloration of underparts. Note: Previously considered (and may still be) conspecific with Flowerpecker Weaver-finch.

DESCRIPTION Sexes differ. **Adult male:** Forehead to crown bright red. Lores, cheeks, ear-coverts to sides of crown and neck olive or earth-brown, finely spotted or tipped with white or pale buff. Hindcrown and nape to mantle, back and scapulars deep brown or olive-brown with paler buffish-brown tips to feathers (some prominently marked with pale tips). Wing-coverts brown or dark earth-brown, often showing buff tips; flight feathers dull or dark olive-brown. Tail is rounded at tip, dark olive-brown. Chin pale buff; rest of underparts rich or deep cinnamon-brown, some with dark or blackish feather tips to flanks. Black and pointed bill is slim or fine, with a curved ridge to upper mandible. Eye red or reddish-brown. Legs and feet dusky brown to greyish or pale brown. **Adult female:** Similar to adult female Flowerpecker Weaver-finch, but has a finely spotted forehead to crown and face and more prominently spotted underparts, which are cleaner, whiter, with spots larger and more widely spaced. **Juvenile:** Very similar to juvenile Flowerpecker Weaver-finch and a slightly paler version of adult male Red-fronted, but without red on head; except for a few small spots or speckles on forehead, face is dark brown finely spotted with orange-buff, crown and back unspotted; underparts pale orange-buff or light buffish-brown, with poorly defined dusky brown bars or tips to virtually all feathers.

GEOGRAPHICAL VARIATION Adult males of race *jamesoni* have entire face and chin chestnut, uniform with rest of underparts.

VOICE Unknown.

STATUS, HABITAT AND BEHAVIOUR A scarce and relatively little-known bird, its nest is unknown. Inhabits forest clearings, edges and scrub, where it forages in dense foliage and dead leaves, usually in the undergrowth or at mid-height level; not known to feed on ground. Usually occurs in pairs or small parties, has been recorded in mixed-species parties. Actions recall a warbler, or forages in dead leaves tit-fashion. Feeds mainly on insects, principally ants and their pupae, also small beetles; occasionally takes some seeds.

DISTRIBUTION *P. r. rubrifrons*: present distribution poorly known but discontinuously from Mount Nimba, Liberia, to (southern Mali? and) south-central Ghana.

P. r. jamesoni: eastern Congo and northern Zaire, Semliki valley north to lower Uelle River and western Uganda.

MEASUREMENTS Wing of female 49; tail c42; tarsus 14; bill 10.

REFERENCE Bannerman (1953).

GENUS *NIGRITA*

Four species. Negro-finches, with well-defined differences in size and bill shape between species. The mouth markings of nestlings and the nesting behaviour place them (with the similarly aberrant *Parmoptila*) at the extreme of the estrildids.

131 WHITE-BREASTED NEGRO-FINCH *Nigrita fusconota*   Plate 34

Africa

Nigrita fusconotus Fraser, 1843, Proc. Zool. Soc. London, 1842, p. 145, Clarence, Fernando Po.

IDENTIFICATION Length 10 cm (4 in). A small warbler-like finch with a glossy blue-black crown, face and tail and pale brown mantle, back and wings. Chin and throat are pure white, rest of underparts duller or off-white. Wings are short and rounded, and tail is graduated with central pair of feathers prominent. Confusion with other species unlikely once seen well. Black-crowned Waxbill (184) is superficially similar, but has entirely different habits, bill shape and, more obviously, a bright red rump.

DESCRIPTION Sexes similar. **Adult male:** Forehead to crown and upper nape, upper lores, cheeks and ear-coverts glossy dark blue (appears black in the field); lower nape, mantle, back and scapulars pale brown, slightly paler or yellowish on mantle and scapulars; lower rump, uppertail-coverts and graduated tail glossy blue-black. Median and greater coverts as scapulars or slightly duller; alula, primary coverts and flight feathers a deep glossy blue-black, except for inner secondaries and tertials, which are brown or pale brown. Chin, throat and sides of lower face pure white; breast, belly and undertail-coverts white, greyish-white or pale grey, but can also show pure white on belly. Black bill is short, pointed and slightly flattened at base, with hooked tip. Eye dark brown to dark red. Legs and feet grey, varying in tone from dark grey to greenish-grey. **Adult female:** On average slightly paler brown on upperparts and less grey on underparts than male. **Juvenile:** Similar to adult, but has crown to nape dull blackish-brown, rump and tail are more dark brown than black, and underparts are washed or tinged with grey or greyish-buff.

GEOGRAPHICAL VARIATION Race *uropygialis* has a much paler, almost buff, whitish-buff or pale buffish-fawn rump, and mantle and back are more tawny than dull brown, with some dark brown tips; legs and feet dark brown. There is also variation within races, as some can be greyish on throat and breast.

VOICE Call is a repeated high-pitched trilling on a descending scale, 'tz-tz-tz-tzeee'. The song is a short phrase, rising and falling, becoming softer and lower in pitch until it ends with separate 'chip-chip-chip' notes or just fades away; usually delivered from the topmost branches of a tall tree; song period April to October.

STATUS, HABITAT AND BEHAVIOUR Fairly common to locally common but nowhere numerous. A bird of gallery forest, forest edges and clearings, including areas of mature forest, secondary growth and understorey scrub, though spends much time in tops of trees where largely overlooked; usually occurs below 1400 m. Singly, in pairs or occasionally small parties. Forages by searching leaves in warbler-fashion. Feeds on a variety of insects and caterpillars, also some fruit, berries, outer oily cases of oil-palm nuts and small seeds.

DISTRIBUTION *N. f. fusconota*: southeast Nigeria, Cameroon, Gabon and Fernando Po south to the Cuanza valley, Angola, and northern Zaire, east through the Central African Republic to south and west Uganda and western Kenya (Mount Elgon and the Kakamega Forest).

N. f. uropygialis: Mount Nimba, Liberia, and southeast Guinea to southern Ghana and southwest Nigeria.

MOVEMENTS None long-distance, but wanders at random throughout range when not breeding.

MEASUREMENTS Wing 49–56; tail 40–47; tarsus 14; bill 9. Wing of *uropygialis* 48–54; tail 44–50.

REFERENCES Bannerman (1953), Bates (1930), Chapin (1954), Serle (1965).

---

132 CHESTNUT-BREASTED NEGRO-FINCH *Nigrita bicolor*   Plate 34
Africa

Pytelia bicolor Hartlaub, 1844, Syst. Verz. Naturh. Samml. Ges. Mus. [Bremen], Abth., p. 76, Gold Coast.

IDENTIFICATION Length 11–12 cm (4½ in). A small, shy or secretive, dark-plumaged bird. It has slate or dark grey (tinged brownish on some) upperparts, with a fairly short black or blackish graduated or fan-shaped tail, and deep chestnut-brown or maroon face and underparts. A fairly conspicuous bird when seen well, causing little confusion with any other species. Male Red-fronted Flowerpecker Weaver-finch (130) is superficially similar, but differs considerably in slim and pointed bill, shape and habits and is also paler (more reddish) below, with dark face mottled or finely spotted with white. Juveniles are also possibly confusable with those of Red-fronted Flowerpecker Weaver-finch, which are smaller and more uniformly orange on underparts.

DESCRIPTION Sexes alike. **Adult:** Forehead, lores, sides of crown, cheeks to rear of ear-coverts, sides of neck and entire underparts a deep chestnut with a tinge of maroon. Forecrown, crown and rest of upperparts a very dark slate-grey, tinged slightly or noticeably brown on some, darker or browner on wings and blacker on tail. Tail rounded at rest, but clearly graduated in flight or when spread. Black bill is short, and deep at base. Eye red or reddish-brown. Legs and feet dark brown. Some adult females are separable from males by thinner band of chestnut or maroon on forehead. **Juvenile:** Generally dull brown or olive-brown with a tinge of grey on upperparts, but has grey-buff on throat, becoming pale brown with a tinge of orange-buff or light chestnut on breast and belly when adult plumage begins to show through in irregular patches. Wings and tail as adult. Eye brown; bill blackish, sometimes paler at base of lower mandible.

GEOGRAPHICAL VARIATION Eastern birds of race *brunnescens* are slightly larger and generally somewhat duller than nominate, more brown or brownish-grey above, especially on crown, mantle and back, and more brown or deep chestnut than maroon on underparts. In eastern Zaire, some males are darker and richer in colour and some females are lighter on underparts (previously separated as *N. b. saturatior*).

VOICE Call is a sad or mournful 'chi-chi-hooeee'. The song is a similar-quality low 'kiyu-kiyu-weh-weh-weh', often delivered from a treetop but also from lower growth.

STATUS, HABITAT AND BEHAVIOUR Common or locally common. Widespread in forest, forest clearings, glades and edges, also found in secondary-growth areas, in trees or woods at edges of cultivation, in thick bush, and mangrove scrub. Usually in pairs or small, occasionally mixed, feeding parties (has been seen in mixed flocks with White-breasted (131) and Grey-headed (134) Negro-finches in the Kakamega Forest in western Kenya), but often alone. Occurs at varying heights, from ground level to treetops, but most commonly in the undergrowth or understorey level; generally shy and easily overlooked. Feeds on a variety of insects and small caterpillars, occasionally small seeds and not infrequently the husks of oil-palm nuts, also ripe fruit of some trees, and has been known to take the eggs of tree frogs.

DISTRIBUTION *N. b. bicolor*: extreme southwest Senegal (and possibly western Gambia), Guinea to Sierra Leone, Liberia (Mount Nimba) and southern Mali to Ghana.

N. b. brunnescens: Principe Island, southern Nigeria and Cameroon to western Uganda, western Kenya (Kakamega Forest) south to northern Zaire and northwest Angola (Quincolungo).

MOVEMENTS Wanders at random throughout the range when not breeding.

MEASUREMENTS Wing 53–59; tail 36–43; tarsus 15; bill 10. Wing of *brunnescens* 57–64; tail 39–45.

REFERENCES Bannerman (1953), Mackworth-Praed and Grant (1960).

---

133 PALE-FRONTED NEGRO-FINCH *Nigrita luteifrons*   Plate 34

Africa

Nigrita luteifrons J. and E. Verreaux, 1851, Rev. Mag. Zool. [Paris], ser. 2, p. 420, Gabon.

IDENTIFICATION Length 11·5 cm (4½ in). A small and somewhat short-billed finch with face and most of underparts entirely black. It has plain grey upperparts with pale yellowish-buff or white forehead, and black or blackish flight feathers and tail. Females are virtually all grey, with some white or yellowish-buff on forehead and black lores and around eyes. **Confusion species:** Very similar (especially adult male) to larger Grey-headed Negro-finch (134), from which it can be separated by shorter and smaller bill, pale forehead and lack of white spots on coverts and tertials; the tail is also slightly shorter. Immatures are unlikely to be separable on their own, apart from by size.

DESCRIPTION Sexes differ. **Adult male:** Forehead variably pale buff, yellowish or pale yellowish-white to grey, becoming plain pale grey on crown and rest of upperparts, slightly darker on mantle, back and scapulars and paler (almost white on some) on rump. Black tail is short and rounded. Median and greater coverts, alula and primary coverts to tertials very deep or blackish-grey; secondaries and primaries black, edged slightly glossy bluish-black. Face from lores over eyes and sides of neck and entire underparts black with a slight deep bluish gloss. Black bill is quite short and thick, with a curved culmen. Eye red. Legs and feet flesh or pinkish-brown to grey-brown. **Adult female:** Forehead lightly off-white or pale buff; rest of upperparts, including sides of neck, plain slate-grey, paler or whitish on rump and uppertail-coverts. Wing-coverts dark grey or blackish-grey; flight feathers black or slightly glossy blue. Tail is black with a slight bluish gloss. Lores and broadly around eye black forming 'spectacles'. Underparts entirely pale grey. Eye yellow, pale grey or whitish. Legs as male, feet pale buff. **Juvenile:** Similar to adult female, but can show white patches on forehead and crown, lacks black around eye, and forehead is uniform with dark crown; upperparts are dull, dark or drab grey, and underparts brownish-grey, tinged with buff in places.

GEOGRAPHICAL VARIATION Birds from Fernando Po, *alexanderi*, are slightly larger, with a slightly thicker bill, and pale yellow or buff of forehead extends to crown and nape; eye is black.

VOICE Call is a faint musical whistling 'choo', repeated every few seconds. The song is a pleasant simple phrase descending in scale.

STATUS, HABITAT AND BEHAVIOUR Uncommon or only locally common, but not uncommon on Fernando Po; easily overlooked where Grey-crowned Negro-finch occurs. Little known and probably under-recorded. Inhabits forest, mainly clearings or forest edge, also found in secondary growth or even open scrub, usually alone or in pairs, and spends much time quite high up in the foliage. Feeds on a variety of insects (particularly scale insects), and has been known to visit flowers, often in company with sunbirds (Nectariniidae), and perform aerial flycatching manoeuvres, though mainly a shy and quiet foliage-searcher; also takes some seeds, ripe fruit such as figs and husks of oil-palm fruits.

DISTRIBUTION *N. l. luteifrons*: southern Nigeria (except the east) to Cameroon and Central African

Republic, northern Zaire, western Uganda (Bwamba Forest), Gabon and northwest Angola (Quincolungo); has also been recorded once (two together) in southern Ghana.

N. l. alexanderi: Fernando Po (Bioko).

MEASUREMENTS Wing 55–61; tail 33–41; tarsus 14; bill 9. Wing of *alexanderi* 58–65; tail 33–40.
REFERENCES Bannerman (1953), Chapin (1954), Serle (1965).

134 GREY-HEADED NEGRO-FINCH *Nigrita canicapilla*   Plate 34

Africa

Aethiops canicapillus Strickland, 1841, Proc. Zool. Soc. London, p. 30, Fernando Po.

IDENTIFICATION Length 15 cm (6 in). Similar to Pale-fronted Negro-finch (133), but distinctly larger (the largest of the negro-finches). Very striking, with black forehead, face, wings and tail; most races have large white spots on tips to coverts and tertials; entire underparts are black. Upperparts from forehead to back grey or dark grey, with pale or white rump (particularly noticeable in flight). **Confusion species:** Very similar to slightly smaller male Pale-fronted Negro-finch, but Grey-headed has black broadly across forehead, and most races have white border to sides of nape and pale grey or whitish rump, together with prominent white spots to tips of coverts and tertials (spots lacking only on West African race *emiliae*, which is mostly outside the range of Pale-fronted.
DESCRIPTION Sexes alike. **Adult:** Forehead, face, sides of neck and entire underparts jet-black. Forecrown whitish and crown and sides of nape pale grey or whitish-grey, forming a border to black. Hindcrown and nape plain grey, becoming slightly darker on mantle, scapulars and back, lower scapulars darker grey with white tips; rump whitish-grey or white; uppertail-coverts dark grey, tipped paler. Black tail is long and slightly rounded. Median and greater coverts black, as are alula and primary coverts, but white tips to some coverts form an irregular or erratic pattern; flight feathers and tertials also black, latter also with white tips. Black bill is broad and flattened at base, quite slender, with a hooked tip to upper mandible. Eye yellow, orange-red, red or reddish-brown. Legs and feet dark brown, dark grey or greyish-brown. Adult female is slightly duskier grey above, with smaller white spots; underparts are generally more smoky-black, but there is considerable individual variation; bill is slightly smaller than male's. **Juvenile:** Almost entirely sooty-grey or dull blackish with a faint indication of adult face pattern and a few faint white spots on tips of some wing-coverts and tertials, also paler or greyish on rump. Size and shape of bill is also a useful field character. Eye light grey.
GEOGRAPHICAL VARIATION West African race *emiliae* is somewhat smaller, lacks white border between black underparts and grey sides of nape, rump is almost the same colour as back and mantle, and white spots on wing-coverts and tertials are greatly reduced to small crescents or only tips of some feathers; similarly in juveniles, white or pale spots are less prominent than in nominate.

Both *angolensis* and *schistacea* have deeper or darker grey on upperparts *diabolica*, in addition to having all sooty-grey upperparts, has very dull black underparts. Both *angolensis* and *diabolica* have well-marked white spots at tips of greater coverts, but these are reduced (or absent) in *schistacea* (especially in east of range). Isolated race *candida* is similar to *schistacea*, but has crown, nape and upper mantle as well as rump whitish or very pale whitish-grey.
VOICE Call is an unmistakable, clear and far-reaching plaintive three-note whistle, 'hooeee, hoooeeee, hooo' or 'tyea-tyea-tyea', usually delivered from a series of preferred songposts within the bird's territory all year round.
STATUS, HABITAT AND BEHAVIOUR Locally common. Found in mature and secondary forest or forest edges or clearings, also in gallery or riverine forest and plantations, especially those near water; has a preference for tall trees, including those in cocoa plantations and oil palms. Occurs at up to 1500 m throughout most of the range, but up to 2150 m in Uganda and 2400 m in southern Sudan and eastern Zaire (though most are found below 1500 m); in Kenya and Tanzania it is exclusively a bird of the highlands, occurring between 1700 m and 3350 m. Solitary, but often in pairs or small parties, frequently associating with sunbirds; occasionally tame or approachable, and considered by some to be inquisitive towards man. Feeds in treetops, creepers and shrubs and rarely near the ground; diet is mainly fruit, including ripe figs and the oily husk of the oil palm, also some insects and caterpillars and occasionally (though apparently not taken by all birds) some small seeds.
DISTRIBUTION N. c. *canicapilla*: southern Benin, southern and eastern Nigeria (unknown in the north) and Fernando Po east through Cameroon to the Central African Republic, western Zaire and Uganda; has also been recorded on the borders of extreme southern Sudan.

N. c. *emiliae*: Guinea and Sierra Leone west to Ghana and Togo; has also been recorded once in southern Mali, in March.

N. c. *angolensis*: southwest Zaire to northwest Angola.

N. c. *schistacea*: southeast Sudan (Imatong Mountains), south and west Uganda, northern Zaire, western Kenya and northern Tanzania.

N. c. *diabolica*: Mount Kenya, through central

and southeast Kenya to Crater highlands and Mount Kilimanjaro, northern Tanzania.

N. c. candida: Kungwe-Mahari Mountains, western Tanzania.

MEASUREMENTS Wing 65–72; tail 42–50; tar-

sus c16; bill 12. Wing of *emiliae* 62–67; tail 39–47.

REFERENCES Bannerman (1953), Lamarche (1981), Mackworth-Praed and Grant (1960), Traylor and Archer (1982).

GENUS *NESOCHARIS*

Three species. Olive-backs, very distinctively patterned in olive-green, black and deep grey, with rounded wings and short tails. Very acrobatic feeders, and one, White-collared Olive-back (136), is adapted to feed entirely on the seeds of one plant. They are possibly most closely related to crimson-wings *Cryptospiza*.

135 FERNANDO PO OLIVE-BACK (Shelley's Olive-back, Little Olive Weaver) *Nesocharis shelleyi*   Plate 35
West Africa

Nesocharis shelleyi Alexander, 1903, Bull. Brit. Ornith. Club, 13, p. 48, Moka, Fernando Po.

IDENTIFICATION Length 8·5 cm (3¼ in). A very small (almost minute), short-winged, short-tailed bird with a glossy black hood and greyish collar; mantle and back are yellowish-olive, becoming golden-yellow on rump, and breast is golden-olive, becoming bluish-grey on rest of underparts. Females are similar, but have whole underside bluish-grey. **Confusion species:** The grey collar and colour of underparts are diagnostic. The very similar White-collared Olive-back (136), with which it is sometimes treated as conspecific, is larger, longer-tailed and separated geographically.

DESCRIPTION Sexes differ. **Adult male:** Entire head to nape, sides of neck, chin and upper throat glossy black; lower nape to sides of neck pale grey or bluish-grey, becoming a thin white band on lower sides of throat. Mantle, back and scapulars yellowish olive-green, becoming golden-tinged on rump and uppertail-coverts. Black tail is square, short and partially hidden by long uppertail-coverts. Wing-coverts and tertials similar to mantle and scapulars but duller; flight feathers dark grey or blackish, edged with olive. Lower throat and breast a deep yellowish-olive, similar to mantle and back; belly, flanks and undertail-coverts bluish-grey. Grey or blue-grey, dark-tipped bill is fairly slender, upper mandible curving to a point. Eye brown. Legs and feet grey, greyish-brown or brown. **Adult female:** Resembles adult male or duller and less yellow, more olive, on upperparts, especially rump and uppertail-coverts; white on sides of neck is reduced to a thin line, and entire underparts below black hood are blue or bluish-grey. **Juvenile:** Like adult female but much duller or more olive, with yellow tones much reduced.

Underparts are tinged brownish, and legs and feet are dark or slate-grey.

GEOGRAPHICAL VARIATION Race *bansoensis* is very similar to nominate, but slightly larger (on average) and somewhat darker olive-green or olive-grey on upperparts.

VOICE Call is a continuous high-pitched twittering of very thin sharp notes, including both loud and soft phrases.

STATUS, HABITAT AND BEHAVIOUR Locally common. Inhabits mountain-forest edges and clearings, also found in plantations (usually cocoa), scrub or bushy savanna; in Cameroon occurs above 1200 m, but on Fernando Po occurs mostly at sea level. An active bird, foraging in tops of thickly leaved trees in small roving parties, rather acrobatic and tit-like in actions, often hanging upside-down (even by one foot); also known to feed low down in tall grass. Its nest or eggs have never been found. Feeds on a variety of small insects and seeds, occasionally some ripe fruit.

DISTRIBUTION *N. s. shelleyi*: Moka highlands, Fernando Po and west Cameroon (Mount Cameroon).

N. s. bansoensis: highlands of Cameroon.

Also occurs on the Obudu plateau, southeast Nigeria, although race involved is not known (probably *bansoensis*).

MEASUREMENTS Wing 42–45; tail 24–25. Wing of *bansoensis* 45–48; tail 28–31; tarsus 14; bill 9.

REFERENCES Bannerman (1953), Mackworth-Praed and Grant (1960).

136 WHITE-COLLARED OLIVE-BACK (Olive Weaver-Finch)
Nesocharis ansorgei   **Plate 35**
Africa

Pytelia ansorgei Hartert, 1899, Bull. Brit. Ornith. Club, 10, p. 26, Wemo [Wimi] River, Toro, Uganda.

IDENTIFICATION Length 10 cm (4 in). Very similar to smaller Fernando Po Olive-back (135), from which it is widely separated geographically. All-black head to chin and throat, distinctive half-collar of grey around nape and white on lower throat and sides of throat are diagnostic. Upperparts deep olive-green, breast and upper flanks similar to upperparts, but belly to undertail greyish. Particularly fond of marshy areas. Unlikely to be confused with Fernando Po Olive-back (considered conspecific by some authorities); latter, apart from differences in range and habitat, has a different bill shape and lacks lower white half-collar.
DESCRIPTION Sexes similar but separable. **Adult male:** Entire head to chin and throat black. Hindneck to sides of neck grey, becoming white on sides of lower neck (below cheeks) and quite broadly across throat, forming an entire two-tone collar. Mantle, back, scapulars, wing-coverts to rump and uppertail-coverts rich or deep olive-green, brighter or tinged with yellow on rump and uppertail-coverts. Flight feathers short, dark grey or blackish, edged with olive-green; tail black. Breast same colour as mantle and back; belly, lower flanks and undertail-coverts pale or light grey. Bill is short and stubby, deep at base, and black (occasionally with blue-grey base). Eye dark brown. Legs and feet dark grey. **Adult female:** Very

similar to adult male but much duller, with less grey on nape and hindneck and entirely grey or greyish-buff on underparts from breast. **Juvenile:** Undescribed, but apparently similar to adult female.
VOICE Call is rarely heard; occasional lisping or 'tsssp' notes recalling a sunbird. The song is a pleasant trill beginning with two short individual notes.
STATUS, HABITAT AND BEHAVIOUR Locally common. A shy and probably much-overlooked species within its small or fairly restricted range. Favours typically marshy areas, streamsides, clearings in damp forest or edges of forest, also in bushes or thickets near water between 1000 m and 1970 m. Occurs in pairs or small family parties. Agile and tit-like in its actions, often holding seedhead in one foot while pecking out seeds parrot-fashion. Feeds on seeds, possibly exclusively of the plant *Melanthera scandens* (syn. *brownei*).
DISTRIBUTION Monotypic. Discontinuously through eastern Zaire, western Uganda, northern Rwanda and recently recorded in extreme northwest Tanzania.
MEASUREMENTS Wing 50.
REFERENCES Chapin (1954), Friedmann (1968), Mackworth-Praed and Grant (1960).

137 GREY-HEADED OLIVE-BACK (White-cheeked Olive Weaver, White-cheeked Waxbill) *Nesocharis capistrata*   **Plate 35**
Africa

Pytelia capistrata Hartlaub, 1861, Journ. f. Ornith., 9, p. 259, Bissao, Portuguese Guinea.

IDENTIFICATION Length 14 cm (5½ in). A small, fairly plump and almost tit-like bird with a distinctive head pattern: grey crown, white face and black chin and throat. Underparts generally grey, contrasting with bright yellow flanks and olive-green upperparts; short, rounded wings and rounded tip to tail. Unlikely to be confused with any other species.
DESCRIPTION Sexes alike. **Adult:** Upper forehead, crown and nape to sides of neck pale grey or bluish-grey; face and across lower forehead silvery-white or very pale grey. Mantle, back and scapulars to rump and uppertail-coverts bright olive or olive-green tinged with yellow; wings the same, but inner webs of flight feathers are brown

or pale brown. Tail as upperparts, but has inner webs brown or grey-brown. Black on chin and throat extends to below cheeks; breast to centre of belly and undertail-coverts pale grey; upper flanks bright yellow, becoming light green on lower flanks. Grey bill is fairly deep at base, short and stubby and with curved culmen. Eye deep red or reddish-brown. Legs and feet dark grey or blackish. In worn plumage, olive becomes darker but tips of feathers more yellow, creating a slightly scaly effect. **Juvenile:** Similar to adult, but with forehead, crown, nape and face all dark grey; olive and grey parts of plumage much darker. Flanks are dull buff-brown or rusty-olive, not yellow. Bill is white or

331

whitish with a dark grey tip and cutting edges, becoming progressively darker with age.

VOICE Generally silent, but has a pleasant song, a soft descending 'chwee-chwee-chwee-chwi'.

STATUS, HABITAT AND BEHAVIOUR Local and nowhere common; relatively little known. Inhabits savanna, bush and thicket areas near marshes or swamps, riparian woodland and forest edges and clearings. Rather acrobatic, and searches in the foliage at all heights in a rather tit- or warbler-like manner; more usually found in the undergrowth in forest. Occurs singly or in pairs. Feeds mainly on small seeds, wild figs or grass seeds (which it takes on the ground), small insects,

e.g. ants, caterpillars, and occasionally small snails.

DISTRIBUTION Monotypic. Guinea, extreme southern Mali and northern Ghana east to southern Nigeria, Cameroon, Central African Republic, northern Zaire, extreme southwest Sudan and northwest Uganda. A vagrant to the Gambia (two records, most recent in May 1968). Has recently (March 1990) been recorded in southwest Uganda (Budongo Forest).

MEASUREMENTS Wing 54–60; tail 42–46; tarsus 15; bill 10.

REFERENCES Ash *et al.* (1991), Chapin (1954).

GENUS *PYTILIA*

Four species. Medium-sized estrildid finches with a thin or slender bill; generally brightly coloured, with red, orange, gold or green in the wings, red rump and tail and barred underparts. The wing structure (emarginations on both webs of the second primary, with a notch on the inner web) also separates them from other estrildids. The palate markings of nestlings are very reduced or absent in some species. Found in typical dry scrub or savanna with trees and thornbush habitat, feeding mainly on the ground. Probably more closely related to *Amadina* than to the initially similar firefinches *Lagonosticta*.

138 CRIMSON-WINGED PYTILIA (Aurora Finch, Aurora Waxbill, Red-winged Pytilia) *Pytilia phoenicoptera*　　Plate 36

Africa

Pytilia phoenicoptera Swainson, 1837, Birds W. Africa, 1, p. 203, West Africa; Gambia, see Hartlaub, 1857, Syst. Ornith. Westafrika, p. 145.

IDENTIFICATION Length 12·5–13 cm (5 in). A small, compact and extremely active finch (as are all pytilias and most related estrildids), with grey or light brownish-grey plumage with distinctive finely barred underparts, and bright red wings, rump and tail. Bill is black in central and western races and red in eastern birds. **Confusion species:** Red in wings and lack of any red on head distinguish it from all other pytilias. Female is similar to female Orange-winged Pytilia (140), but is grey or grey-brown and lacks olive tones.

DESCRIPTION Sexes similar but separable. **Adult male:** Forehead to crown, face and nape grey, with light or paler tips to forehead and sides of head. Mantle, back and scapulars grey, sometimes with some feathers tipped crimson; rump and uppertail-coverts bright crimson. Tail dark brown, broadly edged with crimson. Median and greater coverts pale brown or brownish-grey centrally, to variable extent edged and tipped crimson (together with edges to flight feathers forming bright crimson panel); alula and primary coverts brown; inner webs of flight feathers dark brown or dark greyish-brown, outers bright crimson, with distal third of primaries and all tertials brown (or very lightly tinged red). Chin and throat pale grey-brown or with some slightly darker tips to throat; plain grey on breast, becoming progressively more prominently barred grey and buffish-white from lower

breast to undertail-coverts. Thin and finely pointed bill is black. Eye red. Legs and feet pale or fleshy-brown. In worn or non-breeding plumage, crimson on wings, rump and tail fades to an orange-red. **Adult female:** Very similar to adult male, but generally much browner or brownish-grey; generally paler on underparts, with thin brown and buff-white barring beginning high up on breast. Crimson in wings, rump and tail is often darker or duller and less extensive than on male, but varies individually. **Juvenile:** Very like adult female, but more earth-brown and not especially grey. Barring on underparts is duller and faint on pale buff ground colour, and crimson of wings, rump and tail tends to dull red or orange. Eye brown; bill greyish or brown with a pink or reddish base, darkening with age.

GEOGRAPHICAL VARIATION Race *emini* is indistinguishable in the field from nominate. Race *lineata* (sometimes treated as a separate species, the Red-billed or Red-winged Pytilia) has a bright red bill, brown eye and much heavier barring on underparts; females are very similar to nominate except for red bill, and juveniles have a grey bill which becomes pinkish before turning red.

VOICE Call is an occasional chirp. The song, which is variable, is a repeated series of rattling notes followed by a croaky whistle.

STATUS, HABITAT AND BEHAVIOUR
Locally common, uncommon or scarce. In some areas found on edge of human habitation, while in others an uncommon bird of bush and scrub. Inhabits open acacia woodland and savanna with tall grass, edges or clearings in woods or forest, bamboo thickets, also dense grassland, brush or scrub, occasionally near cultivated areas. Usually occurs alone or in pairs, but often mixes with other small finches or weavers. Often spends long periods sitting quietly in trees. Feeds mainly on the ground, on a variety of seeds, usually of grasses, but also takes some small insects, principally ants and termites.

DISTRIBUTION *P. p. phoenicoptera*: southern and eastern Senegal, and Gambia to Guinea-Bissau discontinuously southeast and east to Guinea, Ivory Coast, Burkina Faso, Ghana, northern Nigeria and Cameroon.

P. p. emini: Cameroon, Central African Republic and northern Zaire to northern Uganda and extreme south of Sudan.

P. p. lineata: western and central Ethiopia.

MOVEMENTS Partial migrant, with birds moving south into eastern Zaire from October to January; has also been seen (including birds carrying nesting material) in southern Mali between November and February.

MEASUREMENTS Wing 56–59; tail of male 35–38, of female 31–35; tarsus c15; bill 10–11.

REFERENCES Goodwin (1982), Mackworth-Praed and Grant (1960).

---

139 RED-FACED PYTILIA (Golden-winged Pytilia, Yellow-winged Pytilia, Red-faced Aurora Finch) *Pytilia hypogrammica*   Plate 36

Africa

Pytelia hypogrammica Sharpe, 1870, Ibis, p. 56, Fantee, Gold Coast.

IDENTIFICATION Length 12·5–13 cm (5 in). A small, short-winged finch of West and central Africa, generally dark grey (males have red face and chin) with fine pale bars on underparts; bright yellow or orange-yellow wings and crimson rump and tail are diagnostic field characters. **Confusion species:** Differs from Crimson-winged Pytilia (138) in colour of wings, red face of male and black in outer tail feathers, together with generally darker plumage. From Orange-winged Pytilia (140) and Green-winged Pytilia (141) also in lack of green or greyish-olive in plumage and in very fine barring on underparts.

DESCRIPTION Sexes very similar but separable. **Adult male:** Forehead to forecrown, sides of face, chin and throat bright deep red or scarlet. Rest of head, nape, mantle, back and scapulars dark grey, tinged with brown; edges to some scapulars may be tinged with yellow; rump and uppertail-coverts red or scarlet-red. Tail is black or blackish, with crimson on outer webs except on outermost pair, central pair entirely crimson. Wings rather short and rounded: median and greater coverts variable between burnished yellow and deep gold, can also be tinged with greenish or orange; alula, primary coverts and flight feathers grey-brown, all edged pale orange or yellow except for entirely grey-brown tertials. Upper breast grey or tinged with light buff, becoming deeper grey with fine white barring on lower breast, belly and flanks; undertail-coverts dark grey or blackish with white tips. Bill is short and pointed and black, sometimes with paler base to lower mandible. Eye red. Legs and feet flesh-pink to pale pinkish-brown. **Adult female:** Similar to adult male, but generally paler and browner and lacks red face; has entire head and face uniform with rest of upperparts, brownish-grey. Wings also as male, but more usually yellow, yellowish-gold or greenish-yellow, but not orange. Underparts slightly paler than on male, pale brown with fine white barring on lower breast, belly and flanks. Note: A very few individuals have yellow of wing-coverts and outer webs of flight feathers replaced with red, and some of breast and crown feathers may be tipped with red. **Juvenile:** Very similar to adult female, but tends to be paler brown, with less olive-yellow in wing; barring on underparts is less distinct. Eye brown; bill blackish.

VOICE Generally silent; the call is unrecorded. The song given by courting males is described as a repeated 'vee-vee-vee'.

STATUS, HABITAT AND BEHAVIOUR Local or scarce and relatively little known. Inhabits open country or savanna with bush, occasional thickets or small woods, derelict (burnt) ground or edges of cultivated areas such as orchards. Usually found alone or in pairs, but occasionally associates with other waxbills or small weavers. Feeds mainly on the ground on grass seeds, millet (in captivity) and insects, mostly ants or termites and their larvae. In the breeding season is a host species to the parasitic Broad-tailed Paradise Whydah (*Vidua orientalis*).

DISTRIBUTION Monotypic. Discontinuously east from Sierra Leone and northeast Guinea to Cameroon (Adamawa plateau), eastern Central African Republic and northwest Zaire.

MEASUREMENTS Wing 55–59; tail 33–36; tarsus 15; bill 10.

REFERENCE Goodwin (1982).

140 ORANGE-WINGED PYTILIA (Red-faced Finch, Yellow-winged Pytilia, Yellow-backed Pytilia, Golden-backed Pytilia)
Pytilia afra Plate 36
Africa

Fringilla afra Gmelin, 1789, Syst. Nat., 1, p. 905, Angola.

IDENTIFICATION Length 11 cm (4¼-4½ in). A small, rather short or dumpy-looking finch, almost shy or skulking in its habits. Olive-green upperparts, slightly duller or more olive on female; male has bright red forehead and face, and both sexes have deep orange in wings and scarlet on rump and tail. **Confusion species:** Male Green-winged Pytilia (141) has a band of green or yellow across breast and heavy grey-and-white barring on rest of underparts; both sexes clearly lack orange in wings.

DESCRIPTION Sexes separable. **Adult male:** Forehead and face to rear of ear-coverts, cheeks and chin blood-red to crimson, variable in intensity; lores greyish. Crown and nape grey, with slightly darker centres to some feathers; mantle, back and scapulars green or yellowish-green, tinged or washed with olive; rump and uppertail-coverts crimson. Most of tail appears darker red, but in fact is red only on outer webs (except on central pair of feathers), inner webs being brown or dark brown. Median coverts as mantle/scapulars or slightly darker, edged or tipped lightly orange, greater coverts orange or bright orange; alula and primary coverts blackish-brown, edged with orange; flight feathers also blackish-brown, broadly edged deep or bright orange on secondaries and base of primaries, with tips blackish; tertials as back, but dark olive on inner webs. Throat to sides of neck and upper breast pale grey; breast olive (can be tinged either yellow or orange), becoming finely barred with off-white on lower breast and more obviously barred on belly, flanks and undertail-coverts; belly can also be white. Bill is short and pointed, red, crimson or pinkish. Eye orange or red. Legs and feet pale pink to pale pinkish-brown or flesh-brown. **Adult female:** Similar to male but lacks any red on head, which is greyish (or slightly olive on forehead), becoming whitish on chin and throat. Mantle, back, scapulars and wings similar to male but duller (especially intensity of orange in wings). Underparts more broadly barred buff or olive-brown and dull white or off-white than on male, bars beginning faintly on lower throat and continuing more noticeably across breast to flanks and undertail-coverts; belly white or whitish. Bill duller than male's, dull red or even brownish (some have orange on lower mandible). **Juvenile:** Very similar to adult female, but generally much duller and browner above, with warm buff-brown edges to wing feathers, and paler and more buff below, with barring more diffuse and less clearly marked. Lower rump and tail dull or drab orange to red, some with pale buff tips to feathers. Bill dusky pink, culmen and tip dark sepia. Eye brown.

VOICE Call is a single flat 'seee'. The song is a piping two- or three-note rattling whistle, often repeated in quick succession.

STATUS, HABITAT AND BEHAVIOUR Uncommon or locally common; widespread. Inhabits scattered bush or dry open country up to 1650 m, also in thornscrub, edge of forest, open or mopane woodland. Occurs in small flocks or family parties, or in larger loose flocks in non-breeding season; often associates with Green-winged Pytilia, but generally prefers moister areas. Flight strong, direct and often level. Feeds mainly on the ground (though readily perches on tops of bushes, grasses and trees), on a variety of grass seeds; also probably takes a number of insects and termites. Breeding host to parasitic Broad-tailed Paradise Whydah (*Vidua orientalis*) and Paradise Whydah (*V. paradisaea*).

DISTRIBUTION Monotypic. Extreme southern Sudan (where rare) and southern Ethiopia south and west to lower Congo, central Angola east through Zaire to northwest Kenya (also old records from central highlands and southwest), Zanzibar, Tanzania, northern Zambia to northeast Botswana, Zimbabwe, Malawi, northern Mozambique and the northern Transvaal, South Africa.

MOVEMENTS Wanders widely in search of seeding grasses in the non-breeding season.

MEASUREMENTS Wing 56–61; tail 32–38; tarsus 14–16; bill (culmen) 10–11·5.

REFERENCES Goodwin (1982), Mackworth-Praed and Grant (1960), McLachlan and Liversidge (1978).

141 GREEN-WINGED PYTILIA (Melba Finch) *Pytilia melba* Plate 36

Africa

Fringilla melba Linnaeus, 1758, Syst. Nat., ed. 10, 1, p. 180, China; amended to Angola by Zedlitz, 1916, Journ. f. Ornith., 64, p. 31; restricted to Luanda by Clancey, 1962, Bull. Brit. Ornith. Club, 82, p. 4.

IDENTIFICATION Length 12–13 cm (4¾–5 in). A small, slim, grey-headed and green-backed finch with a longer tail than other similar finches. Widely distributed throughout most of Africa south of the Sahara (except in tropical forest), and often found in very dry areas. Male has conspicuous red forehead, chin, throat and upper breast; female has an all-grey head. **Confusion species:** Orange-winged Pytilia (140), as its name implies, has bright orange in wing, and males also differ in amount of distribution of red on face and head. Green-backed Twinspot (142) is superficially similar, but is heavily spotted white on black on underparts and lacks red rump and tail.

DESCRIPTION Sexes differ. **Adult male:** Forehead to forecrown, chin and throat (occasionally to upper breast) red; lores grey, rest of head and neck to upper mantle soft or medium grey. Mantle, back, scapulars and upper half of rump green or yellowish-olive; lower rump and uppertail-coverts deep orange-red or carmine-red, extending to central pair of tail feathers (which are dark-tipped) and outer webs of all tail feathers, inner webs being dark brown or blackish-brown. Wing-coverts uniform with scapulars or slightly darker, as are outer webs of flight feathers, inner webs of which are brown or dark brown. Breast greenish or light olive, often tinged lighter (yellower) or duller, but with small pale or white and dark spots showing on lower half and becoming more prominent towards belly; belly and flanks quite strongly barred dark olive and white or off-white; centre of belly often white or off-white, continuing to vent and undertail-coverts. Bill slender and pointed, scarlet or crimson; has dark or dusky culmen in non-breeding season. Eye orange, red or reddish-brown. Legs and feet pale brown, brown or grey-brown. In worn plumage can look rather scruffy, and green areas of plumage become dusky or drab and grey is slightly darker or brownish. **Adult female:** Lacks any red on head or face, and has whole of head to upper mantle pale grey; upper throat pale or off-white, with light grey and white barring from (sometimes) lower throat, becoming darker grey (but not so strongly defined as on male) on belly and flanks. Bill dark brown, darker on culmen and tip, with pale red or pinkish at base of lower mandible. **Juvenile:** Fairly similar to adult female but much duller; green areas dull or drab olive, paler or more yellow on edges of flight feathers, with buff tips to median and greater coverts and edges to tertials. Rump dull rusty-orange. Head and face greyish, tinged with buff, this colour extending to most of underparts (but some show darker crescents, giving quite a scaly appearance); vent and undertail-coverts buffish.

Bill dark, becoming red with age. First-year males acquire red face at an early age.

GEOGRAPHICAL VARIATION The most variable of the pytilias (up to 13 races have been described). Most variation concerns presence or amount of red or grey on face to upper breast, tone of upperparts, and strength of barring on underparts. For field-identification purposes, these races can be separated into two groups: those with red lores (*citerior* and *soudanensis*), and those with grey lores (all others). Races *citerior* and *soudanensis* are the only ones which are distinct and more readily recognisable in the field: males have red on face extending around and behind eye; upperparts of both sexes of *citerior* (which is also paler than more richly coloured *soudanensis*) appear a little paler than in nominate, though this may be due partly to bleaching; underparts are golden-yellow on breast and lightly streaked on barred lower breast and flanks, extending to undertail-coverts in *soudanensis*; belly of some *citerior* can be almost white. The breast-band in *thamnophila* is dull olive, while in *grotei* breast is washed with pinkish-red and centre of belly is white. Other races are visibly more akin to nominate, varying in amount of red on lower throat or breast of males (particularly obvious in *belli*, which also has barred undertail-coverts) and intensity of green on upperparts, particularly *grotei* and *belli*, while *percivali* is paler and less intensely coloured; *thamnophila* has forehead and throat peach-red, with grey on crown and nape. Races *grotei*, *belli* and *soudanensis* can show tinges of red on wing-coverts, especially in fresh plumage. Females of all races are virtually indistinguishable from nominate, but female *soudanensis* is said to be darker, with heavier barring on underparts. Birds from Djibouti have recently been described as a new race/species 'flavicaudata', but no specimens have been collected and only photographs exist. If confirmed, this form is substantially different from others (even allowing for some considerable individual variation within other races): males completely lack red in plumage and have forehead, cheeks, fore half of ear-coverts, chin, throat and upper breast to sides of neck bright golden-yellow, crown to nape and mantle grey, shading into dull greenish-brown on rest of upperparts and wing-coverts. Tail with greenish central feathers and all outers bright golden-yellow, and pink bill; females are similar to male, but with yellow of forehead, face and breast replaced with pale grey, and tail is slightly duller yellow.

VOICE Call is a thin 'see-eh', also a low 'wick' or 'wit' note. The song is an attractive series of quiet trills with occasional whistles, 'trrreeeeeechrrroooooo', often lasting for up to 15 seconds. In race *citerior*, the song consists of a single 'veet' note followed by a short series of whistling and croaking notes.

STATUS, HABITAT AND BEHAVIOUR Common or locally common. Widely distributed throughout drier parts of Africa, usually below 1500 m, avoids tropical forest; usually found in fairly dry open country in thornscrub, thickets or acacia woodland with bushes, even on semi-desert edges, also grassland, savanna and edges of cultivated areas. Often inconspicuous or shy, and feeds unobtrusively in rank grass or thick undergrowth but occasionally in open on roadside edges etc.; rarely flies more than a few metres at a time, even when disturbed. Usually in pairs or small family parties. Feeds on a variety of seeds, mostly of grass and millet, but some insects, especially termites, are also taken. Brood host of Paradise Whydah (*Vidua paradisaea*).

DISTRIBUTION *P. m. melba*: Cabinda, through the Congo and Zaire to Malawi, southwest Tanzania, Namibia and Transvaal, South Africa.

P. m. citerior: northern Senegal to Upper Guinea and southern Mali, Burkina Faso, southern Niger, northern Nigeria, northern Cameroon, southern Chad to west and central Sudan.

P. m. soudanensis: south and eastern Sudan, northeast Uganda, Ethiopia and Somalia, south to Kenya and Mount Kilimanjaro area, northeast Tanzania.

P. m. percivali: southwest Kenya and northern Tanzania.

P. m. belli: southeast Sudan, western Uganda, eastern Zaire, southwest Kenya, Rwanda, Burundi, Tanzania and Malawi.

P. m. grotei: east and northeast Tanzania to southern Malawi, northwest Zimbabwe and northern Mozambique.

P. m. thamnophila: Zimbabwe, southern Mozambique, and northern and eastern South Africa (to Natal).

Other races have been described (see Geographical Variation); in overlapping areas of ranges intermediates occur.

MOVEMENTS Wanders at random throughout range when not breeding; a dry-season visitor to Gambia.

MEASUREMENTS Wing of male 56–62·5, of female 57–62; tail 46–53; tarsus 14–17; bill (culmen) 12–14.

REFERENCES Goodwin (1982), Mackworth-Praed and Grant (1960), McLachlan and Liversidge (1978), Sinclair (1984), Welch and Welch (1986, 1988).

GENUS *MANDINGOA*

One species. Together with the other twinspots in the genera *Hypargos, Euschistospiza* and *Clytospiza*, this forms a group of species which may be closely related to each other but also have apparent affinities outside this group. *Mandingoa* has a more pointed wing and shorter tail than any of the others, and a general plumage pattern similar to that of pytilias and Red-faced Crimson-wing (143).

142 GREEN-BACKED TWINSPOT (Green Twinspot) *Mandingoa nitidula*
Plate 37
Africa

Estrelda nitidula Hartlaub, in Gurney, 1865, Ibis, p. 269, Natal.

IDENTIFICATION Length 10–11 cm (4–4¼ in). A small active finch with olive or deep green upperparts, red or orange face, and boldly spotted with white on black underparts. No other twinspot has green upperparts, and all are generally much darker. **Confusion species:** Orange-winged Pytilia (140) has bright orange in wing and Green-winged Pytilia (141) has extensive area of red on face (male) or an all-grey head (female); both also have red on rump and tail, but neither has distinctive black-and-white spots on underparts.

DESCRIPTION Sexes differ. **Adult male:** Lores and around eye to chin red or deep orange-red. Forehead to crown, nape, mantle, back and scapulars a deep moss- or olive-green; rump and uppertail-coverts a warm golden-olive or tinged with orange. Tail olive-green with blackish inner webs, central pair of feathers entirely olive. Median and greater coverts as scapulars, or slightly dusky or grey edged with olive-green; alula, primary coverts and flight feathers blackish, but all edged with light olive-green. Ear-coverts, sides of neck and throat bright green or olive-green, slightly darker or deeper on breast; lower breast, belly and flanks dark grey to black, boldly spotted with white; vent and undertail-coverts pale olive-green with darker bases. Bill fairly short, slender, pointed, all black or with red at tip. Eye brown or dark brown. Legs and feet pinkish-brown, brown or even purple-brown. **Adult female:** Similar to adult male, though somewhat duller and lacks bright red face; green or olive-green upperparts as male, rump and uppertail-coverts only lightly (if at all) tinged yellow or golden-buff. Tail also as male, but tinged slightly browner. Light yellow or orange/ peachy-buff on lores, cheeks, chin and upper throat, on some to around eye, but rest of face and throat light buff or fawn-brown, becoming greenish-olive on breast. Spotting on lower breast, belly and flanks as male, but black is more dark grey and spots are less distinct. Bill black, with red cutting edges to tip. **Juvenile:** Similar to but much duller than adult female, and lacks spots on underparts; generally greyish-olive above, becoming greener on rump and edges to tail, and grey or drab grey-brown on underparts; face and throat buff or greyish-buff. Young males show tinges of green on breast, and spots appear gradually in an erratic or random fashion.

GEOGRAPHICAL VARIATION Males of race *chubbi* have brighter rich red face, green on breast tinged deep or rich yellow or orange, rump and uppertail-coverts deep or rich rusty-brown tinged with orange, and larger white spots on underparts are often suffused with grey or greyish-green; juveniles have deep green tinge or wash to breast. Male *schlegeli* has a noticeably larger bill, which is all black except for red cutting edges (both mandibles), face is deeper blood-red, breast is tinged either with golden-yellow or with deep orange and belly has greenish wash; upperparts are deep olive-green, tinged with golden or rusty-orange, the latter more prominent on rump (can also be present on sides of neck). Female *schlegeli* is similar to male, more richly coloured on upperparts, tinged with golden-yellow on breast and with dark greenish wash on belly. Both sexes have richly coloured eye-rings, red on male and greyish-blue on female. Juvenile *schlegeli* is darker than nominate race; underparts are darker grey and breast is tinged olive-green. Race *virginiae* is strongly tinged orange or warm orange on upperparts, and rust or orange on rump extends up back; bill is entirely red.

VOICE Call is a chirping or squeaky 'tzeeet' or 'tseeeht', also various other short 'tak' or 'tek' notes; when alarmed or excited has a 'tsit-tsit' note,

occasionally followed by 'terr'. Song is a subdued series of trills interspersed with whistling and call notes.

STATUS, HABITAT AND BEHAVIOUR Very local or rare; seldom seen but possibly overlooked. Widely distributed over much of central and eastern Africa up to 2400 m, generally slightly lower. A shy and unobtrusive bird, spending much of its time in undergrowth of dense riverine or secondary forest, edges of forest, plantations (including those of cassava), tall or rank grassland, evergreen thickets or other dense undergrowth, occasionally on edge of cultivated areas; also occurs in the canopy when trees are seeding. Usually alone, in pairs or small parties feeding low down or on the ground, occasionally in the open on cleared areas such as paths but always near cover, into which it rapidly retreats when disturbed. Feeds on a variety of small seeds, usually grass seeds, and small insects; has also been known to take rice and pieces of cassava and oil-palm husk.

DISTRIBUTION *M. n nitidula*: northern and central Tanzania west to southern Zaire and northern Zambia, south through Malawi and Zimbabwe to northern Mozambique, Natal and extreme northeast Cape Province, South Africa.

M. n. schlegeli: Sierra Leone, southern Guinea, Liberia (Mount Nimba) and Ghana discontinuously east to Cameroon, Uganda and northwest Tanzania and south through Zaire to Angola.

M. n. virginiae: Fernando Po.

M. n. chubbi: southeast Sudan (Imatong, Dongotona and possibly the Didinga Mountains) and southern Ethiopia to Kenya, northern Tanzania, Zanzibar and Pemba Island.

MEASUREMENTS Wing 50–55; tail 28–35; tarsus 13·5–14·5; bill (culmen) 9–11. Weight of male 8–10, of female 7–9.

REFERENCES Goodwin (1982), Mackworth-Praed and Grant (1960).

GENUS *CRYPTOSPIZA*

Four species. Crimson-wings, a group of medium-sized estrildid finches with deep red back, rump and, in most, wings. They have short wings and rounded tail and are generally shy or skulking birds of montane forest, rarely flying more than a metre or two between clumps of vegetation. Their closest relatives are unclear, but they appear to have some affinities with twinspots, bluebills and seedcrackers.

143 RED-FACED CRIMSON-WING (Nyasa Crimson-wing) *Cryptospiza reichenovii*   Plate 39

Africa

Pytelia reichenovii Hartlaub, 1874, Ibis, p. 166, Bondongo, Cameroun.

IDENTIFICATION Length 11–12 cm (4¼-4¾ in). A small, rather dumpy, short-tailed, brightly plumaged but secretive finch with conspicuous eye patches, red on male and buff or yellow on female. Generally deep olive on head and neck, but bright

crimson or deep blood-red on rest of upperparts and extensively onto wings. **Confusion species:** Ethiopian Crimson-wing (144) or female Shelley's Crimson-wing (146), both of which lack prominent red or buff eye patches; also red extends to tertials on Red-faced, but not on Shelley's. Juveniles are probably not safely separable in the field, but Red-faced is generally more olive above and yellowish below. In southern areas of the range confusion is possible with Lesser Seedcracker (149), but latter has an all-red face and chin and red on rump and tail.

DESCRIPTION Sexes differ. **Adult male:** Lores and area around eye bright red or scarlet; rest of face olive or yellowish-olive. Forehead, crown to nape and upper mantle deep or dull olive; rest of mantle, back, scapulars, rump and uppertail-coverts rich or deep blood-red. Tail short and entirely sooty-black. Median and greater coverts as scapulars, deep blood-red, in worn plumage showing dark brown bases; alula, primary coverts and flight feathers dark brown or olive-black, tertials rich or deep blood-red on outer webs and black on inners. Chin and throat yellowish-olive; rest of underparts greenish-olive (some show a patch of rich red or blood-red towards rear of flanks). Bill short and fairly deep at base, pointed and black. Eye dark brown. Legs and feet pinkish-brown or sepia-brown, sometimes tinged with grey. **Adult female:** Very similar to adult male in overall coloration but somewhat duller; red on mantle and upper back is not always bright or complete (dark olive-green feather bases may show through). The distinct pale yellowish-buff or straw-coloured face patch is diagnostic. **Juvenile:** Very similar to adult female but browner, with buff eye patch less clearly defined or absent; red areas of mantle and back are browner or olive-brown or ill-defined, often with olive bases to dull red-tipped feathers on mantle, back, wing-coverts, tertials, rump, uppertail-coverts and flanks. Young males begin to show red facial feathers at an early age.

GEOGRAPHICAL VARIATION Racial distinctions are not noticeable in the field, as individual variation occurs and there are no consistent differences between supposed races. On average, aus-tralis differs in having olive and red areas of plumage slightly paler; some birds of this race (formerly separated as sanguinolentus) show little or no red on face. Birds of race homogenes are darker on upperparts, with dull blackish olive-green, but crown and nape are a paler green and red areas lighter than nominate.

VOICE Generally silent, but has a sharp or high-pitched 'chirp' or 'tzeet' and a loose collection of similar notes. The song is soft (inaudible beyond 3–4 m) and variable, consisting mostly of long drawn-out notes on a descending scale followed by a chirp.

STATUS, HABITAT AND BEHAVIOUR Common or locally common; very shy, secretive and easily overlooked, and rarely seen away from thick or dense cover. Inhabits principally montane evergreen forest, usually between 1000 m and 2100 m but also at lower levels in southern parts of the range. Usually found in pairs or small groups in thick or dense undergrowth, but also occurs along forest edges, clearings, along paths or more especially near streams. Often in mixed flocks or groups with Black-and-white Mannikins (223) or Black-crowned Waxbills (184). Occasionally ventures into old cultivated areas or even millet fields, but seldom away from cover. Feeds mainly on grass seeds, but other small seeds also taken, including millet, maize or balsam; may also take some insects. Usually feeds on the ground, but has been recorded extracting seeds from cones up to 15 m from the ground in conifers (Pinus patula) in Zimbabwe.

DISTRIBUTION C. r. reichenovii: southeast Nigeria (Obudu plateau), western Cameroon and Fernando Po (also said to occur south to northern Angola, but no recent records and this may have been published in error).

C. r. australis: southern Uganda, eastern Zaire (Kivu) and Rwanda, discontinuously south through Tanzania to northeast Zambia, southern Malawi, northeast Zimbabwe and northern Mozambique.

C. r. homogenes: Inyangani highlands south to the Chimanimani Mountains, eastern Zimbabwe, and the adjacent borders of Mozambique, also on Mount Gorongosa, north-central Mozambique.

MOVEMENTS Entirely sedentary.

MEASUREMENTS Wing of male 50–58, of female 50–54; tail 35–42; tarsus 17–19; bill (culmen) 10·5–12. Weight 11·5–15. Wing of homogenes 56·5–58.

REFERENCES McLachlan and Liversidge (1978), Sclater and Moreau (1933).

144 ETHIOPIAN CRIMSON-WING (Abyssinian Crimson-wing)
Cryptospiza salvadorii   **Plate 39**
Africa

Cryptospiza salvadorii Reichenow, 1892, Journ. f. Ornith., 40, pp. 187 and 221, Shoa; amended to Sciolitat, Shoa, by Salvadori, 1884, Ann. Mus. Civ. Genova, 21, p. 180.

IDENTIFICATION Length 11·5 cm (4½ in). A small, shy, dull olive or greyish-olive finch with bright crimson wings, mantle, back and rump. **Confusion species:** Both sexes are very similar to Red-faced Crimson-wing (143), especially the female, but Ethiopian lacks red or buff face patches, is generally greyer on head and breast, and red of plumage is duller. Juveniles are not safely separable in the field. **DESCRIPTION** Sexes differ. **Adult male:** Fore-

head to crown, nape, entire face (to moustachial area) and upper mantle dull or greyish-olive, except for blackish lores; rest of mantle, back, scapulars, rump and uppertail-coverts rich or deep crimson. Black tail is short and slightly rounded. Median coverts red or crimson, greaters similar but with black inner webs often showing; alula, primary coverts, primaries and secondaries blackish-grey, with outer webs of tertials crimson. Chin buff-yellow; rest of underparts greyish-olive, rear of flanks show irregular red or crimson tips. Black bill, short, with curved culmen. Eye dark brown. Legs and feet dark brown. **Adult female:** Very like adult male, but paler greyish-olive and less intensely red; has pale buff lores, chin and throat (but lacks obvious pale face patch of very similar female Red-faced Crimson-wing 143). **Juvenile:** Similar to adult, but has patchy red on scapulars and rump, mantle is olive tinged with brown, and inner secondaries, rump and uppertail-coverts are also less rich or occasionally brown or olive-brown. Probably not safely separable in the field from juvenile Red-faced, but slightly greyer where the ranges overlap.
GEOGRAPHICAL VARIATION Race *kilimensis* is very similar to nominate, but paler or more olive on underparts and darker above. Race *ruwenzori* has greyer, almost plain pale grey head and nape to upper mantle, with area around eyes dull olive; underparts are also lighter and greyer, with buff chin and throat and a tinge of greenish-olive on breast; bill is slightly smaller.

VOICE Call is a soft 'teeep' or variations thereof, 'tseep-tseep' and 'chip-chip'. The song is a repetition of the call, but also has a rarely heard soft and melodic 'dee-goo-goo-day-dee'.
STATUS, HABITAT AND BEHAVIOUR Local. Probably not uncommon but shy and elusive and easily overlooked, as it is easily alarmed and rapidly retreats into cover at first sign of danger. Inhabits forest, especially montane forest, between 1500 m and 3000 m in Kenya, at edges or clearings, usually in undergrowth but occasionally at some height in creepers, also in thickets, bamboo or dense brush, especially along streams or rivers. Usually in pairs or alone, but small (family?) parties of up to six are not unknown. Feeds low down, often partially hidden, or on the ground, principally on grass seeds, but other small seeds such as balsam are taken; possibly also eats small insects.
DISTRIBUTION *C. s. salvadorii*: southern Ethiopia (Shoa Province) to northern Kenya.
  C. s. ruwenzori: Ruwenzori Mountains, eastern Zaire to southwest Uganda.
  C. s. kilimensis: southeast Sudan (Imatong, Dongotona and Didinga Mountains) and northeast Uganda to west and central Kenya and northeast Tanzania.
MEASUREMENTS Wing 54–60.
REFERENCES Goodwin (1982), Williams and Arlott (1980).

145 DUSKY CRIMSON-WING (Jackson's Crimson-wing)
Cryptospiza jacksoni   **Plate 39**
Central Africa

Cryptospiza jacksoni Sharpe, 1902, Bull. Brit. Ornith. Club, 13, p. 8, Ruwenzori.

IDENTIFICATION Length 11·5 cm (4½ in). A small, dumpy and secretive finch with deep red or crimson on face, upperparts and flanks, black or blackish wings and tail, and dark grey underparts. The darkest of the crimson-wings, lacking any olive in plumage; if seen well, red on head divided from rest of red upperparts by grey hindneck is diagnostic of adult. **Confusion species:** The two dusky twinspots (156, 157) are similar, but crimson-wings lack any white or spotting on underparts and are somewhat different in shape.
DESCRIPTION Sexes separable. **Adult male:** Forehead to crown and hindcrown, face and sides of neck deep or rich crimson (variable in extent on crown); nape and hindneck to sides of lower neck dark grey or blackish (but in hand appears paler, and some feathers can be tipped with red). Mantle, back, scapulars, rump and uppertail-coverts deep crimson, often with darker bases showing through. Tail square-ended and black. All wing-coverts and flight feathers black or blackish except outer webs of inner two tertials, which are deep crimson. Chin and throat pale greyish, becoming deep grey or slate-grey on rest of underparts except for a small irregular or incomplete patch of crimson on rear of flanks. Bill short and rather stubby, pointed and black. Eye dark brown; eyelid dull pinkish. Legs and feet blackish or dark olive-brown. **Adult female:** Very similar to adult male, but on average has less (occasionally no) red on crown and sides of nape and neck, and shows more grey or grey-brown; general tone of red upperparts is also lighter, less deep blood-red, and more crimson or with an orange tinge. **Juvenile:** Very similar to adult, but lacks red on head and face and is generally much duller red on upperparts (almost a dingy red on some); underparts entirely grey or slate-grey or tinged sooty-brown, with red on rear of flanks absent or greatly reduced.
VOICE Generally silent, but has a soft 'tzeek' or 'tsit', also a soft trilling 'geegeegeegee'. The song is similar to call notes and seems to be a drawn-out version of these, or with a high-pitched 'peeeee'.
STATUS, HABITAT AND BEHAVIOUR Probably not uncommon, but very little known; has a fairly restricted range. A shy, elusive and localised

bird which is easily overlooked in dense forest undergrowth. Usually found alone or in pairs between 1550 m and 3200 m in thick forest scrub or undergrowth, including bamboo, but emerges into open in adjacent areas to feed on grass seeds, balsam seeds or millet; is always quickly into cover once disturbed.

DISTRIBUTION Monotypic. Mountains (including Ruwenzori range) of eastern Zaire (south to Bukavu) to southwest Uganda, Rwanda and Burundi.
MOVEMENTS Entirely sedentary.
MEASUREMENTS Wing 55–60.
REFERENCE Goodwin (1982).

146 SHELLEY'S CRIMSON-WING (Red-billed Crimson-wing)
Cryptospiza shelleyi   Plate 39
Central Africa

Cryptospiza shelleyi Sharpe, 1902, Bull. Brit. Ornith. Club, 13, p. 21, Ruwenzori.

IDENTIFICATION Length 13 cm (5in). The largest and rarest of the crimson-wings. Male has bright red or maroon upperparts and black wings and tail, while female has an almost entirely olive-green head; the bill is bright red. Like all crimson-wings, very shy and relatively little known; its nest and eggs are unknown in the wild. **Confusion species:** Female likely to be confused with female Red-faced Crimson-wing (143), but latter has noticeable pale buff eye patch (absent or reduced on juvenile), while female Shelley's has a plain olive head (with paler or yellow chin and throat) and a rusty or orange flank patch. Red-faced and out-of-range Ethiopian (144) have more extensive red on wings than Shelley's.
DESCRIPTION Sexes differ. **Adult male:** Forehead, face and rest of head (except chin and throat) to rump and uppertail-coverts and including scapulars rich red or maroon, tinged with mauve. Black tail short and slightly rounded at tip. Wings short and rounded: wing-coverts and flight feathers dark brown or blackish, sometimes showing a green tinge on edge of flight feathers; inner two tertials edged maroon. Chin and throat green or olive-green, with yellowish tinge on lower throat, breast and belly; lower flanks and sides of belly bright orange or orange-brown; undertail-coverts black or lightly tinged olive.
Bill quite prominent or stout with a curved culmen, red with a pinkish-red base. Eye dark brown, with a fine pink eye-ring visible at close range. Legs and feet dark brown. **Adult female:** Similar to adult male, but lacks any red on head, which is entirely olive or slightly greenish, with paler chin and throat; rest of plumage identical to male, but less bright (red is not so deep), and red on scapulars broken or infused with greenish-olive. Bill as male's but slightly smaller, red or reddish-brown, with brown on culmen and base of lower mandible. **Juvenile:** Little known and virtually undescribed; probably very similar to adult female or duller in general tones.
VOICE Call is a series of rapid, high-pitched, rising and falling twittering notes, 'tu-tu-tu-ti-ti-ti', similar to that of some small sunbirds.
STATUS, HABITAT AND BEHAVIOUR Uncommon or scarce resident. In common with other crimson-wings extremely shy, elusive and seldom seen, spending much of its time hidden in deep or dense undergrowth or jungle thickets. Found in thick tangled undergrowth of mountain forest between 1550 m and 3400m. Occurs alone or in pairs, sometimes associating with other crimson-wings (even less likely than latter to be seen in the open in clearings). Feeds on small seeds, mainly balsams, usually on the ground or close to it, also some insects; apparently does not take millet.
DISTRIBUTION Monotypic. Ruwenzori Mountains of eastern Zaire (west to Lake Kivu) and southwest Uganda, south to Burundi and Rwanda.
MEASUREMENTS Wing 66.
REFERENCE Mackworth-Praed and Grant (1960).

GENUS *PYRENESTES*

Three species. Seedcrackers, large-billed and dome-headed estrildids with glossy red plumage. All are closely related to each other and are sometimes treated as representing a racial cline of one species. Of uncertain affinities, but show some structural and plumage features that recall both crimson-wings *Cryptospiza* and bluebills *Spermophaga*.

147 CRIMSON SEEDCRACKER *Pyrenestes sanguineus*   **Plate 40**
West Africa

Pirenestes sanguineus Swainson, 1837, Birds W. Africa, 1, p. 156, West Africa; type marked Senegal by Swainson.

IDENTIFICATION Length 13–14 cm (5–5½ in). A small to medium, sparrow-sized finch, rather plump or dumpy in shape, with distinctive (even in flight) large or medium-sized and deep-based bill and rounded or domed head. Usually found in or near swamps or marshland areas with reeds. Males are dark brown or blackish-brown and red, females mid-brown with less red. **Confusion species:** Very similar to (out-of-range) Black-bellied Seedcracker (148), but male Crimson has brown central upperparts and belly, which are black on Black-bellied. Females and immatures are especially similar (if not identical), but those of Black-bellied tend to be more uniform brown and have more red in tail. Note: Crimson, Black-bellied and Lesser (149) Seedcrackers may well be conspecific and have been treated as such by some African taxonomists, but are here treated as three species largely because of lack of overlap in ranges and existence of well-defined plumage characters; further observations in areas where ranges adjoin, however, may yet reveal them to be conspecific.

DESCRIPTION Sexes differ. **Adult male:** Entire head, face and sides of neck (to nape), chin, throat, breast and flanks bright or deep glossy crimson. Nape, mantle, back, scapulars and short and rather rounded wings earth-brown or dark earth-brown; rump and uppertail-coverts crimson. Tail dark brown with central pair of feathers crimson, all outers with red or reddish edges. Some show black tips or edges to crimson feathers of lower breast and flanks, but otherwise belly, vent and undertail-coverts and undertail are dark brown. The sharply pointed bill is variably large to massive (though in all three seedcrackers individuals with comparatively small bills exist) and triangular, with broad and deep base; it is steel-blue (see also Geographical Variation). Eye dark brown with noticeable white eyelids. Legs and feet brown or olive-brown. **Adult female:** Fairly similar to adult male on belly and wings. Forehead, crown and face to sides of neck, chin and throat crimson; hindcrown, nape and rest of upperparts are mid-brown, apart from crimson rump and uppertail-coverts; tail as male; breast and flanks to undertail-coverts olive-brown. **Juvenile:** Similar to adult female but lacks crimson on head, which is all brown; dull red or crimson only on rump, uppertail-coverts and outer webs of tail. Eyelids yellowish; bill black, with dull yellow at base of lower mandible when newly fledged.

GEOGRAPHICAL VARIATION Large-billed birds in north of range are referred to nominate race. Race *coccineus* is slightly smaller, with a noticeably smaller bill than nominate; adult female is also much less intensely red or crimson, and has nape and flanks washed or lightly tinged with red.

VOICE Call is a sharp 'zeet'. The song is a short, pleasant warble.

STATUS, HABITAT AND BEHAVIOUR Uncommon or scarce; a shy and elusive bird. Lives in swamps, marshes or dense undergrowth and bushes alongside streams, rivers or flooded rice-fields. Rises by a series of twists and turns, to fly off in a rather sparrow-like undulating flight for some distance. Occasionally feeds in the open in pairs or small parties, sometimes in company with bluebills (150–152) on the ground adjacent to cover. Food virtually unknown but presumably seeds, especially those with hard or strong kernels.

DISTRIBUTION *P. s. sanguineus*: southern Senegal and the Gambia to southern Mali and Guinea-Bissau; also Sierra Leone and the Ivory Coast.

P. s. coccineus: Sierra Leone, Liberia and the Ivory Coast.

MEASUREMENTS Wing 69–75; tail 55–60; tarsus 20–21; bill (from feathers) 16–17, breadth (at base) 18. Wing of male *coccineus* 60–68, of female 57–63; tail 44–51; tarsus 17–20; bill (from feathers) 11–13, breadth 11·5–15.

REFERENCES Bannerman (1953), Goodwin (1982), Hall and Moreau (1970), Serle *et al.* (1977), Traylor (1968).

148 BLACK-BELLIED SEEDCRACKER (Rothschild's Seedcracker (*P. o. rothschildi*)) *Pyrenestes ostrinus*

Plate 40

Africa

Loxia ostrina Vieillot, 1805, Ois. Chant., p. 79, India and Africa; restricted to southern Gabon coast by Chapin, 1924, Bull. Amer. Mus. Nat. Hist., 49, p. 439.

IDENTIFICATION Length 15 cm (6 in). Very similar in size, shape and coloration to Crimson Seedcracker (147), with which it may be conspecific, but males are black where Crimson are brown. Females and immatures are more uniform brown than those of Crimson, but apart from range there is little to separate the two species in the field. **Confusion species:** Male is similar to Red-headed Bluebill (152), but has more red on rump and tail and a distinctive triangular bill. Female is told from all bluebills by brown plumage and lack of any white spots on belly and flanks, and from all crimson-wings (143–146) by larger size, brown mantle, back and scapulars and red in tail.

DESCRIPTION Sexes differ. **Adult male:** Entire head, face, neck, chin, throat, and breast to upper flanks deep or bright glossy scarlet. Mantle, back, scapulars and wings jet-black; lower rump and uppertail-coverts crimson. Central pair of tail feathers and edges to all outer feathers crimson, but inner webs jet-black. Underparts from centre of lower breast to belly, lower flanks, undertail-coverts and undertail jet-black. Bill large, deep and broad at base, triangular, with a notch on cutting edge near base; bluish or blue-black (slightly metallic). Eye dull or deep red to reddish-brown; eyelid pale blue. Legs and feet brown or yellowish-brown. **Adult female:** Almost entire head to nape bright red, with feathers on sides of neck, upper flanks and breast also variably tipped red. Mantle, back, scapulars and wings uniform warm olive-brown; rump, uppertail-coverts and tail red as adult male, but inner webs of tail dark or deep rich brown (not black). Underparts from breast warm olive-brown. Bill as adult male. Eye brown or dark brown, with narrow pale blue eyelid. **Juvenile:** Generally dark olive-brown, dull in tone and lacking any red on head or breast; rump and uppertail-coverts dull dark rust or orange, extending slightly onto tail (usually only on central pair of feathers). Bill black, pale yellow at base when recently fledged.

GEOGRAPHICAL VARIATION Some confusion exists over recognition of races: between two and four have been proposed, all of these occur within the same geographic area of distribution separable only on wing and bill measurements, otherwise identical in the field. Several authors recognise *frommi*, which is large in overall size and larger-billed than nominate, and *rothschildi*, which is small and small-billed (or smaller than nominate). Others have also given *maximus* (now regarded as synonymous with *frommi*) and *gabonensis* (now considered synonymous with *rothschildi*). Bill size varies considerably, however, even among birds within a small area, and large-billed males often pair with small-billed females and vice versa; intermediates also occur, but, since both large-billed and small-billed birds predominate, there must be an ecological separation or barrier preventing widespread mixing of individuals with different-sized bills, otherwise populations with more average dimensions would arise. It seems best (at present) to treat all populations as subspecifically recognisable (certainly in the hand if not in the field) where 'classic' types (or those conforming to measured sizes) are found occurring or co-existing within the same geographic area. Within this area it is probable that minor differences in habitat choice or food selection separate or isolate the birds subspecifically, the smaller-billed ones being found in areas containing food not taken by larger-billed birds, which have a dependence on harder-shelled seeds.

VOICE Call is a low metallic 'peenk', also a soft chattering note; alarm or anxiety note a sharp 'terr'. The song is a soft tinkling warble, 'dee-oh-la-dee-day'.

STATUS, HABITAT AND BEHAVIOUR Similar to Crimson Seedcracker, but not always found in marshes or swamps and more likely in dense woods, evergreen forest, forest edges or clearings, usually near water, also in dense foliage and shrubs in gardens. Locally common but shy, and dives into thick cover when alarmed. Usually in pairs or small groups, though communal roosting in tall grass recorded for *rothschildi*. Feeds low down or on the ground, on a variety of hard seeds (large-billed birds) or softer seeds (smaller-billed birds), especially those of sedges (*Scleria* spp.); also takes fruit, grain, rice, a few insects and spiders.

DISTRIBUTION See Geographical Variation. *P. o. ostrinus*: Ivory Coast (east from about Abidjan) and Ghana east through (mostly southern) Nigeria and Cameroon to Uganda and the borders of southern Sudan, south to Gabon, Congo, Zaire, northern Angola and northwest Zambia.

P. o. frommi: Togo east to central Nigeria, Cameroon, northern Zaire and extreme southern Sudan (where rare), Uganda, south through Zaire to northern Zambia; the original (or type) of this race was collected at Kitungulu in southwest Tanzania, but apparently no subsequent records from there.

P. o. rothschildi: Ghana to southern Nigeria, Cameroon to eastern Zaire and extreme southern Sudan, Uganda, south to northern Angola, southern Zaire and Zambia.

May also be a scarce resident in the Kakamega Forest, western Kenya, where a pair seen in December 1990 (and previously rejected records in 1960).

MOVEMENTS Sedentary.

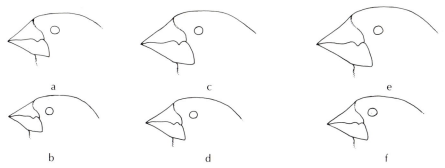

Seedcracker bills showing size variation: (a) P. minor, East Africa); (b) P. minor (Nyasaland); (c) P. ostrinus frommi; (d) P. o. rothschildi; (e) P. sanguineus; (f) P. s. coccineus (Mount Nimba, Liberia).

MEASUREMENTS See also Geographical Variation. Wing 62–74; tail 47–59; bill (from nostril) 10–12·5, breadth 14·5–17·5. Wing of *frommi* 65–74; tail 50–65; bill (from nostril) 12–13·3, breadth 17·5–20. Wing of *rothschildi* 57–68; tail 42–53; tarsus 19; bill (from nostril) 84–11, breadth 10·2–14.

REFERENCES Bannerman (1952), Britton (1980), Chapin (1954), Goodwin (1982), Mackworth-Praed and Grant (1960), Stevenson (1992).

149 LESSER SEEDCRACKER (Nyasa Seedcracker) *Pyrenestes minor*
Plate 40

East Africa

Pyrenestes minor Shelley, 1894, Ibis, p. 20, Zomba, Nyasaland.

IDENTIFICATION Length 13–14 cm (5–5½ in). A small and slim brown East African seedcracker, with less red in plumage than seedcrackers of central and West Africa. Sexes are very similar, with red on face or front of head to breast and red rump and tail, and rest of body and wings mid- or earth-brown. **Confusion species:** Female Black-bellied Seedcracker (148) is extremely similar to male Lesser, but ranges do not (apparently) overlap; Lesser is slightly smaller, with slightly less red on upper breast, and has smaller bill. Brown upperparts and red tail separate it from any crimson-wings, especially Red-faced (143), the only one likely to occur within range.
DESCRIPTION Sexes similar but separable. **Adult male:** Forehead to crown, face (to rear of ear-coverts), chin, throat and upper breast deep or bright red; on some individuals or in worn plumage, red may extend to lower breast or upper flanks. Hindcrown, nape, mantle, back, scapulars and entire wing-coverts uniform mid- or earth-brown with a light olive tinge; flight feathers darker brown, but in worn plumage become paler-edged (and coverts show pale buff tips). Rump and uppertail-coverts deep blood-red, this colour extending to central pair of tail feathers; outer tail feathers dark olive-brown on inner webs, broadly edged scarlet. Sides of lower neck, throat and breast olive-brown (lighter than upperparts) with some buff or greyish tinges. Black bill same shape as other seedcrackers, large or broad and deep at base but more in keeping with size of bird, though both small, large and intermediate bills are known. Eye brown or dark brown with white eye-ring. Legs and feet dark brown or grey-brown. In worn plumage, body is greyish or dull grey-brown. **Adult female:** Similar if not identical in most respects to adult male, but red on head restricted to forehead and to fore part of face, from just behind eyes to cheeks, chin and upper throat; some, perhaps worn individuals, show red on lower throat and breast. **Juvenile:** Very similar to those of other seedcrackers, but slightly smaller or slimmer; generally olive or pale olive-brown, with dull rusty-red on rump and uppertail-coverts.
VOICE Call a sparrow-like 'zeet' or 'tzeet', and a sharp clicking or strident 'quap' alarm note. The song is a soft chittering trill.
STATUS, HABITAT AND BEHAVIOUR Local and uncommon. A shy or scarce inhabitant of hill forest in areas of high rainfall, but also drier forest edges, *Brachystegia* woodland, clearings or bracken-briar thickets with scrub, rank grassy areas or weedy tangles at lower levels between 725 m and 1800 m; usually along streams or rivers. Usually in pairs, low down or on the ground. Feeds on grass seeds and rice, probably as other species of seedcracker.
DISTRIBUTION Monotypic. South and southeast Tanzania to southern Malawi, eastern Zimbabwe and northern Mozambique (north of the Save river).

MOVEMENTS Sedentary.

MEASUREMENTS Wing of male 56·5–62, of female 59–61; tail 49–56; tarsus 17·5–19·5; bill (culmen) 8·5–10·5, width (across base of lower mandible) 9·5–16.

REFERENCES McLachlan and Liversidge (1978), Vincent (1936).

GENUS *SPERMOPHAGA*

Three species: bluebills. The genus has previously been considered as more closely related to weavers or to have affinities with both weaver and estrildid genera (hence weaver-finch), but its members are now classified as true estrildid finches. In wing structure and bill size they bear an initial similarity to dusky twinspots *Euschistospiza* and seedcrackers *Pyrenestes*, but in behaviour they are also closely related to cordon-bleus *Uraeginthus*.

150 GRANT'S BLUEBILL *Spermophaga poliogenys*   Plate 41
Central Africa

Spermospiza poliogenys Ogilvie-Grant, 1906, Bull. Brit. Ornith. Club, 19, p. 32, 20 miles north of Beni, Semliki Valley.

IDENTIFICATION Length 14 cm (5½ in). A shy and extremely skulking ground-dweller. Male is similar in plumage to seedcrackers, especially Black-bellied (148), with bright scarlet on forehead, face to breast and flanks; rest of the plumage jet-black except for bright red rump. Female has grey head and face, with red on throat and breast and white spots in pairs or forming crescents on underparts. **Confusion species:** Differs from both sexes of Black-bellied Seedcracker in having black nape, less triangular and more weaver-shaped bill with blue base at most seasons, and jet-black tail without any red. Red-headed Bluebill (152) is extremely similar, but Grant's has less red on head, black nape, and red on rump and uppertail-coverts slightly brighter. Western Bluebill (151) has black forehead, crown and nape (both sexes). Females are separated from other female bluebills by grey head and face and scaly pattern of upperparts (probably seen well only at close range).

DESCRIPTION Sexes differ. **Adult male:** Forehead and crown, entire face, sides of neck to chin, throat, breast and flanks bright or iridescent red or scarlet. Nape to back, scapulars and entire wings (which are short and rounded) black, with nape, mantle and scapulars glossy black; rump and uppertail-coverts bright red. Black tail is long or fairly long and rather graduated at tip. Underparts (except for glossy red extending to lower breast and upper flanks) jet-black. Bill quite deep at base, with curved culmen, bluish or metallic blue with red or reddish-pink at tip and along cutting edges. Eye brown or dark brown with pale blue eye-ring. Legs and feet dark olive to greenish-brown. **Adult**

female: Entire head and face to upper mantle grey to dark grey; rest of mantle, back and wings deep slate-grey, with glossy black edges and tips forming scaly pattern; rump and uppertail-coverts bright red. Tail as male. Chin, throat and upper breast bright red or orange tinged with red; lower breast, belly and flanks grey or dark grey with small paired white spots, becoming bars on rear of flanks and undertail-coverts. **Juvenile:** A dull version of adult female, but lacking red on throat and breast and white spotting on rest of underparts; has red or dull red on rump and uppertail-coverts. Young females show faint spots on belly and flanks at an early age. Bill bluish or greyish-blue.

VOICE Call a hoarse 'chip' and a melodious 'tyee-dyeeu', the only notes recorded for an otherwise generally silent bird.

STATUS, HABITAT AND BEHAVIOUR Rare. An extremely shy and elusive species, seldom seen, and little is known of its breeding biology. Spends most of its time low down or on the ground in thick undergrowth of heavy primary or secondary forest, occasionally venturing out into clearings but rarely seen in the open. Feeds on seeds (quite large hard-shelled seeds) collected from the ground, also some insects and spiders.

DISTRIBUTION Monotypic. Northern and north-central Zaire (west to Lake Tumba, south to about Kasongo) to southwest Uganda (Bwamba Forest).

MOVEMENTS Resident; birds live within a very small area for most of their lives.

MEASUREMENTS Wing 65–73.

REFERENCES Chapin (1954), Goodwin (1982).

151 WESTERN BLUEBILL (Red-breasted Bluebill, Blue-billed Weaver)
Spermophaga haematina
Plate 41

Africa

Loxia haematina Vieillot, 1805, Ois. Chant., p. 102. Africa; restricted to Gold Coast by Neumann, 1910, Journ. f. Ornith., 58, p. 523.

IDENTIFICATION Length 15 cm (6 in). A scarce, little-known and rarely seen, skulking weaver-finch. Male is all black except for bright red or scarlet chin (lower sides of face in *pustulata*) to breast and upper flanks; female has dusky black face tinged with red, becoming red on breast and flanks with white-spotted belly. Both sexes have a pearl-blue bill with red tip. **Confusion species:** Both sexes differ from Red-headed (152) and Grant's (150) Bluebills in having dark grey or black forehead to nape. Females told from female Grant's also by reddish (not grey) face and more extensive red on lower breast and flanks. Crimson (147) and Black-bellied (148) Seedcrackers are similar, but both have all-red or predominantly all-red heads, while no female seedcracker shows white spots or bars on underparts. Often mistaken for malimbes (*Malimbus* spp.), all but one of which, have thinner and slightly longer weaver-like bills and bright red on forehead to nape; the exception is Grey's Malimbe (*M. nitens*), which has a crescent-like patch of red on throat and upper breast. Note: Considered by some authorities to be conspecific with Red-headed Bluebill.

DESCRIPTION Sexes differ. **Adult male:** Entire head, face and upperparts including wings and tail glossy black. Chin and throat to centre of lower breast and flanks deep or rich scarlet, rest of underparts jet-black. Bill deep at base, triangular but slightly elongated with curved culmen, deep metallic blue or pearl-blue with a red tip and cutting edges in breeding season. Eye dark brown or chestnut-red; eyelids pale or whitish-blue. Legs and feet reddish-brown, brownish-black, dark green or olive. **Adult female:** Forehead and face dark or blackish-maroon or tinged with orange, becoming a deep grey or slate-grey on crown and nape. Mantle and back to rump deep grey or blackish; wings blackish-brown; uppertail-coverts red or reddish, tinged darker or orange, extending to base of tail, with rest of tail dark brown or blackish-brown. Chin and throat as male, but more orange and less intensely glossy red; belly, lower flanks and undertail-coverts black, heavily spotted or barred white. Bill much as male's. **Juvenile:** Young birds can be sexed at an early age: young males are generally dark slate-grey like adult female, and have orange or dull rust-red on uppertail-coverts and are tinged the same on breast and flanks; young females lack or have only very faint reddish

tinge on breast, but show pale white or buffish barring or spotting on belly and flanks.

GEOGRAPHICAL VARIATION Males of race *pustulata* have lores to lower ear-coverts red and joining red of chin and throat on sides of neck, and uppertail-coverts are bright crimson-red; bill has red tip and cutting edges to both mandibles. Females have less red on forehead than nominate, but have brighter orange-red face and crimson-red or orange-red uppertail-coverts. Male *togoensis* are intermediate between nominate and *pustulata*, with a black face but red or orange-red uppertail-coverts, and bill as *pustulata*; females closely resemble *pustulata*, but intermediates occur in areas where ranges overlap.

VOICE Contact note is a fairly sharp (or can be soft to almost inaudible) 'tip', 'tsik', 'tsip' or even a more drawn-out 'tsee'; has a strong *Sylvia* warbler-like 'tack', often repeated as an alarm. The song is a low clucking series of 'tack' notes rising into a trill before dying away, usually given from low thick undergrowth or dense cover; both sexes sing.

STATUS, HABITAT AND BEHAVIOUR Local and probably not uncommon; shy and extremely elusive, easily overlooked. Inhabits dense thickets or edges of forest, secondary forest, bush or over-grown areas such as abandoned cultivation, usually, though not always, near damp ground, but avoids swamp habitat. Usually in pairs or family parties, and often detected by characteristic contact note. Forages low down in undergrowth or on the ground, but not averse to searching creepers or vines on trees. Feeds on a variety of seeds, including rice, also insects, spiders and husks of oil-palm fruit.

DISTRIBUTION *S. h. haematina*: southwest Senegal and west Gambia to southern Mali, south and southeast to Sierra Leone, Liberia and Ghana.

S. h. pustulata: southeast Nigeria (east of lower Niger river), Cameroon, Central African Republic to Congo, western and central northern Zaire and northwest Angola (Quincolungo).

S. h. togoensis: Togo to southwest Nigeria (west of lower Niger river).

MEASUREMENTS Wing 63·5–73; tail 47–56·5; tarsus 20–23; bill (culmen) of male 16·5–19, of female 14–17. Wing of *pustulata* 65–74; tail 49–58.

REFERENCES Bannerman (1953), Goodwin (1982), Louette (1988).

152 RED-HEADED BLUEBILL *Spermophaga ruficapilla* Plate 41

Africa

Spermospiza ruficapilla Shelley, 1888, Proc. Zool. Soc. London, p. 30, Bellima, upper Uele district [Zaire].

IDENTIFICATION Length 15 cm (6 in). Similar to Grant's (150) and Western (151) Bluebills, both of which it overlaps in range, and to Crimson (147) and Black-bellied (148) Seedcrackers in bill size and overall shape and plumage. Male has entire head to throat and breast deep scarlet, uppertail-coverts slightly deeper or darker red and rest of plumage black. Female is similar, but slate-grey above and red (but not so intensely scarlet) with white spots and bars on underparts. **Confusion species:** Differs from Western and Grant's Bluebills in entire head to nape and hindneck being red. Female Grant's is grey on head and face, while male Grant's has black nape and somewhat brighter red on rump and uppertail-coverts and on head and face. Differs from either seedcracker in all-black tail and less massive or longer bill which has red tip and cutting edges. Considered by some authorities to be conspecific with Western Bluebill.

DESCRIPTION Sexes differ. **Adult male:** Entire head to nape and hindneck, sides of neck to chin, throat, breast and upper flanks bright or iridescent scarlet. Mantle, back, scapulars and all wing feathers black, slightly glossy; rump black, uppertail-coverts deep or dark red (darker than head and breast). Tail is slightly rounded, black, and slightly glossy above. Centre of lower breast and upper belly to undertail-coverts black. Bill is large and deep at base, almost triangular but long with curved culmen, light metallic blue or silvery-blue with tip and cutting edges red or reddish-pink. Eye dark brown or reddish-brown, with a narrow blue or bluish eye-ring (unlikely to be seen in the field). Legs and feet dark brown or olive-green. **Adult female:** Very similar to male in overall plumage, but red on head, face and underparts less intense and more suffused with orange; mantle to rump and wings slate-grey (not black), and red on uppertail-coverts is also slightly orange in tone. Tail dark slate-grey. Underparts below red are dark blackish-grey, heavily spotted with small round white spots on belly and flanks, becoming bars on lower belly, vent and undertail-coverts. Bill as male. **Juvenile:** Generally dark or dull grey, males usually darker than females, with a red tinge or heavy wash on face and breast. Young females can show pale or ill-defined spots or bars on belly and flanks at an early age. Bill grey or deep grey, gradu-ally becoming pale blue with a pale tip and pinkish cutting edges.

GEOGRAPHICAL VARIATION Males of isolated race *cana* have black upperparts of nominate dark grey (paler than nominate female), and on some individuals this extends onto nape and hindneck; primaries and secondaries tinged brown, belly black, flanks tinged brownish; red areas are less deep or scarlet but still iridescent, with ginger or rufous feather bases showing through. Female as nominate, but paler grey on upperparts and more barred than spotted with white on lower underparts. Bill of both sexes is bright purple with red tip and cutting edges.

VOICE Generally silent. Call a soft, almost inaudible squeak, a 'seet' or 'tseet' contact note, and a hard, almost chat-like clacking or 'tack' alarm. The song consists of rising and falling chuckling, whistling or flute-like notes ending in a trill.

STATUS, HABITAT AND BEHAVIOUR Widespread, but uncommon or locally common. Shy and skulking, keeping to dense cover or low undergrowth. Found in forest edges or clearings, usually secondary-forest areas, thickets or overgrown areas (up to 2400 m), usually in damp areas though avoids wet swamps or marshes. Often in pairs or small parties, rarely more than five together. Flight slow or sluggish and rather fluttery, but direct; at rest usually keeps a low or horizontal posture and nervously flicks wings and tail. Feeds low down in the undergrowth or on the ground itself, occasionally in the open but always within retreating distance of cover. Feeds on a variety of grass seeds but also some insects, especially termites; race *cana* also feeds on seeds of the plant *Olyra latifolia*.

DISTRIBUTION *S. r. ruficapilla*: extreme southern Sudan, Uganda (mainly forests of west and south), western Kenya (Mount Elgon) to northwest and western Tanzania, west to eastern Zaire and northwest Angola.

S. r. cana: eastern Usambara Mountains, northeast Tanzania.

MEASUREMENTS Wing of male 66–76, of female 68–75; tail of male 53·5–59, of female 48·5–57·5; bill (culmen) 16–19·5. Weight 21–24.

REFERENCES Goodwin (1982), Louette (1988), Moreau and Moreau (1937).

GENUS *CLYTOSPIZA*

One species. One of the twinspots (see also *Mandingoa*, *Hypargos* and *Euschistospiza*). Has distinct chin and throat markings, and spots on underparts are less uniform, becoming bars on lower flanks, belly and undertail. The wing has a long outer primary, and the courtship display suggests that it is closer to those species in *Hypargos*, with which it is allopatric.

153 BROWN TWINSPOT (Monteiri's Twinspot) *Clytospiza monteiri*
Plate 37

Africa

Pytelia monteiri Hartlaub, 1860, Proc. Zool. Soc. London, p. 111, Bembe, Congo district, Angola.

IDENTIFICATION Length 13 cm (5 in). A small grey-headed bird with grey-brown back, bright red rump and blackish tail. Sexes differ slightly in chin and throat markings, but both have diagnostic brown or rich brown underparts heavily spotted and barred with white. The grey head and brown underparts with white spots/bars are diagnostic; all other twinspots have either red breasts, white spots on black on underparts or green upperparts.

DESCRIPTION Sexes differ. **Adult male:** Almost entire head (except for dark lores) is dark grey or slate-grey to nape and sides of neck and chin, with a distinctive bright red stripe from chin to centre of lower throat. Mantle, back, scapulars and wings dull dark brown, wings rather short and rounded; rump and uppertail-coverts dark blood-red. Tail brownish or bronzed brown-black, rounded at sides of tip and appears graduated when spread. Entire underparts below chin and throat warm or rich chestnut-brown, spotted heavily with white on breast and upper flanks and becoming barred on belly, lower flanks and undertail-coverts. Bill short but fairly deep at base with slight curve to culmen, black or grey-blue at base. Eye red or deep red; eye-ring pale blue. Legs and feet flesh-brown. **Adult female:** Almost identical to adult male, but generally paler grey on lores, and red on centre of throat is replaced with white; less rich brown or chestnut on underparts and more orange-red than red on rump and uppertail-coverts. **Juvenile:** Similar to adult female, but browner on head and warmer brown on mantle, back and wings; rump and uppertail-coverts dull red. Underparts light orange-brown or pale brown, tinged with fawn or deep buff, and with some faint white barring on

lower belly and undertail-coverts. Young males are darker on head and underparts than young females. Eye brown; bill blackish.

VOICE Call a sharp and frequently repeated 'vay, vay, vay', often quite intensely loud; alarm is a hard *Sylvia*-like 'teck' or 'tack'. The song, given by the male only during courtship, is a variable series of twittering notes.

STATUS, HABITAT AND BEHAVIOUR Uncommon or locally common. Found in tall grassland savanna or damp thickets, lantana scrub, bush or forest edges and clearings, also edges of cultivation where there is thick cover. Usually occurs in pairs or small, probably family, parties. Feeds almost entirely on the ground, where it shuffles about in a horizontal posture and makes long striding hops. Feeds on a variety of seeds, mostly grass but also some millet; also takes insects, particularly white ants, termites and spiders.

DISTRIBUTION Monotypic. The grasslands of southeast Nigeria, Cameroon, southern Gabon, southern Congo, Cabinda and northwest Angola; also Central African Republic to central and northern Zaire, extreme southern Chad, southern Sudan (north to Bussere), west and southern Uganda and western Kenya.

MOVEMENTS Sedentary, though in recent years the range has extended west into southeast Nigeria and slightly to the east in west-central Kenya.

MEASUREMENTS Wing 55–61; tail 43–55; tarsus 17–18; bill 11–13.

REFERENCES Goodwin (1982), Mackworth-Praed and Grant (1960).

GENUS *HYPARGOS*

Two species. Twinspots (see also *Mandingoa, Euschistospiza* and *Clytospiza*). Strongly spotted (in pairs on individual feathers) with white or pinkish-white on black underparts. The general plumage suggests close affinity to *Euschistospiza*, but may also have strong links with the much larger bluebills *Spermophaga*.

154 ROSY TWINSPOT (Pink-throated Twinspot, Verreaux's Twinspot) *Hypargos margaritatus*　　　　　Plate 37
Africa

Spermophaga margaritata Strickland, 1844, Ann. Mag. Nat. Hist., 13, p. 418, Madagascar; amended to Coguna, Inhambane district, Mozambique, by W.L. Sclater, 1911, Ibis, p. 320.

IDENTIFICATION Length 12–13 cm (4¾–5 in). A small, slender and obvious twinspot, both sexes having black underparts boldly spotted with white (pale pink on male at close range). **Confusion species:** Similar to Peters's Twinspot (155), but paler and not so boldly coloured. Male has pink or deep pink (not bright red) face, throat and breast and brown (not grey) crown and nape. Female Rosy is paler (grey) on breast, and lacks yellow throat and rusty-orange breast of Peters's.

DESCRIPTION Sexes differ. **Adult male:** Forehead to crown and nape a warm brown or gingery-brown, tinged slightly sandy. Mantle, back and scapulars slightly browner and less warm or ginger in tone; lower back and upper rump darker, almost dark brown; lower rump and uppertail-coverts deep pinkish-mauve, extending slightly onto edges of base of tail feathers, tail otherwise dark brown. Wings almost entirely uniform dark brown, edges to greater and primary coverts, flight feathers and tertials slightly warmer or sandy in tone. Lores, over eye to ear-coverts, sides of neck, chin, throat and entire breast deep pink or slightly tinged mauve (especially on lower breast); belly and flanks black, heavily marked (but unevenly spread, mostly on flanks and sides of belly) with large round white spots, some slightly overlapping; undertail-coverts black. On some, spots on upper flanks are pale pink, and on others belly is entirely black. Bill small or short with a fairly deep base, triangular, pointed, black or slaty blue-grey. Eye dark or dark brown, with pale pinkish or blue eye-ring. Legs and feet dark grey or black. **Adult female:** A pale version of male. Forehead to crown and nape warm brown or gingery-brown; mantle, back, scapulars and wings dark brown, with slightly paler edges to coverts; rump and uppertail-coverts to base of tail deep pink, rest of tail black or blackish-brown. Lores to above eyes, cheeks and ear-coverts grey or greyish, tinged with buff-brown, becoming plain grey on sides of neck, chin, throat and breast. Upper belly and flanks black, with large round white spots in pairs, centre of belly to undertail-coverts pale buff or buffish-white. Bill as male. Eye dark; eye-ring pink, pinkish or occasionally pale blue. **Juvenile:** Similar to adult female above, but generally duller or greyish-brown with a reddish tinge to lower rump and base of tail. Pale buffish-brown on breast; generally lacks black belly and white spots, though young males soon begin to show pink or mauve wash and grey or dull buffish-white on belly and undertail-coverts.

VOICE Some calls very similar to those of Peters's Twinspot, but the following are fairly distinct: a soft 'seesee'; alarm a short trilling 'zirr' or 'rrrrreee' or a long high-pitched ringing 'tseeerrrr'. The song is short trilling 'tit, tit tititit' recalling Red-billed Firefinch (161).

STATUS, HABITAT AND BEHAVIOUR Common or locally common. Occurs in thickets, bush, savanna woodland or acacia scrub, usually in (or in the vicinity of) dense tangled growth, even forest edges. Usually in pairs or small family parties, often in mixed flocks with firefinches or waxbills; a shy and elusive bird, easily alarmed, diving into cover at first sign of danger. Feeds on the ground or low down in bushes, on a variety of small seeds and occasionally small insects.

DISTRIBUTION Monotypic. Southern Mozambique (north to the Save river) to eastern Transvaal, eastern Swaziland and northern Natal, South Africa.

MOVEMENTS Generally sedentary.

MEASUREMENTS Wing of male 52–56; tail 50–54; tarsus 15·5–17; bill (culmen) 11–12·8.

REFERENCES Goodwin (1982), McLachlan and Liversidge (1978), Newman (1983).

155 PETERS'S TWINSPOT (Red-throated Twinspot) *Hypargos niveoguttatus*

East Africa

Plate 37

Spermophaga niveoguttata Peters, 1868, Journ. f. Ornith., 14, p. 133, Inhambane, Mozambique.

IDENTIFICATION Length 12–13 cm (4¾–5 in). A small, active but quiet and unobtrusive finch, usually found in lowland bush near water. Male has bright red face to breast and rich brown upperparts, while female has duller brown upperparts, pale face and chin but rich rusty or orange on breast; both sexes have characteristic spotted underparts of all twinspots. Overall very similar to Rosy Twinspot (154), with which it overlaps in the south, but much more widespread.

DESCRIPTION Sexes differ. **Adult male:** Forehead to crown deep grey or lead-grey (faintly tinged with olive in fresh plumage), becoming warm brown or light reddish-brown on lower nape, mantle, back, scapulars and upper rump; lower rump, uppertail-coverts and centre of base of tail deep or rich crimson, rest of tail and all outers black or blackish-brown. All wing-coverts, tertials and edges to flight feathers warm brown or light reddish-brown as scapulars; flight feathers otherwise dull brown. Lores, over eye, sides of neck to upper breast rich red or bright crimson. Belly and flanks black, heavily spotted with large circular white spots, most heavily on flanks and sides of belly; vent and undertail-coverts black, unspotted. Bill quite large or substantial, pointed, black, blue-black or tinged purplish, pale blue-grey at base. Eye brown or reddish-brown, with white or pale blue eye-ring. Legs and feet grey or grey-brown. In worn plumage, grey on head and red on breast much paler. **Adult female:** A pale and more washed-out version of male, with grey or pale grey-brown upperparts (yellowish or pale brown on some); rump and uppertail-coverts to base of tail duller or deeper red. Face pale yellowish-buff from lores over eye to ear-coverts, occasionally tinged with grey on lores and ear-coverts. Chin to lower throat and sides of neck the same, but often suffused with pink or orange; lower throat and breast reddish or rusty orange-brown. Belly and flanks dark grey-black, heavily spotted with white (each spot emarginated with black), spots heaviest or largest on flanks and sides of belly; undertail-coverts dark grey or black. Bill dark grey-black or bluish-black, with paler blue-grey at base. Eye-ring as male but thinner. **Juvenile:** Very similar to adult female above, but browner on the top of head, with face buff and throat, sides of neck and breast russet-brown; belly to undertail-coverts black or greyish-black with some pale tips to feathers.

GEOGRAPHICAL VARIATION All racial variation is slight, and some authorities consider the species to be monotypic with local geographical variation in plumage. Most differences are in plumage tones, are very slight to insignificant in terms of identification in the field, and may not be valid at all times of the year.

VOICE Generally silent, but gives a quiet hissing note; also a 'tseet' is used as a contact call, as is a longer more drawn-out and louder, cricket-like trill 'trree-rree'. The song is a feeble and stuttering trill and continues with short whistling or clucking notes.

STATUS, HABITAT AND BEHAVIOUR Common or locally common; widespread but easily overlooked. Inhabits lowland bush or grassland (generally below 1250 m, but up to 1800 m in parts of the range) and evergreen thickets or acacia scrub, often in tangled or rank grass and undergrowth at edges of secondary forest, near streams or pools, occasionally close to human settlements. Usually in pairs or small parties, and in some areas becomes tame and inquisitive. Often feeds on the ground in the open, but usually not far from cover. Feeds on a variety of seeds, particularly grass, and occasionally small insects.

DISTRIBUTION *H. n. niveoguttatus:* Malawi to Zimbabwe and Mozambique south to Chimonzo and Macia.

H. n. macrospilotus: eastern Zaire, locally throughout eastern Kenya to extreme southern Somalia, south to Tanzania and Malawi *H. n. idius:* eastern Angola and Zambia.

H. n. interior: Zimbabwe.

MEASUREMENTS Wing of male 54–58; tail 48–53; tarsus 16–17·5; bill (culmen) 12–13·5. Weight 15–16.

REFERENCES McLachlan and Liversidge (1978), Newman (1983), Sclater and Moreau (1933).

GENUS *EUSCHISTOSPIZA*

Two species. Twinspots (see also *Mandingoa*, *Clytospiza* and *Hypargos*). Generally dark grey in plumage, and spots on underparts are small (or minute crescents or bars) and restricted to flanks. Genus possibly has closer affinities with *Lagonosticta* species than with other twinspots.

156 DYBOWSKI'S DUSKY TWINSPOT *Euschistospiza dybowskii*

Plate 38

Africa

Lagonosticta dybowskii Oustalet, 1892, Naturaliste, p. 231, upper Kemo River, Oubangi-Chari [Zaire].

IDENTIFICATION Length 12 cm (4¾ in). A small, skulking and little-known dark grey or black finch with a fragmented distribution across grassland and savanna edge of the northern tropical forest belt. The male has crimson-red on mantle to uppertail-coverts, and black belly spotted with white; female similar, but has red on mantle broken with grey and is greyer on underparts. **Confusion species:** Similar to out-of-range Dusky Twinspot (157), but Dybowski's crimson back and bold white spots on flanks are distinctive. All other twinspots lack dark grey head and face. Similar to Dusky Crimson-wing (145), but latter has red on head, lacks white spots on underparts and has a different tail shape (and slightly different behaviour).

DESCRIPTION Sexes differ. **Adult male:** Entire head to lower nape, chin, throat and breast slate-grey. Mantle, back and scapulars to rump and long uppertail-coverts deep crimson-red with grey feather bases often showing through in patches (especially when worn or in non-breeding season). Tail slightly rounded at tip, partly concealed by uppertail-coverts and black, but often shows deep crimson on outer webs. Median and greater coverts dark grey or tinged olive-brown, often with small white spots on tips of outer feathers; rest of wing feathers dark slate-grey, with paler edges when worn. Lower breast dark slate-grey; belly, flanks and undertail-coverts black, with bold white spots, half-spots or crescents on flanks (belly and vent unspotted). Both mandibles curve to a point on black bill. Eye dark red; eye-ring pale grey-blue but can be pink or red. Legs and feet dark grey, black or blackish-brown. **Adult female:** Slightly smaller than male and generally paler grey on head and breast; white spots on flanks are often bordered with black (but this not always noticeable). Red on mantle to uppertail-coverts is deeper or duller crimson and broken by grey feather bases. Eye brown or reddish-brown, eye-ring pale grey. Wings much browner (or more blackish-brown) than male. **Juvenile:** Similar to adult female, but generally slate-grey with rusty or deep reddish-brown patches on mantle to rump; lacks white spots on wholly dark grey underparts. Eye and eye-ring pale grey. Adult plumage is attained (as in most estrildids) within three months of life.

VOICE Call a soft and quickly repeated 'tset' or 'tsit-tsit', also used as an alarm note but much louder, becoming 'tsit-tsit-tsit'. Song consists of a variety of trills and phrases suggestive of a Canary (7), deep bubbling notes of a Nightingale (*Luscinia megarhynchos*) and flute-like phrases of a Blackbird (*Turdus merula*), usually given from cover or when displaying; female also sings, especially if unpaired, a softer version of male's song.

STATUS, HABITAT AND BEHAVIOUR Uncommon and local or scarce; generally little known or recorded; its nest and eggs are unknown in the wild. Inhabits grassy savanna with dense thickets in hilly regions up to considerable elevation in some areas, and in lower regions, in grass clumps near rivers; also found along the edges of forest and some cultivated areas. Occurs in pairs, small groups or family parties; often in mixed feeding flocks with African (162) and Black-bellied (158) Firefinches. Feeds on the ground, principally on grass seeds but also on a variety of small insects, and known habitually to dig in soft earth.

DISTRIBUTION Monotypic. Sierra Leone and Guinea and from Mambilla and Jos plateaux, Nigeria, east to Cameroon, Central African Republic, northern Zaire and southern Sudan (Zande district); possibly also a very scarce resident in southeast Senegal, where recorded twice, in March 1972 and March 1984.

MOVEMENTS Sedentary.

MEASUREMENTS Wing 49–57; tail 39–47; tarsus 16–17; bill 11–12.

REFERENCES Bannerman (1953), Goodwin (1982), Morel and Morel (1990).

157 DUSKY TWINSPOT (Dusky Firefinch) *Euschistospiza cinereovinacea* Plate 38

Africa

Lagonosticta cinereo-vinacea Sousa, 1889, Jorn. Sci. Math. Phys. Nat. Lisboa, ser. 2, p. 49, Quindumbo, Angola highlands.

IDENTIFICATION Length 11·5 cm (4½ in). A small and inconspicuous dark grey finch of high mountain valleys and plateau grassland of Angola. Of all the twinspots this has the smallest spots, with just tips of flank feathers finely spotted with white; all dark grey except for deep blood-red rump and uppertail-coverts and slightly paler red flanks. Easily told from all other twinspots by lack of red on head or breast and by spots on underparts being poorly developed or very small; from very similar Dybowski's Dusky Twinspot (156), with which it does not overlap, also by lack of red on mantle, back and scapulars. All similar crimson-wings, particularly Dusky Crimson-wing (145), and all blue-bills (150–152) have red on head and/or chin and throat.

DESCRIPTION Sexes alike. **Adult:** Entire head, neck and upperparts to lower back dark slate or sooty-grey, with wings slightly browner or with a tinge of brown when worn; rump and uppertail-coverts deep crimson. Tail rounded at tip and black. Chin, throat and breast dark grey or blackish, becoming black on belly and undertail-coverts; flanks and sides of belly deep scarlet or burgundy, slightly paler than rump and uppertail-coverts, and finely spotted or barred with white (but spots or bars are very small and not obvious from any distance).

Bill short and both mandibles curve to a point, black or deep blue-black. Eye red or reddish-brown, and eye-ring pale grey or pale blue or whitish. Legs and feet grey to greyish-black. Adult females are slightly greyer on head and breast and not black. **Juvenile:** Generally dark slate or olive-grey, except for brown wings, dull or deep maroon or crimson rump and uppertail-coverts, and also a pink or reddish wash on unspotted flanks. Bill horn at first, quickly becoming black. Eye brown, with a pale grey or whitish eye-ring. Legs and feet brown.

GEOGRAPHICAL VARIATION Adults of race *graueri* are darker or blacker on grey areas of plumage, especially throat and breast, and red or deep maroon or crimson is brighter, but very few specimens have been examined. Eye-ring purplish-red.

VOICE 'Tsyip, tsyip' is the contact note, becoming louder and more shrill and repeated 'tsvilip' as an alarm. Song, given only during courtship, is a varying series of not very loud or striking notes.

STATUS, HABITAT AND BEHAVIOUR Locally common; birds of race *graueri* are shy, secretive and very little known. Inhabits long grass in high mountain valleys or on plateau grassland with thickets, bush or outcrops of scrub, usually between 1500 m and 1800 m, and *graueri* to 2000 m. Usually alone or in pairs; birds of nominate race occupy same habitat as Red-winged Cisticola (*Cisticola emini*). Feeds on the ground, on a variety of grass seeds and small insects.

DISTRIBUTION *E. c. cinereovinacea*: western and central Angola.

E. c. graueri: southwest Uganda (north to Lake Chahafi and the Impenetrable Forest) to central and eastern Zaire, Rwanda and Burundi.

MOVEMENTS Resident and sedentary.

MEASUREMENTS Wing 50–55.

REFERENCE Goodwin (1982).

GENUS *LAGONOSTICTA*

Nine species. Firefinches: small, with mostly reddish (including pink to crimson-red) plumage, pointed bills, small white spots on sides of breast (except one) and graduated or wedge-shaped tails. Usually dry-country birds of semi-arid grassland, although some prefer vicinity of human settlements or edges of swamps or rivers. Most species are fairly widespread throughout Africa but avoid tropical forest. Probably more closely allied to twinspots *Hypargos* and *Euschistospiza* and cordon-bleus *Uraeginthus* than to initially similar waxbills.

158 BLACK-BELLIED FIREFINCH (Black-billed Firefinch) *Lagonosticta rara*
Plate 43

Africa

Habropyga rara Antinori, 1864, Coll. Uccelli, p. 72, between White Nile and Bahr el Ghazal.

IDENTIFICATION Length 10 cm (4 in). A small and active finch, often in small parties feeding on edge of cultivated areas. Fairly common but not always easily separated from similar species with which it associates. Male is deep wine-red above except for dark brown wings; belly and undertail-coverts black. Female paler buff-brown about head and has browner upperparts. Very similar to several other firefinches, but combination of red on mantle to uppertail-coverts, black on centre of belly and lack of any small white spots is diagnostic. **Confusion species:** Male African Firefinch (162) and Pale-billed Firefinch (163) are both brown-backed, and together with Jameson's Firefinch (164) (does not overlap with latter two in range) have small white spots on side of breast and black only on lower belly, ventral region to undertail-coverts. Females are best separated by dark grey head and chin, dark blood-red loral spot, pale base to bill and black on belly and undertail-coverts. In all cases apart from African Firefinch, where confusion arises colour of bill (especially base) is diagnostic.

DESCRIPTION Sexes differ. **Adult male:** Entire head, nape, mantle and back to face, chin, throat, breast and upper flanks deep blood-red or wine-red, tinged with deep or rich pink on breast and upper flanks; in worn plumage, brown feather bases may show on body. Rump and uppertail-coverts brighter or more red-crimson than back. Tail is thin and appears rounded at tip, black with some red on fringes to bases of feathers. Wings almost entirely uniform dull brown or earth-brown, with some deep red or wine-red edges to median coverts and more faintly on greaters. Underparts from centre of lower breast, belly, rear flanks and undertail-coverts black. Bill small, almost conical, pointed, black with a white, pink or pinkish-red base to lower mandible. Eye brown or dark brown; eye-ring pale, buff or greyish-green. Legs and feet slate-grey. **Adult female:** Forehead, crown, nape and ear-coverts grey, with a dark red spot on lores. Mantle, back and scapulars dull brown with a tinge of dull or deep red (not always present), merging with dull dark brown of coverts and flight feathers;

rump and uppertail-coverts deep crimson. Tail crimson at base, becoming brown or deep brown (not black). Chin and throat buff; breast and upper flanks pinkish, or slightly tinged deeper wine-red towards flanks; upper belly buffish-brown; lower belly, vent and undertail-coverts entirely black or brownish-black. Bill as male. **Juvenile:** A dull buffish-brown on upperparts, with dull or deep crimson on rump and uppertail-coverts; throat buff, becoming buffish grey-brown on rest of underparts, warmer or pale buff on breast (some with a dark wine flush) and paler buff on undertail-coverts. Bill blackish, base of lower mandible pink. Eye-ring pale yellowish.

GEOGRAPHICAL VARIATION Males of race *forbesi* are much brighter than nominate, with red of breast and uppertail-coverts deep or rich bright crimson and feathers of wing-coverts edged with red; jet-black on underparts. Females have head darker grey, chin and throat also grey, and upperparts deeper or brighter wine-red; deeper wine-red on breast and flanks, becoming olive-black on belly and black on undertail-coverts.

VOICE Call a repeated sharp 'chek' or 'tseeay', also a soft nasal 'keeyh' or 'squeer'. Song a variable jumble of low-pitched phrases and a Greenfinch-like trilling ending with a whistling 'tyee-tyee-tyee' or 'tew-tew-tew', very like African Firefinch (162).

STATUS, HABITAT AND BEHAVIOUR Widespread, common or locally common; not always easy to see and becoming scarce towards eastern end of the range. A bird of open country with grassland savanna or with scattered bush, but also favours edges of cultivated areas, often at a considerable elevation. Usually in pairs or small parties, often mixing with other firefinches particularly African. Feeds on the ground, on a variety of small seeds, millet, and also takes some insects, principally termites. A brood host to the Nigerian (or Alexander's) Indigobird (*Vidua funerea nigeriae*).

DISTRIBUTION *L. r. rara*: northern Cameroon and the Central African Republic to northern Zaire, southern Sudan, northern Uganda and western Kenya.

L. r. forbesi: southeast Senegal (rare, three

records) discontinuously to eastern Sierra Leone, Liberia (Mount Nimba) and southern Guinea east to Ghana, and possibly east to central and northern Nigeria.

MEASUREMENTS Wing 46–52; tail 37–41; tarsus 15; bill 10.
REFERENCE Goodwin (1982).

159 BAR-BREASTED FIREFINCH *Lagonosticta rufopicta*   **Plate 42**
Africa

Estrilda rufopicta Fraser, 1843, Proc. Zool. Soc. London, p. 27, Cape Coast castle, Gold Coast.

IDENTIFICATION Length 11 cm (4¼ in). A very small red-and-brown firefinch of West and central African grassland savanna. Sexes alike or almost so; red on head extends to breast, with fine white barring or speckles on breast distinguishing it from very similar Red-billed Firefinch (161). **Confusion species:** Only Brown Firefinch (160) and Red-billed Firefinch share red bill. Brown Firefinch lacks red rump and pink is restricted to face and upper breast. Male Red-billed is extensively red on head, this usually extending (varying in intensity, depending on race) onto mantle, where Bar-breasted has grey-brown forehead and crown and red areas are more mauve-red; spots more crescent-like on Bar-breasted but very small on Red-billed. Juvenile similar to those of Black-bellied (158), Brown and Black-faced (166), and separation is difficult owing to early moult and bill-colour changes, but Bar-breasted always has crimson flush on breast.
DESCRIPTION Sexes alike. **Adult:** Lower forehead, lores and over eye deep pinkish-red, rest of face to ear-coverts and sides of neck, chin and throat the same or slightly paler and less intensely crimson. Upper forehead to crown, nape, mantle, back, scapulars and upper rump uniform greyish earth-brown, fairly dark in tone and becoming olive-brown in worn plumage; lower rump and uppertail-coverts deep blood-red or crimson, this extending to base of tail, especially on bases to central pair of feathers and outer webs of outers (except outermost), with rest of tail dark-brownish-black (tail is short but broad, and rounded at tip). All wing-coverts the same earth-brown as rest of upperparts, but on some birds (in fresh plumage) washed with crimson, especially on tips; flight feathers slightly darker brown. Pinkish-red of face extends to breast and upper belly, but becoming red- or mauve-crimson with small white crescents or faint bars on sides of breast and upper flanks; belly and lower flanks greyish or buffish grey-brown, becoming paler on undertail-coverts. Bill is small, fairly thin and pointed, pink or pinkish-red, but on some darker or brown at base and along culmen. Eye brown or dark brown, eye-ring pale grey or white. Legs and feet flesh-pink, or brown tinged pale pinkish. **Juvenile:** Generally dull earth-brown, with rump and uppertail-coverts as adult but deeper or duller crimson; lacks any red on face, but is washed with crimson or pale pinkish-crimson on breast; flanks and belly are buffish grey-brown, becoming paler or more buffish on undertail-coverts. Bill entirely brown or dusky brown.
GEOGRAPHICAL VARIATION See note below under Distribution. Race *lateritia* is slightly greyer on crown to nape, and has white spots or speckles on sides of breast forming bars, extending quite noticeably across feathers.
VOICE Call a musical twittering and a short, sharp, high-pitched piercing note, also used as a contact; alarm call is low-pitched 'tzet' or 'chuk', very similar to that of Red-billed Firefinch. Song is vigorous and composed of harsh metallic and low nasal notes.
STATUS, HABITAT AND BEHAVIOUR Common or locally common. A widely distributed finch of grassland, bush, acacia savanna and forest clearings, also edges of villages, human settlements or cultivated areas, usually but not exclusively in damp areas or along streams. Quite tame and confiding, but normally within reach of cover; often feeds in mixed flocks, but also occurs in pairs or small family parties or in larger groups in the non-breeding season. Feeds on the ground, on a variety of seeds, usually grass and millet.
DISTRIBUTION *L. r. rufopicta*: Senegal (local in the south and east) and the Gambia discontinuously southeast and east to southern Mali, Guinea, Ivory Coast, Ghana to Nigeria (mostly in the south and central areas), northern Cameroon, the Central African Republic and northern Zaire (Ubangi-Shari district).

L. r. lateritia: southern Sudan (to about 8°N), southwest Ethiopia and northeast Zaire, western Uganda to eastern Kenya.

Note: Regarded by some authorities as monotypic.
MEASUREMENTS Wing 45–51; tail 33–38; tarsus 12; bill 8.
REFERENCE Goodwin (1982).

Lagonosticta nitidula Hartlaub, 1886, Bull. Mus. Hist. Nat. Belg., 4, p. 145, near Lake Tanganyika; amended to Mpala by Chapin, 1954, Bull. Amer. Mus. Nat. Hist., 75B, p. 531.

IDENTIFICATION Length 10 cm (4 in). Similar to but browner than Bar-breasted Firefinch (159), predominantly grey-brown or dusky grey with a mauve-pink breast with small white spots. Sexes slightly different, with females showing less pink (darker bases showing through) on face and throat, but probably not always separable in the field. **Confusion species:** The grey or grey-brown on rump, uppertail-coverts and base of tail is distinctive and separates it from any of the other firefinches or Peters's (155) or Rosy (154) Twinspots, which also have more red or pink on face and breast.

DESCRIPTION Sexes differ slightly. **Adult male:** Forehead grey-brown, occasionally with some pink or pinkish feathers on lower or sides. Crown and nape to rump, uppertail-coverts and wings uniform dull or dark grey-brown, with crown, nape, rump and uppertail-coverts slightly greyer than rest of upperparts; wing-coverts as upperparts, but flight feathers and tertials dark brown. Tail dark brown, almost black in fresh plumage. Lores, over eye to ear-coverts, chin, throat and breast pinkish-red, deeper on breast, with prominent small white spots on sides of breast, spots sometimes joining to form short crescents or bars; sides of breast to flanks and belly grey-brown; undertail-coverts paler or greyish-buff. Bill short and pointed, purple-red, pink or red at base and sides, culmen and tip black. Eye brown or reddish-brown; eye-ring pale blue. Legs and feet grey or dark grey. **Adult female:** Similar to adult male but generally paler, especially in reddish-pink tone of throat and breast, which also is not usually so extensive as on male and is broken by grey feather bases; rest of underparts much paler buff or buffish-brown than male. **Juvenile:** Similar to adult, but lacks any pink or red and is much more buffish-brown above and not so grey on crown or rump; underparts grey-brown on throat and breast, becoming dull buff-brown on belly, flanks and undertail-coverts. Bill black or blackish-purple, with pale pink base to both mandibles.

GEOGRAPHICAL VARIATION Southern *plumbaria* are much greyer and lack any buff-brown tones above or below; the red is less extensive, more of a heavy or purplish-pink wash on face, chin, throat and upper breast but admixed with grey (white spots on sides and lower breast are often entirely on grey, not pink or pinkish-red, feathers).

VOICE Call a sharp chirping 'tsiep, tsiep', 'wit-wit' or 'weet, weet-weet', or a 'tseeb tseeb-sa-seeb' contact call, also a sharp 'tdrrr', 'trrrt-t-t, eet-eet, trr-trrrt' or 'trr-tk-tk-tk' alarm call; in flight utters a 't-rrr' or 'tsa-trr'. Song a high-pitched medley of notes, 'tseekedeetseeeedeetsweee', or a chirping 'weet, weet-weeheet', interspersed with call notes and alarm-like churrs.

STATUS, HABITAT AND BEHAVIOUR Fairly common or local. Found in lowland riverine forest or thickets, reedbeds and generally swamp or damp areas with thick bush and adjacent open areas, but also occurs along edges of evergreen forest up to 1800 m. Shy, and usually in pairs or small parties, often in mixed groups of other small finches feeding in the open. Feeds on the ground, on a variety of small seeds and millet and probably small insects; has been seen foraging in soft damp earth. A brood host to the Violet Indigobird (*Vidua incognita*).

DISTRIBUTION *L. n. nitidula*: central and eastern Angola, southern Zaire and northeast Zambia.

L. n. plumbaria: southern Zambia, south of the Zambezi, east of Victoria Falls, northwest Zimbabwe (along the Zambezi river for about 25 km above Victoria Falls), also extreme northeast Namibia (Caprivi strip) and northern Botswana south to the Okavango.

Treated by some authorities as a race of Bar-breasted Firefinch.

MEASUREMENTS Wing 52–56; tail 35–42·5; tarsus 16; bill (culmen) 9–10·5. Weight 9–11.

REFERENCES Goodwin (1982), McLachlan and Liversidge (1978).

161 RED-BILLED FIREFINCH (Senegal Firefinch, Common Firefinch)
Lagonosticta senegala **Plate 42**

Africa

Fringilla senegala Linnaeus, 1766, Syst. Nat., ed. 12, p. 320, Senegal.

IDENTIFICATION Length 10 cm (4 in). A widely distributed finch throughout virtually the whole of sub-Saharan Africa. Tame and common, invariably the firefinch around human settlements, often into suburban gardens. Male is almost entirely bright red, with a brown back and wings, some small white spots on sides of breast and pale buff on lower underparts. Female is almost entirely plain brown above with a bright crimson rump, and pale buff below. The bill colour is very distinctive. **Confusion species:** Similar to several other species of firefinch, particularly African (162), Pale-billed (163) and Jameson's (164) females, most of which can be separated fairly easily by the more intense red plumage of the latter and extensive reddish-orange on underparts of the former two; neither African nor Jameson's has a red bill. Both sexes of all three species have black on vent and/or undertail-coverts. Bar-breasted Firefinch (159) has a contrasting face pattern (with top of head grey-brown) and breast spots tending more towards bars. Females also told from Brown Firefinch (160) by paler underparts and lack of red or pinkish-red on face (except lores), chin, throat or breast.

DESCRIPTION Sexes differ. **Adult male:** Head, face, neck, sides of neck to chin, throat, breast, upper belly and upper flanks rich rose-red. Centre of hindcrown to centre of nape, mantle, back, scapulars and wing-coverts brown or warm brown, noticeably washed above with red or reddish, especially on wing-coverts; flight feathers and tertials dark brown (some tertials and inner secondaries also occasionally tinged red); rump, uppertail-coverts and outer webs of bases of tail feathers deep or rich scarlet, rest of tail blackish-brown (tail slightly rounded at tip). Some breast-side feathers have small white spots, but this varies individually and spots can be entirely absent. On lower flanks and belly red merges into a buff-brown or a buffish-orange, becoming paler and more buffish on undertail-coverts; undertail red at base. Bill small and pointed, pink or red at sides with a dark culmen. Eye brown or reddish-brown; eye-ring white or pale yellow. Legs and feet brown or pale flesh-brown. **Adult female:** Forehead and crown to lower back including scapulars and coverts mid-brown or buffish-brown. Wings, rump, uppertail-coverts and tail as adult male. Upper lores red, occasionally to behind eye; generally buff-brown or tinged warm brown on sides of face, some birds showing a reddish wash on cheeks and ear-coverts. Underparts light buff, tinged yellow or brown on breast and upper belly; white spots on breast usually more extensive (than on male) across breast and onto flanks. Sides of bill lightly paler red than on adult male. Eye-ring white or silvery. **Juvenile:** Very similar to adult female, but lacks any red on head; also lacks white spots on breast or flanks, and bill is all black. Young males in first winter are duller red on head and breast, and browner (lacking red wash) on mantle, back and coverts.

GEOGRAPHICAL VARIATION Race *rhodopsis* has brown and buff areas paler and more tinged with yellow, especially on mantle and back. Males of *brunneiceps* and *somaliensis* are brighter and females more grey-brown than buffish-brown; in *brunneiceps*, males have fewer (or sometimes no) white spots on sides of breast and females also tend to be less heavily spotted, and the eye is often (if not always) bright orange. Male *ruberrima* have almost entire upperparts (except wings) a purple-red or deep carmine, lower underparts are more grey-brown than buff- or orange-brown, and spotting on sides of breast is small and well spaced; females are like female *brunneiceps*, grey-brown and not buff-brown, but show more red or a reddish wash in plumage. Male *rendalli* have very little red on upperparts, restricted to face, forehead, wing-coverts and rump to base of tail, and rest of plumage is warm brown or russet-brown; on both sexes white spots on breast are more extensive, often across entire breast. There is much individual and geographical variation within the range of any of the races, which has led to more races being described or differentiated, not all of which are reliably separable in the field.

VOICE Generally the commonest call is a soft but thin or high-pitched 'dwee', 'uee' or 'fweet', often repeated as a double note, the alarm is a low-pitched and abrupt 'tzet', 'chuk' or 'clook', often repeated rapidly, and at nest gives rapid series of notes broken by occasional churring; young birds give a repeated 'tset-tet'. Song is a series of soft, rising, twittering whistling notes which include the 'tset' call at the start .

STATUS, HABITAT AND BEHAVIOUR Widespread and common (abundant in places). A noticeable, tame and confiding bird of acacia grassland and scrub, but better known for its fondness for the proximity of human settlements including towns and suburbs, either in gardens or in cultivated areas; natural habitats include thornbush or acacia scrub and dry woodland thickets or undergrowth, often near water; rarely found above 2000 m. Usually in pairs or small parties, often mixed with other firefinches or waxbills, and in larger groups in the non-breeding season. Has been seen feeding on seedheads from an adjacent perch, but like all other firefinches is predominantly a ground-feeder close to available cover. Feeds on a variety of grass seeds and millet or, on rare occasions, small insects. Breeding host to the parasitic Green Indigobird (*Vidua chalybeata*).

DISTRIBUTION *L. s. senegala*: Cape Verde Islands, Senegal and Gambia southeast and east to Sierra Leone, Liberia, southern Mali, northern Ghana and Nigeria to northern and central Cameroon.

L. s. guineensis: coasts of Guinea and Sierra Leone.

L. s. rhodopsis: southwest Mauritania and northern Senegal to Mali, Burkina Faso, Niger (to northern Air province), Chad, Central African Republic, southern Sudan and western Ethiopia (possibly also northwest Kenya).

L. s. brunneiceps: highlands (above 1000 m) of Ethiopia (except eastern Eritrea).

L. s. somaliensis: southeast Ethiopia to central Somalia, eastern Kenya (coastal lowlands) and eastern Tanzania (south to Usambara Mountains).

L. s. ruberrima: extreme southern Sudan (borders of Uganda), Uganda to central and eastern Zaire, northeast Angola, extreme northern Zambia, Malawi, western Tanzania and northern Zimbabwe.

L. s rendalli: central and southern Angola to Zambia, southeast Zaire, Malawi and southern Tanzania (south of about 8° S) south to Mozambique and northern and central Cape Province, northern Orange Free State and Natal, South Africa.

L. s. pallidicrissa: southern Angola to central and eastern Zimbabwe and northern Namibia.

Not all taxonomic authorities agree on the above separation or distribution of races; other races have also been proposed.

MOVEMENTS Some populations move locally or nomadically outside the breeding season. Has also been recorded (*rhodopsis?*) at oases of extreme southern Algeria, where it may be resident.

MEASUREMENTS Wing of male 47–51, of female 45–50; tail 31–38; tarsus 11–12·5; bill (culmen) 8·5–9·5. Weight of male 7·3–12·3, of female 8·1–10·5.

REFERENCES Goodwin (1982), Hollom *et al.* (1988), Urban (1975).

162 AFRICAN FIREFINCH (Dark Firefinch, Blue-billed Firefinch)
Lagonosticta rubricata　　　　　　　　　　　　　　　　　Plate 42
Africa

Fringilla rubricata Lichtenstein, 1823, Verz. Doubl. Zool. Mus. Berlin, p. 27, Terra Caffrorum; restricted to Uitenhage, Cape Province, by Stresemann, 1954, Ann. Mus. Congo, Zool., new ser. 1, p. 81.

Firefinch 'face' patterns: (a) L. landanae; *(b)* L. r. rubricata; *(c)* L. rufopicta; *(d)* L. nitidula, L. senegala; *(e)* L. rhodopareia, L. virata, L. larvata *(f)* L. rara.

IDENTIFICATION Length 10–11·5 cm (4–4½ in). A small red or reddish and brown firefinch with a dark grey crown similar in tone to but much deeper red than Red-billed Firefinch (161), with black undertail-coverts. Not usually so tame or confiding as Red-billed. **Confusion species:** Separated from the similarly widespread Red-billed Firefinch by much darker or deeper plumage, and black undertail-coverts (and belly on male); female is reddish-orange (not grey) on breast and lacks bright pink or red bill. Told from Bar-breasted Firefinch (159) by lack of white barring at sides of breast and by black on undertail-coverts and mainly dark (not red) bill. Separated from Jameson's (164) by much deeper red underparts (not deep pinkish-red) and more white spots on sides of breast, grey crown and nape, and pale base to lower mandible. From Black-bellied (158) by brown, olive-brown or grey-brown (not red) mantle and back and by white spots on sides of breast; Black-bellied female has grey head and face, and both sexes have a much greater extent of black on underparts. Out-of-range Pale-billed (163) is also very similar, but has a brown or crimson rather than grey crown and nape and also pink base to lower mandible (which separates it from pinker-headed races *congica* and *haematocephala* or African).

DESCRIPTION Sexes differ slightly. **Adult male:** Crown, nape and hindneck to sides of neck lead-grey or dull grey, merging into olive-brown mantle, back, scapulars, wing-coverts and tertials, which can also be tinged grey, strongest on mantle; flight feathers slightly darker brown. Rump, uppertail-coverts and outer webs of base of tail deep carmine-red or tinged deep pink on some, rest of tail black. Upper lores to over eye and most of ear-coverts deep or rich red; chin, throat, breast and upper flanks deep bright red, almost scarlet or deep scarlet (on some tinged with pink on face and throat, while others show grey on sides of face). Small white spots on sides of breast and upper flanks; red continues along flanks to sides of rump; centre of belly greyish or brown-grey, becoming black on vent and undertail-coverts. Bill short and pointed, black or blackish-grey with pink base to lower mandible. Eye dark brown; eye-ring pink or pale-pinkish. Legs and feet grey, grey-brown or slightly blackish. **Adult female:** Similar to the adult male, but paler or less intensely coloured. Lower forehead and lores (and, on some, possibly extending very slightly above and behind eye) light scarlet-red, almost enclosed by grey upper forehead, crown, nape, hindneck, sides of neck and ear-coverts, fading on cheeks (but can be tinged with pink). Mantle, back and scapulars as male but slightly paler, wings paler olive-brown; rump, uppertail-coverts and outer webs of base of tail feathers deep carmine, rest of tail blackish. Chin and throat pinkish rose-red, becoming orange-red on breast to upper belly (though tinged quite noticeably pink on some); small white spots on sides of breast and upper flanks usually more prominent than on adult male; flanks tinged pinkish, and belly buff or orange-buff; vent and undertail-coverts black. Bill as adult male, but pale pinkish base not always visible in the field. **Juvenile:** Generally similar to adult female, but lacks any red or pinkish-red on face and underparts; instead has dull brown or dull buffish-brown of upperparts extending to face, and underparts more yellowish-buff, with belly darker brown; rump and uppertail-coverts rich or deep red. Bill short, dark brown or blackish on upper mandible and paler or whitish on lower. First-winter male as adult male, but rear flanks warm buff or honey-buff.

GEOGRAPHICAL VARIATION Male *haematocephala* have pinkish-red suffusion on head and nape, and both sexes have less grey on crown; red on underparts is deeper and more rich ruby; black of undertail-coverts extends to vent and lower belly. Bill of both sexes is blue-grey or steel-blue, with edges and tips to mandibles black. Females of this race are suffused with mauve or brownish-pink on head to nape, and rosy-tinged on underparts and less buffish, except for the buff-brown belly. Birds of race *ugandae* are similarly brightly plumaged, but often have brown on crown and nape. Race *congica* is browner or more earth-brown on upperparts and can show a reddish tinge to crown and nape. The amount of spotting on sides of breast on males of all three races is very variable and absent on some individuals. Male *polionota* is much darker, with forehead to crown and back grey-brown and only slightly, if at all, tinged red, and rump and uppertail-coverts much deeper red than in other races; bill is deep bluish. Female *polionota* is similar to *haematocephala*, with a pinkish-red crown and nape.

VOICE Most frequent calls are a rising trilling twitter, loosely interpreted as 'trrrrrrrrr-t', or a simple 'trrrrrrrr', and a loud ringing 'chew-chew-chew-chew' or 'chwee-chwee-chwee', occasionally 'chub-chub-chub-chub', or a 'feeeu-feeeu', all of which may be followed by a 'wink-wink-wink'; the alarm call is a loud, explosive, hard stuttering 'tchit, tchittick' or 'tchittick-ik', rather like the scolding of a Wren (*Troglodytes troglodytes*). Song, given by both sexes, consists of various ringing notes repeated in a random sequence, interspersed with squeaky whistles, trills and warbles.

STATUS, HABITAT AND BEHAVIOUR Widespread; common or locally common. Inhabits similar terrain to Black-bellied and Red-billed Firefinches, but more likely to be found in more natural or wild habitat, edges of forest or savanna with acacia woodland, scrub or thornbush with tall grass, also in valleys and along streams with thick vegetation, up to 1800–2420 m; not usually so common around human habitation or edge of cultivation as Black-bellied, but not unknown. Occurs in pairs or small groups, often in family parties, and may mix with other firefinches but not known to associate with Jameson's (which is separated by altitude and habitat). Feeds on the ground on areas such as paths or tracks, often in the open but close to cover, into which it dives when alarmed. Feeds on a variety of grass seeds, millet and other small seeds; some insects, particularly ants and termites, are taken. A brood host to Wilson's or Dusky Indigobird (*Vidua funerea*).

DISTRIBUTION *L. r. rubricata*: southern Mozambique south to eastern Transvaal and central Cape Province, South Africa.

L. r. haematocephala: southern and eastern Tanzania to Malawi, northern Zambia (Katanga), extreme eastern Zimbabwe and central Mozambique (south to the Save river).

L. r. congica: Gabon to central and southern Zaire and northeast Angola east to northwest Zambia (Mwinilunga and north and west Katanga).

L. r. ugandae: Cameroon, northern Congo, northern Zaire, Uganda, southeast Sudan to central Ethiopia and central Kenya to northern Tanzania.

L. r. polionota: Guinea-Bissau east to southern Mali, Ghana and Nigeria; also two records in southwest and eastern Senegal, where it may be a scarce resident.

Other races have been described (e.g *hildebrandti*, now considered to be synonymous with *ugandae*) which may well refer to intermediates or intergrades between races. Introduced into the Hawaiian Islands in the 1960s, but no records of it there since the mid-1970s. Several pairs which had escaped from captivity bred in Monterey County, California, in 1964 and 1965, but has failed to become established.

MOVEMENTS Wanders widely at random throughout the range when not breeding (see comment under the race *polionota* above).

MEASUREMENTS Wing 45–50; tail 41–48; tarsus 13–16; bill (culmen) 10–12. Weight of male 9.5, of female 10.

REFERENCES Chapin (1954), Goodwin (1982), McLachlan and Liversidge (1978), Newman (1983), Sclater and Moreau (1933).

163 PALE-BILLED FIREFINCH *Lagonosticta landanae*   Plate 42

Africa

Lagonosticta landanae Sharpe, 1890, Cat. Birds Brit. Mus., 13, p. 283, Landana.

IDENTIFICATION Length 9·5–10 cm (3¾–4 in). Very similar to Red-billed (161), African (162) and Jameson's (164) Firefinches, and may well be a race of the latter, but is here considered a full species as it does not interbreed in the small area of overlap. **Confusion species:** Very similar to *congica* race of African Firefinch, but brighter and deeper red on face, with bright pink or red base to lower mandible. Other differences such as bright plumage and extent of red on head and back are of real use only in direct comparison with African Firefinch or possibly with male Red-billed Firefinch (161), which has a red bill and lacks the black undertail-coverts; Jameson's Firefinch is much deeper red on underparts, and both sexes of all races have a distinctive blue or slate-blue bill.

DESCRIPTION Sexes differ. **Adult male:** Forehead and crown rich russet or reddish rose-brown; nape grey-brown, washed with rose. Mantle, back and wings brown or mid-brown, tinged with grey; rump, uppertail-coverts and outer webs of base of tail deep crimson; rest of tail dark brown or blackish-brown, washed with crimson. Lores and around eye to cheeks as forehead or slightly more crimson, lower cheeks and ear-coverts bright pinkish-red. Chin and throat to breast and flanks bright rose-pink, except for some small white spots each side of breast and on rear flanks; lower breast and belly brown, undertail-coverts black. Upper mandible of bill and tip of lower mandible black, lower bright pink or red at base (some long-dead specimens examined have had upper mandible also pink or red, with black culmen, cutting edges and tip). Eye brown or reddish-brown; eye-ring pink or reddish-pink. Legs and feet dark greyish-green or pale flesh-grey. **Adult female:** Similar to adult female

African Firefinch, but has forehead dull rose, crown grey-brown, mantle greyish-earth or mid-brown and becoming slightly browner on wings, ear-coverts rose-grey, lores to chin peachy-orange, and throat and breast warm russet, tinged red or rosy pinkish-red; undertail-coverts dark or blackish. Face and upper sides of neck are buffish, tinged with deep pink. **Juvenile:** Very similar to same-age African Firefinch, with a pale pink base to dark bill (African lacks red on forehead or pink on cheeks). First-winter male as adult male, but rear flanks are honey-buff or warm buff.

VOICE Undescribed.

STATUS, HABITAT AND BEHAVIOUR Common or locally common within a very limited range. Found in grassland savanna and dry thornbush or acacia plains. Usually in pairs or small parties, occasionally in company with Jameson's Firefinch. Other actions and behaviour as African Firefinch. Feeds mostly on the ground, on small seeds.

DISTRIBUTION Monotypic. Cabinda and the lower Congo to nothwest Angola (south to Canhoca and Pungo Andongo, east to Pedreira and Tembo Aluma on the borders of southern Zaire).

MEASUREMENTS Wing 46–49; tarsus 12; bill (culmen) 8·5.

REFERENCES Chapin (1954), Goodwin (1982).

164 JAMESON'S FIREFINCH (Pink-backed Firefinch) *Lagonosticta rhodopareia*   Plate 43

Africa

Estrelda rhodopareia Heuglin, 1868, Journ. f. Ornith., 16, p. 16, Keren, Bogosland [Eritrea].

IDENTIFICATION Length 10–11 cm (4–4½ in). Very similar to African Firefinch (162), but much more pink in overall plumage, especially underparts and nape to coverts area, which is warm brown or chestnut; no grey in the upperparts at all. Has a very indistinct eye-ring. **Confusion species:** Red-billed Firefinch (161) has a distinctive red bill, and mantle, back and wings are predominantly grey or grey-brown; also has pale buff or greyish-buff undertail-coverts (black on Jameson's). Female Jameson's are much more red or pinkish-red on lores and underparts than female Red-billed, which is grey and with deep crimson only on rump and base of tail and has small white spots on breast and flanks. Combination of wholly dark blue bill and black undertail-coverts separates adult male Jameson's from all other similar firefinches except dark-billed races of African and Kulikoro Firefinch (165). African has (in most races) grey or greyish forehead to hindneck and a prominent eye-ring (indistinct on Jameson's), and bill of Jameson's is usually bluer than African. Jameson's prefers much drier or more arid habitat than African, and is secretive and unlikely to be found near or around human habitation. Both sexes of Kulikoro Firefinch are separated by dark grey crown, nape and upperparts.

DESCRIPTION Sexes differ. **Adult male:** Forehead to face, ear-coverts, sides of neck, chin, throat and most of underparts deep or rich scarlet-red, only lightly tinged pink or pinkish-red. Crown to nape darker red with brown bases to feathers, nape to hindneck slightly pinkish. Mantle, back and scapulars chestnut or rich warm brown; median and greater coverts the same or olive-brown; flight feathers and tertials darker brown with paler brown edges. Rump and uppertail-coverts deep or rich scarlet-red, becoming carmine-pink on outer webs of base of tail, rest of tail sooty-black. Some birds show a few small white spots on sides of breast; flanks slightly duller or more pink than breast; lower belly, vent and undertail-coverts black. Bill short and almost conical, pointed, bluish-grey with a black tip. Eye brown; eye-ring very thin and inconspicuous, pale pink. Legs and feet slate or blue-grey. **Adult female:** Forehead to crown, nape, sides of neck to cheeks and towards base of bill grey or light grey with buffish-brown tinge almost encircling blood-red lores. Mantle, back, scapulars and coverts warm brown tinged with russet or orange, becoming brown and edged warm brown on greater coverts and tertials and dark or deep olive-brown on flight feathers. Rump and uppertail-

358

coverts similar to adult male, bright or deep scarlet-red tinged with pink, continuing onto edges of outer webs to base of tail, with rest of tail blackish. Chin deep carmine-pink, becoming peachy on throat and breast and tinged warm brown on belly and flanks; vent and undertail-coverts blackish. **Juvenile:** Almost entirely warm brown on upperparts, except for dull pinkish-red rump, uppertail-coverts and base of tail feathers; underparts and face buffish-brown (some are reddish-brown or russet-brown on belly). Generally not separable from juvenile African Firefinch in the field. Bill blackish.

GEOGRAPHICAL VARIATION Race *jamesoni* is much more pink or mauve-pink on lower face to throat, breast and flanks, with lores to over eye and chin bright scarlet; crown grey-brown; nape and mantle, back and coverts heavily suffused or washed with red or reddish. Female *jamesoni* is similar to nominate, but has paler scarlet on lores and grey of crown to nape and sides of face tinged pink; throat, breast and flanks buff with pink or mauve-pink tips, and vent and undertail-coverts dark grey (not black). Male *ansorgei* is brighter or much more reddish-pink than other races, while females have large bright red lores to sides of forehead and are also brighter below, but lack reddish tinge to brown mantle, back and coverts; bill is also more blue than in nominate. Males of isolated race *bruneli* have crown and nape plain grey, and mantle, wing-coverts and scapulars much more maroon than pinkish-red; similar to other races below, with face to chin and throat bright red and rest of underparts deep or rich blood-red, slightly tinged with pink. Female *bruneli* is similar to male, but has only a light wash of red on cheeks and ear-coverts, and underparts are similar but slightly paler than on male, with belly slightly brown.

VOICE Very similar to African Firefinch. Contact call a soft 'tsit, tsit', becoming an intensified 'ti-ti-ti-ti', also a soft 'teu' or 'chew'; alarm is a hard rattling or churring trill. Song is either a rapid trilling 'we-we-we-we-we-we' or occasionally a 'weet-weet-weet-weet-weet' and a long thin plaintive 'feeeee' repeated several times.

STATUS, HABITAT AND BEHAVIOUR Common or locally common throughout most of its range, certainly in the south and east. Inhabits dry grassland with thornscrub or bracken-briar and thickets or lightly wooded areas with rank grass and thick undergrowth. Race *bruneli* is found on rocky hillsides with scattered clumps of bushes or thornbush and trees, but always where there is tall grass. In southern Sudan and Ethiopia, occurs in the highlands between 1350 m and 1800 m. Occurs in pairs or small family parties, and differs little in general habits and actions from other firefinches. Feeds low down or on the ground on a variety of grass seeds and the seeds of other small ground-loving plants, also millet and possibly small quantities of insects, mostly ants. Breeding host of Black Indigobird (*Vidua nigerrima purpurascens*).

DISTRIBUTION *L. r. rhodopareia*: highlands of southern or southeast Sudan (east of the Nile), southern Ethiopia to Uganda and northern Kenya.

L. r. jamesoni: southern Kenya south to eastern and southern Tanzania, Malawi, central and eastern Zambia, Zimbabwe, northern Botswana, Mozambique, Transvaal and northern Natal, South Africa.

L. r. ansorgei: Cabinda, lower Congo and south-west Zaire to western Angola (Huila).

L. r. bruneli: southern Chad (possibly also north-east Nigeria).

Note: Race *bruneli* (more recently known as *umbrinodorsalis*) is treated by some taxonomists as a full species, Reichenow's Firefinch.

MEASUREMENTS Wing 46–51; tail 38–45; tarsus 12·5–14; bill (culmen) 9·5–12. Weight 9–10.

REFERENCES Goodwin (1982), McLachlan and Liversidge (1978), Newman (1983).

165 KULIKORO FIREFINCH *Lagonosticta virata*   Plate 43

Africa

Lagonosticta rubricata virata Bates, 1932, Bull. Brit. Ornith. Club, 53, p. 7, Kulikoro, French Sudan.

IDENTIFICATION Length 10 cm (4 in). Very similar to West African race (*polionota*) of African Firefinch (162), with which it may be conspecific. A small finch with dark grey upperparts and pinkish-crimson underparts. The sexes are almost identical but can be told apart in the field. Has a distinctive dark bill (or dark-tipped with slate-blue base). Inhabits a small area of suitable habitat in southern Mali. **Confusion species:** Within native range unlikely to be confused with any other species except Red-billed Firefinch (161), which has red bill and lacks black undertail-coverts. African Firefinch of race *polionota* is very similar, but Kulikoro has distinctive bill and usually has red forehead and grey-brown crown to back and generally has fewer white spots on sides of breast.

DESCRIPTION Sexes similar but separable. **Adult male:** Lower forehead (at close range) has dull or dark reddish feather tips; crown, nape, mantle to back, scapulars and wings drab or slightly dark grey, wing-coverts slightly darker, and flight feathers tinged brownish or olive-brown. Rump, uppertail-coverts and outer edges to base of tail deep or rich scarlet-red, rest of tail brownish-black. Lores, over eye, cheeks and chin deep red, contrasting with paler or more pinkish-red on rest of face and ear-coverts, sides of neck, lower chin and throat, deepening on breast and flanks. Small

359

white spots on sides of breast and upper flanks, variable in extent. Belly and thighs dull grey, becoming black on undertail-coverts. Bill slim and pointed, slightly larger than on other firefinches, dark blue or slate-blue with black tip (often all-black upper mandible). Eye dark brown or black; eye-ring pale yellow. Legs and feet dark grey or grey-brown. **Adult female:** Very similar to adult male (some almost identical) but generally slightly paler, especially on pinkish-red underparts and lores, with cheeks and chin not so intense or contrasting; cheeks often suffused with grey. Bill as adult male. **Juvenile:** Almost entirely grey or pale greyish buff-brown above and buffish below, but with dull crimson-red on rump and uppertail-coverts.

VOICE Most common contact call is a low-pitched and slightly harsh 'kyew', 'kew' or 'kyah', also a long plaintive 'feeeeeeee . . .' occasionally broken into a two-syllable note; alarm is a rattling trill or churr, frequently repeated, also a sparrow-like 'tshek'. Song is a long drawn-out trill and a few short loud high-pitched phrases and whistling notes repeated frequently.

STATUS, HABITAT AND BEHAVIOUR Uncommon or local. Within very limited range (entirely within Mali), found in rocky sandstone areas with bushes, scrub and grass. In most habits very similar to other firefinches, particularly Jameson's (164) and African, to which it is closely related; range overlaps with that of latter. Feeds on grass seeds.

DISTRIBUTION Monotypic. Endemic to Mali, along the Upper Niger river from Mopti south to Bamako and the border with Guinea. Considered by most (not all) taxonomic authorities to be a race of either Jameson's or African Firefinch, but we prefer to treat it as a separate species.

MOVEMENTS Entirely sedentary.

MEASUREMENTS Wing 51; tarsus 10; bill (culmen) 9.

REFERENCES Goodwin (1982), Lamarche (1981).

166 BLACK-FACED FIREFINCH *Lagonosticta larvata*   Plate 43
Africa

Amadina larvata Rüppell, 1840, Neue Wirbelt., Vögel, p. 97, Simen, Abyssinia.

IDENTIFICATION Length 11·5 cm (4½ in). A distinctive firefinch of open savanna grassland with thornscrub. The male has an all-black face to chin and throat, grey crown, warm brown upperparts and pinkish underparts. Females lack black face and have head pale grey-brown. The two central African races are greyer above and below, and pink or mauve in plumage is greatly reduced or absent. **Confusion species:** The male is easily told from other firefinches: dark grey crown, darker body colour and more red at base of shorter tail separate it from similar but smaller Black-cheeked (186) and Crimson-rumped (179) Waxbills. Females are best distinguished by lack of red bill; pale undertail-coverts separate it from all other firefinches except Bar-breasted (159), Brown (160) and Red-billed (161), all of which have red bills.

DESCRIPTION Sexes differ. **Adult male:** Forehead to crown and nape dark grey or slightly darker, washed with reddish-pink on hindneck; from sides of lower (occasionally across) forehead to ear-coverts, chin and upper throat black. Mantle, back and scapulars to wing-coverts slate-grey, or slightly brown when worn; edges to greater coverts, primary coverts, flight feathers and tertials grey-brown; rump, uppertail-coverts, central pair of tail feathers and outer webs to bases of outer tail (except outermost) rich red or blood-red (becoming pinkish when worn), rest of tail black or blackish-brown. Sides of neck to breast, belly and flanks deep pink, slightly tinged with mauve, with a few small white spots on sides of lower breast, which is grey or mauve-washed grey; belly to undertail-coverts black. Bill larger and deeper at base than on other firefinches, slightly more substantial and somewhat weaver-like: deep or dark olive-green on upper mandible and paler green on lower, with dark tip and cutting edges. Eye reddish-brown, with eye-ring pale blue or grey. Legs and feet olive-green or brown or grey-brown. **Adult female:** Entire head and face dark greyish-brown, tinged pink on side of neck. Upperparts similar to adult male but generally more grey-brown, though some are more heavily tinged pink (both above and below) than others. Underparts paler than male, with buff on throat tinged greyish or pinkish, becoming dark vinaceous-brown tinged rose (or tinged light mauve) on breast, with small white spots on sides of lower breast; flanks as breast; belly grey-brown, becoming dark grey or blackish-grey tinged pink on vent and undertail-coverts. **Juvenile:** Generally dull or drab brown all over, but with rump to base of tail as adult but duller or deeper crimson.

GEOGRAPHICAL VARIATION Race *vinacea* is generally paler above, with a softer grey on forehead to crown and with most of upperparts pinkish-mauve; underparts are bright pink, which extends to belly, flanks and vent; bill black, but can also show rose-red patch on each side of base of upper mandible. Females also paler and have a paler grey head, and mantle to scapulars and edges of coverts and flight feathers tinged pink; throat, breast and belly are also tinged pale pink. Male *nigricollis* is entirely dark grey from forehead to lower back, with underparts pale or soft grey from throat to belly and flanks, tinged with lavender-pink across breast; Females are brownish-grey on upperparts and grey-brown on throat and breast, with belly and undertail-coverts much more buffish-brown or dull buff than in other races. Both sexes have face,

360

rump and base of tail as nominate; bill grey or greyish-blue, with black tip and cutting edges. Race *togoensis* is similar to *nigricollis*, but paler on head and breast to belly or slightly browner above, often lacking any pink in plumage.

VOICE Call a weak lisping note. The song is very similar to that of African Firefinch (162).

STATUS, HABITAT AND BEHAVIOUR Widespread but local, and nowhere common. A bird of tall savanna grassland with thickets of scrub and in bamboo at up to 1700 m in northeast Africa, and thornbush, edges of woods and on edge of (disused or overgrown) cultivated areas, often close to water but not exclusively so; in Gambia often associated with bamboo thickets, but has declined in parallel with the removal of bamboo. Occurs in pairs or small groups or family parties, often mixing freely with Red-billed Firefinches and Cordon-bleus (167), but often shy and generally unapproachable. Feeds on the ground or close to it, on a variety of grass seeds, millet and occasionally small insects and spiders. Breeding host to the parasitic Senegal or Green Indigobird (*Vidua chalybeata*).

DISTRIBUTION *L. l. larvata*: southeast Sudan (Boma area) and central and western Ethiopia (excluding Eritrea)

L. l. nigricollis: eastern Cameroon, central and east Central African Republic, northern Zaire, northern Uganda and southern Sudan (west of the Nile), possibly also to southern Ethiopia.

L. l. togoensis: central and northern savannas of Ghana, Togo to northern and eastern Nigeria and northern Cameroon (may be only a non-breeding visitor) to western Sudan .

L. l. vinacea: Senegal (along northern border of Gambia and the east), Gambia, Guinea-Bissau, Guinea to southern Mali (Bamako) and southern Burkina Faso.

MOVEMENTS An occasional non-breeding or dry-season visitor or wanderer to areas where it is not known to breed. Recent records in Burkina Faso in January-March and in northern Ivory Coast in February and March may refer either to non-breeding visitors (as both sets of records are in the dry season) or to a range extension; in neither case is the race known.

MEASUREMENTS Wing 47–54; tail 36–40; tarsus 15; bill 10.

REFERENCES Chapin (1954), Thonnerieux *et al.* (1989), Walsh (1986).

GENUS *URAEGINTHUS*

Five species. Cordon-bleus and grenadiers. The cordon-bleus are slim or slender finches with large areas of pale blue and pale brown back and wings. The grenadiers have long graduated tails and are much more richly coloured, with a purple face and deep blue on rump and underparts. Dry-country species, spending long periods feeding on the ground. Related to true waxbills *Estrilda*, but behaviourally show closer ties to bluebills *Spermophaga*.

167 CORDON-BLEU (Blue Waxbill) *Uraeginthus angolensis* Plate 49
Africa

Fringilla angolensis Linnaeus, 1758, Syst. Nat., ed. 10, p. 182, Angola.

IDENTIFICATION Length 12–13 cm (4¾–5 in). All cordon-bleus are readily identifiable by their pale brown upperparts and blue underparts and tail. The sexes differ slightly, and species are separable by presence of red on cheeks (of males) and extent of blue on face or over head. Most are common, confiding and found on the edges of human habitation. **Confusion species:** Likely to be confused only with the other two cordon-bleus, Red-cheeked (168) and Blue-capped (169). Male Red-cheeked has a clearly marked blood-red, kidney-shaped patch on ear-coverts and is generally warmer brown on upperparts; females are very similar to males, but lack the red cheek spot and generally have less blue on underparts (though on some it extends to forehead). Male Blue-capped has an all-blue head, and both sexes have a bright red bill. In the hand, the inner web of the second primary is prominently notched on Cordon-bleu (notch poorly defined on Red-cheeked).

DESCRIPTION Sexes differ slightly. **Adult male:** Forehead to crown and nape and extending to lower back and wings light or pale brown, slightly warmer on forehead to nape; flight feathers slightly darker than coverts. Rump, uppertail-coverts and tail pale cerulean-blue, darker or greyer on tail, especially central pair of feathers. Lores, over eye to ear-coverts, sides of neck, chin and throat to breast and flanks pale cerulean-blue; lower flanks occasionally paler blue; centre of lower breast, belly and undertail-coverts washed warm buffish or pale pinkish-brown. Bill short and both mandibles curve to a point, grey, mauve-grey or mauve with dark tip and cutting edges. Eye brown or reddish-brown, with pale blue or whitish eye-ring. Legs and feet pale pinkish-brown. **Adult female:** Very similar to adult male in overall plumage, but blue is slightly paler or faded and confined to rump to tail and to face and chin to centre of breast; rest of underparts buff-brown, with ventral area pale buff. Bill as male or occasionally blue-grey. **Juven-**

ile: Very similar to adult female, but duller and paler and bill all dark lead-grey; blue areas paler or powdery cobalt, indistinct or a poorly defined wash, with buff-brown bases showing through on breast and throat of some.

GEOGRAPHICAL VARIATION Most racial variation concerns depth of plumage coloration, in most cases undetectable in the field without direct comparison. Both *damarensis* and *cyanopleurus* are paler on upperparts than nominate and blue colour is paler, while *niassensis* is a brighter blue and is darker or warmer brown on upperparts. More noticeably, females of races *cyanopleurus* and *niassensis* have blue extending along flanks (sometimes meeting with that on sides of rump) as on nominate males; tail of *niassensis* visibly longer (by c8 mm) than in other races.

VOICE Call notes very similar if not identical to those of Red-cheeked and Blue-capped Cordonbleus, a 'weet-weet', 'sweet-sweet-sweet' or 'weety-weet' contact note; the alarm is a harsh stuttering rattle. Song is also fairly similar to that of other two cordon-bleus, but is sweeter and less squeaky in tone, 'kway, kway' or 'cheru, chreu, chittywoo, weeoo, wee' or slight variations thereof.

STATUS, HABITAT AND BEHAVIOUR Widespread, common or occasionally abundant. Found in a variety of open habitats below 1400 m, exceptionally to 1500 m, usually savanna or low grass with tangled undergrowth, rank vegetation, bush, scrub, acacia woodland and edges of cultivation or human habitation; tame and confiding, often feeding in the middle of villages. Usually in pairs or family parties, small or occasionally large flocks often mixed with firefinches or waxbills. Flight low, usually in short bursts, but often (over larger distances) less erratic and more undulating. Feeds on the ground, on a variety of grass seeds and seeds of other low-growing plants; some fruit taken when available and occasionally insects, principally termites (especially in the dry season).

DISTRIBUTION *U. a. angolensis*: São Tomé (where possibly introduced), Cabinda, Congo, southern Zaire, northern Angola, northwest Zambia and northern Zimbabwe.

U. a. cyanopleurus: west and northwest Zimbabwe, northern Botswana to northern South Africa (western Transvaal).

U. a. niassensis: southeast Kenya (Lake Jipe), east, south and southwest Tanzania south through southeast Zaire, Malawi, east and northeast Zimbabwe and Mozambique to Transvaal, northern Orange Free State and northern Natal, South Africa. Also introduced into Zanzibar.

U. a. damarensis: northern Botswana to northern Namibia.

Other races have been described, but intermediates between races occur in overlap areas.

MOVEMENTS Wanders widely throughout the range when not breeding.

MEASUREMENTS Wing 50–56; tail 47–61; tarsus 13–15; bill (culmen) 9–11. Wing of *damarensis* 51–55. Wing of *niassensis* 47–55; tail of male 55–69.

REFERENCES Goodwin (1982), Mackworth-Praed and Grant (1963), McLachlan and Liversidge (1978), Sinclair (1984).

168 RED-CHEEKED CORDON-BLEU *Uraeginthus bengalus* Plate 49

Africa

Fringilla bengalus Linnaeus, 1766, Syst. Nat., ed. 12, p. 323, Bengal; amended to Senegal by Hartlaub, 1857, Syst. Ornith. Westafrika, p. 145.

IDENTIFICATION Length 12·5–13 cm (5 in). More northern distribution than Cordon-bleu (167), with only a small area of overlap, and widely distributed throughout most of West and East Africa apart from heavily forested areas. Males are very similar to Cordon-bleu (167), but with a large, almost blood-red kidney-shaped patch on ear-coverts; pale brown forehead, crown and nape separate it from Blue-capped Cordon-bleu (169). Lone female Red-cheeked are less likely to be separated successfully from Cordon-bleu, but generally have a longer tail; more easily separated from female Blue-capped, which has a red bill, paler or whiter belly and longer tail.

DESCRIPTION Sexes differ. **Adult male:** Essentially, the only field character that needs to be seen is the diagnostic deep red or blood-red kidney-shaped patch on ear-coverts. Otherwise almost the same as Cordon-bleu, but upperparts are slightly warmer brown or more mid-brown, and most tail feathers are much deeper blue than rump and uppertail-coverts; blue of underparts extends along flanks to meet blue on sides of rump. Bill short and pointed, pink or variably reddish-pink, sometimes pinkish-grey with a dark tip. Eye pale brown to reddish-brown; white or pale grey eye-ring. Legs and feet pale or flesh-brown. **Adult female:** Similar to adult male, but lacks red on cheeks or ear-coverts and is generally paler, and has white or pale buff admixed with blue on upper flanks. In worn plumage, blue on face to breast can also show buffish-brown bases to feathers.

Juvenile: Very similar to adult female, but blue is paler and less extensive, especially on juvenile females, where belly and lower flanks are buffish-brown. Bill lead-grey; eye brown.

GEOGRAPHICAL VARIATION Males of all races show considerable individual variation in the intensity of blue, from those with a greenish to turquoise tinge, to those with deep ultramarine-blue, and races are not separable on this alone. Race *ugogoensis* is browner on upperparts, lacks warm tones, and female has greater extent of brown on sides of neck. Race *katangae* is darker or colder brown than nominate, and has very dark red ear-covert patches and pale pink base to bill; females have face, chin and throat blue and buffish-brown on breast and flanks (both *ugogoensis* and *katangae* females have blue restricted to face and bluish tinge to breast, but remainder of underparts are pale buffish-brown). In *brunneigularis*, females have head, face and sides of neck buffish-brown; lores, chin and throat are mottled with blue, which is otherwise restricted to breast and flanks, though some show a deep blue tinge to cheeks and ear-coverts; belly and undertail-coverts are deep buff-brown. Male *littoralis* are smaller, and have smaller or more rounded red facial patch.

VOICE Very similar to Cordon-bleu. Contact note is a weak squeaking 'tsee-tsee' or 'tseu-tseu'; alarm is a rapid, chattering 'che-che-che-che'. Song is a high-pitched whistling 'te-chee-wa-tcheee' or 'sseedeedelee-deedelee-ssee-ssee'.

STATUS, HABITAT AND BEHAVIOUR Common to abundant; widely distributed over most of West and Central Africa up to 1800 m. Overlaps with Cordon-bleu in southeast of the range. Tame and very confiding, living within villages, gardens and the edges of cultivation, otherwise found in savanna with thornscrub, dry acacia woodland (avoids forest and well-wooded areas) or open grassland. Occurs in pairs, small groups or, in the non-breeding season, quite large flocks; usually in single-species flocks but also known to associate with firefinches and waxbills in villages. Feeds mostly on the ground, on a variety of seeds, mainly grass seeds, but also millet and other small plant seeds; occasionally takes insects, mainly termites or ants (has been known also to catch them in flight), and in captivity known to eat small grasshoppers.

DISTRIBUTION *U. b. bengalus*: most of West, central (or north-central) and East Africa, from southwest Mauritania, Senegal and Gambia, southeast and east through southern Mali (south of 16° N), northern Ghana, southern Niger and southern Chad to southern Sudan (south of 16° N, except extreme southeast), Ethiopia south to Uganda and western Kenya (west of the Rift Valley), and from Cameroon to Central African Republic, northern and central Zaire (avoids vast forested areas) to Rwanda.

U. b. brunneigularis: highlands of central Kenya east of the Rift Valley (intergrades in east of the range with *littoralis*).

U. b. littoralis: extreme southern Somalia (where very uncommon) to east and southeast Kenya and northeast Tanzania (intergrades with *ugogoensis* in south of the range).

U. b. ugogoensis: northern to central and west-central Tanzania (to Mount Kilimanjaro in northeast).

U. b. katangae: southern Zaire and extreme eastern Angola to Zambia.

The nominate race may also occur on Santo Antão in the Cape Verde Islands. Other races (e.g. *camerunenesis*, *ugandae* and *schoanus*) have been described, but are now considered synonymous with nominate. It has also been introduced into the Hawaiian Islands, where it is established on Hawaii but probably now extirpated on Oahu.

MOVEMENTS Wanders widely when not breeding.

MEASUREMENTS Wing 48–57; tail 58–64; tarsus 13–14; bill (culmen) 8–9·5.

REFERENCE Goodwin (1982).

169 BLUE-CAPPED CORDON-BLEU (Blue-headed Cordon-bleu)
Uraeginthus cyanocephalus   Plate 49

East Africa

Estrilda cyanocephala Richmond, 1897, *Auk*, 14, p. 157, Useri River, near Mt Kilimanjaro.

IDENTIFICATION Length 13 cm (5 in). All-blue head, breast and flanks to rump and tail, together with warm brown mantle, back and wings and short bright red bill (both sexes) make this an unmistakable finch. Females have brown forehead to nape and pale blue face to breast and flanks, becoming buff then white on underparts. **Confusion species:** Bright blue head of adult male eliminates confusion with any other cordon-bleu or any other African passerine. Females and immatures are not always readily distinguishable from female Red-cheeked (168), but red or pink of bill in adult females is distinctive, as are paler or white underparts. Both sexes of Cordon-bleu (167) have paler blue or powder-blue on face and underparts, with dark bill at all times.

DESCRIPTION Sexes similar but separable.

Adult male: Entire head to lower nape, sides of neck to chin, throat, breast and flanks light cerulean-blue, varying in intensity with changing light. Rump and uppertail-coverts slightly deeper or mid-blue; tail, except for outer feathers, slightly duller blue. Mantle, back and wings warm brown or russet. Centre of lower breast, belly and vent to undertail-coverts buffish or white. Bill short and stout at base, red or scarlet, especially at tip and along cutting edges, paler at base on some. Eye brown to reddish-brown. Legs and feet fleshy-pink or brown. **Adult female:** Forehead to crown pale brown, merging on nape with warm brown (as adult male) rest of upperparts, with wing and tail as adult male. On face, blue extends slightly over eye and sometimes across lower forehead (in the hand may show some blue feather tips on crown),

but otherwise as adult male; sides of belly, lower flanks and undertail-coverts pale cinnamon buff-brown, centre of belly to vent white. Bill is sometimes as intensely red as adult male, but otherwise pale pinkish-red. **Juvenile:** Very like adult female, but much less bright in overall plumage, and blue is less extensive, on some restricted to cheeks or ear-coverts or a wash on otherwise buffish throat and breast. Bill dark greyish. Juvenile males are occasionally identifiable at an early age by blue beginning to show on forehead; attains adult plumage within first five months of life.
VOICE Very similar to Cordon-bleu and Red-cheeked Cordon-bleu. Commonest contact call is a brief or abrupt 'tse-tseeuu', also a high-pitched 'chee-chee-chee'; alarm is a harsh 'tchet' or 'tchrut', often given as 'tchek-tchek-tchek'. Song is a mixture of sweet and plaintive notes, 'teu, skurr, tsee-ee-wee-see-see, skurr, teh-teh'.
STATUS, HABITAT AND BEHAVIOUR

Locally common. A bird of semi-arid and dry desert, thornbush or open grassland with scattered acacias. Usually in pairs or small flocks and often inhabits same areas as Red-cheeked Cordon-bleu, but only rarely found together; a much shyer and less approachable bird than Red-cheeked, and never in or near human habitation. Feeds on the ground, on a variety of seeds, principally grass, but also millet and other small-seeded plants; some insects, such as termites or ants, are also taken.
DISTRIBUTION Monotypic. Southern Somalia (where very uncommon, 12 records) discontinuously west to extreme southeast Sudan (Kapoeta) and south through Kenya (from 2° N) to central Tanzania (south to Dodoma and Kilosa).
MOVEMENTS Moves locally within the range; a breeding-season visitor to southeast Sudan.
MEASUREMENTS Wing 53–59; tarsus 14; bill (from skull) 9·5.
REFERENCE Goodwin (1982).

170 COMMON GRENADIER (Violet-eared Waxbill) *Uraeginthus granatina* Plate 50

Africa

Fringilla granatina Linnaeus, 1766, Syst. Nat., ed. 12, p. 319, Brazil, amended to Angola by W.L. Sclater, 1930, Syst. Av. Aethiop., p. 806.

IDENTIFICATION Length 14–15 cm (5½-6 in). An unmistakable, long-tailed and brightly coloured finch of southern Africa. Sexes differ; females are paler and not so richly marked, but still retain diagnostic head-and-face markings. **Confusion species:** Males are unlikely to be mistaken: no other species has same shape or combination of plumage features. Female is only briefly confusable with much more extensively paler blue Cordon-bleu (167). In East Africa Purple Grenadier (171) is similar in shape, but has much larger areas of deep blue on underparts.
DESCRIPTION Sexes differ. **Adult male:** Forehead and upper lores (to over eye) a band of deep blue; face, lores, cheeks and ear-coverts light violet or purple. Forecrown to nape, sides of neck, mantle, back and scapulars brown, occasionally paler brown or tinged buff on mantle and lower back; rump and uppertail-coverts bright or deep blue. Tail long and pointed, in flight appears graduated, black with deep blue edges to outer feathers. Flight feathers dull or dark brown, edged pale buff or greyish-brown; tertials dark brown, thinly or finely edged with buff-brown; dark brown wing-coverts often overlapped by long scapulars. Chin and throat black; breast, belly and flanks as mantle, rich or deep chestnut-brown; vent black, undertail-coverts deep blue, slightly duller than on upper coverts. Bright red bill deep at base, with curved ridge to upper mandible. Eye red or orange-red; eye-ring bright red. Legs and feet brown or purplish-brown. **Adult female:** A paler and shorter-tailed version of male. Forehead and upper lores pale sky-blue; forecrown to lower nape pale chest-

nut or russet-brown. Face as male, but paler and less intensely coloured. Mantle, back, coverts and wings brown, with slightly paler buffish-brown or greyish edges to greater coverts and flight feathers. Rump and uppertail-coverts blue, less extensive than on adult male. Tail slightly shorter than male's and all black. Underparts almost entirely pale buff or creamy buff-brown, sides of neck to breast tinged with warm brown. Bill as adult male, but slightly smaller and paler or more pinkish-red. **Juvenile:** Initially very similar to adult female, but much duller, with buff or grey-brown on head and face, lacking bright facial tones of adults. Rump and uppertail-coverts deep blue or purple. Bill blackish. Eye brown, eye-ring blackish. Within first six weeks of life, head feathers are moulted and replaced by adult plumage, but rest of adult plumage is not assumed until full moult several weeks later prior to breeding.
GEOGRAPHICAL VARIATION Very little difference between races exists that is recognisable in the field or is more than slight individual variation, but both sexes of *retusa* are smaller and paler, with a correspondingly shorter tail.
VOICE A variety of short contact notes from 'psis' or 'psit' to 'tsyeet', a repeated 'tsit', 'squee' and a wagtail-like 'chissick', also a three-note 'tiu-woo-wee'. Song is a soft or gentle twittering melody and recalls Barn Swallow (*Hirundo rustica*).
STATUS, HABITAT AND BEHAVIOUR Common or fairly common. Has wide distribution across most of the hinterland of southern Africa. Found in dry thornscrub or open acacia woodland of semi-arid country, often far from water; some-

364

times occurs on the edge of cultivated land. Usually in pairs or occasionally small flocks (made up of family groups) in company with waxbills and cordon-bleus. Feeds mainly on the ground, though has been known to feed in bushes or on seeding flower-heads, on a variety of seeds, principally grass, but other plants are taken; also ripe fruit, insects such as termites and ants (particularly in the dry season). A brood host to the parasitic Shaft-tailed Whydah (*Vidua regia*).

DISTRIBUTION *U. g. granatina*: southwest Angola east to southwest Zambia and southern Zimbabwe and south to Transvaal, Natal and northern Cape Province, South Africa (intergrades with *siccata* in northeast Namibia and northern Cape Province).

U. g. siccata: western Angola through Namibia to northern Cape Province, South Africa.

U. g. retusa: known only from the district of Inhambane, southern Mozambique.

Not all authorities recognise more than nominate race.

MOVEMENTS Wanders locally when not breeding.

MEASUREMENTS Wing of male 55·5–60, of female 55–59; tail 61–71; tarsus 15–17; bill 9, (from skull) 10–12. Wing of *retusa* 53–55; tail 62–66·5.

REFERENCE Goodwin (1982).

---

171 PURPLE GRENADIER *Uraeginthus ianthinogaster*   Plate 50

East Africa

Uraeginthus ianthinogaster Reichenow, 1879, Ornith. Centralbl., 4, p. 114, Massa, lower Tana River, East Africa.

IDENTIFICATION Length 14 cm (5½ in). A distinctive brightly plumaged East African finch with a fairly long tail and bright red bill. Males have deep brown head to mantle and breast, with deep blue around eye, on rump and irregularly from breast to undertail-coverts. Females are more uniformly pale brown, with pale blue around eye, small white spots on breast and flanks and deep blue rump. Unmistakable when seen well. Out-of-range Common Grenadier (170) from South Africa has much more extensive facial markings, and males are heavily chestnut-brown over most of body and lack deep blue underparts.

DESCRIPTION Sexes differ. **Adult male:** Forehead to crown, nape, upper mantle, sides of neck to chin, throat and upper breast deep or rich warm russet-brown. Upper lores to over eye and cheeks and ear-coverts deep blue; mid-lores the same or broken by warm brown. Lower mantle, back, scapulars and coverts dull dark brown, with some warm russet edges to coverts; flight feathers dark brown edged warmer brown. Rump and uppertail-coverts deep blue or violet-blue. Tail long and graduated, black, tinged with purple on outer webs of feathers. Underparts below throat deep blue or violet-blue, glossy in tone and broken for most part by rich brown patches on breast and flanks (only tips of feathers blue, with bases brown). Bill deep at base, curved culmen, red or deep pinkish-red or with blackish tip. Eye red, orbital ring also red. Legs and feet dark grey or black. **Adult female:** Forehead to crown and nape warm brown, becoming browner on mantle, back, scapulars and wing-coverts. Flight feathers dark brown. Rump, uppertail-coverts and tail as adult male. Face generally buffish-brown with a broad patch or circle of pale blue around eye; rest of head, sides of neck and almost entire underparts warm buff-brown, tinged peachy-orange on sides of neck and breast,

with small white spots or bars on lower breast and upper flanks; flanks occasionally show a few violet-tipped feathers. Belly pale buff, and vent to undertail-coverts pale buff-brown with darker centres. Bill as adult male but slightly paler or duller, culmen black. Eye red, orbital ring orange. **Juvenile:** Very similar to adult female, but lacks pale blue around eye and spotting on breast and upper flanks, and is generally uniform buff or pale buffish-brown below. Bill black or blackish. As in closely-related Common Grenadier, there is a partial moult of head feathers at a very early age, when head pattern of adult is acquired and rest of plumage is as juvenile; in this plumage upper mandible is mainly black with lower orange-red.

GEOGRAPHICAL VARIATION Not all taxonomic authorities agree on amount of racial separation, and some consider this species monotypic. There is considerable individual variation and intermediate plumages exist. Most races are poorly separated, and the only one perhaps identifiable in the field is race *roosevelti*: generally darker than nominate, with facial area of blue deeper, and (more noticeably) breast occasionally shows a wash of deep blue.

VOICE Call a weak chirp, also a series of buzzing notes often ending with a trill; has a high-pitched rattling alarm; other contact notes as Common Grenadier. Song is a jumble of soft musical notes and harsher buzzes, culminating in a trill; both sexes sing.

STATUS, HABITAT AND BEHAVIOUR Common or locally common. Widely distributed throughout East Africa, in dense thornbush, scrub and dry brush country, often low down in tangled bushes or grass; fond of aloes. Shy or secretive, but can also be fairly tame when used to the presence of humans. Occurs alone or more usually in pairs or small parties, feeding on the ground on a variety of grass seeds and other small seeds, also occasionally insects, such as termites and ants. A breeding host to the parasitic Straw-tailed Whydah (*Vidua fischeri*).

DISTRIBUTION *U. i. ianthinogaster*: central and southern Kenya to northern central Tanzania.

U. i. ugandae: extreme southeast Sudan, southern Ethiopia, discontinuously through Somalia, northern Kenya and northern Uganda.

U. i. roosevelti: highlands of central Kenya.

MOVEMENTS Wanders locally within the range when not breeding.

MEASUREMENTS Wing 56–63; tarsus 12; bill 10.

REFERENCE Goodwin (1982).

GENUS *ESTRILDA*

Fifteen species. Waxbills are small, very active finches, mostly with finely barred buffish plumage and, in some, a distinctive red bill which appears wax-like in texture. Agile and acrobatic feeders, very adept at feeding on growing plants, mainly grasses. Most species are widespread throughout Africa (except tropical forest), but two, Anambra Waxbill (176) and Arabian Waxbill (180), are of extremely limited range. Yellow-bellied Waxbill (175) is occasionally placed in a separate genus *Coccopygia*, havng shorter, rounded tail, brighter plumage and marked differences between sexes. Lavender Waxbill (172) differs from other typical waxbills in its uniform grey plumage and some behavioural features that link it to firefinches *Lagonosticta*.

172 LAVENDER WAXBILL (Lavender Firefinch, Red-tailed Lavender Waxbill) *Estrilda caerulescens*   Plate 47

Africa

Fringilla caerulescens Vieillot, 1817, Nouv. Dict. Hist. Nat. nouv. ed., 12, p. 176, Zone Torride; Senegal designated by W.L. Sclater, 1930, Syst. Av. Aethiop., p. 800.

IDENTIFICATION Length 10 cm (4 in). A small, almost entirely pearl- or dove-grey finch with a short but thickset blackish bill and crimson lower back to rump and base of tail. Unlike any other West African finch (though has similar congeners elsewhere). Sexes are alike, but female separable on call. **Confusion species:** Within its native range unlikely to be confused with any other species, as combination of pale grey and deep reddish or crimson is diagnostic. Cinderella (174) and Black-tailed (173) Waxbills are extremely similar, but both differ in having a black tail and Cinderella has crimson on flanks.

DESCRIPTION Sexes alike. **Adult:** Forehead to crown and upper back including mantle and coverts plain pearl-grey, washed bluish on mantle, scapulars, coverts and upper back. Lower back, rump and long uppertail-coverts (which cover at least half the tail) deep crimson, on some almost blood-crimson; central tail feathers entirely crimson and tips of rest of tail dark grey; flight feathers dark grey, edged pale grey or slightly bluish-grey. Lores to eye black, tapering to point behind eye; ear-coverts, cheeks and chin pale or whitish-grey, becoming pale grey on breast, upper belly and flanks; blackish or sooty-grey on centre of belly (blacker on male than on female) and ventral region. Some very small white spots towards rear of flanks not always visible in the field. Undertail-coverts darker or deeper crimson than uppertail-coverts. Bill quite thick or deep at base, curving to a point, mostly black but pale pink or grey at base. Eye dark brown with black orbital ring. Legs and feet black or blackish-brown. **Juvenile:** Generally a very similar but paler version of adult, with crimson on rump to base of tail much duller red and black lores not so well defined; lacks spots on lower flanks.

VOICE The most common contact call is a short, shrill, high-pitched 'squee', 'tsee' or an explosive 'tseep': female has a distinctive two- or three-syllable 'tseeeht-tseeeht' contact note, male has characteristic 'see-you' response; the alarm is similar to call notes, a longer more drawn-out 'squeep'. The song is a thin and squeaky series of 'see-see-see-swee' notes.

STATUS, HABITAT AND BEHAVIOUR Common or locally common. Found in a variety of habitats, from shrubs (i.e. mimosa) in gardens, roadside verges, bushes in open country, thornscrub, edges of cultivation to dry savanna with short grass and bushes. Usually in pairs or small groups, but larger aggregations are not uncommon; often tame and confiding. Mixes freely with other waxbills and weavers. Flight low, direct and fairly fast compared with other waxbills. Feeds in bushes, trees and on the ground, on a variety of seeds, mainly grass, but also other small plant seeds; also takes some insects and ripe fruit.

DISTRIBUTION Monotypic. Southern Senegal (scarce or local in the north), Gambia and Guinea-Bissau east through southern Mali, southern Burkina Faso, northern Ghana, northern Togo to northern Nigeria (to about 15° N), extreme northern Cameroon, northwest Central African Republic and southwest Chad.

Introduced to Hawaiian Islands (Hawaii and Oahu) in early 1960s and apparently established there, but numbers had declined by 1980 and it is considered unlikely to survive.

MEASUREMENTS Wing 48–53; tail 37–41; tarsus 15; bill 9.
REFERENCE Goodwin (1982).

173 BLACK-TAILED WAXBILL (Black-tailed Lavender-Waxbill, Grey Waxbill) *Estrilda perreini* Plate 47
Africa

Fringilla perreini Vieillot, 1817, Nouv. Dict. Hist. Nat. nouv. ed., 12, p. 179, Malimbe, Portuguese Congo.

IDENTIFICATION Length 11 cm (4¼ in). Very similar in overall plumage to Lavender Waxbill (172), with which it does not overlap in range, but has a black chin, brighter red rump and an all-black, longer, rounded or graduated tail. Found in southern central Africa. **Confusion species:** Cinderella Waxbill (174) is paler, has a bright red base to bill, and red with black smudges on flanks. Yellow-bellied (175) has a bright red lower mandible and pale green or grey-green mantle, back and scapulars.
DESCRIPTION Sexes alike. **Adult:** Very similar in size, shape and plumage to Lavender Waxbill, though is slightly more lead-grey on upperparts. Rump and uppertail-coverts bright red. Black tail long and graduated towards tip. As Lavender Waxbill, has black lores and thin eye-stripe, with cheeks, ear-coverts and throat pale grey. Chin black (but not easy to see in the field). Lacks any white spots on flanks, and has vent to undertail-coverts blackish (greyer on females). Bill grey or greyish-blue at base, with black tip and cutting edges. Eye dark brown or black, with a blackish orbital ring. Legs and feet dark green, grey-green, dark blue-grey or blackish. **Juvenile:** Similar to adult but duller grey, and lacks black eye-stripe behind eye; red on rump and uppertail-coverts dull and dark. Has paler base to bill than adult.
GEOGRAPHICAL VARIATION Birds of race *poliogastra* are slightly paler grey (some are very pale) and have red on rump and uppertail-coverts more glossy, while *incana* also averages marginally paler and occasionally shows small white spots on red or reddish-tipped flanks.
VOICE Contact call is a short 'psee' or 'pseee', or

an explosive 'pseeu-pseeu'; also a variety of whistling notes given in (song?) repetition, often long and drawn-out and followed by more abrupt notes.
STATUS, HABITAT AND BEHAVIOUR Uncommon or scarce; easily overlooked. Inhabits thick damp evergreen scrub or thornbush with areas of tall grass, or forest edges and bamboo thickets, from which it seldom ventures; a shy and very retiring species. Occurs alone or in pairs or in small, probably family, parties. Many habits and actions as firefinches (158–166), with which this, and Lavender Waxbill are sometimes classified. Feeds on the ground and in bushes and trees, on a variety of grass and other small seeds; also takes some insects.
DISTRIBUTION *E. p. perreini*: Gabon and the lower Congo south to northern Angola, east to southern Zaire, northern Zambia and western Tanzania.
E. p. poliogastra: southern Tanzania, southern Malawi (Nyasaland), eastern Zimbabwe and Mozambique to northern Zululand, South Africa.
E. p. incana: southern Zimbabwe to southern Zululand and Natal, South Africa.
MOVEMENTS Probably mostly resident, but *incana* has been known to winter north of its breeding range in southern Mozambique. There is also a record of one outside the present range in central Tanzania.
MEASUREMENTS Wing 47–55; tail 43–49; tarsus 14·5–15·5; bill (culmen) 8–9.
REFERENCES Goodwin (1982), Mackworth-Praed and Grant (1960), McLachlan and Liversidge (1978).

174 CINDERELLA WAXBILL (São Tomé Waxbill)
Estrilda thomensis Plate 47
Africa

Estrelda thomensis Sousa, 1888, Journ. Sci. Math. Phys. Nat. Lisboa, 12, p. 155, São Tomé Island (name takes precedence over) *Estrilda cinderella* Neumann, 1908, Bull. Brit. Ornith. Club, 23, p. 44, Deep Sloot, Benguella, Angola).

IDENTIFICATION Length 11 cm (4¼–4½ in). A much paler and slightly smaller version of Black-tailed Waxbill (173), which it replaces in the west of southern central Africa. Has a bright red base to bill, pink flush on body, and red on uppertail-coverts extends along lower flanks. **Confusion species:** Only possible confusion in the wild is with Black-tailed Waxbill, which it overlaps in northern Angola, but separable by paler grey plumage, pinkish flush to upperparts, breast and upper belly, red or reddish base to bill and deep red on lower flanks. Yellow-bellied Waxbill (175) has red lower mandible and green upperparts.

DESCRIPTION Sexes differ slightly. **Adult:** Forehead to crown, upper back, scapulars and wing-coverts pale, almost washed-out grey (duller on female) with very light pink wash (but can be absent on females or in worn plumage). Flight feathers darker grey than rest of upperparts, but edged with pale grey. Lower back, rump, uppertail-coverts and base of tail dull crimson or blood-red, extending along outer webs of tail; rest of tail black. Face very pale grey or whitish, extending across lower forehead on some, lores jet-black and extending very thinly behind eye. Chin and throat almost white, becoming greyer on breast; upper flanks and upper belly (which has rosy-pink wash) grey, as upperparts. Lower flanks dull crimson, but often show dark or blackish bases to feathers; centre of belly to undertail-coverts blackish. Bill short and pointed, red or reddish-pink to mauve-pink at base with blackish ridge and tip. Eye dark brown, with very thin blackish orbital ring. Legs and feet dark brown or black. **Juvenile:**

Very pale grey, lacking pink tinge to plumage, and shows less black on undertail-coverts, (does not extend along flanks). Bill very pale whitish-pink at base, with rest of bill black.

VOICE Unrecorded in the wild, but captive birds have a soft 'tree' or 'kr' contact note. Song of male is a long drawn-out whistling 'see-eh, see-eh, sueee'; female has a single repeated 'seee'.

STATUS, HABITAT AND BEHAVIOUR Locally common. Occurs in dry habitat, thornbush, scrub and open mopane woodland with grass, also found in riverine forest. Usually in pairs or small parties; many habits much as Black-tailed Waxbill. Feeds on a variety of small seeds, principally grass seeds and millet, but also takes some insects, mainly ants.

DISTRIBUTION Monotypic. Western Angola (Dondo south to Benguela, Huila and Moccamedes provinces) to Cunene river, extreme northern Namibia. Originally described in error as originating from São Tomé, hence the alternative name.

MOVEMENTS Those seen along Cunene river in northern Namibia are presumed to be non-breeding birds wandering in search of food.

MEASUREMENTS Wing of male 48–52, of female 47–51; tail 40–45; tarsus 14; bill (culmen) 8. Weight 6–8.

REFERENCES Goodwin (1982), McLachlan and Liversidge (1978).

175 YELLOW-BELLIED WAXBILL (Swee Waxbill) *Estrilda melanotis*
Plate 47

Africa

Fringilla melanotis Temminck, 1823, Pl. Col., livr. 37, pl. 221, 'Pays de Cafres', eastern Cape Province.

IDENTIFICATION Length 10 cm (4 in). A small, active but somewhat shy and retiring waxbill. Has distinctive plumage: grey crown and nape, olive-green upperparts, bright red rump and black tail; underparts with bright yellow or buff on belly to undertail-coverts. Males of nominate race and *bocagei* have black lower face, otherwise the sexes are scarcely separable. Unlikely to be confused in the field with any other species once seen well; for differences from all-grey Black-tailed (173) and Cinderella (174) Waxbills, see those species.

DESCRIPTION Sexes similar. **Adult:** Forehead to crown and nape deep grey or slate-grey; lores, cheeks and ear-coverts to chin (occasionally upper throat) black. Mantle and upper back, scapulars and coverts dull olive-green, finely barred darker (but visible only at close range); greater coverts tinged with warm brown or orange-rufous (only in *melanotis*); flight feathers dark brown or blackish. Lower back, rump and uppertail-coverts deep or bright red or deep orange-red, more orange in worn plumage. Tail short and square-tipped, black (but

base overlapped by long uppertail-coverts). Lower throat and sides of neck white or buffish, becoming very light grey or buffish-grey on breast; flanks light olive-grey, and rest of underparts creamy-buff or slightly tinged with yellow. Bill small, short and pointed, black on upper mandible, pinkish or red on lower. Eye red, with black or greyish orbital ring. Legs and feet black or dark grey-brown.

Adult female: Very similar to adult male, but lacks black face, which instead is pale grey (slightly paler than forehead to nape); chin and throat to sides of throat white or pale grey, and has pale buff on belly to undertail-coverts. **Juvenile:** Similar to adult female, but much duller or browner, especially on green upperparts, and rump and uppertail-coverts dull orange-red or brownish-orange. Bill black on both mandibles.

GEOGRAPHICAL VARIATION Males of race *bocagei* have slightly more olive-green on upperparts, with fine cross-barring noticeable at close range (extending on some to nape, tertials and flanks); breast is deeper blue or bluish-grey and belly is deep yellow (sometimes with a tinge of green), becoming paler towards undertail-coverts. Females of this race as nominate, but have fine cross-barring on upperparts and yellow on belly to undertail-coverts. Males of races *quartinia*, *kilimensis* and *stuartirwini* (sexes of latter alike) lack black face, but have grey head and face to chin and throat, deepest or most heavily grey in *kilimensis*. Male *kilimensis* have a rusty or light orange wash to belly, while female is yellow from belly to undertail-coverts. In race *quartinia*, both sexes have bright yellow (or slightly tinged with green) belly to undertail-coverts, but there is some variation within populations and those from Sudan are palest; juveniles of this race have brighter orange on rump than nominate.

VOICE Call a weak or soft-sounding 'see-see' or 'swee-swee' or a higher-pitched and explosive 'tswee'; alarm a sharp 'teerrr'. The song is a soft but penetrating 'teeeeeeeit' or 'tuuuuuueeet', but race *quartinia* has a variation on this: 'tee-tee-tee-tee-tuuuueeeh, teekutehleekehleekee'.

STATUS, HABITAT AND BEHAVIOUR Common or locally common. A bird of mainly upland or mountainous areas up to 2400 m, in low undergrowth, bracken-briar or dense grass and brush in scrub, woodland or forest edge, usually in vicinity of water, occasionally at the edge of cultivation or in large gardens; also occurs in coastal bush of Cape Province and at low levels elsewhere; only races *quartinia* and *kilimensis* are restricted to high ground, above 1200 m and 1650 m respectively. Occurs in pairs or small parties, rarely, if ever, in large parties or mixed flocks. Tame, but often inconspicuous and overlooked

until it calls. Feeds in an active and agile manner, clinging to plants and flower-heads also forages on the ground and has been known to take insects in flight. Principal food is grass seeds and millet, but also takes a variety of other small seeds and some insects.

DISTRIBUTION *E. m. melanotis*: Cape Province, Natal and the eastern Transvaal, South Africa, to west and central Zimbabwe.

E. m. quartinia: northeast Uganda and Ethiopia.

E. m. kilimensis: highlands of southeast Sudan (Didinga and Dongotona Mountains) to highlands of eastern Zaire, Uganda, Kenya, Burundi, Rwanda, and Tanzania to eastern Zambia, northern Malawi (south to Nyika plateau) and northern Mozambique; intergrades with *stuartirwini* in Malawi.

E. m. bocagei: Pungo Andongo south to Mossamedes district, western Angola.

E. m. stuartirwini: southern Malawi (Nyika plateau) and the eastern highlands of Zimbabwe to Furancungo, northern Mozambique. Intermediates occur where the ranges overlap. Race *quartinia* is treated as a full species by some authorities.

MOVEMENTS Some seasonal or non-breeding-season movements take place, with birds from high altitudes (in Zimbabwe) moving to lower altitudes; elsewhere, occurs erratically in areas where it does not breed.

MEASUREMENTS Wing 46·5–49; tail 34–39; tarsus 12·5–13·5; bill (culmen) 8–9. Wing of *quartinia* 42–45·5; tail 35–38; tarsus 12–13; bill (culmen) 8–9. Weight 6–6·5.

REFERENCE Goodwin (1982).

176 ANAMBRA WAXBILL *Estrilda poliopareia*   **Plate 46**
West Africa

Estrilda poliopareia Reichenow, 1902, Ornith. Monatsb., 10, p. 185, Congo; restricted to southern Nigeria by Chapin, 1950, Bull. Brit. Ornith. Club, 70, p. 24.

IDENTIFICATION Length 11–12 cm (c4½ in). A very small waxbill of very restricted range in West Africa; an *African Red Data Book* species. Both sexes are generally pale brown above with fine dark barring, with rump and uppertail-coverts scarlet and tail dark brown, and buff or buffish-yellow below. Bright red bill is very obvious. **Confusion species:** Apart from Common (182) and Orange-cheeked (178) Waxbills, no other similar small finch is found within the natural range of Anambra. Both Common and out-of-range Crimson-rumped (179) Waxbills have bright red through eye and over ear-coverts (Anambra lacks any red on head). Common Waxbill lacks red on rump, and has bright red belly and is lightly barred on underparts. Orange-cheeked has distinctly different head pattern. Out-of-range Fawn-breasted (177) has grey head and face, is paler below and has white edges and tips to tail.

DESCRIPTION Sexes alike. **Adult:** Forehead to

crown and nape pale brown with a faint grey tinge. Lores, cheeks, ear-coverts and sides of neck buff or warm brown. Mantle, back, scapulars and wing-coverts warm buff or yellowish-brown, very finely barred darker (usually visible only at close range); flight feathers and tertials dull or deep brown. Rump and uppertail-coverts bright red or scarlet, but some, especially females, are paler and can be tinged orange. Tail slightly graduated or rounded at tip, dark brown but with red on base of central feathers and pale buff edges to outers. Chin and throat pale buff or yellowish-buff, becoming paler on breast, and darker or brownish on belly and flanks (on some males, can be a reddish wash extending to sides of breast). Adult females are generally paler on underparts than males. Bill short, stubby and bright waxy-red. Eye pale or creamy. Legs and feet brown or grey-brown. **Juvenile:** Unknown, but very probably a paler version of

adult without any red on flanks and much duller red on rump.
VOICE A variety of nondescript waxbill-type calls.
STATUS, HABITAT AND BEHAVIOUR Uncommon and little known. Found in tall grass within or on the edges of open deciduous forest, swamps or river banks. Habits almost unknown, but presumed to be similar to those of other closely related waxbills. Feeds actively in tall grass and moves up and down stems with ease; food is principally grass seeds taken from seedheads. A brood host to parasitic Pin-tailed Whydah (*Vidua macroura*).

DISTRIBUTION Monotypic. Restricted to a few sites in southern Nigeria between Niger delta and west to border with Benin (provinces of Agoulerie and Onitsha); first discovered in 1907 in Anambra Creek, Onitsha Province. Considered by some authorities to be a race of Fawn-breasted Waxbill.
MOVEMENTS None known, but, since part of the very small range suffers from considerable flooding in severe rainy seasons, birds must make some short distance movements.
MEASUREMENTS Wing 45–49; tail 37–40.
REFERENCES Bannerman (1953), Collar and Stuart (1985), Serle (1957).

177 FAWN-BREASTED WAXBILL *Estrilda paludicola* Plate 46
Africa

Estrelda paludicola Heuglin, 1863, Journ. f. Ornith., 11, p. 166, middle course of Bahr el Ghazal.

IDENTIFICATION Length 11·5 cm (4½ in). A very small waxbill of central and East Africa. Sexes are similar, with dark grey head and face, warm brown upperparts and deep red rump and base of tail; underparts are pale cream or buffish-white. Has a small bright red bill. Combination of grey on head and face (in most races) and rich warm brown on mantle and back, bright red rump and uppertail-coverts and pale buffish or yellow unstreaked underparts is distinctive. **Confusion species:** Orange-cheeked Waxbill (178) is similar, but has a bright orange face.
DESCRIPTION Sexes alike. **Adult:** Forehead to crown and nape grey or slate-grey, sides of face paler, more ashy-grey. Mantle, back, scapulars and wing-coverts a warm brown or russet-brown, at close range very finely barred; flight feathers darker or blackish with brown edges. Rump and uppertail-coverts deep red, tinged with pink in fresh plumage. Tail graduated at tip, black with white outer edges. Underparts yellowish-buff, creamy or light buff or fawn-brown on breast and somewhat deeper on belly; males in fresh plumage have a pinkish wash; sides of breast and flanks greyish (more extensive on females), undertail-coverts paler, almost white. Bill short and rather stubby, a bright waxy or orange-red. Eye red. Legs and feet dark brown. **Juvenile:** Very similar to adult, but has brown on forehead to crown and rump is duller or tinged with brown; throat white, and is generally paler buff on underparts; bill black.
GEOGRAPHICAL VARIATION Birds of race *benguellensis* have darker grey on head, more clearly defined from brown of mantle, which is darker or deeper in tone than nominate; bright pinkish tinge to lower flanks (occasionally to lower breast) and vent. Race *roseicrissa* has forehead to nape uniform brown with mantle and back, paler or greyer underparts than nominate, and belly usually whiter, and males also have a bright pink tinge to lower flanks and vent. Race *marwitzi* is darker brown above than nominate race, and has grey

chin to breast. Race *ruthae* is pale tawny-brown on upperparts and almost white on underparts. Race *ochrogaster* is quite distinct from nominate and all above-mentioned races: it has forehead to crown and nape brown, and lores, cheeks and area around eye to chin and throat a rich golden-brown, becoming paler golden-buff on breast and flanks; belly and undertail-coverts are as nominate, but some show a few pink tips around vent. Female *ochrogaster* are paler and washed with grey.
VOICE Commonest contact call is a nasal 'tyeek', 'tyeep' or 'tsyee'; alarm is a 'tsyee-krr' or a 'kr-yee-eh'. Song is a harsh 'tek tek tek teketree teketree'.
STATUS, HABITAT AND BEHAVIOUR Common or locally common. A bird of moist or swampy grassland or grass clumps in open bush, forest or clearings, usually near streams, occasionally at edges of human settlements and cultivation; race *ochrogaster* inhabits uplands of Ethiopia (but not found on the open plateau). Occurs in pairs or small flocks of up to about 30, occasionally in larger numbers, often in company with other waxbills. Feeds in the manner of other waxbills, taking food on the ground or from vegetation, mostly small grass seeds or occasionally some insects.
DISTRIBUTION *E. p. paludicola*: northeast Congo, northern Zaire, central and northern Uganda and southern Sudan (to about 11° N) to western Kenya (intergrades with *roseicrissa* in area of overlap on northern shore of Lake Victoria).
E. p. ochrogaster: highlands of extreme eastern Sudan (Baro River to Boma hills) and Ethiopia.
E. p. roseicrissa: southern Uganda to Rwanda, Burundi and northwest Tanzania.
E. p. marwitzi: Iringa highlands to Shinyanga, western Tanzania.
E. p. benguellensis: central Angola (northern Huila to central Malanje), southern Zaire and northern and northeast Zambia to extreme southwest Tanzania.
E. p. ruthae: Bolobo to Lukolela and Kunungu, middle Congo (now Zaire) river, central Zaire.

MOVEMENTS Very little known; some must wander in search of food when not breeding. Has occurred in Central African Republic.

MEASUREMENTS Wing 43–50; tail 39; tarsus 13; bill (culmen) 8.
REFERENCES Carroll (1988), Goodwin (1982).

178 ORANGE-CHEEKED WAXBILL *Estrilda melpoda*   Plate 46
Africa

Fringilla melpoda Vieillot, 1817, Nouv. Dict. Hist. Nat. nouv. ed., 12, p. 177, India and west coast of Africa; restricted to Senegal by Neumann, 1932, Anz. Ornith. Ges. Bayern, 2, p. 154.

IDENTIFICATION Length 10 cm (4 in). A small, active and distinctive plumaged waxbill. Sexes are alike, with grey crown and nape surrounding bright orange face, brown mantle and wings, red or orange-red rump and black tail; underparts very pale grey or buffish. Orange face, present at all ages, is diagnostic and makes it unlikely to be confused with any other species.

DESCRIPTION Sexes alike. **Adult:** Forehead to nape grey, tinged slightly darker on nape and sides of neck. Lores, over eye to ear-coverts and cheeks deep or rich orange (by far the most obvious field character); extent or intensity of orange variable, some are more yellow than orange. Mantle, back and scapulars to wing-coverts deep or warm brown; flight feathers blackish-brown, but tertials and secondaries edged darker brown. Rump and uppertail-coverts red or reddish-orange or slightly paler orange. Tail long and thin when closed, but graduated or wedge-shaped when spread; blackish-brown with some red on edges to feather bases, sometimes with pale tips on outers. Chin and throat whitish, but can be buff or greyish-buff as breast and upper flanks; belly and lower flanks buffish-brown, vent yellowish or pale orange, undertail-coverts pale buff. Bill short and stubby, bright waxy-red or deep orange. Eye brown or reddish-brown. Legs and feet dark brown. **Juvenile:** Very like adult, including face, but generally paler with crown and nape brown or buffish-brown; face and rump paler and less brightly orange. Underparts much more buff than grey of adults, and has black bill.

GEOGRAPHICAL VARIATION There is considerable individual variation throughout species' wide range, especially in intensity of orange on face; some are very pale while others have a deep, almost reddish-orange tone. Only birds in northern Cameroon and around Lake Chad, which are distinctly reddish-orange and paler brown on upperparts, are considered by most authorities to be consistently subspecifically separable, as race

tschadensis. Red-faced birds from Zaire were formerly considered to be separable as *fucata*.

VOICE Contact call is a soft, high-pitched peeping note frequently repeated; also gives an excited 'sree-sree-sree-sree'; alarm call is a shrill 'tsit, tsit' or 'tseet, tseet'. Song is a collection of several short notes 'de-de-de-sweea, sweea, sweea' or a 'tsee-ree-ree, tsee-ree-ree, tsee-ree-ree'.

STATUS, HABITAT AND BEHAVIOUR Common or locally common to abundant. Found in a variety of habitats, from grassland savanna or grassy clearings at the edge of cultivation, to swamps, forest edges, thickets or weedy patches, even in gardens where suitable feeding is available. Usually in pairs or small groups, but sizeable flocks band together in the non-breeding season. Often in flocks of its own kind but does also mix with other waxbills and mannikins, especially at roosts or a common source of food, though it appears to avoid areas where Common Waxbill (182) is numerous. Feeds in tall grass, where it takes seeds from the heads, but also feeds on the ground on a variety of small seeds, mostly of grasses, but some small insects may also be taken.

DISTRIBUTION *E. m. melpoda*: Senegal (scarce in the north) and Gambia and southern Mali south and southeast through West Africa (south of 11° N) to Cameroon, Central African Republic, northern Congo, west and northern Zaire, northern Zambia and northern Angola.

E. m. tschadensis: northern Adamawa, Cameroon, and Lake Chad area, southern Chad.

Intermediates between the two races occur in the areas of overlap. Has also been introduced into Bermuda, Puerto Rico and the Hawaiian Islands (Hawaii and Oahu).

MOVEMENTS Local movements occur in the coastal zones of Ghana and elsewhere in West Africa in the non-breeding season.

MEASUREMENTS Wing 45–50; tail 38–48; tarsus c15; bill c10.
REFERENCES Chapin (1954), Goodwin (1982).

179 CRIMSON-RUMPED WAXBILL *Estrilda rhodopyga*   Plate 44
Africa

Estrilda rhodopyga Sundevall, 1850, Ofv. K. Sv. Vet.-Akad. Forh., 7, p. 126, northeast Africa; restricted to Sennar, see Shelley, 1905, Birds of Africa, 4, p. 206.

IDENTIFICATION Length 10 cm (4 in). One of a group of closely related waxbills, several of which

occur in East Africa: Common (182), Black-rumped (181) and Arabian (180) Waxbills. All have pale or buff-brown upperparts finely dark-barred, a deep red or crimson stripe through eye, and pale buff-brown underparts with variable amounts of fine barring. Crimson-rumped differs in its black bill (with some red at base), crimson edges and tips in wing, unbarred deep crimson rump and buff underparts. Red wing panel, rump and tail also recall Crimson-winged Pytilia (138), which is grey overall, lacks red eye-stripe and has pinkish legs.

DESCRIPTION Sexes alike. **Adult:** Forehead to crown and nape grey or greyish-brown; thin bright red stripe across lores through eye, tapering across top of ear-coverts; rest of face pale cream. Mantle, back and scapulars to median coverts pale brown or buff-brown, very finely or closely dark-barred; edges and tips of greater coverts deep or rich carmine-red, extending on closed wing to edges of inner secondaries and tertials; rest of flight feathers and inner webs of tertials dark brown. Rump and uppertail-coverts deep red or crimson, extending to edges of base of tail; rest of tail dark brown. Chin and throat creamy, becoming deeper buff or buff-brown on breast and flanks, with indistinct barring on flanks to undertail-coverts, which are barred blackish, buff and crimson. Bill short, rather stubby and appears almost black, but at close range has pinkish-red at base of both mandibles. Eye dark brown or deep reddish-brown. Legs and feet blackish-brown. **Juvenile:** Very similar to adult, but duller and lacks barring on mantle, back and underparts, and has duller orange-red on rump and uppertail-coverts; also lacks red stripe through eye and has all-black bill.

GEOGRAPHICAL VARIATION There is a considerable amount of local and individual variation within the range, and some birds are noticeably darker than others, but *centralis* is consistently

darker or browner on upperparts, is also darker on underparts and has deeper red on wings and rump.
VOICE Call a soft 'tyeek' or 'tyeep', or a harsh, nasal 'tcha, tcha-tcha, tchek-tchek-chek'; also a harsh, nasal 'tchair', 'tcherr' or 'tchaee', often becoming a double-note 'tche-tchair'. Song is a long drawn-out version of 'tchair' call but also with some slight variation, i.e. a chattering 'tcha-tcha-tcha-tcha-tcha-tcha-tchurr' recalling Great Tit (*Parus major*).
STATUS, HABITAT AND BEHAVIOUR Common or locally common. Inhabits lowland grassland up to 1650 m with bushes or scrub, forest edges, open acacia savanna, marshes or swamp grassland and edges of cultivated areas. Usually occurs in pairs or small parties feeding together, occasionally mixing with other waxbills, including Common Waxbill, or mannikins. Feeds on seedheads or growing vegetation and on the ground, where it takes a variety of small seeds, mainly grass, but also millet and small quantities of insects and ant larvae. Brood host to Pin-tailed Whydah (*Vidua macroura*).
DISTRIBUTION *E. r. rhodopyga*: Sudan (from Darfur to about Khartoum), Ethiopia and southern Somalia (rare in the north).
 E. r. centralis: southern Ethiopia, southeast Sudan (Equatoria), Uganda, northern and central Zaire, central and southeast Kenya, central and northeast Tanzania to extreme northern Malawi.
MOVEMENTS Wanders widely throughout the range in non-breeding season in search of seeding grasses.
MEASUREMENTS Wing 45–50; tarsus 11; bill 8.
REFERENCE Goodwin (1982).

180 ARABIAN WAXBILL *Estrilda rufibarba*   Plate 18
Arabia

Habropyga rufibarba Cabanis, 1851, Mus. Heineanum, 1, p. 169, Arabia.

IDENTIFICATION Length 10 cm (4 in). The only waxbill of its kind with a black bill and dark blood-red stripe through eye. Has a white face and pale grey-brown upperparts and buff-brown underparts, both finely barred or vermiculated darker, with an all-black rump to tail. Very similar to (but paler and greyer than) closely related Common (182), Black-rumped (181), Black-faced (183) and Crimson-rumped (179) Waxbills of Africa. Within native range, unlikely to be confused with any other species. Female Zebra Waxbill (189) has a bright red bill (but can be dark brown on immatures), upperparts not so soft grey as Arabian and lacks dark stripe through lores and eye. In Africa, Common, Black-faced and Black-rumped Waxbills are much more pinkish-buff on body than plain grey-brown of Arabian, and also have a bright red

bill. Crimson-rumped Waxbill is pale brown on upperparts, lacks pink tinge to body and has dull red in wings.
DESCRIPTION Sexes alike. **Adult:** Upperparts from forehead to nape and wing-coverts and upper rump soft ash-grey or washed grey-brown, with fine close dark barring faintly on nape but more visible on mantle, back and wing-coverts; flight feathers black or blackish. Lower rump and uppertail-coverts black. Tail long and graduated or rounded at tip, black, with white in outer tail feathers (but usually visible only from below). Face has deep or dark crimson (often appears darker) stripe across lores and upper ear-coverts (on some females appears black in the field); rest of face to chin and upper throat silky-white, merging gradually into pale buff-brown of underparts, which are very

closely barred or vermiculated, becoming paler on belly and undertail-coverts. Bill short and almost stubby, in breeding season black with red at base, in non-breeding season bluish-black, but some are pale, greyer or whitish. Eye dark brown or brown. Legs and feet black or blackish-grey. In the hand, females are paler and more buff on belly and vent. **Juvenile:** Generally duller brown or buff-brown on upperparts, with darker wings, and close barring faint or absent. Dark brown or blackish stripe through eye, sometimes not so broad or so complete as on adult. Underparts dull buffish or off-white, but with a buffish-brown wash to belly and flanks. Bill dark grey.

VOICE Most frequent contact notes are a hard buzzing 'dzit', 'dzeet', 'chzit' or 'chee'; in flight, latter note (or similar) is repeated to become a 'chee-chee-chee-chee-chee'. Flocks utter a constant 'tse-tseee', which becomes a noisy chatter.

STATUS, HABITAT AND BEHAVIOUR Rare or local in southern Saudi Arabia and South Yemen, but slightly commoner in North Yemen. Inhabits dry wadis or valleys and rocky hillsides with thick scrub or trees, usually between 250 and 2200 m, mostly above 1000 m, exceptionally to 2600 m; weedy thickets and patches of reeds and tamarisk, often near or within reach of cultivation (mainly cereals), also has a preference for boggy areas or running water. Occurs in pairs, more often in small flocks (in non-breeding season up to 200 together); occasionally associates with Zebra Waxbill, the other waxbill of the region. Tail is often flicked or switched from side to side when excited or alarmed; has a short and rather erratic bouncing flight. Roosts communally in large (often mixed) flocks in bamboo or typha. Quite shy in some areas, but feeds in the open especially when in small flocks. Feeds on reed heads, growing plants and on the ground on grass seeds, maize, millet and other small weed seeds.

DISTRIBUTION Monotypic. The lowlands and Red Sea coast of southwest Saudi Arabia (north to about 20° N), and through the Tihamah and foothills of North Yemen to South Yemen.

MOVEMENTS Generally resident, but some wander locally in the non-breeding season.

MEASUREMENTS Wing 46–49.

REFERENCES Christensen and Porter (1987), Hollom et al. (1988).

---

181 BLACK-RUMPED WAXBILL (Red-eared Waxbill, Grey Waxbill)
Estrilda troglodytes   Plate 44

Africa

Fringilla troglodytes Lichtenstein, 1823, Verz. Doubl. Zool. Mus. Berlin, p. 26, Senegambia.

IDENTIFICATION Length 10 cm (4 in). A very small and active finch of the dry grassland belt of sub-Saharan Africa. Habitually switches its tail from side to side when excited or alarmed. The sexes are alike, with a broad red eye-stripe and generally brown upperparts, slightly paler on mantle and back with indistinct fine or close barring; rump and tail black, latter with white outer feathers. Black rump and tail prominent in flight. **Confusion species:** Crimson-rumped Waxbill (179) has red in wings and red or crimson (not black) rump and uppertail-coverts; it is finely barred above and below, and has a thinner red eye-stripe and black bill. Common Waxbill (182) lacks black rump, and is much more clearly barred both above and below (especially on flanks). Out-of-range Arabian (180) is much greyer, lacks pink tinge to plumage and rose or reddish-pink on belly, and has a black bill.

DESCRIPTION Sexes alike. **Adult:** Forehead to crown and nape uniform deep grey, tinged with pale brown, becoming paler or browner on mantle, back, scapulars and wing-coverts (though some can be tinged warm brown on back); some birds show fine or almost indistinct close barring on nape, mantle and back. Wings plain or uniform mid-brown, flight feathers slightly darker. Rump, uppertail-coverts and tail black; tail rounded or slightly graduated at tip, with white outer webs to outer feathers. Bright red or crimson mask from base of bill through eye and across top of ear-coverts, tapering to a point. Cheeks and lower ear-coverts whitish or pale buff, this extending to chin and throat, the latter washed with pink on males, becoming more noticeably pinkish-buff on lower breast, flanks and upper belly, (pink generally, but not always, lacking or less extensive on females); on males, lower belly and vent reddish-pink, extending on some to breast; undertail-coverts pinkish-white. Bill short, stubby, waxy-red or reddish-orange. Eye brown or reddish-brown. Legs and feet dark or blackish-brown. **Juvenile:** Similar to adult, but paler or duller unbarred buff-brown above and lacks pinkish tinge on underparts; stripe through eye is dark brown or blackish. Bill is black.

VOICE Call is a loud repeated 'cheu-cheu', 'chit-chit' or a 'chihooee'; in flight, flocks constantly give a 'tiup-tiup-tiup'; also has a 'cheeer', 'chee-ey' or a buzzing 'cheea', which may be given when disturbed, alarmed or excited. Song of male is a loud, explosive rising (on second syllable) 'tche-tcheer, che-eeer', or 't,chu-weee' (with second syllable descending); song of female is a shorter but also explosive 'pwich pwich' or an ascending 'pwich cheee'.

STATUS, HABITAT AND BEHAVIOUR Widespread but locally common. Inhabits dry or arid grassland savannas, often in thickets, scrub or thornbush, occasionally on the edge of cultivation (rice-fields), but not generally found in close vicinity of human settlements. Usually in pairs, small groups or occasionally in large flocks, often with other waxbills. Tail often flicked or switched from side to side when excited or alarmed, a habit it shares with Common and Arabian Waxbills. Feeds on the ground or while in vegetation, principally on grass seeds, but millet also taken; has been known to take insects, including midges caught in flight. A breeding host of parasitic Pin-tailed Whydah (*Vidua macroura*).

DISTRIBUTION Monotypic. Senegal, Gambia and Guinea east to southern Mali, Burkina Faso, Ghana, southern Niger, northern Nigeria, northern Cameroon, southern Chad, Central African Republic, extreme northern Congo and northeast Zaire, northwest Uganda, southern Sudan (north to about 12° N), western Ethiopia and western Kenya. Introduced in the mid-1960s into Puerto Rico, where apparently established, and into Hawaii (Oahu), where no sightings since the mid-1970s and now considered to have died out.

MOVEMENTS Mostly sedentary, but some wander in the dry season into areas outside immediate breeding range; recorded twice in Mauritania, singles in November 1978 and November 1980. In Ghana, it is a wet-season breeding visitor to the coastal thicket zone. Possible vagrant to Tenerife, Canary Islands (May 1988), but may also have been an escape from captivity.

MEASUREMENTS Wing 44–50; tail 37–42; tarsus 12–15; bill 8–9.

REFERENCES Bannerman (1963), Browne (1981), Goodwin (1982), Grimes (1987).

182 COMMON WAXBILL *Estrilda astrild* Plate 44
Africa

Loxia astrild Linnaeus, 1758, Syst. Nat., ed. 10, p. 173, Canaries, America, Africa; restricted to Cape Town by W.L. Sclater and Mackworth-Praed, 1918, Ibis, p. 442.

IDENTIFICATION Length 11–13 cm (4¼-5 in). The commonest and most widespread waxbill in Africa. A small finch with bright red bill and deep red stripe through eye. Generally brown or buff-brown with fine but distinct close barring above and below, and a pink or reddish wash to underparts or, on some, a patch in centre of belly; tail entirely dark brown. Sexes are alike, but some can be separated by intensity of colour of underparts, though there is considerable individual and racial variation. **Confusion species:** Very similar to both Black-rumped (181) and Crimson-rumped (179) Waxbills, from which it differs principally in having neither black nor bright crimson rump; its uppertail-coverts and rump are brown or buffish-brown, tinged pink and dark-barred. Differs further from Black-rumped in its more general pinkish tinge, clearly barred plumage and lack of white in outer tail feathers; from Crimson-rumped in its bright red bill and lack of red in wings. Shares same tail-flicking habits as Black-rumped Waxbill. Out-of-range Arabian Waxbill (180) is much greyer and appears finely barred grey and white, lacks any pink in plumage and has black bill. All other waxbills lack red eye-stripe of these four species.

DESCRIPTION Sexes alike. **Adult:** Forehead to nape pale brown or greyish-brown; lores to above and below eye bright red, tapering at rear of ear-coverts; cheeks, lower ear-coverts and sides of neck pale buff. Mantle, back, scapulars and wing-coverts brown, buffish or reddish-brown, closely dark-barred; flight feathers dark brown with pale buff-brown edges, broader on tertials, which can also show some barring. Rump and long uppertail-coverts (which cover base of tail) as back (including dark barring), often tinged pink or pinkish-red. Dark brown tail appears long in flight, often looks ragged and is graduated towards tip, with centre often showing slight barring. Chin and throat pale buff, becoming buff or very lightly buffish-brown or fawn, with fine dark cross-barring on breast to flanks; some have a pink tinge or wash on lower breast and belly; vent and undertail-coverts blackish. Bill short and conical, waxy-red or deep orange-red. Eye brown or reddish-brown. Legs and feet dark brown or black. On adult female, underparts are paler and less likely to be washed or tinged with pink and undertail-coverts are more dark brown than blackish. **Juvenile:** Generally paler or more buff-brown, with only faint cross-barring and very faint pinkish wash on underparts; paler red or reddish-orange stripe from lores through eyes, less broad and extensive across ear-coverts; lower lores blackish. Bill black or blackish, but becomes orange in first winter. Note: For ageing and sexing birds in the hand, see Vowles and Vowles (1987).

GEOGRAPHICAL VARIATION Race *rubriventris* is reddest or richest pink of all the races, adult males having upperparts (especially rump and uppertail-coverts) washed red, cheeks and throat visibly pink and lower breast and belly bright crimson-red; females have a pink wash to underparts, but are less intensely red and closely resemble nominate. Male *damarensis* are paler above, more buffish or greyish-buff, but still show pink tinge on both upperparts and underparts; females lack red on belly and vent and have barred undertail-coverts (as flanks). Race *ngamiensis* is similar in being as pale above, but underparts are more as those of following three races. Both sexes of *cavendishi* have much more noticeable darker barring, face to chin and throat almost white, and a broad red or reddish-pink stripe up the centre of belly; *angolensis* are similar to *cavendishi*, but have a stronger pink wash on upperparts and flanks (though latter race is not so dark as the former); *peasei* are generally a darker brown, with a pale or whitish lower face and only a pink wash on breast and belly, and barring on underparts is restricted to flanks. Birds of race *minor* are greyer in general tone and more clearly barred on upperparts, generally without pink wash or tinge; they have white face and throat and a very small area of pink on belly. Race *occidentalis* also has a white or pale face, but is darker brown (not warm or rufous) on upperparts, occasionally shows fine dark barring extending onto crown, lacks red centre to belly, but has a general pink tinge on lower breast, flanks and belly; *kempi* is very similar, but plain brown above, with more clearly defined barring.

VOICE Commonest call is a sharp, abrupt 'pit' or 'tchick', often repeated when alarmed or excited, also a soft 'chip' and a nasal 'cher-cher-cher'; in flight, flocks give a light twittering note. Song is a low, harsh rising 'tcher-tcher-preeee', 'cher-cher-cher', occasionally followed by a 'dit' note or a descending 'chewi-chee'.

STATUS, HABITAT AND BEHAVIOUR Widespread and common. Favours long grass or savanna habitat, also edges of marshes, swamps, abandoned cultivation, plantations, gardens, villages, often near water or, where suitable grass habitat exists, in open country, at up to 1000 m throughout most of the range but higher in East Africa, particularly Ethiopia, where recorded to 2400 m. Tame and very confiding. Usually in small flocks (breeds in loose colonies), and in larger, straggling flocks when not breeding. Roosts communally in tightly packed groups, either in a line on a grass stem or even on the backs of other birds. Feeds either on the ground or while clinging, sometimes acrobatically upside-down, to living grass stems. Feeds on a variety of grass seeds, but also some small seeds of sedges; occasionally takes small insects, including emerging termites which it pursues in flight to some height. Brood host to Pin-tailed Whydah (*Vidua macroura*).

DISTRIBUTION Found throughout most of Africa south of the Sahara. *E. a. astrild*: southern Botswana to South Africa outside the range of *tenebridorsa*.

E. a. tenebridorsa: eastern Cape Province, southeast Transvaal, eastern Orange Free State,

western Swaziland, Natal and southern Zululand, South Africa.

E. a damarensis: Namibia.

E. a. jagoensis: coastal plain of Benguela, western Angola; introduced into Cape Verde Islands, São Tomé and Príncipe.

E. a. angolensis: plateau of western Angola.

E. a. ngamiensis: eastern Angola to northern Zambia, central, west and south Zimbabwe and northern Botswana.

E. a. schoutedeni: southern Zaire.

E. a. cavendishi: central and southern Tanzania, Malawi, southern Zaire, Zambia and northern and eastern Zimbabwe to Mozambique and the eastern Transvaal and northern Zululand, South Africa.

E. a. minor: southern Somalia (where rare or scarce), eastern Kenya to central and eastern Tanzania (Uluguru Mountains), Mafia and Zanzibar Islands.

E. a. massaica: Kenya (except arid north and northeast) to northern Tanzania.

E. a. occidentalis: southern Mali, Ivory Coast and northwest Ghana to Nigeria, Fernando Po, Cameroon, Central African Republic and Congo to northern central Zaire (middle Congo river).

E. a. rubriventris: coastal Gabon and the lower southwest Congo to northwest Angola.

E. a. kempi: Sierra Leone to Guinea and Liberia.

E. a. peasii: central and southern Sudan to Ethiopia, Uganda, western Kenya, eastern Zaire (Kivu), Burundi, Rwanda and northwest Tanzania.

There is considerable overlap between races and many intergrades and intermediate forms occur. Nominate race has been introduced into Ascension, St Helena, Mauritius, Réunion, Rodriguez, Seychelles, Amirantes, New Caledonia, Tahiti, Oahu (Hawaii), Bermuda and Puerto Rico; also into Brazil, where now locally distributed in seven main areas. Now extinct on Madagascar and Comoros (after earlier introductions). Also recently introduced/released into Portugal, and has since spread into central Spain.

MEASUREMENTS Wing 47–52; tail 50–61; tarsus 14–16; bill (culmen) 9–9·5. Wing of *occidentalis* 45–48; tail 44. Wing of *peasei* 48–52. Wing of *damarensis* 49–53. Wing of *ngamiensis* 46–49·5; tail 46–50; tarsus 12·5–14; bill (culmen) 8–9. Weight 67–74.

REFERENCES Goodwin (1982), McLachlan and Liversidge (1978), Newman (1983), Sinclair (1984), Vowles and Vowles (1987).

---

183 BLACK-FACED WAXBILL *Estrilda nigriloris*   Plate 45
Central Africa

Estrilda nigriloris Chapin, 1928, Amer. Mus. Novit., no. 308, p. 1, Kiabo, Lualaba River, Congo.

IDENTIFICATION Length 10–11 cm (4–4½ in). A rare or scarce endemic of the grasslands of southern/central Zaire. Possibly a race of Common Waxbill (182), but very little is known of its status,

habits or relationships. Very similar in plumage to Common Waxbill, but has short black stripe through eye, and is generally pale buff-brown with dark barring and with deeper mauve-pink wash below; dark red bill. **Confusion species:** Likely to be confused only with Common Waxbill; the two are not known to occur together, though Common is certainly present not far outside the range of Black-faced.

DESCRIPTION Sexes alike. **Adult:** Entire upperparts as Common Waxbill, but with finely marked bars and a pink tinge. The face has a black (not crimson) line across lores, tapering over ear-coverts (in the hand, shows a thin line of pink or white above black). Chin and throat as Common Waxbill, but breast and upper belly have a deep pink or mauve-pink tinge; centre of belly does not have such a well-defined streak of pink or reddish-pink as in most races of Common. Bill short and slightly deeper or more stubby than on Common, deep blood- or dull scarlet-red. Eye dark brown. Legs and feet dull dark brown. **Juvenile:** Undescribed.

VOICE Undescribed (possibly very similar to that of Common Waxbill).

STATUS, HABITAT AND BEHAVIOUR Rare. Confined to the open grasslands and plains of the banks of the Lualaba, southern Zaire. Very little is known of its biology; presumed to be very similar in most respects, including behaviour and habits, to Common Waxbill. Feeds on small grass seeds collected from the ground.

DISTRIBUTION Monotypic. Restricted to the banks of the Lualaba river and the eastern shores of Lake Upemba in southern central Zaire. The total range of the species has been estimated at less than 2600 km². There appear to be no published records since 1950.

MEASUREMENTS Wing 46; tail 45; tarsus 16; bill (culmen) 8–9.

REFERENCES Chapin (1954), Hall and Moreau (1970).

184 BLACK-CROWNED WAXBILL (Blackcap Waxbill) *Estrilda nonnula*
Plate 45

West and Central Africa

Astrilda nonnula Hartlaub, 1883, Journ. f. Ornith., 31, p. 425, Kudurma, eastern equatorial Africa [Equatoria Province, Sudan].

♂ *bill pattern.*

IDENTIFICATION Length 11–12 cm (4½ in). This and Black-headed Waxbill (185) are very similar; often found together and not always easily separated. Both sexes of Black-crowned have a black cap, grey mantle and back with fine blackish barring, blackish wings and tail, and a bright crimson rump; face and underparts are white. **Confusion species:** Much paler grey on upperparts than Black-headed, and has virtually all-white (tinged grey) underparts (to undertail-coverts), whereas Black-headed has black on vent and undertail-coverts and a greater area of wine-red on flanks. Juveniles are more easily separated: Black-crowned is pale grey becoming buff or whitish-buff on underparts, while Black-headed is grey or streaked blackish-grey; neither shows red or on flanks. White-breasted Negro-finch (131) is also similar in plumage, but has different shape, bill and behaviour (never feeds on the ground), and is much darker (and unbarred) grey on mantle and back.

DESCRIPTION Sexes differ slightly. **Adult male:** Lores and forehead to crown and nape jet-black. Hindneck to mantle, back, scapulars and wing-coverts pale ash-grey, finely but clearly barred dark grey or blackish; lower back, rump and uppertail-coverts deep or bright crimson. Black tail quite long and graduated or rounded at tip. Face (except lores) white, this extending to entire underparts except

for a slight greyish tinge on sides of breast, lower breast and flanks; small crimson patch on lower flanks; undertail-coverts tinged greyish (some show faint bars). Bill short and rather stubby with curved culmen, upper mandible mostly black with red sides, lower black with red base. Eye dark brown. Legs and feet dark grey or blackish. **Adult female:** Very similar to male, but can be separated (especially when both sexes are together) by slightly greyer-brown mantle, scapulars and wings; underparts are tinged with grey, and has less crimson on flanks and less red on bill. **Juvenile:** Very similar to adults, with clear-cut black crown and white face, but has unbarred greyish-brown mantle and back; rump is duller or darker red. Underparts are whitish-buff, with pale buff flanks and light grey undertail-coverts. Bill is black.

GEOGRAPHICAL VARIATION Races *elizae* and *eisentrauti* are more silky-grey than white on underparts.

VOICE Contact call is a thin, high-pitched 'tee-tee' or 'tsee-tsee-tsee'; alarm is a harsher 'srree-srree' or 'tsrreee-tsrreee-tsrreee'. Song is a longer or more drawn-out version of contact call and alarm notes, given by male.

STATUS, HABITAT AND BEHAVIOUR Common, very common or locally abundant. Found in a wide range of habitats comprising grassy clearings with bushes and trees, forest clearings or edges, open savanna and even gardens or bushy woodland; occurs at up to 2500 m on rocky mountain slopes with bamboo or tall grasses. Extremely social and often tame, usually in small flocks, though these can number thousands at ripe millet. Feeds either on the ground or in growing vegetation, on a variety of grass seeds, millet and other small seeds, also takes flying termites and probably other small insects; said also to feed on buds in the manner of a Common Bullfinch (118), but this needs confirmation.

DISTRIBUTION *E. n. nonnula*: extreme southeast Nigeria, southern Cameroon through northern Congo, Central African Republic and northern and eastern Zaire to southern Sudan (mainly in Imatong Mountains), Uganda, Rwanda, Burundi, western and central Kenya and northwest Tanzania.

E. n. elizae: Fernando Po.

E. n. eisentrauti: Mount Cameroon, Cameroon.

Note: Closer examination of those in southeast Nigeria may reveal that they are (as some authorities speculate) closer to *elizae* of Fernando Po.

MEASUREMENTS Wing 44–50; tail 40–46; tarsus 11–15; bill 9–10. Wing of *eisentrauti* 50·5–52·5.

REFERENCES Goodwin (1982), Mackworth-Praed and Grant (1960).

185 BLACK-HEADED WAXBILL *Estrilda atricapilla*   Plate 45
West and central Africa

Estrelda atricapilla J. and E. Verreaux, 1851, Rev. Mag. Zool. [Paris], ser. 2, p. 421, Gabon.

IDENTIFICATION Length 10 cm (4 in). Similar to Black-crowned Waxbill (184), but is darker above and has darker or greyer wash on underparts and a black belly and undertail-coverts. Has a black cap, and black bill with a red spot at base of lower mandible. Likely to be confused only with Black-crowned, with which it often associates, but the darker (not pale) grey upperparts and almost all-dark or buffish-grey (not white, except in race *avakubi*) underparts with extensive red or crimson on flanks and black or sooty-grey on belly to undertail-coverts (entirely white or tinged with grey on Black-crowned) are distinctive. Black-headed also lacks any red on the upper mandible.

DESCRIPTION Sexes differ slightly (see races). **Adult male:** Forehead (including lores, and slightly behind eye), crown and nape black. Mantle, back, scapulars and wing-coverts dark grey with fine black barring; flight feathers very dark grey or blackish; rump and uppertail-coverts bright red (not crimson). Tail as that of Black-crowned Waxbill, rounded at tip, entirely black. Face below black cap white, washed with grey (especially on cheeks to throat and sides of neck); breast grey, becoming black on belly to undertail-coverts; flanks quite extensively red (meeting red of rump). Bill more blunt than on Black-crowned, with black upper mandible and tip to lower, latter with a red or reddish-pink spot at base. Eye dark brown. Legs and feet black or blackish. **Adult female:** Generally paler or more grey-brown than adult male, especially on upperparts, and paler red on flanks. **Juvenile:** Very similar to adult female, but mantle and back and lower breast and belly dull dark brown, has rather inconspicuous barring and lacks red (or is only a very faint wash) on flanks. Bill is all black.

GEOGRAPHICAL VARIATION Race *avakubi* has paler or whiter, tinged bluish-grey upperparts and has barring on back and scapulars more broadly spaced; underparts are paler or white on face and throat and dark grey to blackish on belly

to undertail-coverts. Male *graueri* have barring on mantle and back finely or narrowly spaced, and red on rump is darker; females are duller or tinged with olive (similar to juvenile), and have face to upper breast pale whitish-grey and lower breast, belly and flanks are slightly vermiculated.

VOICE Call a soft or weak 'teep' and a faint twittering; otherwise undescribed and probably very similar to voice of Black-crowned Waxbill.

STATUS, HABITAT AND BEHAVIOUR Common or locally common; abundant in some areas. Found in a variety of grassy habitats but usually in or adjacent to forest areas, and not a bird of open grassland savanna. Occurs in tall grass or bamboo thickets in forest clearings or edges at up to 3050 m in the east of the range, where also visits gardens and the edges of cultivation; race *graueri* occurs between 1500 m and 3300 m. Usually in small flocks, though has been known to occur in large flocks where food is plentiful, and often associates with the very similar Black-crowned or occasionally other waxbills. Feeds on the ground in the open on paths or tracks, and usually takes a variety of grass seeds and millet, but also a small quantity of small insects, mainly ants.

DISTRIBUTION *E. a. atricapilla*: extreme southeast Nigeria, southern Cameroon and Gabon through the Congo to northwest Zaire.

E. a. avakubi: southern and central Zaire to extreme northeast Angola.

E. a. graueri: east Zaire to southwest Uganda and discontinuously to Rwanda and west (Mt Elgon) and central Kenya (Mt Kenya and Aberdares).

Race *graueri* was previously known as *kandti* and classed by some authorities as a separate species, Kandt's Waxbill.

MEASUREMENTS Wing 44–49; tail 42–45; tarsus 11·5–15; bill 8–10. Wing of *avakubi* 46–48. Wing of *graueri* 45–46.

REFERENCE Prigogene (1975, 1980).

Fringilla erythronotos Vieillot, 1817, Nouv. Dict. Hist. Nat. nouv. ed., 12, p. 182, India; Kurrichane, western Transvaal, designated by W.L. Sclater, 1930, Syst. Av. Aethiop., p. 802.

IDENTIFICATION Length 12–13 cm (4¾– 5 in). A small brown or grey-brown, pinkish-tinged waxbill with a diagnostic black face patch, warmer pink body and bright red rump, black tail and wings. Good views are needed of the borders of black face and of the belly and flanks before attempting to determine races. Unlikely to be confused with any other species; Black-faced Firefinch (166) is initially similar, but smaller, and blacker both on wings and underparts.

DESCRIPTION Sexes differ slightly. **Adult male:** Forehead to nape dull grey-brown, paler on forehead and (at close range) very finely barred darker, grey on lower nape and sides of neck unbarred; lores to cheeks, ear-coverts and chin jet-black. Mantle, upper back and scapulars similar to crown and nape, but lightly washed with pink or pinkish-mauve and closely barred darker. Median and greater coverts more broadly barred whitish or pale-buff and dark grey or blackish; alula, primary coverts and flight feathers black or blackish, with pale barred edges prominent on inner secondaries and across tertials. Lower back, rump and uppertail-coverts deep or rich crimson. Tail long and graduated at tip, black. Chin black or blackish; throat light mauve-pink tinged with grey and very faintly barred; some lower breast feathers have pink or reddish-pink tips; flanks much deeper reddish-pink, sometimes barred with deep grey; belly and undertail-coverts black. Bill short and conical, black at tip but with bluish gloss at base. Eye red or reddish-brown (some also show a pale pink orbital-ring). Legs and feet black. **Adult female:** Generally duller or paler pinkish-grey, with more grey on body, and red of rump and flanks is intense and also slightly less extensive than on male; belly and undertail-coverts deep grey, not black. Eye brown. **Juvenile:** Similar to adult female, but with more diffuse barring on upperparts or underparts and upperparts tinged with olive; wing is as adult; rump and uppertail-coverts very dark or drab rust-brown. Bill black.

GEOGRAPHICAL VARIATION Race *delamerei* is distinctly different, being much paler grey on head, nape, mantle and sides of neck. Rump and uppertail-coverts are light rose-red (not deep crimson), black face is finely outlined with pale grey or silvery-grey (especially along lower edge), and underparts are grey washed with pinkish-mauve, with flanks slightly deeper pink; females are similar or slightly duller, and lack any dark areas on belly or undertail-coverts. Males of race *charmosyna* (which may be a separate species, see note below) are very similar to *delamerei* but paler, and pink wash is much more obvious, especially on mantle and underparts, which are almost uniform and lack

any brown or black on belly and undertail-coverts; pale silvery edge to black face (with only a thin line of black on upper chin) is clearly defined and broader than in *delamerei*, and barring on wing-coverts and some of the flight feathers is better defined. Female *charmosyne* lack the strong pink tone and are much greyer overall, pink usually (but not always) just as a wash to belly and flanks. Note: There is considerable individual variation. Other races are doubtfully separable in the field, being either paler or more pink or grey; in a species which shows such variability among individuals, it seems better for the purposes of field identification that these are not pursued.

VOICE The main contact call of the male is a series of soft 'tsssp' notes or a thin 'teeh-teeh' or a melodious and slightly rising 'fwooee'; that of the female is a 'psyee-psyee'. Song of the male is a thin and longer version of the 'teeh-teeh' call notes; northern races apparently have a pleasant warbling song.

STATUS, HABITAT AND BEHAVIOUR Common or locally common but nowhere numerous. Found in dry grassland habitat, from open savanna with thornbush or thickets and acacia scrub or woodlands to the edge of cultivation, usually in dry areas but prefers trees. Usually in pairs or small flocks, or in larger gatherings when not breeding. Often silent and secretive, especially when breeding. Feeds on the ground and actively in grasses and low vegetation, on a variety of grass seeds and millet but also insects, e.g. termites, small beetles and caterpillars; ripe fruit is also taken, as are the buds of fruit trees.

DISTRIBUTION *E. e. erythronotos*: southern Zimbabwe (Southern Rhodesia) south to Transvaal, western Orange Free State and northern Cape Province, South Africa.

E. e. soligena: southwest Angola and central Namibia east through Botswana to southwest Zambia, northern Zimbabwe and south to northwest Transvaal and northern Cape Province, South Africa.

E. e. delamerei: Uganda, southern Kenya to central and eastern Tanzania.

E. e. charmosyna: northwest and southwest Somalia, central and southern Ethiopia, extreme southeast Sudan, northeast Uganda and northern and east Kenya (to Tsavo East and West National Parks).

E. e. kiwanukae: southern Kenya from Lake Magadi to Teita, to Olduvai and Dodoma, northern Tanzania.

Note: Some authorities regard the last two races as a full species (*Estrilda charmosyna*), but we prefer to follow others in uniting all races within a single species.

MEASUREMENTS Wing 52–58; tail 53–60; tarsus 13–16; bill (culmen) 9–10·5. Weight 9–9·5.

REFERENCES Goodwin (1982), Hall and Moreau (1970), Mackworth-Praed and Grant (1960), McLachlan and Liversidge (1978), Peters (1968).

GENUS *AMANDAVA*

Three species. Two species, the Red and Green Munias (187, 188), are more closely related than the third, an African species which bears some affinities to the typical *Estrilda* waxbills. Related to each other in plumage patterns and coloration, and nesting behaviour and habitat occupation, these are birds of dense grass or scrub vegetation often near water. Closely similar to the typical waxbills, but (particularly Red and Green) show some affinities with the true munias *Lonchura*.

187 RED MUNIA (Avadavat, Red Avadavat, Strawberry Finch)
Amandava amandava   Plate 54

Southern Palearctic and Oriental

Fringilla amandava Linnaeus, 1758, Syst. Nat., ed. 10, Bengal, by Baker, 1921, Journ. Bombay Nat. Hist. Soc., 27, p. 725.

♂ *Underside of tail showing tail spots.*

IDENTIFICATION Length 10 cm (4 in). A small, compact, red-billed finch of India and southeast Asia. Male has a distinctive breeding plumage of deep or bright red, speckled with small white spots; in non-breeding plumage is dull greyish-brown or greyish-buff, but retains red rump. Female is like non-breeding male, but generally dull greenish or dull olive. Juveniles resemble female, with two thin wingbars and generally plain dull brown upperparts, but uniform brown rump. Combination of small size, active behaviour and bright red plumage with small white spots (or restricted to tips of wing coverts) and dark wings make it unlikely to be confused with any other species.

DESCRIPTION Sexes differ. **Adult male** breeding: Almost entirely red. Forehead, face (except dark lores) to sides of neck, chin, throat, breast, upper belly and flanks rich or bright scarlet; sides of breast and flanks speckled or spotted with white. Crown to nape slightly duller or darker and mottled with olive. Often shows a thin line of white spots below eye. Mantle, back and scapulars dull reddish-brown, with small white spots on scapulars which become larger on lower scapulars. Median and greater coverts dark brown or blackish, edged dull or deep reddish-brown, with small white spots at tips of greaters (also medians and lessers on some); primary coverts and flight feathers blackish-brown, tertials with small white spot at tip of each.

Rump and uppertail-coverts red or crimson and spotted pink or white. Tail blackish-brown, finely tipped (on underside) with white. Lower belly, vent and undertail-coverts dark brown or black, tinged reddish. Bill, short and pointed, bright red (all plumages) with a thin dark line along culmen. Eye red, reddish-brown or orange. Legs and feet flesh or pinky-brown. **Adult male** non-breeding: Very similar to adult female, but uppertail-coverts spotted with white and the white spots on greater coverts larger than on female; face greyish; chin and throat whitish-grey, becoming buff or deep buff-brown on breast, flanks (which can also be greyer), belly and undertail-coverts, with scattered red tips on breast and belly which become progressively widespread as breeding season approaches. **Adult female:** Forehead to crown, nape, mantle and back earth-brown or greyish-brown; scapulars and wings rich brown often tinged with reddish-brown, with small buff spots at tips of median and greater coverts; flight feathers tinged or edged slightly russet-brown. Rump, uppertail-coverts and tail as breeding-plumage male, but usually unspotted or with only a few indistinct small white spots. Lores dark or blackish, with pale buff under eye. Underparts buffish, tinged light orange. **Juvenile:** Fairly similar to adult female in overall plumage, but lacks any red on rump or uppertail-coverts, has no white or buff spotting, and has pale buff tips to median and greater coverts forming double wingbar. Wings dark brown, with broad pale buff tips to tertials. Face is plain grey, some showing broad pale buff eye-ring. Generally more buffish-white below than female, but breast is greyer. Bill dark brown or blackish. First-year males moult into adult non-breeding plumage before acquiring full breeding plumage.

GEOGRAPHICAL VARIATION Race *punicea* differs very slightly: slightly brighter and has smaller white spots, dark line across lores is less distinct or absent. Race *flavidiventris* is much brighter or paler, some breeding males being orange, golden or yellowish-buff below, principally on lower belly and undertail-coverts, and the white spots continue across breast; females are more yellowish-buff on underparts.

VOICE Call usually a thin 'teei' or 'tsi', but also a variety of high-pitched chirps or squeaks given both when perched and in flight. The song is a feeble or weak but high-pitched warble with softer and sweeter twittering notes, given by male usually from top of a reed or similar prominent position.

STATUS, HABITAT AND BEHAVIOUR Common or locally common. Inhabits tall grass, reeds, sugarcane, bushes or scrub, usually in areas near water or marshes, but also found away from water in grassy clearings in forests or on the edge of cultivation, in villages and occasionally in gardens; a lowland species, but occurs at up to 1500 m in Java and Bali and to 2400 m in the Lesser Sundas. Usually in pairs or small flocks of up to 30, in winter in flocks often exceeding 100 birds, occasionally in company with other munias, sparrows or buntings. Roosts communally and socially in reedbeds and sugarcane. Feeds in tall grass or on the ground, on a variety of grass seeds, rice and millet; in captivity known to take a small quantity of insects, e.g. ants and caterpillars.

DISTRIBUTION *A. a. amandava*: central and western Pakistan to southern Kashmir and throughout India (except the east and southwest coastal areas) north to the foothills of the Himalayas, southern Nepal east to Assam and Bangladesh.

A. a. flavidiventris: southwest China (southern Yunnan, possibly also east to Kweichow) south to Burma and the Lesser Sunda Islands (Lombok, Flores, Sumba, Roti and Timor).

A. a. punicea: southeast Thailand, southern Kampuchea, extreme southeast China (southeast Kwangtung and Hainan), Vietnam, Java and Bali.

A common cagebird, and introduced or released into Japan (Honshu and Kyushu), Hawaiian Islands, (Oahu), Fiji (Viti Levu, Vanua Levu), Philippines (Luzon and Manila, but not seen in the wild in recent years), Malaysia (Singapore), Sumatra, Saudi Arabia (Riyadh), northern Egypt (northern Nile valley and Nile delta), southern Israel (Eilat), and Puerto Rico.

MOVEMENTS In the non-breeding season undertakes random movements away from the breeding areas; some birds of nominate race move or migrate considerable distances, to winter in Burma, northern Thailand and Hong Kong. Has also been recorded (doubtless escapes) in Lebanon, Iran, United Arab Emirates (has bred) and Oman; has apparently bred in the wild in Britain, but such birds rarely, if ever, survive a northern winter in the wild.

MEASUREMENTS Wing 45–52; tail of male 35–41, of female 34–39; tarsus 12–13; bill (from skull) 9–11.

REFERENCES Ali and Ripley (1983), Goodwin (1982).

188 GREEN MUNIA *Amandava formosa*   **Plate 54**

India

Fringilla formosa Latham, 1790, Index Ornith., 1, p. 441, India.

IDENTIFICATION Length 10 cm (4 in). A resident and locally distributed endemic finch of central India. Male is bright lime green or greeny-yellow with a bright red bill, and with a pale green rump which contrasts with black tail; yellow underparts and strongly barred black-and-white flanks. Female is similar, but paler on underparts, tinged olive or brownish above, and has less barring on flanks. Virtually the only small finch of its kind and unlikely to be confused with any other species within its natural range; combination of green, yellow and the red bill together with barred flanks is unmistakable.

DESCRIPTION Sexes similar but separable. **Adult male:** Forehead to nape, face and sides of neck pale green or lime-green or lightly olive-green (some have darker tinge on ear-coverts). Hindneck, mantle, back and scapulars olive-green; rump and uppertail-coverts bright yellowish-green or golden-yellow. Tail short and slightly rounded at sides of tip, black. Wing-coverts deep olive, as are edges of flight feathers and tertials; inner webs of flight feathers brownish. Chin and throat pale yellowish, becoming yellow on sides of lower throat and deep or bright yellow on rest of underparts (brightest on undertail-coverts); sides of lower breast and flanks boldly barred with dark (or very dark) olive and white (or buffish-white). Bill short and pointed, bright red or dull crimson. Eye dark brown or reddish-brown. Legs and feet pinkish-brown. **Adult female:** A paler or duller version of male, with olive-grey upperparts; underparts are never so bright as on male and are often tinged or washed with grey on breast, and barring on flanks is paler and less extensive. **Juvenile:** Dull grey-brown above, with tinges of pale green or yellowish-green to edges of flight feathers and rump and uppertail-coverts. Underparts entirely buff but washed or shaded heavier or grey in places, especially on breast; belly and undertail-coverts washed with yellow or yellowish-buff; flanks warm buff and unbarred. Bill black, with bright pink or red along cutting edges.

VOICE Call a constant weak twittering 'seee' or 'swee, swee', and also utters some 'cheep' or 'chirp' notes similar to those of Red Munia (187); alarm notes are louder versions of the same, as is the song, which often ends with a prolonged trill.

STATUS, HABITAT AND BEHAVIOUR Local, locally common or scarce. Found in tall grasslands, sugarcane or open forests with low bushes and scrub jungle, often near water. Very little is known of its habits or behaviour, and much remains to be studied (even from birds in captivity). In the wild it is loosely social and occurs in small flocks or family parties; in the non-breeding season bands together in groups of up to 50. Feeds on the ground but usually in the vicinity of cover, mainly on small grass seeds, but other small seeds and some small insects are also taken (detailed information lacking).

DISTRIBUTION Monotypic. Discontinuous and fragmentary through central and northern India from southern Rajasthan to Maharashtra, east through Madhya Pradesh to Andhra Pradesh and possibly also Bihar; also extralimital records from Lucknow and Lahore in 1916 and more recently from the Vishakhapatnam Ghats, some of which may relate to escapes from captivity.

MOVEMENTS Resident.

MEASUREMENTS Wing of male 46–51, of female 46–50; tail of male 34–39, of female 35–39; tarsus 13–15; bill (from skull) 10–11.

REFERENCES Ali and Ripley (1983), Goodwin (1982).

189 ZEBRA WAXBILL (Gold/Golden-breasted Waxbill, Orange-breasted Waxbill) *Amandava subflava*   Plate 48

Africa

Fringilla subflava Vieillot, 1819, Nouv. Dict. Hist. Nat. nouv. ed., 30, p. 575, Senegal.

IDENTIFICATION Length 9–10 cm (3¾–4 in). Tiny (the smallest of the African Estrildid finches), very active, short-tailed, and with brightly coloured underparts, red eye-stripe (males) and red bill, making this an easily identifiable species. Widely distributed over most of sub-Saharan Africa. Unlikely to be confused with any other species once seen well. Green-winged Pytilia (141) is similar, but has different distribution of red on face and lacks any yellow on underparts (latter instead barred with black and white). **DESCRIPTION** Sexes differ slightly. **Adult male:** Forehead, crown and nape olive, tinged with grey; mantle, back, scapulars and wing-coverts olive, or tinged with pale grey on sides of the neck; flight feathers blackish but edged olive-brown, tertials olive. Rump and uppertail-coverts bright scarlet, sometimes tinged lightly with orange or with black feather bases. Tail short and slightly rounded, dark brown or blackish-brown with thin white tips to all but central pair (usually visible only from below). Lores to over eye and ear-coverts a thin red or scarlet stripe; thin black line from base of bill to eye becomes olive on ear-coverts; fore cheeks and immediately below eye pale yellow. Chin and throat yellow or bright yellow; breast bright orange, or yellow suffused or washed heavily with orange (probably first-year birds), becoming paler on centre of belly (but can be orange or deep yellow here also); sides of breast and flanks barred with dull olive-green and yellow (or white on some), with blackish tips to feathers; undertail-coverts bright or deep orange, merging with scarlet rump. Bill short, conical, bright red or reddish with a black culmen and base of lower mandible. Eye red or dark red. Legs and feet pale brown or flesh-brown. In worn plumage, upperparts, possibly also wings and tertials, become browner or more olive. **Adult female:** Very similar in overall plumage to adult male, but differs in having no red eye-stripe (but lores are black), underparts are generally paler yellow, becoming orange on undertail-coverts, and rump and uppertail-coverts are duller red. Tail is browner; throat and breast are washed with grey, and barring on sides of breast and flanks is less distinct. **Juvenile:** Much duller than adults, generally dull buffish-brown above, with pale buff tips to median and greater coverts forming double wingbar; rump and uppertail-coverts are tinged orange, and underparts are dull buff with a wash of yellow on centre of breast; flanks unbarred. Bill black. Eye brown.

GEOGRAPHICAL VARIATION Southern and eastern birds, *clarkei*, are bright yellow or golden-yellow on underparts (both sexes), with a variable-sized orange patch on breast (adult male).

VOICE Call a short 'cheep' or 'chirp', very similar to that of Red (187) or Green (188) Munias; also has a soft metallic 'zink zink', usually given in flight.

STATUS, HABITAT AND BEHAVIOUR Widespread. Uncommon, locally or seasonally common; less common in West Africa than in East. Inhabits tall grasslands or savannas, swamp or marsh edges, rice-fields and reedbeds, usually adjacent to water, but also feeds in drier areas, especially at edge of (or abandoned) cultivation; occurs at up to 2000 m, or 2400 m in Ethiopia, but generally below 1600 m. Tame and confiding, active and continually on the move; wags tail from side to side as Common Waxbill (182). Usually in small groups or family parties, but when not breeding often in large flocks; roosts communally, often in reedbeds. Feeds on the ground or from stems of tall grasses, which it climbs with ease; feeds mainly on grass seeds or reed-heads, but also takes a few small insects.

DISTRIBUTION *A. s. subflava*: Senegal and Gambia (scarce in west) south to Sierra Leone, east through southern Mali, Burkina Faso, Ghana (where very localised) and Nigeria to southern

Chad, southern Sudan (to about 12° N), Ethiopia, south to southern Cameroon, Central African Republic, Uganda, northern Zaire, Lake Kivu, Rwanda and west Kenya; has also recently colonised parts of southern North Yemen.

A. s. clarkei: Gabon, western Angola, southern Congo and southern Zaire to Zambia, eastern, central and southern Kenya, eastern Tanzania, Zanzibar, Pemba and Mafia Island, Malawi, extreme northeast Namibia (Caprivi), northern Botswana, northeast, central and southern (but not southeast) Zimbabwe, Mozambique and eastern Cape Province and the Transvaal, Orange Free State and northern Natal, South Africa.

MOVEMENTS Partial migrant or nomadic: when not breeding, moves locally or wanders at random throughout the range in search of food.

MEASUREMENTS Wing 40–49; tail 28–36; tarsus 10–12; bill (culmen) 8–9.

REFERENCES Goodwin (1982), Sinclair (1984).

GENUS *ORTYGOSPIZA*

Three species. Quailfinches are small, short-tailed, entirely ground-dwelling finches with lark-like legs and feet, flat claws and long hind toes. They inhabit open grasslands or sandy areas with sparse clumps or tufts of grass, usually not far from water. Very similar to *Amandava* species, particularly the African representative (189), but clearly different in their divergent adaptation to life spent entirely on the ground.

190 AFRICAN QUAILFINCH *Ortygospiza atricollis*   Plate 48
Africa

Fringilla atricollis Vieillot, 1817, Nouv. Dict. Hist. Nat., nouv. ed., 12, p. 182, Senegal.

IDENTIFICATION Length 9·5–10 cm (3¾–4 in). A small and rather dumpy or short-tailed ground-dwelling finch found in sandy areas, and not usually seen or heard until flushed. Similar to Black-chinned Quailfinch (191) and Locust Finch (192), but has dark brown upperparts and lacks red on rump or head. Has strong black-and-white barring on breast and flanks, also shows white tips to outer tail feathers in flight. **Confusion species:** Very similar Black-chinned Quailfinch overlaps with African in some areas, but generally (not exclusively) in different habitat, and has an all-black chin and generally blacker upperparts, and also a brighter red bill. Southern races of African (except *smithersi*) have white 'spectacles' enclosing lores and eye. Locust Finch is much blacker above (especially when comparing females) and female has pale buff or yellowish-buff underparts with barring only at sides of breast and flanks; males have face to breast bright red and show red in wings.

DESCRIPTION Sexes similar but separable. **Adult male:** Forehead black. Crown, nape, ear-coverts and sides of neck grey-brown or darker, with a lighter grey tinge on ear-coverts; lores, cheeks to sides of chin and throat black. Mantle, back, scapulars, wing-coverts, rump and uppertail-coverts brown or chocolate-brown with a greyish wash or tinge (strongest in fresh plumage); edges of median and greater coverts grey or pale buff (especially in worn plumage); flight feathers dark brown with pale edges. Tail short, blackish or very dark grey with white tips to outer feathers. Chin a small square of white. Upper breast finely barred black-and-white, but sometimes shows a brown or brownish-grey or buff area in centre; flanks similar, with barring more widely spaced and white bars bordered with black; upper belly chestnut or rus-set-brown, tinged lightly with orange, becoming paler or whiter on lower belly and shading to orange-buff with brown streaks on undertail-coverts. Bill short, almost conical, all red or reddish-brown when breeding (has a black culmen at other times of year). Eye brown or pale brown. Legs and feet pinkish-flesh or yellowish-brown. **Adult female:** Similar in most respects to adult male, but paler or greyer-brown and lacks the strong plumage tones. Face and throat lack any black, and has entire head grey or grey-brown; breast grey-brown, with barring paler or less intense and more restricted to lower breast; belly to undertail-coverts paler, light orange-buff or buff with a tinge of warm orange. Bill dark brown on upper mandible and orange or reddish-orange on lower. **Juvenile:** Very similar to adult female but paler or duller, with only very little or faint barring on breast and flanks. Bill all dark, or with a tinge of orange at base.

GEOGRAPHICAL VARIATION Races *ansorgei* and *ugandae* are generally plain or unstreaked and darker above and have black on face more extensive (across ear-coverts and onto upper breast), *ugandae* is paler, and has more white on chin and a thin white eye-ring (can be absent from some individuals from southern Sudan). Races *fuscocrissa*, *muelleri*, *smithersi* and *pallida* all have a large white chin spot and white eye-ring, and some (especially southern birds) have slight extensions of latter across upper lores; they also have streaks on upperparts and broader bars of white on breast. Of these races, *fuscocrissa* has the most black on centre of breast and flanks, and occasional spots among the barring; *muelleri* is paler or greyer, more like *ugandae*, but has a white eye-ring, is paler chestnut or brown on lower breast and belly, and has broader bands of white on breast; *smithersi* is the darkest, and has more streaks on upperparts than any of the races; and *pallida*, as its name implies, is consistently paler than all other races (including *muelleri*), with a grey back and white or whitish belly.

VOICE Contact call is a metallic and bell-like 'tir-rilink', 'trillink' or 'chwillink', occasionally run together in a trill, most often given incessantly in flight; also a few similar squeaky or trumpet-like notes given while on the ground. The song is a very rapid series of 'click, clack, clock, cluck' notes, repeated over and over with increasing speed.

STATUS, HABITAT AND BEHAVIOUR Common or locally common, but probably overlooked owing to its shy and retiring nature. Found in areas of grass or tussocks in dry sandy plains or swampy areas, also in standing crops such as corn and in village farmyards where grain has been threshed (has been known to occur on mown grass at airports); usually not far from water. Not usually seen until flushed almost underfoot, or when it utters its very distinctive call; flies steeply up in short jerky movements, to plunge back to land in similar area not far away. On the ground runs or hops in erratic fashion; crouches low and flat out at first sign of danger, taking flight only as a last resort. Usually in small groups or family parties. Feeds entirely on the ground (rarely perches anywhere else, known to do so only after heavy rains cause flooding). Feeds almost entirely on grass seeds; a few small insects and spiders are taken.

DISTRIBUTION *O. a. atricollis*: Senegal and Gambia east to Mali, northern Guinea, Burkina Faso, northern Ghana, northern and central Nigeria (to Lake Chad) and northern Cameroon.

O. a. ansorgei: Guinea-Bissau to Liberia, Ivory Coast and the coastal plain of Ghana.

O. a. ugandae: southern Sudan, Uganda to North Kavirondo, Kenya.

O. a. fuscocrissa: highlands of Ethiopia (above 2000 m).

O. a. muelleri: central and southern Kenya, central Tanzania, extreme north Malawi to northeast Zambia, Zimbabwe and central Mozambique (to Sul do Save), also southwest (and possibly northwest) Angola, central and northeast Namibia and Botswana to southern Cape Province, South Africa.

O. a. smithersi: northeast Zambia to northern Zimbabwe.

O. a. pallida: northern Botswana to western Zimbabwe.

This classification follows that of Traylor (1963). Other races have been described, most of which are doubtfully distinguishable either consistently or in the field.

MOVEMENTS Wanders at random throughout the range when not breeding; race *fuscocrissa* is considered to be a migrant, as it is not present in breeding areas in winter months. Birds (presumably of nominate race) have been recorded in southern Mauritania in February-April 1980 and in southwest Mauritania (along the Senegal river) in December 1980. Also recorded in northern Cameroon, in Mandara Mountains in October 1966 and the Waza National Park in January and June 1967.

MEASUREMENTS Wing 47–58; tail 25–31; tarsus 13–15; bill (culmen) 9–10. Wing of *fuscocrissa* 55–59. Weight 12.

REFERENCES Benson (1955), Browne (1981), de Greling (1972), Goodwin (1982), Louette (1981), Sinclair (1984), Traylor (1963).

191 BLACK-CHINNED QUAILFINCH (Red-billed Quailfinch)
Ortygospiza gabonensis   **Plate 48**
Africa

Ortygospiza gabonensis Lynes, 1914, Bull. Brit. Ornith. Club, 33, p. 131, Gabon.

IDENTIFICATION Length 9–10 cm (3½-4 in). Very similar to African Quailfinch (190), to which it is closely related and with which it overlaps in south and east of its range. Male has an entirely bright red bill and black face and chin, with fairly broad brown fringes to upperparts; females are similar, but lack black on face (which is replaced with grey) and have a darker culmen. **Confusion species:** All races lack the white chin and white markings around eye (of some races) of African Quailfinch. The bill is also brighter scarlet or orange-red than the reddish-crimson or dull red bill of African. Lone juveniles are not separable with certainty.

DESCRIPTION Sexes differ slightly. **Adult male:** Forehead and lores to chin and throat black or slaty-black. Crown and nape to mantle, back, scapulars and wing-coverts brown or dark grey with broad buffish-brown edges, giving a mottled or streaked effect; flight feathers the same, but with broad buff edges and tips. Rump to tail streaked brown with white edges to outer tail feathers. Underparts barred as on African Quailfinch, but lower breast and belly paler yellowish-buff, fading to buff or dull white on lower belly and undertail-coverts. Bill bright red. Eye brown. Legs and feet dull brown or tinged with pink. **Adult female:** Very similar to adult female African Quailfinch, but has all greyish or grey-brown sides of face, chin and throat, and barring may be as strong as on male. Some have entirely brown or dark red bill with red cutting edges, while others have bill more closely resembling that of female African with dusky brown upper and pink or reddish-pink lower mandible. **Juvenile:** Not safely distinguishable on its own from juvenile African Quailfinch.

GEOGRAPHICAL VARIATION There is considerable individual variation, between those which are darker above than nominate and show streaking (*dorsostriata*) and those which are so dark as to have this obscured (*fuscata*), but in others this may scarcely be noticeable in the field. Both *fuscata* and *dorsostriata* are slightly larger than nominate, but this of little use except in the hand. Race *fuscata* is very similar to darker races (particularly *smithersi*) of African Quailfinch: head, upperparts and breast are entirely black or dark slate-grey, belly is deep or dark rufous, and often shows a more orange-red or scarlet bill with black on culmen (separated from African by lack of white chin and brighter red bill).

VOICE Very similar to that of African Quailfinch, but calls when on the ground and when rising are more rasping.

STATUS, HABITAT AND BEHAVIOUR Widespread but locally common. Found in similar habitat to African Quailfinch, at up to 1500 m, but often or more usually in wetter or more moist areas of swamp and avoids both marshes and dry sand-flats; in Gabon occurs on grassy plains which are regularly burnt; in overlap areas occasionally occurs with or not far from African. Has also been recorded in open grass fields at edge of woodland. Usually in pairs or threes (male with two females) or small family parties. Feeds entirely on the ground, on a variety of small grass seeds and occasionally small insects.

DISTRIBUTION O. g. gabonensis: Rio Muni and Gabon to the banks of the River Congo in central Zaire.

O. g. fuscata: northern Angola (occasionally west to Luanda), southern Zaire to Zambia (west of the Luangwa).

O. g. dorsostriata: extreme east Zaire, southern and central Uganda to Rwanda and northwest (and possibly extreme southwest) Tanzania.

Previously considered to be conspecific with African Quailfinch, but considered by some to be a full species.

MOVEMENTS Wanders throughout the range when not breeding.

MEASUREMENTS Wing 48–49; tarsus 14; bill 8. Wing of *fuscata* 52–55. Wing of *dorsostriata* 49–53.

REFERENCES Goodwin (1982), Hall and Moreau (1970), Mackworth-Praed and Grant (1960), Traylor (1963), White (1963).

192 LOCUST FINCH *Ortygospiza locustella*   Plate 48
Africa

Paludipasser locustella Neave, 1909, Bull. Brit. Ornith. Club, 25, p. 25, near Lake Bangweulu; type from upper Luansenshi River, northeast of Lake Bangweulu, *fide* Neave, 1910, Ibis, p. 251.

IDENTIFICATION Length 9–10 cm (3½-4 in). Shares the same ground-loving habits as the two quailfinches (190, 191) and also usually seen only when flushed. Male has bright reddish-orange face to breast and bright orange in wings, otherwise is entirely black except for some red on sides of rump and small white spots on the upperparts; female has duller orange wing patches and generally white underparts, with barring on flanks. Unlikely to be confused with any other species: both quailfinches lack bright orange or red in the plumage, though all three species share the same type of habitat. Rosy (154) and Peters's (155) Twinspots are initially similar to the male, but both are a different shade of red or pink and have bold white or pinkish-white spots on flanks and belly; both are unlikely to be found on the ground in typical Locust Finch habitat.

DESCRIPTION Sexes differ. **Adult male:** Sides of forehead to lores, over eye to face, ear-coverts and sides of neck red or scarlet-red, becoming orange-red on chin, throat and breast. Forehead sooty-grey; crown dark brown to black, becoming dark grey-brown on nape and hindneck. Mantle, back, scapulars, median coverts, inner greater coverts, inner secondaries and tertials black or tinged with grey or dark grey-brown, all with small white spots which extend along edges of inner tertials; inner greater coverts have white tips; outer greater coverts and bases of primaries and secondaries bright or deep orange (becomes duller or paler in worn plumage). Primary coverts black, edged with orange; tips of primaries and inner webs dark brown or black. Rump and uppertail-coverts dark brown to black in centre, with red or reddish-orange at sides. Tail short, dark brown or blackish-brown (with white tips when seen from below). Underparts below breast dark blackish-grey, often with a few small white spots or bars on flanks. Bill short or stubby, in breeding season bright red or reddish-orange with black culmen (upper mandible entirely black when not breeding). Eye yellow or yellowish. Legs and feet light or pale brown. **Adult female:** Forehead, crown and nape dark brown or brownish, tinged grey; mantle, back, scapulars and median coverts the same, with small (smaller than on male) dull white or off-white spots; tips of median coverts, outer greater coverts, primaries and outer secondaries brown or orange-brown; rump to tail as male. Face to sides of neck dark brown, except for a small buffish-white spot on lores. Underparts buff or buffish-white, with sides of breast finely barred black and whitish-buff, becoming more boldly black-and-white on flanks to undertail-coverts. **Juvenile:** Very similar to adult female, but has browner edges to upperparts with a few whitish spots (especially on scapulars); wing-coverts and flight feathers edged warm brown; underparts buff, duller than on female, and breast and flanks entirely barred darker. Bill black or dark brown. Eye dark brown.

GEOGRAPHICAL VARIATION Race *uelensis* lacks white spots on upperparts and flanks.

VOICE Generally silent while on ground, but utters a squeaking 'chip-chip' or a rapid 'tinka-tinka-tinka' especially when rising or in flight.

STATUS, HABITAT AND BEHAVIOUR Widespread, but generally uncommon or only locally common. Inhabits wet grasslands or swamps and open *Brachystegia* woodland, where found in clumps or tufts of grass; absent from dry plains, but has been found on burnt ground and abandoned cultivation up to 2000 m. As the quailfinches, lives entirely on the ground, never perching on trees, bushes or grasses. Usually in pairs or family parties, and may even be found in the same areas as quailfinches; in the non-breeding season forms large flocks, but unlikely to be seen or heard until flushed at close range, when it rises fast and flies with straight (or slightly dipping) flight for a short distance before dropping down. Despite its name, feeds almost entirely on small grass seeds.

DISTRIBUTION *O. l. locustella*: northeast and southwest Angola, southern Zaire to Zambia, Malawi, highlands of central and eastern Zimbabwe, south Tanzania and northern Mozambique (Tete district); also one record from the Okavango, northern Botswana.

O. l. uelensis: northeast Congo and northern Zaire west to about Niangara, northwest of Lake Albert.

MOVEMENTS Wanders widely throughout (and possibly even beyond) the breeding range when not breeding, but makes return movements to breeding area at onset of rains. Vagrant to Kenya: flock of 25, considered to be race *uelensis*, near Alupe, west Kenya on 31 August 1990.

MEASUREMENTS Wing 43–46; tail 27; tarsus 13–14; bill (culmen) 8·5–9.

REFERENCES McLachlan and Liversidge (1978), Sinclair (1984), Stevenson (1992), Vincent (1936).

GENUS *AEGINTHA*

One species. An Australian waxbill, bearing a close similarity in plumage pattern, structure and behaviour to many true waxbills of Africa but closest on geographical grounds to the other Australian Estrildid finches.

193 RED-BROWED FIRETAIL (Red-browed Firetail Finch, Red-browed Waxbill) *Aegintha temporalis*   Plate 63

Australia

Fringilla temporalis Latham, 1801, Index Ornith., suppl., 48, New Holland [Sydney, New South Wales].

IDENTIFICATION Length 11–12 cm (c4½ in). A small finch of eastern Australia, similar in size, shape and coloration to several of the African waxbills but distinguished by its bright red lores and stripe over eye, greenish-olive upperparts and a smudge of golden or yellow on sides of hindneck; rump and uppertail-coverts are bright scarlet. Very unlikely to be confused with any other species within its natural range. Both Beautiful Firetail (195) and Red-eared Firetail (196) are darker below and finely barred.

DESCRIPTION Sexes alike. **Adult:** Forehead to nape plain pencil-grey; on sides of hindneck a small patch of yellow, can be either bright or golden (in fresh plumage) or dull greenish-yellow or greyish (in non-breeding season). Sides of forehead and supercilium to rear of ear-coverts bright red, generally longer on female than on male (but some individual variation); rest of face to sides of neck pale grey. Mantle, back, scapulars and wing-coverts yellowish-olive or olive-green, tinged lightly with yellow on coverts; edges to flight feathers and tertials olive-green or yellowish, rest of flight feathers grey or dark grey. Rump and uppertail-coverts bright scarlet (longest uppertail-coverts extend to centre of tail). Tail graduated, black or blackish-brown. Chin and throat pale grey or whitish-grey, becoming slightly dull or dingy grey on rest of underparts. Bill short and pointed, bright waxy-red with black culmen. Eye dark brown or reddish-brown. Legs and feet pale yellowish or pinkish-brown. **Juvenile:** Much duller than adult, lacks red stripe over face, the rump and uppertail-coverts are dull crimson, and underparts are dull grey with a faint grey-green or olive-green tinge. Bill black.

GEOGRAPHICAL VARIATION Race *minor* has a paler green patch on sides of neck, is paler grey on forehead to nape (grey often extends to upper mantle), and back and wings are slightly paler or brighter than in nominate race; throat, breast and belly are paler and often white. Race *loftyi* has the grey of head and underparts tinged with brown.

VOICE A high-pitched squeaking 'tsee, tsee' or 'seep seep' is the typical contact note; alarm is an abrupt 'tchip', and a cat-like hiss is used in aggressive display. The song consists of a series of long and short versions of the squeaking contact notes all strung together in a varying rhythmic sequence; both sexes sing.

STATUS, HABITAT AND BEHAVIOUR

Common or locally common. Found in a wide variety of habitats, from eucalypt forest and clearings to open woodlands, mangroves, orchards and gardens in parks and cities, where it has become tame and approachable. Actions and behaviour recall those of the African waxbills and firefinches. Usually in pairs or small groups or family parties, especially in breeding season, but in winter often gathers in flocks of up to 300 when it also joins mixed-species feeding flocks, often with Chestnut-breasted Mannikins (246). Usually keeps to cover, but occasionally feeds in the open where predators are less numerous. Feeds either on the ground or from grass-stalks, on grass seeds and those of weeds, also seeds of fruits and berries; occasionally takes small insects.

DISTRIBUTION *A. t. temporalis*: eastern Queensland south to coastal New South Wales, Victoria and eastern South Australia.

A. t. loftyi: Mount Lofty range, Kangaroo Island, South Australia.

A. t minor: Cape York Peninsula (south to the Mitchell river on west coast), northern Queensland.

Has also become established (possibly from aviary escapes) in southwest Australia (Darling range) and has been introduced to the Society Islands, (Moorea and Tahiti) and Marquesas (Nuku Hiva, Ua Huka).

MOVEMENTS Generally sedentary, but loose flocks wander at random in the non-breeding season.

REFERENCES Frith *et al.* (1979), Goodwin (1982).

GENUS *EMBLEMA*

Four species. Firetails, found only in Australia, are very similar in size and shape, all having boldly spotted or finely barred underparts, and red rump and uppertail-coverts. Also similar in behaviour and in distinctive mouth patterns of nestlings.

194 PAINTED FINCH (Painted Firetail Finch) *Emblema picta* Plate 64
Australia

Emblema picta Gould, 1842, Birds Australia, pt. 7 (also Proc. Zool. Soc. London, 10, p. 17), Depuch's Island, Mid-West Australia.

IDENTIFICATION Length 10·5–11·5 cm (4–4½ in). A small and distinctively coloured finch, mainly of dry rugged country. Both sexes are brightly coloured and very similar, but separable when seen well. Both have brown upperparts, red on the face (less on female) and an almost luminous red rump contrasting with a black tail. The underparts are black, with irregular red patches on the belly and white spots (male) on sides of breast and flanks; the female has the breast spotted with white, and the flanks boldly barred with white. Has a loud distinctive call uttered on taking flight.
Confusion species: The black and red plumage should make confusion with any other species unlikely. Crimson Finch (199) is initially similar, but lacks any black and both sexes have all red or reddish faces and a longer red tail.
DESCRIPTION Sexes similar but separable.
Adult male: Forehead, lores, over eye to cheeks bright red or vermilion. Crown, ear-coverts, nape to mantle, back, scapulars, coverts and wings earth-brown, with some head feathers tipped red (and others may have a reddish wash); flight feathers slightly darker brown; rump and uppertail-coverts bright, almost glowing luminous red (very obvious in flight). Tail short and square-tipped (graduated in moulting birds), blackish-brown. Chin and throat red but variable, as blackish feather bases may show through especially in moustachial

area, dividing the red of chin from that of face; throat may also be black (edged with red), as on breast and flanks; sides of breast have small white spots, becoming slightly larger on flanks; centre of belly to undertail-coverts also black, but with irregular patches of red, sometimes as a central stripe from throat to belly. Bill fairly long and slender (for a small finch), base of upper mandible usually black with a red tip, and lower red or reddish-pink, becoming black at base with a small blue spot at each side. Eye pale buff, creamy or white. Legs and feet, pinkish-brown or yellowish-brown. **Adult female:** Much duller than male, with less extensive areas of red; red on face is restricted to lores, cheeks and above bill base, but many show little or none at all, with entire face and head a dull or dark earth-brown. Upperparts similar to male, but very slightly paler on nape, sides of neck and mantle; rump and uppertail-coverts dull red or crimson, often spotted or broken by dark feather tips or edges. Underparts almost entirely black with little (or no) red on belly, but is much more extensively spotted with white on breast and flanks, spots on latter often joining to form bars. Bill as male, but has a smaller area of pale blue at sides of base. **Juvenile:** Similar to adult female, but tinged reddish-brown on upperparts, and rump and uppertail-coverts duller red than on adult; lacks any red on head, throat, breast, underparts are generally dull coal-black, with fewer and less well-defined spots or bars. Bill black, or with a greyish (becoming pinkish) lower mandible.

VOICE Call, a very loud and harsh, rising scratchy 'trut', 'chek-chek' or 'chek-did-did-dit', also a 'ched up, cheddy-up'. The song is a wheezy chattering 'che-che-che-che-che-che-che, werreeeeee-oweeeee' or finishing with 'cheeurr cheeurr'.

STATUS, HABITAT AND BEHAVIOUR Uncommon or locally common. Usually found only in the most suitable habitat, as absent from apparently good habitat within the range. Found typically in stone deserts, gorges and rocky hills with acacia scrub or areas of spinifex, often near water; nearer the coast it occurs in dunes; has been known to occur in orchards or even gardens (in Alice Springs), but usually in areas adjacent to its preferred habitat. Skulks on the ground or among spinifex clumps and often hard to see until flushed, when bright red rump becomes obvious; perches on boulders or even low bare branches. Flight usu-ally fast, low and direct or slightly undulating. Roosts on or near the ground. Usually in pairs, but in the non-breeding season bands together into flocks of up to 30. Makes regular journeys to drink. Feeds principally on seeds of spinifex grass, but may well take other small seeds.

DISTRIBUTION Monotypic. Mid-western coastal areas (between 20° and 25° S), east across the arid interior of central Australia north to the southern Kimberley range and extreme west Queensland (to about 143° E) and south to the Musgrave range (about 26° S), occasionally further south and exceptionally (see Movements) southeast to eastern South Australia.

MOVEMENTS Generally sedentary, but occasionally appears in areas beyond the range normally occupied and establishes temporary populations (often for a number of years). Otherwise, individuals and some groups wander considerable distances across the central deserts of Australia in the non-breeding season.

REFERENCES Goodwin (1982), Slater (1974).

195 BEAUTIFUL FIRETAIL *Emblema bella*

Australia

Plate 64

Loxia bella Latham, 1801, Index Ornith., suppl., p. 44, New Holland [Sydney, New South Wales].

IDENTIFICATION Length 11·5–12 cm (4½-4¾ in). A small but rather plump and relatively uncommon grassland finch. The sexes are very similar but generally separable. Plumage with very close fine black and olive-brown barring, relieved by bright or vivid red rump and uppertail-coverts; belly blackish. Has a bright blue eye-ring and black lores. The only Australian finch found in Tasmania.
Confusion species: Very similar to (out-of-range) Red-eared Firetail (196) of the extreme southwest, but lacks red on ear-coverts, bold black and white (buff on immatures) spotting on breast to belly and barring on undertail-coverts.

DESCRIPTION Sexes similar but separable.
Adult male: Lower forehead and sides of forehead and lores to (or slightly behind) eye black; rest of forehead to crown and nape dull olive-brown, with very fine bars on nape. Cheeks, ear-coverts and sides of neck warm buff-brown with thin or fine dark barring. Mantle, back, scapulars and wing-coverts as crown and nape, but with more pronounced dark or blackish barring or continuous vermiculation. Flight feathers dark grey, tinged with brown, edged olive-brown with darker barring at intervals. Rump and uppertail-coverts bright or vivid vermilion, this extending to sides of some of the tail feathers (especially bases of central feathers); tail otherwise olive-brown with dark barring (especially noticeable at sides) becoming darker or blackish-brown at tip. Chin as ear-coverts and sides of neck, becoming finely barred black (or dark olive) and white on throat to flanks (ground colour of sides of breast and flanks olive-brown); belly to undertail-coverts black. Bill short and pointed, bright red. Eye dark brown, eye-ring pale blue. Legs and feet pale pink or pale pinkish-brown. **Adult female:** Almost identical to adult male, but below has a greater area of buff on face to breast and only undertail-coverts are black. **Juvenile:** Very similar to adult female, but duller and with little or no black around eye. Bill dark or blackish, with pale red or pinkish-red base.

VOICE Call a plaintive, penetrating, piping 'weee', very similar in tone to that of Red-eared Firetail, but usually only monosyllabic; also a phrase of two or three high-pitched notes with descending trill. The song is a drawn-out 'pee-oo, pee-oo, pee-oo'.

STATUS, HABITAT AND BEHAVIOUR Generally scarce or rare, but locally common (more common on Tasmania than in mainland Australia). Found in thick or dense clumps or belts of forest scrub or heathland with thickets and good areas of undergrowth or bracken, often in moist areas such as edges of marshes or swamps; has been known to occur in gardens in Tasmania. Secretive or elusive, and often skulks in thick undergrowth. Usually in pairs or small family parties, but in the non-breeding season bands together in groups of up to 20, often mixing with Red-browed Firetails (193). Hops rapidly through long grass; flight is quick and direct, often into cover. Feeds on the ground and low in vegetation, principally on grass seeds, but also from trees and shrubs such as casuarinas; occasionally takes small insects and snails.

DISTRIBUTION Monotypic. Southeast Australia;

coastal New South Wales, Victoria and southeast South Australia (west to Yorke Peninsula), Kangaroo Island, Tasmania, Flinders Island, and other islands in the Bass Strait (except King Island).

MOVEMENTS Generally sedentary, but wanders locally in non-breeding season.
REFERENCES Goodwin (1982), Pizzey and Doyle (1980), Slater (1974).

196 RED-EARED FIRETAIL *Emblema oculata*   Plate 64
Australia

Fringilla oculata Quoy and Gaimard, 1830, Voy, Astrolabe, Zool., 1, p. 211, King George's Sound, Western Australia.

IDENTIFICATION Length 11·5–12 cm (4½–4¾ in). Very similar to Beautiful Firetail (195). A small, plump and dark finch, with a very restricted range. The sexes are alike, barred above but with bold white spotting on black underparts; has black lores and a distinctive red patch on lower ear-coverts. A shy and secretive species, invariably in cover or long grass and rarely seen in the open. Within its native range very unlikely to be confused with any other species.
DESCRIPTION Sexes alike. **Adult:** Base of forehead dark or blackish-brown; lores dark or blackish, extending around eye and enclosing pale blue or whitish-blue (or even pinkish-blue) eye-ring. Ear-coverts a small bright red patch, which becomes deeper red on males in breeding season; cheeks warm brown. Upper forehead, crown to nape, mantle, back, scapulars and wing-coverts light or medium olive-brown in fresh plumage (becoming tinged with grey when worn), finely barred with black. Flight feathers grey-brown, with broadly spaced black bars across feathers (to tertials). Rump and uppertail-coverts bright scarlet, this extending to bases of most of the central tail feathers; tail otherwise brown, barred darker or blacker at rounded tip. Sides of neck and chin light buff-brown, becoming finely barred on throat and prominently so on upper breast; breast, belly and undertail-coverts black with large white spots, some of which join or overlap; on undertail-coverts, spots merge to become bars. Bill short and stubby almost conical, waxy-red or pinkish-red. Eye brown, red or reddish-brown, eye-ring normally pale blue. Legs and feet dark brown or sometimes paler pinkish-brown. In breeding season, the female's red face patch is always paler, more orange-red (as on non-breeding male), and does not change colour. **Juvenile:** Generally dull brown above, lacks well-defined dark lores to forehead and red ear-coverts patch, barring often poorly defined, and red or deep scarlet of rump and uppertail-coverts is much duller than that of adult; underparts lack bold black and white spotting, and instead are barred with crescents of buff and dark brown. Bill is initially black, but begins to turn red or pinkish-red at an early age.
VOICE Call very similar to that of Beautiful Firetail, but more usually a double note, 'wee-ee' or 'oo-wee'; at close range has a soft 'quirk' or 'quark' contact note. The song consists of many single notes repeated in sequence and rising in scale, to end on a puffing or gasping note; also has a courtship display song based on the call note, 'ooweeee-eu-eu-eu-eu-eu'.
STATUS, HABITAT AND BEHAVIOUR Uncommon or scarce, and population has declined in recent years. Inhabits the undergrowth of thick or large forests, usually along edges of creeks or valleys, also in dense coastal scrub, thickets and paperbark swamps. Occurs alone, in pairs or in family groups, but does not flock in the non-breeding season. A shy, secretive, generally quiet and inconspicuous bird, rarely seen except in slow direct flight from cover to cover. Feeds in low undergrowth or perhaps occasionally on the ground, on grass seeds and the seeds of sedges and similar plants; also casuarina seeds and some small insects.
DISTRIBUTION Monotypic. Endemic to extreme southwest Australia, mainly between 31° S and 121° E in the Darling range and between Esperance and Duke of Orleans Bay.
MOVEMENTS Sedentary; territories are occupied throughout year.
REFERENCES Goodwin (1982), Pizzey and Doyle (1980).

197 DIAMOND FIRETAIL *Emblema guttata*   Plate 64
Australia

Loxia guttata Shaw, 1796, Mujs. Lever., 6, p. 47, Australia [Sydney, New South Wales].

IDENTIFICATION Length 12 cm (4¾ in). A small and brightly coloured finch with very distinctive plumage. The sexes are almost alike: the head is a soft medium-grey with dark brown or black lores, the upperparts grey-brown, with rump and uppertail-coverts very bright or almost luminous red and the tail black; underparts are white with a black breast-band and flanks, the latter boldly spotted with white. Unlikely to be confused with any other species once seen well.

DESCRIPTION Sexes almost alike. **Adult:** Forehead to nape soft grey or medium-grey, merging on upper mantle into grey-brown or grey (tinged quite strongly with olive-brown) mantle, back, scapulars and wing-coverts; flight feathers and tertials darker grey-brown but with olive-brown edges (all coverts and flight feathers become paler or edged with buff when worn); rump and uppertail-coverts deep and bright or luminous scarlet-red. Tail fairly short and square-ended, black. Lores to eye black (not extending beyond eye), ear-coverts and cheeks as crown; moustachial area, chin and throat white; upper breast a thick or broad band of black extending to sides of breast and flanks, latter boldly spotted with white; rest of underparts pure white. Bill short and conical, bright or deep red. Eye red or reddish-brown, orbital ring red or reddish. Legs and feet dark grey or blackish-grey. Adult female is usually separable by the paler or dark brown lores and thinner black breast-band.
Juvenile: Forehead to crown and nape grey-brown, and mantle, back and wings dull buffish-brown; rump bright red. Underparts generally less white and tinged with buff, lacks thick black breast-band but some black-tipped feathers may give an indication of it; sides of breast and flanks barred brown and white with some indistinct spots. Bill is initially black, but soon becomes red or dark reddish.
VOICE Main contact note is a long drawn-out whistling 'twooo-heee', that of male being louder than that of female's; also has a loud buzzing 'zeep' as a threat display (male) or a nest call (female); alarm is a loud 'tay, tay, tay'. The song is a series of low-pitched buzzing or rasping notes.

STATUS, HABITAT AND BEHAVIOUR Uncommon or locally common and probably declining. Found in open eucalypt forests with grassland or acacia scrub or savanna with occasional trees, open country or mallee, also on suburban fringes on golf courses and in orchards, parks and gardens. Usually in pairs or small flocks of up to 30; very social, often joins mixed-species flocks and roosts communally in specially built nests. Feeds on the ground, and hops in long bounding gait with upright stance; apparently does not cling to growing vegetation to feed. Drinks also in a very characteristic pigeon-like manner, taking long sips without a pause, unlike most other finches (which take short individual sips). Flight strong and rapid, usually flies to high or prominent perch when disturbed; rises from the ground with a quail-like whirring sound when flushed. Feeds largely on grass seeds and doubtless on other small seeds as available; occasionally takes small insects and green vegetation.
DISTRIBUTION Monotypic. Eastern and southeast Australia, from about 23° S in Queensland south through New South Wales and Victoria to the Eyre Peninsula and Kangaroo Island (previously occurred further north to the Dawson river in Queensland).
MOVEMENTS Mostly sedentary, but some populations (particularly those breeding at any altitude, e.g. in Grampian Mountains) move north in winter.
REFERENCES Frith et al. (1979), Goodwin (1982).

GENUS *OREOSTRUTHUS*

One species. Mountain Finch has some similarity in shape and in deep red rump and uppertail-coverts to the firetails of Australia, but the feet are large and clearly more adapted for life on the ground. Since nothing is known of its nesting or breeding behaviour or of the mouth patterns of the young, however, it is correctly placed in a monotypic genus.

198 CRIMSON-SIDED MOUNTAIN FINCH (Mountain Firetail)
Oreostruthus fuliginosus   Plate 58
New Guinea

Oreospiza fuliginosa De Vis, 1897, Ibis, p. 389, Mt Scratchley.

IDENTIFICATION Length 13 cm (5 in). A small, plump and inconspicuous undergrowth-dweller of montane forests and high levels in three areas of New Guinea. The sexes are almost alike: chocolate-brown upperparts, with crimson on the uppertail-coverts and on the flanks. Very unlikely to be confused with any other species. Alpine Mannikin (249), found in the same area and habitat, is initially similar when seen briefly, but has white underparts with a dark breast-band and yellow rump.

DESCRIPTION Sexes almost alike but separable. **Adult male:** Entire head, nape, mantle, back, scapulars and wings chocolate-brown, appears dull brown. Flight feathers and tertials dark chocolate brown. Uppertail-coverts bright vermilion-red. Tail fairly short and rounded, black. Chin, throat and sides of neck as head; breast also deep brown, but with crimson or deep red tips to feathers; flanks and sides of belly bright red or crimson with dark brown feather bases showing through (even in fresh plumage); centre of belly to vent and undertail-coverts deep brown. Bill short and almost conical but with curved culmen, can be bright red or coral-red to black on upper mandible and red on lower. Eye reddish-brown, orbital ring grey to yellow. Legs and feet (huge for the size of the bird) brown or dark horn-brown. **Adult female:** Very similar to adult male, but generally much duller or less rich brown in tone: uppertail-coverts duller or darker crimson; underparts more cinnamon or warm buff-brown, with a lighter red on breast and upper flanks. Bill orange-red with black on culmen. **Juvenile:** Very similar to adult female but more cinnamon in overall plumage tones (or orange-brown on young males), especially on underparts; rump and uppertail-coverts dull crimson. Bill black or dark brown, with orange on lower mandible. Eye dark brown.

GEOGRAPHICAL VARIATION Racial differences involve mainly the tone and intensity of the brown plumage, with *hagenensis* and *pallida* both lighter brown above than nominate. Race *hagenensis* is more easily recognisable in the field, the mantle and back are washed with red or crimson, the lower belly with brownish-buff, and vent and undertail-coverts are warm orange-buff, some having crimson tips to undertail-coverts. Race *pallida* is somewhat paler above than *hagenensis*, but this is of little use in the field.

VOICE Call a quiet cat-like mewing note 'huwee', also a canary-like 'sweet'; alarm an explosive 'pit'. The song is undescribed.

STATUS, HABITAT AND BEHAVIOUR Little known and very inconspicuous. Probably not uncommon within its very restricted area, but little seen and under-recorded. Occurs in bamboo, Pandanus palms and other thick undergrowth in deciduous forest clearings, along pathways or at edges of montane forests up to the tree line, between 2200 m and 3780 m, but usually above 2800 m. Occurs alone, in pairs or, more rarely, in small parties, but very quiet and easily overlooked. Feeds in bamboo clumps or on the ground in dense grass, on a variety of small seeds, mainly of grass, but also takes some fruit and small insects.

DISTRIBUTION *O. f. fuliginosus*: mountains of the Wharton range and Mount Victoria in the Owen Stanley range, southeast New Guinea.

O. f. pallidus: northern slopes of Oranje and Hindenburg Mountains, Snow Mountains, Irian Jaya, western New Guinea.

O. f. hagenensis: Mount Hagen and Mount Giluwe and also (probably this race) Porgera area to Tari Gap, central highlands of New Guinea.

MOVEMENTS None known.

MEASUREMENTS Wing 66; tarsus 19; hind toe (excluding claw) 10; middle toe (excluding claw) 15; bill 9.

REFERENCES Beehler *et al.* (1986), Coates (1990).

GENUS *NEOCHMIA*

Two species. Crimson and Star Finches are very similar in plumage and behaviour to the African firefinches *Lagonosticta* or the grenadiers *Uraeginthus*, and have in the past been classed as such.

199 CRIMSON FINCH *Neochmia phaeton*　　　**Plates 58 and 65**
New Guinea and Australia

Fringilla phaeton Hombron and Jacquinot, 1841, Ann. Sci. Nat. Paris, ser. 2, 16, p. 314, Raffles Bay, Northern Territory.

IDENTIFICATION Length 12·5−14 cm (5−5½ in). A small (but looks deceptively large), active and brightly coloured finch of tropical swamps and marshes. The sexes differ, nominate males having bright crimson face and underparts and females having grey on the underparts; the two northern races have white underparts. All are slim or tapering in shape, with a distinctive long, pointed and wedge-shaped crimson tail. Unlikely to be confused with any other species.

DESCRIPTION Sexes differ. **Adult male:** Forehead to nape deep grey, almost slate-grey, with a brownish or olive-brown tinge on hindneck, nape and sides of nape. Mantle, upper back, scapulars and wing-coverts rich crimson overlying brown or grey-brown bases (which show through more in worn plumage); lesser and outer median coverts often browner than rest of wing; flight feathers lead-

grey, with edges and tips tinged with crimson; tertials the same, but more broadly fringed with crimson. Lower back grey or greyish, becoming crimson on graduated wedge-shaped tail, latter with some brown in outer feathers. Entire sides of head to chin, throat, breast, belly and flanks deep crimson, with a scattering of small white spots on sides of breast and flanks; lower belly to undertail-coverts black. Bill (large for the size of the bird) deep at base and with a noticeable curve to culmen, waxy-red or pinkish-red with a bluish-grey base to lower mandible and often a small white spot or patch at the sides. Eye brown, reddish-brown or straw-orange, orbital ring yellow-orange. Legs and feet yellowish or pale tawny or buffish-brown. **Adult female:** Forehead, crown, nape and mantle grey, becoming tinged or heavily suffused with red on scapulars and wing-coverts, though latter are usually grey at tips of medians and greaters; flight feathers and tertials as adult male, but much paler grey-brown; back is tinged with brown or greyish-brown; rump, uppertail-coverts and tail as male, but tail is browner and not so bright red. Lores, over eye, ear-coverts to chin, throat and sides of neck bright red, but paler or lighter than the crimson of male; breast, flanks and belly grey, paler than upperparts and with occasional red tips on upper breast; sides of lower breast and flanks have a scattering of small white spots; undertail-coverts pale grey, tinged with buff. Bill as male, but paler pinkish-red or orange. **Juvenile:** Generally buffish-brown above, with a light wash of red or reddish-brown on coverts, secondaries and tertials; rump and tail duller red or orange-red than on either adult. Face buff or light buff. Underparts are paler than adult's, more buffish on belly and flanks, which lack white spots. Bill black.

GEOGRAPHICAL VARIATION Males of *albiventer* have the lower breast and belly to undertail-coverts white (or slightly creamy on some of the latter), with rest of underparts lighter red than on nominate race, red extending down sides of breast and flanks and heavily spotted with white; upperparts are much paler and more uniform grey-brown from forehead to lower back and wings, and tertials are also tinged pale or light brown. Female *albiventer* is like nominate female but generally paler, and both male and female have a pale blue base to lower (and occasionally upper) mandible. Male *evangelinae* have the upper belly grey, becoming white on lower belly, vent and undertail-coverts, and females have belly and undertail-coverts white; both sexes have base of bill (both mandibles) pale blue.

VOICE Commonest or most usual contact note or flight call is a brisk but descending 'tsee-tsee-tsee-tsee-tsee' or 'che-che-che-che'; alarm a sharp 'chip' or 'pit'. The song is a series of low-pitched rasping notes, 'ra-ra, ra-ra, reee', and ending with a melodious descending treble note.

STATUS, HABITAT AND BEHAVIOUR Common or locally common. The typical habitat is tropical swamps or areas near water with tall grass, cane grass, pandanus or other dense vegetation, or (in New Guinea) savanna woodland with long grass. In recent years in northern Australia, has adapted to human settlements and is found in and around farms, especially at edges of cultivation (in parts of Irian Jaya, New Guinea, visits rice-paddies), roadsides and in tall-growing crops and gardens (where it may be in search of water). Occurs in pairs or family parties (or groups of families), often in association with mannikins, particularly Grey-crowned (241) or Black (247), or other species of grass finches. Constantly on the move, with tail continually switched from side to side or up and down; often aggressive over food. Not usually shy, and easily approachable; when alarmed flies into trees, but flight is generally weak and does not usually fly great distances, preferring instead to travel in short bursts from tree to tree. Feeds in tall grass, in which it is actively adept at clinging (even in wind), also feeds on the ground and catches termites in flight; diet largely grass seeds and other small seeds, occasionally small insects and spiders.

DISTRIBUTION N. p. phaeton: northern Australia from Fitzroy and Derby rivers, east through Northern Territory to the Gulf of Carpentaria and to eastern Queensland south to Rockhampton.

N. p. albiventer: northern Cape York Peninsula, northern Australia.

N. p. evangelinae: southern New Guinea, from Frederik Hendrik Island east to the middle and lower Fly and Oriomo rivers, north to Lakes Murray and Daviumbu.

One other race (iredalei) is recognised in Australia; some authorities consider the distinction of albiventer from evangelinae doubtful.

MOVEMENTS Generally sedentary, but flocks gather in the non-breeding season, involving local movements.

MEASUREMENTS Wing 53; tarsus 11−12; bill (from skull) 9·5−10.

REFERENCES Goodwin (1982), Pizzey and Doyle (1980).

200 STAR FINCH *Neochmia ruficauda*   Plate 65

Australia

Amadina ruficauda Gould, 1837, Synops. Birds Australia, pt 1, Australia [Liverpool Plains, New South Wales].

IDENTIFICATION Length 10−12 cm (4−4¾ in). A small and distinctive red-faced finch of the northern territories, where it occasionally occurs in huge flocks. The sexes are similar: red on head and face, yellowish to olive-green upperparts except for dull red uppertail-coverts and blackish tail, heavily spotted or speckled with white on grey throat, breast and flanks, and with belly light yellowish-buff; the female is duller than the male, with less extensive red on face. Unlikely to be confused with any other species.

DESCRIPTION Sexes similar but separable. **Adult:** Males have forehead to crown, lores, cheeks and fore part of ear-coverts, moustachial area and chin bright red; on females this is lighter red, and usually confined to forehead, lores, cheeks and slightly around eye. Both sexes show small white spots on ear-coverts. Hindcrown, nape, sides of neck, mantle, back, scapulars and wings light yellowish-olive (duller or more greyish-olive on adult female), slightly darker or browner on flight feathers but with paler or green edges;

uppertail-coverts dull scarlet or crimson, with white bars or spots at tips. Central tail feathers have reddish outer edges, and all outers are dull brown or washed pinkish-red. Throat and breast dull olive or yellowish-olive and profusely spotted with white, spots extending onto flanks where they become smaller and less distinct; lower breast, belly and vent yellow or yellowish-buff; undertail-coverts paler or whitish. Bill short, deep at base and with curved culmen, waxy-red or scarlet. Eye orange or orange-reddish. Legs and feet yellow or yellowish-brown. **Juvenile:** Head and frontal part of face greyish-brown; rest of head and upperparts a dull olive or yellowish-olive, tinged brown, and with light buff edges and tips to wing-coverts and edges to flight feathers; rump and tail warm buff-brown, with paler buff spots at tips of feathers, becoming progressively red with age. Chin, breast and flanks buffish or buffish-brown; upper breast and belly to undertail-coverts paler buff. Bill black, but becomes red at an early age.

GEOGRAPHICAL VARIATION Race *clarescens* from the northwest of the range is more yellowish-green above, the red on the face is brighter and extends to crown, and breast and belly to undertail-coverts are yellow; often shows white spots on tips of median and greater coverts. Considerable individual variation in both races, older birds are brighter and more clearly marked than younger ones.

VOICE Call a loud or penetrating 'ssit' or 'seet', also a single 'tlit' or 'tsit' contact note; has a rapid, high-pitched rattle as an alarm or anxiety call. The song is a short and generally very quiet, toneless note repeated frequently.

STATUS, HABITAT AND BEHAVIOUR
Common, locally common or erratically abundant. Usually found in waterside vegetation or in swamps, including damp grassy areas on sandflats with scattered bushes or rushes, but also in irrigated areas such as field of rice or sugarcane; not found in the vicinity of human settlements. Occurs in pairs or small parties of up to 20; loosely communal when breeding. When in flocks flight strong, swift and erratic in direction, often changing course, and formation reminiscent of Starlings (*Sturnus vulgaris*) or waders; otherwise, short-distance flight rather bounding. Feeds in low vegetation, on the seedheads of ripe and ripening spinifex, on the ground on a variety of grass seeds, but also takes some insects such as ants and termites which it catches in flight. As Diamond Firetail (197), drinks in a pigeon-like manner.

DISTRIBUTION *N. r. ruficauda*: central Queensland, around and to the north of Rockhampton; formerly more extensively south to Namoi river, central New South Wales.

N. r. clarescens: northern Western Australia from Shark Bay northeast to the Kimberley range, discontinuously east to the Gulf of Carpentaria to about 14° S on Cape York, northern Queensland.

MOVEMENTS Generally sedentary, but some local movements undertaken by flocks in non-breeding season.

REFERENCES Goodwin (1982), Pizzey and Doyle (1980).

GENUS *POEPHILA*

Five species. Grass finches, including Zebra and Double-barred Finches. Two species, Long-tailed and Black-throated Finches, are very similar to each other in appearance and behaviour. All are birds of open grasslands or savannas of the dry semi-desert interior of Australia. The relationships of the genus are uncertain, but probably close to both the true munias *Lonchura* and Gouldian Finch *Chloebia*.

201 ZEBRA FINCH (Spotted-sided Finch) *Poephila guttata*   Plate 65
Indonesia and Australia

Fringilla guttata Vieillot, 1817, Nouv. Dict. Hist. Nat. nouv. ed., 12, p. 233, Moluccas [Timor].

IDENTIFICATION Length 10 cm (4 in). A small, stocky, active, social and noisy finch; common and well known as a cagebird. The male is grey with a black-and-white 'teardrop' in front of the eye, warm brown ear-coverts, white rump, black and white at base of tail, fine black-and-white barring on the throat and breast (*castanotis*), or throat and breast pale greyish-buff with black central band (*guttata*), and rich brown flanks spotted with white. The female is duller grey above, with the 'teardrop' less well defined, and has buffish underparts. Virtually unique and unlikely to be confused with any other species of finch, but one or two other Australian birds such as whitefaces (*Aphelocephala*) share a similarly marked face pattern.

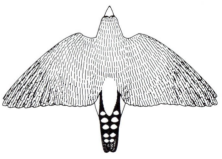

DESCRIPTION Sexes differ. **Adult male:** Forehead to nape and sides of neck grey or light grey,

becoming grey-brown on mantle, back and scapulars; wing-coverts dark grey with paler buff-brown edges; flight feathers also dark grey; centre of lower rump white, sides grey or dark greyish; long uppertail-coverts broadly barred black and white. Tail brownish-black, but overlapped at base by long uppertail-coverts. Lores to moustachial area white, enclosed by black border from base of bill to below eye creating a fine 'teardrop' effect; cheeks and ear-coverts warm brown or light chestnut. Chin, throat and breast pale grey, tinged buffish, with a black breast-band across centre of breast, thinner or tapering narrowly at sides; sides of lower breast and flanks warm or rich chestnut with small white spots, rest of underparts white or creamy-white. Bill short and rather stubby, bright orange to red. Eye deep red or orange-red. Legs and feet pink or pinkish-orange. **Adult female:** A plain version of adult male, lacking warm brown cheeks and ear-coverts, barred chin to breast, black breast-band and chestnut flanks; instead is plain grey above with white lower rump, and dull greyish-buff below, whiter on lower belly and undertail-coverts. Retains the strongly barred long uppertail-coverts and the black border to white 'teardrop' on face. Bill paler than that of male, orange or orange-yellow. **Juvenile:** Very similar to adult female, but upperparts more heavily tinged with buffish-brown, which becomes greyer with age; white 'teardrop' on face is not always bordered with black. Bill entirely black.
GEOGRAPHICAL VARIATION The better-known race castanotis from Australia has chin, throat and upper breast finely barred with grey, white and black, with centre of breast a more solidly black band tapering towards the sides; upperparts dark grey-brown with wing-coverts and flight feathers dark grey. The 'teardrop' effect on face usually much better defined than in nominate guttata.

VOICE The usual contact call is a sharp 'tya', 'teea' or 'tcheea', somewhat like a toy trumpet in tone and strength, with varying degrees of emphasis, also more loudly by male than by female; large flocks make a considerable cacophony when they all call. The song is a frequently given variable series of nasal call notes interspersed with chattering trills.
STATUS, HABITAT AND BEHAVIOUR Common to locally abundant. Occurs in most habitats except wet or damp coastal forests, prefers areas of dry brush, scrub and open woodlands, plains, saltmarshes, edges of cultivation, orchards, parks and gardens; always in vicinity of water. Very tame and approachable. Occurs in pairs and huge flocks, gregarious and highly social, especially at waterholes. Hops easily on the ground; flies fast and direct, with only slight undulations. Feeds in vegetation and from grass stems, more usually on the ground, on a variety of grass seeds and shoots, also some insects such as ants and termites, the latter even caught in the air. Drinks in a pigeon-like manner, often several times a day, but can go long periods without water.
DISTRIBUTION P. g. guttata: entire Lesser Sunda Islands chain from Lombok to Komodo, Timor and Luang, Indonesia.
P. g. castanotis: Australia except for the sclerophyll forests and rainforests; does not breed (though occurs in breeding season) north of 15° S.
Introduced onto Kangaroo Island in 1937, but failed to become established.
MOVEMENTS Generally sedentary, but wanders nomadically in search of food in winter and water in drought years.
REFERENCES Goodwin (1982), Pizzey and Doyle (1980).

202 DOUBLE-BARRED FINCH (Bicheno Finch) *Poephila bichenovii*
Plate 66

Australia

Fringilla bichenovii Vigors and Horsfield, 1827, Trans. Linn. Soc. London, 15, p. 258, Shoalwater Bay and Broad Sound, southern Queensland.

IDENTIFICATION Length 10–11 cm (4–4¼ in). A small and distinctively marked finch of northern and eastern Australia. The sexes are alike, with a white and owl-like face bordered by a thick black band and another across the lower breast against the otherwise all-white underparts; brown of crown becomes greyer on mantle, and has fine black-and-white pattern on wings. The races are easily separable by the colour of the rump. Very unlikely to be confused with any other finch once the distinctive face pattern and breast-bands are seen. Other Australian birds, e.g. Banded Whiteface (*Aphelocephala nigricincta*) and White-fronted Chat (*Ephthianura albifrons*) (neither of which overlaps

in range), have similar black breast-bands but otherwise bear no similarity to Double-barred Finch.
DESCRIPTION Sexes alike. **Adult:** Forehead black; crown and hindcrown a warm brown or gingery-brown, becoming paler on nape and hindneck; mantle, back and scapulars fawn or greyish-brown, finely barred or vermiculated darker. Wing-coverts and flight feathers blackish and finely edged with small white spots, presenting a fine-chequered pattern on closed wing; tips of primaries unspotted. Lower back a band of black above pure white rump and uppertail-coverts. Tail black or blackish with a tinge of brown. Lores, over eyes,

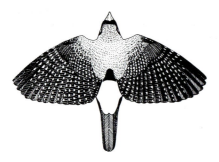

cheeks, ear-coverts, sides of neck, chin and throat pure white, completely encircled by a thin band of black; breast pure white with some fine grey barring at sides, with black band across lower breast; belly and flanks creamy-white; undertail-coverts black. Bill short, stubby and conical, greyish or steel-blue. Eye dark brown. Legs and feet grey, dark grey or greyish-blue. Some females are separable by thinner breast-band and less pure white (more creamy) face. **Juvenile:** Much browner or more buff-brown on upperparts and lacks the strong or bold black-and-white wing pattern of adult (black is replaced by dull buff-brown bars). Underparts are pale buff or with a wash of pale brown, with indistinct bands (some have breast-band present only at sides, becoming complete with age).

GEOGRAPHICAL VARIATION Race *annulosa* has very obvious black rump and uppertail-coverts; the races interbreed in overlap areas.

VOICE The usual contact call is a long drawn-out toy-trumpet-like 'tiaat, tiaat', similar to but longer than that of Zebra Finch (201). The song is also similar to that of Zebra Finch, but generally softer and more repetitive.

STATUS, HABITAT AND BEHAVIOUR Common, widespread or locally common. Found in dry or semi-arid open country, dry grass plains with woodlands or scrub, open forests or edges of cultivation; in more recent years has taken to living in close proximity to human settlements and on waste ground, parks, orchards and gardens. Highly social and occurs usually in parties or small flocks (often largely of immatures), or in larger flocks in non-breeding season. Roosts communally in nests specially built for the purpose. Flight weak and slightly bounding; rarely flies long distances, preferring to retreat into cover when disturbed. Feeds on the ground or among seeding grasses, also takes the seeds of small plants. Drinks in a pigeon-like manner.

DISTRIBUTION *P. b. bichenovii*: eastern and northeast Australia, from eastern Northern Territory, Cairns, Cape York Peninsula south through Queensland to New South Wales and northern Victoria to the Murray river.

P. b. annulosa: northern and northwest Australia from King Sound, Western Australia, east through the Kimberley range to the Gulf of Carpentaria (east of this area the two races interbreed).

MOVEMENTS Generally sedentary, but some flocks roam at random in search of water in the dry season.

REFERENCES Frith *et al.* (1979), Pizzey and Doyle (1980).

203 MASKED FINCH *Poephila personata*   Plate 66
Australia

Poephila personata Gould, 1842, Birds Australia, pt. 6, Port Essington, Northern Territory.

IDENTIFICATION Length 12·5–13·5 cm (4¾–5 in). A drab or soberly plumaged finch of northern Australia with several easily recognisable field characters, most obvious of which is the large, almost Hawfinch-like yellow bill. Has brown or gingery-brown upperparts with a white rump and black tail. Black forehead to chin and white (eastern birds) or buffish-brown throat; distinctive black flank patch and white undertail-coverts. **Confusion species:** Both Long-tailed (204) and Black-throated (205) Finches share the same feature of a black lower flank patch, black lower back and white rump (except one race of Black-throated), and black tail. Long-tailed, however, also has a pale yellow bill and both also have plain grey (not rich warm brown) heads with black lores and a black chin and throat patch; Black-throated also has a rounded (not tapering) tip to the tail, while Long-tailed has thin, wispy, extended central tail feathers in fresh plumage.

DESCRIPTION Sexes alike. **Adult:** Lower fore-head and sides of forehead, lores and chin black; centre of forehead to hindcrown a warm dark brown, fading on nape to a lighter warm brown on mantle, back, scapulars and wing-coverts; alula and primary coverts dark brown; flight feathers and tertials dull brown, with paler or slightly warm brown edges to primaries. Rump and centre of uppertail-coverts white; sides of uppertail-coverts and entire tail (which tapers to a point at tips of central pair) black. Sides of face and almost entire underparts are a soft or light buff-brown, but tinged slightly warm. Lower flanks and thighs a large black patch which tapers towards belly; centre of belly and all undertail-coverts white. Bill large, triangular and almost Hawfinch-like but not excessive in proportion to the bird, bright yellow or orange-yellow. Eye dark brown or reddish-brown. Legs and feet bright pink or pinkish-red. Adult females are separable (usually when accompanied by male) by being duller or paler, especially on underparts, with black on face and lower flanks less extensive.

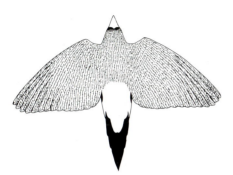

Juvenile: A dull buff-brown version of the adult, but lacks black face mask and has a black bill with yellowish base for the first few weeks of life.

GEOGRAPHICAL VARIATION Race *leucotis* has a greater extent of rich warm brown on crown and nape, continuing as a wash over mantle, back and wings; fore part of the ear-coverts, cheeks and the sides of chin and throat are white or whitish, and central flanks immediately above the black patch are white. The bill is paler yellow on average than that of nominate race.

VOICE Contact call is a low or flat nasal 'tat' or 'tiat', often repeated as a double note, also a loud 'tsit' or 'tya' call like Zebra Finch (201); flocks give a rapid series of high-pitched greeting calls. The song is very similar to that of Zebra Finch, but the phrases are louder and more individually clear.

STATUS, HABITAT AND BEHAVIOUR
Common or locally common. A bird of dry open woodland, grassy areas with trees, often in or near farms and human settlements (especially when water easily available); in parts of the range a common roadside bird, and found in trees in main streets of large towns in the northern territories. Usually in small parties of up to 30, with breeding birds forming loose colonies; in the dry season many band together in much larger numbers, often several hundred strong. Roosts in nests specially built for the purpose. Mixes freely with other finches, usually Long-tailed and Black-throated. Feeds on the ground, on a variety of grass seeds but also pursues and somewhat clumsily catches insects in the air and takes spiders, ants etc. Drinks in a pigeon-like manner, and habitually comes to water twice a day.

DISTRIBUTION *P. p. personata*: northern Australia, from the Kimberley range (mostly the eastern part) east through Northern Territory to the southern shore of the Gulf of Carpentaria to about 140° E.

P. p. leucotis: northern Australia, from Cape York and the eastern shore of the Gulf of Carpentaria south to about 19° S.

MOVEMENTS Sedentary, but large flocks gather in search of water in drought years.

REFERENCES Goodwin (1982), Pizzey and Doyle (1980).

204 LONG-TAILED FINCH *Poephila acuticauda*   Plate 66

Australia

Amadina acuticauda Gould, 1840, Proc. Zool. Soc. London, 1839, p. 143, Derby, Northwestern Australia.

IDENTIFICATION Length 15–16·5 cm (6–6½ in). An active and very distinctive finch with fine long tail streamers, of the dry grasslands of northern Australia. Has a pale yellow bill, grey head, black lores, chin and throat, pale grey-brown or fawn-brown upperparts, white rump and black tail. Shares the same black lower-flank patch as Masked (203) and Black-throated (205) Finches. **Confusion species:** The only likely confusion is between immatures of this and Black-throated Finch: in the very small area of overlap, juvenile Black-throated has greyer head, less black on chin and throat, and richer brown upperparts.

DESCRIPTION Sexes alike. **Adult:** Forehead to nape and face very pale bluish-grey, slightly paler on sides of head (or even white on ear-coverts) and neck; lores black. Hindneck pinkish buff-brown, becoming slightly browner on mantle, back, scapulars and wing-coverts; flight feathers dark brown, edged paler, but outer primaries have thin white edges for about half their length; lower back a band of black or blackish-brown; rump and uppertail-coverts white. Tail fairly long and tapering, with the two thin central feathers projecting at

least as far again in thin wispy or wire-like streamers (longer on male than on female), black. Chin, throat and upper breast a pear-shaped black patch (smaller on females than on males). centre and sides of breast, flanks and belly warm pinkish-buff, with a triangular-shaped black patch each side of lower flanks (slightly larger on male than on female), tapering towards vent; undertail-coverts white. Bill fairly short but quite prominent, almost triangular but with slightly curving ridges to both mandibles, variable from pale yellow to orange. Eye red or reddish-brown. Legs and feet bright pink to orange-red. **Juvenile:** A duller version of the adult, with a pale reddish-buff tinge to upperparts; tail shorter than adult's and lacks projecting central feathers; face, as adult's, but lores to eye brown or dark brown, cheeks and ear-coverts smudged greyish, and smaller chin-and-throat patch dark brown. Bill black or very dark grey in first-year plumage.

GEOGRAPHICAL VARIATION Northwestern race *hecki* has a more orange or orange-red bill than nominate, but considerable individual variation exists in both races and birds in the northwest

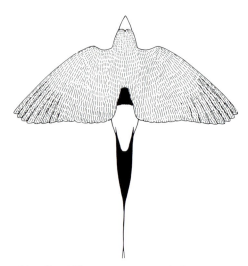

with yellow bills may not necessarily be of nominate race.

VOICE Contact note is a soft 'tet', often given in flight, and a louder or far-carrying mournful and descending 'peew' or 'we-woooooh', also a loud whistling 'thwirrr'; alarm a rapid rising 'cheek-chee-chee-cheek'. The song is a series of quiet or soft notes, followed by a couple of flute-like notes and ending with a variation of the contact note, 'tu-tu-tu-tu-tu, woo-wah-weee'.

STATUS, HABITAT AND BEHAVIOUR
Common or fairly common. Found in eucalyptus woodland with dry grassy open plains or savanna with scattered trees and bushes, often near water. Occurs in pairs, or more usually in small to large flocks (up to many thousands at waterholes in times of drought); often mixes with Masked Finch. Roosts in small nests specially constructed for the purpose. Constantly active, but very agile and quite graceful or delicate in its movements. Feeds almost entirely on the ground, on a variety of ripe and ripening grass seeds, but also takes termites and catches flying ants or flies on the wing. Drinks in a pigeon-like manner.

DISTRIBUTION *P. a. acuticauda*: northern Australia east of Wyndham, through the northern Northern Territory east along the Gulf of Carpentaria to the Leichhardt river and south to Mount Isa, northern Queensland.

P. a. hecki: northwest Australia, from Roebuck Bay through the Kimberley range to Wyndham.

Opinions differ firstly on the validity of subspecies *hecki* (given the considerable variation in bill colour of nominate race), and, secondly, on how closely related Long-tailed Finch is to the allied Black-throated Finch.

MOVEMENTS Sedentary, though in years of prolonged drought many thousands gather at available water.

REFERENCES Frith *et al.* (1979), Goodwin (1982), Pizzey and Doyle (1980).

205 BLACK-THROATED FINCH (Parson Finch) *Poephila cincta*
Plate 66

Australia

Amadina cincta Gould, 1837, Proc. Zool. Soc. London, 1836, p. 105, Upper Hunter River district, New South Wales.

IDENTIFICATION Length 10 cm (4 in). Very similar to Long-tailed Finch (204), with which it meets but does not overlap in range. A stocky or robust-looking finch with a distinctive pale grey head and prominent black bill and bib; warm brown upperparts, white (or black) rump and short black tail. Shares the same black lower-flank patch (but smaller) as the previous two species. **Confusion species:** Only likely confusion is between juveniles of this and Long-tailed Finch (which see) where the ranges meet in northern Queensland.

DESCRIPTION Sexes alike. **Adult:** Forehead to nape soft pearl-grey with a slight bluish tinge; cheeks, ear-coverts and sides of neck paler or more silvery-white; lores jet-black. Lower nape and upper mantle a warm pink, almost salmon-pinkish,. becoming uniform smooth fawn or very light cinnamon-brown on lower mantle, back, scapulars and wings; flight feathers brown, with paler outer edges and tips; lower back a thin band of black; rump and uppertail-coverts white. Tail short and rounded at sides of tip, black. Chin, throat and upper breast black (individually variable

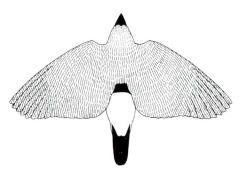

in extent, but generally smaller on females); rest of breast, belly and flanks warm light orange or cinnamon-brown, except for black patch on lower flanks tapering towards belly; centre of belly and thighs to undertail-coverts white. Bill as Long-tailed Finch with a slight curve to culmen, dark grey or blackish. Eye brown or reddish-brown. Legs and feet pink, bright pink or orange-red. **Juvenile:** Very similar to adult but duller, and with a generally buffish-brown wash to upperparts and underparts; chin-and-throat patch dull, more blackish-brown than on adult.

GEOGRAPHICAL VARIATION Race *atropygialis* has rump and uppertail-coverts entirely black; also slightly paler and generally more pink on upperparts and underparts, slightly greyer on wings, and head is paler silvery-grey than in nominate race.

VOICE Calls very similar to those of Long-tailed Finch, but lacks the variety of contact notes, has the same soft 'tet' note but also a fairly hoarse whistling 'tweee' or 'weet'; alarm a soft 'beck-beck-beckadeck'. The song is also similar but more hoarse and softer or lower in pitch than that of Long-tailed.

STATUS, HABITAT AND BEHAVIOUR Fairly or locally common, less common in south of range. Found in open woodlands or, in some areas, more dense and mature woods, also scrub and thornbush or open savannas, invariably close to water; generally avoids settlements, but occasionally found on the edge of cultivation. Habits in general much as Long-tailed Finch, but tends not to form such large flocks; loosely social in small flocks of up to 30. Feeds on grass seeds on the ground or while perched on seedheads; also catches small flying insects in flight and takes spiders and ants. Drinks in a pigeon-like manner.

DISTRIBUTION *P. c. cincta*: eastern Australia, from extreme northern New South Wales north and northwest through Queensland to about 17° S and west to about the Leichhardt river.

P. c. atropygialis: northeast Australia, Cape York Peninsula south to about Normanton and east to Cairns.

The two races interbreed in a wide area of overlap.

MOVEMENTS Usually sedentary, but has occasionally occurred in new localities to the south of its present range.

REFERENCES Frith *et al.* (1979), Goodwin (1982), Pizzey and Doyle (1980).

GENUS *ERYTHRURA*

Ten species. Parrotfinches are small, almost entirely green (except one species) birds with short rounded wings and tail, the head or face is variably blue, red or green, and all but one species have red on rump and on centre of tail. Originally forest birds, many are now found on (if not dependent on) edges of cultivation. The most distinctly recognisable group of Estrildid finches, confusable with no other finches in size, shape or coloration. Of uncertain affinities, but possibly descended from the same distant ancestor as *Chloebia* and (some) *Lonchura*.

206 GREEN-TAILED PARROTFINCH (Bamboo Parrotfinch, Tawny-breasted Parrotfinch) *Erythrura hyperythra*　　Plate 56

Malay Archipelago

Chlorura hyperythra Reichenbach, 1862–63, Singvögel, p. 33, New Guinea [Java].

IDENTIFICATION Length 10 cm (4 in). A small and rather slim finch with short wings and tail, of the jungle and bamboo forests of mountains of southeast Asia, Indonesia and the Philippines. Deep green upperparts and tail, with blue forehead; face and underparts warm buff-brown, or darker orange-brown becoming paler towards undertail-coverts; sides of breast green or blue in some races. Unlikely to be confused with any other species.

DESCRIPTION Sexes differ slightly. **Adult male:** Lower forehead a thin band of black or blackish; rest of forehead to crown a deep blue, often inconspicuous and difficult to see in the field. Crown and nape to lower back including short rounded wings deep green, except for very dark brown flight feathers with greenish outer edges; rump and uppertail-coverts dull bronze or orange (some can be golden-yellow in fresh plumage). Tail short and rounded, with central feathers bright green, outers dark brown or blackish but edged deep green. Face and almost entire underparts rich warm or cinnamon buff-brown, heaviest on face and breast, becoming paler or lighter tawny or buff-brown on undertail-coverts; sides of breast and flanks pale leaf-green or moss-green. Bill deep at the base, pointed, black or blackish-grey. Eye dark brown or black, with pale buff or bluish orbital ring. Legs and feet pink, flesh-pink or pinkish-red. **Adult female:** Lower forehead brown, and the blue deeper or duller and on restricted to forecrown (less extensive than on adult male); generally a much duller green on upperparts. **Juvenile:** Similar to adult female but paler, and forehead is entirely green (lacks blue). Bill yellow, with a dull black tip.

GEOGRAPHICAL VARIATION Most races are smaller than nominate, with smaller bills. Race *brunneiventris* is similar to nominate, but has a shorter bill, hindcrown and nape to rump and tail are uniform bright green, and underparts lighter cinnamon-buff with green of sides of breast and upper flanks tinged bright blue or azure-blue; *microrhyncha* is similar, but has less blue on forehead, and underparts are paler buff and washed with green or deep green. In *borneensis*, the blue on forehead extends to hindcrown, the uniform upperparts can be variably deeper, paler or slightly yellowish-green, and is deeper buff or orange-buff on breast, becoming washed with green on sides of breast and flanks. Birds in southern Sulawesi, formerly separated as *ernstmayri* (now regarded as synonymous with *microrhyncha*), differ chiefly in having less blue on forehead, with upperparts yellowish-green (particularly noticeable on rump). Race *intermedia* has the blue on forehead much paler or duller than in other races; upperparts are yellowish-green, this extending to uppertail-coverts (which are washed with orange) and central tail feathers; the underparts are warm gingery-buff, with sides of lower breast, flanks and sides of undertail-coverts green. Female *malayana* is also yellowish-green on upperparts, and has ginger underparts tinged with yellowish-buff (male is unknown).

VOICE The contact call given in flight is a high-pitched, hissing 'tzit-tzit' or 'tseet-tseet', very similar to that of other parrotfinches, otherwise generally silent; fledglings have a 'srreet-srreet' call note. The song is a series of soft, almost inaudible notes followed by four musical or bell-like notes often repeated; when singing, the bird holds its head with bill horizontal and turns it from side to side.

STATUS, HABITAT AND BEHAVIOUR A rare resident in mountain forest, usually found between 1000 m and 3000 m, but some races occur much lower (down to 300 m on Lombok). Race *malayana* is known from only three individuals; the type (a single female collected in January 1902) and two other females seen in November 1904. Found principally in bamboo jungle, but also open clearings in woods or edges of forests; also occurs in ricefields in Borneo and possibly elsewhere. Occasionally in pairs, but more usually in small (family?) parties or flocks. Feeds on the ground, on bamboo seeds, grass seeds, seeds of *Polygonum chinense*, rice and small fruits; may also take some insects.

DISTRIBUTION *E. h. hyperythra*: Java.

E. h. brunneiventris: north Luzon and Mindoro, Philippines.

E. h. borneensis: Sarawak and Sabah.

E. h. malayana: Cameron highlands, Perak-Pahang boundary, Malaysia.

E. h. intermedia: Lombok, Sumbawa and Flores, Lesser Sunda Islands.

E. h. microrhyncha: Latimodjon Mountains, south-central Sulawesi, Matinan Mountains, northwest Sulawesi, and Mount Lompobattang, southern Sulawesi.

A poorly known species and some races may, on closer examination, not be considered acceptable (e.g. *obscura* is now considered synonymous with *intermedia*, and *ernstmayri* synonymous with *microrhyncha*).

MEASUREMENTS Wing of *brunneiventris* 61; tail 39; tarsus 14; bill 10. Wing of *malayana* 58–60; tail 34–35; tarsus 14–16.

REFERENCES Goodwin (1982), Smythies (1981), White and Bruce (1986).

207 PIN-TAILED PARROTFINCH *Erythrura prasina*   Plate 56
Oriental

Loxia prasina Sparrman, 1788, Mus. Carlsonianum, fasc. 3, pl. 72 and 73, Java.

IDENTIFICATION Length of male 15 cm (6 in), of female 11·5–12 cm (4½ in) One of the more distinctive and widespread parrotfinches. The male is deep green above, with a bright red rump and sharply pointed tail with extensions to central feathers; face to upper breast blue, lower breast and flanks buff with bright red patch on belly. The female is smaller, shorter-tailed and duller, and lacks central tail projections, blue face and red on belly. **Confusion species:** The combination of blue face and red belly and rump to tail distinguishes it from Green-tailed Parrotfinch (206); other similar parrotfinches are all outside range.

DESCRIPTION Sexes differ. **Adult male:** Forehead, around eye to cheeks, chin, throat and upper breast a deep cobalt-blue, slightly paler or greyer on throat (and some individuals have paler faces); lores jet-black. Crown and nape to mantle, back, scapulars and wing-coverts deep green, slightly paler on sides of nape; flight feathers dark brown or blackish, finely edged pale green; tertials similar or olive-green, but finely edged and tipped yellowish; lower rump, uppertail-coverts and central tail feathers bright scarlet. Tail graduated and central feathers extend about 5 cm (2 in) beyond tip, outer feathers dull red, becoming blackish on extreme outers (but see note below). Breast, sides of breast and flanks to undertail-coverts deep or warm gingery-buff, tinged with blue or green on upper breast; centre of lower breast and belly to vent bright red. Bill strong and rather powerful-looking for a finch, dark grey or blackish. Eye brown, with pale grey or greyish-buff orbital ring. Legs and feet brown or pale flesh-pink. **Adult female:** Almost entire upperparts from forehead to upper back and wings dull greenish, slightly darker on crown; flight feathers dark brown or blackish, finely edged pale green; rump, uppertail-coverts and tail dull or deep scarlet, slightly duller than on male (tail is much shorter than male's, but still pointed). Face mostly dull green, with cheeks to sides of neck buffish or washed with powder-blue on lores and ear-coverts. Underparts almost entirely dull buff, peachy-buff or greyish-buff, with a tinge of pale blue on sides of breast. Note: A colour phase exists in which the red rump to tail

(both sexes) and on underparts (male) is replaced by bright yellow. **Juvenile:** Very similar to adult female but duller or greyer-green above, except for red rump to tail (dull orange-red rump may appear brown or brownish in the field), and pale dull buff below. Base of lower mandible yellowish. Young males show extended central tail feathers (with rounded tips) at an early age, and full adult plumage is attained within three months of life.
GEOGRAPHICAL VARIATION Male *coelica* have a much greater extent of blue on breast, the red belly patch extends to lower breast and the rich buff area is restricted to flanks and undertail-coverts. Females have blue on cheeks, ear-coverts, lores, throat and breast.
VOICE Contact call is a loud or high-pitched 'tseet-tseet' or 'tsit-tsit', similar to that of other parrotfinches; also has a sharp 'teger-teter-terge'. The song is fairly similar to that of Green-tailed Parrotfinch, but with less musical and more clinking or chirping notes.

STATUS, HABITAT AND BEHAVIOUR
Seasonally or locally common (especially at times of rice harvest), otherwise rare; generally shy and relatively unknown, possibly under-recorded. Found from the plains up to 1500 m in forests, mainly along edges or in secondary growth, but usually in bamboo. Usually in small flocks but also frequently occurs in huge flocks or swarms, especially when rice is available (in some areas becomes a major local pest). In the wild known to eat only rice and bamboo and grass seeds, but in captivity eats smaller seeds of grasses and millet.
DISTRIBUTION *E. p. prasina*: discontinuously through Thailand, northern and central Laos and Malaysia to Sumatra and Java.
    E. p. coelica: Borneo.
MOVEMENTS Partial migrant and nomadic; in winter, some move north to Tenasserim, southern Burma. Otherwise occurs erratically from season to season at areas of seeding bamboo.
REFERENCE Goodwin (1982).

208 GREEN-FACED PARROTFINCH (Manila Parrotfinch) *Erythrura viridifacies*   **Plate 58**

Philippines

Erythrura viridifacies Hachisuka and Delacour, 1937, Bull. Brit. Ornith. Club, 57, p. 66, Vicinity of Manilla, Luzon.

IDENTIFICATION Length 12·5 cm (5 in). A bird of very restricted distribution in the Philippines. Virtually all green except for bright red uppertail-coverts and tail, latter with darker tip. The tail is graduated, with thin central extension of about 3 cm (1 in). **Confusion species:** Within its native range occurs with, and likely to be confused only with, the initially similar (in size and shape) Green-tailed Parrotfinch of race *brunneiventris* (206), but colours of underparts and tail separate it at all times.
DESCRIPTION Sexes differ. **Adult male:** Entire head, upperparts and wings deep grass-green, slightly darker or dark green on edges of the wing-coverts, tertials, lower back and rump; flight feathers blackish, finely edged with green, short rounded wings; uppertail-coverts and tail bright scarlet, with tip of tail graduating to a point and becoming slightly darker red. Centre of chin and throat dark green or can be uniform with rest of underparts, which are paler, more leaf-green except for pale yellowish-buff thighs and undertail-coverts. Bill short and sharply pointed, slate-grey or black. Eye brown or dark brown, with pale grey orbital ring. Legs and feet pale pink or pinkish-brown. **Adult female:** A duller and greyer-green bird than adult male, especially on underparts, and yellowish-buff on lower belly, vent and undertail-coverts. **Juvenile:** Very similar to adult female, but

much paler buff or yellowish on underparts. Juvenile males have a longer tail than juvenile females and are somewhat brighter in colour.
VOICE Contact call is a typical 'tseet-tseet' or 'tsit-tsit'. The song is also similar to that of Green-tailed Parrotfinch, but slightly sharper or harder; it has also been described (from captive birds) as a quiet flowing 'deedeedeedee' followed by a chattering 'day day day day – day day' and ending with a grating 'gray-gray-gray-ray-day-lay-gray'.
STATUS, HABITAT AND BEHAVIOUR
Scarce, rare or little known; erratically or seasonally common in large flocks in areas where food is abundant. Found generally above 1000 m along forest edges or in lowland open grasslands or savanna with thickets or bamboo stands. Feeds on bamboo or grass seeds. Little is known of its ecology or breeding, and its nest has never been found.
DISTRIBUTION Monotypic. Endemic to Luzon and Negros Islands, Philippines (may also occur on Mount Apo, Mindanao).
MOVEMENTS Occasionally or erratically occurs in eruptions to the adjacent lowlands.
MEASUREMENTS Wing 58; tail 46; tarsus 15; bill (from skull) 12, (from feathers) 9.
REFERENCES Dickinson *et al.* (1991), Goodwin (1982).

209 THREE-COLOURED PARROTFINCH *Erythrura tricolor* Plate 56
Indonesia

Fringilla tricolor Vieillot, 1817, Nouv. Dict. Hist. Nat. nouv. ed., 12, p. 233, Timor.

IDENTIFICATION Length 9–10 cm (3½-4 in). A small, short-tailed and practically unknown finch of restricted range in Indonesia. Very distinctive, with deep green upperparts, bright red tail and cobalt-blue face, breast and belly, becoming paler or turquoise on undertail-coverts. Unlikely to be confused with any other parrotfinch in the wild, as it is the only one found within its very small range. **DESCRIPTION** Sexes differ slightly. **Adult male:** Forehead and over eye to face, chin, throat and breast a deep royal-blue, glossy on face and throat; sides of breast to belly and flanks a paler blue. Blue on forehead merges gradually across crown (and nape) with the deep or rich green of upperparts (exceptionally, some have a wash of blue on mantle and wing-coverts); lower rump and uppertail-coverts and base of (short but pointed) tail bright red, tip and outer edges of tail brown. Wings green as upperparts but tinged yellow, with yellow-green edges to coverts and tertials; alula, primary coverts and flight feathers blackish-brown, finely edged with yellowish-green. Blue of underparts becomes paler or fades to dull greenish-blue on lower flanks (upper flanks green) and pale turquoise on vent and undertail-coverts. Bill short, almost conical with a fairly deep base, slate-grey or black. Eye dark brown, with pale blue or pale grey orbital ring. Legs and feet pale pink. **Adult female:** Paler than adult male, with face to throat and breast pale or light turquoise, becoming a dull greyish-blue on belly and washed with green on flanks; upperparts are less intense or rich green, and uppertail-coverts and base of tail orange-red. **Juvenile:** Like adult female but paler and duller still, almost grey-green above and buffish below with a strong tinge of green on throat, breast and flanks; thighs buff. Bill as that of adult, but smaller and with a yellow lower mandible in the first few weeks of life.
VOICE Very similar to but less harsh than that of Blue-faced Parrotfinch (211), a sharp 'seet seet'.
STATUS, HABITAT AND BEHAVIOUR Very little known. Status unknown. Occurs in thickets in grasslands, bamboo and eucalyptus forest edges from sea-level to 1400 m; usually in pairs or small family parties. Breeds in tops of coconut palms. Actions, behaviour and food probably very similar to those of other parrotfinches.
DISTRIBUTION Monotypic. Lesser Sunda Islands of Timor, Tanimbar, Wetar, Babar, Damar and Romang.

210 MOUNT KATANGLAD PARROTFINCH (Red-eared Parrotfinch, Mindanao Parrotfinch) *Erythrura coloria* Plate 56
Philippines

Erythrura coloria Ripley and Rabor, 1961, Postilla, Yale Univ. no. 50, p. 18, Mount Katanglad, Malaybalay, Bukidnon, Mindanao.

IDENTIFICATION Length 10 cm (4 in). A small, short-winged and short-tailed, all deep green finch with distinctive blue and red face markings; has limited distribution on high ground in central Mindanao. **Confusion species:** Unlikely confusion in the wild is with Green-tailed Parrotfinch (206), which has a green crown, upperparts and wings. Outside its relatively limited range confusion possible with Pin-tailed (207), from which it differs in size and in having red on ear-coverts, deep green underparts and a blunt-tipped tail; Three-coloured (209) also lacks red on ear-coverts and is extensively blue on underparts (both sexes). **DESCRIPTION** Sexes almost alike. **Adult male:** Forehead to forecrown, lores, cheeks and fore part of ear-coverts deep cobalt-blue; rear ear-coverts bright red. Crown to nape, sides of neck and upperparts to rump dark green. Wing-coverts and edges of flight feathers and tertials slightly darker green; alula, primary coverts and flight feathers blackish, edged finely with green; leading primaries edged pale green. Uppertail-coverts and base of tail bright red, tail becoming duller towards rather blunt tip. Chin has a few dark blue feathers (unlikely to be seen in the field), otherwise underparts almost entirely uniform dark or deep moss-green; thighs buff. Bill short, black or blackish-grey. Eye brown or dark brown, orbital ring pale grey or bluish. Legs and feet pale pink or flesh-brown. **Adult female:** Very similar to male, but has slightly less blue on face and red on ear-coverts is slightly less extensive and more orange than red (becoming deeper with age). **Juvenile:** Almost uniform dull pale green version of adult, with no blue or red on head and with duller or browner tail. Bill yellow, with a dark tip.
VOICE Call very similar to that of other parrotfinches, a high-pitched 'tseet-tseet' or 'tsit-tsit'. The song is undescribed.
STATUS, HABITAT AND BEHAVIOUR Scarce

or very uncommon within its very small range. Found only in tall grass and seeding plants in clearings and forest edges between 1150 m and 1600 m on mountains in central Mindanao. Roosts in trees in forested areas. Feeds on the ground and in vegetation on seeds of various grasses, herbaceous plants and bamboo; occasionally takes small insects.

DISTRIBUTION Monotypic. Endemic to the mountain ranges of Mount Katanglad and Mount Apo, central Mindanao, Philippines.
MEASUREMENTS Wing 53; tail 38; tarsus 17; bill 11.

211 BLUE-FACED PARROTFINCH *Erythrura trichroa*   Plate 57
Australia, Indonesia, Pacific Islands

Fringilla trichroa Kittlitz, 1835, Mem. Acad. Imp. Sci. St Petersbourg, 2, p. 8, Ualan [Kusaie], Caroline Islands.

IDENTIFICATION Length 11–12·5 cm (4½-5 in). A small and virtually all deep green finch with red or reddish-brown tail and deep violet-blue forehead and face; more often heard than seen. Widely distributed throughout many of the islands from Indonesia east to Micronesia and the northeastern tip of Australia. **Confusion species:** Overlaps with Green-tailed Parrotfinch (206), which is easily separated by tail colour and by lack of blue on face (present only on forehead); separated from Papuan Parrotfinch (212), which occurs alongside it in parts of New Guinea and with which it is almost identical, principally by size and tail length (see that species). Also overlaps in the east with Red-headed Parrotfinch (214), and juveniles of the two possibly confusable (see that species).
DESCRIPTION Sexes similar. **Adult male:** Forehead and forecrown to cheeks and ear-coverts deep or rich violet-blue; lores to base of bill black or blackish. Crown, nape and sides of neck to upper mantle deep green, sides of neck often tinged or washed with yellow. Mantle, back, scapulars and wing-coverts rich or deep green; flight feathers dark brown with fine yellowish or pale yellowish-green edges. Rump, uppertail-coverts and tapering tail rich or deep blood-red, brighter on uppertail-coverts and central tail feathers (which are slightly longer than the rest), outer tail feathers duller red and outermost dull brown or blackish with only a reddish tinge on outer edge. Underparts slightly paler or brighter green than upperparts (some show a grey wash on belly and undertail-coverts in worn plumage); thighs buffish-brown. Bill stout, black. Eye dark brown, with pale or bluish-grey orbital ring. Legs and feet pale brown or pinkish-brown.
Adult female: Generally duller or paler than adult male, with some buff or buff-brown feathers on underparts; blue on face is less extensive, yellow tinges on hindcrown, nape and upper mantle are less prominent, and red on rump to base of tail is much duller and more reddish-brown.

In worn plumage, both sexes show grey or slightly bluish-grey tips to feathers. **Juvenile:** A dull version of adult, but lacks blue on face and forehead (which is acquired gradually through blue tips to feathers); underparts greyish-green or buffish on belly. Bill entirely pale yellow at first, and darkens from tip inwards.
GEOGRAPHICAL VARIATION There is very little noticeable difference among the many races, and most are probably not separable outside their ranges; some races are probably invalid (though present information is insufficient to determine this), as individual differences and wear make birds even within the same population highly variable. The present classification of races centres on intensity of face or body plumage. Race *sigillifera* is less conspicuously tinged yellow or golden on hindcrown, nape and upper mantle and is more uniform dark green, and underparts are tinged bluish. Both *modesta* and *woodfordi* are very similar to *sigillifera*, but have a mauve-blue tinge (less extensive in *woodfordi*) and a slightly longer bill; *modesta* is paler on underparts than nominate, and *woodfordi* has paler, more yellowish-orange colour on rump to tail (as does race *pinaiae*). The bill of *pelewensis* is also large and thick-based, and the underparts are tinged pale blue. Races *clara* and *cyanofrons* are brighter, with the blue more extensive on crown, and the body uniformly bright leaf-green; *cyanofrons* has a relatively blunt-tipped bill and the blue face is tinged noticeably mauve. Race *eichhorni* has more extensive blue on face, and the red on rump is tinged with orange (as in *clara* and *sanfordi*).
VOICE Call a typical parrotfinch 'tsit-tsit' or 'stit-stit-stit-sti-it-it', also a faint insect-like high-pitched 'tip, ti-tu' or 'ti-tu-tu', a thin metallic 'tink' and a descending trill 'teerrrr', alarm a series of high-pitched notes. The song begins with the metallic trilling call, continues with a loud or shrill series of notes, several of which are repeated at intervals, and ends with a rising whistle.
STATUS, HABITAT AND BEHAVIOUR Locally variable in abundance, and probably often overlooked owing to its inconspicuous nature: in northern Australia a seldom seen resident; in New Guinea it is considered rare to see it, though frequently caught in mist-nets; but considered fairly common on eastern Caroline Islands. Inhabits rainforest, mangrove or eucalypt forest clearings and edges (usually between 1000 m and 3000 m in New Guinea, elsewhere at lower levels), where it is

found in scrub and undergrowth (on Palau Islands occurs most often in ironwood groves), also grasslands and edges of cultivation; has also been recorded on open pastures and airfields. Occurs singly, in pairs or in small (occasionally larger) flocks at all levels from the treetops to the ground or mid-level in bamboo, tall grass or herbaceous plants; often in company with Papuan Parrotfinch on New Guinea, and elsewhere in mixed-species foraging parties in the non-breeding season. Race *sigillifera* is confined to patches of rainforest, while *cyanofrons* has adapted to areas of human occupation and occurs in forest clearings, gardens, plantations and edges of roads. Race *pelewensis*, first described (from a single specimen) in 1922, has been seen on only two occasions since, both in 1976 (a total of only six birds); as there is apparently plenty of suitable habitat (the same as that for other races), the reasons for its scarcity remain unknown. Flight usually level and direct. Feeds on the ground and in growing vegetation, mainly on grass seeds, though bamboo seeds, casuarina seeds, small berries and occasionally insects taken; in New Guinea, becomes abundant when bamboo is seeding. Often flies some distance to water, and regularly does so several times a day.

DISTRIBUTION *E. t. trichroa*: Caroline Islands: Kusaie Island.

E. t. sanfordi: Latimodjon Mountains, south-central Sulawesi; has also been recorded in the Lore Lindu National Park, north-central Sulawesi.

E. t. modesta: northern Moluccas: Ternate, Tidore, Halmahera and Batjan.

E. t. pinaiae: southern Moluccas: Ceram and Buru.

E. t. sigillifera: Cape York, northeast Australia, from Princess Charlotte Bay south to Cairns and Ravenshoe; highlands of New Guinea, Manam Island, Karkar Island, Tagula Island, New Britain and New Ireland, Goodenough Island, Sudest, Dampier and Vulcan Island.

E. t. eichhorni: Bismarck Archipelago: St Matthias Island, (Mussau and Emira).

E. t. pelewensis: Palau Islands: Babelthuap, Eil Malk, Micronesia.

E. t. clara: Caroline Islands: Truk, Ponape, Pohnpei, Kosrae.

E. t. woodfordi: Guadalcanal Island and Solomon Islands.

E. t. cyanofrons: Banks Islands: Santa Maria; New Hebrides: Aoba, Ambrym, Lopevi, Efate, Erromanga, Tanna and Anneitum; Loyalty Islands: Lifu and Mare.

Possibly also present on a number of smaller islands not individually listed.

MOVEMENTS Sedentary, but some local, nomadic or altitudinal movement in the non-breeding season (especially with mixed parties of feeding birds or when bamboo is seeding). Those from the higher levels in New Guinea and Australia descend to lower levels; there may also be some movement from New Guinea to northern Australia.

MEASUREMENTS Wing 55–60. Wing of *modesta* 62–65.

REFERENCES Blakers *et al.* (1984), Frith *et al.* (1979), Goodwin (1982), King (1981), Pratt *et al.* (1987), White and Bruce (1986).

212 PAPUAN PARROTFINCH *Erythrura papuana*   Plate 58

New Guinea

Erythrura trichroa papuana Hartert, 1900, Novit. Zool., 7, p 7, Arfak Mountains.

IDENTIFICATION Length 13·5–15 cm (5½-6 in). Very similar to (but larger than) Blue-faced Parrotfinch (211), with which it overlaps in mountainous forests in three separate areas of New Guinea. The larger size, longer tail and rather larger bill should be pointers for separation, but unless seen well it may not always be possible to eliminate Blue-faced. **Confusion species:** Unlikely to be confused with any species other than Blue-faced Parrotfinch.

DESCRIPTION Sexes differ slightly. **Adult male:** In most respects a larger, longer-tailed version of Blue-faced Parrotfinch, but on most the deep blue on face and forehead extends onto crown and around eye and across ear-coverts. Hindcrown to wing-coverts and upper rump are deep green, lower rump, uppertail-coverts and tail bright or deep red; central tail feathers extend prominently about 7–8 cm (2½ in) beyond rest of tail. Flight feathers dark brown, edged with pale or bright green, broadly on secondaries. Feathers of chin and upper throat are tipped and tinged bluish; rest of underparts entirely green or deep green. Bill

large dark grey or blackish. Most closely resembles race *sigillifera* of Blue-faced, but has longer wings (than any other parrotfinch) and a larger, more robust bill; other differences which have been proposed (e.g. colour tones of body plumage) are not constant. **Adult female:** Very similar to adult male, but has less blue on head (not extending behind eye on crown) and has a pale green chin and throat with bluish tinge or tips to throat feathers. Almost identical to female Blue-faced Parrotfinch, but generally larger or more plump, with a bigger bill. **Juvenile:** Not safely separable from juvenile Blue-faced in the field, but larger bill should be diagnostic in good view.

VOICE Contact calls are very similar to those of Blue-faced Parrotfinch, including the loud trilling call. The song is a series of contact calls ending with two long trills, the first rising and the second falling, 'tsee-tsee-tsee . . . . .srrr . . . .srrrr'.

STATUS, HABITAT AND BEHAVIOUR Scarce or generally uncommon and relatively little known. Found in forests (including secondary forests), forest edges and clearings with tall grass, between

900 m and 2600 m. Often occurs with the very similar Blue-faced Parrotfinch, but usually at lower altitudes; usually singly or in pairs, never in flocks (unlike Blue-faced). Feeds in trees, usually at the top or mid-level, in fruit trees, especially on figs or fig seeds, also in oaks and in flowering trees; doubtless other seeds are taken.

DISTRIBUTION Monotypic. Widely but sparsely distributed throughout the mountains of New Guinea. In Irian Jaya, found in the Vogelkop (in the Arfak and Tamrau ranges) and Wissel Lakes area; in Papua New Guinea, found in the Thurnwald range and around Telefomin on the upper Sepik river, also in the southeast from Okapa and Aseki east to Aguan and Adelbert Mountains.

MOVEMENTS Probably sedentary.

MEASUREMENTS Wing 65–70; tarsus 14; bill (from feathers) 13.

REFERENCES Coates (1990), Goodwin (1982).

213 RED-THROATED PARROTFINCH *Erythrura psittacea*   Plate 57

New Caledonia

Fringilla psittacea Gmelin, 1789, Syst. Nat., 1, p. 903, New Caledonia.

IDENTIFICATION Length 9–10 cm (3½-4 in). A small, lively and fairly common brightly plumaged finch of extremely limited distribution. Sexes almost identical. Bright red on forehead, forecrown to ear-coverts, chin, throat to upper breast and on rump to tail; rest of plumage uniform dark green or bottle-green, slightly paler or tinged greyer on lower underparts. The only parrotfinch in New Caledonia and thus unlikely to be confused with any other species. Elsewhere, the entirely red face to centre of crown and throat and the pointed red tail are diagnostic.

DESCRIPTION Sexes almost alike. **Adult male:** Forehead to forecrown, ear-coverts, cheeks to chin, throat and upper breast bright red; lores dark brown or blackish. Crown and nape to upper rump deep or dark bottle-green extending onto wing-coverts; flight feathers blackish-brown but with bright green edges and tips, becoming slightly yellowish-green on edges of primaries (fading short of tips); tertials slightly deeper green than upperparts. Lower rump, uppertail-coverts and centre of tail bright blood-red or scarlet, becoming duller or darker red towards outer edge of tail, with outermost feathers brown and edged or tinged red. Tail graduated, with elongated central feathers coming to a blunt tip. Underparts as upperparts, but can also appear a deep sea-green; some also have a pale grey wash to belly and undertail-coverts. Bill fairly stubby with a curved culmen, black or blackish. Eye dark brown. Legs and feet pale pink or pale brown. **Adult female:** Almost identical to adult male, but has been described as paler or duller and with red on chin and throat less extensive. From skin measurements, females are smaller than males. **Juvenile:** Lacks any red on forehead or face (but first-winter birds often show red tips to front of face, chin and throat); is generally green on upperparts and dull or dingy yellowish-green below. Rump, uppertail-coverts and tail as adult, but very much duller, almost a dull orange or orange-pink in tone, and tail slightly shorter. Bill yellow or pale yellow, with blackish tip.

VOICE All calls (including the high-pitched trills) and the song are very similar to those of Blue-faced Parrotfinch (211), but song has less of a rising and falling quality and is more of a single whistling note repeated.

STATUS, HABITAT AND BEHAVIOUR Widespread and fairly common within its restricted range. Found in open areas of forest edges or clearings, bushes, scrub or trees, often at or near edges of cultivation, plantations or even gardens. Usually in pairs or small family parties or in flocks of up to 20. Feeds in growing vegetation and on the ground, on seeds of a wide range of herbaceous plants (mainly those bearing dicotyledonous seeds), but also on grass seeds and some insects, including small grasshoppers and termites, the latter caught in flight.

DISTRIBUTION Monotypic. New Caledonia.

REFERENCE Goodwin (1982).

214 RED-HEADED PARROTFINCH (Royal Parrotfinch) *Erythrura cyaneovirens*   Plate 57

South Pacific Islands

Geospiza cyaneovirens Peale, 1848, US Exploring Exped., ed. 1, Birds, p. 117, Upolu, Samoa.

IDENTIFICATION Length 10 cm (4 in). A small but rather robust, short-tailed and thick-billed finch from islands in the southwest Pacific. Adults are bluish-green with green wings and a red crown and face, and bright red on rump and tail. Considerable variation among races, individuals and according to state of the plumage. **Confusion species:** Adults are unlikely to be confused with any other parrotfinches within the native range. Pink-billed Parrotfinch (215) is larger, with an obvious pale pink or horn-coloured bill, black face and blue on crown. In the New Hebrides confusion is possible between juveniles and those of Blue-faced Parrotfinch (211), but Red-headed's larger and more robust bill and Blue-faced's lack of blue or bluish in the plumage should enable separation of any individual showing variation in plumage.

DESCRIPTION Sexes similar in some races (possibly separable in the field). **Adult male:** Forehead to crown and nape, cheeks and ear-coverts deep blood-red; hindcrown, nape and face often tipped with blue; lores dark brown or blackish. Mantle, back and scapulars to rump sea-green. Tail short, stubby and rounded, red or blood-red on central feathers, outers darker or browner on inner webs and red on outer edges. All wing-coverts as scapulars or greener; flight feathers dark brown or brownish-black, but edged finely with pale or yellowish-green. Chin and throat deep blue, becoming bluish-green on breast and sea-green on belly and pale green on flanks; undertail-coverts almost always deep green. Bill large, stout and deep at base, with curved culmen, black or blackish-grey. Eye dark red or reddish-brown, orbital ring grey. Legs and feet pink or pinkish-brown. **Adult female:** Very similar to adult male, but possibly less bright in overall tone. **Juvenile:** Juveniles (like most juvenile parrotfinches) are immediately recognisable by their yellow bills (which turn orange or orange-red before attaining the black of adults) with dark tip. Forehead to hindcrown is blue, tipped dull red, which turns red gradually with appearance of more extensively red tips (birds 6–12 months old may have multicoloured face and head, or red on forehead to forecrown and blue on face). Rest of plumage is similar to that of adult, but generally much more green than blue. Full adult plumage is attained in second winter (at approximately 20 months old).

GEOGRAPHICAL VARIATION Race *gaughrani* is very similar to nominate, but the red on head, face and tail is deeper or brighter, nape is less intensely blue, upperparts (including wings) are also greener and generally lack the blue tinge to plumage. Adult male *regia* (considered a full species, Royal Parrotfinch, by some taxonomic authorities) has a bright scarlet forehead to crown, nape and face; sides of nape, mantle and upper back are deep cobalt-blue becoming deep green with a bluish tinge on lower back and wings; rump and uppertail-coverts are bright red or vermilion, becoming duller on central tail feathers and brown on outers (which have reddish outer webs), tip of tail can also be dark brown or blackish. Entire underparts are deep cobalt-blue, becoming bluish-green on lower belly and flanks, with thighs buff-brown. Legs and feet dark brown. Females are similar, but the blue on mantle and breast is less extensive and less intense and mantle, back, wings, breast and flanks are predominantly green. Juveniles are bright or deep green on upperparts, pale on underparts, and the red on rump and uppertail-coverts is much duller or less intense than on adult; forehead and face is initially blue or grey-blue, this gradually replaced by red duller than that of adult plumage, which is not fully attained until late in

second calendar-year. A mutant or colour-phase of *regia* has the red in plumage replaced by straw-yellow. Race *efatensis* is probably inseparable (outside its native range) from *regia*. Both sexes of *serena* (which may now be extinct through destruction of its habitat) are very similar to *regia*, but have blue restricted to a band around nape and hindneck to chin, throat and breast (also some blue tinges on wing-coverts), with rest of upperparts and underparts mainly deep moss-green, slightly more yellow-green than in nominate; juveniles have forehead, crown and face to chin grey or grey-blue, with rest of plumage deep green except for red uppertail-coverts and tail. Males of the race *pealii* (considered by some authorities to be a full species, Fiji Parrotfinch, but here treated as conspecific with *cyaneovirens* and within the boundaries of variation shown by other races and individuals) have forehead to crown or hindcrown and face deep or rich scarlet and upperparts a deep green and lacking blue or bluish tinge (except possibly some blue tips on hindcrown and nape); uppertail-coverts are bright scarlet, and the tail has bright red central feathers with brown outers (some red or reddish-buff only in outer edges). Chin and throat black or blackish, becoming dark cobalt-blue on lower throat and turquoise on upper breast, fading to light green on rest of underparts. Females are generally less bright in overall plumage, and some may be separable in the field (have less red on head, and the green on sides of hindcrown reaches eye). The bill of this race (both sexes) is shorter and stubbier, and some have pinkish-grey legs and feet. Exceptional individuals (apparently a natural mutation) have entire head and face blue and are thus very similar (if not identical outside native range) to Blue-faced Parrotfinch, though latter has a longer and thinner, pointed tail. Juvenile *pealii* are similar to those of other races (see above), but lack red tips to forehead and crown (as in nominate) and have face and throat blue or blue-grey, gradually becoming red through appearance of red feather tips over following 20–24 months; bill yellow or yellowish, with a dark band at or near tip.

VOICE Call a high thin 'seep'; other calls very similar to those of the Blue-faced Parrotfinch, including the sharp or shrill trilling notes. The song is also very similar to that species and to that of Red-throated Parrotfinch (213), with a whistling note or a double note repeated for several seconds.

STATUS, HABITAT AND BEHAVIOUR Uncommon or locally common. In Samoa, a shy or retiring bird found mainly in rainforests, secondary forest or plantations; in New Hebrides also found in areas of cultivation, and in Fiji found additionally in grasslands, pastures, rice-fields and also parks and city gardens. A social or gregarious bird, occurring in pairs, small parties or flocks of up to about 30, but *regia* is rarely found in more than small family groups. Generally shy or wary, and takes cover at slightest sign of danger. Flight usually quite fast and undulating, often at considerable height; usually lands in the top of a tree (where it prefers to feed) and moves downward in search of food. Feeds high in treetops, usually on wild fig seeds (*regia* almost exclusively so) or on the seeds of casuarinas or other plants, also in vegetation, where it searches actively and with agility for grass seeds and rice; also takes some insects and their larvae, including caterpillars and spiders.

DISTRIBUTION *E. c. cyaneovirens:* Savaii and Upolu, Western Samoa.

E. c. gaughrani: Savaii, Western Samoa.

E. c. regia: Banks Island (Santa Maria) and Vanuatu (northern New Hebrides).

E. c. efatensis: Aneitum and Efaté, New Hebrides.

E. c serena: Aneitum Island, southern New Hebrides.

E. c. pealii: Fiji: Kandavu, Viti Levu, Vanua Levu and Taveuni.

MEASUREMENTS Wing of *gaughrani* (type specimen) 64; tail 32; bill 13; tarsus 18. Wing of *efatensis* 61–66·5. Wing of *serena* 65–67·5.

REFERENCES Dupont (1972), Goodwin (1982), Pratt *et al.* (1987).

215 PINK-BILLED PARROTFINCH *Erythrura kleinschmidti*　　Plate 57
South Pacific Islands (Fiji)

Amblynura kleinschmidti Finsch, 1879, Proc. Zool. Soc. London, p. 440, Viti Levu.

IDENTIFICATION Length 11 cm (4½ in). A relatively large and robust parrotfinch, with a prominent pale pink bill much larger than that of other parrotfinches. Has a black face, blue crown and nape and bright red rump, otherwise is almost entirely olive-green. Endemic to mature forests of Vitu Levu in the Fiji Islands, where unlikely to be mistaken for any other species; race *pealii* of Red-headed Parrotfinch (214) is the only other parrotfinch found within the range.

DESCRIPTION Sexes alike. **Adult:** Forehead to forecrown, lores and chin black, on some extending to just behind eye; ear-coverts pale green or yellowish-green. Crown blackish, becoming a deep or rich blue on nape; sides of the neck deep green or grass-green, tinged yellowish; mantle, back, scapulars and rump dark green; uppertail-coverts bright or brilliant red or scarlet. Tail short or somewhat stunted and rounded at tip, black. All wing-coverts and tertials as scapulars; flight feathers blackish-brown, finely edged with bright or pale green. Underparts deep green or grass-green, slightly paler than upperparts, in fresh plumage showing yellow or golden-yellow on sides of breast. Bill fairly deep at base, longer and more tapering than on any other parrotfinch, pale pink or whitish-pink; some (perhaps sub-adults or non-breeders) have a dark or black tip. Eye brown or reddish-brown. Legs and feet flesh-pink or fleshy-brown. **Juvenile:** Very similar to adult, but with a dark tip to otherwise pale orange bill; slightly duller or tinged brown on upperparts and underparts, with rump and uppertail-coverts duller or more orange.

VOICE Contact call is a typical parrotfinch 'tsee-tsee' or a 'high rather thin but carrying' single or

Individuals with dark-tipped bills are thought to be immatures.

repeated 'cheee cheee cheee'; also gives a series of clicking sounds.

STATUS, HABITAT AND BEHAVIOUR Scarce or locally common. Found only in mature rainforests or recently in secondary forest from sea-level up to about 915 m. Generally not so highly sociable or gregarious as other parrotfinches; usually alone, in pairs or in small family parties, but in non-breeding season freely joins mixed-species feeding flocks which rove through the forest understorey. Feeds mainly in trees but also on the ground, on figs, flower buds, fruit (including berries), and a variety of insects which it seeks or pursues in manner of a shrikebill (*Clytorhynchus*), vigorously probing bunches of dead leaves and cracking open dead tree-fern leaf stems with its powerful bill.

DISTRIBUTION Monotypic. Endemic to Vitu Levu Island, Fiji.

MOVEMENTS Usually sedentary within a small area of rainforest, but in non-breeding season joins mixed-species flocks.

REFERENCES Clunie (1973), Pratt *et al.* (1987).

GENUS *CHLOEBIA*

One species. Gouldian Finch is the most brightly coloured finch of the Estrildid group. The structure and plumage provide conflicting signs as to its nearest relatives, the depth of colour suggests some affinity with the two long-tailed grenadiers of Africa, its behavioural, vocal and some plumage details, together with the mouth tubercules of nestlings, show some relationship with the parrotfinches *Erythrura* and (some) of the true munias *Lonchura*, on wing structure the grass-finches *Poephila*; some authors have suggested on plumage similarity (not pattern) ties with Java Sparrow (254).

216 GOULDIAN FINCH *Chloebia gouldiae*   Plate 65
Australia

Amadina gouldiae Gould, 1844, Birds Australia, pt. 15, pl. 88 (also Proc. Zool. Soc. London, 12, p. 5.), Victoria River, Northern Territory.

IDENTIFICATION Length 12·5–14 cm (5–5½ in). An unmistakable bird with a very rich or striking plumage of intense brilliance in both sexes, but males are more highly or deeply coloured. Widely kept in captivity, where it produces colour variants. No races, but three colour variations exist which differ in head pattern from red-headed to golden- or black-headed, the latter being by far the commonest (outnumbering red-headed 3:1); there are also differences in the males between large circular or oval breast patch. Very unlikely to be mistaken for any other species.

DESCRIPTION Sexes differ slightly. **Adult male:** Forehead to crown, face and chin to upper throat either (i) all jet-black, (ii) bright or deep red except for black chin and throat, or (iii) rich, deep yellow or orange-yellow except for black chin and throat. Hindcrown, sides of nape to sides of throat and lower throat a complete band of turquoise-blue; nape green or pale green. Mantle, back, scapulars and upper rump rich or deep grass green fading to paler turquoise blue on lower rump and uppertail-coverts. Tail long and graduated with central pair of feathers having fine elongated projecting points, entirely black. All wing-coverts and flight feathers grey or greyish-brown, but most of coverts, secondaries and tertials are overlain by the long green or grass-green scapulars so that only dark tips of primaries show; edges of primaries finely yellow or green. Chin (and upper throat) black; a fine (almost invisible) band of turquoise across throat above a large and almost circular or oval patch of purple (on red-headed birds it is pinkish, tinged slightly with purple) on breast; lower breast, flanks and belly yellow (brightest on lower breast); vent, thighs and undertail-coverts white. Bill deep at base, quite strong-looking (for the size of the bird), very pale or bone colour with red or reddish tip (orange-yellow-headed birds have yellowish tip). Legs and feet light yellow or pale straw. **Adult female:** Similar in overall plumage to male (in each respective colour phase), but generally much duller and lacking brilliance or intensity of male. On red- and golden- or yellow-headed birds, the black is more extensive on sides of chin and throat; also much paler or washed-out on underparts, with the breast patch pink or deep pink. Lacks the very long central tail feathers, but has a shorter central projection beyond rest of tail feathers. **Juvenile:** Head and face grey, slightly darker on lores and tinged with olive on nape and sides of neck. Mantle, back and scapulars a dull olive-green; rump and uppertail-coverts pale greyish-green, tinged light buff; wings and tail greenish, but wings (as on adults) largely covered by long scapulars. Has a very short tail, lacking long black feathers or elongated central tips of adults. Chin pale greyish, becoming buffish-brown (quite warm) on throat and breast on immature male but greyish or dull greyish on young female; flanks and upper belly yellowish; lower belly to undertail-coverts white. Often breeds at an early age in 'immature' plumage. Bill short and stout, dark grey upper and tip to lower mandible, with pale pink base to lower.

VOICE A single 'sit' or 'ssit' is the usual contact call, often given as a short series of notes, occasionally uttered as a drawn-out 'sree' or 'sreet'; alarm a similar but sharper 'set-set'; young birds may give a 'dyit' note. The song is a high-pitched, almost inaudible continuous series of whispering, hissing or whining notes and low clicking sounds.

STATUS, HABITAT AND BEHAVIOUR Scarce or locally (seasonally?) common; has declined considerably in northern Queensland and south of the Gulf of Carpentaria, the widespread burning of grass in the range being considered the principal reason. Black-headed birds are most frequent (about 75% of the population) and golden- or yellow-headed birds very rare (one in several thousand). Inhabits dry grassy plains with scattered trees, often near water or in tall bushes or other vegetation along rivers, creeks or streams; in the wet season takes to woods and scrub, particularly with spinifex; avoids human habitation. Highly social, usually in small parties or flocks, and nests loosely colonially; occasionally in large flocks when not breeding. Often active throughout the day, and frequently sunbathes. Usually shy and secretive, and takes cover when disturbed or alarmed; often flicks its tail in an agitated manner. Feeds in tall grass or scrub (rarely on the ground), on a variety of grass and plant seeds, especially sorghum; in the rainy season readily chases and takes flying insects.

DISTRIBUTION Monotypic. Northern Australia, from King Sound east through the Kimberley range to the southeast Gulf of Carpentaria, Leichhardt river region, eastwards (more thinly spread) through northeast Queensland to about Charters Towers.

MOVEMENTS Sedentary and partially migratory, with regular southward movement during the wet season; breeds in southern part of the range during the rainy season and retreats northwards in winter.
REFERENCES Frith *et al.* (1979), Goodwin (1982).

GENUS *AIDEMOSYNE*

One species. Plum-headed Finch is of uncertain affinities. Similar in size and some actions to the species within *Neochmia*, may possibly be closer to the distant African silverbills or Madagascar Munia (219–221) in bill structure, but the display is similar to that of some Asian munias and the spots on wings and rump also connect it to the Star Finch in *Neochmia* and the Pictorella Finch in *Lonchura*.

217 PLUM-HEADED FINCH (Cherry Finch) *Aidemosyne modesta*
Plate 62

Australia

Amadina modesta Gould 1837, Synops. Birds Australia, pt 1, pl. 10, Upper Hunter River, New South Wales.

IDENTIFICATION Length 10–11 cm (4–4¼ in). A small brown waxbill-sized finch, with sombre brown upperparts, white spots on the wings and bars on the rump and uppertail-coverts. Has a dark reddish-brown cap (smaller on female), black lores and the male and black chin (latter white on female). The white underparts are closely barred with brown. Sociable and often in large flocks.
Confusion species: Possible confusion likely with Spotted Munia (229), but Plum-headed's white face and dark cap (and chin of male), together with fine barring (not chevrons) and black (not yellowish) tail, should separate it.
DESCRIPTION Sexes similar. **Adult male:** Forehead to crown dark reddish-brown, appearing almost chocolate-brown in the field (becomes black in worn plumage); lores to slightly behind eye black, lower lores to cheeks white; ear-coverts and sides of neck white, finely barred with brown. Hindcrown and nape to mantle, back and scapulars pale brown or light tawny-brown, tips of lower scapulars white; rump deeper or warmer brown, lower rump and uppertail-coverts all broadly edged and tipped white, forming thin bars. Tail graduated, with elongated black central feathers pointed, all outer feathers tipped with white, decreasing in extent towards centre of tail. Lesser coverts as upperparts but with small or fine white tips (which often show as spots), median coverts the same but with darker or blackish-brown subterminal spots, greater coverts slightly warmer brown, tipped with white; alula, primary coverts and flight feathers dark or blackish-brown, flight feathers edged warmer or sandy-brown; tertials uniform with upperparts, broadly edged white on tips of outer webs. Chin to upper throat deep reddish-brown or black; lower throat and sides of throat, breast, flanks and upper belly white, closely barred with brown; centre of belly, vent, thighs and undertail-

coverts uniform white. Bill small and waxbill-like, black with a paler or bluish base to lower mandible. Legs and feet pale pink or flesh-brown. **Adult female:** Very similar to adult male except for a duller cap, often divided from the black lores by a thin white supercilium; chin and upper throat white or off-white (not black), and plumage generally duller with less prominent (or less complete) barring on underparts. **Juvenile:** Similar to adult female. Crown and forehead brown, dull buff supercilium, lores grey-brown; upperparts plain brown (warmer than adult), lacking spots on scapulars; rump and uppertail-coverts loosely barred buff and brown. Wings as adult, but tips of tertials, greater coverts and median coverts cream (not white). Underparts diffusely barred brownish. First-year birds assume dark cap in spring, and are usually whiter (often without any barring) below; spots on tips of wing-coverts, white on adults, are buffish on first-year birds.
VOICE Contact call is a single 'tlip', 'tleep' or 'tyeet', occasionally uttered as a double note or as a more drawn-out note; alarm also a single or double note, 'tyait'. The song begins with an almost inaudible series of high-pitched chirps, followed by gargling notes which become louder, and ends with flute-like notes.
STATUS, HABITAT AND BEHAVIOUR Scarce or locally common, occasionally abundant; irruptive, and in some areas within the range very erratic in occurrence. Found in open woodlands and tall savanna-type grasslands and reeds, often near water or swamps; also occurs in scrub or thickets on lowland plains, though appears to avoid the coastal plains. A highly sociable bird, often in pairs but more usually encountered in winter in rather noisy flocks which can number several hundred; mixes freely with other finches in non-breeding season, especially Double-barred Finch (202);

tame and generally approachable. In the breeding season usually alone or in pairs and quiet or inconspicuous. Flight fairly fast or rapid, only slightly undulating. Feeds on the ground or by climbing stems of plants or grasses, mainly on a variety of grass seeds but also known to take small insects. Makes frequent visits to drink.

DISTRIBUTION Monotypic. Eastern Queensland east of Winton and south from about Townsville through eastern New South Wales to about 35° S, though appears to avoid the coastal plains.

MOVEMENTS Partial migrant in varying numbers, moving north in the non-breeding season and returning south to breed in summer; occasionally occurs north to Atherton, north Queensland, in winter and has occurred in northern Victoria in summer. Also very nomadic over a wide area in both breeding and non-breeding seasons.

REFERENCES Frith *et al.* (1979), Goodwin (1982), Pizzey and Doyle (1980).

GENUS *LONCHURA*

Thirty-five species. Munias and mannikins are finches with a generally short or graduated tail and comparatively stout bill. They feed principally in grassland-type vegetation on seeds. Within this genus are found species from Africa east to Australia and the remote Pacific islands. Some authors have separated the African species, all three silverbills and the Madagascar Munia into a subgenus within the genus.

218 INDIAN SILVERBILL (White-throated Munia) *Lonchura malabarica*

Plate 51

Arabia and Oriental

Loxia malabarica Linnaeus, 1758, Syst. Nat., ed. 10, 1, p. 175, India; restricted to Malabar by Baker, 1926, Fauna Brit. India, Birds, ed. 2, p. 89.

Note: This and African Silverbill (219) are two poorly (or unconvincingly) separated species which may in time, with the spread and eventual merging of the ranges, produce recognisable hybrids in parts of the Middle East. At such time they may warrant reclassification as a single species, but for the present are treated here (in agreement with most current taxonomic authorities) as two separate species.

IDENTIFICATION Length 10 cm (4 in). A small, slender, brown and white waxbill-sized finch with a distinctively shaped grey or blue-grey bill. Generally pale sandy or caramel-brown on upperparts, with black wings, white rump and black tail; the underparts are almost entirely white or silvery-white, except for a buffish wash on the flanks. **Confusion species:** African Silverbill is very similar, but has prominent black rump and uppertail-coverts; it also has a slightly larger bill, darker face lacking thin supercilium, darker chin and throat, faint barring or vermiculations (usually visible only at close range) on wing-coverts, tertials and across lower back, and a slightly shorter tail. For differences from the initially similar White-rumped Munia (225), see that species.

DESCRIPTION Sexes alike. **Adult:** Forehead to crown sandy-brown with small or fine dark feather centres; face a light sandy or yellowish-buff, except for white or whitish lores and area over eye. Hindcrown and nape uniform light sandy-brown, becoming slightly darker on mantle, back and scapulars; rump and uppertail-coverts white. Tail fairly long and distinctly graduated, with elongated central feathers projecting to a point, black. Median and inner greater coverts sandy-brown; outer greaters, alula, primary coverts, secondaries (except inner secondaries, which are blackish-brown) and all primaries black; tertials sandy-brown with pale buff tips. Underparts almost entirely silvery-white, except for buffish-brown wash on extreme sides of breast and sides of lower neck (shoulders) and slightly more heavily on flanks, which are faintly barred. Bill distinctive, deep at base, conical, with slight curve to culmen, pale grey or greyish-blue. Eye brown or dark brown, with grey orbital ring. Legs and feet pinkish or light purplish-grey. In worn plumage often looks paler, duller or generally greyish, and bill is darker. **Juvenile:** Similar to adult, but distinguished by brownish-buff face. The rump is mottled with buffish-brown and tip of tail is more rounded (without elongated central feathers). The breast is buffish (not white), lacks the faint barring on flanks, and wings and tail have brown edges.

VOICE Contact call is a sharp 'cheep', often repeated; also a soft 'seesip', a trilling 'zip-zip' and a harsh 'tchwit'. The song is a rambling series of twittering 'cheep' or 'chirp' notes.

STATUS, HABITAT AND BEHAVIOUR Common or locally common. Usually a dry-country or forest-edge bird, inhabits open grasslands, savannas, scrub, semi-desert, open woodlands and the edges of cultivation. Very social, usually in flocks of varying size; breeds and roosts communally. Characteristically flicks or switches its tail from side to side when active, excited or alarmed. Feeds on the ground but also in vegetation, actively feeding in an agile manner from seedheads, often on or beside paths, tracks or clearings in grassland; majority of food is the small seeds of grasses and sedges, but also takes millet and rice, small insects and their eggs or larvae.

DISTRIBUTION Monotypic. Eastern Province of Saudi Arabia, Abu Dhabi and the eastern United Arab Emirates, northern Oman, southeast Iran, southern Baluchistan to lowland peninsular India (up to 1200 m), southern (terai) Nepal, Sikkim to west and central Bangladesh, and northern, eastern and southeast Sri Lanka. The range is slowly expanding westwards and now breeds in some of the desert oases of eastern central Saudi Arabia and at Eilat, southern Israel; the first (3) records for Jordan occurred in March 1989 and November 1990.

MOVEMENTS Partial migrant; a summer visitor to some parts of the range, e.g. Chitral, northern Pakistan. Non-breeding flocks wander at random throughout the range and into remote deserts and mountain ranges.

MEASUREMENTS Wing of male 55–58, of female 53–57; tail of male 39–56, of female 41–50; tarsus 13–15; bill (from skull) 10–11. Weight 10–14.

REFERENCES Ali and Ripley (1983), Harrison (1964), Hollom *et al.* (1988).

219 AFRICAN SILVERBILL *Lonchura cantans* Plate 51
Africa and Arabia

Loxia cantans Gmelin, 1789, Syst. Nat., 1, p. 859, Africa; restricted to Dakar, Senegal, by W.L. Sclater and Mackworth-Praed, 1918, Ibis, p 440.

See note on previous species regarding the taxonomic relationships of these two silverbills.

IDENTIFICATION Length 10 cm (4 in). Very similar in size, shape and general plumage to Indian Silverbill (218), from which it is poorly or weakly separated. Overlaps in range with Indian (and may interbreed in southern Arabian states in the near future). **Confusion species:** For differences from Indian Silverbill see below. Unlikely to be confused with any other species of African finch; all similar waxbills are darker, have a smaller or thinner bright red bill and a red stripe through eye.

DESCRIPTION Sexes alike. **Adult:** As Indian Silverbill, but has a darker or browner or more sandy-brown face which is more uniform with crown and nape compared with generally pale or whitish-buff lower face (and over eye) of Indian; general tone of upperparts is slightly more buffish sandy-brown, with fine buff-brown bars or vermiculations on inner greater coverts, tertials and (rather obscurely) across lower back (all generally visible only at close range). The most obvious difference in the field is the black rump and uppertail-coverts (uniform with tail). Tail same shape (but shorter) and colour as Indian Silverbill's but some female African may show a brown or reddish-brown tinge in tail. Chin and throat light sandy-brown or sometimes slightly browner, with darker feather centres on chin; breast light or pale buff, sides of breast and flanks washed a light sandy-brown; belly, vent and undertail-coverts buffish-white. The bill is slightly larger and marginally longer than on Indian, bluish-grey or slightly paler. Eye dark, with distinctive pale blue (not grey) orbital ring. **Juvenile:** Similar to adult above, but with light buff edges (and tips) to tertials, lacks vermiculations and has brown edges to otherwise black tail; chin and throat faintly barred. Bill much as adult.

GEOGRAPHICAL VARIATION Race *orientalis* is slightly darker or deeper sandy-brown on upperparts, with close barring somewhat more pronounced, face is less buff, and underparts are also paler. Interbreeds with nominate where ranges overlap in East Africa.

VOICE Calls very similar to those of Indian Silverbill. The song is a rapidly repeated, gently rising and falling trill of single and then slurred double notes.

STATUS, HABITAT AND BEHAVIOUR Widespread but locally common. Restricted to dry or arid savanna zones, where it inhabits thornscrub, open acacia woodland and edges of cultivation, usually near (or within flying distance of) water. Tame and easily approachable. Highly social and usually in flocks, the size of which depends on season; in the non-breeding season often in large roosting flocks, but occasionally recorded alone or in pairs; where the ranges overlap often in mixed flocks with Grey-headed Silverbill (220). Feeds mostly on the ground (rarely on growing vegetation), on a variety of small grass and weed seeds; also takes a few small insects.

DISTRIBUTION *L. c. cantans*: central Mauritania (Atar), Senegal and Gambia (where scarce) east and southeast to southern Mali (north to 17° N), Niger (Air province), Chad, Burkina Faso, northern Ghana, Nigeria and northern Cameroon to south Sudan, possibly also in extreme north Zaire.

L. c. orientalis: extreme southeast Egypt (Gebel Elba), east Sudan, southwest Saudi Arabia (Red Sea coastal lowlands and foothills of the Hejaz and Asir, north to Jeddah, about 22° N), southwest Oman (Dhofar), the Tihamah of North Yemen and possibly into South Yemen, south through Ethiopia (except Red Sea islands) and Somalia to Kenya, north-east Uganda and northeast Tanzania (exceptionally south to Dodoma). Occurrences in Saudi Arabia and elsewhere in the Gulf States may possibly refer to escapes from captivity or to escapes now breeding in the wild. Has been introduced into Hawaiian Islands, where now widespread from Hawaii to Oahu; also introduced into Puerto Rico in early 1960s and apparently locally common. In 1965 a pair successfully bred on Merritt Island, Florida.

MOVEMENTS In the non-breeding season flocks roam in nomadic fashion throughout the range. Has occurred in southern Algeria, at Tamanrassat (April 1970).

MEASUREMENTS Wing 50–57; tail 37–44; tarsus c12; bill 9·5–10.

REFERENCES Etchécopar and Hüe (1967), Goodwin (1982), Hall (1970), Hollom et al. (1988).

220 GREY-HEADED SILVERBILL *Lonchura griseicapilla*   Plate 51
East Africa

Pitylia caniceps Reichenow, 1879, Ornith. Centralbl., 4, p. 139, Massa, Tana River, Kenya.

IDENTIFICATION Length 11·5 cm (4½ in). A small and distinctive East African finch with a relatively small range. Similar to African Silverbill (219) in size, but with a grey head and white-speckled face; pinkish-brown upperparts, with white rump and uppertail-coverts; wings and tail black, tail shorter and without elongated central feathers of African, with which it sometimes occurs. **Confusion species:** Adults are unlikely to be confused with any other species; immatures are probably confusable with those of African Silverbill, but white (not black) rump is immediately distinctive. **DESCRIPTION** Sexes alike. **Adult:** Forehead to nape and sides of neck grey or almost silver-grey; face (except blackish lores) the same but with forehead (and slightly over eye), cheeks, ear-coverts, chin and upper throat finely tipped white or silvery-white, creating a very fine speckled pattern. Mantle, back and scapulars warm brown, tinged pink in fresh plumage (fading to pale brown when worn); rump and uppertail-coverts pale creamy or white. Tail slightly graduated with rounded tip, black, tips of outer two feathers often white. Median and greater coverts warm or dark brown, often edged or tipped slightly paler; alula, primary coverts and flight feathers black on outer edges, browner or blacker-brown on inner webs; tertials as median and greater coverts. Lower throat usually blacker than grey upper; rest of underparts peachy-orange tinged with pink or buffish-brown, paler on vent and undertail-coverts. Bill similar in shape to that of African Silverbill, but slightly shorter, bluish-grey or darker on upper mandible. Eye dark, with pale greyish orbital ring. Legs and feet dark grey or blackish, soles whitish. **Juvenile:** Paler or duller than adults. Generally buffish-grey on head and face, and lacks white tips to face, chin and throat (gradually assumes these in first-winter/first-summer plumage); mantle, back and scapulars also pale brown or buffish-brown; rump and uppertail-coverts creamy-buff; tertials have pale buff fringes; and underparts are paler buff-brown than on adults. Bill slightly darker than adult's.

VOICE Contact call is a high-pitched weak trill, alarm a longer drawn-out version of this note. The song is similar to the call notes, but begins with soft and whispering notes and becomes louder towards the end.

STATUS, HABITAT AND BEHAVIOUR Common, locally common or uncommon. Inhabits dry bush grasslands and acacia or thornscrub country, occasionally found on the edge of cultivated areas. Gregarious and social in small flocks, often mixing with African Silverbill in areas of overlap. Regularly comes to waterholes and streams to drink. Feeds on a variety of small grass seeds and other small weed seeds; apparently also takes small quantities of insects, especially when feeding young.

DISTRIBUTION Monotypic. Southern Ethiopia (rare) through Kenya (where uncommon, most records from south) to northern and central Tanzania (exceptionally east to Dar es Salaam).

MOVEMENTS Generally resident, but wanders widely at random in the non-breeding season; a dry-season visitor in small numbers to extreme southeast Sudan.

MEASUREMENTS Wing 55–62; tarsus 15; bill (from feathers) 9.

REFERENCE Goodwin (1982).

221 MADAGASCAR MUNIA (Madagascar Mannikin, Bib-finch)
Lonchura nana   Plate 51
Madagascar

Pyrrhula nana Pucheran, 1845, Rev. Zool. [Paris], 8, p. 52, Madagascar.

IDENTIFICATION Length 9·5–10 cm (3½-4 in). Restricted to Madagascar. A tiny greyish-brown finch, with dark lores separated by a pale area from the black 'bib'; has pale yellow rump and uppertail-coverts contrasting with a black tail. The underparts are pinkish-buff or tinged with grey, reddish-buff on flanks, with dark tips forming crescents on sides of breast and flanks. Within its native range unlikely to be confused with any other species.

DESCRIPTION Sexes alike. **Adult:** Forehead to crown pale grey, becoming duller grey on crown; nape and sides of neck brownish-grey. Lores black, cheeks and malar region pale or creamy-white (tinged duller or greyer in worn plumage); ear-coverts pale grey as forehead. Mantle, back and scapulars brown or greyish-brown; rump and uppertail-coverts pale yellow, rather dull in tone or with black feather bases showing. Tail fairly short and graduated, with central pair of feathers longer than the others (but do not project), black or blackish-brown. Median coverts and inner greater coverts uniform with scapulars; outer greaters, alula, primary coverts and flight feathers blackish-brown; tertials paler grey-brown towards tip. Chin and upper throat a bib-like patch of black; rest of underparts pinkish-buff or pinkish tinged with grey, slightly more reddish on flanks and undertail-coverts, with feather tips to breast, sides of breast and flanks darker (form spots or crescents). Bill short, stout and conical, blackish upper mandible, lower reddish or pale pink-horn. Eye dark, with paler orbital ring. Legs and feet pink or flesh-pink. When sexes together, males can be separated by their heavier or deeper plumage coloration. **Juvenile:** Generally dull warm brown above with less

grey than on adult, some showing fine darker mottling on crown and nape; rump and uppertail-coverts pale buff or buffish-brown, tinged with reddish; tail brown or brownish-black. Underparts buffish-brown, slightly duller, sometimes with some dark mottling on breast and flanks. Adult plumage is not assumed until first summer (or slightly later).

VOICE Call a soft 'pit' and a more metallic drawn-out 'pitsri'. The song is a short purring or rattling burst of notes, often repeated.

STATUS, HABITAT AND BEHAVIOUR Widely distributed; common or locally common (especially in north). Occurs in a variety of habitats from sea-level to about 2000 m, in forests or forest edge, woodlands, scrub, grasslands with bushes to plains, marshes, edges of cultivation and in some areas also in villages. Usually in pairs, small flocks or family parties; also occurs in mixed flocks with other seedeaters. Very waxbill-like in many of its habits and actions. Feeds actively in vegetation and on the ground, principally on grass seeds and other small seeds, but relatively little studied in the wild; possibly also takes some insects and their larvae.

DISTRIBUTION Monotypic. Endemic to Madagascar, mainly in northern half, though there are less frequent records for the whole island (those from the south are widely scattered).

MOVEMENTS Resident and sedentary.

MEASUREMENTS Wing 44; tarsus 11; bill (from feathers) 7.

REFERENCES Dee (1986), Goodwin (1982).

222 BRONZE MANNIKIN *Lonchura cucullata* Plate 52
Africa

Spermestes cucullata Swainson, 1837, Birds W. Africa, 1, p. 201, West Africa; type from Senegal.

IDENTIFICATION Length 9–10 cm (3½-4 in). A small, short-tailed and compact little finch with a thickset bill; common and widespread over much of Africa. An incessant nest-builder, and almost always in small flocks in which most birds are likely to be related to each other. Has an entirely black head to chin, throat and centre of breast. Mantle, back and wings dark brown, tinged greyish, scapulars glossed with green, rump and uppertail-coverts barred black-and-white. Has white underparts except for large smudges of black on sides of breast, becoming black crescents on flanks. Considerable individual variation in plumage resulting from age or abrasion. **Confusion species:** All three African mannikins (excluding Madagascar (221)) are very similar on a brief view, but can be easily separated once seen well. Black-and-white Mannikin (223), including chestnut-backed race *nigriceps*, has a greater amount of pure black on head, face, chin, throat and upper breast and (in *nigriceps* and *poensis*) fine white bars across base of flight feathers; nominate race also lacks black-and-white barring on rump and uppertail-coverts (on *nigri-*

ceps and *poensis*, rump and uppertail-coverts finely barred). Magpie Mannikin (224) is larger, with a bigger bill, has a warmer brown mantle, back and wings, lacks barring on rump and uppertail-coverts, has white on upper breast (black restricted to chin and throat), and the bars on sides of breast and flanks often become a smudged area (instead of individual bars or crescents).

DESCRIPTION Sexes alike. **Adult:** Forehead to crown, nape, face, sides of neck, chin, throat and centre of breast black or blackish-brown, with a slight purplish gloss or sheen on face and sides of breast (some also have the crown glossy black). Mantle, back and scapulars brown, tinged or washed slightly with grey or buffish-grey in worn plumage; outer scapulars dark brown, glossed with bottle-green; rump and uppertail-coverts broadly barred black-and-white. Tail short and rounded, black-brown. Lesser, median and greater coverts dull dark brown, almost dark chocolate-brown, with paler or warm brown fringes and tips; alula, primary coverts and flight feathers black, all finely edged browner, more broadly so on inner secondaries; tertials warm brown with darker inner webs. Underparts from sides of breast almost entirely white; sides of lower breast and flanks barred brown (or dark brown), forming broad crescents extending along flanks; central flanks blackish, glossed with bottle-green; undertail-coverts white, finely barred blackish-brown. Bill short and rather stubby or deep at base, black upper mandible, pale greyish or bluish-grey lower. Legs and feet black or blackish-grey. **Juvenile:** Entirely pale or dull buff-brown, with head and face dark brown and with buffish grey-brown on chin, throat and breast. Mantle, back, scapulars and wings brown, with some buffish-brown edges and tips to coverts and secondaries; flight feathers otherwise dark brown. Rump, uppertail-coverts and tail as adult, though rump may be duller or pale buff-brown; underparts buffish, with browner-buff on sides of lower breast and flanks. Bill all dark greyish-horn.

GEOGRAPHICAL VARIATION Race *scutata* is slightly more extensively barred on upper flanks and lacks any solid glossy black patch; the rump and uppertail-coverts are finely or less noticeably barred black-and-white and may appear all dark. Generally lacks any gloss or sheen on sides of breast. Where the ranges meet or overlap, intermediates occur.

VOICE Call a wheezy or buzzing 'tsek' or 'chik, chik, chikka'. The song is a series of 'chi-chu, che-ri-hit' notes run together or frequently repeated.

STATUS, HABITAT AND BEHAVIOUR Common and widespread. Occurs from sea-level up to 2150 m, but more usually below 1500 m, in open or semi-open woodland country with bushes, scrub, edges of cultivation, marshes or swamp edges; a common bird in and around gardens, villages and towns. In parts of the range (principally in West Africa) considered a pest as it feeds on rice and grain crops. Very social, almost always in parties or flocks (which appear to be dominated by a single adult male); often associates with waxbills

and other mannikins. Spends long periods nest-building, both for breeding and for roosting; the whole flock is involved in the construction of the roost nest, which may be dismantled and reassembled daily. Very prolific, raising several broods a year. Tame and often very approachable, taking alarm only at the last moment. Body contact between members of the flock is frequent during roosting or even while perched, and pairs often indulge in allopreening. The short wings and tail and rather rounded body give it a weak or fluttering flight, often appearing uncertain of its direction (especially when flushed from the ground); rarely flies long distances. Feeds on the ground or from stems of long grass (even, apparently, upside-down) mostly on grass seeds including millet but in some areas also eats considerable quantities of rice or grain; takes termites and flying ants in flight and may well eat other insects; has also been seen taking nectar and strands of filamentous green algae.

DISTRIBUTION *L. c. cucullata:* Senegal and Gambia to Sierra Leone and east to Guinea, southern Mali (to 14° N), southern Burkina Faso, Ghana, Nigeria, Cameroon, Central African Republic to Uganda, south and southwest Sudan and west Kenya; south through Gabon, Congo to northwest Angola, also São Tomé and Principe.

L. c. scutata: west Ethiopia and eastern Sudan south through Kenya, Tanzania, Zanzibar, Pemba Island, Mafia Island, Comoro Islands, west to southern Zaire, Zambia, Malawi, Zimbabwe to northern and eastern Angola, Mozambique, eastern Transvaal, Natal and eastern Cape Province, South Africa.

Has also been introduced into Puerto Rico.

MOVEMENTS Wanders widely at random throughout the range in search of ripening food.

MEASUREMENTS Wing 47–51·5; tail 30–35; tarsus 11–12·5; bill (culmen) 9–10.

REFERENCE McLachlan and Liversidge (1978).

223 BLACK-AND-WHITE MANNIKIN *Lonchura bicolor*   Plate 52

Africa

Amadina bicolor Fraser, 1843, Proc. Zool. Soc. London, 1842, p. 145, Cape Palmas, Liberia.

IDENTIFICATION Length 9·5–10 cm (3¾–4 in). Very similar in size, shape and build to Bronze Mannikin (222), but has blacker plumage and slightly longer bluish bill. Upperparts generally black (except races *nigriceps*, *woltersi* and *minor*, which have deep chestnut on mantle, back and wings) with a glossy green tinge and with variable amount of black-and-white barring at base of flight feathers. Chin, throat and breast also black, flanks barred with black, rest of underparts white. Has a distinctive thin whistling call in flight. **Confusion species:** For differences from Bronze Mannikin, see that species. Black-backed birds are unlikely to be confused with any other small African finch, and

all races, including the brown-backed, are unlikely to be confused with any other species once the diagnostic black-and-white barring on wing is seen. Brown-backed birds generally are much warmer or richer brown than the other species of African mannikin.

DESCRIPTION Sexes alike. **Adult:** Entire head and upperparts to rump and tail jet-black with a faint glossy green sheen (except on tail). All wing-coverts jet-black; flight feathers black, tertials also jet-black with two small white spots on lower two. Chin, throat and breast black, flanks barred black and white, rest of underparts pure white. Bill fairly deep at base, with curved culmen, bluish-grey or occasionally greyish-horn. Legs and feet dark olive or blackish. **Juvenile:** Generally dull brown on head, face and upperparts; primaries and tail black or blackish-brown, primaries finely edged white at base. Sides of neck grey or grey-brown, becoming buffish on chin and throat, pale buff on breast and pale peachy-buff on flanks; belly and undertail-coverts pale buff or whitish.

GEOGRAPHICAL VARIATION Race *poensis* is very similar to nominate, but has a large patch of black-and-white barring extending across bases of primaries, secondaries and lower two tertials; rump and uppertail-coverts are also finely barred or spotted (on tips) with white, and the black feathers on lower and sides of the breast are finely tipped white in fresh plumage. The three races *nigriceps*, *woltersi* and *minor* are often referred to as (or treated as a separate species) the Red-backed Mannikin, all having the mantle, back, wing-coverts and tertials chestnut or deep chestnut-brown; head, face, chin, throat and breast are jet-black, and the flanks are also slightly less barred but more spotted with black on white; *minor* is the smallest race and has faint brown and black bars at base of flight feathers. Juveniles of all three races are generally a lighter or warmer reddish-brown, especially on mantle, back and scapulars.

VOICE Contact calls are a soft 'kip' (given with bill closed) and a short piping or whistling 'seeet-seeet', usually given in flight; alarm call is a short harsh note. The song is a short series of contact notes run together.

STATUS, HABITAT AND BEHAVIOUR Common or locally common. Occurs in grass-lands, savanna with bushes or thickets, forest edges and clearings, edges of cultivation often near marshes, swamps or moist areas, up to 1500 m or exceptionally to 2200 m. Generally occurs in less open areas than Bronze Mannikin, with which it often mixes on edges of (and less frequently in)

towns and villages; also often found with Common Waxbill (182). Usually in small flocks of up to 100. All other habits are fairly similar to those of Bronze Mannikin. Food also as latter, but spends more time foraging on grasses, plants or in bushes; feeds on seeds etc., and takes more insects than Bronze Mannikin (including termites in flight); has been seen taking filamentous algae and also feeds on oil-palm.

DISTRIBUTION *L. b. bicolor*: Guinea-Bissau southeast and east to Guinea, southern Mali (to about 12° N), Sierra Leone, Liberia (Mount Nimba), Ghana, Togo, discontinuously through Nigeria (except for coastal area) to Cameroon.

L. b. poensis: Cameroon and Fernando Po south to north Angola and east through the Congo, Central African Republic and Zaire to extreme southern Sudan (Lotti forest), southwest and south Ethiopia, Uganda, western Kenya, Rwanda, Burundi and Tanzania.

L. b. nigriceps: southern Somalia, central and eastern Kenya, eastern Zaire, Tanzania, Zanzibar, Pemba Island, Mafia Island, northeast Zambia, Malawi, northern and east Zimbabwe and Mozambique to eastern Transvaal and Natal, South Africa.

L. b. minor: southern Somalia.

L. b. woltersi: southeast Zaire and northwest Zambia.

Intermediates between the races occur in overlap areas.

MOVEMENTS Usually sedentary, but some may wander locally or to lower altitudes in non-breeding season. A vagrant to southwest Senegal (ten together, January 1977).

MEASUREMENTS Wing 47–51·5; tail 30–33; tarsus 12–13·5; bill 11–12. Wing of *poensis* 48–54. Weight of male 8–9·5, of female 6·5.

REFERENCES Goodwin (1982), Morel and Morel (1990), Savalli (1989), Sinclair (1987), Slater (1974).

224 MAGPIE MANNIKIN *Lonchura fringilloides* Plate 52

Africa

Plocus fringilloides Lafresnaye, 1835, Mag. Zool. [Paris], 5, pl. 48, India; amended to Liberia by Hartlaub, 1857, Syst. Ornith. Westafrika, p. 147.

IDENTIFICATION Length 13 cm (5 in). Similar in shape to Bronze (222) and Black-and-white (223) Mannikins, and with noticeably much larger or heavier weaver-like bills. General black-and-white appearance, with black on head to nape, face, chin and throat, white breast and upper flanks usually a black or blackish smudge, becoming barred with black-and-white and chestnut on lower flanks. Upperparts warm dark brown, with fine pale buffish edges to mantle and back. **Confusion species:** The extent of black on head, chin and throat makes it unlikely to be confused with either of the two smaller African mannikins, Bronze and Black-and-white. Unlikely to be confused with

other species of African finch once the bill is seen well.

DESCRIPTION Sexes alike. **Adult:** Forehead to nape, face to chin and throat black with a deep bluish sheen or gloss. Mantle and back dark brown, tinged slightly reddish, with pale buff central streaks and tips with subterminal dark spots on mantle; scapulars warm dark brown, with pale buff shaft streaks on lower scapulars. Generally appears much darker or blacker above in worn plumage. Rump and uppertail-coverts black, also with slight bluish or bluish-green gloss. Tail fairly short and rounded, black. All wing-coverts and tertials similar to scapulars, but medians have pale shafts in fresh plumage; flight feathers dark brownish-black.

Underparts generally white, becoming creamy-white on undertail-coverts; sides of lower breast/upper flanks black, becoming barred with black, white and chestnut on lower flanks (but individual bars may not always be apparent, and often appears as a continuation of upper flanks with white and chestnut tips showing). Bill large and heavy-looking, deep at base and longer than on other African mannikins, black or blackish-grey on upper mandible, bluish or pale grey on lower; in direct comparison, females are separable by slightly smaller bill. Legs and feet dark grey or black. **Juvenile:** Upperparts generally dull or drab buffish-brown, with forehead, face and crown darker grey-brown and rump and tail blackish-brown; mantle, back and scapulars are buff-brown with fine buff streaks or tips; median and greater coverts have thin pale buff tips forming two pale wingbars (quickly abraded), tips to tertials and secondaries also pale buff in fresh plumage. Chin and throat pale buff; rest of underparts pale peachy-buff, with a deeper or buffish-brown patch on sides of breast and flanks. Adult plumage is assumed within the first three months of life.

VOICE Contact call is a loud chirruping 'pee-oo, pee-oo'; has a thin 'cheep' alarm call and a 'tsek' note. The song is a single short note similar to the contact note, frequently repeated.

STATUS, HABITAT AND BEHAVIOUR Generally uncommon, locally common or scarce. Occurs at up to 1000 m (2000 m in south Sudan) in clearings or edges of forests, including riverine forests and bamboo thickets, bush (often fairly thick or rich vegetation) and grasslands with scrub, often in mango trees, and nests in (introduced) conifers. Usually in loose flocks, though never so large as those formed by Bronze and Black-and-white Mannikins (with which it occasionally associates); roosts communally in reeds, tall grasses or bamboos. Feeds in growing vegetation (rarely seen on the ground), on a variety of seeds, mostly of grasses but also some rice and millet; in south of range has a liking for the seeds of Bindura bamboo (*Oxytenanthera abyssinica*).

DISTRIBUTION Monotypic. Southern Senegal and west Gambia southeast and east to southern Mali, Guinea, Sierra Leone, Ghana, Togo, Nigeria, Cameroon, Central African Republic, southern Sudan, Gabon and discontinuously through the Congo and north, central and eastern Zaire, west Uganda, southern and extreme southeast Kenya, Tanzania, Zanzibar, Malawi, Zambia, northeast Zimbabwe and Mozambique to extreme east Transvaal, Swaziland and east Natal, South Africa. Has also been recorded in northern Angola, and once in southern Ethiopia (July 1971).

MOVEMENTS Most are sedentary, but some are semi-nomadic (especially in south of range) and wander at random in search of food.

MEASUREMENTS Wing 57·5–64; tail 33–39; tarsus 13·5–15·5; bill (culmen) 15–17·5.

REFERENCES Ash (1973), Goodwin (1982), Sinclair (1987).

225 WHITE-RUMPED MUNIA (Striated Munia, Hodgson's Munia, White-backed Munia, Sharp-tailed Munia; Bengalese Finch (avic.))
Lonchura striata　　　　　　　　　　　　　　　　　**Plate 54**
Oriental and marginally southeast Palearctic

Loxia striata Linnaeus, 1766, Syst. Nat., ed. 12, p. 306, Bourbon Island [Réunion] in error; Ceylon designated by Baker, 1926, Fauna Brit. India, Birds, ed. 2, p. 83.

IDENTIFICATION Length 10–11·5 cm (4–4½ in). A small black-and-white finch with a wide distribution from the Himalayas to Malaysia. Adults have dark chocolate-brown upperparts, with a square white (or buffish-white) rump, and pale shaft streaks on crown, nape, mantle, back and coverts. Underparts blackish-brown on chin to breast, white on belly and flanks, with brown or reddish-brown undertail-coverts. Juveniles (which are very unlikely to be seen on their own for long) are buff-brown on the head, face, breast and most of upperparts, paler buff on rest of underparts. **Confusion species:** The white rump and black head to breast are diagnostic of adults, and make species unlikely to be confused with any other Asiatic finch. Note: The domesticated or aviary-bred form (Bengalese Finch), which has now been produced in a range of colour mutations, derives from this species, most probably from races *acuticauda* or *swinhoei*.

DESCRIPTION Sexes alike. **Adult:** Forehead to lores, face, sides of neck, chin, throat and breast dark chocolate-brown. Crown, nape, mantle, back and scapulars brownish-black, slightly warmer than head and face and with fine pale buff central shaft streaks; rump an almost square patch of white; uppertail-coverts blackish-brown with buff shaft streaks. Tail wedge-shaped, pointed, black. Median and greater coverts as scapulars, but with pale central shafts to inner feathers; alula and primary coverts black, latter with buff edges; flight feathers also black or blackish, with brown edges to secondaries and outer webs of tertials. Lower breast, belly to vent and flanks creamy-white, rear of flanks dark chocolate with buff shaft streaks, thighs brown or reddish-brown; undertail-coverts brown or dark reddish-brown, often with pale buff tips, longest feathers blackish. Bill short and typical of mannikin/munia genus, blackish upper mandible, blue-grey lower. Legs and feet dark or bluish-grey. **Juvenile:** Generally pale buff-brown on forehead to back, with some very fine (almost invisible in the field) central shaft streaks on mantle and scapulars; rump very pale buffish or pale buffish-brown; tail blackish-brown. Wing-coverts as mantle, back and scapulars, but with some pale buff edges and tips; flight feathers brown, edged pale buff-brown. Lores dull or drab sandy-brown; sides of face and neck a warm sandy-brown, this extending to chin and throat, with paler or buff tips on breast; rest of underparts pale peachy-buff. Bill blackish. As in other *Lonchura* species, juveniles attain adult plumage within the first three months of life.

GEOGRAPHICAL VARIATION Andaman and Nicobar Islands races *fumigata* and *semistriata*, respectively, are generally darker or blackish-brown above and more creamy-buff below and generally lack any pale shaft streaks; some have reddish-brown tips to breast feathers and uppertail-coverts. Birds from northern India and Nepal eastwards (*acuticauda*, *swinhoei* and *subsquamicollis*) are distinctly different from others. Race *acuticauda* has pale buff-brown cheeks, ear-coverts and sides of neck, and the rump is tinged or washed buff-brown and faintly barred in fresh plumage; the breast is dark chocolate-brown with reddish-brown tips on upper breast or whitish-buff tips (creating a scaly effect) on lower breast, and belly and flanks are greyish and very finely streaked with pale brown; the bill on some is uniform grey. Race *swinhoei* is similar to *acuticauda*, but with slightly paler or warmer brown upperparts and with prominent pale buff streaks on mantle, back and scapulars, and uppertail-coverts are warm tawny or sandy-brown; the cheeks and ear-coverts to breast are warm ginger with darker tips to the feathers (forming short bars on breast); belly and flanks are greyish and finely streaked with brown, and thighs and undertail-coverts are rufous or light reddish-brown. Race *subsquamicollis* is intermediate in plumage between the last two races, but all three interbreed in areas of overlap and intermediates (together with variations within the races) occur. Juveniles vary slightly in the extent or intensity of brown, buff-brown or pale areas.

VOICE Has a weak or feeble and plaintive peeping or a twittering 'tr-tr-tr', 'prrrit' or a 'brrt' call. The song is a series of twittering notes rising and falling in tone.

STATUS, HABITAT AND BEHAVIOUR Common or locally common; widespread. Occurs in a wide variety of open dry scrub or lightly wooded country, from clearings and edges of forest to grasslands, edges of cultivation (especially rice-paddies and stubble) and gardens; occurs at up to 1800 m in Taiwan and to 2000 m in Malaysia. Highly social, usually in small flocks of 15–50 birds, often larger in non-breeding season. Roosts communally in dense thickets or sugarcane, often in company with Spotted Munias (229) and weavers (Ploceidae). Feeds mainly on the ground or climbs agilely in growing vegetation to take seeds from the seedheads; feeds mostly on seeds of grasses, but also takes rice and has been known to take filamentous algae (*Spirogyra*) from dry pools.

DISTRIBUTION *L. s. striata*: southern India from southeast Gujarat, Madhya Pradesh and southern Bihar to the lowlands of Sri Lanka.

L. s. acuticauda: southeast Kashmir and northern India to Nepal, Sikkim, Bhutan, Assam, Arunachal Pradesh, Nagaland, Manipur, Bangladesh, Burma and northern Thailand.

L. s. fumigata: Andaman Islands.

L. s. semistriata: Nicobar Islands.

L. s. subsquamicollis: extreme southeast Burma and southern Thailand through west Yunnan, south China to Cambodia, Laos and South Vietnam to Hainan; south to Malaysia, Sumatra and Bangka.

L. s. swinhoei: southern China from southeast Szechwan to southern Shensi, east to Kiangsu south to Kweichow, Kwangsi, Kwangtung (including Hong Kong) and Taiwan.

It is also established on Okinawa, Ryukyu Islands, but origins of the birds there are unclear.

MOVEMENTS A resident over most of its range, occurring from sea-level up to 900 m, but in the breeding season occurs at up to 2100 m in the Himalayas or 1500 m in Burma and China.

MEASUREMENTS Wing of male 51–56, of female 52–57; tail of male 35–42, of female 35–39; tarsus 13–14; bill (from skull) 12–14. Weight 9·5–13. Wing of male *acuticauda* 49–55, of female 51–54; tail of male 38–46. Wing of *fumigata* and *semistriata* 48–51. Wing of *swinhoei* 46·5–50.

REFERENCES Ali and Ripley (1983), Goodwin (1982).

226 JAVAN MUNIA (Javanese Mannikin, Javanese White-bellied Munia) *Lonchura leucogastroides*   Plate 53

Indonesia

Munia leucogastroides Horsfield and Moore, 1856, Cat. Birds Mus. East India Co., 2, p. 510, Java.

IDENTIFICATION Length 10–11·5 cm (4–4½ in). A small munia of restricted range. Generally dull or drab brownish, with a distinctive black fore face, chin, throat and breast, white lower breast and dark brown or blackish undertail-coverts. **Con-** fusion species: Very similar to White-bellied Munia (231), with which it overlaps in parts of the range, but Javan has paler brown upperparts, generally lacks (or has only faintly indicated) pale shaft streaks on mantle and back, has white flanks (blackish-brown on White-bellied) and lacks the yellow-edged feathers in tail.

DESCRIPTION Sexes alike. **Adult:** Forehead and lores, front of cheeks, moustachial region, chin, throat and upper breast blackish, tinged with purple. Crown and nape to mantle, back and scapulars medium-brown, in fresh plumage mantle and back showing faint pale or whitish central shaft streaks; rump and uppertail-coverts blackish-brown, often with purple tinge or sheen. Tail graduated, with central feathers slightly elongated and pointed at the tip, blackish-brown with outer feathers dull medium-brown. Median and greater coverts slightly darker brown than scapulars; alula and primary coverts dull dark brown. Blackish-purple on upper breast sharply divided from pure white on lower breast, belly and flanks; thighs dark brown; undertail-coverts blackish-brown, tinged with purple. Bill short and stout, blackish or dark grey upper mandible and pale greyish-blue lower. Legs and feet grey or blue-grey. **Juvenile:** Similar to adult, but front of face and chin to breast warm brown; rest of underparts light buff, or peachy-buff on breast. Upperparts uniform chocolate-brown on crown and nape to mantle, back and wings.

VOICE Call a high-pitched 'pi-i', 'pee-ee-eet' or 'tyee-ee-ee'. The song is a pleasant purring or a series of characteristic 'prreet' notes.

STATUS, HABITAT AND BEHAVIOUR Locally common to abundant. Generally occurs in lowland (up to 1500 m) grassland or bushy areas, often in scrub and secondary-growth areas on the edges of cultivation, rice-paddies and gardens. As most munias usually found in pairs, small family parties, or in larger flocks in non-breeding season, often mixing with other seedeaters and munias (possibly hybridises with White-rumped Munia (225) in south Sumatra. Perches and feeds low down in vegetation or on growing plants and on the ground, mainly on grass seeds and rice.

DISTRIBUTION Monotypic. Southern Sumatra (where possibly introduced) Java, Bali and Lombok. Has also been introduced into Singapore.

MOVEMENTS Generally sedentary.

MEASUREMENTS Wing 48–51; tail 32–40; tarsus 13–14; bill 10.

REFERENCES Goodwin (1982), van Marle and Voous (1988).

227 DUSKY MUNIA (Dusky Mannikin) *Lonchura fuscans*   Plate 53

Malay Archipelago

Spermestes fuscans Cassin, 1852, Proc. Philadelphia Acad., 6, p. 185, Borneo.

IDENTIFICATION Length 10 cm (4 in). A small and entirely dark or brownish-black munia with slightly paler tips to some feathers; the pale grey base to bill is very distinctive. Restricted to Borneo and several small outlying islands. Unlikely to be confused with any other species as its uniform plumage is diagnostic. The local race of White-bellied Munia (231) (*castanonota*) on Borneo has rufous-chestnut upperparts and a white belly and vent.

DESCRIPTION Sexes alike. **Adult:** Entirely brownish-black above and below, but with darker tips and paler bases creating a scalloped pattern; some birds have a purple sheen to head, face and breast. Albino or leucistic birds have been found in the highlands of Borneo. Bill stout, with black or blackish-grey upper mandible and pale grey or bluish-grey lower. Legs and feet grey or greyish-blue or pale blue. **Juvenile:** Very similar to adult, but more drab or uniform blackish-brown without any of the dark tips or crescents of the adult plumage. Bill is entirely black.

VOICE Call a shrill 'pee pee', a thin 'chirrup', and a quick low 'teck, teck' uttered in flight.

STATUS, HABITAT AND BEHAVIOUR Common to abundant. Occurs in grasslands, scrub, edges of forests, river banks, cultivation, especially rice-paddies, also in gardens in towns and cities wherever suitable food is available. Very secretive and mouse-like, spending a lot of time on the ground; clambers up plants to reach the seedheads; when alarmed, sometimes 'freezes' instead of flying off. As many other munia species roosts communally, often in nests, either disused breeding nests or those specially constructed for the purpose. Generally keeps low in vegetation or feeds on the ground, on small grass seeds, reed seeds and rice.

DISTRIBUTION Monotypic. Borneo and the outlying islands of Natuna and Banguey (Banggi), and Cagayan Sulu (southwest Philippines).

MOVEMENTS Sedentary.

MEASUREMENTS Wing 48–51; tail 45; tarsus 11–12; bill (from skull) 11–13, (from feathers) 10.

REFERENCE Smythies (1981).

228 MOLUCCAN MUNIA (Moluccan Mannikin, Black-faced Munia)
Lonchura molucca　　　　　　　　　　　　　　　　　　**Plate 53**
Malay Archipelago

Loxia molucca Linnaeus, 1766, Syst. Nat., ed. 12, p. 302, Moluccas; restricted to Ambon.

IDENTIFICATION Length 9·5–11 cm (3¾–4½ in). A small black-and-white munia of restricted distribution, initially very similar to White-rumped Munia (225), with which it does not overlap. Adults have entire head and face to chin, throat and breast black, with nape and sides of neck, mantle, back and scapulars brown; rump white, barred with black crescents, wings blackish-brown and tail black. The underparts are white, thinly barred with black. Within its native range unlikely to be confused with any other species. Told from similar (but out-of-range) White-rumped Munia by the finely barred rump and underparts (not always visible at a distance, and worn birds may show only partially barred areas).

DESCRIPTION Sexes alike. **Adult:** Forehead to hindcrown, face, chin, throat and upper breast black. Nape, hindneck and sides of neck to mantle, back and scapulars medium-brown; rump white, finely barred darker with small blackish crescents; uppertail-coverts and tail black. Median and greater coverts as scapulars or darker rufous; alula, primary coverts and flight feathers blackish-brown. Underparts from lower breast white, thinly or finely barred with dark or brownish-black crescents. Bill stout and rather short, upper mandible black or blackish-grey, lower grey or bluish-grey. Legs and feet pale grey. **Juvenile:** Forehead and lores dull dark brown; cheeks and ear-coverts to chin and throat pale buff, thinly barred darker. Crown, nape and upperparts warm brown, and median and greater coverts and tertials have paler buff tips; rump pale buff, and often shows some barring as adult. Chin, throat and upper breast buffish-brown, with duller brown barring on lower throat and breast; rest of underparts buffish or pale buff, also with faint traces of barring (usually on undertail-coverts) which becomes progressively widespread with moults to adult plumage.

GEOGRAPHICAL VARIATION Three races (nominate, *propinqua* and *vagans*) were previously recognised, but were poorly defined, with very little constant difference visible in the field (except for *propinqua* on Sumbawa, Flores, Sumba and Pantar, in which breast barring reduced or completely absent) or recognisable in the hand. We follow White and Bruce (1986) in treating species as monotypic.

VOICE Generally silent, but has a short 'tr,tr' call.

STATUS, HABITAT AND BEHAVIOUR Abundant, common or locally common. Occurs in rice-paddies, grasslands, bushes and scrub at edges or clearings in forests up to 1000 m, also on edges of cultivated areas. Usually in pairs, family parties and groups. Tame and not at all shy of man. Feeds principally on grass and small weed seeds, but many details of its habits unknown.

DISTRIBUTION Monotypic (see above). Sulawesi: Talaud, Sangihe, Siau, Ruang, Tobea, Tukangbesi, Salayar, Kalao, Kalaotoa, Tanahjampea, Peleng. Moluccas: Morotai, Halmahera, Ternate, Batjan, Obi, Sula, Buru, Seram, Ambon, Seram Laut, Watubela, Tayandu, Kai. Lesser Sunda Islands: Penida, Sumbawa, Flores, Paloe, Sumba, Pantar, Timor, Tanimbar, and Lembongan and Kangean Islands (north of Bali).

MEASUREMENTS Wing 48; tarsus 12; bill 10.

REFERENCES Goodwin (1982), White and Bruce (1986).

---

229 SPOTTED MUNIA (Spice Finch, Nutmeg Mannikin, Spotted Mannikin, Scaly-breasted Munia) *Lonchura punctulata*　　**Plate 53**
Oriental and marginally southeast Palearctic

Loxia punctulata Linnaeus, 1758, Syst. Nat., ed. 10, p. 173, Asia; restricted to Calcutta by Baker, 1926, Fauna Brit. India, Birds, ed. 2, p. 91.

IDENTIFICATION Length 10 cm (4 in). A small reddish-brown munia, widely distributed in many races throughout the Oriental region. Adults have plain reddish-brown on forehead to crown and face; mantle and back less reddish; wings, rump and uppertail-coverts yellowish, barred with brown, becoming straw-yellow on base of tail. Underparts boldly spotted or scaled with white on black, giving a very strong pattern. Juveniles almost entirely buffish-brown, darker above. **Confusion species:** The warm brown or reddish-brown on head to chin, paler brown upperparts, and brown-barred rump and uppertail-coverts separate this species from the superficially similar White-rumped Munia (225). The blackish bill of juveniles is useful in separating them from those of Chestnut (235) and White-headed (236) Munias.

DESCRIPTION Sexes alike. **Adult:** Entire head

and face (except slightly darker brown lores to behind eye) to nape deep reddish- or chestnut-brown becoming browner with indistinct pale buff streaks on mantle, back and scapulars; rump pale buffish-brown, barred or spotted darker brown; uppertail-coverts yellowish or straw-yellow. Tail short and wedge-shaped with pointed central tail feathers; base overlain by long uppertail-coverts, rest of tail dark brown in centre but edges to central and all outer feathers golden-brown or yellowish. Median and greater coverts as scapulars; alula and primary coverts dark chestnut-brown; flight feathers also dark brown, but edged paler or medium-brown, tertials warmer or reddish-brown. Chin, throat and upper breast rich reddish- or deep chestnut-brown as head and face. Breast, including sides of breast, to flanks and sides of belly scaled or spotted, with white centres and blackish fringes; centre of belly, vent and undertail-coverts creamy-white. Bill short, stout with curved ridge to upper mandible, lead-grey, blue-grey or black, lower mandible blue-grey and usually paler at base. Eye dark brown, orbital ring grey. Legs and feet grey or bluish-grey. In worn or non-breeding plumage generally much duller or paler, with yellowish (or greenish-yellow) on tail and uppertail-coverts reduced or absent and tail brown or dark brown.

Juvenile: Generally tawny or warm buffish-brown on head, face and upperparts; rump to tail olive-brown, with yellowish centre and warmer brown outer edges to tail. Chin to breast and flanks paler buff or peach-buff, belly pale cream; lacks the scales or spots of adult, but some show very slight or faint warm brown streaks on lower throat and breast. Pale buffish-brown eye-ring. Bill dark greyish-horn or blackish, with pale flesh-pink base to lower mandible.

GEOGRAPHICAL VARIATION Most racial variation involves the tone, extent or intensity of chestnut or reddish-brown on head and face, the brown on upperparts, and the shape of the white markings on breast and flanks (some differences are appreciable only in the hand). Race *subundulata* is darker, more brownish, on head, with face and throat more uniform, rump olive-grey, and yellow on tail duller and tinged with olive-green. Dull brown face of *topela* extends to lower throat and white spots or scales on underparts are more oval and less intensively white, as also on *cabanisi*, which is dull brown above with only a small amount of yellow on uppertail-coverts. Both *fretensis* and *nisoria* are similar to *subundulata*, but are more like nominate in having reddish-brown on face and throat; *nisoria* has grey on rump; *baweana* has narrower edges to breast and belly feathers, the chestnut on chin and throat is not so extensive as in other races, and the white on belly to undertail-coverts is more extensive; *blasii* is darker on head and has broad black fringes and shaft streaks on lower breast and flanks; *blasii*, *sumbae* and *particeps* all have a greenish or olive tinge to upper surface of tail.

VOICE Contact call is a repeated 'kitty-kitty-kitty', also occasionally given as 'kit-eeeeee', alarm is a similar 'ki-ki-ki-ki-ki-teeee'; also has a harsh 'chup' or 'tret-tret', often repeated rapidly. The song is a soft and virtually inaudible melody of high flute-like whistles and low-pitched slurred notes; can be given by either sex.

STATUS, HABITAT AND BEHAVIOUR Abundant, common or locally common. Occurs in a wide variety of open or semi-open habitats from sea-level up to 2000 m in India and Nepal, 2200 m in parts of Wallacea and 2275 m in Bhutan, mostly in grasslands or rice-paddies with bushes, trees or scrub, edges of forest or jungle, cultivated areas (in crops), parks and gardens. Very sociable, usually in flocks; nests communally, often in large numbers (up to several hundred). Also roosts in large gatherings, often with other munias and weavers (Ploceidae), in thick foliage, either in old nests or in ones specially constructed. Frequently flicks tail and wings. Feeds on the ground or from growing plants (especially rice); takes mainly grass seeds and other small weed seeds, lantana berries, and also known (in captivity) to take millet and scraps of bread. Widely trapped for Buddhist religious purposes in southeast Asia (where referred to as 'rice-birds').

DISTRIBUTION *L. p. punctulata*: most of India north to southern Punjab (absent from extreme northwest India and Assam) and Sri Lanka, to southern Nepal and Sikkim.

L. p. subundulata: Assam, Bhutan and west Burma.

L. p. yunnanensis: northeast Burma and southwest China from south Szechwan to west and southwest Yunnan.

L. p. topela: southern China from south Yunnan east to Kiangsi and Fukien, Taiwan and Hainan, northern Thailand, Laos, Cambodia/Kampuchea and Vietnam.

L. p. cabanisi: Philippines: Luzon Is, Mindoro, Panay, Palawan, Cebu and Calauit.

L. p. fretensis: southern (peninsular) Thailand, Malay peninsula, Sumatra, Batam, Bangka, Belitung and Nias.

L. p. nisoria: Java, Bali, Lombok and Sumbawa.

L. p. sumbae: Lesser Sunda Islands: Sumba.

L. p. blasii: Lesser Sunda Islands: Flores, Lomblen, Sawu, Timor, Kisar, Romang, Leti, Babar and Tanimbar.

L. p. particeps: north and south-central Sulawesi.

L. p. baweana: Bawean Island, Java Sea.

Has been introduced into Australia, where now well established and occurs almost continuously along east coast from Sydney to Cooktown, northern Queensland; also to Okinawa, where now well established as a breeding bird. Race *topela* has also been introduced into Ryukyu Islands, Hawaii (all main islands), Mauritius, Réunion and the Seychelles; and *cabanisi* has been introduced into Yap (where common) and Palau, Caroline Islands, but has not been seen at latter locality since the 1940s. Also introduced into Puerto Rico (status uncertain), and has bred (1964 and 1965) in southern Florida, latter as a result of escapes from captivity.

MOVEMENTS Generally resident and sedentary. A lowland bird over much of its range, but some races occur up to considerable altitudes; generally found above 1500 m only in period June-October.

Race *topela* may be a winter visitor to southeast Burma.

MEASUREMENTS Wing of male 54–58, of female 53–59; tail of male 32–45, of female 33–45; tarsus 14–16; Bill (from skull) 11–13. Wing of male *nisoria* 52–54, of female 49–53; tail of male 34–40, of female 32–40; bill (culmen) 9–

12. Wing of male *fretensis* 51–53, of female 50–52; tail 32–42; bill (culmen) 11–12. Wing of *particeps* 48–51; tail 28–38; bill (culmen) 10–11. Wing of *baweana* 50–52; tail 35–38; bill (culmen) 10–11. Weight 12–15.

REFERENCES Goodwin (1982), Hoogerwerf (1963).

230 RUFOUS-BELLIED MUNIA (Sri Lanka Hill Munia, Rufous-breasted Munia) *Lonchura kelaarti*

Plate 54

Oriental

Munia kelaarti Jerdon (ex Blyth MS), 1863, Birds India, 2, p. 356, Ceylon.

IDENTIFICATION Length 10 cm (4 in). A small dark brown munia with a black face, chin, throat and upper breast. Top of head and upperparts brown or medium-brown with fine, relatively indistinct pale shaft streaks, rump blackish but spotted with white, uppertail-coverts dark with yellow or greenish-yellow edges and tips, tail black; underparts vary between the two races. Confusion with any other species unlikely. Juveniles may resemble those of other species, but the barring on underparts is distinctive.

DESCRIPTION Sexes alike. **Adult:** Forehead blackish-brown, becoming paler or browner on crown, nape, mantle, back and scapulars, all feathers with fine or indistinct pale buff central shafts (not always visible in the field); rump blackish-brown, spotted or barred finely with white; uppertail-coverts dark brown, edged yellowish, gold or even greenish-yellow. Tail wedge-shaped, with longest central feathers pointed, black. Median and greater coverts dark brown with paler shaft streaks; alula, primary coverts, tertials and flight feathers blackish-brown, finely edged with brown. Face almost entirely black from base of bill to ear-coverts and to chin, throat and centre of breast; sides of neck and breast dull buff or pinkish-buff, lightly tinged sandy in fresh plumage; lower breast, belly, flanks and undertail-coverts whitish, spotted with dark brown or black. Bill short and stout, with curved culmen, upper mandible dark grey or blackish, lower prominently pale or bluish-grey at base, becoming blackish at tip. Legs and feet blackish or bluish-grey. **Juvenile:** Entire upperparts dark brown or tinged warm brown, lacking pale edges or tips on rump and uppertail-coverts. Face medium-brown, with pale buff tips or central shaft streaks on ear-coverts; chin and throat pale buff or greyish, with dark tips forming small or short bars; breast, belly and flanks pale or buffish-brown with faint indication of spotting of adult plumage; undertail-coverts have black bars.

GEOGRAPHICAL VARIATION Race *jerdoni* has entire underparts uniform pinkish-buff or

sandy-buff, with only a faint pattern of darker spots on undertail-coverts; in worn plumage underparts are greyer and show grey fringes and tips or bars on feathers, the rump is warm rufous. Juveniles are similar to those of nominate, but have much paler buffish underparts.

VOICE Contact call is a high-pitched nasal 'tay'; also gives a typical munia chirp. The song is an almost inaudible series of five notes.

STATUS, HABITAT AND BEHAVIOUR Locally common or scarce within fairly small areas of distribution. Occurs generally between 600 m and 2100 m, but in some of the wetter areas in Sri Lanka occasionally/rarely down to 200 m, in grassland with lantana scrub, bushes or thickets, edges of forests, clearings and cultivated areas (including tea and coffee plantations), usually in more moist or wetter areas than White-rumped Munia (225). Usually in pairs, groups or small (probably family) parties, and often forms mixed flocks in non-breeding season with Spotted (229) and White-rumped Munias. Most habits as those of other munias, but said also to have a rather high undulating flight. Feeds low down or on the ground, on a variety of small seeds, principally grass seeds, grain and rice.

DISTRIBUTION *L. k. kelaarti*: highlands of central and southwest Sri Lanka.

L. k. jerdoni: southwest India from southern Karnataka, through Kerala to western Tamil Nadu; also the Vishnakhapatnam district, Eastern Ghats, Andhra Pradesh.

Note: Those from the Eastern Ghats area were previously considered to represent a separate race, *vernayi*.

MOVEMENTS A partial or local migrant, occurring on high ground above 2100 m in summer.

MEASUREMENTS Wing of male and female 54–58; tail of male 38–42, of female 36–42. Weight 12–17. Wing of male *jerdoni* 56–59, of female 57–59; tail of male 37–43, of female 36–39; tarsus 14–15; bill (from skull) 13–14.

REFERENCE Henry (1971).

231 WHITE-BELLIED MUNIA (White-breasted Mannikin)
Lonchura leucogastra
Plate 53
Oriental

Amadina leucogastra Blyth, 1846, Journ. Asiat. Soc. Bengal, 15, p. 286, Malacca.

IDENTIFICATION Length 9·5–11·5 cm (3¾–4½ in). A small, thick-billed munia with a fairly short mustard-yellow tail. Black or blackish-brown (with a gloss in fresh plumage) on face, upperparts, chin, throat and breast; distinctive white belly to vent, with blackish undertail-coverts. The upperparts have fine, thin buffish shaft streaks. **Confusion species:** Clearly lacks a white band across the rump at any age. Very similar to Javan Munia (226), with which it (possibly) overlaps in southern Sumatra, but White-bellied has much darker or chocolate-brown upperparts with thin but prominent white or pale buff shaft streaks on mantle, back and scapulars; Javan has white (not barred or smudged with black) flanks and a brown or dull brown, pointed (not rounded) tail that lacks any yellow or dull yellow edges.

DESCRIPTION Sexes alike. **Adult:** Forehead to crown and entire face dark or blackish-brown. Nape, mantle, back and scapulars as crown, but with fine pale buff shaft streaks, some back feathers often showing pale buff tips; rump and uppertail-coverts blackish-brown, often with a purple sheen in fresh plumage. Tail short, wedge-shaped and blunt at tip, dark brown feather centres broadly edged with mustard-yellow or yellowish-brown, more broadly on central pair than on outers. Median and greater coverts as mantle and scapulars; alula, primary coverts and flight feathers brownish-black, very slightly darker than coverts. Chin and throat to upper breast brownish-black as face; flanks also brownish-black but broadly tipped white; some feathers on lower breast (usually at sides) also show white tips, centre of lower breast, belly and vent creamy-white; undertail-coverts dark or blackish-brown, with purple sheen in fresh plumage. Bill stout and proportionately larger than on other munias, blunt-tipped, black or blackish-grey upper mandible, lower paler grey or bluish-grey, blackish towards tip. Legs and feet grey or dull grey. **Juvenile:** Generally similar to adult but duller brown, and dark brown on wings; belly and vent more buffish or dull buffish than white. Tail has reduced amount of dull yellow on outer feathers.

GEOGRAPHICAL VARIATION Most racial variation involves size of bill, prominence of shaft streaks on mantle, back, scapulars and wing-coverts, and extent of black on chin to breast and flanks. Race *castanonota* is much more obviously

separable in the field (apart from by its isolated range) by the chestnut hindcrown to mantle, back and wings and the blacker-brown on face, chin, breast and flanks.

VOICE Call a soft cheeping 'chee-ee-ee' or a piping 'prrit prrit', higher-pitched than calls of White-rumped (225) and Spotted (229) Munias.

STATUS, HABITAT AND BEHAVIOUR Locally common or scarce. Occurs in bushes or scrub, generally in semi-open areas such as forest edges, clearings, villages or cultivated areas, but also known to occur in fairly thick forest. Occurs in pairs or small flocks of up to ten or in company with White-rumped Munia, but also more often encountered on its own than other munias. Other habits generally typical of the munias, but this species appears to be relatively unknown and rather little studied. In Borneo, where rare or local in occurrence, it is apparently shy, often solitary, always skulking in rice etc. Food, small seeds of grasses, weeds or rice.

DISTRIBUTION *L. l. leucogastra*: southeast Burma (Tenasserim), southern (peninsular) Thailand, peninsular Malaya (absent from Singapore) and Sumatra (where status uncertain).

L. l. everetti: Luzon, Mindoro, Calayan, Camiguin Norte, Cantanduanes and Polillo, Philippines.

L. l. manueli: southern Luzon, Basilan, Biliran, Bohol, Bucas, Camiguin Sur, Carabao, Cebu, Dinagat, Guimaras, Leyte, Marinduque, Mindanao, Negros, Pujada, Panay, Romblon, Samar, Semirara, Siargao, Sibuyan, Siquijor and Tablas, Philippines.

L. l. palawana: Palawan, Balabac, Culion, Calamian, and Sulu Archipelago, Philippines, also north and east Borneo.

L. l. smythiesi: Kuching, southwest Sarawak.

L. l. castanonota: southern Borneo.

MOVEMENTS Generally resident, but in Borneo also makes local movements or migrations that are not fully understood (a migrant to upland areas where it is not known to breed). A rare visitor to west Java (has bred); one collected at Jasinga, near Bogor, west Java.

MEASUREMENTS Wing 53; tail 41; tarsus 13; bill 12.

REFERENCES Hoogerwerf (1949), King *et al.* (1975), Mackinnon (1988), Smythies (1981).

232 STREAK-HEADED MANNIKIN (Streak-headed Munia) *Lonchura tristissima*
Plate 59

New Guinea

Munia tristissima Wallace, 1865, Proc. Zool. Soc. London, p. 479, northwest New Guinea.
   Possibly conspecific with the following species, White-spotted Mannikin (233).

IDENTIFICATION Length 10 cm (4 in). Endemic to New Guinea, where similar to (but separable from) other island endemic mannikins. Generally all dark, with pronounced pale streaks on forehead, face, crown, nape and upper mantle, slightly warmer brown on mantle, back and wing-coverts, and has a prominent square pale or dull yellow patch on rump. Flight feathers and tail black or blackish-brown. **Confusion species:** Black Mannikin (247) is all black without any streaking, and has bright orange-yellow uppertail-coverts to base of tail. White-spotted is much lighter or warmer brown above and below, with a whitish face, chin and throat, prominent pale buff streaks on forehead to nape, and white spotting on mantle and back and tips of median and greater coverts.
DESCRIPTION Sexes similar. **Adult male:** Forehead, ear-coverts and sides of neck to nape and upper mantle dull dark brown with fine pale buff streaks (quite prominent at close range); lores and cheeks black. Mantle, back and scapulars brown, or deep warm brown, the back sometimes tipped paler, lower back black or blackish-brown; rump a square patch of biscuit-yellow or dull yellowish; uppertail-coverts black. Tail graduated to pointed tip, black. Median and greater coverts as mantle and scapulars with rich dark brown fringes, both sets of coverts often (in fresh plumage) showing pale buff tips and rufous fringes; alula, primary coverts and flight feathers blackish-brown, inner secondaries and tertials edged warm brown on outer webs and tipped pale buff. Underparts blackish-brown with darker bases to feathers; some birds are paler than others or show brown or reddish-brown tinges on breast (with pale buff bases) and flanks. Bill stout and fairly thick or deep at base, with curved culmen, blue-grey on both mandibles. Legs and feet blackish or bluish-grey. **Adult female:** Very similar to adult male but slightly paler, and buff streaks on crown and ear-coverts are wider, more prominent and extensive; centres to scapulars paler, and sides of breast show paler buff bases. **Juvenile:** A paler or duller brown version of adult, from which very difficult to separate. Generally lacks streaks on head and face for first few weeks or months of life (or streaks very fine, and present on crown and face only).
GEOGRAPHICAL VARIATION Very few racial differences noticeable, as all three races show some individual variation within the respective populations; most racial variation concerns the tone of the chestnut to dark brown of body and the amount or intensity of streaks on head and face.
VOICE Usual contact call is a thin buzzing 'tseed', slightly rising in tone, also a sharp 'jjbb'.
STATUS, HABITAT AND BEHAVIOUR Locally common. Occurs at up to 1700 m along edges of forests, usually in patches of grass, shrubs or scrub including villages and gardens in towns, but never far from forest. Occurs in flocks of varying size from five to 30, usually in smaller numbers when breeding. Generally shy or wary. Food mostly grass seeds or other small plant seeds, occasionally takes small insects.
DISTRIBUTION *L. t. tristissima*: Vogelkop Mountains, northwest New Guinea.
   L. t. hypomelaena: Weyland Mountains, central New Guinea.
   L. t. calaminoros: Oranje and Nassau Mountains, east to Noord river, southern New Guinea, and northern New Guinea from Mamberano to Hydrographer Mountains and Karkar Island.
MOVEMENTS Largely sedentary.
MEASUREMENTS Wing 49; tarsus 14; bill (from feathers) 9.
REFERENCE Beehler *et al.* (1986).

233 WHITE-SPOTTED MANNIKIN (White-spotted Munia) *Lonchura leucosticta*
Plate 59

New Guinea

Munia leucosticta d'Albertis and Salvadori, 1879, Ann. Mus. Civ. Genova, 14, p. 88, Fly River, 300 miles, New Guinea.

IDENTIFICATION Length 10 cm (4 in). A New Guinea endemic of very restricted range. Similar to Streak-headed Mannikin (232), with which it is sometimes considered conspecific, but easily separable in the field. Has a pale or whitish face, chin and throat, and fairly broad or well-marked streaks on forehead, crown and nape becoming small white spots on mantle and wing-coverts; flight feathers dark brown, tail black, rump and uppertail-coverts a band of bright yellow.

Underparts warm rufous-brown. **Confusion species:** For differences from the initially similar (but much darker) Streak-headed Mannikin, see that species. Other 'white-headed' mannikins from New Guinea, Grey-crowned (241), Grey-banded (239) and Grey-headed (240), are all much paler in general, especially about the head, lack any white spotting and have yellow or orange-yellow tails.

DESCRIPTION Sexes almost alike (but possibly separable in the field). **Adult male:** Forehead to nape dark brown, broadly and prominently streaked pale buff or white, the streaks on forehead often very close together; lores, cheeks and ear-coverts white or very pale buff to creamy-buff (but bases of feathers brown or warm brown). Sides of neck to mantle, back and scapulars dark chocolate-brown or deep chestnut-brown with unevenly distributed white spots, lower back darker brown; rump and uppertail-coverts a band of pale yellow or pale orange, the longer uppertail-coverts black. Tail wedge-shaped and slightly longer than on most other New Guinea mannikins, blunt at tip of central pair, black. Median and greater coverts slightly warmer rufous than scapulars, with a white spot at tip of each covert feather; alula, primary coverts and flight feathers dull dark brown, inner secondaries and tertials edged warm brown (some show white subterminal spot at tips of tertials). Chin and upper throat white or whitish-buff, lower throat warm rufous, rust-brown or deep orange with a few white tips or crescents; breast, belly to vent and flanks warm rufous or rust-brown, with a few small white spots or tips on sides of breast; vent to undertail-coverts blackish-brown; thighs rufous-

buff. Bill stout and with curved ridge to upper mandible, pale grey or greyish-blue. Legs and feet dark grey or blackish. **Adult female:** Generally duller than adult male, with the white more broken or scaly, but has slightly more individual white spots on breast; undertail-coverts may be tipped and edged with pale or brown (entirely blackish-brown on male). **Juvenile:** Almost entirely earth-brown, darker above than below, with both uppertail- and undertail-coverts very dark brown; a few short, pale buff-white streaks on crown, ear-coverts and throat, and a few small white spots on sides of breast and on tips of median and greater coverts forming double wingbar. Bill grey. Orbital ring grey. Legs and feet grey.

VOICE Call a distinctive 'peep' and a short nasal buzzing note, continually given in flight.

STATUS, HABITAT AND BEHAVIOUR Fairly or locally common within restricted range. Found in clumps or stands of tall grass, savanna and bamboo along forest edges, clearings or along streams, river banks or marshes, usually at fairly low altitudes. Occurs in pairs or small flocks. Feeds low down or on the ground, on grass, weeds and other small plant seeds.

DISTRIBUTION Monotypic. Southern New Guinea from Noord river east to Turama river, Gulf province.

MOVEMENTS Entirely sedentary.

MEASUREMENTS Wing 48; tarsus 14–15; bill (from feathers) 8–9.

REFERENCES Beehler *et al.* (1986), Restall (1989).

234 CHESTNUT-AND-WHITE MANNIKIN (Coloured Finch, Five-coloured Munia, Chestnut-and-white Munia) *Lonchura quinticolor* Plate 55

Indonesia

Loxia quinticolor Vieillot, 1807, Ois. Chant., pl. 54, p. 85, Timor.

IDENTIFICATION Length 11–12·5 cm (4½-5 in). A small and rather distinctive mannikin from a very restricted range in Indonesia. Head and face to chin and upper throat very dark brown or dark chestnut, upperparts warm brown, slightly darker on wings, and rump, uppertail-coverts and most of tail golden-brown. Underparts white, except for black thighs, vent and undertail-coverts. Within its native range unlikely to be confused with any other species.

DESCRIPTION Sexes alike. **Adult:** Forehead, crown and lores to cheeks, chin and throat dark chestnut, tinged slightly plum-chestnut on chin; ear-coverts slightly lighter, with paler brown shaft streaks; hindcrown and nape also slightly paler brown, tipped with grey. Mantle, back and scapulars warm chestnut-brown; rump and uppertail-coverts golden-brown or deep golden-orange. Tail graduated or wedge-shaped with elongated central feathers blunt at tip, similar in tone to rump and

uppertail-coverts or slightly darker or browner on central feathers and at tip. All wing-coverts, edges to flight feathers and tertials uniform with scapulars, inner webs of primaries and secondaries dull or dusky brown. Underparts below throat pure white, except for dark brown thighs and dull black, vent and undertail-coverts. Bill stout and with curved culmen, blue or pale bluish-grey on both mandibles. Legs and feet grey or dark grey. In worn plumage much darker, and rump may also be brown (or browner than described above). **Juvenile:** Forehead to nape dark olive-brown; face and lores greyish, with some pale shaft streaks on face and especially on ear-coverts; rest of upperparts similar to the head or slightly paler or more buffish-brown, with rump and tail warm olive-brown. Underparts pale or dull buffish, tinged with orange-buff across breast and on undertail-coverts.

VOICE Contact note is a repeated 'veeveevee' or a similar 'geev-geev-geev'. The song is a longer series of the call note followed by almost inaudible high-pitched whispering trills and whistling notes.

STATUS, HABITAT AND BEHAVIOUR
Uncommon or local. Occurs in coastal scrub, grasslands, edges of cultivation and rice-paddies (and edges of montane forest on Flores). Little known; many actions and behaviour probably much as other mannikins. Usually singly or in pairs, rarely in flocks, and avoids contact with others of genus. Food also unknown, but probably small grass seeds.

DISTRIBUTION Monotypic. Lesser Sunda Islands: Lombok, Sumbawa, Flores, Alor, Sumba, Roti, Timor, Sermata and Babar.

REFERENCE Goodwin (1982).

235 CHESTNUT MUNIA (Chestnut Mannikin, Black-headed Munia, Tricoloured Mannikin, Tricoloured Munia, Tricoloured Nun) *Lonchura malacca* Plate 55

Oriental and marginally extreme southeast Palearctic

Loxia malacca Linnaeus, 1766, Syst. Nat., ed. 12, p. 302, China, Java and Malacca in error; Belgaum, India, designated by Baker, 1926, Fauna Brit. India, Birds, ed. 2, p. 78.

IDENTIFICATION Length 11–12·5 cm (4½–5 in). A fairly small and distinctive munia with a wide distribution and several easily recognisable races. Adults are identified by the all-black head, chin, throat and upper breast (except *ferruginosa*, which is white-headed). Upperparts including wings and tail rich or warm light chestnut-brown. Birds from southern India have white underparts (except for black vent and undertail-coverts), while populations from further east are light or warm chestnut above and below. Immatures lack the black head, face and undertail-coverts. Within their native ranges most races are unlikely to be confused with any other species. Race *ferruginosa* is separated from the very similar White-headed Munia (236) by the greater extent of black on the underparts to chin, throat and breast, and also has the white of head much more clearly or sharply defined than that on White-headed. Juveniles are separated from juvenile Spotted Munia (229) by wholly blue or greyish-blue bill.

DESCRIPTION Sexes almost alike (but possibly separable in the field). **Adult male:** Entire head to nape, sides of neck, chin, throat and centre of breast jet-black. Mantle, back and scapulars rich or warm chestnut-brown; rump and uppertail-coverts similar or darker, with a deeper chestnut tone. Tail wedge-shaped with slightly rounded tip, central feathers longest and slightly pointed, warm brown to light chestnut with pale yellow, yellowish-gold or orange-yellow edges, broadest at bases of the outer feathers. Median and greater coverts as scapulars; alula, primary coverts and flight feathers darker or duller brown, but flight feathers edged warm brown or chestnut, broadest (or even tinged slightly yellowish) on tertials. Sides of upper breast to centre of lower breast, upper belly and flanks creamy-white (some show fine blackish centre streaks); centre of belly to vent, thighs and undertail-coverts black. Bill quite large and stout, entirely pale grey or bluish-grey with culmen often darker than rest of bill. Eye dark brown or dark

Juvenile moulting to adult plumage. Many mannikin flocks contain birds in transitional plumage.

reddish-brown, indistinct orbital ring pale grey or mid-grey. Legs and feet grey or greyish-blue. **Adult female:** Similar to adult male, but undertail-coverts brownish-black; also generally paler and duller brown on upperparts, with less pale yellow or yellowish in tail. Bill comparatively smaller than male's. **Juvenile:** Generally buffish-brown, with a brown or grey-brown forehead to nape, dark lores, dark brown-grey ear-coverts and pale buff chin and throat; upperparts and wings are light or warm buffish-brown, rump and uppertail-coverts olive-brown, tail browner or darker brown (initially without pale yellowish edges). Breast warm buff or buffish-brown, paler or generally whitish- to yellowish-buff on rest of underparts. Bill at first dull blackish-grey, becoming blue or bluish 'lavender-grey' towards gaining adult plumage. Orbital ring pale buff.

GEOGRAPHICAL VARIATION All races except nominate have chestnut underparts so that they become warm brown both above and below; also the black on vent and undertail-coverts is reduced and often has some dark or brown tips, and the uppertail-coverts and edges of the tail feathers are usually brighter than in nominate race, paler, yellowish-golden or even orange, contrasting with reddish-brown rump. Juveniles are very similar to those of nominate, but average slightly darker, more warm buff-brown on underparts. Within the races there are also minor variations. Race *rubroniger* in fresh plumage has uppertail-coverts and edges to base of tail more reddish or maroon (but wears to yellowish or yellowish-gold). Races *sinensis* and *deignani* lack the black on vent to undertail-coverts, and the latter race has the longer uppertail-coverts and edges to base of tail feathers tinged bright orange. Races on the Philippines are quite noticeably different: *formosana* has forehead, lores and face dark brown or blackish-brown, crown, nape and sides of neck tinged with grey, chin and throat black, and the black on vent to undertail-coverts extends from belly (females have paler brown or more grey-brown head than males); *jagori* is highly variable within its area of distribution, and can be very similar to *formosana*, but generally brighter or richer chestnut with forehead, crown and nape greyish-brown or black (black-crowned birds also show a large area of black from belly to undertail-coverts); *brunneiceps* is a poorly defined race, very similar to greyish-brown-headed birds of *jagori* and not always separable in the field. Race *ferruginosa* is entirely different from all the foregoing races and very similar to White-headed Munia, with entire head and face pale buffish or white (in worn plumage) or with buffish-brown on nape and sides of neck (in fresh plumage); the black of chin, throat and breast often joins across lower breast with that on vent and undertail-coverts, otherwise flanks and sides of belly are rich chestnut as are upperparts. Juveniles of this race are generally entirely dull or dingy brown.

VOICE Contact call is a weak or reedy 'peekt' or 'pee-eet'; in flight gives a triple 'chirp' note; call of nominate *malacca* is a whistling 'veet veet'. The song is an almost inaudible series of bill-snapping notes followed by 'silent' singing (with no sound emerging) and ending with faint but long drawn-out whistling notes.

STATUS, HABITAT AND BEHAVIOUR
Locally common. Occurs from sea-level up to 1500 m (or 2100 m in southern India), in or at edges of marshes or swampland, reedbeds, grasslands or rice-paddies, cane-fields or in scrub at edges of mangroves or cultivated areas; in some areas a forest-edge species. Usually in pairs or small flocks in breeding season, forming much larger flocks when not breeding. Often nests in association with Streaked Weaver (*Ploceus manyar*). In non-breeding season often forms mixed flocks with Spotted Munias, though some island races (e.g *ferruginosa*) rarely in anything other than single-species flocks. Wings make a loud or prominent whirring noise in flight. Roosts either in old nests or in large communal roosts in reedbeds or cane-fields. Feeds on the ground, on a variety of grass seeds and rice; in some areas, race *ferruginosa* is regarded as a serious pest at rice-gathering.

DISTRIBUTION *L. m. malacca*: southern India from the Tapi river east to about Raipur and Sri Lanka.

L. m. rubroniger: northern India from Haryana east to northern Bihar and lowlands of southern and eastern Nepal (extends north to the Kathmandu valley).

L. m. atricapilla: southeast Nepal and northeast India from Bihar, northern Orissa and West Bengal, Assam, east through Bangladesh, Manipur, Nagaland to Burma and northwest Yunnan, southwest China.

L. m. deignani: southwest Yunnan and southwest China (possibly also to Hainan Island), discontinuously through northern and central Thailand to southern Laos, central and southern Vietnam.

L. m. sinensis: discontinuously through southern (peninsular) Thailand and Malaya, to the lowlands of Sumatra (including islands in the Riau and Lingga archipelagos).

L. m. batakana: mountains of northern Sumatra.

L. m. formosana: Taiwan and the Philippines: Batan, Calayan, Fuga, Ivojos, north Luzon and Sabtang.

L. m. jagori: Philippines (almost throughout entire archipelago except northern Luzon), Halmahera (where possibly introduced), Sulu Islands, Palawan Island, Borneo (including Natuna), northern and central Sulawesi including Togian, Muna and Butung.

L. m. brunneiceps: Makassar district, southern Sulawesi.

L. m. ferruginosa: Java and Bali.

Has also been introduced into Australia (around Sydney), and escaped cagebirds have now become established on Okinawa and parts of Honshu, Japan. Also introduced into Hawaiian Islands (Oahu and Kauai), Caroline Islands, (Palau), Marianas (Guam) and Puerto Rico; in 1965 a pair bred on Merritt Island, Florida, but has not become established.

MOVEMENTS Generally sedentary, but flocks and family parties often wander in search of food following the monsoons.

MEASUREMENTS Wing of male 53–59, of female 53–56; tail of male 32–39, of female 31–36; tarsus 15–16; bill (from skull) 13–14. Weight 10–15.

REFERENCES Goodwin (1982), White and Bruce (1986).

236 WHITE-HEADED MUNIA (Pale-headed Mannikin) *Lonchura maja*
Plate 55

Oriental

Loxia maja Linnaeus, 1766, Syst. Nat., ed. 12, p. 301, East Indies; restricted to Malacca by Robinson and Kloss, 1924, Journ. Nat. Hist. Soc. Siam, 5, p. 362.

IDENTIFICATION Length 11·5–12 cm (4½ in). A pale or white-headed munia similar to race *ferruginosa* of Chestnut Munia (235), with which it overlaps in Java and Bali. Entire head to chin and throat white; nape, sides of neck and breast buffish-white, tinged light brown. Upperparts, including wings, dark warm brown or chestnut. Tail bright chestnut or reddish-brown. Lower breast pale brown, belly darker, becoming blackish-brown on undertail-coverts. **Confusion species:** Race *ferruginosa* of Chestnut Munia has extensive black on chin, throat and breast and has much sharper contrast between head colour and upperparts. Juveniles are paler about the head than juvenile Chestnut and have reddish-brown (not olive-brown) rump; generally warmer brown or more rufous-tinged than juvenile Spotted Munia (229). No other munias in the native range have white or whitish heads; Pale-headed Munia (237) from Sulawesi and the Lesser Sundas is very similar, but with paler peachy-orange underparts (juveniles are greyer on head and face but otherwise probably inseparable on their own). For differences from the initially similar New Guinea finches Grey-banded (239) and Grey-headed (240) Mannikins, see those species.

DESCRIPTION Sexes similar. **Adult male:** Entire head to nape, face, chin and throat pale whitish or creamy-buff, lower nape and sides of neck (to breast) similar but more clearly tinged or washed with light buffish-brown; in fresh plumage hind-crown and nape have vinaceous tinge. Mantle, back and scapulars warm brown or dull chestnut; rump and uppertail-coverts dark chestnut-brown. Tail wedge-shaped, rounded at tip with two central feathers longest, dark brown on central feathers, outers reddish-brown or bright chestnut tinged with yellow at edges. All wing-coverts and edges to flight feathers uniform with scapulars, inner webs to flight feathers dark brown. Breast as nape and sides of neck or tinged slightly greyer; lower breast and belly brown, becoming darker or blackish-

brown on vent and undertail-coverts. Bill stout and thick at base, with curved culmen, grey or greyish-blue with white or whitish tip and cutting edges. Legs and feet dark grey or blue-grey. **Adult female:** Very similar (if not identical) to adult male and not always separable; generally paler or duller, and head is washed with buffish-brown (males in worn plumage look exactly the same). **Juvenile:** Head and face buffish-brown or pale greyish-buff. Upperparts generally light tawny, with warm or reddish-brown on rump, uppertail-coverts and tail; underparts generally buff, palest on chin and throat and darkest on undertail-coverts. Bill pale blue or grey-blue. Legs dark grey.

VOICE Contact call is a soft, piping 'puip', 'peekt' or 'pee-eet', fairly similar to that of Chestnut Munia but much higher-pitched and lacking reedy tone. The song is a high-pitched and constantly repeated tinkling 'heeheehee' etc.

STATUS, HABITAT AND BEHAVIOUR Fairly or locally common resident. Occurs in similar habitat to Chestnut Munia, at up to 1500 m (in Java and Bali) in marshes, swamps and reedbeds, tall grassy areas of cultivation, and in some areas, gardens. Roosts in reedbeds or cane-fields. Usually in pairs, or in small or large flocks, and occurs in large mixed flocks with other munias during the rice harvest; breeds in colonies or loose groups. Tame and rather easily approached. Feeds on the ground and in or on growing plants, mostly on small weed seeds and grass seeds.

DISTRIBUTION Monotypic (although some authorities recognise two other races). Southern (peninsular) Thailand, Malay peninsula, Singapore and Penang, Sumatra, Simeulue, Nias, Java and Bali.

MEASUREMENTS Wing 54; tarsus 13; bill (from feathers) 11.

REFERENCES Goodwin (1982), King *et al.* (1975).

237 PALE-HEADED MUNIA (Pallid Finch) *Lonchura pallida* Plate 55

Indonesia

Munia pallida Wallace, 1863, Proc. Zool. Soc. London, p. 495, Lombok and Flores.

IDENTIFICATION Length *c* 9–10 cm (3½-4 in). A small pale-headed finch of Sulawesi and the Lesser Sundas, very similar to White-headed Munia (236) but ranges do not overlap. White head and face, becoming tinged with grey or grey-brown on nape and breast; upperparts are warm dark brown, with rump and uppertail-coverts chestnut, and

underparts light peachy-orange. **Confusion species:** Very similar to a number of other white- or pale-headed munias (none of which occurs within same range): White-headed Munia has darker, brown underparts and black undertail-coverts, and white on head is usually slightly more extensive; race *ferruginosa* of Chestnut Munia (235) has black chin to breast and black undertail-coverts and generally is much richer brown or more chestnut-brown; juveniles of all three species are probably inseparable on their own. For differences from very similar New Guinea finches, Grey-banded (239) and Grey-headed (240) Mannikins, see those species.

DESCRIPTION Sexes similar. **Adult male:** Forehead to crown and face pale buff or buffish-white; nape, hindneck and sides of neck slightly greyer or in fresh plumage tinged buffish-brown, merging into warm or deep brown of mantle, back and scapulars. Rump and uppertail-coverts (which cover short tail feathers) a bright or rich deep reddish-chestnut; in worn plumage tips of uppertail-coverts become orange-yellow. Tail short and rounded at tip, warm brown with orange edges to outer feathers. Median and greater coverts as upperparts; primary coverts and edges to secondaries and tertials paler, more gingery-brown; primaries and centres to secondaries brown. Chin and throat as face or tinged slightly duller or greyer; breast as nape and sides of neck or grey tinged with brown, lower breast, belly to vent and flanks pale peachy-orange; undertail-coverts similar to rump and uppertail-coverts but slightly duller. Bill deep at base, with curved culmen, grey or bluish-grey. Legs and feet dark grey. **Adult female:** Similar to adult male, but very slightly duller above and below (but rump, uppertail- and undertail-coverts as male). **Juvenile:** Very pale grey-brown on fore-head, crown to face and nape; mantle, back, scapulars and rump pale brown or slightly duller, uppertail-coverts slightly warmer brown; edges to tail feathers warm ginger, centres darker. Median and greater coverts pale brown, as are edges to secondaries and tertials; primaries and centres to secondaries brown. Chin and throat to upper breast pale buff or whitish, becoming pale warm or orangey-buff wash on flanks and slightly heavier on belly and undertail-coverts.

GEOGRAPHICAL VARIATION Race *subcastanea* is slightly darker and browner, but differences between the two races are very slight and may not be constant owing to individual variation. Sometimes treated as monotypic.

VOICE Undescribed.

STATUS, HABITAT AND BEHAVIOUR Common within a very restricted range. Occurs in paddy-fields, dry scrubland, grasslands and fallow fields or edges of cultivation up to 1400 m. Often in company with Moluccan (228) and Spotted (229) Munias. Feeds on grass seeds, rice and small seeds. Actions and behaviour as other munias.

DISTRIBUTION *L. p. pallida:* central and southwest Sulawesi, Madu, Kalaotoa and the Lesser Sunda Islands: Lombok, Sumbawa, Flores, Roti, Alor, Sawu, Dao, Kisar, Romang, Sermata and Babar.

L. p. subcastanea: known only from lower Palu valley, Gulf of Palu, north-central Sulawesi.

REFERENCE White and Bruce (1986).

238 GREAT-BILLED MANNIKIN (Grand Munia) *Lonchura grandis*
Plate 60

New Guinea

Munia grandis Sharpe, 1882, Journ. Linn. Soc. London, Zool., 16, p. 319, Taburi, Astrolabe Mountains, Southeastern New Guinea.

IDENTIFICATION Length 12 cm (4¾ in). A very distinctive and comparatively large mannikin with a very large bill. All-black head to nape and underparts, except for a patch of light chestnut on sides of lower breast and flanks; upperparts chestnut-brown or tinged brighter, with orange or yellow on rump, uppertail-coverts and tail. Unlikely to be confused with any other species within its native range.

DESCRIPTION Sexes alike. **Adult:** Entire head and face (to underparts) black, relieved only by bright red or reddish-brown eye. Mantle, back and scapulars light chestnut, tinged slightly orange; rump and long uppertail-coverts variable from light chestnut to orange, edged with yellow or yellow-ish-gold. Tail wedge-shaped with pointed central feathers, dark brown on central pair of feathers, with edges to outers yellow, yellowish-gold or on some tinged with greenish. Median and greater coverts as scapulars or very slightly darker chestnut; alula, primary coverts and flight feathers darker chestnut-brown, with edges of tertials broadly warm brown. Underparts entirely black, apart from a thin patch of light chestnut on sides of lower breast and flanks. Bill clearly very large, deep at base, with curved culmen, pale greyish or whitish-blue. Legs and feet dark greyish-blue. Adult female is slightly but noticeably smaller and shorter than male. **Juvenile:** Almost uniform brown or medium-brown above, with paler or buffish-brown rump and tail; light buff underparts, or darker buff-brown on throat and upper breast. Bill large and distinctive, dark grey or paler along cutting edges.

GEOGRAPHICAL VARIATION Most races separated geographically by only very short distances, isolated from each other by ridges or lines of hills dividing the valleys where they occur. Most variation concerns bill size, the depth of the brown or chestnut on upperparts and the tone of the yellow edges to uppertail, and are of little use for field purposes. Races are generally separable on range, as very few (if any) overlap.

VOICE Contact note between the sexes is a sharp metallic 'peep' or 'pi-pi'; also a sharp 'tink tink' uttered occasionally and a plaintive 'quire'.

Uncommon or locally common. Usually found in lowland rank grasslands, swamps, marshes, edges of lagoons and rice-fields, also in cane-fields; in some parts of the range occurs in gardens. Mostly sedentary, from sea-level to the lowlands and hills up to 600 m, exceptionally to 1300 m. Occurs in pairs, or in small or medium-sized flocks of up to 300. Occasionally (in southeast of range) mixes with flocks of Grey-headed (240) and Chestnut-breasted (246) Mannikins. A probable hybrid between latter and Great-billed has been seen in the wild. Feeds mostly on the ground or on floating vegetation, mostly on seeds of marsh grasses; occasionally takes small insects.

DISTRIBUTION *L. g. grandis*: southeast New Guinea, on south coast west to Hall Sound and to Upper Watut river on northern coast.

L. g. ernesti: northern New Guinea from Ramu and Sepik valley to Astrolabe Bay.

L. g. destructa: northern New Guinea, Hollandia district.

L. g. heurni: northern New Guinea, Idenberg and Mamberamo valleys.

MEASUREMENTS Wing 51; tarsus 15–16; bill (from feathers) 12.

REFERENCES Beehler *et al.* (1986), Coates (1990), Restall (1989).

239 GREY-BANDED MANNIKIN (Arfak Mannikin) *Lonchura vana*
Plate 61

New Guinea

Munia vana Hartert, 1930, Novit. Zool., 36, p. 42, Kofo, 2000 m, Arfak Mountains, New Guinea.

IDENTIFICATION Length 10 cm (4 in). A shy and little-known mannikin of very limited distribution in the northwest of New Guinea. Has a pale buff or greyish-white head, dull brown upperparts and wings and pale yellow rump and tail. A thin band of grey across the lower breast separates the pale brown breast from the warm brown or rufous-brown belly to undertail-coverts. **Confusion species:** The ranges of the other two species of white-headed mannikins from New Guinea, Grey-headed (240) and Grey-crowned (241), do not overlap with (or are adjacent to) the range of this species. Grey-crowned has a black chin and throat (and undertail-coverts) and bright orange underparts; nominate Grey-headed lacks any warm brown and is pale grey below, becoming darker grey and with black undertail-coverts (race *scratchleyana* is paler, with brown upperparts and buff-brown on flanks). Elsewhere, White-headed (236) and Pale-headed (237) Munias have an initial resemblance, but lack the bright yellow uppertail-coverts and bright orange underparts.

DESCRIPTION Sexes alike. **Adult:** Forehead, forecrown to face, chin and throat whitish-buff or greyish-white. Hindcrown, nape and sides of neck brownish, tinged with grey at tips, becoming warm earth-brown on mantle, back and scapulars; rump and uppertail-coverts bright yellow (in fresh plumage), becoming duller or straw-yellow (when worn). Tail wedge-shaped, the longest central feathers pointed at tip, dark brown or blackish on central feathers and broadly pale or bright yellow on outer webs of all outer feathers. All wing-coverts as scapulars; flight feathers dark brown, or edged slightly warmer brown on outer edges of tertials. Breast brown or muddy grey-brown, with a band of grey across lower breast separating it from the warm orange-brown or light chestnut on belly, flanks, thighs and vent to undertail-coverts, the latter slightly darker (often tipped with black). Bill stout and deep at base, with curved culmen, grey, dark grey or bluish-grey. Legs and feet dark grey or blackish. **Juvenile:** Generally brown on upperparts, but with a grey-brown tinge to head and face; underparts dull greyish-buff on breast, becoming a pale yellowish wash on flanks and belly.

VOICE A thin, rather high-pitched 'ts ts ts'.

STATUS, HABITAT AND BEHAVIOUR A scarce and shy resident of grasslands on hillside or mountain slopes between 1800 m and 2100 m. Very little known about its habits, food, breeding or social behaviour.

DISTRIBUTION Monotypic. Restricted to the middle levels of the Arfak and Tamrau Mountains in the Vogelkop of northwest New Guinea and around the Anggi lakes.

REFERENCE Beehler *et al.* (1986).

240 GREY-HEADED MANNIKIN (Grey-headed Munia) *Lonchura caniceps*
Plate 61
New Guinea

Munia caniceps Salvadori, 1876, Ann. Mus. Civ. Genova, 9, p. 38, Naiabui, Hall Sound.

IDENTIFICATION Length 10 cm (4 in). A small mannikin of restricted distribution in southeast New Guinea. Has a pale buff or greyish head, and darker grey underparts becoming black on undertail-coverts; mantle, back and wings dark reddish-brown or chocolate-brown, with bright yellow or golden-yellow rump and uppertail-coverts (overlying brown tail). See comments under Grey-banded Mannikin (239); no other white-headed mannikin in New Guinea overlaps with this species. The immature is similar to that of Chestnut-breasted Mannikin (246), but separable by size, darker bill and lack of any dark streaks on face.

DESCRIPTION Sexes alike. **Adult:** Entire head and face to nape, sides of neck, chin, throat and upper breast pale buffish or light grey. Mantle to lower back and scapulars dark chocolate-brown; rump, uppertail-coverts and wedge-shaped tail bright yellow or on some bright orange-yellow (central pair of tail feathers can be dark brown, usually noticeable only towards tip). All wing-coverts and tertials similar to scapulars but browner, and edges to tertials slightly warmer; flight feathers dull brown or tinged dark grey. Lower breast to belly, upper flanks and thighs dull grey, becoming darker grey on lower belly, vent and lower flanks; undertail-coverts black. Bill deep at base, generally stout (though smaller in comparison with other mannikins/munias), with curved culmen, dark grey or bluish-grey. Legs and feet dark grey or blackish-grey. Adult female as adult male, but somewhat duller in overall plumage (probably noticeable only when a pair present).

Juvenile: Very plain and more sandy-brown on the head and paler and lighter sandy-brown on upperparts, wings darker brown and generally pale buff below; also lacks bright yellow or golden tones of rump to tail, which are replaced with buff.

GEOGRAPHICAL VARIATION Race *scratchleyana* is much warmer brown on upperparts, the crown often shows some slight streaking, and rump and uppertail-coverts to base of tail are pale yellow; underparts are tinged slightly warm buff or reddish-buff to rear of flanks, light brown on belly with the black sharply demarcated only on undertail-coverts. Race *kumusii* is paler above than nominate, but has belly to vent and thighs dark or slate-brown.

VOICE Usual call is a frequently repeated 'teee' or a lower-pitched 'tooo'; when in flocks gives a rapid 'seee seee seee'.

STATUS, HABITAT AND BEHAVIOUR Fairly or locally common. Occurs in a variety of grassland and savanna habitat from sea-level to 2200 m, in swamps and marshes, forest edges, clearings with tall grass and scrub to rice-fields, open grassy areas such as airfields or even gardens in villages, roadsides in towns and cities (including Port Moresby). Usually in flocks of various sizes, generally larger in non-breeding season (but numbers fluctuate between seasons); often in huge numbers in the dry season (June-October) when seeding grasses are plentiful. Often in company with Chestnut-breasted and other mannikins; hybrid Grey-headed X Chestnut-breasted have been recorded in the wild. Feeds in vegetation and on the ground, on a variety of grass seeds. General actions and behaviour as other species of mannikin, but breeding and social behaviour little known.

DISTRIBUTION *L. c. caniceps*: southeast New Guinea, southern coast from Yule Island and Hall Sound to Port Moresby district.

L. c. scratchleyana: southeast New Guinea, Malalaua and Kupriano Mountains; possibly also this race occurs on the northern watershed of the central mountains of Garaina, Chirima Valley and Myola.

L. c. kumusii: southeast New Guinea, Kumusi river to upper Musa river.

MOVEMENTS Makes random or nomadic movements in non-breeding season.

MEASUREMENTS Weight 8.

REFERENCES Beehler *et al.* (1986), Coates (1990).

241 GREY-CROWNED MANNIKIN (Grey-crowned Munia, White-crowned Munia) *Lonchura nevermanni*
Plate 59
New Guinea

Lonchura nevermanni Stresemann, 1934, Ornith. Monatsb., 42, p. 101, Merauke.

IDENTIFICATION Length 11·5 cm (4½ in). One of three species of endemic New Guinea mannikins each with a pale buff head and face and a very small or restricted range, none of which overlaps with others. Very similar in size and shape to the other two, Grey-banded (239) and Grey-headed (240). Grey-crowned is distinctive, with orange on rump and rich orange-brown underparts except for black chin and throat and undertail-coverts.

DESCRIPTION Sexes almost alike (females separable when birds in pairs). **Adult male:** Forehead, crown and face pale buff or buffish-white. Hindcrown, nape and sides of neck grey, but obscured or spotted with dull pale brown edges and tips. Mantle, back and scapulars medium or dark earth-brown (in fresh plumage shows pale greyish tips to mantle and back); lower back warmer brown, merging into rufous-brown on rump and yellow or deep golden-yellow on uppertail-coverts. Tail short, wedge-shaped with elongated and pointed central feathers, central pair brown in centre but broadly edged yellow, with broad yellow edges to all outer feathers. Median and greater coverts slightly darker brown than scapulars; alula, primary coverts and flight feathers slightly duller brown or greyer on inner webs; tertials with broad warm brown or rufous-brown edges. Chin and throat (to sides of throat) black; breast, belly and flanks deep or warm reddish- or orange-brown, occasionally (in fresh plumage) with pale buff tips to breast, and some have a paler centre to belly; thighs, vent and undertail-coverts black. Bill stout or stubby with curved culmen, bluish-grey on upper mandible and pale grey on lower. Legs and feet dark grey or bluish grey. **Adult female:** Very similar to adult male, but has much darker brown lores, cheeks and lower ear-coverts, with pale shaft streaks on upper ear-coverts; forehead and crown tipped buff, with brown edges to hindcrown and nape (palest part of head is usually forehead and cheeks). Chin and throat dark brown (not black). **Juvenile:** Head, face and upperparts generally medium-brown or earth-brown, slightly paler or warmer on rump and uppertail-coverts; underparts are warm or rich buff-brown, without any dark areas on throat or undertail-coverts. First-year birds have dark brown on chin and throat (often with paler or browner tips showing); the white head and face of adult male is apparently not attained until second calendar-year.

VOICE Contact call a short and soft 'eeb' or 'deet', occasionally more drawn out into a 'drooeeet', recalling piping note of Common Bullfinch (118). The song is apparently completely inaudible to human ears, and is given with the head turning from side to side.

STATUS, HABITAT AND BEHAVIOUR Locally common or common. Occurs at up to 1800 m, in tall grass and reeds, mostly in lowland savanna, marshes, reedbeds, grassy riverside banks and rice-fields (even on floating mats of grasses). Usually in pairs or small family parties or in larger flocks, occasionally in mixed flocks with Crimson Finches (199) and Black Mannikins (247). Has hybridised in the wild with latter, with which it may be conspecific. Feeds mostly on the ground, usually in cover of tall grasses, on a variety of small grass seeds; some insect food may possibly be taken, as captive-bred birds have been successful only with the addition of insects or their larvae to their diet.

DISTRIBUTION Monotypic. Southern New Guinea from Kurik and Mapa, Irian Jaya, north to Lake Daviumbu and Balimo, east to the lower Fly river.

MEASUREMENTS Wing 52; tarsus 12; bill (from feathers) 10.

REFERENCE Goodwin (1982).

242 NEW BRITAIN MANNIKIN (Hooded Mannikin/Munia) *Lonchura spectabilis*
Plate 62

New Guinea

Donacicola spectabilis P.L. Sclater, 1879, Proc. Zool. Soc. London, p. 449, New Britain.

IDENTIFICATION Length 9·5 – 10·5 cm (3¾–4¼ in). A small munia endemic to New Guinea, with an all-black head and face to chin and upper throat, and warm brown upperparts with yellow or golden-yellow on rump and tail. Underparts vary with race, from all white (nominate) to light buff-brown (*gajduseki*) to warm cinnamon-brown (*sepikensis*). **Confusion species:** Entirely black head sharply demarcated from mantle and breast makes it easily distinguishable from the high-altitude Alpine Mannikin (249), which also shows a dark bar or band across centre of breast. Grand Valley Mannikin (248) has a greater extent of black on breast, sides of breast and flanks, and the black on the head merges with the brown upperparts. Race *sepikensis* is very similar to the (out-of-range) New Ireland Mannikin (243) from the Bismarck archipelago.

DESCRIPTION Sexes almost alike (possibly separable in the field). **Adult male:** Entire head, face, chin and throat black, except for a thin pale grey orbital ring. Mantle, back and scapulars a light chestnut or warm brown, occasionally with some black tips to feathers of upper mantle; rump and uppertail-coverts deep orange or golden-orange. Tail short and wedge-shaped, reddish-brown or chestnut on central pair of feathers and reddish-orange on outers, all edged with yellow-orange. All wing-coverts as scapulars; flight feathers darker or duller brown, but edges to tertials warm brown. Breast white, becoming pale cream or buffish-white on belly and flanks (in worn plumage, sides of breast and flanks may show pale or fine dark bars); thighs, lower flanks and undertail-coverts black. Bill stout and deep at base, with curved culmen, pale bluish-grey or light grey. Legs and feet dark grey, bluish-grey or blackish. **Adult female:** As adult male, but very slightly duller on rump and tail, and upperparts are more brown than chestnut. **Juvenile:** Lores and face blackish, with some very fine paler streaks on ear-coverts, becoming brown or dark brown on crown, nape and sides of neck. Mantle to rump and wings plain warm brown, uppertail-coverts buffish-brown. Chin and throat black or blackish with extensive pale or buff tips; rest of underparts dull off-white or buffish, with a dull or dingy wash on breast, vent and undertail-coverts. Bill uniformly dark grey-blue or blackish.

GEOGRAPHICAL VARIATION Most racial variation concerns the colour of underparts, the brown tones of upperparts and the intensity of yellow or gold on rump and uppertail-coverts. Race *mayri* is lighter brown above, sharply demarcated on nape from black of head and generally paler straw-yellow on rump and uppertail-coverts; also has a white breast with a buff or yellowish tinge to rest of underparts, and a smaller grey-blue bill. Race *wahgiensis* is similar to *mayri*, but has a pale greyish or bluish-grey bill; *gajduseki* is deep buffish-brown on breast, flanks and belly; *sepikensis* has rich cinnamon-brown (very similar to that of upperparts) on breast, belly and flanks, and rump and uppertail-coverts are deep orange-brown. Birds from the region of Karimui (not so far racially named or separated from other races) have a charcoal-brown head, reddish-brown or straw-coloured uppertail-coverts and buff on breast and belly.

VOICE Typical call note is a 'geeb' or 'eeb' (when given by many in a flock, creates a tinkling sound); *sepikensis* has a thin, down slurred 'zeee zeee'. The song, partly inaudible to human ears, is given by the bird in almost full excited animation, and appears to consist of clicking and 'weee' notes and long drawn-out whistles repeated several times in rising and falling sequences.

STATUS, HABITAT AND BEHAVIOUR Common or locally common. Occurs in lowland to mid-level and up to 2500 m in grasslands, savanna or tall grass with scrub, also in cane grass and gardens with tall grasses. Usually occurs in flocks of up to 40 birds, occasionally much larger, and at onset of breeding season large flocks of females visit beaches to obtain calcium; roosts communally in nests specially built for the purpose (and different from breeding nests). In the eastern highlands hybridises with Alpine Mannikin. Generally tame or confiding. Feeds mostly on grass seeds or pollen taken from the seedheads of growing plants, especially millet; also known to take small amounts of filamentous algae from surface of pools.

DISTRIBUTION *L. s. spectabilis*: New Britain, Long and Rooke Islands.

L. s. wahgiensis: eastern New Guinea, in central and southern highlands from Lake Kopiago east to Aseki; the populations in the Wau valley and Huon peninsula are also considered to be of this race.

L. s. gajduseki: central New Guinea, in Karimui basin and eastern highlands west to Tari.

L. s. mayri: northern New Guinea, in Cyclops mountains and the lowlands of Hollandia.

L. s. sepikensis: northeast New Guinea, East Sepik province.

More information is needed on the distribution of the various races and their relationships with closely related species (with which they occasionally hybridise): such information will determine the future racial divisions in this poorly understood spread of subspecies.

MOVEMENTS Generally sedentary.

REFERENCES Beehler *et al.* (1986), Goodwin (1982), Jonkers and Roersma (1990).

243 NEW IRELAND MANNIKIN (New Ireland Finch)
Lonchura forbesi   **Plate 62**

New Guinea

Munia forbesi P.L. Sclater, 1879, *Proc. Zool. Soc. London*, p. 449, Topia, New Ireland.

IDENTIFICATION Length 11 cm (4¼ in). A short-tailed and large-billed mannikin of very restricted distribution. Generally very little known, social and breeding behaviour virtually unknown. Head and face black; upperparts dull brown, becoming chestnut on edges to wings, and rump to tail brown, fringed with yellow or yellowish-gold. Underparts pale or light warm chestnut, often with pale silvery tips to breast or blackish tips to belly and flanks; undertail-coverts blackish. Within its small range unlikely to be confused with any other species of mannikin; similar to New Britain Mannikin (242), with which it does not come into contact, but closest race of New Britain (nominate *spectabilis*) has white breast, belly and flanks and black chin and throat and vent to undertail-coverts.

DESCRIPTION Sexes alike. **Adult:** Entire head to nape and sides of neck black. Mantle, back and scapulars deep chestnut-brown; rump and uppertail-coverts orange-yellow or yellowish-gold, and wedge-shaped tail with pointed central feathers similar, with brown or orange-brown central feathers and brownish-yellow edges to all outers. All wing-coverts as scapulars; flight feathers dull dark brown but finely edged lighter brown, tertials broadly edged warm or chestnut. Chin and throat black; breast and belly to flanks light cinnamon or reddish-buff, with some slight silvery tips to breast (in fresh plumage) or blackish tips to belly and flanks (in worn plumage); thighs and undertail-

430

coverts black. Bill large, stout and deep at base, black, paler or greyer at base of lower mandible. Legs and feet dark grey or tinged bluish. **Juvenile:** Similar to adult, but with head and face brown and forehead to nape streaked with buff-brown. Upperparts are paler brown, and pale yellowish-brown on rump and uppertail-coverts; underparts pale buff-brown, with faint buffish-brown wash on flanks.

VOICE Undescribed, but apparently similar to that of other New Guinea mannikins.

STATUS, HABITAT AND BEHAVIOUR Scarce or locally common. Occurs in lowland grassland up to 1000 m. Usually in flocks or small (family) parties. Feeds on small seeds of grasses. Other actions and habits little known.

DISTRIBUTION Monotypic. New Ireland, east Bismarck archipelago.

MOVEMENTS Sedentary.

244 HUNSTEIN'S MUNIA *Lonchura hunsteini*   Plate 61
New Guinea (Bismarck archipelago)

Donacicola hunsteini Finsch, 1886, Ibis, p. 1, New Ireland.

IDENTIFICATION Length 10–11 cm (4–4¼ in). A small, short-tailed and rather plump-looking munia of very restricted distribution. Generally very dark all over except for the mottled head, face and nape (which are pale grey or silvery-grey, finely spotted with black) and the reddish or orange-yellow rump to tail feathers. Females are less intensely black than males. Within native range unlikely to be confused with any other small all-dark munia with pale head and bright rump. Grey-headed Mannikin (240) and Thick-billed Munia (251) are both superficially similar but geographically isolated.

DESCRIPTION Sexes almost alike (when in pairs probably separable). **Adult male:** Forehead to nape pale grey or silvery-grey with fine black or dark grey centres to feathers, giving a slightly mottled effect; crown and nape whiter, with only very fine dark centres; cheeks and ear-coverts darker, with only a few well-spaced silvery-white tips; lores jet-black. Mantle, back and scapulars coal-black, but mantle can be washed with grey; rump, deep or warm chestnut-brown; uppertail-coverts golden-yellow. Tail short and slightly or bluntly wedge-shaped, central feathers as uppertail-coverts but all outers dark brown or blackish. All wing-coverts dark brown-black as scapulars; flight feathers brownish-black, but edged paler or with dark grey (paler still in worn plumage). Underparts entirely coal-black, in worn plumage with pale crescents to tips of throat, breast and flank feathers. Bill stout and deep at base, black or greyish-black, with a slightly bluish sheen in breeding plumage. Legs and feet blackish or dark grey. **Adult female:** Similar to adult male but is less intensely black, more charcoal-grey, and has brighter or cinnamon-brown uppertail-coverts; often shows small white spots or bars on lower flanks. **Juvenile:** Generally dark or dark brown, with pale or buffish-brown underparts.

Head, face and neck dark brown, with pale or ash-grey tips to forehead, crown and nape, and ear-coverts streaked with pale buff. Mantle, back and wing-coverts dull brown, and rump to tail also brownish but tinged with yellow at edges of feathers. Wing-coverts as mantle, with darker or blacker brown centres to feathers; flight feathers blackish-brown. Chin and throat blackish or blackish-brown; breast brown, streaked with buff, and belly yellowish-buff. Some sub-adults are dull or dusky brown, with a pale head and face.

GEOGRAPHICAL VARIATION Race *nigerrima* is much blacker or more uniform black in appearance, lacking grey tips to feathers of crown and nape, but the underparts are often tipped with buffish or pale brown. The bill is black with a dark grey base to lower mandible; legs and feet dark slate-blue.

VOICE Call a high, thin 'peep' or 'peep-peep' etc., also a more flute-like 'pee' or 'pee-ip'.

STATUS, HABITAT AND BEHAVIOUR Locally common. Occurs in lowland grasslands including airfields. Feeds on small seeds of grasses and other plants. Very little studied, and its social or breeding behaviour virtually unknown. On Pohnpei (Caroline Islands), where introduced in 1920s, a common roadside bird often forming large flocks and feeding in grasslands and cultivated areas (in some areas has become an agricultural pest).

DISTRIBUTION *L. h. hunsteini*: Kaveing district, northern New Ireland, eastern Bismarck archipelago.

L. h. nigerrima: New Hanover, northeast Bismarck archipelago.

Introduced in 1920s to Pohnpei, Caroline Islands (Micronesia), but race involved unknown.

REFERENCES Coates (1990), Pratt *et al.* (1987).

245 YELLOW-RUMPED MANNIKIN (Yellow-rumped Finch) *Lonchura flaviprymna*

Plate 63

Australia

Donacola flaviprymna Gould, 1845, Proc. Zool. Soc. London, p. 80, Victoria River, Northern Territory.

IDENTIFICATION Length 10 cm (4 in). A rather stout, short-tailed mannikin of northern Australia. Adults have pale buff or whitish head, rich brown upperparts, golden-yellow rump to tail, and yellowish underparts with black on undertail-coverts. Very similar to three white- or pale-headed mannikins in New Guinea from which it is geographically separated. In northern Australia, interbreeds frequently with Chestnut-breasted Mannikin (246) and produces hybrids which are probably fertile. Within native range adults are unlikely to be confused with any other species. Juveniles are sometimes inseparable in the field from juvenile Chestnut-breasted, but latter tends to be duller brown above with a dark grey-brown tail and with a pale or whitish-buff chin and throat and a warm orange-buff pectoral band. Juvenile Star Finch (200) is slimmer, with a much finer and more pointed bill, some grey on face and breast, and upperparts tinged with olive.

DESCRIPTION Sexes alike. **Adult:** Entire head pale buff or creamy-white, but in worn plumage whole head and face dull buffish or white. Mantle, back, scapulars and upper rump warm dark brown (in worn plumage some grey or grey-brown tips show on mantle and back); lower rump and uppertail-coverts bright or warm golden-yellow. Tail short, wedge-shaped, with dark brown central feathers and tips to most of outers, edges to all outers yellowish-gold. Median and greater coverts brown, edged warm brown or chestnut; alula and primary coverts dark brown; flight feathers and tertials dark brown, edged warm brown or cinnamon-brown. Chin and throat whitish, pale buff or tinged with cream; breast tinged with light orange; belly and flanks pale yellowish or straw, becoming paler on lower belly and lower flanks; vent and undertail-coverts black. Bill large, stout, silvery-grey or light bluish. Legs and feet pale grey or bluish-grey. **Juvenile:** Generally entirely warm or light cinnamon-brown with a paler or tawny rump and light brown tail, and dark grey lores and bill. Underparts almost entirely pale buffish-brown.

VOICE Very similar to that of Chestnut-breasted Mannikin. Call is a bell-like 'treet' or 'tlit' of varying length for contact or alarm. The song begins with bill-clicking followed by a harsh or hoarse set of notes, and ends with a series of long drawn out whistles.

STATUS, HABITAT AND BEHAVIOUR Scarce, but locally common (or occasionally abundant). Prefers tall rank grasses, savannas or reeds, often found near water in mangroves, on open plains or with scattered trees and bushes, also at edges of cultivation such as rice-fields. Highly social and found in small or large flocks, often mixing with Chestnut-breasted Mannikin (with which it freely interbreeds); also breeds in mixed colonies with latter. Feeds principally on ripe and half-ripe grass seeds, small seeds, and has been known to take rice.

DISTRIBUTION Monotypic. Northern Australia from (about Derby and) Kimberley range, Western Australia, east through Arnhem Land to about 135° E in Northern Territory.

MOVEMENTS Largely sedentary but also nomadic, and some move south (to southern edge of the range) to breed in January-March; in dry or drought years occurs in numbers in some coastal areas.

REFERENCE Frith *et al.* (1979).

246 CHESTNUT-BREASTED MANNIKIN (Chestnut-breasted Munia) *Lonchura castaneothorax*

Plates 60 and 63

Australia and New Guinea

Amadina castaneothorax Gould, 1837, Synops. Birds Australia, pt 2, pl. 21, Interior of New South Wales.

IDENTIFICATION Length 9·5–10 cm (3¾–4 in). A distinctively coloured mannikin with a black face, chin and throat and a warm orange-brown breast-band bordered below by a black band across inner breast. Upperparts and tail very similar to those of Yellow-rumped Mannikin (245), with which it is often found in the dry interior of northern Australia and with which it often interbreeds

(producing hybrids which are probably fertile). Adults unlikely to be confused with any other species; lone juveniles are difficult to separate with certainty in the field from those of Yellow-rumped, but Chestnut-breasted has greyer crown to nape, darker or grey-brown upperparts, dark or grey-brown tail, and a buff-brown band across breast.

DESCRIPTION Sexes almost alike. **Adult male:**

Forehead to nape light grey or pale buff-brown, mottled with paler silvery-grey tips; entire face to over eye, lores and sides of neck black or blackish-brown, with some very fine buffish-brown streaks on cheeks and ear-coverts. Mantle, back and scapulars warm chestnut or reddish-brown, often with pale buff or greyish tips to upper mantle in fresh plumage; rump and uppertail-coverts golden-yellow or deep orange (tinged browner in worn plumage), longest uppertail-coverts paler yellow. Tail wedge-shaped but blunt or more graduated than on other mannikins, drab or dull brown centrally with golden-yellow edges. All wing-coverts uniform with scapulars; alula and primary coverts darker brown; flight feathers dark brown, edged with reddish-brown or chestnut. Chin and throat black, sharply demarcated along lower edge of throat from the bright orange or light chestnut breast, which is bordered below by a broad band of black across centre of breast; belly to vent white, extending to flanks, which are barred with black or brown crescents on lower flanks; thighs and undertail-coverts black. Bill stout, heavy, pale or light bluish-grey. Legs and feet grey, bluish-grey, purplish or blackish. In worn plumage looks altogether paler and duller, especially on head and upperparts. **Adult female:** As adult male but generally paler and duller, with much paler breast and a comparatively thinner dividing line between orange of breast and white of belly. **Juvenile:** Head and face greyish or greyish-buff, with some pale buff streaks on ear-coverts; upperparts cold brown tinged with grey, wing-coverts and flight feathers darker. Underparts washed light buffish, with a buff-brown or orange-brown pectoral band; chin and throat pale buff or whitish-buff, occasionally with a few dark bars on lower throat. Bill horn or slaty-grey, with a pale buff or yellow spot at base of lower mandible.

GEOGRAPHICAL VARIATION Race *assimilis* is slightly darker in colour. Race *ramsayi* is deeper or richer in general and has completely black face and throat, brown or brownish-black crown scalloped with fine buff tips, the rump is more rufous-brown, becoming golden-yellow or yellowish-buff on uppertail-coverts, and the flanks have more extensive (towards belly) or bolder black-and-white barring; immatures are also slightly darker than those of nominate, with indistinct dark brown streaks on crown, and face, chin and throat are dark brown streaked with buff, upperparts are somewhat darker or deeper tawny-brown, and rump and uppertail-coverts are warm tan or tawny-brown. Race *boschmai* has paler brown (light or tan) breast and a wash or tinge of chestnut on flanks. Race *sharpii* is slightly smaller, and has the forehead buffish-white and crown and nape pale buffish-grey, the rump and uppertail-coverts reddish or warm brown, flanks are extensively barred, and edges of tail feathers are golden-yellow or tinged reddish.

VOICE Very similar to that of Yellow-rumped

Mannikin. Call is a 'tit', 'tlit' or 'treet', when given by a feeding flock, it may be slightly more drawn out and of quite bell-like quality. The song is a long series of high-pitched notes, 'weeeeee eeeeeee, tuee tuee (etc.), cheeouk cheeouk cheeouk, ching-ching-ching (etc.)'.

STATUS, HABITAT AND BEHAVIOUR Common, locally common or scarce. Occurs at up to 1200 m in a wide variety of grassland or scrub habitat, from stands of tall savanna grass to swamp or marsh vegetation, mangroves, wetlands, scrub or thornbush thickets, cane- or rice-fields and edges of other crops or on the edges of towns and villages, often near water. Very social, usually in flocks of up to several hundred (especially in non-breeding season), and often mixes with other finches and mannikins, including Crimson Finch (199), Red-browed Firetail (193) and Yellow-rumped Mannikin in Australia and Grey-headed Mannikin (240) in New Guinea; interbreeds with latter two species. Roosts communally in grass or reedbeds. Flight normally short and bounding, but in large flocks flies fast with shallow undulations, the flock often twisting and turning together. Feeds on the ground or in vegetation, often holding ears of grass or crop under its feet while feeding; eats mainly small grass seeds, millet, sorghum and rice, also takes termites (in flight) and probably other insects.

DISTRIBUTION *L. c. castaneothorax*: eastern Queensland (and islands in the southern Torres Strait) east of the Gulf of Carpentaria, south through eastern New South Wales to about Sydney.

L. c. assimilis: Northern Territory west of the Gulf of Carpentaria, west to the Kimberley range (about 125° E), including Melville Island and Groote Eylandt.

L. c. uropygialis: Geelvink Bay, northwest Irian Jaya, New Guinea.

L. c. sharpii: northern New Guinea from Astrolabe Bay to Humboldt Bay, east to the upper Watut river, Morobe province, and Manam Island.

L. c. boschmai: Wissel Lake, central Irian Jaya, New Guinea.

L. c. ramsayi: southeast New Guinea from the Kumusi river to Bereina area, also the D'Entrecasteaux archipelago; west on the south coast to Hall Sound.

Birds from Australia have also been introduced into New Caledonia, the Society Islands, (Bora Bora, Raiatea, Moorea, Tahiti) and the Marquesas (Hivaoa, Tahuata, Mohotani).

MOVEMENTS Resident, nomadic or partially migratory; in New Guinea, individuals have been known to travel up to 70 km in the non-breeding season.

MEASUREMENTS Wing 54; tarsus 10·5; bill (from feathers) 9·5. Wing of *sharpii* 46. Wing of *ramsayi* 48.

REFERENCES Goodwin (1982), Pizzey and Doyle (1980).

Lonchura stygia Stresemann, 1934, Ornith. Monatsb., 42, p. 102, Mandum, upper Bian River, southern New Guinea.

IDENTIFICATION Length 10·5–11 cm (4–4¼ in). Small, virtually all-black mannikin of very restricted range in southern New Guinea. Has yellowish-orange rump to uppertail-coverts and a pale blue-grey bill; females average duller or browner on the wings. Within its native range the all-black plumage makes it unlikely to be confused with any other species; Streak-headed Mannikin (232), which also occurs within the range, looks black at a distance, but at closer range the brown on mantle, back and coverts and streaks on the head will be obvious.

DESCRIPTION Sexes similar. **Adult male:** Almost entirely glossy black (but becomes browner with wear or abrasion), tinged with brown on wings, with flight feathers edged blackish-brown; underwing-coverts pale cream or whitish. Rump and uppertail-coverts vary from pale yellowish to rich golden-yellow. Tail wedge-shaped, with elongated, pointed central feathers which are black centrally, becoming yellow on edges, all outers black with yellow on outer edges. Bill stout and with a curving culmen, grey or bluish-grey. Legs and feet dark grey. **Adult female:** Generally duller black and not so glossy as male; browner on wings and upperparts, with chestnut band on upper

rump. **Juvenile:** Generally drab brown or grey-brown on head and upperparts, including rump and uppertail-coverts, but rump can also be warm buffish-brown; tail feathers are not so pointed as those of adult, and all tail feathers are narrowly edged very pale yellow. Crown and nape feathers have pale buff shaft streaks and dark or blackish tips, and ear-coverts are blackish-brown with pale buff or whitish centre streaks. Breast a paler grey or buffish-grey with uneven dark feather tips, rest of underparts pale buff or washed peachy-buff.

VOICE Undescribed.

STATUS, HABITAT AND BEHAVIOUR Locally common. Found in lowland grasslands and reeds, swampy grasslands, floating mats of grass in swamps or marshes, also drier savannas at sea-level; in some areas an occasional visitor to rice-paddies. Usually in small flocks of up to 20, often mixed with Grey-crowned Mannikins (241) (with which it has been known to hybridise) and with Crimson Finches (199). Feeds on the ground or in vegetation, on seeds of grasses.

DISTRIBUTION Monotypic. Kurik and Mandum to Lake Daviumbu, western Trans-Fly region, Papua New Guinea.

248 GRAND VALLEY MANNIKIN (Black-breasted Munia, Grand Valley Munia) *Lonchura teerinki*   Plate 60

New Guinea

Lonchura teerinki Rand, 1940, Amer. Mus. Novit., no. 1072, p. 14, Bele River, 2200 m, 18 km north of Lake Habbema.

IDENTIFICATION Length 10 cm (4 in). A small brown-and-white mannikin restricted in distribution to a few valleys and mountainsides in northwest New Guinea. Has a black face, breast and flanks with some brown streaking along lower flanks, rich or deep warm brown upperparts, with rump and uppertail-coverts golden or straw-yellow, and blackish-brown tail with yellow edges to central feathers. Whitish underparts with black undertail-coverts. **Confusion species:** Within its native range likely to occur only with New Britain Mannikin (242), with which it comes into contact in part of its range; Grand Valley Mannikin has black on breast and flanks (unmarked white, buff or cinnamon on New Britain) and the black on nape merges with the brown of mantle (sharply demarcated on New Britain Mannikin). Snow Mountain Mannikin (250) is similar on upperparts, but has throat and breast warm yellowish-buff and

is strongly barred on sides of breast and flanks.

DESCRIPTION Sexes almost alike (possibly separable in pairs). **Adult male:** Forehead and lores blackish-brown becoming deep or dark warm brown on crown and nape to mantle, back and scapulars (with pale tips to mantle and back in fresh plumage); rump and uppertail-coverts golden or yellowish-straw. Tail graduated, yellowish-brown, central feathers longer than the dark brown or blackish-brown outer feathers, some with paler or lighter brown edges. Median and greater coverts as scapulars, but edged and tipped slightly warmer; alula, primary coverts and flight feathers the same, or edged with warm brown or light chestnut; tertials duller, but broadly edged warm brown. Face, sides of neck, chin, throat and breast black, continuing as glossy black onto sides of lower breast and flanks; the latter have brown or blackish-brown blotches, often appearing to join along the flanks

in long streaks (may also show some reddish-brown spots on flanks); rear of flanks and undertail-coverts plain black; belly to vent white. Bill stout, with curved culmen, pale blue with lead-grey tip and cutting edges. Legs and feet grey or dark slate-grey. **Adult female:** Very similar to adult male but duller, not so black on face and breast, and the black on sides of breast and flanks not so extensive, with the brown broken into individual patches or bars; centre of belly and vent tinged light buffish. Bill slightly smaller than that of male. **Juvenile:** Generally brown on upperparts, with light brown or light tan-brown on rump, uppertail-coverts and edges of tail feathers. Chin and throat warm brown or orange-buff, becoming dull or greyish-brown on breast; rest of underparts pale buffish, with pale orange-buff on flanks.
GEOGRAPHICAL VARIATION Race *mariae* has the black extending across the head and face (not dark brown) and a deeper or richer brown on mantle, back and scapulars.
VOICE Contact note is a typical 'teu', repeated

frequently; also gives a dry, rising 'twy' and a sparrow-like chirrup.
STATUS, HABITAT AND BEHAVIOUR Uncommon or scarce. Occurs between 1200 m and 2200 m in grasslands, weed or scrub patches, secondary-growth areas including abandoned gardens and edges of clearings or cultivation, even in villages. Very poorly known, and little information available on social or breeding behaviour. Occurs in flocks, as is typical of all mannikins. Probably feeds on grass seeds and other small seeds.
DISTRIBUTION *L. t. teerinki*: Grand Valley, the Balim and Bele river valleys and northern slope of Mount Wilhelmina, central Snow/Oranje Mountains, west-central New Guinea.
   L. t. mariae: central Snow Mountains of western Irian Jaya, northwest New Guinea.
MOVEMENTS Sedentary.
MEASUREMENTS Wing 53; tarsus 12; bill (from feathers) 9.
REFERENCES Beehler *et al.*(1986), Goodwin (1982), Restall (1989).

249 ALPINE MANNIKIN (Eastern Alpine Mannikin, Alpine Munia)
Lonchura monticola   Plate 61

New Guinea

Munia monticola De Vis, 1897, Ibis, p. 387, Mt Scratchley.

IDENTIFICATION Length 12 cm (4½-4¾ in). A fairly large (larger than most) or plump mannikin from high altitudes of southeast New Guinea. A striking bird with an all-black head and face merging across the nape with brown or buffish-brown upperparts; wing-coverts warm brown, slightly darker on edges of flight feathers, rump chestnut and uppertail-coverts pale yellow. Underparts white, with a prominent black band across centre of breast to upper flanks. Unlikely to be confused with any other mannikin, as no others are found at such high altitude. New Britain Mannikin (242), found at low to mid-level, has clear-cut black hood and no warm brown on upperparts.
DESCRIPTION Sexes alike. **Adult:** Forehead to crown and face to ear-coverts, chin and upper throat black, blackest on forehead. Hindcrown, nape and lower sides of neck brown or grey-brown with a darker tinge, becoming paler mid-brown or warm buffish-brown on mantle, back and scapulars and chestnut on rump; uppertail-coverts pale lemon or straw-yellow. Tail wedge-shaped, tips of longest central feathers rounded at tip, blackish with bright yellow edges to all feathers. All wing-coverts bright warm brown or dull chestnut; flight feathers brown, edged as on coverts and broadly so on outer edges of tertials. Lower throat to belly and sides of body white, except for a broad band of black across centre of breast and continuing down flanks (where often appears broken or as bold black bars); thighs, vent and undertail-coverts black. Bill fairly stout and deep at base, with curved culmen, pale blue or greyish-blue. Legs and feet pale grey-

brown or bluish-grey. **Juvenile:** Generally brown on head and upperparts; crown, nape and face have some dark, dusky or blackish feather centres and are tipped pale buff; rump and uppertail-coverts contrastingly warm buff-brown or pale chestnut. Chin and throat black, but mottled or flecked with white tips; breast buffish-white, tinged duller or grey-brown (dark band across breast becomes apparent at an early age); rest of underparts buffish-white, except for peachy to reddish wash on flanks and undertail-coverts. Bill dark grey or blue-grey.
VOICE Typical call notes are distinctive and unlike those of other New Guinea mannikins: has a distinctive rattling, buzzing note and a thin 'see see see' uttered in flight.
STATUS, HABITAT AND BEHAVIOUR Common within limited range. Occurs at high altitude between 2700 m and 3900 m, in alpine grasslands and in rocky or boulder-strewn pastures with stunted bushes. Usually in small flocks of up to 50, and individual flocks may comprise same-aged birds; has been known to associate with Grey-headed Mannikins (240) at Myola (2000 m), and may have hybridised with New Britain Mannikin. Generally shy and unapproachable. Flight stronger and more direct than that of lower-level mannikins. Feeds on the ground or in vegetation, usually on small grass seeds.
DISTRIBUTION Monotypic. Mountains of the Wharton and Owen Stanley ranges east to Myola, southeast New Guinea.
MOVEMENTS Generally resident.

MEASUREMENTS Wing 62; tail 57; tarsus 17; bill (culmen) 9.

REFERENCES Beehler *et al.* (1986), Coates (1990), De Vis (1897).

250 SNOW MOUNTAIN MANNIKIN (Western Alpine Mannikin)
Lonchura montana **Plate 60**
New Guinea

Lonchura montana Junge, 1939, Nove Guinea, new ser., 3, p. 67, Oranje Mountains, 4150 m, New Guinea.

IDENTIFICATION Length 11 cm (4¼-4½ in). A fairly distinctive high-altitude mannikin from the mountains of central New Guinea. Has a black face and chin, with warm or rich brown upperparts, warm brown coverts and black wings; rump and (short) uppertail-coverts are pale yellow and the tail black. Lower throat, breast and sides of throat warm gingery-brown, rest of underparts white with prominent blackish bars on lower breast and flanks; undertail-coverts black. **Confusion species:** Confusion possible with Grand Valley Mannikin (248), but latter has much more extensive black on head, face and breast and lacks the individual barring on flanks. Chestnut-breasted Mannikin (246) has more black on the face and similar underparts, but has a black (dividing) band across lower breast. Neither species is likely to be found at the same altitude as Snow Mountain.
DESCRIPTION Sexes similar. **Adult male:** Forehead to crown, extending to sides of crown behind eyes and to cheeks, fore ear-coverts, chin and upper throat black. Nape and hindneck deep brown, becoming warmer or deeper brown on mantle, back and scapulars, slightly paler on lower back; rump and short uppertail-coverts pale lemon-yellow. Tail rather short but wedge-shaped, black but with yellow at edges of base. Median and greater coverts warm brown; alula and primary coverts dark brown, finely edged with warm brown or warm earth-brown; flight feathers dark brown or blackish-brown, edged with warm brown. Chin and upper throat black; sides of neck and rear of ear-coverts warm buff, lower throat and upper breast warm gingery-brown; lower breast, belly and flanks white, with thin blackish-brown bars;

belly to vent white or whitish, undertail-coverts black. Bill stout and with curved culmen, pale grey or lead-grey. Legs and feet grey or dark slate-grey. **Adult female:** In direct comparison with male, female is paler straw-yellow on breast, the black face mask is more clear-cut on throat and does not merge into breast, and the black on top of head is restricted to forehead. **Juvenile:** Generally dull brown above. Dark cold brown lores, forehead, crown and nape; more olive or slightly paler olive or warmer brown on mantle and back, with wings dark brown; pale tan olive-brown rump, becoming pale buff-brown on uppertail-coverts. Tail black. Chin dark cold brown, throat dull muddy brown, becoming dull orange-brown in a band across breast; rest of underparts washed dingy creamy-buff (begins to show a few dark bars at an early age).
VOICE Undescribed.
STATUS, HABITAT AND BEHAVIOUR Common or locally common within very limited range. Found at high levels, generally above 3000 m and up to 4100 m, in wet or boggy grasslands in alpine plateaus, stunted shrubs or scrub and edges of cultivated fields. Usually in flocks of up to 20 in both breeding and non-breeding seasons. Social and breeding behaviour little known; apparently nests in long grass near water, but nest has never been found. Perches in trees and tree-ferns. Feeds on the ground, on small seeds of grasses and herbs.
DISTRIBUTION Monotypic. Snow Mountain range, west of the Balim gorge, western central New Guinea; extralimital to Mount Capella, Papua New Guinea.

251 THICK-BILLED MUNIA (New Britain Finch, Buff-bellied Mannikin, Buff-bellied Black Mannikin) *Lonchura melaena* **Plate 62**
New Britain

Munia melaena P.L. Sclater, 1880, Proc. Zool. Soc. London, p. 66, Kabbakadai, New Britain.

IDENTIFICATION Length 10–11 cm (4–4¼ in). A fairly large, dark munia with a large bill and very limited distribution. Head and breast black, becoming brownish-black with a tinge of rust on upperparts; rump and tail reddish or rusty-brown

with a tinge of golden. Underparts black, with a broken-edged patch of deep buffish-cinnamon or pale orange on belly. **Confusion species:** Only confusion likely to arise is with New Britain Mannikin (242), which has a black hood, warm brown upperparts and pale or creamy-buff underparts. Juveniles may not be so easy to separate, but juvenile New Britain Mannikin is paler or pale buff below and has a smaller bill.

DESCRIPTION Sexes alike. **Adult:** Entire head and face to nape, sides of neck, chin, throat and upper breast black. Mantle, back and scapulars blackish-brown, tinged with rusty-brown; rump and uppertail-coverts rich reddish, tinged gold or rusty-orange. Tail short and slightly wedge-shaped, pointed at tips of central feathers, dark brown with reddish-yellow edges, outer feathers dark brown with paler or more orange or reddish-yellow edges. Median and greater coverts as upperparts; alula, primary coverts and flight feathers black. Black continues from breast onto flanks and to vent and undertail-coverts; lower breast and belly rich or deep buffish-cinnamon or pale orange-buff, with some dark tips forming broken bars or crescents on flanks and sides of belly. Bill large, very stout or prominent, curving ridge to upper mandible, dark grey or blackish with distinctive blue-grey base to lower mandible. Legs and feet dark grey. **Juvenile:** Generally has dark brown upperparts with reddish-brown rump and uppertail-coverts; underparts light brown. Bill is smaller than adult's.

GEOGRAPHICAL VARIATION No races described, but birds on Buka in the Solomon Islands are darker or deeper brown or chestnut on mantle, back and wings, the rump and uppertail-coverts are deep reddish-chestnut, and lower breast, belly, flanks and thighs are reddish-buff, the flanks barred with black.

VOICE Undescribed.

STATUS, HABITAT AND BEHAVIOUR Fairly common or locally common. Occurs in rank grasslands with bushes or scrub, also in swamp vegetation, at up to 1200 m. Often in flocks of up to 20, and appears to breed almost throughout the year. Feeds on the ground, on grass seeds, and possibly also other small seeds.

DISTRIBUTION Monotypic. New Britain, Bismarck archipelago and Buka in the Solomon Islands (latter population discovered only in 1981).

MOVEMENTS Possibly nomadic within its very limited range.

MEASUREMENTS Wing 54; tarsus 16; bill (from feathers) 13.

REFERENCES Coates (1990), Goodwin (1982).

252 PICTORELLA FINCH *Lonchura pectoralis*   Plate 63
Australia

Amadina pectoralis Gould, 1841, Proc. Zool. Soc. London, 8, p. 127, Derby, northwest Australia.

IDENTIFICATION Length 11−11·5 cm (4¼-4½ in). A small and distinctive grey finch with a black face and throat, from northern Australia. Crown and upperparts mainly grey or silvery-grey, with browner wings and brown rump and tail. Breast blackish partially (female) or entirely (male) obscured by broad silvery-white tips; rest of underparts rich or deep pinkish-buff. **Confusion species:** Chestnut-breasted Mannikin (246), however, has rich brown upperparts and yellowish rump and uppertail-coverts.

DESCRIPTION Sexes similar (but separable in the field). **Adult male:** Forehead to nape pale grey, tinged with brown; sides of forehead pale buff or pinkish-buff from bill to rear of ear-coverts and sides of nape. Mantle, back and scapulars as crown; rump, uppertail-coverts and tail (rounded at tip) darkish brown. Median and greater coverts as scapulars, with small white spots at tips often forming a row; alula, primary coverts and flight feathers brown or dark brown, with edges to flight feathers and tertials warm brown. Lores, cheeks and ear-coverts to chin, throat and sides of throat black (in fresh plumage shows a purple sheen); throat (especially lower throat) has small white spots, but in worn plumage often shows brown shaft streaks or spots; upper breast with black feather bases obscured by bright white tips, appearing closely barred (but also shows as an almost

white patch). Rest of underparts rich or warm pinkish-buff, but some (in worn plumage) lack pink on centre of belly and vent; sides of lower breast and upper flanks show some black-and-white spots or small crescents; undertail-coverts as belly or paler, sometimes showing darker tips (crescents). Bill slimmer, slightly longer and more pointed than on typical munias with only slight curve to upper mandible, grey or blue-grey, with culmen darker grey. Legs and feet bright flesh-pink or fleshy-brown.

Adult female: Very similar to adult male but paler on underparts, which are generally warm buff, and with fewer and smaller white spots on tips of median and greater coverts. Face and throat are more brownish-black (becoming greyer in worn plumage), and has more fine white spots on lower throat than male; breast is more clearly black, with white tips appearing as fine close scallop marks.

Juvenile: Generally dull brown or buffish-brown on upperparts, darker or warmer brown on face, and pale buffish-grey on throat and upper breast, with remainder of underparts pale peachy-buff; wings and tail are brown, with warm or rich buff edges and tips to coverts and flight feathers. Bill dark brown or blackish, with pale buffish-horn base to lower mandible.

VOICE Contact call is a soft and fairly sparrow-like 'chip', 'pik' or 'tscheep', often drawn out into a penetrating 'tlit' or 'tleet'. The song is extremely short and simple, a very brief 'giee' repeated at two-second intervals.

STATUS, HABITAT AND BEHAVIOUR Uncommon or locally common: declining in parts of the range. Found in open woodlands, grasslands, savannas with scattered trees and bushes, including spinifex plains, and often in tall grass near water, also at edges of cultivation; decline may be due to the frequent burning and destruction of habitat for the development of cattle stations. Usually in pairs, small groups or large flocks, the latter especially in non-breeding season. Frequently mixes with both Yellow-rumped (245) and Chestnut-breasted (246) Mannikins and Zebra Finches (201). Rather wary or unapproachable. Feeds in vegetation and on the ground, usually on a variety of grass seeds and to some extent rice, but readily takes insects (including termites, beetles and spiders) and also catches insects in flight; has been seen to feed on filamentous green algae from the side of a pool. Drinks by rapid sipping and by sucking.

DISTRIBUTION Monotypic. Northern Australia from about King Sound east through the Kimberley range (south to about 20° S) to the eastern shore of the Gulf of Carpentaria; also (formerly continuously) east from about the Robinson river to the Barkly Tableland east to about Croydon and Richmond, northern Queensland.

MOVEMENTS Nomadic and wanders widely inland in summer, returning towards coastal districts at the start of the dry season; has occurred north to the Edwards river (along the Cape York region), where it may also have bred.

REFERENCES Blakers et al. (1984), Frith et al. (1979), Goodwin (1982).

GENUS *PADDA*

Two species. Java Sparrow and Timor Dusky Sparrow are closely related to the *Lonchura* finches (with which they have frequently been classified) in bill shape, structure, voice and behaviour, but are slightly larger and share a very clearly defined plumage pattern; they also differ from the *Lonchura* in the palate pattern of the nestlings. Both have very restricted natural ranges in the wild, but Java Sparrow has been widely introduced throughout the world.

253 TIMOR DUSKY SPARROW *Padda fuscata*   Plate 73

Indonesia

Loxia fuscata Vieillot, 1807, Ois. Chant., p. 95, pl. 62, Timor.

IDENTIFICATION Length 13 cm (5 in). Similar in overall plumage pattern to Java Sparrow (254), with white cheeks and black cap and chin, but rest of plumage is brown or chocolate-brown with mostly white underparts. Within native range unlikely to be confused with any other species. Considerably different (brown, not grey, and lacks coral-red bill) from initially similar Java Sparrow.

DESCRIPTION Sexes alike. **Adult:** Forehead to nape and sides of crown black; lower lores, cheeks and ear-coverts white. Lower nape and hindneck to mantle, back, scapulars, rump and uppertail-coverts chocolate-brown, tinged with purple (on some, rump is grey or grey-brown). Tail slightly rounded at tip, dark or deep rich brown, undertail whitish. All wing-coverts and tertials chocolate-brown, with paler buff edges and tips in worn plumage; alula, primary coverts and flight feathers all deep chocolate-brown with darker or blackish inner webs. Chin and sides of upper throat (below white face patch) black or blackish-brown; throat and breast chocolate-brown, tinged purple (slightly warmer than that on upperparts), bordered below with a broad band of black; rest of underparts pure white. Bill strong and sparrow-like with curved culmen, more pointed than on munias, bluish or steel-grey. Eye dark brown, pale blue orbital ring. Legs and feet pale brown. **Juvenile:** Generally very pale brown or fawn-brown overall, with a paler or lighter buffish face, throat and breast, and only lores and top of ear-coverts are dark brown; throat and breast warm orange-buff, rest of underparts white or whitish. Bill dark grey.

VOICE Contact call 'chip' or 'tsip', similar to but quite distinguishable from that of Java Sparrow. The song is a rapid series of call notes run together, 'chip chip chip chipchipchipchip', or a more garbled version, 'clik clik clik clikliklikliklikli', often repeated several times.

STATUS, HABITAT AND BEHAVIOUR Local or locally common. Occurs singly, in pairs or in family parties (up to 12) in lowland scrub, grasslands and saltflats, also frequently on the edges of cultivation, mainly rice-paddies. Often in company with Red Munia (187). Feeds principally on small grass seeds and seeds of other plants, including thistles, also some rice. Apparently still widely trapped for the cagebird trade.

DISTRIBUTION Monotypic. Lesser Sunda Islands: Timor and (adjacent) Semau and Roti islands.

MOVEMENTS None known, but has only recently been recorded on Roti.

REFERENCES Restall (1989), White and Bruce (1986).

254 JAVA SPARROW *Padda oryzivora*

Plate 73

Indonesia

Loxia oryzivora Linnaeus, 1758, Syst. Nat., ed. 10, 1, p. 173, Asia [Java].

IDENTIFICATION Length 17 cm (6¾ in). Very distinctive; one of the most common and widespread cagebirds, readily recognised throughout the world by its distinctive plumage. Introduced into many areas of the world, though has not always become established. Within its native range now rather scarce owing to continued depletion of the wild population for the avicultural trade. Unlikely to be confused with any other species. The superficially similar Timor Dusky Sparrow (253) is chocolate-brown with a pale grey bill.

DESCRIPTION Sexes alike. **Adult:** Forehead, upper lores, crown and nape black; lower lores, cheeks and ear-coverts pure white, bordered below by a fine line of black on sides of neck to chin. Mantle, back, scapulars and rump pale bluish-grey, becoming blackish on uppertail-coverts. Tail graduated or rounded at tip (when perched, appears square-ended), black. All wing-coverts as scapulars, and flight feathers slightly darker or more slate-grey. Chin and sides of upper throat black; throat, breast and upper belly pale grey, sharply demarcated across upper belly from the pale pink or light mauvish-pink belly, flanks and ventral region; lower flanks and undertail-coverts creamy-white. Bill large and deep at base, prominent, deep pink or coral-pink with pale pinkish or whitish at tip and on cutting edges. Legs and feet deep pink or flesh-pink. **Adult female:** Usually inseparable from male in the field (and also in the hand), but in known pairs shows very slightly smaller and paler bill. **Juvenile:** Generally a pale buffish-brown bird with pinkish-buff face and dark grey crown. Upperparts pale buff-brown, with warmer or darker brown edges and tips to pale grey coverts, secondaries and tertials. Chin and throat whitish or pale buff, becoming a heavier buff-brown or spotted with the same colour on breast; yellowish-buff on the lower breast and belly. Bill slightly smaller than adult's, black or blackish-brown with pale pink base to both mandibles.

GEOGRAPHICAL VARIATION No races known, but white, pied and fawn forms occur in captivity.

VOICE Contact call is a liquid-sounding 'tup', 't,luk' or 'ch,luk', also a sharp 'tack'; alarm is a harsh-sounding version of contact call. The song is a series of bell-like notes followed by trilling and clucking sounds, often ending with a long drawn-out metallic whistling note.

STATUS, HABITAT AND BEHAVIOUR Scarce or generally uncommon within its native range in Java and Bali (largely through considerable numbers having been trapped, and either eaten locally or exported to satisfy avicultural demands). In the wild prefers lowland (up to 1500 m) grass-lands or open woodlands with grass or scrub, but also edges of cultivation, gardens and suburban towns. Highly social, and often in large flocks in rice- or cane-fields, trees or thickets; at other times found in pairs or small flocks. Is or was considered a pest species owing to its invasion of rice- or maize-fields in numbers. Feeds in growing vegetation or on the ground, mostly on grass seeds, fruits or small insects, but also regularly takes rice and maize.

DISTRIBUTION Monotypic. Java, Bali and Bawean. Now introduced and/or escaped (and has formed feral populations) in many parts of southeast Asia, including parts of India (Calcutta, Madras), Sri Lanka (around Colombo), Burma (apparently became established around Tenasserim, but may now be extinct), Thailand (Bangkok), Malaya (including Singapore), Sumatra, Borneo, Sulawesi, Ambon (Moluccas) and Lesser Sundas (Lombok and Sumbawa), Fiji (Viti Levu, Vanua Levu and Taveuni), Philippines (Guimaras, Luzon, Mindanao, Panay, Samar, Cebu, Pan de Azucar, Calagnaan and Negros), Taiwan, eastern China from Kiangsu south to Kwangsi and Hong Kong, Japan (Honshu and southern Kyushu), and South Vietnam; also Christmas Island, Cocos Keeling Islands; Zanzibar and Pemba; Hawaii (Oahu, Kauai and Hawaii), Puerto Rico and Florida (Miami); formerly on Guam, Mauritius and Comoro Islands.

MOVEMENTS Largely sedentary, but makes local movements when flocks gather at cultivated rice-fields when rice is ripening.

MEASUREMENTS Wing 68; tail 50; tarsus 19; bill 18.

REFERENCE Goodwin (1982).

GENUS *AMADINA*

Two species. Cut-throat and Red-headed Finches are generally more sturdy or robust in appearance than other estrildids, with a thick or deep-based bill and sandy body plumage barred or spotted darker. Species of dry or semi-arid country. They have been widely regarded in the past as closely allied to the weavers (hence Cut-throat Weaver), but on the basis of the mouth markings and downy young are probably nearest to the *Pytilia*, though the shape of the bill also shows some similiarity to the *Lonchura* genus.

255 RED-HEADED FINCH (Paradise Sparrow) *Amadina erythrocephala*
Plate 50

Africa

Loxia erythrocephala Linnaeus, 1758, Syst. Nat., ed. 10, p. 172, Africa; restricted to Angola by Edwards, 1751, Nat. Hist. Birds, 4, p. 180.

IDENTIFICATION Length 12–13 cm (4¾–5 in). A distinctive finch from southern Africa. Male has an all-red head and face (except lores), sandy-brown or grey-brown upperparts, and slightly darker wings with pale sandy or buff tips to coverts and edges to tertials. Dark or grey-brown tail has white spots on tips of outer feathers. Underparts heavily barred or scaled. Females lack any red on the head, and are uniform grey-brown or sandy on head, face and upperparts and prominently barred or scaled below. **Confusion species:** The heavily barred underparts separate this from the mostly smaller Estrildid finches and also from Red-headed Quelea (*Quelea erythrops*), which is similar in size and has a similar head pattern to adult male. Most confusion likely with Cut-throat Finch (256), but all-red head of males, together with prominently barred underparts (more broken or in crescents on Cut-throat), white spots to tips of outer tail feathers and plain upperparts (and plain head of adult female) are distinctive.
DESCRIPTION Sexes differ. **Adult male:** Forehead to nape, cheeks, ear-coverts, chin and throat rich red, almost blood-red, with some brown tips to hindcrown, nape or sides of nape (in worn plumage, crown, nape and face become a rusty-orange); lores pale grey or sandy-buff. Mantle, back and scapulars sandy-brown or greyish sandy-brown, this extending to rump and uppertail-coverts, which have slight or fine dark subterminal bars and pale or whitish tips (prominently on uppertail-coverts). Tail graduated towards tip, dark grey or brown with white tips to outermost feathers. Median and greater coverts greyish or sandy-brown (slightly darker in tone than the paler scapulars), each feather subterminally dark with a pale sandy spot at tip; alula, primary coverts and flight feathers deeper sandy-brown, edged pale sandy-buff, tertials the same with broad sandy-buff fringes. Underparts pale buff or white-buff with thin or fine black tip to each feather, giving a scalloped appearance on breast and belly; on flanks the bars or scallops become more widely spaced, with warm sandy-buff bases, extending to thighs and vent; undertail-coverts pale creamy. Bill short, stout, with curved culmen, brownish-horn, pale buffish

or brown, tinged pinkish in breeding season. Eye brown, orbital ring pale grey. Legs and feet pinkish-brown. **Adult female:** A plain version of adult male (lacks any red on head), but can show some orange or rust tones to the otherwise pale grey-brown crown, nape and sides of neck. Upperparts slightly greyer than on male, and bars and tips on uppertail-coverts not so prominent. Underparts similar to those of male, but less intensely marked sandy-buffish (not white) subterminally and barring more individually spaced (appears less scaly than male); centre of belly pale sandy-buff. **Juvenile:** Very similar to adult female, but generally paler and more buffish and barring on underparts not so distinct; rump and uppertail-coverts barred at tips. Juvenile males can show some orange tints to head and face at an early age, but others develop this at moult into adult plumage in first summer.
GEOGRAPHICAL VARIATION Race *dissita* is slightly darker and less sandy on upperparts, and not so white on throat.
VOICE Typical call is a harsh 'chuk, chuk', also a sparrow-like 'shep' or 'tsep', or a 'zree zree' given in flight; alarm a sharp 'tek' or 'tak', also a hissing anger note. The song is a series of soft munia-like churring or buzzing notes.
STATUS, HABITAT AND BEHAVIOUR Common. Inhabits dry grasslands, savanna and thornscrub (has been recorded in semi-desert scrub), edges of broad-leaved woodlands, edges of cultivation and settlements. Usually in pairs, small groups or larger flocks of up to 1,000, often (in east of the range) in company with Cut-throat Finch. Flight often in short undulations, but also fast and/or in shallower bounds. Feeds on the ground on grass seeds, also takes termites. Makes regular daily visits to waterholes to drink.
DISTRIBUTION *A. e. erythrocephala*: northwest Angola south to Namibia, Botswana (except the north), southwest Zimbabwe to Cape Province, western Transvaal and Natal, South Africa.
    A. e. dissita: Drakensberg escarpment, eastern Cape Province to southern Natal, South Africa.
MOVEMENTS Nomadic, and wanders widely throughout the range in non-breeding season.
MEASUREMENTS Wing 70–75; tail 46–55; tar-

sus 14–17; bill (culmen) 11–12·5, depth 10.
Weight 24.

REFERENCES Goodwin (1982), McLachlan and Liversidge (1978), Newman (1983).

256 CUT-THROAT FINCH *Amadina fasciata* **Plate 50**
Africa

Loxia fasciata Gmelin 1789, Syst. Nat., p. 859, no locality; Senegal designated by Vieillot, 1805, Ois. Chant., p. 90.

IDENTIFICATION Length 11–12 cm (4½–4¾ in). A very scaly or closely barred finch found over much of Africa outside the tropical-forest zone. Both sexes have a very finely barred head, but male has a distinctive semicircle of red stretching from ear-coverts to throat (hence the name Cut-throat). Rest of plumage buffish or sandy-brown with some warm buff edges and tips and dark bars, crescents or chevrons. Tail black. **Confusion species:** Once the diagnostic head-and-face pattern of adult male is seen, unlikely to be confused with any other species. Lone females may initially be confused with female or juvenile Red-headed Finch (255), but sandy plumage and fine barring on head and upperparts of female Cut-throat will separate it from the more uniform Red-headed.

DESCRIPTION Sexes differ. **Adult male:** Forehead to nape and sides of nape finely or closely barred black on pale sandy-buff, the feathers being sandy-brown or pale sandy-buff at base with fine black tip; lores, cheeks and chin white or whitish-buff; ear-coverts to centre of throat a band of crimson-red; sides of neck to lower throat creamy or whitish with some fine black tips. Mantle, back and scapulars slightly darker or more heavily sandy than crown, but barred and spotted at intervals with blackish subterminal crescents and pale warm sandy-buff tips to scapulars; rump and uppertail-coverts closely barred with whiter or paler tips, forming a black-and-white barred pattern. Tail slightly rounded at tip, dark brown or brownish-black with white tips to all feathers, some of which (especially on central feathers) wear down; outermost tail feathers broadly tipped white and outer webs also white. Median and greater coverts sandy-grey (similar to colour on scapulars), with black subterminal barring and pale sandy-brown tips forming indistinct wingbars; alula and primary coverts dark grey-brown; flight feathers dark grey-brown, with warm pale brown or buffish-brown edges and tips. Breast and flanks sandy-brown with black crescents or chevrons; lower breast and belly a patch of chestnut or warm brown; thighs pale or light brown; vent and undertail-coverts pale buff-brown with light sandy-brown tips. Bill short, conical, pointed, pale creamy-horn or whitish, grey or tinged with pinkish or light bluish-grey. Legs and feet pale flesh-pink. **Adult female:** Very similar to adult male except for absence of red on face-to-throat area. Entire head and face as on forehead to nape and sides of neck on adult male. Upperparts and underparts similar to those of male, but lacks chestnut lower breast and belly patch; usually has more black marks on feather tips often forming complete bars, especially on underparts, which are paler or lighter buff; dark bars usually continue to undertail-coverts, but belly and vent sometimes unmarked. **Juvenile:** Juvenile males closely resemble adult male, but are more sandy or warm buff in general, with tips to median and greater coverts prominently pale sandy or buff and edges of secondaries also broadly pale sandy; the red 'cut-throat' appears at an early age, but is broken by black-and-white tips; bars on crown and back, the back is poorly marked, or unmarked on mantle and underparts are also poorly marked in comparison with adult. Juvenile females are as adult female, but crown bars are thinner; centre of mantle usually unmarked or only faintly barred; pale fringes to wings as on juvenile male, and fewer black marks on face and throat; underparts less marked, occasionally unmarked.

GEOGRAPHICAL VARIATION There is considerable individual variation (often due to wear), but in general East African birds *alexanderi* are slightly duller or greyer, with the black markings (on upperparts and underparts) usually broader than in nominate race and tips not so pale sandy or buff, and the chestnut patch on belly of male is smaller and not always so obvious. Southern African *meridionalis* has the head and face greyish or pale whitish (not sandy or pale buff-brown), tipped or finely barred with black, and is generally darker or deeper sandy-brown on upperparts and underparts; has a band of white across lower throat, and breast is more heavily marked than in nominate; it also has a slightly smaller bill. Other races have also been described.

VOICE Generally most calls are rather sparrow-like chirps and fairly similar to those also made by Saxaul Sparrow (257); nesting pairs have a loud 'kee-air'; otherwise gives a thin 'eee-eee-eee' in flight. The song is a low-pitched humming or buzzing broken by low toneless warbling notes, often repeated without a break.

STATUS, HABITAT AND BEHAVIOUR Common or locally common. Prefers dry brush country, mopane woodland, acacia savanna, semi-desert with scattered trees or scrub, often at edge of cultivation and villages; generally occurs below 1500 m, exceptionally to 2100 m. Makes frequent or regular visits to drink. Usually in groups or flocks of varying size, but also encountered in isolated pairs; pair bond very strong, and lone females unlikely to be far from a male. Mixes freely in non-breeding season, often in company with Red-headed Finch in south of the range, and in large flocks containing queleas and weavers. Hops or walks on ground. Feeds on a variety of (mainly grass) seeds; also eats termites.

DISTRIBUTION *A. f. fasciata*: Senegal and Gambia southeast and east to southern Mali (to about 17° N), Burkina Faso, Niger, northern Nigeria, northern Cameroon and Chad to central Sudan, northeast Uganda and northwest Kenya.

A. f. alexanderi: southeast Sudan, Ethiopia and Somalia, south through Kenya to central and southern Tanzania.

A. f. meridionalis: central and southern Malawi, southern Zambia, Zimbabwe, central and south Mozambique, east Botswana (possibly also to southern Angola and northeast Namibia) to western Transvaal and northern Orange Free State, South Africa.

MOVEMENTS Generally resident, but wanders widely at random in search of food in non-breeding season; a dry-season visitor to northern Ghana and southern Nigeria; in the south of the range, occasionally wanders south to Natal and the eastern Cape Province. Ringing recoveries in Zimbabwe have shown that some move considerable distances, with one recovery 285 km north-north-east of its original point of capture.

MEASUREMENTS Wing 63–70; tail 39–42; tarsus 12·5–14; bill (culmen) 10–12.

REFERENCES Goodwin (1982), Irwin (1981), Newman (1983).

GENUS *PASSER*

Twenty-one species. Sparrows, widespread and global in distribution, include some species that are specialised and restricted in range and feeding requirements. Most are sexually dimorphic, but in the grey-headed species of Africa the sexes are identical. Sometimes regarded as part of the Ploceidae family, which includes the weavers, whydahs and indigobirds, largely because of their complex nest structures and feeding behaviour.

257 SAXAUL SPARROW *Passer ammodendri*   Plate 67
East Palearctic

Passer ammodendri Gould, 1872, Birds of Asia, pt 24, pl. 15, Turkestan [Djulek, above Kzyl Orda, on the Syr Darya, Hartert, 1904, Vög. pal. Fauna, p. 158].

IDENTIFICATION Length 14–16 cm (5½–6¼ in). A pale sandy or grey-brown sparrow, adult male with a very distinctive head-and-face pattern. A bird of remote desert areas and oases in central Asia. Adult male has black forehead to nape and chin to throat, with patch of pale warm brown on sides of crown to nape, and the face is pale or greyish; upperparts, depending on the race, are pale grey or sandy-brown streaked with black (extending onto rump in nominate race). Females are very pale buff or greyish sandy-brown, with dark streaks on mantle and back. Both sexes have pale tips to median and greater coverts forming double wingbar. Unlikely to be confused with any other sparrow.

DESCRIPTION Sexes differ. **Adult male:** Centre of forehead to nape and hindneck black (in fresh plumage shows pale edges and tips); sides of lower forehead pale or whitish, becoming pale tawny or sandy on sides of crown and broadly onto nape; lores to slightly behind eye and thinly along rear of ear-coverts black; cheeks and ear-coverts pale grey or buffish-grey. Mantle and back grey or brown-tinged grey (paler in worn plumage) and streaked with black, heaviest and often forming a partial collar or shawl on upper mantle; scapulars only lightly streaked; rump and uppertail-coverts dingy grey-brown, lightly streaked darker. Tail thin and slightly indented at tip, dark brown, edged and tipped paler greyish-buff or light brown. Median coverts black at base, broadly tipped white, greaters dark brown to blackish at base, broadly edged grey or grey-brown and tipped pale whitish or buff; alula dark brown with fine white edge; primary coverts dark brown, edged finely with pale creamy-buff, tips all dark brown; flight feathers dark brown, primaries finely edged white or pale buff with a small whitish or pale buff panel at base of inners, secondaries similar and broadly edged pale buff, tertials broadly edged and tipped pale buff. Chin and throat (or upper throat) black, sometimes extending slightly onto upper breast, sides of chin and throat white; sides of breast and flanks tinged grey or buffish, rest of underparts pale or dull off-white. Bill black. Legs and feet pale brown or pinky-brown. **Adult female:** Generally grey-brown, streaked darker, with black on forehead, crown and nape; mantle and back loosely streaked dark or blackish; rump and uppertail-coverts plain unstreaked grey. Tail slightly paler brown than adult male, and all feathers edged finely with buff. Wings similar to male but slightly duller brown; dark bases to coverts are rather broadly tipped pale buff and form double wingbar. Pale sandy-buff supercilium, thin and not always well defined; dark eye-stripe to rear of ear-coverts; cheeks and ear-coverts greyish or smudged dull grey-brown. Chin and throat variable from grey or pale grey to dark grey (not always visible), becoming pale buff, dingy or off-white on rest of underparts; flanks often washed buffish-brown. Bill pale yellowish at base of both mandibles, with dark or blackish tip. **Juvenile:** Juvenile and first-winter are very similar to adult female, but lack any dark on throat, and the crown is generally not so dark or blackish as on adult.

GEOGRAPHICAL VARIATION Male *nigricans* are similar to those of nominate race in general plumage, but have much blacker and somewhat more extensive streaks on mantle and upper back, and rump and uppertail-coverts spotted with black; females are similar to those of nominate. Male *stoliczkae* have upperparts including edges to coverts and flight feathers predominantly cinnamon, warm sandy or sandy-buff, with mantle and back as heavily spotted and streaked (in worn plumage) as in nominate, but rump and uppertail-coverts plain light brown or grey-brown; sides of crown and more broadly on nape are a warm gingery-brown, much deeper or heavier in tone than in either of preceding races; underparts are as nominate, but also show faint broad bluish-grey stripes on sides of breast and flanks. In fresh (winter) plumage the black on crown and nape is obscured by brown or grey-brown tips, and nape often appears entirely cinnamon or warm gingery-brown. Female *stoliczkae* are not so cinnamon or warm sandy and look much plainer, except for broad pale sandy supercilium, slight streaks on mantle, and broad warm sandy-buff edges to coverts and especially tertials and secondaries; chin and throat white or pale buff. Within all three races there is some slight variation in intensity of plumage tones among populations. Some birds of the previously separated race '*timidus*' (now included within *stoliczkae*) have slightly longer or deeper bill. Other races have been proposed or formally recognised, but are now considered to be synonyms of the presently recognised races.

VOICE Call a melodic chirping and a short whistle.

STATUS, HABITAT AND BEHAVIOUR Common, locally common or abundant; recent evidence from Mongolia indicates that drying-out of large areas and land-use changes or intensification of agriculture have reduced the amount of habitat available and probably caused a retraction in the range. A bird of deserts, oases and desert river valleys, also into foothills; usually not far from saxaul (*Arthrophytum haloxylon*), tamarisk or poplar thickets, also found at or near the edges of desert settlements. A shy or wary bird, spending much time hidden within foliage and often difficult to approach. In winter associates with mixed flocks of Spanish (259), House (258) or Tree (274) Sparrows. Feeds mainly on seeds of saxaul and other shrubs, also those of available plants, and takes insects in spring; the young are fed principally on insects, mostly weevils, grasshoppers, small beetles and caterpillars; around human settlements feeds on spilled grain. Makes regular trips to drink, often flying some way to do so.

DISTRIBUTION *P. a. ammodendri*: Russian Turkestan, southeast and east of the Aral Sea, along the course of the middle and lower Syr Darya, Kazakhstan north to 47° N and south to about 40° N, also extreme northern Uzbekistan; also south of Lake Balkhash from 45° N along the Ili river to Issyk Kul; and along the middle course of the Amu Darya to about 56° E south to the border with (but not known to breed within) northern Iran.

P. a. stoliczkae: west Sinkiang from Kashgar, east along the foothills of the Tien Shan range, south to the Kunlun range (though probably absent from the Takla Makan desert) to the foothills of the Astin Tagh, extreme northern Kansu, Ningsia to west Inner Mongolia (Gobi and Ordos deserts); also western Gobi desert, southern Mongolia.

P. a. nigricans: northern Sinkiang from north Dzungaria, about 48° N to about 90° E and south to the Manas river valley, northwest China.

MOVEMENTS Mostly resident or sedentary, but in non-breeding season undertakes local movements and numbers at breeding sites fluctuate. Occurs as a winter visitor to extreme northeast Iran and the foothills of the Paropamisus, northwest Afghanistan.

MEASUREMENTS Wing of male 72−81, of female 71−78; tail 63−69·5; tarsus 19−20; bill (culmen) 10−13. Wing of male *stoliczkae* 78−82, of female 75−76. Wing of female *nigricans* 73·5−81. Weight 25−27.

REFERENCES Densley (1990), Flint *et al.* (1984), Summers-Smith (1988).

258 HOUSE SPARROW *Passer domesticus*　　　　Plate 67
Holarctic and Oriental (with introductions elsewhere)

Fringilla domestica Linnaeus, 1758, Syst. Nat. ed. 10, p. 183. Sweden.

IDENTIFICATION Length 15 cm (6 in); races vary from 14 cm in the south of the range to 18 cm in the north. One of the world's most widespread and best-known species. Has flourished widely largely as a result of successfully adapting to and benefiting from the activities of man; absent only from parts of China (except the extreme north), northern Siberia, Japan, Indo-China, Thailand, Malaysia, west Australia, Alaska, most of northern Canada and Newfoundland, Greenland, Iceland, northern tropical forests of South America, most of Africa (except the southern third) and Madagascar. **Confusion species:** The grey crown of the male distinguishes it from Tree (274) (both sexes),

Spanish (259) and Cinnamon (262) Sparrows. Tree Sparrow is also distinguished by less extensive amount of black on the throat (none on the breast) and by the dark patch on the ear-coverts. Male Sind Jungle Sparrow (260) also has less black on throat and upper breast, as well as a much greyer nape and sides of nape and a warm brown lower back and rump. Confusion most frequent with Spanish Sparrow, but latter's brown (not grey) crown, extensive black on breast and flanks and bold black and brown streaks on mantle and back should enable separation when dealing with pure birds. The position is complicated, however, by the 'Italian Sparrow' (currently considered) a race of Spanish Sparrow, which has probably evolved from a long history of hybridising with House Sparrow and now stabilised; current hybrids between the two species exist in northwest Africa, southern Italy and some Mediterranean islands. Female and immature House Sparrows are extremely similar to those of Spanish and Sind Jungle Sparrows, and some individuals may not always be separable. Female Spanish generally looks somewhat more substantial or slightly robust, with a much larger bill than female House; it has well-defined or broadly pronounced pale buff supercilia, and golden or bright buff 'tramline' streaks bordered boldly with black on mantle and back; the underparts are diffusely but noticeably streaked on breast and flanks (underparts of female House are plain dingy). Female Sind Jungle Sparrow is slightly smaller than female House, and generally has a well-defined pale or creamy-buff supercilium that often extends to sides of nape; other differences (which depend on time of year and/or state of plumage) are its paler or whiter throat and a warmer buff or sandy-buff tone to rump.

DESCRIPTION Sexes differ. **Adult male:** Forehead to centre of nape and hindneck dull or dark grey; lores black, often extending slightly below and behind eye; small or thin white post-ocular spot; cheeks and ear-coverts dingy, off-white to grey (white or whiter in fresh plumage); sides of crown from behind eye to sides of nape chestnut-brown. Mantle and upper back warm brown, boldly and broadly streaked with black, edges to centre of mantle and back paler buff or golden-brown in fresh plumage; scapulars black, with broad warm brown or chestnut edges and tips; lower back and rump grey-brown, greyer in worn plumage; uppertail-coverts similar, with darker centres. Tail quite long, thin and notched at tip, dark brown or blackish-brown with fine pale buff or buffish-brown edges. Lesser coverts uniform bright reddish-chestnut, extending to medians, which have thin subterminal band of black and broad white tips; greater coverts dark brown or blackish, broadly edged warm brown or bright chestnut and tipped pale buff or golden-buffish; alula black; primary coverts blackish, edged warm brown or chestnut; flight feathers blackish with a small pale brown patch at base of inner primaries, edges to secondaries pale or light brown; tertials similar but often paler, especially towards tip. Chin, throat and centre of breast black, rest of breast grey; flanks,

belly and undertail-coverts pale or dingy grey or washed with buff. Bill black in breeding season. Legs and feet brown or dark brown. In winter, following autumn moult, the black on breast is broken up with pale grey tips, nape and sides of neck become greyish, and edges and tips to upperparts are paler buff-brown. Bill brown or pale brownish-horn with yellow base. **Adult female:** Forehead and upper lores to crown and nape generally dull sandy-brown; pale buffish-brown supercilium behind eye (occasionally begins slightly in front of or just over eye); thin dark or dull sandy-brown eye-stripe; cheeks and ear-coverts dull or dingy grey or greyish with buff tinge. Mantle, back and scapulars similar to crown, with broad dark streaks; sides of mantle and back have pale creamy or yellowish-buff centres bordered by blackish edges, and scapulars have dark brown at base, rump and uppertail-coverts dull sandy or dingy brown in worn plumage. Tail uniform brown with slightly paler edges. Median coverts dark brown at the base, becoming warm brown and fairly broadly tipped pale buff or sandy-buff; greater coverts dark brown, edged warm or deep sandy-brown and tipped slightly paler brown; alula black or blackish-brown; primary coverts similar, edged browner; flight feathers dark brown, edged with buff or warm buff-brown; tertials similar, edged paler towards the tip. Underparts buffish-brown, centre of belly whitish or pale buff; undertail-coverts the same or paler. Bill brown or brownish-horn with yellow basal half to lower mandible. **Juvenile:** Very similar to adult female, but generally has much broader buff-brown edges to feathers of upperparts and dingy-brown underparts. Generally looks very scruffy (similar to adults in moult), with loose feathering. Chin and throat tend to be white or whitish on young females and grey on males, but not all are separable. Supercilium tends to be more buffish or dull buff than the buffish-brown of adult females' and some young birds have quite well-defined supercilia and a thin whitish post-ocular stripe. Bill usually much paler than that of adult female, pale yellow or straw with a dark horn base. First-year birds are similar, if not identical, to adults, adult plumage is usually assumed in the post-nuptial moult in June-October, but some, perhaps birds from later broods, may not moult into adult plumage until approaching their first summer. It is quite usual in autumn to find various states of plumage in flocks made up of differently aged individuals (even by a few weeks).

GEOGRAPHICAL VARIATION There is very little racial variation that can be detected in the field; most variation concerns the intensity of the plumage coloration (on males) and differences (in millimetres) in size. The races can, however, be divided into two groups, each of whose members show common characteristics: races *domesticus*, *tingitanus*, *biblicus*, *niloticus* and *persicus* form the Palearctic group, while those of the races *indicus*, *rufidorsalis*, *hyrcanus*, *bactrianus*, *parkini* and *hufufae* form the Oriental group. Birds of the Palearctic group are predominantly grey (not white) on cheeks, ear-coverts and underparts, and those of the Oriental group are smaller in size (generally with smaller bills), have whiter or paler grey cheeks and underparts, and the chestnut plumage is of a more reddish-brown tone. Race *parkini* has slightly more extensive black on the breast than other races.

VOICE Call, possibly the most commonly known bird sound over most of the world, a typical monotonous 'chirrup' or 'chirp' note, at times can sound like a 'chissick' or 'tissip'; also a soft 'swee swee' or 'dwee'. When alarmed or excited has a rolling 'chur-r-r-it-it-it'; also a shrill 'chree' often given at approach of a predator. The song is a monotonous series of the call note interspersed with similar notes, 'chirrup cheep chirp'.

STATUS, HABITAT AND BEHAVIOUR Common practically everywhere throughout its vast range. In both its natural and its introduced range it has successfully occupied a niche alongside human habitation. Its love of urban and suburban environments is such that many birds probably never come into contact with a natural habitat other than a city garden or town square. Has become so well adapted to the built-up environment that it has even been seen feeding at night on the 80th floor of the Empire State Building in New York City; frequently enters factories and warehouses in search of food, especially remarkable being the birds that lived and bred 640 m down a coal-mine in South Yorkshire, England, living on food provided by miners. Apparently absent only from large tracts of equatorial rainforest, deserts and tundra. In parts of eastern Asia it appears to be successfully repelled and replaced (even in cities, towns and villages) by the Tree Sparrow, and in such areas where it does occur it is a bird of open country. Besides its preference for human habitation and settlements (farms and similarly cultivated areas), it can occur in almost any habitat from sea-level to 4500 m where food is available; in warmer climates (e.g. Mediterranean basin, the Middle East and east Australia) it exists quite happily and independently away from man. Social and gregarious, usually living in small or loose colonies; following the breeding season family groups gather at feeding areas, where flocks (often in grain or stubble fields in autumn) can number many hundreds or thousands and in some areas can soon become a nuisance by damaging ripening crops. Roosts communally, often in hedges, trees or woods; the largest roost in Britain was estimated at about 19,000 birds near London at the end of August 1949 (small by comparison with the 100,000 at the same time of year in Egypt in 1931). Feeds principally on seeds and readily takes to cultivated crops, especially cereals, millet, rice and sorghum, but favours oats and wheat; also takes the seeds of a variety of wild plants, particularly docks, chickweed, herbs and a number of grasses and will take almost anything suitable offered by way of household scraps. In spring, feeds on buds and sprouting leaves of fruit trees. Feeds on the ground and in vegetation, also chases insects (principally flies, flying ants and moths, rarely butterflies), which it catches in flight. Nestlings are fed almost entirely on insects and/or their larvae, with aphids, weevils, grasshoppers and caterpillars providing the greatest share of their diet, but have such a wide-ranging diet (can be supplemented by a variety of items, from seeds and berries to insects, molluscs and crustaceans) that it is no surprise that it easily survives and prospers alongside mankind.

DISTRIBUTION *P. d. domesticus*: Europe, north to Lapland and the Kola Peninsula, west to the British Isles, south to Portugal and Spain, almost continuously east through southern Europe to the Balkans and most of CIS (USSR) (except the northern tundra region north of the Arctic Circle east of 80° E), south to Mongolia, Amurland and northern Manchuria.

P. d. tingitanus: northwest Africa from Morocco east to Tunisia, northwest Libya and Cyrenaica, in the south to the oases of southern-central Algeria.

P. d. biblicus: Turkey and Cyprus to the southern Caucasus, south through the Middle East to Sinai and west and north Saudi Arabia east to Iraq and west Iran.

P. d. hufufae: eastern Arabia to Oman.

P. d. niloticus: northeast Africa, from Alexandria and the Suez Canal, Egypt, south to northern Sudan.

P. d. rufodorsalis: Sudan, along the Nile to the Blue Nile and lower White Nile.

P. d. persicus: central Iran (south of the Elburz Mountains) to southern Afghanistan and western Baluchistan.

P. d. indicus: northeast Saudi Arabia, southern Iran and Baluchistan to southern Afghanistan, west Pakistan, peninsular India (to about 1500 m and exceptionally to 2000 m), lowlands of Nepal, Sikkim, Bangladesh to Burma (south to Rangoon) and Sri Lanka.

P. d hyrcanus: northern Iran from south Caspian to the Elburz range.

P. d. bactrianus: south-central Asia, east of the Caspian to the Syr Darya valley, east of the Aral Sea to the Tarbagatai range, Dzungarian Ala Tau, Ili and Manas rivers, south through Tadzhikstan to Afghanistan and northern Baluchistan, Pakistan in the west and Kashgaria in the east.

P. d. parkini: Karakoram and Himalayas, from east Afghanistan and Baltistan through Kashmir and northwest India to southwest Tibet, Nepal and Sikkim.

Races hybridise commonly and widely where ranges overlap; also hybridises with nominate and *italiae* races of Spanish Sparrow, more rarely with Tree Sparrows. Introduced and thriving in North and South America (north to Yukon and North-West Territories, discontinuously south to Tierra del Fuego and the Falklands), Juan Fernandez, (some) Caribbean Islands, Bahamas, Azores, Cape Verde Islands (São Vicente), Ascension, coast of Mauritania, Senegal and Gambia (and up to c160 km inland along the Senegal river), southern Africa north to Zambia, Malawi, southern Zaire and Tanzania, Kenya (Mombasa area) (possibly also Mogadishu, Somalia), Zanzibar, Comoros, Amirantes, Seychelles, Mauritius, Maldives, Andaman Islands, Christmas Island, east Australia, Tasmania, New Zealand, Hawaii, New Caledonia and

Easter Island, also possibly elsewhere as the range increases. For full map of House Sparrow distribution and introduction areas, see Summers-Smith (1988).

MOVEMENTS Most populations and races are sedentary, or move only locally over short distances (less than 10 km) in non-breeding season; those in more arid areas move some distance when there is a shortage of water. Post-breeding dispersal of juveniles also takes place on a localised basis, few immatures surviving long enough to replace their parents or colonise new areas adjacent to their natal area. Some evidence that adults, in years of high productivity and low mortality, undertake movements of up to 500 km, and birds crossing the North Sea in autumn are thought to be involved in such movements. Only two races, *bactrianus* and *parkini*, are truly migratory, moving south from the breeding ranges in Afghanistan, Turkestan and the Himalayas to the plains of northwest Pakistan and northern India.

MEASUREMENTS Nominate. Wing (UK) of male 71–82, of female 71–76, (Europe) of male 67–89, of female 70–86; tail of male 55–64·6, of female 52–65; tarsus of male 17–24, of female 16–25; bill (culmen) of male 10–14, of female 10·5–14·5. Weight (Europe) of male 27·7–39·5, of female 24–39·5. For complete biometric data see Summers-Smith 1988.

REFERENCES Brooke (1973), Summers-Smith (1980, 1988).

259 SPANISH SPARROW (Willow Sparrow) *Passer hispaniolensis*
Plate 67

Palearctic, Oriental and marginally Arabia

Fringilla hispaniolensis Temminck, 1820, Man. d'Orn., ed. 2, p. 353, Algeciras, southern Spain.

IDENTIFICATION Length 15–16 cm (6–6¼ in). A rather large-looking sparrow, appearing quite substantial in build with a fairly large or heavy-looking bill. Breeding-plumage males are boldly marked, with a rich brown forehead to nape, white face, and heavy black streaks on underparts often merging into a solid black area on breast; upperparts also streaked blackish, with warm brown on wings. Females are similar to the slightly smaller female House Sparrow (258), but have several fairly characteristic features: slightly larger bill, long pale supercilium, pale 'braces' on sides of mantle, and small spots or streaks on underparts, with a whitish belly. Juveniles are unlikely to be separable from same age House Sparrow in the field unless showing some adult features.

DESCRIPTION Sexes differ. **Adult male:** Forehead to crown, nape and lower sides of neck deep chestnut or reddish-brown; short white line across upper lores, black over eye, and a small postocular patch of white; lores and slightly behind eye black; cheeks, ear-coverts and sides of neck white. Mantle, back and scapulars streaked boldly and heavily with black, edged pale or warm buff-brown, with pale buff or golden-buff braces down sides of mantle and back; rump and uppertail-coverts greyish-brown or dingy sandy-brown with darker centres. Tail quite long and slightly indented at tip, dark brown, edged paler buffish-brown at base. Lesser and median coverts deep chestnut or rich reddish-brown, tips of medians broadly white; greater coverts black, broadly edged chestnut or rich brown and finely tipped white; alula black; primary coverts dark to blackish-brown, edged lighter or warmer brown; flight feathers black or blackish-brown, with pale brown or sandy patch on base of primaries, and all secondaries and tertials edged pale sandy or warm brown. Chin, throat and breast black in full breeding plumage, sides of lower breast and flanks heavily and boldly streaked with black (some more heavily or solidly streaked than others); centre of lower breast, belly to undertail-coverts pure white or tinged slightly with pale grey. Bill stout and quite prominent, black in breeding season. Legs and feet pale pinkish or fleshy-brown. In autumn and early winter much duller, with broad yellowish-buff tips obscuring or partially covering the feathers of forehead, crown, nape, mantle, back and scapulars; the line above eye and ear-coverts is duller; wings much as in breeding plumage, but have broad buff edges to flight feathers; underparts remain streaked with black, but extensively edged and tipped with grey or whitish-buff. Bill dark horn or dull yellowish at base, with dusky tip. **Adult female:** Slightly larger but duller version of adult female House Sparrow. Forehead to crown, nape and sides of neck dull grey-brown; long pale creamy or sandy-buff supercilium, slightly paler (or sandy-) brown than on female House Sparrow and also much longer and better defined over ear-coverts to sides of nape, or to rear of ear-coverts; eye-stripe grey-brown, fairly broad, usually present only behind eye; lores, cheeks and ear-coverts pale grey-brown, but lores may be tipped darker. Mantle, back and scapulars grey-brown, tinged slightly sandy, fairly heavily streaked darker, with pale 'braces' (bordered by long dark edges) at sides of mantle; rump and uppertail-coverts dull grey-brown, lightly or faintly streaked darker. Tail brown or deep grey-brown, finely edged paler grey or sandy-grey. Lesser coverts as scapulars; median coverts black or blackish at base, prominently edged and tipped white; greater coverts dark brown, broadly edged pale sandy-buff or sandy-brown and tipped pale buff; alula dark brown; primary coverts dark

446

brown, paler at base and edged buffish-brown; flight feathers and tertials dark brown, with small square pale buff patch at base of primaries, and edges to secondaries and tertials sandy-buff (pale greyish-buff in worn plumage). Chin and throat white or pale buff, but can also be grey; breast, sides of breast and flanks pale greyish-buff, lightly but visibly spotted or streaked darker (dark feather shafts); belly to undertail-coverts whitish, often smudged greyish. Bill similar to that of non-breeding adult male, yellow or straw-yellow at base and on lower mandible, with dull or dusky brown upper and tip. **Juvenile:** Very similar to juvenile House Sparrow and lone birds are not always separable in the field, but generally well-defined supercilium often a good guide.

GEOGRAPHICAL VARIATION 'Italian Sparrow' *italiae* is now regarded as a race of Spanish rather than (as previously) of House Sparrow. Male *italiae* show characters of both Spanish and House Sparrows, having head and face of Spanish and chin to breast, underparts and rump of House, but a number of hybrid House x Spanish populations exist (particularly in southern Italy and parts of Tunisia and Algeria) which show variations in features between the two species, particularly black on mantle and some streaks on flanks or a cline towards typical Spanish Sparrow characters. In moult or non-breeding plumage, the chestnut of crown to nape is similar to true Spanish but obscured by yellowish-buff feather tips. Female *italiae* are probably not safely separable outside native range; they closely resemble nominate female but (as female House) lack dark streaks on the underparts. Race *transcaspicus* is inseparable from nominate in the field except by range, but in fresh plumage some (especially females) are paler than nominate, and the chestnut on males is not so bright.

VOICE Calls are very similar to those of House Sparrow but variable in pitch, usually slightly higher or more metallic in tone, 'chweeng chweeng' or a squeaky 'cheela-cheeli', but more typically 'chirrup' call is deeper or more resonant; also 'chee-chee-chee' and rolling 'chrr-r-r-i-t-t' similar to House Sparrow. Song also very similar to House Sparrow's, but more of a rolling or rhythmic 'chuet-chuet-chuet-tchuet'.

STATUS, HABITAT AND BEHAVIOUR Common or locally common (though apparently declining in Spain). A bird of open country, often in dry or arid areas but also in vicinity of wetlands, occurs in olive groves, open woodlands, date-palm plantations, hedges or roadside trees, usually adjacent to cultivated areas; in winter occurs in open country with scattered bushes or scrub. In areas where House Sparrow is absent, freely occurs as an urban or suburban bird frequenting built-up areas and gardens; roosts in large numbers in trees in town squares. Colonial in both nesting and roosting habits, winter flocks may contain up to a thousand birds; a Spanish x Tree Sparrow has been recorded in Malta (in December 1975). Generally shy; even when feeding in crops tends to fly off for some distance when disturbed. In all other respects behaves as House Sparrow (but see Movements). Feeds on the ground or in vegetation, mainly on seeds, both of grasses and of cereals (principally wheat, millet, barley and oats), leaves, fruit and some insects, mainly caterpillars, flying ants, grasshoppers and crickets; young are fed principally on insects until fledging.

DISTRIBUTION *P. h. hispaniolensis*: Cape Verde Islands, Canary Islands, Madeira, east-central Portugal (Tagus valley), central to south and southeast Spain, extreme southwest France, Sardinia, southern Yugoslavia east to the Danube delta between Romania and Moldavia, south through Albania, Bulgaria and mainland Greece; in North Africa, from Morocco east through northern Algeria to southeast Tunisia, northwest Libya and Cyrenaica.

P. h. italiae: Italy, Sicily, Corsica, Malta and Crete.

P. h. transcaspicus: Turkey, Cyprus, Syria, Lebanon and Israel south to northern Sinai (extreme northeast Egypt); eastern and southeast Caucasus (north to Terek river) through northwest to central and eastern Iran, to central and north Afghanistan and north through Turkmenia and Uzbekistan to the Aral Sea and eastern Kazakhstan to Lake Alakol, also in the Tarim basin to about 84° E, between the Tien Shan and Kunlun ranges, west Sinkiang, west China.

Has attempted to breed in Kuwait (1955), and in 1991 bred at three sites in Saudi Arabia. Hybridises commonly and widely with House Sparrow in areas of overlap.

MOVEMENTS Outside breeding season, individuals and flocks disperse or wander at random, often for considerable distances, in search of food. In northern parts of range appears to be a migrant, with breeding birds north of the Mediterranean moving south to parts of North Africa, along northern edge of the Sahara, down the Nile valley and into northern Sudan, the northern Hejaz and irregularly to northern and eastern Saudi Arabia and the UAE, Iraq, Kuwait, Oman, southern Iran, southern Afghanistan to Pakistan, Kashmir (where may occasionally breed) and Ladakh, also northwest India from the Punjab to Rajasthan east to Uttar Pradesh. A scarce and irregular winter visitor to United Arab Emirates; vagrant to Majorca (August 1971), England (four records), Norway (two records), northern Yugoslavia (island of Pag, Slovenia, autumn 1959), Bahrain (February 1992) and Nepal (three records).

MEASUREMENTS Wing (Europe) of male 73–81, of female 74·5–77·5, (northwest Africa) of male 74–83, (Canary Islands) of male 76–80; tail of male 49–56, of female 49–53; tarsus 19–21; bill (culmen) 13–16·5. Wing of *italiae* 73·5–82. Wing of male *transcaspicus* 73–87, of female 73–82; tail of female 48–55; bill (culmen) of female 13–14. Weight (CIS) of summer male 24·5–27·5, of female 23·7–37·8; (India) of winter of female 18–28.

REFERENCES Jennings (1991), Sultana *et al.* (1975), Summers-Smith (1988).

Passer pyrrhonotus Blyth, 1844, Journ. Asiat. Soc. Bengal, 13, p. 946, Bahawalpur, Sind.

IDENTIFICATION Length 13 cm (5–5¼ in). A small sparrow with a restricted distribution (virtually confined to Pakistan). Smaller and slimmer than House Sparrow (258), males have all-grey crown to nape and sides of the neck, with upperpart markings more distinct or cleaner than on male House Sparrow and the rump bright reddish-brown; the face is grey, much greyer than on races *bactrianus* and *indicus* of House, which are white and have more brown on nape and sides of neck, duller upperparts (lack the warm or bright reddish-brown) and a much larger bib. Females are also very similar to female House, but slimmer and smaller, with supercilium pale buffish-brown and usually well defined over ear-coverts and sides of nape.

DESCRIPTION Sexes differ. **Adult male:** Forehead to hindneck and sides of neck pale lead-grey; line above bill and lores to behind eye black; cheeks and ear-coverts ashy-grey; sides of crown (from above eye) to sides of nape warm chestnut or reddish-brown. Mantle, back and scapulars rich or warm brown, becoming chestnut on scapulars, heavily streaked with black, with pale or warm buffish-brown 'tramlines' on sides of back and mantle bordered with black (bases of scapulars black); lower back and rump warm or deep reddish-brown; uppertail-coverts grey. Tail grey-brown, finely edged pale buffish-brown. Lesser coverts as scapulars, median coverts black at base and broadly tipped white; greater coverts black or blackish-brown, broadly edged with warm brown or chestnut, tipped pale buffish-brown; alula dark grey or black; primary coverts the same, with pale buff-brown edges; flight feathers blackish, finely edged buffish or sandy-brown (broadly on secondaries), with small sandy-buff panel at base of primaries; tertials edged warm or golden buff-brown. Centre of chin and throat a small straight-edged black bib, extending slightly onto upper breast; sides of chin, throat and neck white; breast grey or pale greyish, rest of underparts washed with grey or greyish-buff, flanks washed buff-brown; undertail-coverts whitish. Bill small, typically sparrow-like, black in breeding season but brown on upper mandible and yellowish-horn on lower in winter. Legs and feet yellowish-brown. **Adult female:** Very similar to but slimmer and smaller than female House Sparrow. Only likely visible differences (apart from smaller size) in the field are: slightly greyer tone to head and face; pale creamy-buff supercilium from over eye to nape; pale buffish-brown 'braces' bordered by black on sides of mantle and back; lower back and rump pale buffish-brown; chin and throat white or whitish against a grey or greyish wash on rest of underparts. **Juvenile:** Similar to adult female, and probably inseparable (except by size and shape) from juvenile House Sparrow.

VOICE Most calls are similar to those of House Sparrow, but generally softer or less strident; the chirp is more of a 'chup' note. The song is also as that of House Sparrow, but softer and interspersed with warbling twitters and a sharp or high-pitched note like that of White Wagtail (*Motacilla alba*).

STATUS, HABITAT AND BEHAVIOUR Locally common. Occurs in riverine lowlands, mainly of the Indus and its tributaries, but also in adjacent pockets of suitable habitat; a bird of tamarisk and acacia scrub with tall grass or reeds along rivers, pools, rice-paddies, swamps or marshes, invariably in close association with water. Sociable and loosely colonial and found in small flocks of up to 20, often occurring with House Sparrows when feeding near human habitation, but as a rule does not associate with man or his cultivation. Breeds in tall trees and roosts in thickets, scrub or tamarisk, usually in or adjacent to water. Feeds on the ground and in vegetation, on grass seeds and the seeds of small weeds, with a particular preference for *Polygonum plebeja*; some insects and caterpillars are also taken.

DISTRIBUTION Monotypic. Extreme southeast Iran, Pakistan and extreme northwest India (Punjab); virtually restricted to the floodplains of the River Indus, the delta and its major tributaries the Sutlej and Ravi rivers (north to about 34° N).

MOVEMENTS None known or recorded, but there are records in Baluchistan (southeast Iran), so must make some small-scale movements.

MEASUREMENTS Wing of male 62–70, of female 62–67; tail of male 47–57, of female 48–54; tarsus 15·5–19; bill (culmen) 11–12·5.

REFERENCE Ali and Ripley (1983).

261 SOMALI SPARROW *Passer castanopterus*

East Africa

Plate 70

Passer castanopterus Blyth, 1855, Journ. Asiat. Soc. Bengal, 24, p. 302, Somaliland.

IDENTIFICATION Length 13–14 cm (5–5½ in). The common sparrow of Somalia. Males are very distinctive, with brown crown, nape, scapulars and wing-coverts and grey (streaked darker or blackish) on mantle and back; the rump is plain grey. Face creamy-yellow or yellowish, with a black bib extending onto the upper breast; rest of underparts washed with yellow or more heavily marked, depending on race. Females and immatures closely resemble female House Sparrow (258), but are more extensively sandy-brown and relatively less streaked with black (though this may not be constant) and have a broad pale creamy-buff supercilium. **Confusion species:** Females and immatures are likely to be confused with those of House Sparrow, but latter (apart from one isolated record) does not (yet) occur within the native range of this species. For general differences between females of Somali and House Sparrows, see below.

DESCRIPTION Sexes differ. **Adult male:** Forehead to crown, nape and partly sides of neck rich or deep chestnut; lores to slightly behind eye black; cheeks and ear-coverts pale creamy-yellow. Mantle and back (partly to edge of scapulars) grey, streaked with black or dark grey centres; lower back and rump grey, becoming darker on uppertail-coverts. Tail dark grey with brown or buffish-brown edges. Lower edge of scapulars and all wing-coverts rich or warm chestnut; alula and primary coverts black, the latter edged brown or pale brown; flight feathers black or blackish, with small pale creamy-buff patch at base of primaries, and edges to secondaries pale buffish-brown, becoming warmer brown on edges of tertials, which are pale buffish at tip. Chin and throat black, extending slightly onto upper breast and flecked with white in fresh plumage; rest of underparts dull off-white or pale buffish-grey in worn plumage. Bill black in breeding season, otherwise brown or brownish-horn. Legs and feet pale or pinkish-brown. **Adult female:** Very similar to female House Sparrow, from which it differs chiefly in sandy-brown upperparts with fairly well-spaced blackish streaks on sides of mantle and back; long pale creamy-buff supercilium above and behind eye, often extending to sides of nape; face greyish, tinged with sandy-brown; chin and throat white, but rest of underparts creamy-buff or washed with pale yellow. Bill pale yellow or straw-coloured at base, with dusky brown tip. **Juvenile:** Very similar to adult female, but generally paler or more sandy-buff, with fairly broad buff edges to wing-coverts

and flight feathers; underparts paler than on female, with less yellow.

GEOGRAPHICAL VARIATION Males of the race *fulgens* have the forehead, crown and nape brighter chestnut; the yellow on cheeks, ear-coverts and underparts is brighter and more prominent.

VOICE Call a disyllabic 'chirrup', not generally distinguishable from that of House Sparrow. Song undescribed, but very probably as, or similar to, that of House Sparrow.

STATUS, HABITAT AND BEHAVIOUR Common or very common; uncommon in northern Kenya. Occurs at up to 1500 m (lower in Kenya) in dry, arid, open plains with scattered bushes, scrub or cultivation, also along rocky coasts with cliffs; in some areas fills the niche occupied elsewhere by House Sparrow and freely occurs in towns and villages, where it lives in and around houses. Like most sparrows a gregarious or sociable bird, nesting in loose colonies but roosting and gathering in non-breeding season in large flocks. Many habits are similar to those of House Sparrow. Feeds on the ground, on grain, seeds (even taking them from animal droppings) and household scraps; also some insects, principally termites and caterpillars, on which the young are fed until fledging.

DISTRIBUTION *P. c. castanopterus*: Somalia south to Mogadishu, west to about 41° E in eastern Ethiopia.

P. c. fulgens: extreme southwest Ethiopia to about 200 km south of lake Turkana, east to Mount Karoli, northwest Kenya.

Although the House Sparrow does not occur within the range of Somali (except for one record of three, presumed ship-assisted, in Mogadishu, November 1981), a hybrid Somali x House Sparrow was collected in 1980 from a breeding site at the extreme southern edge of breeding range of Somali Sparrow.

MOVEMENTS Sedentary in breeding season but nomadic at other times, mainly in south of range, where it roams in search of feeding areas and occurs in some areas where it is not normally present.

MEASUREMENTS Wing of male *castanopterus* 70–75, of female 67–70. Wing of male *fulgens* 66–68, of female 62·5–67.

REFERENCES Ash and Colston (1981), Summers-Smith (1988).

Fringilla rutilans Temminck, 1835, Pl. Col., livr. 99, pl. 588, Japan.

IDENTIFICATION Length 14–15 cm (5½-6 in). A bright or warm rufous sparrow of the uplands and mountains of central and eastern Asia. Males have the upperparts almost entirely rich cinnamon or rufous-brown, with blackish streaks down mantle and back; double wingbar; white face and small black bib; two races are yellow on face and underparts. Females are similar to but darker than female House Sparrow (258), with mantle and back streaked with black; prominent broad pale buff supercilium extends to sides of nape and is given some emphasis by the equally broad dark eyestripe, which extends as far as supercilium. **Confusion species:** Within its native range likely to be confused only with Tree Sparrow (274), both sexes of which have a prominent black patch on an otherwise white face, a pale or whitish collar, paler brown and more heavily streaked upperparts, and lack the rich cinnamon tones of Cinnamon Sparrow.

DESCRIPTION Sexes differ. **Adult male:** Forehead to crown and nape rich reddish-brown or russet-brown; short and thin whitish line above lores to behind eye; lores to behind eye black; lower lores, cheeks and fore part of ear-coverts white, rear of ear-coverts greyish-white. Mantle and back as crown, fairly heavily streaked black or blackish, with two thin pale buff lines down centre of upper mantle and back in fresh plumage; scapulars the same, but lower scapulars unstreaked; rump and uppertail-coverts rich reddish-brown or russet-brown, with tips of longest uppertail-coverts grey. Tail dingy or grey-brown, with edges and tips finely light or pale buff. Lesser coverts plain or uniform russet-brown; median coverts black at base, broadly tipped white; greater coverts blackish, broadly edged buff or pale buff-brown, tipped pale buff; alula and primary coverts dark brown, the latter edged paler brown; flight feathers dark or blackish-brown, with a small pale buff or whitish patch at base of primaries, and edges to secondaries light buffish-brown, paler on inner secondaries; tertials similar, broadly edged warm brown and tipped pale buff. Chin and throat black, forming a short bib extending slightly onto centre of upper breast; rest of underparts dingy grey or off-white, washed with buff, paler on undertail-coverts. Bill typical of sparrow, fairly small, black in breeding season. Legs and feet pale or pinkish-brown. In winter, becomes slightly paler, more orange or reddish-orange, on upperparts and greyer on face and underparts; some grey feathers also show on crown; the black chin and throat is often obscured by white tips, especially at edges. Bill pale brown or brownish-horn on upper mandible with yellowish-horn lower. **Adult female:** Similar to but in several ways fairly distinct from

female House Sparrow; generally much darker and more olive-brown on head. Crown grey, but forehead, sides of crown and nape are dark; long and distinctive, fairly broad creamy-white (or buffish in worn plumage) supercilium from over eye to sides of nape, where it curves downwards, emphasised by broad dark or blackish-brown stripe through eye to nape; rest of face white or tinged pale buffish. Mantle and back brown, edged sandy and streaked dark or blackish, with thin, short, pale creamy or buff 'braces' bordering black on mantle and upper back; scapulars virtually unstreaked; lower back and rump tinged with warm gingery-brown. Lesser coverts plain, as scapulars; median coverts dark brown or blackish at base, with broad white or buffish tips forming a broad wingbar (much broader than on female House Sparrow); greater coverts blackish on inner webs, edged with sandy-buff and tipped pale buffish, forming a thin second wingbar; alula and primary coverts black or blackish; flight feathers dark brown or blackish, with a small whitish or dull yellowish-buff patch at base of primaries, and edges to secondaries and tertials buff or warm buffish-brown. Underparts white or pale buffish, except for warm buffish-brown tinge on flanks. Bill pale greyish or yellowish at base of both mandibles, with a dusky or dark brown culmen and tip. **Juvenile:** Very similar to adult female, but generally duller with less olive and more sandy or sandy-buff, especially on crown and nape, tips of median and greater coverts, also paler areas on face, supercilium; underparts are white or tinged with pale buff. First-autumn and first-winter males are like adults but browner, the chestnut is not so intense, and the throat patch or bib is dusky (not black).

GEOGRAPHICAL VARIATION Male *cinnamomeus* and *intensior* have tinges of yellow on face, lower sides of throat and underparts, paler in *intensior*, which usually shows only a pale wash on cheeks and underparts but has a darker or heavier russet tone to upperparts; *cinnamomeus* is quite heavily tinged with yellow on cheeks, sides of throat and underparts, but breast and flanks are greyish. In worn plumage, however, all races are much paler, greyish or dingy buff on face and underparts than in fresh plumage. Female *intensior* are also darker or deeper brown on upperparts.

VOICE Call a single 'cheeep' or 'chilp', somewhat sweeter and more musical and softer than that of House Sparrow, also a 'swee . . . swee'; in alarm or aggression utters a rapid 'chit-chit-chit'. The song is a 'cheep-chirrup-cheweep' or 'chwe-cha-cha', frequently repeated.

STATUS, HABITAT AND BEHAVIOUR Common or locally common (scarce in some parts of the range). Mainly, but not entirely, a bird of upland or mountainous areas, in summer up to 4000 m (to 4550 m in Tibet), where it occurs in lightly forested areas or open woodlands of oak, rhododendron or alder, also edge of cultivated areas; in winter occurs in river valleys, grasslands or scrubby areas near cultivation. In areas where House Sparrow is absent, it readily replaces it and becomes a bird of villages or towns. In the breeding season generally in pairs or small loose flocks, in winter in larger flocks; appears not to form mixed-species flocks. Most habits are similar to those of House Sparrow, but has a preference for open, exposed perches. In winter roosts communally in trees and bushes. Feeds on the ground or in vegetation, principally on grain (barley), rice and the seeds of small plants, also some berries and insects; the young are fed almost exclusively on insects and their larvae.

DISTRIBUTION *P. r. rutilans*: south Sakhalin to Japan, South Korea, eastern Manchuria; and in central, eastern and southern China, from Shantung to eastern Shensi, south to east Szechwan, Kweichow, Hunan and Kwangtung, and Taiwan.

P. r. intensior: southwest China from northwest Szechwan and south Tsinghai to Yunnan, west to Assam, Manipur and northern Burma (south to Karenni), Laos and northwest Tonkin, Vietnam.

P. r. cinnamomeus: northeast Afghanistan east through the Himalayas of Kashmir, northwest India to central Nepal and Sikkim (rare), Assam, Bhutan, Arunachal Pradesh, northeast India and southern and southeast Tibet.

Intermediates between the races occur where the ranges meet or overlap.

MOVEMENTS An altitudinal migrant, birds breeding in the higher parts of the range moving down to below 2000 m in winter, and most leave Tibet between November and April. In winter to southern Japan, and has also occurred on the southern Kurile Islands, Quelpart Island (South Korea), Izu Islands, Ryukyu Islands, and Askold Island (Ussuriland); a rare winter visitor to north Thailand.

MEASUREMENTS Wing of male (west Himalayas) 68–76, (central and east Himalayas) 73–82, of female 68–77; tail 43–49; tarsus 16·5–17; bill (culmen) 11–13. Weight 18–22·5. Wing of male *intensior* 68–75·5, of female 67–72·5; tail of male 46–51, of female 46–50; tarsus 16–18. Weight 19.

REFERENCE Summers-Smith (1988).

263 PEGU SPARROW (Plain-backed Sparrow) *Passer flaveolus*
Plate 68

Oriental

Passer flaveolus Blyth, 1844, Journ. Asiat. Soc. Bengal, 13, p. 946, Arakan.

IDENTIFICATION Length 14 cm (5½ in). A brightly coloured and fairly distinctive bird; both sexes lack any streaks. Adult male has a pale yellowish forehead, grey crown and nape, warm rufous-brown sides to the crown, unstreaked mantle and scapulars, and greyish back to tail; face yellowish, black bib, and yellowish underparts tinged with grey. Female is like a plain, unstreaked female House Sparrow (258), but with a fairly prominent pale buffish supercilium, pale bill and yellowish underparts. Both sexes are unlikely to be confused with other sparrows; lack of any streaks is distinctive (hence the alternative name of Plain-backed Sparrow).

DESCRIPTION Sexes differ. **Adult male:** Lower forehead (to upper lores) and over eye pale yellow, merging across upper forehead into grey infused with yellow on crown to nape; sides of neck to upper mantle grey or dark greyish; upper lores to just behind eye black; cheeks pale yellow, ear-coverts pale grey. Sides of nape from behind eye to sides of upper neck rich warm brown or chestnut; lower mantle, scapulars and lesser coverts chestnut; back to rump grey or greyish, tinged with yellow; uppertail-coverts slightly darker. Tail dark grey or grey-brown, finely edged paler. Median coverts whitish or dull yellow or with olive at bases; greater coverts black, broadly edged grey or greyish tinged yellow, tips pale grey; alula and primary coverts black, finely edged pale yellowish; flight feathers black, finely edged dull yellowish, more broadly so on inner secondaries and edges to tertials. Centre of chin and throat black, forming a small bib, extending slightly to centre of upper breast, sides of chin and throat pale yellow; breast, sides of breast and flanks pale grey, tinged or washed yellow, rest of underparts washed yellow. Bill fairly stout, black in breeding season, brown or brownish in non-breeding season. Legs and feet brown, pale brown or pinkish-brown. **Adult female:** Like female House Sparrow but lacking any streaking. Almost entire upperparts from forehead to rump and uppertail-coverts are dull sandy-brown, tinged with grey or light greyish. Wings have a distinctive white wingbar formed by broad white tips to median coverts (which also have black bases); greaters dark brown but edged paler or warmer buffish-brown, with pale buff or buffish-brown tips. Face rather plain buffish or warm sandy-buff, with dark eye and broad pale sandy or creamy-buff supercilium extending to sides of nape, with dark grey-brown eye-stripe. Underparts almost entirely pale creamy or yellowish, tinged with grey on breast, sides of breast and flanks; undertail-coverts paler or whitish. Bill pale pinkish-horn. **Juvenile:** Very similar to adult female but slightly paler, with more buff on underparts.

VOICE Most calls and song notes are very similar

to, but slightly louder or harsher than, those of House sparrow; the frequent 'fillip' or 'chirrup' has the second syllable rather slurred, and the alarm is a deeper 'chu-chu-weet' than that of House.

STATUS, HABITAT AND BEHAVIOUR Common, locally common or scarce in some areas. A bird of open country and clearings at up to 1500 m on edges of forests, isolated clumps of trees or plantations, often near water or coastal areas (including islands), also cultivation and edges of villages to town and city suburbs, but generally a more rural bird than Tree Sparrow (274) in eastern Asia. Usually occurs in small or loose colonies of up to ten pairs, occasionally in larger numbers, but in winter flocks of up to 100 gather at feeding areas. Feeds mainly on the ground (but also in bushes and other vegetation), on grain, rice and seeds of shrubs, casuarinas and small plants; some insects are taken, and the young are fed mostly on insects (including aphids, bugs and caterpillars) until they fledge.

DISTRIBUTION Monotypic. Northern Burma south through Thailand to north Malaysia, east to Laos, Campuchea and central and south Vietnam (north to Annam region). In the Malay peninsula the range has expanded southwards this century and is now just to the north of Kuala Lumpur.

MOVEMENTS Largely resident, but some birds or populations move into new feeding areas for the winter while others roam at random in search of food.

MEASUREMENTS Wing of male 68–75, of female 64–71; tail of male 53–64, of female 48–60; tarsus 18–20; bill (culmen) 11–12. Weight of male 17–22, of female 17–23.

REFERENCE Summers-Smith (1988).

264 DEAD SEA SPARROW *Passer moabiticus*   Plate 70
Palearctic

Passer moabiticus Tristram, 1864, Proc. Zool. Soc. London, p. 169, Palestine.

IDENTIFICATION Length 11·5–13 cm (4¾ in). A small and distinctive sparrow. The male has a dark grey head and neck except for a long white/pale buffish-brown supercilium, black lores, chin and throat, white submoustachial streak, and pale yellowish patch or spot on sides of neck. Upperparts sandy-brown, streaked darker or blackish, with rich brown or chestnut on median and greater coverts. Underparts are pale greyish or tinged with yellow (*yatii*). Females are sandy-brown above, with pronounced darker streaks and a well-defined pale supercilium (eastern race also more yellowish on underparts). Distinctive head and upperparts plumage, size and shape make it unlikely to be confused with any other species.

DESCRIPTION Sexes differ. **Adult male:** Forehead to crown, cheeks, ear-coverts and nape dark ash-grey, paler grey in worn plumage; thin pale whitish supercilium in front of eye, broadening behind eye and becoming warm buffish-brown over ear-coverts; lores to eye black; submoustachial area white. Mantle and back warm sandy-brown or light chestnut, quite heavily streaked with black; scapulars greyer, also streaked with black, lower scapulars edged light brown; rump dark grey, tinged with warm brown, becoming darker grey on uppertail-coverts. Tail slightly notched or forked at tip, dark brown or blackish, finely edged light brown or buffish-brown. Lesser coverts black, finely tipped white; median and greater coverts rich chestnut, tips to greaters pale buff or whitish, in worn plumage tips to medians become finely pale buff or buffish-brown; alula and primary coverts black, the latter edged finely with pale buff; flight feathers and tertials black, broadly edged pale or light sandy and often forming a panel (mainly on secondaries), broader and warmer brown on edges to tertials. Centre of chin and throat black, forming a bib; sides of throat white, becoming a yellow spot or patch on sides of lower throat; breast pale greyish, becoming heavier on sides and upper flanks; rest of underparts pale greyish-white; undertail-coverts white with tips reddish-buff; thighs black. Bill small, black or dark grey in breeding season. Legs and feet pale pinkish-brown. In fresh plumage, head, crown, nape, lower back and rump are tinged with sandy-brown; often shows white tips to some of throat feathers. Bill brown or pale brownish on lower mandible, dark brown on upper. **Adult female:** Like a small female House Sparrow, but much cleaner-looking. Lores to ear-coverts sandy-grey, with broad well-defined pale buff or bright yellow or sandy-buff supercilium behind eye extending to nape. Upperparts sandy-brown, palest or brightest on mantle and scapulars, streaked, with black and pale braces down each side of mantle/upper back. Bases to median coverts blackish-brown, tipped pale grey in first-summer and second-winter plumage, becoming black at bases with bright chestnut tips on older birds; greaters similar, but tips pale sandy-buff; edges to tertials warm sandy-buff. Chin and throat pale buff or whitish, with faint pale yellow spot or small patch on side of neck; underparts pale buffish or white, washed buffish or sandy-brown on flanks; thighs sandy-brown. Bill pale straw at base, dark grey or black on culmen and tip of both mandibles. **Juvenile:** Similar to female but not so brightly coloured, and with fairly broad buff edges to wings; lacks yellow spots on sides of neck, and supercilium is duller and not so well defined.

GEOGRAPHICAL VARIATION Males of race *yatii* are slightly paler or more sandy-brown on upperparts; the underparts are pale yellow, heaviest or yellowish-brown on breast and flanks. Also has broader warm sandy-brown edges to black (or darker than in nominate) tertials and tail feathers. In winter, the head, nape, lower back and rump are tipped buffish-brown and chin and throat feathers are tipped with white. Female *yatii* are slightly paler or more sandy-brown, with a whitish-buff supercilium, and have the underparts pale yellow or yellowish-buff; the thighs are pale buff or very slightly yellowish.

VOICE Generally silent, but becomes extremely noisy (in display and defence of territory) at onset of breeding season. Usual note is a 'chet-chet-chet-chet', occasionally given as a harsher 'chip-chip-chip' or a slurred 'chiz-chiz-chizz', and, in addition to the usual range of chirps, rattles and churrs, has a liquid 'chrelp'. The song is a far-carrying and rhythmic 'chillung-chillung-chillung' or 'tweeng-tweeng-tweeng'; like House Sparrow (258), often indulges in social singing, with many birds collecting together often at pre- (or post-) roost gatherings.

STATUS, HABITAT AND BEHAVIOUR Locally common or common; disjunct and widely scattered range. Occurs in tamarisk and other bushes, poplars or scrub (including reedbeds in some areas), often in river or waterside areas near deserts. Occurs in loose or scattered flocks and breeds colonially (often in tamarisks), with up to 100 nests in close proximity, though most colonies are smaller. In winter usually in flocks of between 50 and 100, occasionally in company with House or Spanish (259) Sparrows. A wary or rather flighty bird, very alert and usually within distance of cover if danger threatens. Feeds on the ground but more usually in vegetation, mainly on seeds of grasses, herbs, sedges and shrubs, including tamarisks or suaeda, but also on a variety of insects.

DISTRIBUTION *P. m. moabiticus*: discontinuously through southern Turkey, Cyprus (from 1980), Israel and Jordan (mostly at sites along the Jordan valley from Eilat to Hula), Iraq and southwest Iran.

P. m. yatii: eastern Iran and southwest Afghanistan.

MOVEMENTS Migratory, partially migratory or dispersive away from breeding areas in winter months. Wandering birds are frequently recorded at several localities away from the breeding area, e.g. high numbers at Eilat in southern Israel, and the breeders of southern Turkey are absent from the colony in the winter. Wintering areas of nominate race are largely unknown (most records are from southern part of breeding range), and may be in as yet undiscovered areas to the south of the breeding range, or the birds may undertake extensive random or nomadic wanderings in search of food. A flock of 200–250 wintered in Bahrain in 1991/92, and at the same time several were recorded in the UAE (first records) and elsewhere in the Gulf. Birds of race *yatii* from southwest Iran and Afghanistan winter in northern Baluchistan. A vagrant to Greece (20, east coast of Rhodes, early October 1972) and Egypt (south Sinai, October-November 1987).

MEASUREMENTS Wing of male 57·5–66·5, of female 58·5–62; tail of male 47·5–59·5, of female 47·5–56; tarsus 15·5–18; bill (culmen) 8·5–10·5. Weight 11–17. Wing of male *yatii* 62–68, of female 60–65·5; tail 48–55·5; tarsus 16·5–17·5; bill (culmen) 8·5–10·5. Weight 14–17.

REFERENCE Hirschfeld *et al.* (1992).

265 RUFOUS SPARROW (Great Sparrow (South Africa))
Passer motitensis   Plate 69
Africa

Passer motitensis A. Smith, 1848, Ill. Zool. S. Afr., Aves, pl. 114, 60 miles south of Orange river; restricted to near Hopetown, northern Cape Province, by Macdonald, 1957, Contr. Orn. W. South Africa, p. 157.

IDENTIFICATION Length 15–16 cm (5½-6 in). Initially resembles a larger version of House Sparrow (258). Considerable variation within the range covered by the races (see below), but nominate males have grey crown to nape, bordered by rich brown sides of nape; upperparts deep chestnut, streaked darker, with plain rich brown or rufous rump very obvious in flight; face as House Sparrow but with small black bib not extending onto breast. Other races vary in intensity of plumage coloration and in presence or absence of a black eye-stripe bordering the upper edge of the white (or grey) ear-coverts. Females are fairly distinctive but also very variable in grey or brown tones. **Confusion species:** Most races are very similar to (but larger than) Iago Sparrow (266), with which Rufous Spar-

row is extremely unlikely ever to come into contact. All Rufous Sparrows can be told from the slightly smaller House by their head-and-face pattern: mainly the extent of grey on nape and sides of neck and (on some) onto mantle, white (when present) above the lores, and shape and extent of supercilium and eye-stripe; all Rufous Sparrows have plain warm or tawny shoulders to scapulars (and lesser coverts).

DESCRIPTION Sexes differ. **Adult male** (nominate): Forehead to hindneck and sides of neck ashy-grey; sides of forehead whitish, sides of crown and nape (from behind eye) to sides of upper neck rich brown or chestnut; upper lores black; thin black eye-stripe along top edge of ear-coverts; lower lores white, becoming pale ashy-grey on cheeks and ear-coverts. Mantle, back, scapulars and rump rich brown or rufous, boldly streaked with black on mantle and upper back; uppertail-coverts dark brown. Tail dark brown, with paler brown edges to outer feathers. Lesser coverts as scapulars; median coverts black or blackish at base, broadly tipped white; greater coverts dark brown, broadly edged with warm buff-brown and tipped buffish-brown; alula and primary coverts black, edged with brown or pale brown; flight feathers dark brown or blackish-brown, with a small patch of buff or sandy-brown at base of primaries, edged thinly with buff or warm buffish-brown, becoming warmer and broader on edges of tertials, with tips of tertials pale buff. Chin and throat black; rest of underparts whitish or washed with grey, tinged with buffish-brown on flanks. Bill quite large or stout with pronounced curved culmen, black in breeding season, brown or brownish-horn in winter. Legs and feet brown or reddish-brown. **Adult female:** Similar in pattern to adult male but forehead to crown and nape slightly paler or browner-grey; thin whitish and pale buff supercilium across upper lores to eye, becoming tinged with warm or creamy buff-brown and extending to nape, where it curves towards sides of neck; upper lores black, becoming a black or dark eye-stripe across top and rear of ear-coverts; cheeks and ear-coverts pale grey or off-white. Mantle and back warm brown, streaked with black, scapulars to lesser coverts the same but unstreaked and upper mantle tinged lightly with grey; lower back and rump warm brown; uppertail-coverts and tail grey-brown. Median coverts black at base, broadly tipped pale buff or white; greater coverts dark brown with pale or sandy buff-brown edges and tips; alula, primary coverts, flight feathers and tertials all as adult male, except edges are generally paler or more buffish-brown. Chin and throat dingy grey or tinged with grey or an indistinct or ill-defined bib, often obscured by whitish or grey tips; rest of underparts dingy grey, paler on centre of belly. Bill black, blackish or dark grey at base. **Juvenile:** Juveniles of both sexes are similar to adults, but paler on upperparts and sides of crown and nape. Juvenile females possibly not always told with certainty, but juvenile males have dark grey bib and a strong wash of tawny-buff on the extended warm buff-brown supercilium (curving round onto sides of nape).

GEOGRAPHICAL VARIATION Most racial variation involves either the intensity or depth of the plumage tones or the presence/absence of a dark eye-stripe along the top and rear of ear-coverts. Of the races in southern Africa, *benguellensis* is slightly paler than nominate, with cheeks and ear-coverts all white (not tinged with grey); male *subsolanus* has ear-coverts darker grey than in nominate and generally has darker brown or chestnut on sides of head and upperparts, with underparts grey and slightly streaked. In East Africa, *rufocinctus* has cheeks and ear-coverts very grey, lacks the dark eye-stripe (below supercilium and rear of ear-coverts), the grey on crown and nape (of both sexes) merges on upper mantle into the brown of upperparts, the back and

rump are rich or warm chestnut, contrasting slightly with mantle and scapulars, and also has a fairly prominent pale eye; females have chin and throat dark grey. Race *shelleyi* is paler than any other race, less warm brown or chestnut on upperparts and warmer tawny-brown, with the grey or grey-brown of crown and nape extending considerably onto mantle; the back is grey-brown, streaked darker, and contrasts with the bright chestnut lower back and rump; the dark eye-stripe is well defined, black or blackish (both sexes). Female *shelleyi* is like a paler (or duller, especially about head) version of adult male, with a dark grey (not black) bib. Both sexes of *cordofanicus* from northeast Africa are very similar to each other and also to those of nominate race, with pale grey on forehead to hindneck and sides of nape, white face and sides of forehead, thin dark or blackish eye-stripe, and pale brown or tawny supercilium to rear of ear-coverts; chin to upper breast black (adult male) or grey (adult female); perhaps the greatest difference shown by this race from all others is the clean white underparts. Individuals of race *insularis* are closer in some respects to those in East Africa (*rufocinctus*): males are generally dark grey (except for white on face), the grey of forehead continues over crown, mantle and back to rump and uppertail-coverts, and only the scapulars (and lesser coverts) are warm brown, with mantle and upper back streaked; the black bib is slightly more extensive (to centre of breast), while the rest of the underparts are grey to the sides of the breast and flanks, paler or whiter on lower breast, belly and undertail-coverts. Female *insularis* are also darker, generally a dingy or drab grey (recalling a dull female or immature House Sparrow), with only a tinge of brown or buffish-brown behind eye or on sides of nape; there is also a trace of white in front of eye and a fairly broad dark eye-stripe from lores to sides of nape; as on adult male, the scapulars and the edges to coverts and particularly to tertials are tinged warm buff-brown; underparts are pale ashy-grey or whitish, without any trace of a bib; the bill is black.

VOICE All calls are initially recognisable as very similar to those of House Sparrow but has a more metallic or twangy version, 'chereep chereeoou', or 'churr-chirrup' or a single 'chirititit' or 'chissick', slightly deeper in tone than those of House sparrow. The song is also as that of House Sparrow, but contact notes between pairs are described as a thin 'chee-ti-cheet, ti-cheet-it' or 'chee-wee'.

STATUS, HABITAT AND BEHAVIOUR Common or locally common. A bird of dry or arid areas, often with grasslands or savannas; some races replace House Sparrow as the tame bird of gardens in towns and villages, while others shun virtually all contact with human settlements. In South Africa, the three southern races are shy or wary birds of dry acacia veld, preferring trees to bushes or scrub, and are never found in or near towns or villages. In East Africa, *rufocinctus* occurs in acacia savanna and open plains, but also in villages and on the edge of cultivated areas; it is frequently found in towns, where it becomes a typical 'house' sparrow; *cordofanicus* shares similar dry-area habitats, but generally is less frequently found on open plains or open savannas; *shelleyi* also has similar habitat requirements to *rufocinctus*, preferring arid plains, semi-desert areas, savannas and open woodlands and areas of cultivation, but is not generally found in and around towns and villages. Generally not so sociable or gregarious as other sparrows; in breeding season occurs in pairs, usually sparsely distributed, and in non-breeding season occurs alone or in small flocks. Feeds either in vegetation or (more especially *rufocinctus* and *shelleyi*) on the ground principally on a variety of seeds, including grain and small weed seeds; takes some insects (on which the young are fed until fledging) and in towns and villages household scraps.

DISTRIBUTION *P. m. motitensis*: Botswana south to northern Cape Province, South Africa, and Transvaal.

P. m. benguellensis: southern Angola (from about 8° S) to Namibia (to about 20° E).

P. m. subsolanus: southern Zimbabwe (where scarce and status uncertain) to the Transvaal, northern Orange Free State and northwest Swaziland, South Africa.

P. m. cordofanicus: extreme eastern central Chad through Darfur and Kordofan Provinces, central and west Sudan.

P. m. shelleyi: northeast Uganda to southeast Sudan (where rare), possibly also northwest Kenya, through southern and east Ethiopia to the border with northwest Somalia.

P. m. rufocinctus: Rift Valley highlands (between 1000 m and 3000 m), from Eldoret in central Kenya east to Tsavo West and the Taita hills, south to the Serengeti, Mount Kilimanjaro and Arusha, northern Tanzania.

P. m. insularis: Socotra and Abd-al-Kuri Islands (off Somalia).

The first three races interbreed widely in 'overlap' areas to such an extent that clear boundaries between the races have yet to be determined. Note: This species has several widely dispersed and disjunct populations. The relationship between these sparrows and the similar Iago Sparrow from the Cape Verde Islands is discussed at some length by Summers-Smith (1988); for identification (and not taxonomic) purposes, we here follow the treatment of races/species proposed therein.

MOVEMENTS Generally resident or sedentary, but some birds, especially those in South Africa, undertake nomadic or random wanderings in the non-breeding season (December-May).

MEASUREMENTS Wing of male 82–88, of female 79–85; tail 56–67; tarsus 18–21; bill (culmen) 13–15. Weight of male 34–358, of female 306–32. Wing of male *rufocinctus* 70–85, of female 73–81. Wing of male *shelleyi* 70–78, of female 68–73. Wing of male *cordofanicus* 74–81, of female 69–76. Wing of male *insularis* (Socotra) 72–80, (Abd-al-Kuri) 69–73; tail c58; tarsus 19–22.

REFERENCE Summers-Smith (1988).

266 IAGO SPARROW (Cape Verde Sparrow, Rufous-backed Sparrow) *Passer iagoensis*   Plate 69

Cape Verde Islands

Pyrgita iagoensis Gould, 1838, Proc. Zool. Soc. London, 1837, p. 77, Sãnto Tiago, Cape Verde Islands.

IDENTIFICATION Length 125–13 cm (5 in). Endemic to the islands of the Cape Verde group. Very similar to several races of Rufous Sparrow (265), with which it shares some characteristics and, most probably, a common ancestor. Males have black crown to upper nape merging into grey on nape and mantle and, on some, to upper back; sides of crown and nape warm brown, scapulars similar but streaked with black, wings and tail as on Rufous Sparrow; face white, with a small black eye-stripe along top of ear-coverts, and small black bib restricted to chin and throat. Female very like female House Sparrow (258), grey or greyish with a fairly prominent or well-defined supercilium.

Confusion species: Within its native range occurs only with House and Spanish (259) Sparrows, thus unlikely to be confused with any races of the very similar Rufous Sparrow. Female and juvenile female more likely to be confused with those of House Sparrow, but have neater appearance, long well-defined supercilium, warmer brown on shoulders/lesser coverts area, pale buffish braces on sides of streaked mantle and back and white or whitish chin, throat and sides of neck and face.

DESCRIPTION Sexes differ. **Adult male:** Forehead, crown and hindcrown black or blackish-grey, becoming grey on upper nape, hindneck and sides of neck and extending onto mantle and, on some, to centre of back. Sides of lower forehead a small line or patch of white; upper lores to below eye black, continuing as an eye-stripe; cheeks and ear-coverts white. Sides of crown from behind eye and extending around sides of nape rich brown or cinnamon. Scapulars and sides of back warm brown or light chestnut, sides of mantle, lower back and lower scapulars streaked heavily with black; lower back and rump rich warm brown or chestnut; uppertail-coverts grey or brown-tinged grey, becoming dark brown on tail, edges to tail thinly buffish-brown. Median coverts black, broadly tipped white; greaters brown or dark brown, edged paler brown, all tipped pale buffish-brown; alula and primary coverts dark brown or blackish, the latter edged slightly buffish;

flight feathers dark brown or blackish, with a small sandy-buff panel at base of primaries, and edges to secondaries pale buffish-brown, becoming warmer on edges to tertials, which are tipped white. Chin and throat a small square patch of black; sides of breast and flanks grey; rest of underparts off-white or washed grey. Bill thinner and smaller than on Rufous Sparrow, black in breeding season, brown or brownish-horn in non-breeding. Legs and feet brown or flesh-brown. **Adult female:** Very similar to female House Sparrow, but considerably different from females of any race of Rufous Sparrow. Almost entirely grey-brown on upperparts including wings, but slightly darker on forehead and crown, greyish on cheeks and ear-coverts and slightly warmer brown on nape and sides of neck; sides of mantle have pale creamy 'braces', but mantle and back otherwise streaked with black or blackish; rest of wings as adult male (including white tips to median coverts, not so broad as on male), but generally duller brown, edged sandy-buff. Prominent pale creamy-buff supercilium from upper lores, broadening behind eye over ear-coverts and curving down behind ear-coverts; fairly broad or prominent dark eye-stripe. Chin, throat and moustachial area white or whitish, becoming pale grey or greyish on rest of underparts; flanks tinged lightly with buff. Bill pale yellowish at base, becoming dusky or darker towards tip. **Juvenile:** Very similar to adult female, but young males can be separated at an early age by the warm brown or cinnamon supercilium (pale creamy on young females), warmer brown mantle, back and scapulars (often tinged with grey), and traces or beginnings of a black bib on chin.

VOICE Calls similar to those of Rufous Sparrow, but slightly higher in pitch, usually a twangy 'cheesp, chew-weep' or 'chew-leep', also a slurred 'chirrp' and a sibilant 'chisk' note from female, all given in addition to the more typical House Sparrow-like chirps and churrs. The song is a series of call notes strung together, 'cheep chirri chip cheep chirri chip cheep'.

STATUS, HABITAT AND BEHAVIOUR

Common or fairly common (within restricted range). Found in a variety of habitats at up to 1200 m, mostly on open dry desolate plains of lava or in gorges or cliffs, also on edges of cultivation and (less evenly distributed) in urban parks, squares and gardens, where it occurs with House Sparrow but not, it appears, where Spanish Sparrows occur. A social and gregarious bird occurring in small loose colonies in breeding season and in larger flocks at other times. On the ground, runs or hops rapidly and actively in search of food. Generally tame and approachable; shares many habits and actions with House Sparrow. Feeds on the ground or in vegetation, on grain (maize), grass seeds and also household scraps, occasionally some insects (e.g. flying ants), and the young in the nest are fed principally on insects. There is some evidence that it may take shoots or buds of cereal crops, causing some damage.

DISTRIBUTION Monotypic. Cape Verde Islands (except Fogo). Some authorities consider that this species could also be easily included within the races of Rufous Sparrow (265), as the level of variation is proportionately no more than is already found within the present division of the races of that species. However, since this is an island endemic and thus unlikely to come into contact or hybridise with any of the races of Rufous, and has developed distinguishing characters which put it at some distance from other sparrows, we follow Mackworth-Praed and Grant (1963) and Summers-Smith (1988) in treating this as a full species (note also that Mackworth-Praed and Grant treat some races of Rufous Sparrow, notably *rufocinctus* and *insularis* as full species).

MOVEMENTS None, sedentary; exceptional record of one at Bougouni, Mali.

MEASUREMENTS Wing of male 57–69, of female 55–61; tail of male 48–58, of female 43–52; tarsus of male 17–21, of female 18–19; bill (culmen) 125–16.

REFERENCES Bannerman (1968), Hall and Moreau (1970), Lamarche (1981), Mackworth-Praed and Grant (1963), Summers-Smith (1988).

267 CAPE SPARROW *Passer melanurus* Plate 69
South Africa

Loxia melanura P.L.S. Muller, 1776, Syst. Nat., Suppl., p. 153, Cape of Good Hope; restricted to Cape Town by Macdonald, 1957, Contr. Orn. W. South Africa, p. 157.

IDENTIFICATION Length 14–16 cm (5½–6¼ in). A brightly coloured and distinctive sparrow of southern Africa. Male is easily told by its almost all-black head, with a long broad white band from behind eye encircling the ear-coverts; unstreaked warm brown or chestnut upperparts, dark brown wings and tail; underparts greyish. Female similar except for the head, which is a paler or shadow version of the male's with white on sides of throat. **Confusion species:** Adult male is virtually unmistakable, and the face pattern and plain chestnut

upperparts of the adult female and/or juvenile make any lasting confusion unlikely. Southern Grey-headed Sparrow (272) is slightly larger and more plump, with an all-grey head and larger black bill.

DESCRIPTION Sexes differ. **Adult male:** Forehead to crown, upper nape and entire face black; nape, lower sides of neck and upper mantle grey; sides of crown from behind eye/supercilium area to sides of nape white, curving onto sides of neck and ending abruptly on sides of lower throat/upper breast (but on some, white lines of both sides appear almost to meet). Upper mantle lightly tinged grey, but otherwise mantle, back and scapulars to rump plain or uniform chestnut-brown; uppertail-coverts grey, tipped paler. Tail dark brown, tinged with grey, and edged thinly with pale greyish. Lesser coverts as scapulars; median coverts black at base, broadly tipped white (less broad in worn plumage); greater coverts dark brown, edged and tipped pale buffish-brown (off-white in fresh plumage); alula and primary coverts black, the latter with greyish edges at base; flight feathers dark or blackish-brown, with a small pale sandy, buffish or whitish patch at base of primaries, and edges to secondaries warm buff in fresh plumage (paler or duller when worn), tertials tipped pale buff in fresh plumage. Chin and throat to centre of breast black; rest of underparts pale ashy-grey, whitish or washed with buff. Bill black in breeding season, but dark brown or horn-brown at other times. Legs and feet dark or blackish-brown. **Adult female:** Similar to adult male in overall plumage, but black of head is grey and head has slightly different pattern. Forehead to crown dark grey, becoming paler on nape, upper mantle and sides of neck; lower mantle, back and scapulars to rump warm brown or chestnut, slightly duller or darker than on male; uppertail-coverts grey. Tail greyish-brown. Wings as adult male. Face grey, with a pale creamy or creamy-buff supercilium which begins thinly on upper lores, continues over eye, where it broadens and curves onto sides of nape (latter are grey and obscure the pattern), continuing onto sides of neck below ear-coverts (or on some across lower throat); pale buff, creamy or whitish moustachial stripe often joins pale area on sides of neck. Chin, throat and upper breast pale grey; rest of underparts pale buffish, tinged with pale grey or tinged buffish-brown on flanks. Bill dark or blackish-horn, paler at base in non-breeding season. **Juvenile:** Very similar to adult female; young males develop a dark face and throat at an early age.

GEOGRAPHICAL VARIATION Male *damarensis* are less warm brown or chestnut on upperparts, and the black on crown and nape is tinged with brown; females are also slightly paler. Race *vicinis* is slightly larger than nominate; males have a more contrasting black-and-white head pattern, and females are generally darker than nominate.

VOICE Calls generally as those of House Sparrow (258), but more mellow and musical; apart from the usual range of 'chirrup' or 'chissick' calls, has a loud and far-carrying 'tweeng' or 'twilleeng'. The song is a distinctive jerky and repetitive series of notes, rendered as 'chip, chollop, tlip, tlop' or 'chip cheerup, chip cheerup', or variations on this such as 'chip chroop'.

STATUS, HABITAT AND BEHAVIOUR Common or locally very common. Found in a variety of open grassland habitats from savanna to open acacia woodland thickets, also in very dry or arid areas where there are trees, but usually within distance of water; also found on the edge of cultivation (where often considered a pest) and in villages and suburban parks and gardens. Occurs in isolated pairs and small loose flocks or colonies in breeding season, but in winter non-breeding flocks can number up to about 200. Freely mixes, especially at a food source, with other species, particularly Cape Weaver (*Ploceus capensis*) and bishops (*Euplectes*), and in suburban or built-up areas appears to co-exist quite well with the introduced House Sparrow. Tame and generally confiding. Roosts communally in specially built nests. Feeds on the ground or in vegetation in typical sparrow fashion, on grain (particularly wheat), grass seeds and the small seeds of weeds, also buds and shoots of fruit trees and grapes; takes some insects (particularly caterpillars), and the young are fed mainly on insects until fledging.

DISTRIBUTION *P. m. melanurus*: Cape Province (except the east) and southern Orange Free State, South Africa.

P. m. vicinis: eastern Cape Province, Transkei to Lesotho, eastern Orange Free State, western Natal, southern Transvaal and western Swaziland, South Africa.

P. m. damarensis: coastal southwest Angola (to Benguela) through Namibia (absent from Damaraland), west, southern and eastern Botswana (avoids the Kalahari) and extreme south Zimbabwe to northern Transvaal, northwest Orange Free State and northern Cape Province, South Africa.

MOVEMENTS Generally resident or sedentary; most movements in non-breeding season are of relatively short distance or duration, and are mainly to and from food. Has been recorded as a vagrant to Harare district, Zimbabwe.

MEASUREMENTS Wing of male 72–85, of female 73–80; tail of male 55–64, of female 52–60; tarsus 17·5–21; bill (culmen) 13–16. Weight of male 17·4–24·6, of female 17·3–21. Wing of male *vicinis* 80–86, of female 77–82; tail of male 61–65, of female 59–63·5; bill (culmen) 14·5–16. Weight of male 25–34, of female 22–38.

REFERENCES Maclean (1984), Summers-Smith (1988).

Fringilla grisea Vieillot, 1817, Nouv. Dict. Hist. Nat. nouv. ed., 12, p. 198, United States [in error]; Senegal, Lafresnaye, 1839, Rev. Zool., p. 95.

Note: The classification here follows that proposed by Hall and Moreau (1970) and Summers-Smith (1988) in treating the previously considered races of one polymorphic species as five separate species. This and the following four species are all extremely similar, and differ only in geographic location and (subtly but significantly) in fine details of plumage. The sexes are identical in all five species. Grey-headed Sparrow, which ranges over much of West and Central Africa, is further divided into closely similar races, all of which are separable (with some effort or patience) in the field.

IDENTIFICATION Length 15 cm (5¾–6 in). See note above. The house or village sparrow over much of Africa, with many of the characters or actions of House Sparrow (258). Head is entirely grey – pale or darkish ash-grey – with brown or rich brown lower mantle and back and light chestnut on scapulars and wing-coverts; has a generally small (or absent) white wing patch on tips of inner median coverts, and a whitish throat contrasting with pale grey (or in one race entirely white) underparts. **Confusion species:** For differences from other species in the 'grey-headed sparrow' group, i.e. Swainson's (269), Parrot-billed (270), Swahili (271) and Southern Grey-headed (272), see those species. The features that best distinguish this species from the others are: races *griseus* and *ugandae* have white on chin and throat and grey on breast, flanks and belly (race *laeneni* has all-white underparts); bill smaller than that of Parrot-billed Sparrow.

DESCRIPTION Sexes alike. **Adult:** Forehead to crown, nape, face and sides of neck pale ash-grey; dark grey lores to around eye and slightly onto ear-coverts. Mantle and upper back grey-brown, becoming reddish-brown or light chestnut on scapulars, lower back and rump; uppertail-coverts brown or edged with light buff-brown. Tail quite long and square-ended, brown, edged paler brown. Lesser coverts as scapulars; bases to median coverts the same, tips to inner feathers broadly white or entire inner medians white or with tips to some or all of outers also white; greaters dark brown, broadly edged and tipped warm or light chestnut (shows as a continuation of chestnut upperparts); alula and primary coverts dark brown, finely edged warm buffish-brown; flight feathers blackish-brown, thinly edged brown or buffish-brown on primaries, becoming broader and more warm brown or chestnut on secondaries and tertials. Chin and throat white, contrasting with grey breast and flanks, slightly paler on belly, vent and undertail-coverts. Bill fairly stubby but both mandibles curve to a point, black or very dark brownish-horn, becoming grey-brown with yellow base to lower mandible in non-breeding season. Legs and feet grey-brown or tinged slightly pinkish. **Juvenile:** Very similar to adult but slightly duller, with some dark streaks on mantle and sides of back,

and lacks any white on wing-coverts. Bill paler than on adult, more brown or brownish-horn.

GEOGRAPHICAL VARIATION Race *ugandae* is generally much darker in overall tones, with head, nape and face much deeper grey (in worn plumage grey-brown) and mantle to rump, wing-coverts and edges to flight feathers more rust-brown than chestnut; underparts are also slightly darker or greyer than in nominate. At the opposite extreme, *laeneni* is a much paler bird, with head, nape and face paler grey, mantle to rump pale or fawn-brown or slightly sandy-brown, and entire underparts virtually white.

VOICE Call and song are either an individual 'chip', 'cheerp' or 'chirp' or a series loosely strung together in a rather tuneless 'cheep chirp cheep chirp' etc.; also has the rolling churr alarm typical of many sparrows.

STATUS, HABITAT AND BEHAVIOUR Common and widely distributed. Occurs at up to 2000 m in a wide variety of habitats, from arid bush and scrub to open plains and savannas with trees, light deciduous woods to the edges of cultivation and in and around towns and villages; generally a bird of humid areas, but northern *laeneni* is found in dry or arid areas on the edge of the Sahara. Sociable, noisy and mainly the 'house sparrow' over much of western and central Africa. Breeds in loose colonies but in remote areas also occurs in pairs or small groups, and in winter usually in flocks of up to 50 but larger numbers of several times that are not unknown; also roosts communally in bushes, scrub and trees. Feeds on the ground or in vegetation, on cereals, grass seeds, berries and fruit, and also some insects (on which the young are mainly fed), especially termites and flying ants; in towns and villages readily takes household scraps.

DISTRIBUTION *P. g. griseus*: West Africa, from Senegal and Gambia east to southern Chad, northern Cameroon, northern Central African Republic and most of south Sudan (except the east and southeast), south to northern Gabon.

P. g. laeneni: Mali to extreme northern Cameroon and west-central Sudan.

P. g. ugandae: extreme northern Ethiopia, Sudan south through Uganda and most of the Rift Valley to Malawi, Zaire, eastern Congo, northern and

northeast Angola, and in the east to southwest and southeast Kenya, central and northeast Tanzania.
MOVEMENTS Generally sedentary or makes short-distance foraging movements, but in winter flocks become more nomadic and wander considerably, often appearing in areas where species does not breed.

MEASUREMENTS Wing of male 79–90, of female 75–87; tail of male 55–65, of female 53–67; tarsus 20–21; bill (culmen) 14–16. Weight of male 20–26, of female 20–28. Weight of male *laeneni* 24–30, of female 26–31.
REFERENCES Hall and Moreau (1970), Summers-Smith (1988).

269 SWAINSON'S SPARROW *Passer swainsonii*   Plate 71
East Africa

Pyrgita swainsonii Rüpell, 1840, Neue Wirbelt., Vögel, p. 94, Abyssinia.

IDENTIFICATION Length 16 cm (6¼ in). Extremely similar to Grey-headed Sparrow (268), with which it comes into contact in northern Ethiopia. **Confusion species:** Much darker or greyer on head, face, nape and underparts than race *ugandae* of Grey-headed, and entirely lacks any white or pale areas on chin; pale chestnut rump contrasts with dull brown mantle and back. Swahili Sparrow (271) is also very similar, but paler on chin; does not come into contact with Swainson's. On northern and western borders of the range Swainson's may interbreed with race *ugandae* of Grey-headed (individuals with intermediate features have been recorded), and on southern border may also interbreed with Parrot-billed Sparrow (270).
DESCRIPTION Sexes alike. **Adult:** As Grey-headed Sparrow, except for much deeper or darker grey on head, face (slightly darker mark from lores through eye) to nape and sides of neck. Mantle, back and scapulars dull or dingy brown, contrasting with bright chestnut (in fresh plumage pale chestnut) rump and uppertail-coverts. Wings and tail as Grey-headed, with warm brown shoulders or lesser coverts; white patch equally variable in size as on Grey-headed, but usually duller or off-white. Underparts entirely grey or deep pencil-grey, lacking any white or pale on chin, throat, breast or flanks. Bill (as Grey-headed, but slightly finer or smaller) black. Legs and feet as Grey-headed. **Juvenile:** Very similar to adult, but with paler bill and lacks any white on median coverts.
VOICE Call very similar to that of Grey-headed Sparrow, but perhaps slightly more musical or liquid, 'chirrip' or 'chirri-up', in addition to the more usual 'chirp' notes.
STATUS, HABITAT AND BEHAVIOUR Common or fairly common. Occurs in much the same type of habitat as Grey-headed, including up to 4500 m on the Ethiopian plateau; otherwise the 'house sparrow' of towns, villages, cultivation but also occurs in bush and scrub away from human habitation. Other habits, social behaviour and food as Grey-headed Sparrow.
DISTRIBUTION Monotypic. Extreme northeast Sudan (Port Sudan and the Red Sea coast), Ethiopia, northern Somalia and north-central Kenya (south to Marsabit).
MOVEMENTS Largely sedentary, but may wander short distances in search of food in non-breeding season.
MEASUREMENTS Wing of male 80–92, of female 80–88; tail 64–72; tarsus 19–20; bill (culmen) 13–15·5. Weight 27·3–35·2.
REFERENCES Summers-Smith (1988), Urban (1975).

270 PARROT-BILLED SPARROW *Passer gongonensis*   Plate 71
East Africa

Pseudostruthus gongonensis Oustalet, 1890, Gongoni, near Mombasa, Kenya.

IDENTIFICATION Length 18 cm (7 in). In general appearance very similar to Grey-headed (268) and Swainson's (269) Sparrows, clearly larger and has a much bigger or more bulbous bill than any of the other grey-headed species. Head to nape, face and underparts grey or dark grey, tinged very lightly with brown or grey-brown, and no white or pale area on chin or throat; mantle, upper back and scapulars dull brown and rump bright chestnut; wing-coverts also bright chestnut, and with a large white patch on inner medians (or variably across tips of outer medians). Overlaps with race *ugandae* of Grey-headed Sparrow in the west of the range.
DESCRIPTION Sexes alike. **Adult:** Entire head to nape, face, sides of neck and entire underparts deep grey or brown-tinged grey, underparts more clearly tinged buffish-brown; the only feature of the head and face is the very slightly darker grey lores to slightly behind eye. Mantle, back and scapulars dull brown, nape and upper mantle suffused with grey; lower back and rump bright chestnut; uppertail-coverts and tail brown or brownish, with warm buff-brown edges (especially at base of outer feathers). Wings similar to those of Grey-

459

headed and Swainson's, with bright chestnut coverts contrasting with darker brown flight feathers and tertials, with a correspondingly larger white patch on inner median coverts. Bill very obvious, large, bulbous and rather 'Roman-nosed', black or blackish-grey. Legs and feet pale brown or pale fleshy-brown. **Juvenile:** Paler and browner (less grey) on head, face and underparts. Lower back and rump pale chestnut with pale buff feather edges; wings duller brown (not chestnut), and median-covert patch pale tawny-buff or absent. Bill slightly smaller than adult's, and paler or yellowish at base.

GEOGRAPHICAL VARIATION No races currently recognised, but in overlap areas in north and west of the range, where it comes into contact and interbreeds with Swainson's and Grey-headed Sparrows respectively, individuals with intermediate characters occur (have smaller and less bulbous bill and are paler or buffish on belly). Overlaps in south of the range with Swahili Sparrow (271), but apparently does not interbreed.

VOICE In addition to the similar chirp and churring notes of other grey-headed sparrows, has a somewhat lower-toned 'choop' note.

STATUS, HABITAT AND BEHAVIOUR Common or locally common. A bird of dry or arid places or savannas with scattered thornbush or scrub, and found much less in towns, villages or settlements (except in some more northerly parts of range) than other grey-headed sparrows. Occurs in pairs or small groups, rarely larger flocks, though in breeding season in some areas common sources of food attract up to 20–30 individuals. A shy or rather unapproachable bird, not generally frequenting human habitation. Feeds on the ground, on a variety of seeds, probably of heavier or more durable quality than other 'grey-headed' sparrows are capable of tackling; otherwise known to take a variety of scraps at picnic sites in game reserves.

DISTRIBUTION Monotypic. Extreme southeast Sudan, southern Ethiopia (Shoa province) and southern Somalia throughout Kenya to extreme northeast Tanzania.

MEASUREMENTS Wing of male 89–102, of female 85–96; tail of male 59–69; bill (culmen) of male 16–18·6, of female 16·7–19·6.

REFERENCE Summers-Smith (1988).

271 SWAHILI SPARROW *Passer suahelicus*   **Plate 71**

Africa

Passer griseus suahelicus Reichenow, 1904, Vög. Africa, 3, p. 231, Bussissi [Mwanza district, Tanganyika Territory].

IDENTIFICATION Length 16 cm (6¼ in). Very similar to the other grey-headed sparrows, especially race *ugandae* of Grey-headed (268) and Parrot-billed (270). Smaller and with a smaller bill than latter, and darker on underparts than Grey-headed and with much greyer mantle and upper back and pale grey or whitish-grey on chin and throat.

DESCRIPTION Sexes alike. **Adult:** Forehead to crown, nape, mantle, face and sides of neck grey, slightly darker on lores and through eye. Back and scapulars grey or grey-brown, contrasting with warm brown or light brown lower back and rump; uppertail-coverts and tail dark brown, edged paler brown at base of tail. Wings as on other species of grey-headed sparrows with white inner median-covert patch or variably a bar across tips of up to five or six feathers, otherwise coverts and edges to secondaries and tertials dull chestnut-brown. Underparts mostly grey, with paler or whitish area on belly; some have a pale ashy-grey on chin and throat (often invisible in the field). Bill smaller than on Parrot-billed Sparrow, black. Legs and feet pale brown or pale fleshy-brown. **Juvenile:** Similar to adult, but lacks any white on median coverts.

VOICE Generally silent; call and song are undescribed.

STATUS, HABITAT AND BEHAVIOUR Locally common. Found in grassland with acacias or scattered trees, scrub or open woodlands; also on the edge of cultivation and in villages and towns, but not so frequently as Grey-headed Sparrow. Habits and social behaviour much as other grey-headed sparrows. Feeds on the ground, on a variety of small seeds, but little is known of its diet (presumed to be much as that of its close relatives). Has been known to take food (scraps) put out at lodges in game reserves.

DISTRIBUTION Monotypic. Southern or southwest Kenya (north to Lake Magadi) through west Tanzania to northern and central Malawi and extreme northwest Mozambique.

MOVEMENTS None recorded; generally resident or sedentary.

MEASUREMENTS Wing of male 83–91, of female 81–89; bill (culmen) of male 15–15·5, of female 14·6–15·8.

REFERENCE Summers-Smith (1988).

272 SOUTHERN GREY-HEADED SPARROW *Passer diffusus* **Plate 71**
Africa

Pyrgita diffusa A. Smith, 1836, Rep. Exped. Cent. Africa, p. 50, between the Orange river and the tropic; restricted to 'near Kuruman' by Macdonald and Hall, 1957, Ann. Transvaal Mus., 23, p. 35.

IDENTIFICATION Length 15·5–16 cm (6–6¼ in). Similar to other grey-headed sparrows, but more easily recognisable by the pale grey or off-white underparts, giving it a paler appearance by comparison. Head and face also rather pale grey or tinged grey-brown, becoming pale brown or fawn on upperparts, which contrast with warm brown or chestnut lower back, rump and wing-coverts. The white patch or bar across medians is somewhat larger or more pronounced in this species. **Confusion species:** Only very small areas of overlap with Grey-headed Sparrow (268). Adult female Cape Sparrow (267) has a well-defined pale or creamy supercilium and patch on side of neck and a grey chin and throat, but lacks the bright chestnut lower back and rump.

DESCRIPTION Sexes alike. **Adult:** Forehead to nape, sides of neck and face pale ash-grey, tinged slightly buffish-brown, slightly darker or greyer from base of bill through eye and across ear-coverts. Mantle, upper back and scapulars pale brown or fawn-brown, tinged grey; lower back and rump bright warm brown or chestnut; uppertail-coverts and tail brown, edged slightly paler or buffish on edges to base of tail; slightly (but noticeably) longer in tail than Swahili Sparrow (271). Wings very similar to those of other grey-headed sparrows, with chestnut lesser coverts and bases of median and greater (or inner greater) coverts and edges to secondaries and tertials; white patch or bar on median coverts is somewhat larger or more extensive (by a few millimetres) than on Grey-headed. Chin, throat and upper breast very pale greyish (white on some), becoming whiter on rest of underparts. Bill slightly finer or more slender at base than on other grey-headed sparrows, also (in areas of overlap) comparatively slimmer than on Swahili Sparrow, black, or dark brownish-horn in non-breeding season. Legs and feet pale pinkish-brown. **Juvenile:** Very similar to adult, except that mantle, back and scapulars are streaked darker and the patch on median coverts is absent, reduced or tinged with buffish.

GEOGRAPHICAL VARIATION Eastern birds are progressively darker or warmer brown on upperparts, with *mozambicus* deeper in tone (but still paler than Grey-headed Sparrow). Northern *luangwae* darker on crown, mantle and rump, also slightly paler grey on face, breast and flanks (probably imperceptible in the field without direct comparison), and are smaller overall, with slimmer bill.

VOICE Generally silent, but has a softer and more musical 'chirp', 'cheep chirp' or 'chirrup' than that of House Sparrow (258). The song is a series of call notes strung together into a tinny or high-pitched 'chirrip cheeu chiriri,titt cheeu'.

STATUS, HABITAT AND BEHAVIOUR Common and widespread. Found on dry open plains, grasslands or savannas with scattered acacias or other trees, thornbrush and scrub, generally avoids forests or dense woodlands; frequently occurs in villages and towns, but more often found away from human habitation and cultivation than Grey-headed Sparrow, especially where Cape Sparrow is dominant. Occurs in pairs or small parties in loose colonies, and in winter small flocks consisting of several family parties may band together; freely mixes with Cape and House Sparrows, especially when feeding. Most habits and actions as those of other grey-headed sparrows, but a characteristic of this species is that it walks as well as hops on the ground. Feeds mainly on the ground, on a variety of seeds and insects, but has also been known to feed on nectar from aloes.

DISTRIBUTION *P. d. diffusus*: west and south Angola, northern Namibia (north of 24° S), southern Zambia to Zimbabwe and southern Mozambique south through Botswana to Natal and most of South Africa except western Cape Province.

P. d. mozambicus: east and southeast Tanzania (including Zanzibar and Pemba Island) to northern Mozambique.

P. d. luangwae: upper Luangwa valley, eastern Zambia.

MOVEMENTS Generally sedentary, but may make short-distance foraging movements when not breeding.

MEASUREMENTS Wing of male 79–88, of female 73–82; tail 55–65; tarsus 16–19; bill (culmen) 13–15. Weight of male 20·4–27·5, of female 19·5–25·4.

REFERENCES Maclean (1984), Oatley and Skead (1972), Summers-Smith (1988).

Fringilla simplex Lichtenstein, 1823, Verz. Doubl., p. 24, Ambukol on the Nile, Sudan.

IDENTIFICATION Length 13–14 cm (5–5½ in). A very distinctive pale sandy or pale grey sparrow, males appearing initially like a washed-out House Sparrow (258) with a small black bib, white face and very pale wings, rump and tail. Females of nominate race are more sandy-coloured than males and lack any distinctive head or face pattern or a black bib, whereas those of race *zarudnyi* are similar to males. Primarily a bird of the desert edge in wadis or oases, and occurs where there is vegetation (generally avoids open rolling dunes). Unlikely to be confused with any other species of sparrow in its native habitat: male is more likely to be briefly mistaken for a small shrike, particularly Lesser Grey (*Lanius minor*) in flight, while female could be mistaken for a small lark, before typical sparrow habits and actions become apparent.

DESCRIPTION Sexes differ. **Adult male:** Forehead to crown, nape, mantle, back and scapulars very pale grey or sandy yellowish-grey, though some show a varying amount of light warm buff or gingery-brown on forehead, sides of crown and scapulars; lores to just behind eye black or tipped finely with brown; cheeks and ear-coverts to sides of neck white. In fresh plumage mantle and back have paler tips. Lower back, rump and uppertail-coverts creamy-white. Tail black, but broadly edged and central feathers tipped creamy-white. Lesser coverts as scapulars; median coverts entirely white, greaters black at basal half, broadly tipped white; alula and primary coverts black, alula very finely tipped white, the latter with white bases; flight feathers dark grey or blackish, finely edged pale grey, white or creamy-white (broadest on secondaries), and with a small white patch or panel across bases of primaries (often obscured by pale edges to rest of primaries); tertials black or blackish, edged white or pale sandy-brown. (In flight, the black on greater and primary coverts shows as a dark bar and the dark tips to flight feathers surround the pale or whitish area of bases.) Chin and throat black, extending slightly to centre of upper breast; rest of underparts pale buff, whitish or tinged with very pale grey on flanks. Bill black in breeding season, becoming dull brown or blackish-brown at other times. Legs and feet pale pinkish or pinkish-brown. **Adult female:** Forehead to crown, nape, mantle, back and scapulars pale or creamy-sandy (bleaches paler); face pale sandy or creamy-buff, slightly paler or more buffish than head and mantle (in fresh plumage some have white or whitish lores); lower back and rump paler or whiter than upper back and mantle, becoming whiter or creamy-white on uppertail-coverts and edges to base of tail; tail grey or greyish, edged pale or creamy-white. Wings generally very pale: lesser and median coverts white or creamy-buffish;

greater coverts pale or creamy-sandy with paler tips; alula and primary coverts dark grey, broadly edged white, the latter also tipped with white; flight feathers dark grey, broadly (broadest on secondaries) edged pale creamy or creamy-sand, with pale or paler base to primaries whiter than rest of pale edges (often merges with edges to primaries); tertials darker or browner on inner webs. Underparts pale or whitish, tinged lightly with sandy-buff on sides of breast and flanks. Bill brown, pale brown, or with a pale yellow base to lower mandible. **Juvenile:** Very similar to but slightly duller or more dingy than (and doubtfully separable in the field from) adult female. First-winter birds resemble the respective adults but are duller, and first-winter males have poorly developed amounts of black on chin and/or throat.

GEOGRAPHICAL VARIATION Males of race *zarudnyi* are slightly greyer on upperparts (forehead to back and rump) and whiter on underparts; lores to eye area is blacker. Female *zarudnyi* are similar to the males, with sandy-grey upperparts, paler on rump and tail, but have black lores to slightly behind eye, and the black of 'bib' is replaced with blackish-brown; flight feathers are also blackish-brown on inner webs. Both sexes are also slightly smaller than nominate, and have smaller, more stubby or rounded bills.

VOICE Generally silent outside breeding season. Has a soft 'chu', repeatedly given, and a high-pitched 'chip chip', as well as the more usual chirping calls of House Sparrow. The song, given only by male, is a musical melodious trill, in quality recalling a Linnet (72) or the rolling trills of a Greenfinch (44).

STATUS, HABITAT AND BEHAVIOUR Not common; local and resident, but not always present in areas where known to occur. Favours edges of deserts, in sandy plains with scattered trees or scrub or in oases, wadis or date palms; in some areas of western Sahara occurs in and around human settlements. Usually in pairs or small groups; outside breeding season also occurs in small flocks of up to ten birds (though up to 50 are not unknown). Generally more shy and retiring than other sparrows, spending long periods of time (especially in the heat of the day) in the shade of trees, particularly palms (where it hides in the tops); roosts in similar habitat. Feeds on the ground, principally on the seeds of awn grass (*Aristida pungens* or *A. pennata*), which it grasps while hovering and pulls to the ground, also the seeds of other desert plants, spilled grain and a variety of insects including flies, spiders, beetles, small moths and caterpillars; the young are fed on insects until they fledge.

DISTRIBUTION *P. s. simplex*: widely scattered into discrete or disjunct populations throughout the

Sahara desert from southern Morocco, central and southern Algeria to southwest Tunisia, central Libya, south to northern Chad, northern Niger, northern Mali and western Mauritania; also recently recorded again in Sudan (where it was considered extinct).

P. s. zarudnyi: southern Turkmenistan, Karakum (Black Sands) desert and extreme western Uzbekistan Kyzylkum (Red Sands) desert, (CIS); formerly occurred in central Iran (Great Sands desert or Dasht-e-Lut, Kuhistan), but no records from there this century and now considered probably extinct.

MOVEMENTS Some populations may be resident or sedentary, but outside breeding season some undertake local wanderings or random dispersal (mainly in search of food) as birds are not always present near breeding areas. An accidental or unusual visitor to north Libya and southern Egypt (records at two sites, October to December 1968).

MEASUREMENTS Wing of male 72–81, of female 69–77; tail of male 54–66, of female 50–67; tarsus 19–20; bill of male 9–11·5, of female 9–10·5. Weight of male 19–20, of female 18–21. Wing of male *zarudnyi* Wing; male 69–74, of female 68–72.

REFERENCES Densley (1990), Summers-Smith (1988).

274 TREE SPARROW *Passer montanus*   Plate 68
Palearctic and Oriental (with introductions elsewhere)

Fringilla montana Linnaeus, 1758, Syst. Nat., ed. 10, p.   183, in Europe; restricted to Bagnacavallo, Ravenna, Italy, by Clancey, 1948, Bull. B.O.C., 68, p. 135.

IDENTIFICATION Length 14 cm (5½ in). A common and distinctive sparrow with a brown crown and nape, complete white collar, white face with a black patch on lower ear-coverts, and a small black bib. Rest of upperparts similar to House Sparrow (258), but slightly warmer brown, often much cleaner-looking and with a double wingbar and brown rump. Has a distinctive call which is higher-pitched and somewhat more metallic in tone than that of House Sparrow. Over much of its range replaces latter as an inhabitant of cities, towns and villages, especially in east and southeast Asia, where House Sparrow is absent. **Confusion species:** Immediately recognisable by the plumage of head and face, which separates it from male House Sparrow. No other brown-headed sparrow with a white face within or adjacent to the range has a dark ear covert spot (present in all ages and plumages, though less well defined on juveniles). Male Spanish (259) is separated by heavy black streaks on upperparts and on chin to breast and flanks; race *italiae* of Spanish has brown head, white face and a reduced amount of black on upper breast, but still lacks the ear-covert patch and has white extending over eye.

DESCRIPTION Sexes alike. **Adult:** Forehead to crown and upper nape rich deep chestnut (or reddish-brown in worn plumage); hindneck a complete white collar; lores to around eye black, continuing along top of ear-coverts; cheeks and ear-coverts white, except for very distinctive (kidney-shaped) patch of black or dark brown; mantle, back and scapulars warm brown, streaked heavily with black; lower back, rump and uppertail-coverts plain or uniform pale brown to fawn-brown (becomes browner in worn plumage). Tail dark brown, edged thinly with buff or light greyish-buff. Lesser coverts rich brown or chestnut; median coverts black at base, broadly tipped white; greaters black or blackish this mostly concealed by broad warm brown or light chestnut edges and pale buff or whitish tips; alula black; primary coverts black, edged warm brown; flight feathers black or blackish, edged with pale golden-brown, thinly on primaries but more broadly on secondaries, with paler golden-brown or buffish-brown patch at base of inner primaries; tertials the same, broadly edged warm brown and tipped white or whitish. Chin and throat black, this sometimes extending to sides of lower throat; rest of underparts greyish or dingy white, sides of breast and flanks tinged with light buffish-brown; undertail-coverts paler, or with brown tips to some feathers. Bill black in breeding season, paler in winter with yellow or pale yellowish base. Legs and feet pale brown or pale pinkish-brown. **Juvenile:** Very similar to adult but duller or dingy, with more buffish-brown tones to upperparts and wings; forehead to crown duller brown, with dark tips; chin and ear-covert patch grey and rather poorly defined, cheeks and face also flecked with grey. Bill yellowish at base.

GEOGRAPHICAL VARIATION There is very little distinctive variation among the races throughout the extensive range; most differences involve intensity of plumage colours and (minimally) size. Race *dilutus* is the palest (paler than nominate), with pale sandy-brown upperparts (except head), and some show a greyer-sandy tone to rump. Race *tibetanus* is similar to *dilutus* but slightly darker, and is the largest of all the races. Race *saturatus* is deeper brown or more richly coloured than nominate and has a larger and slightly longer bill. Race *malaccensis* is also darker and deeper in colour than nominate and thus similar to *saturatus*, but is smaller, and some show heavier dark streaks on upperparts (but note that even within the ranges of these races there is some variation between different populations); *hepaticus* is similar to the previous race but distinctly reddish-brown on head, upperparts and lesser/median coverts, and also

463

more heavily tinged buffish-brown below. Race *transcaucasicus* is similar to nominate but duller or greyer, with less rich or warm brown tones to upperparts, and paler or whiter on underparts (especially belly).

VOICE Call is similar to that of House Sparrow, but much harder and somewhat more abrupt and higher-pitched, 'chip' or a distinct sharp 'tet', often given as a dry 'tet-tet-tet' in flight; also has a very distinctive metallic 'tsooit' (or variations), given both when perched and in flight. The song is a repeated series of the call note interspersed with 'tsooit', 'tsveet' or 'tswee-ip' notes.

STATUS, HABITAT AND BEHAVIOUR
Common almost throughout its extensive range; locally common in areas where it has been introduced. In western parts of the range, over much of Europe, it is a bird of open or lightly wooded country, the edge of cultivated areas, hedgerows and parkland, only occasionally venturing into towns or villages; in the east and in isolated parts of the range where House Sparrow is entirely absent or only a migrant, it is a close associate of man, living to all degrees as House Sparrow does in Europe and throughout much of its range. In areas where there is some overlap between the two species, e.g. in southern and central Asia, both species may be found occupying towns and villages or House Sparrows occupying the countryside around towns and villages that support breeding Tree Sparrows. In some parts of the range, e.g. Mongolia, it occurs where there are no trees, while in others it is truly a montane bird, being found up to 4270 m in Nepal. Occurs in pairs throughout the year, though more generally it is loosely colonial and is found in small flocks even during breeding season, while in winter it frequently occurs in larger numbers and readily mixes with flocks of finches, buntings and House Sparrows, especially at common sources of food (e.g. in Europe, in autumn stubble or weed fields). Also roosts communally in trees, hedges etc. Generally shy and more retiring than House Sparrow, to which in most other respects it is very similar. Hybrids between House and Tree sparrows are frequently recorded, and a hybrid Tree x Spanish Sparrow was recorded in Malta in December 1975. Feeds on the ground or in trees, bushes and other vegetation (e.g. weedy patches), on a variety of grass seeds and seeds of other small plants (in Europe includes chickweed and goosefoot), cereals, spilled grain; also takes considerable quantities of insects, including aphids, caterpillars, weevils, beetles and grasshoppers, and the young are fed principally on insects until they fledge.

DISTRIBUTION *P. m. montanus*: Europe, from Britain (though sparsely distributed in Scotland and mainly coastal in Ireland) to Norway and Sweden (absent from much of the interior), Finland (very scarce) to the Baltic Republics, and much of the CIS (north to the Kola Peninsula) north to about 68° N (or 72° N along the Pechora and Yenisei river valleys) and east to the Lena river and the Sea of Okhotsk; in the south, from Portugal (except the south) and Spain (except the southwest) east along the northern Mediterranean including Sicily and Malta, (absent from southern Greece and from Yugoslavia except Bosnia and Macedonia) to central and northern Turkey, northern Caucasus to the north Caspian Sea and northern Kazakhstan (north of the Pamirs, Tien Shan and Altai ranges) to northern Mongolia, Manchuria (south to Liaoning) and northern Korea.

P. m. transcaucasicus: southern Caucasus from Black Sea coast of Georgia to Baku, Caspian Sea coast of Azerbaijan, south to Armenia and Gorgan, northern Iran.

P. m. dilutus: extreme northeast Iran, Afghanistan, northern Pakistan (Gilgit) to Kashmir, and into Himachal Pradesh, northwest India; in the north through Uzbekistan and Tadzhikstan to Sinkiang (south to Kashgaria), northwest China, northern Mongolia and most of China from eastern Kansu to Manchuria and south to Hong Kong and eastern Szechwan.

P. m. tibetanus: northern Himalayas from Nepal, Sikkim, Bhutan, Arunachal Pradesh and Tibet, through Szechwan to northern Tsinghai and Kansu (east of *dilutus*), northwest China.

P. m. saturatus: Sakhalin (except the north) to Kuril Islands, Japan, South Korea and Taiwan.

P. m. malaccensis: southern Himalayas from Uttar Pradesh, northwest India, and Nepal, through Assam, Bangladesh and Burma east to Yunnan, Thailand, Laos, Vietnam and Hainan south to Malaysia, Sumatra, Java and Bali.

P. m. hepaticus: northeast Assam to northwest Burma.

Other races (at least 15) have been described, most of which are intermediate between those given above. Formerly bred on Faroes; has also bred on Malta and Gozo, and may still breed on Zembra (off Tunisia) where last reported in 1953. Has been introduced into Sardinia; the USA, where resident within 80-km radius of St Louis, Missouri, occasionally to west-central Illinois and Kentucky; Eastern Ghats, Andhra Pradesh, India; parts of Indonesia (Sulawesi, Ambon and Buru); Lombok, Flores and Sumba in the Lesser Sundas; Philippines (*saturatus*) originally introduced into Luzon, now all sizable inhabited islands); Micronesia, on Mariana Islands, Marshall Islands (Kwajalein) and Caroline Islands (Yap); and in southeast Australia from Hunter river valley, New South Wales, west to Dimboola, Victoria. Apparently self-introduced by boat from Hong Kong (*dilutus*) or Singapore (*malaccensis*) to Borneo and Brunei, where now locally thriving. Introduced into Bermuda, Andaman Islands and New Zealand in late 19th century, but unsuccessful (probably owing to competition with introduced House Sparrow) and now considered extinct.

MOVEMENTS Sedentary, partially migratory or erratic. Numbers breeding in Britain fluctuate markedly, from common to abundant in some years to very few in others; can usually be found in certain favoured localities, but numbers at edge of range appear to be dependent on cyclic fluctuations or movements of birds from Europe or areas of high density. Nominate race is a passage migrant or winter visitor (in varying numbers) to the Balearics, Corsica, Malta, the coast of Yugoslavia and some Adriatic islands, Crete and occasionally to Cyprus and Iraq; birds of race *dilutus* move south in winter and reach the Makran coast of southern Baluchistan and Pakistan, and in east of range movements of up to thousands have been recorded along the east coast of China; birds of race *saturatus* move south, and are absent in winter months from most of Sakhalin. A vagrant to Gibraltar, Algeria, Tunisia, Egypt, Israel and Dubai.

MEASUREMENTS Wing of male 65–76, of female 65–74; tail of male 50–58, of female 49–59; tarsus 16–18; bill (culmen) 13–14. Weight of male 20·2–30, of female 21–27·4. For further details on biometrics of all races, see Summers-Smith (1988).
REFERENCES Sultana *et al.* (1975), Summers-Smith (1988).

275 SUDAN GOLDEN SPARROW *Passer luteus*   Plate 70
Africa

Fringilla luteus Lichtenstein, 1823, Verz. Doubl., p. 24, Dongola, Sudan.
  Note: The retention of this and the following species as separate species follows the treatment by Hall and Moreau (1970).

IDENTIFICATION Length 12–13 cm (4¾–5 in). A distinctive small sparrow ranging widely over dry savanna and semi-desert of the southern Sahara. Males have pale lemon-yellow head, face, rump and underparts, with a rich chestnut mantle and back; blackish wings edged with rufous and two whitish wingbars. Females are sandy-brown on upperparts, finely streaked darker, and with a pale yellowish supercilium, and a yellowish wash on face and underparts. **Confusion species:** Confusion possible with the similar (but isolated) Arabian Golden Sparrow (276), but adult male of latter is more noticeably intensely deep yellow and lacks any warm brown or chestnut and female is greyer (not sandy) and unstreaked on upperparts. Female Sudan's lack of any grey or heavy, bold streaking on mantle and back and its warm sandy-brown tones make it unlikely to be mistaken for other sparrows, the relationship with which is readily apparent in habits and behaviour. Confusion possible with escaped canaries, all of which, however, lack any bright chestnut tones.
DESCRIPTION Sexes differ. **Adult male:** Forehead to nape, face, sides of neck and underparts rich or deep lemon-yellow (some may show paler lores and grey tips to ear-coverts). Mantle, back and scapulars bright chestnut; rump yellow (grey or greyish tinged with yellow in non-breeding season), becoming greyish-yellow on uppertail-coverts (greyer on longest coverts). Tail slightly notched or forked, brown or dark brown, finely edged paler buff-brown. Lesser coverts as scapulars; median and greater coverts black, with white tips forming double wingbar (may be reduced or absent in worn plumage); alula and primary coverts black, or latter may be finely edged with yellow; flight feathers black or blackish, with a small pale or sandy-buff patch at bases of primaries, and edges to secondaries broadly warm brown or rufous; tertials the same, more broadly edged and tipped pale or yellowish-buff. Underparts from centre of belly to vent and undertail-coverts may be white or whitish. Bill black in breeding season, brown or brownish-horn upper mandible and paler lower in winter. Legs and feet flesh-pink or pinkish-brown. **Adult**

female: Generally a warm sandy-buff bird with yellowish face and underparts. Forehead to crown, nape, mantle, back and scapulars warm sandy-buff or a light ginger tone (mantle and scapulars streaked darker); pale sandy or yellowish-buff supercilium from base of bill and over ear-coverts, bordered by thin dark eye-stripe; cheeks and ear-coverts dull or dingy sandy-buff. Rump and uppertail-coverts dull greyish-sandy. Tail dark grey, edged pale buffish. Lesser coverts as scapulars; bases to medians black, tips broadly buff, and greaters black, broadly edged and tipped with buff, forming double wingbar; alula and primary coverts black, latter edged slightly pale buff; flight feathers dark grey or blackish, with a small pale buff patch at base of primaries, and edges to inner primaries and secondaries buff or pale buff, becoming broadly edged on tertials. Chin and throat yellowish, becoming yellowish-buff on rest of underparts; belly to undertail-coverts white or whitish. Bill pink in breeding plumage, becoming pale grey or greyish-horn in non-breeding season.
Juvenile: Very similar to adult female, but greyer on head, nape and face, and underparts also generally much paler. First-winter males develop chestnut bases to feathers at a fairly early age, and bases to medians and inner webs of greaters are black (or blacker than on females) with pale sandy-buff tips (duller in worn plumage). Bill as adult female, or dusky or greyish-horn at tip on first-winter males. Some first-year birds can have blue legs.
VOICE Call a distinctively different but sparrow-like 'chirp', 'schilp' or a disyllabic 'tchirrup', but in flight also gives a redpoll-like rhythmic 'che-che-che', rapidly repeated. The song is a sparrow-like repetition of the call notes.
STATUS, HABITAT AND BEHAVIOUR Common to abundant. A bird of dry arid scrub and thornbush, sparse savanna, but also in areas where cereal cultivation (via irrigation) is being developed; not generally found in towns or villages, but often roosts collectively in trees in towns, villages or even cities (e.g. Khartoum, Sudan). Highly social and gregarious, breeds colonially and

465

generally occurs in flocks of up to 100, but some roosts can number several hundred thousands; frequently occurs in mixed flocks with the smaller species of weaver (*Ploceus*) or Red-billed Quelea (*Quelea quelea*). On the ground hops or runs, and other habits typical of the sparrow family. Feeds on the ground and in vegetation, principally on grass and small weed seeds, cereals, millet or sorghum (rice taken only after being de-husked); also small quantities of fruit, berries and insects, mainly ants, weevils, bugs and caterpillars; the nestlings are fed mainly on insects until they fledge, breeding season being timed to coincide with onset of rains, though in dry season or drought years some young have been raised on a diet consisting principally of small seeds.

DISTRIBUTION Monotypic. Mauritania and northern Senegal, east through northern Mali (between 14° 30′ and 14° 17′N), extreme southern Algeria, extreme north Burkina Faso, Niger and north-central Chad to northern and central Sudan and extreme northern Ethiopia.

MOVEMENTS Highly mobile and extremely nomadic, remaining to breed in an area only when conditions favourable. Wanders in non-breeding season intermittently north and south of range given above; a regular non-breeding-season visitor to northern Nigeria and north Cameroon, has also occurred in southern Egypt (where bred) and central Ethiopia; vagrant to Gambia.

MEASUREMENTS Wing of male 60–70, of female 58–67; tail of male 46–50, of female 45–50; tarsus 17–18; bill (culmen) 10–11·5. Weight av. 14.

REFERENCES Bannerman (1953), Hall and Moreau (1970), Summers-Smith (1988).

276 ARABIAN GOLDEN SPARROW *Passer euchlorus* Plate 70

Arabia and Africa

Auripasser euchlorus Bonaparte, 1851, Consp. Av., 1 (1850), p. 519, 'Abyssinia, Arabia'; type from Kunfuda, Arabia.

IDENTIFICATION Length 13 cm (5 in). An unmistakable bright golden-yellow sparrow of very restricted range. Males are a deep, bright or golden-yellow, with a large dark eye, domed head, pale yellow wing-coverts and black flight feathers and tail; duller in non-breeding season, with tinges of buffish-brown or cinnamon on head and nape. Females are greyish, unstreaked on mantle, but with warm yellow on face and nape; underparts are grey or paler than on similar female Sudan Golden Sparrow (275). **Confusion species:** Does not (yet) meet or overlap with Sudan Golden (though every possibility that it soon will: the gap between the two in east Ethiopia and Djibouti is about 75 km), adult males of which have deep chestnut on mantle, back and scapulars and lack deep yellow tones or pale yellow edges to wing-coverts. Females and juveniles are similar to those of Sudan Golden Sparrow, but are buffish-brown with some slight streaking on mantle and scapulars. Both sexes are distinguished from small weavers by the bright yellow plumage, domed head, short stubby bill, and longer and straight-edged/square-ended tail; all similar-plumaged weavers, e.g. Rüppell's (*Ploceus galbula*) have long streaks on upperparts and males have black faces in breeding season. Escaped canaries are not usually so intensely golden-yellow with jet-black flight feathers.

DESCRIPTION Sexes differ. **Adult male:** Entire head, face, nape, mantle, back and scapulars to rump, uppertail-coverts and underparts deep golden-yellow. Tail black, broadly edged whitish. All wing-coverts and alula pale yellow, with greyish inner webs on coverts; primary coverts black or blackish with pale yellow bases and edges; flight feathers black, edged white or whitish, and with a small patch of white at bases of primaries; tertials black, broadly edged white or very pale yellow. Bill black in breeding season, otherwise grey or pale grey (can be tinged pale pink). Legs and feet pale pinkish-brown. In non-breeding plumage, head and nape are duller and tinged with buffish-brown or cinnamon and mantle and scapulars are pale grey; wing-coverts lose their yellow edges and are pale greyish. **Adult female:** Forehead to crown greyish-brown, tinged warm yellow or sandy; upper lores and sides of forehead to supercilium pale or light yellow; thin dark eye-stripe often present only behind eye; cheeks and ear-coverts pale buff, yellow, pale yellow or tinged sandy and extending to nape (hindcrown and nape can also be yellowish or warm sandy-buff in breeding plumage). Mantle, back and scapulars to rump and uppertail-coverts grey, tinged or lightly washed with yellow. Tail dark grey, edged paler. Lesser coverts as scapulars; median coverts dark or blackish at base, broadly tipped dull or yellowish-buff; greater coverts dark grey or blackish, broadly edged and tipped pale buff; alula and primary coverts the same, very finely edged with pale buff; flight feathers dark grey or blackish, finely edged pale buff and with a small pale patch at base of primaries. Chin and throat yellow or pale yellow, extending to centre of breast, or grey on centre and sides of breast and flanks; belly to vent washed pale yellowish or grey; undertail-coverts white. Bill pale grey or pinkish at base, becoming dark grey along cutting edges and tip. **Juvenile:** Similar to adult female, but generally greyer and with some slight mottling on mantle and back; lacks yellow tones except for a pale yellowish wash on face, throat and breast, becoming off-white on belly and flanks.

VOICE Call very similar to that of Sudan Golden

Sparrow and clearly also to House Sparrow (258), but appears to lack the redpoll-like quality to flight calls; call is a softer and more subdued 'chirp', and flocks calling together give a whispering twitter.

STATUS, HABITAT AND BEHAVIOUR Common or locally common. Found in similar habitat to Sudan Golden Sparrow: dry or arid country, savannas or in acacia or thornscrub up to 600 m; when not breeding, occurs almost entirely in areas of cereal cultivation and edges of towns or villages. Also highly social, and occurs in small flocks throughout the year, in non-breeding season forming flocks numbering hundreds or occasionally thousands; breeds and roosts colonially. Frequently associates with House Sparrow or Rüppell's Weaver. Feeds on the ground or in vegetation, on much the same items as Sudan Golden Sparrow, but has a preference for millet, sorghum and maize fields.

DISTRIBUTION Monotypic. Southwest Saudi Arabia (coastal Red Sea lowlands north to about 22° N, and the Tihama), western North Yemen, southwest South Yemen (Aden), Djibouti and the adjacent areas of eastern Ethiopia and northwest Somalia.

MOVEMENTS Sedentary in some areas but otherwise nomadic; wanders in non-breeding season (usually in search of food), but in some years breeds continuously in one area, only to abandon it in favour of elsewhere in later years.

MEASUREMENTS Wing of male 57–64, of female 55–64; tarsus 15–16; bill (to skull) 10–12·5, (to feathers) 7–8·5. Weight 12–16·8.

277 CHESTNUT SPARROW *Passer eminibey*   **Plate 70**
Africa

Sorella eminibey Hartlaub, 1880, Journ. f. Orn., 28, p. 211, 325, Lado.

IDENTIFICATION Length 11·5 cm (4½ in). A small sparrow of much of East Africa which has close affinities to the golden sparrows (275, 276). In breeding plumage male is almost entirely deep chestnut, with a slightly darker face and black wings and tail; non-breeding males have the chestnut broken by flecks and tips of white on upperparts and black centres to mantle and scapulars, while underparts are white or pale buff with chestnut tips or crescents. Females are closer to other female sparrows, with grey head, warm buff-brown supercilium, chin and throat, black streaks on mantle, and warm brown scapulars to rump; underparts off-white or washed with warm buff. **Confusion species:** Adult male in breeding or non-breeding plumage is virtually unmistakable; only the much larger, longer-billed, black-headed male Chestnut Weaver (*Ploceus rubiginosus*), which has bright white tips to the coverts and the edges of flight feathers, is likely to cause brief confusion. Females and immatures are more likely to be confused with those of other sparrows, especially Rufous Sparrow (265) of race *rufocinctus*, but the plumage of head, face, scapulars and especially underparts should enable separation; immatures are more difficult, especially lone birds and those outside range, as confusion with House Sparrow (258) possible, but tones of supercilium, scapulars (including lesser coverts) and rump are good indicators.

DESCRIPTION Sexes differ. **Adult male** (breeding plumage)**:** Entire head, face and body to both uppertail- and undertail-coverts rich or deep chestnut, slightly darker or blacker on forehead, face, chin and throat. Tail dark brown or blackish, edged warm buff-brown or light chestnut. Lesser and median coverts as upperparts; greater coverts black, broadly edged chestnut and tipped slightly paler or lighter chestnut; alula black; primary coverts black, edged warm chestnut at bases; flight feathers black, with small pale buff or light buff-brown patch at base of primaries; edges to primaries light buff, becoming chestnut on secondaries and tertials, broadest on tertials, which have pale buffish or light brown tips. Bill black or blackish. Legs and feet pale brown. Non-breeding adults in the breeding season have fine pale whitish or buff tips to the chestnut feathers of nape, mantle, breast and belly and also pale yellowish-brown base to the dark-tipped bill. In non-breeding season, much of the chestnut plumage is lost through wear, abrasion or bleaching and the bird looks altogether very untidy or ragged: upperparts are flecked or tipped paler or with pale buff, sides of mantle and scapulars have black centres or bases, and edges to wing-coverts become much paler buff; face is finely speckled with whitish tips, and broad white tips obscure much of the chestnut on breast, belly and flanks or reduce it to odd patches; bill is generally pale or light brown with a dusky or dull grey-brown tip. **Adult female:** Forehead to crown, nape, sides of neck and upper mantle grey or grey-brown; lores grey or greyish, but feathers at base of bill tipped lightly with buff or orange-brown; warm buff-brown supercilium over eye to rear of ear-coverts; cheeks and ear-coverts pale buff or tinged with grey. Lower mantle and back grey-brown, becoming warm brown or chestnut on scapulars, with bold black streaks or feather centres to mantle and upper scapulars; lower back and rump warm brown; uppertail-coverts and tail brown, tail edged finely with warm buff (especially at base). Lesser and median coverts chestnut as scapulars; greaters dark or blackish-brown, edged and tipped brown or pale buff-brown; alula black; primary coverts dark brown, edged pale buff-brown at base; flight feathers dark brown, with a small pale buff panel at base of primaries, and edges to primaries thinly pale buff, becoming broader on secondaries and tertials, tips of latter pale buff. Chin and throat warm buff-brown or light chestnut; breast and flanks washed light warm buff-brown; belly, vent and undertail-coverts white. Bill pale yellowish, with dusky grey tip and cutting edge to both mandibles. **Juvenile:** A paler or duller version of adult female. Forehead to crown, nape and upper mantle dull grey or ashy-brown, back and mantle slightly browner with black streaks; scapulars and lesser coverts washed with warm buff-brown (but lighter than on adult female); rump also warm buff-brown; pale buff tips to median and greater coverts; pale yellowy or pinky-buff supercilium over and behind eye, with slight continuation to rear edge of ear-coverts. Bill generally pale yellowish-horn. First-winter birds are similar to juveniles, with progressively more dark chestnut showing and darker tips (forming crescents) on breast and flanks.

VOICE Call a subdued chirping, otherwise unrecorded; males at the nest give a high-pitched twittering trill.

STATUS, HABITAT AND BEHAVIOUR Common or locally common. Inhabits dry grasslands or savannas with bush or scrub, acacia thickets, near marshes or papyrus swamps, often in or near towns and villages. Occurs in pairs or small groups, occasionally associating with queleas (*Quelea*) or small weavers but usually only at a common source of food. Breeds colonially or loosely colonially; sometimes parasitises nests of weavers (*Ploceus*) or social weavers (*Pseudonigrita*). Feeds on the ground, on a variety of grass and weed seeds, also takes household scraps and insects; the young are fed mostly on small insects until they fledge.

DISTRIBUTION Monotypic. Western Sudan (Darfur province), discontinuously southeast to southwest Ethiopia (with a northeastward extension up the Rift Valley), eastern Uganda, through Kenya (mainly the Rift Valley and the west) to extreme southwest Somalia and south to north-central Tanzania.

MOVEMENTS Generally resident or sedentary, though some undertake extensive nomadic wanderings in non-breeding season; has occurred outside the range given above, in northern Uganda and east to Dar-es-Salaam, eastern Tanzania.

MEASUREMENTS Wing of male 60–65, of female 57–60; tail c40; tarsus c15; bill c10.

REFERENCE Summers-Smith (1988).

GENUS *PETRONIA*

Six species. Petronias are related to the sparrows but have specialised habitat requirements, being usually found in drier or more arid areas of semi-desert scrub, cliffs, gorges or wadis. Somewhat more squat and robust in appearance than most of the species within *Passer*.

278 PALE ROCK SPARROW *Petronia brachydactyla*   Plate 72
Palearctic and Arabia

Petronia brachydactyla Bonaparte, 1851, Consp. Av., 1 (1850), p. 513, 'Arabia, Abyssinia'; type from Kunfuda, western Arabia.

IDENTIFICATION Length 14 cm (5½ in). A rather featureless and dull sandy bunting- or lark-like bird, recalling an unstreaked Corn Bunting (*Miliaria calandra*) in its size, somewhat dumpy shape and song. The upperparts are pale sandy or sandy-grey, with pale buff edges to coverts and secondaries; the wings are long and reach well beyond uppertail-coverts. The white tips to tail feathers are a good identification point. Poorly defined pale buff supercilium and a pale submoustachial stripe. The pale, stout bill is a good field character, as are the pale orange-brown legs and feet. In flight, the long wings are especially noticeable. **Confusion species:** Likely to be confused with the smaller and darker female and juvenile Yellow-throated Sparrow (279), which see for differences.

DESCRIPTION Sexes alike. **Adult:** Forehead to nape pale sandy or sandy-grey; poorly defined pale or sandy-buff supercilium from upper lores over eye, fading over ear-coverts; lower lores to below eye also pale buff, giving the dark eye a pale surround; cheeks and ear-coverts grey-brown or paler; pale buff-brown moustachial streak, with a pale buff submoustachial and darker malar stripe. Mantle, back, scapulars and rump as crown and nape, uppertail-coverts slightly darker or browner. Tail dark grey-brown, thinly edged paler buff and tipped pale or whitish-buff (except central pair of feathers), and generally paler on undertail. Lesser coverts as upperparts; median coverts dark or brown at base, broadly tipped pale buff, greaters similar with fine pale buff edges and broader pale tips, forming double wingbar; alula dark brown; primary coverts pale buffish with darker edges and tips; flight feathers dark brown, finely edged and tipped lighter or sandy-buff, more broadly so on secondaries and tertials (appears as a pale panel on closed wing). Chin and throat whitish or pale buff, paler than the fawn-grey on breast and flanks; belly, lower flanks and vent washed pale buff; undertail-coverts white. Bill stout and somewhat lark-like with a pronounced curve to culmen, pale creamy or pale sandy on both mandibles. Legs and feet bright pale or rich orange-brown and very obvious. In winter, the fresh plumage is slightly darker or deeper sandy-brown in tone than the worn or faded plumage of summer. **Juvenile:** Very similar to adult but generally paler or more sandy, especially the pale tips and edges to coverts and secondaries; bases to median coverts paler, and bill has dusky brown tip and cutting edges.

VOICE Call a high-pitched, nasal 'twee' or 'zweee' or 'twee-oo'; also a soft trill or churr given in flight. The song is a distinctive monotonous buzzing recalling a flat or rather tuneless Corn Bunting or a cicada, a rising 'tss tss tss tsseeeeeeei' or 'tee-zeeeze-zeeezeeei', usually given from top of a rock or bush from March onwards.

STATUS, HABITAT AND BEHAVIOUR Locally common or occasionally abundant, with erratic occurrences in some areas. Found on grassy plains or hillsides with rocky outcrops, also in arid stony semi-deserts and wadis; in some areas, occurs in considerable numbers as cultivated millet is ripening, and can become a pest. Occurs in pairs or loose flocks; semi-colonial, but in non-breeding season flocks can number several hundred. Feeds on the ground or in vegetation, on a variety of seeds, grass seeds and other small weed seeds, but also on millet and other cultivated seed-bearing crops.

DISTRIBUTION Monotypic. Southeast Turkey, Syria and Lebanon south to Mount Hermon, Israel; also Armenia east through Iran to Baluchistan. Has also bred United Arab Emirates (1988).

MOVEMENTS Migratory. Moves south in autumn through Iraq, Jordan, UAE and Oman to winter in southern Iraq (occasionally or infrequently west to southern Israel and Sinai), western Saudi Arabia, Ethiopia and Sudan south to about 12° N; vagrant to Dagestan (north of the Caucasus), Egypt (six records) and Yemen. Leaves breeding areas from end of July, with southward movements in autumn from late August to October and northward return movements from February to May; has been noted singing and even attempting nest-building while on passage.

MEASUREMENTS Wing of male 90–102, of female 86–94; tail 42–52; bill 12·5–13·5. Weight 21–25.

279 YELLOW-THROATED SPARROW *Petronia xanthocollis*   Plate 72
Palearctic and Oriental

Fringilla xanthocollis Burton, 1838, Cat. Coll. Mamm. Birds Mus. Fort Pitt, Chatham, p. 23, Ganges between Calcutta and Benares.

IDENTIFICATION Length 13–14 cm (5–5½ in). A generally grey sparrow with relatively few distinctive features. More of a tree-loving species than other petronias. Adult male is grey on head and upperparts with a warm brown or chestnut patch on lesser coverts; broad white tips to median coverts and thinner pale tips to greaters, but these can be lacking or obscured; chin and throat are white, with a bright yellow spot on lower throat in fresh plumage. Females are duller and lack the chestnut (replaced by warm brown) at bend of wing; the yellow throat spot is also much reduced or entirely absent. **Confusion species:** Slimmer and much greyer than Pale Rock Sparrow (278), with broad white tips to median coverts and slightly thinner tips to greaters, male with bright chestnut lesser coverts, both sexes and all ages with a white throat, and adults with yellow or a trace of yellow on lower throat. Bush Petronia (283) is similar but slightly smaller, lacks the broad white tips to median coverts, and adult male has a well-defined warm brown supercilium curving onto sides of nape (pale or warm buffish-brown on females and juveniles respectively). Yellow-spotted Petronia (280) of East Africa is also similar in having grey head and upperparts with a yellow spot in centre of lower throat, but lacks the wingbars or the chestnut on lesser coverts (was previously considered a race of Yellow-throated Sparrow).

DESCRIPTION Sexes similar but separable. **Adult male:** Entire head and upperparts to rump and uppertail-coverts grey, becoming slightly paler or buffish-grey in worn plumage. Tail rather short and slightly notched at tip, dark grey, thinly edged paler or buffish. Lesser coverts rich warm brown or chestnut, but often obscured by grey scapulars; median coverts brownish-grey at bases and broadly tipped white, greaters dark grey, edged paler and tipped pale buff or whitish, forming double wingbar; alula and primary coverts dark brown, the latter edged slightly paler at base; flight feathers dark brown or brownish-grey, edged paler buff or buffish-grey on secondaries; tertials the same or slightly browner, and edged broadly pale buff. Face with a faint or pale suggestion of a supercilium over lores to eye or slightly beyond, but often uniform with sides of crown; lores and eye-stripe dark grey or brownish-grey; cheeks and ear-coverts plain grey or greyish-buff (as upperparts). Chin, throat and sides of throat off-white; centre of lower throat a spot of bright yellow, variably extending to sides of lower throat or centre of upper breast; breast and flanks washed pale grey; belly, vent and undertail-coverts white or whitish-buff. Bill rather long and slender for a sparrow, black in breeding season, but otherwise pale yellow on upper mandible or pinkish at base of lower with dark or dusky tip to both. Legs and feet grey or grey-brown. **Adult female:** Very similar to adult male, but lesser coverts are warm brown to grey-brown, not chestnut; tips to median coverts pale buff (not white, but still has a double wingbar), and yellow throat spot much reduced or completely absent. Bill as that of adult male in non-breeding season. **Juven-**

ile: Very similar to adult female, but slightly more buffish and lacks any yellow on lower throat; has a paler face with a well-defined supercilium, and pale buffish-brown edges and tips to wing-coverts and warm buff-brown edges to secondaries.

GEOGRAPHICAL VARIATION Race *transfuga* is slightly more sandy-grey than plain grey in general plumage tones, and edges to wing-coverts are paler and chestnut on lesser coverts lighter, but overall may show very little difference in the field from nominate race.

VOICE Most calls are very similar to those of House Sparrow (258) in tone but slightly softer or more tuneful, 'chilp' or 'chirrup', as well as the more usual harsh churring notes. The song is a fairly distinctive and rhythmic 'chilp chalp cholp', uttered endlessly from a favoured song perch.

STATUS, HABITAT AND BEHAVIOUR Common or locally common. Occurs in a variety of wooded habitats, from dry forests, jungles, scrub, groves, hedges to oases and date palms; often near cultivation or villages. Usually found in pairs or small groups, but in non-breeding season occasionally in flocks of up to 100, also in mixed flocks with House Sparrows and Black-headed Buntings (*Emberiza melanocephala*). Roosts communally in hedges and hawthorn scrub. On the ground recalls a finch, with a slightly hesitant hopping gait. Undulating flight is rather more dipping than that of other sparrows. Feeds in trees and on the ground, on a variety of seeds, princi-pally grass and weed seeds, grain, rice, berries and ripe fruit, also insects, including ants, weevils, beetles and caterpillars; also takes nectar of certain plants (at such times, forehead often becomes stained golden-yellow).

DISTRIBUTION *P. x. xanthocollis*: eastern Afghanistan to central and northern Pakistan, India (north to Uttar Pradesh up to about 1400 m), east to Bihar and lower West Bengal and south throughout the peninsula) to lowland Nepal.

P. x. transfuga: southeast Turkey, discontinuously through Iraq to United Arab Emirates, northern Oman and east to southern Iran, Baluchistan and southern Afghanistan to Sind and the Punjab, southern Pakistan to Haryana, Rajasthan and Gujarat, northwest India.

MOVEMENTS Sedentary or partially migratory. Breeders in Turkey, Iraq, east Afghanistan and northwest India move south, southeast or east (from Oman) to winter in India; recorded on passage in Kuwait, and has been recorded in winter in Oman. A vagrant to Malta (November 1912 and March 1971), Israel (May 1982), east Saudi Arabia, Bahrain, and Sri Lanka (October 1876). Breeders arrive on territory from March to early May, and depart for wintering areas from September (occasionally August) to November.

MEASUREMENTS Wing of male 77–89, of female 76–85; tail of male 43–52, of female 43–55; tarsus 16–18; bill (from skull) 13–16. Weight 15–20.

280 YELLOW-SPOTTED PETRONIA *Petronia pyrgita*   Plate 73
Africa

Xanthodina pyrgita Heuglin, 1862, Journ. f. Orn., 10, p. 30, Bogos Mts, slopes of the Barca Valley, Eritrea.

Note: The splitting of this species from *P. xanthocollis* follows the classification of African petronias into a superspecies group, as proposed by Hall and Moreau (1970).

IDENTIFICATION Length 15 cm (6 in). Grey or grey-brown petronia of the scrub and bush of lightly wooded country in northern tropical Africa. Similar to but slightly paler than Yellow-throated Sparrow (279) of Asia and Arabia (of which some authorities consider it a race). Lacks Yellow-throated's white or pale wingbars and the brown or chestnut patch on lesser coverts; the yellow spot on throat is paler and reduced in size. **Confusion species:** Bush Petronia (283) is generally browner and has a well-defined supercilium in all plumages: adult male has a pale or white chin and throat, and a warm brown supercilium curving onto sides of nape; female has a white throat patch surrounded by grey, and a broad pale buff supercilium; juvenile is much more buffish-brown and resembles juvenile House Sparrow (258). For differences from the similar but geographically separated Yellow-throated Sparrow, see that species.

DESCRIPTION Sexes very similar but separable. **Adult male:** Entire head, face, nape to sides of neck and mantle plain light grey or greyish-brown; thin dark eye-stripe and pale indistinct area behind eye to over ear-coverts. Mantle, back, scapulars and rump also plain or uniform grey-brown; uppertail-coverts slightly browner. Tail dark brown, with fine pale grey or greyish-buff edges to outer feathers. Median and greater coverts grey-brown, edged and tipped with pale buff, more broadly or noticeably on greaters; alula and primary coverts dark brown; flight feathers also dark brown, edged with pale buff, more broadly edged and tipped pale buff on tertials. Chin and throat white, with a bright yellow spot on lower throat (but not always present or prominent); breast very pale buffish-grey or washed with grey; rest of underparts off-white or tinged with buff or pale buffish-brown. Bill quite prominent and slender, upper mandible brown, lower paler or brownish-horn. Legs and feet blue or bluish-grey. **Adult female:** Very similar to adult male, but slightly smaller and usually with less (and less intense) yellow on throat. **Juvenile:** Very similar to adult, but with some fine or indistinct darker grey streaks or mottling on mantle and upper back;

wing-coverts and flight feathers have buff edges and tips.

GEOGRAPHICAL VARIATION Race *pallida* is slightly paler or more buffish-brown on head to mantle, back and rump; underparts are white or creamy-white with a buffish wash on breast.

VOICE Generally silent, but occasionally makes sharp or high-pitched sparrow-like 'chillip', as well as a more usual 'chirp' note.

STATUS, HABITAT AND BEHAVIOUR Common or locally common, but nowhere numerous. Occurs in dry or arid grasslands or steppes with acacia and thornscrub with light open woodland at up to 1800 m, more often in trees than on the ground, but also found on the edge of cultivation. Occurs in pairs or small parties, often in association with small weavers, e.g. Rüppell's (*Ploceus galbula*), or bishops (*Euplectes*). Feeds on

the ground but more often in trees, on seeds, fruit, berries, also insects, for which it forages in rather tit-like fashion in the foliage.

DISTRIBUTION *P. p. pyrgita*: southern Ethiopia, Somalia, west through Kenya to extreme southeast Sudan and northeast Uganda (Kidepo Valley National Park to Debasien Game Reserve), and in northeast Tanzania from Arusha south to Pangani.

P. p. pallida: southern Mauritania and northern Senegal, discontinuously east through Mali and Niger to Chad and central Sudan (to the White Nile).

MOVEMENTS Largely sedentary, but wanders throughout the range outside breeding season.

MEASUREMENTS Wing of male 87–97, of female 86–90. Wing of *pallida* 81–91.

REFERENCE Hall and Moreau (1970).

281 ROCK SPARROW *Petronia petronia* Plate 72
Palearctic

Fringilla petronia Linnaeus, 1766, Syst. Nat., ed. 12, p. 322, Northern Italy.

IDENTIFICATION Length 14–15·5 cm (5½-6 in); *intermedia* 17 cm (6½-6¾ in). A distinctively marked and rather plump or squat sparrow, with a bold black-and-white striped head pattern and a small (not always present or obvious) yellow spot on centre of lower throat/upper breast. In fresh plumage, has white tip to the (fairly short) tail and the undertail-coverts are grey-brown with broad pale tips. A fairly noisy bird with a high-pitched or ringing call note among its more usual sparrow-like chirping notes. **Confusion species:** Only possible confusion is likely to be with a poorly seen female House Sparrow (258); head pattern of Rock is diagnostic, and it is slightly shorter-tailed and with a broader wing base, features more easily noted in flight than at rest.

DESCRIPTION Sexes alike. **Adult:** Lower central forehead to hindcrown pale buff to white, sides of forehead to sides of crown and nape broadly blackish-brown, forming prominent striped head pattern. Broad pale creamy supercilium from eye to sides of nape, broad dark brown eye-stripe extending to rear of ear-coverts; lores brown with pale or buffish tips; light or pale buff area below eye, and cheeks and ear-coverts pale grey or streaked lightly with pale buff; thin dark moustachial stripe, pale buffish submoustachial stripe, and thin dull or buffish-brown malar stripe. Nape, hindneck and sides of neck grey-brown. In fresh plu-

mage, mantle, back and scapulars tawny-brown, streaked darker, with pale buff 'braces' on sides of mantle enclosed by dark streaks; rump and uppertail-coverts pale grey-brown, with darker centres to uppertail-coverts. Tail fairly short, grey-brown, with pale buff-brown edges and fairly prominent pale buff or white subterminal spots to all feathers (visible mostly in flight). Lesser coverts pale grey or grey-brown, tipped darker grey; median coverts dark brown, finely edged pale buff or whitish; greaters dark brown, edged paler grey or greyish-buff and finely tipped with white or pale buff; alula and primary coverts dark brown, the latter with fine pale buff edges at bases; flight feathers dark brown, edged with pale buff, broadest on secondaries and tertials, with a small panel or patch of pale creamy-buff at base of inner primaries; tertials also tipped pale buff or whitish in fresh plumage. Chin and throat whitish-buff; lower throat to centre of upper breast a spot of pale yellow (often covered by upper throat feathers, absent in worn plumage, and seen well only on displaying birds); breast, flanks and belly pale buff or whitish with prominent brown or olive-brown streaks, heaviest on flanks; undertail-coverts dark olive or olive-brown at base, with broad white tips. Bill rather stout or deep at base, pale yellow on most of lower mandible, with grey or greyish-horn upper (except for pale area at sides of base) and dusky tip. Legs and feet pale brown or pinkish-brown. **Juvenile:** Similar to adult, but warmer or more sandy-brown in general tones of upperparts, and with pale buff tips to median and greater coverts forming slightly more prominent double wingbar; tips of tertials are paler than on adult, streaks on underparts are not so heavy or prominent, and also lacks any yellow on a generally grey-washed lower throat and upper breast.

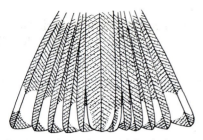 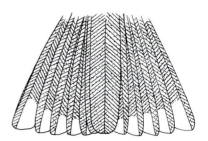

Tail pattern (from above) of Rock Sparrow P. petronia *(left) and Pale Rock sparrow* P. brachydactyla.

GEOGRAPHICAL VARIATION Overall, there is relatively little variation among the different races or populations that can be detected in the field, as most differences relate to comparative features or to the intensity of the grey to sandy tone of the plumage. Of the seven races recognised, only nominate and *puteicola*, *brevirostris* and to some extent *barbara* are likely to be separable in the field. Birds of race *puteicola* are the palest or most sandy-coloured, with very fine or thin dark streaks on the underparts, and have the largest bill (in mm) of any race; *intermedia* is, as its name implies, intermediate between nominate and *puteicola*; *brevirostris* has less clear-cut or less well-defined markings on head and mantle, and a short thick bill; race *barbara* is paler and greyer (as is *exigua*), with the greyest birds in the east of the range (and merging at the western end of the range with birds of nominate race), and on average has a larger bill than other races (except *puteicola*).

VOICE A variety of calls, many of which are similar (or vaguely so) to those of House sparrow, but also has some distinctive, inquisitive, metallic notes 'dliu', 'viep' or 'vi-viep'; in flight gives a 'sup' or 'doui' note; also a very characteristic sharp and metallic 'cheeooee' or 'pee-uoo-ee'. The song appears to be a loose collection of the call notes repeated.

STATUS, HABITAT AND BEHAVIOUR Locally common. A bird of barren hills and mountainous regions, where it occurs in rocky outcrops, gorges, ravines, scree slopes and in arid regions and edges of deserts at up to 2500 m in North Africa and 3000 m in China; also at lower elevations in villages (occupied or otherwise) with ruins, wells or ancient structures, hollow trees, or in winter on adjacent farmland. Sociable and usually in pairs, small flocks or loose colonies, breeds in colonies of up to 100 pairs; often in close association with House Sparrows, and in Spain has been found sharing a river bank with a colony of Bee-eaters (*Merops apiaster*). On the ground it runs and hops in lark-like manner, but spends a lot of time calling or 'singing' from high vantage points; flight strong and typically sparrow-like. Feeds on the ground but also in vegetation, on seeds, mainly grass and small weed seeds, but also grain and fruit, berries and insects, particularly caterpillars or grubs, on which the young are fed until they fledge.

DISTRIBUTION *P. p. petronia*: southern Europe, from Portugal and Spain to Balearic Islands, southern France (north to Charentes and the Rhone valley), southern Switzerland (rare) to Italy, Corsica, Sardinia and Sicily and southern Yugoslavia (southern Dalmatia) to Albania, Greece, southern Bulgaria and western Turkey; also Morocco.

P. p. barbara: Algeria (south to Saharan Atlas), north and east Tunisia to western Libya (Tripolitania) south to about 31° N.

P. p. madeirensis: Madeira, Porto Santo, Desertas and the western Canary Islands.

P. p. puteicola: Anti-Lebanon range southern Syria, northern Israel and Jordan (may also have bred in Iran).

P. p. exigua: central and eastern Turkey to northern Caucasus (to lower River Don) and northwest and northern Iran.

P. p. intermedia: north Caspian (east of the Volga) to the southwest Kirghiz steppes, east of the Caspian to central and east Iran, to northern Afghanistan, Pakistan (Gilgit) and Kashmir, north through Tadzhikstan to Bukhara, Uzbekistan, the Pamirs and the Tien Shan to the Dzungarian Ala Tau, east to the Bogdo Ola Shan and in Sinkiang from Kashgaria to the western Kunlun range.

P. p. brevirostris: eastern Siberia from the Russian Altai, through Mongolia to northwest Manchuria, northern China south through west Hopeh, Inner Mongolia, Ningsia to west Kansu, Tsinghai and Szechwan (to about 32° N).

MOVEMENTS Sedentary, partial migrant or altitudinal migrant, some moving to lower levels or away from breeding areas in winter. Birds of race *puteicola* disperse or wander at random throughout the range; *exigua* move south to winter in east and southwest Iran and Iraq; *intermedia* occurs south to Iraq, southern Afghanistan, northern Baluchistan and northern Pakistan (south to Kohat). A vagrant to Gibraltar (September 1973), Malta, Cyprus, Yugoslavia (Slovenia), the Azores (1903) and England (June 1981).

MEASUREMENTS Wing 93–100; tail 48–54; bill 14–16.; Wing of *exigua* 100–104; tail 53–55; bill 15–16.; Wing of *puteicola* 100–105. Wing of *intermedia* 97–108; tail 57–60; tarsus 18·1–19; bill (from skull) 15–18. Weight 26–37.

REFERENCES Moore and Boswell (1956), Vaurie (1956).

282 SOUTHERN YELLOW-THROATED SPARROW (South African Rock Sparrow) *Petronia superciliaris*   Plate 73
South Africa

Gymnorhis superciliaris Blyth, 1845, Journ. Asiat. Soc. Bengal, 14, p. 553, South Africa; restricted to Cape Town by Grant and Clancey, 1953, Ostrich, 24, p. 128.

IDENTIFICATION Length 15–16 cm (6–6¼ in). A fairly large and distinctive sparrow of southern Africa. Adults have broad creamy or pale buff (buff-brown on juveniles) supercilium extending to sides of nape and emphasised by a broad dark eye-stripe; double wingbar is also prominent both on adults (except in worn plumage) and juveniles, but the yellow throat spot is unlikely to be seen in the field unless birds are displaying. Rarely or infrequently on the ground. **Confusion species:** Streaky-headed Seedeater (27) is initially similar with bold white supercilium, but has an entirely dark face and clearly marked brown-and-white streaks on forehead to nape, and also lacks pale wingbars. White-browed Sparrow-Weaver (*Plocepasser mahali*) has a very broad, bulging, supercilium but a blackish forehead and crown, very broad white tips to the wing-coverts and a white rump. Unlikely to be confused with any other southern African sparrow.
DESCRIPTION Sexes alike. **Adult:** Forehead to crown, nape and hindneck deep earth-brown; broad whitish (or pale buff) supercilium from upper lores to behind ear-coverts and sides of nape; lores buff or dark brown, broadening into dark brown eye-stripe underlining pale supercilium; cheeks and ear-coverts pale buffish-brown. Mantle, back and scapulars slightly paler or warmer earth-brown, streaked darker brown; rump and uppertail-coverts greyish earth-brown, or slightly paler buff or greyish on uppertail-coverts. Tail dark brown with fine pale or warm buffish-brown edges. Lesser coverts as scapulars; median coverts brown or dark brown at bases, broadly tipped white or pale sandy-buff (tips can be absent in worn plumage); greater coverts dark brown, edged with warm brown and tipped pale buff; alula and primary coverts dark brown; flight feathers dark brown or blackish-brown, finely edged pale buffish-brown, becoming warmer brown on inner secondaries and tertials; lower edges and tips of tertials pale buff or whitish. Chin and throat white; in breeding season, lower throat/upper breast shows a small patch or spot of bright yellow (reduced, absent or concealed at other times of year); sides of throat and breast pale buffish-brown, extending to flanks; rest of underparts washed with

buff or pale greyish. Bill quite large or robust in appearance, dark brown upper mandible, paler, lighter or warmer brown lower. Legs and feet dark grey. **Juvenile:** Very similar to adult but upperparts generally warmer brown (streaked dark brown), with supercilium and (broader) edges to flight feathers buff-brown and tips to coverts buffish. Underparts cleaner or paler and lacking any yellow spot; face and sides of breast to flanks washed pale buffish-brown.
VOICE Call a sparrow-like chirp but sharper, 'chick chick', and a rapid rising trill 'trrreeep' or 'chreep-chreep-chreep'. The song is described as short and pleasant.
STATUS, HABITAT AND BEHAVIOUR Common or locally common. Occurs at up to 1730 m in acacia grasslands, thornscrub, light deciduous woodland, *brachystegia* woodland and in trees near rivers or streams; not infrequently on edges of villages, orchards and farms, but shy and usually avoids the presence of humans. Generally solitary, in pairs or loosely social in breeding season, more often in small flocks in non-breeding season. Rarely on rocks or even the ground, but when it is walks with fairly rapid gait, does not hop in the usual sparrow manner. Flicks or flashes tail feathers when alarmed or agitated. More usually feeds in trees and tall bushes than on the ground, forages along branches for insects and their larvae; also takes seeds when on the ground.
DISTRIBUTION Monotypic. Southern Congo and southern Zaire east to southern Tanzania (north to about 5° N), south through Angola and Zambia to northeast Namibia (Caprivi strip), north and east Botswana, Zimbabwe, Mozambique and eastern South Africa (northern, east and southeast Cape Province, northern and eastern Transvaal, western Orange Free State, Swaziland and Natal).
MOVEMENTS Generally sedentary, but some may wander in search of food or move to lower altitudes outside breeding season.
MEASUREMENTS Wing of male 89–98, of female 86–91; tail of male 55–63, of female 52–59; tarsus 18–20; bill (culmen) 13·5–14·5. Weight 27.
REFERENCE Chapin (1954).

283 BUSH PETRONIA (Lesser Rock Sparrow) *Petronia dentata*

Plate 72

Africa and Arabia

Xanthodira dentata Sundevall, 1850, Ofv. K. Sv. Vet.-Akad. Forh., 7, p. 127, northeast Africa; type from Ronga [Abu Saad] on the Blue Nile, Sudan.

IDENTIFICATION Length 13 cm (5in). A small and rather featureless sparrow of dry semi-desert scrub and wadis. Generally warm or grey-brown above; chin and throat white (with a small spot of yellow on lower throat in breeding plumage) bordered by light buffish-grey, and underparts buffish or off-white. Females have some darker streaks on mantle and back. The only feature of note is the broad curving supercilium, warm brown or light chestnut on male and pale buffish or pale cream tinged with warm brown on female. **Confusion species:** Only possible confusion is with Yellow-spotted Petronia (280), which is larger and has an almost plain grey head and face with only a faintly indicated supercilium. Bush Petronia is slightly darker or browner than Yellow-spotted, and at all times has a pale or white chin and throat; female and juvenile are easily separated by the clearly defined or obvious supercilium and mantle streaks. Female and juvenile House Sparrows (258) lack the clear-cut white or pale chin and throat, have less well-defined supercilia, and have more heavily streaked upperparts with contrasting paler buff 'braces'.

DESCRIPTION Sexes differ. **Adult male:** Forehead to crown and nape grey; supercilium pale buff from upper lores to eye, becoming warm brown or light chestnut behind eye to nape, where it curves behind ear-coverts; lores, cheeks and ear-coverts grey or lightly tinged with greyish-buff, but some (possibly sub-adults or non-breeding adults) are pale buff on cheeks to ear-coverts. Hindneck, mantle, upper back and scapulars warm brown or cinnamon-brown, becoming tinged grey-brown in worn plumage; rump and uppertail-coverts duller greyish or olive-brown. Tail fairly short, dark grey or greyish-brown, finely edged paler and tipped buffish or buffish-white. Lesser coverts as scapulars; median coverts dark brown with paler buff tips; greaters brown or grey-brown, edged paler or warmer brown on outers, tips paler buffish and form thin wingbar; alula and primary coverts dark brown; flight feathers dark brown, finely edged paler or buffish-brown, with ill-defined pale patch at base of primaries, and secondaries more broadly edged pale buff. Chin and throat white or pale buff, with a yellow spot or small patch on lower throat (but often obscured, reduced or absent); sides of throat to breast and flanks pale grey or light greyish-buff, becoming whitish on belly, lower flanks and undertail-coverts. Bill sparrow-like but slightly longer, black in breeding season, becoming dark brown with pale horn base to lower mandible in non-breeding season. Legs and feet grey, bluish-grey or greyish tinged with brown. **Adult female:** Very similar to adult male in general plumage, but

slightly lighter or paler brown; has some dark centres to mantle and upper back. Most noticeable difference is the pale cream or creamy-buff supercilium beginning over (or just in front of) eye and extending to sides of nape; face is slightly paler grey, and bill has a yellowish or flesh pink base to lower mandible. The yellow on lower throat is (when present) only weakly indicated or much paler than that of adult male. **Juvenile:** Much more brown or warm brown than adults, and recalls a female or immature House Sparrow. Upperparts from forehead and crown to wings are a light or warm brown; some dark centres or streaks on mantle, back and scapulars; warm buff brown edges to greater coverts and flight feathers, with two pale wingbars formed by pale buff tips to median and greater coverts. Supercilium pale buffish, tinged with light buff-brown (but brighter, generally longer and better defined than on House Sparrow). Face pale or light brownish-buff, with darker buff-brown on rear of ear-coverts and sides of neck; dark buff-brown malar stripe encloses white or pale whitish chin and throat. Rest of underparts greyish or buffish-brown (no yellow on throat), but some show a row or necklace of dark spots across lower throat and are generally paler on flanks and whiter on belly and undertail-coverts. Bill as adult female.

GEOGRAPHICAL VARIATION Race *buchanani* has paler upperparts than nominate, but intermediates between the two races also occur.

VOICE A soft sparrow-like 'chewee' given in flight; also some very sparrow-like chirruping notes. The song is a fast twittering 'triup-triup-triup-triup' and a more bunting-like rising and falling 'chu-chu-chu-chu'.

STATUS, HABITAT AND BEHAVIOUR Locally common. Occurs in dry or arid areas of semi-desert wadis or valleys with scrub, tree savannas or sparsely vegetated hillsides, also found on the edge of cultivation, usually below 1500 m (or slightly higher, to 1900 m in Yemen). Most often in trees, rarely but not exceptionally on the ground. Usually alone, in pairs or in small groups, but large flocks often congregate where food is abundant. Tame and fairly confiding, often spending long periods sitting in the top of a tree or bush; occasionally flicks its tail in a sparrow-like manner. In flight recalls a sparrow, with fast and direct but bounding flight. Feeds in trees and bushes, on insects (particularly fond of immature stages of locusts) and seeds.

DISTRIBUTION *P. d. dentata*: Senegal and Gambia (where scarce), south to Sierra Leone, east through southern Mali, Burkina Faso, northern Ghana, southern Niger and northern and central

Nigeria to northern Cameroon, northern Central African Republic, central and southern Sudan, north Uganda, west and central Ethiopia and North Yemen south to western South Yemen.

P. d. buchanani: Zinder province to Lake Chad, southern Niger.

MOVEMENTS Sedentary or partial migrant. Seasonally common in south of the range and south to southern Ivory Coast (where increasing) and southern Nigeria between November and February; breeds in the dry season and wanders widely throughout the range outside this.

MEASUREMENTS Wing of male 71–87, of female 72–77; tail 42–46; bill 10–11. Wing of *buchanani* 76–82.

REFERENCE Hollom *et al.* (1988).

GENUS *MONTIFRINGILLA*

Seven species. Snow finches are specially adapted to life at high altitudes and in areas of extremely low temperatures and often with little visible sign of sustenance; several species have adopted a symbiotic breeding relationship, sharing the burrows of mouse-hares. All show varying amounts of white in the wing and sides of the tail. Some, undoubtedly, spend their entire lives out of sight of man.

284 SNOW FINCH *Montifringilla nivalis*   Plate 20
Palearctic

Fringilla nivalis Linnaeus, 1766, Syst. Nat., ed. 12, p. 321, Switzerland.

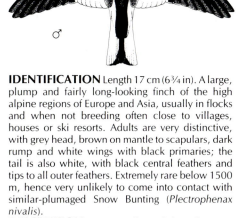

♂

IDENTIFICATION Length 17 cm (6¾ in). A large, plump and fairly long-looking finch of the high alpine regions of Europe and Asia, usually in flocks and when not breeding often close to villages, houses or ski resorts. Adults are very distinctive, with grey head, brown on mantle to scapulars, dark rump and white wings with black primaries; the tail is also white, with black central feathers and tips to all outer feathers. Extremely rare below 1500 m, hence very unlikely to come into contact with similar-plumaged Snow Bunting (*Plectrophenax nivalis*).

DESCRIPTION Sexes similar. **Adult male** (summer)**:** Entire head and face pale grey or bluish-grey, except for whitish eye-ring, all-black lores and pale or whitish submoustachial stripe. Mantle, upper back and scapulars warm or rich brown, with paler brown edges and tips to feathers; lower back, rump and uppertail-coverts black or blackish-brown with brown or greyish-brown tips; sides of rump white. Tail long, central feathers black, all outers white with black tips, forming a terminal band. Wings long with a long primary extension: all coverts pure white except innermost two to three greaters, which are as scapulars but edged paler (shows only at close range in flight); alula black; primary coverts white at base, tipped black; all primaries black, but innermost white on inner web and tip, all secondaries mainly white; tertials dark brown, fringed pale buffish-brown, with white outer webs to bases of outer two. Chin and throat black with white tips (shows as a mottled black-and-white 'bib'); breast pale brownish-grey; rest of underparts pale greyish-white, or white on undertail-coverts, flanks often tinged with buff. Bill stout and quite deep at base, pointed, black with small amount of yellow at base of lower mandible. Legs and feet black. **Adult female:** In summer, very similar to adult male, but has a poorly defined and smaller grey 'bib' with bases of feathers black, and head is browner; rump, uppertail-coverts and outer primaries are blackish-brown; the white in wings is less extensive with black tips to primary coverts, also some dark tips to lesser coverts and dark bases to median coverts; scapulars are uniformly dark or blackish-brown; the tail has more black on those feathers adjoining central pair. Bill brownish-yellow at base with black tip. **Adult winter:** The sexes are alike. The head is paler grey, or greyish-white on nape and sides of neck; mantle and back are mottled with dark brown centres and pale edges; scapulars are uniformly dark or blackish-brown; tertials are also blacker than in summer, and have white or buffish-white tips, and tips of primaries are also white; chin and throat are white or pale grey. Bill yellow with dusky or dark tip. **Juvenile:** Similar to adult female, but has head and face to sides of neck buffish-brown, with darker or greyer lores and forehead to crown; inner greater coverts, inner secondaries and tertials are fringed pale orange-buff; primary coverts dark brown, and secondaries edged dark brown. Tail has pale orange-buff fringes to the white or whitish outer feathers. Chin dull grey, and breast to flanks pale or dull buffish-brown. Bill all yellow, as winter adult. Legs and feet pale yellowish-brown.

475

Undergoes complete moult into adult plumage in autumn.

GEOGRAPHICAL VARIATION Race *alpicola* has crown and nape brown or brownish-grey, the same as mantle, back and scapulars, which are paler brown than in nominate race; the 'bib' is more solidly black, and the bill slightly larger. Race *kwenlunensis* is similar to *alpicola*, but paler and lighter fawn-brown on upperparts; in the hand, the bill and wing measurements are smaller. Race *henrici* is the darkest race, with upperparts (including crown) earth-brown with dark rust-brown centres to mantle and back, and the underparts are much greyer except for flanks, which are grey-brown.

VOICE Call a sharp or strident nasal 'pschieu' or 'pchie', usually given in a flock in flight, also a 'tsee' and a softer 'pruuk' or 'kiek'; alarm a 'pchurrt'. The song is a monotonous repetition of 'sitticher sitticher', delivered either from the top of a rock, crag or building or during male's circular songflight on slowly fluttering wings.

STATUS, HABITAT AND BEHAVIOUR Common or locally common. A bird of high mountains on the rocky slopes and gullies between the vast snow-fields and the tree line, on cliffs, scree slopes and around or near buildings, including ski resorts. Occurs in pairs or small loose flocks in breeding season, but outside this in larger flocks (exceptionally up to several hundred), often in company with other snow finches and the two mountain finches (75, 76). On the ground hops or runs quickly; rarely flies great distances, but when forced has a swift bounding flight on fairly long but narrow wings. Generally tame and confiding, often coming to food put out by tourists. Perches readily on rocks but rarely if ever on trees, except dwarf junipers in some areas. Feeds entirely on the ground, on a variety of seeds of alpine plants and grasses and small insects; nestlings are apparently fed entirely on insects until they fledge.

DISTRIBUTION *M. n. nivalis*: central and southern Europe: west and east Pyrenees, the Alps from southern France, through Switzerland to southern Bavaria, Germany and Austria, and south in the northern Appennines and Abruzzi Mountains, northern Italy, also southern Yugoslavia to northern Greece.

M. n. alpicola: Taurus Mountains and southern central plateau, Turkey, and the Caucasus south to Armenia, to west and north Iran, northern Afghanistan and the Hindu Kush, north through the Pamirs and Tadzhikstan to the Kirghiz range in the Tien Shan east to west Sinkiang and the Bogdo Ola Shan, the Dzungarian Ala Tau, the Tarbagatai range, Russian Altai east through Mongolia to the Gobian Altai.

M. n. kwenlunensis: western Kunlun range through the Astin Tagh to Lop Nor, Sinkiang, west China.

M. n. henrici: Tibet, north to Buckhan Boda Shan range and central Tsinghai, west China.

MOVEMENTS Generally resident up to 3300 m in the Alps, up to 1820 m in the Taurus range, central Turkey, up to 3500 m in the Abruzzi, northern Italy, up to 2900 m in the Russian Altai, up to 3100 m in the Caucasus and up to 5150 m in Tibet. In winter, generally moves to slightly lower levels depending on snowfall, but in the eastern Pamirs (Tadzhikstan), where there is little snow in winter, birds are present at high levels up to 4500 m all year round. A vagrant to Heligoland (1849), the Canary Islands, Malta (October 1970), Sicily (October 1976), Egypt and Iraq (March 1945).

MEASUREMENTS Wing of male 103–121·5, of female 108–114·5; bill (from skull) 13–14, (from feathers) 11. Wing of male *alpicola* 111–122, of female 110–115; tail 66–71; bill (from skull) of male 16–17·5, of female 15–16·5. Wing of *kwenlunensis* 102–120. Weight of male 31–34, of female 31–33.

REFERENCE Dementiev and Gladkov (1951–54).

285 ADAMS'S SNOW FINCH (Tibet Snow finch, Black-winged Snow Finch *Montifringilla adamsi*   Plate 20

Eastern Palearctic

Montifringilla adamsi Adams, 1858, Proc. Zool. Soc. London, p. 482, Ladak.

IDENTIFICATION Length 17 cm (6½ in). Very similar to the closely related (confusion species) Snow Finch (284), but much browner on head, neck and underparts and shows less white in wings in flight. In overlap areas (Kashmir and Tibet), the species are usually separated altitudinally.

DESCRIPTION Sexes alike. **Adult:** Forehead to crown grey-brown; face (except for faint, pale buffish-brown and grey-brown lores), hindcrown and nape similar or slightly browner, with slightly darker centres to feathers; submoustachial area pale buffish. Upper mantle greyish buff-brown, becoming warmer brown with slightly darker brown feather centres on lower mantle, back and

scapulars; rump and uppertail-coverts dark brown, longest coverts tipped white. Central tail feathers blackish-brown, outer edges white, all outers white with black tips (and some distal edges), edges to inner feathers yellowish-buff. Lesser coverts grey or buffish-brown, edged slightly paler; median coverts dark brown, fringed broadly with white; greaters almost entirely white, but some can show brown on inner webs or spots towards tip; alula dark brown; primary coverts white with fine brown or blackish-brown tips; primaries dark or blackish-brown, all finely edged with white or pale buff, secondaries blackish at base, and with distal half of the feathers pale or whitish-buff (outers have

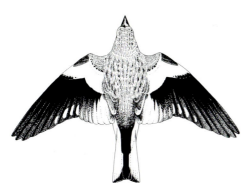

increasing amounts of blackish-brown); tertials dark brown, fringed paler buff-brown. Chin and throat (extending slightly onto upper breast) black, tipped finely with white; breast and sides of breast creamy-buff with a grey wash; rest of underparts pale whitish-buff, undertail-coverts white. Bill stout and fairly deep at base, pointed, black in breeding season, pale yellowish or horn with dark culmen and tip in non-breeding season (in the breeding season, some females have a dark brown bill with black tip and with yellow at base of lower mandible). Legs and feet black. In winter becomes slightly paler, with more buffy edges to plumage. In April and May some (possibly first-summer birds) have pale edges to scapulars and broad white tips to inner primaries and lower (largest) tertial, while on others (probably adults) these are completely abraded. **Juvenile:** Very similar to non-breeding adult, but warmer buff-brown and slightly more uniform on head and upperparts; tips to medians and edges and tips to inner greaters pale buff-brown (inner greaters have dark brown inner webs), edges to scapulars and tertials warm buff-brown, inner secondaries buffish-brown, and primaries broadly fringed warm buff-brown. Tail with black central feathers and tips to (most) outers, but outers otherwise pale buffish or orange-buff. Chin and throat greyish, rest of underparts pale or buffish-white. Bill yellowish-horn with dark tip.

GEOGRAPHICAL VARIATION Race *xerophila* is generally paler and with streaks on mantle and back less distinct than in nominate.

VOICE Call a sharp or strident 'pink pink' like that of Chaffinch (1) and a soft mewing note; large flocks keep up a constant soft twittering, recalling

Linnet (72). The song is a distinctive single note repeated rather monotonously and delivered from the top of a rock or boulder, or while hovering (rising and falling) with wings and tail outspread or in parachuting display flight.

STATUS, HABITAT AND BEHAVIOUR Uncommon or scarce. Occurs on barren mountaintops or boulder-strewn plateaux of the Tibetan semi-desert biotope, usually between 3500 m and 5200 m, often in the vicinity of streams; also steppes, terraces, rocky slopes or cliffs above river valleys. Nests in rocky screes or stone walls. Often occurs near villages, and frequently feeds in grazing and cultivated fields. Sociable and usually in pairs or family parties during breeding season, but flocks in winter often contain up to 3,000; can be very tame and approachable. On the ground walks and runs in a lark-like manner; perches on the ground and on rocks, boulders etc. Flight swift, buoyant and undulating; often indulges (throughout year) in striking butterfly-like display flights and wheeling manoeuvres. Courtship display flight in spring is particularly impressive and elaborate, with somersaults, vertical drops, stiff wingbeats, and wing-claps below the body. Feeds on the ground, often at edges of melting patches of snow, on a variety of small insects and on seeds of alpine plants.

DISTRIBUTION *M. a. adamsi*: Kashmir (Ladakh), Nepal (Mustang and Dolpo districts), northern Sikkim and southern Tibet east to eastern Tsinghai (south of the Koko Nor) and Szechwan, central China.

M. a. xerophila: Humboldt range of the northwest Nan Shan south to Buckhan Boda Shan and west to about 84° E in the Astin Tagh ranges, Sinkiang, west China.

MOVEMENTS None long-distance, but part of the population makes short-distance movements away from breeding area, often altitudinally down to neighbouring valleys; large flocks have been noted in December and March at Sikkim at 4600 m, in southeast Tibet at 4400 m, and in October around Ladakh at 4000 m.

MEASUREMENTS Wing of male 109–117, of female 106–115; tail 66–75; tarsus 21–22; bill (from skull) 16–17·5.

REFERENCES Henderson and Hume (1873), Walton (1906).

286 MANDELLI'S SNOW FINCH (White-rumped Snow Finch)
Montifringilla taczanowskii   **Plate 21**

Eastern Palearctic

Montifringilla taczanowskii Przewalski, 1876, Mongol. Strana Tangut, 2, p. 81, pl. 11, Tetunga and Kuku Nor Steppe.

IDENTIFICATION Length 17 cm (6½ in). A large and distinctive snow finch from the high plateaux of Tibet and western China, the only snow finch with a white rump. The size, pale grey, dark-streaked mantle and coverts and diagnostic white

rump make confusion with any other snow finch unlikely.

DESCRIPTION Sexes alike. **Adult:** Forehead and supercilium to nape and hindneck whitish-buff; crown and nape grey or grey-brown, slightly duller or greyer on sides of neck. Mantle, back and scapulars pale grey-brown, streaked darker brown, with white or pale buff edges to feathers; rump white; uppertail-coverts fawn-brown. Central tail feathers dark brown, outer feathers black at base with black decreasing inwardly, becoming white for most of distal half. Lesser coverts pale grey; median coverts dark or blackish-brown, tipped with white; outer greater coverts dark brown, edged with pale buff or tinged buffish-brown, inner greaters more extensively white; alula and primary coverts blackish; flight feathers blackish-brown, the first primary broadly edged with white and inner primaries more finely edged, secondaries broadly edged with pale buff or white in fresh plumage and broadly tipped white, and broad white panel at base of the secondaries and inner primaries (shows in flight); tertials the same, edged pale buffish-brown and tipped with white. Lores black, becoming a thin dark eye-stripe behind eye; cheeks and ear-coverts white or pale grey. Chin and throat (to sides of throat) white; breast and flanks washed grey or greyish-buff; belly to undertail-coverts creamy or white. Bill stout and deep at base, pointed, pale yellowish (or slightly duller in non-breeding season) with dusky or blackish tip. Legs and feet black. In worn plumage, the head and nape become paler, mantle and back darker, and the white edges to flight feathers are reduced. **Juvenile:** A warmer buff-brown version of adult, with crown dark brown and nape and hindneck grey-brown; fringes to mantle, back and scapulars warm brown or buff-brown; rump dull or off-white and uppertail-coverts brown. Tail black on central feathers, with outers pale buffish-brown towards tips. Tips of median coverts pale

buff; edges to greaters buff-brown, tipped pale buff or whitish; edges to secondaries pale buffish or buff-brown.
VOICE Call a sharp and resounding 'duid duid'. The song is a short but loud 'duid ai duid, duid, duid, ai'. Has an elaborate lark-like display flight and a courtship dance on the ground which involves 'drumming'.
STATUS, HABITAT AND BEHAVIOUR Common or locally common. Occurs between 3800–4900 m on high stony plateaux and steppes or edges of marshes in close association with colonies of mouse-hares or pikas (*Ochotona melanostoma*), in whose burrows it shelters, roosts and breeds. Often alone but also occurs in pairs or loose colonies, and in winter gathers into larger flocks; frequently occurs in mixed flocks with Red-necked Snow Finch (288). Shy and generally unapproachable; on the ground has a very erect or upright stance and runs well. When landing, characteristically bows and bobs its tail. Feeds on the ground, on insects and small seeds.
DISTRIBUTION Monotypic. Discontinuous in Tibet (Gartok area) and southeast Tibet to west Szechwan and north to the Koko Nor and the Nan Shan ranges, Tsinghai, western China.
MOVEMENTS Generally sedentary between 3800 m and 5500 m, but some move to slightly lower altitudes following heavy falls of snow in winter. Infrequently recorded in Sikkim and Ladakh (Kashmir) in winter.
MEASUREMENTS Wing 101–109; tail 68–73; tarsus c22; bill (from feathers) c14–15.
REFERENCES Przewalski (1876), Schäfer (1938).

287 PÈRE DAVID'S SNOW FINCH *Montifringilla davidiana*   Plate 21
Eastern Palearctic

Pyrgilauda davidiana Verreaux, 1871, Nouv. Arch. Mus. Hist. Nat. (Paris), 6 (1870), p. 40, Mountains of Chinese Tibet; type from the plains of Mongolia in the Ourato.

IDENTIFICATION Length 15 cm (6 in). A comparatively small snow finch of northwest China and Inner Mongolia. Generally pale or light buff-brown; adults have a distinctive black forehead, lores, chin and throat, light warm brown upperparts, becoming duller on rump and uppertail-coverts, and are paler or buffish below.
Confusion species: Adults are unlikely to be confused with any other snow finch (bear greatest similarity to the endemic Theresa's Snow Finch (290) of Afghanistan); lone juveniles are best separated from similar-aged Red-necked (288) and Blanford's (289) Snow Finches by lack of a supercilium or white areas on face **DESCRIPTION** Sexes alike.
Adult: Forehead to forecrown black (forecrown has pale brown tips), narrower on females; lores to chin and slightly under eye black; cheeks, ear-coverts and sides of neck washed pale brown or fawn; pale light buff supercilium to rear of ear-coverts. Crown to nape light brown or tinged warm buff-brown; nape

fawn-brown, becoming buffish-brown with darker brown feather centres on mantle, back and scapulars; lower back, rump and uppertail-coverts uniform pale brown. Tail short, central feathers blackish-brown, all outers except outermost white or smudged grey or dark grey with only a subterminal band of white below broad black tips (in worn plumage, tips become pale buff). Lesser and median coverts uniform fawn-brown; greater coverts the same fringed with pale buff; alula blackish edged buff; primary coverts the same, but white at bases; flight feathers blackish-brown, first primary broadly edged white, outer primaries edged white only at base, secondaries and inner primaries edged white and tipped pale buffish or white. Chin and throat to centre of breast black (on females, black restricted to chin and throat, about half of that shown by males), sides of chin and throat white; breast washed off-white or with a buffish wash; belly and undertail-coverts white.

Bill conical and fairly small, pointed, black or blackish with a pale or yellow base to both mandibles. Moulting birds in autumn show very little black on forehead, and the black on chin and throat is largely obscured by pale or buff tips. **Juvenile:** A pale version of adult but lacking any black on face, which is generally pale buff; forehead to crown, lores, chin and throat grey. Wings as adult, but with broad pale sandy-buff or warm buff-brown edges and tips (lacks any white). Bill pale yellow, with dusky tip to both mandibles.

GEOGRAPHICAL VARIATION Race *potanini* is much paler or more sandy buff-brown on upperparts, and shows less contrasting dark centres on lower mantle and upper back.

VOICE Undescribed.

STATUS, HABITAT AND BEHAVIOUR Locally common, but generally scarce or restricted. Occurs on flat or slightly undulating plateaux and semi-steppe plains or valleys or deserts between 1000 m and 3000 m, usually close to water such as springs, streams or rivulets. Usually in pairs or loose colonies, but flocks in winter can number 200 individuals. Associates closely with small burrow-dwelling rodents, sousliks or marmots, particularly mouse-hares (*Ochotona melanostoma*), whose burrows it shares for shelter, roosting and nesting; is also capable of digging small holes in the ground or enlarging those of rodents. In winter becomes tame, and often found in or around human settlements and cattle pens, where feeds on the snow-free areas. Has a habit of perching on small mounds of earth or stones, wing-flicking in wheatear-fashion to survey the surroundings (eg when a predator is present). Food is mainly insects, including butterflies, beetles, flies and their larvae, also the seeds of grasses and those of low plants.

DISTRIBUTION *M. d. davidiana*: Inner Mongolia (from Suiyuan) south through Ningsia and Kansu to south and east of the Koko Nor, Tsinghai, west China.

M. d. potanini: discontinuously from southeast Russian Altai range, through Outer Mongolia to Hulun Nor, Heilungkiang, northeast China to about 104° E; in the south reaches the foothills of the Gobian Altai, Mongolia.

MOVEMENTS Generally sedentary; most movements are usually random wanderings outside breeding season. Flocks in autumn and early winter have been known to associate with Lapland Buntings (*Calcarius lapponicus*) and Shore Larks (*Eremophila alpestris*) which are descending to lower levels. A vagrant to Sikkim: one in a flock of Brandt's Mountain Finches (76) at 3000 m in March 1952.

MEASUREMENTS Wing 84–86; tail c43; tarsus c17; bill (from skull) c12.

REFERENCE Ali and Ripley (1983).

288 RED-NECKED SNOW FINCH (Rufous-necked Snow Finch)
Montifringilla ruficollis   **Plate 21**
Eastern Palearctic

Montifringilla ruficollis Blanford, 1871, Proc. Asiat. Soc. Bengal, p. 277, Kangra Lama Pass, Sikkim.

IDENTIFICATION Length 15 cm (6 in). A distinctive snow finch of Tibet and northwest China. Adults have white face and forehead, divided by black lores and rich reddish-brown or chestnut rear ear-coverts and sides of neck; rest of the plumage light brown, streaked darker on mantle and scapulars. The wings have two white wingbars formed by the tips of the coverts. Juveniles are like a faded or duller version of adult, with only a tinge of orange on sides of nape and pale buffish-brown tips to coverts. **Confusion species:** Likely to be confused only with the similar Blanford's Snow Finch (289) but adults lack latter's distinctive black 'horns', chin and upper throat; juvenile Blanford's are generally whiter on the face and greyer on chin, and have uniform (or with ill-defined centres) mantle and scapulars.

DESCRIPTION Sexes alike. **Adult:** Lower forehead whitish or pale grey, becoming grey-brown or warm brown on crown, with sides of crown white; lores to slightly below and slightly behind eye black (often appearing to continue along top of ear-coverts); cheeks white, with a fairly long black moustachial stripe; rear of ear-coverts reddish or chestnut-brown, becoming ginger or cinnamon on sides of nape and neck. Mantle, back and scapulars deep brown with pale buffish or warm buff edges; lower back to rump and uppertail-coverts uniform warm buff-brown. Tail dark brown on central feathers and white or whitish on all outers (some, especially the inners, have grey on bases), with tips to all outer feathers dark brown (recalling wheatear). Lesser coverts pale brown, edged pale greyish; median coverts dark brown, broadly tipped with white; greaters brown, broadly tipped white; alula and primary coverts blackish-brown; flight feathers blackish-brown, outermost primaries edged with white and the rest finely edged with warm buff, secondaries edged warm buffish-brown, and bases of secondaries and inner primaries broadly white for half their length (shows as a broad panel in flight); tertials brown, becoming buffish-brown at edges. Chin and throat pure white; breast to belly and flanks white, sides of breast often gingery-buff; undertail-coverts white. Bill small and rather like that of Linnet (72), with both mandibles coming to a point, black or dark slate-blue in breeding season (and probably for most of year). Legs and feet black. **Juvenile:** Rather sparrow-like, with brown forehead, crown and nape. Hindneck, mantle and back warm buff-brown, finely streaked darker. Pale or white upper lores to upper eye, becoming faintly ginger at or near supercilium; lores to eye and along top of ear-coverts dark brown; cheeks white or whitish, ear-coverts and sides of nape light warm ginger; moustachial stripe poorly defined, grey or pale greyish. Rump and uppertail-coverts grey-brown. Tail brown, but most of outer feathers edged rich or warm buff (only the outermost two have white in outer webs). Greater coverts dark brown, edged and tipped brown or buffish-brown; all flight feathers dark brown, the outermost primary finely edged pale or white and all others edged light or buffish-brown, with pale bases to secondaries and inner primaries as on adults; tertials brown or dark brown, edged light or warm buff. Underparts off-white, but tinged or washed gingery-buff on sides of breast.

GEOGRAPHICAL VARIATION Race *isabellina* is paler or greyish on upperparts and tinged buffish-yellow (isabelline).

VOICE Call a soft and repeated 'duuid' or 'dooooid', and a chattering alarm call recalling Magpie (*Pica pica*). Like other species of snow finches, it has an elaborate display flight accompanied by buzzing and rushing noises.

STATUS, HABITAT AND BEHAVIOUR Locally very common to abundant. Inhabits high, barren stony steppes or rolling grassy plateaux or slopes intersected by rocky gullies or ravines between 3800 m and 5000 m, where it is found in the breeding season in close association with mouse-hares or pikas (*Ochotona melanostoma*), in whose burrows it breeds (also breeds in rock fissures and holes); in recent years has also developed a preference for rubbish tips near human habitation. A confiding bird, during breeding season found in pairs; outside breeding season more likely to be found in small flocks, when it ranges over a wide variety of mountainous terrain, often in company with Mandelli's (286) or Blanford's Snow Finches. Flight is weak and low, and rarely over long distances. Feeds on the ground, on a variety of small seeds and insects.

DISTRIBUTION *M. r. ruficollis*: disconintuous in west Tibet (Gyanima-Lejondak), also from north Sikkim across east Tibet to eastern Tsinghai (Koko Nor and the Humboldt range of the southern Nan Shan), western China.

M. r. isabellina: southern Sinkiang to northwest Tsinghai (Astin Tagh to the Koko Nor), western China.

MOVEMENTS None long-distance, but may disperse to lower altitudes in winter; has occurred near Darjeeling in October.

MEASUREMENTS Wing 91–101; tail 55–58; tarsus 19–20; bill (from feathers) 10–11.

REFERENCES Ali and Ripley (1983), Schäfer (1938).

289 BLANFORD'S SNOW FINCH (Plain-backed Snow Finch)
Montifringilla blanfordi
Plate 21

East Palearctic

Montifringilla blanfordi Hume, 1876, Stray Feathers, 4, p. 487, Borders to the north of native Sikkim.

IDENTIFICATION Length 15 cm (6 in). Similar to Red-necked Snow Finch (288), with which it often associates, but stands much more erect. Adults have a distinctive black-and-white head-and-face pattern and more uniform sandy-brown upperparts; juveniles have white face and grey lores and crown. **Confusion species:** Likely to be confused only with the initially similar Red-necked Snow Finch (288), but lacks latter's rich chestnut on sides of nape and rear of ear-coverts and has only warm ginger nape and sides of neck; Red-necked lacks Blanford's black chin and throat. Lone juveniles may be difficult to separate, but Blanford's is generally pale, lacking any strong streaks on upperparts, and has a whiter face with grey chin and only poorly defined wingbars at tips of coverts.

DESCRIPTION Sexes alike. **Adult:** Forehead to forecrown white, with central forehead a spur of black from base of bill to forecrown; crown to nape pale brown, with some blackish tips on crown; hindneck and sides of neck warm sandy-buff, on some becoming ginger or cinnamon; lores black, with blackish horn or 'spur' rising in front of eye

to sides of crown; thin black eye-stripe across top of ear-coverts; short pale buff supercilium behind eye; cheeks and ear-coverts white. Mantle, back and scapulars to rump and uppertail-coverts light brown or fawn-brown with slightly darker centres. Central tail feathers brown or greyish-brown, outers white with grey or dark grey smudges, tipped with black or subterminally black with pale buffish-brown or white (white usually only on outers) tips. Lesser and median coverts pale grey-brown; greaters as scapulars, with rather warm buff edges; alula and primary coverts dark brown; outer primaries brown, inners and secondaries dark brown and edged white or ashy except for innermost, which are broadly edged white at base and form a pale panel across secondaries and inner primaries (shows well in flight); tips to all secondaries and inner primaries pale buff; tertials brown, with warm buff edges and pale whitish tips. Chin and upper throat black; rest of underparts off-white or washed pale creamy, with a band of warm peachy-buff or ginger extending down from sides of neck across breast in breeding season. Bill dark bluish-horn or blackish, fairly small or conical. Legs and feet black. In worn plumage, head and upperparts become greyer through wear, as do greater coverts. **Juvenile:** Forehead to crown and nape grey-brown, but some nape feathers tinged warm buff. Mantle, back and scapulars pale brown, heavily tinged sandy or warm buffish-brown. Tail similar to adult, but edged (except for outers) warm buff-brown. Flight feathers also similar to those of adult, but with warmer edges to secondaries and tertials (but lacks white tips). Face buffish or pale buff, with some brown spots on cheeks and ear-coverts. Chin and upper throat grey or greyish; rest of underparts off-white or pale buff. Bill pale yellowish, or with dark upper mandible and tip to lower.

GEOGRAPHICAL VARIATION Race barbata is greyer on upperparts and lacks the ginger tinge, while ventorum is even paler grey above, with a tinge of yellow on sides of nape.

VOICE Generally silent, but has a constant and rapid twittering call given by birds both on the ground and in flight.

STATUS, HABITAT AND BEHAVIOUR Locally common but sparsely distributed. Occurs on dry, sandy steppes or hillsides with stunted grass between 4200 m and 5000 m, exceptionally on cultivated or tilled land. Usually in pairs or small flocks in breeding season, associating with colonies of voles or mouse-hares (*Ochotona melanostoma*), in whose holes or burrows it nests; in winter in large flocks, often associating with other finches, sparrows and Red-necked Snow Finch. A confiding and active bird, behaves in a sparrow-like manner; on the ground runs rapidly while foraging for food. Has a rising and hovering stiff-winged display flight, with quivering and whirring wingbeats while hovering. Feeds mainly on seeds of grasses and dwarf or stunted alpine plants.

DISTRIBUTION *M. b. blanfordi*: discontinuous in west Tibet (Kum Bulak to Rupshu), in southwest Tibet (Ding Tso) and Karakoram range, possibly also in Ladakh, also northern Sikkim, southeast Tibet (approximately 78° E) and western China north to the Buckhan-Boda Shan, central Tsinghai.

M. b. barbata: mountains of northeast Tsinghai, south of the Koko Nor to the Nan Shan, western China.

M. b. ventorum: southeast Sinkiang to western Tsinghai (Moskowski Mountains to the western edge of the Zaidam Basin), western central China.

MOVEMENTS Sedentary at high elevations (even during severe winters), but the appearance of birds at lower altitudes in autumn and winter in Ladakh and east Sikkim suggests that some undertake altitudinal movements.

MEASUREMENTS Wing of male 90–97, of female 94–97; tail of male 49–56, of female 45–50; tarsus 19–20; bill (from feathers) 10–12.

290 THERESA'S SNOW FINCH (Meinertzhagen's Snow Finch, Afghan Snow Finch) *Montifringilla theresae* Plate 21

Afghanistan

Montifringilla theresae Meinertzhagen, 1937, Bull. Brit. Orn. Club, 58, p. 10, Shibar Pass, northern Afghanistan.

IDENTIFICATION Length 13·5–15 cm (5¼-6 in). A scarce and very little-known species from the Hindu Kush, discovered only in 1937. Adults are grey-brown, with black lores and chin and some streaking on mantle and scapulars, and plain warm buff-brown rump; pale or white tips to median and greater coverts. Juveniles are undescribed. **Confusion species:** The black face of the adult and the general grey-brown plumage, together with the lack of large areas of white in the wing, makes confusion with Snow Finch (284), which it overlaps in range, unlikely. Adult male recalls Desert Finch (82) in general plumage, but is greyer, with dark streaks, and the black face is slightly more extensive; Desert is pale uniform sandy-grey, with bright pink edges to coverts forming a pale bar across the wing in flight. The black face recalls that of Père David's Snow Finch (287), from which it is widely separated geographically.

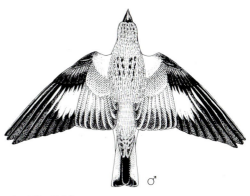

♂

DESCRIPTION Sexes similar but separable. **Adult male:** Lower forehead and lores black; cheeks, ear-coverts and sides of neck pale greyish-buff; rest of forehead to crown pale grey (in worn plumage shows darker centres to feathers). Nape and hindneck pale grey-brown; mantle, back and scapulars similar, but slightly more heavily tinged with buff and with dark brown centres to feathers; rump and uppertail-coverts buffish brown, longest uppertail-coverts with black or blackish-brown centres. Central tail feathers dark or blackish brown, all outers white, fairly heavily smudged greyish subterminally, and tipped dark brown or black. Lesser coverts grey or greyish with dark centres; median coverts white, but outers have dark bases; outer greaters blackish, becoming browner on inners, with inners broadly bordered and tipped pale buff-brown; alula and primary coverts black or blackish-brown; flight feathers dark brown to blackish, primaries finely edged greyish-brown, with basal half of all secondaries and all but outermost three primaries forming a broad panel of white, and tips to secondaries also white; tertials dark brown, edged and tipped pale buff. Chin, upper throat and sides of lower throat black, centre of lower throat whitish; rest of underparts pale buff or washed very light buffish-brown. Bill longer than on other snow finches, pointed, greyish-horn or black. In winter, loses the black on face but retains black bill; mantle, back and scapulars appear almost uniform (dark centres are obscured by broad grey-brown edges), underparts are whitish-grey tinged with brown, and flanks are more visibly tinged with brown. **Adult female:** Very similar to adult male, or more generally buff-brown than grey; the black on face is restricted to lores, chin and upper throat (but this can be obscured by pale buff tips to feathers).

White wing panel is not so extensive across wing, and is often duller and not white, and median coverts are pale grey, tipped with buff. **Juvenile:** Undescribed, but probably very similar to adult female in winter.

VOICE Undescribed.

STATUS, HABITAT AND BEHAVIOUR Scarce or locally common within a very small area of distribution. Occurs in the high mountains and passes of the northern Hindu Kush, between 2575 m and 3000 m, on open stony hillsides and plateaux, where it associates closely with sousliks (*Citellus fulvus*), in winter descends to valleys and the edges of cultivated areas. Usually alone or in pairs during breeding season, and in larger flocks in winter, when mixes freely with Snow Finches, Adams's Snow Finches (285), Shore Larks (*Eremophila alpestris*) or Rock Sparrows (281). Flight is direct and not bounding. Feeds on the ground, on the seeds of *Carex pachystilis*, *Convolvulus divaricatus* and *Thuspeinantha persica*; also takes some insects, particularly weevils and ants.

DISTRIBUTION Monotypic. Endemic to the northern and central ranges of the Hindu Kush, Afghanistan (Shibar, Sabz and Unai Passes, Bamian), between approximately 67° and 69° E.

MOVEMENTS In winter descends to lower levels, also occasionally moves north into Badghyz and Karabil, southeast Turkmenia (CIS).

MEASUREMENTS Wing of male 84·5–99, of female 87–96; bill of male 14–15, of female 13–15. Weight of male 23–35, of female 24–28.

REFERENCE Wood et al. (1978).

GLOSSARY OF TERMS

Acacia – evergreen tree or shrub of the genus *Acacia*, very thorny with small compound leaves; widespread in Africa.

Accidental – refers to an extremely unusual occurrence of a species outside its normal range (see also vagrant).

Afrotropical – Africa south of the Tropic of Cancer, formerly called the Ethiopian faunal region.

Allopatric – of species (or subspecies) with ranges which do not overlap.

Altitudinal migrant – species which breeds at high altitudes (in mountains) and moves to lower levels and valleys in non-breeding season.

Arboreal – tree-dwelling.

Austral – living in the southern hemisphere.

Austral migrant – bird which moves north in non-breeding season.

Australasia – Australia, New Zealand and the adjacent islands.

Brachystegia – broadleaved tree of the genus *Brachystegia*, widespread in southern Africa.

Brood-host – species which are host to parasitic breeding species (latter make no nests themselves but deposit their eggs in the nests of others).

Carpal – the bend or wrist joint of the wing, where the wing-coverts meet the flight feathers.

Colonial – nesting or roosting in tight colonies; species which are loosely colonial have nests more widely spaced.

Conspecific – of the same species.

Crop – thin-walled extension above the oesophagus in which food is stored or partly digested before passing through the oesophagus to the gizzard.

Endemic – restricted or confined to a specific country or region.

Flight feathers – the longest feathers of the wing, usually considered to be the secondaries and primaries but also includes the tertials.

Genus – a classification or taxonomical term referring to a group of similar species which are considered to be related; the first name in any species' scientific name, e. g. *Fringilla*, *Estrilda* etc., is the generic name; genera are grouped into families.

Graduated tail – where the longest tail feathers are the central pair and the shortest the outermost, with those in between intermediate in length.

Gregarious – living in flocks or communities.

Holarctic – comprises the Nearctic and Palearctic faunal regions.

Irruption – an irregular or exceptional movement or migration into a new area in search of food, usually consisting of large numbers of birds moving over a short period of time.

Local – occurring or common within a small or restricted area.

Miombo – open broadleaved woodland where trees of the genus *Brachystegia* dominate.

Monotypic – species in which there are no subspecies.

Montane – mountainous.

Mopane – a broadleaved woodland or scrub habitat in which the tree (or shrub) *Colophosphermum mopane* dominates.

Morph – a colour phase of a species, usually comprising small numbers of individuals within the range.

Nearctic – North American faunal region, north of the Tropic of Cancer, and includes Greenland.

New World – North, Central and South America, the western hemisphere.

Nomadic – of a wandering or erratically occurring species which has no fixed territory when not breeding.

Nominate – the main or first-named race of the species, that which has its racial name the same as the specific name, e. g. *Fringilla coelebs coelebs*.

Old World – Europe, Asia and Africa, the eastern hemisphere.

Oriental – the southeast Asian faunal region, usually considered as lying between 68° and 135°E and between 32°N and 10°S.

Palearctic – Europe, Asia south to the Himalayas, North Africa, the Middle East and northern Arabia.

Parkland – open woodland with well-spaced trees, little scrub or secondary growth and with a short-grass ground cover.

Passerine – a species of the order Passeriformes, birds which habitually sing or call and have three toes forward and one hind toe.

Pectoral band – a band of colour over or across the breast.

Plantations – groups of trees (usually exotic or non-native species) planted in close proximity to each other for timber or crop.

Race – subspecific populations of bird within a geographical area, similar to the originally described form (nominate race) but differing in several respects (plumage, length or coloration), though not to the extent of being considered a separate species.

Resident – a sedentary species, found within the same area all year.

Rictal bristles – bare feather shafts at the base of the bill.

Riparian – living on or attached to river banks.

Subspecies – see Race

Symbiotic – of two differing organisms (e. g. bird and mammal) living together.

Sympatric – of species or subspecies where ranges overlap.

Taxonomy – the study of the classification of living organisms.

Terrestrial – living or occurring mainly on the ground.

Territory – an area established by a bird and defended against intrusion by others (usually of the same species), used mainly in the breeding season.

Vagrant – an extreme rarity in a region outside its normal range, usually recorded only once or twice in the region in question.

Vermiculated – finely barred or marked with fine or narrow wavy lines, usually visible only at close range.

Wingbar – bar on wing formed by pale or white tips to the median or greater coverts.

Wing-coverts – tracts of feathers on the forearm of the wing covering the bases of the flight feathers.

BIBLIOGRAPHY

Ali, S (1962) *The Birds of Sikkim*. Oxford University Press, Delhi.

—(1978) *Field Guide to the Birds of the Eastern Himalayas*. Oxford University Press, Delhi.

—**and Ripley, S D** (1983) *Handbook of the Birds of India and Pakistan*. Compact edition. Oxford University Press, Delhi.

Archer, S G, and Godman, E M (1961) *The Birds of British Somaliland and the Gulf of Aden*. Edinburgh.

Armani, G C (1983) *Guide des Passereaux Granivores*. Neuchâtel Paris.

Ash, J S (1979) A new species of serin from Ethiopia. *Ibis* 121: 1–7.

—(1973) Six species of birds new to Ethiopia. *Bull. B.O.C.* 93: 3–6.

—**and Colston, P** (1981) A House x Somali Sparrow *Passer domesticus* x *Passer castanopterus* hybrid. *Bull. B.O.C* 100: 291–294.

—**and Gullick, T** (1989) The present situation regarding the endemic breeding birds in Ethiopia. *Scopus* 13:90–96.

—**and**—(1990) *Serinus flavigula* rediscovered. *Bull. B.O.C.* 110(2): 81–83.

—**and Miskell, J E** (1983) Birds of Somalia, their habitat, status and distribution. *Scopus* Special Supp. No. 1.

—**and** —(1981) Present abundance of the Warsangli Linnet *Acanthis johannis*. *Bull. B.O.C.* 101: 396–398.

—, **Coverdale, M A C, and Gullick T M** (1991) Comments on the status and Distribution of Birds in W Uganda. *Scopus* 15: 24—29.

Bannerman, D A (1953) *The Birds of West and Equatorial Africa*. 2 Vols. Edinburgh.

—**and Bannerman, W M** (1963) *Birds of the Atlantic Islands*. Vol. I. Edinburgh.

—**and** —(1965) *Birds of the Atlantic Islands*. Vol. 2.

—**and** —(1966) *Birds of the Atlantic Islands*. Vol. 3.

—**and** —(1968) *Birds of the Atlantic Islands*. Vol. 4.

Barthel, P H, Hanoldt, W, Habatsch, K, *et al.* (1992) Der Mongolengimpel in der Westpaläarktis. *Limicola* 6: 265–286.

Bates, G L (193) *Handbook of the Birds of West Africa*. London.

Bates R S P, and Lowther, E H N (1952) *The Breeding Birds of Kashmir*. Oxford University Press, Bombay.

Bates, J M, Parker, T A, Capparella, A P, and Davis, T J (1992) Observations on the campo, cerrado and forest avifaunas of eastern Dpto Santa Cruz, Bolivia, including 21 species new to the country. *Bull. B.O.C.* 112(2): 86–98.

Beehler, B M, Pratt, T K, and Zimmerman, D A (1986) *Birds of New Guinea*. Princeton.

Belthoff, G R, and Gauthreaux, S A (1991) Partial migration and differential winter distribution of House Finches in the eastern United States. *Condor* 93: 374–382.

Benson, C W (1947) Notes on the Birds of southern Abyssinia. *Ibis* 29–50.

—(1955) New forms of Pipit, Longclaw, Robin-chat, Grass-warbler, Sunbird, Quail-finch and Canary from Central Africa. *Bull. B.O.C.* 75: 101–109.

Bibby, C J, and Charlton, T D (1991) Observations on the San Miguel Bullfinch. *Acoreana* 7: 297–304.

—, —, and Ramos, J (1992) Studies of West Palearctic Birds 191. Azores Bullfinch. *Brit. Birds* 85: 677–680.

Bishop, K D, and King, B (1986) The Sunda Serin *Serinus estherae* in Sulawesi. *Kukila* 2(4): 90–92.

Blakers, M, Davies, S F J, and Reilly, P N (1984) *The Atlas of Australian Birds*. Melbourne.

Bond, J (1979) *Birds of the West Indies*. London.

Bowden, C G R, and Brooks, D J (1987) The Yemen Linnet in North Yemen. *Sandgrouse* 9: 111–114.

Brazil, M A (1991) *The Birds of Japan*. Christopher Helm, London.

Britton, P L (ed.) (1980) *Birds of East Africa*. Nairobi: EANHS.

Brooke, R (1973) House Sparrows feeding at night in New York. *Auk* 90: 206.

Browne, P W P (1981) New Bird Species in Mauretania. *Malimbus* 3: 63–72.

Carroll, R W (1988) Birds of the Central African Republic. *Malimbus* 10: 177–199.

Catley, G P, and Hursthouse, D (1985) Parrot Crossbills in Britain. *Brit. Birds* 78: 482–505.

Cave, F O, and Macdonald, J D (1955) *Birds of the Sudan*. Edinburgh.

Chalmers, M L (1986) *Annotated Checklist of the Birds of Hong Kong*. WWF Hong Kong.

Chapin, J P (1950) A new race of *Estrilda paludicola* from the Congo River. *Bull. B.O.C.* 70: 23–25.

—(1954) *Birds of the Belgian Congo*. Vol. 4. New York.

—(1959) The behaviour of the Olive Weaver-finch *Nesocharis ansorgei*. *Ostrich supp.* 3: 230–232.

Christensen, S, and Porter, R F (1987) The Arabian Waxbill in North Yemen. *Sandgrouse* 9: 98–101.

Clancey, P A (1964) *The Birds of Natal and Zululand*. Edinburgh.

—(1968) The southern forms of *Serinus canicollis* (Swainson). *Bull. B.O.C.* 88: 21–24.

— (ed). (1980) *S.A.O.S. Checklist of southern African birds*. Southern African Ornithological Society, Johannesburg.

—(1985) *The Rare Birds of South Africa*. Johannesburg.

Clement, F A (1992) Recent records of birds from Bhutan. *Forktail* 7: 57–73.

Clunie, F (1973) Pink-billed Parrot Finches near Nailagosakelo Creek, southern Viti Levu. *Notornis* 20: 202–209.

Coates, B J (1990) *The Birds of Papua New Guinea*. Vol. 2.

Collar, N J, and Stuart, S N (1985) *Threatened Birds of Africa and related Islands*: The ICBP/IUCN Red Data Book. Part 1. Cambridge, UK.

—and Andrew, P (1988) *Birds to Watch*: The ICBP World Check-list of Threatened Birds. ICBP Technical Publication No. 8. Cambridge.

—, Gonzaga, L P, Krabbe, N, et al. (1992) *Threatened Birds of the Americas*. The ICBP/IUCN Red Data Book, Part 2. Smithsonian Institute.

Dee, T J (1986) *The Endemic Birds of Madagascar*. ICBP Report. Cambridge.

de Greling, C (1972) New records from northern Cameroon. *Bull. B.O.C.* 92: 24–27.

Delin, H, and Svensson, L (1988) *A Photographic Guide to the Birds of Britain and Europe*. Hamlyn, London.

Dementiev, G P, and Gladkov, N A (1951–54) *The Birds of the Soviet Union*. 6 Vols. Moscow.

Densley, M (1990) Desert Sparrows in Morocco. *Brit. Birds* 83: 195–201.

—(1990) Saxaul Sparrow in Mongolia. *Dutch Birding* 12: 5–9.

de Schauensee, R M (1984) *The Birds of China*. Oxford University Press, Oxford.

—**and Ripley, S D** (1940) Zoological results of the George Vanderbilt Sumatra Expedition 1936–39. Part 1, Birds from Atjah. *Proc. Acad. Nat. Sci. Philadelphia* 111: 311–368.

De Vis, C W (1897) Diagnoses of thirty-six new or little-known birds from British New Guinea. *Ibis* III: 371–392.

Dickinson, E C, Kennedy, R S, and Parkes, K C (1991) *The Birds of the Philippines*. BOU Check-list No. 12.

Dupont, J (1972) Notes from western Samoa, including the description of a new Parrot Finch (*Erythrura*), *Wilson Bulletin* 84: 375–376.

Eames, J C, and Robson, C R (1992) *Vietnam Forest Project; Forest Bird Surveys*. ICBP Report No. 51.

Edwards, E P (1972) *A Field Guide to the Birds of Mexico*. Sweet Briar, Virginia.

Ehrlich, P R, Dobkin, D S, and Whege, D (1988) *The Birders Handbook: A Field Guide to the Natural History of American Birds*. New York.

Elgood, J H (1982) *The Birds of Nigeria: an annotated check-list*. BOU Check-list No. 4.

Erard, C (1974) Taxonomie des Serins à gorge jaune d'Ethiopie. *Oiseau et R.F.O.* 44: 308–323.

Etchécopar, R D and Hüe, F (1967) *The Birds of North Africa*. Edinburgh.

Everett, M J (1987) The Arabian and Yemen Serins in North Yemen. *Sandgrouse* 9: 102–105.

Farrand, J (Jnr), *et al.* (1985) *The Audubon Society Master Guide to Birding*. 3 vols. A A Knopf, New York.

Finsch, O (1886) On two new species of birds from New Ireland. *Ibis* (4): 1–2.

Fjeldså, J, and Krabbe, N (1990) *Birds of the High Andes*. Svendborg, Denmark.

Fleming, R L (Snr), Fleming, R L (Jnr), and Bangdel, L S (1979) *Birds of Nepal*. 2nd edition. Avalok Publishers, Kathmandu.

Flint, V E, Boehme, R L, Kostin, Y V, and Kuznetsov, A A (1984) *A Field Guide to Birds of the USSR*. Princeton University Press, New Jersey.

Friedmann, H (1968) The Olive-weaver Finch *Nesocharis ansorgei ansorgei* in Uganda. *Bull. B.O.C.* 88: 135–138.

Frith, H J (ed). (1979) *Complete Book of Australian Birds*. Reader's Digest, Sydney.

Gantlett, S (1990) Parrot Crossbill Variation. *Birding World* 3: 349.

George, W G (1964) A Peruvian race of *Spinus crassirostris*. *The Condor* 66: 248–249.

Ginn, P J, McIlleron, W G, and Milstein P le S (1990) *The Complete Book of Southern African Birds.* Cape Town.

Godfrey, W E (1979) *The Birds of Canada.* National Museums of Canada, Ottawa.

Good, A I (1952) *The Birds of French Cameroon.* Science Naturelles, Series 2. L'Institute François d'Afrique Noir.

Goodwin, D (1982) *Estrildid Finches of the World.* BM(NH), London.

Grant P J (1980) Judging the size of birds. *Brit. Birds* 73: 227–8.

—(1983) Size-illusion. *Brit. Birds* 76: 327–334.

—**and Mullarney, K** (1989) *The New Approach to Identification.* (Published privately).

Grant, P R (1964) A New Subspecies of Lesser Goldfinch from Mexico. *The Condor* 66: 512514.

Grimes, L G (1987) *The Birds of Ghana: an annotated Check-list.* BOU Check-list No. 9.

Gyldenstolpe, N (1924) *Zoological results of the Swedish Expedition 1921.* Stockholm.

Hall, B P (1970) A new record for Algeria. *Bull. B.O.C.* 90: 136.

—**and Moreau, R E** (1970) *An Atlas of Speciation in African Passerine Birds.* BM(NH), London.

Harrap, S, and Millington, R (1991) Identification Forum: Two-barred Crossbill. *Birding World* 4: 55–59.

Harris, A, Tucker, L, and Vinicombe, K E (1989) *The Macmillan Field Guide to Bird Identification.* Macmillan, London.

Harrison, C J O (1964) The taxonomic status of the African Silverbill *L. cantans* and Indian Silverbill *L. malabarica. Ibis* 106: 462–468.

Henderson, G, and Hume, A O (1873) *Lahore to Yarkand.* London.

Henry, G M (1971) *A Guide to the Birds of Ceylon.* 2nd edition. London.

Herremans, M (1990) Taxonomy and Evolution in Redpolls *Carduelis flammea hornemanni*: a multivariate study of their biometry. *Ardea* 78(3): 441–458.

Hirschfeld, E, Morris, R, Andrew, I, and Andrew, J (1992) In 'Around the Region'. *OSME Bull.* 29: 36.

Hollom, P A D (1959) Notes from Jordan, Lebanon, Syria and Antioch. *Ibis* 101: 183–200.

Hollom, P A D, Porter, R F, Christensen, S, and Willis, I (1988) *Birds of the Middle East and North Africa.* Poyser, Calton.

Hoogerwerf, A (1963) A new race of the Spotted Munia *Lonchura punctulata* (Linn). *Bull. B.O.C.* 83: 36–40.

Howard, R, and Moore, A (1980) *A Complete Checklist of the Birds of the World.* Oxford.

—**and** —(1991) *A Complete Checklist of the Birds of the World* (revised edition). Academic Press, London.

Howell, S N G, and Webb, S (in prep) *A Guide to the Birds of Mexico and North Central America.*

Irby Davis, L (1972) *A Field Guide to the Birds of Mexico and Central America.* University of Texas, Austin.

Irwin, M P S (1981) *The Birds of Zimbabwe.* Harare.

Jennings, M C (1991) Recent Reports. *The Phoenix* 8: 7–9.

Jones, P J, and Tye, A (1988) *A Survey of the Avifauna of São Tomé and Principé.* ICBP Study Report No. 24.

Jonkers, B, and Roersma, H (1990) New subspecies of *Lonchura spectabilis* from East Sepik Province, Papua New Guinea. *Dutch Birding* 12: 22–25.

Jonsson, L (1982) *Birds of the Mediterranean and Alps.* Croom Helm, London.

—(1992) *Birds of Europe with North Africa and the Middle East.* Christopher Helm, London.

King B, Woodcock, M, and Dickinson, E C (1975) *A Field Guide to the Birds of South-east Asia.* London.

King, W B (1981) *Endangered Birds of the World.* ICBP Red Data Book. Washington DC.

Knox, A G (1975) In Nethersole-Thompson, D. *Crossbills.* Poyser, Berkhamsted.

—(1976) The Taxonomic Status of the Scottish Crossbill, *Loxia sp. Bull. B. O. C.* 96: 15–19.

—(1988) The Taxonomy of Redpolls. *Ardea* 76: 1–26.

—(1990) Identification of Crossbill and Scottish Crossbill. *Brit. Birds* 83: 89–94.

Koepcke, M (1964) *The Birds of the Department of Lima, Peru.*

Lamarche, B (1981) Oiseaux du Mali. *Malimbus* 3: 73–102.

Land, H C (1970) *Birds of Guatemala.* Pennsylvania.

Lansdown, P, Riddiford, N, and Knox, A (1991) Identification of Arctic Redpoll *Carduelis hornemanni exilipes. Brit. Birds* 84: 41–56.

Louette, M (1981) The Birds of Cameroon: an annotated Check-list. *Ac. West. Let. Sch. K. Belgie.*

—(1988) Additions and Corrections to the Avifauna of Zaire (3). *Bull. B.O.C* 108(3): 112–120.

Ludlow, F (1951) The Birds of Kongbo and Pome, south-east Tibet. *Ibis* 93: 547–580

—**and Kinnear, N B** (1933) On the Ornithology of Chinese Turkestan. *Ibis* 3: 658–694.

McLaren, I A, Morlan, J, *et al.* (1989) Eurasian Siskins in North America—distinguishing females from green morph Pine Siskins. *American Birds* 43(5): 1268–1274

Mackinnon, J (1988) *Field Guide to the Birds of Java and Bali.* Jakarta.

Mackworth-Praed, C W, and Grant C H B (1960) *Birds of Eastern and North Eastern Africa.* Vol. II. London.

—**and**—(1963) *Birds of the southern third of Africa.* Vol. 2. London

—**and**—(1981) *Birds of West Central and Western Africa.* Vol. II. London.

Maclean, G (1984) *Roberts Birds of South Africa.* 5th edition. Johannesburg.

Martins, R P (1987) The Golden-winged Grosbeak in North Yemen. *Sandgrouse* 9: 106–110.

McLachlan, G R, and Liversidge, R (1978) *Roberts Birds of South Africa.* 4th edition. Cape Town.

Medway (Lord), and Wells, D R (1976) *The Birds of the Malay Peninsula.* Vol. 5. Penerbit University, Malaya.

Meinertzhagen, R (1954) *The Birds of Arabia.* Edinburgh.

Mild, K (1990) *Bird Songs of Israel and the Middle East.*

Molau, U (1985) Gråsiskkomplexet i Sverige. *Vår Fågelvärld* 44: 5–20.

Moore, H J, and Boswell, C (1956) Field observation on the birds of Iraq. *Iraq Nat. Hist. Mus. Publs.* 1956 No. 9, 10. 1957 No. 12.

Moreau, R E, and Moreau, W M (1937) Biological and other notes on some East African birds. *Ibis* (14)1: 152–174.

Morel, G, and Morel, M-Y, (1990) *Les Oiseaux de Sénégambie.* Paris.

Neufeldt, I A, and Vietinghoff-Scheel, E V (1978) *Kozlowia roborowskii* (Przewalski). In Dathe, H, and Neufeldt, I A (eds.) *Atlas der Verbreitung Palaearktischer.* Vögel no. 7, Akademie Verlag, Berlin.

Newman, K (1983) *Newman's Birds of Southern Africa.* Johannesburg.

Newton, I (1972) *Finches.* London.

Niethammer, G (1967) On the breeding biology of *Montifringilla theresae. Ibis* 109: 117–18.

Nikolaus, G (1989) Birds of South Sudan, *Scopus* Special Supp. No. 3.

Oatley, T B and Skead, D M (1972) Nectar feeding by South African birds. *Lammergeyer* 15: 65–74.

Ogilvie-Grant, W R (1895) On the Birds of the Philippine Islands, Part V. *Ibis* 433–463.

Olsson, V (1964) Studies of less familiar birds 126. Parrot Crossbill. *Brit Birds* 57: 118–123.

Osmaston, B B (1925) The Birds of Ladakh. *Ibis* I: 663–719.

Paludan, K (1959) On the Birds of Afghanistan. *Vidensk. Medd. dansk naturh. Foren.*

Panov, E N, and Bulatsova, N Sh (1972) On the coexistence of Trumpeter and Mongolian Finches in Transcaucasia. *Byull. Mosk. Obschch. Ispyt. Prir. Otd. Biol.* 77: 86–94.

Paz, U (1987) *The Birds of Israel.* Croom Helm, London.

Peters, J L, *et al.* (1934–1987) *Check-list of Birds of the World.* Cambridge, Massachusetts.

Peterson, A T, and Stotz, D F (1992) Review of Sibley and Monroe (1990) *Distribution and Taxonomy of Birds of the World. Ibis* 134: 306–8.

Peterson, R T (1961) *A Field Guide to Western Birds.* Houghton Mifflin, Boston.

—(1980) *A Field Guide to the Birds East of the Rockies.* Houghton Mifflin, Boston.

—and Chalif, E L (1973) *A Field Guide to Mexican Birds.* Houghton Mifflin, Boston.

Pizzey, G, and Doyle, R (1980) *A Field Guide to the Birds of Australia.* Sydney.

Pratt, H D, Bruner, P L, and Berrett D G (1987) *The Birds of Hawaii and the Tropical Pacific.* Princeton.

Prigogine, A (1975) The status of *Estrilda kandti* and *Estrilda atricapilla graueri. Bull. B.O.C.* 95(1): 15–18.

—(1980) Etude de quelques contacts secondaires au Zaïre oriental. *Gerfaut* 70: 356–384.

Pyle, P, Howell, S N G, Yunick R P, and DeSante, D F (1987) *Identification Guide to North American Passerines.* Bolinas.

Przewalski, N (1876) *Mongolia and the Tangut Country.* London.

Restall, R L (1975) *Finches and Other Seed-eating Birds.* London.

—(1989) Reminiscences of Rare Munias. Part I. *Avicultural Magazine* 95: 129—141. Part II. 95: 192—209.

Ridgely, R S, and Tudor G (1989) *The Birds of South America*. Vol. I. Oxford.

Savalli, U M (1989) Black and Mannikins *Lonchura bicolor* eating algae. *Scopus* 13: 136.

Schäfer, E (1938) Ornithologische Ergebnisse zweier Forschungsreisen nach Tibet. *Journ. f. Ornithologie* (Sonderheft): 1—349.

Schuchmann, K-L, and Wolters, H E (1982) A New Subspecies of *Serinus estherae* (Carduelidae) from Sulawesi. *Bull. B.O.C.* 102(1): 12—14.

Sclater, P L, and Hudson, W H (18881889) *Argentine Ornithology*. 2 Vols. London.

Sclater, W L and Moreau R E (1933) Taxonomic and Field Notes on Some Birds of north-eastern Tanganyika Territory (Part V). *Ibis* 75: 399—440.

Scott, D A (1992) Around the Region. *OSME Bulletin* 29: 42.

Sergeant, D E, Gullick, T, Turner, D A, and Sinclair, J C (1992) The rediscovery of the São Tomé Grosbeak in south-western São Tomé. *Bird Conservation International* 2: 157—159.

Serle, W (1957) A Contribution to the Ornithology of the Eastern region of Nigeria, Part 2. *Ibis* 99: 628—685.

—(1965) A 3rd Contribution to the Ornithology of the British Cameroons. *Ibis* 107: 230—246.

—, **Morel, G J, and Hartwig, W** (1977) *A Field Guide to the Birds of West Africa*. London.

Shaw, A M T H (1936) *Birds of Hopei Province*. Peking.

Shirihai, H (1989) Photospot 27: Sinai Rosefinch. *Brit. Birds* 82: 52—54.

Sibley, G C, and Ahlquist J (1991) *Phylogeny and Classification of Birds*. Yale University Press.

—**and** —**Monroe, B L** (1991) *Distribution and Taxonomy of Birds of the World*. Yale University Press.

Sinclair, I (1984) *Field Guide to the Birds of Southern Africa*. London.

Slater, P (1974) *A Field Guide to Australian Birds*. Vol. 2. Adelaide.

Smythies, B E (1981) *The Birds of Borneo*. 3rd edition. Kuala Lumpur.

—(1986) *The Birds of Burma*. Liss, Hampshire.

Stepanyan, L S (1990) *Conspectus of the Ornithological Fauna of the USSR*. Moscow.

Stevens, H (1925) Notes on the Birds of the Sikkim Himalayas. *J. Bombay Nat. Hist. Soc.* 30: 352—379.

Stevenson, T (1992) First record of the Black-billed Seed-cracker *P. ostrinus* in Kenya. *Scopus* 15: 133—134.

—(1992) First record of the Locust Finch *Ortygospiza locustella* in Kenya. *Scopus* 15: 32.

Sultana, J, Gauci, C, and Beaman, M (1975) *A Guide to the Birds of Malta*. Valetta.

Summers-Smith, J D (1980) House Sparrows down coal mines. *Brit. Birds* 73: 325—327.

—(1988) *The Sparrows*. Calton.

Svensson, L (1984) *Identification Guide to European Passerines*. 3rd edition. Stockholm.

—(1992) *Identification Guide to European Passerines*. 4th edition. Stockholm.

Terres, J K (ed), et al. (1980) *The Audubon Society Encyclopedia of North American Birds.* New York.

Thonnerieux, Y, Walsj, J F, and Bartoli, L (1989) L'Avifaune de la Ville Ougadougou et ses Environs (Burkina Faso). *Malimbus* 11: 7–38.

Traylor, M A. In Paynter R A (ed.) (1968) *Peters' Checklist of Birds of the World.* Vol. XIV. Cambridge (Mass.) USA.

—(1963) Revision of the Quailfinch *Ortygospiza atricollis. Bull. B.O.C.* 83: 141–146.

—**and Archer, A L** (1982) Some results of the Field Museum 1977 Expedition to South Sudan. *Scopus* 6: 5–12.

Troy, D M (1985) A Phenytic Analysis of the Redpolls *Carduelis flammea flammea* and *Carduelis hornemanni exilipes. Auk* 102: 82–96.

Urban, E K (1975) Weight and longevity of some birds from Addis Ababa, Ethiopia. *Bull. B.O.C.* 95(3): 96–98.

Van den Berg, A, and Blankert, J J (1980) Crossbills *Loxia curvirostra* with prominent double wingbar. *Dutch Birding* 2: 33–36.

van den Elzen, R (1985) Systematics and Evolution of African Canaries and Seedeaters (Aves: Carduelidae). *Proc. Intern. Symp. African Vertebr.* Bonn.

Van Marle, J G, and Voous, K H (1988) *The Birds of Sumatra.* BOU Check-list No. 10.

Vaurie, C (1949) Notes on some Asiatic Finches. *Am. Mus. Novitates* No. 1424:24–28.

—(1956) Systematic Notes on Palearctic Birds No. 19. Fringillidae. *Am. Mus. Novitates* No. 1775: 19–21.

—(1956) Systematic Notes on Palearctic Birds No. 20. *Am. Mus. Novitates* No. 1786.

—(1958) Systematic Notes on Palearctic Birds No. 33. A second review of *Carpodacus puniceus* with a study of its plumages and a supplementary note on *Emberiza schoeniclus. Am. Mus. Novitates.* No. 1898.

—(1959) *The Birds of the Palearctic Fauna.* 2 vols. Witherby, London.

Vincent, J (1936) The Birds of Northern Portuguese East Africa (Part X). *Ibis* (6): 48–120.

Voous, K H (1977) *List of Recent Holarctic Bird Species.* BOU, London.

—(1978) The Scottish Crossbill: *Loxia scotica. Brit. Birds* 71: 3–10.

Vowles, G A, and Vowles, R S (1987) Ageing and sexing of the Waxbill in southern Portugal. *Ringing & Migration* 8: 119–120.

Walsh, J F (1986) Notes on the Birds of the Ivory Coast. *Malimbus* 8: 89–93.

Walton, H J (1906) On the birds of Southern Tibet (Part II). *Ibis* XXII: 225–256.

Welch, G R, et al. (1986) *Djibouti II, Autumn '85.* Privately published report.

—**and Welch H J** (1988) A new subspecies of *Pytilia melba* from Djibouti, East Africa. *Bull. B.O.C.* 108: 68–70.

Wetmore, A, and Swales, B H (1931) *The Birds of Haiti and the Dominican Republic.* US Govt Printing Office, Washington.

Whistler, H (1923) A Note on the Birds of Spiti. *Ibis* 611–629.

—(1925) The Birds of Lahul, NW Himalya. Part VIII. *Ibis* 152—208.

—(1925) A Note on the Weavers and Finches of the Punjab. *Journ. Bombay Nat. Hist. Soc.* XXX: 177—188, 406—417.

—(1930) On the Birds of the Rawalpindi District. *Ibis* (6): 67- 112.

—(1940) Unusual plumage sequence in a passerine bird. *Ibis* 4: 151—153.

White, C M N (1963) *A revised check-list of African Flycatchers, tits, tree creepers, sunbirds, white-eyes, honey eaters, weavers and waxbills.* Lusaka.

—**and Bruce, M D** (1986) *The Birds of Wallacea: Sulawesi; the Moluccas and Lesser Sunda Islands, Indonesia.* BOU Check-list No. 7.

Williams, J G (1957) The juvenile plumage of *Warsanglia johannis. Bull. B.O.C.* 77: 157.

—**and Arlott, N** (1980) *A Field Guide to the Birds of East Africa.* London.

Williamson, K (1961) The taxonomy of the redpolls. *Brit. Birds* 54: 238—241.

Witherby, H F, Jourdain, F C R, Ticehurst, N F, and Tucker, B W (1938—41) *The Handbook of British Birds.* 5 Vols. Witherby, London.

Wood, B, Madge, S C, and Waller, C S (1978) Description, moult and measurements of *Montifringilla theresae. Bull. B.O.C.* 98: 35—36.

Woods, R W (1982) *Falkland Islands Birds.* Anthony Nelson, Oswestry.

—(1988) *Guide to Birds of the Falkland Islands.* Anthony Nelson, Oswestry.

INDEX

Figures in bold refer to plate numbers.

495